T3-BQR-947

WORLD ENCYCLOPEDIA OF PARLIAMENTS AND LEGISLATURES

WORLD ENCYCLOPEDIA OF PARLIAMENTS AND LEGISLATURES

Sponsored by

Research Committee of Legislative Specialists,

International Political Science Association

and

Commonwealth Parliamentary Association

Edited by

George Thomas Kurian

Consulting Editors

Lawrence D. Longley

Thomas O. Melia

VOLUME I

CONGRESSIONAL QUARTERLY INC.
Washington, D.C.

1414 22nd Street, N.W., Washington, D.C. 20037

Book design and production by Kachergis Book Design, Pittsboro, North Carolina

Printed and bound in the United States of America

The paper used in this publication meets the minimum requirements of the American National Standard for Information Sciences—Permanence of Paper for Printed Library Materials, ANSI Z39.48-1984.

LIBRARY OF CONGRESS CATALOGING-IN-PUBLICATION DATA

World encyclopedia of parliaments and legislatures / sponsored by Research Committee of Legislative Specialists, International Political Science Association [and] Commonwealth Parliamentary Association; edited by George Thomas Kurian ; consulting editors, Lawrence D. Longley and Thomas O. Melia.

p. cm.

Includes bibliographical references (p.) and index.

ISBN 0-87187-987-5 (set : alk. paper). — ISBN 1-56802-365-0 (vol. 1 : alk. paper). — ISBN 1-56802-366-9 (vol. 2 : alk. paper)

1. Legislative bodies—Encyclopedias. 2. Comparative government—Encyclopedias. I. Kurian, George Thomas. II. Longley, Lawrence D. III. Melia, Thomas O. IV. International Political Science Association. Research Committee of Legislative Specialists. V. Commonwealth Parliamentary Association.

JF511.W67 1998

328'.03—dc21

97-30226

CONTENTS

PREFACE

The twentieth century has witnessed the triumph of parliamentary democracy. This achievement has come at great cost—nearly three hundred coups, more than one hundred revolutions and civil wars, and two world wars. In 1901, when the century was dawning, there were only a half-dozen parliamentary democracies in the world, including the United States, the United Kingdom, and four European countries. Even these parliamentary systems were far from full-fledged because neither women nor certain racial minorities enjoyed suffrage and the elites still controlled the levers of power. But as the century is drawing to a close, the numbers are reversed. There are more than 180 countries with viable and functioning parliaments and only a dozen or so nations with weak, moribund, or suspended legislatures. It is true that in terms of population, the picture is less heartening: China, with one-fifth of the global population, is outside the camp, along with Nigeria, the most populous country in Africa, North Korea, Cuba, and more than a dozen African nations. Nevertheless, more than two-thirds of the world's population lives under parliamentary democracies, and this percentage is likely to increase in the twenty-first century.

The *World Encyclopedia of Parliaments and Legislatures* is a record of the state of parliamentary democracy around the world. It looks at the development of the parliamentary form of government in more than 190 countries, including those where such a development has been arrested by political events. As the first encyclopedia on parliaments and legislatures worldwide, it provides a comprehensive survey of one of the central institutions of modern political life. It also provides the basis for the comparative study of parliaments and legislatures in terms of their history as well as their present functions and procedures. As a reference book it provides accurate and definitive treatment of an important subject consistent with the highest standards of scholarship. But it attempts to go further and convey something of the vitality and excitement of the world of parliaments and legislatures.

Parliaments have evolved differently from the other two branches of government. Absolute monarchy is historically the oldest and the most universal form of government, indigenous to virtually every country. On the other hand, parliaments in their modern form are comparatively recent phenomena, the oldest dating to the seventeenth century. They are indigenous only to a handful of European and North American countries. In advanced and mature political systems parliaments are organically linked to other branches of government and are grounded in the political ethos of the country. But they are a Western import in many developing and former communist countries. In this group of countries parliaments were not part of the original architecture of power but were add-ons introduced by colonial powers or instituted at the time of independence. In Middle Eastern Islamic countries and communist countries parliaments are actually alien institutions without any roots in the political and legal matrix of society.

Governments have not existed—and cannot exist—without some form of executive and some form of judiciary, but they can exist without parliaments. In countries where they are not indigenous but were introduced from outside, parliaments are highly vulnerable to being suppressed or abolished by a hostile executive supported by the military. Among the first acts of a military-backed dictatorship are to abolish the constitution and suspend the legislature. Only a minority of developing nations have escaped this experience at some time in their history.

The parliaments profiled in this encyclopedia fall into two groups. The first are *evolved*, or strong, parliaments and the second are *imposed*, or weak, parliaments. Evolved parliaments are those institutions that have developed over the course of time in countries where the political and legal climate favors discourse and consensus and where there are deep-rooted traditions favoring public participation in government. Imposed parliaments are those institutions that were established in former colonial countries at the time of formal independence in an effort to legitimize existing regimes. In these countries there are no historical parliamentary traditions to draw upon. In many cases the executive is so entrenched that it has no desire to share power with an equal body.

EDITORIAL ORGANIZATION AND STRUCTURE

The classic architectural maxim, form follows function, is applicable to the architecture of encyclopedias. The reader needs a clear understanding of the organizing principles used in writing the entries and in presenting the information.

In general, information in each country section is arranged according to a standard, but not rigidly uniform, pattern. This classification system is central to this work and has been adhered to throughout except where the need for clarity of presentation or the nature or absence of information required modification in the scheme. This organizational system has been designed not only for ease of consultation but also to provide a comparative framework essential to the study of international institutions.

The cutoff date for this work is June 30, 1997. Every effort has been made to make the data current as of that date. Political and economic data change rapidly, but information on parliaments tends to be relatively stable and, except in countries subject to coups and revolutions, the country profiles will remain valid for many years.

The spelling of country names follows common international usage. Thus Palestine is used although the name is not universally recognized. Numerous countries without a functioning parliament have been included. Some of these countries, like the Holy See, never had a parliament, but others, like Afghanistan and Nigeria, had short-lived parliaments that became casualties of civil wars and coups. In these cases the entries explain the circumstances in which parliaments withered and died. Each entry relates to a single country, except in the case of the Commonwealth of Independent States, Non-Slavic, in which nine states of the former Soviet Union are treated together. The rationale is to facilitate a comparative study of their democratic institutions in light of their common starting point.

Each country parliamentary profile shares a common topical basis, and authors of all major and many middle-level countries have tried to address these elements:

- Historical background
- Constitutional provisions on parliament
- Elections; current party positions; seats; term of office; membership
- Sessions; annual calendar; recess; dissolution
- How laws are made; reading of bills; amendments; volume of legislation; quorum; private bills
- Debates; official record; voting procedures
- Budget
- Committees; power and procedures; public hearings
- Relations with the executive; monitoring executive performance; interpellations; ombudsman
- Executive vetoes; overriding executive vetoes
- Speaker
- Party caucuses and groups; majority and minority leaders and whips; party discipline
- Multicameral parliaments; relations between chambers
- Parliamentary library and research
- Parliamentary privileges and immunities; recall, expulsion, and resignation
- Parliamentary pay and perquisites
- Parliamentary ethics; discipline
- Judicial functions of parliament
- Architecture; physical description of parliamentary buildings
- Parliamentary media; broadcasting of proceedings
- Constitutionality of laws; emergency powers
- Bibliography

Within this topical framework, the slant and focus of the articles vary according to the political climate of the country. Legislatures function as part of a rich and varied tableau of powerful social movements, political identities, and economic forces. Appropriately, the emphasis in each article is on the political environment. In many countries there is a dichotomy between the constitutional and normative position of parliament and its powers in actual practice. There are parliaments with enormous powers in theory but none in practice. For countries with weak parliaments, the authors try to illustrate the reasons for the erosion of their constitutionally mandated powers.

The second part of the encyclopedia consists of fourteen interpretative essays offering vibrant analyses of salient aspects of parliamentary activity. They are global overviews tying together many of the issues, problems, and trends noted in the country profiles. Because of the dominant influence of the British Westminster model of parliaments, legislatures throughout the world share many features and characteristics, and these entries illustrate the evolution of these common traits. Many of the unfamiliar terms used in the encyclopedia are explained in a glossary which has been prepared by Congressional Quarterly editors.

ACKNOWLEDGMENTS

An encyclopedia is the work of many hands. During the gestation of this project, I was privileged to work with a great team of contributors and associates, and also a great team of editors. It was a particular pleasure to work with Dave Tarr, executive editor at Congressional Quarterly Books. From the beginning he provided tremendous encouragement and inspiration, and his commitment to the project and the direction he provided proved invaluable. Also closely associated with the project at CQ were Jerry Orvedahl and Ann Davies; their unobtrusive efficiency kept the project on track and helped make the passage from manuscript to print remarkably smooth. It would be difficult to find two editors so dedicated to working harmoniously with authors and so unfailingly courteous.

The contributors to this encyclopedia are distinguished scholars, many of them the top legislative specialists in the world, and they have generously invested time and effort in the work. I am grateful to them. I am also particularly grateful to Lawrence D. Longley, who, as consulting editor, was one of the staunchest supporters of the project and who was instrumental in providing the sponsorship of the Research Committee of Legislative Specialists of the International Political Science Association. Thomas O. Melia, also a consulting editor, brought with him an intimate knowledge of the parliamentary systems of the developing world and persuaded many of his colleagues at the National Democratic Institute to contribute articles. Andrew Imlach, who represented the Commonwealth Parliamentary Association on the editorial board, was a wellspring of advice and wise counsel, and he secured for the encyclopedia a number of essays on parliaments in Commonwealth countries.

Above all, my unbounded gratitude goes out to Annie, my beloved wife and faithful companion, for her constant encouragement and support.

George Thomas Kurian

EDITORIAL BOARD

ALPHABETICAL LIST OF ARTICLES

TOPICAL ESSAYS

ABOUT THE SPONSORS

THE COMMONWEALTH PARLIAMENTARY ASSOCIATION

The Commonwealth is a free association of fifty-one countries uniting a quarter of the world's population through a community of interests and institutions and common ideals, chief of which is a commitment to democratic government. Evolving from the old British Empire, the Commonwealth today is a complex network of official and unofficial relationships of which the oldest is membership in the Commonwealth Parliamentary Association (CPA).

The CPA was founded in 1911 as the Empire Parliamentary Association (EPA) when parliamentarians from the United Kingdom and the five dominion parliaments of the British Empire met to establish a forum through which they could exchange ideas and discuss political and procedural issues. As the British Empire evolved to become the Commonwealth, and individual colonies and dominions developed into self-governing nations, the EPA became the Commonwealth Parliamentary Association in 1948. Its imperial emphasis was transformed into a global mission to strengthen the parliamentary system and democratic institutions.

The EPA was formed as a vehicle to advance imperial foreign policy. But since the dominions followed the Westminster model of parliamentary government, the focus soon shifted to professional interests. By 1913 branches of the EPA had been formed at Westminster and in the five dominions, with the British branch serving as headquarters. Following World War I, the EPA began to publish in 1920 the *Journal of the Parliaments of the Empire,* which later became the *Parliamentarian,* the official journal of the CPA today. In the 1930s the EPA expanded to include legislatures of other colonies and territories in India, Africa, and the Caribbean; by the outbreak of World War II the membership had risen to twenty.

Meanwhile, the British Empire was changing. The Balfour Declaration of 1926 described the free association of nations under the British monarch as the British Commonwealth. The passage of the Statute of Westminster in 1931 recognized the right of the dominions to become fully sovereign. In 1947 a major change took place in the nature of the association when the Constituent Assembly of newly independent India adopted a republican constitution but expressed a strong desire to remain in the Commonwealth and in the EPA. A meeting of Commonwealth prime ministers in 1949 agreed to India's continued membership on the basis of its acceptance of the British monarch "as the symbol of the free association of independent nations and, as such, Head of the Commonwealth." This statement became the basis of the official relationship underpinning the modern Commonwealth. The EPA became the CPA in 1948, and a year later established the International Secretariat as a body distinct from the United Kingdom branch.

Under Section I of its constitution, the CPA exists to "promote knowledge of the constitutional, legislative, economic, social, and cultural aspects of parliamentary democracy." Its membership is constitutionally confined to practicing Commonwealth democracies whose legislatures are competent to enact public laws. No stipulation is made as to the type of the democratic system. Most member assemblies follow the Westminster model with variations to suit local traditions and circumstances. Some follow a presidential system. Some countries have a multiparty system, while others do not. In some countries, representatives are popularly elected; others have systems combining appointive, traditional, and inherited elements. If a member country ceases to have a democratic government, it is automatically excluded from CPA membership.

By 1997 the CPA had expanded to include active branches in 126 national, state, provincial, and territorial parliaments and legislatures with a membership of more than 12,000 parliamentarians. Membership spans assemblies in all the continents.

The CPA's principal governing body is the General Assembly, which meets annually in one of the member countries. The General Assembly elects an executive committee composed of a chair, president, vice president, treasurer, three representatives each from seven regions and four representatives from Asia, the largest region. The annual parliamentary conference is the principal mechanism for bringing together the more than three hundred presiding officers, ministers, and parliamentarians representing member parliaments. The conference discusses issues and developments in the conduct of parliamentary affairs, but there is no formal voting on issues. Summary reports of each discussion, elucidating the main points of agreement and disagreement, are circulated to the Commonwealth heads of government and opposition leaders as well as to officials of the United Nations, the Commonwealth Secretariat, and other international and intergovernmental organizations. The CPA works in tandem with the Commonwealth Secretariat in monitoring elections. It recommends to the Commonwealth secretary general the names of parliamentarians to serve on Commonwealth Election Observer missions, which report on the propriety of elections and the legitimacy of the governments elected.

The CPA bolsters the democratic system through programs designed to assist parliaments and individual representatives. At the institutional level, it assists emerging democracies in their transition to a popularly elected, responsible government. At the individual level, it serves as a professional development body. It exposes representatives to legislative procedures, practices, and policies of other Commonwealth democracies and fosters respect for cultural differences and social traditions impinging on parliamentary activities.

In addition to its official journal, the *Parliamentarian,* the CPA publishes a series of professional reports and studies, including an *Election Observation Handbook,* a study of the barriers facing women in politics, an analysis of the steps parliaments could take to improve the credentials of their representatives, and special studies on such issues as the security of small states, parliamentary scrutiny of public expenditures, and regulations and practices governing the integrity of parliamentarians.

The CPA maintains at its London headquarters a Parliamentary Information and Reference Center, which responds to requests from members, parliaments, governments, and interested observers. It has an extensive collection of foundation documents, such as constitutions, standing orders, and reports on parliamentary development, augmented by on-line databases.

The Commonwealth's democratic philosophy was enunciated in 1971 by the Singapore Declaration, which affirmed that all peoples should be free politically to frame the society in which they live. This tenet has guided the CPA for more than eight decades. The CPA has served as an effective agent in expanding parliamentary democracy in a multicultural world with differing political traditions and levels of economic development.

Arthur R. Donahoe
Secretary General
Commonwealth Parliamentary Association
Suite 700, Westminster House, 7
Millbank, London SW1P 3JA
Telephone: (071) 799 1460
Fax: (071) 222 6073

RESEARCH COMMITTEE OF LEGISLATIVE SPECIALISTS

The Research Committee of Legislative Specialists (RCLS) of the International Political Science Association comprises more than 180 scholars from thirty-nine countries engaged in legislative research. The network includes individuals interested in national, cross-national, and subnational aspects of parliaments and legislatures throughout the world.

Founded in 1971, RCLS organizes regular international gatherings of parliamentary and legislative specialists. Three recent meetings were the conference on "The Changing Roles of Parliamentary Committees" in Budapest; the conference on "The New Democratic Parliaments" in Ljubljana, Slovenia; and the workshop of "Parliamentary Scholars and Parliamentarians" in Oxfordshire, England. Proceedings of these workshops and conferences have been published in a book series titled *Working Papers on Comparative Legislative Studies.*

Since 1991 RCLS has published the *International Newsletter.* Each issue features a section called "Scholarly Extensions" that presents summaries of research efforts. Periodically, RCLS also publishes a membership directory and research register.

Lawrence D. Longley
Lawrence University
Appleton, WI 54912
Telephone: (920) 832 6673
Fax: (920) 832 6944

CONTRIBUTORS

Ervand Abrahamian, *Baruch College of the City University of New York*

Attila Ágh, *Budapest University of Economics*

Ariffin Omar, *Universiti Sains Malaysia*

David Arter, *University of Aberdeen*

Abdo Baaklini, *State University of New York at Albany*

Stanley Bach, *Congressional Research Service of the U.S. Library of Congress*

Gerald Benjamin, *State University of New York at New Paltz*

Roger Berry, *National Democratic Institute*

R. C. Bhardwaj, *Lok Sabha, India*

Roger Bobacka, *University of Aberdeen*

Zoey L. Breslar, *Academy for Educational Development*

Kimberly Mahling Clark

Gary W. Copeland, *University of Oklahoma*

Raymond Copson, *Congressional Research Service of the U.S. Library of Congress*

Maria Sofia Corciulo, *University of Rome*

Brian F. Crisp, *University of Arizona*

William W. Culver, *State University of New York at Plattsburgh*

Da-chi Liao, *National Sun Yat-sen University*

Richard Dale, *Southern Illinois University*

Erik Damgaard, *Aarhus University*

Roger H. Davidson, *University of Maryland at College Park*

Dámaso de Lario, *Embassy of Spain, London*

Lieven De Winter, *Université Catholique de Louvain*

Mary-Jane Deeb, *Middle East Journal and American University*

Guilain Denoeux, *Colby College*

Gavin Drewry, *University of London*

Mark S. Ellis, *American Bar Association*

Ömer Faruk Gençkaya, *Bilkent University*

Benjamin Feit, *National Democratic Institute*

Lawrence S. Finkelstein, *Northern Illinois University*

David Fleischer, *Universidade de Brasilia*

Christopher Fomunyoh, *National Democratic Institute*

Takis Hadjioannou, *House of Representatives, Cyprus*

Magnus Hagevi, *Göteborg University*

Tatsunori Isomi

Keith Jackson, *University of Canterbury, New Zealand*

Jacek Jedruch, *International Commission for the History of Representative and Parliamentary Institutions*

Kevin Johnson, *National Democratic Institute*

Christopher M. Karlsten, *Congressional Quarterly*

Zillur R. Khan, *University of Wisconsin—Oshkosh*

Harvey F. Kline, *University of Alabama*

George Thomas Kurian

Eve R. Ladmann, *University of Buenos Aires*

Philip Laundy, *House of Commons, Canada*

Rett R. Ludwikowski, *Catholic University*

Jose Magone, *University of Hull*

Gregory S. Mahler, *Kalamazoo College*

Erin Martin, *National Democratic Institute*

Raj Mathur, *University of Mauritius*

Didier Maus, *International Institute of Public Administration and University of Paris*

Timothy S. McCoy, *National Democratic Institute*

Thomas O. Melia, *National Democratic Institute*

Albert P. Melone, *Southern Illinois University*

Michael L. Mezey, *DePaul University*

Mya Saw Shin

Jim Nichol, *Congressional Research Service of the U.S. Library of Congress*

Philip Norton, *University of Hull*

Eunan O'Halpin, *Dublin City University*

Walter J. Oleszek, *Congressional Research Service of the U.S. Library of Congress*

David M. Olson, *University of North Carolina at Greensboro*
Jerry A. Orvedahl, *Congressional Quarterly*
Chan Wook Park, *Seoul National University*
Samuel C. Patterson, *Ohio State University*
Jan Pelle, *Erasmus Universiteit Rotterdam*
Andrejs Penikis, *Columbia University*
Gerald G. Reed, *Office of the Tennessee Secretary of State*
Alfredo Rehren, *Pontificia Universidad Católica de Chile*
Thomas F. Remington, *Emory University*
Socorro L. Reyes, *Center for Legislative Development, The Philippines*
William H. Robinson, *Congressional Research Service of the U.S. Library of Congress*
Alejandro Rodriguez, *Florida International University*
Cristina Rodriguez-Acosta, *Florida International University*
Allan Rosenbaum, *Florida International University*
Wilma Rule, *University of Nevada, Reno*
Paul S. Rundquist, *Congressional Research Service of the U.S. Library of Congress*
Michael Rush, *University of Exeter*
Thomas Saalfeld, *University of Kent at Canterbury*
Amir Santoso, *University of Indonesia*
Günther Schefbeck, *Parliament of Austria*
Edward Schneier, *City College of the City University of New York*
David W. Schodt, *St. Olaf College*
Malcolm Shaw, *University of Exeter*
Donald R. Shell, *University of Bristol*
Carol Jean Smetana, *U.S. Department of State*
Robert Springborg, *MacQuarie University*
Amy J. Standefer, *United Nations Verification Mission in Guatemala*
Carlyle A. Thayer, *Australian Defence Force Academy*
Adrian Vatter, *University of Bern*
David Welsh, *University of Cape Town*
Martin Westlake, *European Commission*
David M. Wood, *University of Missouri—Columbia*
Sheldon Yett, *Catholic Relief Services*
Wendy I. Zeldin, *U.S. Library of Congress*
Joseph F. Zimmerman, *State University of New York at Albany*

PARLIAMENTS AND LEGISLATURES

National parliaments vary in size and shape, in tenure, in powers and functions, in autonomy, and in procedures and traditions. The Inter-Parliamentary Union, a renowned world organization of parliaments, counted 180 national parliaments operating in May 1997. Their sessions run from about 10 days to 225 days a year, and they count between 13 members (the Parliament of Tuvalu) and 2,978 members (the Chinese National People's Congress). Their official names differ, and their status differs from country to country. Nevertheless, all are quite recognizable as parliamentary assemblies. In this introduction we explore these ubiquitous, remarkable institutions, examining their history, common features, functions, and operation as deliberative or policy-making bodies.

Accordingly, we conceive "parliament" broadly and inclusively. Parliamentary houses have country-specific monikers—the Japanese Shugi-in, the German Bundestag, the Danish Folketinget, the French Assemblée Nationale, the Ulsyn ikh Khural in Mongolia, the Hungarian Országgyülés, the British House of Commons, the U.S. Senate. At the same time, parliamentary institutions share general labels. Some are called "national assemblies," others "legislatures," and still others "parliaments." It would be a mistake to overemphasize these nominal differences in terminology; the terms employed in each country may merely reflect historical happenstance.

The varying names given to representative assemblies indicate that these institutions do, in fact, play different constitutional, legal, and political roles in their respective societies. The roots of the words themselves call forth differing images of the responsibilities of these bodies. Parliaments derive their generic name from the same origins as the French verb *parler* (to talk), identifying themselves as places for discussion or debate. *Legislature,* derived from the Latin root referring to bringing forth laws, connotes a body with influence over the laws of the land. A national assembly brings the people of a nation together in some sense, with the purpose for assembling left undefined. For that reason, many people prefer the name "national assembly" to refer to the range of these institutions, but historically "parliament" is the most common and accepted term. In this essay, we speak primarily of parliaments and legislatures, without drawing a sharp formal distinction in the application of different names to the representative institution.

We explore parliamentary life first by surveying the institutions' historical development. Then we define and discuss the characteristics of parliaments. Next, we explore the functions performed by parliaments in various societies. Finally, we consider how parliaments operate within their polity and how they interact with other parts of the political system.

Before turning to these considerations, we pause to recount how two scholars introduce their studies of these institutions. In an essay on legislatures, Nelson W. Polsby highlights the difficulty of coming to grips with these bodies: "There occasionally arises a natural confusion among scholars because sometimes lawmaking is done outside legislatures, and sometimes legislatures do things other than lawmaking" (Polsby 1975, 258). Even more expansive in his reflections on the complexity of this task is Gerhard Loewenberg, who prefaces various analyses of these institutions by saying:

> Parliament is a paradoxical institution. Medieval in origin, it exists in nearly all contemporary political systems. Although associated with democracy, it has also had its place in aristocracies and dictatorships. Regarded as an ideal instrument of representation, it has at times been composed of instructed as well as autonomous members, who have been variously chosen by birth or appointment as well as by election. . . . In view of the variety of forms which the parliament has taken, the contrasting cultures in which it has appeared, and the tenacity with which it has confounded the prophets of its demise, few generalizations about the institution seem safe (Loewenberg 1971, 1).

THE HISTORICAL DEVELOPMENT OF PARLIAMENTS

The establishment of national assemblies might seem to have followed from the notion that citizens, however legally and politically defined, should have some say in or influence over national policy. In fact, this idea came relatively late to parliamentary development. The evolution of parliaments is properly understood as the result of persistent struggles over power, influence, and obligation (Marongiu 1973, 109).

Traces of representative assemblies can be found in the earliest of recorded history. Councils of nobility began to wrestle power from kings in Greece during the seventh century B.C., a tendency that ultimately led to a dispersion of power and greater control by the nobility over its own civic affairs. Over the next century power continued to become more widely shared. An Athenian citizens' assembly emerged, soon to be reorganized by Solon, as an institution that foreshadowed the establishment of a Council of Four Hundred intended to direct the "business of the state" (Hooper 1967). Years later, as the Roman Empire grew, similar patterns developed. The Roman nobility first demanded respect, consultation, and even the right to approve initiatives, and, gradually, it received these in exchange for the satisfaction of the more short-term needs of the executive. As wealth spread, so did the desire for political and governmental influence. These emergent citizen assemblies slowly but inexorably acquired legitimacy.

As the Roman Empire began deteriorating in the first century A.D., so did the role of assemblies. They became meaningless in the context of a power vacuum. But as the Dark Ages evolved into the Middle Ages, and as local kings began to accumulate power, mutual dependency of nobles and monarch again began to arise. The earlier pattern was very much repeated. Kings, acquiring greater responsibility and obligations, became more dependent on the support of the nobility. And, as the nobility was asked to contribute more and more, it demanded, first, consultation, and then the right of approval. In Spain *cortes,* parliamentary precursors, developed in a formal way and even provided representation for the third estate, the vassals, by the middle of the twelfth century (Wilkinson 1972). The notion of representation in these early assemblies was undeveloped and perhaps completely unknown (Post 1973). Participants in the assembly were loyal to the king while acting out of self-interest, rather than acting in behalf of others (Post 1973, 99). The developing relationship between kings and the nobility was epitomized in this era by the signing of the Magna Carta by King John of England, in 1215. Thereafter, parliamentary institutions emerged elsewhere in Europe. German examples can be found by 1255, and in France the Estates General convened in 1302 (Stubbs 1972, 110).

These bodies—which might be considered "preparliaments" because they were not truly representative institutions—became established and evolved into more powerful councils for four reasons (Marongiu 1973). First, over time these councils gained sufficient confidence and self-awareness to enable them to move beyond their previous bounds. Second, at some point kings decided to seek the advice and consent of chancellors as *representatives* of their villages and towns. Third, various groups formed unions, organized, and developed strength so they could effectively demand representation. Fourth, parliaments evolved more fully as they watched neighboring institutions emerge and succeed.

Critical to the institutional evolution of these assemblies was their capacity to serve as representative bodies. Those assembled had to accept the responsibility of acting on behalf of others. That transformation required these bodies to shift their focus from the king to their constituents. This innovation required two developments. It required a psychological revision of representatives' sense of loyalty to and responsibility for their constituents. And it required a mechanism to ensure that the institution would be maintained. The institutional mechanism was to be found in successful modes of selecting representatives. It would be necessary for the represented to have some say in choosing who would speak and act in their behalf.

Elections emerged as the mechanism through which constituencies could select their own representatives. As election mechanisms evolved, who should be represented and who should control the selection process came to be more clearly defined. Initially, participation in elections was very limited. The development of the modern parliamentary system hinged on expansion of the suffrage (Gerlich 1973). Defining the effective electorate for representative democracies is a recent experience for political entities, and the struggle continues. Eighteenth-century progress in expanding the suffrage to increasing numbers of male voters was followed by later additions to electorates, some belated. For instance, most of the world's women won voting rights only within the past century.

Political thought eventually caught up with the evolution of parliaments. Seventeenth-century philosophers John Locke, Thomas Hobbes, and many others ultimately developed the intellectual justification for liberal democracies and the notion of representation. Nonetheless, it is a reasonable reading of history to conclude that the development of parliaments had more to do with the exercise of self-interested power than with the power of ideas.

PARLIAMENTS AND THEIR CHARACTERISTICS

The range of institutions that we call parliaments, both historically and in the contemporary world, leaves scholars unable to agree upon an entirely satisfactory definition of their meaning. Parliaments are ubiquitous, in part because they are not simple to classify and hence defy easy definition. The conception of parliament is not constrained by an ethnocentric notion of what one should look like. Rather, we accept that various polities adopt and adapt governing institutions like parliaments, often with mixed results. Because the consequences of institutionalization may vary in different societies, parliaments can come to look quite different from one another both structurally and functionally. A functional definition of parliament is irreparably flawed because such a definition has no hope of meeting the requirement of being both reasonably inclusive and exclusive of these institutions. Polsby asks two questions in addressing the definitional difficulties:

> (1) How are we to discuss a legislature that is relatively uninfluential in the making of laws in a given political system? (2) What distinguishes a legislature that engages in lawmaking—as well as all the other varied activities that may be attributed to it—from other sorts of institutions that, in greater or lesser measure, do likewise? (Polsby 1975, 259)

Polsby resorts to a structural definition of parliaments, partly out of necessity and partly because structural criteria allow for the use of observable—empirical—phenomena in determining whether a body can be classified as a parliament. Accordingly, scholars can seek "observable regularities" and can explore the functions performed by various parliaments (p. 262). Polsby's definition becomes a "mélange of characteristics—officiality, a claim on legitimacy based on links with the people, multi-memberedness, formal equality, collective decision making, deliberativeness" (p. 260). Following a similar line of reasoning, Loewenberg concludes that all parliaments share two characteristics: "(1) their members are formally equal to one another in status, distinguishing them from hierarchically ordered organizations; and (2) the authority of their members depends on their claim to representing the rest of the community, in some sense of the protean concept, representation" (Loewenberg and Patterson 1979, 3).

Parliaments, furthermore, can be considered "to be a group of individuals operating on behalf of others in a binding and legitimate manner and making decisions collectively but with formal equality" (Copeland and Patterson 1994, 153). This definition suggests a variety of both structural characteristics and functions that are emblematic of these bodies. We now turn to consider relevant structural characteristics of parliaments and shall address functional features thereafter.

Because a parliament is composed of a group of assembled individuals, the nature of the organization once assembled is important. For the sake of efficiency, human groups commonly organize themselves hierarchically. In marked contrast to this conventional organizational tendency, parliaments are flat organizations. Two points are important here. The first is that members share formal equality. The second is that the hierarchy that does exist in various parliaments is very modest. In a formal sense, members of parliaments are considered equals. When parliament acts, when it makes decisions, it does so through the process of members casting votes. Within these bodies, the votes of individuals carry the same putative weight. Now, we can be pretty sure that in no human organization are individuals truly equal in the weight of their decisions or influence or in garnering the benefits of organizational membership. In parliaments, that tenet is no less true than in other areas; some members have more influence than others, and some of this influence differential is based on organizational position or status. Nevertheless, compared with other kinds of organizations—bureaucracies, corporations, armies, political parties—the structure of parliaments is relatively flat. Those in the executive cabinet are close to backbenchers; speakers are not far removed from members; and committee chairs sit among the rank and file.

While we have identified parliaments as bodies of equals, we should ignore neither the great variations that exist in how equality is practiced nor the significant variations in how power is dispersed across these bodies. In one body a speaker may be quite powerful, while in another he or she occupies a largely symbolic or honorific position. A committee chair in one parliament may be at the center of a powerful issue network that controls public policy within its domain, while in another body the chair may command few advantages and exert little influence. Such structural differences, along with their causes and consequences, are central to the proper understanding of the nature of parliamentary institutions. The important fundamental observation is that parliaments tend to have relatively flat organizational structures and memberships formally composed of equals.

Parliaments are called upon to make decisions for a polity. In most cases, they are part of a constitutional process whose unfolding is authoritative, legitimate, and binding. Commonly, decisions rendered concern matters both of public policy and of the selection of the nation's executive.

Within these areas there is a substantial disparity in how decisions are made and the influence of the parliament in reaching them.

Consider the fundamental distinction between parliamentary and presidential systems. Variations abound, but in parliamentary systems the legislative body, rather than the electorate, bears responsibility for selecting the nation's chief executive. Although parliament may be little more than a conduit for the voice of the people, more often it exercises considerable discretion—when delicate and agonizing coalition-formation processes precede the choice of prime minister. Most parliaments have the constitutional capacity to remove the executive through a vote of no confidence, although there are many variations in the specific nature of this prerogative. In this regard, Germany is particularly interesting: a constructive vote of no confidence is required in parliament to remove a chancellor, meaning that an alternative leader must have been agreed upon.

In presidential systems, by contrast, the legislature has little or no influence over the choice or removal of the executive. These systems tend to have more clearly delineated and separated powers as well as independent lines of responsibility and accountability. More will be said on this topic later, but it is important to recognize that the most important decision of many parliamentary bodies is the selection of the executive.

Parliaments almost always play some role in the processes of making public policies and enacting laws. In some cases, their level of participation is largely pro forma, with little or no debate and no real doubt as to the outcome. In other cases, parliament's legislative influence is great. As a rule, the laws of a land are passed through its parliament; that is, there is generally a formal aspect to law making that includes some action by the parliament. Beyond that aspect, legislatures' roles range from those of puppets of the regime to those of major players in a nation's policy making. The U.S. Congress is understandably held up as the leading example of an activist body that has substantial influence over the content of legislation, but there are other examples of "strong" legislatures, including those in many of the constituent states of the United States of America and in the Scandinavian countries (Damgaard 1992, 1994). At the opposite pole are those authoritarian polities in which legislators could attempt to exercise independent influence only with some substantial risk to their personal well-being. Most parliaments are between the extremes where influence may be subtle, but where it is, nevertheless, real enough.

Where policy influence is genuinely exercised by the legislature, the center of internal power will vary. Power may be found within the formal leadership of the body. This situation is most likely to occur in a presidential system such as France or Finland. Committees are also a potential location for substantial influence, as in Italy or the United States. Committee influence may be derived from individual members' expertise, from the ability to control the flow of legislation, from control of resources, or through some independent legislative authority (as in Italy, Cotta 1994). Specialization is generally considered to be key to the ability of committees to be influential in the policy-making process. The controlling parliamentary party is a third place where power may be developed. For example, Germany is dominated by the *fraktionen* (party caucuses), argues Schüttemeyer, claiming they control "the selection and formulation of policies, the negotiation of legislation, the steering of the parliamentary process, [and] the allocation of resources for effective representation. . . ." (Copeland and Patterson 1994, 51).

Another critical characteristic of parliaments is that the individuals in those bodies are representatives. The consequences of the representative nature of these bodies are many and will be explored later. What is important here is that parliamentarians are present to act on the behalf of others—in a formal sense. Their selection is generally by election. Elections may be fair and competitive, biased and unfair, or patently rigged. The votes cast in these elections may be personal votes for individual candidates, votes for a particular party, or choices dominated, if not determined, by the selection of the executive. But the representational link is nearly always established by way of election. A variation from popular election is the selection of representatives to the national assembly by officials of lower units of government. The German Bundesrat exemplifies an upper chamber selected by lower units in the federal system, with members having explicit responsibility for linking those units (the *Lander*) to the national government. There are other bases for representation as well, with perhaps the most visible one being nobility, as in the anachronistic British House of Lords.

In general, there is a geographic basis for representation in national assemblies. The purpose of this geographic basis is to link representatives with specific groups of constituents. Like everything else, there is substantial variation in this linkage among differing electoral systems. At one end of the continuum is the single-member district system, often employing relatively small geographical units, like that in the United Kingdom to elect members of the House of Commons. At the other end are the more distant relationships embedded in a system invoking quite large multiple-member districts, the most striking being the case of Israel where the 120 members of the Knesset are elected in a single multimember district consisting of the entire country. In the former case, one person is entrusted with the representation of a specific and discrete constituency. In the latter case, the geographic linkage is weakened both by the size of the constituency and by overlapping responsibilities for representation of it. In the most extreme cases, national lists are used in some proportional electoral systems in a way that leaves some representatives without substantial geographic ties. These national lists are rosters of parliamentary candidates chosen by the political party organizations and offered on election ballots throughout the country. Even in proportional systems, elected representatives may still seek to develop more specific geographic linkages. In Costa Rica, for example, those elected to the National Assembly divide their multimember districts into smaller geographic units and allocate responsibilities for providing benefits to those units among fellow partisans (Taylor 1992).

Representatives are almost always selected to serve a discrete term and must return to their constituents for reelection upon completion of that term. The British House of Lords and the Canadian Senate are conspicuous exceptions to this general practice; their members enjoy hereditary or lifetime appointments. Electing representatives for a fixed term of office serves a variety of purposes, but primary among them is accountability. Term lengths vary, but commonly they range from two to six years. Short terms of office are intended to keep representatives closer to their constituents and to ensure greater accountability. Longer terms generally allow representatives greater discretion and flexibility.

Most parliaments permit elected representatives to serve an unlimited number of terms, but in many cases there are limits to service. Costa Rica, Mexico, and the Philippines prohibit legislators from serving consecutive terms. In the 1990s the United States is engaged in a debate over the appropriateness of limits on the number of terms one can serve in its Congress.

We will return to both representation and electoral systems, but for now it is important to understand the general representative characteristic of parliamentary bodies. In general, parliamentarians are elected to act on behalf of constituents in subnational units. They serve a term and must be reelected if they are to continue in that role.

Eligibility and selection requirements common to democratic electoral processes mean that most parliamentarians are not typical, in a descriptive sense, of their nation's general populations or electorates. As a general rule, legislators tend to share traits in common with the elite in a society rather than reflecting the variety of race and ethnicity, gender, social status, economic class, and occupational station found in the society. But a second general rule is that legislatures today are considerably more diverse than they have been in the past.

It is difficult to get good data regarding the racial and ethnic makeup of national assemblies. Some anecdotal evidence, though, seems strong and representative of the overall picture. In Nicaragua, representation of the 15 percent of the people who are black and indigenous is minuscule—three of ninety-three representatives in 1986 and two in 1990. In Costa Rica, representation by black and indigenous people has been virtually nonexistent—only one of fifty-seven representatives in 1986 and none in 1990 (where population estimates for these people range from 4 to 10 percent). In Australia, only one aboriginal has ever been seated in the national representative assembly. New Zealand is a prime example of a parliament in which a small number of seats is reserved for a designated minority group. There, four seats (less than 5 percent of the body) are designated for the indigenous Maoris, who constitute about 20 percent of New Zealand's total population (see Saint-Germain 1994).

Universally, women have been substantially underrepresented in national parliaments. In most otherwise democratic countries of the world, suffrage was extended to women only in the twentieth century. Women have had the right to seek parliamentary election in Switzerland since 1971, in Kenya and Morocco since 1963, and in Brazil, Egypt, Greece, the Netherlands, and Peru only since the 1950s. Given the remarkably recent extension of voting rights to women in many nations, it should come as no surprise that women are seriously underrepresented in parliaments (Nelson and Chowdhury 1994). In only a handful of nations are as many as one-quarter of parliamentary memberships composed of women. In the overwhelming number of countries, women make up little more than a small minority (see Lovenduski and Norris 1993).

The pattern of representation for workers, less educated citizens, and those with generally lower status is very similar to the pattern described for women. In many societies, suffrage has been restricted on the basis of socioeconomic class. Even when voting rights ultimately are granted, lower classes may remain underrepresented. It is well known that individuals in the professional, managerial, white-collar, and business occupations account for the vast majority of the members of parliaments. By the same token, lawyers are also vastly overrepresented in the parliaments of most polities (see Loewenberg and Patterson 1979, ch. 3). Although there are marked occupational and social class biases in the composition of parliamentary bodies, upper-class dominance in the older assemblies of Europe has diminished substantially over the past century (as in the case of France; see Dogan 1967).

Unmistakably, parliaments do not mirror the societies in which they are found, but their memberships have become more diverse as the suffrage is expanded. That is not to say that expansion of the suffrage is a sufficient condition and will alone lead to more representative parliaments, but it does appear to be a necessary condition. Barriers other than voting rights may constrain the representation of groups in parliaments. Moreover, many of the other strictures on parliamentary representation, such as constraints on groups' access to the ballot or insufficient resources for effective campaigning, may prove more insurmountable to excluded groups.

PARLIAMENTS AND THEIR FUNCTIONS

In the preceding discussion of the structural characteristics of parliaments, we implied a variety of functions that might properly be traced to the structural features of parliamentary organizations. We need to explore the more significant of these functions. We have observed that purely functional analysis of parliaments can be problematical because there is no function or set of functions either exclusively parliamentary or universally undertaken by parliaments. Moreover, functional interpretations of parliaments may be confounded by invoking similar but overlapping concepts with inconsistent usage. Yet, despite the pitfalls and limitations of a functional approach to parliaments, it remains true that parliaments, like all human organizations, do engage in recurring activities that have systematic consequences. Our task is to examine these recurring, consequential activities that help to define parliaments as political institutions (see, for instance, Jewell and Patterson 1966).

Conventionally, parliaments are said to perform three key functions: linkage, or representation; legitimation; and policy making, or addressing the problems of the polity. We consider each of these and then entertain other functions either less universally fulfilled by parliaments or less critical to the polity.

Representation

Parliaments, as we have noted, evolved from councils seeking personal influence over the executive. Eventually these councils came to have as their function acting on behalf of others. Over time, the justification for their existence and the nature of the institution became intimately connected with their standing as representative assemblies. In fact, many use the term "representative body" as a synonym for parliaments. The primary basis for the legitimate authority of these bodies is that they are representative—institutions operating in behalf of the larger body politic.

But to know that parliaments are representative institutions is only to scratch the surface of the conceptual and analytical problem; "representation" is a complex, slippery concept. In a formal sense, representation refers to the fact that some individuals are selected out of a larger body to operate on behalf of that constituency. Much of the thinking on representation, though, takes a much narrower view, reflecting a bias toward what one scholar calls a "demand input" model of representation (Wahlke 1971, 142–150). According to this model, the primary role of constituents is to make demands, primarily policy demands, on their representatives, who then act on those demands in a more or less satisfactory way. The process is profoundly one way. Constituents make their demands known; representation occurs when elected officials act upon constituents' demands.

While this model is unsatisfactorily incomplete, it captures an element critical to any notion of representation. The questions that naturally arise from the demand-input model are, "how, and how well, does this form of representation take place." Central to answering these questions is the role of elections. We do not want to confuse elections with representation, but elections generally are the strongest way to ensure an effective representational link, and they are, of course, the formal way of selecting most representatives. Thereby, the nature of the election has great impact on the nature of representation. Although elections are critical, there is reasonable agreement that they are not fully effective as mechanisms of control. The list of the shortcomings of elections as control mechanisms is long, but leading the list are the lack of competitiveness in some elections and the lack of voters' ability to make them work as needed.

The competitiveness of parliamentary elections is critical to the development of an effective system of representation. Many parliaments, we know, lack the independent capacity to influence the political outcomes that matter most to a society. One method of ensuring that parliaments lack that independent capacity is by controlling their memberships. In a number of countries, for instance, all or most of the members of the upper houses of bicameral parliaments are appointed by the head of state, not by independent election. Therefore, whether elections are fair says much about the nature of representation in a political system. On the one hand, fair and competitive elections are a way to ensure that parliamentarians are responsive to or represent the citizens of a nation. On the other hand, unfair and uncompetitive elections usually ensure responsiveness to some other power, usually an autocratic executive. In short, unfair elections do not work to ensure citizens' control.

Because nominally parliamentary institutions may be selected through elections of questionable integrity, Loewenberg and Patterson (1979) suggest that the notion of representation as a key function of parliaments is too narrow a conceptualization of this theoretical construct to give the complete picture. They elaborate upon the linkage function of representatives—the two-way relationship between constituents and the legislature. Parliamentarians serve as a critical link between the government and the citizenry. The success of this link may strongly affect the health of the polity even if elections do not function so as to ensure the congruence required by the demand-input conceptualization of representation. We will return to this broader notion of representation after completing the investigation of the demand-input model.

Fair elections can serve as mechanisms to promote responsiveness to constituent demands in a variety of ways. Under one model, voters can choose parliamentary candidates who mirror characteristics that voters consider critical. Farmers might elect farmers, for example. Once these elected representatives are in office, they will naturally tend to act on behalf of their constituents because they are like them in some central attribute. Unfortunately, there are serious problems with this model. First, elected representatives are not mirror images of the populace. Second, being like one's constituency in some descriptive manner is neither a necessary nor a sufficient condition for operating on behalf of that constituency. A farmer, for example, might act like a banker, or a banker might very effectively act on behalf of farmers.

A second method by which elections might serve to ensure that elected officials operate on behalf of their constituents requires that voters make carefully informed judgments about who will most likely and most often act in the desired manner and cast their vote accordingly. Theoretically, if the voters err or change their preferences, or if the elected officials change, these representatives can be removed from office when they stand for reelection. These confirming or disconfirming elections may well combine both prospective and retrospective judgments about who is the most appropriate representative.

There are, in reality, two general mechanisms by which voters can make these judgments. The first is personal. Voters evaluate candidates as individuals and cast their votes accordingly. Representatives gain office by virtue of a personal relationship with the constituency. The second derives from the responsible parties model. In this case, representation is filtered through a political party. When a party dominates the nomination of candidates, voters may respond more strongly to partisan cues than to the quality or characteristics of individual candidates. In most instances, citizens' electoral judgments reflect the combined influence of personal and party votes.

Regardless of the vehicle, empirical research on the ability of voters to exercise the discretion available to them leaves open serious questions about whether they can actually operate in a manner that facilitates this critical link. The inadequacies of voters are problematic for the responsible parties model, but they are critical for the personal vote model. For either model to work, voters must have developed their own views on a topic, candidates or parties must develop alternative views for presentation to the voters, voters must see and understand party differences, voters must judge which positions best reflect their own views, and finally voters must somehow weigh all issues and reach a reasonable overall judgment. The systematic research on this matter, although it focuses primarily on U.S. elections, shows that voters fail at every step of the way (for example, Hurley and Hill 1980). In addition, although the requirements of voters might appear to be less stringent when they are trying to evaluate parties rather than candidates, Wahlke (1971) shows that the evidence is just as strong that the responsible parties model is also inadequate for ensuring this type of responsiveness. In short, the overwhelming evidence indicates that voters are incapable of ensuring quality representation through the ballot box alone.

What that conclusion means for representation is unclear. In an effort to develop further the concept of representation, Eulau (Wahlke, Eulau, et al. 1962, 267–286) builds on the critical distinctions among styles and focuses of representation noted by the eighteenth-century British philosopher and statesman Edmund Burke. By style, Eulau means the three representational roles played by the legislator: delegates, trustees, and politicos. The delegate role is the one that first comes into play in the demand-input model of representation. Representatives, playing the delegate role, will substantially endeavor to bend to the instructions of their constituents. Delegates do not exercise independent judgment or utilize their own consciences in their voting. If only delegate-representatives were elected, the responsibility of the voters would be diminished greatly, and their burdens would be transferred to the representatives. The problem here is that few representatives are pure delegates, and even those who seek to fulfill that role often find the task impossible when they discover their inability routinely and confidently to ascertain constituent views. The second role, that of trustee, is played by representatives who feel that they should exercise discretion and utilize their own judgment on their constituents' behalf. Under this unfolding of the representatives' role, the application of the demand-input model of representation is even more questionable. Indeed, empirical work suggests that it is fairly rare to find representatives playing a pure trustee role and indicates that many legislators combine roles, playing what Eulau and his colleagues label the "politico" role.

The distinctions among these roles become more complex when one considers them across political systems. Parliaments in polities with strong parties or that are divided into multimember districts are likely to draw few delegates because representatives will generally take their cues from other sources. Still, many variations are found. Costa Rica, for instance, has strong parties and multimember districts; therefore, most legislative voting reflects a trustee role filtered through the parties. Yet their members still feel compelled to act as delegates by providing benefits to artificially defined geographic constituencies.

Representation, Eulau observes, may also be understood in terms of its focus. Elected officials may attempt to represent varying constituencies. Eulau distinguishes between a national focus, on the one hand, and a local or district focus, on the other. Variations within parliaments do develop in these terms, but even greater differences—based on their historical development and crucial features of their electoral systems—can be unearthed across systems. Those representing large, multimembered districts are less likely to follow constituency imperatives slavishly and are more likely to have a national focus. But this certainly is not necessarily true: representatives of large districts may have those interests very much at the forefront of their minds.

Richard Fenno's research on the U.S. House of Representatives (1978) suggests that this notion may be too simplistic. Elected officials may well focus on portions of their constituency. Interestingly, Fenno found members of Congress responding in varying ways to geographic, reelection, primary, and personal constituencies. Indeed, members of parliaments are quite capable of making sophisticated judgments about portions of their constituencies. The focuses of representation may be segmented so that representatives tend to be responsive to a number of different components. Fenno's analysis of the U.S. Senate suggests that the linkage between representatives and their constituents evolves as the result of continued negotiations or exchanges taking place primarily during election campaigns and involving understandings which are, of course, ultimately subject to a vote of the people (Fenno 1996).

Such conceptual and theoretical elaborations of the concept of representation leave us many unresolved problems with the demand-input model. That conception of representation suggests that parliamentarians, the parliament, and ultimately the regime receive support primarily when the represented are content with the decisions made by the parliament. When citizens are fully satisfied with policy, they offer specific support and will continue to provide that support as long as they are satisfied. But Easton and others have called attention to the notion of "diffuse support," a generalized commitment or attachment to the system that is not dependent on any specific decisions made (1965, 273–274). Wahlke, for one, advocates a system-support model—one focusing on diffuse rather than specific support (1971).

Diffuse support ebbs from more nebulous factors. Wahlke's analysis calls attention to the efficacy of a more general notion of representation as the basis for diffuse support. Moreover, it is in the provision of the intangibles of representation that parliaments tend to excel. Parliamentary systems promote the development of symbolic attachments to the community and provide a sense of participation in decision making. Process rather than outcome matters most to the represented; symbols are important.

Elections are critical to diffuse support, but they are critical in a manner that is quite different from that for specific support. For the latter, elections are a way to try to ensure that representatives are properly informed regarding constituents' opinions and that they will act as desired. Elections are important to diffuse support because they are emblematic of a representational process that both values the authority of citizens and allows them to participate in the process.

Similarly, Eulau and Karps (1977) develop this aspect of representation by building on Hanna F. Pitkin's notion of representatives acting in a responsive manner. They identify four types of responsiveness that combine to constitute representation. The first three fit within the demand-input model of representation: (1) policy responsiveness, referring to public issues; (2) service responsiveness, referring to intervention with various parts of the government on behalf of constituents, most notably with the bureaucracy; and (3) allocation responsiveness, referring to obtaining benefits for representatives' constituencies.

A fourth type of responsiveness, called "symbolic responsiveness" by Eulau and Karps, "involves public gestures of a sort that create a sense of trust and support in the relationship between representative and represented" (p. 241). This mode of responsiveness is more symbolic and psychological than the others, but it is critical to maintaining system support. Ilter Turan, applying these concepts to Turkey, carries them even further (1994). Historically, he concludes that the Turkish legislature has played a critical role in that political system by institutionalizing symbolic responsiveness. That resource provided continuity and support for the polity in periods otherwise characterized by instability. Over time, symbolic responsiveness also facilitated the evolution of other types of responsiveness.

It is impossible to overstate the importance of the representational processes of parliamentary institutions. Parliaments are uniquely qualified to play various representational roles. The diffuse support accorded to such parliaments is critical to the ability of the system to survive. There is no single look of representation; there is no pervasive method for representation to be provided within a parliamentary system; and, there is no universally desired form of representation. What is critical is that parliaments perform this function in some way. Variations are found for a variety of reasons that merit careful consideration, but the bottom line is that representation and parliaments are so intertwined that it is difficult to imagine one without the other.

Legitimation

The legitimation function of parliaments is intimately entwined with their function of representation. Legitimation is the public recognition and acceptance of the right of parliament, and the government generally, to act in some manner and the corresponding obligation of citizens to abide by that action. Not only does this function embrace parliament, but it also comprehends the government and its policies and has critical ramifications for the ability of a polity to survive. If the legitimation function is working, at a minimum it results in the perception that parliament is acting properly on behalf of the citizens. If that perception occurs, it becomes possible to transfer parliamentary legitimacy to the entire governmental system. Finally, the undertakings or policies of the government will be perceived as legitimate outcomes of the activities of parliament and government. Because order in modern societies is generally maintained through the somewhat nebulous perception that the government and its actions are legitimate, this function is critical to a polity.

If legitimacy is built upon public perception, how does the legitimacy of parliaments arise? Parliamentary legitimacy is grounded in the representative character of the body. Although there are exceptions, the primary basis for this status is the way elections ensure that representatives will operate on behalf of the citizens. Other, less cogent foundations for legitimacy include the historical heritage of the institution or ideological claims, giving us, for example, the National *People's* Congress in China.

By themselves, fair elections do not ensure that legitimacy will be conferred upon the parliamentary system. For it to gain legitimacy, activities within the parliament must be seen as fair and appropriate. The importance of the equality of membership criterion is evident when one considers that parliamentary activities themselves must be perceived as fair. A well-known story about Abraham Lincoln has his entire cabinet opposing him on one of his initiatives. But he announces the votes, "Twelve nays and one aye, the 'ayes' have it." That decision-making rule may work in executive branches, but if parliaments operated in that manner the value of representation would be severely diminished. The legislative process must be, and must be seen to be, grounded in fair procedures. The legitimacy of parliaments hinges upon the perception that the rules are unbiased and that the majority has a reasonable capacity to work its will.

For a legitimate parliament to transfer that legitimacy to the broader political system requires that the citizens of a nation see parliament as having a reasonable and appropriate role in the decision making in the system. A parliament bearing no substantial role in the political process and in making binding decisions may be perceived as meaningless. At the same time, even legitimate parliaments may not contribute to the legitimacy of the governmental system. In fact, the legitimizing role of parliaments hinges on the wide range of parliamentary activities that the public values and accepts as a proper basis for the legitimacy of the entire polity. Perversely, perfunctory legislative sessions, pro forma votes on legislation, and rubber-stamping the selection of the executive may be found acceptable by a public willing to confer legitimacy on a weak assembly. Such a public may even be willing to condone the transfer of parliament's legitimacy to the regime.

Once the legitimacy of the government is established, it is a short step to ensuring that the actions of the government are considered legitimate and merit respect. In most systems, that legitimacy is conferred by formal action on the part of the parliament. Legislation that deals with most substantial policies is subject to a vote in parliament and becomes law only after engendering majority support. Variations abound as to what laws are subject to parliamentary action and what are the acceptable mechanisms of enactment. And the influence of the parliament may be great or very limited, within an overarching facade of parliamentary authority.

Conferral of legitimacy on political regimes is so fundamental that even autocrats may attempt to establish or reestablish parliaments in an effort to consolidate their own power. But governing solely by coercion is difficult if not impossible in modern societies; hence, the establishment of even a modest amount of legitimacy is critical to the ability to sustain power.

Addressing the problems of the polity

A parliament designed to represent society at large and perceived as legitimate provides a natural forum for addressing problems that confront a polity. How parliament goes about coping with problems that require collective action varies dramatically from society to society, but parliaments are the political institutions peculiarly suited to serve as the arena for policy confrontation and action. The application of the policy-making function is the nearly universal role of parliaments in the formal enactment of legislation into law.

Parliament's husbandry in enacting legislation may be expanded to include influencing or even determining the content of that legislation. The U.S. Congress is at one extreme on the world continuum of legislative influence—having the capacity to draft its own legislation and enact laws even over the opposition of the executive. At the other extreme are any number of assemblies that might attempt to affect the content of legislation only at great personal risk. But most parliamentary institutions are somewhere between these poles. In recent decades, parliaments have tended to increase in institutional strength and importance. Far from a world in which there is a "decline of parliaments," in many polities today (as in such cases as Italy or the countries of Scandinavia) parliaments are institutionally stronger and more heavily utilized because political executives find it difficult to act with unity and dispatch (see Bryce 1921, Crick 1964, and Robins 1994).

Beyond the legislative process, parliaments may come to be relied upon to address fundamental societal problems, such as that of nation building in newly independent states. The Kenyan parliament provides a pertinent illustration of nation-building efforts (see Loewenberg and Patterson 1979). Kenyan parliamentarians are well known to the citizenry, travel between the core and the periphery of the nation, and serve as a two-way communications link. They deliver to their constituents both the benefits that can be forthcoming from the central government and the government's demands for taxes, service, and support. In so doing, MPs promote a sense of affiliation with national government as well as a sense of responsibility for adhering to its dictates.

Representation in one or both houses of a parliament may be designed to give both voice and authority to a segment of society that is otherwise left out of the system and requires special attention. This special representative purpose may be served through some form of federalism, with representation in a subnational assembly to provide a voice for some racial, ethnic, or religious minority. Perhaps as many as twenty national parliaments, about 15 percent of these institutions around the world, explicitly reserve seats exclusively for representatives with specific descriptive characteristics (Laundy 1989).

A more subtle way that parliaments work to ameliorate the problems in a society is commonly labeled the "catharsis," or "safety valve," function. All societies exhibit cleavages of one kind or another, often precipitating violent disagreements. Parliaments provide a forum where voice can be given to these disagreements so that they can be resolved through nonviolent or acceptable forms of political decision making. Losers in a conflict are more likely to accept their fate if they feel they have been heard and were provided with a reasonable opportunity to have a say in the outcome.

In his analysis of the Brazilian National Congress, Robert Packenham identifies and explores yet another way in which a parliament may resolve conflict (1970). The "exit" function is utilized when normal methods of decision making fail. Under these circumstances, the Brazilian Congress was given unusual responsibility to develop a solution to a problem or to resolve an impasse. To break an impasse, the legislative body is handed a discrete task and asked to help the polity handle it when normal approaches have failed or, perhaps, when there is too much risk involved in the decision.

Other significant functions

Because parliaments fulfill so many different functions and because the value of each varies dramatically from society to society, it is risky to identify three primary functions or to develop a comprehensive list of functions. The three functions just discussed—representation, legitimation, and addressing problems—are considered critical both because of their centrality to the institution and because of how commonly they are performed. But there are other very significant functions that merit attention.

One set of functions—interest articulation, aggregation, and mobilization—overlaps substantially with both the representation and the problem-addressing functions. Basically, these highly related functions begin with the notion that there are varying interests in society and that these interests generally need and will gain expression. Parliaments provide a forum and a purpose for articulating those interests. Both the selection process for legislators and the law-passing function provide motivation for articulating varying interests. They also provide mechanisms and a focus to draw many interests into a smaller number of aggregated interests and to mobilize those interests to achieve their political goals. These functions are generally viewed as important for political parties, but they apply to parliamentary institutions as well.

Oversight of the executive is also a critical parliamentary function performed in quite different ways in different systems. In traditional parliamentary systems, oversight is so powerful that it includes both the selection and the removal of the executive. Where selection and removal powers are nonexistent or weak, oversight tends to be limited to review of the activities of the executive. Such reviews may be narrow in scope, taking the form of intervention on behalf of specific constituencies, or entail a more general review of administrative activities. In the latter case, committee hearings or budgetary deliberations provide the most common venues for oversight.

Other common and significant parliamentary functions include the recruitment and training of political officials. Commonly, parliamentary service is the initial point of entry into politics for many individuals, and it is the environment where budding politicians first learn about the processes and substance of politics. Political campaigns and legislative debates, in specific, and the linkage function, in general, make parliaments great educational institutions (see Muir 1982). The open character of most legislatures, fermenting and extolling the expression of alternative viewpoints, provides information, opinion, and competing judgments that help educate members and the public at large. Finally, while it has been alluded to in many contexts, it should be made explicit that in many polities legislators perform direct constituent services through intervention with agencies of the executive branch. Because they are key links between individual citizens and the central government, representatives are the officials to whom citizens often look for help when they are experiencing difficulties.

Parliamentary activities vary in scope and depth from one polity to another, and because the functions of parliament are not immutable or requisite, parliaments exhibit admirable complexity and variety. What makes parliaments such vibrant institutions is that their nature fosters a capacity to serve many differing and critical functions in a society. What they actually do depends on the vagaries of a national history, cultural norms, institutional preferences, political structures, and the peculiar range of alternatives perceived to lie in the future.

PARLIAMENTS IN THEIR ENVIRONMENTS

Having developed some sense of parliaments as institutions, what they are and what they do, we turn to the task of outlining how the character and activities of parliaments vary according to the environments in which they find themselves. Specifically, the character of parliaments depends on the electoral system, relations with the nation's executive, and the shape and imperatives of the political party system.

Electoral systems

We have abundantly alluded to the importance of electoral systems to parliamentary bodies. Elections are at the core of establishing the character of parliaments. Almost universally, legislators are selected by direct or indirect election. But the dynamics of those elections can be quite diverse. Where citizens elect representatives directly, the tie of the members of parliament to their constituencies is straightforward. But indirect elections tie the representative to an intermediary (the electors) rather than directly to the people. Where the intermediary is a subnational agency or assembly, representatives may be responsive primarily to the subnational units that elected them. In fact, indirectly elected officials commonly have no discretion in casting their votes, or they are subject to easy recall should they depart from the mandate given to them by the intermediaries to whom they are accountable. In general, indirect elections are constitutional arrangements designed to protect specific elements of society. We see, then, Chinese assemblymen chosen indirectly to protect the interests of the ruling communist elite; French senators chosen by local electoral colleges to represent local communities; and U.S. senators, throughout the nineteenth century, chosen by state legislatures to defend states' rights.

Direct elections more specifically tie the representative to the citizenry, but variations in this type of system abound. We have noted that frequent elections in small, single-member districts strengthen the personal link between the representative and the represented. Generally, the most important distinctions are due to differences in the requirements for election and the number of representatives chosen in each district. In single-member districts, candidates may gain office either by plurality or majority vote. In single-member districts with a plurality-vote requirement, a small number (usually, two) of relatively centrist parties tend to provide the competition, if any, as in the United States where almost all national and state legislators are either Republicans or Democrats. Entrance is difficult for new or small parties because they have to gain more votes than all of the competing parties, and thus they lack real bargaining power. The primary exception to this rule is when smaller parties have a concentrated geographic base—and these exceptions abound. Majority systems, though, give greater power to small parties. Depending on how the system moves toward a second election, small parties find themselves able to bargain with larger parties, trading support in some areas for representation in others. France has utilized a two-election system in various ways throughout the history of the Fifth Republic, but one constant outcome has been the survival of many fluid parties.

Multimember districts tend to have a proportional basis for representation of the parties. Depending on the specifics of the system, lists of candidates are provided by the parties, and candidates on the party lists win seats in parliament in proportion to the party vote. The larger the district, the more effectively the mathematics work out, but rules do vary. Germany, for example, provides for single-member districts but also utilizes national lists to bring the party proportions into balance. But Germany, like most proportional systems, also establishes a minimum percentage of the vote that a party must receive in order to gain representation in the parliament. Proportional systems tend to reflect better the diversity in a society resulting, often, in a larger number of parties seated in the parliament.

Relationship with the executive

To understand the legislature in a given political system, one must look at its relationship with the executive. On the one hand, we have presidential systems with independent executives, and on the other, we have parliamentary systems (here, using *parliamentary* in a technical sense—also periodically referred to as cabinet government or prime ministerial government) that have a fusion of executive and legislative personnel.

Presidential systems tend to have a marked separation of powers and duties as between the executive and legislative branches, but the critical distinction is in the methods of selection and removal. In presidential systems, the times and manner of choosing legislature and executive are distinct and separate. Different ballots may be used for elections to the two governmental branches, and choices lie in the hands of different constituencies. The rules of selection typically entail differences in electoral rules, dates of elections, and lengths of terms, all intended to put distance between the legislature and the president. In presidential systems, removal of executives before their terms expire is difficult or impossible. Generally, presidents are not accountable to the legislature for their job performance, and they can be removed only when found to have violated some sacred code of legal, ethical, or constitutional conduct.

The fact that a legislature exists in a presidential system tells us a lot about the way it will operate, but it tells us little about legislative power and influence. Legislatures in presidential systems may be vibrant and influential, but more commonly they are tools of a powerful central figure who has great discretion to perform independently.

Parliamentary systems are those in which the chief executives arise from among the ranks of the parliament's membership, are subject to selection by parliament, and may be removed from office simply because the body no longer has confidence in them. In some cases, the choice of a prime minister is obvious, but in others it may be difficult to find someone who can garner majority support. In political systems with strong parties and with a limited number of parties, parliamentary elections may revolve around candidates preselected to serve as prime minister, should their party receive a majority. In this case, parliamentary voting is instrumental—merely a way to select the chief executive. Great Britain provides the most ready example of this dynamic. No-confidence votes are very rare, resulting from either an intraparty squabble that may actually be resolved elsewhere or a divisive issue that splits parties in a critical way.

Most parliamentary elections in multiparty systems are less determinant of who will serve as the next prime minister than are elections in Great Britain. If no party receives a majority, there may be a number of viable candidates for prime minister. The question is which one can put together a coalition of parties and members so as to gain majority support. Alternatively, members of parliament may agree to allow a minority government when no stable majority coalition can be formed. When a majority coalition emerges, there may be limits on how long that majority can be maintained. Votes of no confidence or prime ministerial resignations are fairly common in some systems, as in Italy where cabinet reshuffling and prime ministerial changes are especially frequent. When these occur, a new majority, a new cabinet, and hence a new prime minister might develop. Depending on the rules of the body, its customs and traditions, and the political situation, a new election might be called. With a new election, the citizenry of a nation is afforded an opportunity to develop a new majority in parliament. Accordingly, elections may aggregate interests in a way that gives a new majority, and thus a new government, a clearer direction and, perhaps, a mandate to undertake a program of action.

As in presidential systems, the power of the representative assembly in parliamentary systems varies dramatically among democratic societies. Parliament may have essentially no independent role in the selection of the prime minister, where strong party discipline minimizes its independent impact on the choice of executive and on the legislative process altogether. Or the cabinet may find itself incapable of acting independently because it lacks the capacity to ensure majority support within parliament. As a result, parliament itself might be the location where critical policies are discussed, bargains struck, and decisions made.

Party systems

A third critical environmental component that interacts with the previous two, and that greatly influences the way parliaments work, is the political party system. Two aspects of the party system merit focused attention: the number of parties and their strength. The number of parties in the field has several obvious consequences for the legislative process. The ability to legislate depends upon putting together a majority of votes. When there is a larger number of parties, that majority is likely to be a multiparty coalition, an aggregation composed of members of more than one political party. Because building coalitions across parties is more difficult than constructing majorities within a party, the problem of governing becomes more complex with multiple parties than with a two-party system. Another implication of having multiple parties in parliament is that the legislative institution then becomes the location where preferences are aggregated. In a two-party system, preferences are aggregated by the parties where one is confident of achieving majority status. In that event, aggregation takes place outside parliament. Where no party has a majority in parliament, aggregation of preferences tends to occur among competing political forces within the halls of parliament.

The number of parties represented in a parliament is a more critical factor in parliamentary systems than in presidential systems. Parliamentary systems are built upon the supposition that the prime minister has majority support, at least tacitly. Absent that support, a vote of no confidence can remove prime ministers from office. In reality, minority governments are not at all uncommon. Erik Damgaard's (1994) work on Scandinavian parliaments illustrates the remarkable capacity of parliaments to adapt to unusual political circumstances. These Nordic representative assemblies have grown in influence because more and more important decisions are necessarily made in the bosom of parliament rather than by the executive.

Parliamentary parties are naturally important and influential in relation to their strength of numbers, their moral force, and their ideological cohesiveness. Parties are strong if they can maintain the support of voters or control processes for nominating candidates. They also are strong if they can hold the votes of their members in the legislative arena. Party voting is the ultimate reflection of disciplined and strong parties. Strong parties allow for a coherence of position and for greater assurance and predictability in the legislative process.

CONCLUDING OBSERVATIONS

Parliaments are remarkably diverse in appearance and role. Their influence in societies tends to flourish because of the special function they perform as the most representative of all political institutions, with both unusual capacity and unparalleled opportunity to serve the state and the people. Parliaments are very recognizable institutions. And, yet, the world's family of parliaments is composed of individual institutions variegated in size, shape, scope, and power. Each is unique in the impress of its institutional history, its overall constitutional structure, and the needs of its society.

In this introduction, we have sought to define and identify parliaments by their structures and to highlight the varied functions they fulfill in societies. The most significant of those identified are representation, legitimation, and policy making, or addressing problems. Moreover, we have explored how differences in constitutional systems affect the way parliaments operate. The full richness of the institution can be appreciated only when exploring them in detail, parliament by parliament, representative by representative, constituency by constituency. So doing heightens awareness of the importance of representative assemblies in institutionalizing free government and strengthening democratic societies.

Gary W. Copeland and Samuel C. Patterson

REFERENCES

Bryce, James. 1921. *Modern democracies.* New York: Macmillan.

Copeland, Gary W., and Samuel C. Patterson, eds. 1994. *Parliaments in the modern world: Changing institutions.* Ann Arbor: University of Michigan Press.

Cotta, Maurizio. 1994. The rise and fall of "entrality" of the Italian parliament: Transformations of the executive-legislative subsystem after the Second World War. In *Parliaments in the modern world: Changing institutions,* ed. Gary W. Copeland and Samuel C. Patterson. Ann Arbor: University of Michigan Press.

Crick, Bernard. 1964. *The reform of Parliament.* London: Wiedenfeld and Nicolson.

Damgaard, Erik. 1994. The strong parliaments of Scandinavia: Continuity and change of Scandinavian parliaments. In *Parliaments in the modern world,* ed. Gary W. Copeland and Samuel C. Patterson. Ann Arbor: University of Michigan Press.

———, ed. 1992. *Parliamentary change in Nordic countries.* Oslo: Scandinavian University Press.

Dogan, Mattei. 1967. Les filières de la carrière politique en France. *Revue Française de Sociologie* 8: 468–492.

Easton, David. 1965. *A systems analysis of political life.* New York: Wiley.

Eulau, Heinz, and Paul D. Karps. 1977. The puzzle of representation: Specifying components of responsiveness. *Legislative Studies Quarterly* 2: 233–254.

Fenno, Richard F. 1996. *Senators on the campaign trail: The politics of representation.* Norman: University of Oklahoma Press.

———. 1978. *Home style: House members in their districts.* Boston: Little, Brown.

Gerlich, Peter. 1973. The institutionalization of European parliaments. In *Legislatures in comparative perspective,* ed. Allan Kornberg. New York: McKay.

Hooper, Finley. 1967. *Greek realities: Life and thought in ancient Greece.* New York: Scribner's.

Hurley, Patricia A., and Kim Quaile Hill. 1980. The prospects for issue voting in contemporary congressional elections: An assessment of citizen awareness and representation. *American Politics Quarterly* 8: 425–449.

Jewell, Malcolm E., and Samuel C. Patterson. 1966. *The legislative process in the United States.* New York: Random House.

Laundy, Philip. 1989. *Parliaments in the modern world.* Aldershot, U.K.: Dartmouth.

Loewenberg, Gerhard. 1971. The role of parliaments in modern political systems. In *Modern parliaments: Change or decline,* ed. Gerhard Loewenberg. Chicago: Aldine-Atherton.

Loewenberg, Gerhard, and Samuel C. Patterson. 1979. *Comparing legislatures.* Boston: Little, Brown.

Lovenduski, Joni, and Pippa Norris, eds. 1993. *Gender and party politics.* London: Sage.

Marongiu, Antonio. 1973. From pre-parliament to parliament. In *Medieval representative institutions,* ed. Thomas N. Bisson. Hinsdale, Ill.: Dryden Press.

Muir, William K., Jr. 1982. *Legislatures: California's school for politics.* Chicago: University of Chicago Press.

Nelson, Barbara J., and Najma Chowdhury, eds. 1994. *Women and Politics Worldwide.* New Haven, Conn.: Yale University Press.

Packenham, Robert A. 1970. Legislatures and political development. In *Legislatures in developmental perspective,* ed. Allan Kornberg and Lloyd D. Musolf. Durham, N.C.: Duke University Press.

Polsby, Nelson W. 1975. Legislatures. In *Handbook of political science,* ed. Fred Greenstein and Nelson A. Polsby. Reading, Mass.: Addison-Wesley.

Post, Gaines. 1973. Medieval parliaments a consequence of the revival of Roman law. In *Medieval representative institutions,* ed. Thomas N. Bisson. Hinsdale, Ill.: Dryden Press.

Robins, Lynton. 1994. Chronicles of decline. *Parliamentary Affairs* 47: 310–313.

Saint-Germain, Michelle A. 1994. Representation in Costa Rica and Nicaragua. In *Electoral systems in comparative perspective: Their impact on women and minorities,* ed. Wilma Rule and Joseph F. Zimmerman. Westport, Conn.: Greenwood Press.

Stubbs, William. 1972. Stubbs on the development of parliaments in Europe. In *The creation of medieval parliaments,* ed. Bertie Wilkinson. New York: Wiley.

Taylor, Michelle M. 1992. Formal versus informal incentive structures and legislative behavior: Evidence from Costa Rica. *Journal of Politics* 54: 1055–1073.

Turan, Ilter. 1994. The Turkish legislature: From symbolic to substantive representation. In *Parliaments in the modern world,* ed. Gary W. Copeland and Samuel C. Patterson. Ann Arbor: University of Michigan Press.

Wahlke, John C. 1971. Policy demands and system support: The role of the represented. In *Modern parliaments: Change or decline,* ed. Gerhard Loewenberg. Chicago: Aldine-Atherton.

Wahlke, John C., Heinz Eulau, William Buchanan, and Leroy C. Ferguson. 1962. *The legislative system: Explorations in legislative behavior.* New York: Wiley.

Wilkinson, Bertie, ed. 1972. *The creation of medieval parliaments.* New York: Wiley.

WORLD ENCYCLOPEDIA OF PARLIAMENTS AND LEGISLATURES

AFGHANISTAN

OFFICIAL NAME: Islamic State of Afghanistan (Pashtu, De Afghanistan Islami Doulat; Dari, Doulat-e-Islami Afghanistan)
CAPITAL: Kabul
POPULATION: 22,664,000 (1996 est.)
DATE OF INDEPENDENCE: August 19, 1919 (from the United Kingdom)
DATE OF CURRENT CONSTITUTION: None
FORM OF GOVERNMENT: Transitional
LANGUAGES: Pashtu, Dari, Uzbek, Turkmen
MONETARY UNIT: Afghani
FISCAL YEAR: March 21–March 20
LEGISLATURE: None
NUMBER OF CHAMBERS: —
NUMBER OF MEMBERS: —
PERCENTAGE OF WOMEN: —
TERM OF LEGISLATURE: —
MOST RECENT NATIONAL ELECTION: —
MINIMUM AGE FOR VOTING: —
MINIMUM AGE FOR MEMBERSHIP: —
SUFFRAGE: —
VOTING: —
ADDRESS: —
TELEPHONE: —
FAX: —

A landlocked country in Central Asia *(see map, p. 519)*, Afghanistan has been rent by military conflict almost without stop since 1979, when Soviet armed forces entered the country to prop up the Marxist government that had come to power in a military coup the year before. The legislature established in 1988 by the Marxist regime, the National Assembly (Meli Shura), was dissolved in April 1992 following the regime's ouster by *mujaheddin* fighters. There is no functioning parliament in Afghanistan today, and the possibility of establishing a constitutional and democratic government is remote.

BACKGROUND

Conquered by Alexander the Great (329–327 B.C.), Jenghiz Khan (c. 1220), Tamerlane (late fourteenth century), and others, Afghanistan was at the crossroads of Persian, Indian, and central Asian civilizations. In the nineteenth century the land of present-day Afghanistan remained the scene of conflict and intrigue, as Great Britain and Russia vied for influence in the region. An agreement signed in 1907 by those two powers granted Great Britain foreign policy prerogatives over a nominally independent Afghanistan. After World War I the emir of Afghanistan freed his country of British influence by invading British India, which induced the British to grant full Afghani independence through the Treaty of Rawalpindi in 1919.

From 1919 until 1973 the country was ruled by traditional Islamic emirs, some of whom styled themselves "king" and undertook limited modernization in politics, social relations, and economic development. In July 1973 Mohammad Zahir Shah was overthrown by military officers who, in league which a small but restive middle class, blamed the king for a failing economy, recurrent famine, and insufficient political reforms.

The Republic of Afghanistan proclaimed in 1973 under Lt. Gen. Mohammad Daoud Khan lasted five years. Daoud was overthrown April 27, 1978, in a left-wing military coup. The coup plotters announced the formation of the Marxist Democratic Republic of Afghanistan and the appointment of Nur Mohammad Taraki, secretary general of the People's Democratic Party of Afghanistan, as prime minister. An appointed Revolutionary Council was formed in lieu of a legislature. Taraki, possibly with Soviet backing, almost immediately became engaged in a power struggle with Hafizullah Amin, whose hardline policies toward the increasingly restive Muslim tribes was fueling the organization of antigovernment *mujaheddin* guerrilla bands.

SOVIET INVASION AND AFTERMATH

Taraki died under mysterious circumstances sometime in late September 1979. Soviet troops entered the country three months later, and Amin was killed during the initial intervention, also under mysterious circumstances. The Soviet Union installed Babrak Karmal to power, but the *mujaheddin* were no more amenable to Karmal than they had been to Amin. The Soviet military fought side-by-side with Afghani government troops in a futile effort to protect the regime until February 1989, when they withdrew.

In April 1988, in preparation for the Soviet withdrawal, the governments of the United States, Pakistan, Afghanistan, and the Soviet Union signed a series of agreements that provided for, among other things, the formation of a representative legislature, the National Assembly (Meli Shura). The *mujaheddin,* however, holding the upper hand on the battlefield and distrusting the government, refused to participate in the elections. In May 1988 the Revolutionary Council was abolished and the National Assembly assumed its functions. But the National Assembly was never a functioning legislature, and it was eclipsed within months by a newly created Supreme Council for the Defense of the Homeland.

The Marxist regime, headed by Mohammad Najibullah, who had succeeded Karmal in May 1986, fought on without direct Soviet military involvement until April 1992. *Mujaheddin* forces compelled Najibullah's resignation on April 16 and entered the capital, Kabul, at the end of the month. They abolished the National Assembly that had been established in 1988 and created a fifty-member Leadership Council.

Fitful attempts made between 1992 and 1994 to hold national elections and convene a legislature fell victim to civil war. The *mujaheddin* had never been a monolithic fighting force. Like Afghanistan itself, the *mujaheddin* were divided by ethnicity (Pashtun, Tajik, Hazara, and Uzbek, primarily), by region (the regions corresponding to ethnicity), by clan and tribe, and by religion (the country is roughly 84 percent Sunni and 15 percent Shiʿa, and there is divergence even among members of these branches of Islam). Indeed, even at the height of Soviet involvement the various factions spent much energy fighting one another.

In 1994 a potent new force, Taliban (meaning "Islamic theology students"), arrived on the scene with little warning, vowing to install a traditional Islamic government. Formed by theology students studying in the neighboring provinces of Pakistan, Taliban steamrolled through government opposition. The predominantly Pashtun (and southern) Taliban overthrew the largely Tajik (and northern) Leadership Council, capturing Kabul in September 1996. But Taliban faces potent opposition from rival ethnic groups and clans, and the civil war continues to simmer.

George Thomas Kurian

ALBANIA

OFFICIAL NAME: Republic of Albania (Republika e Shqipërisë)
CAPITAL: Tirana
POPULATION: 3,249,000 (1996 est.)
DATE OF INDEPENDENCE: November 28, 1912 (from the Ottoman Empire)
DATE OF CURRENT CONSTITUTION: Adopted April 29, 1991 (interim)
FORM OF GOVERNMENT: Parliamentary democracy
LANGUAGES: Albanian (official), Greek
MONETARY UNIT: Lek
FISCAL YEAR: Calendar year
LEGISLATURE: People's Assembly (Kuvënd Popullore)
NUMBER OF CHAMBERS: One
NUMBER OF MEMBERS: 155
PERCENTAGE OF WOMEN: —
TERM OF LEGISLATURE: Four years
MOST RECENT LEGISLATIVE ELECTION: June 29 and July 6, 1997
MINIMUM AGE FOR VOTING: 18
MINIMUM AGE FOR MEMBERSHIP: 21
SUFFRAGE: Universal and direct
VOTING: Optional
ADDRESS: People's Assembly, Tirana
TELEPHONE: (355 42) 32 003
FAX: (355 42) 27 949

The Republic of Albania, a mountainous country situated in southeastern Europe on the Balkan peninsula *(see map, p. 749),* ended nearly five decades of communist domination and isolation in 1991. Since then, though beset by economic difficulties, political turmoil, and accusations of electoral fraud, Albania has been a parliamentary democracy with a unicameral legislature and a president as head of state and prime minister as head of government.

HISTORICAL BACKGROUND

After the Roman Empire was divided into eastern and western parts in A.D. 395, Albania came under control of the Byzantine (Eastern) Empire. In the fifteenth century the Ottoman Turks invaded the area, and Albania was incorporated into the Ottoman Empire in the second part of that century (though the Turks never fully controlled the entire territory of modern Albania). Albania finally gained independence in 1912. The selection of a German prince as Albania's king resulted in internal strife that lasted until the outbreak of World War I, in 1914. The war brought periods of Italian, Greek, Serbian, and Austrian occupation that drained the country economically and contributed further to Albania's enormous hardships.

Reestablished in 1920, Albania was proclaimed a constitutional monarchy in 1928, under King Zog I. The constitution provided for a two-chamber parliament composed of the Council, whose members were appointed by the king, and the elected Chamber of Deputies.

Albania was occupied by Italy during World War II. The Soviet Union's military successes during the war strengthened the Albanian Communist Party, headed by Enver Hoxha, a young teacher educated in the West. At the end of 1945, with the war over, the Albanian communists called a meeting of a Constituent Assembly, which, on January 11, 1946, proclaimed the establishment of the People's Republic of Albania. Two months later, on March 14, the country's first communist constitution was adopted. In the late 1950s the country's relations with the post-Stalinist Soviet Union cooled, and an alliance with China brought a period of isolation for the country. In 1977 Albania adopted a second postwar constitution that emphasized the great progress made toward communism. To highlight this transformation, the constitution added the word *socialist* to the name of the state, and the country became the People's Socialist Republic of Albania.

When Ramiz Alia, Hoxha's successor as president and first secretary of the ruling Party of Labor, assumed power in 1985, many people hoped he would follow Soviet leader Mikhail Gorbachev's example and bring reforms. Contrary to these expectations, the situation in Albania remained essentially the same, with the personality cult established by Hoxha still dominating.

The first outright challenges to the communist regime came in late 1990. President Alia announced that the elections of March 1991 would be by secret ballot and multichoice, but he refused to allow multiparty elections. On December 8, 1990, student protests erupted at Tirana University. The protests evolved into a pro-democracy movement, and on December 11, President Alia agreed to meet with the student leaders. As a result of this meeting and of mounting demonstrations, Alia authorized the formation of opposition parties.

THE DRAFT CONSTITUTION

The constitution-making process began in the fall of 1990, when a parliamentary commission was formed to draft a new constitution. The first draft was completed in December 1990, and work on a second draft proceeded as the country moved toward the spring 1991 elections. Disputes over the second draft, dated March 1991, focused on several issues: separation of powers, regulation of economic activity, human rights protections, the judiciary, and constitutional courts.

The framework describing the basic philosophical concepts of the Albanian constitution was not clear, however. The March 1991 draft referred to Albania as a "state of law" that was "based on social justice, the protection of human rights and freedoms, and on political pluralism" (Article 2). This concept in a classical sense comprises the idea of division of powers, the most venerated principle of Western constitutionalism. In contrast, socialist constitutional jurisprudence usually rejected the doctrine of division of powers as incompatible with the idea of parliamentary supremacy. In fact, the doctrine of division of powers was irreconcilable with the totalitarian leadership of the communist parties and, as such, could not be among the major principles of socialist constitutionalism. Unlike some constitutional drafts in other new east central European democracies, such as Bulgaria, Poland, or the Czech Republic, the Albanian draft did not recognize this principle explicitly. It referred to the People's Assembly, the country's unicameral legislature, as "the supreme organ of state power," whereas the Council of Ministers was not referred to as the executive power but, as is typical in socialist constitutions, was called "the supreme executive organ."

The Albanian draft set up a framework for a parliamentary system in which the two branches of government, the legislative and the executive, were more or less fused. The legislature was, however, as in all socialist countries, by far the supreme organ, able to vote the executive out of office without a national election by the people. The People's Assembly also had the exclusive right to adopt and amend the constitution, to adopt statutes, and to elect the president and the Council of Ministers. The imbalance between the governmental bodies did not matter under the communist regime, when the apparently powerful legislature and weak executive were, in fact, under the control of the Communist Party. In the new postsocialist parliamentary system, however, the constitutionally confirmed frailty of the executive bodies would likely result in the impotency of the whole decision-making process.

The drafters clearly wanted to keep the concept of ownership of property close to the socialist model. Although the draft stated that private property could be expropriated only for public needs and that the state did not have a monopoly over ownership, public ownership was still privileged. Land and underground resources were the property of the state. There were no declarations of the marketization of the economy. In fact, the draft contained numerous references to "central planning" as a mechanism to harmonize national and local interests. Such phrases are reminiscent of the traditional rhetoric of communist constitutions.

FORMATION OF PARTIES AND THE FIRST FREE ELECTIONS

The Democratic Party—made up of students and intellectuals—was the first opposition party to form. Six other parties formed before the spring 1991 elections: the Republican Party, the Democratic Front, the environmentalist Greens, the procommunist Agrarian Party, the Albanian Women's Committee, and Omonia, the Democratic Union of the Greek Minority.

The first multiparty parliamentary elections since the communists took over in 1944 took place in two rounds, on March 31 and April 7. As predicted, the communists, acting under the pretense of reform, were victorious at the ballot box, receiving the vast majority of their support from rural areas. The Democratic Party received most of its support from cities, including the capital, Tirana. These elections resulted in a 250-member parliament consisting of both hardline communists and moderates. The communist Party of Labor held 168 seats—more than a two-thirds majority.

President Alia, surprisingly, failed to win a seat. The apparent upset was not, however, the end of his political career. A new draft constitution, introduced by Alia and the Party of Labor immediately preceding the March 31 elections, stated that the National Assembly could elect anyone as president as long as the candidate met all requirements for being elected a deputy. The draft constitution did not explicitly require that the person be a member of parliament. Because the Party of Labor won a parliamentary majority, it had sufficient strength, in April 1991, to push through a temporary "Law on the Major Constitutional Provisions," despite resistance from the opposition. After passing this interim constitution, it elected Alia as president.

GOVERNMENT UNDER THE INTERIM CONSTITUTION

The interim constitution is still far from Western standards, and, like the March 1991 draft, has a number of inconsistencies. For example, Article 3 recognizes the principle of division of powers. Typical of socialist constitutionalism, however, the constitution refers to the People's Assembly and the president as "the supreme organs of state power" and to the government as "the supreme organ of state administration." This language seems to suggest that the executive and legislative branches are not "the powers," but rather are organs of a unified power and, therefore, "not divided" powers.

The interim constitution recognized Albania's inclination to develop market mechanisms, but it used ambiguous language that may discourage foreign investment. Although it says the country's economy is based on diversity of ownership and free initiative, it also declares that the economy is regulated by the state.

The interim constitution increased the power of the president but left presidential prerogatives vague and relationships with the People's Assembly unclear. The president is the head of state and "represents the whole unity of the people" (Article 24). Still, the president is elected by the People's Assembly, not directly by the people. The right to nominate candidates for the presidency is reserved to a group of at least thirty deputies. In the case of multiple nominations, the number of candidates is reduced to two by consecutive ballots of the Assembly. In the first round, a winning candidate must receive a two-thirds majority of the votes of all deputies. In the second round, an absolute majority suffices for election. Candidates must be of Albanian nationality, at least forty years old, and eligible to be elected as a deputy to the People's Assembly. The president is elected for a five-year term and cannot serve more than two terms.

Under the interim constitution, the president is granted the right to appoint the chair of the Council of Ministers, accept the chair's resignation, and between sessions of the Assembly appoint and discharge the members of government. On the other hand, the Council of Ministers is controlled by the People's Assembly, and appointments of the president are subject to its approval. The president can request that the People's Assembly reexamine a law it has passed, but he can return a law only once.

The president may be discharged or released for violation of the constitution, betrayal of the republic, or reasons of health. The motion to remove the president must be submitted to the People's Assembly by a group of at least one-fourth of the deputies. The decision requires a vote of two-thirds of the deputies. The president cannot hold any other public office.

As long as it is not within the last six months of the president's term, the president, after consulting with the chair of the Council of Ministers and the chair of the presidium of the Assembly, can dissolve parliament. The circumstances in which parliament may be dissolved are unclear, however; the president is allowed to act only if the Assembly's "composition does not allow the performance of the functions of the Assembly" and makes it impossible to run the country.

The Council of Ministers, which includes the chair (the prime minister), vice chair (deputy prime minister), ministers, and others as defined by law, is "the highest executive and legislative organ." Performing their executive functions, the ministers may issue decisions, ordinances, and instructions. Similar acts issued by the president require the countersignature of the chair of the Council of Ministers or of the proper minister. The interim constitution does not specify the legislative functions of the Council of Ministers.

Ministers respond collegially for the acts of the council and individually for the acts of their institutions. The council has the following powers: it directs domestic and foreign policy; issues declarations, ordinances, and instructions in compliance with the constitution; coordinates and monitors local administrative organs; adopts security measures; reaches international agreements; devises economic and social plans; decides on the division or unification of administrative territorial units; adopts environmental protection measures; and invalidates the illegitimate acts of the ministries and other central organs of state administration.

PARTIES, ELECTIONS, AND DEPUTIES

Parties may be freely formed in Albania. To submit a national list of electoral candidates, a party must register candidates in thirty-three districts in nine regions of the country. The state contributes set amounts to party campaigns. Fifty percent of the state's contribution is granted in proportion to the number of nationwide votes received by the party in the previous election. Fifty percent of the set amount is divided among the parties in proportion to the number of candidates registered.

In 1992 an amendment to the constitution decreased the number of deputies from 250 to 140, which subsequently was raised to 155. Under the current regulation 115 seats are directly elected and 40 seats are allocated according to proportional representation.

Franchise laws guarantee electoral rights to all citizens at least eighteen years old, disqualifying those convicted of a crime and those declared mentally incompetent by a court. Citizens twenty-one years of age or older are eligible to be nominated as candidates for election if they live permanently in Albania or if they declare that they will live in the country permanently after the election. Nomination requires four hundred signatures from the district in which the candidate runs.

Deputies elected to the People's Assembly enjoy immunity. They cannot be controlled, detained, arrested, or prosecuted without the consent of the Assembly. They may be detained in cases in which they have committed an apparent and grave crime. Deputies may not be held legally responsible for actions and stands adopted while performing their duty as deputy.

THE LEGISLATIVE PROCESS AND JUDICIAL REVIEW

The parliament meets at least four times per year. The sessions convene on the decision of the presidium or as requested by the president of the republic, the Council of Ministers, or one-fourth of all of the deputies. The presidium consists of the chair and two deputy chairs.

In addition to its controlling functions over the government and central agencies of the state, the People's Assembly defines the main direction of the internal and foreign policy of the state; adopts, amends, and interprets the constitution; approves economic programs and the state budget; and ratifies and denounces political and military treaties, border agreements, and fundamental human rights and duties of citizens. The Assembly also grants amnesty and decides on referendums, wars, and states of emergency. It elects and discharges the president of the republic. Additionally, the parliament elects, appoints, and discharges the Supreme Court and the attorney general.

The People's Assembly elects from among its ranks permanent and temporary commissions. The permanent commissions examine draft laws and control the legality of the executive acts of the president and of the ministers. The temporary commissions are created for certain questions submitted by the Assembly.

Legislative initiative lies with the president, the Council of Ministers, every deputy, and groups of at least 20,000 citizens with voting rights. Laws and other acts of the People's Assembly are deemed adopted when voted on by a majority of the present deputies; at least one-third of the total membership of the Assembly must be present. Constitutional laws require the vote of a qualified majority of two-thirds of all the deputies. Laws are declared in the official legislative gazette no later than fifteen days after their adoption.

In April 1992 the People's Assembly amended the Law on the Major Constitutional Provisions, adding a chapter on the judiciary and the Constitutional Court. The drafters adopted the German model of a "mixed," concrete, and abstract judicial review of legislation. Review can be initiated by the highest executive officials, a group of one-fifth of the deputies, local courts, local governments, or any person claiming a violation of fundamental constitutional rights.

The court also has broad power to interpret the constitution and the laws and to investigate the legality of elections and charges against the president of the republic. It has jurisdiction over disputes of competency between the constitutional powers and over the constitutional status of political parties and other political and social organizations. The court seems to have only suspensory power regarding laws, and its decisions are final with regard to other normative acts at the substatutory level. Nonetheless, the court apparently tries to assert more power and actively intervenes in the legislative policy of the People's Assembly.

THE 1992 PARLIAMENTARY ELECTIONS AND AFTERMATH

As a result of unsuccessful attempts by several governments to cope with the political turmoil and grave economic problems besetting Albania, parliamentary elections were scheduled for March 22, 1992. Although the Democratic Party won these elections, predictably defeating the Social Democratic Party, it inherited a country in serious economic trouble, with large numbers of hungry and unemployed people, rising inflation, and widespread crime. The Democratic Party gained control over 62 percent of the seats in the People's Assembly, giving Albania's parliament the largest democratic majority in eastern Europe. Thus the 1992 elections brought the country's first anticommunist takeover since 1944. The Democratic Party leader, Sali Berisha, was appointed by parliament as Albania's first noncommunist president. Much to the satisfaction of the Democrats, on April 4, 1992, President Alia resigned before the parliament could remove him from office.

After joining the International Covenant on Civil and Political Rights in October 1991, the government attempted to demonstrate its respect for the covenant's basic freedoms of expression and assembly. It gave all parties access to the media and allowed rallies to be held by opposition parties. Although no major irregularities were noted, socialist leaders complained that some of their meetings were disrupted by opponents.

The election law became a point of serious conflict in 1992. The law, which was passed in February 1992, basically prevented ethnic parties from participating in elections. The Greek minority viewed this law as directed toward Omonia, the political and cultural organization of the ethnic Greeks, who had won five parliamentary seats in the 1991 elections. Omonia protested against the law, locally and abroad, but was not allowed to participate in the elections. In response, Omonia leaders created the Unity for Human Rights Party, which was approved by the government and was successful in fielding candidates in the ethnic Greek areas of southern Albania. Albanians, in turn, denounced the treatment of the Albanian minority group in Greece.

As he promised following the 1992 elections, President Berisha pursued economic reform in Albania by way of "shock therapy." Through strict adherence to reforms suggested by the International Monetary Fund, Berisha created 100,000 jobs in the private sector, increasing agriculture production by 20 percent and reducing the inflation rate to zero in June 1993. Despite these gains, Albania is far from being economically prosperous, and its people are unhappy with the current economic policy.

As in other new democracies in east central Europe, the Albanians began turning to the former communist parties. The Albanian Socialist Party, the former ruling party, has continued to amass support. It has adopted a social democratic platform through which it supports a market economy and multiparty democracy, at the expense, however, of a slower pace of economic transition and a temporary reopening of state-run factories to create jobs. Moreover, party leaders consider their members to be the country's true new democrats and accuse Berisha's government of moving toward a dictatorship.

The biggest clash between Berisha's Democratic Party and the former communists came as a result of the July 28, 1993, People's Assembly vote to lift the immunity of Deputy Fatos Nano, former premier of Albania and chair of the Socialist Party. On July 30 Nano was arrested for abuses of power and falsification of official documents. Additionally, eight former leading communists and four former lower-ranking officials were arrested. In response to these arrests, the opposition Socialist Party demanded the release of their leader. Even foreign diplomats took issue with these arrests, suggesting that a return to authoritarian methods could seriously impede the reforms that Berisha has so rigorously pursued. In April 1994 Nano was found guilty of theft of state property and sentenced to twelve years in prison. In May began the trial of former president Alia, who had been under house arrest since October 1992.

THE NEW CHARTER OF RIGHTS AND FURTHER CONSTITUTIONAL DEVELOPMENT

Under communist rule, Albania had perhaps the worst human rights abuses in Europe. After the downfall of communism, Albania moved away from its isolationism and sought to reform itself. The 1991 interim constitution (the Law on the Major Constitutional Provisions) guaranteed the right of citizens to change their government by free, general, direct, and secret ballot. It also provided for political pluralism and required that political parties be independent from state institutions and not ethnically or religiously based. In fact, however, international observers showed concern over an increase in the number of human rights violations committed by the police in Albania, particularly after the elections of 1992.

To improve the situation, the Constitutional Commission drafted a new bill of rights, which was passed in March 1993 by a majority of the parliament. The Charter of Rights states that freedoms can be restricted only by law and for reasons enumerated in the constitution. Except for ambiguity in some of the criteria allowing for infringement of human rights, such as the "protection of morals," the charter looks impressive. In June 1995 Albania joined the Council of Europe, and in August 1996 the parliament ratified the European Convention on Human Rights and the European Convention for the Prevention of Torture. It still is a cause for concern, however, that Albania's record in human rights protection does not match the formal international obligations and constitutional guarantees.

The Constitutional Commission worked through 1992 and 1993, but little progress was made toward a complete draft. Finally, in November 1994 the president submitted a new version of the constitution to the parliament. It was criticized by the opposition for vesting too much power in the president and for not ensuring the judiciary's independence. The president attempted to bypass the parliament by holding a referendum; more than 60 percent of the voters opposed the move. In February 1995 the Constitutional Court ruled that submitting the constitution to a referendum before asking the parliament to vote violated the interim constitution, which requires a two-thirds majority vote in the People's Assembly for the approval of a new constitution.

Soon after the referendum an opposition group composed of members of the Socialist Party, the Party of Democratic Alliance, the Social Democratic Party, and the Party for the Protection of Human Rights prepared a new draft of the constitution. Berisha attacked it as unconstitutional.

On May 26 and June 2, 1996, new elections to the People's Assembly were held. The Democratic Party won the elections, securing 122 of 140 seats in parliament. The Socialist Party won only 10 seats, the Republican Party, 3; the Party for the Protection of Human Rights, 3; and the National Front, 2.

International observers and the opposition in Albania expressed concerns about violations of the electoral process and other irregularities. Despite a resolution of the European Parliament condemning the violations and urging Berisha to hold new elections, and a resolution of the Council of Europe denouncing the use of force, the new parliament was convened on July 1. The Socialist Party, which announced the new Assembly illegitimate, did not take its seats. In August the imprisoned Nano urged the opposition to continue boycotting parliament to force Berisha to continue discussions.

The new parliament had been in place only six months when financial crises led to violent antigovernment protests beginning in January 1997. Within two months Berisha was forced to appoint a member of the opposition Socialist Party as prime minister. Still, riots persisted that the army proved incapable of suppressing, leading to the introduction of an international peacekeeping force. The president called April 21 for new elections, which were held June 29 and July 6. Berisha's Democratic Party lost almost one hundred seats in the parliament, while the Socialist Party secured an overwhelming majority.

Albania faces significant challenges on its road to democracy.

Rett R. Ludwikowski

BIBLIOGRAPHY

Biberaj, Elez. "Albania, the Last Domino." In *Eastern Europe in Revolution,* edited by Ivo Banac. Ithaca, N.Y.: Cornell University Press, 1992.

Ludwikowski, Rett R. *Constitution Making in the Region of Former Soviet Dominance.* Durham, N.C., and London: Duke University Press, 1996.

ALGERIA

OFFICIAL NAME: Democratic and Popular Republic of Algeria (al-Jumhuriyah al-Jaza'iriyah al-Dimuqratiyah al-Sha'biyah)

CAPITAL: Algiers

POPULATION: 29,183,000 (1996 est.)

DATE OF INDEPENDENCE: July 3, 1962 (from France)

DATE OF CURRENT CONSTITUTION: Adopted November 28, 1996; effective December 8, 1996

FORM OF GOVERNMENT: Parliamentary democracy

LANGUAGES: Arabic (official), French, Berber

MONETARY UNIT: Algerian dinar

FISCAL YEAR: Calendar year

LEGISLATURE: Parliament

NUMBER OF CHAMBERS: One. National People's Assembly (Majlis Ech Chaabi al-Watani). The 1996 constitution also provides for a second chamber, the Council of the Nation

NUMBER OF MEMBERS: 380
PERCENTAGE OF WOMEN: 2.9
TERM OF LEGISLATURE: Five years
MOST RECENT LEGISLATIVE ELECTION: June 5, 1997
MINIMUM AGE FOR VOTING: 18
MINIMUM AGE FOR MEMBERSHIP: 28
SUFFRAGE: Universal and direct
VOTING: Optional
ADDRESS: National People's Assembly, 18 boulevard Zirout Youcef, Algiers
TELEPHONE: (213) 73 86 00
FAX: (213) 74 03 89

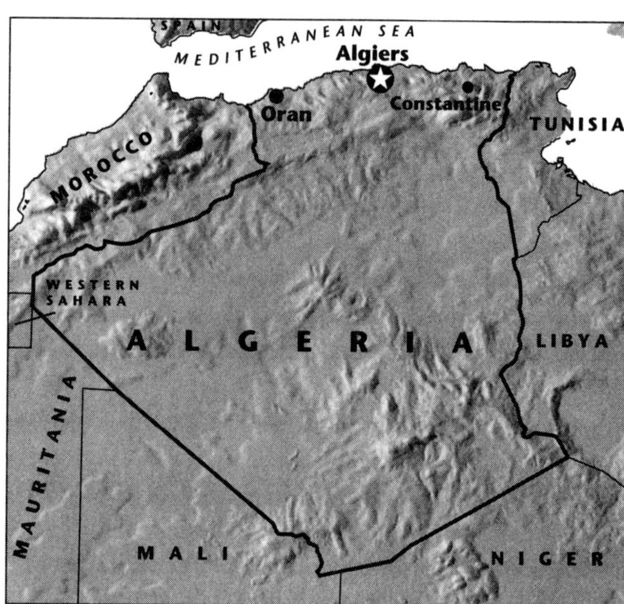

Algeria, a north African nation, won independence from France in July 1962 after 132 years of colonial rule. For much of the postindependence period the country was under military rule until an Islamist movement challenged it in free and fair elections in 1992. The government annulled the elections, and the resulting civil war between Islamist groups and the army has caused the deaths of tens of thousands of people.

The legislature was suspended in 1992, but a new constitution was adopted in late 1996, and elections to a new National People's Assembly were held in June 1997.

HISTORICAL BACKGROUND

A French colony from 1830 to 1962, Algeria won its freedom after fighting an eight-year war of independence. Ahmed Ben Bella became Algeria's first president and head of its single party, the National Liberation Front (FLN). On September 20, 1962, Algerians elected their first National Assembly. Six days later the Assembly elected Ben Bella as its prime minister and gave the nation its official name: the Democratic and Popular Republic of Algeria. A national constitution was drafted that set up a socialist regime in Algeria that would last until 1989.

On June 19, 1965, Colonel Houari Boumedienne, the defense minister, overthrew Ben Bella in a bloodless coup and seized power. He suspended the National Assembly and the constitution and transferred all political power to a military-led Council of the Revolution. Boumedienne became president and prime minister, heading the FLN as his predecessor had. His political base was the military and a technocratic elite that emerged after independence. The state took over control of the economy and nationalized almost all industrial and agricultural enterprises.

At the national level the major political institutions were the FLN and the parallel state apparatus. At the regional and local levels, administrative bodies and assemblies took their directives from the FLN and the state. Until 1976 there was no parliament, constitution, or any form of popular political participation.

In 1976 a national charter was approved by a nationwide referendum that reaffirmed the socialist nature of the state and the one-party system as represented by the FLN. A 199-article constitution based on the principles of the charter was drafted that same year, reestablishing the National People's Assembly as a unicameral legislative body and giving the executive the dominant role in the state. The Assembly named Boumedienne the chief executive, president, prime minister, commander in chief of the armed forces, minister of defense and national security, and secretary general of the National Liberation Front.

In February 1977 elections for the National People's Assembly were held, and although all candidates were members of the FLN, they represented diverse social and occupational groups. When Boumedienne died in December 1978, a special party congress chose Col. Chadhli Benjedid to replace him. He ran unchallenged in a national election and received 94 percent of the vote. In 1985 he was reelected in a similar way.

POLITICAL REFORM

Benjedid undertook major economic and political reforms. He liberalized the economy, encouraged privatization, opened the country to limited foreign investment, and supported domestic private investment. He appointed a number of prime ministers such as Mohamed Cherif Messadia, Mouloud Hamrouche, and Sid Ahmed Ghozali rather than retaining those powers for himself as his predecessors had. By 1987 he had moved away from socialism and adopted a free market approach to the economy. That same year he allowed the Algerian League of Human Rights to form and various independent political organizations critical of the government to operate freely. Despite these reforms there was deep dissatisfaction, and major strikes and riots broke out in October 1988. The military was used to put down the riots, and hundreds died in the confrontations.

Benjedid introduced further reforms. In February 1989 a new constitution was drafted by the National People's Assembly and approved by a national referendum. In the referendum, 78 percent of the electorate participated, of which 75 percent approved of its provisions. The new constitution no longer referred to Algeria as a socialist or one-party state. It separated religious institutions from the state and allowed for the formation of political associations. The National Liberation Front's powers were diminished as it became only one of a number of such political organizations, and reference to its unique position in the Algerian political system was dropped from the new text. The 1989 constitution also emphasized the powers of the executive, giving him the right to appoint and dismiss prime ministers and exercise supreme authority over the military. The prime minister's role was defined in terms of defense and external security.

THE ROAD TO CIVIL WAR

As it had been in the 1976 constitution, the National People's Assembly remained unicameral. Deputies were elected for a five-year term by universal suffrage for Algerians older than twenty-five. Although the 1976 constitution allowed for multiple candidates for a single parliamentary seat, all candidates had to be FLN members. The 1989 constitution abolished this restriction and allowed candidates from different parties to compete for parliamentary seats. Electoral districts were created based on proportional representation. To be awarded a seat, one had to win a simple majority of the vote. Nationally, if no party won a majority, the one with the highest number of votes was awarded 51 percent of the seats. The rest were divided among the other parties that had received at least 7 percent of the total vote, in proportion to their winnings. In 1991 the National People's Assembly increased the number of seats to 430 from 261.

New legislation subsequently legalized political parties, and more than fifty were formed in the next two years. In June 1990 municipal and provincial elections took place—the first free and fair elections since Algeria's independence. The Islamic Salvation Front (FIS), which comprised a number of militant Islamic groups opposed to Benjedid's government, got the lion's share of the vote, spelling the demise of the National Liberation Front. In July 1991 Benjedid resigned as secretary general of the FLN, which had broken into several factions after the elections.

National elections were held in December 1991. More than fifty political parties participated, but the FIS was the clear winner in the first round. Two hundred seats had to be decided in the second round of the elections set for January 16, 1992. It was apparent that the FIS would again win, and by more than the two-thirds majority needed to transfer parliamentary powers from the Benjedid regime to the Islamist opposition. Fearful of such a transfer of power, the military, headed by Maj. Gen. Khalid Nizar, the minister of defense, called for the suspension of the second round of elections and the resignation of the president. Benjedid resigned on January 11, 1992.

The military then created the High Security Council, an advisory council to Prime Minister Sid Ahmed Ghozali, headed by Nizar and Maj. Gen. Larbi Belkheir. The council took over power, voided the December 1991 electoral results, and suspended all political institutions. It then created the High Council of State, headed by an old independence leader, Mohamed Boudiaf, who had been in exile for more than thirty years, to act as a transitional government.

To protest such policies, Islamists fought back in mass demonstrations and with acts of violence against government forces. A state of emergency was imposed, the National Assembly was suspended, the Islamic Salvation Front was banned, and local and municipal assemblies controlled by Islamists were dissolved. There were mass arrests and imprisonment of FIS leaders. The country fell into civil war as Islamists began a campaign of assassinations and violence first against government forces and then against civilian targets. The government responded with ruthless military force. On June 29, 1992, Boudiaf was assassinated, allegedly by a member of the military. By 1993 more radical Islamist groups such as the Islamic Armed Group had emerged, and the casualties of the civil war rose to an average of five hundred a week.

COUNTRY IN CRISIS

The National Consultative Council was created in February 1992 to act in place of the disbanded National People's Assembly. In 1993 a five-member High Council of State was created to govern the country until the end of that year. It then turned over its powers to the 200-member National Transitional Council, which became the new government of transition. The council did not include Islamists or members of major political parties such as the FLN or the Front of Socialist Forces. In January 1994 former general Liamine

Zeroual was appointed president by the military leaders and chose a prime minister to head the transitional council. Although the constitution was not suspended, the state of emergency imposed since the beginning of the crisis allowed those in power to circumvent it.

In November 1995 four candidates representing the government, the moderate Islamists, the Berbers, and the independents ran for president in national elections. Officially, 74.9 percent of the electorate voted, and Zeroual won with a 61.3 percent majority.

The government held a national referendum on a new constitution in 1996 that strengthened the powers of the president, created a bicameral legislature, and explicitly denied any organization with a religious, regional, or ethnic agenda the right to form a political party or run a candidate for office. There was not much enthusiasm for the new constitution, but according to official results, it was approved. Legislative elections were held in June 1997, but the militant Islamist opposition was not allowed to participate. Violence continues.

Mary-Jane Deeb

BIBLIOGRAPHY

Deeb, Mary-Jane. "Islam and the State in Algeria and Morocco: A Dialectical Model." In *Islamism and Secularism in North Africa,* ed. John Ruedy. New York: St. Martin's, 1994.

———. "Radical Islam and the Politics of Redemption." *Annals of the Academy of Political and Social Sciences* 548 (November 1992): 52–65.

Entelis, John P., and Philip C. Naylor, eds. *State and Society in Algeria.* Boulder, Colo.: Westview Press, 1992.

Mortimer, Robert. "Islamists, Soldiers, and Democrats: The Second Algerian War." *Middle East Journal* 50 (winter 1996): 18–39.

Zartman, I. William, et al., eds. *Political Elites in Arab North Africa: Morocco, Algeria, Tunisia, Libya, and Egypt.* New York: Longman, 1982.

ANDORRA

OFFICIAL NAME: Principality of Andorra (Principat d'Andorra)
CAPITAL: Andorra la Vella
POPULATION: 73,000 (1996 est.)
DATE OF INDEPENDENCE: 1278
DATE OF CURRENT CONSTITUTION: Adopted March 14, 1993; effective May 4, 1993
FORM OF GOVERNMENT: Constitutional coprincipality
LANGUAGES: Catalan (official), French, Castilian
MONETARY UNIT: No local currency. Both the French franc and Spanish peseta are legal tender
FISCAL YEAR: Calendar year
LEGISLATURE: General Council of the Valleys (Consell General de las Valls)
NUMBER OF CHAMBERS: One
NUMBER OF MEMBERS: Twenty-eight
PERCENTAGE OF WOMEN: 7.1
TERM OF LEGISLATURE: Four years
MOST RECENT LEGISLATIVE ELECTION: February 16, 1997
MINIMUM AGE FOR VOTING: 18
MINIMUM AGE FOR MEMBERSHIP: 18
SUFFRAGE: Universal and direct
VOTING: Optional
ADDRESS: Consell General, Casa de la Vall, Andorra La Vella
TELEPHONE: (33) 82 12 34
FAX: (33) 86 12 34

Andorra, a small state of approximately 180 square miles, is located in southwestern Europe, between France and Spain *(see map, p. 627)*. The General Council of the principality is an ancient institution, but until 1993 the country had no formal constitution.

The first constitution came into effect on May 4, 1993. It legalized the formation of political parties, and within the first year a number of political parties were formed to contest the December 1993 elections. According to the constitution neither the president nor members of the Executive Council may be members of the legislature. Of the twenty-eight councilors of the General Council, fourteen are elected by a single national constituency and the remainder are elected by the seven parishes, each of which has two representatives. The governing organ of the General Council is the Sindicatura, headed by the syndic general, or speaker.

George Thomas Kurian

ANGOLA

OFFICIAL NAME: Republic of Angola (República de Angola)
CAPITAL: Luanda
POPULATION: 10,343,000 (1996 est.)
DATE OF INDEPENDENCE: November 10, 1975 (from Portugal)
DATE OF CURRENT CONSTITUTION: Effective November 11, 1975
FORM OF GOVERNMENT: Transitional democracy
LANGUAGES: Portuguese (official), Bantu, other languages
MONETARY UNIT: New kwanza
FISCAL YEAR: Calendar year
LEGISLATURE: National Assembly (Assembléia Nacional)
NUMBER OF CHAMBERS: One
NUMBER OF MEMBERS: 223
PERCENTAGE OF WOMEN: 9.5
TERM OF LEGISLATURE: Four years (current Assembly's term extended)
MOST RECENT LEGISLATIVE ELECTION: September 29–30, 1992
MINIMUM AGE FOR VOTING: 18
MINIMUM AGE FOR MEMBERSHIP: 35
SUFFRAGE: Universal and direct
VOTING: Optional
ADDRESS: National Assembly, Caixa Postal 1204, Luanda
TELEPHONE: (244 2) 33 83 22
FAX: (244 2) 33 11 18

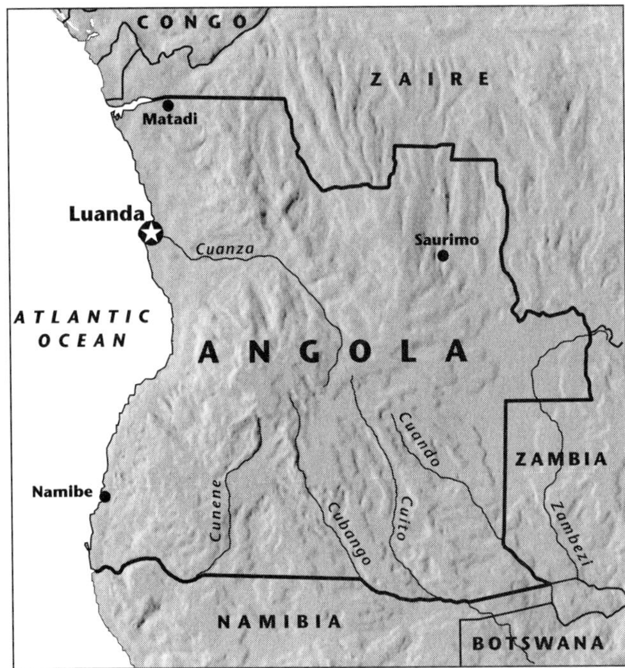

The Republic of Angola, which is located in southwest Africa on the Atlantic coast, achieved independence from Portugal in 1975 after fifteen years of armed struggle. During the first five years of its existence, the new republic was ruled by a Marxist Revolutionary Council. The first legislature, called the People's Assembly, was set up on November 11, 1980, and the Permanent Committee of Parliament held its first meeting two days later.

Although the term of the first Assembly was only three years, it sat until 1986 because of the unsettled conditions created by the civil war between rival groups that had raged in the country since independence. A second Assembly was convened in 1986 and served until 1992. Like the first, the second was a single-party legislature with no opposition. Following a peace agreement signed in Washington in June 1991 by the various Angolan factions and brokered by the United States and the Soviet Union, the first multiparty elections were held in 1992, when the Second Republic came into being. Constitutional amendments allowing multiparty elections were adopted in April 1992.

All 220 seats up for election (three seats reserved for overseas citizens were left unfilled) are filled by proportional representation and closed party-list balloting; 130 candidates are selected from a single nationwide constituency, and the remainder from eighteen five-seat constituencies. In contrast with the First Republic's People's Assembly, deputies in the new National Assembly are full-time paid members.

The National Assembly is elected for a term of four years. It convenes in ordinary annual sessions for eight months from October 15 to June 15. Special sessions may be convened by the president of the National Assembly, the standing committee of the National Assembly, or one-third or more of deputies. The standing committee assumes legislative powers between sessions. The National Assembly meets in a building originally built as a theater, renovated and enlarged to accommodate seven hundred people.

LEGISLATIVE PROCEDURES

Bills may be initiated by parliamentary groups (discussed below), by individual deputies, or by the government. Draft bills, called *projects,* are submitted in writing to the president of the chamber, who transmits them to the respective committees. On the basis of committee recommendations, projects are included by the president of the chamber in the agenda for the next plenary session. At this stage amendments may be introduced by any member, and the project is returned to the committee for further deliberations.

When a project returns to the plenary session, it is debated and voted on. Priority is given to government bills. On passage the bill is signed by the president and published in the official gazette. Amendments to the constitution require a vote of at least two-thirds of the full membership. Such amendments may be proposed by any ten deputies, and they follow the same legislative path as regular bills. Parliamentary proceedings are broadcast except when the sessions are closed to the public.

Much legislative work is done by parliamentary committees, of which there are three types: permanent working committees, temporary committees, and investigative committees. The political composition of each committee reflects the party composition of the National Assembly.

Ministers and state secretaries may attend plenary sessions of the National Assembly and take part in its discussions. Senior government officials also may be asked to take part in the discussions or to explain technical details of programs and projects. The prime minister, who is appointed by the president, and cabinet members are expected to attend all plenary sessions when a motion of confidence or censure is being considered or when the national budget or national plan is being debated.

In the National Assembly of the Second Republic, unlike in the People's Assembly of the First Republic, there are more than twelve political parties, each of which constitutes a parliamentary group when it has more than three party members. The president of the National Assembly keeps a record of the groups and notes changes in membership as reported by the group leaders. The rights of deputies during debate are spelled out in the standing orders, which establish procedural rules.

The decisions of the National Assembly are taken by simple majority. The president of the chamber controls the order and duration of debates as well as the method of voting. Voting is normally by show of hands. Nominal voting by alphabetical order or by secret ballot may be adopted on important matters. Parliamentary control over the administration is exercised through interpellations (requests for information or clarification from cabinet members and officials), as well as through investigative committees charged with independent inquiry into any government sector or activity.

Deputies enjoy the full range of parliamentary immunities, including freedom from arrest, unless the National Assembly lifts that immunity. They also enjoy honorariums specified in the constitution, free medical assistance, the right to own a pistol, and other perquisites. Deputies lose their legislative mandate if they are incapacitated, desert their political group, or are absent for a long period without reason. The National Assembly may revoke a mandate when a deputy is convicted of a serious crime, fails to attend the chamber without due reason, or leaves the country for more than forty-five days without permission.

CIVIL WAR RESUMED

The formal parliamentary procedures adopted by the National Assembly belied the country's descent back into civil war. In the presidential balloting conducted concurrently with the parliamentary elections in 1992, Josí Eduardo Dos Santos of the Popular Liberation Movement of Angola–Party of Labor (MPLA-PT) narrowly led Jonas Savimbi of the National Union for the Total Independence of Angola (UNITA) after first-round balloting. Before the second round could be scheduled, Savimbi proclaimed the elections rigged and resumed war against the government. The battle raged for another four years despite on-again, off-again peace talks.

Under strong international pressure, Savimbi finally in 1996 began to adhere to some provisions of a peace plan that he had signed in November 1994. But by 1997 he still was resisting the complete demobilization of UNITA's military forces, UNITA deputies had not taken up their mandates in the National Assembly, nor had UNITA filled the government positions accorded it under the peace plan.

George Thomas Kurian

ANTIGUA AND BARBUDA

OFFICIAL NAME: Antigua and Barbuda
CAPITAL: Saint John's
POPULATION: 66,000 (1996 est.)
DATE OF INDEPENDENCE: November 1, 1981 (from the United Kingdom)
DATE OF CURRENT CONSTITUTION: Effective November 1, 1981
FORM OF GOVERNMENT: Constitutional monarchy
LANGUAGE: English (official)
MONETARY UNIT: Eastern Caribbean dollar
FISCAL YEAR: April 1–March 31
LEGISLATURE: Parliament
NUMBER OF CHAMBERS: Two. House of Representatives; Senate

NUMBER OF MEMBERS: House of Representatives, 19 (17 directly elected, 1 ex officio, speaker); Senate, 17 (appointed)

PERCENTAGE OF WOMEN: House of Representatives, 5.3; Senate, 17.6

TERM OF LEGISLATURE: Five years

MOST RECENT LEGISLATIVE ELECTION: March 8, 1994

MINIMUM AGE FOR VOTING: 18

MINIMUM AGE FOR MEMBERSHIP: 21

SUFFRAGE: Universal

VOTING: Optional

ADDRESS: Parliament Building, Queen Elizabeth Highway, St. John's

TELEPHONE: (1809) 462 4822

FAX: (1809) 462 6724

Antigua and Barbuda consists of three islands in the Caribbean Sea: Antigua, the smaller Barbuda, and the rocky uninhabited islet of Redondo. They lie along the outward edge of the Leeward Island chain in the West Indies *(see map, p. 303)*. The islands were under British rule from the seventeenth century until 1981, when they received independence. The country continues to be a member of the British Commonwealth. The constitution states that Antigua and Barbuda is "a unitary sovereign and democratic state" with the British monarch as head of state represented by a governor general.

Parliament consists of a seventeen-member appointed upper house (Senate) and a nineteen-member lower house (House of Representatives), which includes seventeen elected members, the attorney general ex officio, and the speaker if he or she is not a member by election. Senators are appointed by the governor general, eleven on the advice of the prime minister, four on the advice of the leader of the opposition, one at the governor general's discretion, and one on the advice of the Barbuda Council, the principal organ of local government on the smaller island. The term for members of Parliament is five years. The attorney general does not have the right to vote.

The prime minister and cabinet remain in office only as long as they enjoy the confidence of the House. On the passage of a no-confidence motion, the prime minister is required to resign or to advise the governor general to dissolve Parliament within seven days.

The islands are divided into seventeen single-member constituencies. The age of voting is eighteen.

George Thomas Kurian

ARGENTINA

OFFICIAL NAME: Argentine Republic (República Argentina)

CAPITAL: Buenos Aires

POPULATION: 34,673,000 (1996 est.)

DATE OF INDEPENDENCE: Declared July 9, 1816 (from Spain)

DATE OF CURRENT CONSTITUTION: May 1, 1853

FORM OF GOVERNMENT: Parliamentary democracy

LANGUAGE: Spanish (official)

MONETARY UNIT: Peso

FISCAL YEAR: Calendar year

LEGISLATURE: National Congress

NUMBER OF CHAMBERS: Two. Chamber of Deputies (Cámara de Diputados); Senate (Senado)

NUMBER OF MEMBERS: Chamber of Deputies, 257 (directly elected); Senate, 72 (indirectly elected until 2001)

PERCENTAGE OF WOMEN: Chamber of Deputies, 25.3; Senate, 2.8

TERM OF LEGISLATURE: Chamber of Deputies, four years (one-half of members elected every second year); Senate, nine years (one-third of members elected every third year)

MOST RECENT LEGISLATIVE ELECTION: Chamber of Deputies, May 14, 1995; Senate, December 10, 1995

MINIMUM AGE FOR VOTING: 18

MINIMUM AGE FOR MEMBERSHIP: Chamber of Deputies, 25; Senate, 30

SUFFRAGE: Universal

VOTING: Compulsory, with some exceptions

ADDRESS: Chamber of Deputies, Calle Rivadavia 1864, 1033 Capital Federal; Senate, Calle Hipólito Yrigoyen 1835, Capital Federal

TELEPHONE: Chamber of Deputies, (541) 370 7100; Senate, (541) 953 3081

FAX: Chamber of Deputies, (541) 954 1100; Senate, (541) 953 5746

The Argentine Republic is the second-largest nation in South America. Its fertile plains, extending throughout the southeastern part of the continent to the Atlantic littoral, are capable of producing great agricultural wealth. Argentina is a federal republic with a presidential system of government, a bicameral legislature, and a judiciary.

HISTORICAL BACKGROUND

The Spanish colony of Río de la Plata (today the Argentine Republic) set up its first autonomous government on

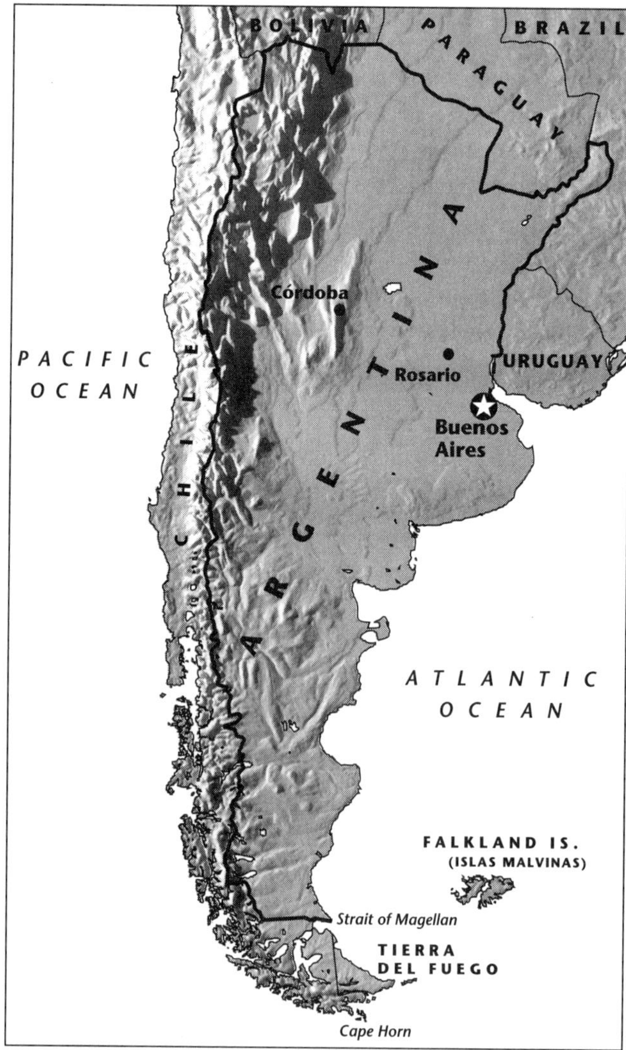

May 25, 1810, two years after Napoleon had invaded Spain and deposed the Spanish king. The first major congress met in 1813 to draft a constitution. On July 9, 1816, Argentina declared its independence in the city of Tucumán under the name of the United Provinces of Río de la Plata. The declaration was followed by several years of confrontation between the defenders of provincial autonomy and the supporters of central government concentrated in Buenos Aires.

From 1829 to 1852 Juan Manuel de Rosas, governor of the province of Buenos Aires, controlled most of the country, enjoying far broader support than any of his predecessors. After Rosas was overthrown in 1852, federalists and centralists agreed on a federal constitution embodying a presidential and representative government based on that of the United States. The constitution of 1853 has remained in effect since its adoption. Major amendments made in 1949 at the behest of President Juan Perón were repealed in 1956.

The first Congress under the new constitution assembled at the city of Paraná on October 22, 1854, without delegates from the province of Buenos Aires, which had refused to join the new federation. Six years later Buenos Aires was incorporated by armed force, but the federal authorities agreed to a constitutional revision that underscored the federal character of the government and satisfied some of the concerns of the residents of Buenos Aires.

An electoral reform law passed in 1912 provided for a secret and compulsory ballot for all male citizens and created a list of voters designed to prevent fraud and electoral manipulation. The first elections under universal male suffrage took place in 1916 and brought to power Hipólito Yrigoyen, a member of the middle-class Radical Party and a strong opponent of the previous regime.

The constitutional system was interrupted in 1930 by the republic's first coup d'état, under the leadership of Gen. José Félix Uriburu, who occupied the presidency until 1932. A succession of democratic and military governments governed until 1983. Congress was closed by the military in 1930–1932, 1943–1945, 1955–1957, 1962–1963, 1966–1972, and 1976–1983.

In 1946 Juan Domingo Perón was elected president. Appointed in 1943 to head the labor department, Perón built his political power on the labor unions and a welfare program that became the centerpiece of his Workers Party, later renamed the Peronist Party and now known as the Justicialista Party, a name coined by Perón. A constitutional convention in 1949 reformed the constitution to provide for presidential reelection. Perón was duly reelected in 1951 but was overthrown by a coup in 1955.

A law introducing female suffrage was passed in 1947. In the election of 1951 the Peronist Party included thirty women among its candidates for senators and deputies.

In 1976 the military took power in another coup d'état. Congress was closed for seven years, the longest suspension since its founding, and leftist groups were persecuted in a "dirty war" in which thousands of people were abducted and killed by the military.

An unsuccessful attempt to reclaim the Falkland (Malvinas) Islands from Great Britain weakened the military's hold on power. On December 10, 1983, Raúl Alfonsín was elected president in a free election. In 1989 his administration was succeeded democratically by that of President Carlos Saúl Menem, who was reelected in May 1995. During these years Argentina slowly recovered its economic health.

CONSTITUTIONAL PROVISIONS AFFECTING THE LEGISLATURE

The constitution of the Argentine Republic has been amended six times since its adoption in 1853. The most recent amendments, made in 1994, affected the structure and functions of the Congress.

The Congress consists of two houses. In the lower house, the Chamber of Deputies, the number of representatives is proportional to the population, but each province has at least five deputies. Since 1995 the Senate has comprised seventy-two senators, three from each province and three from the city of Buenos Aires. Within each province, two senators represent the political party with a majority of votes in that province and the other represents the largest minority. The federal vice president is the president of the Senate and votes only to break a tie.

Under the constitution, the Congress approves the federal budget and accounts; makes laws about customs, customs duties, and direct taxes; writes the civil, commercial, criminal, mining, and labor codes; passes laws on naturalization, bankruptcy, and the counterfeiting of currency and public documents; coins money and regulates its value; fixes the standard of weights and measures; regulates the free navigation of rivers; borrows money; regulates the use of state-owned lands; issues subsidies to the provinces; regulates commerce with foreign nations and among the provinces; makes arrangements to determine the nation's borders and determines those of the provinces; establishes courts below the level of the Supreme Court; grants general amnesties; and raises and supports armies and authorizes them to leave the country.

Some of these powers have never been exercised or have been taken over completely or partially by the executive, such as power over the country's foreign debt, declaration of a state of siege, and federal intervention in the provinces. Other powers are shared with the executive branch. Congress approves or disapproves treaties made by the president, approves by absolute majority treaties of regional integration that delegate functions and jurisdiction to supranational organizations, ratifies the president's denunciation of any of the human rights treaties included in the constitution in the 1994 reform, authorizes the executive branch to declare war or to make peace, approves or suspends a state of siege or federal intervention in the provinces declared by the executive branch during a congressional recess, accepts or rejects the resignation of the president or vice president, and declares the need for new elections.

Powers shared with the provinces include making laws necessary for the prosperity of the state and the people's development through the promotion of business, investment, immigration, education, and job-creation and levying certain joint taxes.

Congress has the power to declare a state of siege in a province to protect the republican form of government. It may order federal intervention in a province or in the city of Buenos Aires to enforce the free exercise of republican institutions. It may also authorize the use of military force to contain insurrections or repel invasions.

Members of Congress cannot be prosecuted for the views and opinions they express in the legislature. They may not be arrested except when caught in the act of committing a crime; upon arrest, the member's chamber must be notified. The resignation of a member of Congress is accepted by an affirmative vote of half plus one of the members present in the chamber. A member may be expelled by a two-thirds vote of the members present. Members may not be recalled by their constituencies between elections.

The Supreme Court has assumed a role, authorized by legislation, in interpreting treaties and federal law and determining their constitutionality. It has appellate jurisdiction over the lower courts and provincial courts where federal matters are at issue. In the cases that come before them, the Supreme Court and the lower courts are expected to review the actions of the other two branches in the light of the constitution. Although Supreme Court decisions are not formally binding as precedent, they are usually followed by lower courts.

PARTIES AND ELECTIONS

Deputies are elected to four-year terms by direct vote using the d'Hondt system of proportional representation. After each census, the Congress sets the basis of representation; in 1994 there was one deputy for every 161,000 inhabitants (plus an additional deputy for each remainder of at least 80,500 people), for a total of 257 deputies. Regardless of population, no province has fewer than five deputies. Half of the chamber stands for election every two years.

In 1995 the number of senators was raised by constitutional amendment from forty-eight to seventy-two. By the same amendment, Senate elections will be direct beginning in 2001, and senators will serve six-year terms, with half of the body standing for election every three years. Presently, senators are elected by the provincial legislatures for nine-year terms.

Deputies and senators can be reelected indefinitely. When a vacancy occurs, the provincial government calls for elections to fill the seat. To appear on the ballot, candidates must be endorsed by a political party. Parties are required to give equal opportunities to male and female candidates. Parties must be officially recognized.

The two main political parties are the Radical Civic Union and the Justicialista Party. The Radical Civic Union is the descendant of the Radical Party founded in 1890 by Leandro N. Alem and Hipólito Yrigoyen to fight electoral fraud. The Justicialista Party represents Juan Perón's "third position" between capitalism and communism. Many other political parties are represented in Congress. Some of these are national parties; others operate primarily at the provincial level.

Deputies must be at least twenty-five years old and have been Argentine citizens for four years. Senators must be thirty years old and have six years of Argentine citizenship. In both cases, candidates must be natives of the province in which they seek election or must have resided in that province for the last two years. Senators must have a minimum income, the amount of which is specified in the constitution.

Members of the clergy and provincial governors may not serve in the legislature. Legislators may not serve in the cabinet or in any other federal office. In 1994 nearly half the members of Congress were lawyers. The average age of deputies was fifty-one; the average age of senators was fifty-six. The lower house contained thirty-seven female deputies, of whom just three chaired committees.

ORGANIZATION AND OPERATIONS OF PARLIAMENT

The national Congress has met in the city of Buenos Aires since 1862. Its first building was inaugurated in 1864 in the central Plaza de Mayo. In 1898 Italian architect Victor Meano began the construction of a new building in which the Congress has met since 1906. Meano's building, finally completed in 1946, has strong Greek and Roman influences that are clearly revealed in its monumental columns. It stands at one end of the Avenida de Mayo, at the other end of which lies the Casa Rosada, the president's residence. A high copper-covered dome makes the Congress visible from many parts of the city.

The Hall of Lost Steps, said to be named for impatient visitors waiting to see members of Congress, leads to the Chamber of Deputies. The chamber is arrayed in a semicircle with three rows of balconies reserved for the general public. The Senate chamber is smaller than that of the Chamber of Deputies. The benches are arranged in a semicircle and surrounded by two public galleries. In both houses, members' seats are equipped with microphones that may be switched on and off as needed. The system allows the president of the chamber to switch off any microphone at any time.

The president opens the parliamentary year with a speech on the state of the nation in which he or she presents policy recommendations. In Argentina's history as a republic, only President Hipólito Yrigoyen has declined to follow this practice, which is enshrined in the constitution.

The chambers meet simultaneously, though separately, in ordinary sessions from March 1 to November 30. The president may extend sessions or call for extraordinary sessions during the recess (December 1 to February 28). While Congress is in session neither house may adjourn for more than three days without the consent of the other. Preliminary sessions take place before March 1. These are not provided for in the constitution but are authorized in the legislature's rules of procedure. Plenary sessions are held on Wednesday, Thursday, and Friday. Most legislators return to their provinces on weekends. At the close of 1996 Congress had met for 114 ordinary legislative sessions. Had it met without interruption since its founding in 1854 it would have completed 142 sessions.

The two houses of Congress assemble jointly as the Legislative Assembly to announce the election of the president and vice president, to hear the president and vice president take the oath of office, to hear the president's annual message, to accept or reject a president's or vice president's resignation, and to declare the need to elect a new president. No provision is made for dissolving the legislature.

The Congress may require ministers, including the head of the cabinet, to appear before it. At least once a month, the head of the cabinet must appear in each chamber to discuss new events. Ministerial appearances have no formal consequences but their political effects may be considerable. The chambers frequently request written reports from the executive.

The Congress employs more than six thousand people. Each chamber has its own facilities and services, including a dining room. The printing office, established in 1919, the library, and the health service are shared by the two chambers. A thirteen-story annex houses offices for deputies, committees, and caucuses, as well as an auditorium.

Journals have been kept since the first session of Congress. Sessions are recorded and transcribed by a staff of more than sixty stenographers, and a file of magnetic tapes is kept. Under the supervision of the Office of Parliamentary Information, a unit of the Chamber of Deputies whose professional staff are selected through a competition, the Congressional Printing Office publishes a bulletin of new bills, an agenda for each session that includes the text of bills being considered by the committees, and a journal of floor debates. The journal and the *Trámite Parlamentario* of the Chamber of Deputies, which reports on the progress of legislation, are available to the general public by subscription;

the others mentioned are for internal distribution. The printing office also publishes, largely for internal consumption, a review of committee proceedings and a legislative gazette containing the text of new laws and of legislation that has gained at least preliminary approval. Other publications cover legislative research, parliamentary law and procedure, and the final text of laws.

Since the end of the last century, the news media have paid close attention to debates on important issues, which have been excerpted and analyzed in the newspaper, *La Nación*. The political humor and the caricatures of newspapers such as *El Mosquito* and *Caras y Caretas* were born in the same era. Today, reporters covering the legislature work from special press boxes. Legislators are frequently interviewed, especially by television news programs that offer widely watched political analysis. Legislators know that cultivating the press pays off in good publicity.

The parliamentary library responds to legislators' questions and to research issues dealt with in legislation. The library may also answer questions from the other two branches of government and from the public. It has up-to-date national and international holdings. The Office of Legislative Reference, a unit of the library, performs research for Congress. It has databases of new library holdings, legislative analyses, and bill status. The office has agreements with information centers around the world for the exchange of data. It has published a large number of research studies.

Congress's attendance-taking and vote-counting system was modernized in 1984. Each member of Congress carries a key imprinted with a personal code number. A central computer registers the legislator's presence and sends the information to a pair of signboards that the president uses to determine whether a quorum exists. On roll-call votes, lights next to each member's name glow green for a yes vote, red for a no vote, and yellow for an abstention.

With the exception of some special sessions, floor debates are not televised. A closed-circuit television system allows members of Congress and their staff to follow floor deliberations from their offices. Cameras are automatically controlled from a central console. A speaker system is used to broadcast debates from the floor.

Members of Congress are paid a salary for their services by the federal government. They also receive an allowance of two and one-half times their salary for living and entertainment expenses. Members whose place of residence is more than one hundred kilometers from Buenos Aires receive an additional housing allowance.

Each chamber has the power to punish its members for disorderly conduct, to apply fines or other methods of punishment in cases of unjustified absence from sessions, to expel members who commit morally reproachable acts after taking office, and to suspend members against whom legal proceedings reach the trial stage.

LEGISLATION

Both houses of Congress, as well as the president, may introduce legislation, but bills on taxation and military service must originate in the Chamber of Deputies. Citizens, too, may introduce bills, except in fiscal, budgetary, and criminal matters or to amend the constitution or approve a treaty. Citizens' bills must be considered during the term in which they are introduced.

Bills, which must include a statement of purpose as well as proposed articles of law, are sent first to an appropriate committee to be discussed in depth. Once approved, bills move to the floor, first for general discussion and later for more thorough debate. If a bill is not approved unanimously in committee, majority and minority reports are brought to the floor. Following debate, voting occurs. A bill may be given preliminary approval and referred back to the committee for more work, or it may be given full approval. Once approved, a bill is sent to the other house. If rejected by either chamber, the bill may not be reintroduced during the parliamentary session.

Once approved by both chambers a bill is sent to the president for signature or veto. Congress has the option, however, of submitting legislation directly to the people. If passed by referendum the bill becomes law and is not subject to presidential veto. Congress is considering legislation to implement provisions of the 1994 constitutional reform related to the referendum process.

In the event the second chamber amends a bill, the originating chamber may restore it to its original form by a two-thirds vote. There is no provision for conference committees to reconcile different versions of a bill. To override a presidential veto, a two-thirds majority of the chamber that introduced the law is required, along with a like majority of the second chamber acting on the same version of the bill.

In addition to its exclusive right to introduce bills related to taxation and military service, the Chamber of Deputies alone may call for a referendum on particular bills. The Senate has exclusive jurisdiction over laws dealing with revenue sharing between the federal government and the provinces and with public policy on economic development within Argentina. The Senate also approves the president's appointments of judges, ambassadors, and high military officers.

Between December 1983, when Congress reconvened after a seven-year hiatus, and October 1994, it passed 1,276 bills. The annual volume of legislation varied from a low of

24 bills in 1989 to 183 in 1986. Bills originating in the executive branch are more likely to become law than those originating in Congress.

An absolute majority of each chamber constitutes a quorum to do business. A smaller number may demand the attendance of absent members. Failure to attend a session may result in a penalty specified in the rules of each house.

LEADERSHIP, COMMITTEES, AND HEARINGS

Every member of Congress is assigned to at least one standing committee. Parliamentary rules establish the number of committees and their jurisdiction. In 1994 the Chamber of Deputies had thirty-eight committees comprising from eighteen to thirty-three members. There were forty Senate committees comprising from five to fifteen senators. Among the most important committees are those devoted to budget and finance, labor, and foreign relations.

Special committees are charged with issues such as modernization of the functions of the parliament and regulation of river traffic between provinces. Public hearings are seldom held, and records of public hearings are not kept. Bills for the establishment of mandatory public hearings have not been successful.

Congress has investigative powers in connection with its essential functions. It may delegate this power to special committees to investigate specified activities or events. On occasion such committees have abused their investigative powers. Search warrants and subpoenas of documents require special court orders.

Joint committees of the two houses are responsible for approving or rejecting the president's annual budget report, overseeing the privatization of state companies, and supervising the operation of the congressional library, among other things.

The rules of the Chamber of Deputies state that the president of the chamber for that year is to be elected in the preliminary session. The president plays a role similar to that of the speaker of the U.S. House of Representatives. Presidents may be reelected for as long as their party controls the chamber. The Senate elects a provisional president to replace, when necessary, the federal vice president, who serves as president of the Senate. The powers and duties of the leaders of both chambers are similar: to call sessions and direct debate, to set the agenda, to put bills to a vote and publish the results, to prepare the budget of the chamber, to appoint and remove the chamber's staff, to see that the rules of procedures are observed, and to break tie votes.

Legislators from each party form a party caucus to choose their leaders, assign members to committees, deal with political questions, and decide whether to support legislation. At the end of 1994 there were twenty-two caucuses in the Chamber of Deputies and ten in the Senate. With the exception of the caucuses of the Radical Civic Union and the Justicialista Party, most are made up of a small number of legislators—sometimes only one. The leaders of the party caucuses resolve differences between versions of legislation approved by the two houses of Congress. Acting together with the president of the Chamber of Deputies, they also schedule floor debates.

Party caucuses employ an informal whip system; only occasionally do they leave their members free to vote. Disobedient members may be expelled from the party and thereby lose their seat in the chamber. The view that legislators' seats belong to the parties rather than to the individual members has given rise to debate. Although members are not elected as individual candidates but as part of lists prepared by the political parties, some scholars believe that the method of nomination is less important than the fact that each member is *elected* by the people.

Interest groups have influenced congressional decisions. Their most important techniques of influence are direct lobbying, financial contributions to electoral campaigns, sharing research and technical information, and drafting legislation.

RELATIONS WITH THE EXECUTIVE

The president has ten days to sign or return a bill to the Congress in whole or part or to take no action, in which case the bill becomes law. If a partial veto does not alter the bill's unity, in the opinion of the Supreme Court, that part of the bill that is approved may be promulgated. A two-thirds vote of both houses is required to override a presidential veto. Presidential vetoes, particularly of private bills, have been common in Argentina. In recent years Congress has very rarely overridden a veto.

The president's annual budget bill, once approved by the cabinet, is sent to Congress, where it is examined by the Budget and Finance Committee. Traditionally, Congress ran late in its consideration of the annual budget bill. In recent years, however, the bill has been approved before the beginning of the fiscal year.

Certain powers of Congress are shared with the executive branch. The sharing encourages the two branches to coordinate policy and allows each to serve as a check on the other. The Congress cannot delegate its legislative functions to the executive branch, however, except in cases of public emergency and even then only within preassigned limits. If the president exercises legislative powers in cases of serious emergency, the head of the cabinet must send the decree to a bicameral standing committee for approval.

Presidents Alfonsín and Menem resorted to decrees with great frequency even when Congress was in session. The Supreme Court has accepted this development.

The 1994 constitutional reform gave Congress the power to review the administration's performance. Based on an annual review by the General Audit Office, the director of which is appointed by the opposition party with the greatest number of seats, Congress issues a report on the government's management of the nation's economy and finances.

The reform also established the office of ombudsman to ensure that constitutional rights were protected against acts or omissions of the government. The ombudsman is appointed or removed by a two-thirds vote of each chamber and has the same immunities as legislators. The term of office is five years with the possibility of reappointment to one additional term.

The Chamber of Deputies has exclusive power to bring impeachment charges against the president, vice president, head of the cabinet, cabinet ministers, and members of the Supreme Court for crimes or misconduct while in office. Two-thirds of the members present must vote to initiate the process; the same proportion is required for impeachment. The Senate has the exclusive power to try the impeached official. Judgment does not extend further than to remove the accused from office, but the individual is subject subsequently to the jurisdiction of the courts. Three presidents have been subject to motions for impeachment, but no president or vice president has ever been impeached or removed from office through impeachment.

Eve R. Ladmann

BIBLIOGRAPHY

De Riz, Liliana, and Eduardo Feldman. *Guia del Parlamento Argentino.* Buenos Aires: Fundación Friederich Ebert, 1988.

Fennell, Lee C. "Reasons for Roll Calls: An Exploratory Analysis with Argentine Data." *American Journal of Political Science* 18 (May 1974): 359–403.

Kirkpatrick, Jeane. *Leader and Vanguard in Mass Society: A Study of Peronist Argentina.* Cambridge, Mass., and London: MIT Press, 1971.

Ladmann, Eve R. de. "El proceso político: Relaciones entre el Congreso y el PE." In *Documentos y Conclusiones.* Vol. 1. Buenos Aires: Imprenta Congreso, 1991.

Molinelli, N. Guillermo. *Presidentes y Congresos en la Argentina: Mitos y realidades.* Buenos Aires: Ediciones Gel, 1991.

Pellet Lastra, Arturo. *El Congreso por dentro.* Buenos Aires: Saint Claire Editora, 1991.

Smith, Peter H. *Argentina and the Failure of Democracy: Conflict among Political Elites, 1904–1955.* Madison: University of Wisconsin Press, 1974.

ARMENIA

See Commonwealth of Independent States, Non-Slavic

AUSTRALIA

OFFICIAL NAME: Commonwealth of Australia

CAPITAL: Canberra

POPULATION: 18,261,000 (1996 est.)

DATE OF INDEPENDENCE: January 1, 1901 (federation of UK colonies)

DATE OF CURRENT CONSTITUTION: Adopted July 9, 1900; effective January 1, 1901

FORM OF GOVERNMENT: Parliamentary democracy

LANGUAGES: English, native languages

MONETARY UNIT: Australian dollar

FISCAL YEAR: July 1–June 30

LEGISLATURE: Federal Parliament

NUMBER OF CHAMBERS: Two. House of Representatives; Senate

NUMBER OF MEMBERS: House of Representatives, 148; Senate, 76

PERCENTAGE OF WOMEN: House of Representatives, 15.5; Senate, 30.3

TERM OF LEGISLATURE: House of Representatives, three years; Senate, six years (half of membership elected every third year)

MOST RECENT LEGISLATIVE ELECTION: March 2, 1996

MINIMUM AGE FOR VOTING: 18

MINIMUM AGE FOR MEMBERSHIP: 18

SUFFRAGE: Universal and direct

VOTING: Compulsory

ADDRESS: Parliament House, Canberra, A.C.T. 2600

TELEPHONE: Federal Parliament, (616) 277 71 11

FAX: House of Representatives, (616) 277 20 58; Senate, (616) 277 31 99

Located southeast of Asia between the Indian and Pacific Oceans, the island continent of Australia and nearby island Tasmania make up the Commonwealth of Australia. On January 1, 1901, federation of the six Australian colonies of the then British Empire formed the commonwealth.

Australia is a constitutional monarchy and a parliamentary democracy. The titular head of state is the reigning British monarch, with the functions of head of state vested in the governor general. Australia has a bicameral legislature and an independent judiciary. The prime minister and cabinet, who constitute the executive branch, are members of the legislature.

THE CONSTITUTION AND PARLIAMENT

A written constitution established the Commonwealth of Australia and created the Federal Parliament. The constitution provides for a Parliament comprising the queen, who is represented by the governor general, and two chambers—the Senate and the House of Representatives. Constitutional provisions determine how the governor general is to be appointed and the powers of that office in summoning and dissolving Parliament; how the two chambers are to be constituted and their members elected; what the qualifications of senators and members of the House of Representatives are; and how vacant seats in the two houses are to be filled. The Parliament is given the power to make laws governing how senators and members are elected and to change the numbers of each.

The constitution provides for equal numbers of senators from each state regardless of size or population. Senators are elected for a term of six years, and elections for half the Senate take place every three years. Members of the House of Representatives are elected in proportion to the population of each state. The number of members must be as near as practicable twice the number of senators. Each term of the House of Representatives is limited to three years. Each house has the right to determine its own procedures and to exercise control over its own proceedings.

The Parliament is vested with the legislative power of the commonwealth but can make laws on only those matters specified in the constitution. The commonwealth is given exclusive legislative powers in some areas, but in others both the commonwealth and the states can legislate. In cases of conflict, commonwealth law has precedence. The states retain legislative powers over all matters not specifically listed in the constitution.

Commonwealth and state laws are likely to be struck down if they breach any of the prohibitions and guarantees contained in the constitution. For example, section 92 of the constitution requires that trade, commerce, and intercourse among the states be absolutely free. Any commonwealth or state law that abridged this freedom would be unconstitutional.

The constitution also provides for certain types of financial legislation, including limits on the Senate's ability to initiate or amend such legislation. Where the Senate may not make amendments, it may request the House to make amendments and decline to pass the bill until they are made. In all other respects the Senate has the same lawmaking powers as the House of Representatives, including the power to reject legislation.

There are two ways of altering provisions of the constitution, including those relating to Parliament. A few provisions contain the words "until the Parliament otherwise provides," and an act of Parliament can supersede them. To change the constitution itself, a bill proposing a constitutional amendment must be passed by both houses, or in specific circumstances, twice by the one house. The proposal must be then put to the direct vote of the people by means of a referendum. To be successful the proposal must be approved by a majority of voters and by majorities of voters in a majority of states.

PARLIAMENT HOUSE AND THE LIBRARY OF PARLIAMENT

Parliament House, Canberra, stands on Capital Hill at the apex of the parliamentary triangle. Opened in May 1988 in the bicentennial year of European settlement of the Australian continent, it is one of the largest buildings in the Southern Hemisphere.

Parliament's functions are accommodated along two axes that intersect at the members' hall in the center of the complex. To the north, along Canberra's land axis, lie the public and ceremonial spaces—the forecourt, great verandah, foyer, great hall, and members' hall—and nineteen committee rooms and the ministerial or executive government wing. To the east are the House of Representatives chamber and surrounding offices for members and staff; to the west, the Senate chamber and offices for senators and staff, as well as accommodation for most of the national capital's media corps.

Seating for the members of both chambers forms a horseshoe around a central table, a departure from most other legislative chambers, which seat their members either on opposite sides of the room directly facing one another or fanned around a central dais or rostrum. The focal point of each chamber is the chair of the presiding officer. Members of the governing party or parties sit on the right of the chair, and members of the nongoverning party or parties and independents sit on the left. All senators and members are allotted a seat. Except for certain senior officeholders, senators and members speak standing from their allotted places. There are large open galleries on all four sides of each chamber from which proceedings can be observed.

The establishment of a Library of Parliament broadly modeled on the U.S. Library of Congress was one of the first steps the Federal Parliament took in 1901. For sixty years the parliamentary library also served as a de facto national library.

The parliamentary library has become one of the most significant legislative libraries in the world. A research division employing subject specialists was established in 1966 and extended the range of reference and information services provided to senators and members to include analysis, interpretation, and comment on issues.

The parliamentary library has a staff of more than two hundred and a principal clientele of 224 senators and members. The personal staff of senators and members, the staff of parliamentary committees, officers of the Parliament, and the press gallery in Parliament House have access. Direct services are not provided to executive departments, other organizations outside the Parliament, or the public. Requests from constituents for information or research services are not accepted, but advice on alternative sources is provided.

ELECTIONS

Australian citizens who are eighteen years old or older are eligible to enroll to vote, and enrollment and voting are compulsory. Those who do not comply may be fined. Voting is by secret ballot, and all elections are supervised by the Australian Electoral Commission.

In general elections for members of the House of Representatives, voters choose one person to represent each electoral district. When a vacancy occurs in the House because of a member's death, resignation, or any other reason between general elections, a by-election is held in that member's electoral district.

A preferential system of voting is used. The voter ranks all candidates for his or her electoral district in order of preference by placing a number (1, 2, 3, and so on) in a square opposite the name of each candidate. To be successful, a candidate must receive more than 50 percent of the votes cast. If no candidate has such a majority when the first preferences are counted, the candidate with the fewest first preferences is removed from the count, and his or her second preferences are distributed—that is, the votes are allocated to the candidate marked "2" on the ballot paper. If necessary this process is repeated, with candidates progressively eliminated from the count and their votes redistributed.

There are 148 seats in the House of Representatives. One member represents each electorate. The districts vary greatly in size because their boundaries depend on population distribution. The smallest electorate in the thirty-eighth Parliament was Wentworth (10 square miles), and the largest was Kalgoorlie (849,200 square miles). In the 1996 general election there was an average of about 78,750 voters in each electorate.

The term of office of each member of the House of Representatives is the life of the Parliament to which he or she is elected, that is, no more than three years from the date of its first meeting following a general election.

In Senate elections voters choose a number of senators to represent their state or territory, and each state or territory votes as one electorate. Senate elections are usually held at the same time as general elections for the House of Representatives. Whenever a vacancy occurs in the Senate, it is filled until the end of the former senator's term by a person chosen by the Parliament of the state or territory the former senator represented. If possible, the replacement must come from the same political party as the senator being replaced.

A system of proportional representation is used to elect senators. Voters may rank each candidate in their order of preference as in elections for the House, or they may vote for candidates from a particular party or group. The method of counting votes ensures that the proportion of seats each party or group wins is virtually the same as the proportion of votes gained. There is thus greater opportunity for the election of minority parties and independents than in the House.

Each state of Australia is represented by twelve senators, and the Northern Territory and the Australian Capital Territory are each represented by two senators. State senators usually serve six years, with half of the senators facing re-election every three years. When there is a disagreement between the two houses and both are dissolved as a prerequisite to full elections for both houses, half the senators elected in these circumstances have only a three year term, with a resolution of the Senate determining the division into three-year and six-year senators. Territory senators are elected for the duration of one term of the House of Representatives. Senators' terms begin on July 1 following their election, except in the case of a dissolution of both houses, when the term begins on July 1 preceding the election.

SESSIONS

A Parliament commences on the first sitting day following a general election and concludes either at dissolution or at the expiration of three years from the first meeting of the House of Representatives. A Parliament may consist of one or more sessions, each session being terminated by a prorogation or the end of the Parliament. In recent years there have been no prorogations, and there has been only one session in each Parliament.

As a continuing body, the Senate prefers to use the term session rather than Parliament, so the first session of the 38th Parliament was the 66th session of the Senate.

The House of Representatives sits for sixty to seventy days each year, and the Senate, approximately eighty to eighty-five. The sittings are divided into periods—February to March, May to June, and August to December. Parliament usually sits Monday to Thursday for two weeks in succession followed by a break of two weeks, then another two weeks of sitting, and so on.

The most common way for a Parliament to be terminated is by the dissolution of the House of Representatives by proclamation of the governor general acting on the advice of the prime minister. Six Parliaments have been terminated by the simultaneous dissolution of the House and the Senate, and one Parliament ended because of the expiration of time.

When only the House of Representatives is dissolved, senators are discharged from attendance until the day appointed for holding the next sitting of Parliament. Dissolutions of the House are usually timed to permit general elections for the House of Representatives to be held at the same time as pending elections for half the Senate.

A recess is technically the period between sessions of the Parliament or the period between the close of a session by prorogation and the dissolution or expiry of the House. The several weeks between the three periods of sitting each year are popularly known as recesses, although they are more correctly referred to as adjournments.

HOW LAWS ARE MADE

All commonwealth laws must be passed by both houses of Parliament. The powers of the two houses are essentially identical, but the Senate cannot initiate or amend specified financial legislation. It can, however, ask the House to amend bills it cannot amend itself and can reject any bill.

In either house a member intending to introduce a bill normally gives written notice, which is listed on the notice paper. Or a senator or member may introduce a bill by leave, that is, with the unanimous consent of all senators or members present. Notice or leave is unnecessary for appropriation, supply, or taxation bills, which may originate only in the House of Representatives. Bills introduced by members or senators who are not ministers or parliamentary secretaries are known as private members' or private senators' bills. Any member or senator may introduce such a bill, but few are passed.

Legislative proceedings differ slightly in the two houses, but both include first reading (introduction); second reading (debate of the bill in principle); consideration in detail (called the committee of the whole stage in the Senate), when a bill may be amended; and third reading (final passage). In both houses a bill may be referred to a standing committee, although this is not common in the House of Representatives. A minister can declare a bill urgent and seek the agreement of the House or the Senate to a motion allotting time for the completion of the consideration of particular stages.

After a bill has passed one house, the presiding officer sends it with a message to the presiding officer of the other house. Bills are introduced into the other house when the presiding officer reads the message. Amendments or requested amendments made to a bill by the other house are considered in detail by the originating house. Where there are disagreements, messages pass between the houses seeking agreement on the bill's final form. If the houses cannot agree, a bill may be laid aside.

When a bill has passed both houses in identical form it is presented to the governor general for assent. At this point it becomes an act of Parliament, although it may not take effect until later. About two hundred acts are passed each year, and in recent years about 15 percent have originated in the Senate.

Under the constitution, proposed laws must be assented to by the governor general before becoming law. By convention governors general do not withhold their assent to proposed laws. They may, however, return any proposed law to the house from which it originated, together with any amendments they recommend. Traditionally these amendments are limited to correcting minor drafting errors.

COMMITTEES

Each house of Parliament appoints committees from among its own members. There are standing committees, which stand—or remain—for the life of any one Parliament. There are select committees, which are appointed to inquire into a particular matter and cease to exist at the conclusion of that inquiry. There are statutory committees, established by acts of Parliament, which exist until such acts are repealed. There are many domestic committees. There are also joint committees composed of senators and members of the House of Representatives.

The majority of Senate committees are standing committees, although at any time there may be several select committees. There are usually six to eight members of a Senate committee.

Legislative and general purpose standing committees make up the largest group of Senate committees. To represent the political composition of the Senate, each of eight subject areas has a References Committee and a Legislation Committee. Each pair of these committees has overlapping membership and a shared secretariat. The chair has a casting vote. The work of the Legislation Committees includes examining the annual appropriation and expenditure of government departments and agencies.

Other committees of note include the Scrutiny of Bills and the Regulations and Ordinances Committees, which examine all proposed legislation and delegated legislation to ensure that they conform to certain principles, mainly those concerned with civil liberties. There are also a number of committees concerned with internal matters, including the Privileges Committee.

The Selection of Bills Committee, established in 1990, advises the Senate on which bills should be considered by a specific committee or committees. The number of bills referred to the Senate's legislative and general purpose standing committees and select committees has increased in recent years. The committees have no power to amend bills referred to them but may recommend amendments or advise the Senate that bills should not be changed.

Aware that ultimate power resides in the Parliament, Senate committees monitor the way the government administers the law. They scrutinize government expenditure and decision making and examine and report on important or controversial issues. They systematically inquire into the annual reports of government departments and statutory bodies.

House committees

The nine House of Representatives general purpose standing committees established (since 1987) at the commencement of each Parliament inquire into and report on any matters referred to them by the House or a minister, including any prelegislation proposal, bill, motion, petition, vote or expenditure, other financial matter, report, or paper. Among them these committees of the House review most government activity, with each committee covering a particular spread of subjects and thus a number of related government departments and authorities. The Joint Com mittee on Foreign Affairs, Defense, and Trade makes a general purpose standing committee unnecessary for those areas. Annual reports of government departments and statutory authorities are automatically referred to the appropriate committee.

The House has a range of housekeeping committees concerned with its powers and procedures or the administration of Parliament. These more or less parallel those of the Senate, and, concerned with the operation of the Parliament as a whole, usually meet jointly with the equivalent Senate committee.

Committees are normally composed of members from the various parties in proportion to the numerical strength of each party in the House. Thus, government members form a majority on each committee. In practice each House of Representatives committee is chaired by a government member and has an opposition member as deputy chair. The members of each committee are selected or elected within the political parties, and their names are then put forward by the party whip.

Joint committees draw their membership from and report to both houses of Parliament, enabling members and senators to work together on the same matter. All statutory committees such as the Public Works and Public Accounts Committees are joint committees.

Investigations

The direction and extent of a committee's investigation are determined by its terms of reference. Committees do not have powers of their own—they possess only the authority delegated to them by the houses themselves. Each house has very wide prerogatives of inquiry, which include the power to probe into any matter of public interest and to acquire whatever information it considers necessary to discharge its constitutional responsibilities. Committees can summon witnesses and compel them to attend and produce relevant documents.

Unless held in secret, all committee inquiries are open to the public. Committees usually advertise their terms of reference and invite written submissions, which may be followed by oral testimony. Witnesses are rarely compelled to attend hearings. A committee usually invites people or organizations to provide relevant documents and to make oral or written submissions. Because committee hearings provide a forum in which individuals and groups may put their views directly to the Parliament, the opportunity to appear is usually welcomed. The proceedings of committees are recognized as proceedings of Parliament and thus have the same privileges and immunities as Parliament itself.

Public hearings can be held anywhere in Australia. Committees take Parliament to the people by traveling to areas relevant to their inquiries. Senate committees may not meet in public while the Senate is sitting except with the permission of the Senate.

THE BUDGET

Parliament has ultimate control over government finances because taxes, borrowing, and expenditure must be authorized by legislation. The government has the financial initiative, and only it can request that an appropriation be made or increased or propose to impose or increase taxation.

For constitutional reasons the annual appropriations for executive government expenditure are contained in two appropriation bills—one covering ordinary annual expenditure, which the Senate cannot amend, and one covering capital expenditure, which the Senate may amend. A separate appropriation covers expenditure by the Parliament. The appropriation bills introduced on budget day in May authorize expenditure for the following financial year commencing on July 1.

There is no special budget procedure in the House of Representatives. The budget depends on passage of the main appropriation bill for the year, which essentially follows the same stages as any other bill. Proceedings start with the speaker announcing a message from the governor general recommending that an appropriation of revenue be made for the purposes of the ordinary annual expenditure bill. The treasurer then presents the bill to the House, and it is read a first time. The treasurer moves the second reading and delivers the second reading speech on the bill. This is the budget speech in which the treasurer compares the estimates for the current financial year with actual expenditure, reviews the economic condition of the nation, and states the anticipated income and expenditure for the next financial year including taxation measures.

After debate on the ordinary annual expenditure bill has been adjourned, the treasurer presents the budget papers and the other appropriation bills. Other business may include introduction of related bills, presentation of related documents, ministerial statements to explain budget decisions, and customs and excise tariff proposals.

The second reading debate on the ordinary annual expenditure bill is the budget debate, which normally continues over several weeks. This is an opportunity for members to speak on a wide range of issues because the usual rule of relevance is relaxed for this debate. When the bill is being considered in detail, the House examines the proposed expenditure of each government department as listed in a schedule to the bill. A department's expenditure may be considered separately or grouped with other departments. The bill is then read a third time and sent to the Senate.

Senate consideration of the budget begins before the appropriation bills are received from the House. On budget day a minister presents copies of the budget papers to the Senate and makes a statement outlining the budget measures. Debate takes place on the motion to take note of the statement and papers, and the proposed expenditure of government departments is referred to Senate legislation committees for examination and report. During committee hearings, Senate ministers and senior government officials are questioned on current and proposed expenditure. The legislation committees report their findings to the Senate because the Senate considers the budget legislation after it has passed the House.

If the appropriation bills do not pass before the financial year begins, the Parliament may pass supply bills to provide funds in the interim.

Bills authorizing funding for specific purposes may be introduced at any time, and such appropriations may be indeterminate in both amount and duration. Appropriations not restricted in application to one financial year, and thus not subject to the annual supervision and control of the Parliament, are known as standing appropriations. A large proportion of government expenditure is funded by this means.

EXECUTIVE POWER AND THE PARLIAMENT

Under the constitution the executive power of the commonwealth is vested in the queen of Australia and is exercisable by her representative in Australia, the governor general. By convention, the governor general acts in accordance with advice provided by ministers of state led by the prime minister. These ministers of state are usually referred to as the government. The constitution requires that ministers of state be members of the Parliament.

Under the Australian system of parliamentary government, the party or coalition of parties that possesses the confidence of the majority of members of the House of Representatives forms the government. The government must resign if it loses this confidence. But if it maintains the confidence of its party members in the House, in practice the government is assured of the support of the House for the term of the Parliament. This backing also means that government bills will usually pass the House and that, although members use the opportunities available to investigate and scrutinize the operations of government, in all normal circumstances the majority will, at the end of the day, support the government.

Government control of the House of Representatives exists for two reasons. First, the single-member preferential system used for elections for the House of Representatives makes it very likely that one party or coalition will win a majority of seats in the House. Second, tight discipline within Australian political parties ensures that members of the government party or coalition in the House continue to support the government.

It is rare for the government to control the Senate, because the proportional voting system used for Senate elections makes it difficult for the government party or coalition to obtain a majority there. Therefore the government is not usually assured of the Senate's continuing support. In addition, the government must win support from nongovernment senators, usually the minor parties and independents, before the Senate will agree to pass a government bill. If the opposition party or coalition is able to gain the support of the minor parties and independents, the Senate may reject or amend government bills. Again, because the Senate is not controlled by the government, it is able to investigate government policies and activities closely.

Each sitting day during question time, ministers in each house may be questioned on any aspect of the administration of their departments, proceedings in Parliament they oversee, or public affairs with which they are connected. Questions are asked directly without notice, with the opportunity to ask questions alternating between government and opposition senators or members. Written questions on notice may also be submitted for written response.

The government may also be examined at other times—for example, during time set aside for raising matters of public importance, during general debates such as that which takes place when each house adjourns for the day, and, in the House of Representatives, during the budget and address-in-reply debates.

The opposition party or coalition allocates primary responsibility for examining particular areas of government policy and administration to certain of its members, who are known as shadow ministers. It is usually these shadow ministers who, for example, ask the opposition's questions without notice to government ministers during question time or raise matters of public importance. But other members of the opposition party or coalition also study the government, often in their capacity as members of parliamentary committees.

Other institutions that oversee the operations of the executive government include the Australian National Audit Office and the commonwealth ombudsman. The National Audit Office carries out financial audits of commonwealth departments and agencies and assesses whether they are being administered efficiently and effectively. The commonwealth ombudsman investigates complaints about the administrative actions of the executive government departments and agencies. These investigations may reveal defective administration that the ombudsman recommends departments and agencies remedy.

THE SPEAKER AND PRESIDENT OF THE SENATE

The speaker of the House of Representatives and the president of the Senate are the principal office holders of their respective houses. They are their houses' representatives, chairs, and ministers in terms of the support they provide. The presiding officers' authority is derived from their respective houses of Parliament, to which their duty lies and to which they are answerable.

Each presiding officer is the spokesperson for his or her house in its relations with the other constituent parts of the Parliament, the executive, the judiciary, and with other outside bodies and people. On behalf of their houses, they receive delegations from other Parliaments and special visitors. On formal occasions they represent their houses and play central ceremonial roles. In these capacities presiding officers uphold the dignity and authority of the houses of Parliament and protect the rights and privileges of the houses.

When chairing meetings of the houses, the presiding officers must ensure that the rules of parliamentary procedure as embodied in the standing orders and practice of the respective houses are applied. They interpret and enforce the standing orders, respond to members' or senators' points of order, and give rulings when necessary.

Standing orders provide substantial disciplinary powers to the presiding officers. For a minor infringement a member or senator may be called to order or warned. For a major offense or persistent defiance of the chair, a motion for the member's or senator's suspension may be brought. The penalty increases each time within a calendar year a member or senator is suspended—twenty-four hours on the first occasion, three (House) or seven (Senate) sitting days on the second, and seven (House) or fourteen (Senate) sitting days on the third and subsequent occasions. The speaker can also direct a disorderly member to withdraw from the House for one hour.

Presiding officers have ultimate responsibility, alone and jointly, for the administration of Parliament and the operation of Parliament House. The speaker is, in effect, minister for the Department of the House of Representatives, and the president of the Senate, minister for the Department of the Senate. Each has a role analogous to that of a minister of state in relation to a government department and may be questioned on matters of parliamentary administration. The speaker and the president are jointly responsible for the administration of the three parliamentary service departments—the Joint House Department, the Department of the Parliamentary Library, and the Department of the Parliamentary Reporting Staff.

PARTIES

The leader of the majority party or larger party in a coalition commanding a majority in the House of Representatives is the prime minister, and the leader of the largest opposition party is the leader of the opposition. Leaders of the same parties in the Senate are the leader of the government in the Senate and leader of the opposition in the Senate regardless of whether the government has a majority in that chamber.

Members and senators who belong to the Labor Party form the parliamentary Labor Party, often known as the caucus. The term caucus is not generally used for other parties.

All parties have caucus or party meetings during sitting weeks, usually at times when the houses are not sitting. These meetings provide the forum for discussing internal party policy, parliamentary activity, and parliamentary tactics; resolving internal disputes; electing officers; and exerting backbench pressure on and communicating with party leaders. Coalition partners may hold separate and joint party meetings. Separate Senate and House of Representatives party meetings are also held.

Party loyalty and discipline are strong in the major parties, and members and senators of those parties generally vote in accordance with the party decision unless a conscience vote is permitted. Failure to vote along party lines on important issues may seriously jeopardize a member's or senator's chances of reelection if the party withdraws its support. Parties have been willing to use this sanction, and serious breaches of party discipline are rare. The governing party uses discipline to control the House of Representatives. Party members do not ordinarily act individually in the Parliament, where they usually exhibit party solidarity, but they have many opportunities to express their views within the party. Senators of the non-Labor parties have historically exercised greater freedom, and members of minor parties in the Senate do not necessarily vote with their parties.

Each party has whips for each house whose main function is to provide administrative support to their parliamentary parties. Outside the chambers the whips may provide the clerical back-up for such matters as coordinating party committees, arranging nominations to parliamentary committees, and organizing party balloting.

Whips perform many tasks, including arranging the number and order of participants in debate (the list of speakers is not binding on the chair), ensuring the attendance of party members for divisions and quorum calls, arranging pairs for members or senators who are absent from parliamentary sittings, and acting as tellers in divisions. They also assist their respective party managers of business in negotiations on the government's legislative program. In the House of Representatives the chief government whip has the authority to expedite certain motions relating to the sitting arrangements and the business of the House.

DEBATES

Members and senators have opportunities to take part in debates other than those on legislation. These include debates on parliamentary committee reports, papers presented to the House and Senate, statements made by ministers, matters of public importance or urgency, and motions moved by private members or senators. An adjournment debate is scheduled at the end of every sitting in each house, during which individual members or senators may raise any matter they choose.

The chair allocates the call, which in practice alternates between government and nongovernment members or senators. Time limits apply to speeches in most instances and are generally more restrictive in the House than in the Senate.

The standing orders set down some rules to control debate; others are based on convention or tradition. Restrictions on the content of debate in both chambers include matters not relevant to the question, except where specifically permitted; matters listed on the notice paper for future debate; references to previous debate, unless relevant to the matter under discussion; reference to proceedings in the other house, unless relevant to the matter under discussion; tedious repetition; references to the queen and her representatives that are disrespectful or made for the purpose of influencing debate; unparliamentary language; offensive words against either house, member, senator, or the judiciary; and matters before, or listed to come before, a court of law.

Decisions are made by the chair asking those supporting the motion to say "aye" and those against it to say "no." Most decisions are made on the voices. If more than one challenges the chair's opinion of the vote, the question is decided by a formal vote.

Formal votes are taken by the members or senators dividing for and against the question. When a division is called, the chair instructs the clerk to ring the bells to summon those not present to the chamber. The bells are rung for four minutes throughout Parliament House, accompanied by flashing green or red lights to indicate the House of Representatives or Senate, respectively.

After the bells stop, the chair orders the doors of the chamber locked and states the question, directing the "ayes" to the right of the chair and the "noes" to the left. Members or senators take seats on the appropriate side of the chamber, and the chair appoints tellers to record the names of those voting. The chair announces the result.

Transcripts of the debates of both houses are published in *Commonwealth Parliamentary Debates* (Hansard). The Parliament's other official records are the *Votes and Proceedings* of the House of Representatives and the *Journals of the Senate*.

RELATIONS BETWEEN CHAMBERS

The Senate and the House of Representatives function as distinct and independent units. Each undertakes its responsibility in relation to proposed legislation independently of the other. Each house is solely responsible for its own procedures and for resolving any matters relating to its powers, privileges, and immunities. Each has established its own committee system. Each house employs its own staff to assist its members in performing their duties. In addition, the constitution provides that no member of one house may sit as a member of the other house.

The independence of the Senate and the House of Representatives from each other is also manifested in relations between the houses. For example, the power of each house to call people to appear before it (or one of its committees) does not extend to calling members of the other house. In the same way, Senate estimates committees do not examine the appropriations for the House of Representatives.

The constitution provides a way to resolve disagreements between the houses over proposed legislation. If the House of Representatives passes a proposed law and the Senate rejects that proposed law or passes it with amendments to which the House of Representatives will not agree, and if after three months the same thing happens again, then the governor general may dissolve both houses of Parliament. If after the ensuing election the houses still cannot agree, then the governor general may convene a joint sitting of the members of the Senate and the House of Representatives. The proposed law is deemed to have been passed by both houses of Parliament if an absolute majority of members of Parliament approve the proposed law at the joint sitting.

Formal communications between the Senate and the

House of Representatives are usually undertaken by message between the president of the Senate and the speaker of the House. Most messages relate to proposed legislation. Messages may contain a proposed law initiated by one house that it wishes to send to the other house for concurrence. If the other house amends the proposed law, it will send a message to the initiating house containing the proposed law and the amendments it has made.

PARLIAMENTARY PRIVILEGES AND IMMUNITIES

The constitution provided that the powers and immunities of the Senate and the House of Representatives and of the members and the committees of each house should be those of the House of Commons of the United Kingdom until the commonwealth Parliament itself defined them. The Parliament did this in 1987 when it enacted the Parliamentary Privileges Act. This statute declared that the powers and immunities existing before its enactment were to continue, subject to some significant alterations.

Each house of Parliament has the power to require the attendance and service of its members, to regulate its internal affairs and procedures free of interference by the courts, to institute inquiries and to require the attendance of witnesses and the production of documents, and to punish those guilty of committing offenses against it. The failure to comply with an order of the Senate or the House of Representatives made in pursuance of one of its powers may be punished.

A senator or member of the House of Representatives can present a motion that an offense has been committed or that the Committee of Privileges of the relevant house consider whether a person has committed an offense. If the house agrees to this motion, its committee investigates the matter. When undertaking an inquiry, the privileges committee of each house seeks to ensure that the subjects of the inquiry are treated fairly. The Senate has passed formal resolutions on this matter.

The Committee of Privileges reports to its parent house. The house then decides whether or not an offense has been committed and may resolve to punish the offender. Offenses may be punished by reprimand, fine, or imprisonment. Alternatively, a house may decide not to punish an offense if, for example, it considers the offense minor. The Parliamentary Privileges Act of 1987 sets limits on the penalties a house may impose for offenses. The maximum term of imprisonment a house may impose is six months. A person may not be both fined and imprisoned for the same offense.

Where a house resolves to imprison a person, the resolution of the house and the warrant to commit the person to prison must set out the particulars of the offense committed. This allows a court to review the decision of the house to determine whether the person's conduct constituted an offense.

Members of Parliament are immune from certain laws that would unduly restrict their performance in Parliament. These immunities are enforced by the courts when cases come before them involving parliamentarians. Parliamentary immunities are limited in number and effect. The most important relates to freedom of speech and ensures that no member of a house of Parliament may be called to account for what he or she says in that house (or one of its committees) other than by that house itself. Thus, when speaking in the Parliament members are immune from suit or prosecution in the courts under the laws relating to defamation. This immunity is also extended to people giving evidence before a House of Parliament or one of its committees. Members of Parliament are also exempt from appearing before a court or tribunal as a witness or juror when Parliament is sitting or for five days before and after a sitting day.

The Senate provides an opportunity for redress to people who believe that they have been referred to in the Senate in a way that damages their reputation or interests or invades their privacy. Such a person may make a submission to the president of the Senate. The president passes this submission to the Committee of Privileges, which may recommend either that the Senate take no action or that a reply by the person be published by the Senate or incorporated in the *Hansard*. The committee does not make any judgment about the truth of the statements made in the Senate or in the response. The Senate then decides whether to accept the committee's recommendation or not.

MEMBERS

A senator or member of the House of Representatives may resign by writing to the president of the Senate or the speaker of the House of Representatives.

Neither house of Parliament possesses the power to expel one of its members. However, the constitution provides that a senator or member of the House forfeits his or her place in the Parliament in a number of circumstances—for example, if he or she becomes a citizen of a foreign country, is convicted of committing an offense punishable under the law of the commonwealth or of a state by imprisonment for one year or longer, becomes an undischarged bankrupt, or obtains a pecuniary interest in any agreement with the Australian Public Service other than as a member of an incorporated company consisting of more than twenty-five members.

Under the constitution Parliament determines members' pay. Senators and members of the House are entitled to a base salary, an electorate allowance, and a number of other allowances. The base salaries of members of Parliament are tied to the salaries of officers of the Australian Public Service. The size of the electorate allowances paid to members of the House of Representatives increases with the size of their electorate. All senators receive the same electoral allowance, which is equal to the allowance paid to members of the House of Representatives with the smallest electorates. Other benefits and allowances relate to travel on parliamentary business both within Australia and overseas and to office expenses such as postage and telephone. The Remuneration Tribunal, which determines the salary entitlements of a wide range of public officials, determines the size of allowances but not the base salary.

All members of Parliament are required to contribute a fixed percentage of their salaries and allowances (including any additional salary they receive as a parliamentary office holder or minister) to the Parliamentary Contributory Superannuation Scheme. Members of the House of Representatives who serve four terms and senators who serve two terms are entitled to a pension on completing their stint in Parliament. The rate of their pension entitlement is calculated as a proportion of their total ending salaries and allowances and increases with the length of their service in Parliament. Members may also receive up to 50 percent of their pensions as a lump sum. Members of Parliament who do not serve the required number of terms to qualify for a pension are entitled to a lump sum comprising their contributions plus interest. A pension is also payable to the spouse of a member of Parliament who dies in office, regardless of the length of that member's service.

Senators and members of the House of Representatives who hold parliamentary offices are entitled to a salary in addition to that which they receive as members of Parliament. These offices include the speaker of the House of Representatives and the president of the Senate, the leader of the opposition, the leader of the opposition in the Senate, government and opposition whips in the House of Representatives and in the Senate, and the chairpersons of all parliamentary committees.

The salaries of individual ministers are paid in addition to their salaries as members of Parliament. The Remuneration Tribunal regularly reviews the level of salaries and allowances to be paid to ministers and recommends alterations to them, but it is the executive government that decides whether the recommendations should be adopted. Salaries vary according to each minister's level of responsibility.

Under the standing orders of each house, the Senate and the House of Representatives may suspend senators or members who persistently and willfully obstruct the business of the relevant house, are disorderly, use objectionable words and refuse to withdraw them, persistently and willfully refuse to conform to any standing order, or persistently and willfully disregard the authority of the chair.

A house may also punish a parliamentarian for any act that interferes with the authority or functions of a house or committee or with another member's duties. Accepting bribes, misleading a house or committee, or willfully disturbing them fall under this category. Offenses may be punished by reprimand, fine, or imprisonment.

Senators and members of the House of Representatives are required to make a statement to the respective registrar of all registrable interests that the senator, member, spouse, or dependent children hold, including share holdings in companies, directorships of companies, real estate, debts, bonds, and many other types of assets and liabilities. Only the interest needs to be registered, not the value of the interest. Failure to provide this information would constitute an offense. Each house has established a housekeeping committee to oversee the operation of its register of interests.

PARLIAMENT AND THE MEDIA

Radio broadcasts of the proceedings of Federal Parliament began in 1946. By law, the Australian Broadcasting Corporation, an independent statutory corporation funded by the commonwealth, is required to provide radio broadcasts of the proceedings of Federal Parliament in accordance with determinations of the Joint Statutory Committee on the Broadcasting of Parliamentary Proceedings. Broadcast days are allocated to each house to give them approximately equal broadcast time. A parliamentary broadcasting network has been established for this purpose.

Although television broadcasts of certain parliamentary proceedings had been permitted for some years, it was not until 1990 that televising parliamentary proceedings was authorized permanently. The Australian Broadcasting Corporation is allowed to broadcast the Senate's question time, and television stations may use excerpts of Senate proceedings. The House of Representatives authorized the live broadcast and rebroadcast of its proceedings on television. It also established a housekeeping committee to monitor televising of its proceedings. Both houses resolved that public hearings of their committees may be broadcast only with the committee's permission.

The Sound and Vision Office of the Department of Parliamentary Reporting Staff records the proceedings of the Senate and the House of Representatives for television and radio. This office then provides broadcast-quality television footage and radio coverage to television and radio networks. The guidelines of each house restrict, for example, the use of wide angle shots, requiring cameras to focus on the senator or member who is speaking.

Television stations may use footage of proceedings of each house only in accordance with guidelines contained in the resolutions authorizing the televising of each house. The guidelines of each house require that material should be used only for fair and accurate reports of proceedings and may not be used for ridicule or satire, in advertising of any type, or in election campaigns. Reports of proceedings must provide a balanced presentation of differing views.

Australian Broadcasting Corporation statistics indicate that over a twelve-week period more than twelve million people, more than two-thirds of Australia's population, watch at least ten minutes of parliamentary proceedings on television.

Parliament of the Commonwealth of Australia

BIBLIOGRAPHY

Barlin, L. M., ed. *House of Representatives Practice.* 3d ed. Canberra: Australian Government Publishing Service, 1997.

Evans, Harry, ed. *Odgers' Australian Senate Practice.* 7th ed. Canberra: Australian Government Publishing Service, 1995.

Lloyd, C. J. *The Parliament and the Press.* Carlton: Melbourne University Press, 1988.

Lucy, Richard. *The Australian Form of Government: Models in Dispute.* 2d ed. South Melbourne: Macmillan, 1993.

Millar, Ann. *Trust the Women: Women in the Federal Parliament.* Rev. ed. Canberra: Department of the Senate, 1994.

Reid, G. S., and Martyn Forrest. *Australia's Commonwealth Parliament, 1901–1988.* Carlton: Melbourne University Press, 1989.

Rydon, Joan. *A Federal Legislature: Australian Commonwealth Parliament 1901–1980.* Melbourne: Oxford University Press, 1986.

Singleton, G., et al. *Australian Political Institutions.* 5th ed. Melbourne: Longman, 1996.

Solomon, David. *The People's Palace: Parliament in Modern Australia.* Carlton: Melbourne University Press, 1986.

Souter, Gavin. *Acts of Parliament: A Narrative History of the Senate and House of Representatives.* Carlton: Melbourne University Press, 1988.

AUSTRIA

OFFICIAL NAME: Republic of Austria (Republik Österreich)
CAPITAL: Vienna
POPULATION: 8,023,000 (1996 est.)
DATE OF INDEPENDENCE: October 30, 1918 (from Austro-Hungarian Empire)
DATE OF CURRENT CONSTITUTION: Adopted October 1, 1920; effective November 10, 1920
FORM OF GOVERNMENT: Parliamentary democracy
LANGUAGE: German
MONETARY UNIT: Austrian schilling
FISCAL YEAR: Calendar year
LEGISLATURE: Organs of the federal legislation
NUMBER OF CHAMBERS: Two. National Council (Nationalrat); Federal Council (Bundesrat)
NUMBER OF MEMBERS: National Council, 183 (directly elected); Federal Council, 64 (indirectly elected)
PERCENTAGE OF WOMEN: National Council, 26.8; Federal Council, 20.3
TERM OF LEGISLATURE: National Council, four years; Federal Council, term of individual members varies from five to six years, as determined by the province they represent
MOST RECENT LEGISLATIVE ELECTION: National Council, December 17, 1995
MINIMUM AGE FOR VOTING: 18 before calendar year in which election is held
MINIMUM AGE FOR MEMBERSHIP: 19 before calendar year in which election is held
SUFFRAGE: Universal
VOTING: Optional
ADDRESS: Parliament, Dr.-Karl-Renner-Ring 3, A-1017 Vienna
TELEPHONE: (431) 401 10
FAX: (431) 401 10 2537

Austria, located in the heart of Europe *(see map, p. 265)*, emerged as a republic from the Austro-Hungarian Empire in 1918. The federal constitution, dating to 1920, establishes a federal state with a parliamentary system of government, the federal government being politically responsible to the Nationalrat, which is the federal legislative organ elected directly by the people. The other of the two organs of federal legislation is the Bundesrat, whose members are delegated by the legislative bodies of the federal provinces.

HISTORICAL BACKGROUND

When the Austro-Hungarian Empire fell apart in 1918, the Republic of Austria emerged as one of its successor states. The state was founded on October 30, 1918, by the Provisional National Assembly, an interim parliament consisting of those members of the House of Representatives of the Imperial Council who represented German-speaking electoral districts. On November 12, 1918, the republic was proclaimed. After the boundaries of the state had been determined by the Treaty of Saint-Germain in 1919, the Constituent National Assembly elected on February 16, 1919, began work on a definitive constitution, which was adopted on October 1, 1920, and entered into force on November 10 of that year.

Under the provisions of the federal constitution, the Nationalrat and the Bundesrat were vested with the federal legislative power. The federal government was made politically responsible to the Nationalrat, and until 1929 it was elected by the Nationalrat as well. Through the 1929 amendment of the federal constitution, the federal president—who from then on was to be elected directly by the people—was entrusted with appointing the federal government. The members of the federal government, however, could be dismissed by a vote of no confidence by the Nationalrat.

The 1929 amendment expressed the reservations of bourgeois politicians about the system of parliamentary government. The amendment also reflected an increasing hostility between left- and right-wing political parties, which manifested itself even more vividly in the streets. When the three presidents of the Nationalrat resigned on March 4, 1933, after a controversial vote, the federal government under Christian Social chancellor Engelbert Dollfuss seized the opportunity and declared that the Nationalrat had incapacitated itself; thenceforth it governed by decree. Social Democratic opposition was suppressed in the civil war of February 1934. The authoritarian system established by a new constitution decreed by the federal government on May 1, 1934, lasted until March 12, 1938, when German troops occupied the country. Now Austria had to pay the price for having suppressed the opposition instead of working toward the cooperation of all anti-fascist forces.

After World War II the Republic of Austria declared its independence on April 27, 1945. Austria remained under Allied occupation until 1955, when the State Treaty of Vienna was concluded. On December 19, 1945, the day the newly elected Nationalrat assembled for the first time, the federal constitution as amended in 1929 entered into force again. Austrians and the Austrian political parties had learned their lesson. From 1945 on, a fundamental consensus based on the principles of parliamentary democracy characterized the political system.

CONSTITUTIONAL PROVISIONS ON PARLIAMENT

The Austrian federal constitution establishes the Republic of Austria as a federal state. According to the federal principle, the constitution divides two of the three classical functions of government—legislation and administration—between the *bund* (federation) and the *länder* (federal provinces), but the *bund* has exclusive power over the judiciary. The extent of federalism is determined by the distribution of legislative and administrative powers between the *bund* and the *länder* in Articles 10–15 of the federal constitution. As a whole, the federal character of the republic proves to be rather weak, especially since the power to determine or change the distribution of powers remains with the *bund*.

Federal legislation (and enactment of constitutional laws) falls within the competence of the Nationalrat (National Council) and the Bundesrat (Federal Council) as two organizationally separate bodies, not as constituents of a bicameral parliament. Legislative powers are distributed unequally between these two bodies.

Articles 24–33 of the constitution contain the organizational and institutional provisions for the Nationalrat, Articles 34–37 for the Bundesrat, and Articles 38–40 for the Bundesversammlung (Federal Assembly).The Federal Assembly is a parliamentary body in its own right, consisting of the members of the Nationalrat and the Bundesrat and given some specific competences, such as swearing in the federal president. Legislative procedure (Articles 41–49b), the share of the Nationalrat and the Bundesrat in the federal executive power (Articles 50–55), and the status of the members of the Nationalrat and the Bundesrat (Articles 56–59a) are also constitutionally prescribed. Articles 23a–23f, which were inserted by a 1994 amendment when Austria joined the European Union (EU), govern Nationalrat and Bundesrat participation in Austrian decisions about EU projects.

Further provisions on parliament are spread throughout the constitution, such as the regulations for the vote of no confidence (Art. 74) or the Court of Audit (Articles 121–126d), which as an organ of the Nationalrat is entrusted with monitoring the *bund's* administration of public funds.

ARCHITECTURE AND FACILITIES

The Austrian parliament building was designed by the Danish architect Theophil Hansen and built in the years 1874–1884 to accommodate both houses of the Austrian Reichsrat (Imperial Council).

The parliament building was constructed in the classical style. To Hansen, this style represented timeless beauty and was thus the only valid form for the country's most important monumental construction. It also represented classical Greece as the cradle of democracy. According to Hansen's plan, the two mighty, cube-shaped wings accommodating the plenary debating chambers of the House of Representatives (Abgeordnetenhaus) and the House of Lords (Herrenhaus) were to be connected by a long central structure with a protruding portico. A columned hall stood at the center of the entire building. On December 4, 1883, the first sitting of the House of Representatives took place, and on December 16, 1884, the House of Lords assembled for the first time in the new parliament building.

The front view of the parliament building reflects Hansen's architectural concept. The (northern) wing to the right accommodates the debating chamber of the former House of Representatives, and the (southern) wing to the left, the debating chamber of the House of Lords. The southern wing was heavily damaged in the Second World War; today, the former debating chamber of the House of Lords, in its renovated form, serves for the plenary sittings of the Nationalrat.

The lower tracts connecting the wings with the central structure accommodate the offices of the presidents of the Nationalrat, parliamentary committee rooms, and the offices of the parliamentary administration as well as of the parliamentary groups. The columned hall recalls the Parthenon on the Acropolis of Athens; it forms the center of the parliament building and was originally intended as a meeting place for the members of the two houses of the Reichsrat. Today it serves for special events.

As building materials, Hansen attempted to obtain marble and stone from the several crownlands of the monarchy to express their close relationship to parliament. The twenty-four monolithic columns of the large hall, each weighing more than sixteen tons, were made of marble from the Adnet quarries in the province of Salzburg, and the floor plates were made of Istrian karstic marble (today the peninsula of Istria belongs to the Republic of Croatia).

The debating chamber of the former House of Representatives in the northern wing is largely preserved in its original form, having escaped damage in World War II, and serves today for the sittings of the Federal Assembly as well as for joint ceremonial and commemorative meetings of the Nationalrat and the Bundesrat. The hall is in the style of a Greek theater. Along the front wall are the chair of the House, the rostrum, and government bench. Seats for the members of parliament (MPs) are arranged in a semicircle. The Carrara marble statues on the front wall lie between columns and pilasters made of Untersberg marble and represent Roman statesmen; the frieze painting by Friedrich Eisenmenger shows the genesis of state life. The pediment group symbolizes the daily routine.

The former debating chamber of the House of Lords, which had accommodated the sittings of the Nationalrat between 1920 and 1934, was totally burned out at the end of the Second World War, and the figural ornamentation seemed beyond repair. Between 1953 and 1956 the debating chamber of the Nationalrat was reconstructed with a modern, functional interior built from plans prepared by the architects Max Fellerer and Eugen Wörle.

Since June 8, 1956, the Nationalrat has held its meetings in this hall. The three presidents of the Nationalrat alternately preside over meetings from the chair along the front wall of the hall. The government bench from which members of the federal government may take the floor is in front. The MPs speak from the rostrum in front of the government bench. The seats for the MPs are arranged in a semicircle. The loges for the federal president, the members of the Bundesrat, the diplomatic corps, and journalists are located on the balcony above. Seats for the general public are on the gallery.

In 1920 what had been the assembly hall for members of the House of Lords, between the columned hall and the present debating chamber of the Nationalrat, was adapted as a debating chamber for the Bundesrat. The interior dates mainly from 1961.

Taking turns, the president of the Bundesrat or the two vice presidents preside over the meetings from the chair, with the government bench in front subdivided to allow room for the rostrum. The seats for the members of the Bundesrat are arranged in a semicircle. The benches reserved for the general public are in both corners at the front of the hall.

PARTIES AND ELECTIONS

Nationalrat elections

The Nationalrat is elected by the people in accordance with the principle of proportional representation through equal, direct, secret, and personal suffrage for men and women who have reached the age of eighteen before January 1 of the election year. Voting is not compulsory. Eligible for election are all men and women who before January 1 of the election year have reached the age of nineteen. Only a court sentence can exclude one from the right to vote and from eligibility.

The Nationalrat consists of 183 members. For election of the Nationalrat, the country is divided into nine constituencies, whose boundaries correspond to the boundaries of the nine federal provinces. These provincial constituencies are subdivided into forty-three regional constituencies. The number of deputies to be elected in each provincial and regional constituency is determined in proportion to the number of citizens who in the last census had their principal residence in a particular constituency and the number of citizens living abroad entered on the electoral register of a local community in that constituency.

Each party contesting the election may, but need not,

submit lists of candidates at the provincial and regional constituency levels as well as at the federal level. The number of candidates entered on each of these lists may exceed (at the provincial and regional levels double) the number of seats to be distributed. Voters cast ballots for a list. The seats are allocated to the parties standing for election through three distribution procedures: The first allocation takes place at the level of the regional constituencies; the second, at the level of the provincial constituencies. In both allocations, the Hare method is used. Often, some seats remain undistributed after the first two allocations. The final allocation, for the whole federal territory, is carried out according to the d'Hondt formula to ensure proportional balance. In this final step, all 183 seats are distributed among those parties that either won a seat in a regional constituency or reached the 4 percent threshold at the federal level for seating candidates; the seats not distributed through the first two allocation formulas are distributed to the parties to bridge the difference between the number of seats a party has already gained at the regional and provincial levels and the number of seats the party is entitled to according to its nationwide share of the vote.

This system of distributing seats dates to the electoral reform of 1992. When used in the Nationalrat elections of 1994 and 1995, it proved better at translating the constitutional principle of proportional representation into action than the system used before.

The other objective of the electoral reform of 1992—to deepen the relationship between the electorate and the elected by an improved preferential vote system—was not as well realized. Furthermore, the chance of voters upsetting the order of the party list is small.

Vacancies arising between general elections are filled by the "next-in-line" candidate on the list of the party that held the seat.

The most recent Nationalrat elections, held after the premature dissolution of the Nationalrat elected in 1994, were conducted on December 17, 1995. In two electoral districts, balloting had to be held again on October 13, 1996, after the Constitutional Court had allowed an electoral challenge. The Social Democratic Party gained six seats, winning seventy-one with 38.06 percent of the vote, and the Austrian People's Party held steady at fifty-two seats with 28.29 percent of the vote. The Freedom Party won forty-one seats, for a net loss of one, with 21.89 percent of the vote. The Liberal Forum also lost one seat, falling to ten seats, with 5.51 percent of the vote; and the Greens dropped from thirteen seats to nine, with 4.81 percent of the vote.

Bundesrat elections

The members of the Bundesrat are elected by the legislative bodies of the federal provinces (*ländtage,* or diets), for the duration of their respective legislative terms. They need not be members of the diet by which they are delegated but must be eligible for it. The election must follow the principles of proportional representation and must be based on the results of the latest election to the provincial diet. As an exception to this principle, at least one seat must fall to the party with the second highest number of popular votes in the election.

The diets elect a substitute member for each member they delegate to the Bundesrat. This substitute becomes the member's *ex lege* successor if the member's seat becomes vacant.

The Bundesrat has no permanently fixed number of members. After each census (usually taken every ten years) the federal president determines how many members each province may elect. The province with the most citizens has twelve seats. Each of the other provinces has as many members as correspond to the ratio between the number of its citizens and that of the most populous province, the minimum of seats being three.

Based on the 1991 census, the Bundesrat has had sixty-four members since 1993. Since the 1996 provincial election, the Austrian People's Party has held twenty-six, the Social Democratic Party twenty-four, and the Freedom Party fourteen seats in the Bundesrat.

PARLIAMENTARY PROCEEDINGS

Sessions and annual calendar

Each Nationalrat serves four years, calculated from the day of its first meeting. The legislative period started on January 15, 1996, will end no later than January 14, 2000.

Every year the federal president convenes an ordinary session of the Nationalrat, which lasts from mid-September to mid-July of the following year. At the request of the federal government or of one-third of the members, the federal president is obliged to convene an extraordinary session of the Nationalrat. The president of the Nationalrat convenes the chamber's sittings according to the program of work he draws up after consulting with the Conference of Presidents. The federal government or a qualified minority of the members can ask the president to convene a sitting within a session.

The federal government has to call general elections in time to ensure that the newly elected Nationalrat can meet on the day after the end of the fourth year of a legislative period. The Nationalrat can also decide to dissolve itself, or the federal president may dissolve the Nationalrat on proposal of the federal government (the federal president has not done this since 1945).

The Bundesrat is permanently in session. The president of the Bundesrat convenes sittings after consulting with the Conference of Presidents. A qualified minority of the members of the Bundesrat or the federal government can, however, oblige the president to convene a sitting.

How laws are made

There are several ways to introduce a law in the Nationalrat. Most laws adopted by the Nationalrat originate as bills submitted by the federal government. The federal ministry concerned drafts a bill and then asks other ministries, the administrations of the federal provinces, and interest groups for their comments. Then the respective member of the federal government submits it to the Council of Ministers. Only after the Council of Ministers adopts it unanimously is the bill submitted to the Nationalrat, where it is distributed to all members.

The second most important form of proposing a law is the private member's motion submitted to the Nationalrat, which requires the support of a minimum of five members of the Nationalrat. Occasionally, proposals of laws are submitted as bills of the Bundesrat or of one-third of its members or as a popular initiative that must be supported by 100,000 voters or one-sixth of the voters from each of three provinces. Except for the committee responsible for petitions and citizens' initiatives, Nationalrat committees, in connection with a matter referred to them for deliberation, can submit a motion for the adoption of a federal law to the plenary.

Motions by a committee of the Nationalrat may be passed on to second reading without further deliberations in committee, but all other bills are either referred to a committee for preliminary deliberation or undergo a first reading (that is, a discussion of the general outline of the bill) in plenary before being referred to a committee. In the committee or subcommittee the bill may still be modified completely. The committee report to the Nationalrat forms the basis for deliberations in plenary, and further amendments can be adopted during the second reading. During the third reading, however, amendments are limited to eliminating contradictions, orthographic and typing errors, or grammatical deficiencies. In practice, however, most major amendments are adopted in the committee. Deliberations in plenary serve to present decisions made in the committee to the general public and allow members to speak for or against the bill.

As a rule, the quorum required for a decision in the Nationalrat is one-third of its members, and an absolute majority of the votes cast is necessary for adoption. Federal constitutional acts and constitutional provisions contained in simple federal laws, however, require a quorum of one half of the members and a two-thirds majority of the votes cast.

After a bill passes the Nationalrat, it goes to the Bundesrat when that body has the right to object to or approve that kind of law. Certain laws, such as the Federal Finance Act or legal provisions for federal property, become federal law without going to the Bundesrat. The Nationalrat can overrule a Bundesrat objection by adopting the law a second time, for which a quorum of one-half of its members is required. If the Nationalrat, in response to a Bundesrat objection, modifies its original legal enactment, the Bundesrat must act on it again. Laws restricting the legislative and executive powers of the provinces, laws modifying the provisions of the federal constitution for the Bundesrat, or proposed federal framework acts establishing a deadline of less than six months or more than twelve months for adopting provincial legislation require the consent of the Bundesrat to enter into force.

The quorum and majority requirements in the Bundesrat are similar to those in the Nationalrat.

After a bill passes into a federal act of parliament, to put it into force the federal president must sign it, the federal chancellor must countersign it, and the law must be announced in the *Federal Law Gazette*. The constitution does not grant the federal government veto power over enactments of the Nationalrat. Authentication by the federal president and countersignature by the federal chancellor only certify the constitutionality of the procedure by which a federal law has been enacted. A federal act of parliament becomes effective either on the date figuring on the act itself or, if there is no such date, on the day after it appears in the *Federal Law Gazette*.

Budget procedures

The Federal Finance Act (including the federal budget estimates) constitutes the legal basis for managing the federal economy. At least ten weeks before the fiscal year ends, the federal government must submit to the Nationalrat the draft of a federal finance act for the next fiscal year. After an introductory speech by the minister of finance and its first reading, the draft is referred to the budget committee for preliminary deliberation. The second and third readings take place in the plenary of the Nationalrat.

If the federal government has not submitted the draft of a federal finance act to the Nationalrat in time, the chamber's members can move to introduce a draft. Should the federal government later submit its draft, the Nationalrat can vote to adopt it as the basis for its debates.

If the Nationalrat does not adopt a federal budget before the new fiscal year begins and makes no temporary provision for funding, revenue will be raised in accordance with the fiscal laws in force. If the federal government has submitted the draft of a federal finance act, expenditure is made pursuant to this draft until a federal finance act enters into force but only during the first four months of the fiscal year. If the federal government has not submitted a draft, or the first four months of the fiscal year have expired before the draft becomes an act, expenditure is made according to the amounts budgeted in the previous federal finance act.

Every year the Court of Audit prepares the federal financial accounts and submits them to the Nationalrat. After preliminary deliberation in the Budget Committee, the Nationalrat may, if the committee's report is favorable, give these accounts its sanction in the form of a federal law, which, as the federal finance act, is enacted without participation of the Bundesrat.

Debates, official records, and voting

As a rule, a plenary meeting of the Nationalrat starts with question time or, at the beginning of a week of sittings, with a debate on a topical issue related to the federal executive proposed by a parliamentary group. Thereafter the meeting follows the agenda.

Debate on a particular item of the agenda may be opened by the rapporteur elected by the committee or, in his or her place, the chair or vice chair of the respective committee. MPs may then ask for the floor. If there are requests for leave to speak in favor of and against the committee motion, supporting and opposing speakers are called up alternately to address the house. Limits can be set for the length of speeches. Motions for resolution may be submitted in the course of debates in plenary but must relate to the matter at issue. After the debate, votes are taken on the motion submitted by the committee or on other motions that may have been submitted during the debate.

As a rule, voting is by standing to signify "aye" or remaining seated to indicate "no." The rules of procedure also provide for electronic voting. Members present in the chamber must not abstain. Before the vote any member may request that the president announce the number of ayes and noes once the vote has been taken.

Members may also request, or the president may order, that separate votes be taken on individual parts of a question. This gives members the opportunity to vote according to their personal views on specific parts of a bill. Under certain circumstances, the roll call and secret ballot may be used. Debates can also be requested by a parliamentary minority or the house on urgent questions or motions, on a written answer to a question addressed to a member of the federal government, on a motion to set a deadline for a committee to report on a particular item of business, on a motion to set up an investigating committee, and on procedural motions. There has been a statutory time limit on most of these debates since 1996.

Bundesrat meetings also usually start with question time and then proceed to the agenda. Each debate is opened by the committee rapporteur or, if he or she is absent, by the chair or vice chair of the committee; then the members entered on the list of speakers are given the floor. Unlike Nationalrat debates, provincial governors as well as members of the federal government may take the floor in the Bundesrat. Motions for resolutions germane to the subject at issue may be submitted in the course of the debate. In the Bundesrat voting is usually by show of hands. As in the Nationalrat, there may be votes by roll call or secret ballot.

Official records of all sittings of the Nationalrat and the Bundesrat are kept by staff appointed by the parliamentary administration. These records are limited to the items of business deliberated on, the issues voted on, the results of the votes, and the decisions made. If objections to the official record are raised, the president rules on them.

Verbatim records are made of the public sittings of the Nationalrat and the Bundesrat and published (since October 1946 all sittings have been public). The speakers are given the opportunity to make editorial corrections in their speeches; the president rules on the admissibility of such corrections. With a few exceptions, the items of business are published as attachments to records.

Broadcasts of proceedings

The department of the parliamentary administration responsible for liaison with journalists operates a press release service, which may be subscribed to. This information is also available on the parliament's World Wide Web server *(http://www.parlinkom.gv.at)*, which also offers Parliamentary Research Service information on parliamentary business and the MPs. The professional association of parliamentary journalists assists the Parliamentary Administration in accrediting reporters. Special seats on the balcony of the Nationalrat debating chamber are reserved for these journalists.

The Austrian Broadcasting and Television Corporation (ORF), an independent public company, broadcasts the proceedings. Besides the reports on the regular news broadcasts, there is a biweekly program on parliamentary events. Only important sittings are broadcast live.

ORGANIZATION AND STRUCTURE

Committees

Both the Nationalrat and the Bundesrat have established standing committees for preliminary consultations. Most matters must be referred to a committee before being deliberated in plenary, except for state treaties, which may be submitted directly to the plenary of the Nationalrat unless one of its members objects. The plenary may then set a deadline for a committee to report, after which the matter must be included in the agenda of the plenary even if the committee has not concluded its work yet.

As the proportional composition of the committees corresponds to that of the plenary, and as the parliamentary groups delegate their experts on the various policy areas to the respective specialized committees, substantial decisions on the matters at issue are generally made in the committees. Because the committee meetings are not open to the general public and subcommittee meetings are confidential, talks can be more constructive than in the plenary.

Besides those committees primarily entrusted with preliminary deliberation of bills and other parliamentary business, there are other standing committees with special functions, such as the Incompatibility Committee, which decides if MPs must give up other jobs while serving in the legislature. The Main Committee of the Nationalrat carries out the chamber's duties in certain executive functions and in the decision making on EU projects. The Budget Committee is also responsible for monitoring the budget.

Public hearings of experts and other witnesses before committees deliberating important bills and state treaties have been allowed since Nationalrat procedures were amended in 1996. Committees are also now responsible for final deliberation of reports by the federal government or its members, and these meetings are open to the general public as well.

The right to set up committees to investigate the federal government is restricted to the Nationalrat. The courts and all other authorities are required to comply with their requests for investigations and the procurement of evidence, and all public agencies have to produce documentation. The investigating committees confine themselves to fact-finding and evaluation of these facts from a political perspective. If an investigating committee so decides, the president of the Nationalrat may admit representatives of the media to the hearing of witnesses and experts.

Office of Speaker

From among its members the Nationalrat elects its president, as well as its second and third presidents. The president conducts the business of the Nationalrat and enforces the rules of procedure. He or she has authority over the Parliament Building, appoints the staff of the parliamentary administration, and has full authority over them. With the second and third presidents, the president prepares the Nationalrat budget. These three act for the federal president in case of his or her incapacity (for more than twenty days or pending a decision on the deposition of the federal president by referendum) and if the federal presidency falls vacant.

Chairmanship of the Bundesrat changes every six months, following the alphabetical order of the names of the federal provinces. In each case, the Bundesrat is chaired by the delegate placed first on the list of members representing the diet of the province entitled to chairmanship at the time given. The person chairing the deliberations has the title of president of the Bundesrat. Every six months, the Bundesrat elects from among its members two vice presidents. The president convokes the sittings of the Bundesrat and chairs them, taking turns with the vice presidents.

In both the Nationalrat and the Bundesrat there is a kind of steering committee called the Conference of Presidents, which comprises the Nationalrat president, the second president, the third president, the chairs of the parliamentary groups, the president and the vice presidents of the Bundesrat, and the chairs of Bundesrat factions, respectively. The Conference of Presidents deliberates on the agendas and the times of plenary sittings and committee meetings, the program of work, and so on and thus contributes to consensus in parliamentary work.

Party caucuses and leadership

In the Nationalrat, at least five MPs of the same party that participated in the election are required to form a parliamentary group (MPs of different parties may form a parliamentary group only with the approval of the Nationalrat). In the Bundesrat members may form factions in the same way. The groups of the Nationalrat and the factions of the Bundesrat belonging to the same party form a common parliamentary group, which receives financial assistance to support its parliamentary activities according to the Financing Act for Parliamentary Groups.

The chairs of the parliamentary groups are usually elected for the four-year term of the Nationalrat. Chairs of governing coalition groups link the federal government and the Nationalrat, usually taking part in the cabinet meetings, for example. Opposition party leaders also customarily act as chairs of their parties' parliamentary groups.

Parliamentary groups help formulate parliamentary objectives. Individual MPs specialize in matters that the committees to which they are delegated will deliberate, and their recommendations or the formal decisions of the respective groups based on these recommendations serve as a guide for the voting behavior of the other group members in the plenary. Members of parliament have no legal obligation to adhere to any group or party policy when voting, but the party-list electoral system implies a political obligation to the principles of the party on whose list they are elected. In regional matters MPs have increasingly felt a commitment to their constituencies.

Relations between chambers

Legislative power is vested in the Nationalrat, which represents the will of the people through direct elections based on proportional representation.

For this reason, the Bundesrat is merely given the right to make a suspensive veto against bills passed in the Nationalrat. The federal government also depends politically on the Nationalrat rather than the Bundesrat. The more important oversight powers, such as the right to establish investigating committees, are conceded exclusively to the Nationalrat. The Bundesrat is given only minor powers, such as the right of interpellation (to question formally an official action or policy of a member of the government). The Court of Audit, which monitors government spending, is subordinate to the Nationalrat, not to the Bundesrat.

In practice, the Bundesrat has used its suspensive veto powers less to represent the interests of the federal provinces than to support the position of its majority party. When Nationalrat and Bundesrat majorities are politically identical, the Bundesrat acts only as a revising chamber, pointing out textual errors in legal enactments of the Nationalrat.

The position of the Bundesrat is weaker than that of the Nationalrat in administrative matters as well. The president of the Nationalrat is in charge of personnel for both houses. Separate legislative services for the Nationalrat and the Bundesrat are established, but all other services are shared. The president of the Nationalrat also assigns space in the Parliament Building. Only the debating chamber and some offices have been permanently assigned to the Bundesrat. Most other facilities are shared.

The powers of the Bundesrat have been slowly increased over the last decades, but a reform of that house remains on the political agenda.

EXECUTIVE-LEGISLATIVE RELATIONS

The largely ceremonial head of the Austrian state is the federal president, who is elected by direct popular vote to a six-year term. The federal government, though appointed by the federal president, politically depends on the confidence of the Nationalrat. If under Article 74 of the federal constitution the Nationalrat passes a vote of no confidence in the federal government or its individual members, the federal president is obligated to remove them from office. The federal president does not depend on the confidence of the Nationalrat, but the Nationalrat can move that the Federal Assembly hold a referendum on his or her dismissal.

The Nationalrat has the power to bring charges against members of the government for violations of the law, which are to be dealt with by the Constitutional Court. The Federal Assembly may also bring suits against the federal president by a two-thirds majority for violations of the federal constitution.

The federal government must count on a majority in the Nationalrat, and a federal government can be formed only if supported by such a majority. Minority governments in the history of the Austrian Republic have been very short-lived.

In this way the classic concept of separation of powers has undergone substantial changes in the parliamentary system as compared with the system of the constitutional monarchy: No longer are parliament and government contrasted with each other, but parliamentary majority and government are instead on one side and the parliamentary opposition on the other. The task of the parliamentary opposition is to monitor the government and present political alternatives. Although in the classic model of separation of powers the controlling function was exclusively vested in parliament as a whole, that is, in the parliamentary majority according to the majority principle, under the circumstances of the party state in a modern parliamentary system certain controlling instruments are to be transferred to parliamentary minorities, or new controlling instruments are to be created. This political principle has characterized the development of Nationalrat procedure since 1961, when question time was introduced. In 1975 the parliamentary minority was given its first opportunity to commission an audit at the Court of Audit. The majority still controls efficient oversight instruments such as the right to set up investigating committees, however.

Both the Nationalrat and the Bundesrat have the right of interpellation. The constitution provides for two forms: written or oral questions to the federal government or one of its members. Written questions must be seconded by at least five MPs in the Nationalrat and three in the Bundesrat. Oral or written replies must be made within two months; as a rule they are made in writing. Should it prove impossible to provide the information desired, reasons must be given. The Nationalrat and the Bundesrat may discuss the reply to a written question under certain circumstances. In principle, every sitting of the Nationalrat and the Bundesrat starts with question time, when members may exercise their right of interpellation by addressing brief oral questions to the members of the federal government.

In the Nationalrat the motion or request for immediate treatment of a written question is made before the chamber has entered upon the agenda; the question is then dealt with after the agenda is exhausted but not later than 3 p.m. If in the Bundesrat the immediate treatment of a written question is requested before the chamber enters into the agenda, the president may decide to have the question dealt with at the end of the sitting but not later than 4 p.m. The member of the federal government queried is obliged to make an oral reply or take a position on the subject after the reasons for the question have been given. The matter is then put to a debate. The urgent question is thus one of the most important means by which parliamentary minorities can force a debate; however, the 1988 and the 1996 amendments of the rules of procedure of the Nationalrat have restricted the use of this instrument by parliamentary minorities.

As an organ of the Nationalrat, the Court of Audit oversees all economic activities of the federal government. It is also entrusted with auditing foundations, funds, and institutions administered by agencies of the federal government and enterprises in which the federal government holds at least 50 percent of the share or equity capital.

The Court of Audit reports to the Nationalrat annually and may make interim reports and proposals for action. The Court of Audit also carries out special investigations when called on to do so by the Nationalrat or a qualified minority of at least twenty members (however, no further special audit may be demanded by a minority, if three such audits are pending).

Several laws require the federal government to submit annual reports on important matters. The Nationalrat or the Bundesrat can request additional reports through a resolution.

The Nationalrat also deals with the annual report of the Ombudsman's Office. The three members of the Ombudsman's Office are elected by the Nationalrat for six years and are charged with examining complaints on alleged federal misadministration. They also help with the petitions and citizens' initiatives submitted to the Nationalrat.

A specific feature of the Austrian system of parliamentary government is the share of the Nationalrat and of the Bundesrat in federal executive power. In this way, for example, certain ordinances by the federal government or a federal minister need the approval of the Main Committee of the Nationalrat.

Moreover, although the constitution empowers the federal president to conclude state treaties, all those of a political nature or that change or add to legislative acts or the constitution require the approval of the Nationalrat. The Bundesrat has the same rights as it has with regard to legal enactments of the Nationalrat.

The Nationalrat and Bundesrat may also draft resolutions on the exercise of the executive power. Motions for resolution submitted by members of the Nationalrat or the Bundesrat may be independent items of business or may be filed in the course of a debate about another issue to which they are germane. Moreover, in the Nationalrat it may be decided or moved that an independent motion for resolution brought in at the same time be addressed immediately; the procedure is the same as that for the urgent consideration of a written question.

These resolutions of the Nationalrat and the Bundesrat are expressions of the chamber's political will. The executive branch has no obligation to heed them.

Since Austria became a member of the EU, the Nationalrat has been entitled to information and cooperation, the maintenance of its competences being in principle incumbent on its Main Committee; the Bundesrat, as well, is entitled to information and cooperation and may entrust its EU Committee with these rights. Thus, the member concerned of the federal government will immediately inform the Nationalrat and the Bundesrat of all EU projects, giving them the opportunity to give their opinion.

If members of the federal government receive a Nationalrat opinion on an EU project that is to be realized by a federal law or that aims at enacting a directly applicable legal act in matters that ought to be regularized by a federal law, they are bound to these opinions during the deliberations and votes within the organs of the EU. The member may deviate from it only for urgent reasons of foreign and integrative policy and after the Nationalrat has dealt with the matter again. If the legal act being prepared by the EU would mean an amendment of the federal constitution, deviation is allowed only if the Nationalrat does not oppose it in time.

An opinion by the Bundesrat on an EU project binds the federal government if the project has to be carried out by a federal constitutional law subject to the approval of the Bundesrat because the legislative and administrative competences of the provinces would be bypassed. From such an opinion, the member of the federal government may deviate only for urgent reasons of foreign or integrative policy.

Since the Social Democratic Party and the People's Party formed a coalition in January 1987, the Nationalrat's influence on policy has increased. Many important legislative decisions have been made at the parliamentary rather than the governmental level. The Nationalrat's powers in EU matters have introduced a new element into the relationship between parliament and the executive, for example.

PARLIAMENTARY LIBRARY AND RESEARCH

The Parliamentary Research Service comprises four departments—Information and Publications; Library; Documentation of Literature; and Parliamentary Documentation, Archives, and Statistics—that serve parliament and the public.

Information and Publications oversees publishing and general information activities. The Parliamentary Library, the reading room of which was modernized in 1994–1995, holds more than 250,000 single volumes and more than 600 current periodicals, as well as microfiches and CD-ROMs. Documentation services deal with parliamentary documentation proper and literature produced outside parliament but containing information relevant to the members in the exercise of their duties. The Parliamentary Archives preserve and organize the work of both houses of the Reichsrat, of the Provisional and Constituent National Assemblies, as well as of the Nationalrat and the Bundesrat of the Republic of Austria.

STATUS OF MEMBERS

Privileges and immunities

The members of the Nationalrat and Bundesrat are guaranteed freedom of vote and speech.

As long as they are in office, the MPs may be arrested for criminal offenses—the case of apprehension in the act of committing a crime excepted—only with the consent of the house. Legal action without the consent of the house may be taken against MPs only if it is manifestly not connected with their political activity. In all other cases the authority concerned has to ask the house if legal action may be taken. This kind of immunity expires with the term of office.

The penal code makes insulting the Nationalrat or the Bundesrat a punishable offense, which is to be dealt with by the courts of law after the house has authorized them to do so.

MPs cannot be recalled; their mandate therefore expires with the end of the term of office, death, resignation, or expulsion.

Members of the Nationalrat may resign their seats through the Federal Electoral Authority, which informs the president of the Nationalrat. Members of the Bundesrat may resign by announcing their intentions to the president of the diet of the province that elected them.

Members may be expelled for failing to take the official oath; delaying taking their seats for thirty days, remaining absent from the sittings of the house for thirty days without valid reason and failing to obey the president's public announcement to appear or justify the absence within another thirty days; losing eligibility (ensuing from a sentence for a criminal offense); or failing to give up an incompatible occupation. On decision of the house or of the Incompatibility Committee the president of the house applies to the Constitutional Court, which pronounces on expulsion. Since 1945, however, no member of the Nationalrat or of the Bundesrat has been expelled.

Pay and perquisites

Legislative pay and retirement benefits are undergoing a radical change. Remuneration of MPs had been linked to the salaries of the highest ranking civil servants. This link meant that MPs' pay depended on their length of service. MPs had to contribute 13 percent of their remuneration and were, at age of fifty-five and after ten years' service, entitled to a pension of between 48 and 80 percent of their ending salaries.

The proposed pay system fixes $8,000 as the monthly remuneration for the members of the Nationalrat. Members of the Bundesrat receive half that. The rate of increase of this basic amount is linked to the increase in the per capita income of Austrian (private and public) employees. MPs then would come under general compulsory social insurance regulations and have the opportunity to contribute to a private pension fund.

CONSTITUTIONALITY OF LAWS AND EMERGENCY POWERS

The Constitutional Court determines the constitutionality of laws. The Administrative Court, the Supreme Court, an appeal court, an independent administrative tribunal, a provincial government, one-third of the members of the Nationalrat, one-third of the members of the Bundesrat, or individuals alleging direct infringement of their constitutional rights may ask the Constitutional Court to decide whether or not a federal law is unconstitutional. If the law is deemed unconstitutional, it is rescinded; the Constitutional Court may set a deadline for this rescission to give the Nationalrat time to amend the law.

Until the end of the 1970s the Constitutional Court used its power of judicial review of legislation only sparingly but has since been more aggressive. The Nationalrat, meanwhile, has guarded several of its legal enactments against judicial review by inserting constitutional provisions. There is only one limit to such action by the Nationalrat: Amendments of the principles of the federal constitution also require the approval of the people in a referendum (and it is incumbent upon the Constitutional Court to state whether such principles are amended).

The federal constitution does not contain provisions for declaring a state of emergency. But if it becomes necessary to prevent obvious and irreparable damage to the community at a time when the Nationalrat is not assembled, cannot meet in time, or is impeded from action by events beyond its control, the federal president is entitled to make provisional ordinances, but he or she may do so only at the recommendation of the federal government with the consent of the standing subcommittee of the Main Committee of the Nationalrat. Every ordinance issued in this way must be submitted to the Nationalrat without delay for approval.

Günther Schefbeck

BIBLIOGRAPHY

Lauber, Volkmar, ed. *Contemporary Austrian Politics.* Boulder, Colo.: Westview Press, 1996.

Müller, Wolfgang C. "Changing Executive-Legislative Relations in Austria (1945–1992)." *Legislative Studies Quarterly* 18 (1993): 467–494.

———. "A Vote for Stability: The Austrian Parliamentary Elections of 1995." *Electoral Studies* 15: 410–414.

Müller, Wolfgang C., et al. "Austria: Party Government within Limits." In *Party and Government: An Inquiry into the Relationship between Governments and Supporting Parties in Western Liberal Democracies,* ed. Jean Blondel and Maurizio Cotta. London: Macmillan, 1996.

Pelinka, Anton, and Fritz Plasser, eds. *The Austrian Party System.* Boulder, Colo.: Westview Press, 1989.

Schefbeck, Günther. *The Austrian Parliament.* Vienna: Federal Ministry for Education and Cultural Affairs, 1995.

AZERBAIJAN

See Commonwealth of Independent States, Non-Slavic

B

BAHAMAS

OFFICIAL NAME: Commonwealth of the Bahamas
CAPITAL: Nassau
POPULATION: 259,000 (1996 est.)
DATE OF INDEPENDENCE: July 10, 1973 (from the United Kingdom)
DATE OF CURRENT CONSTITUTION: Effective July 10, 1973
FORM OF GOVERNMENT: Constitutional monarchy
LANGUAGE: English
MONETARY UNIT: Bahamian dollar
FISCAL YEAR: Calendar year
LEGISLATURE: Parliament
NUMBER OF CHAMBERS: Two. House of Assembly; Senate
NUMBER OF MEMBERS: House of Assembly, 40 (directly elected); Senate, 16 (appointed)
PERCENTAGE OF WOMEN: —
TERM OF LEGISLATURE: Five years
MOST RECENT LEGISLATIVE ELECTION: March 14, 1997
MINIMUM AGE FOR VOTING: 18
MINIMUM AGE FOR MEMBERSHIP: House of Assembly, 21; Senate, 30
SUFFRAGE: Universal
VOTING: Optional
ADDRESS: House of Assembly, P.O. Box N3003, Nassau; Senate, P.O. Box N7147, Nassau
TELEPHONE: House of Assembly, (1242) 32 21001; Senate, (1242) 32 22427
FAX: House of Assembly, (1242) 32 88294; Senate, (1242) 32 88294

The Commonwealth of the Bahamas, a Caribbean nation that comprises about seven hundred islands and more than two thousand cays and rocks, extends from the east coast of Florida in the United States to Cuba *(see map, p. 303)*. A former British colonial territory, the Bahamas attained internal self-government in 1964 and full independence in 1973. Still a member of the British Commonwealth, the Bahamas acknowledges the British monarch as sovereign. A prime minister is head of government, and a governor general has mainly ceremonial duties.

The country's parliamentary tradition dates to 1729, when the first House of Assembly was established. Adult suffrage, however, was not introduced until 1962. The bicameral Parliament consists of a nominated upper house (Senate) and an elected lower house (House of Assembly). Of the sixteen members of the Senate, nine are appointed by the governor general on the advice of the prime minister, four on the advice of the leader of the opposition, and three on the advice of both the prime minister and the leader of the opposition. The House of Assembly has forty members (their number having been reduced from forty-nine prior to the 1997 elections), who are elected in single-member constituencies by simple majority vote. Members in both the House and the Senate serve for five years unless dissolved sooner. A Constituencies Commission reviews the demarcation of constituencies on the basis of population and recommends adjustments at intervals of not more than five years. Suffrage is universal.

The two leading political parties on the island are the Progressive Liberal Party, which led the Bahamas to independence in 1973 and continued to rule until 1992, and the Free National Movement, which has ruled since then. In the March 1997 elections, held five months before the term of the House of Assembly was due to expire, the Free National Movement increased its majority. After the election, the Free National Movement held thirty-four seats, and the opposition Progressive Liberal Party, six.

George Thomas Kurian

BAHRAIN

OFFICIAL NAME: State of Bahrain (Dawlat al-Bahrayn)
CAPITAL: Manama
POPULATION: 590,000 (1996 est.)
DATE OF INDEPENDENCE: August 15, 1971 (from the United Kingdom)
DATE OF CURRENT CONSTITUTION: Adopted May 26, 1973; effective December 6, 1973
FORM OF GOVERNMENT: Absolute monarchy
LANGUAGES: Arabic, English, Farsi, Urdu
MONETARY UNIT: Dinar
FISCAL YEAR: Calendar year
LEGISLATURE: Consultative Council (Majlis al-Shura)
NUMBER OF CHAMBERS: One
NUMBER OF MEMBERS: 30 (appointed)
PERCENTAGE OF WOMEN: —
TERM OF LEGISLATURE: —
MOST RECENT LEGISLATIVE ELECTION: December 7, 1973
MINIMUM AGE FOR VOTING: —
MINIMUM AGE FOR MEMBERSHIP: —
SUFFRAGE: —
VOTING: —
ADDRESS: —
TELEPHONE: —
FAX: —

An absolute monarchy situated in the Persian Gulf, Bahrain is an archipelago of thirty-five islands *(see map, p. 743)*. The country became a protectorate of Great Britain under a treaty signed in 1861.

Bahrain's only constitution, which came into force in 1973, provided for a unicameral National Assembly of thirty members elected for four-year terms by popular vote. About thirty thousand voters participated in the first election. Since political parties are illegal, all 114 candidates ran as independents, but the thirty elected members were almost equally divided among conservatives, moderates, and radicals. The National Assembly also counted as members the members of the royal cabinet. Soon the prime minister found himself on a collision course with the new legislature, and it was dissolved in August 1975. It has not been reconvened since. In 1993 a Consultative Council of thirty members was set up. It has no legislative powers and is merely a rubber stamp.

George Thomas Kurian

BANGLADESH

OFFICIAL NAME: People's Republic of Bangladesh (Ganaprojatantri Bangladesh)
CAPITAL: Dhaka
POPULATION: 123,063,000 (1996 est.)
DATE OF INDEPENDENCE: Proclaimed March 26, 1971 (from Pakistan)
DATE OF CURRENT CONSTITUTION: Adopted November 4, 1972; effective December 16, 1972
FORM OF GOVERNMENT: Parliamentary democracy
LANGUAGE: Bengali (official), English
MONETARY UNIT: Taka
FISCAL YEAR: July 1–June 30
LEGISLATURE: National Parliament (Jatiya Sangsad)
NUMBER OF CHAMBERS: One
NUMBER OF MEMBERS: 330 (300 elected; 30 seats reserved for women)
PERCENTAGE OF WOMEN: 9.1
TERM OF LEGISLATURE: Five years
MOST RECENT LEGISLATIVE ELECTION: June 12, 1996
MINIMUM AGE FOR VOTING: 18
MINIMUM AGE FOR MEMBERSHIP: 25
SUFFRAGE: Universal and direct
VOTING: Optional
ADDRESS: National Parliament, Parliament House, Sher-e-Banglanagar, Dhaka 1207
TELEPHONE: (880 2) 81 16 00
FAX: (880 2) 81 22 67

A country in southern Asia bordering the Bay of Bengal, Bangladesh was until 1947 part of Great Britain's India holdings *(see map, p. 319)*. Between 1947 and 1971 Bangladesh was an eastern province of Pakistan, with which it did not and does not now share a border. Bangladesh gained its independence from Pakistan in 1971 following massive civil strife and a brief war in which Bangladesh was aided by India. Since 1971 Bangladesh has had serious difficulties in consolidating democratic rule.

The growth of a parliamentary culture was stunted in the former British colony in part by the failure of the 1956 Pakistani constitution to achieve a workable blend of presidential and parliamentary forms of government, resulting in frequent gridlock between the chief executive and parliament and an inability to resolve long-standing cultural, linguistic, and economic issues as well as questions of local political autonomy. The stalemate gave Maj. Gen. Ayub Khan, chief of staff of the Pakistani army, the excuse to stage a bloodless coup in 1958, promising to "put the ship of state on an even keel" and starting a long trend of military rule in Pakistan and, later, Bangladesh.

In the presidential election of 1964, Ayub won by a three-to-one margin over his strongest challenger. For the next four years the civilianized military leader completely dominated the parliamentary process, turning the legislature into a glorified debating club in spite of its being designated by the constitution as the supreme law-making body. The constitution incorporated a quasi-presidential form of government, making the executive branch separate from the legislative branch but at the same time giving the indirectly elected chief executive the authority to convene as well as to dissolve the 156-member parliament, one half of whose members were elected through an electoral college of 40,000 electors from East Pakistan and the rest by the same number of electors from West Pakistan.

Notwithstanding the trappings of parliamentary democracy (questions, resolutions, adjournment motions, and so on), parliament in reality was guided by an irremovable chief executive. But the question and motion privileges of parliamentarians became increasingly effective means of registering the mounting frustrations of the people of both East and West Pakistan, which ultimately climaxed in a mass uprising in both parts of the country against the Ayub regime. The uprising forced an ailing Ayub to transfer power in 1969, rather hurriedly, to another military leader, Yahya Khan, the chief of staff of the Pakistani army. In so doing, Ayub reneged on his earlier commitment to a political settlement of conflicts over the issue of states rights.

In the parliamentary elections of 1970, a Bengali political party, the Awami League, unexpectedly won an absolute majority of seats in the Pakistani National Assembly (167 of 312, the number of seats having been increased under the 1962 constitution). The Awami League had campaigned on a platform that called for renegotiating relations between the central government in Islamabad and the provinces. Even though the parliament had been largely eviscerated over the years by the military regime, its control by East Pakistanis caused the military to be concerned. On March 1, 1971, the first session of the new parliament was postponed indefinitely by the ruling junta of Yahya.

Incensed by the high-handedness of the military leadership, Awami League leaders started a mass movement overriding directives of the martial law regime. The army's violent reaction to the civil disobedience was periodically interrupted by what seemed to be stalling strategies of Pakistani political leaders and General Yahya until March 25, 1971. The Pakistani military junta's bloody crackdown on East Pakistan's movement for greater states' rights provoked a mass insurgency against the junta, which resulted in the 1971 Indo-Pakistani war and the subsequent independence of East Pakistan as the new nation of Bangladesh.

WEAKNESS OF THE POLITICAL CULTURE

Lacking steady growth in its democratic political culture, due chiefly to the external and internal colonialism of the British and Pakistanis, respectively, Bangladesh has struggled to institute a parliamentary form of government. Progress has been sporadic and at times explosive.

Recourse to force for resolving the political conflicts with Pakistan also had a negative impact on democratic institution building. During the civil-cum-independence struggle, a majority of Bengali parliamentarians either went underground or crossed over to India, and very few took active part in the armed struggle. This created a questionable image of them in the eyes of those Bengalis who had waged the battle. Their lack of direct involvement in the struggle tended to distance the parliamentarians, including the top political leadership, from the realities of postwar independence shaped largely by the public experience with the struggle and its resulting consequences. Moreover, after independence was achieved, the parliamentarians hurried back and seemed overly eager to exercise control over scarce resources. This created an environment of mistrust, underscored by growing opposition to the Awami League. Sheikh Mujibur Rahman and other parliamentarians must have sensed that mistrust because in the 1972 constitution a provision was incorporated that stipulated the automatic expulsion of any parliamentarian who votes against party directives or resigns from the party after getting elected.

Mistrust breeds uncertainty, and the drive for unneeded security measures further distanced the representatives from the constituents. For example, under the Special Powers Act, a carryover from British rule, a suspect could be incarcerated without a warrant signed by a judge or magistrate and without bail for six months before bringing formal charges and producing the suspect for trial. The preventive detention measure has survived and so has the draconian measure against crossover voting in parliament.

Notwithstanding the democratic aspirations of the people of Bangladesh, incumbents have generally undermined the electoral process. Incumbent government parties in particular, and parliamentarians in general, tend to use public resources in order to remain in power. As a result, most parliamentary and presidential elections have been orchestrated by the party in power in its favor, with questionable use of government functionaries and facilities, coercion and fraud, and often political violence.

Having experienced unfair electoral practices, opposition parties and candidates have found it expedient to follow suit. Furthermore, grave political uncertainty is sometimes created when losers in genuinely fair elections in some constituencies refuse to accept the results, inciting their supporters to violence.

PARLIAMENT AND THE CONSTITUTION

The parliamentary form of government in Bangladesh is rooted in the constitution of 1972. Since its adoption, more than a dozen amendments have been added to the constitution, the most important being the fourth, fifth, eighth, twelfth, and thirteenth. The fourth amendment, adopted in 1975, transformed the Bangladesh government from an Indian-type parliamentary government to the French presidential form and established a one-party system. The fifth amendment renounced secularism as one of the basic principles of state policy and incorporated a verse from the Koran in the preamble. Islam was declared the state religion in the eighth amendment, and the twelfth amendment repealed the fourth amendment and returned the Bangladesh government to its original parliamentary form. The thirteenth amendment provided for caretaker governments for holding general elections every five years or when necessary.

The Bangladesh parliament, according to the 1972 constitution as amended, resembles more the Indian parliament than the British. Indeed, the executive power of the republic is vested in the prime minister. But there is a president, indirectly elected by parliament every five years, who acts in accordance with the advice of the prime minister. The president is empowered to appoint the leader of the majority as prime minister, accept the prime minister's resignation for lack of majority support, or dissolve parliament upon the prime minister's advice. Like in the American presidential form, it takes only a majority vote to impeach the president and a two-thirds majority vote to remove him or her from office. The fourth amendment, which has since been repealed, had required a two-thirds majority to impeach and three-fourths majority to remove the president.

The constitution provides for a unicameral parliament, vesting in it all legislative powers and allowing delegation of rule-making powers to any person or authority. The membership of parliament was set by the original constitution at three hundred elected members and fifteen nominated seats reserved entirely for women. Through proclamation in 1978, the number of seats reserved for women was increased to thirty.

The constitution authorizes the president to summon parliament after a general election, prorogue it during emergencies, and dissolve it on the advice of the prime minister. Notwithstanding the presidential power to summon parliament, the constitution stipulates the summoning of parliament within thirty days after the declaration of the results of any general election. Without presidential action, automatic dissolution of the parliament occurs five years from the date of its first meeting.

In addition to the prime minister and his or her cabinet, the leadership of the unicameral parliament includes a speaker and a deputy speaker elected at its first session. The speaker or deputy speaker vacates office if he or she ceases to be a member of parliament, becomes a minister, or is removed by a vote of absolute majority. In the absence of the president, the speaker exercises the functions of the president, and the deputy speaker performs the speaker's functions during the period. The speaker and deputy speaker cannot preside while a motion for their removal is being discussed, but they have the right to take part in the proceedings of parliament during the removal considerations. The parliamentary leadership also includes the leader of the opposition, deputy leaders of government and opposition parties, and ranking members heading the standing committees of parliament.

Standing committees of parliament include a Public Accounts Committee, a Committee of Privileges, and other standing committees created by parliament to examine draft bills (at the specific request of the government party), review the enforcement of laws and propose appropriate enforcement measures, investigate administrative activities referred to them by parliament, and perform any other functions as assigned. Parliament by law confers on committees the power to enforce attendance of witnesses, examine them under oath, and compel the production of documents.

The constitution, in the tradition of Western legislative institutions, upholds the parliamentary immunity of its members and proceedings against any charges in any court of law. The constitution authorizes parliament to have its own Secretariat located within the parliament building, which was designed by the American architect Louis Kahn, reportedly using the same scale as the Taj Mahal of India. Surrounded by a thousand acres of green sprinkled with water-filled channels and moats, the parliament building has become a major tourist attraction. It took about twenty years to complete the project.

The legislative procedure for drafting a bill and enacting it into law follows the Western democratic model. For many years, however, a major difference between Pakistani and Western parliaments was the lack of any provision for direct or indirect involvement of parliamentary committees in the law-making process. A 1997 parliamentary reform measure for the first time required the involvement of special parliamentary committees in processing every bill.

Every proposal in parliament must be in the form of a bill. The successful passage of any bill except a money bill involves its presentation to the president after it is passed by a majority of members present and voting (sixty being the quorum). The president must assent to the bill or return it to parliament requesting it to reconsider the bill in whole or in part or to consider any amendment specified by him or her. If the president fails to act within fifteen days he or she will be deemed to have given assent. If the president returns the bill to parliament for its reconsideration, and if parliament passes the bill with or without amendment by a simple majority of votes, provided there is a quorum of sixty, the bill will be presented for the president's assent. If the president fails to assent within seven days, he or she will be deemed to have assented. At the end of this process the bill becomes law and is called an act of parliament.

The absence of an absolute presidential veto, even during the primacy of the presidential form of government—between adoption of the fourth and twelfth amendments (1975–1991)—underscores the essentially parliamentary rather than presidential slant of Bangladesh's legislative process. However, approval of a bill by parliament after the president has returned the bill to it was made significantly more difficult by the Second Proclamation Order No. IV of 1978. The order, passed during the presidency of Ziaur Rahman, required an absolute majority rather than a simple majority of votes to pass a bill over a presidential veto. Rahman, unsure of gaining an absolute majority in the parliamentary election of 1979 for his Bangladesh Nationalist Party, perhaps considered it prudent to insert that limitation in the constitution.

Money bills, which require certification by the speaker before their presentation for presidential approval, deal with all forms of tax; borrowing of money; and the consolidated fund, which includes all revenues, loans, and money received in repayment of loans. The constitution delineates the fiscal policy-making process of parliament. The budget is presented annually by the finance minister and, according to the constitution, must show separately the sums required to meet expenditures charged on the consolidated fund and the sums required to meet other proposed expenditures from the consolidated fund. Over the years an unwritten practice has been established whereby the finance minister also presents a second budget, called the Annual Development Program, which is based heavily on external economic assistance involving soft loans and outright grants, which make up between 82 and 86 percent of the development budget.

Interestingly, the constitution stipulates that expenditures charged on the consolidated fund may be discussed by, but not submitted to the vote of, parliament. Other expenditures must be submitted as "demands for grants," and parliament is empowered to assent to, disavow, or vote for a reduction of the amount specified in the demand for grants. A supplementary budget, if necessary, is provided for in the constitution, under which the president is empowered to authorize expenditures from the consolidated fund. Notwithstanding certain limitations, parliament is given power to authorize by an act of parliament the withdrawal of moneys from the consolidated fund for the purposes for which such grants are made.

Serious charges of misuse of fiscal powers have been leveled consistently against different governments by opposition parties. Ironically, a strong ombudsman provision incorporated in the original 1972 constitution has not been put in operation by any parliament. Neither has any parliament since 1972 had the will to delete the constitutional provision. Perhaps like American legislators, Bangladeshi parliamentarians see the institution as having the potential to diminish their power by limiting the role of legislative committees in investigating governmental corruption, including electoral coercion and vote fraud. Another reason for not making the constitutional provision for a powerful ombudsman into a political reality may be the resistance of the powerful bureaucracy to instituting such a potentially effective mechanism of control. In this a strange alliance can be seen between the bureaucracy and political leaders, who have been advocating the reduction in the power and size of the bureaucracy. The apparent self-interest-driven alliance seems to have included the nouveaux riches, who shy away from any effective probe into certain questionable business and banking practices.

It is doubtful that a powerful, independent Election Commission, as provided for under the 1972 constitution and strengthened by two 1994 acts of parliament and the thirteenth amendment in 1996, would be able to allay the fears of opposition parties. Given the power of incumbency, opposition parties understandably believe that the only way a free and fair election could be held is through a neutral caretaker government, which became reality under the thirteenth amendment.

Indeed, the election of 1991, conducted by a neutral caretaker government, shows how a free and fair election monitored by neutral poll watchers from within and abroad, whose security is protected by the government, could bring about widespread, violence-free participation from different political parties and factions. The June 12, 1996, elections, held under the second caretaker government, reinforce that view.

RESTORING CONFIDENCE IN THE ELECTORAL PROCESS

Political instability and vote fraud were endemic throughout the 1970s and 1980s in Bangladesh. Two presidents were assassinated: Sheikh Mujibur Rahman in a 1976 military coup, which began a period of military dominance that would last into the 1990s, and Maj. Gen. Ziaur Rahman in an unsuccessful 1981 coup by an opposition military group. Zia was succeeded by his vice president, Abdus Sattar, who was in turn overthrown in 1982 in a bloodless coup orchestrated by Lt. Gen. Hussain Mohammad Ershad. Ershad suspended the constitution and declared martial law. The constitution was restored November 10, 1986, after parliamentary and presidential elections in May and October, respectively, that were rife with corruption.

Public resentment of Ershad and his National Party rose through the last years of the decade as corruption flourished. In order to clear the electoral environment of fraud and violence, demands were made by Bangladeshi leaders for neutral elections to be held by an interim government. A framework for instituting a caretaker government was put in place through the concerted efforts of the two largest political parties: the Bangladesh Nationalist Party (BNP) and the Awami League. Ershad was to hand over power to a neutral, nonpartisan vice president. The vice president would serve as an acting president until the election of a new president. The acting president would appoint an interim cabinet from a slate of nominees submitted by the major parties. The interim government would be responsible for holding parliamentary elections within three months from its inception. After the election, the interim government would hand over power to the leader of the majority of parliamentarians, namely the prime minister.

In keeping with the framework, Ershad was forced in December 1990 to hand over power to Justice Mohammad Shahabuddin, the politically neutral chief justice of the Supreme Court of Bangladesh, under pressure of a mass movement. In preparing for the election, the interim government constituted an impartial Election Commission of three Supreme Court justices, with the senior-most serving as chair. In verifying voter registration data, the commission reduced the total number of voters by ten million (16.1 percent), from 61.3 million to 51.3 million, for "false registrations," which included nonexistent and underage persons. The interim government also ordered an interdistrict transfer of all career district administrators, preventing them from being influenced by vested interests, and ordered strict enforcement of 1972 electoral rules, which imposed serious legal and administrative sanctions on officials and workers supervising the polling centers for impropriety and fraud. And the interim government invited election monitoring teams from the British Commonwealth countries and elsewhere to oversee the electoral process. The elections of March 1991 were adjudged universally to be the most free and fair in the history of Bangladesh.

Political commentators and some newspapers had expected an edge for the Awami League in the 1991 elections because of its organizational strength vis-à-vis the BNP at the grass roots, an advantage which did not materialize. Awami League, with a secular nationalism platform, secured 88 seats as against 140 for the BNP, which has an Islamic orientation. But the margin of popular votes separating the Awami League from the BNP was less than 1 percent. The Awami League and its breakaway faction, BAKSAL, which had aligned with the Awami League in the electoral fight along with seven other minor political parties and which in August 1991 merged with the Awami League, together won more popular votes than the BNP.

The rightist Bangladesh Islamic Assembly, an ultrareligious party, won eighteen seats in the parliamentary election. Perhaps its success was partially due to its last-minute alliance with the BNP. The outcome was electorally significant not because Bangladesh Islamic Assembly received eight more seats than it had in the 1986 election but because its 18 seats together with the BNP's 140 enabled the latter to claim 28 of the 30 seats reserved for women (Bangladesh Islamic Assembly claimed the other 2 seats), thus giving the BNP the majority needed to form the government and an absolute majority of seats (168) in the 330-seat parliament.

The National Party managed to win thirty-five seats. Its leader, Ershad, the deposed president who was later convicted for the possession of an unlicensed firearm, won in five constituencies even though serving a prison term of ten years for his conviction.

Although twelve parties and three independent candidates out of sixty-three parties and hundreds of independents contesting the 1991 election won seats in parliament, the outcome held out hope of a two-party system emerging to offer the people a greater opportunity for political stability and a possible end to military takeovers of the civilian government. The possibility of gridlock between the BNP and opposition parties had not been anticipated. But that is what happened.

Allegations that the BNP committed vote fraud in an early 1994 by-election, coupled with the "poll losers syndrome" of opposition party members, led to renewed and intensified demands that the BNP government commit to stepping down in favor of a neutral, caretaker government to conduct the general elections scheduled for January 1996. The government of Prime Minister Khaleda Zia refused to submit such a bill to parliament, citing her constitutional duty to hold elections, and all parliamentary opposition parties began to boycott sessions. Parliament remained stalemated from March 1994 until December 28, 1994, when all opposition MPs submitted resignation papers. In November 1995 President Abdur Rahman Biswas dissolved parliament at Zia's request. During the eighteen month impasse, the opposition parties, principally the Awami League, stoked the fires of discontent by calling some seventy-five work stoppages.

The January 1996 elections were postponed by the government due to yet another election-related work stoppage that turned violent, leading to twenty-five people being injured. When elections were finally held on February 15, 1996, the opposition parties boycotted, and the BNP won 205 of 207 contested seats. The elections were marked by low turnout (estimated at 15 percent), widespread violence (between fourteen and nineteen killed and several hundred injured), and allegations of extensive vote fraud.

Khaleda Zia formed her government soon after the elections of February. Amid unrelenting pressure to step down, she asked parliament to pass a constitutional amendment giving the president the right to form a caretaker government. On March 26 parliament complied, and on March 27 she resigned. Mohammad Habibur Rahman, a former chief justice, was sworn in as interim president three days later, and new elections were scheduled for June.

In the June 12 balloting, the Awami League won 146 of 300 elective seats, and the BNP won 116. Despite the allegations made by losing candidates and some party officials of voting irregularities, most observers hailed the elections as free and fair. Turnout was estimated by the Election Commission at 76 percent, a record high for Bangladesh attributed in large part to the interim government's mobilization of more than four hundred thousand troops and security personnel to deter violence.

After the three major parties had given up sixteen parliamentary seats that their leaders had won by running in multiple constituencies (National Party, 5; BNP, 6; Awami League, 5), the Awami League had 141 seats in parliament; it needed 143 of 284 parliamentary seats to form a government. With the support of A. S. M. Rab of the National Socialist Party and an independent MP, Awami League secured the needed majority, averting a possible constitutional crisis. In order to strengthen its parliamentary position, Awami League formed a coalition with the National Party, which had won twenty-seven elective parliamentary seats (after giving up five multiple constituency seats). Ironically, Ershad, the leader of the National Party, was released from prison and took his seat in parliament on June 23. The Awami League's Sheikh Hasina was named prime minister the same day.

CONCLUSION

The constitutional amendment allowing for a nonpartisan, caretaker government for the specific purpose of holding a general election every five years holds out hope for the future stability of Bangladeshi politics. In this the democratic aspirations of the people confront the political reality of the incumbents' propensity to use the powers and resources of the state to ensure electoral victory. As mentioned earlier, the ruling party's gestures of good intention—coalition government, strengthening of the Election Commission, and so forth—were not enough to allay the fears of the opposition parties about government-instigated electoral violence and vote fraud.

Democracy is a slow and frustrating process through which the legitimate hopes, aspirations, expectations, and demands of the people are transformed into tangible programs of action. Impatience and a lack of moderation and balance can undermine the democratic process, which can lead to rule by demagogues or autocrats. Even if the recent emergence of democracy reflects the people's power and determination, there is no guarantee for its continuation as a viable system. The events of 1975 and 1982 can be repeated. It is imperative, therefore, for the leaders of democratic forces to tread cautiously, charting a course of moderation, equity, and fair play by which certain basic values needed to nurture it, such as education, dignity of labor, and commitment to maintaining and raising civic consciousness, can be deeply imbedded in the collective psyche of the people.

Zillur R. Khan

BIBLIOGRAPHY

Khan, Zillur R. *Leadership in the Least Developed Nation: Bangladesh.* Syracuse, N.Y.: Maxwell School of Citizenship and Public Affairs, Syracuse University, 1983.

———. *The Third World Charismat: Sheikh Mujib and the Struggle for Freedom.* Dhaka: University Press, 1996.

BARBADOS

OFFICIAL NAME: Barbados
CAPITAL: Bridgetown
POPULATION: 257,000 (1996 est.)
DATE OF INDEPENDENCE: November 30, 1966 (from the United Kingdom)
DATE OF CURRENT CONSTITUTION: Effective November 30, 1966
FORM OF GOVERNMENT: Constitutional monarchy
LANGUAGE: English
MONETARY UNIT: Barbados dollar
FISCAL YEAR: April 1–March 31
LEGISLATURE: Parliament
NUMBER OF CHAMBERS: Two. House of Assembly; Senate
NUMBER OF MEMBERS: House of Assembly, 28 (directly elected); Senate, 21 (appointed)
PERCENTAGE OF WOMEN: House of Assembly, 10.7; Senate, 28.6
TERM OF LEGISLATURE: Five years
MOST RECENT LEGISLATIVE ELECTION: September 6, 1994
MINIMUM AGE FOR VOTING: 18
MINIMUM AGE FOR MEMBERSHIP: 21
SUFFRAGE: Universal
VOTING: Optional
ADDRESS: Parliament, Parliament Buildings, Bridgetown
TELEPHONE: House of Assembly, (1809) 426 3712; Senate, (1809) 426 5331
FAX: (1809) 436 4143

Barbados, the easternmost of the Caribbean islands (*see map, p. 303*), on November 30, 1966, became one of the first nations of the region to receive its independence from the United Kingdom. The country remains a member of the British Commonwealth.

The constitution of the newly independent Barbados incorporated several institutions and traditions that had been part of ordinary practice prior to independence, as well as other institutions of the British system of government (sometimes called the Westminster model). Among these are the Office of the Prime Minister, the office of the leader of the opposition, the Privy Council, the governor general, the practice of party discipline, and votes of confidence. The bicameral Parliament is made up of the House of Assembly (the lower house) and the Senate (the upper house).

As the British model would suggest, executive authority in Barbados rests with the governor general, acting on behalf of the British sovereign and "on the advice" of the prime minister. The prime minister is assisted by a cabinet, although the prime minister clearly is the most important figure in the executive branch.

The constitution recognizes the relationship between the legislative and executive branches of the government. It indicates that the governor general shall appoint as prime minister the member of the House of Assembly who in his or her judgment is "best able to command the confidence of a majority of the members of that house." It also recognizes the ability of the House of Assembly to fire the prime minister and requires the governor general to revoke the appointment if the prime minister does not resign following a vote of no confidence.

PARLIAMENTARY ELECTIONS AND ORGANIZATION

The constitution includes three sections on Parliament: the first focuses on the composition, the second on the powers and procedures, and the third on sessions. The constitution also establishes the ground rules for elections. Barbados has a multiparty system, with the Barbados Labour Party, the Democratic Labour Party, and the National Democratic Party having significant blocs in the House. Many independent candidates run for office as well.

In the House of Assembly elections for the five-year terms take place in twenty-eight single-member districts and are based upon a direct-election, simple-majority voting system. Vacancies arising between general elections are filled through by-elections held within ninety days. Voting is not compulsory.

The Senate has twenty-one members, twelve appointed by the governor general on the advice of the prime minister, two appointed by the governor general on the advice of the leader of the opposition, and seven appointed by the governor general "acting in his discretion" to represent "religious, economic, or social interests or such other interests as the governor general considers ought to be represented." Senators must be citizens of Barbados, at least twenty-one years of age, and must have been resident in Barbados for one year prior to appointment. Specific guidelines are included in the constitution governing conditions under which individuals are not eligible to be senators and conditions under which Senate seats held by individuals might become vacant.

To vote, individuals must be at least eighteen years of age and have Barbados citizenship (or Commonwealth citizenship if they have had residence in the country for three years before elections). They also must have residence in a specific district for three months prior to the election. The grounds for disqualification as a voter are insanity, imprisonment, or being under a death sentence.

To be a candidate for office, individuals must be qualified voters and must be twenty-one years of age, have Barbados citizenship, and have had residence in the country for more than seven years. To be a candidate, an individual must be nominated by four voters and make a deposit equivalent to US$125, which is reimbursed if the candidate is elected or obtains more than one-sixth of the total votes cast in the district. Individuals cannot be candidates if they have undischarged bankruptcy, allegiance to a foreign state, imprisonment exceeding six months, conviction for a felony or for an offense involving dishonesty, or if they have been convicted of electoral fraud. Candidates for elected office also cannot be public officers, members of armed or police forces, judges, director of public prosecutions, or the auditor general.

OPERATIONS

Parliament is granted broad powers in the constitution to "make laws for the peace, order and good government of Barbados." Each house establishes its own procedures. The Senate, for example, elects its president and has established a quorum of eight members plus the presiding officer.

The election of the speaker and the deputy speaker are the first order of business for the House at the beginning of each Parliament. The speaker has a great deal of discretionary power in the legislative session to regulate debate and parliamentary questions, keep order during the legislative process, and decide on the appropriateness of topics for extended discussion.

Bills may be introduced in either house, with the usual exception of money bills, which may be introduced only in the popularly elected House of Assembly. A bill becomes law after it has passed both houses of Parliament and has been signed by the governor general.

The Senate is clearly the weaker of the two legislative bodies in Barbados. The standing orders of the legislature provide that if a bill is passed by the House of Assembly in two successive sessions and is sent to the Senate more than a month before the end of the session—and each time the Senate rejects the bill—the bill may be submitted to the governor general for assent despite the lack of approval of the Senate.

The legislative procedure is substantially the same in Barbados as in most other Commonwealth nations. There is a first reading for each bill, followed by an interval of "not less than five days" between the first and second readings of a bill (unless the House votes to waive that provision). After bills have been read a second time, they can be sent to a standing committee or a committee of the whole house for further study. Following the committee stage, a third reading takes place in front of the entire House; during the third reading no amendments of a material character may be proposed in the legislation.

Gregory S. Mahler

BIBLIOGRAPHY

Anderson, Thomas D. *Geopolitics of the Caribbean: Ministates in a Wider World.* New York: Praeger, 1984.

Hoyos, F. A. *Barbados: A History from the Amerindians to Independence.* London: Macmillan Education, 1976.

BELARUS

OFFICIAL NAME: Republic of Belarus (Respublika Belarus)

CAPITAL: Minsk

POPULATION: 10,416,000 (1996 est.)

DATE OF INDEPENDENCE: Declared August 25, 1991 (from the Soviet Union)

DATE OF CURRENT CONSTITUTION: Effective November 28, 1996

FORM OF GOVERNMENT: Parliamentary democracy

LANGUAGES: Belarusian (official), Russian

MONETARY UNIT: Belarusian rubel

FISCAL YEAR: Calendar year

LEGISLATURE: National Assembly

NUMBER OF CHAMBERS: Two. Chamber of Representatives; Senate (also known as the Council of the Republic)

NUMBER OF MEMBERS: Chamber of Representatives, 110 (directly elected); Senate, 64 (56 indirectly elected; 8 appointed)

PERCENTAGE OF WOMEN: —

TERM OF LEGISLATURE: Four years

MOST RECENT LEGISLATIVE ELECTION: May 1995, to the defunct Belarusian Supreme Soviet

MINIMUM AGE FOR VOTING: 18

MINIMUM AGE FOR MEMBERSHIP: Chamber of Representatives, 21; Senate, 30

SUFFRAGE: Universal

VOTING: Optional

ADDRESS: National Assembly, 220 010 Minsk

TELEPHONE: (375 172) 29 35 14

FAX: (375 172) 27 37 84

Belarus, smallest of the three Slavic successor states to the Soviet Union, is one of the more politically conservative of the new republics. It was slow to adopt democratic insti-

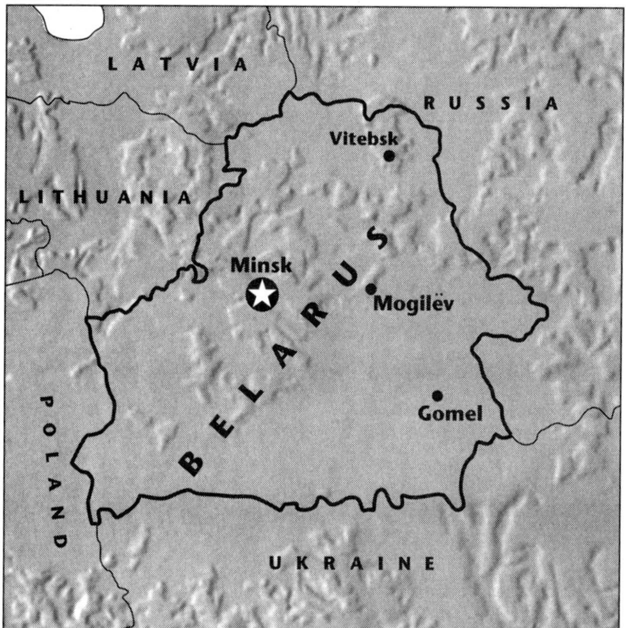

tutions and procedures and has undergone substantial constitutional turmoil since gaining independence in 1991.

HISTORICAL BACKGROUND

Throughout the thirteenth, fourteenth, and fifteenth centuries the territory that is modern-day Belarus was part of the Grand Duchy of Lithuania. Belarusian was the official language of the Grand Duchy (or Principality) of Lithuania until it was replaced by Polish in 1697. With the creation of the Commonwealth of Poland and Lithuania through the Union of Lublin in 1569, Belarus came under Polish domination. When Russia, Prussia, and Austria partitioned the Commonwealth in 1772, 1793, and 1795, Russia acquired the entire territory of Belarus. Following the 1917 Russian Revolution, Belarusian nationalists formed a Rada (council) to push for independence, but their efforts were defeated by the invading Germans. By 1918 most of Belarus was occupied by Germany. In 1919, however, the Bolsheviks reoccupied Belarus.

From 1918 to 1921 Belarus was caught in the middle of the Russo-Polish War. The Riga Treaty of 1921 ending the war divided Belarus into three parts: the western portion was ceded to Poland, central Belarus was established as a nominally independent Belarusian Soviet Socialist Republic (BSSR), and the eastern territories temporarily became part of the Russian Federation until their reunification with the BSSR in 1922 upon the formal proclamation of the Union of Soviet Socialist Republics (USSR). The Russian invasion of Poland in 1939 returned the western part of Belarus to Soviet control, and those lands were annexed from Poland by the USSR at the end of the war. From the end of World War II until 1990, all of present-day Belarus was under Soviet domination as a socialist republic of the USSR.

During the 1960s and 1970s the Belarusian culture was "russified," which led to diminishing use of the Belarusian language in education and the media. Opposition to the communist regime in Belarus first began to coalesce in reaction to Moscow's suppression of Belarusian language and culture. Throughout the 1980s intellectuals in Belarus pressed for Belarusian-language schools and greater input into environmental issues; the environment became an especially sensitive issue after the 1986 Chernobyl nuclear power plant disaster, which affected a large part of southeastern Belarus.

The only true political opposition to the Communist Party, the Belarusian Popular Front, emerged in 1988. Although restricted in all aspects of political life, the popular front had moderate success against the Communist Party in 1989, when it persuaded voters to reject some of the Communist candidates to the Supreme Soviet. The popular front persuaded the government to approve a law that made Belarusian the official language, although the provisions were to be enacted over a period of ten years.

The Belarusian Popular Front was not officially permitted to participate in the March 1990 elections to the Belarusian Supreme Soviet. Instead, its members joined other proreform political groups, and the new coalition (Belarusian Democratic Bloc) won 32 of the 360 seats in the Belarusian Supreme Soviet. The Communist Party won 86 percent of the vote.

The Belarusian Communist Party remained a steadfast supporter of the central regime. Only after the failed putsch in Moscow on August 19, 1991, did the Belarusian leadership move to break away from Moscow. On August 25, 1991, Belarus declared its independence, and soon after the Supreme Soviet voted to rename the Belarusian Soviet Socialist Republic the "Republic of Belarus."

After achieving independence, Belarus was dominated by a conservative majority of former communist officials. Many of the deputies elected in March 1990 under the undemocratic Soviet system were reluctant to implement reforms and tended to be nostalgic for a close political and economic union with the former Soviet Union. Although Belarus had embraced multiparty democracy in theory, in practice the opposition was weak; the most active opposition after independence continued to come from the deputies of the reform-minded Belarusian Popular Front. In the spring of 1992 the Supreme Soviet ignored a petition containing 447,000 signatures calling for new elections. More serious events occurred in the fall of 1993, when strikes and a political protest of 30,000 people led the Supreme Soviet to assemble army troops.

The reform-minded chair of the Supreme Soviet, Stanislav Shushkevich, advocated rapid mass privatization. By 1993 the conflict between Shushkevich and the conservative majority of the Supreme Soviet had become pronounced. The most controversial issue involved establishing closer military and economic ties with Russia and the Commonwealth of Independent States. The Supreme Soviet wanted them; Shushkevich was against them. The Supreme Soviet voted to sign a new treaty on collective security with the Commonwealth. After surviving a vote of no confidence in July 1993, Shushkevich was ousted as chair on January 26, 1994, only a few days after U.S. president Bill Clinton visited Belarus and praised Shushkevich for his leadership. Alexander Lukashenka, the head of the anticorruption committee of the Supreme Soviet, had accused Shushkevich of corruption and mismanagement. Shushkevich was replaced by conservative hard-liner Mechyslav Hryb.

Hryb and the conservative majority of the Supreme Soviet, however, could not hold out indefinitely against popular demands for change. With the economy declining and public resentment escalating, the Soviet-era Belarusian Supreme Soviet voted on March 1, 1994, to create the post of president. Two weeks later, on March 15, a new constitution was adopted that retained the Supreme Soviet, and presidential elections were scheduled for June.

Six candidates qualified for the presidential ballot: Prime Minister Vyacheslav Kebich; Shushkevich; Lukashenka; Zenon Paznyak, chair of the Belarusian Popular Front; Vasily Novikov, chair of the Belarusian Communist Party; and Alexander Dubko, chair of the Union of Collective Farms. The first round of voting took place on June 23, 1994, and approximately 80 percent of the eligible voters participated. Lukashenka polled 45 percent of the votes cast; Kebich polled 17 percent; Paznyak, 13 percent; and Shushkevich, 10 percent. In the second round of voting, on July 10, Lukashenka overwhelmed Kebich, capturing 85 percent of the vote. Lukashenka's election was not viewed favorably among Western observers. He had displayed a very conservative economic and political agenda, which centered on derailing privatization and pushing for union with Russia.

By the end of 1994 Lukashenka's government had begun to splinter. Reform-minded deputy prime minister Viktar Gonchar resigned his post, and others soon followed. Parliamentary Deputy Sergei Antonchik (a Lukashenka supporter) demanded the resignation of the president's closest advisers because of allegations of corruption. Lukashenka refused to accept their resignations and initiated censorship of the major Belarusian newspapers, which had attempted to print the corruption report.

In November 1996 President Lukashenka initiated a referendum on a new draft constitution designed to strengthen the presidency dramatically at the expense of parliament. The United States declared the referendum "illegal." The Organization for Security and Cooperation in Europe refused to send observers to the poll, and the Council of Europe denounced the presidential draft constitution. Although the referendum favored the constitution, no diplomats from European embassies accepted Lukashenka's invitation to attend the signing ceremony of the new constitution on November 28, 1996. Three justices from the Constitutional Court resigned in protest of the new constitution. The court has declared the referendum to be nonbinding.

THE CONSTITUTION

The 1996 constitution created a National Assembly (parliament) with two chambers: the Chamber of Representatives, comprising 110 deputies; and the Senate (also referred to as the Council of the Republic), with 64 senators. The National Assembly replaced the unicameral Belarusian Supreme Soviet.

Deputies are elected on the basis of universal, direct vote. Any citizen of Belarus at least twenty-one years of age may be elected to the Chamber. The president may liquidate the Chamber in case of political gridlock following a finding by the Constitutional Court that the Chamber has committed a grave breach of the constitution.

The Senate is the chamber of territorial representation. Eight of the Senate's sixty-four members are selected from each of the seven regional legislatures (including the city of Minsk). Eight additional members are appointed by the president. The regional candidates must also be approved by the president's representatives in the regions. A citizen of Belarus at least thirty years of age and living in the territory of the respective region or in the city of Minsk for at least five years may become a member. The members of both chambers have a four-year term and are elected at the same time. Parliament meets for only 170 days each year.

Among the powers granted to the Chamber of Representatives by the constitution are the power to consent to the president on appointing the prime minister; initiate a vote of no confidence in the government by a one-third vote; impeach the president by a two-thirds vote on the basis of a similar decision by the Senate; and interpret the constitution. It is unclear whether the Constitutional Court or the Chamber of Representatives has the final word on interpreting the constitution. Yet, the fact that the latter is involved at all with interpreting the constitution violates the doctrine of separation of powers.

The Senate has the authority to approve or deny draft laws passed by the Chamber of Representatives; consent to the president's appointment of the chair of the Supreme Court, the general prosecutor, the chair of the Constitutional Court, members of the Supreme Economic Court, the chair of the Central Committee on Elections, and the chair and members of the Board of the National Bank; elect six judges of the Constitutional Court; elect six members of the Central Committee on Elections; and cancel decisions of local soviets.

ELECTIONS AND PARTIES

The March 1990 elections to the Supreme Soviet were generally met with apathy and disinterest among the voting population, due at least in part to the fact that at the time the Communist Party was the best organized political party and also controlled the media. The party won a landslide victory, gaining 90 percent of the seats. In December 1991 the Communist Party of Belarus was reconstituted as the Party of Communists-Belarusian. The party has since gained popularity owing to nostalgia for the relative stability experienced under Soviet rule.

The Soviet-era Supreme Soviet elected in 1990, after extending its own term beyond its original mandate, finally declared elections for May 1995. In advance of the elections, a new Law on Elections was adopted that reduced the number of Supreme Soviet deputies from 360 to 260. It also required all deputies to be elected by majority vote and eliminated the 50 seats reserved for veterans and invalids. Because of strict election regulations regarding the required voter turnout, only 18 of the 260 seats were filled in the first round of elections, conducted on May 14, 1995. Two weeks later an additional 102 seats were filled. However, the two rounds of voting failed to produce the two-thirds quorum needed to convene the new Supreme Soviet. After two further rounds of voting in 1995, an additional 78 deputies were elected, bringing the number of duly elected deputies to 198. Candidates from the Communist Party collected the largest number of seats with 42. The Agrarian Party received 33; the United Civic Party of Belarus obtained 9; the Party of People's Accord won 8; several smaller parties gained 11; and independent candidates accounted for 95 seats. The remaining 62 seats were left vacant.

At the first-round elections of May 14, Lukashenka successfully initiated a referendum in which citizens voted in favor of forging closer integration with Russia; giving the Russian language state status; and giving Lukashenka the power to dissolve parliament.

The new Supreme Soviet, with a complement of only 198 deputies, held its inaugural session in January 1996. Symanyon Sharetski, leader of the Agrarian Party, was appointed chair. Later in 1996 one additional independent deputy was elected to the Supreme Soviet, resulting in a total of 199 deputies. The realignment of independent candidates and parties into factions resulted in several major groups: Accord (sixty-two deputies); Agrarians (forty-six); Civic Action (eighteen); "Union of Labor" Social Democrat Faction (eighteen); Belarusian Communist Party (forty-five); and independents (ten).

The new Supreme Soviet met for only eleven months, having been supplanted by the bicameral National Assembly created by the November 1996 constitution. On November 29, 1996, President Lukashenka signed a bill terminating the authority of the Supreme Soviet. A day earlier, the Chamber of Representatives had opened its first extraordinary session, which, pending elections to the new body, comprised 110 members of the Supreme Soviet who had supported Lukashenka.

The United Civic Party of Belarus was founded in October 1995, combining two parties: the Democratic Party and the Civil Party. It has strong support among intellectuals and is committed to democratic development and de-emphasizing nationalism. The party advocates market reforms, human rights, and the rule of law.

The Belarusian Social-Democratic Union was founded in March 1991 and has sixteen chapters throughout Belarus. The party models itself after the German Social Democratic Party. The Belarusian Peasant Party, founded in February 1991, focuses primarily on the interests of agricultural workers and favors private farming.

The Belarusian Popular Front has been very active. The front is more of an umbrella organization than a party. It was first established in October 1988. It is open to any individual or party who shares a basic belief in a democratic, independent Belarus. The front is also known for its nationalistic stance on Belarusian ethnicity and language. The leaders of the popular front fled to the United States in March 1996, where they sought political asylum based on their persecution by the Belarusian government.

Three other parties also have significant followings. The Party of the People's Accord, founded in April 1992, is closely tied to other democratic parties. It maintains a centrist political philosophy. The Slavic Assembly endorses a larger Slavic entity comprising Belarus, Russia, and Ukraine. The party's platform of bilingualism (it supports both Russian and Belarusian as official state languages) has much popular support. And the Liberal Democratic Party is an extremist sister party to the Russian ultranationalist party of the same name led by Vladimir Zhirinovsky.

PARLIAMENTARY PROCEEDINGS

Legislative calendar

Parliament has two regular sessions. The first session begins October 2 and continues for up to 80 days. The second session begins on April 2 and continues for up to 90 days (total of 170 days per year). Parliament may be summoned to an extraordinary session by the president or by a two-thirds majority of the complete membership of each of the chambers. The extraordinary sessions are "opened" and "closed" by decrees of the president, thus the president has an opportunity to dismiss the session if he or she is not in favor of members' decisions.

The Chamber of Representatives and Senate elect their respective chairs from among their members. Sittings are open to the public and media unless a majority of the deputies votes to close the proceedings. Sessions are held in both the Russian and Belarusian languages. Two-thirds of the total number of listed deputies comprise a quorum.

Legislative process

During the past several years parliament has been operating under temporary rules of procedure. Since the constitutional referendum of November 1996, the Chamber of Representatives has adopted the "Temporary Rules of Procedure for the Chamber of Representatives." Senate rules have not yet been adopted.

The right to initiate legislation in parliament is vested by the constitution in the deputies of both chambers, the government, the president, and citizens eligible to vote who form a bloc of at least fifty thousand people. Only the president or the government can initiate bills involving the budget and taxation. The president may also propose laws to parliament that he or she considers urgent. The proposed law must be considered by both chambers within ten days of the submission. Parliament cannot amend the proposed law; it can only vote "yes" or "no."

A draft law is discussed first in the Chamber of Representatives and then in the Senate. A draft law is then forwarded to the appropriate committee in the Chamber of Representatives. The committee discusses the draft and can include input from the president, the Senate, and the public. The committee votes on whether the draft law is "necessary" for the republic. This is only a recommendation to the full Chamber of Representatives, since a committee cannot, on its own, "kill" the draft.

Draft laws normally undergo two readings before the Chamber of Representatives. The draft law is submitted to the deputies at least three days prior to the first reading. During the first reading, the proposer and the leading committee assigned to the draft legislation report to the entire chamber on the proposed legislation. After conclusion of debate on the first reading, the deputies may accept or reject the draft law. If alternative bills on the same issue are read, deputies can decide by a majority vote which shall proceed to a second reading. A bill rejected in its original form can be amended or resubmitted to the committee for further research or rewording. The product of the reworking is subjected to a new first reading. A bill accepted by the deputies can either be sent back to the committee for "minor" reworking (the bill would then move directly to a second reading) or be sent directly to a second reading. During the first and second readings, deputies can submit in writing suggested amendments to the chair.

At the second reading, the sponsor of the bill begins the debate, followed by committee members and then deputies. The title and each article of the bill are debated and voted upon. A final vote on the entire draft law is then taken. If part or all of the draft bill is rejected, the draft bill is either sent back to the committee for further reworking or amended directly during the second reading (the proposed amendments must be submitted in writing).

After the draft bill is passed by the Chamber of Representatives, it is forwarded within five days to the appropriate Senate committee for analysis and then to the full Senate for a vote. There is only one reading in the Senate, and the bill is voted in its entirety. A vote must be concluded within twenty days.

If the draft bill is rejected by the Senate, it is sent back to the Chamber of Representatives. The chambers then create a joint commission to reconcile differences. Once the draft emerges from the conciliatory commission, it goes through the two readings in the Chamber of Representatives. As provided for in the temporary rules, the draft bill does not have to be sent back to the Senate (this procedure will probably be amended). If the joint commission cannot resolve the differences, the president may request the Chamber of Representatives to take a final decision. The draft law is considered adopted by the Chamber of Representatives if two-thirds of the members vote in favor of the law.

Voting in both the Chamber of Representatives and the Senate is generally open, but it may be conducted in secret if a majority of the deputies vote to do so. Decisions are ordinarily adopted by a show of hands. In certain enumerated procedures, voting may be done through electronic ballot. If a vote is taken by a show of hands, an exact count may not be necessary if the outcome is obvious and there is not a specific demand by one of the deputies. A legislative history is kept, and all debates in the Chamber of Representatives and the Senate are recorded electronically and by a stenographer. Committee debates are summarized in official minutes.

A bill becomes law after its adoption by both the Chamber of Representatives and the Senate by a majority of their respective members. The draft law is considered approved by the Senate if it has not been decided upon within twenty days, or within ten days regarding an urgent matter presented by the president.

An adopted law is presented to the president for signature within ten days. The president has two weeks to sign the law or can allow the law to come into effect by taking no action. The president can return the text of the law with his or her objections to the Chamber of Representatives. The Chamber must reconsider the law within thirty days, and after approval by at least two-thirds of Chamber members, submit the law with the president's objections to the Senate. Within twenty days the Senate can pass the amended law with no less than two-thirds of the members. If both chambers override the president's objections, the president is obligated to sign the law within five days or the law shall come into force.

Budget

The Council of Ministers is responsible for developing the budget. It submits the proposed budget to the president, who then presents it to parliament. Parliament refers the draft budget to all standing committees. Each standing committee is able to submit changes or recommendations to the proposed budget. Once the standing committees have approved the budget, it is open to debate among the entire parliament.

Broadcasting of proceedings

Almost all sessions of the Chamber of Representatives and Senate are open to both the public and the media unless determined otherwise by a majority vote of the deputies or senators, respectively. Open sessions are broadcast on television and radio, and all information regarding the sessions and their agenda is published in a parliamentary bulletin. Detailed reports prepared by the Secretariat are also available in special publications.

The problem is not that parliament is inaccessible to the media, it is that the media in Belarus tend to be in large part under the control of the government. President Lukashenka has imposed nearly complete censorship over state media. For instance, all major publishers still use state printing presses. Lukashenka used this power to stop the printing of the independent newspapers *Belarusian Business Gazette, Name,* and *Popular Freedom.* There are no independent television stations, and all major publications and radio stations are heavily subsidized. Under a 1996 law, the president has unlimited air-time on television and radio.

ORGANIZATION AND LEADERSHIP

Committees

As of March 1997 new rules of procedure had not been adopted. Under the temporary rules, the Chamber of Representatives and the Senate form permanent standing committees, temporary committees, and other bodies to draft legislation and decide on issues within the scope and operation of the chambers. Deputies may serve as members of a maximum of two standing committees. Each committee is chaired by a single deputy who is elected by a majority vote of the committee. The chair presides over the committee for the full four-year term. In the event that a chair is no longer able to fulfill the duties of the position, he or she may resign. The chairs of the Chamber of Representatives and the Senate, the first deputy chair, and ministers of the republic are prohibited from chairing committees.

According to the temporary rules of procedure, committee responsibilities include drafting legislation, promoting the implementation of new laws and regulations, and controlling the activities of state agencies and institutions. New committees are formed through resolution of the entire parliament, and existing committees are dissolved in the same manner. All deputies are permitted to work on any committee. The vote in committee, however, is reserved only to those who are permanent members.

Temporary committees are formed by resolution of the Chamber of Representatives or Senate and exist until the assignment they oversee is completed. A temporary committee has the right to obtain any documents, materials, or testimony from government and public agencies, companies, institutions, and organizations. The Chamber of Representatives and Senate may also create investigating, auditing, and other committees to approach various problems. They operate in a manner similar to temporary committees.

According to the existing temporary rules of procedure, deputies have the right to form permanent and temporary groups. Deputies' groups must notify the speaker in writing of the proposed group's objectives and tasks. The chair then informs all deputies of the group's foundation. The existing rules of procedure do not require any other information or conditions to create a new political or other group in parliament. Once formed, a group of at least twenty deputies has the right to take the floor of parliament during debates. In addition, at the request of a group with at least twenty deputies, the Chamber of Representatives or the Senate must circulate among the deputies written materials prepared by the group as an official document of the session.

Party caucuses

In theory, the Belarusian parliament should contain many diverse factions, since the broader political arena is diverse. At present, however, there is very little separateness among the parties in the new parliament. The Chamber of Representatives voted overwhelmingly at its first sitting in support of the president's initiatives, including banning from the Chamber several dozen deputies who had dissented. However, political caucuses do exist among parties and sometimes within blocs of parties. These groups have a fluid membership, and their membership may overlap with membership within deputy groups. As of early 1997 the major party caucuses included the Communist Party, the Agrarian Party, and the Civic Action Party.

Office of Chair

The first session of a newly elected parliament is presided over by the chair of the Central Election Committee until the election of the respective chairs. The chairs are elected by majority vote. Duties of the chairs include opening and closing sessions; organizing debates; putting draft laws to a vote; announcing questions, information, and statements; signing minutes; and monitoring debates.

A deputy, a group of deputies, or a standing committee of the Chamber of Representatives or Senate may request a formal explanation of any action taken by one of the republic's governing bodies or officials. The request for explanation may be lodged with the chairs, the republic Council of Ministers, or any other authority appointed or elected by parliament. The chair forwards the request to the body or official to whom it is directed. The body or official must, within three days, give a written or an oral answer to the question at a session of parliament.

STATUS OF MEMBERS

The constitution provides deputies of the Chamber of Representatives and the members of the Senate immunity for expressing their views and exercising their powers. However, they are not protected from "charges of defamation and insult" in speeches before parliament. Considering that the president's honor and dignity are protected by the constitution, it is unlikely that members of parliament will risk criticizing the president. All deputies and members are also immune from criminal prosecution, pursuant to the constitution and the Act of Status of a People's Deputy of the Republic of Belarus.

A deputy or member cannot be arraigned on criminal charges or arrested or otherwise deprived of personal liberty without permission of a majority of the respective chamber unless caught in the act of committing state treason or another capital crime. Criminal prosecution may only be instituted by the prosecutor general with the permission of parliament. Furthermore, all deputies and members are protected from retention or search of their person or their belongings, including baggage, means of transport, residence, and telephone calls. A deputy or member is prosecuted by the Supreme Court. Yet, despite these protections, Lukashenka attempted to negate deputies' immunity in August 1995, so that he could arrest a deputy who had been critical of the president.

Deputies and members of parliament are paid a salary of approximately $100 a month. The rules of procedure do not specify ethical standards of conduct. There are only general references to ethical conduct in the rules. For instance, during parliament sessions, deputies are prohibited from using rude and improper language or calling for unlawful or violent action.

No quality legislative research library exists for parliament. Individual government institutes and commissions maintain limited library collections. Parliamentarians also have access to the neighboring National Public Library.

THE EXECUTIVE

Under the new constitution, the president occupies a near authoritarian position. The constitution creates an executive that is more powerful than the presidents in nearly every other system with a strong presidency. The desired separation of powers and checks and balances between the branches of government have been supplanted with the domination of one branch—the executive.

According to the new constitution of November 1996, the president is "the head of state, the guarantor of the constitution . . . and of the human and civil rights and freedoms." The president is also accorded broad, generalized powers including the authority to "protect the sovereignty of the Republic of Belarus, its national security, and territorial integrity; ensure political and economic stability, continuity, and interaction between the government authorities; perform mediation between the government, the state, and society." Since there is no longer any real separation of powers, the president can use the office's constitutional authority to justify nearly every presidential act. The president even has the power to call unilaterally for popular referenda. Even the concept of judicial review is minimized since the constitution gives the president the authority to object to parliament's interpretation of the constitution.

The constitution extends even further the powers of the

president by setting forth a remarkably detailed twenty-eight-point provision granting extraordinary powers to the president. For instance, the president can unilaterally appoint and dismiss members of government, except the prime minister. He or she can appoint six members of the Central Election Commission and dismiss the chair of the Committee of State Control and the entire Board of the National Bank. The president appoints and dismisses the leaders of local executive and administrative organs. The president can essentially control the judiciary with additional constitutional powers to dismiss the chair of the Supreme Court and the general prosecutor; and dismiss, with consent of the Senate, the chair and justices of the Constitutional Court and Supreme Economic Court. He can also appoint the chair and six members of the Constitutional Court (without Senate consent) and appoint all other judges without legislative confirmation.

The president's powers cannot be delegated to any other official or body. The president can also cancel acts of the government, control adherence to legislation by local bodies of management, suspend decisions of local soviets, form and chair the Security Council, and declare martial law without any approval by parliament. Even minor and relatively unimportant constitutional powers such as granting citizenship must be handled by the president.

In legislative functions, the president has supreme power. The president has the right of legislative initiative as well as the right to veto the legislative acts of parliament. Parliament plays a significantly lesser role vis-à-vis the president on legislative matters. The president is also able to issue and enforce decrees and directives that are binding on the entire country. Since the president's strength is so significant and the parliament's strength so weak, the presidential power to issue decrees and directives is absolute. Other powers usually vested with the legislature belong to the president. By a majority vote, the two chambers of parliament can give the president authority to "issue decrees having the status of law."

The president also holds a broad item veto over laws passed by the legislature. A proposed law can be signed by the president and go into effect, excluding the provisions that the president found objectionable. The veto may be overridden by a two-thirds vote of the two chambers. A three-fourths vote would be required to override presidential vetoes of constitutional amendments and interpretations and "key laws."

The constitution also gives the president authority to terminate the Chamber of Representatives or the Senate in case of a Constitutional Court verdict indicating "grave violation of the constitution." The decision to terminate is at the discretion of the president.

There is an executive department in the form of a Council of Ministers. The executive power is executed by the government, which is the Council of Ministers. The prime minister is appointed by the president upon consent of the Chamber of Representatives. If the Chamber refuses two candidates, the president may appoint an acting prime minister, dismiss the Chamber, and call for new elections.

The president is substantially protected from impeachment. Impeachment of the president requires a two-thirds vote of the senators and a majority vote of the full Chamber of Representatives. The president is also essentially protected from liability for any wrongdoing. And the president is immune from all civil action or criminal prosecution.

Under the Law on Elections, the president must be thirty-five years old and have resided in Belarus for at least ten years. The president serves a term of five years and may hold office for only two terms. In order to be nominated, a candidate must receive the endorsement of seventy parliamentary deputies or 100,000 eligible voters. The nomination of candidates must begin seventy-five days before the elections and end forty days before the voting. All registered candidates have equal access to financial, technical, and media support through the Central Commission for Presidential Elections.

JUDICIAL FUNCTIONS

The constitution states that judges are independent and subordinate only to the law. In reality, there is very little evidence that judicial independence is protected under the constitution. The basis for dismissal of judges from office is "determined by law." Since the constitution defers much legislative authority to the president, the concept of judicial independence is greatly weakened.

The president appoints the chair and members of the Supreme Court and the prosecutor general upon the consent of the Senate. This constitutional provision alone might be acceptable; however, the president also appoints the chair (with consent of the Senate) and six members of the Constitutional Court, which does not require any approval by the legislature. The president also has complete discretion on appointing judges of lower courts, who do not hold lifetime appointments. He or she can also dismiss the chair and justices of the Constitutional Court and the Supreme Economic Court, with the consent of the Senate.

According to the rules of procedure, the Supreme Court, chair of the Supreme Economic Court, and prosecutor general must report at least once a year to parliament on their activities. The information submitted by the Supreme Court is forwarded to parliament's Committee for Law Enforcement and Crime Control, which is responsible for "analyzing and judging" the court's activities.

CONSTITUTIONALITY OF LAWS

In accordance with the constitution, the Constitutional Court determines the constitutionality of statutes. The twelve judges of the court are supposed to be qualified specialists and are limited to a single eleven-year term. The chair and five judges are selected by the president; six judges are elected by the Senate.

The new constitution has significantly restricted access to the Constitutional Court. Standing is now limited to the president, the Supreme Court, cabinet, and the Supreme Economic Court. Parliamentary committees, blocs of deputies, and the procurator of the Supreme Council can no longer initiate cases before the court.

In addition, neither a nongovernmental body nor an individual can petition the court to review an act based on its constitutionality. The court can no longer initiate its own consideration of the validity of acts of the president, the legislature, the Supreme Court, and the cabinet. In fact, because the court had ruled several of Lukashenka's decrees to be unconstitutional, Lukashenka replaced decrees with "presidential rulings," which cannot be brought before the court.

The constitution may be revised on the initiative of no fewer than 150,000 citizens who are eligible to vote, no fewer than forty deputies of the National Assembly, the president, or the Constitutional Court. Constitutional amendments are considered valid if at least two-thirds of each chamber votes in favor of the proposed amendments.

Mark S. Ellis

BIBLIOGRAPHY

Analysis of the Draft Constitution of the Republic of Belarus with Alterations and Amendments. Washington, D.C.: American Bar Association, Central and East European Law Initiative, October 15, 1994.

"Belarus." *East European Legislative Monitor* 1, no. 6 (October 1996).

Markus, Ustina. "Belarus Elects Its First President." *RFE/RL Research Report* 3, no. 30 (July 1994).

———. "Lukashenka's Victory." *Transition* 1, no. 14 (August 11, 1995).

BELGIUM

OFFICIAL NAME: Kingdom of Belgium (Koninkrijk België, Dutch; Royaume de Belgique, French; Königreich Belgien, German)

CAPITAL: Brussels

POPULATION: 10,170,000 (1996 est.)

DATE OF INDEPENDENCE: October 4, 1830 (from the Netherlands)

DATE OF CURRENT CONSTITUTION: February 7, 1831

FORM OF GOVERNMENT: Constitutional monarchy

LANGUAGES: Dutch, French, German

MONETARY UNIT: Belgian franc

FISCAL YEAR: Calendar year

LEGISLATURE: Parliament

NUMBER OF CHAMBERS: Two. House of Representatives (Abgeordnetenkammer, Chambre des Représentants, Kamer van Volksvertegenwoordigers); Senate (Senat, Sénat, Senaat)

NUMBER OF MEMBERS: House of Representatives, 150 (directly elected); Senate, 71 (40 directly elected; 31 indirectly elected)

PERCENTAGE OF WOMEN: House of Representatives, 12.0; Senate, 22.5

TERM OF LEGISLATURE: Four years

MOST RECENT LEGISLATIVE ELECTION: May 21, 1995

MINIMUM AGE FOR VOTING: 18

MINIMUM AGE FOR MEMBERSHIP: House of Representatives, 21; Senate, 21

SUFFRAGE: Universal

VOTING: Compulsory

ADDRESS: Palace of the Nation, 1008 Brussels

TELEPHONE: House of Representatives, (32 2) 519 81 11; Senate, (32 2) 501 70 70

FAX: House of Representatives, (32 2) 512 65 33; Senate, (32 2) 514 06 85

The Belgian Parliament was founded in 1831 by the National Congress, the constituent assembly that defined the institutions of the new state created after the successful 1830 rebellion against Dutch dominance. The founders opted for a representative constitutional monarchy with a—for the time—quite liberal constitution, protecting most modern civil rights and liberties.

Apart from measures democratizing the composition of the chambers, until 1993 the constitutional form of the Belgian Parliament had not undergone important modifications, in spite of several waves of significant constitutional reform launched in the 1970s and 1980s. However, the 1993 reform which completed the transformation of the unitary state into a complex federal system also modified the struc-

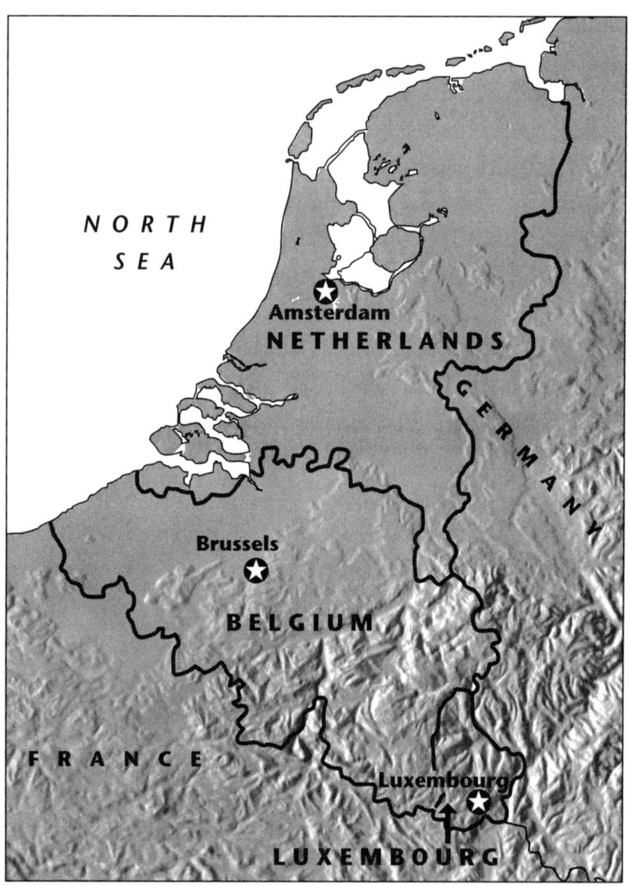

ture, composition, and functioning of Parliament. As these changes were implemented only after the 1995 general elections, it is too early to evaluate to what extent the fundamental changes have affected the actual functioning of the chambers and MPs' behavior.

THE CONSTITUTION

The National Congress opted for a bicameral system, in which the Senate originally constituted a more aristocratic and conservative element than the House of Representatives. From the beginning, both chambers were symmetrical in terms of their main functions (government making, legislation, control) and organization. Due to the democratization of suffrage, their composition has also grown highly similar. In the 1993 constitutional reforms, the Senate lost several of its competencies, although its party composition remains congruent to that of the House. Now only the House can invest or dissolve a government, vote the budget, and allow interpellation of ministers. All government bills are introduced in the House. Yet the Senate remains with the House equally competent for constitutional reforms, regional and community matters, ratification of treaties, and the organization of the judiciary. It is exclusively competent for conflicts between the national and regional/community legislatures. Hence, the Senate evolved into a "reflection chamber" and a forum where the federal and regional/community levels of government meet.

Legislative power is shared by the two chambers and the monarch (in practice, the Council of Ministers). Individual MPs as well as government ministers can introduce bills.

Since 1970, all MPs have been required to indicate at the beginning of each legislative term, by taking the oath either in Dutch or French, whether they belong to the Dutch or French-speaking linguistic group, as some specific policies require 'linguistically qualified' majorities.

COMPOSITION OF PARLIAMENT

Elections

The House is composed of 150 representatives, all directly elected through a proportional representation system in twenty multimember constituencies of variable magnitude (212 representatives were elected in thirty constituencies before 1995). The post-1995 Senate has become a chamber of regional representation, comprising 71 members, of whom 40 are directly elected in two constituencies, the Flemish and Francophone communities, that only overlap in the Brussels region. There, 21 representatives of the communities are appointed to the federal parliament—the Flemish Parliament and the Francophone Community Council each nominating ten members, and the Council of the German-speaking Community nominating one. The other ten senators are coopted by the first two types of senators (before 1995 there were 106 directly elected senators, 51 senators appointed by the provincial councils, and 26 senators coopted by the previous two types). Contrary to upper houses in other federal systems, the number of senators representing different regions and communities is roughly proportional to the number of inhabitants of each subunit.

The party composition of the two chambers has been very similar, corresponding closely to the parties' strength in general elections (held simultaneously for both chambers). The main difference between the chambers in composition had been age: representatives had to be at least twenty-five years old, and senators forty. In 1995 the minimum age was brought down to twenty-one for both.

Due to the proportional electoral rules, in practice voters only decide on the number of seats a party will receive, not on who will fill the seats. Only a candidate's place on his or her constituency's party list and the electoral success of the party affects the candidate's chances of election. This system contributes to the grip that constituency and national parties exercise over their MPs.

Current party positions

The Belgian party system is now characterized by extreme fragmentation. It started out as a two-party system in the nineteenth century, opposing Catholics and Liberals basically on the issue of the religious neutrality of the bourgeois state. After the emergence of the socioeconomic, left-right cleavage and the breakthrough of the Socialists at the end of that century, a three-party system functioned until at least 1965, in which the three traditional parties, Christian Democrats, Socialists, and Liberals alternately shared governmental offices in different coalition combinations. In the 1960s and 1970s the number of parties represented in Parliament rose drastically. First the regional parties broke through, among them the People's Union in Flanders, the Walloon Party in Wallonia, and the Democratic Front of French-Speakers in the Brussels region.

The growing saliency of the linguistic and regional cleavage internally divided the three traditional unitary parties, each splitting into two organizationally and programatically autonomous Flemish and French-speaking branches: the Christian Democrats cleaved into the Flemish-speaking Christian People's Party and the French-speaking Christian Social Party; the Socialists split to form the French-speaking PS and the Flemish-speaking SP; and the Liberals split into the Flemish Liberals and Democrats and the French-speaking Liberal Reformation Party. At the end of the 1970s another wave of expansion of the party system occurred, with the emergence of the Flemish separatist and antimigrant Flemish Bloc, the Democratic Union for the Respect of Labor, and the ecologist parties (AGALEV and ECOLO). By 1981 fourteen parties were represented in Parliament. During the 1980s the Belgian Communist Union, the Walloon Party, and the Democratic Union for the Respect of Labor had lost their last representatives in Parliament, and thus a small reduction of the party system occurred. However, the 1991 general election introduced more newcomers: the extreme-right National Front and the libertarian ROSSEM, which did not win a seat in 1995. In Belgium there are no national parties any more. All parties are homogeneous Flemish or Francophone and only present themselves in the Flemish or Francophone constituencies.

Both chambers have a general assembly room in the shape of a hemisphere. Ministers are seated on the front benches in the middle or, if present in high number, on the second row of the central front benches. MPs are seated by party: traditionally the socialists are seated on the left, the Christian democrats on the right, the liberals in the middle. MPs of the smaller parties sit behind the traditional parties, in the last rows of the back benches.

Membership

Members of the House of Representatives and of the Senate are elected for four-year terms on the same day. In practice, the average length of postwar legislative terms has been three years, as most elections are held early.

Most incompatibilities stem from the principle of separation of powers. MPs can be a member of only one chamber at a time. MPs cannot be concurrently employed by the executive or judicial branches, which excludes from parliamentary membership national civil servants, judges, teachers in the federal public school system, clergy of the four religions subsidized by the state, fully state-employed lawyers, tax collectors, or government commissioners in enterprises. Other offices that are incompatible with membership in Parliament include the office of governor; vice governor; member of the board of the public broadcasting company, economic public enterprises, or certain financial institutions; member of the European Parliament; the regional and community legislatures or provincial councils; and member of certain official oversight committees. Although the combination of ministerial portfolio with parliamentary office was very common (87 percent of ministers also served in Parliament between 1945 and 1984), since 1995 this overlap is prohibited. MPs appointed ministers are replaced, but their replacements will have to step down if the minister wants to take up his or her seat in Parliament again, for instance due to a coalition change.

Architecture

The Belgian Parliament is situated in the heart of the capital. The chambers are housed in separate wings of an eighteenth century palace, combining luxury and prestige with lack of comfort and tightness. Each wing comprises a general assembly, committee rooms, library and archives, institutional staff offices, and a few common reading rooms for MPs. Only a few leading MPs have a personal office in the building. In 1985 a spacious adjacent building was annexed (now called the "House of the Parliamentarians") that offers each MP a private office and each parliamentary group meeting rooms and office space. Groups of up to thirty persons are admitted to the palace; request must be made one month before a visit. Visits and guides are free.

LEGISLATION

Parliamentary calendar

A parliamentary term (legislature) is divided into sessions. Each "ordinary" session starts on the second Tuesday of October. If due to elections a new parliament starts on a different day, the monarch will call the chamber in "extraordinary" session. Each chamber should gather at least forty days per session. In practice, the chambers will recess around July 20. Yet, since sessions formally only close on the eve of a new session, the chamber can always be called to convene, even while in recess. Since 1993 the House has invited the government on the third Tuesday of September to present its main policy orientations for the coming year, a "state of the union" that is followed by a debate. Other fixed moments in the parliamentary calendar concern the presentation and voting of budget bills. After four years Parliament is dissolved de jure, and general elections are held. Yet, of the sixteen elections following the first postwar election, only three were not held early.

How laws are made

Two kinds of bills are introduced in the Belgian Parliament. A bill introduced by the government is called a "legislative project," and a bill introduced by an MP or several MPs is called a "legislative proposal." Legislative proposals can be introduced by one or more representatives as well as senators, each in their respective chamber. In order to become law, a bill has to go through many stages.

Contrary to legislative proposals, legislative projects go through additional preparliamentary stages. The responsible minister prepares a "draft legislative project" which is usually discussed within the cabinet. This draft is submitted to the Legislation Section of the Council of State for prior advice about the constitutionality of the project. After incorporating any changes resulting from that advice, the draft project goes back to the cabinet for approval. Then it is submitted for the signature of the king and sent to the House.

In parliament, a draft bill follows a path prescribed in detail:

- Bills are introduced by handing them over to the speaker of the chamber concerned.
- Legislative projects are referred directly to the appropriate House committee. A legislative proposal, however, has to be formally taken into consideration by the Plenary Assembly of the chamber in which it was introduced. It is not taken into consideration and therefore not discussed if, for instance, the Assembly estimates it violates the constitution.
- After being considered by the Plenary Assembly, legislative proposals are referred for examination to the appropriate committee. Upon explicit request of the authors, a legislative proposal is taken into consideration for inclusion on the committee agenda and for publication in the *Parliamentary Documents.* Legislative projects and budgets are included automatically and have priority of discussion over legislative proposals. Given the heavy workload of committees, most legislative proposals sent to a committee are never put on its agenda.
- Once put on the committee agenda, a bill will be discussed in the committee. The author of a legislative proposal who is not a member of the committee that considers it can attend committee meetings in which the bill is discussed.
- Amendments to legislative proposals or projects can be introduced by committee members as well as by the government. Amendments have to be approved by a majority of the committee.
- One committee member is charged with making a report to the Plenary Assembly summarizing the committee debates on the bill. Committees are not obliged to report back to the plenary session in a given time, and therefore a large majority of legislative initiatives die in committee. Bills receiving a positive report are referred to the Plenary Assembly of their chamber for discussion. If the bill was treated in public committee meetings, no more plenary general discussion is held.
- Then the text of the bill as it was adopted by the committee is debated, amended by individual MPs and the government, and voted in the plenary session. The author can briefly develop and explain his or her amendment, upon which the chamber decides if it is necessary to refer the amendment back to the committee and therefore to suspend the plenary deliberation.
- At the end of the discussion and the (re-)introduction of amendments, the bill is voted first article by article, then as a whole.

Under the old symmetrical bicameral system, if a bill was accepted by the plenary of one chamber, it was sent to the other, which repeated steps three to eight. If the version of the bill approved by the first chamber was also passed by the second, it was sent to the monarch for royal approval, published by the *Official Record,* and became law.

If the second chamber modified the version approved by the first, the bill was referred back to the latter, where steps three to eight were to be repeated; the bill was sent back and forth between the two chambers until they both voted the same version of the bill. There were no rules to stop the potentially endless back-and-forth process—nothing akin to a conference committee or conciliation procedure. Although in principle this legislative path could be extremely time-consuming and inefficient, in practice majority parties exerted strong pressure on their MPs in order to resolve differences between the chambers.

Under the new asymmetrical bicameral system, except for matters for which the Senate is equally competent, bills adopted by the House are examined in the Senate only if fifteen members ask within one week to do so. If a bill is "revoked," the Senate has one month to examine it and propose amendments. The bill is then sent back to the House, which can accept or reject the Senate's amendments. If the House adds amendments of its own, the Senate has three days to examine those; the Senate also can formulate new amendments and send the bill back to the House. The House then takes a final decision on the bill, if necessary after having amended it again. Hence, the House has the final word on all bills, those first introduced in the House, which is the case for government bills, as well as those stemming from senatorial initiative. In the case of the latter, a proposal accepted by the Senate is sent to the House, which can amend it and send it back to the Senate, which will examine the amendments and can introduce new ones. The bill is then transferred back to the House, which takes a final decision on the bill.

In most matters, therefore, the House has the final say. In the case of conflicts on matters on which the chambers are equally competent, a joint conciliation committee is established, composed of an equal number of representatives and senators. It decides issues in one of two ways, either by an overall two-thirds majority vote, or by a "double" simple majority of the senators as well as of the representatives that constitute the joint committee.

Government and private member bills

Like in most other Western states, in Belgium the initiation of legislation is largely usurped by the executive. A large majority of bills approved by Parliament are introduced by the government, rather than by individual MPs, in spite of the fact that the number of bills introduced by representatives tends to increase every year. Thus the weak lawmaking performance is due to the low success rate of private member bills: roughly speaking, about nine of every ten bills introduced originate from parliamentary initiative. Yet, contrary to most government projects, only one of every ten proposals becomes effective law. Still, some improvement has occurred: in the 1960s, one of every five enacted bills originated in parliament; in the 1990s the ratio rose to about one in three.

The low success rate of legislative proposals is due first to the detailed and comprehensive policy agreements reached between the majority parties (usually between four and six), which to a large extent predefine the legislation to be initiated by the government and enacted by Parliament in the following legislative term. Majority MPs have very little leeway to amend these legislative projects, as this would destabilize the delicate agreement reached between coalition parties. In principle, only private member bills that do not cover an area discussed in the governmental program and on which the other coalition parties can agree have a chance to become law. Second, the content of legislative proposals is often demagogic, aiming simply at increasing certain government expenditures and transfers or reducing taxation. The successful proposals usually are of little policy relevance. Third, since the majority controls most leadership positions in the chambers and therefore can set the agenda of the general assembly and the committees, governmental projects usually enjoy priority treatment. Fourth, some of the most valuable proposals are usurped by the government, which will introduce a project with similar content, thereby rendering the proposal obsolete. Fifth, given the increasing complexity of the decision-making process and the need for rapid decisions, the executive is sometimes granted special powers that further undermine the law-initiating and law-making role of Parliament. In addition, given the consociational nature of Belgian decision-making processes, delicate or extremely controversial matters are often transferred from the parliamentary arena to "round table conferences," where party leaders conclude special pacts which Parliament is forced to ratify later on without any modification. Finally, in many socioeconomic matters Parliament's legislative initiation is bypassed by the agreements reached in the neocorporatist arena between trade unions, employers, agricultural and middle class organizations, and the government.

Debate and voting

Debate can occur in the Belgian Parliament on nearly any matter raised by the government in parliament: following the presentation of a new governmental program, governmental or ministerial declarations, interpellations, presentations of general and departmental budgets, and during the reading of bills and the ratification of international agreements. Often, plenary debate is used for attracting media attention to major points that MPs already made in committee sessions, and plenary debate offers an opportunity for the opposition to challenge ministers. Yet its effect on the outcome of the parliamentary decision-making process is limited, given the strong voting discipline.

The constitution stipulates that each decision of each chamber has to be taken by an absolute majority with at least half of the MPs present. Nominal votes are cast electronically, by pushing the agree, disagree, or abstain button of the voting box each MP has on his or her desk. Votes on the complete text of a bill, investiture votes, and votes on declarations that engage the government's responsibility are always taken nominally. Votes on individual articles of bills and internal business are usually taken by sitting and standing, and votes regarding the nomination of members to parliamentary leadership positions are always secret.

For each nominal vote, parliamentary records present an alphabetical list of those who voted for and against and those who abstained. Those who abstain can explain their "blank" vote, referring to the content of the matter or to technical reasons (such as pairing with an absent MP).

Apart from the two-thirds supermajority required for passage of constitutional revisions, there is a so-called alarm bell procedure to protect the interests of linguistic minorities. When at least three-quarters of the members of one of the linguistic groups in a chamber introduce a motion objecting to a particular bill (after the committee report on the bill and before a final vote in the plenary), parliamentary procedure is suspended. The Council of Ministers, which is equally composed of Flemish- and French-speaking members, has to pronounce itself on the alarm-bell motion within thirty days and invite the chamber to reach a decision on an amended version of the disputed bill based on the opinions of the Council.

Linguistic minorities are further protected by "special majority laws." Unlike ordinary laws, legal rules affecting certain matters explicitly enumerated in the constitution (modifying borders, competencies and statutes of the provinces, the linguistic communities and regions) must be passed by a majority in each linguistic group in each chamber, with a majority of members of each linguistic group present. The total number of votes cast in favor of the bill by both linguistic groups taken together must constitute two-thirds of the votes cast.

Budget procedures

Before the 1989 budgetary reforms, budgets were usually introduced at the last moment and rushed through the chambers by the government and its majority, most of the money already having been spent before the final budget was approved. Since then, the government has presented its fiscal, economic, and social policy objectives in the general budget statement, on which a parliamentary debate is held before the vote on the actual budget law. This law, which the House has to approve no later than the last day of October of the same year, comprises the Ways and Means Budget and the General Budget of Expenditures. The latter contains both an estimate of the different items of expenditure and an authorization to proceed with the expenditures listed by program, for every department of the central administration. The appropriations are further allotted within each program by Administrative Budgets for the various ministerial departments. The Ways and Means Budget gives an estimate of all revenues of the state and empowers the government to levy taxes during the relevant fiscal year, to raise nonfiscal revenues, and to borrow. These two main budgets are examined by the Finance Committee, while departmental budgets are also examined by the corresponding committees. Each budget bill approved by a committee has to be discussed and approved by the Plenary Assembly.

During the first three months of each fiscal year, the government carries out a budgetary review in order to assess whether any adjustments are needed in the Ways and Means Budget and the departmental budgets. Before the end of June, the ensuing amendments must be approved by the House.

The budget process ends with parliamentary approval of the Law on Accounts, which includes the financial report of the Audit Office. To that effect, a bill has to be introduced in Parliament in October of the following fiscal year. Whereas the vote on this bill was originally intended to assess governmental policy, in practice the vote is often taken several years later, rendering it a mere formality, as the responsible government is usually no longer in office. In addition, the Audit Office's report covers only the regularity and legality of governmental expenditures, and not their efficacy.

Official record

The verbatim version of discussions in the Plenary Assembly (containing also interpellations, oral and urgent questions, motions, governmental declarations, plenary votes, and voting declarations) is contained in the *Parliamentary Annals* of the House and the Senate, published a few weeks afterward in the language originally used (French or Dutch). Both chambers also publish a bilingual summary of debates the following day *(Analytical Reports)*. The original and subsequent versions of a bill, its amendments, committee reports, and advices of the Council of State are published in *Parliamentary Documents.* Bills approved by parliament and signed by the monarch are published in the *Belgian Official Gazette,* upon which they have force of law. In the past few years, the House has also published the *Annual Report,* offering quantitative and qualitative information on its activities, composition, and resources.

ORGANIZATION AND STRUCTURE

Committees

Committees in both chambers are permanent and specialized, usually corresponding in number and competence to the main ministerial departments. In the current term (1995–1997), the House counted, in addition to ten permanent departmental committees, three internal affairs committees (accountancy, statutory rules, and parliamentary reform), three specific functional committees (naturalizations, petitions, persecutions), and four advisory and control committees (European affairs, party finance, police, emancipation). In the Senate there are six departmental committees and three advisory and control committees. In addition, a few extraordinary committees and some temporary subcommittees are usually created every legislative term to deal with comprehensive packages of legislation within restricted time frames.

Committee members are formally nominated by the General Assembly. In practice the parliamentary groups choose their candidates for the seats allotted proportionally to each group, and the party selections are declared nominated by the Assembly. Most permanent House committees count eighteen permanent members and twenty-five substitutes; those of the Senate, fifteen and twenty-two, respectively. Each MP of a recognized group has to be a member of at least one committee. The small groups that are not formally recognized can send a delegate to each committee, who is not allowed to vote. Committee chairs are also assigned proportionally.

Within parliamentary groups, committee assignments are decided by the leader. At the beginning of a legislative term, the group leader will draw up a slate trying to satisfy all members. In case of conflicting demands, seniority usually decides. Generally, specialization, factional affiliation, and regional background are also taken into account in making committee assignments. Every committee member (and his or her substitute) can be replaced by another member of the group upon notification by the group leader of the speaker of the chamber. Therefore, group leaders can replace committee members against their will.

The main role of committees is the passage of legislation (including budget bills). In order to pass a bill, proposal, or decision, a majority of committee members has to be present, of which an absolute majority has to vote in favor. Until 1985 all committee meetings were held behind closed doors. Since then, the House has started gradually opening committee meetings to the public. After the 1993 statutory reforms, open meetings have become the rule rather than the exception. By 1997 more than two-thirds of the meetings were public. Since 1993 MPs who are not members of a committee have been permitted to attend meetings, participate in debates, and even introduce amendments. Ministers can be assisted by civil servants or personal staff members, and MPs can also receive backing by their personal or group advisers.

In principle, for each bill examined a report is drafted containing a summary of the committee discussions; the names of participants are mentioned only for matters discussed in public meetings. The report's conclusion on a bill presents only the opinion of the majority of committee members. The verbatim minutes of nonpublic meetings are not published, in extensive or summarized form.

Committees can—in order to prepare their legislative work—gather advice and ask for documentation from persons or institutions not belonging to Parliament. Until recently, the number of hearings was extremely low, but in the past few years hearings have become more frequent. For committee hearings held in public, the minutes are reproduced in the *Parliamentary Annals*.

Until the 1980s committees of investigation were quite uncommon, due to the attitude of majority MPs who—in solidarity with the government—were reluctant to allow investigations that could embarrass a minister or the entire government. In addition, even when a committee of inquiry suggested that a minister was politically responsible for certain failures, ministers did not resign as long as they were supported by their party. Whereas the House established only nine such committees between 1880 and 1988, since then they have been established on the average of about one a year. They have developed into an alternative instrument of parliamentary oversight and have gained considerable publicity.

Directing bodies

There are several directing bodies, the most relevant politically being the Office of Speaker and the Conference of the Presidents of the Parliamentary Groups. The conference comprises the speaker of the chamber, the vice chairpersons, and the leader of each parliamentary group. The prime minister can assist personally or send a representative, and committee chairs can also be invited to attend conference meetings. The conference meets weekly and decides—usually by consensus—on the agenda of the chamber, the time each group is allocated for debate, the holding of interpellations, the regulation of parliamentary activities, and long-term planning. It gives advice on several matters, including the composition and functioning of the committees.

The speaker is in principle elected by an absolute majority in a secret vote, but until recently most appointments were in practice made by acclamation. The nomination of chamber speakers is part of the coalition negotiations over ministerial posts. The president of a chamber is responsible for the enforcement of internal rules and discipline. He or she judges the permissibility of private member bills, motions, and questions, and formulates the matters to be voted upon, brings them to a vote, and announces the decisions of the chamber. The president usually chairs an important permanent committee as well as most internal affairs committees. Finally, the president sets the plenary agenda, after mandatory consultation with the Conference of Group Presidents.

Politically less significant are the vice chairs (who replace the chairs in case of absence), the secretaries (MPs who primarily control voting procedures), the Quaesture (responsible for managing the chambers in terms of personnel, infrastructure, budget, and ceremony), and the Griffie, or secretariat, composed of civil servants (who deal with committees, plenary sessions, parliamentary records, archives, and research and documentation). The chair, vice chairs, and secretaries—together with the leaders of the parliamentary groups—constitute the Bureau.

Party caucuses and groups

In most parties, rules restrict the initiative of individual MPs quite severely: MPs have to ask permission from their group or its leader to introduce private member bills or amendments, hold interpellations, and support bills sponsored by another party. In practice the group leadership also has to agree with initiatives MPs take inside committees. The parliamentary group meets weekly in order to discuss the initiatives members intend to take, the parliamentary agenda, and current political problems. Usually, the group specialists explain the matters currently under review in their committees and the matters to be voted upon in the plenary session.

The group leader is the group's main liaison with the national party executive. Being a member of the latter, the group leader communicates its decisions to his or her back benchers and also informs the national party executive about the issues at stake in the parliamentary arena and warns the party executive about backbench discontent. In most governmental parties, the group leader attends the weekly informal meetings between the party leadership and the party's ministers, at which the party's positions in the next cabinet meeting are defined. In Parliament the group leader is the main spokesperson of the party, appoints the group's spokesperson for important debates, and selects the candidates for intralegislative offices and committees. Within the group, the leader coordinates the discussion on which positions to take in the matters to be voted upon in the Thursday afternoon voting session. He or she enforces discipline and decides on sanctions. Finally, the group leader is the manager of the group secretariat and often plays an important role in the party research center.

Parliamentary groups are collectively responsible to the party. In most parties, group leaders have to submit to their party executive a report on the activities of the parliamentary group and its members. In case of excessive absenteeism and other abuses, the national party can decide to contact an MP's constituency party and suggest that it deselect the member.

Due to the necessity of permanent government support, voting discipline is very strong among majority parliamentary groups. Discipline is reinforced by formal and informal party constraints. First, the statutes of all parties accord final decision-making power to their national conference. This supreme decision-making body endorses the coalition policy agreement, binding the entire party, including the MPs, to the government. Between conferences, decision-making power is delegated to the Party Executive, of which usually only a minority of MPs are members. That most ministers and party presidents were MPs and therefore attended the meetings of their parliamentary group further enhanced party control over the group's decision making. Although voting behavior is almost exclusively determined by party, MPs are not constantly coerced to vote and act in ways that differ from their own opinion. Usually, groups are ideologically cohesive enough to vote in a disciplined manner without the use of sanctions.

The poor staffing of individual MPs, in contrast to the relatively well subsidized party research centers, reinforces MPs' dependency on their party organization. In each party research center (which is financed mainly by the parliament's subsidies to the groups and individual MPs), specialized policy preparation committees operate. In most policy areas, a group of permanent experts and volunteer specialists prepare the party's policy proposals in collaboration with specialist MPs. MPs often rely on information and technical assistance provided by their research center for drafting their private member bills, amendments, and interpellations. Thus MPs are to a large extent dependent on their party's brain trust, in case they do not rely on alternative resources (like the research centers of pressure groups).

LEGISLATIVE-EXECUTIVE RELATIONS

Government support has become a permanent duty for majority MPs as far as voting on legislative projects, investiture declarations, and motions of confidence and censure is concerned. This stems from the complexity of the coalition formation process, which is often characterized by many setbacks. Usually after several months, a formateur, nominated by the king, will eventually manage to conclude an encompassing and detailed coalition agreement and will be nominated prime minister. The new government presents its program and ministerial team before the House. After the debate on the governmental program, the government has to win the investiture vote (by a simple majority, excluding abstentions, with a quorum of half of the MPs). Until this final stage, the parliamentary groups as such are not involved in government formation. Moreover, since the coalition program and configuration are negotiated and approved by the national party conferences of the respective coalition parties before the government seeks the investiture by Parliament, a negative vote by majority MPs would openly defy the decisions of their party's supreme decision-making body. Thus, during the investiture debate, majority MPs may criticize some governmental intentions as contained in its program, but very few dare to follow this up with a negative vote.

The role of parliamentary groups and individual MPs is equally limited in coalition maintenance and collapse. Since 1947 not a single cabinet has fallen due to a defeat on a confidence vote in Parliament. Usually, internal governmental cohesion collapses due to interparty and intraparty conflicts, and cabinets resign before Parliament has a chance to formally register a cabinet's failure.

The constitutional reform of 1993 further reduced parliament's role in government dissolution. When the House rejects a motion of confidence introduced by the government and introduces the name of a new prime minister within three days, the government has to resign. If the House does not name a new prime minister, the chambers will be dissolved. The House can also take the initiative to unseat the government, by voting a motion of censure, whereby at the same moment a new prime minister is named ("positive vote of censure"). If it does not name an alternative prime minister, the government can carry on or even ask the monarch to dissolve the House. Finally, when a government resigns for other reasons, the monarch can also dissolve the House if a majority in the House agrees. The dissolution of the House also causes the dissolution of the Senate.

The other main tools of government control, parliamentary questions and interpellations, are increasingly used. Yet, in spite of this increasing activism, the majority's duty to support the government considerably undermines Parliament's control function.

There are three types of parliamentary questions: written, oral, and urgent. After an MP has read his or her oral or urgent question and the minister has answered, no debate is held, and no motions can be tabled. Oral questions are introduced in written form some days before "question time" (Thursday afternoon), whereas urgent questions can be introduced orally during a plenary meeting. In the House such questions are posed increasingly in public committee meetings rather than in the Plenary Assembly. Written questions must be answered within twenty working days and are published in the *Bulletin of Questions and Answers.*

Questions concern demands for clarification or confirmation. They aim at exposing neglect, abuse, or ill application of the law and sometimes suggest improvements and reform. They can force a minister to voice an opinion on delicate matters. Yet, in spite of their substantial control potential, about half the questions concern only demands for information and are often inspired by mere electoral and publicity-seeking motives, giving an MP written proof that he or she has taken to heart a matter raised by constituents or client pressure groups. Since ministers' answers to oral and urgent questions are not followed by debate, the oversight utility of questions is limited. Also, many ministers fail to give a prompt answer to written questions.

Interpellations of ministers represent the classical and most powerful tool of parliamentary control in Belgium. Interpellations can aim at obtaining information from the government, question the policy of a particular minister, and sometimes also criticize general governmental action. In principle, matters of local or special interest are excluded, although in practice these have become more numerous. The House increasingly relegates such interpellations to public committee meetings, and only those of general importance are still held in the plenary.

On average, one out of three interpellations is followed by a motion. Members of the opposition usually introduce a motion of censure, while majority members traditionally counter with a motion demanding the "return to the pure and simple order of the day." The motion to return to the order of the day has voting precedence on motions of censure and annuls all other motions. Thus, majority MPs are not obliged to express themselves on the political problem raised during the interpellation; this is a face-saving device in case the government or a minister's reply has failed to satisfy the House.

In spite of public needs for administrative recall and the introduction of ombudsmen in other public institutions, only in 1997 did the House establish a parliamentary ombudsman service. One of the reasons for its reluctance was the fact that Belgian MPs themselves are very active case workers. The prominence of this role is related to a clientelistic political culture, to the lack of other sources of administrative redress, and to the wide variety of services MPs can offer, since most sectors of public life are subject to party patronage.

PRIVILEGES, IMMUNITIES, AND RESOURCES

No MP can be prosecuted or arrested without the approval of his or her chamber, unless caught in the act of committing a crime or violence. The chamber can order that detention or prosecution be suspended during the session or throughout the term. Given the recent wave of corruption accusations, the immunity provisions will most likely be changed in the near future, facilitating interrogation of MPs.

Formally, MPs do not get an allowance, only an indemnity. In 1997 the indemnity amounted to about US$80,000 a year. MPs can travel free on all state-operated or state-contracted means of transport. They receive prestamped envelopes and can send free mail to public administrations and officeholders.

As far as individual staffing is concerned, only beginning in 1981 was each MP allocated funds for employing a full-time secretary. In 1995 funds were added for each MP to hire one university-trained assistant, but in many parties these new assistants have been pooled and work for the party research center. The secretariats of the parliamentary groups are not very well staffed either. Yet, in spite of their poor institutional staffing, MPs manage to mobilize help from a wide variety of sources, mainly the research centers of parties and interest groups, which makes MPs even more dependent on these organizations.

In 1995 the House counted only 477 permanent employees, of which over a quarter were university-trained. Of the university-trained aides, only those working for the Service for Studies, Documentation, Statistics, and Archives (about three dozens) and the Library of Parliament (a dozen) can provide intellectual assistance to individual MPs. Each permanent committee has one secretary-archivist. Until a few years ago, none of these House bodies were computerized.

JUDICIAL FUNCTIONS OF PARLIAMENT

The judicial powers of the Belgian Parliament include the power of the House to indict members of the government and have them tried by the Court of Cassation (used for the first time only in 1994), the right of each chamber to determine the conditions of eligibility of its members, and the right to establish committees of investigation. Such committees have the same powers as an examining magistrate, including use of subpoena and hearing witnesses under oath.

THE MEDIA AND BROADCASTING PROCEEDINGS

The parliamentary press has a specific tribune overlooking the Plenary Assembly of each chamber. Most national newspapers have a full-time parliamentary correspondent. Still, apart from major debates and incidents, coverage is rather poor, in the written press as well as on radio and television.

In order to boost one's political career through national media coverage, an MP has to develop good relations with political journalists. The relationship between politicians and political journalists in Belgium has often been described as symbiotic. MPs and political journalists belong—together with ministers, party and pressure group leaders, and their personal staffs—to a small political in-crowd of about fifteen hundred people. Many know one another from university, share the tensions of political crises, and visit the same bars, restaurants, receptions, and so forth.

Until the 1980s several chief editors of the national newspapers served as civil servants of the House and were responsible for the plenary session minutes. Hence, they were physically at the center of parliamentary debate and had been privileged "parliament watchers" for decades. Their advice on parliamentary matters, techniques, and strategies was often sought and highly appreciated. In addition, given the strong ties between newspapers and the three ideological pillars (Christian democrat, socialist, and liberal), the opinion of the chief editor of a pillar newspaper often served as the final judgment on a political matter.

CONSTITUTIONALITY OF LAWS AND EMERGENCY POWERS

In Belgium, the Arbitration Court and the Council of State are the arbiters of the constitutionality of legal rules. Ordinary courts cannot review the constitutionality of laws, but they exercise judicial control over administrative actions.

The Legislation Section of the Council of State verifies the constitutionality of bills. As an advisory body, its decisions are nonbinding. Government-initiated bills containing general rules must be submitted to the Council of State. In other cases the advice of the Council of State is purely optional (only 20 percent of all rules are submitted to the Council of State). Hence, the council basically serves to improve the technical quality of legislative work and to preserve the rule of law. Although it has no formal power in the legislative process, the advice of the Council of State has gained moral weight since the 1970s, when constitutional reforms began to dominate the political agenda.

The Court of Arbitration enjoys genuine competence of judicial review. It can determine whether legislative rules are enacted in compliance with the allocation of powers determined by the constitution. Since the 1988 constitutional reforms, the court has also been able to review the compliance of laws with three fundamental constitutional rights: equality, nondiscrimination, and freedom of education. The court exercises its jurisdiction on the one hand through annulment proceedings that may be initiated by the executive or legislative bodies of the various levels of government (federal, regional, community) or by any legal or moral person; and on the other hand, through requests for preliminary rulings initiated by ordinary courts if cases pending before them present conflicts between legislative rules and constitutional and legislative standards.

Through special powers, Parliament can accord the government large competencies over a broad range of policies for a fixed period of time. In that period Parliament cannot alter decisions taken under this system. Between 1926 and 1986 the government ruled with special powers for about 15 percent of the time. In nearly all cases, the special powers covered a broad range of economic, social, budgetary, and financial policies.

Lieven De Winter

BIBLIOGRAPHY

De Winter, Lieven. *The Belgian Legislator.* Florence: European University Institute, 1992.

———. "MPs and Parliamentary Groups in Belgium: Slaves of Partitocracy?" In *Behind Closed Doors: Parliamentary Party Groups in European Democracies,* ed. Knut Heidar and Ruud Koole. London: Routledge, 1997, forthcoming.

———. "Parliament and Government in Belgium: Prisoners of Partitocracy." In *Parliaments and Executives in Western Europe,* ed. Philip Norton. London: Frank Cass, 1997, forthcoming.

———. "Intra- and Extra-Parliamentary Role Attitudes and Behaviour of Belgian MPs." *Journal of Legislative Studies* 3 (1997): 128–154.

Macmullen, Andrew. "Citizens and National Parliamentarians in Belgium." In *Representatives of the People?* ed. Vernon Bogdanor. Aldershot: Gower, 1985.

BELIZE

OFFICIAL NAME: Belize
CAPITAL: Belmopan
POPULATION: 219,000 (1996 est.)
DATE OF INDEPENDENCE: September 21, 1981 (from the United Kingdom)
DATE OF CURRENT CONSTITUTION: Effective September 21, 1981
FORM OF GOVERNMENT: Constitutional monarchy
LANGUAGES: English (official), Spanish, Creole
MONETARY UNIT: Belize dollar
FISCAL YEAR: April 1–March 31
LEGISLATURE: National Assembly
NUMBER OF CHAMBERS: Two. House of Representatives; Senate
NUMBER OF MEMBERS: House of Representatives, 29 (directly elected); Senate, 8 (appointed)
PERCENTAGE OF WOMEN: House of Representatives, 3.4; Senate, 37.5
TERM OF LEGISLATURE: Five years
MOST RECENT LEGISLATIVE ELECTION: June 30, 1993
MINIMUM AGE FOR VOTING: 18
MINIMUM AGE FOR MEMBERSHIP: 18
SUFFRAGE: Universal
VOTING: Optional
ADDRESS: National Assembly Building, Belmopan, Cayo District
TELEPHONE: (501 8) 22141
FAX: (501 8) 23889

Belize, known as British Honduras until 1973, lies on the east coast of Central America, between Mexico and Guatemala *(see map, p. 526)*. Colonized by the British in the seventeenth century, it became a formal British colony in 1862 and gained its first legislative assembly under a new constitution in 1954. In 1981 Belize became the last country on mainland North America to become independent. It remains a member of the British Commonwealth, with the British monarch as head of state.

Under the 1981 constitution, Belize has a bicameral legislature, the National Assembly, consisting of two chambers. The Senate (upper house) has eight nominated members, and the House of Representatives has twenty-nine members who are elected in single-member constituencies by simple majority vote. Of the senators, five are appointed by the governor general on the advice of the prime minister, two on the advice of the leader of the opposition or a person of comparable stature, and one in consultation with the Belize Advisory Council. The term of the National Assembly is five years. In both the Senate and the House, a person who is not a member may be named as presiding officer.

The two major political parties in the National Assembly are the United Democratic Party (sixteen seats), the government party, and the People's United Party (thirteen seats), the opposition. Prior to the June 1993 elections, the ruling and opposition roles had been reversed, with the People's United Party holding a slim majority.

George Thomas Kurian

BENIN

OFFICIAL NAME: Republic of Benin (République du Benin)
CAPITAL: Porto-Novo
POPULATION: 5,710,000 (1996 est.)
DATE OF INDEPENDENCE: August 1, 1960 (from France)
DATE OF CURRENT CONSTITUTION: Approved December 2, 1990
FORM OF GOVERNMENT: Limited parliamentary democracy
LANGUAGES: French (official), Fon, Yoruba, tribal languages
MONETARY UNIT: CFA franc
FISCAL YEAR: Calendar year
LEGISLATURE: National Assembly (Assemblée Nationale)
NUMBER OF CHAMBERS: One
NUMBER OF MEMBERS: 83
PERCENTAGE OF WOMEN: 7.2
TERM OF LEGISLATURE: Four years
MOST RECENT LEGISLATIVE ELECTION: March 28, 1995
MINIMUM AGE FOR VOTING: 18
MINIMUM AGE FOR MEMBERSHIP: 25
SUFFRAGE: Universal and direct
VOTING: Optional
ADDRESS: Assemblée Nationale, B.P. 371, Porto-Novo
TELEPHONE: (229) 21 31 29
FAX: (229) 21 56 61

The Republic of Benin, a small country in West Africa *(see map, p. 447)*, established itself in the early 1990s as a pioneer among francophone African countries in developing a democratic multiparty political order. This was reflected most vividly in the composition and operation of its legislature after the election of February 1991. Indeed, the instinct for participation and diversity then prevailing in Benin resulted in a legislature in which twenty-one parties divided up just sixty-four seats. With the shifting alliances among the many parties, the president of the republic only occasionally could command a reliable majority.

Throughout its four-year term the National Assembly struggled with limited success to establish the bureaucratic infrastructure and staff resources that would enable it to professionalize its work. Then, in mid-1994, in a high-stakes showdown with the president over the state budget, the legislature asserted its right to a significant voice in the country's governance. Perhaps more important—in a country whose political history since independence in 1960 had been characterized by violence, military rule, and a repressive one-party regime—the confrontation was referred to the Constitutional Court established in 1993 and partially resolved there. In March 1995 Benin held its second multiparty elections, under a revised electoral code.

POLITICAL BACKGROUND

Benin was a part of French West Africa until it obtained self-governing status in 1958, followed by independence in 1960. Known officially as Dahomey until 1975, Benin during the first twelve years of independence was characterized by extreme political unrest. After numerous coups and failed elections, army major Mathieu Kerekou forced his way into power in 1972. In December 1974 Kerekou declared Dahomey a Marxist-Leninist state, and over the course of the next fifteen years he attempted to restructure the government, the economy, and the society along Marxist-Leninist lines. In December 1975 the country was renamed the People's Republic of Benin.

The Central Committee of the People's Revolutionary Party of Benin (PRPB), closely modeled after political parties in the Soviet bloc, played the primary role in national decision making throughout Kerekou's tenure. In November 1979 the Revolutionary National Assembly, a nominal legislature, was created. The PRPB presented the only set of candidates and was elected, with 97.5 percent of the electorate officially voting. The Assembly, which merely rubber-stamped Kerekou's proposals, was duly reelected in 1982, 1984, and 1989.

Late in 1989, facing escalating charges of widespread corruption within the regime and near total financial collapse, the Kerekou government yielded to domestic and international pressure and adopted an unprecedented course of radical reform. By year's end, as communist governments in central and eastern Europe were stepping aside, Kerekou began a similar process in Benin. In December the government announced that Marxism-Leninism was being abandoned and convened in February 1990 a semisovereign national conference in the capital of Porto Novo. Some 488 delegates from more than fifty organizations took part. Archbishop Isadore De Souza presided over an extraordinary assembly which, over the course of nine days, plotted a wholly new and distinctly democratic course for the nation. So successful was the exercise at effecting peaceful reform that the national conference model soon was emulated in other African states.

The conference formed an interim High Council of the Republic, which counted among its twenty-seven members three former presidents of Benin who had returned to Benin as leaders of opposition parties. Nicéphore Soglo, a former World Bank official, was named interim prime minister. Kerekou, now politically weaker, remained as president.

In April 1990 a preliminary constitution providing for a

multiparty system was drafted. The constitution balanced the executive with several institutions, including a multiparty legislature, an independent judiciary, an advisory economic and social council, and a High Commission on Broadcasting and Communications to safeguard the free circulation of information and ideas. In December the proposed constitution received 80 percent approval in a nationwide referendum.

RECENT ELECTIONS

On February 17, 1991, the people of Benin elected representatives to the legislature according to a proportional representation system. The entire country was treated as a single constituency, and no threshold (minimum number or percentage of votes required for receiving a seat in parliament) was applied. As a result, numerous small parties won single seats, and the largest party (a coalition of three parties running under a single banner) won just twelve seats.

In the presidential race, thirteen candidates presented themselves in the first round on March 10. The two top finishers (interim prime minister Soglo and the former head of state Kerekou) entered a runoff election two weeks later, which Soglo won with 68 percent of the vote. On April 4, 1991, he was inaugurated for a term of five years.

In the legislative elections held on March 28, 1995, thirty-one parties ran candidates for the enlarged eighty-three-seat National Assembly. Eighteen multimember districts elected three-to-five deputies each to the Assembly.

In the March 1996 presidential elections former dictator Mathieu Kerekou was elected to the presidency, making Benin the first African country to oust a democratically elected incumbent president via the ballot box.

ORGANIZATION AND OPERATIONS OF PARLIAMENT

Deputies to the National Assembly must be at least twenty-five years old, a Beninese citizen by birth (or a naturalized citizen for at least ten years), and a resident of the country for at least one year. Deputies are elected for four-year terms.

The legislature meets in the National Assembly Building in Porto Novo, the capital. The plan to renovate the Old Colonial Governor's Palace, however, includes new legislative chambers.

The governing bureau of the Assembly includes a president, first and second vice presidents, first and second treasurers, as well as first and second parliamentary secretaries. All are elected from the membership. The bureau, which meets once a week during ordinary sessions and more often if necessary, has administrative responsibilities in organizing the Assembly's work and that of the committees. It determines the parliamentary agenda and duration of each session and generally ensures the organization of individual plenary sessions.

The Assembly's five permanent committees are composed of a president, vice president, first and second rapporteurs, and a secretary (usually of diverse party affiliation), and several other members. The committees are: Law, Administration, and Human Rights; Finance; Planning, Infrastructure, and Production; Education, Culture, Employment, and Social Affairs; and External Relations, Cooperation, Development, Defense, and Security.

The Assembly has established itself as the preeminent forum for spirited debate over matters of national interest, such as privatization of state-owned enterprises. The privatization of the national brewery, for example, developed into a major debate, largely because of the symbolic loss of public ownership of the popular national beer.

Under the constitution of December 1990, the National Assembly exercises legislative power and oversees the activities of the government. The Assembly has the power to determine its own rules, but it is obliged to convene two plenary sessions annually—one in the first half of April and the other in the second half of October, neither to exceed three months. The Assembly also can meet in extraordinary session at the request of the president of the republic or at the request of a majority of deputies. Extraordinary sessions last no longer than fifteen days, although in fact the Assembly met almost continuously in 1993 and 1994.

Any deputy named to one of the eighteen ministerial posts forfeits his or her parliamentary seat. The prime minister may not hold any other public office.

The constitution delineates in considerable detail the respective rights and responsibilities of the National Assembly and the president in determining the national budget. For example, it appears to prevent the adoption by the legislature of any amendments to expenditure laws proposed by the executive without offsetting reductions, or increases, in the income to the state. The constitution also requires the Assembly to adopt only budgets that are balanced. If the budget is not settled at the start of a fiscal year, the president may request parliamentary concurrence to receive and spend money according to "provisional twelfths"—in effect, monthly continuances to spend according to the previous year's budget.

Because Benin is heavily dependent on funding provided by foreign donors and multilateral financial institutions, the government must negotiate its annual budget with the International Monetary Fund (IMF). This situation leaves the government little room to compromise if the National Assembly perceives different national priorities (and has not been included in the talks with the IMF).

Christopher Fomunyoh and Thomas O. Melia

BHUTAN

OFFICIAL NAME: Kingdom of Bhutan (Druk-yul)
CAPITAL: Thimphu
POPULATION: 1,823,000 (1996 est.)
DATE OF INDEPENDENCE: August 8, 1949 (from the United Kingdom and India)
DATE OF CURRENT CONSTITUTION: None
FORM OF GOVERNMENT: Absolute monarchy
LANGUAGES: Dzongkha (official), Tibetan dialects, Nepalese dialects
MONETARY UNIT: Ngultrum
FISCAL YEAR: July 1–June 30
LEGISLATURE: National Assembly (Tshogdu)
NUMBER OF CHAMBERS: One
NUMBER OF MEMBERS: 150 (105 directly elected, 45 appointed)
PERCENTAGE OF WOMEN: 2.0
TERM OF LEGISLATURE: Three years (terms are staggered)
MOST RECENT LEGISLATIVE ELECTION: No general elections; members are elected at various dates
MINIMUM AGE FOR VOTING: Each family has one vote in village-level elections
MINIMUM AGE FOR MEMBERSHIP: 25
SUFFRAGE: Universal
VOTING: —
ADDRESS: Tshogdu, P. O. Box 139, Convention Center, Thimphu
TELEPHONE: (975) 222729
FAX: (975) 224210

Long isolated by its mountainous terrain, Bhutan is located in the eastern Himalayas, between Tibet and India *(see map, p. 141)*. Bhutan was an independent kingdom as early as the mid-sixteenth century and came under British influence in the mid-nineteenth. Upon Britain's withdrawal from neighboring India following World War II, Bhutan came under the influence of India, which plays a role in Bhutanese foreign policy under a treaty signed in August 1949.

The Tshogdu was established in 1953. It meets at least once a year in spring (May to June) or autumn (October to November), but in recent years it has tended to meet for longer sessions. The size of the membership has remained constant over the years, although in principle the number of members is based on the population of the electoral districts and is subject to periodic revision.

Of the 150 members of the Tshogdu, 105 are elected by popular consensus (formal voting is used, however, in the event of a deadlock). Ten seats are reserved for the monasteries, and they are filled by the central and regional ecclesiastical bodies; one seat is reserved for commerce and industry (filled by the Bhutan Chamber of Commerce and Industry); and the remainder are occupied by government officials appointed by the king.

The elected members are not elected simultaneously, and there are overlaps in tenure. The speaker is elected by the members. The Tshogdu enacts laws, advises the king and the Council of Ministers on all constitutional matters, and debates important issues. Decisions are reached by consensus, but there is provision for a ballot on controversial issues. In theory, the Royal Advisory Council and the Council of Ministers are accountable to the Tshogdu. Political parties are outlawed in the kingdom, but some opposition parties are based in Kathmandu, Nepal.

George Thomas Kurian

BOLIVIA

OFFICIAL NAME: Republic of Boliva (República de Bolivia)
CAPITAL: La Paz (seat of government); Sucre (legal capital)
POPULATION: 7,165,000 (1996 est.)
DATE OF INDEPENDENCE: August 6, 1825 (from Spain)
DATE OF CURRENT CONSTITUTION: February 2, 1967
FORM OF GOVERNMENT: Parliamentary democracy
LANGUAGES: Spanish (official), Aymará (official), Quechua (official)
MONETARY UNIT: Boliviano
FISCAL YEAR: Calendar year
LEGISLATURE: Congress (Congreso)
NUMBER OF CHAMBERS: Two. Chamber of Deputies (Cámara de Diputados); Senate (Senado)
NUMBER OF MEMBERS: Chamber of Deputies, 130; Senate, 27
PERCENTAGE OF WOMEN: Chamber of Deputies, —; Senate, —
TERM OF LEGISLATURE: Four years
MOST RECENT LEGISLATIVE ELECTION: June 1, 1997
MINIMUM AGE FOR VOTING: 21 (18 if married)
MINIMUM AGE FOR MEMBERSHIP: Chamber of Deputies, 25; Senate, 35
SUFFRAGE: Universal and direct
VOTING: Optional

ADDRESS: National Congress, La Paz
TELEPHONE: Chamber of Deputies, (591 2) 36 73 03;
Senate, (591 2) 37 50 56
FAX: (591 2) 34 16 49

Named for Simón Bolívar, the liberator of South America from Spanish rule, the Republic of Bolivia is located in west central South America, where it straddles the Andes Mountains *(see map, p. 536)*. Although Bolivia is constitutionally a republic with a bicameral legislature, the country's recent history has been marked by extraordinary periods of political instability in its democratic institutions.

POLITICAL BACKGROUND

Constitutional turmoil was the norm in Bolivia in the nineteenth and early twentieth centuries, when new constitutions were promulgated no less than a dozen times. Through the 1980s elected civilian governments were routinely expelled by military coups. As a result, legislative institutionalization was episodic, and the frequent interruptions of democratic rule undermined the development of a functioning and assertive legislature.

The end to military rule in Bolivia in the summer of 1982 and the return to office of the Congress elected (and then suspended by the coup) in 1980 marked the beginning of a period of democratic stability that has been reinforced by democratic stabilization among most of Bolivia's neighbors. Building on more than a decade of continuous operation, covering three presidential election cycles, legislative organization and operations have begun to assume a degree of stability and permanence not evident in earlier periods of Bolivian independent government.

ELECTIONS

Bolivia possesses a bicameral Congress composed of a 130-member Chamber of Deputies and a 27-member Senate. Deputies and senators, who are elected simultaneously for four-year terms, are required to be Bolivian citizens by birth and to have fulfilled their military service. Deputies must be at least twenty-five years of age, senators thirty-five. Deputies and senators must be nominated by a recognized political party or civic organization.

Members of the Chamber of Deputies are selected by a mixed electoral system that combines election of most deputies from single-member districts, with additional seats filled on the basis of proportional representation. In 1997 all seats in the Chamber of Deputies were filled through elections in single-member districts. In the Senate three senators are chosen from each of the nine administrative departments, with two seats going to the party receiving the largest number of votes and one seat to the party receiving the second greatest number of votes.

Civil servants, police, and military officers on active service, as well as active members of the clergy, are ineligible under the constitution for legislative service. The ban against selection of civil servants also extends to government contractors and managers, directors, agents, or representatives of state-owned corporations and enterprises that are organized on a mixed public-private ownership basis or otherwise receive state subsidies. Finally, any person convicted and sentenced to a prison term is barred from election to either chamber unless the Senate has voted formally to restore the person's civil rights.

The two chambers have no authority to review contested elections. Such challenges are submitted to the national electoral court, which has plenary authority to rule on the validity of election returns.

LAW MAKING

The Chamber of Deputies and the Senate share legislative responsibility in most policy areas. Each possesses, however, a number of unique powers to initiate policy actions.

The constitution gives the Chamber of Deputies priority in financial matters: fixing expenditures of the government departments, considering economic development plans submitted by the president, authorizing loans backed by the faith and credit of the state, and issuing contracts for the exploitation of national resources. The chamber also considers legislation on the size and composition of the military in peacetime. Legislation related to any of these matters must be introduced, considered, and approved in the Chamber of Deputies before the Senate can begin consideration. The Senate's power of amendment on these measures is not limited, however.

The Chamber of Deputies also is authorized to propose to the president three candidates to head each of the state-owned enterprises; the president selects the finalist. The Senate proposes to the president three candidates for comptroller general of the republic from which the president chooses. In addition, the Senate proposes three candidates for each vacancy on the Supreme Court of Justice. The Chamber of Deputies then elects the justice from among the three candidates.

In most other legislative matters the Chamber of Deputies and the Senate have equal responsibilities and powers. A bill passing one chamber may be amended by the other and returned to the first chamber for further action. The initiating chamber may agree to the second chamber's changes, clearing the bill for the president. It may, however, further amend the measure or refuse to accept the second chamber's changes. In either event a joint session is convened and the various alternatives are brought to a vote with senators and deputies voting individually. As a result, a unified Chamber of Deputies usually prevails against the Senate. If one chamber passes a bill and the second chamber takes no action within two weeks, the first chamber is permitted to request a joint session at which the disputed measure is put to a vote by the entire Congress.

The president of the republic retains a key power over state finances, thus minimizing the ultimate power of the legislative branch. The annual government budget is submitted to Congress by the president. If both houses of Congress do not enact the budget (in either submitted or amended form) within thirty days, the budget as submitted by the president is deemed enacted into law.

ORGANIZATION AND OPERATION OF THE LEGISLATURE

The legislative work of Congress is confined to a 90-day annual session. Congress can, however, on its own initiative or pursuant to presidential order, extend the session to 120 days. Only actual meeting days are counted against the limit.

Between annual sessions of Congress a bicameral management committee handles the institutional and operational interests of the legislative branch. Chaired by the vice president of the republic, the committee comprises nine senators and eighteen deputies, including the presidents of each chamber. It has constitutional authority to act on all matters that fall within the constitutional power of Congress, including the authority to summon the entire Congress or either chamber into extraordinary session.

The vice president of the republic serves not only as president of the Senate but also as president of Congress. As a consequence of this largely ceremonial power, the vice president is able to pursue legislative objectives that span the interests of either chamber. For example, since 1992 the vice president has appointed and headed a bicameral committee on legislative modernization that has served as the focal point for internal operational and administrative reforms in both the Chamber of Deputies and the Senate. The bicameral committee also is Congress's sole agent in dealing with aid-granting institutions financing the reforms.

Each chamber is subject to the direction of a *mesa directiva* (literally, a directing table) comprising the president of the chamber and the heads or designees of each of the political parties represented in the chamber. The *mesa* is responsible for developing an overall schedule for the annual session and for each daily session of the chamber. It also determines conditions for debate on bills and for debate on proposed amendments to bills on the daily session agenda. Members of the *mesa* share a variety of administrative responsibilities in the chamber—for example, supervising legislative services and preparing legislative documentation.

The constitution requires the presence of an absolute majority of members in either chamber before legislative business can commence each day. Delays in beginning daily sessions occur frequently while the parties seek to produce the requisite quorum. The absence of a quorum at any point in the daily session can cause the immediate suspension of the session.

Both chambers have appointed a wide array of permanent and temporary committees. Members typically serve on three or more committees, although members serving on committees with big workloads or committees with highly salient subject responsibilities may serve on fewer. Legislation is routinely submitted to the appropriate committee or committees for review and recommendations. Committees have the authority to request information related to proposed legislation (and to government operations generally) from executive officials and to request their appearance before committees of either chamber.

Committees have no full-time staff; most share support personnel lent to them from the central administrative service units of the chamber. Some committees use specialists working under short-term contract to assist them in particularly complex technical matters, and it is becoming more common for committees to request executive officials (including the comptroller general) to lend suitably skilled staff to the committee for specialized work. The absence of extensive permanent staff support limits the amount of documentation committees can produce, and it is rare that a committee issues transcripts of committee hearing testimony or that legislative reports of committees provide extensive analysis of bills reported to the chamber.

The committee and administrative systems in both chambers have not developed extensive institutional supports. The tradition continues in both chambers of annual rotation of committee assignments. Thus legislators have little opportunity to develop their subject expertise in the areas covered by their committees. Similarly, the administrators of the chamber, including the *oficial mayor* (major official), serve brief terms, usually only one year. This tenure limit originated in the desire to minimize the opportunity for fraud or embezzlement of the chamber's financial resources, but it also prevents any long-term internal reorganization under the supervision of managers having some degree of continuity.

SELECTION OF THE PRESIDENT AND VICE PRESIDENT

The Bolivian Congress possesses a right that has grown increasingly important since the return to stable democratic traditions. Under the constitution the president and vice president are elected upon receiving a majority of the national popular vote. In the event, however, that no presidential ticket receives an absolute majority of the votes cast, the election devolves upon Congress. The Chamber of Deputies and the Senate sit jointly, but each member votes individually.

In the presidential elections held in 1985, 1989, and 1993, no candidate received a majority of the popular vote. In each instance, the presidential candidates began negotiations in an effort to form a congressional coalition that would provide the majority vote needed. In two cases, the congressional voting and private negotiations were long. In the 1993 elections the candidate finishing second, Gen. Hugo Bánzer, announced that he was prepared to accept the election by Congress of the leading candidate in the popular vote, Gonzalo Sánchez Losado, because of the size of Sánchez's plurality. In a show of national unity, Sánchez approached the third candidate, Max Fernández, about obtaining Fernández's support in the congressional voting. In return, Sánchez offered to name a member of Fernández's party to the cabinet. The result was a consensus selection of the president by Congress reflecting the private negotiations among party chiefs.

When Congress is unable to muster a majority for one of the leading presidential candidates, it is free to choose someone else for the presidency. This it did in the face of a protracted deadlock in 1979–1980, when it ultimately selected Senate president Walter Guevara Arze as interim president pending a call for new elections. Six months later the military deposed Guevara, but public opposition to the coup, combined with the refusal of Congress to accept coup leader Col. Alberto Busch as president, ultimately forced all claimants to step aside. The eventual result was a significant strengthening of democratic institutions because of visible public support in the face of great danger, and the stature of Congress was greatly enhanced because of its role in the opposition to Busch.

ETHICS, IMMUNITIES, AND CONSTITUTIONAL RESTRAINTS

Each chamber has the power to revoke by a two-thirds vote the electoral mandate of a duly sworn member for violation of chamber rules or violation of ethical standards of behavior.

The constitution provides absolute immunity from prosecution for opinions expressed by deputies and senators in the performance of their official duties. Immunity from arrest or prosecution can be waived only by a two-thirds vote of the chamber in which a deputy or senator serves. Deputies and senators may not be sued or required to give bond during a period beginning sixty days before the meeting of Congress; this limited immunity applies only for the duration of an annual session.

The constitution expressly bans deputies and senators from purchasing or leasing public property, acquiring contracts for public works or sale of supplies to the state, or receiving any other financial benefit from the state by virtue of their office. Violations of these constitutional bans can be enforced by a resolution canceling a deputy or senator's electoral mandate and passed by the legislator's own chamber by a majority vote.

According to the constitution, a member of Congress is eligible for selection as president or vice president or for appointment as a minister of state or as an accredited diplomat. The member's rights and privileges as a deputy or senator are suspended, however, for the duration of his or her service in the executive post. Upon relinquishing such an executive post, the deputy or senator may return to the Congress if the term for which he or she was elected has not yet expired. If a member of Congress is appointed to the judiciary or is named to head a state-controlled corporation, the leave of absence provision does not apply and the deputy or senator must resign from Congress.

Paul S. Rundquist

BIBLIOGRAPHY

Hudson, Rex A., and Dennis M. Hanratty. *Bolivia: A Country Study.* Washington, D.C.: Government Printing Office, 1991.

Malloy, James M. "Democracy, Economy, Crisis, and the Problems of Governance: The Case of Bolivia." *Studies in Comparative International Development* 26 (1991): 37–57.

BOSNIA-HERZEGOVINA

FORM OF GOVERNMENT: Federal state comprising two independent entities—the Federation of Bosnia and Herzegovina and the Republic of Srpska

CONSTITUTION: Adopted 1995 as part of the Dayton Peace Agreement

PRESIDENCY: Three-person presidency—one Croat and one Bosniac directly elected by Federation voters; one Serb directly elected by Republic of Srpska voters

LEGISLATURE: Bicameral Parliamentary Assembly

LOWER HOUSE: Forty-two-member House of Representatives. One-third of members (fourteen) directly elected by Republic of Srpska voters; two-thirds of members (twenty-eight) directly elected by Federation voters

UPPER HOUSE: Fifteen-member House of Peoples. Five Serbs elected by National Assembly of the Republic of Srpska; five Croats and five Bosniacs elected by the House of Peoples of the Federation

FEDERATION OF BOSNIA AND HERZEGOVINA

FORM OF GOVERNMENT: Federal entity comprising eight cantons and a number of municipalities

CONSTITUTION: Adopted 1994 and subsequently amended to conform with the 1995 constitution of Bosnia and Herzegovina

PRESIDENCY: One person, directly elected in Federation-wide election

LEGISLATURE: Bicameral Federation Assembly

LOWER HOUSE: 140-member House of Representatives directly elected by party list in Federation-wide elections

UPPER HOUSE: House of Peoples. Members elected by cantonal legislatures: thirty Bosniac delegates, thirty Croat delegates, and a number of "other" delegates as determined by the ratio of "other" delegates to Bosniac and Croat members in the eight cantonal legislatures

REPUBLIC OF SRPSKA

FORM OF GOVERNMENT: Unitary entity

CONSTITUTION: Adopted 1992 and subsequently amended to conform with the 1995 constitution of Bosnia and Herzegovina

PRESIDENCY: One person, directly elected by voters in the Republic of Srpska

LEGISLATURE: Unicameral National Assembly of eighty-three directly elected members

Bosnia-Herzegovina, formerly a constituent of Yugoslavia *(see map, p. 749)*, is a federal state comprising two independent entities: the Federation of Bosnia and Herzegovina and the Republic of Srpska. Each of the three entities—Bosnia-Herzegovina, the Federation of Bosnia and Herzegovina, and the Republic of Srpska—has a constitution, legislature, and executive.

HISTORICAL BACKGROUND

The area of modern-day Bosnia and Herzegovina came under Roman rule in the second century B.C., ending the rival territorial ambitions of the Thracians, Illyrians, Celts, and Greeks. The division of the Roman Empire in 395 A.D. brought the region under the control of the Byzantine emperor in Constantinople. In the fifth century, Slavic tribes from the Carpathian Mountains began regularly settling in the Balkan Peninsula, establishing a firm Slavic presence in the area.

As Catholicism dominated the western area of Croatia in the ninth century, the eastern region of Serbia adopted Eastern Orthodox Christianity, leaving the Bosnian area as a buffer between the two religious groups. In the eleventh century, the Bosnian principality of Rama struggled to create its own regional identity. Despite the efforts of Byzantium to control the Bosnian region, Bosnian rulers of the fourteenth century temporarily established a powerful Bosnian state. In 1389 the Ottoman Empire thwarted the efforts of Stjepan Tvrtko, self-proclaimed tsar of the Bosnians and Serbs, to unify Bosnian and Serb lands. Bosnia finally succumbed to Ottoman rule in 1463. Twenty years later, the Ottoman Turks gained control of Herzegovina (an Austrian border duchy since 1448) and confirmed their domination over the region. From the fifteenth to the nineteenth centuries, the Ottoman Empire ruled Bosnia and Herzegovina through a system that allocated responsibility for religious groups to the leader of each group. Many Bosnians converted to Islam to maintain control over their property and became members of the Muslim ruling class. Persecution of Christians through heavy taxation, a Koran-based legal system, forced conversion to Islam, and, for girls, servitude in harems, contributed to hostile uprisings and violent repression.

Also during the fifteenth through the nineteenth centuries, the northern Hapsburg Empire encouraged Serb settlement of the bordering Krajina region to prevent the expansion of the Turks. As the Ottoman Empire began to crumble, the 1878 Congress of Berlin gave the Hapsburg Empire administrative rights in the six regions of Bosnia and Herzegovina (Sarajevo, Travnik, Bihać, Dinja Tuzla, Banja Luka, and Mostar).

In 1908 Austria-Hungary officially annexed Bosnia and Herzegovina as a province to counter the threat of Serbian expansion. The empire reversed the Ottoman policy of Muslim privilege. Political organizations were banned and the nationalistic tendencies of Serbs and Croats were suppressed. The Austro-Hungarian Empire attempted to insulate Bosnia and Herzegovina from the influence of its increasingly disgruntled neighbors—Croatia and Serbia—while trying to prevent the creation of a Muslim state. Tensions in the area erupted when a student member of the Serb nationalist Black Hand organization, Gavrilo Princip, assassinated Archduke Francis Ferdinand, heir to the Hapsburg monarchy, and his wife, Sophie, during a visit to Sarajevo. Austria-Hungary, supported by Germany, subsequently declared war on Serbia, igniting World War I.

Despite siding with the losing Austrians during World War I, Bosnia and Herzegovina joined the newly formed Kingdom of Serbs, Croats, and Slovenes in 1918. The kingdom lasted until 1929, when King Alexander established a royal monarchy. The area of Bosnia and Herzegovina, no longer recognized as a political region, was divided into four administrative units. Agrarian reforms freed peasants from the Muslim-led feudal hierarchy, but the centralized, Serb-dominated government dissatisfied many Muslims, Croats, and Slovenes.

A coalition government of Serbs, Muslims, and Slovenes took control in 1939 after the assassination of King Alexander in France. Tensions between the Serbs and the Croats steadily increased until the outbreak of World War II. Croats collaborated with German and Italian fascists and formed the Independent State of Croatia, forcing the Serbs to vacate the region in order to create a "Greater Croatia." The Serbs countered with aggression by both the nationalist Četnik organization, led by Draza Mihajlović, and the communist Partisan movement, led by Josip Broz Tito. At the end of the war, Tito's partisans led the formation of the Federal Republic of Yugoslavia, comprising Serbia, Croatia, Slovenia, Macedonia, Montenegro, and the reunited region of Bosnia and Herzegovina.

Throughout the period of communist rule, Tito and his League of Communists of Yugoslavia suppressed nationalist sentiments and forcibly promoted an ideology of "unity and brotherhood." The 1974 constitution increased the autonomy of each member republic. The death of Tito in 1980 brought a powerful resurgence of long-suppressed nationalistic sentiments. Unlike the five other, ethnically more homogenous, constituent republics, Bosnia and Herzegovina comprised significant numbers of Muslims, Serbs, Croats, and people of mixed ethnicity. In an attempt to increase their ranks, both the Serbs and the Croats claimed the Bosnian Muslims to be either converted Serbs or converted Croats. The Muslims resisted being identified with either group and claimed the right to a Muslim state within Bosnia and Herzegovina.

Because of its relative strength within the federal republic, Serbia sought to reassert the dominance of the federal government over the individual republics through legal, economic, communication, and voting reforms. Serbia also campaigned to reunify the decentralized League of Communists. By 1990 ethnic Serbs in Croatia and Bosnia had begun planning for a "Greater Serbia." Relations between the member republics rapidly disintegrated, culminating in the secession of Slovenia and Croatia in 1991.

In Bosnia and Herzegovina, dissatisfied Serb delegates in the regional Assembly deserted the coalition government and walked out during initial discussions of the region's independence. Following the example set by Slovenia and Croatia, the Muslim-dominated Assembly of Bosnia and Herzegovina declared independence in December 1991. A referendum held two months later, boycotted by Serbs, confirmed the country's independence. In April and May, the United States, the European Union, and the United Nations joined in recognizing the independence of the Republic of Bosnia and Herzegovina.

Following the declaration of sovereignty by the Republic of Bosnia and Herzegovina, the Bosnian Serbs declared the formation of the Serbian Republic of Bosnia and Herzegovina. Initially, Bosnian Croats remained united with the Bosnian Muslims in the Republic of Bosnia and Herzegovina against the rebel Serbs, despite proposals to Croatia from Serbian leader Radovan Karadžić to partition Bosnia. Bosnian government forces joined with Bosnian Croats to recapture the southern city of Mostar from the Bosnian Serbs. President Franjo Tudjman of Croatia, acting in support of Bosnian Croats, signed a cooperation treaty with the president of Bosnia and Herzegovina, Alija Izetbegović, and formed a joint defense committee against the Bosnian Serbs. However, the cooperation did not last long, and the Bosnian Croats declared independence for the Croatian Union of Herzeg-Bosna (a year later renamed the Croatian Republic of Herzeg-Bosna) in the area west of Mostar.

Relations between Bosnian government and Bosnian Croat forces broke down in October 1992, as Bosnian Croats, backed up by Croatian army troops, took over Mostar and other towns in Croatian-held areas of Bosnia. The Bosnian government battled both the rebel Serbs and rebel Croats for almost a year before the Bosnian Muslim government and the Bosnian Croats renewed their cooperation against the Bosnian Serbs. In March 1994, under international pressure, Prime Minister Haris Silajdžić of Bosnia and Kresimir Zubak, leader of the Bosnian Croats, met in Washington to sign an agreement creating the Federation of Bosnia and Herzegovina ("Federation"). Bosnian president Izetbegović and Croatian president Tudjman then signed a second agreement that established a loose confederation between the new Bosnian Federation and Croatia.

The new Federation, approved by the Bosnian Assembly on March 31, 1994, was designed to replace the governance structure of the Republic of Bosnia and Herzegovina. The Bosnian Federation held together, albeit precariously, despite political and military tensions between Bosnian Muslims (Bosniacs) and Bosnian Croats.

In December 1995 the Dayton Peace Agreement was signed by the governments of Serbia, Croatia, and Bosnia-Herzegovina, bringing a formal end to the war in Bosnia. The agreement called for the continuance of a single Bosnia-Herzegovina state based on a new constitution.

CONSTITUTIONAL PROVISIONS ON PARLIAMENT

Bosnia and Herzegovina comprises two autonomous entities: the Federation of Bosnia and Herzegovina and the Republic of Srpska. There are three constitutions in force in Bosnia and Herzegovina. The Constitution of the Federation of Bosnia and Herzegovina (1994; hereafter referred to as the "Federation constitution") established the Federation government and eight cantonal governments. The Constitution of the Republic of Srpska (1992) set forth the legal principles, rights, and duties upon which that republic is based and the powers of the respective bodies within the Republic of Srpska. The 1995 Constitution of Bosnia and Herzegovina governs the two entities within the state.

Bosnia and Herzegovina

The 1995 constitution of Bosnia and Herzegovina was part of the Dayton Peace Agreement. It replaced the previous constitution of the Republic of Bosnia and Herzegovina and governs the relations between the two entities (the Federation of Bosnia and Herzegovina and the Republic of Srpska). The constitutions of the Federation and the Republic of Srpska, adopted in 1994 and 1992, respectively, were subsequently amended to bring them into compliance with the 1995 constitution.

The government of Bosnia and Herzegovina is headed by a three-person presidency which comprises a representative of the Bosnians, a representative of the Croats, and a representative of the Republic of Srpska. Bosnia and Herzegovina has a Parliamentary Assembly comprising two chambers: a House of Representatives and a House of Peoples.

The House of Peoples is made up of fifteen delegates. One-third of the delegates (five) are selected from the Republic of Srpska, and two-thirds (five Croats and five Bosniacs) are selected from the Federation. The delegates from the Federation are selected, respectively, by the Croat and Bosniac delegates to the House of Peoples of the Federation. Delegates from the Republic of Srpska are selected by the National Assembly of the Republic of Srpska.

There are forty-two members in the House of Representatives. As with the House of Peoples, one-third of the House of Representatives delegates come from the Republic of Srpska, and two-thirds are elected from the Federation. Each chamber of the Parliamentary Assembly of Bosnia and Herzegovina must convene in Sarajevo no more than thirty days after the selection or election of members. Although the first election to the House was held in September 1996, parliament's first session was not held until January 1997.

The Parliamentary Assembly has the responsibility to enact legislation necessary to implement decisions of the presidency; establish and approve a budget for the operations of the institutions of Bosnia and Herzegovina; and consent to the ratification of all international treaties. Other duties may be assigned to the Parliamentary Assembly by mutual agreement of the Federation of Bosnia and Herzegovina and the Republic of Srpska.

Each chamber adopts its internal rules by a majority vote of its members. In 1997 each chamber adopted provisional rules of procedure. There are also provisions in the constitution that regulate some important aspects of the legislative process.

Each chamber selects from among its members one Serb, one Bosniac, and one Croat to serve as its chair and deputy chairs. The position of chair automatically rotates among the three selected persons every eight months. At no time can the chair of both chambers represent the same constituent people.

In each chamber, the chair and deputy chairs comprise the Collegium of Chair and Deputy Chairs. The collegia have the responsibility to prepare the proposed legislative agenda, to provide the delegates at least seven-days' notice of each session sitting, and to ensure that draft legislative proposals are presented to the appropriate committees of the respective chambers. In case of undue delays in the legislative process, either chamber may call for a joint meeting. Both collegia are expected to make their best effort to overcome deadlocks.

All legislation requires the approval of both chambers. Unless otherwise proposed by the initiator of the draft legislation, a bill is first introduced in the House of Representatives. However, laws may be initiated in either chamber. Laws may be proposed by any member of parliament, by one or more committees, by any member of the presidency, or by the Council of Ministers. Upon approval by one chamber, the draft law is transferred within seven days to the other chamber, which may approve the legislation or return it to the originating chamber with suggested amendments. The originating chamber then sends the proposed law back to the other chamber, with or without the suggested amendments, for a final vote. The law is considered adopted when signed by the chairs of both chambers.

During deliberation, the chair of the respective chamber gives the floor to the requesting delegates. The presentation of a draft law is limited to ten minutes, and debate is limited to five minutes per delegate. Votes are normally taken by a show of hands. Upon request, votes can be taken by roll call in alphabetical order. If the chair is a Serb, the alphabetical order of the Cyrillic alphabet is followed. If the chair is a Bosniac or a Croat, the alphabetical order of the Latin alphabet is followed.

Decisions are made by a majority of those present and voting. In the House of Peoples, 9 delegates comprise a quorum, provided that at least 3 Bosniac, 3 Croat, and 3 Serb delegates are present. In the House of Representatives, 22 members comprise a quorum. The delegates and members are supposed to make their best effort to see that these majorities include at least one-third of the votes of the delegates and members from the territory of each entity. Absent this proportional vote, the Collegium of Chair and Deputy Chairs for the relevant chamber meets to obtain approval from one-third of the members from each entity within three days of the vote. If those efforts fail, a vote is taken by a majority of those present and voting, providing that the dissenting votes do not include two-thirds or more of the delegates or members elected from either entity.

A proposed decision of the Assembly may be declared to be "destructive of a vital interest" of the Bosniac, Croat, or Serb delegates by, respectively, three Bosniac, three Croat, or three Serb delegates of the House of Peoples. A proposed decision requires approval in the House of Peoples by a majority of each of the Bosniac, Croat, and Serb delegates present and voting. When a majority of one of the above groups of delegates objects to declaring a decision "destructive of a vital interest," the chair of the House of Peoples must convene a joint commission comprising three delegates—one from each group—to resolve the issue. If the joint commission fails to resolve the issue within five days, the matter is referred to the Constitutional Court for a decision. If the court finds no procedural violations, the proposed decision is sent back to the House of Peoples for a vote at its next sitting.

Decisions of the Assembly come into effect after publication. Both chambers publish a complete record of their deliberations, and these deliberations are generally held in a public forum. Amendments to the constitution require a majority vote by delegates of the House of Peoples; there must be a two-thirds vote in the House of Representatives.

The constitution provides that the House of Peoples (excluding the first elected House) may be dissolved by either the presidency or by a majority of its members. The majority must include a majority of delegates from at least two of the three ethnic groups.

Members of the Parliamentary Assembly cannot be held liable for criminal or civil acts carried out within the scope of their duties in the Assembly. However, any individual who has been indicted or sentenced by the International War Crimes Tribunal for the Former Yugoslavia is banned from running or holding a seat in the Assembly.

The Federation of Bosnia and Herzegovina

Several agreements followed the original Federation Agreement signed in Washington in March 1994 by the Bosnian prime minister and representatives of the Bosnian Croats. The Vienna Agreement, negotiated in May 1994, amended the Federation constitution by adding a new section regarding cantons and establishing criteria for defining the territory of Bosnia and Herzegovina. The Petersberg Agreement, signed in Bonn, Germany (March 10, 1995), set forth a framework for implementing the Federation. The agreement also set a date of April 15, 1995, for the creation of all cantons not already created within Bosnia and Herzegovina. Yet, as of 1996, Tuzla Podrinje was the only confirmed, fully functioning canton. The Constitution of the Federation of Bosnia and Herzegovina, as amended by the subsequent agreements, claims for the Federation all powers and responsibilities that are not reserved for the institutions of Bosnia and Herzegovina.

The Federation is based upon the relationships among the Federation government, eight smaller cantonal governments (four Muslim-dominated cantons, two Croat-dominated cantons, and two mixed cantons), and still smaller municipal governments. For instance, the 1994 Federation constitution established exclusive responsibilities for the Federation Assembly (a bicameral body comprising a House of Peoples and a House of Representatives), including electing the Federation president and vice presidents; approving the selection of the cabinet; authorizing any use of military force by the Federation; authorizing cantons to conclude agreements with states and international organizations; adopting the budget of the Federation; and enacting legislation to levy taxes and impose other necessary financing instruments.

Joint Federation and cantonal responsibilities include issues of human rights; health; environmental policy; transport and communication infrastructure; social welfare policy; citizenship; immigration and asylum; and use of natural resources. All powers not expressly granted to the Federation are reserved for the cantons, particularly in matters regarding police; education and cultural policy; housing; public services; local land use; local energy production; regulation of radio and television facilities; implementation of social welfare policy; and finance of cantonal activities.

The Federation Assembly is made up of a 140-member House of Representatives and a House of Peoples comprising 30 Bosniac delegates, 30 Croat delegates, and a number of "other" delegates (primarily Serb) as determined by the ratio of "other" delegates to Bosniac and Croats in the cantonal legislatures. Four years is the maximum term of each house. Members of the House of Representatives are elected directly by eligible voters in Federation-wide elections. Voters cast a single, secret ballot for any registered party. Political parties must receive at least 5 percent of the vote to be allocated seats in the House of Representatives. Before each election, each registered party publishes a list of candidates. The members of the House of Representatives from each party are the persons highest on that party's list.

In contrast, members of the Federation House of Peoples are elected from members of the cantonal legislatures. The number of delegates allocated to each canton is proportional to the population of the canton. However, there must be at least one Bosniac, one Croat, and one "other" delegate from each canton that has at least one such member in its legislature. Each house of the Federation Assembly must select from among its members a chair and a deputy chair who represent different constituent groups.

The House of Representatives of the Federation and the House of Peoples of the Federation met on November 6, 1996. The delegation from the Federation to the Bosnia and Herzegovian House of Peoples was selected during this initial sitting.

As of February 1997, the rules governing the Federation Assembly were the 1994 Rules for the Federation Constitutional Assembly. New rules were expected to be adopted.

Votes in each house of the Federation are passed by a simple majority unless otherwise specified under the constitution or by law. Each house is required to approve "necessary" legislation within a "reasonable time" of its approval in the other house. When the prime minister decides that one house is delaying its decision, he or she may convene a joint conference, comprising up to ten members from each house, to develop a position acceptable to both houses.

When the president decides that the legislature is unable to enact necessary legislation, he or she may, with the concurrence of the vice president, dissolve either or both houses. The president is also required to dissolve the legislature when it fails to adopt the budget of the Federation.

Decisions that concern the "vital interest" of any of the constituent peoples require, in the Federation House of Peoples, the approval of a majority of the Bosniac and Croat delegates. This constitutional provision can be invoked by a majority vote of the Bosniac or Croat delegates. If a majority of the remaining delegates opposes the invocation of this provision, a joint commission of the Bosniac and Croat delegates is established to resolve the issue. If the commission is unable to resolve the issue within one week of the provision's invocation, the question is determined by the Constitutional Court in an expedited procedure.

Amendments to the constitution can be proposed by the president with concurrence of the vice president, by a majority of the House of Representatives, or by a majority of the Bosniac and Croat delegates in the House of Peoples. To be adopted, proposed amendments require the following majority: in the House of Peoples, a simple majority of the Bosniac delegates and a majority of the Croat delegates; in the House of Representatives, a two-thirds majority.

Each house deliberates in open sessions and publishes a record of its deliberations and decisions. Members of both houses are protected from any criminal or civil liability regarding acts carried out within the scope of their respective authority. No member of either house may be detained or arrested by any authority in the Federation without the approval of that house.

The Republic of Srpska

The unicameral National Assembly of the Republic of Srpska comprises eighty-three members who are elected for a term of four years through direct, secret ballot. The National Assembly is presided over by a president and two vice presidents, who are elected from among its members for a term of four years. The president convenes the Assembly and chairs its sittings. The president of the Assembly is required to call a session on the demand of one-third of the total number of representatives or on the demand of the president of the Republic of Srpska. The Republic of Srpska's National Assembly had not adopted its operational rules by early 1997. A new set of rules was expected to be passed in 1997.

In accordance with the constitution of the Republic of Srpska, decisions in the Assembly are made by majority vote of all deputies, unless a special majority is required by the constitution. The right to introduce bills, other regulations, or general enactments is vested in the representatives, the government, the president of the republic, or a least three thousand voters. The National Bank can also propose laws relating to monetary policies. Within seven days of the passing of a law by the National Assembly, the president is required to declare the law by decree. During this time, the president may also require the Assembly to reconsider the law. If the Assembly readopts its decision, the president is required to declare the law. Laws come into force no earlier than the eighth day from the day of publication in the official gazette. The Assembly amends the constitution, enacts laws, passes on the budget, announces referenda, holds elections for the president, and elects and dismisses high-ranking officials.

Representatives enjoy immunity. They may not be criminally prosecuted, punished, or detained for opinions expressed or votes cast during National Assembly sittings. A representative cannot be detained without the approval of the Assembly, unless he or she has been caught in the act of committing a criminal offense that carries a penalty of more than five years' imprisonment. No representative can be subject, without the approval of the National Assembly, to criminal proceedings after he or she has invoked parliamentary immunity. The president of the Republic of Srpska, the government, representatives, and voters in excess of three thousand may introduce bills and regulations to the National Assembly.

The mandate of the National Assembly may be reduced by a proposal of thirty members and a subsequent vote by two-thirds of all members. Elections must then be called within sixty days of the decision to shorten the mandate. This reduction may not take place during a state of war. The mandate of the government is also shortened as a result of the National Assembly's reduced mandate.

ELECTIONS AND PARTIES

The first postwar elections were held in Bosnia on September 14, 1996. They were monitored by the Provisional Election Commission of the Organization for Security and Cooperation in Europe (OSCE), which also was responsible for formulating the rules and regulations for the election. Citizens residing within Bosnia and Herzegovina and refugees residing outside Bosnia and Herzegovina were permitted to vote in the election. Elections were held for the House of Representatives of Bosnia and Herzegovina (in the Federation and the Republic of Srpska), the National Assembly of the Republic of Srpska, the president of the Republic of Srpska, the Federation presidency, and the House of Representatives of the Federation.

One-third of the forty-two members elected to the House of Representatives of Bosnia and Herzegovina were from the Republic of Srpska. The Serbian Democratic Party of Bosnia and Herzegovina (SDSBiH) gained nine seats; the Muslim Party of Democratic Action (SDA), three; and People's Union of Peace, two. In the Federation, where two-thirds of the seats (twenty-eight) were selected, the SDA captured sixteen seats, followed by the Croat Democratic Party, eight; Party for Bosnia and Herzegovina, two; and United List of Bosnia-Herzegovina, two.

For the House of Representatives of the Federation, thirteen parties ran in the September elections, but only six acquired seats: United List of Bosnia and Herzegovina, eleven; SDA, seventy-eight; Croatian Rights Party, two; Croat Democratic Party of Bosnia and Herzegovina, thirty-six; Democratic People's Union, three; and Party of Bosnia and Herzegovina, ten.

Elections for the eighty-three-member National Assembly of Srpska also took place. Sixteen political parties vied for seats; nine parties won seats: Serb Democratic Party, forty-five; SDA, fourteen; People's Union for Peace, ten; Serb Radical Party, six; Democratic Patriotic Party, two; Party for Bosnia and Herzegovina, two; Serb Party of Krajina, one; Serb Patriotic Party, one; and a coalition of several parties, two.

In 1990 the Communist Party in Yugoslavia had given way to the smaller nationalist parties of the republics, including the Croatian Democratic Union of Bosnia and Herzegovina (HDZBiH), named after Franjo Tudjman's party in Croatia; the Muslim Party of Democratic Action (SDA), led by Alija Izetbegović; and Radovan Karadžić's Serbian Democratic Party of Bosnia and Herzegovina (SDSBiH), modeled after the SDS in the Croatian region of Krajina. Although there are more than fifty-five political parties in Bosnia and Herzegovina, the HDZBiH, SDA, and SDSBiH continue to play the most important role. They dominated the September 1996 elections.

The SDA, led by Izetbegović, was founded on two main principles. The party chose religion as the vehicle to implement its first goal of strengthening Muslim nationalism. By appealing to the feature certain to distinguish the SDA from other parties, the SDA was able to rally the majority of Muslims behind the banner of Islam. The second goal was promoting the preservation of a multinational and multireligious state.

The HDZBiH was initially founded on the principle of keeping the borders of Bosnia and Herzegovina inviolate. However, as Bosnian Croats cooperated with Bosnian Serbs, inviolate borders appeared to be merely a step in creating a "Greater Croatia." The HDZBiH has not given up on the idea of an independent Herzeg-Bosna. The president of Croatia, Franjo Tudjman, controls the party.

The SDSBiH was initially created in Croatia by Croatian Serbs to combat rising Croat nationalism. By 1991 the SDS in Bosnia had declared three areas of Bosnia as "Serb Autonomous Regions" and made plans to link them with similar self-declared Serb regions in Croatia to form a new republic. It is widely recognized that the SDSBiH was being influenced, if not directed, by Serbia. Members of the SDSBiH walked out of the Republic of Bosnia and Herzegovina Assembly in October 1991 and formed their own Serb Assembly in the city of Pale in Bosnia. Radovan Karmić was the leader of this party until he stepped down prior to the September 1996 elections. Had he not stepped down, his party would have been unable to participate in the elections due to his status as an indicted war criminal.

SESSIONS OF THE PARLIAMENTARY ASSEMBLY OF BOSNIA AND HERZEGOVINA

The 1995 constitution of Bosnia and Herzegovina provides that each house of the Parliamentary Assembly must meet within thirty days of the election. However, the initial session of the first postwar Assembly did not take place for more than three months after the elections. Each chamber convenes in ordinary sessions as called by the chair or at the request of either of the deputy chairs. Delegates are required to attend the sessions of the Parliamentary Assembly as well as meetings of any committees on which they serve.

Under the Federation constitution, the House of Representatives must convene within twenty days of the promulgation of election results. Delegates in the House of Peoples, elected from the members of the cantonal legislatures, must likewise convene within twenty days of the elections of the cantonal legislatures. The first sessions of the Federal House of Peoples and the Federal House of Representatives took place more than a month after the elections, in November 1996.

The constitution of Srpska is silent as to the annual number of sittings for the National Assembly. The 1992 constitution simply provides that the Assembly shall convene "permanently."

Two official journals record the work of the Assemblies. The *Official Gazette of Bosnia and Herzegovina* reports on the activities of the bicameral Bosnia and Herzegovina Parliamentary Assembly. The *Gazette* is published in the Bosniac, Croat, and Serbian languages. The *Official Gazette of the Federation of Bosnia and Herzegovina* documents the work of the bicameral Federation Assembly. The *Gazette of the Federation* is published in the Bosniac and Croat languages.

Each of the three constitutional assemblies (Bosnia-Herzegovina, the Federation, and the Republic of Srpska) is in the process of adopting new procedural rules which will maintain old or establish new committees. The Federation has the most established committee structure because of its relative longevity vis-à-vis the other two assemblies.

The Rules of Procedure of the Federation House of Peoples has established the following permanent working bodies: the Committee for Economy and Industry; the Committee for Agriculture and Forestry; the Committee for Finance; the Committee for Labor, Health Care, and Social Security; the Committee for Education, Science Culture, and Physical Culture; the Committee for Building, Housing and Municipal Services; the Committee for Political Organization; and the Committee for Justice.

The Federation House of Representatives provides for the following standing working bodies: the Committee for Economic Relations and Development; the Committee for Finance; the Committee for Internal Policy; the Committee for Education, Science, and Culture; the Committee for Health Care and Social Welfare; the Committee for Building, Housing, and Municipal Services; and the Mandate-Immunity Commission.

The state of Bosnia and Herzegovina in early 1997 adopted procedural rules creating new working committees. The committees are identical for both chambers of the Parliamentary Assembly and include the Committee for Constitutional and Legal Affairs; the Committee of Foreign Affairs; the Committee on Foreign Trade and Customs; the Committee for Finance and Budgetary Affairs; the Committee on Human Rights, Immigration, Refugees, and Asylum Issues; the Committee on Transportation and Communications; the Committee on Administrative Issues; and the Committee on Verification. Both chambers may establish additional committees and may draft legislation concerning their respective subject jurisdictions.

Each committee in the House of Peoples comprises at least three, six, or nine members, with an equal number of members from each of the three constituent peoples. Each committee in the House of Representatives comprises at least three and not more than ten members. Two-thirds of the members are delegates elected from the territory of the Federation, and one-third are delegates elected from the Republic of Srpska. Each party that does not have a representative in a particular committee may participate in the discussions of that committee, although without having the right to vote. Each committee meets at least once a week or at the request of any of its members.

Joint meetings of the committees in both chambers can be held to debate an issue of mutual importance. The decision to convene jointly is made by a majority of the members of the relevant committees. Each committee votes independent of the other.

The committees of each chamber review and comment on draft legislation within their subject jurisdiction. Decisions are taken by a majority of those present and voting, provided that at least one-half of the members of the committee are present.

The constitution of Bosnia and Herzegovina states that

the Parliamentary Assembly is responsible for adopting an annual budget proposed by the president. If the Assembly fails to adopt the proposed budget before the start of the budgetary period, the budget of the previous year will be used.

Under the constitution of Srpska, the National Assembly of Srpska is responsible for the budget and annual balance sheet.

Under the Federation constitution, the Federation Assembly is responsible for adopting the budget before the beginning of the budgetary period. If it fails to do so, the president must dissolve the legislature.

THE EXECUTIVE BRANCH

The presidency of Bosnia and Herzegovina

The constitution provides for a three-member presidency of Bosnia and Herzegovina: one Bosniac and one Croat, each elected directly from the Federation, and one Serb president directly elected from the Republic of Srpska. The term of the first presidency is two years. Subsequent presidencies will have a term of four years, governed by a yet-to-be-enacted election law.

Elections for the presidency of Bosnia and Herzegovina were held in September 1996. The Bosnian presidency winner was Alija Izetbegović (SDA). The Croatian presidency winner was Kresimir Zubak (HDZBiH). The Serbian presidency winner was Momčilo Krajišnik (SDSBiH).

The presidency is charged with establishing its own rules of procedure. The constitution establishes the selection process for the chair of the presidency. The presidency endeavors to adopt all decisions by consensus. A dissenting member of the presidency may declare a presidency decision "destructive of a vital interest" of his or her entity. Such a decision is referred immediately to the assembly of the relevant entity (to the National Assembly of the Republic of Srpska or the House of Peoples of the Federation). If the declaration is confirmed by a two-thirds vote of the relevant parliamentary body within ten days of the referral, the challenged presidency decision does not take effect.

The powers of the presidency include presenting the annual budget to the Parliamentary Assembly and executing parliamentary decisions; and negotiating treaties, with the consent of the Parliamentary Assembly. The presidency is also charged with appointing, subject to the approval by the House of Representatives, a chair of the Council of Ministers. The chair has the power to appoint a minister of foreign trade, a foreign minister, and other ministers as may be appropriate, who take office upon the approval of the House of Representatives.

The president of the Federation of Bosnia and Herzegovina

The House of Peoples has the responsibility to nominate both the president and vice president, who serve alternating one-year terms as president and vice president during a four-year period. Successive presidents may not be from the same constituent people. The Constitutional Court may remove the president or vice president after two-thirds of the Federation Assembly has voted that the official violated the oath of office or is otherwise unworthy to serve.

The president, with the concurrence of the vice president and with the consultation of the prime minister (or nominee), nominates cabinet ministers for approval by the House of Representatives. The president, acting on a request of the prime minister, with the concurrence of the vice president, may also remove members of the cabinet.

The powers of the president include nominating the government, officers of the military, and judges of the Federation courts and signing decisions of the Federation Assembly.

The president of the Republic of Srpska

The president of the Republic of Srpska is elected by direct, secret ballot and is limited to two consecutive terms, of five years each. Duties of the president include proposing candidates for the president and justices of the Constitutional Court and the prime minister; granting pardons; and promulgating laws through ordinances.

A 1996 amendment to the constitution also provides for the election of vice presidents. Only one vice president will be elected in the first elections. The election for vice president will take place simultaneously with that for the president. Moreover, both positions will be selected from the same list and will have a term of five years, with a maximum two consecutive terms. The president will determine which vice president will replace him or her during a temporary absence.

In the event the National Assembly is unable to convene because of unusual circumstances, the president can enact measures, so long as they do not infringe upon the constitution or law.

THE GOVERNMENT

Bosnia and Herzegovina

The chair of the Council of Ministers is nominated by the presidency and approved by the House of Representatives. The chair of the Council of Ministers is responsible for proposing candidates for foreign minister, foreign trade minister, and other ministerial posts. The chair's nominations for these ministerial posts must be approved by the House of Representatives. These ministers, in addition to the chair, comprise the Council of Ministers. The chair is also responsible for nominating deputy ministers, who are also approved by the House of Representatives. No more than two-thirds of all ministers can be appointed from the territory of the Federation.

The Federation of Bosnia and Herzegovina

The prime minister serves as the head of government, aided by a deputy prime minister and cabinet ministers. Each minister and respective deputy minister must represent different constituent parties. The deputy prime minister is designated to serve as either defense minister or foreign minister.

The Federation prime minister is responsible for executing and enforcing Federation government policies and laws; proposing and making recommendations concerning legislation; and preparing budgetary proposals for the Federation Assembly. The president and the prime minister are jointly responsible for conducting foreign affairs within guidelines provided by the legislature.

Under the Federation constitution, Croats must occupy at least one-third of the ministerial positions. Cabinet decisions concerning the vital interest of any of the constituent peoples, as determined by at least one-third of the ministers or the Constitutional Court, require a consensus.

The Republic of Srpska

The government of the Republic of Srpska comprises the prime minister, deputy prime minister, and ministers.

The prime minister is nominated by the president. He or she, in turn, nominates candidates for the other ministerial positions. The prime minister may alter the composition of the government upon the opinions of the president of the republic and the president of the National Assembly; the National Assembly must be notified of this change. The candidate for prime minister presents his or her program and proposes the list of ministers to the National Assembly.

The government is elected by a majority vote of the Assembly. A proposal by the prime minister to dismiss a member of the government requires a majority vote of all representatives in the National Assembly for approval. If the prime minister resigns or is dismissed, the government is deemed to have resigned. If the president of the republic perceives a crisis in the functioning of the government, the president may, with the initiative of twenty members of the National Assembly and after getting the opinions of the president of the National Assembly and prime minister, force the prime minister to resign. If the prime minister refuses, the president of the republic is empowered to release the prime minister of his or her duties.

The National Assembly may also take a vote of no confidence in the government. A proposed no-confidence vote can be submitted by no fewer than twenty members of the Assembly. A government that resigns, has been voted no confidence, or has been dissolved by the National Assembly will continue in office until an election for a new government takes place. The president must nominate the prime minister within ten days of the resignation, expiration of mandate, or vote of no confidence in the prior government. Elections for the government must then take place within forty days after the nomination by the president of the republic.

Ministries as well as other state agencies are responsible for the administration of the republic. Ministries are given the authority to carry out policies, laws, and other laws put forth by the president, National Assembly, and government.

STATUS OF MEMBERS AND PARLIAMENTARY RESOURCES

The national library in Sarajevo and most university libraries were destroyed during the war. There is a major international effort to build and refurbish libraries. The Administrative Service performs research and technical and administrative duties for Federation Assembly members. The service is divided into three units: a Secretariat (which covers both chambers), the Office of the President and Vice President of the House of Peoples, and the Office of the President and Vice President of the House of Representatives.

The three parliaments have not yet passed new regulations on compensation for their members. At least for the Federation Assembly, members continue to be paid under rules established in a prewar republic law. Pursuant to this law, members receive reimbursement for travel to Sarajevo for parliamentary sessions, hotel costs while attending sessions, transportation within Sarajevo, and food; they also receive salary during parliamentary sittings.

The procedural rules for Bosnia and Herzegovina state that delegates of both chambers receive the same compensation, based on attendance for each day that a chamber is in session or a committee is meeting.

CONSTITUTIONALITY OF LAWS AND EMERGENCY POWERS

Bosnia and Herzegovina

The constitution of Bosnia and Herzegovina provides for a Constitutional Court, which comprises nine members. Four justices are elected by the House of Representatives of the Federation; two justices are selected by the National Assembly of the Republic of Srpska; the remaining three justices are selected by the president of the European Court of Human Rights, after consultation with the presidency. The three justices appointed by the president of the European

Court of Human Rights must not be citizens of Bosnia and Herzegovina or neighboring states. The president of the European Court of Human Rights appointed three justices in November 1996: Hans Danelius (Sweden); Louis Favoreu (France); and Joseph Marko (Austria). The constitution allows the Parliamentary Assembly to alter the method of appointing the three justices by the president of the European Court of Human Rights after the initial five-year appointment. All of the justices are initially appointed for a single term of five years, after which justices will be appointed to serve until the age of seventy years or until they are removed for cause.

The Constitutional Court has original jurisdiction over disputes arising under the constitution between Bosnia and Herzegovina and an entity or entities; between entities; or between institutions in Bosnia and Herzegovina. The Constitutional Court also has appellate jurisdiction over issues arising out of the constitution from any court in Bosnia and Herzegovina. The court must determine whether a law is compatible with the constitution and the European Convention on Human Rights and Fundamental Freedoms. All decisions of the court are final and binding. One-fourth of the members of either chamber of the Parliamentary Assembly or one-fourth of either chamber of an entity legislature may refer an issue to the court.

Although the constitution of Bosnia and Herzegovina does not specifically mention emergency powers, it does provide the presidency with the power to "perform such other function as may be necessary to carry out its duties."

The Federation of Bosnia and Herzegovina

The constitution of the Federation includes provisions for a new Federation judiciary and establishes a Constitutional Court, Supreme Court, and a Human Rights Court. The constitution provides that courts shall operate independently and autonomously and that Federation law will govern as necessary to provide uniformity, due process, and basic guarantees of justice. Cantonal legislatures may adopt complementary local rules, and each court may adopt any subsidiary rules that do not contradict Federation law.

The Federation constitution provides for an equal number of Bosniac and Croat judges on each court of the Federation as well as appropriate representation of "others." The president, with the concurrence of the vice president, nominates all Federation judges for approval by a majority of the Federation House of Peoples. Judges appointed under the Federation constitution serve a five-year probationary period, after which they may be reappointed and serve to the maximum age of seventy. The Supreme Court is the highest court of appeals in the Federation for questions of constitutional and Federation law, except issues that fall within the exclusive jurisdiction of the Constitutional Court or the Human Rights Court.

The Human Rights Court consists of three judges—one Bosniac, one Croat, and one "other." Additional judges may be appointed by the Federation Assembly if necessary to avoid delayed disposition of cases. The Human Rights Court presides over cases involving constitutional or other legal provisions concerning human rights and fundamental freedoms. The court is authorized to grant whatever relief it deems appropriate, and its decision is final and binding.

The Federation constitution provides for a Constitutional Court. The primary role of the nine-member Constitutional Court is resolving disputes between cantons; between cantons and the Federation government; between a municipality and its canton or the Federation government; and between or within any of the institutions of the Federation government. The constitution requires that for the first five years, three of the nine seats be filled by foreigners chosen by the president of the International Court of Justice. The judges initially selected to serve were from Nigeria, Syria, and Belgium.

The Federation Constitutional Court is authorized to review federal laws or proposed laws at the request of the president, vice president, prime minister, or one-third of the members of either house of the Federation Assembly. It is empowered to review cantonal law upon request of a cantonal president or one-third of the members of the legislature of a canton. The Constitutional Court may also decide on constitutional questions that arise in the Supreme Court, the Human Rights Court, or a cantonal court.

The government is authorized to promulgate decrees having the force of law in response to national emergencies when the legislature is unable to do so. The decrees cannot derogate the rights and freedoms provided for in the constitution. A decree can be issued for up to thirty days, unless the legislature votes to terminate the decree. After the automatic termination of a decree, it may not be extended, reinstated, or repeated without the approval of the legislature.

The Republic of Srpska

The constitution provides that the Constitutional Court decide whether the laws and regulations are in conformity with the constitution. The court has seven justices who are appointed for a single eight-year term. The president of the court is elected by the National Assembly for a three-year term.

Any person may submit an initiative for a proceeding before the Constitutional Court as to issues of legality and constitutionality. The National Assembly, government, president, and other bodies and organizations may initiate a proceeding according to the law. The Constitutional Court can also initiate a proceeding. Any law found to be unconstitutional will be considered void as of the date the court issues its decision.

In the event of a state of war, or an immediate threat of war, the president can pass enactments normally reserved for the Assembly's jurisdiction. Once the Assembly convenes, the presidential enactments are submitted for its approval.

MEDIA AND BROADCASTING OF PROCEEDINGS

The Federation constitution guarantees the freedom of the media and press, and, with the exception of the government press center, media agencies operate freely and independently. The award-winning Sarajevo daily paper, *Obsloboqienje,* has continued its operations despite production difficulties imposed by the war. The Federation constitution also lists freedom of the press as a fundamental freedom of the Federation.

The Bosnia and Herzegovina constitution also provides for freedom of expression. The constitution of the Republic of Srpska sets forth the freedom of public expression. Although the constitution guarantees freedom of communication, this may be limited by a court order if it is deemed crucial for criminal proceedings or for the Republic of Srpska's security.

The Office of the High Representative in Bosnia (OHR), a body created by the Dayton Accord and approved by the UN Security Council, and other international bodies have been active in promoting an independent media. For example, the OHR, Organization for Security and Cooperation in Europe, and the European Monitoring Commission have been working toward the establishment of an independent and self-sufficient publishing house in the Republic of Srpska.

Bosnia's first independent television station, the Open Broadcast Network, began broadcasting on September 7, 1996. TV-IN, a joint venture company that represents independent journalists in Bosnia and Herzegovina and five commercial television stations, was also launched in late 1996.

Mark S. Ellis

BIBLIOGRAPHY

Pomfret, John, and Christine Spolar. "Bosnian Election: Voting Mostly a Peaceful Occasion," *Washington Post,* September 15, 1996.

"Post-Dayton Bosnian Parliament Holds First Sessions." *This Week in Bosnia,* January 6, 1997.

BOTSWANA

OFFICIAL NAME: Republic of Botswana
CAPITAL: Gaborone
POPULATION: 1,478,000 (1996 est.)
DATE OF INDEPENDENCE: September 30, 1966 (from the United Kingdom)
DATE OF CURRENT CONSTITUTION: Effective September 30, 1966
FORM OF GOVERNMENT: Parliamentary democracy
LANGUAGE: English (official), Setswana
MONETARY UNIT: Pula
FISCAL YEAR: April 1–March 31
LEGISLATURE: National Assembly
NUMBER OF CHAMBERS: One
NUMBER OF MEMBERS: 47 (40 elected, 4 co-opted, 2 ex officio, plus the speaker)
PERCENTAGE OF WOMEN: 8.5
TERM OF LEGISLATURE: Five years
MOST RECENT LEGISLATIVE ELECTION: October 15, 1994
MINIMUM AGE FOR VOTING: 21
MINIMUM AGE FOR MEMBERSHIP: 21
SUFFRAGE: Universal
VOTING: Optional
ADDRESS: National Assembly, P.O. Box 240, Gaborone
TELEPHONE: (267) 355 681
FAX: (267) 313 103

A landlocked nation in southern Africa, the Republic of Botswana is regarded as one of the few democratic systems on the continent. The West sees Botswana as an example of economic—especially free market—growth, but this was not always the case. The country originally had little wealth except from cattle ranching, and the British valued it primarily as a strategic stepping-stone along the Cape-to-Cairo route. Only after independence in 1966 did copper, diamond, and nickel mining fuel economic growth.

A parliamentary democracy, Botswana vests executive power in the president, assisted by a vice president and cabinet. The National Assembly is the supreme legislative body and elects the president. The government must consult the House of Chiefs on all matters relating to the chieftaincies and changes to the constitution. The judicial system includes magistrate's courts and the High Court.

HISTORICAL BACKGROUND

For the first thirty-five years after it became a protectorate in 1885, Bechuanaland, the colonial name for Botswana, was governed by the British without a territorial legislature. Providing only meager governmental services, the British relied on the African chiefs, who had their own tribal councils. In 1920 British authorities established protoparliaments in the form of two racially segregated advisory councils, one for the whites, the European Advisory Council, and one for the Africans, the Native Advisory Council, restyled the African Advisory Council in 1940.

These bodies began meeting separately in 1921 at the Imperial Reserve in Mafikeng (then called Mafeking), South Africa, under the chairmanship of the Bechuanaland Protectorate resident commissioner, who served as speaker as well as senior administrative officer in the territory. Not only were there separate protoparliaments in Mafikeng, the administrative headquarters for the protectorate, but tribal chiefs also represented the Batswana, as the Africans of the protectorate were known. In the beginning the African Advisory Council included only six of the eight principal tribes, but by 1940 all eight were represented on the council. Membership grew from thirty in 1921 to thirty-eight in 1951.

Elections under the banner of political parties or movements were not characteristic either of the African or the white chamber. The tiny white population of the protectorate was located in territorial blocs where freehold tenure was permitted. To be elected to the European Council, members had to be British subjects who were property owners or licensed merchants who had resided in the protectorate for five years. They served three-year terms and constituted the unofficial part of the mini-legislature.

In 1921 the council began with six unofficial members, but by 1948 their number had expanded to eight. The resident commissioner appointed six official members, none of whom had a vote. Neither council had unfettered jurisdiction, and neither developed an extensive staffing service. Their focus was on local—rather than colonial and foreign policy—concerns, although they did make clear their feelings about partial or total incorporation into the Union of South Africa, which was the paramount issue for the legitimacy and future of the protectorate. The whites would have preferred this territorial realignment, but Africans opposed it. Nevertheless, the council did provide the rudiments of political and administrative training to elements of the local elite. After the close of the Second World War, to which Bechuanaland contributed a sizable number of troops, the pace of political change increased.

By 1950 a Joint Advisory Council was formed to bridge the two separate councils. This new institution had four official and sixteen unofficial members evenly divided between the European and African Advisory Councils. Chaired by the resident commissioner, the joint committee met twice a year in Mafikeng. Ten years later, with decolonization well under way throughout the rest of anglophone, or English-speaking, Africa, the protectorate received a constitution, which, in turn, provided for a Legislative Council. This new institution replaced both the Joint Advisory Council and the European Advisory Council, and the African Advisory Council was reconstituted as the African Council. The African Council, which functioned from 1961 until 1964, was a more inclusive body than the African Advisory Council had been and incorporated elected members in addition to the chiefs of the eight major tribes.

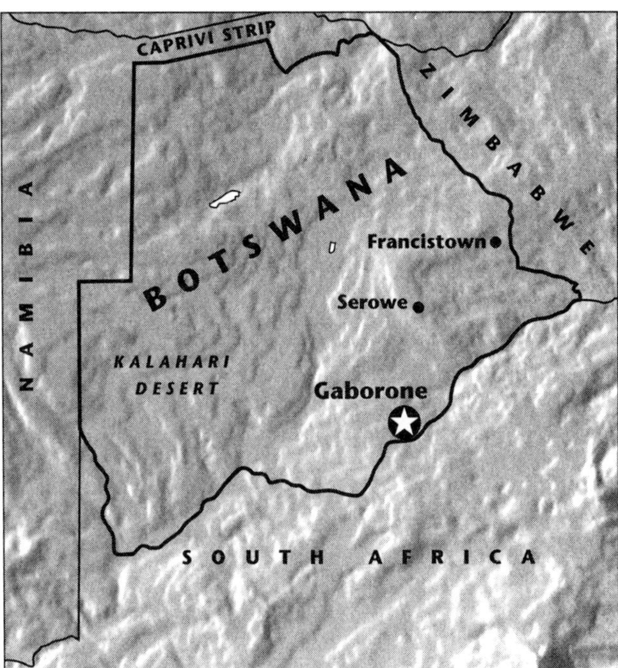

The Legislative Council, which provided for parity between the African and white communities (each being allotted ten members) as well as for the small Asian community (one member), had only modest powers, but it continued to serve as a political socializing mechanism once political parties formed in the protectorate in 1959. These parties began to attract the politically able, educated, and ambitious Batswana who found inadequate opportunities to apply their talents in the traditional political system and who were deeply impressed by the pace of decolonization and concerned about the status of Africans in neighboring white-ruled countries.

By 1963 a new constitution provided for self-government—the penultimate phase of British colonial rule. Not only were elections held for the Legislative Assembly (which replaced the Legislative Council), with fully functioning political parties contesting the thirty-one seats, but the administrative headquarters of the protectorate also moved from Mafikeng to Gaborone, where a raft of government offices was constructed. The Bechuanaland (now Botswana) Democratic Party of Seretse Khama emerged the clear victor of the March 1965 general election with twenty-eight seats; the opposition Bechuanaland (now Botswana) People's Party secured the other three seats.

Three weeks later self-government began, and Khama became the first (and only) prime minister of the protectorate. During this period an independence conference took place in London, an independence constitution was drawn up, and the Legislative Assembly began to operate. On September 30, 1966, the country became independent and joined the British Commonwealth of Nations. An uneven bicameral system—the constitution called for the creation of the House of Chiefs and the restyling of the Legislative Assembly as the National Assembly—was developed, and the president was designated as both head of state and head of government.

THE CONSTITUTION, ELECTIONS, AND SESSIONS

The thirty-eight articles of the constitution that concern parliament are grouped together as the fifth chapter of the constitution, wedged between the parts devoted to the executive and the judicial branches of government. The chapter is, in turn, subdivided into six parts, one of which concerns the House of Chiefs. The remaining five parts deal with the National Assembly and cover such topics as membership and officers, powers, interpretation, parliamentary procedure, and duration. There are ten additional articles in the schedule to the constitution concerning the election of specially elected members of the National Assembly.

Botswana uses the traditional British plurality (or first-past-the-post) method of election for members of parliament. Originally there were thirty-one single-member constituencies, but now there are forty. In the 1994 election the Botswana Democratic Party garnered twenty-seven of the forty elective seats in the National Assembly, and the opposition Botswana National Front won the other thirteen. Five other parties competed in that election, but none was able to capture a single seat. Members of parliament are elected to five-year terms (or less if the president dissolves parliament or if parliament passes a motion of no confidence in the government). The constitution provides that the MPs can, in turn, elect up to four other members known as specially elected MPs. The government can use these members to strengthen its position in the National Assembly or to provide a seat to a government MP defeated in the general election. Furthermore, although he or she cannot vote, the attorney general is a member of parliament, and the president is also an ex officio member.

Each year the National Assembly meets for roughly 105 days, and each of the parliaments (ordinarily a five-year span) is broken into sessions, which are subdivided into meetings. The constitution stipulates that at least one session must be held every year. Each session, which entails three meetings, runs six to nine weeks. While in session the National Assembly sits Monday through Friday (except for public holidays) beginning at 2:30 p.m., although the first sitting of each session begins at 3:30 p.m. The sittings, which are conducted in English, begin with questions for oral answer.

These questions last for about thirty minutes, and the business of the National Assembly ends at 4:00 p.m. to allow brief committee meetings and to enable the MPs to meet their constituents or representatives of various groups. Work resumes at 4:30 p.m. and continues until about 7:00 p.m. unless a motion has been moved and passed to go beyond that hour. The president of Botswana speaks at the beginning of each session of a specific parliament. The president's synopsis of government policy, in turn, is followed by a debate on his or her address in the National Assembly, along the lines of British parliamentary practice.

HOW LAWS ARE MADE

The building housing the National Assembly is at the end of a long mall, with four government office buildings at right angles to the National Assembly along the length of the rectangle. At the other end are a statue of the late president Khama (1921–1980) and a preindependence war memorial. Following the British Westminster model, the chamber of the National Assembly has front and back benches facing one another, with the speaker's chair and the clerk's table (with the mace) separating the government and opposition benches.

Because of the overwhelming number of government MPs and the small number of opposition members, some of the government MPs are seated on the left of the speaker, among the opposition. When the president of Botswana, who is an ex officio MP, attends sessions of the National Assembly, he or she is seated to the right of the speaker in a chair of his own, called the state chair, and not among the cabinet members on the treasury bench, as is the British custom.

Passage of legislation in the National Assembly follows

the traditional Westminster model of three readings for each bill, with the second reading the critical one in which the broad structure of the proposed legislation is debated. Details are examined during the committee stage, which follows successful passage of the second reading. At this point, the National Assembly reconstitutes itself as a committee of the whole house, with the speaker acting as chair of the house in committee. The president can veto a bill the National Assembly has passed, but this veto can be overridden if the National Assembly passes the bill once again within six months after the president has returned it without signature.

Provided that he or she does not dissolve the National Assembly at that point, the president must give assent within three weeks to the legislation that the National Assembly has passed once again following the veto.

COMMITTEES

The National Assembly selection committee appoints members of parliament to various committees according to the balance of political parties in the National Assembly. There are specialized and general committees, reflecting both older British and contemporary legislative organizational patterns. Specialized committees include Finance, Public Accounts, and Law Reform, and the general include the House, Standing Orders, Subsidiary Legislation, Privileges, and National Assembly Staff. The 1966 standing orders of the National Assembly referred to the Committee of Selection, the House Committee, the Public Accounts Committee, and the Finance Committee as sessional select committees, but other committees were termed special select committees. These committees vary from five to ten members of parliament, with the speaker serving as chair of the Standing Orders and National Assembly Staff Committees.

During the Seventh Parliament, the National Assembly established sessional select committees on Foreign Affairs, Defense, and Security.

THE PRESIDENT, PARLIAMENTARY OFFICERS, AND THE HOUSE OF CHIEFS

The political system of Botswana incorporates elements of the American and British systems. During the brief self-government era (from March 1965 to September 1966), there was a prime minister who operated as a head of government-to-be, but that office was abolished and replaced by a presidency that fused the functions of head of government and head of state. The stipulation that the president be an elected member of parliament was changed to provide ex officio MP status for the president, who is elected by the members.

Candidates for parliament must indicate which presidential candidate they will back. To be elected president, one must receive the support of more than half the MPs elected in the general election. The National Assembly thus serves as an electoral college for the president, who is indirectly elected and has no specific constituency, unlike the British prime minister.

The president is responsible for naming a vice president and members of the cabinet from the ranks of the MPs, and he or she does not need the approval of the National Assembly either to appoint or to dismiss members of the cabinet. The attorney general, unlike the president, enjoys no right to vote in the Assembly. Usually, the president speaks only at the opening of the National Assembly—where he delivers an address comparable to the British monarch's speech from the throne in the House of Lords or the American president's state of the union address—or at the dissolution of the National Assembly. The proclamation of the dissolution is published in the government gazette. A cabinet office, which subsumes an economic and a business committee as well as the cabinet secretariat, supports cabinet members in their work. Following standard British practice, the National Assembly has the power to pass a motion of no confidence in the government, but given the strength of the Botswana Democratic Party in the National Assembly, such an occurrence is very unlikely and would require exceptional support from the backbenchers of the party.

Botswana does not completely follow the tradition of either the British House of Commons or the U.S. House of Representatives for eligibility to serve as speaker of the National Assembly. There is no constitutional stipulation that the speaker of the National Assembly be either a regularly or specially elected member of parliament, so presumably the Assembly can elect a nonpartisan figure as its presiding officer. Indeed, it selected a missionary physician, Dr. Alfred M. Merriweather, as its first speaker. In 1989 M. P. K. Nwako was elected as the first MP to serve as speaker of the National Assembly.

The constitution obliges the National Assembly to elect a deputy speaker, and when neither the speaker nor deputy speaker is available, the Assembly is to elect a member other than an assistant minister, minister, or vice president to preside over that particular sitting. By a two-thirds majority vote the Assembly can remove either the speaker or deputy speaker, or both, from their positions. The speaker presides over the debates of the National Assembly, ensuring the smooth flow of business, maintaining courtesy in language and deportment, and ruling on points of order. To fulfill such functions, the speaker is expected to be impartial.

According to the constitution, the parliament of Botswana is composed of the National Assembly and the president, so it could technically be regarded as unicameral. Yet, the fifth chapter of the constitution establishes the House of Chiefs, an essentially advisory body not comparable to the British House of Lords. The House of Chiefs might be considered a modification and extension of the former African Advisory Council or African Council. Its scope and power are issue-specific and embrace traditional African group concerns, such as customary law, African courts, leadership, tribal property, and tribal organization and leadership, as well as proposed constitutional amendments. Composed of fifteen members—four of whom are elected, three specially elected, and the remainder ex officio—the House of Chiefs must meet annually and whenever it needs to advise the National Assembly on bills concerning those topics. Members of the House of Chiefs, like their counterparts in the National Assembly, may raise questions for ministerial answer.

PARLIAMENTARY REPORTING

Coverage of the sessions of parliament is the responsibility of the clerk of the National Assembly, who supervises publication of the verbatim official report, commonly called *Hansard,* following the British tradition. Summaries of many of the debates and questions are published in the *Botswana Daily News* as well as in the weekly private press, which is quite independent of the government and receptive to the views of the opposition and Botswana Democratic Party backbenchers.

Radio Botswana covers the proceedings irregularly, and its reporters may interview members outside parliament. Radio Botswana also enables MPs to have their remarks in the National Assembly broadcast in Setswana, the language of the majority of the population, after they have spoken in the chamber. So far, there is no television broadcasting service in Botswana to offer live coverage of the debates.

Richard Dale

BIBLIOGRAPHY

Mokobi, Charles G. "The New Parliament of Botswana." *The Parliamentarian* 71 (April 1990): 106–107.

Morton, Fred, and Jeff Ramsay, eds. *The Birth of Botswana: A History of the Bechuanaland Protectorate from 1910 to 1966.* Gaborone: Longman Botswana, 1987.

Sillery, Anthony. *Botswana: A Short Political History.* London: Methuen, 1974.

BRAZIL

OFFICIAL NAME: Federative Republic of Brazil (República Federativa do Brasil)

CAPITAL: Brasília

POPULATION: 162,661,000 (1996 est.)

DATE OF INDEPENDENCE: September 7, 1822 (from Portugal)

DATE OF CURRENT CONSTITUTION: Approved September 2, 1988; effective October 5, 1988

FORM OF GOVERNMENT: Parliamentary democracy

LANGUAGE: Portuguese (official), Spanish, English, French

MONETARY UNIT: Real

FISCAL YEAR: Calendar year

LEGISLATURE: National Congress (Congresso Nacional)

NUMBER OF CHAMBERS: Two. Chamber of Deputies (Câmara dos Deputados); Federal Senate (Senado Federal)

NUMBER OF MEMBERS: Chamber of Deputies, 513; Federal Senate, 81

PERCENTAGE OF WOMEN: Chamber of Deputies, 6.6; Federal Senate, 7.4

TERM OF LEGISLATURE: Chamber of Deputies, four years; Federal Senate, eight years (one-third and two-thirds of the members are elected alternately every four years)

MOST RECENT LEGISLATIVE ELECTION: November 15, 1994

MINIMUM AGE FOR VOTING: 16 (optional); 18 (mandatory registration)

MINIMUM AGE FOR MEMBERSHIP: Chamber of Deputies, 21; Federal Senate, 35

SUFFRAGE: Universal and direct

VOTING: Compulsory

ADDRESS: Chamber of Deputies, Palacio do Congresso Nacional, 70000 Brasília, D.F.; Federal Senate, Palacio do Congresso Nacional, 70 165-900 Brasília, D.F.

TELEPHONE: Chamber of Deputies, (5561) 318 51 51; Federal Senate, (5561) 311 41 41

FAX: Chamber of Deputies, (5561) 318 21 07; Federal Senate, (5561) 612 03 56

The only Portuguese-speaking South American nation, Brazil is the largest country on the continent and the fifth largest in the world, occupying almost half the entire area of South America. Despite the country's great wealth of natural resources, many Brazilians live in extreme poverty. Brazil today is a federal republic with a president as head of state and government, a bicameral legislature, and an independent judiciary.

HISTORICAL BACKGROUND

Brazil became a Portuguese colony when navigator Pedro Alvares Cabral formally claimed it in 1500. After Napoleon conquered Portugal in 1808, the Portuguese court of Dom João VI fled to Rio de Janeiro, making Brazil a kingdom. The court remained in Brazil until 1820. The following year, the Portuguese legislature, or Cortes, was convened and acted to return Brazil to its former status as a colony, an attempt that did not please the Brazilians. Before most Brazilian deputies elected to the Cortes reached Lisbon, however, João VI's second son, Dom Pedro, who had been left behind as regent, declared Brazil's independence on September 7, 1822, and took its throne as Dom Pedro I.

A constitutional convention was called in 1824, but the autocratic Dom Pedro I dissolved it and promulgated his own constitution, which remained in force until 1889. In 1831 he was compelled to abdicate in favor of his five-year-old son, Dom Pedro II, who assumed the throne in 1840 after a period of regencies. Until the advent of the Brazilian Republic in 1889, Brazil was a constitutional monarchy patterned on the British model, complete with Conservative and Liberal Parties.

During the empire, the legislature was bicameral: the Chamber of Deputies was elected by two-stage, indirect elections, and the Senate was composed of three representatives from each state named to life terms by the emperor. During this period, the legislature had little effective political power.

In 1891 a second constitutional convention drafted a republican constitution very close to the federal U.S. model. Senators were elected to staggered nine-year terms; deputies, to three-year terms; and the president of the republic, to a four-year term, all by direct vote. The presidency tended to alternate between the two most powerful states, Minas Gerais and São Paulo, and in effect political power rested with five or six powerful states.

The 1930 liberal revolution led by Getúlio Vargas, who would remain as president and virtual dictator until 1945, deposed the president and closed Congress. After the state of São Paulo initiated a short civil war in 1932, new elections were held in 1933, and a constituent assembly drafted the 1934 constitution. During the 1930s Brazil experimented with a limited form of functional representation. The Vargas government, officially styled the *Estado Novo,* or New

State, suspended Congress again in 1937 and granted Vargas dictatorial powers in an attempt to pull the country out of the Great Depression.

After the Brazilian Expeditionary Force returned from the battlefields of Italy, where they had fought with the Allied Forces "against dictatorship," pressures for elections increased until Vargas was deposed in October 1945, just before the December elections. The 1946 constituent assembly drafted a liberal constitution, which retained a bicameral Congress with three senators from each state and proportional representation for the lower house. Fearing renewed domination by Minas Gerais and São Paulo, the small, less-developed periphery states imposed a system of representation that inflated their delegations and decreased those of the larger states.

During 1945–1964 Congress enjoyed considerable political power and was on the verge of achieving a more progressive majority when the military seized the government in April 1964 and moved quickly to reduce congressional powers. Congress lost all control over the budget and autonomy over the election of its presiding officers (whose reelection was prohibited). Reelection of committee chairs was also prohibited. The military ruled until 1985.

A civilian president, José Sarney, was indirectly elected in 1985, and a new constituent assembly was elected in 1986. The 1988 constitution, which was revised in 1995, restored most congressional prerogatives. In 1989 Brazil held its first direct elections for president since 1960. Fernando Collor was elected but was impeached for corruption in 1992. His vice president, Fernando Cardoso, served out the term and was himself elected president in 1994.

CONSTITUTIONAL PROVISIONS

With presidential sanction, the constitution allows Congress control over taxation, financial, and currency matters; budget approval and national planning; changes in the armed forces and civil service; national and subnational territorial questions; concession of amnesty; federal government reorganization; and awarding and renewal of television and radio concessions.

Congress alone has final approval of treaties and declarations of war. Only it can authorize the president and vice president to leave the country for more than fifteen days, approve states of defense or siege or federal intervention in the states, and exercise legislative veto over executive branch regulations. Members of Congress set their own salaries and those of the president and cabinet ministers, judge the president's annual accounts, and provide legislative oversight on executive branch operations. Congress nominates two-thirds of the members of the National Accounting Court, approves executive branch nuclear energy policies, approves referendums and plebiscites, and authorizes mining and hydroelectric projects on Indian lands and sale of parcels of public lands of more than 2,500 hectares.

The constitution grants the Chamber of Deputies exclusive powers to authorize impeachment proceedings against the president, vice president, or cabinet ministers by a two-thirds vote of its membership and to elect members to the Council of the Republic.

The Federal Senate's exclusive powers include authority to impeach the president, vice president, or cabinet ministers by a two-thirds vote and try and judge members of the Supreme Court, the general prosecutor, and legal counsel general for crimes of responsibility. The Senate alone can approve by secret vote presidential appointments to the Supreme Court, Superior Court of Justice, and National Accounting Court and appointment of governors of territories, presidents and directors of the central bank, the legal counsel general, and ambassadors. Only the Senate can approve foreign treaties and agreements and increase internal and external debt ceilings (for federal, state and municipal governments) and elect members to the Council of the Republic.

THE LEGISLATURE

Congressional elections have been held regularly every four years since 1950, even during the twenty-one-year military government. The 513 members of the Chamber of Deputies are elected every four years. Senators serve eight-year terms, and three members represent each of the twenty-six states and the Federal District of Brasília. Senate elections are staggered.

Deputies must be at least twenty-one years old, and senators, thirty-five. Candidates must be native-born or naturalized Brazilian citizens and cannot have been convicted of a major crime. Blood relatives (up to the fourth degree) of executive branch office holders are ineligible to run for office unless the related official resigns six months before the election. If a potential candidate for legislative office holds any important executive branch office, he or she must resign six months before the election.

Senators are chosen in statewide elections by simple majority. Each senator has an alternate, who may temporarily or permanently fill a vacancy. Each party may register one or two slates, depending on how many seats are up for election that year.

Federal deputies are elected under a modified d'Hondt system of proportional representation. The 1988 constitution stipulates that each state have a minimum delegation of eight deputies, regardless of the size of its population. São

Paulo, the largest state, has a cap of seventy deputies. Ten states benefit from the inflated minimum. Each São Paulo deputy represents 296,786 voters, and each deputy from Roraima, the smallest state, represents just 14,986 voters.

Normally, senators and deputies arrive in Brasília on Monday afternoon or Tuesday morning and depart for their home states on Thursday evening or Friday morning. Plenary sessions are held on Tuesday, Wednesday, and Thursday afternoons or evenings. Committee meetings, party caucuses, and other activities are usually held in the mornings. When necessary, the governing boards attempt to mobilize quorums for marathon Monday through Friday sessions to reduce an overloaded docket or pass urgently needed measures.

The current Congress building was inaugurated in April 1960, when Brazil's capital was moved to Brasília from Rio de Janeiro. The Senate and Chamber are housed in a modern-style building designed by architect Oscar Niemeyer. A series of staff support offices for the presiding officers and party leaderships adjoin each chamber, and each has a series of annexes with space for administrative staff, standing committees, library and research staff, medical services, data processing center, members' offices, and printing office.

Each four-year legislative session begins on February 1, when new deputies and senators are sworn in. The next day, the presiding officers of each house are elected. The annual calendar is divided into two sessions: March 1 through June 30 and August 1 through December 5. The president of the republic or the Congress itself may convene special sessions during recesses. The July recess is automatically canceled if the annual budget targets have not been approved by June 30. If the final budget is not approved by December 5, the session does not necessarily continue into the rest of December and January.

Joint sessions of Congress are held in the Chamber of Deputies, with the president of the Senate presiding.

MEMBERS' IMMUNITY AND BENEFITS

Immunity for federal, state, and municipal legislatures covers most crimes, including homicide, felonies, robbery, corruption, and libel. Only if an absolute majority of the respective chamber decides to strip a member's immunity at the request of prosecutors can a member be tried, and only the Supreme Court may try members of the National Congress.

In early 1995 more than one hundred requests to prosecute members of Congress languished in the files of the Senate and Chamber presidents, who have the right to decide whether or not to transmit such requests to the floor for action. Thus members are rarely stripped of their immunity, and they are almost never convicted by the Supreme Court.

There are no recall procedures in Brazilian election laws. Members of Congress are on occasion expelled from their respective parties, but they do not lose their mandates. If a party has strong internal discipline, it may force a member to resign or take a leave of absence to allow an alternate to be seated as deputy or senator.

All members of Congress receive four round-trip air tickets to their home state each month. Both senators and deputies have rent-free, four-bedroom apartments or paid hotel accommodations provided in Brasília. All members have access to mail, telephone, telex, and printing office privileges. Senators have larger offices and staffs than do deputies. Each senator has an official car and driver, and deputies have access to the chamber car pool. The governing boards of each house and their respective party leaders, whips, and committee chairs have additional staff, office space, franks, automobiles, and so on.

At the end of each legislative session, members' pay is set for the next period. Although the 1988 constitution grants Congress the autonomy to set its own pay scale, these decisions are usually articulated within the executive branch budget proposal. Pay has fixed and variable components. In 1995 fixed pay was the equivalent of US$4,000 a month, and the variable based on the proportion of days present was $6,000, or a total of $10,000 a month. Each member of Congress also receives $20,000 a month for office staff.

Members and their families have comprehensive medical and hospitalization coverage, and members may draw a minimum retirement benefit after only eight years of service.

HOW LAWS ARE MADE

The president, senators, deputies, and members of the Supreme Court may all introduce legislation. Under the 1988 constitution, laws may also be proposed by popular initiative.

The president may opt to introduce a law in the form of a provisional measure, similar to provisions in the French and Portuguese constitutions. The measure immediately goes into effect for thirty days while Congress deliberates. If no action is taken during this period, the law ceases to exist. However, the president can sign another provisional measure renewing or altering the original ad infinitum. Since 1989 a flood of these measures has inundated Congress and clogged the normal legislative process.

Once a bill has been introduced, it goes to the appropriate subject committee, then to the Finance Committee, and finally to the Constitution and Justice Committee of the appropriate house, where its constitutionality is judged. Committees were granted increased powers under the 1988 constitution and may kill or pass a bill. Only complicated floor procedures can bring a bill out of committee. The 1988 constitution gave the Supreme Court the prerogative to judge the constitutionality of laws passed by Congress and sanctioned by the president.

A bill is amended during committee deliberations, and the reporter may offer a new substitute bill. A bill reported out of committee has a first reading on the floor and may receive a new series of amendments. Again, the floor reporter may offer a substitute bill. Internal rules also allow a general yes-no vote to be taken on the bill. If it passes, specific votes may be taken on certain previously marked items. Quorums for opening sessions are 10 percent of the membership. Voting on normal laws needs an absolute majority present; decisions are by an absolute majority of that quorum.

Congress may pass various ordinary legislation, complementary laws, or delegated laws. Complementary laws "regulate," or apply, articles of the constitution. To pass "difficult" articles of the 1988 constitution, legislators left some three hundred in very vague form, rendering them not automatically applicable and the constitution essentially unfinished. (More than two hundred articles are still not applicable.) For such constitutional articles to be activated, complementary laws must be passed by an absolute majority of the members of the respective house. A delegated law is the result of a presidential request for the delegation of authority to legislate and execute on certain specific questions. Congress may also issue legislative decrees, which go into effect without presidential sanction.

After one house passes a bill, it goes to the other, where the same process begins again. If a different version of the bill is voted out, it is considered amended, and no conference committee is convened. Instead, the bill returns to the original house, where it may be submitted to a simple yes-no vote with no amendments. Sometimes the college of leaders established in 1988 to ease negotiations acts as a conference committee and may mark up the bill through negotiations and submit it to the original chamber for an item-by-item vote. If it is finally passed, the bill goes to the president for sanction and publication in the daily record.

The National Congress may amend the constitution. Two separate three-fifths majority votes in each house must approve amendment proposals. Congress promulgates amendments so approved directly, without presidential sanction. One-third of the membership of each house, the president, or fourteen of the state assemblies may introduce proposals for amendments.

Articles governing the federal system of government; secret, direct, universal, and periodic voting; the separation of powers; and basic individual human rights cannot be amended.

COMMITTEES

The Senate has seven standing committees, each of which has a president and one vice president. Twenty-five to thirty senators are assigned to each committee. The Chamber of Deputies has sixteen standing committees, each of which has a president, three vice presidents, and twenty-five to fifty-three members.

Committee assignments rotate every two years. A deputy or senator may receive more than one committee assignment. Each year the largest parties rotate the committee chairs in proportion to their size and importance. Alternates are also assigned to each committee. Once a committee chair has been designated for a party, its floor leader names the chair. During their short terms, committee chairs have considerable power to name reporters for each bill, determine agendas, and decide procedures. The 1988 constitution enhanced the powers of committees, which can kill bills, summon ministers to testify, and conduct certain investigations.

Special congressional investigating committees may also be installed by a petition signed by at least one-third of the membership (27 senators or 171 deputies). One-third of the membership of each house can convene a joint committee.

Investigating committees have 120 days to address specific subjects. They have summons and contempt powers; can subpoena bank, telephone, and credit card records and request court orders for search and seizure of evidence; and can requisition the services of specialists. They do not have indictment powers. All evidence and recommendations are turned over to prosecutors for further action. If members of Congress are involved in misdeeds, the investigating committees may recommend that their respective houses expel them.

In 1993 a joint committee investigated the so-called Budgetgate scandal of the Joint Budget Committee and discovered a massive scheme of extortion, kickbacks, rigged bidding, and cost overruns. Its final report recommended expulsion of seventeen members of Congress, further investigation of another twenty-two, special investigations within the executive branch, and two new investigating committees to look into campaign finance and the activities of large construction companies. Seven members were eventually expelled and four resigned. President Itamar Franco set up an executive branch investigation committee, which his successor dissolved before final conclusions were reached. A Senate committee was set up in March 1995 to study the construction companies.

Joint congressional committees are constituted to consider each provisional measure the president introduces.

THE BUDGET

Brazil's fiscal year coincides with the calendar year, and each new budget is supposed to take effect on January 1. During the first half of the year's legislative session (March 1–June 30), Congress considers the annual budget targets plan. Once the plan has been approved, the president submits the detailed budget proposal in the second semester (August 1–December 5).

After the 1964 takeover, one of the military's first actions was to strip Congress of budget power. Congress retained the nominal power to approve annual budgets but was not allowed to alter the president's proposal. With the 1988 constitution, Congress regained most of its powers to modify the proposed budget, but the portion available for such rearrangements is only about 15 percent after entitlements and other fixed items are accounted for. For example, internal and external debt servicing amount to about 50 percent of each budget.

Instead of proceeding through the respective standing committees of both houses, in 1995 the annual budget targets and detailed budget proposal were sent to a joint budget committee of twenty-one senators and sixty-three deputies proportionally representing the parties in Congress. This number was reduced after Budgetgate. This committee has a president and final reporter, which alternate between a senator and a deputy and the two largest parties—the Brazilian Democratic Movement and the Liberal Front—each year. The joint committee is divided into eight subcommittees by subject areas, each with a subreporter.

After Budgetgate, the rules were changed, sharply reducing the number of budget amendments allowed each member of Congress. Before these changes, lobbyists representing municipalities, diverse groups, and especially construction companies swarmed the corridors of Congress during the amendment filing period gathering signatures for amendments they had drafted.

The Joint Budget Committee's final report is submitted for approval to a joint session of Congress with no amendments, but some item votes are allowed. After presidential approval, which always includes some line-item vetoes, the budget is published in the daily record. During the fiscal year, the executive branch may introduce supplemental budget appropriations, which was commonplace during periods of high inflation.

In March 1994 Congress passed a sweeping social emergency fund in preparation for the economic stabilization plan that would produce Brazil's new, revalued currency, the *real*, on July 1. This measure gave the president almost total impoundment and transfer powers over the 1994 and 1995 budgets to curb spending to reduce current account deficits. It was extended through June 1997.

A joint session of Congress finally passed the 1994 budget on October 19 after nearly ten months of contingency operations. The 1995 budget passed quickly.

The Joint Budget Committee usually holds no hearings. Thus monitoring by nongovernmental organizations (and other civil organizations) is difficult.

THE EXECUTIVE AND THE LEGISLATURE

Executive-legislative relations have always been difficult in Brazil. Some presidents such as Juscelino Kubitschek (1956–1960) have had easier relations with Congress than others because they had been members of Congress, spoke the same language, had solid support majorities, and, in particular, governed during periods of rapid economic growth.

The two branches have very different mandates. The president is elected by a direct popular vote, concentrated in the more developed center and south. Congress is elected to represent states through the unequal representation system, which favors the underdeveloped regions to the north and west. During the period 1945–1964, presidents had five-year mandates, and congressional elections were every four years.

This lack of shared purpose came to a head with the 1960 election of President Jânio Quadros, who tried to govern with a minority in a Congress elected in 1958 and who would have had to wait until 1963 for the installation of a new legislature. His resignation in August 1961 plunged the country into an institutional crisis that resulted in the 1964 military coup.

Members of Congress expect deferential treatment from cabinet ministers and other high officials, who normally receive ten to twenty politicians a day requesting executive branch appointments, implementation of public works programs, and disbursements for tasks completed. In difficult economic times, such requests are not easily fulfilled.

The Brazilian president has extensive line-item veto powers, down to removing a word or a comma, and there is no time limit for sanctioning or vetoing proposed legislation. Congress also has no time limit for deliberating presidential vetoes. The latter are placed on the legislative agenda in chronological order, and scheduling votes by joint sessions of Congress is the prerogative of the president of Congress. To override a veto an absolute majority of the joint membership is needed.

Seven-member executive boards comprising a president, two vice presidents, and four secretaries preside over the Senate and the Chamber of Deputies. Four alternates are chosen. Each of the four secretaries has a designated administrative jurisdiction. The governing boards are elected for two-year terms at the outset and middle of each legislative session and cannot serve consecutive terms.

Although attempts have been made to curb the nearly imperial powers of the presidents of the Senate and Chamber of Deputies, internal rules provide them with great authority to set legislative agendas, make major administrative decisions, modify the day's legislative calendar, decide all procedural challenges, and determine what goes to the floor (and when) and what should be merely filed. The president of the Senate and a mix of other board members from each house preside over joint sessions of Congress.

PARTIES

Since 1987, when the Brazilian Democratic Movement Party alone had an absolute majority in the Constituent Assembly, the party system has become fragmented. In 1995 it took the three largest parties to compose an absolute majority (257) in the Chamber of Deputies, and six parties to surpass the three-fifths necessary (308) to pass constitutional amendments.

In 1995 eleven parties were represented in the Senate, and eighteen in the Chamber. Each party has its floor leader, and, depending on the size of the party, a certain number of whips (called vice leaders). At the start of each annual session, each party delegation caucuses to elect or reelect its leader and whips. Each leadership is allocated office space and budget for staff, postage, telephone, telex, and office equipment and supplies in proportion to the size of its delegation.

During difficult negotiations in the unicameral Constituent Assembly in 1988, a college of party leaders was established that greatly enhanced and accelerated the approval of difficult questions. Since 1989 the college of leaders has been maintained as an informal institution and has become very important for setting agendas, negotiating controversial legislation, striking political bargains, and especially establishing floor voting procedures. If a bargain is struck for the floor vote, for example, it becomes a symbolic vote of the floor leaders, and a roll call vote is avoided.

Of the eight major parties, only the Liberal Front Party and the Workers' Party have consistent party discipline so that if their leaders strike a bargain the delegations will stand behind them and vote together. Brazil's party legislation allows floor leaders to close a question, obliging all members to vote the indicated position under penalty of being expelled from the party, but such penalties are rarely applied.

DEBATES AND VOTING

Each plenary session has a previously elaborated daily agenda, which includes a mixture of communications from party leaders, short and long speeches, debate on bills introduced, and voting on bills. Past attempts to modify internal rules have aimed at establishing fixed monthly agendas, with separate weeks reserved for debate, voting, committee sessions, and so on.

Each house has an ethics committee, with one member designated ethics prosecutor. Ministers and other executive branch officials may receive interpellations—formal questions of official actions, policies, or personal conduct—from members of Congress at plenary sessions or spontaneously offer to be questioned in the form of written requests for information or convocation for testimony and questioning before standing committees. There are, however, no hard sanctions for noncompliance.

Debates on the floor of each house and committee sessions must abide by certain rules of courtesy and parliamentary decorum. If these rules are broken, members may be subject to reprimand, suspension, or expulsion.

Four types of voting procedures are used. If the college of leaders so decides, a poll of the leaders present is taken, even without the necessary minimum quorum of members present. Three types of roll-call votes are possible. In electronic voting, the member activates a box under the desk by an access code and votes "yea", "nay," or "abstain." The results are immediately posted on a big scoreboard. For a traditional roll call, the first secretary of the chamber calls out the name of the member, requests a verbal declaration of vote, and duly notes the result. In a roll-call vote by secret paper ballot, the member receives a previously printed ballot, marks it, and deposits it in a ballot box.

The official record of the Congress is printed five days a week as a section of the *Federal Register,* the official record of the federal government, which publishes the records of the three branches. The official congressional record has subsections for the Senate and Chamber and records all debates, committee reports, voting results, and administrative decisions. Members can revise their speeches, however, and on occasion the president of the respective chamber may ask a member to delete offensive sections from a speech to avoid official reprimand.

The Senate is considered the chamber of review for legislation passed by the Chamber of Deputies, and many deputies consider the Senate an impediment to their more popular mandate. Before the 1987–1988 constituent assembly, some deputies proposed a unicameral legislature for Brazil. During the opening sessions of the assembly in February 1987, a proposal not to seat the twenty-three senators elected in 1982 was defeated. Fearing these threats, in December 1986 the Senate defeated a bill passed by the Chamber that would have made the Senate and Chamber refrain from electing presiding officers and constituting their own committees during 1987–1988 and that required legislative committees of deputies and senators be constituted to deliberate important measures on demand.

David Fleischer

BIBLIOGRAPHY

Ames, Barry. "The Congressional Connection: The Structure of Politics and the Distribution of Public Expenditures in Brazil's Competitive Period." *Comparative Politics* 19 (1987): 147–171.

Baaklini, Abdo I. *The Brazilian Legislature and the Political System.* Westport, Conn.: Greenwood Press, 1992.

Fleischer, David. "The Brazilian Congress: From 'Abertura' to 'New Republic.'" In *Political Liberalization in Brazil,* ed. Wayne Selcher. Boulder, Colo.: Westview Press, 1986.

———. "The Constituent Assembly and the Transformation Strategy: Attempts to Shift Political Power from the Presidency to the Congress." In *The Political Economy of Brazil: Public Policies in an Era of Transition,* ed. Larry Graham and Robert Wilson. Austin: University of Texas Press, 1990.

———. "Government and Politics." In *Brazil: A Country Study,* ed. Rex Hudson. Washington, D.C.: Library of Congress, 1997.

Schneider, Ronald M. *Order and Progress: A Political History of Brazil.*Boulder, Colo.: Westview Press, 1991.

BRUNEI

OFFICIAL NAME: State of Brunei Darussalam (Negara Brunei Darussalam)
CAPITAL: Bandar Seri Begawan
POPULATION: 300,000 (1996 est.)
DATE OF INDEPENDENCE: Independent sultanate declared January 1, 1984
DATE OF CURRENT CONSTITUTION: September 29, 1959 (suspended)
FORM OF GOVERNMENT: Absolute monarchy
LANGUAGES: Malay (official), English, Chinese
MONETARY UNIT: Brunei dollar
FISCAL YEAR: Calendar year
LEGISLATURE: Legislative Council (Majlis Meshuarat Negeri)
NUMBER OF CHAMBERS: One
NUMBER OF MEMBERS: 21 (all appointed)
PERCENTAGE OF WOMEN: —
TERM OF LEGISLATURE: —
MOST RECENT LEGISLATIVE ELECTION: March 1965
MINIMUM AGE FOR VOTING: —
MINIMUM AGE FOR MEMBERSHIP: —
SUFFRAGE: —
VOTING: —
ADDRESS: —
TELEPHONE: —
FAX: —

The Sultanate of Brunei lies on the northwest coast of the island of Borneo in the Pacific Ocean *(see map, p. 335)*. A British protectorate since 1888, it gained internal self-government and a constitution in 1959 and full independence in 1984. Brunei's oil-based economy makes it one of the world's richest nations.

As an Islamic autocracy, Brunei currently has no legislative institutions as such. The 1959 constitution vested all power solely in the sultan and created an appointive Legislative Council to advise the sultan. Under pressure from Great Britain for a more representative government, ten of the twenty-one seats in the Council were made elective, and elections were held to fill those seats in 1962 and 1965. The constitution was suspended in 1970, however, and the Legislative Council reverted to its original appointive, advisory character.

The sultan is also advised by a Council of Ministers along with a Privy Council and Religious Council. Although there is no electoral process, a few political parties have been legally formed and later dissolved; their activities and status are unclear.

George Thomas Kurian

BULGARIA

OFFICIAL NAME: Republic of Bulgaria (Republika Bulgariya)
CAPITAL: Sofia
POPULATION: 8,613,000 (1996 est.)
DATE OF INDEPENDENCE: Declared October 5, 1908 (from Ottoman Empire)
DATE OF CURRENT CONSTITUTION: Adopted July 12, 1991; effective July 13, 1991
FORM OF GOVERNMENT: Parliamentary democracy
LANGUAGE: Bulgarian
MONETARY UNIT: Lev
FISCAL YEAR: Calendar year
LEGISLATURE: National Assembly (Narodno Sobranie)
NUMBER OF CHAMBERS: One
NUMBER OF MEMBERS: 240
TERM OF LEGISLATURE: Four years
MOST RECENT LEGISLATIVE ELECTION: April 19, 1997
MINIMUM AGE FOR VOTING: 18
MINIMUM AGE FOR MEMBERSHIP: 21
SUFFRAGE: Universal and direct
VOTING: Optional
ADDRESS: National Assembly, Sofia
TELEPHONE: (359 2) 8401
FAX: (359 2) 80 33 46

A Balkan country, Bulgaria emerged from four and a half decades of communist rule to form a parliamentary democracy with a unicameral National Assembly *(see map, p. 749)*. Bulgaria's communist regime of Todor Zhivkov fell on November 10, 1989, after forty-five years of one-party dominance.

At the time of Zhivkov's fall there was a very small middle class, a weak economy, no supportive civic culture, and no competing political parties. Because the Bulgarian Communist Party (BCP) had possessed a constitutional monopoly on political power, there was little reason after its fall to expect the rapid development of strong competing political parties capable of organizing public discourse and laying the groundwork for effective government. Yet following the peaceful November 1989 coup d'état, a responsible party system began to take shape. The Union of Democratic Forces (UDF) emerged as a powerful, though at times unwieldy, counterforce to the politically sophisticated former communists, who began calling themselves the Bulgarian Socialist Party (BSP). And a third party—the Movement for Rights and Freedom (MRF), a primarily Turkish ethnic organization—played a broker role between the two major parliamentary forces.

The National Assembly is a raucous yet fragile institution. Party unity, particularly of the UDF, exhibits serious fractures that bring into question the long-term viability of parliamentary democracy in Bulgaria. Yet given the perseverance of Bulgarian politicians in and out of the National Assembly, a negative prognosis would be premature and unwarranted. Indeed, there is justification for guarded optimism that parliamentary democracy can be consolidated.

ORGANIZATION AND STRUCTURE OF PARLIAMENT

On July 13, 1991, Bulgaria's new constitution came into force. The constitutional framers clearly intended to create a basic law to protect human rights. It features a law-governed state within a framework of separation of powers. Lawmaking power is vested in a unicameral legislature called the National Assembly. Consisting of 240 members elected by a system of proportional representation, parliament conducts its business in the picturesque center of Sofia at Narodno Sobranie Square. The parliament building is a handsome, architecturally eclectic, rectangular structure located near the imposing national cathedral and the country's most prestigious university.

Organization of parliament

Members of the National Assembly are elected for a four-year term. Any Bulgarian citizen who does not hold another citizenship, is above twenty-one years of age, and is not on trial or in prison is eligible for election. Those candidates for a National Assembly seat who hold a state post must resign upon the registration of their candidacy. In keeping with the principle of separation of powers, any member of parliament shall not occupy another state post; if selected as a government minister, parliamentarians are required to cease serving as members of the National Assembly. Such persons are replaced for the period during which they function as ministers by the next person on the party slate for the National Assembly election. When such persons are dismissed as ministers they resume their parliamentary duties and their replacements are relieved as members of the National Assembly. Members of the National Assembly are obliged by the constitution to follow their own conscience in performing their duties.

Members of the National Assembly may form parliamentary groups by party or political affiliation. The rules of the Assembly require that, with certain exceptions, at least twenty members are necessary to form a parliamentary group. The National Assembly sits in three sessions per year. It does not sit during the Christmas holiday season, from December 22 until January 10, and for ten days during the Easter holidays. It does not sit in August. It normally sits on Wednesdays and Thursdays from 3:00 p.m. until 8:00 p.m. and on Fridays from 9:00 a.m. until 1:00 p.m.

National Assembly sessions are held in public excepting circumstances involving important state interests. The public may be admitted to the building with a special pass and must clear armed police and metal detectors. The media are present during sessions, and Bulgarian radio and television frequently carry live broadcasts throughout the country. Private sessions are held upon a motion of the chair of the National Assembly or one-tenth of the members of parliament or upon a request from the Council of Ministers. After listening to the justification for the motion, the National Assembly votes to decide whether a private session should be held.

The constitution empowers the National Assembly to pass, amend, and rescind laws; pass the state budget bill and the budget report; establish taxes and their size; schedule the elections for president of the republic; resolve on the holding of a national referendum; elect and dismiss the prime minister and, on his motion, the members of the Council of Ministers; effect changes in the government on a motion from the prime minister; elect and dismiss the governor of the Bulgarian national bank and the heads of other institutions established by law; approve state loan agreements; resolve on the declaration of war and conclusion of peace; and approve any deployment and use of Bulgarian armed forces outside the country's borders and the deployment of foreign troops on the territory of the country or their crossing of that territory, on a motion from the president or the Council of Ministers. The National Assembly may introduce martial law or a state of emergency on all or part of the country's territory, grant amnesty, institute orders and medals, and establish official holidays. The National Assembly also possesses considerable authority in the ratification of international agreements and treaties.

The president of the republic may return a legislative enactment for further consideration to the National Assembly along with his or her justification. The new passage of such a bill requires the concurrence of a majority of all the members of the National Assembly. As a further check, the Constitutional Court possesses the authority to declare unconstitutional acts of the National Assembly and other institutions. Disputes come to the Constitutional Court on the petition of no fewer than one-fifth of the members of the National Assembly, the president, the Council of Ministers, the Supreme Court of Cassation, the Supreme Administrative Court, or the chief prosecutor.

Structure of parliament

The chair of the National Assembly is elected by secret ballot on the nomination of any member of the body or by a parliamentary group. The chair's formal powers include announcing and assigning bills and other motions to appropriate committees; ensuring that the committees and members of the National Assembly are afforded appropriate working conditions; adopting standing orders for the premises of the National Assembly; administering the budget of the National Assembly; authenticating the verbatim records of the National Assembly sittings; determining the seating arrangements for the members by parliamentary groups, the members of the Council of Ministers, and the president and the vice president; administering the rules of the National Assembly; and determining the schedule of positions and appointing and dismissing the staff of the National Assembly. Assisting the chair of the National Assembly in the performance of these duties is an advisory body consisting of the deputy chair, the parliamentary group leaders, and the chairs of the various legislative committees.

The National Assembly has both standing and special committees. The eighteen standing committees are Legislative Committee; Economic Committee; Budget and Finance Committee; Administrative Division and Local Government Committee; Foreign Policy Committee; National Security Committee; Labor and Social Security Committee; Human Rights Committee; Committee on the Control of the Political Parties' Revenues, Expenditures, and Property; Agricultural Committee; Committee on Culture; Education and Science Committee; Committee on Religious Affairs; Committee on Radio and Television; Environmental Committee; Health Care Committee; Youth, Sports, and Tourism Committee; and Complaints, Suggestions, and Petitions Committee.

No member may belong to more than two committees simultaneously, and no member may be a chair or deputy chair of more than one standing committee. Standing committee membership is based on proportional representation of the parliamentary groups. The leaders of these committees are designated by the members of the National Assembly on an open ballot on the motion of the chair of the National Assembly in consultation with the leaders of the various parliamentary groups. Each standing committee may contract for expert services to conduct studies and to aid in the performance of its duties. Moreover, the standing committees may create subcommittees and working committees. The Legislative Committee has the special responsibility to consider all bills introduced in the National Assembly and to render an opinion on their compliance with the constitution.

On those Fridays when the National Assembly is in session, each member of the National Assembly has the right to address no more than two questions at the same sitting to the prime minister or to other members of the Council of Ministers. Notice of the questions is given forty-eight hours in advance. Ministers must answer the questions put to them within fourteen days of their submission. This may be done either orally or in writing. After a question has been answered by the minister to whom it was directed, the asking parliamentarian is entitled to ask two supplementary questions. The answer is undebatable, meaning no reply may be made on it. The member, however, is granted two minutes to indicate whether he or she is satisfied with the response.

There are two circumstances in which the National Assembly may conduct a vote of no confidence in the cabinet. First, the cabinet itself may request that the National Assembly take a no-confidence vote on its overall policy or on specific grounds. The motion is carried if more than half the members of the National Assembly present and voting cast their vote for it. Second, one-fifth of the members of the National Assembly may move a reasoned draft resolution of no confidence either of the prime minister or the Council of Ministers. In this instance, the no-confidence resolution is carried if more than half of all members of the National Assembly vote for it.

FORMATION OF PARLIAMENTARY DEMOCRACY

On November 10, 1989, reform-minded persons within the BCP caused the downfall of the forty-five-year totalitarian regime of which they were prominent members. With a view toward personal survival, they wanted to avoid the age-old Bulgarian practice of overthrowing regimes violently and in the process guarantee themselves a place in the political life of a new democratic Bulgaria.

End of one-party rule

On November 17, 1989, the National Assembly, still in the hands of the Communist Party, elected Petur Mladenov, then secretary general of the Central Committee of the BCP, as president of the State Council of Bulgaria, replacing the long-time dictator, Todor Zhivkov. In short order, the cabinet underwent a shake-up, and several hard-line members were replaced. But these changes were criticized as not going far enough. Critics from within and outside the Communist Party called for radical change, including the abolishment of Article 1 of the constitution, which granted the Communist Party the leading role in society. BCP functionaries hotly debated this matter, and several more leadership changes occurred in the months following Zhivkov's ouster.

Anticipating the inevitability of a multiparty system, the new leadership, anxious to align itself with the forces of change, moved to eliminate the party's political monopoly. The Politburo and the Council also disbanded the party's propaganda agency within the armed forces. The party leadership was prepared to work out the details for a transition to democracy. This posture presupposed that the Communist Party would at least have to share power with opposition forces. They agreed to the establishment in late December 1989 of national roundtable talks that would facilitate the process. Roundtable members represented a variety of movements and fledgling political parties opposing the Communist Party. These groups organized under the single banner of the Union of Democratic Forces (UDF). The Communist Party, renamed the Bulgarian Socialist Party (BSP), and its allies represented the UDF's opposition. By mid-March 1990 the roundtable talks had yielded a series of agreements necessary for the country to proceed peacefully toward democracy. Among their accomplishments, roundtable participants agreed to the election of a new parliament that would serve simultaneously as a constitutional convention.

The first parliamentary elections

After considering a variety of proposals designed to strengthen the competing forces, BSP representatives agreed with the UDF on a unique system of mixed representation. It provided for the election of two hundred members in single-member voting districts based on the principle of majority vote. A system of proportional representation would account for an additional two hundred seats. Each voter had the right to two votes: one for a single-member election district and the other for multimember districts under a party list. Political parties or other groups with a membership of at least five hundred had the right to nominate candidates.

By May 7, 1990, no fewer than fifty-six political parties and movements had registered for the national elections that were held on June 10 and 17, 1990. These parties included spin-offs from the old Communist Party and many so-called democratic parties with a variety of platforms for changing Bulgarian society.

During roundtable negotiations, BSP leaders had pushed for early elections, ostensibly to hasten reform. Yet this was also a tactic to capitalize on BSP political strengths. At first the UDF resisted the suggestion. Finally, however, it acceded to the wishes of not only the former communists but of the United States secretary of state, James Baker.

To the consternation of the many political novitiates in the opposition, the Bulgarian Socialist Party won the election. The BSP profited from the mixed electoral system. While it received 47 percent of all votes, it obtained 57 percent of the seats in the National Assembly. There was a large divergence between the votes in the large cities, where the UDF was strongest, and in rural Bulgaria, where the former communists were still strong. Because the BSP was the best organized party, it garnered more seats in the single-member districts than its competitors. Nevertheless, there was also bad news for the BSP. In all thirteen districts where there were run-off elections, UDF candidates defeated their BSP opponents.

Formation of the government

For the second time since the ouster of Todor Zhivkov, the leader of the Bulgarian Socialist Party and chair of the Council of Ministers, Andrey Lukanov, was called upon to form a government. Once again, he headed a one-party government. Although Lukanov appealed for a cabinet with representatives from the other political forces, opposition members refused to join his government. They claimed that the Socialists were too reluctant to accept radical change. There was also a widespread belief among the opposition that the Socialists had no intention of dismantling existing totalitarian structures. Consequently, Lukanov's government closely mirrored the previous one. But the prime minister insisted that his government would not be partisan. Instead, his government would be guided by the desire to seek national consensus.

Lukanov's government lasted just a few months before it fell on November 28, 1990. Parliamentary and public forces, including a major trade union, made it difficult for the Lukanov government to function. The Socialists faced criticism for the activities of the late totalitarian regime, with many anticommunists demanding retribution for the misdeeds of the past. The severe economic conditions common to all of eastern Europe at the time were also central to the collapse of Lukanov's Socialist government. Politicians of all stripes, including Lukanov, thought that a new government enjoying the support of all national political forces was necessary at this juncture.

On December 7, 1990, President Zhelyu Zhelev proposed to the Grand National Assembly a new prime minister. A lawyer of long standing and without party affiliation, Dimitur Popov was thought an appropriate person to form a coalition government. Many in the Popov cabinet had not served in government before as head of a ministry. Popov named as deputy prime ministers a member of the BSP, a member of the Bulgarian Agrarian Party (BZNS), and a UDF politician.

The Grand National Assembly together with the government was charged with tackling national problems, including the transition to a market economy, while simultaneously devising a new constitution. Many observers now believe that constitution making so preoccupied the Grand National Assembly that it unduly sacrificed progress toward privatization of the economy and solving the nation's other problems. Yet despite protests, walk-outs, and hunger strikes, the Popov government managed to remain in power until after the promulgation of the new constitution in July 1991 and the successful parliamentary elections of October 1991.

Meanwhile, the fragile UDF coalition comprising parties and movements with different agendas and flamboyant leaders underwent a crisis. The accusation was made that its charismatic leader, Petur Beron, had been an informer for the secret police in the days of the old regime. The charge came from the forceful leader of the Podkrepa Labor Confederation, Konstantin Trenchev. Many persons believe that this charge was inaccurate and grossly unfair to Beron. But only a few UDF notables came to Beron's defense, and the result was the effective retirement from politics of one whom many believed to be a gifted leader.

The UDF leadership role then went to Philip Dimitrov, a relatively obscure lawyer in his thirties but a person of enormous energy, passion, and considerable intellect. Dimitrov stressed a desire to hold parliamentary elections as early as May 1991. Prior to holding new elections, however, the National Assembly revamped the election law, abandoning the system of mixed representation. The new election law provided that only parties receiving at least 4 percent of the votes would be entitled to representation in parliament, and the law allotted all seats based on proportional representation.

New parliamentary elections

Elections for the new parliament were held in October 1991. For the first time since the communists seized control of the government after World War II, the opposition won an election. Although thirty-eight parties and coalitions had registered for the 1991 parliamentary elections, only three succeeded in entering the National Assembly. The UDF received 34.36 percent of the votes and 110 of the 240 seats. The BSP received 33.14 percent of the votes and 106 seats. Finally, the MRF received 7.55 percent of the votes and 24 seats.

The 4 percent rule deprived the nation of some of its most gifted leaders. Some losers had been instrumental in the national roundtable talks and had played key roles in the creation of the July 1991 constitution. Among those excluded was Petur Dertliev, leader of the Bulgarian Social Democratic Party and a person often spoken of as the father of the constitution. Also defeated were thoughtful public figures such as Petko Simeonov, the leader of the Liberal Party; Milan Drenchev, the head of the Nikola Petkov Bulgarian Agrarian Party; and Ivan Glushkov of the Christian-Agrarian Party. All of these persons had been instrumental in the roundtable deliberations, the roundtable in the Grand National Assembly that framed the new constitution, or both.

The October 1991 parliamentary elections brought to political prominence the Turkish ethnic party, the MRF. The MRF figured heavily in the ability of the two major parties to form a government. The BSP had hoped to keep the MRF off the ballot for the October elections. BSP supporters claimed that Article 11(4) of the constitution forbids political parties of an ethnic, racial, or religious nature. In a series of judicial opinions, the courts permitted the MRF to remain on the ballot and to participate in the elections.

Government instability

There was good reason for the BSP to fear the influence of the MRF. The Zhivkov regime had persecuted the ethnic Turk population from the 1960s on, prompting the creation of the National Turkish Liberation Movement in 1985. Subsequently, many of its leaders went to jail, including Ahmed Dogan, a highly charismatic leader in the postcommunist period. MRF officials claim that its activities were one reason why the totalitarian regime fell in November 1989. It turned out that the BSP fears were warranted, at least with respect to the creation of the new government after the October 1991 elections. Dogan's parliamentary forces supported the election of a UDF government.

Despite the UDF victory, Dimitrov's government suffered not only the opposition of the BSP but, within a year, serious fractures within UDF ranks as well. Center-oriented parties gradually reappeared within parliament. Deputies from the three parliamentary groups declared themselves independent and started establishing organizational structures for their own independent parties. The UDF had twenty-nine defectors, whereas the more disciplined BSP and MRF had far fewer. Because of these defections and the attendant lack of party discipline, the UDF lost its parliamentary majority, and the BSP supported the clamor for a new cabinet. There were calls for a government of experts that might deal with the nation's problems in a nonpartisan way, and a growing consensus developed for preterm general elections.

Dimitrov's government managed to survive its first no-confidence vote, on July 24, 1992. The MPs of the ruling UDF, in cooperation with the members of the MRF, unanimously voted against the no-confidence motion sponsored by the BSP. Yet perceptible cracks appeared in the UDF armor. A representative of the MRF proclaimed that the UDF should not take MRF support for granted; the MRF demanded that progress be made toward democratization of Bulgarian society. Further, Stefan Savov, the UDF chair of the National Assembly, barely survived a vote to oust him from that position. On September 17 the MRF made a motion for his early dismissal. At the same time, President Zhelev, an original UDF leader, expressed dissatisfaction with the UDF leadership in parliament. The rift between Zhelev and members of his own party in parliament became not only a matter of disagreement about policy and tactics but also personal. In fact, in a primary battle during the summer of 1996, Zhelev lost his bid for reelection to a UDF-backed candidate.

In late October 1992 the Dimitrov cabinet resigned under strong pressure from both the BSP and the MRF. On November 20 the National Assembly repelled an attempt to reinstate Dimitrov as prime minister. The vote was 124 against and 104 for his return to power. The BSP then attempted but failed to form a government. This was followed by attempts within the UDF to propose a candidate for prime minister that the MRF could abide. Finally, the MRF proposed Lyuben Berov, an ecomonic adviser to President Zhelev and a professor of economics, as the new government leader. The MRF did not ask for any cabinet positions in return for its support.

Berov proposed a government of experts. The leadership of the BSP expressed a willingness to support Berov, but Dimitrov objected. In the end, 23 of the 110 UDF members of parliament bolted party ranks to support Berov, and with the support of the BSP and the MRF Berov was elected prime minister on December 30, 1992. The small group of UDF parliamentarians that had defied Dimitrov later formed a separate parliamentary group, the New Alliance for Democracy.

While criticizing Dimitrov's government for making mistakes, Berov expressed his commitment to the program of the previous government. He lauded the UDF as the political force behind the transition to democracy and a market economy. Nonetheless, Dimitrov denounced the Berov government because it was in fact distancing itself from UDF policies. He also announced that the UDF would act as stiff opposition to the government in parliament.

By late June 1993 the Berov government found it necessary to make some cabinet changes. Though the government was able to win parliamentary endorsement of these changes by a 126 to 84 vote, the UDF group voted against the cabinet because the changes were the result of bargaining with the BSP. The UDF leadership declared that the parliamentary group would boycott the plenary sessions in protest and would only take part in meetings of parliamentary commissions and in voting on certain laws dealing with dismantling the totalitarian system. Moreover, it expelled from its ranks Marin Todorov Dimitrov, who was relieved of his post as minister of science, education, and culture in the Berov cabinet.

The boycott also increased tension between the UDF leadership and the former UDF leader, President Zhelev. He condemned the boycott as a serious mistake that would only heighten tensions and pleaded that greater tolerance was required. Viewing him as something of a traitor to the prodemocracy cause he once championed, some UDF activists demanded Zhelev's resignation.

A month later the UDF called for early general elections. Dimitrov argued that since the start of the boycott of plenary sessions on June 23, the National Assembly had been functioning without adequate representation. Dimitrov pointed out that parliament was making decisions without a quorum and MPs were voting using absent MPs' cards. Nothing came immediately of this suggestion for early elections. Yet it was plain that the Berov government would continue to have difficulties maintaining power.

MRF leader Dogan complained publicly that the Turkish ethnic movement was tired of balancing parliamentary forces. Its aim was to prevent political dominance by either the BSP or the UDF. For a year following the parliamentary elections of 1991, the MRF aligned with the UDF. When relations between the MRF and UDF became strained, however, Dogan's forces supported the nonpartisan government of Berov; it did so in concert with the BSP and the UDF breakaway faction, the New Union for Democracy. Remaining true to its original position, the MRF through Dogan expressed concern that if the BSP gained control over the government and parliament, the MRF would react negatively.

By November 1993 the UDF had initiated four no-confidence votes in the Berov government. Each time the government survived, although its support in parliament continued to erode. One explanation for the survival of the Berov government was that no single party wanted to take control of the government because of the difficult economic and social problems facing the country. No party wanted to be blamed for failure. Indeed, the Berov government carried on until the National Assembly accepted its resignation on September 8, 1994, by a vote of 219 to 4 with 1 abstention.

Under the terms of the constitution, parliament has three chances to form a government. If it is unable to form a new government, the president must appoint an interim cabinet and call elections within two months. President Zhelev first asked BSP leaders to form a new government. They declined, saying that a strong and resolute government would be impossible given the partisan configuration of parliamentary seats. Perhaps, too, BSP leaders were aware that public opinion was beginning to swing in their direction. An October 1994 public opinion survey indicated that the BSP was in a good position to win a majority of parliamentary seats.

Zhelev then turned to the most vociferous opponent of the Berov government. The UDF coalition was divided on the issue because some favored new elections. On September 21 the UDF rejected Zhelev's offer to form a new government. President Zhelev turned last to a small centrist group, the New Choice Party (NCP). On September 29 the NCP proposed former defense minister and presidential adviser Dimtar Loudzhev as prime minister. Loudzhev looked for coalition partners. But the two major forces remained in support of early elections, forcing the third parliamentary election since the downfall of the Zhivkov regime and testing again the resolve of Bulgarians to proceed along a democratic course.

General elections were held on December 18, 1994. The BSP gained eighteen additional seats, giving it an absolute majority in parliament. It formed a parliamentary group with left-wing agrarians and ecologists called the "Democratic Left." The UDF lost forty-two seats, and the MRF lost eight, or 33 percent, of its seats. Two new parties gained access to parliament by obtaining the requisite 4 percent of the popular vote: the Popular Union won nineteen representatives in parliament, and the Bulgarian Business Bloc acquired thirteen seats.

In the next two years, 1994 to 1996, the BSP government, headed by the thirty-five-year-old economist Zhan Videnov, survived several no-confidence votes. The country suffered from high inflation, increasing crime, and grain-storage and banking crises. By December 1996, however, the faltering economy and allegations of corruption and mismanagement had become too great for Videnov to withstand, and he resigned. BSP attempts to form a new government were complicated by ever widening popular protests against BSP leadership. After thirty days of mass antigovernment rallies and in the face of opposition-party resistance to continued BSP rule, the Socialists acquiesced on February 4 to early elections.

In the new elections, conducted on April 19, 1997, the UDF captured 52.3 percent of the vote and 137 of the parliament's 240 seats. The BSP fell to 58 seats, while the Union for National Salvation took 19, the Euroleft took 14, and the Bulgarian Business Bloc won 12.

CONCLUSIONS

Legislative systems everywhere require a modicum of trust and respect among their participants to carry on their daily business in a fruitful manner. The transgressions of the past make it difficult for many Bulgarians to accept a working relationship with the former communists because they believe that adequate retribution has yet to take place. Yet the roundtable talks provided for accommodation without repeating the regrettable cycle of bloodshed and vendetta characteristic of Bulgaria's political history.

To be sure, self-taught lessons in democracy are not always well understood while participants in the process are experiencing them. Certainly, boycotts by parliamentary groups do not speak well for the institutionalization of democratic process. It may be that the concept of a loyal opposition is not yet fully appreciated. Nonetheless, the National Assembly is performing its lawmaking functions, albeit imperfectly at times, while bridging the various social, economic, ethnic, and political cleavages that threaten national unity.

Continuing economic hardships for the population make the task all the more difficult. Nonetheless, political parties regularly compete and in the process define areas of agreement and disagreement. The very existence of parliament may be helping produce attitudes among relevant publics and elites that the constitutional system adopted by the Grand National Assembly in July 1991 has earned their support and that democratic institutions have a moral right to exist.

Albert P. Melone

BIBLIOGRAPHY

Drumeva, Emilia. "A New and Original Election System in Bulgaria—June 1990." In *Law in a Fast-Changing Society,* ed. Silvy Chernev. Sofia, Bulgaria: St. Kliment Ohridski University Press, 1994.

Kolarova, Rumyana, and Dimitr Dimitrov. "Electoral Laws in Eastern Europe: Bulgaria." *East European Constitutional Review* 3 (spring 1994): 50–55.

Melone, Albert P. "Bulgaria's National Roundtable Talks and the Politics of Accommodation." *International Political Science Review* 15 (1994): 257–273.

———. *Creating Parliamentary Government: The Transition to Democracy in Bulgaria.* Columbus: Ohio State University Press, 1998, forthcoming.

———. "The Struggle for Judicial Independence and the Transition Toward Democracy in Bulgaria." *Communist and Post-Communist Studies* 29 (1996): 231–243.

Mishler, William, and Richard Rose. "Support for Parliaments and Regimes in the Transition Toward Democracy in Eastern Europe." *Legislative Studies Quarterly* 19 (1994): 5–32.

Troxel, Luan. "Bulgaria: Stable Ground in the Balkans?" *Current History* (November 1993): 386–389.

Tzvetkov, Plamen S. "The Politics of Transition in Bulgaria: Back to the Future?" *Problems of Communism* (May–June 1992): 34–43.

BURKINA

OFFICIAL NAME: Republic of Burkina (Burkina Faso)
CAPITAL: Ouagadougou
POPULATION: 10,623,000 (1996 est.)
DATE OF INDEPENDENCE: August 5, 1960 (from France)
DATE OF CURRENT CONSTITUTION: Adopted June 2, 1991; effective June 11, 1991
FORM OF GOVERNMENT: Limited parliamentary democracy
LANGUAGE: French (official), many indigenous languages
MONETARY UNIT: CFA franc
FISCAL YEAR: Calendar year
LEGISLATURE: Parliament (Parlement)
NUMBER OF CHAMBERS: Two. National Assembly (Assemblée Nationale); House of Representatives (Chambre des Représentants)
NUMBER OF MEMBERS: National Assembly, 107 (directly elected); House of Representatives, 178 (appointed or indirectly elected)
PERCENTAGE OF WOMEN: National Assembly, 3.7; House of Representatives, 11.9
TERM OF LEGISLATURE: National Assembly, five years; House of Representatives, three years
MOST RECENT LEGISLATIVE ELECTION: National Assembly, May 24, 1992; House of Representatives, December 28, 1995
MINIMUM AGE FOR VOTING: 18
MINIMUM AGE FOR MEMBERSHIP: 21
SUFFRAGE: Universal
VOTING: Optional
ADDRESS: Parliament, BP 6482 Ouagadougou 01
TELEPHONE: (226) 31 46 84
FAX: (226) 31 45 90

Known as the Republic of Upper Volta upon achieving independence of France in 1960, Burkina, a landlocked country in western Africa *(see map, p. 447)*, experienced instability and military rule for much of its first three decades. The country adopted its present name in 1984.

The first elections to the new National Assembly under the 1991 constitution were held in May 1992 and resulted in a true multiparty legislature of 107 members representing ten political parties; twenty-seven parties had participated in the elections. The Organization for People's Democracy—Labor Movement, an amalgam of former communist parties active in Burkinabe politics for years, controlled seventy-eight seats. The party ran as part of the Popular Front, which includes three smaller parties. The party with the next-highest number of seats, the National Convention of Progressive Patriots—Social Democratic Party, elected thirteen members.

The 107 members of the National Assembly are elected in thirty multimember constituencies of two-to-seven seats corresponding to Burkina's provinces. Burkina citizens age eighteen or over who have fulfilled their military obligation and are not disqualified by criminal conviction may vote. Voting is conducted on the basis of proportional representation and party lists.

The House of Representatives, although created by the 1991 constitution, was not formed until December 1995. The 178 members of the House serve three-year terms. All of the 178 members are either appointed or indirectly elected to represent different constituencies, including provincial legislatures, societal organizations, the military, cultural organizations, the Protestant and Catholic communities, and other groups.

Legislative procedures and practices are modeled on those of the French parliament. Both government and parliamentary members can initiate legislation. Two sessions are held annually.

George Thomas Kurian

BURMA

OFFICIAL NAME: Union of Burma
CAPITAL: Yangon
POPULATION: 45,976,000 (1996 est.)
DATE OF INDEPENDENCE: January 4, 1948 (from the United Kingdom)
DATE OF CURRENT CONSTITUTION: January 3, 1974; suspended September 18, 1988
FORM OF GOVERNMENT: Military dictatorship
LANGUAGE: Burmese
MONETARY UNIT: Kyat
FISCAL YEAR: April 1–March 31
LEGISLATURE: None
NUMBER OF CHAMBERS: —
NUMBER OF MEMBERS: —
PERCENTAGE OF WOMEN: —
TERM OF LEGISLATURE: —
MOST RECENT LEGISLATIVE ELECTION: May 27, 1990, for new constituent assembly that never convened
MINIMUM AGE FOR VOTING: —
MINIMUM AGE FOR MEMBERSHIP: —
SUFFRAGE: —
VOTING: —
ADDRESS: —
TELEPHONE: —
FAX: —

Burma is located in Southeast Asia *(see map, p. 735)*. In the early twentieth century the Burmese began to develop a parliamentary system while under British colonial administration. The state held elections in the 1920s, and home rule was introduced in the 1930s. Soon after gaining independence, however, the military began to dominate politics.

Following the military coup of September 18, 1988, the 492-member People's Assembly was abolished. A general election was held on May 27, 1990, to elect members to a new 492-member constituent assembly. In the elections, the National League for Democracy, whose de facto leader is Nobel Peace Prize winner and dissident Aung San Suu Kyi, secured 59.9 percent of the votes and 392 seats; the National Unity Party, 21.2 percent of the votes and 10 seats; Shan Nationalities League for Democracy, 1.7 percent and 23 seats; Arakan League for Democracy, 1.2 percent and 11 seats; 23 minor parties and independents, 16.9 percent and 49 seats. (Seven seats were not filled due to instability in the voting districts.) The military government set aside the results and disqualified, arrested, or drove into exile most of the successful candidates. As a result, the assembly has never met.

For electoral purposes the country is divided into 14 states or divisions; they, in turn, are divided into 314 townships based on population, and townships are divided into ward or single-member constituencies numbering 492. Members of the People's Assembly and constituent assembly were elected by simple majority vote.

George Thomas Kurian

BURUNDI

OFFICIAL NAME: Republic of Burundi (Republika y'u Burundi, Kirundi; République du Burundi, French)
CAPITAL: Bujumbura
POPULATION: 5,943,000 (1996 est.)
DATE OF INDEPENDENCE: July 1, 1962 (from UN trusteeship under Belgian administration)
DATE OF CURRENT CONSTITUTION: Adopted March 13, 1992 (suspended)
FORM OF GOVERNMENT: Transitional, army-backed regime
LANGUAGE: Kirundi (official), French (official), Swahili
MONETARY UNIT: Burundi franc
FISCAL YEAR: Calendar year
LEGISLATURE: National Assembly (Assemblée Nationale)
NUMBER OF CHAMBERS: One
NUMBER OF MEMBERS: 81
PERCENTAGE OF WOMEN: —
TERM OF LEGISLATURE: Five years
MOST RECENT LEGISLATIVE ELECTION: June 29, 1993
MINIMUM AGE FOR VOTING: —
MINIMUM AGE FOR MEMBERSHIP: —
SUFFRAGE: Universal and direct
VOTING: —
ADDRESS: National Assembly, Palais de Kigobé, B.P. 120, Bujumbura
TELEPHONE: (257 22) 233 641
FAX: (257 22) 233 663

Burundi, a small, densely populated country in east central Africa *(see map, p. 261)*, has been politically unstable since its independence from Belgium in 1962. Deep social divisions between the majority Hutu and minority Tutsi thwarted recent efforts to establish multiparty democratic rule and plunged the country into a civil war. In 1996 Burundi reverted to military rule after a bloodless coup d'état; the new regime suspended the country's constitution and temporarily dissolved the National Assembly.

After reactivation in 1993 following a six-year hiatus, Burundi's National Assembly faced a series of crises and challenges that by early 1995 had eviscerated its position as the supreme legislative authority in the country. The Assembly had barely begun to function in October 1993 when its president and several of its members were killed during an attempted military coup that also took the life of Burundi's first democratically elected president. Another tragedy in April 1994—a shot-down aircraft—claimed the life of his successor and sent political leaders scrambling to avert a feared ethnic bloodbath. Negotiations among the principal political forces to name the country's new president effectively excluded the legislature. The government that took office in late 1994 disregarded the 1993 legislative election results. Emphasizing intercommunal consensus over the integrity of the constitution and the political institutions, the negotiated accord obliged the Assembly to ratify its own emasculation. Conflict in 1995 and 1996 prevented the Assembly from effectively operating; by the July 1996 coup the Assembly had ceased to play an appreciable role in the country's political management.

POLITICAL BACKGROUND

Even before it gained independence from Belgium in 1962, Burundi already was divided along the ethnic lines that would scar the country throughout its postcolonial independence. Although the origins of ethnic distinction in Burundi are subject to debate, some historians believe that, beginning in the fifteenth and sixteenth centuries, members of the Tutsi ethnic group entered the region and subjugated the indigenous Hutu and Twa. The Tutsis established a feudal caste system under which the majority Hutus tilled the land, and the Tutsis owned the cattle. There was, however, a degree of openness in the local caste system. A custom known as *kwihutura* permitted certain wealthy Hutus to enter the ranks of the Tutsi. Inversely, impoverished Tutsis could fall to the status of Hutu.

Precolonial Burundi was ruled by a king who hailed from a class of nobility called the *ganwa*. The *ganwa* considered themselves separate from the ethnic groups. Some historians argue, however, that there was no real ethnic difference between the *ganwa* and the Tutsis and refer to the *ganwa* as a Tutsi subgroup. While Hutus were allowed access to the royal court by holding positions such as judge, counselor, and doctor, Tutsis possessed a higher status in the monarchical system.

In 1916 Belgium occupied the country, wresting control from the Germans, who had first colonized Burundi in the 1880s. In 1923 the League of Nations awarded the Belgians a mandate over the country, which was extended as a United Nations trusteeship in 1946. The Belgians followed the Germans' practice of indirect rule through the country's existing monarchy, which was headed by King Mwambutsa IV. At the same time, the colonial power reorganized Burundi's administrative structure by replacing Hutu and Tutsi chiefs with *ganwa*. Believing the minority Tutsi ethnic group to be more capable of governing, the colonial administrators provided education and government positions almost exclusively to the Tutsis. The Hutus, deprived of Western education, continued to be excluded from government.

As Burundi moved toward independence, political parties began to form. In 1958 Mwambutsa's son, pro-independence leader Prince Louis Rwagasore, founded the Union for National Progress (UPRONA), which won a landslide victory in the September 1961 legislative elections organized by the United Nations. The all-Hutu People's Party came in second. Just weeks later, however, Rwagasore was gunned down in Bujumbura.

Burundi became independent as a parliamentary monarchy on July 1, 1962. But without the prince's unifying influence, politics in the country soon became delineated along ethnic lines. In the Assembly, the People's Party joined with Hutu members of UPRONA to form the Monrovia Group, while Tutsi members of UPRONA formed the Casablanca Group. In the May 1965 legislative elections, the first after independence, the Hutus won twenty-three of thirty-three parliamentary seats. An increasingly authoritarian Mwambutsa, however, refused to name a Hutu as prime minister. On October 18, 1965, disgruntled Hutu army officers attempted to overthrow the government. The coup attempt resulted in the execution of many Hutu political leaders, including the president and two vice presidents of the National Assembly and two government ministers, after Hutus killed an estimated five hundred Tutsis. In July 1966 Mwambutsa IV was deposed by his son, Ntare V.

Burundi's monarchy was overthrown on November 28, 1966, by Capt. Michel Micombero, who had served as Ntare V's prime minister. Micombero declared the First Republic, made UPRONA the only legal political party, and dissolved the National Assembly. The Assembly was replaced by a committee of military officers who were predominantly Tutsi, although Micombero's first cabinet was 50 percent Hutu. The discovery of a Hutu-led coup plot in 1969, however, unleashed further purges of Hutus from the army and government. Finally, in 1972 another Hutu uprising resulted in ruthless suppression by the government and military. More than 200,000 Burundians, mainly Hutus, were estimated to have been killed in that round of interethnic violence. Educated Hutus who did not flee were virtually wiped out, and hundreds of Hutu army officers were executed. Four years later, on November 1, 1976, Micombero was forced from power during a bloodless coup led by Lt. Col. Jean-Baptiste Bagaza, a fellow Tutsi, who established the Second Republic.

The Bagaza regime initiated agrarian reforms aimed at ending Burundi's feudal landholding and labor systems. Among other things, Tutsi overlords were required to cede much of their land to Hutu peasants. Little progress, however, was made toward political liberalization. Although initially Bagaza had decided to dissolve UPRONA, the party was reconstituted in 1979, and the 1981 constitution formalized UPRONA's position as the country's only legal political party. Moreover, the constitution provided that the UPRONA president alone could be a candidate for president. A sixty-five-member National Assembly also was established, with fifty-two deputies to be elected and thirteen to be appointed by the president. When the first elections in seventeen years were held on October 22, 1982, all the candidates (two per district) were selected by UPRONA's central committee, based on nominations by local UPRONA committees. Government control over individual liberties engendered opposition from the country's powerful Catholic Church, which advocated farther-reaching reforms. In response, Bagaza closed down religious schools, clinics, and some parish churches. In September 1987 Bagaza was overthrown while traveling abroad. Maj. Pierre Buyoya seized power and established Burundi's Third Republic.

Initially, the Third Republic, drawing its support from a small circle of Tutsi elites, differed little from its two predecessors. But after renewed ethnic conflict in northern Burundi in 1988, Buyoya undertook a series of political reforms. He established a new government and restored the post of prime minister, to which he appointed a Hutu, Adrien Sibomana. Buyoya also moved toward equal representation of Hutus and Tutsis on the Council of Ministers. A National Commission of Inquiry and National Unity, comprised equally of Hutu and Tutsi members, was appointed in October 1988 to address the issue of interethnic relations. The commission's work resulted in the Charter of National Unity, which called for national reconciliation and guaranteed equal rights for all citizens. The charter was approved by 89 percent of voters in a national referendum in February 1991. A multiethnic commission also was formed in 1991 to study and promote a national discussion on democratization and to draft a new constitution. The constitution was ratified by the Burundian electorate in a March 1992 referendum. President Buyoya then established two commissions to oversee the country's democratic transition. The Technical Commission was to draft the electoral code and devise a plan of election administration; the National Consultative Commission was to provide a forum for dialogue between the government and political parties on important democratization and election-related issues. A law governing political parties was promulgated in April 1992.

Nine parties competed in the presidential and legislative elections held in June 1993, but only two turned out to matter. The Burundian Democratic Front (FRODEBU), a predominantly Hutu political party, captured more than two-thirds of the seats in the eighty-one-seat National Assembly, with UPRONA securing the remaining seats. FRODEBU's presidential candidate also won handily—Melchior Ndadaye was inaugurated on July 10, 1993, as Burundi's first democratically elected president. Ndadaye, a Hutu, sought to include the previously dominant minority ethnic group by naming Sylvie Kinigi, a Tutsi, as his prime minister. The largely Tutsi army, however, remained restless with the large number of Hutus at the upper echelons of government; rumors of military coup plots began circulating even before Ndadaye took office and continued in the months that followed. On October 21, 1993, Ndadaye and several of his close advisers, including the president of the National Assembly, were assassinated during an attempted military coup. Remaining government members fled into hiding while the military held power for less than one week. Tens of thousands of people died in the subsequent interethnic violence. With assistance from the United Nations, the Organization of African Unity, and the international donor community, relative calm and political stability eventually returned to Burundi. The National Assembly reconvened in December 1993 as the country began to reestablish its young democratic institutions.

ORGANIZATION AND OPERATION OF THE NATIONAL ASSEMBLY

The National Assembly of Burundi, which had functioned only nominally under the one-party military regimes, was temporarily suspended after the 1987 coup. The 1992 constitution established a unicameral legislature composed of representatives elected to five-year terms on a proportional basis from party lists in sixteen multimember districts. The number of seats in the Assembly, currently eighty-one, is fixed by law and apportioned to the country's districts on the basis of population. Independent candidates are allowed to compete for parliamentary seats. Elected deputies are forbidden from simultaneously holding positions in the Assembly and government.

Two annual parliamentary sessions are required by the constitution. The first session begins on the first Monday in April; the second begins on the first Monday in October. Each session cannot exceed two months' duration. Extraordinary sessions can be convoked by the president, prime minister, or a majority of Assembly members. According to Assembly rules, plenary meetings take place each week during the mornings and afternoons of Tuesday, Wednesday, Thursday, and Friday. At the request of the president of the republic, the prime minister, or one-tenth of members, the Assembly may hold closed-door plenaries. Minutes of parliamentary meetings are to be published in the country's official gazette.

Assembly meetings take place in the parliamentary chambers of Kigobé Palace, a large yellow and white structure located about a mile north of central Bujumbura, the capital. The palace's grandiose architecture, with boxy, inset windows and a flat roof, reflects its North Korean origins. The Assembly shares the palace with the country's Constitutional Court and, as such, does not yet possess its own permanent meeting site. Budgetary constraints have kept staffing and equipment to a minimum; virtually no office space exists for individual members.

The leadership of parliament, comprising a president, vice president, and a secretary general for each parliamentary caucus, is elected at the first meeting of the first session. Eight members are required to form a parliamentary caucus.

Five permanent parliamentary committees have been established: Political, Administrative, and Legislative Affairs; Economic Affairs, Production, and the Budget; Social, Family, and Cultural Affairs; Human Rights; and Defense and National Security. Special committees are created upon request by the government or Assembly. Each permanent committee is composed of at least twelve members; special committees have ten members. Committees are headed by a president, vice president, and secretary and, in the case of the Committee on Economic Affairs, a rapporteur-general. Assembly members cannot be president of both a permanent and a special committee.

Both the government and Assembly members can propose legislation, and each can amend the other's proposed legislation. Government ministers are allowed to participate in Assembly debates. Parliamentary debate on the budget begins at the start of the Assembly's October session. If a budget is not adopted by December 31, an extraordinary session can be called within fifteen days. If the extraordinary session fails to produce a new budget, the constitution allows the government to establish the budget by decree.

The 1992 constitution vests in the National Assembly the right to hold votes of confidence in the government, although this power was relinquished in 1994. Assembly members also have the right to question government ministers, either verbally or in writing.

RECENT POLITICAL DEVELOPMENTS

The Assembly had just met for its first session after the June 1993 elections when the coup attempt took place in October. When it finally reconvened in an extraordinary session on December 16, the Assembly was faced with electing new parliamentary leadership and new members to replace those who had been killed during the violence. Sylvestre Ntibantunganya, former minister of foreign relations, was elected as the Assembly's new president; new members were chosen from party lists used for the 1993 parliamentary elections.

The Assembly also confronted the issue of reestablishing

Burundi's presidency. Partisan conflicts, procedural maneuvering, and inexperience impeded the Assembly's ability to reach agreement on a new president. On January 14, 1994, government and opposition leaders signed the Kigobé Accords, which designated Cyprien Ntaryamira as the country's new president. The accords also awarded 40 percent of ministerial posts to the opposition, which now comprised UPRONA and several other small, primarily Tutsi political parties not represented in the National Assembly. Some opposition parties, however, petitioned the Constitutional Court to review the procedure by which Ntaryamira had been chosen. As early indications pointed to a ruling against the government, five of the court's seven members were dismissed by the minister of justice on January 29 before they could issue a verdict on the petition. Opposition parties called for a general strike in Bujumbura, and violence soon erupted throughout the city. After intense pressure from the international community and warnings of widespread violence, all political parties finally reached agreement on Ntaryamira, and the new president took office on February 5.

Barely two months later, Ntaryamira died when the plane carrying him and Rwandan president Juvénal Habyarimana was shot down over Kigali. Thus, Assembly members were once again thrust into the national debate on a new president. The Assembly was effectively marginalized, however, as Burundi's political leaders spent the next six months debating the composition and role of a new government as well as the designation of a new president. These talks ultimately resulted in an agreement between UPRONA and eight other parties, on the one hand, known as "the opposition," and FRODEBU and three other parties, on the other, known as "the forces of democratic change." The convention, as it was styled, was signed on September 10, 1994, and established consensus institutions to govern the country during a four-year transition period. A National Council of Security, composed of high-ranking government officials and political party representatives, was created and given the power to review presidential actions related to, among other things, the promulgation of laws and revision of the constitution. National Assembly representation on the council was not foreseen under the convention. Furthermore, the convention required Burundi's prime minister to belong to "a party other than the president's" and invested in the prime minister the power to countersign all legislative acts.

The convention also awarded the opposition parties 45 percent of ministerial posts, ambassadorial appointments, and governorships. The National Assembly was obliged to guarantee the "strict application" of the convention, but it was stripped of its constitutional prerogative to hold votes of confidence in the government during the transition period. Some Burundians complained that the convention was undemocratic because it ignored the will of the electorate by giving the opposition, which had captured less than one-fifth of parliamentary seats, a disproportionate share of political power. Nevertheless, the Assembly accepted the convention and on September 30 formally approved interim president Sylvestre Ntibantunganya as president of the republic.

On December 1, 1994, the Assembly elected Jean Minani of FRODEBU as its president to replace Ntibantunganya. UPRONA members objected to Minani's election, claiming that he had urged Hutus to organize massacres of their Tutsi compatriots after the October 1993 coup attempt. UPRONA members withdrew from parliament, and opposition ministers refused to participate in the new government. The impasse, which again brought political activity in Burundi to a standstill, was resolved only after Minani agreed to step down. Léonce Ndikumana, former acting executive secretary of FRODEBU and an outspoken supporter of Minani, was chosen as the new Assembly president on January 12, 1995. Ndikumana told reporters after his election that the Assembly would actively monitor the government and seek to ensure that neither the government nor the political parties interfere with the Assembly's work.

Events in Burundi soon spiraled out of control, however. Civilian and military authorities, faced with increasing civil strife, lost their ability to govern effectively and ensure the national security. Despite repeated efforts to mediate the crisis, by mid-1996 Burundi had lost any semblance of government authority and was embroiled in a civil war that threatened to unleash all-out genocide. In July 1996 elements of Burundi's army, itself divided into several political camps, seized power, suspended the constitution, dissolved the National Assembly, and reinstalled Pierre Buyoya as president. International sanctions forced Buyoya to reopen the National Assembly, although many FRODEBU members refused to participate and thwarted the strongman's efforts to restructure the Assembly.

Timothy S. McCoy

BIBLIOGRAPHY

Lemarchand, René. *Burundi: Ethnocide as Discourse and Practice.* Washington, D.C.: Woodrow Wilson Press Center, 1994.

Watson, Catharine. "Transition in Burundi: The Context for a Homecoming." Washington, D.C.: U.S. Committee for Refugees, September 1993.

C

CAMBODIA

OFFICIAL NAME: Kingdom of Cambodia (Preah Reach Ana Pak Kampuchea)
CAPITAL: Phnom Penh
POPULATION: 10,861,000 (1996 est.)
DATE OF INDEPENDENCE: November 9, 1953 (from France)
DATE OF CURRENT CONSTITUTION: Adopted September 21, 1993; effective September 24, 1993
FORM OF GOVERNMENT: Constitutional monarchy
LANGUAGE: Khmer (official), French
MONETARY UNIT: Riel
FISCAL YEAR: Calendar year
LEGISLATURE: National Assembly (Radhsphea Ney Preah Recheanachakr Kampuches)
NUMBER OF CHAMBERS: One
NUMBER OF MEMBERS: 120
PERCENTAGE OF WOMEN: 5.8
TERM OF LEGISLATURE: Five years
MOST RECENT LEGISLATIVE ELECTION: May 23–28, 1993
MINIMUM AGE FOR VOTING: 18
MINIMUM AGE FOR MEMBERSHIP: 21
SUFFRAGE: Universal and direct
VOTING: Optional
ADDRESS: National Assembly, Phnom Penh
TELEPHONE: (855) 23 427 768
FAX: (855) 23 427 769

Cambodia, an ancient Southeast Asian kingdom *(see map, p. 735)*, experienced over two decades of civil war and strife beginning in the late 1960s. Under the terms of the United Nations peace plan signed in October 1991 by the Khmer Rouge, the Cambodian People's Party, the United National Front for an Independent, Neutral, Peaceful, and Cooperative Cambodia (FUNCINPEC), and the Khmer People's National Liberation Front, Cambodia became a constitutional monarchy. By mid-1997, however, the two parties that dominated the coalition government formed in 1993 had ceased to cooperate. Politics was becoming increasingly violent, with assassinations commonplace, and law and order had nearly disintegrated as the coalition parties became armed camps.

Legislative power is vested by the 1993 constitution in the 120-member National Assembly, the members of which are elected for a term of five years by universal adult suffrage. Executive power is vested in the prime minister, who is designated by the king at the recommendation of the chair of the National Assembly and who commands a majority in the National Assembly. Members of the National Assembly must be Cambodian citizens over twenty-one years of age. The National Assembly may not be dissolved before its term expires unless the royal government has been dismissed twice within twelve months. The National Assembly may dismiss cabinet ministers or remove the royal government from office through a censure motion passed by a two-thirds majority vote.

The National Assembly is required to meet in ordinary session at least twice a year, each session lasting at least three months. Extraordinary sessions may be convoked by the king upon request of the prime minister or by a majority of the National Assembly. Members of the National Assembly enjoy immunity from arrest, detention, or prosecution, but the immunity may be lifted in certain cases.

Laws passed by the National Assembly are subject to review by the Constitutional Council, which also has the right to interpret the constitution and settle electoral disputes. The Constitutional Council consists of nine members, of whom one-third are elected by the National Assembly, one-third are appointed by the king, and one-third are nominated by the Supreme Council of the Magistracy. Members of the Constitutional Council serve nine-year terms, with three members retiring every three years.

The first elections under the UN peace plan were held on May 23–28, 1993. The new Assembly, meeting as a Constituent Assembly, adopted the constitution promulgated on September 21, 1993. Following the 1993 National Assembly elections, FUNCINPEC held fifty-eight seats; the Cambodian People's Party (formerly the Communist Party) held fifty-one seats; the Buddhist Liberal Democratic Party, ten seats; and MOLINAKA, a breakaway faction of FUNCINPEC, one seat. The royal government represents a coalition of all four parties, but the two largest parties predominated.

In 1997 the co-prime ministers, Prince Norodom Ranariddh of FUNCINPEC and Hun Sen of the Cambodian People's Party, ceased to function effectively as head of government. The National Assembly had no plans to convene, the legislative elections scheduled for 1998 were in doubt, and political rallies invariably ended in violence. In July 1997 parliamentary government ceased completely when Hun Sen staged a coup and Ranariddh fled the country.

George Thomas Kurian

CAMEROON

OFFICIAL NAME: Republic of Cameroon (République du Cameroun)
CAPITAL: Yaoundé
POPULATION: 14,262,000 (1996 est.)
DATE OF INDEPENDENCE: January 1, 1960 (from UN trusteeship under French administration)
DATE OF CURRENT CONSTITUTION: Adopted May 20, 1972; effective June 2, 1972
FORM OF GOVERNMENT: Parliamentary democracy
LANGUAGES: French (official), English (official), twenty-four major African language groups
MONETARY UNIT: CFA franc
FISCAL YEAR: July 1–June 30
LEGISLATURE: National Assembly (Assemblée Nationale)
NUMBER OF CHAMBERS: One
NUMBER OF MEMBERS: 180
PERCENTAGE OF WOMEN: —
TERM OF LEGISLATURE: Five years
MOST RECENT LEGISLATIVE ELECTION: May 17, 1997
MINIMUM AGE FOR VOTING: 20
MINIMUM AGE FOR MEMBERSHIP: 23
SUFFRAGE: Universal and direct
VOTING: Optional
ADDRESS: Assemblée Nationale, Yaoundé
TELEPHONE: (237) 23 40 70
FAX: (237) 22 57 24

Cameroon, a West African country that occupies the great bend where the continent begins its bulge westward *(see map, p. 261)*, is the only African country that was under three colonial masters. It was a German protectorate until 1916, when it was divided between the French and British.

Cameroon's multiple colonial heritage is reflected in its political institutions. The 1972 constitution created a federal republic under a strong presidential executive and a weak unicameral legislature, the National Assembly. The president is head of state and government. The National Assembly comprises 180 members elected by universal suffrage for a term of five years, which may be extended or shortened by the president.

Although the legislature is subordinate in practice to the executive, the constitution goes to great lengths to specify its powers and define its relations with the president. Laws are passed by a simple majority of those present, except when they are read a second time at the request of the president of the republic; then an absolute majority is required.

The National Assembly meets twice a year in two sessions, one of which is a budget session; each session lasts not more than thirty days. The Assembly may be summoned to extraordinary sessions of not more than fifteen days.

Bills may be introduced either by the president of the republic or by any member. The National Assembly may empower the president to legislate by means of ordinance or decree for a limited period or for a given purpose. The president has the right to address the National Assembly, and cabinet members have the right to participate in its debates. Sections 27–29 of the constitution deal with the conduct of legislative business, the setting up of boards of inquiry into governmental activity, and the publication of laws in the *Official Journal of National Assembly Debates.*

The Bureau of the Assembly is charged with the legislative agenda. One sitting per week is devoted to oral questions. The constitution also authorizes the use of referendums. The National Assembly has the right to amend the constitution by a simple majority, except in the case of a presidential veto, which may be overridden only by a two-thirds majority. All bills are sent first to parliamentary or standing committees for consideration except presidential bills, which are exempt from committee scrutiny. The Supreme Court has the right to review the constitutionality of legislation.

National Assembly members receive no salary but enjoy certain perquisites, such as medical care, subsidized meals, and free transportation. Members enjoy certain immunities but may be warned, censured, admonished, or suspended for breach of parliamentary regulations.

Despite the constitution's explicit creation of a multiparty system, the country remained a de facto one-party state until 1990. After 1990 parties proliferated; forty-five parties and three thousand candidates competed in the May 1997 elections. The dominant Cameroon People's Democratic Movement won an outright majority of 109 seats; the major opposition party, the Social Democratic Front, won 43. A number of parties split the remaining seats.

George Thomas Kurian

CANADA

OFFICIAL NAME: Canada
CAPITAL: Ottawa
POPULATION: 28,821,000 (1996 est.)
DATE OF INDEPENDENCE: July 1, 1867 (from the United Kingdom)
DATE OF CURRENT CONSTITUTION: Patriated April 17, 1982
FORM OF GOVERNMENT: Constitutional monarchy
LANGUAGES: English (official), French (official)
MONETARY UNIT: Canadian dollar
FISCAL YEAR: April 1–March 31
LEGISLATURE: Parliament
NUMBER OF CHAMBERS: Two. House of Commons; Senate
NUMBER OF MEMBERS: House of Commons, 301 (directly elected); Senate, 104 (appointed)
PERCENTAGE OF WOMEN: House of Commons, 21.3; Senate, 15.4
TERM OF LEGISLATURE: Five years
MOST RECENT LEGISLATIVE ELECTION: June 2, 1997
MINIMUM AGE FOR VOTING: 18
MINIMUM AGE FOR MEMBERSHIP: House of Commons, 18; Senate, 30
SUFFRAGE: Universal
VOTING: Optional
ADDRESS: House of Commons, Ottawa, Ontario K1A OA6; Senate, Ottawa, Ontario K1A OA4
TELEPHONE: House of Commons, (613) 996 3611; Senate, (613) 992 2493
FAX: House of Commons, (613) 992 3674; Senate, (613) 992 7959

Canada, whose ten provinces and two territories straddle northern North America, is a constitutional monarchy and parliamentary democracy. The constitution of Canada, embodying the essential institutions of the British system of government, provides for the monarchy and its representative, the governor general; the Parliament and its three components—the British monarch represented by the governor general, the appointed Senate, and the elected House of Commons; the lieutenant governors of the provinces, who are appointed by the federal government; and the division of powers between the federal and provincial levels of government.

HISTORICAL BACKGROUND

The Parliament of Canada came into being on July 1, 1867, when the four original provinces—Quebec, Ontario, Nova Scotia, and New Brunswick—united to form the first federal country in what was then the British Empire. Canada's parliamentary tradition predates the creation of the federation, however; Great Britain's North American colonies had long had elected assemblies. But popular representation was not sufficient to allay the prevailing discontent because the colonial government did not regard itself as being responsible to the elected assemblies. Moreover, the governor of each colony chose his own advisers, over whom the assemblies had no control. The resulting grievances led to rebellion in Upper Canada (Ontario) and Lower Canada (Quebec) in 1837. The British government responded by appointing Lord Durham governor general of the British North American colonies with a mandate to restore order and make recommendations for their constitutional future. The famous Durham Report contained two recommendations of particular importance. First, it proposed the establishment of responsible government based on the conventions of the British parliamentary system. The British governor, on all internal questions, was required to act on the advice of a council responsible to the elected assembly of the colony. In 1848 Nova Scotia became the first Canadian colony to enjoy responsible government.

Lord Durham's second major recommendation was less successful. He proposed that Upper and Lower Canada be united as the Province of Canada. He was motivated by the belief that the assimilation of the French-speaking population into the larger anglophone community would reduce the potential for conflict. But, although the Province of Canada was granted responsible government in 1840, French Canadians strongly resisted all attempts to assimilate them, and the recognition of their legitimate aspirations was a crucial factor in the launching of negotiations to form a Canadian federation, which resulted in the 1867 enactment by the British Parliament of the British North America Act, as the original Canadian constitution was called.

Within less than a century the original four provinces were joined by six more: Manitoba (1870), British Columbia (1871), Prince Edward Island (1873), Saskatchewan and Alberta (1905), and Newfoundland (1949). Canada also includes the Yukon and Northwest Territories which, like the provinces, have their own legislatures. The federation and the provinces are each autonomous within their spheres of jurisdiction, some powers being exclusive, some being shared.

The constitution assumes, without making specific reference to them, that the conventions of the British constitution will underlay the system of government. Thus, no reference is made to three of the most fundamental elements of the Canadian system: the prime minister, the head of the government; the cabinet, the supreme policy-making body; and political parties, the bedrock of the modern parliamentary system. The Constitution Acts contain no word on the convention whereby the cabinet is collectively responsible to the elected House of Commons, no reference to the fact that a government can be forced to resign if it loses the confidence of the House of Commons, and no reference to the important role played by the party system in the parliamentary process.

Although the Canadian federation enjoyed responsible government after its inception, it was not until 1931, with the adoption of the Statute of Westminster by the British Parliament, that Canada became a truly independent country. This act gave statutory effect to a declaration adopted by the Imperial Conference of 1926 that defined the United Kingdom and the other self-governing states of the then British Empire as "autonomous communities within the British Empire, equal in status, in no way subordinate one to another in any aspect of their domestic and external affairs, though united by a common allegiance to the Crown, and freely associated as members of the British Commonwealth of Nations."

Despite passage of the Statute of Westminster, vestiges of colonialism continued to cling to Canada's constitutional fabric. Amendments to the constitution had to be enacted by the British Parliament, although it acted only at the request of the Canadian government. In 1949 the Parliament of Canada acquired the power to amend those provisions of the constitution dealing exclusively with the federal authority, except those touching on the duration and annual meeting of Parliament.

The involvement of the British Parliament in the amendment of the constitution was a consequence of the failure, over the years, of the federal and provincial authorities to agree on an amending formula. There was reluctance at the provincial level, most notably in Quebec, to strengthen the federal government's scope for initiative in proposing constitutional amendments. For decades the federal and provincial governments had tried to find an acceptable amendment formula that would enable the constitution to be "patriated"—that is, removed from the legislative jurisdiction of the British Parliament and rooted in Canada. After a breakthrough in 1982—preceded by much intense and acrimonious debate, a court challenge, and a great deal of lobbying against the federal government's proposals—the federal government eventually won the support of all the provincial governments except that of Quebec, and the text of a bill for transmission to the British Parliament was adopted by the Parliament of Canada. The Canada Act 1982, incorporating the Constitution Act 1982 as a schedule, finally brought to an end the archaic process that for so long had tied Canada to its colonial origins. The former British North America Act and its amendments are now styled the Constitution Acts 1867 to 1982.

The principal changes effected by the Constitution Act 1982 were the incorporation of an amending formula and the Canadian Charter of Rights and Freedoms. Under the complex amending formula, most constitutional changes would require affirmative resolutions of both houses of Parliament and of the legislatures of at least two-thirds of the provinces that have at least 50 percent of the population of all the provinces. The amendment of certain provisions, including those affecting the monarchy, would require unanimity. The Charter of Rights and Freedoms guarantees the equality of all individuals before the law and outlaws discrimination based on race, national or ethnic origin, color, religion, sex, age, or mental or physical disability. Special provisions deal with language rights and the equality of Canada's two official languages, English and French.

THE MONARCHY

Many Canadians find it bewildering that the British monarch also is the Canadian monarch and regard this as yet another vestige of colonialism. Although both offices are held by the same person, the Canadian monarchy is separate and distinct from the British monarchy. This constitutional nicety lies at the root of Canada's sovereignty as an independent nation: in all matters relating to the governance of Canada the British monarch is advised exclusively by Canadian ministers and the British government retains no powers whatsoever over Canadian affairs.

Although the monarch is constitutionally the head of the Canadian state, the monarch's representative, the governor general, is for all practical purposes the de facto head of state. In 1947 all the prerogative powers of the Crown related to Canada were delegated to the governor general by letters patent, giving legal effect to what had been custom. The governor general is appointed by the Canadian government, and since 1952 all those who have held the office have been Canadian.

In Canada's parliamentary system executive power lies with the prime minister and the cabinet. The governor general, the head of state, appoints the prime minister, the head of government, but this normally is a foregone conclusion since he or she appoints the leader of the party that wins the general election or, should the prime minister die or resign, the leader chosen by the party in power to succeed to that office. The governor general has no will but that of his or her ministers, all the powers of the Crown being exercised in conformity with this convention. Prerogative powers such as the summoning and dissolving of Parliament are, in all normal circumstances, exercised on the advice of the prime minister. A bill passed by the two houses of Parliament requires the royal assent to become law, but in practice this has become a mere formality.

Although it might be argued that the governor general, like the British monarch, is nothing but a figurehead, there is more substance to the office than might appear. Separation of the head of state from the head of government protects the former from being tainted by any scandal that might attach to a government. This enables the governor general to stand aloof from political controversy and represent the nation on a higher plane. Furthermore, a reserve power resides in the Crown, the use of which could be justified only in the event a government committed a flagrant abuse of its own power. For example, should a prime minister after an election defeat refuse to resign or to call Parliament together, the governor general would have a duty to summon Parliament and force the defeated government to meet the elected House of Commons. It is almost inconceivable that such a situation might arise, yet in Australia, whose parliamentary system is similar to that of Canada, a constitutional crisis arose in 1975 which culminated in the governor general dismissing the government.

THE STRUCTURE AND FUNCTIONS OF PARLIAMENT

Parliament is the central institution of the Canadian system of government, and its fundamental structure has remained unchanged since 1867. Modeled on the British Parliament, the Canadian Parliament has an appointed Senate equivalent in many respects to the hereditary House of Lords; the House of Commons is fully elected like its British namesake.

System of checks and balances

The Canadian Parliament was structured according to the principle of checks and balances. The Senate is intended to represent the regions of Canada, thus balancing the elected Commons where representation is determined by the size of a province's population, which gives an overwhelming advantage to the larger provinces. The provinces themselves, however, have never been equally represented in the Senate.

The Senate is regarded by most people today as an anachronism and completely inconsistent with modern concepts of parliamentary democracy. But in 1867 an upper house consisting of men of mature age representing the property-owning classes was seen as a necessary counterbalance to a popularly elected chamber. It must be remembered, however, that Canada was formed before the attainment of universal adult suffrage and that political philosophy has changed radically since those days. Although attempts have been made to reform the Senate during the intervening years, none has ever come to fruition.

The Senate enjoys powers almost equal to those of the House of Commons, but with some exceptions. First, bills proposing expenditure or taxation must originate in the House of Commons. The House of Commons always has maintained that the Senate has no right to amend or reject a money bill, but the Senate has never accepted this interpretation of the lower house's financial privilege. Second, the amending formula in the Constitution Act 1982 provides that in the majority of cases the Senate cannot veto a constitutional amendment but only can delay it for 180 days. Finally, the government is accountable to the elected House of Commons, which could force a government to resign by adopting a resolution of no confidence or by defeating the government on a fundamental issue—for example, by rejecting its budget. An adverse vote in the Senate would not have the same effect unless a prime minister chose to make it an electoral issue.

Thus, the House of Commons is the true repository of power within the parliamentary system—indeed, within the government itself as long as a government controls an overall majority in the Commons. The primacy of the House of Commons is reflected in the fact that the prime minister and the vast majority of the cabinet are members of the Commons, elected for a constituency like every other member. Every province hopes to be represented in the cabinet, but the smaller provinces cannot expect to have more than one cabinet minister. The most populous provinces are more widely represented, and the claims of major cities like Toronto and Montreal are unlikely to be overlooked when cabinet appointments are made. Usually at least one senator serves in a modern cabinet, although between 1957 and 1962 there were no senators at all in the cabinet. On occasion, prime ministers have appointed senators to the cabinet to represent provinces where the governing party had failed to elect any, or a sufficient number of, members.

Women in Parliament

Although all legal barriers to the representation of women in Parliament have long since been removed, they remain disadvantaged in numerical terms. For many years after the first woman was elected to the House of Commons in 1921, the number of women in both houses remained insignificant, and even today it is hardly overwhelming. After the June 1997 elections, 16 women were serving in the 104-member Senate, and 64 of the 301 members of the House of Commons were women. The first woman to be appointed a cabinet minister was Ellen Fairclough, in 1957, and in recent years Canadian cabinets have invariably included women. Two women have served as speaker of the Senate: Muriel McQueen Fergusson (1972–1974) and Renaude Lapointe (1974–1979). The only woman to serve as speaker of the House of Commons, Jeanne Sauvé (1980–1984), was later appointed governor general. In 1993 Progressive Conservative Kim Campbell served briefly as prime minister but was defeated along with her party at the general election held in October of that year.

Functions of Parliament

In Canada the people elect the government, and the government is responsible to the elected house of Parliament. Parliament is the essential institution in the system of government, and the House of Commons is the essential institution of Parliament. The bulk of the legislation dealt with by Parliament is initiated by the government, and, although a certain amount of time is set aside for private members' business, very few private members' bills ever reach the statute book. Most of the time of the Commons is devoted to government business because the responsibilities of government in this day and age extend into virtually every area of public activity. The government is therefore committed to a certain program of measures and policies, the legislation and financial authority required to implement them being matters for the approval of Parliament, and predominantly the House of Commons.

The functions of Parliament fall into six categories, largely exercised by the House of Commons but also shared with the Senate. First, it is a representative institution; every member of the House of Commons is directly accountable to his or her constituents. Second, because Canada has no ombudsman at the federal level, every member is in effect an ombudsman with the duty of offering assistance or advice to constituents who have problems with officialdom. Third and fourth, of fundamental importance are the legislative function, since only Parliament can pass laws, and the financial function, since only Parliament can authorize expenditure and taxation. Fifth, through the critical function, largely exercised by the opposition parties, government activities are monitored and ministers are called to account. Sixth, the deliberative function permits Parliament to debate and consider all issues brought before it and register decisions by means of a vote. Finally, allied to their representative function, members have a duty to inform their constituents of what Parliament is doing, explain the purpose and effect of legislation, justify their own and their parties' positions, and respond to any questions that constituents may care to raise.

THE SENATE

The Senate originally consisted of seventy-two members, with twenty-four assigned to each of what were then the three regions of Canada: Ontario, Quebec, and the Maritime provinces. In 1915 the four western provinces became a region for the purpose of representation in the Senate, and each was given six senators. A further six were accorded to Newfoundland when that province entered the federation in 1949, and in 1975 the Yukon and Northwest Territories were each given one Senate seat. Thus, the normal size of the Senate today is 104 members, but the regional balance has been considerably upset. In terms of population, the four Atlantic provinces are generously represented in relation to the four western provinces, whose combined population is about three times that of the Atlantic provinces. It also is arguable whether the four western provinces fit logically into a single region since British Columbia possesses characteristics that are not shared by the three prairie provinces—Manitoba, Saskatchewan, and Alberta. A provision of the constitution requires that no province have fewer members of the House of Commons than it has senators. Prince Edward Island is the principal beneficiary of this protection.

The constitution provides for the appointment of four or eight additional senators, representing equally the four regions of Canada, should it prove necessary to resolve an impasse between the two houses. This provision has been invoked only once, on the initiative of Prime Minister Brian Mulroney in 1990, when the Liberal opposition in the Senate tried to block passage of the Goods and Services Tax Bill after it had been adopted by the House of Commons. The additional eight senators provided the Progressive Conservative government with the bare majority it needed to secure passage of the bill by the Senate.

Qualifications for appointment

Senators are appointed by the governor general on the advice of the prime minister. Successive prime ministers have not been able to resist the temptation to turn the Senate into a house of patronage. Only rarely has an appointment to the Senate not been politically motivated.

Senators originally were appointed for life, but an amendment to the constitution in 1965 introduced a retirement age of seventy-five applicable to all senators appointed after the new provision took effect.

The constitution provides that a senator must be at least thirty years of age and own freehold property with a net value of $4,000 and real and personal property valued at $4,000 over and above all debts and liabilities. A senator also must reside in the province for which he or she is appointed and, in the case of Quebec, must reside and own the required property in one of the original twenty-four electoral districts of the former province of Lower Canada. These requirements have remained unchanged since 1867. The property qualifications do not amount to much by today's standards, but in 1867 they ensured that a senator would be a person of reasonable wealth and substance.

Role of the Senate in the legislative process

For most of its existence the Senate has accepted a passive role in the legislative process, recognizing that it does not have a popular mandate. But it has flexed its muscle on more than one occasion. In 1913 it refused to pass the Naval Bill, forced through the House of Commons by means of closure, on the grounds that it was an issue for the electorate to decide. In 1961 it declined to give a third reading to a bill to dismiss the governor of the Bank of Canada. This gave the governor the opportunity to be heard in his own defense before a Senate committee after the House of Commons had declined to summon him before one of its own committees. In 1988 the Senate refused to pass the legislation giving effect to the free trade agreement between Canada and the United States until it had been submitted to the people at a general election. The government of Brian

Mulroney, which had negotiated the agreement, was reelected and the legislation went through. The attempt to block the Goods and Services Tax Bill in 1990 was the most dramatic example of the Senate's use of its powers and led to some of the unruliest scenes ever witnessed in the Canadian Parliament.

While the Senate seldom rejects bills outright, it frequently proposes amendments to bills sent up by the House of Commons where the majority of legislation originates. Even when amendments to money bills have been proposed by the Senate—although the House of Commons denies its right to do so—the Commons sometimes has accepted them with the proviso that the matter not be taken as a precedent. (The Senate concedes that it cannot constitutionally propose increases in expenditure or taxation.) When Senate amendments lead to improvements in legislation, the House of Commons may accept them as such. If the Senate insisted on an amendment that the Commons rejected, it would be required by its rules to send a message to the Commons explaining the reasons for its insistence, and, in the event of a deadlock, provision exists for a conference between the two houses. This procedure, however, has been used only rarely, the last time in 1947.

Although the number of bills originating in the Senate is not great, those that do frequently deal with highly complex or technical matters such as bankruptcy or company law. The Senate has more time than the House of Commons to deal with such legislation, and the experience of many senators in the fields of finance, business, and the law provides the expertise required to produce sound legislation in areas of great importance. Virtually all private bills—bills promoted by private organizations such as professional associations, as distinct from public bills which are national in scope—are introduced in the Senate. The volume of private legislation has decreased considerably since passage of the Divorce Act in 1968, which ended the practice of requiring an individual act of Parliament for every divorce.

Because of the frequent late arrival of bills referred from the House of Commons, the Senate adopted the informal practice of considering the content of some legislation in advance of its adoption by the House of Commons. In 1991 this practice was formalized by the adoption of a rule providing that the leader or deputy leader of the government in the Senate may give notice of a motion to refer the subject matter of a bill to a special committee or a named standing committee.

It also has long been a practice to consider estimates of expenditures in the Senate Finance Committee once they have been presented to the House of Commons. Such work thus can be undertaken well in advance of the passage of the appropriation bills through the House of Commons, and, although such procedures are unorthodox, they help to promote the efficiency of the Senate's work.

A great deal of the work of the Senate is accomplished by its committees, through which it has launched major investigations into significant social and economic issues such as poverty, aging, agriculture, the mass media, relations with other countries, and the operations of government departments.

Leadership

The speaker of the Senate is appointed by the governor general on the prime minister's advice and serves for the duration of a Parliament. Regardless of which party is in the majority in the Senate, the speaker always is appointed from the governing party. The speaker has a deliberative vote like any other senator but no casting vote. In the event of a tie, the question is decided in the negative.

The deputy speaker is elected by members of the Senate for the duration of a Parliament. If the governing party is in the minority in the Senate, the deputy speaker is almost certain to be an opposition member. Two assistant deputies serve for the duration of a parliamentary session.

At the time of the crisis over the Goods and Services Tax Bill, the speaker was in great disfavor with the Liberal opposition because, in the absence of any formal powers, he used certain strategies to assist the passage of the bill. In view of the manner of the speaker's appointment, it is an interesting argument as to whether his first loyalty should have been to the Senate itself or to the political party and the prime minister to whom he owed his appointment. So acrimonious were relations between the parties at the time that the opposition members refused to participate in the committee that considered changes to the rules.

The chief permanent officer of the Senate, called clerk of the Senate and clerk of the Parliament, is equal in rank to the permanent head of a government department, also known as a deputy minister. But unlike the latter the clerk is not a member of the public service. Parliament recruits its own staff, and their separation from the public service underlines Parliament's independence from the government itself. The full designation of the clerk of the Senate reflects the Senate's symbolic status as the upper house, although it is in fact the less powerful of the two houses.

Senate rules

In 1991 the rules of the Senate were substantially revised as a direct result of the chaos and disorder that attended the debates on the Goods and Services Tax Bill. Previously the rules had been characterized by a high degree of flexibility since it was expected that the Senate would conduct its proceedings with decorum and that the need for rules would be minimal. There were no time limits on speeches, no mechanism for limiting the length of debates, and no fixed hours of adjournment. The speaker had no disciplinary powers and very little power to control debate, and could rule on a question of order only if asked to do so.

During the debates on the Goods and Services Tax Bill in 1990, the Liberal opposition went to great lengths to obstruct the bill, making interminable speeches in order to prolong debate and forcing the Senate to sit round the clock. Their tactics were unprecedented, and parliamentary behavior on both sides of the Senate reached an all-time low. The opposition justified its actions with the claim that the new tax was highly unpopular in the country and that an election should be held before it was imposed. But passage of the bill, as noted earlier, was eventually forced by the creation of eight new government Senate seats.

The revised rules provide for a time limit on most speeches of fifteen minutes, although the leader of the government and the leader of the opposition are entitled to unlimited time in most debates. If no agreement on time limits can be reached between the parties, the leader or deputy leader of the government may give notice of a motion to allocate a specified number of days or hours to any stage of any item of government business, provided debate on that stage already has been adjourned.

The amended rules also provide for fixed hours of sitting. The automatic hour of adjournment is midnight except on Friday, when it is 4:00 p.m. A sitting commences at 2:00 p.m. except on Friday, when it begins at 9:00 a.m.

The new rules greatly increase the powers of the speaker, who can now act on his or her own initiative to enforce the rules and control breaches of order. Should grave disorder arise, the speaker is empowered to suspend the sitting for not more than three hours. Among other things, the speaker rules on points of order, limits the interventions of senators speaking to points of order, and determines when a sufficient argument has been made to decide a matter.

Many of the changes to the rules were influenced by the practice of the House of Commons, but in spite of the strengthening of the powers of the speaker of the Senate, there remains a significant difference between that leader's powers and those of the speaker of the House of Commons. In the Senate any ruling of the speaker can be appealed from the floor and overturned by an immediate vote.

Compensation and perquisites

Senators are entitled to the same salaries as members of the House of Commons, together with one-half of the tax-free expense allowance accorded to House members and most of the same benefits and perquisites.

THE HOUSE OF COMMONS

When the first Canadian Parliament met on November 6, 1867, the House of Commons consisted of 181 members. The constitution provides for a readjustment of representation in the House of Commons following each decennial census, the first of which took place in 1871. Electoral boundaries commissions were first established in 1964 to ensure a fair and objective approach to the redistribution of Commons seats. A complex formula is applied to guarantee that, to the extent possible, there is not too great a discrepancy among the various constituencies in the size of their electorates. Yet underpopulated provinces and regions also are to be fairly represented.

Of the 295 seats in the House of Commons prior to the 1997 elections, Ontario and Quebec, the two most populous provinces, accounted for well over half. A bill adopted in 1994 by the Commons, which would have postponed a further redistribution of seats until after the next election, was amended by the Senate so that the size of the House of Commons would increase to 301 for the next election.

Elections and parties

Members of the House of Commons are elected from single-member constituencies (ridings) by the "first-past-the-post" system: the candidates receiving more votes than any of their opponents are declared elected. The minimum voting age was twenty-one until 1970, when it was reduced to eighteen. In 1960 the last remaining restrictions on the voting rights of aboriginal peoples were removed.

The electoral system is simple and straightforward but does not usually produce a result that is proportionately representative. Governments are able to win substantial majorities with considerably less than 50 percent of the popular vote, and minor parties are unlikely to win many seats unless their support is concentrated in certain regions of the country.

At the federal level only two parties have ever formed the government, the Liberals and the Progressive Conservatives. Since 1921, however, more than two parties always have been represented in the House of Commons, sometimes as many as five. The New Democratic Party, a left-leaning, social democratic party, has for many years been a significant force in Canadian politics and until 1993 enjoyed third-party status in the House of Commons. The 1993 election, which returned the Liberals to power, created a political upheaval at the federal level because two of Canada's major national parties were decimated at the polls. The

Progressive Conservatives, who had formed the previous government, were reduced to two seats. The New Democrats managed to win nine seats, but both they and the Progressive Conservatives lost official party status since a minimum of twelve members is required to qualify for the advantages that official party status confers.

The beneficiaries of the upheaval were two relatively new regionally based parties which had had minimal representation in the previous Parliament. The Bloc Québécois, a party dedicated to the independence of Quebec, and which only fielded candidates in that province, won fifty-four seats and, ironically, became the official opposition with national responsibilities. The Reform Party, a right-wing protest movement with its roots in the western provinces, won fifty-two seats, the vast majority of them in Alberta and British Columbia. These parties became, then, the two main opposition parties at the federal level, the governing Liberals being the only national party with any federal strength.

In June 1997 the Liberal Party suffered a loss of 22 seats but still maintained a slim majority in the 301-member body. The Reform Party gained 8 seats, raising its total to 60, but the Bloc Québécois lost 10, falling to 44 seats. The New Democats and Progressive Conservatives were the primary beneficiaries of the election, winning 21 and 20 seats, respectively, to regain their official party status.

Speaker of the House of Commons

The speaker, who is an elected member of the House of Commons, is elected by secret ballot by members of the Commons. The speaker serves for the duration of a Parliament. Under the procedure in place since 1986, at the opening of Parliament the chair is taken, until the election of the speaker, by the member who, outside of cabinet ministers, party leaders, or other parliamentary officeholders, has the longest period of unbroken service as a member of the Commons.

The standing orders provide for no nominating procedure. Instead, all members who do not wish to be candidates must so inform the clerk of the Commons in writing, all being eligible unless they are cabinet ministers or party leaders. Balloting continues until one candidate emerges with an absolute majority. The clerk of the Commons is responsible for the balloting procedure and for counting the ballots. No business is transacted until the Commons has elected a speaker.

Should a speaker resign during a Parliament, he or she remains in the chair during the election of a successor. In the speaker's absence, the deputy speaker presides.

The conventions related to the British speakership are largely observed in Canada. Once elected, the speaker presides with complete impartiality, does not participate in debate, and only votes in the case of a tie—not according to his or her own inclinations but in conformity with long-standing precedents. If possible the speaker votes in such a way as to leave the issue open to further debate; if not, in favor of the status quo, unless the issue is one of confidence in the government, in which case the speaker would probably vote to sustain the government.

Unlike in Great Britain where the speaker, once elected, resigns from his or her political party, the Canadian speakership is not as completely detached from party affiliation. The one speaker who succeeded in shedding his political associations was elected to the chair three times, but subsequent speakers found themselves unable to follow this precedent, mainly because of the importance of having a party label when contesting a seat in the general election. Nevertheless, Canadian speakers detach themselves from party influence in every other way. They do not attend party meetings or caucuses, and during a general election campaign they never enter the debate on the political issues of the day. Because of these disadvantages, speakers seeking reelection in their constituencies sometimes have gone down to defeat.

The speaker is not a political leader and plays no part in the organization of the business of the Commons, but he or she is the senior presiding officer of the Commons, assisted by the deputy speaker and two other deputies, and the position is one of great prestige. The speaker is the guardian of the privileges of the Commons collectively and of the members individually.

The speaker also interprets the rules and practice of the Commons and rules on points of order. Should a question of privilege be raised, the speaker decides whether the matter is of sufficient importance to be taken into immediate consideration. If yes, the matter is usually referred to the committee that deals with cases of privilege, although the Commons is free to debate the matter immediately. Should a member request an emergency debate, the speaker decides whether the request conforms to the necessary criteria. Allowance of questions of privilege and emergency debates are the only two areas in which the speaker's decision may have an effect on the order of business. If in the course of debate or the question period a matter is raised that is *sub judice* (before the court) it is the speaker who, in the final resort, decides whether discussion of the matter should be allowed.

In controlling debate the speaker is equipped with disciplinary powers should a member use unparliamentary language or act in a disorderly manner. A breach of discipline is normally dealt with by calling a member to order, or demanding that an offensive expression be withdrawn. If a member persists in defying the authority of the chair, the speaker can order the offending member to withdraw from the chamber for the remainder of the sitting. If in the course of a speech a member persists in irrelevance or repetition to be deliberately obstructive, the speaker may order the member to discontinue the speech.

Among the speaker's other procedural duties are control of the question period and the selection and grouping of amendments at the report stage of a bill.

The speaker, who has extensive administrative responsibilities as head of the House of Commons establishment, is equivalent to a minister in charge of a government department. The speaker's responsibilities consist, among other things, of representing the Commons in all its dealings with outside institutions, receiving foreign diplomats and other distinguished visitors, heading delegations visiting other countries, representing the House of Commons in its dealings with government departments, and maintaining regular contact with ministers and Commons leaders of the various parties.

The speaker ranks fifth in the official order of precedence following the governor general, prime minister, chief justice, and speaker of the Senate. In addition to the salary and allowances due a member of Parliament, the speaker receives emoluments similar to those of a cabinet minister, as well as the use of an official country residence within easy reach of Parliament Hill.

House of Commons operations

The directing authority of the House of Commons is the Board of Internal Economy, provided for under the Parliament of Canada Act. It is composed of the speaker, who serves as chair; the deputy speaker; two ministers of the government; the leader of the opposition or a member appointed by the leader; and four backbenchers—two from the governing party, one from the official opposition, and one from the third-largest party provided it has at least twelve members in the Commons. The board is the employer of the staff of the Commons, who are independent of the public service, and the controller of the parliamentary premises. It determines the administrative and financial policy of the Commons, the conditions of service of the staff, and the services required by members in the fulfillment of their functions.

The chief permanent officer of the Commons is the clerk, who, like his or her counterpart in the Senate, has the status of a deputy minister, the permanent head of a government department. The clerk reports to the speaker and is accountable to the Board of Internal Economy and the Commons as a whole. As head of the parliamentary establishment, under the speaker, the clerk has wide-ranging administrative and financial responsibilities and serves as the speaker's and members' principal adviser on the procedure and practice of the Commons. The clerk also is the custodian of all parliamentary papers and records, and he or she authenticates by signature the texts of bills and the daily votes and proceedings (minutes); oversees the preparation and distribution of the daily order paper (agenda); and calls the first meetings of the standing committees at the start of each session so they can elect their chairs.

PARLIAMENTARY PRIVILEGE

The privileges of the Senate and the House of Commons collectively and of their members individually are derived from the constitution and the Parliament of Canada Act. They are closely allied with those enjoyed by the British House of Commons. In fact, both the constitution and the Parliament of Canada Act provide that the privileges, immunities, and powers of the Canadian Parliament shall not exceed those of the British House of Commons.

The collective privileges of each house include the right to regulate their own proceedings; to institute inquiries and to order the production of papers and the attendance of witnesses for the purpose of the inquiry; to judge questions of privilege without the intervention of the courts; to punish breaches of privilege and contempt whether committed by members or "strangers" (neither members nor staff); and to control the access to the public galleries, committee rooms, and parliamentary premises in general.

For individual members, the importance of parliamentary privilege rests essentially on two factors. The first, freedom of speech, gives members immunity from the laws of defamation for anything said in the Commons and its committees. Witnesses testifying before committees are equally protected. Second, any act designed to obstruct, threaten, intimidate, or harass a member in the performance of his or her duties is a punishable offense, subject to the penal jurisdiction of the house concerned. Parliamentary privilege is not designed to give members advantages not enjoyed by their fellow citizens, but only to provide them with the protection they need to carry out their functions without hindrance. For example, the speaker would not permit a member facing a criminal charge to evade arrest by using parliamentary premises as a refuge and would probably order the sergeant-at-arms to take the offender into custody and hand him or her over to the police (the police are not empowered to arrest a member on parliamentary premises without the authority of the speaker).

Related to parliamentary privilege is the offense of contempt, which covers a variety of acts tending to bring Parliament or its members into disrepute or diminish their authority.

Privilege has never been precisely defined, as each house reserves the right to decide whether its privileges have been breached or not. The courts recognize the exclusive jurisdiction of Parliament in this area, but the potential for conflict between Parliament and the courts nevertheless exists. If parliamentary privilege is pleaded as a defense in a case brought before a court, the court must determine the validity of the claim, which involves a judgment as to how far the limits of privilege extend.

Although Parliament has rarely invoked its penal jurisdiction, it is less hesitant to proceed against its own members when they offend. The most recent case occurred on October 30, 1991, when a member of the House of Commons was reprimanded by the speaker for attempting to seize the mace as a protest against adjournment of the Commons. Each house also has the right to expel its own members for grave offenses. An expelled member is not disqualified from running as a candidate for election or reelection to the House of Commons and, if successful, could legally sit as a member.

Members are exempted from jury service and from appearing in court as witnesses, but the latter immunity is often waived in the interests of justice. The principle underlying these immunities is that a member's parliamentary duties take precedence over all else.

THE OPENING OF PARLIAMENT

Section 5 of the Constitution Act 1982 provides that Parliament and each provincial legislature shall sit at least once every twelve months, but in practice both Parliament and the legislatures meet far more frequently. Parliament sits throughout the year with regular recesses, and each Parliament usually consists of more than one session—the series of sittings that takes place from its opening until its termination by prorogation—but no fixed convention is observed for the duration of a session. Every session is opened by the governor general.

The ceremony attending the opening of Parliament after a general election follows British tradition very closely. The first business of the House of Commons at the first session of a new Parliament is the election of the speaker. The members assemble in their chamber on the appointed day and await the arrival of the Gentleman Usher of the Black Rod, an officer of the Senate whose symbol of office is an ebony rod surmounted by a golden lion rampant. Black Rod knocks three times on the door, and, on being admitted, delivers a message to Commons members desiring their presence in the Senate chamber. Members proceed to the bar of the Senate, where they are instructed by the speaker of the Senate to return to their own chamber and elect their speaker. This they do, and after an adjournment another message is received from Black Rod desiring their further attendance in the Senate chamber. Black Rod leads the procession to the Senate followed by the sergeant-at-arms of the House of Commons bearing the mace—the symbol of the royal authority which, being delegated to each house, also becomes the symbol of parliamentary authority—the newly elected speaker, the clerks-at-the-table, and the other members accompanying the speaker. The speaker informs the governor general of his or her election and claims the privileges of the Commons, principal among which is freedom of speech. The speaker of the Senate, replying on behalf of the governor general, confirms the privileges. The governor general then reads the speech from the throne opening the parliamentary session.

The speech read by the governor general is prepared by the government. It reviews the affairs of the nation and outlines the government's legislative intentions. It will form the basis of the first major debate to take place in the new session.

A similar ceremony takes place whenever a new session is opened, but since the speaker is elected for an entire Parliament, the election formalities are observed only at the opening of the first session of a Parliament.

PARLIAMENTARY PROCEDURE

Parliamentary procedure in Canada consists of four elements: the traditional practice, which has evolved and been refined over the centuries and which may be described as the common law of Parliament; the standing orders, which have codified certain practices, introduced new rules, and modified old ones; the precedents arising from decisions of successive speakers; and convention, for which no rules can be found and which, while setting no precedents, arises from agreements and arrangements among the parties designed to facilitate the passage of business.

A fundamental principle of parliamentary procedure is that debate can take place only when a properly framed, clearly worded motion is before the house. Various kinds of motions may be introduced: substantive motions, which are self-contained and stand on their own; ancillary motions, which depend on an order of the day, such as the motion that a bill be read a second or third time; subsidiary motions, such as amendments to motions before the house, including subamendments to amendments; dilatory motions, designed to delay proceedings, such as motions to adjourn the house or to adjourn the debate; and motions for limiting debate such as previous question, closure, and allocation of time motions. Once adopted, a motion becomes a resolution of the house.

Some motions, such as substantive motions, require notice; others, such as amendments to motions already under debate, do not. Motions dependent on orders of the day are moved when those orders are called since the government has exclusive control of the order of its own business. Some motions, such as dilatory motions, are not debatable.

Amendments must be strictly relevant to the motions they propose to amend, and, similarly, subamendments must be relevant to amendments. Amendments to bills must not exceed the scope of the bill itself or negate its principle. Motions that are wide in scope offer more flexibility for the scope of amendments.

The standing orders of the House of Commons place time limits on speeches, which vary according to the nature of the debate; exemptions are provided as well—for example, in general the prime minister and leader of the opposition are allowed unlimited time. In most debates members are given the floor for thirty minutes, twenty minutes for the speech itself and ten minutes for the questions and comments from other members about the speech.

Members can speak only once on a motion before the House except for the mover, who has the right of reply. Exceptions are sometimes made if a member wants to clarify a misunderstanding. The seconder of a motion may speak later if he or she does not immediately follow the mover. If an amendment is moved, members who already have spoken on the main motion may speak again on the amendment. The rules are relaxed in committee, where members are not limited in the number of times they may speak. Speeches made when Parliament convenes as the Committee of the Whole are limited to twenty minutes, but if a bill is under consideration, the time often is used as a question-and-answer period between the member who has the floor and the minister in charge of the bill. In standing and legislative committees the rules of the house apply to the extent to which they are applicable, but the proceedings are conducted much more informally.

At the conclusion of the debate on any motion before the house, the speaker puts the question by means of a voice vote. The speaker then declares his or her opinion on whether the yeas or nays have it. If five or more members rise, a division—recorded vote—takes place. To be entitled to vote, a member must have been present in the chamber when the question was put. After the votes have been counted and verified, the clerk of the House reports the result to the speaker, who declares the motion carried or lost, as the case may be. The results of recorded votes are entered in the *Votes and Proceedings* and the official report of debates *(Hansard)*. Before the question on a main motion is put, amendments and subamendments must be disposed of. The main motion, if carried, will be put to the house or committee as amended.

THE COMMITTEE SYSTEM

Much of the work of Parliament is undertaken by the committees in the Senate and the House of Commons. Committees fall into five categories: committees of the whole, which consist of all members of the House of Commons; standing committees, which address specific subject areas and mandates and are listed in the rules of the Senate and the standing orders of the House; legislative committees, which undertake clause-by-clause study of bills and are set up as required; special committees, which are appointed on an ad hoc basis to undertake a specific inquiry; and joint committees, which consist of members of both houses sitting together.

Committees of the whole house once were used extensively. Before the procedural reforms instituted by the House of Commons in the 1960s most of the financial business was conducted in the Committee of the Whole, and almost all bills were referred to a Committee of the Whole for clause-by-clause study. Today, most bills are referred to standing committees or legislative committees. The Committee of the Whole is used mainly to consider bills that the parties have agreed to expedite.

In both houses most standing committees have a specific subject mandate, and while their mandates are not identical, they cover more or less the same ground: foreign affairs, finance, transport, agriculture, fisheries, environment, and so forth. Among them, the subject-oriented committees cover the various departments of government, and the Commons committees may initiate inquiries into the management, organization, expenditure plans, policy objectives, and overall effectiveness of the departments assigned to them. The comparable Senate committees pursue their inquiries in response to a specific reference from the Senate itself.

In addition to the subject-oriented committees, the standing committees of the Senate include the Committee on Privileges, Standing Rules, and Orders and the Committee on Internal Economy, Budgets, and Administration, the latter equating with the Board of Internal Economy of the House of Commons. The Senate Committee of Selection nominates members to serve on the various committees and a senator to preside as speaker pro tempore. In the House of Commons the Standing Committee on Procedure and House Affairs has a wide range of duties including review of the standing orders and practice of the Commons, administration of the Commons, provision of services and facilities for members, private members' business, and the broadcast of the proceedings of the Commons and its committees. It also nominates the members of the other committees. Of particular importance is the Standing Committee on Public Accounts, which oversees government expenditures. The Liaison Committee, composed of the chairs of the standing committees and the Commons chairs or vice chairs of the joint committees, apportions the funds authorized by the Board of Internal Economy to meet the expenses of committee activities.

In the House of Commons the speaker's three deputies, together with a number of members selected by the speaker and drawn from both government and opposition parties, form a panel of chairs from whom the chairs of legislative committees are drawn. Chairs of standing committees are in most cases government members, except the chair of the Public Accounts Committee, and they are expected to take an active part in directing the proceedings of their committees. The chairs of legislative committees play a more detached role, taking no position on the merits of the bill being considered by the committee.

The Senate and the House of Commons have three joint committees. The Joint Committee on the Library of Parliament oversees the effectiveness, management, and operation of the library. The Joint Committee on the Scrutiny of Regulations examines the subordinate legislation issued by the executive under the authority of various acts of Parliament and indicates where the executive may have exceeded its powers. Finally, the Joint Committee on Official Languages reviews the federal government's official language policies and programs and considers the reports of the commissioner of official languages on alleged violations of language rights and on the quality of services provided by the federal government in the two official languages, English and French.

THE LEGISLATIVE PROCESS

Bills may be introduced in either the Senate or the House of Commons, but the vast majority are introduced in the Commons. Every bill must complete its passage in both houses and receive the royal assent before it can become law. Bills fall into three categories: public bills introduced by the government; public bills introduced by private members; and private bills, which are sponsored by private organizations and are subject to a different procedure.

Most of the legislation considered by the Commons emanates from the government, or more precisely a government department. Once agreement has been reached about the form a bill should take, the Ministry of Justice drafts the measure, and it is considered and approved by the whole cabinet before being introduced in the Commons by the minister responsible. All bills with financial implications are government bills. Those proposing an expenditure must be accompanied by a recommendation signed by the governor general. Bills proposing taxation are based on ways and means resolutions, which only can be moved by a minister. Private members' bills with financial implications are therefore unacceptable and would be ruled out of order. The effect of this restriction is to keep financial planning under the control of the government, which is responsible for determining priorities and apportioning available resources. It is also for this reason that when financial measures and proposals are considered in Parliament and its committees, amendments proposing increases are out of order, but amendments proposing reductions are not. Should the government itself wish to propose an increase in expenditure or taxation, another royal recommendation or ways and means resolution, as the case may be, would be required. All bills involving finance must be introduced in the House of Commons.

In the Senate and House of Commons government bills and private members' bills are subject to the same legislative process. At the point of introduction there are two formal stages at which no debate or vote takes place: the motion for leave to introduce the bill and the first reading of the bill. Between these stages the member in charge of the bill is permitted to describe briefly its objectives—private members, but not ministers, normally take advantage of this right. The first reading is the authorization to publish the bill and the stage at which the bill enters the public domain.

At the second reading the principle of the bill is debated. Certain amendments to the bill may be moved at this stage, but not amendments of detail. These amendments usually propose postponing consideration of the bill with the intention of defeating it; "reasoned amendments" spell out the objections of a bill's opponents.

After the second reading a bill may be referred to a legislative committee, a standing committee, or the Committee of the Whole in the Commons for clause-by-clause consideration. A bill normally is referred to the Committee of the Whole when the parties have agreed to expedite its passage. In that case they probably will have agreed to a resolution to suspend the standing orders so that various stages of the bill can be taken on the same day. At the committee stage amendments may be moved to any or every clause, and the committee reports the bill to the house with or without amendment, as the case may be.

In the House of Commons a further stage—known as the report stage—may take place with the speaker in the chair. Further amendments, of which notice is required, can be moved, and those previously discussed in committee or aimed at restoring the original text also may be proposed. No report stage takes place if the bill has been referred to the Committee of the Whole in the Commons. At this stage the speaker is empowered to select and combine amendments and also may group them for voting purposes. This very crucial power calls for shrewdness and discretion because in the past the report stage has been used for obstructive purposes. The power to select and combine is designed not only to frustrate outright obstruction but also to give priority to those amendments held important by parties in the Commons. The report stage is mainly an opportunity for members who were not members of the committee to move their own amendments, and it is very unlikely that the speaker will select an amendment discussed and rejected by the committee. The power to combine enables the speaker to group together amendments that have a similar purpose, which reduces the debating time since the standing orders allow a member to speak only once for a maximum of ten minutes on each amendment or each group of combined amendments. Should recorded votes be demanded on any report stage amendments, the voting procedure is postponed until the end of the report stage, when the votes are taken successively. After the report stage a nondebatable motion is made that the bill as amended be concurred in. If no amendments are moved at the report stage, this step becomes a formality and the third reading of the bill may be taken immediately.

The third reading stage is similar to the second reading, and the same kind of amendments can be moved. A motion to recommit the bill for further consideration of detail in a committee also would be in order. Debate at third reading is sometimes waived if the bill is not very controversial. If adopted at third reading, the bill will have completed its passage in the house in which it was introduced. It is then referred to the other house, where it passes through a similar process. If the other house proposes amendments, they are communicated to the house in which the bill originated, which may accept or reject them. Should the two houses fail to agree on the final form of the bill, it would fall. Provision exists for a conference to take place between the two houses in the event of an impasse, but such conferences are rare, the last one having taken place in 1947. In practice, one house or the other normally will concede its objections and allow the bill to pass.

In 1994 changes were made to the standing orders of the House of Commons. With these revisions, bills may be referred to a standing, legislative, or special committee for pre-study prior to second reading, the stage at which the main debate on principle traditionally has taken place. The debate on a motion for referral to a committee is limited to three hours, speeches are limited to ten minutes, and a speaking order is laid down. If the motion, which must be made by a minister and is not subject to amendment, is adopted, no second reading debate takes place. When the committee reports the bill back to the House, a report stage ensues at which amendments can be moved. On completion of the report stage a formal vote takes place on a motion for second reading, which is not debatable, and, if adopted, the bill proceeds to third reading. Related to this new process is a procedure whereby a committee may be appointed or instructed to prepare and bring in a bill on a specified matter, recommending its principles, scope, and general provisions. This procedure is available to private members as well as ministers, but if the necessary motion is made by a private member, it is subject to the draw and other provisions relating to private members' business. If such a motion is moved by a minister, it may be debated for ninety minutes, speeches being limited to ten minutes.

The final stage in the legislative process is the royal assent, which is signified at a ceremony in the Senate chamber based on a centuries-old tradition. The House of Commons is visited by the Gentleman Usher of the Black Rod, who requests members to attend at the bar of the Senate to witness the ceremony.

PRIVATE MEMBERS' BUSINESS

In the House of Commons one hour a day is devoted to the consideration of private members' business, which consists of bills and motions. Because a private member's bill may contain no financial implications, a private member wishing to present any proposal involving expenditure or an increase in taxation would do so through a motion that calls on the government to consider the proposal in question. Such a resolution, if adopted, would be simply an expression of opinion by the Commons and would not be binding on the government. Many private members' bills and motions are introduced, but only a limited number are actually debated on the floor of the Commons, and even fewer ever come to a final vote. Forty-eight hours' notice is required for introduction of private members' bills, and two weeks must elapse between first and second reading. Two weeks' notice is required of a private member's motion before it may be moved in the House.

The precedence of items of private members' business is decided by a draw of an equal number of bills and motions, to a maximum of twenty. Further draws take place when the items in the order of precedence have been reduced to no less than ten. Every item on the order of precedence is guaranteed a one-hour debate, but if no vote is taken by the end of the hour it is dropped from the order of precedence unless it has been selected as a votable item. Six votable items (three bills and three motions) are selected from the twenty on the order of precedence by a subcommittee of the Standing Committee on Procedure and House Affairs, which may hear the arguments of the members sponsoring the items. It then makes its selection according to a number of criteria. Votable items are not dropped from the order of precedence after a one-hour debate but may be returned to the Commons for further consideration. If bills pass second reading, provision is made for them to pass through all the stages of the legislative process until final vote at third reading. If a private member's bill completes its passage in the House of Commons, it is referred to the Senate like any other bill. A private member's bill introduced in the Senate is not subject to the procedure just described, but if adopted and referred to the Commons it is automatically placed at the bottom of the order of precedence. Far more private members' bills are introduced in the House of Commons than in the Senate.

A private bill is introduced through a petition signed by the bill's promoters and is presented in Parliament by a member who has agreed to sponsor it. Most private bills are introduced in the Senate, although they may originate in either house. Like public bills they are considered in principle at second reading and referred to a committee if adopted. If a measure is opposed, its promoters and those opposed to it may be represented by counsel who argue their cases before the committee. The committee reports to the respective house, and the bill is then subject to the normal legislative process. In the House of Commons private bills are considered during the time allotted to private members' business.

FINANCIAL PROCEDURE

Parliament, and in particular the House of Commons, spends a great part of its time considering financial matters, control of the purse being at the heart of the parliamentary system. Most government legislation has financial implications, but the greater part of Parliament's financial business concerns "supply," which covers the government's projected expenditures and the appropriations required to finance the operations of the departments and agencies of government, and "ways and means," which concerns the raising of revenue, largely by means of taxation. All expenditure and taxation must be authorized by legislation. For supply, this is done by enactment of the annual appropriations bills that authorize interim supply—the granting of a certain proportion of the funds requested on account—the main estimates, and any supplementary estimates that may be introduced later. The first hints of taxation proposals usually appear in the annual budget brought forward by the minister of finance, but they also can result from separate initiatives. All such proposals are first authorized by ways and means resolutions, which can be voted on but not amended or debated. The adoption of a ways and means resolution is the authority to bring in a bill giving legislative sanction to its provisions. Legislative authority also is required to enable the government to borrow money.

Appropriations bills, ways and means bills, and borrowing authority bills are all subject to the normal legislative process, although amendments may only propose reductions, not increases, in the sums of money or incidence of taxation proposed. Appropriations bills, however, frequently are not debated, and the standing orders provide that all their stages may be taken on the same day. Time limits apply to the business of supply, and the provisions of the appropriation bills will have been considered, although not exhaustively, in the Commons and its committees during the course of the session, in accordance with the procedure explained here. The debate at the second reading of a borrowing authority bill is limited to two days.

The fiscal year runs from April 1 to March 31 of the next year and therefore does not correspond with the dates of a parliamentary session, which can be of variable length. Usually one budget is presented to Parliament each year, but on occasion two have been brought down within the space of a year. There is no fixed date for presentation of the budget, although it is usual to present it in February since the main estimates of expenditure must be presented no later than March 1. The budget speech of the minister of finance broadly reviews the economic situation and the measures the government proposes to raise the revenues required. The minister then introduces any ways and means motions that may be required in light of taxation proposals.

Once presented, the main estimates are referred to the various subject-oriented committees that oversee the government departments for study within the allotted time frame (the estimates must be reported back to the House by May 31). The committees are empowered to summon the appropriate ministers and departmental officials as witnesses and to report their findings to the Commons, which may include recommendations to reduce, but not increase, the appropriations of the department concerned. Any committees failing to report by May 31 lose the opportunity to make a report at all, although the leader of the opposition may move to permit an extension to consider the estimates of a particular department or agency. The pressure of time, then, is undoubtedly one factor tending to limit Parliament's control of the purse.

While the committees are reviewing expenditure estimates, the business of supply is being addressed on the floor of the Commons itself. For this purpose the fiscal year is divided into three supply periods or "semesters," ending respectively on June 23, December 10, and March 26. During this period twenty "supply days" or "allotted days" are set aside on which the official opposition and the third largest recognized party may raise for debate any matter falling within the jurisdiction of the government. The standing orders provide that interim supply, usually one-quarter of the total amount of the main estimates, must be put to a vote in the Commons no later than March 26 since the government requires the money to finance its operations pending the final adoption of the main estimates by June 23. The adoption by the Commons of the interim supply motion is followed by the introduction and adoption of an appropriations bill. Adoption of interim supply does not imply approval of the various proposals contained in the estimates as a whole.

No more than eight of the twenty allotted days may be used to debate votable motions (known as "non-confidence" motions), which, if carried, would force resignation of the government. These allotted days, together with the opportunity given to committees to study the estimates in some detail, respect the time-honored principle, enshrined in British parliamentary tradition, of the right of the Commons to address their grievances before granting supply. While the opposition parties are free to select departmental estimates, or the reports received from the committees, as the subjects for debate on allotted days, the tendency has been to move motions that raise specific issues on which the government is vulnerable to criticism and that reflect the priorities of the opposition parties.

Given the pressures of parliamentary time, the opportunities available for parliamentary scrutiny of proposed government expenditure probably are as extensive as could reasonably be expected. A government with a parliamentary majority, however, is assured of carrying its budget and its estimates through the House of Commons, and because of the deadlines enshrined in the standing orders it will not be embarrassed by delays. Before the procedural reforms of the 1960s there were no deadlines, and the opposition parties were able to hold the government ransom by threatening to prolong debate. Reforms implemented in subsequent years greatly strengthened the government's control of the business of the Commons.

Parliamentary oversight of public expenditure does not cease with the final approval of the estimates. Through its Standing Committee on Public Accounts, the House of Commons also oversees the actual expenditures, ensuring that monies have been spent according to the appropriations approved and that examples of waste or improper use of funds are highlighted in the committee's reports. The Public Accounts Committee, which always is chaired by a member of the official opposition, is assisted in this task by the auditor general, who publishes an annual report that reviews the public accounts and who works with the committee as its adviser. He or she also may issue additional reports in the course of the year. The committee is authorized to summon senior departmental officials as witnesses to account for their administration of the funds entrusted to them. The auditor general, although appointed by the government, is an officer of the House of Commons and only can be removed by the adoption of a joint resolution of both houses of Parliament. The auditor general's report always generates great public interest and is given wide coverage in the press.

QUESTION PERIOD

As an exercise in public accountability, the daily question period is a feature of particular importance in the procedure of the Canadian House of Commons. The rules of the Senate also provide for a question period.

The rules of both houses recognize two kinds of questions: the written question, of which notice is required and which appears on the order paper, and the oral question, which is asked in the Commons without notice. Members genuinely seeking information use written questions, and in the House of Commons they can request a reply within forty-five days. The oral question period, which the House of Commons runs every day for forty-five minutes, is in reality a period of confrontation between the government and the opposition parties and is the only part of the parliamentary day when a full attendance of members can be expected in the chamber itself, except when a vote is taking place.

The majority of the cabinet ministers, including the prime minister, usually are present for the question period.

In theory all members have an equal right to ask questions of government ministers, but the main opposition parties enjoy priority during the question period, and the speaker recognizes very few government members and only occasionally a member from a party with fewer than twelve members. The questioning of ministers is aimed at exposing government weaknesses, attacking their most controversial policies, probing possible scandals, and generally embarrassing ministers to the extent possible. Ministers for their part will justify their actions and policies, reject the assertions of the questioners, and seize any opportunities to ridicule their opponents.

By convention the leader of the opposition, or someone designated by the leader, is entitled to the first question followed by two supplementaries. He or she is followed by another member of the official opposition, who asks one question and one supplementary, and then by the leader of the third party, whose question also is followed by two supplementaries. The speaker then alternates between the two main opposition parties and occasionally recognizes a member of the government party and perhaps a member of one of the smaller minorities.

The fundamental rule underlying question period is that questions must deal with matters falling under ministerial responsibility. In theory, oral questions must deal with matters of urgency; should be designed only to elicit information; should not be argumentative or preceded by preambles or expressions of opinion; should not repeat questions already asked; should not be based on hearsay or on newspaper reports; and should not anticipate orders of the day. But if all these rules were applied, the question period would be far less exciting.

One of the speaker's most important duties is controlling the question period so that the exchanges do not exceed the bounds of decorum. Ministers cannot be forced to answer questions, and the ministers replying do not necessarily have to be those to whom the questions are addressed. Points of order and questions of privilege must not be raised during the question period to ensure there is no encroachment on the allotted forty-five minutes.

The fifteen minutes preceding the question period are devoted to "members' statements" on local, national, or international affairs—the only restriction: no personal attacks.

DISSOLUTION OF PARLIAMENT

The constitution provides that every House of Commons shall continue for not more than five years from the day of the return of the writs following a general election. Parliament may, of course, be dissolved sooner and usually is. The composition of the Senate is not affected by a dissolution of Parliament, although it cannot meet until a new Parliament is summoned.

The dissolution of Parliament, while constitutionally a royal prerogative exercised by the governor general, is normally a power only exercised on the advice of the prime minister. In normal circumstances the prime minister will decide the timing of a dissolution—a time usually favorable to the prospects of the government and the prime minister's party. The resignation of a government could be forced if it suffered a defeat on an issue of confidence, such as the rejection of its budget, but this is only likely to happen in circumstances of minority government. Even the question of what constitutes an issue of confidence is not entirely clear cut, as the prime minister is entitled to make this determination in situations that leave room for doubt. The power of dissolution is therefore a significant weapon in the prime minister's political arsenal, and a way of keeping his or her own followers in line, among other things. Calls are often heard, when parliamentary reform is discussed, for more independence for backbenchers and a relaxation of party discipline to allow for more free votes. Such proposals, regardless of the lip service often paid to them during election campaigns, are not very realistic in the context of the parliamentary system as practiced in Canada. No prime minister is likely to smile on any reform that would make a difficult task even more difficult. And in any case members are free to take an independent line if they are prepared to accept the political risks.

THE PARLIAMENT BUILDINGS

Parliament Hill is the focal point of the city of Ottawa, the federal capital of Canada. Ottawa is situated in the province of Ontario, just at the Quebec-Ontario border. The site is said to have been chosen by Queen Victoria during the period when the two provinces were united as the Province of Canada. The Parliament buildings consist of the Centre Block, which houses the chambers of the Senate and the House of Commons; the East Block; and the West Block. In recent years a number of major buildings in the immediate vicinity have been taken over to provide office space for members and their staffs.

Construction of the three buildings began in 1859, and on June 8, 1866, the last session of the Parliament of the Province of Canada was convened in the Centre Block. The first Parliament of the federation of Canada met there for its first session on November 6, 1867.

The Senate chamber and furnishings are distinguished by the color red, those of the House of Commons by the color green. This follows the tradition of the British Parliament, where the same colors are associated with the House of Lords and House of Commons, respectively. Each chamber also has its own distinctive decor.

Because the official languages of Canada at the federal level are English and French, simultaneous translation is provided in both chambers for members and the visitors seated in the various galleries. The proceedings of the House of Commons have been broadcast live by radio and television since 1977. Committee proceedings are broadcast on a selective basis.

THE LIBRARY OF PARLIAMENT

The Library of Parliament, circular in form, is one of the showpieces of Parliament Hill. It is a striking example of gothic architecture, the interior adorned with magnificent carved wooden panels and a marble statue of the young Queen Victoria in the center facing the main entrance. Within "the ring," as it is known, librarians and other staff members sit ready to deal with the immediate inquiries of parliamentarians.

The library is equipped with the most modern technology, including a computerized catalogue and access to many databases. It provides a wide range of services to parliamentarians, and its professional staff includes, in addition to librarians, research officers representing disciplines such as law, economics, sociology, political science, and the natural sciences. Press clipping and various documentation services are provided, and everything from immediate responses to straightforward inquiries to detailed research studies are available to individual parliamentarians, parliamentary committees, and parliamentary delegations.

Philip Laundy

BIBLIOGRAPHY

Beauchesne, Arthur. *Beauchesne's Rules and Forms of the House of Commons of Canada, with Annotations, Comments and Precedents.* 6th ed. Edited by Alistair Fraser, W. F. Dawson, and John Holtby. Toronto: Carswell, 1989.

Dawson, R. M. *The Government of Canada.* 7th ed. Edited by Norman Ward. Toronto: University of Toronto Press, 1987.

Franks, C. E. S. *The Parliament of Canada.* Toronto: University of Toronto Press, 1987.

Fraser, John A. *The House of Commons at Work.* Montreal: Les Editions de la Chenelière, 1993.

Laundy, Philip. *The Office of Speaker in the Parliaments of the Commonwealth.* London: Quiller Press, 1984.

Mackay, R. A. *The Unreformed Senate of Canada.* Toronto: University of Toronto Press, 1963.

Maingot, Joseph. *Parliamentary Privilege in Canada.* Toronto: Butterworths, 1982.

Mallory, J. R. *The Structure of Canadian Government.* Agincourt, Ont.: Gage Publishing, 1984.

Stewart, John B. *The Canadian House of Commons: Procedure and Reform.* Montreal: McGill-Queens University Press, 1977.

White, Randall. *The Voice of Region: The Long Journey to Senate Reform in Canada.* Toronto: Dundurn Press, 1990.

CAPE VERDE

OFFICIAL NAME: Republic of Cape Verde (República de Cabo Verde)
CAPITAL: Praia
POPULATION: 449,000 (1996 est.)
DATE OF INDEPENDENCE: July 5, 1975 (from Portugal)
DATE OF CURRENT CONSTITUTION: Adopted September 25, 1992
FORM OF GOVERNMENT: Transitional democracy
LANGUAGES: Portuguese, Crioulo
MONETARY UNIT: Cape Verde escudo
FISCAL YEAR: Calendar year
LEGISLATURE: National People's Assembly (Assembléia Nacional Popular)
NUMBER OF CHAMBERS: One
NUMBER OF MEMBERS: 72
PERCENTAGE OF WOMEN: 11.1
TERM OF LEGISLATURE: Five years
MOST RECENT LEGISLATIVE ELECTION: December 17, 1995
MINIMUM AGE FOR VOTING: 18
MINIMUM AGE FOR MEMBERSHIP: 18
SUFFRAGE: Universal and direct
VOTING: Optional
ADDRESS: Assembléia Nacional Popular, Caixa Postal No 20-A, Achada de Santo Antonio, Praia
TELEPHONE: (238) 61 55 10
FAX: (238) 61 43 30

The Cape Verde Islands are situated in the Atlantic Ocean off the northwest coast of Africa *(see map, p. 447).* The islands were under Portuguese control from the fifteenth century until 1975, when full independence followed a brief period of transitional government. The Second Republic of Cape Verde came into being on September 25, 1992, with the promulgation of a new constitution that ushered in, for the first time in the country's history, a democratic form of government. The constitution vested substantial legislative powers in the unicameral parliament, the

National People's Assembly, and strengthened its role with regard to the president.

The National People's Assembly holds two sessions a year, each lasting an average of thirty days. Members receive no salary but receive some compensation for lost income, as well as free postage, medical benefits, and subsidized lodging and meals. The Assembly has a permanent bureau that directs political affairs and sets the legislative agenda.

Members speak from the main rostrum during debates. The ballot is by show of hands, and the quorum is an absolute majority. The proceedings of the National People's Assembly are recorded in the *Acta das Sessoes.* Much of the legislative work is done in standing and ad hoc committees. Among the standing committees, the most important is the Committee on Legal and Constitutional Affairs, which considers the constitutionality of laws. Committees may summon public officials.

The prime minister is responsible to the Assembly, and the Council of Ministers comprises Assembly members. The president may, under certain circumstances, dissolve the Assembly.

In each of the sixteen constituencies, a minimum of two members are elected, with additional members apportioned according to population. In December 1995 five parties fielded candidates. Winners were determined by the d'Hondt system of proportional representation. The Movement for Democracy won a decisive majority of fifty seats; the African Party for the Independence of Cape Verde, which had ruled until 1991, remained the principal opposition party, with twenty-one seats.

George Thomas Kurian

CENTRAL AFRICAN REPUBLIC

OFFICIAL NAME: Central African Republic (République Centrafricaine)
CAPITAL: Bangui
POPULATION: 3,274,000 (1996 est.)
DATE OF INDEPENDENCE: August 13, 1960 (from France)
DATE OF CURRENT CONSTITUTION: Adopted January 7, 1995
FORM OF GOVERNMENT: Transitional democracy
LANGUAGES: French (official), Sango, Arabic, Hunsa, Swahili
MONETARY UNIT: CFA franc
FISCAL YEAR: Calendar year
LEGISLATURE: National Assembly (Assemblée Nationale)
NUMBER OF CHAMBERS: One
NUMBER OF MEMBERS: 85
PERCENTAGE OF WOMEN: 3.5
TERM OF LEGISLATURE: Five years
MOST RECENT LEGISLATIVE ELECTION: August 22 and September 19, 1993
MINIMUM AGE FOR VOTING: 18
MINIMUM AGE FOR MEMBERSHIP: 25
SUFFRAGE: Universal and direct
VOTING: Optional
ADDRESS: Assemblée Nationale, B.P. 1003, Bangui
TELEPHONE: (236) 61 54 02
FAX: (236) 61 55 60

Land-locked and isolated in almost the geographic center of Africa *(see map, p. 261)*, the Central African Republic is a new democracy in which the National Assembly is striving to establish itself as a competent partner of the executive in governing the country effectively. The first thirty-three years of the country's independence were beset by single-party authoritarianism, military rule, and the peculiar despotism of the self-proclaimed emperor Bokassa. But from the competitive and fair elections of 1993 emerged a National Assembly composed of several parties, which have established the foundation for a pluralist political order.

POLITICAL BACKGROUND

Known as Ubangi-Chari while a territory within French Equatorial Africa, the Central African Republic gained self-governance in 1958 under the leadership of Barthélemy Boganda, founder of the Social Evolution Movement of Black Africa. After Boganda's death in March 1959 his nephew, David Dacko, replaced him as the country's leader, first as prime minister and then as president when the Central African Republic won independence from France on August 13, 1960. Two years later Dacko imposed a one-party system. On January 1, 1966, the president was overthrown by a military coup staged by his cousin, Col. Jean Bédel Bokassa. After a decade as head of state, Bokassa declared himself emperor on December 4, 1976. The "imperial constitution" Bokassa promulgated anticipated the creation of a national assembly, but no elections were ever organized.

In September 1979, with French military assistance, Bokassa was deposed and replaced by former president Dacko, who later agreed to hold elections on March 15, 1981. The official results of the elections gave Dacko 50 percent of the vote against chief rival Ange-Félix Patassé, who received 38 percent. Opposition parties denounced the election, claiming that the results were rigged; in the days that followed, violence and civil unrest erupted in the capital. No parliamentary elections were held.

Gen. André-Dieudonné Kolingba took advantage of the political breakdown to stage a military coup in September and overthrow President Dacko. Kolingba ruled for the remainder of the 1980s despite several coup attempts and recurring underground efforts to organize political alternatives to the regime. The constitution promulgated in 1986 provided for a single political party, a strong presidency, and an advisory role for a National Assembly. In February 1987 the Central African Democratic Assembly (RDC) was created as Kolingba's ruling party, and in the elections of July 1987 all 142 candidates for the fifty-two seats in the National Assembly were members of the RDC.

Gen. Kolingba's government, like many others in the region, came under popular pressure in 1990 and 1991 to adopt a more open political system. The resurgence of a vocal and persistent political opposition after a decade of suppression led to the convening in August 1992 of the Grand National Debate, a version of the national conferences held in other African countries. By the end of the month, the National Assembly had enacted the constitutional amendments and electoral code that had emerged from the conclave. The formal political structure put in place strongly resembled the semipresidential, semiparliamentary structures of France's Fifth Republic.

ELECTIONS OF 1993 AND THEIR AFTERMATH

After a failed attempt to conduct elections in October 1992 (the failure stemming from lack of proper preparation at several levels), pressure from opposition political parties and donor countries helped to put the democratic process back on track. Eventually, elections were held in August and September 1993 following further delays in preparations and changes in the government and other administrative structures.

In the presidential balloting of August 22, none of the eight candidates obtained an absolute majority, and a second round was scheduled for September 19 between the two leading vote-getters: Ange-Félix Patassé and Abel Goumba, who qualified for the runoff with 37.3 percent and 21.7 percent of the vote, respectively. Patassé won the runoff with 52 percent of the vote. When Gen. Kolingba received just 12 percent of the vote in the first round, he tried to annul the results through a presidential decree that altered the makeup of the supreme court. But bowing to pressure by France and other countries, Kolingba relented, and Patassé was sworn in as president on October 22, 1993, for a six-year term.

In the legislative elections, also held in two rounds, on August 22 and September 19, 1993, the Movement for the Liberation of the Central African People (MLPC), the party of President Patassé, won thirty-three of the eighty-five seats. It constituted the nucleus of the parliamentary majority. Allied with the MLPC were three smaller parties: the Movement for Democracy and Development, formed after the elections by five independent followers of former president David Dacko; the Liberal Democratic Party, with seven seats; and the Alliance for Democracy and Progress, with six seats. The Social Democratic Party and National Convention each won three seats and then fused to qualify as a parliamentary group. The parliamentary opposition consisted of the party of former president Kolingba, the Central African Democratic Rally, with fourteen seats, and the Patriotic Front for Progress, led by Goumba, with seven seats. The remaining seats were divided among four minor parties and independents.

President Patassé appointed Jean-Luc Mandaba of the MLPC as prime minister in a broad-based cabinet composed of seventeen ministers and two secretaries of state. Mandaba, however, was ousted in April 1995 when the National Assembly voted no confidence in the government, alleging corruption and maladministration. Mandaba was replaced by Gabriel Koyambounou, who in turn was replaced by Jean-Paul Ngoupande in June 1996 in the wake of an unsuccessful army coup that was put down with the aid of French troops.

Unrest in the military continued to ferment, however. It derived in part from lack of regular pay, growing popular disaffection with the Patassé administration, and tribal rivalries. Patassé, of the northern Baya tribe, was unpopular with military factions from the southern Yakoma tribe, who supported General Kolingba, himself a Yakoma. Following a ten-week-long army mutiny and related tribal violence, Patassé, the rebel army faction, and Patassé's political opponents signed an agreement January 25, 1997, calling for the restoration of democracy and constitutional government.

ORGANIZATION AND OPERATION OF THE NATIONAL ASSEMBLY

The National Assembly meets a few kilometers from the center of the capital, Bangui, in a building constructed by North Koreans during the era of the one-party state in the Central African Republic. The plenary hall is organized as a vast auditorium with galleries. A half dozen smaller rooms suitable for committee meetings are available; offices are provided only for the members of the Bureau.

The constitution (as amended in August 1993) provides for a unicameral, eighty-five-member National Assembly, elected in single-member constituencies on the basis of a two-round majority system. If no candidate receives more than 50 percent of the vote in the first round, then every candidate with more than 10 percent of the vote qualifies for the second round. The candidate with a plurality in the runoff wins the seat. In 1993 the second round coincided with the presidential runoff. Citizens eighteen years and older may vote.

Assembly members are elected for five-year terms unless the Assembly is dissolved earlier by the president. The constitution also provides for an Economic and Regional Council, which acts as an advisory body to the National Assembly on economic, social, cultural, and developmental issues referred by the president. Half its members are appointed by the president; the other half are elected by the National Assembly. Members of the Council serve for a six-year term.

The Assembly is led by a committee of eleven deputies, known as the Bureau, elected by secret ballot from among the elected deputies. It is composed of a president, three vice presidents, two secretaries, a treasurer, and four members. The Bureau is the legislature's liaison with the other branches of government. It meets every Friday to settle the next week's schedule.

Seven permanent committees serve the National Assembly: Foreign Affairs; Defense; Administrative and Interior; Economy, Finance, and Planning; Education; Social Affairs; and Natural Resources and the Environment. Each committee has between seven and fifteen members and can meet only if over half its members are present. Committee meetings are closed to the public.

The Assembly's rules of procedure call for open plenary sessions, recorded votes, and publication of the minutes of plenary sessions. In reality, however, none of these standards were consistently upheld in the first eighteen months the Assembly met. In theory, drafts of legislation, amendments, and committee reports are available to the public through the Assembly's protocol office. In late 1994, however, leaders of civic organizations and journalists complained that requests for such documents were not consistently being met. Moreover, the Bureau occasionally decides to bar the public from controversial plenary sessions.

The general practice of the Assembly is to announce and publish only the final tally of votes taken in plenum. The president of the National Assembly can call for a roll-call vote in which each deputy's vote is recorded, but this rarely has been done.

The Assembly's rules of procedure require that all proceedings be recorded by a stenographer and that the minutes of a preceding session be read at the beginning of the next session. Although the Assembly has two stenographers on staff, their notes have not regularly been transcribed.

PARLIAMENTARY RELATIONS WITH THE EXECUTIVE

As it currently operates, the National Assembly is a reactive body whose schedule and agenda are largely determined by the executive branch. Although the constitution allows bills to be introduced by deputies or the government, almost every bill considered by the Assembly has been proposed by the executive branch rather than by legislators.

Assembly deputies often claim that they must rely on the government to initiate bills because they lack the necessary technical expertise and the resources to hire staff. Resources available in the Assembly's library are extremely limited. Although deputies in other countries have attempted to overcome similar problems by soliciting the advice of experts at local universities or by hiring university students as interns, deputies in the Central African Republic have been slow to embrace these approaches.

Ministers and other executive branch officials are questioned by deputies during weekly plenary sessions, coordinated by the Bureau working closely with the minister in charge of parliamentary affairs. Procedures for parliamentary questioning have not been formalized, although the Bureau has agreed to submit in advance to government ministers all questions to be asked. The weekly questioning of ministers is broadcast live on local radio. Since many voters do not speak French, this session often is held primarily in Sango, the predominant local language.

Thomas O. Melia and Sheldon Yett

CEYLON

See Sri Lanka

CHAD

OFFICIAL NAME: Republic of Chad (République du Tchad)
CAPITAL: N'Djamena
POPULATION: 6,977,000 (1996 est.)
DATE OF INDEPENDENCE: August 11, 1960 (from France)
DATE OF CURRENT CONSTITUTION: Approved March 31, 1996
FORM OF GOVERNMENT: Transitional democracy
LANGUAGES: French (official), Arabic (official), Sara, Sango, more than one hundred other languages and dialects
MONETARY UNIT: CFA franc
FISCAL YEAR: Calendar year
LEGISLATURE: National Assembly (Assemblée Nationale)
NUMBER OF CHAMBERS: One
NUMBER OF MEMBERS: 125
PERCENTAGE OF WOMEN: —
TERM OF LEGISLATURE: Four years
MINIMUM AGE FOR VOTING: 18
MINIMUM AGE FOR MEMBERSHIP: 25
MOST RECENT LEGISLATIVE ELECTION: January 5 and February 23, 1997
SUFFRAGE: Universal and direct
VOTING: Optional
ADDRESS: Assemblée Nationale, Palais du 15 Janvier, B. P. 1, N'Djamena
TELEPHONE: (235) 51 48 14
FAX: —

The Republic of Chad is a landlocked country in central Africa *(see map, p. 261)*, once part of France's colonial French Equatorial Africa. Soon after gaining independence in 1960, Chad became a one-party state. Since independence the country's troubled and frequently violent political history has precluded an effective or functioning legislature.

Between independence in 1960 and a coup in 1975 that led to a military regime, Chad had a unicameral National Assembly composed of 105 deputies elected for five-year terms from a single slate of candidates drawn up by the ruling party. The speaker of the National Assembly was second in importance only to the president of the republic. The chamber was subdivided into ten commissions. The National Assembly met twice a year, in April and October, for sessions of forty-five days each, with one session devoted to the budget. Members of the legislature served as deputies at large and enjoyed full immunity from arrest or prosecution. The president could address the National Assembly at any time and deliver a state of the nation message at the opening of the first session each year. For the first nine years, the country lacked both a printing press and an official gazette, and no permanent records were maintained of the laws passed by the Assembly.

Although the 1962 constitution mandated a strong presidency, the National Assembly had countervailing powers including the right to override presidential vetoes with a two-thirds majority and to pass a motion of censure or a vote of no confidence against the government. The president could dissolve parliament except during the last six months of his term of office. Emergency ordinances proclaimed by the president between sessions had to be submitted to the next session of parliament.

The normative powers and procedures of the Assembly, however, masked an unstable political system. Ethnic conflicts compounded by religious, regional, economic, and political differences contributed to an insurgency movement in the north of the country in the mid-1960s. These antigovernment forces, united under the banner of the Chad National Liberation Front (Frolinat), continued to battle the central government after the 1975 military coup.

Frolinat military successes forced the military government to accept a coalition governing arrangement in 1979. But Frolinat splintered. One faction, the Armed Forces of the North (FAN), headed by Hissein Habré, resumed battle with the coalition government. FAN overthrew the regime in June 1982 and instituted a one-party system. A new constitution was adopted by referendum in December 1989, and elections to a new National Assembly were held in June 1990. Six months later, on December 3, Habré was overthrown by a splinter group of FAN, and the new regime of Idriss Déby suspended the constitution and in early 1991 put forth an interim national charter. At that point, the country had been without a parliament for more than a decade.

The Déby government oversaw the adoption of the current constitution on March 31, 1996. Déby was elected president on July 3, 1996, and legislative elections were held in two rounds on January 5 and February 23, 1997. More than six hundred candidates representing thirty parties contested the elections; ten parties won seats, with the Patriotic Salvation Movement of President Déby winning a slim majority of sixty-three seats. Twenty-five members of the 125-member National Assembly are elected in single-member constituencies on an absolute majority vote, and one hundred are elected on the basis of party list voting in thirty-four multimember constituencies.

George Thomas Kurian

CHILE

OFFICIAL NAME: Republic of Chile (República de Chile)
CAPITAL: Santiago
POPULATION: 14,333,000 (1996 est.)
DATE OF INDEPENDENCE: September 18, 1810 (from Spain)
DATE OF CURRENT CONSTITUTION: Adopted September 11, 1980; effective March 11, 1981
FORM OF GOVERNMENT: Parliamentary democracy
LANGUAGE: Spanish
MONETARY UNIT: Chilean peso
FISCAL YEAR: Calendar year
LEGISLATURE: National Congress (Congreso Nacional)
NUMBER OF CHAMBERS: Two. Chamber of Deputies (Cámara de Diputados); Senate (Senado)
NUMBER OF MEMBERS: Chamber of Deputies, 120 (directly elected); Senate, 47 (38 directly elected, 9 appointed)
PERCENTAGE OF WOMEN: Chamber of Deputies, 7.5; Senate, 6.5
TERM OF LEGISLATURE: Chamber of Deputies, four years; Senate, eight years (one-half of members elected every four years)
MOST RECENT LEGISLATIVE ELECTION: December 11, 1993
MINIMUM AGE FOR VOTING: 18
MINIMUM AGE FOR MEMBERSHIP: Chamber of Deputies, 21; Senate, 40
SUFFRAGE: Universal
VOTING: Compulsory
ADDRESS: Chamber of Deputies, Valparaiso; Senate, Abda Pedro Montt, Valparaiso
TELEPHONE: Chamber of Deputies, (56 32) 697 00 22; Senate, (56 32) 697 07 40
FAX: Chamber of Deputies, (56 32) 23 26 51; Senate, (56 32) 23 05 31

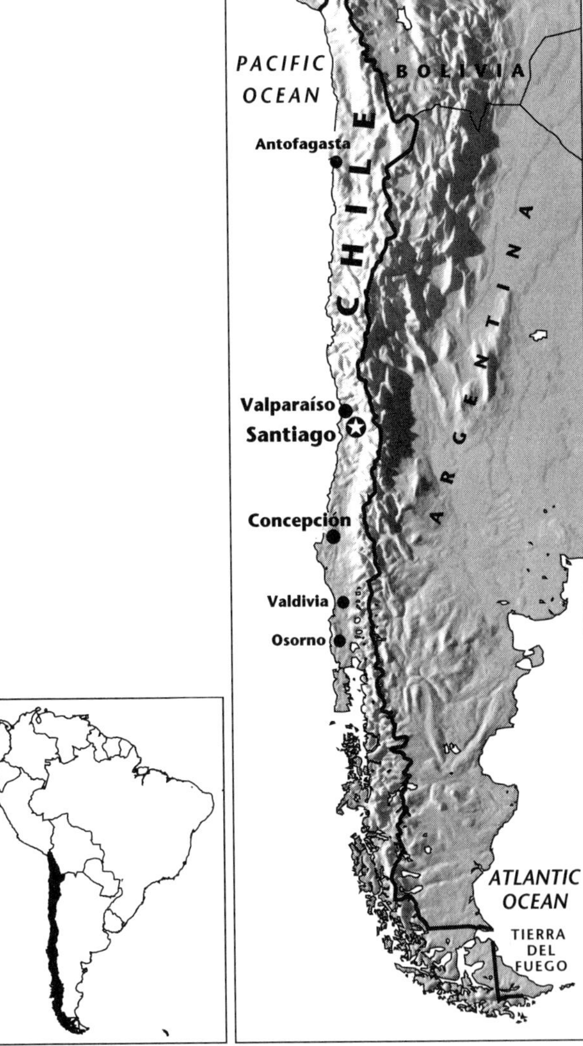

Occupying the southern half of the western littoral of the continent of South America, the Republic of Chile emerged in 1990 from more than seventeen years of dictatorship under Gen. Augusto Pinochet Ugarte. During that period, Chile's economy recovered from earlier disruptions, but the National Congress remained dissolved. Today, the bicameral legislature functions as one of three branches in Chile's presidential system of government.

HISTORICAL BACKGROUND

Notwithstanding its restricted ability to initiate legislation, Chile's National Congress stands as a symbol of democratic governance. After witnessing the collapse of representative institutions in 1973, today's parliamentarians recognize their responsibility to build and maintain respect for democratic process. The forty-eighth Congress convened on March 11, 1990, after a lapse of nearly seventeen years. Shouldering their leadership role in the "democratic transition," they left behind years of military rule for a new era of "redemocratization" under the constitution of 1980.

On September 21, 1973, the military dissolved Congress after assuming constitutional, executive, and legislative powers. The ensuing military years (1973–1990) had two legislative phases. The first began with the coup and the formation of a governing junta. That phase lasted until March 11, 1981, when the constitution of 1980 went into effect. During these years legislation took the form of "decree laws" written by the junta's legislative committees.

After 1981, with the same legislative committees in operation, the junta claimed a constitutional basis for its rule, and laws were no longer implemented as decrees. In a plebiscite held on October 5, 1988, the Chilean people denied President Pinochet an eight-year term under the new constitution. General elections were held in 1989, and on March 11, 1990, the forty-eighth Congress convened in the course of the inauguration of the democratically elected president.

To its supporters, the 1980 constitution corrected the "excesses" of the multiparty political system that had culminated in the 1973 crisis by establishing presidential control over a legitimate legislative process and providing constitutional protection for political minorities. To its critics, these same "protections," taken together with the strong presidential constitution, meant that restoration of the country's representative democratic tradition was less than complete.

Chile's democratic tradition is rooted in a long history of legislative evolution from the initial unicameral body of 1811 through formation of a bicameral institution after 1822 and the consolidation of the Chamber of Deputies and Senate in the constitution of 1833. Since 1833 Congress has provided a forum for public debate of the day's issues.

On three occasions impasse in these debates led to national crisis. In 1891 a fight with the executive arose over congressional budgetary authority and economic policy. Facing congressional intransigence, President José Manuel Balmaceda threatened to rule by decree. Congress responded by refusing to approve the 1891 budget, and Balmaceda ordered Congress closed. Congressional forces won the ensuing civil war, and Balmaceda committed suicide. The next thirty years of congressional dominance are often referred to as the Parliamentary Republic.

A second legislative crisis emerged in 1924 when Congress resisted the progressive legislative agenda of President Arturo Alessandri. Congress finally enacted Alessandri's legislation under threats of military action. Alessandri then resigned, believing his independence had been compromised. One important outcome of the period was the constitution of 1925, which restored the presidential system of government and established a system of proportional representation for both legislative houses.

In 1973 the country divided over the policies of President Salvador Allende, a Marxist. Congress and Allende could neither cooperate nor maintain a working relationship. Agreements between the political parties gave way as an energized minority pushed to "build socialism" with or without the collaboration of Congress. With the economy in shambles, the armed forces assumed power. Led by General Pinochet, the military, using surprising levels of force, restored civil order to the country and began reforming the country's economic and political institutions, including Congress. During the years of authoritarian government the state sector of the economy shrank as market-oriented institutions took on a new vigor. Meanwhile, the military replaced political parties as the broker for conflicting interests.

The memory of 1973 continues to haunt Chilean legislative life. Believing that the country foundered on fragmented ideological politics, the conservative authors of the constitution of 1980 built in features to ensure that in the future leftist policy initiatives would be tempered by legislative checks. Today, the ideological level of Chile's political parties is far lower than in 1973, and compromise is no longer a repulsive concept. With its two broad coalitions encompassing five major political parties, Congress once again serves as the nation's forum, where consensus over the country's future is built.

COMPOSITION OF CONGRESS AND ELECTIONS

The Chamber of Deputies consists of 120 members elected by direct vote for a four-year term. Candidates must be citizens, at least twenty-one years of age, high-school graduates, and residents of their electoral district for at least two years. To establish residence in a provincial district, it is common for politicians in Santiago to claim residence at a summer home or the home of a friend.

The country is divided into sixty congressional districts, with two deputies elected from each district through a "binomial majority" system. Candidates appear on the ballot grouped in lists of two by party or by coalition list. Voters cast a vote for one of the names on a list. For both candidates on a list to win, they must have, together, twice the votes of the next highest list. Failing that, the top candidates from the top two lists win. Not uncommonly, the number-two candidate on the most popular list receives more votes than the winning candidate on the second most popular list.

On one hand the electoral system is criticized as being disadvantageous to small parties while exaggerating the representation of large parties (but not majority parties). On the other hand that is exactly what its designers had in mind. The goal of the electoral system is to push the country toward a system of two coalitions, and perhaps someday two major political parties.

The Senate has thirty-eight members elected for eight-year terms, plus nine designated, or appointed, senators. Ex-presidents who served at least six years continuously become senators for life. Two elected senators represent each of nineteen senatorial districts that follow the lines of the country's numbered regions, one to thirteen north to south, with six regions, including the metropolitan region, divided into two electoral districts.

The issue of a Senate based on regions and not population is an old one in Chile. The current regional representation reverses the popular basis found in the constitution of 1925. To obtain staggered senatorial terms candidates from uneven districts were elected for just four years in the 1989 election, while those from even districts and the metropolitan Santiago region stood for full eight-year terms. Senators are elected by the same binomial majority system as deputies. The eligibility requirements are the same as for deputies except for age, which is forty years.

The center-left Coalition of Parties for Democracy, made up of five parties, held seventy seats in the forty-ninth Congress (1994–1998), against forty-six seats held by the center-right Union for Progress in Chile (plus four center-right independents). The largest single parties are the Christian Democrats on the center-left, with thirty-seven seats, and the rightist National Renewal Party, with twenty-nine seats. The same two parties are dominant in the Senate, where the smaller parties are less well represented than they are in the Chamber of Deputies. The Communist Party holds no seats in the legislature.

Congressional elections fall under the 1987 law on political parties, which was modified in 1989 after the experience of the 1988 plebiscite and general elections. The law requires that if in any given election a political party falls below 5 percent of the national vote it loses its recognition as a party eligible to field candidates in elections. Once recognition is lost, the party must go through a petitioning process to regain its legal status. In the December 1993 election the once powerful Radical Party and the newer Social Democrat Party fell below 5 percent. On August 6, 1994, they merged to form the Radical Social Democratic Party.

Congressional salaries are tied to those of ministers of state. In 1994 salaries were approximately $10,000 per month, plus staff allowances.

THE NATIONAL CONGRESS AND THE CONSTITUTION OF 1980

In 1978 General Pinochet created a group of distinguished citizens, including former president Jorge Alessandri, to propose and implement a political plan to change the country's institutional structure. The resulting document outlined a path for return to democracy. It was approved in a 1980 plebiscite.

The 1980 constitution reinforced the Chilean tradition of strong presidential governance but went farther than any previous document by confining Congress to an overtly passive role. The president became, in effect, the dominant legislator. The executive controls the legislative agenda, drafts most bills, and has absolute control over taxing and spending. Congress is restricted to introducing legislation having no direct spending implications.

The new constitution established a process of slow redemocratization—a "protected democracy"—by including a number of measures intended to limit the ability of any governing majority to stray too far from the course set for the country in the 1980s. The principal measure was the introduction of appointed senators, also known as "institutional senators." The intention is to make any constitutional reform impossible without the agreement of the appointed senators and of conservatives in the Senate. The constitution's authors expected these nonelected senators to check the legislative majority, thereby ensuring protection of pluralism and individual liberty. Institutional senators are appointed by the president, the Supreme Court, or the National Security Council from among qualified former presidents, former members of the Supreme Court, former university presidents, and other former government officials, including military and police leaders.

In addition to appointed senators, the constitution establishes other limits on Congress. The most noteworthy are the Constitutional Tribunal and the requirement that certain laws related to the political rules of the country pass by supermajorities ranging from four-sevenths to three-fifths of the members of both houses. The seven-member tribunal exists to adjudicate conflicts between the legislative and executive branches and to judge the constitutionality of laws prior to their promulgation. There is no appeal of tribunal decisions.

Critics among the governing coalition view these "counterweights" as antidemocratic devices designed to prolong the transition to full democracy. The center-left political parties argue that Chile will become fully democratic only when they are removed. To their supporters, who have been in the opposition since 1990, the counterweights guarantee a political balance in the country and ensure that the radical policies of the early 1970s will not return.

The 1980 constitution assigns two exclusive powers to the lower house: legislative oversight and the authority to decide whether impeachment charges made against top governmental authorities have merit. The Senate has exclusive power to judge the substance of impeachment charges. The Senate also authorizes international travel by the president under some circumstances, reviews presidential resignations, and may declare the incapacity of the president or president-elect. Together the two houses have the power to approve or reject international treaties presented to them by the president and the responsibility to comment on executive declarations of a state of siege.

CHILE'S CONGRESS BY THE SEA

The post-1990 Congress works in modern quarters in the port city of Valparaiso. The congressional complex incorporates an advanced technological infrastructure and contains offices for all members of Congress. The building consists of 60,000 square meters of space and is divided into areas of administrative support and legislative work. The Chamber of Deputies occupies the east wing, and the Senate the west. The tower space between them is divided between the houses.

The move to Valparaiso was controversial. All acknowledge that a new structure was needed. The issue was, and still is, where. By the mid-twentieth century the old legislative palace in Santiago, built in 1857 and damaged by an earthquake in 1906, had insufficient space for Congress; deputies and senators had taken offices all over the city. The palace is neither structurally sound nor easily susceptible to modernization.

Supporters of the decision to put Congress two hours by car from Santiago cited the national goal of decentralization and "deconcentration" of the country. Detractors have claimed that the marginalization of Congress was given a spatial dimension by the move out of Santiago.

Most members of parliament maintain their families in Santiago. They travel back and forth weekly, and in some cases daily. Ministers called to testify before committees lose nearly the entire day in travel. Documents move slowly between the executive and legislative branches. At the same time the congressional leadership has resisted granting legal status to faxed documents and has rejected teleconferencing as a means to cut down on ministerial travel. From Congress's viewpoint, respect and deference come with original documents and face-to-face meetings. Perhaps the issue is not whether Congress will return to Santiago, but when.

The historical collection of the congressional library has remained in Santiago. The new building in Valparaiso contains facilities that support current legislative needs. In 1990 the World Bank and the European Union funded a major modernization project to complement the skeleton information system in the new Congress building, but the effort was initially delayed by discussion between the two houses and the library about where it should reside and who should "own" both the project and the resulting shared information system. The project, completed in 1996, left Congress with an excellent national and institutional network consisting of 1,160 connections in Valparaiso, 76 in the library, and 170 in legislators' district offices. The project included a powerful World Wide Web site.

SESSIONS

Elections were held in 1989 for the 1990–1994 legislature, and in 1993 for 1994–1998. Sessions of Congress are divided into ordinary and extraordinary terms. The ordinary session begins on May 21 and ends on September 18. The president may convene an extraordinary session during the last ten days of the ordinary session or anytime during the parliamentary recess from September 19 until May 20. In practice the president always calls an extraordinary session for the "recess" period. Since 1990 such sessions have been at least as long as the ordinary sessions and have generated more than twice as much legislation. The president sets the agenda for the extraordinary sessions. Serving as a member of Congress is now a full-time profession, and legislators scrutinize all bills.

The public is free to observe all deliberations, unless declared secret. Demonstrations, however, are totally prohibited. Both the Chamber of Deputies and the Senate do most of their work in committee.

Moving Congress to the coast seems to have solved one old problem—lack of a quorum in the Chamber of Deputies. The minimum number of deputies required for sitting and passing legislation is one-third. Attendance is a public issue that is given regular coverage in the press, and the law provides that a financial penalty is to be assessed on all absent deputies if a quorum is called and not met. (This has yet to happen under the new constitution.) From 1990 to 1994 average attendance in both houses reached 83.5 percent, as compared to 40.5 percent in 1973.

HOW LAWS ARE MADE

Bills are introduced either by presidential initiative or upon individual motions by members of Congress, with up to ten coauthors in the Chamber and five in the Senate. In the forty-eighth Congress (1990–1994), just 2 percent of successful legislation started with a parliamentary motion. Midway through the forty-ninth Congress that rate was much higher.

Legislators are severely restricted with respect to the areas in which they may initiate bills. The president has exclusive jurisdiction to originate bills related to altering the political and administrative structure of the country, as well as all budget and finance legislation. The budget-related restrictions are not new to the 1980 constitution, which merely closed loopholes that had allowed for a more active congressional budgetary role prior to 1973. All budget bills must be sent by the executive to the Chamber of Deputies, which serves as the "chamber of origin." Bills relating to amnesty and pardons must start in the Senate.

Once a bill is introduced it is assigned to a committee after a first reading. The committee prepares a general report leading to a second reading and a general discussion of the bill's ideas. At this time all or part of the bill may be accepted or rejected. If there are no concerns or amendments the bill is considered approved and goes to the other chamber. If objections are raised or amendments are proposed the bill goes back to committee for detailed review. The committee then prepares a second report and the bill returns to the full body. This step may be skipped with support of two-thirds of the members present. The report in any case takes the bill back for a third and final reading. Since 1990 the Chamber of Deputies has originated 75 percent of all bills, whether proposed by the executive or by individual members.

The president has the power to give priority to executive legislation. There are three levels of priority: simple (Congress has thirty days to finish work on the bill), *suma* (which reduces the time to ten days), and immediate (three days). The president can raise or lower the priority of legislation even after it has been introduced. Thus the president controls the legislative agenda, and congressional motions are often postponed from session to session.

The budget process has special characteristics. The executive must send the budget for the coming fiscal year (January 1 to December 31) to Congress by September 30. If not approved or rejected within sixty days, it stands as if approved in the form presented to Congress. Congress cannot raise or lower estimated revenues and cannot increase spending. It can only reject or lower specific spending items.

The legislative process leads to three possible results. First, a bill may be approved in its totality in the originating chamber and sent to the other house—the "revising chamber"—for debate. Second, a bill may be approved as amended and then move ahead as above. Third, a bill may be rejected in its totality in the originating chamber, in which case it does not go to the other house and cannot be reintroduced for a year. It is important to keep in mind the severe restrictions on revenue and spending bills, which generally cannot be amended.

In the revising chamber the same process is followed as in the originating chamber, and the bill may be approved, modified, or rejected. If the bill is modified, it is sent back to the originating chamber for further consideration. If it is then rejected, the bill goes to a joint committee for discussion. If the joint committee reaches a compromise, both chambers must vote on the resulting bill. In the absence of a compromise, the originating chamber may insist on its version if it has the votes of two-thirds of its members and the support of the president. Bills approved by both chambers are sent to the president for signature and promulgation in the official gazette.

In calculating the majority needed for approval, modification, or disapproval of a given piece of legislation, senators and deputies who are suspended through a judicial process or are out of the country with constitutional approval are not part of the count. There are several types of votes. Public votes may be by raised hands or by roll call. Roll-call votes must be requested in writing by government ministers or heads of committees before debate is finished, or they may be taken by agreement of the house through a show of hands. Bills dealing with salaries and compensation, including pensions and promotions, are voted on in secret.

Lobbying Congress has a very low priority for Chilean interest groups and associations. Because most legislation originates in the executive and votes follow party lines, pressure to initiate, alter, or stop specific legislation is largely focused on the executive in Santiago.

STAFF AND COMMITTEES

In the Chamber of Deputies each of the sixteen permanent committees consists of thirteen members. Seats on the committees are proportional to the number of seats in Congress held by each political party. The permanent committees include one on domestic policy, regionalization, planning, and social development and another on foreign relations, interparliamentary affairs, and Latin American integration, in addition to the usual array of other committees (on finance, defense, health, and so on). The Senate has eighteen permanent committees, most of which correspond directly to an equivalent in the lower chamber.

Each committee carries out legislative and oversight responsibilities with the help of one administrative secretary and an assistant. A staff career ladder that went into effect in 1995 culminates in the positions of secretary of the chamber, supported by a "prosecretary," and a head committee secretary who supports the deputy who chairs the committee. The head committee secretary processes general paperwork but rarely performs legislative research.

Each member of Congress enjoys a variety of legislative support services and an allowance for personal advisers. Most choose to hire staff to assist them in their political activities, since their marginal policy role does not justify employing staff to draft legislation. For the most part career congressional staff provide technical support. Most of these staff are lawyers. Specialists on the substance of policy are in short supply. Committee staff administer the work of their committee but are not in a position to provide research support or to initiate oversight efforts.

Additionally, each party has advisers who are available for consultations, but such services are mostly reserved for top party leadership. Private think tanks have ties to the various parties. The majority coalition benefits from the party assistance program of a think tank known as Corporación 2000. The Freedom and Development Institute exists for the opposition coalition. Both groups have offices in the congressional buildings. The Catholic University of Valparaiso's Legislative Research and Assistance Center stands out as an excellent effort at independent cross-party training and support for Congress. The center produces Chile's best congressional publication series.

CONSTITUTIONAL REFORM AND MODERNIZATION

In the mid-1990s the topic of congressional reform galvanized frustrated deputies and senators in the governing coalition. Many members of Congress had campaigned expecting to serve in an active and strong legislative body, only to realize once in office that they served in a modern but weak institution. One result of that weakness is low morale. The executive, on the other hand, fears that Congress may become irresponsible if it is given more initiative, particularly in the area of the budget, and the appointed senators and the opposition coalition are committed to resisting major constitutional change.

Within the governing Coalition of Parties for Democracy, splits exist between those favoring "hard reforms" and those preferring a pursuit of "soft reforms." The hard reforms include abolishing the appointed senators, modifying the Constitutional Tribunal so that five of the seven seats are appointed by the political majority, replacing the binomial electoral system with the old proportional system, and restructuring the National Security Council, which advises the president and has extensive military representation. The council also has the power to appoint senators and members of the Constitutional Tribunal. As a vestige of military influence it is much disliked in some political sectors.

The soft reforms include allowing Congress to set its own agenda, increasing the congressional role in the budget process, strengthening legislative oversight, and generally introducing efficiencies into the legislative process. Proponents of the soft position see dealing with the hard reforms as a waste of time due to the power of the appointed senators and the center-right coalition's ability to block major constitutional changes. Instead, the soft position focuses on achievable economic and social programs.

The presidential campaign of 1993 sharpened the related issues of constitutional reform and congressional modernization. The Christian Democratic Party, concerned about the politically disruptive nature of the reform issue, initially sought to leave constitutional change for late in President Eduardo Frei's six-year term (1994–2000), after the party's social and economic projects had been put in place. Coalition partner Jorge Schaulsohn, leader of the Party for Democracy, shares these concerns. A contrary view is held by the Socialist Party leader, Camilo Escalona, whose party is also a part of the governing coalition. He wants constitutional reforms, particularly elimination of the appointed senators and restoration of proportional representation, to take priority over all else.

In August 1994 President Frei sent to Congress a package of six reforms entitled "parliamentary modernization." The package included reform of the electoral system from binomial to proportional representation, phasing out of appointed senators, increased flexibility in the legislative process, increased congressional oversight powers, presidential power to call plebiscites in the face of an impasse with the legislative branch, and modification of the role and powers of the Constitutional Tribunal. This combination of reforms reflected an internal compromise within the governing coalition. Quick resistance from the center-right opposition, however, led to its defeat in the Senate and subsequent withdrawal. A new plan emerged to stretch out the reforms and send them for action a few at a time over the coming years. The first such minipackage was sent to Valparaiso in October 1994. It paired modernization of the legislative process (generally supported by the opposition) with elimination of appointed senators in 1998 (opposed by the opposition). This round of constitutional proposals split the National Reform Party and raised questions of discipline in all parties. The "modernization" reforms continued to lead off each legislative year and continued to fail in the Senate. In 1997 President Frei tried a new approach and sent each reform as a separate bill.

A central part of modernization involves increasing legislative oversight powers. The Socialist Party is particularly concerned that increasing legislative oversight without eliminating the appointed senators will create a "legislative dictatorship" by a conservative minority. By creating a package, however, the two reforms must go through together or fail together.

Passage of any reform will require at least two votes from the opposition. The constitution requires a three-fifths majority (seventy-two votes) in the lower house for these constitutional reforms, and since March 1994 the Coalition of Parties for Democracy has had seventy votes. The opposition parties are calling for disciplined votes on all reforms. In the Senate the governing coalition has fewer votes. Passage of any of the hard reforms seems unlikely.

RELATIONS WITH THE EXECUTIVE

The institutionalization of present-day executive-legislative relations started in 1953 during the second presidency of Carlos Ibañez, whose effort to start a congressional liaison office did not prosper due to top-level unwillingness to force coordination upon government ministers. Until the administration of President Patricio Aylwin each ministry handled its own relations with Congress. Bills, messages, and requests from committees to testify were sent back and forth without consistent executive coordination. President Aylwin brought Edgardo Boeninger (a former rector of the University of Chile and minister of education in the cabinet of Eduardo Frei) and Pedro Correa (long-time administrative head of the Senate before 1973) into the presidential general secretariat to create a Legislative Office to track executive-legislative communications. President Frei has required that all ministry-drafted bills, as well as any communication with Congress, must pass through the Legislative Office, allowing the president to coordinate priorities and resolve disputes between ministries. Fifteen lawyers staff the office.

In the current Frei administration a committee made up of the heads of each political party in the governing coalition meets in the Ministry of the Interior every Monday to coordinate the weekly legislative agenda. Given that most congressional votes occur along party lines, once the party leadership reaches agreement, a bill arrives in Congress virtually preapproved. This situation constitutes an inherent conflict with the principle of congressional independence, a principle that party leaders within the coalition otherwise profess. The staff of the Legislative Office also meet with opposition parliamentarians to inform and listen.

From the executive's perspective, members of Congress at times lack good judgment. For personal and political reasons, motions are sometimes made to initiate legislation known to be unconstitutional, often in matters related to the budget, which, under the constitution of 1980, cannot be initiated by Congress. The politics of this effort consist of testing the constitutional budgetary limits.

The first Office of Information opened in the Chamber of Deputies in 1940, and in the Senate in 1949. The function of the offices was to acquire reports and background information from the ministries and agencies of the government at the request of each house. The law provided for penalties for individuals withholding requested information. These offices never prospered, but with the reopening of Congress they have taken on a more vigorous role, especially in the Chamber of Deputies. Using modern information technology, the Chamber office not only provides research support but also informs the public through a broad series of publications. The Senate office remains traditional and somewhat passive.

Executive-legislative relations entered a period of some tension in 1993 as the Information Office of the Chamber of Deputies became the center of a debate concerning oversight powers and the power to request information intended to improve legislation. Some ministries, particularly the Ministry of the Interior, have resisted requests for information forwarded by the Information Office, which has developed the capacity to respond to legislators' needs for information as the institution seeks to strengthen its legislative role as well as its oversight role. Originally purely administrative, the arguments now turn on constitutional issues.

PARLIAMENT AND MEDIA

Since 1853 Congress has published proceedings, which are carried in many newspapers.

The transmission of videotaped reports and the broadcast of proceedings began in 1990 as part of general coverage of Congress. After a public bidding process, cable transmission began in September 1994 for central metropolitan Chile. Full coverage of proceedings from all angles (as opposed to podium shots alone) began to generate debate among members of Congress concerned about images of empty seats, bored looks, and the possibility that what the public observed would not add to the prestige of the lower house. The Chamber worked out a set of informal rules restricting televised images to the immediate surroundings of the deputy speaking, the podium, and the public galleries.

Overall press coverage of legislation is fairly complete and keeps the public well informed. Coverage focuses on speeches and the content of bills. Most reporting does not look into the process itself, nor does it investigate independently the adequacy of legislative proposals.

William W. Culver

BIBLIOGRAPHY

Agor, Weston. *The Chilean Senate: Internal Distribution of Influence.* Austin: University of Texas Press, 1971.

Bronfman Vargas, Alan, Felipe de la Fuente Hulaud, and Fernando Parada Espinoza. *El Congreso Nacional: Estudio Constitucional, Legal y Reglamentario.* Valparaiso, Chile: Centro de Estudios y Asistencia Legislativa, Universidad Católica de Valparaiso, 1993.

Collier, Simon, and William F. Sater. *A History of Chile, 1808–1994.* New York and Cambridge: Cambridge University Press, 1996.

Estévez Valencia, Francisco, ed. *Manual del Congreso Nacional: Historia, Funciones y Atribuciones.* Santiago de Chile: Instituto Democracia, Educación y Acción Social, 1992.

Munck, Gerardo. "Authoritarianism, Modernization, and Democracy in Chile." *Latin American Research Review* 29 (1994): 188–211.

CHINA

OFFICIAL NAME: People's Republic of China (Zhonghua Renmin Gongheguo)
CAPITAL: Beijing
POPULATION: 1,210,005,000 (1996 est.)
DATE OF CURRENT CONSTITUTION: Effective December 4, 1982
FORM OF GOVERNMENT: Communist dictatorship
LANGUAGE: Various dialects of Chinese; official Modern Standard Chinese is based on Mandarin (north China) dialect
MONETARY UNIT: Yuan
FISCAL YEAR: Calendar year
LEGISLATURE: National People's Congress (Quanguo Renmin Daibiao Dahui)
NUMBER OF CHAMBERS: One
NUMBER OF MEMBERS: 2,978
PERCENTAGE OF WOMEN: 21.0
TERM OF LEGISLATURE: Five years
MOST RECENT LEGISLATIVE ELECTION: March 1993
MINIMUM AGE FOR VOTING: 18
MINIMUM AGE FOR MEMBERSHIP: 18
SUFFRAGE: Universal and indirect
VOTING: Optional
ADDRESS: National People's Congress, Great Hall of the People, Tiananmen Square, Beijing
TELEPHONE: (86 1) 63 09 95 19
FAX: (86 1) 63 09 79 14

Located in East Asia and having the world's largest population, the People's Republic of China (PRC) was founded on mainland China by the Chinese Communist Party in 1949. The National People's Congress (NPC) is the supreme legislative body, according to the 1982 constitution. Although still under the influence of the Chinese Communist Party, the NPC has in recent years begun to display some independence.

The NPC is the largest unicameral legislature in the world, with a membership limit of three thousand delegates who are indirectly elected by people's congresses at the provincial (or equivalent) level for five-year terms. The NPC meets once a year, usually in March, for a two-week session. The major components of the NPC are a Presidium, which supervises the yearly NPC session; a Standing Committee, which, as the permanent organ of the NPC, meets on average once a month to enact laws when the NPC is not in session; and several special committees.

Prior to the enactment of the 1982 constitution, reformers had proposed reducing the size of the NPC and introducing bicameralism. They generally agreed that the lower house should reflect representation on the basis of population, but they differed on what the nature of the upper chamber should be. One of the suggestions put forward at the time called for a three-hundred-member Regional Chamber and a seven-hundred-member Chamber of Social Professions and Occupations.

HISTORY

After gaining power over mainland China in 1949, the Chinese Communist Party (CCP) leadership followed the models of the Paris Commune and the worker, peasant, soldier soviet system of the USSR, and also utilized the experience gained in local government in various communist-held areas of China before 1949 to set up a legislature. However, the model of the Soviet Union's Supreme Soviet was not adopted. In September 1949, at the first plenum of the Chinese People's Political Consultative Conference (CPPCC), a body that comprised representatives of fourteen "patriotic parties" and also "independent democratic personages," the NPC was adopted as the basic representative institution of China. Until the NPC was established, however, the CPPCC carried out the authority of the planned legislative body as a provisional state organ, and its decisions had the force of law. After the NPC was established in 1954 and a constitution and electoral law were in place, the CPPCC became merely an advisory organ.

In 1953 China held people's congresses at different levels; in September 1954 the first National People's Congress was convened. At the initial session of the NPC, the PRC adopted its first constitution, which reaffirmed the people's congress system. In the three years following the convening of that first session, both the NPC and its Standing Committee worked to further industrialization and reform through the adoption of a number of important laws, regulations, and decrees. As a result, government organs, and procedures governing the functions of the organs, were gradually set up.

The years 1954–1956 have been characterized as a period of healthy development of the people's congress system. But 1957 marked a turning point in the fortunes of the NPC. Early that year, Mao Zedong initiated what came to be known as the Hundred Flowers movement to encourage people to criticize openly the party and the state; however, soon after the NPC meeting was held (June 26–July 16), the PRC leadership launched a sweeping Anti-Rightist Campaign to crack down on the critics. From that time until the onset of the Cultural Revolution in 1966, the NPC weath-

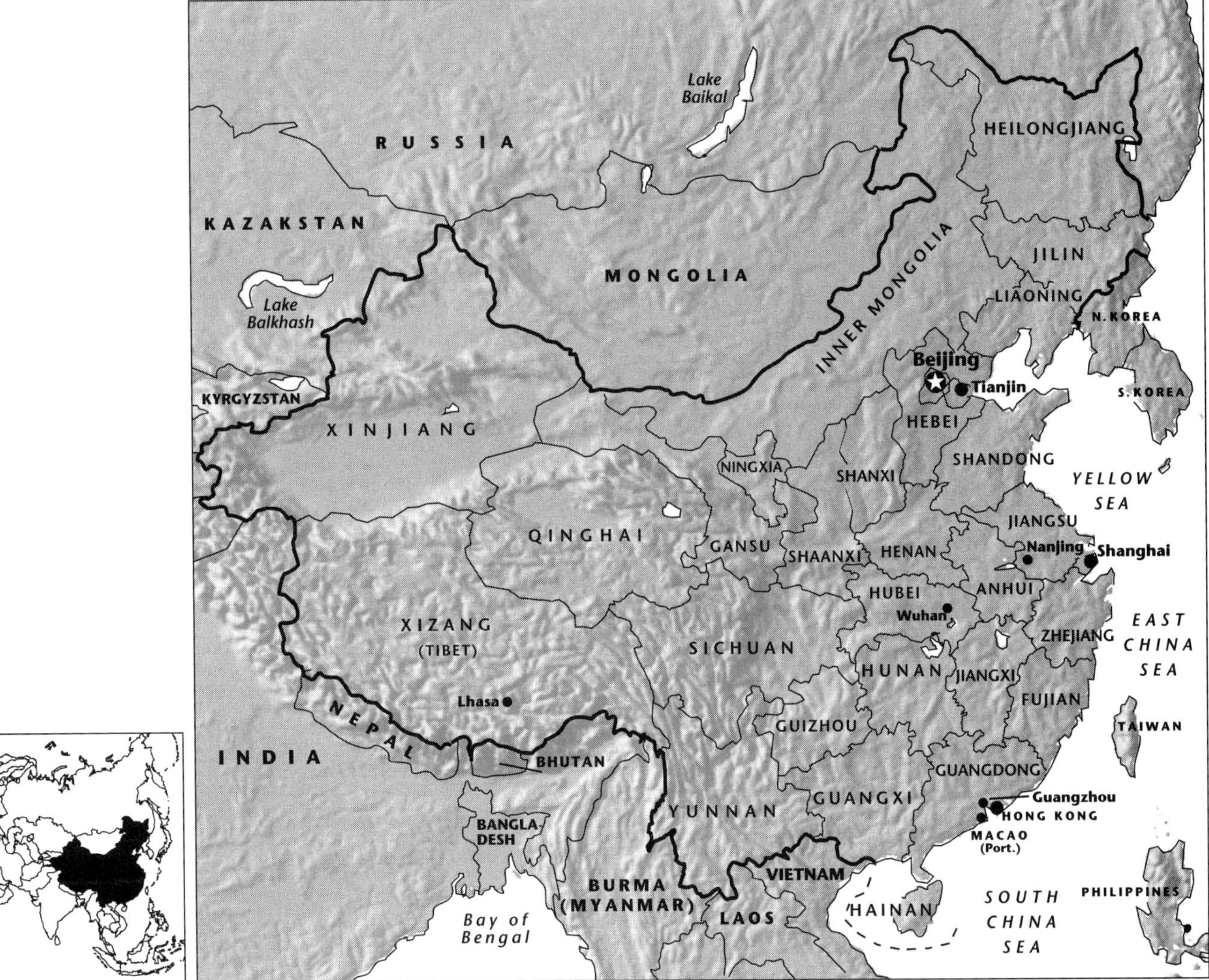

ered a stormy period. Neither the NPC nor its Standing Committee was able to exercise its functions and powers as stipulated in the constitution. In some years the NPC was not convened; in other years, although it convened, little actual work was accomplished, making the sessions merely a formality. Between 1962 and the onset of the Cultural Revolution in 1966, although the functioning of the NPC and its Standing Committee improved slightly, it never reached the level attained from 1954 to 1956. The NPC Standing Committee held its last meeting on April 26, 1966.

The period from May 1966 to October 1976—the Cultural Revolution years—saw the dismantling of China's entire legal system. During that decade, the NPC was almost completely destroyed. After July 1966 the NPC suspended its functions until 1975. In these ten-some years, not a single meeting of the Standing Committee was held, nor did the Third NPC ever meet, and so the NPC and its Standing Committee existed in name only.

In January 1975 the first session of the Fourth NPC convened, just prior to the October 1976 downfall of the Gang of Four (the powerful leftist clique headed by Jiang Qing, wife of Mao Zedong, which held sway during the Cultural Revolution). The Congress elected new leadership, but otherwise the revival of the NPC's functions was tenuous and limited. At the meeting, the constitution was revised, with emphasis placed on leftist ideas that were thereby given legal confirmation; among the changes, the Chinese Communist Party supplanted the government. The Standing Committee of the Fourth NPC held only two meetings, and each one lasted but three days.

In March 1978 the first session of the Fifth NPC convened. It adopted a revised constitution and revived certain basic principles embodied in the 1954 constitution. The constitution confirmed the NPC as the state's supreme organ. However, the 1978 constitution was not completely divorced from the ideas of the Cultural Revolution, such as the supremacy of class struggle and adherence to the theory of continuous revolution. At the end of 1978 the CCP held the third plenum of the Eleventh Party Congress. At the party meeting, the leadership emphasized that in order to protect socialist democracy, the socialist legal system would have to be strengthened. This meeting was significant in laying the foundation for the development of what has come to be called China's socialist democracy and legal system.

In July 1979, at the second session of the Fifth NPC, the election law of the NPC and of local people's congresses of various levels was revised, as was the organic law of the local people's congresses of various levels and of local government. Among other changes, standing committees were established in people's congresses at the county level and above. In December 1982, at the fifth session of the Fifth NPC, a new constitution was adopted that contains important improvements in the people's congress system. Subsequently, the NPC and its Standing Committee met regularly, and the various special committees of the NPC also gradually resumed their constitutionally assigned duties. Since 1979 the NPC has adopted not only a new constitution but also many important laws and revisions of laws. The NPC Standing Committee and the special committees have become more visible, and NPC activities have gradually become institutionalized and normalized.

THE CONSTITUTION

The NPC, the highest organ of state authority, exercises legislative power along with its permanent body, the Standing Committee. The NPC has, among other powers, the power to amend the constitution and to supervise its implementation; to enact and amend the basic laws of the state governing criminal offenses, civil affairs, state organs, and other matters; and to make decisions on the appointment and removal of leading personnel of state organs. This last power specifically includes election and removal of the constituent personnel of the Standing Committee of the NPC; election of a Presidium to conduct the NPC session; election and removal of the president (literally, the chairman) and vice president of the PRC; selection of a premier after his or her nomination by the president of the PRC, and, based on their nomination by the premier, selection of the vice premiers, state councilors, various ministers, chairs of various commissions, the auditor-general, and the secretary-general (the NPC also has the right to remove the above-mentioned personnel); election and removal of the Central Military Commission chair and members; election and removal of the president of the Supreme People's Court; and election and removal of the procurator-general of the Supreme People's Procuratorate.

The NPC is empowered to make decisions on other important state matters as well. According to the constitution, it is to examine and approve the state budget and national economic and social development plan; establish provinces, autonomous regions, and municipalities under the direct control of the central government; make decisions on special administrative regions; decide on questions of war and peace; oversee central state organs; change or annul inappropriate decisions of the Standing Committee; and, under a catch-all provision, exercise any other functions that the highest organ of state power should exercise. Among several other functions and powers, the NPC Standing Committee has the right to supervise the work of the State Council, the Central Military Commission, the Supreme People's Court, and the Supreme People's Procuratorate and to hear their work reports.

In contrast to the U.S. constitution, which is based on the principle of the separation of powers, the Chinese constitution follows the principle of "democratic centralism." This concept, derived from Leninist-Stalinist principles of organization of the Communist Party of the Soviet Union, characterizes a system in which the government maintains centralized administrative power while the people, through representative bodies (in theory), exercise influence over government policies. Like many Western European parliaments, China's NPC is guided by the principle of parliamentary supremacy, according to which the parliament is the highest legislative as well as constitutional authority, in charge of supervising other constitutional organs. Thus, as the highest state organ, in theory the NPC's power is supreme (in fact, the CCP continues to exercise ultimate power in China); all other state organs are accountable and subordinate to it. However, the degree of supervision it exercises would seem to exceed that of Western parliaments. For example, NPC authority over the judiciary is of a sort seldom held by Western legislatures, which typically abide by the principle of judicial independence. The NPC, by means of interpellation, investigation, letters from the people, or other channels, can exercise power over the judiciary. It periodically elects judicial officials and has the power to remove judges and procurators. In Western democracies, unless judges are found guilty of violating the law, the parliaments cannot remove them.

Although Western parliaments have the power to supervise government organs, they typically do not exercise the comprehensive control that can be wielded by the NPC, which supervises short-, middle-, and long-term national economic and social development plans as well as the work of all important government organs (for example, through the submission of annual reports). Moreover, the NPC is accorded the authority to exercise any power that it deems it should exercise. Western parliaments typically do not have unlimited power.

A second difference between the Chinese NPC and Western parliaments is that NPC deputies are indirectly elected, whereas in Western-style democratic countries, in most cases, the members of the lower house of parliament are directly elected by the voters. Western legislators typically serve full time; NPC deputies serve part time and have only the responsibility of attending the NPC meeting once a year for about two weeks, after which they return to their regular employment. Whether a deputy can be a candidate at the next Congress depends on whether he or she is deemed to have representative or "progressive" qualities.

Third, the NPC conducts its activities under the leadership of the CCP. It is a creation of the CCP and remains under its control, and at all levels the party committee is above the people's congress of the corresponding level. Thus, the CCP can issue instructions to the NPC, can examine and approve NPC decisions and approve important legislation of the NPC and the lower people's congresses, and can make important decisions on appointment and removal of personnel. As a result, the NPC has been viewed as a rubber stamp of CCP policies. Only in recent years has the NPC begun to show some independence, in the sense that there is more real discussion and debate and there are dissenting votes on bills proposed for passage, but multiparty politics do not play a role.

In Western countries, by contrast, political parties, depending on their strength, control the parliament in varying degrees. If a political party wins a majority in the legislature as a result of its election campaign, it can establish its leadership position in the parliament, but the power of parliament comes first, above the power of the party leadership within it, and a political party must exercise its power through the parliament. As far as political parties are concerned, in addition to the all-powerful Chinese Communist Party, there are eight "democratic parties" in China of long standing. These include the Revolutionary Committee of the Chinese Kuomintang, the China Democratic League, the China Democratic National Construction Association, the Jiusan Society, the China Association for Promoting Democracy, the Chinese Peasants and Workers Democratic Party, the China Zhi Gong Dang, and the Taiwan Democratic Self-Government League. However, these parties have virtually no power. It follows that there are no party caucuses or groups, or whips and majority and minority leaders in the NPC.

Fourth, the NPC and people's congresses at all levels have a standing committee because the full body only meets once a year for a short duration. This arrangement is not found in Western parliaments, especially bicameral systems, whose two houses can only exercise their legislative powers jointly.

Fifth, once a member of a Western parliament has been elected, the voters usually do not have much power to remove him or her. This is because the members require a certain degree of protection in order to be able to exercise their rights independently. The NPC, by contrast, in theory gives the people the right to remove their representatives (in fact, it is the CCP that exercises this power).

The exercise by the NPC and its Standing Committee of their legal supervisory function—that is, their supervision of the enactment and implementation of state and local laws—has come under criticism in recent years from Chinese legal scholars. One line of criticism has to do with people's congress deputies, who, at all levels, state and local, have the power to elect responsible personnel of administrative and judicial organs as well as to propose, discuss, and vote on resolutions. To improve their supervisory function, it has been argued in Chinese legal circles that more attention be paid to their ability to exercise their actual functions. Moreover, at present, voters are usually only given information about a candidate's age, profession, current position, and general background, rather than about the person's political capabilities. The candidates are not given the opportunity to make speeches or to express their views on how they would achieve their goals and what they would do for the people if elected. Candidates do not meet with voters, nor are opinion polls conducted. Once in office, people's congress deputies have been found to lack first-hand information about such matters as social problems, the kinds of laws that need to be enacted, and how laws are being implemented, as well as time and adequate funds to conduct investigations in the field.

A second criticism is of the requirement that the NPC examine local regulations for conflict with the constitution and national laws. Because the NPC meets only once a year for a period of about two weeks, it is unrealistic that it be expected to consider questions of unconstitutionality. In fact, neither the NPC nor its Standing Committee has ever addressed such issues. Although the Standing Committee is charged with assessing constitutionality, it has never found any law unconstitutional. A related problem is the lack of a suitable organ to supervise the Standing Committee itself to make sure that the legislation it adopts does not violate the constitution. At present, only the NPC can exercise that supervision; critics of the NPC believe that a special organ charged with examining laws for unconstitutionality should be established.

A third criticism is that local laws need be sent to the Standing Committee only for the record; administrative regulations (legislation enacted by the local administrative organs rather than by the legislature) are not even sent for the record. Thus, although one of the Standing Committee's functions is to supervise lower-level legislation, it has not been fully exercising that function. A related criticism is that the legislative powers of the central and local governments have not been clearly stipulated in the form of law. Some jurists believe that local people's congresses should have more leeway to adopt local laws reflecting the special circumstances of their region, while at the same time they should take measures to ensure that their powers are not in conflict with those of the central legislature.

Fourth, the wisdom of having a constitutional provision that calls for a legislative organ, the NPC Standing Committee, to interpret the constitution and laws has been questioned. Giving the Standing Committee the power both to legislate and to interpret the law, it is argued, is in conflict with the general principle that there be a division of labor among state organs.

ELECTIONS AND MEMBERSHIP

Every five years there are new elections to the NPC, held two years prior to the expiration of a given term. The Eighth NPC runs from 1993 to 1998; the Ninth from March 1998 to March 2003.

NPC deputies are elected indirectly, by the people's congresses of provinces, autonomous regions, and municipalities under the direct control of the central government (all of which are at the "provincial" level in the administrative hierarchy). Deputies to the people's congresses of these provincial-level divisions, cities that are divided into districts, and autonomous prefectures are elected by the people's congresses at the next lower level. Deputies of people's congresses of cities that are not divided into districts, municipal districts, counties, autonomous counties, townships, nationality townships, and towns are directly elected. NPC deputies who represent the military are elected by the military, under its own separate procedures. Deputies representing Taiwan Province are selected from among people of Taiwanese origin in different provinces, autonomous regions, municipalities under the direct control of the central government, and the People's Liberation Army. There should be "an appropriate number" of women deputies to the NPC and to local people's congresses (and their percentage is to be gradually increased; as of late 1996, women comprised 21 percent of people's congress members) and of returned overseas Chinese (whose number is relatively large). PRC citizens who reside abroad but who are in China during the election of deputies to the people's congresses below the county level may participate in such elections held in their ancestral home town or in the place where they lived before going abroad. The number of deputies elected from the Hong Kong and Macao Special Administrative Regions and the related electoral procedures were to be separately formulated. On March 14, 1997, the fifth session of the Eighth NPC adopted a resolution establishing procedures for electing thirty-six Hong Kong Special Administrative Region deputies to the Ninth NPC.

The election of NPC deputies is under the charge of the NPC Standing Committee, which determines the number of seats and how they are to be allocated. It allocates seats to the provinces, autonomous regions, and municipalities directly under the central government based on the principle that each rural deputy will represent four times the number of people represented by each urban deputy; the number it allocates for election by minority nationalities will depend on the population and distribution of each minority nationality, and minorities with exceptionally small populations are guaranteed at least one deputy.

Under a resolution adopted at the fifth session of the Eighth NPC, the number of deputies elected to the Ninth NPC is not to exceed three thousand. The resolution also stipulates that there be at least 15 deputies for each province and autonomous region with a very small population; 13 for persons of Taiwanese origin; and 265 for the People's Liberation Army. The resolution further calls for about 12 percent of the membership to be reserved for ethnic minorities, for the election of an increased percentage of female deputies, and for 35 deputies to be elected from among overseas Chinese.

The term of an NPC is five years. A term runs from the starting date of the first conference of a congress to the day when the first conference of the next NPC convenes. The NPC deputies represent the supreme power of the state and exercise that power collectively.

According to the constitution and the law, NPC deputies have the right to propose bills, make suggestions, and offer criticisms and other views; to remove people from their posts; to interpellate the State Council or its ministries; and to conduct investigations in connection with matters to be deliberated by the NPC. No action can be taken against the deputies in connection with their remarks or the way they vote, and when the NPC is in session or in recess, deputies cannot be arrested or tried for a criminal offense without special permission.

NPC delegates have the obligation to be models of observance of the constitution and laws, to conscientiously exercise their functions, and to preserve state secrets. In their own work and other social activities, they must try to make sure that the constitution and laws are faithfully observed. They are to have close contact with the units that elected them as well as the masses with the aim of listening to and reflecting their views and demands.

The Standing Committee of the Sixth NPC (1983–1988) enacted a document entitled "Several Views Regarding the Strengthening of Contacts Between the Standing Committee and the Deputies." The purpose of the document was to help make liaison more regularized and institutionalized. (Connections between the Standing Committee and the standing committees of provincial level people's congresses were also to be strengthened.) The Standing Committee and various special committees were to hold symposia or special meetings for the deputies, so that they could directly hear their views. The Standing Committee, in examining important bills and in making decisions on important matters, was, when necessary prior to making a final decision, to solicit the views of all or some of the deputies and send its draft decisions to them for their information. When the Standing Committee holds its meetings, those deputies who are more familiar with certain topics on the agenda were to be invited to attend the meeting and to participate in the discussion, albeit without a vote. If the Standing Committee and the various special committees conduct investigations in connection with particular bills or other important matters, certain knowledgeable deputies were to be invited to participate. And the work unit of the Standing Committee was to be made responsible for examining various suggestions, criticisms, and views expressed by the deputies and for responding to them.

For the first ten years of its existence, the NPC comprised 1,226 representatives. In 1964, however, their number was more than doubled, to 3,040 members, making the NPC by far the largest unicameral legislature in the world. As was noted above, a 1986 amendment to the 1982 Electoral Law reduced the limit of 3,500 deputies to 3,000, and the total number of deputies elected to the Eighth NPC was reported to be 2,977.

PARLIAMENTARY PROCEEDINGS

Calendar

The NPC meets once a year, in the first quarter of the year, in a session convened by the Standing Committee. The Standing Committee may convene an NPC session at any time it deems necessary, or a session may be convened when a proposal to do so is made by more than one-fifth of the deputies to the NPC. One month before an NPC is convened, the Standing Committee notifies the deputies of the date of the session and of the main items on the proposed agenda. If an NPC session is specially convened, this stipulation does not apply.

Each NPC typically has lasted about two weeks, although in 1955 there was a twenty-six-day session, and in 1975, a five-day session. Authorities prefer a session of ten days, to reduce costs and the inconvenience caused to Beijing residents. Despite attempts to professionalize the legislature by lengthening the sessions and holding two per year, traditional arguments against "professional politicians who stand above the masses" prevailed, and longer sessions were labeled "inappropriate," so sessions have continued to be annual, two-to-three-week events.

According to the Organic Law of the NPC, prior to each NPC, a preparatory meeting is to be held, with the participation of all NPC deputies, under the auspices of the Standing Committee of the previous NPC. For example, the preparatory meeting of the Seventh NPC was held under the auspices of the Standing Committee of the Sixth NPC. The primary tasks of the preparatory meeting are to elect the Presidium and the secretary-general and to adopt the agenda of the NPC.

The Presidium, the leading organ of the NPC, presides over NPC sessions. The Presidium elects some of its members to rotate as executive chairs of the NPC sessions. Standing chairs are elected from among the Presidium members to convene and preside over Presidium meetings. The Presidium, which normally consists of about 150 members, is responsible for organizing the NPC meeting and for resolving any procedural problems. The first meeting of the Presidium, convened by the chair of the NPC Standing Committee, focuses on solving procedure-related problems, such as making a preliminary examination of bills and deciding whether they should be placed on the agenda. Subsequent meetings are convened by the standing chairs. The Presidium comprises leaders of the party and the government (including the leader of the CCP Central Committee, the president and vice president of China, and the NPC Standing Committee chair and vice chairs); responsible persons from the various democratic parties, industry, and commerce and "patriotic persons" without political affiliation; responsible persons from the central CCP, political, and military organs as well as people's groups; members of NPC special committees; model workers, "progressive" personages, and prominent intellectuals; representatives of minority nationalities whose number is above one million; responsible persons of the People's Liberation Army; and delegations of each province, autonomous region, and municipality under the direct control of the central government.

NPC deputies are grouped into delegations based on the units that elected them, and each delegation elects a head and deputy heads. Prior to the NPC meeting, delegations discuss matters brought up by the Standing Committee. Delegations either meet as a whole or break up into small groups.

The mission of the plenary meeting, which is the full annual conference of the NPC, is to listen to reports of the Standing Committee, the State Council, the Supreme People's Court, and the Supreme People's Procuratorate; to make resolutions; and to vote on bills. The plenary meeting also makes decisions on the election and removal of personnel of the central state organs and on other important matters.

Since 1959 NPC sessions have convened in the Great Hall of the People, situated on the western side of Tiananmen Square, the largest public square in the world. The building measures 1,017 feet from north to south and has a marble hall that is 328 feet long. It took only ten months to complete during 1958–1959; workers, students, cadres, and professionals were mobilized to carry out the construction. The main assembly room can accommodate ten thousand people, and banquet rooms are on a similar scale, seating five thousand. Reception rooms for holding interviews with foreigners are named after China's twenty-seven provinces and decorated accordingly. The hall also contains art objects donated by the provinces. Because of the huge size of the assembly room, meetings have been described as more formal and less lively than those that had been held in the 1950s in the smaller Huairentang in Zhongnanhai (a walled compound in central Beijing where China's top leaders live and work). The Great Hall is open to the public when the NPC is not in session, which means for almost the whole year, except for a couple of weeks (usually in March).

How laws are made

The NPC adopts laws and resolutions by a majority vote of all the deputies. The Standing Committee enacts and amends those laws that do not have to be enacted by the NPC. The president of the PRC promulgates statutes pursuant to NPC and Standing Committee decisions. A law is typically promulgated on the same day that it is adopted. Some laws—those that deal with administrative affairs of certain government departments—are adopted for trial implementation only and are not promulgated as such.

The Presidium of the NPC, the Standing Committee and the special committees of the NPC, the State Council, the Central Military Commission, the Supreme People's Court, and the Supreme People's Procuratorate may submit bills or proposals to the NPC. A delegation or a group of thirty or more deputies may also submit bills or proposals.

For bills proposed by the state organs noted above, the Presidium of the NPC decides whether they should be turned over to the various delegations of the NPC or to the delegations and relevant special committees for deliberation. The result of the deliberations is reported to the Presidium, which may, after its own deliberation, decide to put the bills or proposals to a vote at a plenary meeting.

For bills or proposals of a delegation or a group of deputies, the Presidium may decide to put them on the NPC agenda, or it may make that decision after referring them to the relevant special committees for deliberation and receiving their opinions. If prior to the NPC vote the sponsor requests that the bill be withdrawn, deliberation will be terminated immediately, with the Presidium's approval.

Revision of the constitution can only be made on the basis of a proposal from the NPC Standing Committee or more than one-fifth of the deputies of the NPC; two-thirds of the deputies must vote for the revision. Amendment of basic laws governing criminal offenses, civil affairs, state organs, and other matters is to be carried out by the NPC. The Standing Committee amends all other laws, but it may also amend, when the NPC is not in session, laws enacted by the NPC, as long as the basic principles of such laws are not contravened.

From 1990 to the end of August 1995, the NPC adopted seventy-seven resolutions on laws and legal issues. The NPC accelerated the pace of its work, especially since 1993, with the commencement of the Eighth NPC. During the sixth and seventh sessions, on average, the NPC adopted about ten pieces of law each year, whereas in 1993 alone the NPC adopted twenty. As of the end of November 1994, the NPC and its Standing Committee had adopted seventeen items of law—fifteen laws and two decisions relating to questions of law. In the 1995 legislative year, the Standing Committee examined twenty-eight draft laws and decisions and adopted fifteen; it also ratified eleven treaties, pacts, and agreements. The twelfth session of the Eighth NPC Standing Committee broke the previous record for the number of laws and resolutions adopted at a single session by passing seven on February 28, 1995. In 1996 the legislature examined thirty-one laws and decisions and approved twenty-two, leaving about thirty laws to be formulated, examined, and adopted by March 1998 if the Eighth NPC were to meet its legislative goals. In addition, the duration of NPC sessions has been extended. The third session of the Eighth NPC began on March 5, 1995, five days earlier than the opening of the second session, which itself was held ten days earlier than the opening of the first session. The 1997 session met from March 1 through March 14.

The volume of local legislation has also been large. In the past, on average, about 150 local laws and regulations were adopted each year; in 1993, 348 items were adopted, and in the first seven months of 1994, 393 pieces of legislation were adopted.

The NPC can meet only if more than two-thirds of the deputies are in attendance.

Budget procedures

According to the constitution, one of the functions and powers of the NPC is to examine and approve the state budget and the report on its implementation. When the NPC is not in session, its Standing Committee reviews and approves any partial adjustments to the budget that are shown to be necessary in the course of its implementation. It is the State Council's function to draw up and implement the budget.

The state budget is part of the PRC's system of separate budgeting, implemented at five levels of government. There is a system of revenue sharing between central and local authorities, and there should be a balance between revenue and expenditure in the budgets at all levels. The central government budget consists of the budgets of various central departments, including units under their direct jurisdiction, and includes the revenues turned in to the central authorities by the localities and the finances the central authorities return to the localities. A departmental budget is defined as the budgets of various units under a given department's jurisdiction; a unit budget is the revenue and expenditure budget of state organs, social organizations, and other units that is included in the departmental budget.

The State Council's duties in drafting and implementing the budget are set forth in the Budget Law. The council drafts central budgets and final accounts, submits reports to the NPC on these draft budgets, and consolidates and forwards the budgets submitted by provincial, autonomous regional, and municipal governments to the NPC Standing Committee for the record. It arranges for the implementation of the central and local budgets, determines the use of central budgetary reserve funds, makes plans for revising central budgets, and oversees budget implementation by various central departments and by local governments. The State Council modifies or revokes improper decisions and decrees on budgets and final accounts made by various central departments and local governments and submits reports to the NPC and the Standing Committee on the implementation of the central and local budgets.

China has a dual-budget system, adopted in 1992, for which the procedures of compilation and implementation are stipulated by the State Council. Under this system, state revenues and expenditures are divided into a regular budget and a construction budget. The regular budget, which is drafted first, includes general revenues received by the state as the manager and owner of assets. These revenues are used for regular government spending on national security, education, science, culture, and public health and to meet other social needs. A balance between revenues and expenditures is sought, with any surplus used for economic construction. The construction budget covers revenues specified for use in construction and direct expenditures on construction, in line with what the government can afford, with deficits to be made up through treasury bonds and bank loans.

The State Council's financial department submits the main contents of the central draft budget to the NPC Finance and Economic Committee for preliminary examination one month before the NPC session opens every year. At the NPC session, the State Council delivers a report on the draft budgets for the central government and local governments. The NPC examines these draft budgets as well as reports on their respective execution, examines and approves the central budget and the report on its execution, and alters or nullifies any improper resolutions of the NPC Standing Committee on the budgets or final accounts. The NPC Standing Committee supervises the execution of the central budget and the local budget, examines and approves plans for readjusting the central budget, and examines and approves the central final accounts. It nullifies any administrative rules and regulations, decisions, or decrees made by the State Council on the budgets or final accounts that contravene the constitution or the law. It also nullifies any local rules, regulations, and resolutions adopted by provincial, autonomous regional, and municipal people's congresses or their standing committees on budgets and accounts that contravene the constitution, the law, or administrative rules and regulations.

Plans for revising the central government budget must be submitted to the NPC Standing Committee for examination and approval, and no budget may be revised without approval. Budget revision is defined as the introduction of partial changes to increase the total expenditure so that it exceeds the total revenue in the previously approved budget where revenue and expenditure are balanced, or to increase the amount of debt to be raised under the previously approved budget, when extraordinary circumstances in implementing the NPC-approved central budget or budgets approved by local people's congresses at all levels dictate additional expenditure or reduced revenue.

The State Council prescribes the time when draft final accounts are to be prepared by governments, departments, and units at all levels after every budget year comes to an end. Once the State Council has approved the draft final accounts prepared by its financial department for the central government, it submits them to the NPC Standing Committee for examination and approval. The NPC and its Standing Committee supervise budgets and final accounts of the central government and local governments.

Debates and voting

NPC deputies do not really have much say in the revision of laws. In deliberating revisions, Standing Committee members air their views, and then the organ in charge of the subject matter expresses its opinions. These views are forwarded to the special committees or to the Presidium, whose members try to reach agreement, then the proposed revised bill is sent to the full Congress for a vote. Since NPC deputies are not full-time legislators, it is unavoidable that they are unable to make much of a contribution to the formulation of legislation and typically just express their views as a formality. Still, as was noted above, there does seem to be an increase in the expression of different points of view among the deputies.

Deputies who wish to speak at the plenary session of the NPC can each give two speeches, the first lasting not more than ten minutes and the second not more than five. They must register beforehand with the Secretariat, and the NPC executive chair arranges the order of speeches. Spontaneous remarks may only be delivered with the permission of the executive chair. The time limits on speeches are only for explanation of bills and relevant reports. In delegation plenary sessions and delegate group meetings, no legal provision exists on time limits, which are left to the discretion of the presiding member.

At Presidium meetings, Presidium members and delegation heads or delegates elected by a delegation may each speak twice, for not more than fifteen minutes the first time and not more than ten the second, but the speaking time may be extended as deemed appropriate by the chair of the meeting. Deputies may not be held legally responsible for speeches and votes made at NPC meetings.

The constitution, the Organic Law of the NPC, and the NPC Rules of Procedure provide that deputies have the right to address questions to the State Council or the ministries and commissions under it and to receive either an oral or written reply. The receiving organs must answer the questions in a responsible manner. Interpellators may make a written request of inquiry, but it must be submitted by a delegation or group of thirty or more deputies, and the target of the inquiry, the questions to be asked, and the substance of the inquiry must be clearly indicated. If the Presidium decides the inquiry may be made, the responsible person of the department questioned will provide a verbal or written response. If the delegates or delegation that lodged the inquiry remain unsatisfied with the response, they can demand further inquiry, and, if instructed by the Presidium, the department concerned must give another reply. Written answers to inquiries are signed by the head of the organ questioned; they may be printed for distribution at the NPC, at the discretion of the Presidium.

Laws are formally published in the *Gazette of the Standing Committee of the National People's Congress of the People's Republic of China,* compiled by the General Office of the NPC Standing Committee. Texts of laws and decisions on treaties, announcements of the appointment or removal of state officials, and announcements having to do with NPC-related matters (such as deaths, results of by-elections, travel reports, and so forth) are also included. The Legal Affairs Commission has compiled and published the *Compendium of Laws and Regulations of the People's Republic of China* on an annual basis since 1979. The General Office also compiles a compendium of committee papers of each NPC. In January 1994 the bimonthly *National People's Congress Work Bulletin,* published by the Standing Committee's General Office, was launched.

It may be noted that during the NPC session, special bulletins are issued that record the views expressed at deputies' group meetings. The bulletins are compiled, printed, and circulated among the deputies by the bulletin group under the NPC Secretariat. Fewer than four thousand copies of each bulletin are produced. Since about 1986 the bulletins have come to be more substantive, with the inclusion of different views and forthright criticism of government work reports.

Plenary session resolutions must be passed by more than half of all deputies; constitutional revisions require approval by more than two-thirds of all deputies. The outcome of a vote is announced on the spot by the chair of the session. As for voting methods, the Presidium determines whether the ballot, a show of hands, or other method (for example, a voting machine) will be used in deciding on a proposal. Voting must be by ballot when revising the constitution. The Presidium also decides on the type of vote necessary to win the result, typically a simple majority of all deputies.

Judicial functions of parliament

The NPC has the power to elect and to remove from office the president of the Supreme People's Court and the procurator-general of the Supreme People's Procuratorate. The NPC Standing Committee has the power to interpret the constitution and supervise its enforcement. It supervises the work of the Supreme People's Court and the Supreme People's Procuratorate. The Standing Committee also has the power to annul administrative rules and regulations, decisions or orders of the State Council that contravene the constitution or the law as well as local regulations or decisions that contravene the constitution, the law, or the administrative rules and regulations. At the recommendation of the president of the Supreme People's Court, the Standing Committee has the power to appoint or remove vice presidents or judges of the Supreme People's Court, members of its Judicial Committee, and the president of the Military Court; similarly, at the recommendation of the procurator-general, it has the power to appoint or remove the deputy procurators-general and procurators of the Supreme People's Procuratorate, members of its Procuratorial Committee, and the chief procurator of the Military Procuratorate. It also has the power to approve the appointment or removal of chief procurators of the people's procuratorates of provinces, autonomous regions, and municipalities under the direct control of the central government.

Broadcasting of proceedings

Sessions of the NPC are open to the public, but closed sessions may be held when necessary by decision of a meeting of the Presidium and all the delegation heads. The NPC sessions hold news conferences and make news announcements.

During the first session of the Eighth NPC, domestic and overseas reporters alike were permitted to observe the voting procedures for China's top leadership, including the election of Qiao Shi and other leaders of the NPC itself, Jiang Zemin as president (Jiang is the first leader since 1959 to be concurrently head of the CCP and head of state), and Rong Yiren as vice president.

On December 13, 1994, journalists were permitted to cover the NPC Standing Committee's chairmanship meeting for the first time since the founding of the people's congress system. The move is part of reforms being made in the NPC Standing Committee's news release procedures. In addition, as of the eleventh session of the Standing Committee of the Eighth NPC, held December 21–29, 1994, the regular news briefing on the meeting's agenda, typically held beforehand, was to be replaced with a news conference or briefing held after the meeting.

COMMITTEE STRUCTURE

The Standing Committee of the NPC

The Standing Committee is the permanent organ of the NPC. When the NPC is in recess, the Standing Committee exercises the supreme power of the state. It is under the supervision of the NPC and is responsible for submitting reports to it. The Standing Committee supervises the work of the State Council, the Central Military Commission, the Supreme People's Court, and the Supreme People's Procuratorate, and the heads of the last three organs submit reports to the Standing Committee. When the NPC is not in session, the State Council reports on its work to the Standing Committee.

The Standing Committee consists of a chair and a number of vice chairs, a secretary-general, and a number of members. The Standing Committee elected at the inaugural session of the Eighth NPC, held March 15–31, 1993, included a chair, about 20 vice chairs, 1 secretary-general (who is also a member), and 134 members. Standing Committee members are elected from among the deputies by the Presidium. After discussion and consultation with various delegations, the Presidium decides on a list of candidates, taking into consideration the views of the majority of deputies. The constituent personnel of the Standing Committee (the chair, vice chairs, and members; "members" does not include the chair and vice chairs) are then elected by the whole NPC. By law, the Standing Committee is to have an appropriate number of minority nationality delegates. For example, the Seventh NPC Standing Committee had twenty-one members who represented fourteen different minority nationalities.

The term of Standing Committee members is the same as that of NPC members, except that the term concludes when the first conference of the subsequent NPC convenes, to ensure a smooth transition. The chair and the vice chairs may not serve more than two consecutive terms. Constituent personnel are not allowed to hold any state administrative position or any judicial or procuratorial position, so that the Standing Committee may be better able to exercise its oversight function. If anyone, be it the chair or a vice chair or member, wishes to hold a position in any of the above-mentioned organs, he or she must resign from the Standing Committee.

Under the constitution, the primary functions and powers of the Standing Committee include the power to enact laws other than those enacted by the NPC; to interpret the constitution and the law (not only the laws it enacts itself, but also the laws enacted by the full NPC); to exercise supervisory power, including legal supervision of and administrative authority over central executive and judicial organs; to interpellate (when the Standing Committee is in session, ten or more of its constituent personnel may jointly direct interpellations to state organs); to make decisions on important matters; to decide on personnel of state organs when the NPC is not in session, but with a more limited scope (the Standing Committee does not exercise the right of election and recall, it has only the right to make appointments and to remove persons from their posts); to exercise other functions and powers conferred on it by the full Congress. In addition, the Standing Committee is in charge of elections of NPC deputies and convenes the NPC. When the NPC is not in session, the Standing Committee directs the work of the special committees.

Standing Committee Conferences

The chair of the Standing Committee presides over the Standing Committee and is responsible for convening the Standing Committee conferences. The vice chairs and the secretary-general of the Standing Committee assist the chair. If entrusted by the chair, the vice chairs may act on his or her behalf in exercising certain functions and powers. If the chair is not able to work due to poor health or if the position of chair becomes vacant, then an acting chair is chosen from among the vice chairs by mutual consultation. The acting chair serves until either the chair has regained health or a new chair is elected.

There are three forms of Standing Committee conference: conferences of the whole Standing Committee, conferences of small groups (for example, the Standing Committee is divided into small sections and each has a conference), and joint conferences of groups.

The functions of the plenary Standing Committee conference are to decide what is to be put on the agenda and to listen to explanations of bills and to reports made by the State Council, State Council committees, various ministries, the Supreme People's Court, the Supreme People's Procuratorate, as well as by delegations of the NPC when they have made visits abroad or attended international conferences. The conference also votes on bills, personnel matters, and other proposed resolutions and on reports made by various special committees. The committee under the Standing Committee on the evaluation of delegates' credentials votes on the reports made by the State Council and its subordinate units and on reports made by the Supreme People's Court and the Supreme People's Procuratorate on their work. If necessary, it votes and makes a resolution. In accordance with the procedures governing Standing Committee meetings, if those who comprise the Standing Committee or invited attendees wish to speak at the plenary meeting, the speech may not exceed ten minutes. If prior permission is granted, this time limit may be extended. In voting on bills, ballots can be cast anonymously or by a show of hands or by other means. At present, generally speaking, an electronic machine is used to record votes.

In order to give members the opportunity to express their views fully, the chair of the Standing Committee may convene sectional Standing Committee conferences. Those who attend the sectional meetings include regular Standing Committee members as well as invited guests. These sectional meetings can be chaired by either a vice chair or a member of the Standing Committee. At the sectional meetings, questions can be raised by people on certain questions related to a bill. The units that proposed the bill may send their representatives to the meeting to listen to the views expressed and to answer any questions.

A joint sectional meeting is called to have further debate on a bill when there are differing views on it. A participant who makes a remark for the first time on a given question is limited to fifteen minutes; for a second remark on the same issue, speaking time is limited to ten minutes. Such restrictions can be lifted with the Standing Committee chair's prior consent.

Generally speaking, a Standing Committee conference, consisting of the delegate who presides over the conference and a quorum, is held every two months, and each meeting lasts for seven-to-fifteen days. The Standing Committee conference is convened by the chair. The chair may entrust a vice chair to preside over the meeting. A quorum is the majority. Conference invitees may include responsible personnel of the State Council, the Central Military Commission, the Supreme People's Court, and the Supreme People's Procuratorate; the vice chairs, members, and advisers of various special committees of the NPC who are not the regular members of the Standing Committee; the chair or vice chairs of the standing committee of the people's congresses of various provinces, autonomous regions, or municipalities under the direct control of the central government; deputies of the NPC who have a connection with the bill, at the special invitation of the conference chair; and responsible personnel of other relevant units.

The chairman's conference is convened and presided over by the chair of the Standing Committee. At his or her request, a vice chair can preside on the chair's behalf. The agenda of the chairman's conference is submitted by the secretary-general of the Standing Committee and approved by the chair. The document adopted by the chairman's conference is issued in the name of the Standing Committee secretary-general or his or her deputy. Based on a decision by the chairman's conference, with the consent of the secretary-general, news releases can be made regarding matters deliberated at the chairman's conference.

The chairman's conference is composed of the chair of the Standing Committee, the vice chairs, and the secretary-general. The deputy assistant secretary-general can attend the meeting but does not have a vote. With the consent of the chair or the vice chair responsible for administrative affairs (that is, the first vice chair), other responsible personnel of relevant units may also be invited to attend the conference.

The chairman's conference decides on the date and duration of the Standing Committee conference and on the proposed agenda, and it proposes what is to be put on the agenda for the full Standing Committee to consider when the Standing Committee conference is in session. If there is an interpellation motion made by ten or more members of the Standing Committee, the chairman's conference asks the relevant special committees or the Standing Committee to examine and approve it. If the interpellation is approved, then a decision is made as to whether the response from the relevant organs is to be made orally or in writing at either the Standing Committee meeting or the special committee meeting. The chairman's conference decides whether a report is to be made and whether a certain motion should be sent to the special committees first for examination or whether it is to be deliberated by the Standing Committee conference directly. The chairman's conference also decides whether a state organ's work report submitted to the Standing Committee should first be sent to the relevant special committee for examination and whether the views on such reports are to be made by the special committees. And the conference leads and coordinates the work of various special committees. When the NPC is in recess, the conference selects the vice chairs of individual special committees as well as their members if there are vacancies.

Administrative organs of the Standing Committee

The primary work organs of the Standing Committee are its Secretariat, General Administrative Office, and Legislative Affairs Commission. The mission of such offices is to carry out the work of the NPC conference, the Standing Committee conference, and the chairman's conference. They also support the various special committees and do work for the deputies of the NPC as well as individual members of the Standing Committee.

Under the direction of the chair of the Standing Committee, the Secretariat carries out the day-to-day business of the Standing Committee. The head of the Secretariat is the secretary-general of the Standing Committee. It is jointly led by deputy secretaries-general. Vice chairs of the various special committees are also members. The functions of the Secretariat are to understand various issues and find ways to deal with them; to serve as liaison among the various special committees of the NPC, the General Administrative Office of the Standing Committee, as well as the Legislative Affairs Commission; to be responsible for personnel matters and propose plans for setting up any legislative-related organs; and to carry out any assignments given by the chair of the Standing Committee. Conferences of the Secretariat, to be chaired by the secretary-general, typically meet every two weeks. In addition to Secretariat members, responsible personnel of various government organs may be invited to attend. Minutes are kept, and a summarized record is sent in the name of the secretary-general to other participants for reference.

The General Administrative Office, led by the Secretariat of the Standing Committee, carries out assignments of the Standing Committee. It comprises nine offices: the Bureau of Secretaries, the Research Office, the Liaison Office, the Foreign Affairs Bureau, the Press Bureau, the Letters and Visitors Bureau, the Personnel Bureau, the Bureau for Management of the Great Hall of the People, and the Administrative Management Bureau.

1) Bureau of Secretaries. The bureau carries out secretarial work of a general nature. It participates in making plans and doing other preparatory work for the convening of the Standing Committee chairman's conference, the Standing Committee conference, and the NPC conference. It makes arrangements for the organization of the Standing Committee's investigation groups. It is also responsible for compiling the *Standing Committee Gazette* and for the printing, management, and delivery of conference documents and of documents issued by the General Office. The Bureau of Secretaries conducts an exchange of documents between the Chinese Communist Party Office and other state organs. It is in charge of the preservation of the NPC archives. It also carries out secretarial work for the secretary-general and the deputy secretaries-general.

2) Research Office. The primary function of the Research Office is to conduct research and respond to inquiries on behalf of the Standing Committee and the various NPC special committees. For certain important questions on the agenda of the Standing Committee, the office conducts research and supplies all relevant materials, both domestic and foreign, and submits a report on such topics on the agenda. It is also responsible for issuing bulletins and express bulletins for the NPC conference and the Standing Committee conference. The office participates in drafting the work report of the Standing Committee.

3) Liaison Office. The primary function of this office is to liaise with the standing committees of the people's congresses of various provinces, autonomous regions, and municipalities under the direct control of the central government. It is to understand the situation of local people's congress work, grasp the election situation, reflect the views of individual deputies, and respond to the criticisms, sugges-

tions, and views of the deputies on their handling of such matters. The office receives letters from deputies and also makes arrangements for deputies to make field investigations.

4) Foreign Affairs Bureau. This bureau has the day-to-day responsibility of seeing to it that the foreign affairs activities of the leadership of the Standing Committee are handled properly. It is responsible for making preparations for receiving foreign dignitaries and foreign parliamentary groups visiting China and for translating and gathering materials for the use of the leadership. It also prepares a plan for conducting the foreign affairs activities of the legislature. The bureau participates in bilateral and international parliamentary organizations, and on behalf of the Standing Committee it conducts liaison activities with the foreign embassies in China as well as with foreign organs in order to promote international exchange. It is also responsible for handling correspondence regarding foreign affairs matters for the NPC.

5) Press Bureau. The Press Bureau was established in May 1987. Its purpose is to keep the leadership of the Standing Committee apprised of the news and its import, both domestic and foreign, and to strengthen the Standing Committee's publicity work. It is also responsible for supplying the news in summarized form to the leadership of the Standing Committee. It issues press releases and handles foreign propaganda work on behalf of the Standing Committee and the General Office of the Standing Committee. The bureau receives foreign correspondents and acts as coordinator of different press units for the duration of the NPC conference.

6) Letters and Visitors Bureau. The primary function of this bureau is to handle letters from the public that are sent to the Standing Committee and its leaders. It is responsible for representing the popular view on certain important questions to the Standing Committee and to the party leadership. Typically, it receives complaints having to do with civil disputes, court decisions, and prison sentences. According to the March 1996 NPC Standing Committee Work Report, in the past year 67,600 letters had been handled and 13,746 visitors had been received.

7) Personnel Bureau. This bureau handles budgetary matters and the transfer, appointment, evaluation, retirement, and security of those who work for the NPC.

8) Bureau for Management of the Great Hall of the People. Prior to May 1989, the management of the Great Hall was under the General Office of the Central Committee of the CCP; since May 1989, it has been under the General Office of the NPC Standing Committee. The Great Hall is used by both the party and the state for important occasions and for holding various kinds of meetings. The primary functions of the bureau are to make arrangements for party and state leaders to receive guests, hold conversations, have meetings, and receive foreign dignitaries as well as to hold ceremonies for the signing of important documents. The Great Hall can also be used by government organs, people's organizations, and military groups for holding conferences.

9) Administrative Management Bureau. This bureau is responsible for handling the day-to-day practical administrative matters of the NPC, the NPC Standing Committee, the chairman's conference, the special committees, and the General Office of the Standing Committee.

The precursors of the Legislative Affairs Commission were the Law Office of the 1950s and the Legislative Commission, instituted in 1979. The Legislative Commission had 180 full-time staff members, of whom 160 were professionals; after 1979, the size of the Legislative Affairs Commission was increased sixfold. The primary functions of the commission are to draft laws on behalf of the Standing Committee; in conjunction with the relevant government agencies, draft and revise other laws that are to be examined by the Standing Committee; make suggestions on the revision of proposed draft laws submitted by various government organs under the State Council, paying special attention to the coordination of different laws as well as their parameters; send the draft laws to various government organs and other places to solicit their views and, when necessary, hold symposia on the more controversial issues, and also do research on certain aspects of the laws; when the NPC and its Standing Committee examine draft laws, furnish all relevant useful material in order to show the views voiced by different organs and also provide foreign legal materials for comparison; propose revisions in draft laws based on the views expressed by different government units and by the Standing Committee; answer questions from different government units and localities.

The Legislative Affairs Commission has a chair, a number of vice chairs, a secretary-general, and a number of deputy secretaries-general. It has a General Administrative Office, which convenes meetings, handles daily routine affairs, and issues and distributes documents; a Research Office, comprising about two dozen professional researchers divided into two specialized groups, one on comparative and foreign laws and the other on Chinese law, as well as a Subordinate Materials Office responsible for distributing materials to the Legislative Affairs Commission's four specialized offices; an Office of Civil Law, Office of Criminal Law, Office of State Law and Administrative Law, and Office of Economic Law. The four specialized offices have between fifteen and thirty members each. They are responsible for ensuring that draft laws are consistent with existing laws, drafting amendments under the Law Committee's guidance, formulating certain types of laws not drafted under the Legislative Affairs Bureau of the State Council, and polishing laws recommended by the State Council before handing them on to the Law Committee. In addition, they reach outside the unit to arrange provincial investigations, solicit opinions from officials, hold conferences, and write reports for the Standing Committee and the Law Committee.

Special committees and other committees

The constitution stipulates that the National People's Congress establish a Nationalities Committee, a Law Committee, a Finance and Economic Committee, an Education, Science, Culture and Public Health Committee, a Foreign Affairs Committee, an Overseas Chinese Committee, and such other special committees as are necessary. These special committees work under the direction of the Standing Committee of the National People's Congress when the Congress is not in session.

The special committees examine, discuss, and draw up relevant bills and draft resolutions under the direction of the National People's Congress and its Standing Committee. Special committees are responsible to the NPC and are under the direction of the Standing Committee when the NPC is not in session.

The special committees are permanent work organs of the NPC. Each special committee is composed of a chair, vice chairs, and members. Candidates for these positions are nominated by the Presidium and approved by the NPC. When the NPC is not in session, the Standing Committee may have certain NPC deputies fill vacancies on the special committees and also appoint vice chairs. The nomination is made by the Standing Committee chair and approved by the Standing Committee. The special committees may have a certain number of experts as advisers, appointed or removed by the NPC Standing Committee, who may attend meetings and express their views.

The special committees submit bills related to their particular functions to the NPC Presidium or to the Standing Committee; deliberate on bills and proposals received from the Presidium or the Standing Committee; examine apparent conflicts between the constitution and laws and certain administrative laws and regulations, decisions, and decrees issued by the State Council; and examine the administrative laws and regulations issued by the subordinate organs of the State Council as well as the local people's congress enactments and decisions and orders and report on any conflict of laws to the Standing Committee. They examine interpellations of the NPC Presidium or the Standing Committee, listen to replies from the government organs, and, when necessary, report on such matters to the Presidium or the Standing Committee; conduct investigations and do research on work-related issues and send any recommendations resulting therefrom to the NPC or its Standing Committee.

The NPC Organic Law mentions six special committees by name, and others have also been created. The Internal Affairs and Judicial Committee came into being in March 1988, six years after the law's enactment.

The First, Second, and Third NPC, starting from 1954, each set up a Nationalities Committee, but it later became defunct until a decision was made in 1979, at the second session of the Fifth NPC, to re-establish it. In March 1988, at the first session of the Seventh NPC, the number of members of the Nationalities Committee stood at twenty-two. The primary functions and responsibilities of the Nationalities Committee are to enact and oversee the laws on autonomous nationality regions, strengthen legislative work on nationalities, and ensure that laws regulating nationality issues are thoroughly implemented; make suggestions on nationality questions and organize investigation groups and send reports on its findings to the Standing Committee, and assist the local governments in the autonomous areas in enacting local laws and regulations; examine bills sent from the NPC and its Standing Committee and report back their views on them; investigate important reforms to be carried out in minority nationality areas and send reports on its findings to the Standing Committee and the Standing Committee chairman's conference; strengthen ideological work on Marxism-Leninism and the thought of Mao Zedong regarding the minority nationality areas; learn from other countries in handling minority nationality issues, compile relevant materials, and conduct exchanges with foreign parliamentary groups; make an effort to expand the functions and powers conferred on the committee by the constitution.

The Law Committee was established at the first session of the Sixth NPC in 1983. Its primary functions are to examine draft laws that are submitted to the NPC or its Standing Committee for adoption, make suggested revisions, and also participate in the actual drafting; examine bills submitted to the NPC and the Standing Committee and report back its findings; do research and conduct investigations as part of the legislative process and submit its views.

The Internal Affairs and Judicial Affairs Committee was first established on March 24, 1988, during the first session of the Seventh NPC, with twenty members. Its main role is to supervise the work of the judiciary, the primary functions being to examine bills or matters requiring interpellation that deal with internal judicial affairs sent by the NPC or its Standing Committee; examine or participate in the drafting of relevant laws; examine administrative laws and regulations as well as local laws and regulations dealing with internal judicial affairs; investigate the implementation of laws and constitutional provisions by the internal judicial affairs organs; listen to reports of the various organs in charge of internal judicial affairs; conduct interparliamentary communications work; and see that the work of the committee, especially personnel matters and work procedures, is correctly carried out.

The Finance and Economic Committee was first established in 1983 at the first session of the Sixth NPC. Its primary functions are to understand the annual state budget and monitor its implementation; examine bills on financial and economic matters submitted by the NPC and its Standing Committee; and visit important areas to investigate how economic laws are being implemented. It also conducts research on and investigates important financial and economic questions and submits suggestions and proposals based on this work to the NPC and its Standing Committee.

First established at the first session of the Sixth NPC in 1983, the Education, Science, Culture, and Public Health Committee conducts research, examines and participates in the drafting of laws on education, science, culture, and public health; exercises oversight by conducting investigations into whether such laws are properly implemented, and advances the reform and development of educational, scientific, cultural, and public health-related enterprises; examines and makes suggestions on bills relevant to the committee's expertise; and listens to reports from relevant government organs, conducts research on important issues, and proposes changes in the handling of those issues when called for.

The Foreign Affairs Committee was established at the first session of the Sixth NPC in 1983 with ten members. Since the Sixth NPC it has been divided into three sections, for the (former) Soviet Union, Eastern Europe, and Africa; for Western Europe and the Americas; and for Asia, Oceania, and North Africa. The committee is responsible for conducting research on, examining, and participating in drafting bills on foreign affairs; maintaining communication with counterpart committees of foreign parliaments; and doing investigative and research work.

The Overseas Chinese Committee was established at the first session of the Sixth NPC in 1983. The committee examines bills and draft laws and participates in drafting laws having to do with Overseas Chinese, ensures that Overseas Chinese policy is duly implemented, and in general furthers work related to Overseas Chinese.

The main task of the Committee on Evaluating the Qualifications of Deputies is to make sure that the qualifications of NPC deputies meet the prescribed standard. The committee has a chair and a number of vice chairs. The chair and the other members are nominated by the chairman's conference of the NPC Standing Committee and confirmed or rejected by a vote of the full Standing Committee.

LEGISLATIVE–EXECUTIVE RELATIONS

The State Council is described in the constitution as "the executive body of the highest organ of state power" and the "highest organ of state administration." Its term of office is the same as that of the NPC, and the premier, vice premiers, and state councilors may not serve more than two consecutive terms. The constitution stipulates that, among its other functions and powers, the State Council is to submit proposals to the NPC or its Standing Committee.

The constitution provides that the NPC Standing Committee is to exercise supervision over the work of the State Council. One means of supervision is that the State Council must submit yearly reports on national economic and social development plans and on the state budget to the NPC for its examination and approval; if partial adjustments need to be made in the course of execution, the State Council submits revised programs for Standing Committee examination and approval. The NPC is empowered to elect the president and the vice president of the PRC, who are largely figureheads, and to choose the premier of the State Council upon the president's nomination. It also makes decisions on the appointment of officials below the level of premier, including the vice premiers, state councilors, ministers in charge of ministries or commissions, the auditor-general and the secretary-general of the State Council, based on nominations submitted by the premier. The NPC has the power to remove all of the above-named officials of the executive. In addition, the NPC or its Standing Committee decides upon the establishment, dissolution, or merger of ministries and commissions of the State Council that are proposed by the premier.

The constitution prescribes that it is the right of NPC deputies and members of the Standing Committee, during Congress sessions or committee meetings, to address questions to the State Council or its ministries and commissions, in accordance with procedures prescribed by law. The executive bodies must provide answers in a responsible manner. According to the Organic Law of the NPC, a delegation or group of thirty or more deputies may address written questions to the State Council and its ministries and commissions. The Presidium decides whether to refer the questions to the organs concerned for written replies or to ask the leaders of the organs to reply orally at meetings of the Presidium, the relevant special committees, or the relevant delegations. If the replies are to be given at Presidium or special committee meetings, the head of the delegation or of the group of deputies who addressed the questions may also attend.

In late 1994 there were reports that NPC leaders were making a new bid for power, the boldest since the legislature was established in 1954, by claiming the NPC to be the protector of the constitution and the embodiment of the will of the country. According to Chinese constitutional scholars there had been frequent conflicts between legislators and government officials over the substance of new laws, causing delays in the enactment of some laws. At the March 1995 plenum, a stir was created when only 63 percent of NPC members voted in favor of a candidate's premiership, perhaps the lowest show of support in NPC history. In addition, there were significant shows of dissent against an education law (with only 25 percent voting in favor), a banking law, and the reports presented by the Supreme People's Court president and the procurator-general (17 and 20 percent, respectively). However, the dissent indicated not so much a challenge to the state and the CCP as a desire for greater participation in the political process. Another watershed of the meeting was Premier Li Peng's admission in his Government Work Report that the high rate of inflation in 1994 was partly due to government errors.

According to the PRC constitution, the NPC Standing Committee decides on the imposition of martial law throughout China or in particular provinces, autonomous regions, or municipalities under the direct control of the central government. The executive body, the State Council, has the power to impose martial law in parts of provinces, autonomous regions, and municipalities under the direct control of the central government.

STATUS OF MEMBERS AND PARLIAMENTARY RESOURCES

The Legislative Affairs Commission, as the primary research arm of the NPC, has a small library. However, its collection does not compare in size to institutions like the Diet Library of Japan or the Library of Congress of the United States.

No deputy to the NPC may be arrested or placed on criminal trial without the consent of the Presidium of the current NPC session or, when the NPC is not in session, without the consent of the Standing Committee. If a deputy is caught in the act of committing a crime and detained, the public security organ that detained him or her must immediately report the matter to the Presidium or the Standing Committee.

Deputies are subject to supervision by the units that elected them, and those units have the power, through prescribed procedures, to recall the deputies they elected. The Electoral Law stipulates that the recall of a deputy elected by a people's congress must be approved by a majority vote of all the deputies of the Congress or by a majority vote of all the standing committee members when the people's congress is not in session. A deputy to be recalled may attend the recall vote meetings to state his or her views or submit a written statement. The recall resolution is to be reported to the standing committee of the people's congress at the next higher level for the record. Specific recall procedures are stipulated by the standing committees of the provincial, autonomous regional, and directly centrally controlled municipal people's congresses.

The Presidium, more than three delegations, or more than one-tenth of the delegates can propose the recall of an NPC Standing Committee member. After the Presidium submits the case to the various delegations for discussion, it is put to a vote at the plenary session. Alternatively, an investigation committee can be organized, at the suggestion of the Presidium and decision of the plenary session, whose report will be used by the next NPC session in making a decision. It is also stipulated that the recall is to be based on reasons that are clearly spelled out, with relevant data provided. Before the recall is put to a vote, the target of the action has the right to plead his or her case at a meeting of the Presidium and at the session or to argue it in writing. His or her arguments are printed and distributed at the session by the Presidium.

NPC deputies may submit their resignations to the standing committee of the people's congress that elected them. The Presidium refers requests to resign made by a member of the NPC Standing Committee to various delegations for discussion and seeks a decision at the plenary session. If the request is made when the NPC is not in session, it will be referred to the Standing Committee for consideration and action. If the Standing Committee accepts the resignation, it reports the matter for confirmation at the next NPC session.

The constitution prescribes that NPC deputies must play

an exemplary role in abiding by the constitution and the law and keeping state secrets, and in public activities and other work help enforce the constitution and law. It also states that no one on the NPC Standing Committee may hold office in any of the state administrative, judicial, or procuratorial organs. No punishments are prescribed in the rules, which state only that those who seriously violate the rules "should examine their conduct at a Standing Committee chairmanship meeting."

China does not yet have a "sunshine" law. Prior to the convocation of the second session of the Eighth NPC, a group of deputies from several delegations demanded that NPC vice chairs who are party members, state councilors, ministers of various commissions and ministries, or members of the CCP Central Committee Politburo, among others, provide an account of their own economic status as well as that of their dependents and relatives (and in addition the latter's political and working conditions). However, when some of the deputies tried to submit a joint motion along these lines to the NPC, the Presidium (which exercises control over the Congress by means of CCP units in the delegations) and party committees of some delegations contended that the motion was out of order. Nevertheless, there is a draft Law on Disclosure of Property and Income. Its formulation was placed on the legislative agenda in early 1994 by the Standing Committee of the Eighth NPC, and by August 1994 the State Ministry of Supervision had begun work on the draft. It was expected that the law would be passed in 1996, but that did not materialize. However, in March 1997 the General Office of the CCP Central Committee and the State Council issued rules requiring "leading cadres"—among others, those serving in people's congresses at and above the county level—to report on several categories of their activities. For example, they must report on the building, trading, or leasing of privately owned living quarters by themselves, their spouses, or their children; on their own weddings and on their or their children's marriage to a foreigner; on private trips abroad; on the operations of small businesses run by their spouse or children, and so on.

Wendy I. Zeldin

BIBLIOGRAPHY

Bunge, Frederica M., and Rinn-Sup Shinn, eds. *China: A Country Study.* 3d ed. Foreign Area Studies Series. Washington, D.C.: American University, 1981.

Cheng, Joseph Y. S. "How To Strengthen the National People's Congress and Implement Constitutionalism." *Chinese Law and Government* 16, no. 2–3 (summer-fall 1983): 88–122.

Chiu, Thomas, Ian Dobinson, and Mark Findlay. *Legal Systems of the PRC.* Hong Kong: Longman, 1991.

Dowdle, Michael. "Realizing Constitutional Potential." *China Business Review* 23, no. 6 (November-December 1996): 30–37.

Nelson, Daniel, and Stephen White, eds. *Communist Legislatures in Comparative Perspective.* Albany: State University of New York Press, 1982.

O'Brien, Kevin J. *Reform Without Liberalization: China's National People's Congress and the Politics of Institutional Change.* New York: Cambridge University Press, 1990.

———. "China's National People's Congress: Reform and Its Limits." *Legislative Studies Quarterly* 13 (August 1988): 343–374.

———. "Legislative Development and Chinese Political Change." *Studies in Comparative Communism* 22, no. 1 (spring 1989): 57–75.

Tanner, Murray Scot. "Organizations and Politics in China's Post-Mao Law-making System." In *Domestic Law Reforms in Post-Mao China,* ed. Pitman B. Potter. Armonk, N.Y.: M.E. Sharpe, 1994.

COLOMBIA

OFFICIAL NAME: Republic of Colombia (República de Colombia)

CAPITAL: Santa Fe de Bogotá

POPULATION: 36,813,000 (1996 est.)

DATE OF INDEPENDENCE: 1819 (from Spain)

DATE OF CURRENT CONSTITUTION: Adopted July 5, 1991

FORM OF GOVERNMENT: Parliamentary democracy

LANGUAGE: Spanish

MONETARY UNIT: Colombian peso

FISCAL YEAR: Calendar year

LEGISLATURE: Congress (Congreso)

NUMBER OF CHAMBERS: Two. Chamber of Representatives (Cámara de Representantes); Senate (Senado)

NUMBER OF MEMBERS: Chamber of Representatives, 163; Senate, 102

PERCENTAGE OF WOMEN: Chamber of Representatives, 11.7; Senate, 6.9

TERM OF LEGISLATURE: Four years

MOST RECENT LEGISLATIVE ELECTION: March 13, 1994

MINIMUM AGE FOR VOTING: 18

MINIMUM AGE FOR MEMBERSHIP: Chamber of Representatives, 25; Senate, 30

SUFFRAGE: Universal and direct

VOTING: Optional

ADDRESS: Congreso, Capitolio Nacional, Santa Fe de Bogotá

TELEPHONE: Chamber of Representatives, (571) 283 46 66; Senate, (571) 341 16 27

FAX: Chamber of Representatives, (571) 284 04 67; Senate, (571) 284 55 60

One of the world's major coffee exporters, the Republic of Colombia, in northwest South America, has coasts on both the Pacific and Atlantic Oceans. Struggling to overcome a legacy of violence and corruption, Colombia has long been plagued by illegal drug trafficking that has disrupted society and created conflict with other countries, particularly the United States. The country is now a presidential republic with a bicameral legislature. The president serves as both chief of state and head of government.

HISTORICAL BACKGROUND

Soon after the 1830 breakup of the Gran Colombia Federation—formed by Colombia, Venezuela, and Ecuador following independence from Spain in 1819—a tradition of civilian, elective government began in Colombia. Democratic government meant party government with elections for both president and Congress. In the nineteenth century there were three dictatorships, only one of which was a military one. None lasted more than a year and a half, and partisan opposition ended them all.

In the twentieth century the elected president Laureano Gómez (in office from 1949 to 1953) governed like a dictator. The only military dictatorship was that of Gen. Gustavo Rojas Pinilla (1953–1957), followed by a one-year caretaker military government as a transition to civilian rule. Throughout Colombian history the military and national police have been feared as potential foes of elective government and the parties.

The nature of elected governments from the time the Liberal and Conservative Parties were established at the end of the 1840s until 1958 affected the national Congress. Called "sectarian democracy" by some Colombian scholars, the political regime was one in which the dominant party maintained power through fraud and occasional violence. Party animosities were played out in Congress. For example, the son of Conservative president Laureano Gómez Alvaro once passed out whistles to Conservative members to use whenever a Liberal tried to speak. Members of Congress carried firearms, and there was at least one exchange of fire in the congressional chambers.

Since 1930 the Colombian Congress has met fairly regularly in both ordinary and special sessions. On November 9, 1949, at a time of high partisan violence, Conservative president Mariano Ospina Pérez closed Congress. President Laureano Gómez reopened it on October 31, 1951. Congress met only six days during the 1952–1953 session and even fewer during the military dictatorship of Rojas Pinilla.

After 1949 Colombia lived almost constantly under what was known as a "state of siege," during which various constitutional rights were suspended. Congress usually continued meeting, however, although the chief executive had the right to issue decrees that had the force of law.

Congress met regularly after civilian government resumed in 1958, and total days in session (both ordinary and special) varied between 138 (1958–1959) and thirty-eight (1968–1969). But between 1958 and 1974, under the compromise National Front government, the constitution divided Congress equally between members of the Liberal and Conservative Parties. Members of other parties were excluded from all public posts, including Congress. Not surprisingly, the two reigning parties tended toward factionalism because each would have 50 percent of the seats regardless of electoral results. This parity ended in 1974, and the Liberal Party has had a majority of the congressional seats ever since.

After a decade of violence by drug dealers, guerrillas, and paramilitary groups that made homicide the leading cause of death and Colombia the world murder-rate leader, in 1991 a Constituent Assembly met and wrote a new constitution to replace that of 1886, one of the oldest in Latin America.

REFORM

By the 1980s it was apparent that the Colombian Congress was not functioning effectively. By 1991 when the Constituent Assembly met, if there was one part of the Colombian political system that leaders considered broken and in need of fixing, consensus was that it was the national Congress. Members of Congress seemed more concerned with their individual well-being than with that of the nation. Absenteeism was high, in part because members could also be elected to departmental assemblies and town councils; "principal" members left Congress to be replaced by their alternates; foreign trips at taxpayers' cost were common; and pork barrel legislation (not for projects but for the congressional members to funnel directly to their supporters) was passed each session.

The argument to reform Congress came from all parts of the political continuum. Although there were disagreements from some groups (the Democratic Alliance—April 19 Movement, or M-19, a former guerrilla group arguing for a unicameral Congress, for example), the consensus was that changes to the institution were needed in the new constitution to make Congress a more effective branch of government.

Thus the 1991 constitution tried to lead to the election of more responsible members of Congress while giving it more power. Under the 1886 constitution, individual politicians could hold posts in all three levels of legislatures at the same time: the national Congress, departmental assembly, and municipal council. The national Congress typically ground to a halt when the assemblies began their short sessions. And the lack of a residency requirement might mean that a politician represented one area of the country in the Congress, sat on a city council, and was a member of the assembly in yet another area of the country. The 1991 constitution made it impossible for an individual to be on more than one legislative body at the same time.

The power of Congress was further increased by allowing it to hold votes of censure against government ministers. This right to censure, it was argued, would make the president more likely to consult with Congress. In addition, Congress was given more initiative in the budgetary process than it had before.

Finally, the 1991 constitution instituted the concept of the "state of exception," eliminating the state of siege, which the president, under the constitution of 1886, had the right to declare in cases of foreign wars or internal disturbances. The upper house of Congress, the Senate, would have to approve any extension of the states of exception. There were no time limits on the states of siege, and since the 1940s Colombia had been governed through them more often than not. Under states of siege the president could rule by decree, although the Council of State reviewed all decrees to make sure that they were constitutional.

A state of exception constrained the president much more than the state of siege because human rights and liberties could not be denied and branches of government could not be suspended. As soon as the causes of the exceptional state ended, so must the exceptional powers. Most important, the president could declare the state of exception for only ninety days a calendar year, after which it could be extended another ninety days by a vote of the Senate.

Displeasure with the old structure was so intense that the Constituent Assembly deposed the Congress elected under the old constitution. A new Congress was elected in October 1991 and began sessions in 1992. Few feel it behaved very differently from the Congress under the constitution of 1886. Even pork barrel legislation, through sleight of hand by calling the measure something different, was passed. A second congressional election under the new constitution took place in 1994.

ELECTIONS, MEMBERSHIP, AND TERMS OF OFFICE

Under the constitution of 1886 the electoral district for Congress was the department. Each department had two senators, plus an additional senator for each 200,000 inhabitants. The department also had two members in the lower house, plus an additional one for each 100,000 people. Terms in both houses were four years.

The constitution of 1991 left the lower house (the Chamber of Representatives) based on departments, although its size was reduced to 163 members. Each department has at least two members, plus an additional member for every 125,000 inhabitants over 250,000. The 102-member Senate, however, is elected by a national constituency, thus favoring minor parties. Members of the Constituent Assembly were explicit in wanting a constitutional arrangement that would encourage minority parties. The term of office for both houses is four years.

The electoral system used for both houses is a proportional representation list system in which voters cast ballots for the entire party list. If a list has the right to two senators, for example, the first two on the list are elected. To complicate matters, the list system encourages multiple lists. If any list receives less than one-half of the electoral quotient (defined as the total number of votes divided by the number of seats), those votes are assigned to the list with the same label that received the most votes. Furthermore, under the constitution of 1886 both principal members and alternates were elected. If any principal decided not to attend

Congress, the first alternate took the principal's place. The constitution of 1991 did away with alternates; now if an elected member of either house cannot attend Congress, he or she is replaced with the first person on the list who was not awarded a seat on the basis of the number of votes.

The new Congress includes representatives of minority communities. As stated in the constitution, the Senate has two members elected by the indigenous communities; Congress can pass a law giving the lower house as many as five representatives of "ethnic groups and political minorities." A law passed in 1992 gave two such members to the black communities.

The 1994 Senate election showed that the Colombian system under the new constitution is much more open than before—and perhaps confusing. Thirty-six political parties offered 251 lists of candidates (with 1,978 aspirants) for the Senate (not including the two indigenous senators). Only two of the lists for Senate elected more than one candidate (two each), which meant that 98 lists were represented in the new Senate. Distribution was fifty-three Liberals, twenty-four Conservatives, two Indians, one Christian, and eighteen from other movements.

The number of candidates for the lower house was even larger. There were 674 lists (with 3,355 hopefuls) for the 163 positions, not counting the two black representatives. Eighty-nine Liberals, fifty-four Conservatives, two M-19s, and sixteen others were elected.

CONGRESSIONAL OPERATIONS AND LEGISLATION

Congress meets in a neoclassical building that was completed in 1925, after nearly eighty years of construction. It occupies the southern side of Plaza Bolívar, the principal square of downtown Bogotá, sharing it with the national cathedral on the eastern side and the Palace of Justice on the northern perimeter. Just south of the Congress building is the Nariño Palace, in which the president resides.

Sessions

Under the constitution of 1886 Congress convened on July 20 each year and had regular 150-day sessions. If work was not finished, the president called extraordinary sessions during which only executive proposals could be considered. Bills, however, either were passed in forms quite different from those in which they had been proposed or were defeated. Ministers were questioned on the floor of the two houses and could be cited if they failed to attend. The reformers of 1991 increased annual sessions to two, the first from July 20 to December 16, and the second from March 16 to June 20.

Law Making

With two exceptions, laws may originate in either house of Congress. Tax laws must be initiated in the lower house, and laws having to do with international relations must be introduced in the Senate. One of the commissions in each house first considers any proposal made to Congress. This is the first debate. Any proposal passed at the commission level goes to the floor of the respective house for a debate. The author of a proposal can request that it be considered by the full house, even if not approved by the commission. Should the two houses pass legislation in different forms, an ad hoc committee with members from both houses redrafts the legislation, which then must be approved by each of the houses. If a proposal is passed by both houses in their second debates or after ad hoc committee resolution of differences, it is sent to the president for signature.

Although before 1991 the Colombian Congress was one of the more powerful in Latin America, it was never equal to the president. The legislative body could alter executive proposals, or even block them completely, but rarely did it initiate legislation. Over the years its authority diminished. The 1968 constitutional reform took power from Congress by giving the president the authority to declare any initiative urgent and giving Congress only thirty days to defeat it. Congress could not amend such urgent bills. In addition, all economic bills had to originate in the executive branch. Under the new constitution, the Colombian president can still declare a piece of legislation urgent. In such cases, each house has a maximum of thirty days to consider the executive proposal, which must be placed on legislative agendas with priority over other items.

The constitution of 1991 also introduced the idea of popular initiative, making it possible for 5 percent of the registered voters or 30 percent of the members of town councils or departmental assemblies to propose legislation. The first such legislation introduced, and later passed, in this fashion prescribed higher penalties for kidnapping.

After both houses of Congress pass a bill, it is sent to the president. If the president objects to any proposal, the bill is returned to the house in which it originated with the president's objections within six to ten days, depending on the length of the bill. A majority vote of the members of each house can override the president.

Some of the most important laws passed by the first Congress under the new constitution were the anti-kidnapping law, the first divorce law for both civil and church marriages, a law setting up a civil service bureaucracy, and a measure reforming higher education.

Commissions

As amended, the constitution of 1886 called for commissions in each house of Congress in eight areas: constitutional matters; foreign relations and defense; treasury and public credit; budget; education and public health; public works; social assistance and labor; and decentralized institutes. These commissions did not develop power comparable to committees in the U.S. Congress for several reasons, among them the lack of adequate staff, the high rate of congressional turnover from one term to another, and even greater turnover on the commissions.

The constitution of 1991 does not establish specific congressional commissions but does state that Congress will pass a law that will determine the number of committees, the size of their congressional membership, and the matters that they will consider.

Budget

Each year the executive branch must submit a national budget to the Congress, which debates it in joint meetings of the respective budget committees of the two houses. Congress can neither increase the amounts proposed by the executive for a budget category nor add an expense not thus proposed. It can, however, reduce or eliminate budgetary proposals of the executive branch. If Congress does not pass the proposed budget, it automatically goes into effect. If the executive does not propose a budget, the one approved for the previous year continues in force.

MEMBERS

People ineligible for election to Congress include those who have served prison terms, unless they were for political crimes; individuals who served as supervisory public employees during the year before the election; representatives of interest groups in the six months before the election; individuals who signed contracts with the government in the six months before the election; members of Congress who have been expelled; relatives of political, civil, administrative, or military authorities; and relatives of people who are candidates of the same party for the same elections.

Rules were established to make Congress more professional. Members can no longer hold other public posts, and alternate members are no longer permitted. Any member who resigns or is expelled is replaced by the person from his or her party next on the list of candidates. Members of Congress can make foreign trips paid for by governmental funds only for specific purposes approved by a vote of three-quarters of the members of the respective chamber. Nepotism rules make it impossible for the family of a member of Congress to hold any governmental post. Members of Congress must state their economic interests to avert conflict of interest. Most important, pork barrel legislation was ended. To avoid the continuing problem of absenteeism, the new constitution stated that any member of Congress who missed six votes in plenary sessions would be expelled. The Council of State decides who has violated these rules.

Members of Congress cannot be legally charged for the opinions they state or for their votes. Any crime alleged against a member of Congress is tried privately by the Penal Section of the Supreme Court. Congress in turn can impeach the president, the national prosecutor, and members of the Supreme Court and the extreme council of the judiciary. The accusation is made by majority vote of the lower house, and conviction is by a two-thirds vote of the Senate.

In 1996 this impeachment power was considered in the case of President Ernesto Samper Pizano. Samper had been accused of having received money from the Cali cocaine syndicate during his 1994 presidential campaign. Much to the dismay of the national prosecutor and the U.S. ambassador, on June 12 the Chamber of Representatives voted 111–43 against indicting the president.

PROBLEMS OF LEADERSHIP AND RESOURCES

The Colombian Congress has suffered a lack of leadership. Every year each house of Congress elects a governing board, with the stipulation that no member can be elected more than once during a four-year term. Elected heads of the two houses tend to be well-known Liberal Party leaders, but their leadership time tends to be short. Furthermore, because the Liberal Party is based on regional personalities more than national leadership, the leaders of the Chamber of Representatives and Senate often do not get along well.

For the same reasons, party caucuses have had limited importance, especially within the Liberal Party. Subgroups of the Conservative Party, such as the New Democratic Force and National Salvation Movement, have had more cohesion, albeit around the respective founders of the group rather than a leader within Congress.

The Colombian Congress is slow in developing a modern communications system, the lack of which endangers its autonomy and legislative independence. Each member of Congress can hire up to six aides but has a budget of only about $3,300 a month to do so. Almost all members have modern computers, but there is no electronic network for either communication or data consultation. The congressional library is rarely used, perhaps because it is not systematically organized. Nor is there a systematic archive of previous laws and projects.

The inability to make photocopies in large quantities and the lack of fax facilities except for a few offices are also problems. Using thirty-year-old recorders and electric typewriters, staff members take a week to transcribe debates. As a result, the technical quality of bills and monitoring of executive performance depends exclusively on the personal knowledge and hard work of individual members of Congress. Members often turn to others within the legislature who are experts in certain fields. They also present bills on which they received assistance from members of the executive branch, economic interest groups, or others.

Harvey F. Kline

BIBLIOGRAPHY

Hoskin, Gary, Francisco Leal, and Harvey F. Kline. *Legislative Behavior in Colombia.* Buffalo, N.Y.: Special Studies, Council on International Studies, State University of New York at Buffalo, 1976.

Kline, Harvey F. *Colombia: Democracy under Assault.* Boulder, Colo.: Westview Press, 1995.

Martz, John D. *The Politics of Clientelism: Democracy and the State in Colombia.* New Brunswick, N.J.: Transaction Press, 1996.

COMMONWEALTH OF INDEPENDENT STATES, NON-SLAVIC

Armenia, Azerbaijan, Georgia, Kazakstan, Kyrgyzstan, Tajikistan, Turkmenistan, and Uzbekistan comprised the "southern tier" of the former Union of Soviet Socialist Republics. Moldova, which is among the western newly independent states, along with Belarus and Ukraine, as a smaller, non-Slavic CIS member, is included here as well.

These states inherited Soviet-style legislatures upon the breakup of the Soviet Union at the end of 1991 (Georgia's legislature was under siege because of civil war). These legislatures, however, had undergone some restructuring as a result of constitutional changes introduced in 1988 at the instigation of Soviet Communist Party general secretary Mikhail Gorbachev. The changes called for increased legislative powers, including regularly convened working sessions.

Elections to the new republic legislatures occurred in 1989–1990. Elections were multicandidate though not multiparty, in line with Gorbachev's reform program. Candidates officially ran under either Communist Party or nonparty labels. Candidates endorsed by popular fronts (which were not allowed to register as political parties), however, often won seats. In other cases, reformist Communist Party candidates defeated officially backed Communist Party candidates.

Members of these unicameral legislatures (called *Supreme Soviets)* sat for five years. The legislatures possessed a presidium to guide their work, chairs, and various committees and commissions as determined by the membership. In some cases the chairs selected by the members were, as suggested by Gorbachev, the first secretaries of the republic communist parties, though in Georgia the members chose a nationalist popular front leader as chair, and in Moldova they chose a Communist Party member supported by the popular front.

After the breakup of the Soviet Union there were calls in many of the new states to revamp legislative structures and to elect new members, but sitting legislators usually were successful in blocking efforts to shorten their terms. In Kyrgyzstan, for instance, although a new constitution was enacted in May 1993 which called for new legislative elections, legislators refused to step down prematurely. Finally, in late 1994 Kyrgyz president Askar Akayev engineered the dissolution of the legislature and ordered new elections to be held in early 1995. Early elections occurred in Moldova in February 1994 to replace its communist-era legislature and in March 1994 in Kazakstan.

The predominant feature of the legislatures elected in 1994–1995 was their transitional nature. In Kazakstan and Kyrgyzstan, for example, even basic issues concerning the unicameral or bicameral structure of the legislatures remained subject to review even after the promulgation of new constitutions. Many of the legislatures also demonstrated their transitional nature by embodying features reminiscent of communist-era bodies, such as presidiums and councils of elders (long-tenured deputies) that formerly had controlled proceedings and even issued laws or decisions on their own authority. Moreover, they lacked a fully democratic legal culture, with deputies often more interested in debate than in detailed legislative work.

Although most constitutions stressed that legislators were not to serve in other, lower-level legislatures, hold government offices, or engage in other activities that erod-

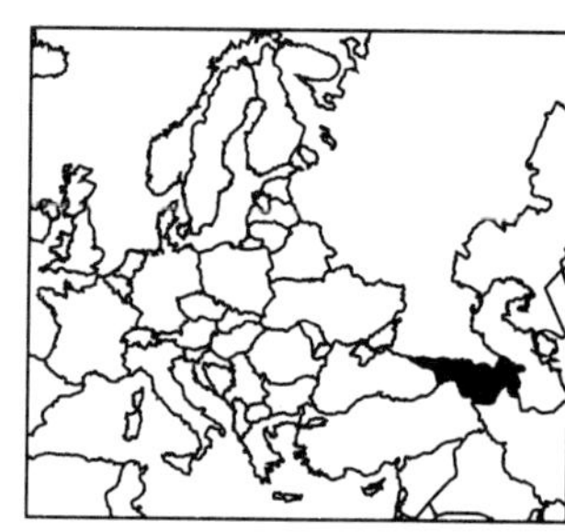

ed their professionalism, many deputies were unable to devote full time to legislative duties, mainly because of low pay. Quorums were sometimes difficult to achieve. Professional staffs were small, and legislative research services were lacking or rudimentary.

Despite these drawbacks, the legislatures in most of these southern-tier states and Moldova appeared, at least on paper, as potentially more effective law-making and oversight bodies than their predecessors. Most were standing bodies holding regular sessions and were free to determine the length of their sessions and whether to convene emergency sessions. Internal structure, such as committees and procedures, were also freely determined. Although elections were often marred by irregularities, most of these legislatures were also more reflective of the political and social makeup of the population than had been the pre-1994–1995 legislatures. Exceptions included the Tajik and Turkmen legislatures, which were designed as rubber stamps for the powerful executives in those states.

ARMENIA

OFFICIAL NAME: Republic of Armenia (Hayastani Hanrapetoutioun)
CAPITAL: Yerevan
POPULATION: 3,464,000 (1996 est.)
DATE OF INDEPENDENCE: September 23, 1991 (from the Soviet Union)
DATE OF CURRENT CONSTITUTION: Adopted July 5, 1995
FORM OF GOVERNMENT: Presidential
LANGUAGES: Armenian, Russian
MONETARY UNIT: Dram
FISCAL YEAR: Calendar year
LEGISLATURE: National Assembly (Azgayin Zhoghov)
NUMBER OF CHAMBERS: One
NUMBER OF MEMBERS: 190
PERCENTAGE OF WOMEN: 6.3
TERM OF LEGISLATURE: Four years
MOST RECENT LEGISLATIVE ELECTION: July 5 and 29, 1995
MINIMUM AGE FOR VOTING: 18
MINIMUM AGE FOR MEMBERSHIP: 25
SUFFRAGE: Universal and direct
VOTING: Optional
ADDRESS: National Assembly, 19 Marshal Baghramyan Ave., 375095 Yerevan
TELEPHONE: (374 2) 58 82 25
FAX: (374 2) 52 98 26

A unicameral Supreme Soviet consisting of 260 members was elected in May 1990 by voting districts. Its powers and the structure and functions of the political system were enumerated in a communist-era constitution approved in 1978 and later amended. In the absence of a postindependence constitution, the government's legitimacy rested on the 1990 Law on the Presidency and the 1991 Law on Parliament. The latter created a multiparty system. The president and the legislature clashed repeatedly over proposed constitutional drafts, with the legislature calling for a parliamentary system and the president for a strong presidential system. Another draft constitution proposed by Communist Party legislators called for resurrecting a socialist state.

No party had a legislative majority. The largest group of deputies, numbering fifty-five, belonged to the president's party, the Armenian National Movement (ANM), which advocated market reforms. In the spring of 1995 the ANM formed an electoral bloc with the Christian Democratic Union, the Union of Armenian Intellectuals, and a rump of the Democratic Liberal Party. The main opposition parties were the Armenian Revolutionary Federation (ARF/Dashnaktsutyun) and the Armenian Communist Party (ACP). The ARF had eighteen legislators, advocated slower economic reforms, and opposed what it termed authoritarian government methods.

Polls in late 1994 showed increasing popular support for the ARF. It formed an electoral bloc, called the Union of National Accord, with the National Democratic Union, the Union for National Self-Determination, the Democratic Party, and the Union of Constitutional Law. The ACP was represented by twenty-four legislators and called for confederation with Russia and re-creation of a command economy. The chair of the Supreme Soviet was ANM official Babken Ararktsyan.

Many legislators boycotted sessions to protest government actions; the frequent lack of quorums slowed the implementation of much legislation. In December 1994 the assassination of former Yerevan mayor Ambartsum Ealstyan, a former ANM official who had joined the opposition National Democratic Union, led to the resignation of about fifty legislators, with others suspending their participation. These actions seriously eroded the legislature's remaining effectiveness.

In early December 1994 President Levon Ter-Petrosian suspended the activities of the ARF, accusing it of involvement in terrorism, and closed its offices and newspapers. Its eighteen legislative members were allowed to continue their duties. In January 1995 the Armenian Supreme Court upheld the ban on the ARF for six months, precluding its participation in July 1995 legislative elections.

In mid-March 1995 the Armenian legislature approved a law setting elections to a new National Assembly on July 5, 1995. The National Assembly has 190 deputies, with 40 elected by party lists and the remainder on the basis of first-past-the-post contests in single-member districts.

International observers reported many campaign and voting irregularities in connection with the July elections. Observers from the Organization for Security and Cooperation in Europe (OSCE, formerly CSCE) judged the elections "free but not fair," in part because the main opposition party, the ARF, was banned from participation, the government dominated campaigning, the Central Electoral Commission appeared heavily progovernment in its decisions, and security officers constituted a chilling presence in many voting places. Also, electoral committees in the localities were overwhelmingly filled with members of the ruling ANM, raising the question of bias during the registration of parties and candidates. Voting irregularities reported on election day by the international observers included the violation of secret voting and pressure in voting places to cast a ballot for certain parties or candidates. Twenty of the forty seats allocated through party-list voting went to the Republic Bloc led by the ANM, followed by eight seats won by a women's party composed mostly of wives of ANM officials, six seats won by the ACP, three seats won by the National Democratic Union, and three seats won by the Union for National Self-Determination. In all, the Republic Bloc and other progovernment parties won 166 of 190 seats, while the opposition won only 18, and independents, 4 (2 seats were undecided).

A new Armenian constitution was approved at the same time as the Armenian legislative elections. The draft constitution had been drawn up by a commission headed by Ter-Petrosian. It provides for a strong presidential system of government with a weak legislative system. Members of the opposition had called unsuccessfully for a parliamentary system with strong legislative powers. The president's draft was approved on July 5, 1995, by 68 percent of the voters. It grants the president power to appoint and remove the prime minister, judges, and prosecutors and gives him liberal grounds to dissolve the legislature, declare martial law, and limit human rights by declaring a state of emergency.

AZERBAIJAN

OFFICIAL NAME: Azerbaijan Republic (Azarbaijchan Respublikasy)

CAPITAL: Baku

POPULATION: 7,677,000 (1996 est.)

DATE OF INDEPENDENCE: August 30, 1991 (from the Soviet Union)

DATE OF CURRENT CONSTITUTION: Adopted November 12, 1995

FORM OF GOVERNMENT: Parliamentary democracy

LANGUAGES: Azeri (official), Russian, Armenian

MONETARY UNIT: Manat

FISCAL YEAR: Calendar year

LEGISLATURE: National Assembly (Milli Mejlis)

NUMBER OF CHAMBERS: One

NUMBER OF MEMBERS: 125

PERCENTAGE OF WOMEN: 12.0

TERM OF LEGISLATURE: Five years

MOST RECENT LEGISLATIVE ELECTION: November 12 and 26, 1995

MINIMUM AGE FOR VOTING: 21

MINIMUM AGE FOR MEMBERSHIP: 25

SUFFRAGE: Universal and direct

VOTING: Optional

ADDRESS: National Assembly, Parliamentary Avenue 1, Baku 370152
TELEPHONE: (994 12) 39 97 50
FAX: (994 12) 93 49 43

Growing demonstrations against Azerbaijani Communist Party (ACP) rule caused the Soviet government to intervene militarily in Azerbaijan in January 1990, suppressing the opposition and placing Ayaz Mutalibov in power. Violence in Azerbaijan, linked to the efforts of its mainly ethnic Armenian enclave of Nagorno-Karabakh to secede and join Armenia, caused the February legislative elections to be postponed to September 1990. The ACP, in the face of a state of emergency that prevented effective campaigning and its harder line in regard to Nagorno-Karabakh, won about 80 percent of the seats in the 360-seat Supreme Soviet (not all seats were filled because of civil conflict).

But the ACP formally disbanded one year later, in September 1991, during a wave of popular revulsion against the role it had played in supporting the August coup against Mikhail Gorbachev. Mutalibov, after resigning from the ACP, was popularly elected to the presidency in an election that opponents denounced as fraudulent. Opposition deputies, including those of the Azerbaijani Popular Front (APF), united in a democratic bloc. A subset of the Supreme Soviet, called the National Council, was formed in November 1991 as a consultative body; it was composed of seventy deputies (later numbering fifty to fifty-two deputies), equally divided between conservative and opposition deputies.

In May 1992 the Supreme Soviet tried to restore Mutalibov, who had been forced to resign the presidency in March 1992 because of APF and popular discontent with his handling of the Nagorno-Karabakh dispute, to power. The APF foiled this attempt, and the National Council rescinded the decisions of the Supreme Soviet. Discredited and under duress, the Supreme Soviet voted to cede its powers to the National Council. Popular front leader and president Abul'faz El'chibey, who had succeeded Mutalibov by popular election on June 7, 1992, was ousted in June 1993, and the National Council transferred his presidential powers to Heydar Aliyev, a former ACP head, pending new presidential elections in October 1993.

Many violations of legislative immunities occurred. The speaker of the National Council, Isa Qambar (Gambarov), who had stepped down on June 13, 1993, to allow Aliyev to become speaker, was arrested on the floor of the legislature three days later, and only subsequently was stripped of his legislative immunity and mandate. He was vaguely charged with "abuse of power." Other APF deputies were stripped of mandates, and a Musavat deputy was severely beaten in early 1994 in the legislative building.

Under Aliyev's guidance, deputies of the Supreme Soviet attended sessions of the National Council as observers without the right to vote. In early October 1994 Aliyev reconvened the National Council to approve a state of emergency to defeat an alleged coup attempt. Aliyev also used the Council to secure the ouster of alleged coup plotter and prime minister Suret Huseynov and to ratify a high-profile oil agreement with a Western consortium.

Elections to a new, 125-member, unicameral National Assembly (Milli Mejlis) were held on November 12, 1995. Twenty-five of the seats were allocated through a proportional party list vote, and one hundred through single-member district balloting. Eight parties were allowed to take part in the party list voting in the legislative elections, but of them only the APF was clearly an anti-Aliyev party. The eight were the New Azerbaijan (NAP), APF, Azerbaijan Democratic Independence (ADIP), National Independence (NIP), Azerbaijan Democratic Proprietors (ADPP), Motherland, Azerbaijan National Statehood (NSPA), and Alliance for Azerbaijan parties. Parties excluded from the ballot included the Azerbaijani Communist Party, Musavat, Islamic Party, and others. All parties are small; NAP is the largest with 100,000 members claimed. NAP was formed in November 1992 by Aliyev and encompasses many of his former ACP supporters. NIP broke off from APF in early 1992, and ADIP broke off from NIP in late 1993. NIP views itself as a moderate nationalist party in "loyal opposition" to Aliyev, whereas ADIP is staunchly pro-Aliyev. ADPP was formed in 1994 as a pro-Aliyev and proreform party. Musavat, formed in 1912, supports close ties with Turkey. The pro-Iranian Islamic Party calls for an Islamic state.

Aliyev's NAP won most of the legislative races. The elections were marred by the harassment and exclusion of most opposition parties and candidates from participation and by rampant irregularities, such as the open stuffing of ballot boxes, according to international observers. Aliyev's NAP candidates ran unopposed in many electoral districts because of the exclusion of opposition candidates. Campaign advertising by most parties was severely restricted on state-owned television, while Aliyev received extensive coverage. Some observers stressed that the elections marked some progress in holding a multiparty vote.

The Azerbaijani constitution was approved by 91.9 percent of voters in a referendum held along with the November 12 legislative election. (Following two weeks of public debate in October, the final draft was to be completed in three-to-four days and published ten days prior to the referendum; in fact, it was completed just before the referendum.) The constitution strengthens presidential power, establishes the new unicameral legislative system, declares Azeri the state language, proclaims freedom of religion and a secular state, stipulates ownership over part of the Caspian Sea, and gives Nakhichevan Autonomous Republic (an exclave of Azerbaijan) quasi-federal rights. The president appoints and removes cabinet ministers (the legislature consents to the president's choice of prime minister), submits budgetary and other legislation that cannot be amended by the legislature but only approved or rejected within fifty-six days, and appoints local officials. Impeachment of the president by the legislature is extremely difficult.

GEORGIA

OFFICIAL NAME: Republic of Georgia (Sakartvelos Respublika)
CAPITAL: Tbilisi
POPULATION: 5,220,000 (1996 est.)
DATE OF INDEPENDENCE: April 9, 1991 (from the Soviet Union)
DATE OF CURRENT CONSTITUTION: Adopted October 17, 1995
FORM OF GOVERNMENT: Presidential
LANGUAGES: Georgian (official), Russian, Armenian, Azeri
MONETARY UNIT: Lari
FISCAL YEAR: Calendar year
LEGISLATURE: Parliament (Sakartvelos Parlamenti)
NUMBER OF CHAMBERS: One
NUMBER OF MEMBERS: 235
PERCENTAGE OF WOMEN: 6.8
TERM OF LEGISLATURE: Four years
MOST RECENT LEGISLATIVE ELECTION: November 5 and 19, 1995
MINIMUM AGE FOR VOTING: 18
MINIMUM AGE FOR MEMBERSHIP: 25
SUFFRAGE: Universal and direct
VOTING: Optional
ADDRESS: Georgian Parliament, 8 Rustaveli Avenue, 380018 Tbilisi
TELEPHONE: (995 32) 93 51 13
FAX: (995 32) 99 95 94

Georgia's first multiparty legislative elections were held in October 1990 and resulted in a victory for the proindependence party coalition Round Table-Free Georgia. The coalition, headed by academic and dissident Zviad Gamsakhurdia, won 155 seats in the 250-seat Supreme Soviet. The Georgian Communist Party won only 64 seats despite its adoption of a nationalistic stance, marking a sharp reversal of its previous dominance in the legislature. Ethnic minority parties were effectively disenfranchised by a rule prohibiting regional parties; secessionist sentiments in Abkhazia and South Ossetia, therefore, were not represented. Gamsakhurdia was selected by the deputies to serve as chair of the legislature and was popularly elected president of Georgia in May 1991.

During 1991 Gamsakhurdia's increasingly authoritarian and erratic attempts to remake Georgian society and politics led to growing opposition. Primary among this opposition were parties and paramilitary groups associated with the National Congress, an alternative "legislature" formed in October 1990 to push for independence. These groups spearheaded a general assault to overthrow Gamsakhurdia in December 1991, forcing him to flee the country in early January 1992. A Military Council formed by paramilitary and national guard leaders and others assumed power and suspended the Soviet-era constitution (substituting a 1921 constitution), dissolved the legislature, and declared emergency rule. Former Georgian leader Eduard Shevardnadze was invited in early March 1992 by the Military Council to return to Georgia, where he headed a civilian State Council (replacing the Military Council), which was to rule until legislative elections could be held. This executive and legislative body was dissolved in October 1992, after the elections.

Despite boycotts from nine electoral districts in Abkhazia, Mingrelia, and South Ossetia which sought to secede from Georgia, and reported voter irregularities, a new unicameral legislature of 235 members named the State Council was elected on October 11, 1992, in voting generally judged by international observers as free and fair. Forty-seven parties participated in the campaign, with many combining into blocs. Regional parties were not allowed. Four blocs, consisting of twenty parties, won seats. The largest number of seats—twenty-nine—was won by the Peace Bloc, indicating the factiousness of the new legislature.

The elections heralded the creation of a political system in which the legislative chair served as the highest official; the presidency was abolished. The election law provided for the popular election of the chair, who could not be a member of a political party. Shevardnadze, who ran uncontested, was elected chair of the legislature, gaining 95 percent of the popular vote. Two days after convening on November 4, the new legislature granted Chairman Shevardnadze wide-ranging powers as head of state pending completion of a new constitution. Work on a new constitution began in early 1993 but was slowed by civil turmoil.

Relations between the legislative and executive branches have been contentious. In August 1993 the cabinet resigned after the legislature rejected its budget. In the face of widespread legislative accusations of dictatorial methods, Shevardnadze resigned on September 14, 1993. The legislature refused to accept his resignation, however, after crowds surrounded the legislative building and demanded Shevardnadze's reinstatement. Shevardnadze agreed to rescind his resignation if the legislature approved a two-month state of emergency and recessed for two months. It met temporarily on September 27, however, in the face of Abkhazia's fall to insurgent forces. Reconvening on November 25, the legislature extended the state of emergency but refused Shevardnadze's call for it to extend its recess.

Other legislative challenges to Shevardnadze's rule occurred in August and September 1994. In the former case, a quorum could not be achieved to convene a special session, and in the latter, the State Council finally rejected opposition calls for Shevardnadze's resignation. In early 1995 the legislature appeared hamstrung in its efforts to draft a new election law to govern legislative elections planned for late 1995.

Work on a new constitution had begun in early 1993 and was finally approved by the legislature on August 24, 1995. Shevardnadze and most legislators felt that democratic principles required that the constitution be approved prior to, rather than simultaneously with, elections to a new legislature created by the constitution. The new constitution reestablishes a strong presidency, though it affirms a balance of executive and legislative powers more equitable than that reflected in most other new constitutions approved by former Soviet republics. It establishes a unicameral, 235-member legislature elected by single-member constituencies (85 seats) and party lists (150 seats). The post of prime minister is abolished; government ministers are responsible to the president, who is assisted by a state minister. The speaker of parliament is barely mentioned in the constitution; the speaker's only specified powers are to sign bills and serve as acting president in case the president is indisposed or dies. Federal and local government provisions were not included, with agreement that they would be added when the territorial integrity of Georgia has been assured.

Voting for the new legislature took place on November 5, 1995, simultaneous with the presidential race. The elections were judged "consistent with democratic norms" by international observers. Shevardnadze was elected to the new post of president (the old post having been abolished after former president Gamsakhurdia was ousted in January 1992), winning 74.3 percent of the vote in a six-man race. Legislative and presidential voting were described by international observers as generally "free and fair," though violations were reported in Ajaria.

Only three of the fifty-four parties running in the legislative races received at least 5 percent of the party-list vote, the minimum required to win seats, though other parties won representation through constituency races. Political parties that won representation based on their share of the party-list voting include Shevardnadze's Georgian Citizens' Union (gaining more than 500,000 of about 2 million party-list votes cast), the opposition National Democratic Party (garnering 169,000 votes), and the progovernment Revival Union (146,000 votes), headed by Aslan Abashidze, chair of the Ajarian Republic legislature. The United Communist Party, an umbrella party, just failed to gain enough votes to win party-list seats. Among the other parties that participated in the party-list vote were the Union of Traditionalists, the "21st Century" bloc (including Gamsakhurdia supporters), and the Socialist Party, each of which garnered around 4 percent (80,000–90,000 votes) and failed to win representation via the party-list voting. Fourteen minor opposition parties that failed to gain any seats in the legislative races created a Coordinating Council to pursue common policies, including participating in the September 1996 legislative election in Ajaria. Most of the minor political parties and groups characterize themselves as in opposition to the Shevardnadze government.

The parties have formed eight legislative factions; the largest is the Citizens' Union faction, with more than 110 members (almost 50 percent of the members of the legislature). Although it is the ruling party in the legislature, the Citizens' Union faction has at times objected to some of Shevardnadze's policies. The speaker is Zurab Zhvania, former Greens Party head and now a leader of the Citizens' Union.

KAZAKSTAN

OFFICIAL NAME: Republic of Kazakstan (Kazakstan Respublikasy)

CAPITAL: Almaty

POPULATION: 16,916,000 (1996 est.)

DATE OF INDEPENDENCE: December 16, 1991 (from the Soviet Union)

DATE OF CURRENT CONSTITUTION: Adopted August 30, 1995

FORM OF GOVERNMENT: Presidential

LANGUAGES: Kazak (official), Russian

MONETARY UNIT: Tenge

FISCAL YEAR: Calendar year

LEGISLATURE: Parliament

NUMBER OF CHAMBERS: Two. Assembly (Majlis); Senate (Senat)

NUMBER OF MEMBERS: Assembly, 67 (directly elected); Senate, 47 (40 indirectly elected, 7 appointed)

PERCENTAGE OF WOMEN: Assembly, 13.4; Senate, 8.5

TERM OF LEGISLATURE: Assembly, four years; Senate, four years (half of senators turn over every two years)

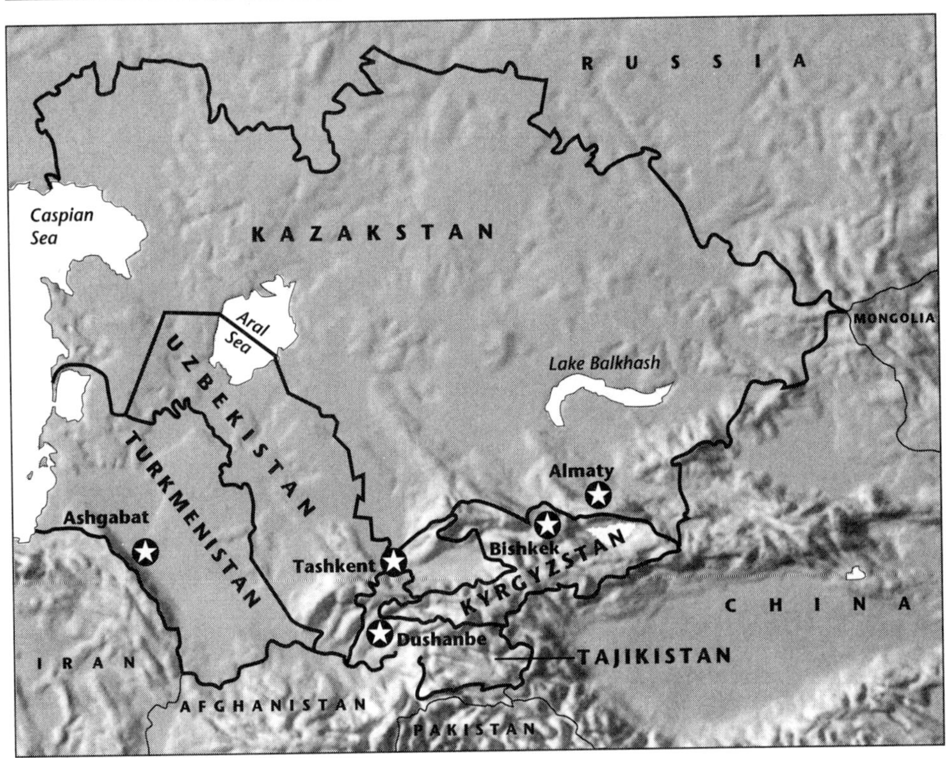

MOST RECENT LEGISLATIVE ELECTION: Assembly, December 5 and 9, 1995
MINIMUM AGE FOR VOTING: 18
MINIMUM AGE FOR MEMBERSHIP: 25
SUFFRAGE: Universal
VOTING: Optional
ADDRESS: Parliament House, 480091 Almaty
TELEPHONE: (732 72) 62 39 48
FAX: (732 72) 63 94 90

The Soviet-era Supreme Soviet was elected in March 1990, consisting of 360 members. Despite Gorbachev's reforms, in Kazakstan many legislative candidates stood unopposed. Kazakstan also followed Gorbachev's nonreformist policy of reserving seats for the Communist Party and affiliated organizations. As a result, fewer than two dozen of the winning legislators had not run on the Communist Party ticket. Before the elections, in February 1990, Nursultan Nazarbayev, head of the Kazak Communist Party, had had himself elected to the new post of chair of the Supreme Soviet, but after the legislature convened in April, he had it elect him to the newly created post of president of Kazakstan. About seventy of the deputies worked full time on legislative duties. There were seventeen standing committees, with a legislative staff of about 140.

The Soviet-era Supreme Soviet (or Supreme Kenges) on January 28, 1993, approved a new constitution that established a unicameral legislature. The Supreme Soviet was to finish out its normal term before the new legislature was elected.

In early December 1993, 43 deputies of the old Supreme Soviet, supporting Nazarbayev's call for early legislative elections, resigned their mandates. On December 8, the Supreme Soviet in closed session agreed to dissolve itself and to transfer supreme legislative power to Nazarbayev pending new elections it set for March 8, 1994. It remained in session until mid-December, however, to pass an election law and other statutes.

Under the electoral law, 135 members of the new 177-member Supreme Soviet would be elected from territorial constituencies, and 42 from a "state list" of presidentially picked candidates. Almost 700 candidates were registered, including 64 on the state list. From the state list, two members would be elected to represent each of nineteen regions in Kazakstan, plus the cities of Almaty and Leninsk. Nazarbayev voiced the hope that the constitution might eventually be amended so that the state list members could become part of an upper legislative chamber, formed on regional and ethnic grounds.

The Electoral Commission approved the credentials of 754 candidates to contest the 135 popularly chosen seats. Nazarbayev chose 64 candidates to contest the 42 state list seats. Election observers from the Conference on Security and Cooperation in Europe judged the elections not free and fair. It noted that many independent candidates had been disqualified from running, the state list was not democratic, the campaign was very short, media coverage was sometimes constrained, and many voters cast ballots for relatives and friends. Ethnic Kazak were overrepresented among the winning candidates, securing 56 percent of the seats (105), whereas ethnic Russians were underrepresented, securing only 27 percent of the seats (49). Ethnic Kazaks represent about 40 percent of the population, and ethnic Russians about 38 percent. Several parties and civic organizations won seats, including the Kazak People's Unity Union (Nazarbayev-supported, 33 seats), Trade Union Federation (11 seats), People's Congress (9 seats), Socialist Party (8 seats), the Lad Slavic Society (4 seats), Peasant Union (4 seats), and other parties and groups (7). A large number of candidates won seats as independents (59), relying on personal, regional, or ethnic ties, particularly ties to Nazarbayev.

The legislature in 1994 repeatedly expressed a lack of confidence in the economic policies of the government and opened an investigation into governmental corruption, using its broad constitutional power to question cabinet members on the execution of laws and raise with the president the issue of releasing a cabinet member (Article 88). These actions contributed to the resignation of the government in October. However, a new cabinet was formed that differed only partly from the old and that pledged to continue the reform course.

Upon appeal by a losing legislative candidate, the Kazak Constitutional Court in March 1995 ruled that the March 1994 legislative election was invalid because it violated the principle of "one person, one vote." Constituencies had not been drawn up representing approximately equal populations, and confused voting procedures resulted in electors voting for several candidates. On March 11 Nazarbayev noted that the decision was in accordance with the constitution and dissolved the legislature. Critics charged that the dissolution served Nazarbayev's purposes since it eliminated a legislature that opposed his policies. All legislative powers were to be exercised by the president pending new legislative elections, planned for mid-1995. A transitional government also was formed. Many former deputies formed an anti-Nazarbayev electoral bloc in anticipation of the new elections.

A final draft constitution was submitted to referendum on August 30, 1995. According to a number of international observers, many proposed changes to the constitution that had been suggested by democracy and human rights advocates during the discussion phase were not incorporated into the draft, and the referendum turnout and results were "exaggerated." Compared to the 1993 constitution, the 1995 constitution increases the powers of the presidency and reduces those of the legislature, and it places less emphasis on protecting human rights. The new constitution creates a bicameral, 114-member legislature, with an upper house (the Senate) designed to enhance regional, clan, and ethnic representation. As fleshed out by an October 1995 presidential edict, the legislature does not control the budget or the legislative agenda, cannot initiate changes to the constitution, and cannot exercise oversight over the executive branch. If the legislature fails within thirty days to pass an "urgent" bill brought by the president, the president may issue the bill by decree. Whereas the president has broad powers to dissolve the legislature, it may only remove the president for disability or high treason. An extraconstitutional, quasi-legislative 327-member People's Assembly comprising various cultural and ethnic leaders acts as a propaganda forum for Nazarbayev.

Elections to the lower house (the Assembly) were held December 5 and 9, 1995, and were judged by international observers as largely "free and fair," although some problems were evident. These included an onerous fee required to register as a candidate, inflation of turnout rates, and family voting. Forty deputies of the forty-seven-member Senate were indirectly elected by regional legislatures (termed *maslikhats),* and seven were appointed by Nazarbayev. Deputies to the sixty-seven-member Assembly, or *Majlis,* were directly elected by district. The two opposition parties allowed to campaign alleged government harassment and voting irregularities.

Six parties competed in the December 1995 legislative races. Progovernment parties participating included the Party of National Unity (SNEK), Democratic Party, Cooperation Party, and National Rebirth Party. Opposition parties included the Communist Party and People's Congress Party, the latter formed by poet and environmentalist Olzhas Suleymenov. The oppositionist National Democratic Party (the political arm of the Kazak nationalist movement Azat), the Republican Party (which calls for creation of a multiethnic multiparty democracy that will elevate Kazak culture and "decolonize" Kazakstan), and the previously progovernment Socialist Party (formerly the Kazak Communist Party, which now advocates a slowdown of economic reforms) boycotted the election as illegitimate.

SNEK, formerly a social movement created by Nazarbayev to support his presidency, has the largest number of deputies in the legislature. The Democratic Party, Cooperation Party, and National Rebirth Party were formed in 1995 as pro-Nazarbayev parties. The Communist Party, re-registered in July 1994, has advocated Stalinist policies, including re-creating the Soviet Union, and was warned by the government in May 1996 that it might lose its registration. Registration requires personal information from at least three thousand members, which many fear to provide. The Alash (a Kazak nationalist party) and Social Democratic Parties refuse to register.

The new legislature convened in January 1996. The chair of the Senate is Omirbek Baygeldiyev, and the chair of the Assembly is Marat Ospanov. Baygeldiyev noted that, to contain costs, the chambers shared a "minimized bureaucracy," and deputies' staffs had been eliminated, signifying weak legislative oversight and initiative powers. In June 1996 legislators rejected a government bill widely unpopular among their constituents restricting or eliminating many pension benefits, part of the president's "anticrisis" economic reforms, causing the government to force a vote of confidence. If the legislature voted confidence in the government, the bill would be deemed adopted. If it did not vote confidence, the president could dismiss either the legislature or the cabinet. Nazarbayev warned that he would not dismiss the government. The legislature, in an indication of its weakness vis-à-vis the presidency, yielded and voted confidence by a wide margin on June 12.

KYRGYZSTAN

OFFICIAL NAME: Kyrgyz Republic (Kyrgyz Respublikasy)
CAPITAL: Bishkek
POPULATION: 4,530,000 (1996 est.)
DATE OF INDEPENDENCE: August 31, 1991 (from the Soviet Union)
DATE OF CURRENT CONSTITUTION: Adopted May 5, 1993
FORM OF GOVERNMENT: Presidential
LANGUAGES: Kyrgyz (official), Russian (official)
MONETARY UNIT: Som
FISCAL YEAR: Calendar year
LEGISLATURE: Supreme Assembly (Togorku Kenesh)
NUMBER OF CHAMBERS: Two. Assembly of People's Representatives (El Okuldor Palatasy); Legislative Assembly (Myizam Chygaru Palatasy)
NUMBER OF MEMBERS: Assembly of People's Representatives, 70; Legislative Assembly, 35
PERCENTAGE OF WOMEN: Assembly of People's Representatives, 1.4; Legislative Assembly, 11.4
TERM OF LEGISLATURE: Five years
MOST RECENT LEGISLATIVE ELECTION: February 5 and 19, 1995
MINIMUM AGE FOR VOTING: 18
MINIMUM AGE FOR MEMBERSHIP: 25
SUFFRAGE: Universal and direct
VOTING: Optional
ADDRESS: Supreme Assembly, 207-209 Abdimomunov Street, 722003 Bishkek
TELEPHONE: (733 12) 22 23 08
FAX: (733 12) 22 60 35

Upon independence, supreme legislative power in Kyrgyzstan was exercised by the 350-member Supreme Soviet, elected on February 25, 1990. In these elections, seventy candidates ran unopposed, and 95 percent of the deputies elected were members of the Kyrgyzstan Communist Party (KCP), though many subsequently supported reforms. The legislature was relatively ineffective as a deliberative and oversight body since it met only twice a year for a total of four weeks, though committees worked between sessions. About ten deputies worked full time on legislative affairs. There were ten standing committees, with a total legislative staff of about sixty.

In April 1990 the legislature elected Absamat Masaliyev, long-time Communist Party boss, to the new post of chair of the Supreme Soviet. He called for the creation of the executive post of president, following Gorbachev's lead. In the summer of 1990 ethnic riots in the Osh region led to mass demonstrations in the capital, Bishkek, against KCP rule and to demands for the ouster of Masaliyev. When the Kyrgyz Supreme Soviet convened in extraordinary session to elect a president in October 1990, a democratic bloc of deputies narrowly defeated Masaliyev's bid. This democratic bloc and other supporters of reform urged USSR Supreme Soviet deputy and president of the Kyrgyz Academy of Sciences Askar Akayev to return to Kyrgyzstan from his legislative duties in Moscow, and after repeated voting they elected him to the newly created post. Masaliyev resigned as legislative chair in December.

A new constitution was promulgated in May 1993. This constitution, the product of months of executive-legislative branch negotiations and consultations with many international experts, called for a unicameral, 105-member legislature. The two sides agreed that current legislative and executive branch officeholders could serve until 1995, delaying legislative reforms and reducing the president's term in office.

In early September 1994 Akayev's supporters in the legislature—who constituted a slim majority of 168 of 323 sitting deputies, most of whom were local administrators—boycotted the last session of the legislature before the expiration of its mandate in February 1995. Their boycott prevented formation of a quorum, causing the dissolution of the legislature. Opponents of Akayev alleged that the dissolution was intended to squelch a legislative investigation into government corruption and to open the way for Akayev to create a more malleable legislature. Akayev took over legislative powers pending elections and moved quickly to decree economic reforms that had been blocked by the legislature. He decreed legislative elections be held by the end of the year and a referendum be held on October 22 to approve amendments to the constitution, including provisions revamping the legislative system. He argued that legislative and other provisions of the May 1993 constitution were too idealistic for Kyrgyz conditions and that a transitional period was needed before a Western-style democracy was created. Although this amendment process contravened the existing constitution, the referendum was approved by more than 80 percent of the voters.

The constitutional amendments created a two-chamber legislature termed the Supreme Assembly (Togorku Kenesh): a Legislative Assembly, with thirty-five members that would serve continuously and represent "all people"; and a seventy-member Assembly of People's Representatives, which would meet in regular sessions and represent territorial interests. The Legislative Assembly would be the lawmaking chamber, while the other chamber would approve the budget and confirm presidential appointees. In general, the amendments reduced the powers of the legislature. Whereas the May 1993 constitution had called for the legislature to determine the basic form of domestic and foreign policy, the amendments gave broad prerogatives to the executive branch. The amendments also removed the power of the legislature to approve all ministerial appointments, giving it the power to confirm only the prime minister. The constitutional provisions approved in sketchy form in the October referendum were published in greater detail for popular debate in January 1995 and were to be given final form and approval by the newly elected legislature.

More than a dozen parties were legally registered at the time of the legislative elections, rescheduled by Akayev to occur on February 5, 1995. Almost all parties fielded candidates. However, the lack of a developed party system was reflected in the low percentage—less than 20 percent—of the almost one thousand candidates who ran under party labels. The population tended to respond more to the ethnic and regional qualifications of candidates rather than to party labels.

The greatest proportion of candidates were directors of state enterprises and members of the Social Democratic Party and the KCP. Candidates were required to receive over 50 percent of votes to be elected, and a voter turnout of over 50 percent in a district was required. Partly because of the many candidates and the awkward electoral requirements, campaigning and voting were marred by irregularities and confusion, including the assassination of one candidate. Few candidates were elected in the first round of voting, and further rounds were held over several weeks. The Social Democratic and Republican People's Parties won the largest proportion of party-contested seats, with the KCP showing poorly. Ethnic Kyrgyz dominated the winners. Akayev criticized the electoral process, stating that he would have preferred a mixed system of voting that included party lists, a social organization list, and quotas for women and ethnic minorities, so that the legislature was more representative of society. The legislature convened in March 1995.

In September 1995 Akayev's supporters submitted a petition signed by 1.2 million people (52 percent of the voting age population) urging the legislature to approve holding a referendum on extending Akayev's term to the year 2001. Indicating some independence, the legislature rejected the petition, spurring Akayev to announce a presidential election for December 24, 1995. Thirteen candidates registered, but ten were disqualified, leaving Akayev, former speaker Medetken Sherimkulov, and Communist Party head Masaliyev. Akayev handily won reelection to a five-year term.

Still dissatisfied with the scope of his presidential powers vis-à-vis the legislature, Akayev in December 1995 ordered another constitutional referendum to be held February 10, 1996. About 95 percent of voters approved the referendum. The changes give Akayev greater powers to veto legislation, dissolve the legislature, and appoint all ministers (except the prime minister) without legislative confirmation, while making legislative impeachment of the president more difficult. The legislature confirms the prime minister and high judges. The changes also address rivalry between the two legislative chambers by more carefully delineating their functions.

MOLDOVA

OFFICIAL NAME: Republic of Moldova (Republicii Moldova)
CAPITAL: Chisinau
POPULATION: 4,464,000 (1996 est.)
DATE OF INDEPENDENCE: August 27, 1991 (from the Soviet Union)
DATE OF CURRENT CONSTITUTION: Adopted July 28, 1994
FORM OF GOVERNMENT: Parliamentary democracy
LANGUAGES: Moldovan (official), Russian, Gagauz
MONETARY UNIT: Leu
FISCAL YEAR: Calendar year
LEGISLATURE: Parliament (Parlamentul)
NUMBER OF CHAMBERS: One
NUMBER OF MEMBERS: 104
PERCENTAGE OF WOMEN: 4.8
TERM OF LEGISLATURE: Four years
MOST RECENT LEGISLATIVE ELECTION: February 27, 1994
MINIMUM AGE FOR VOTING: 18
MINIMUM AGE FOR MEMBERSHIP: 18
SUFFRAGE: Universal and direct
VOTING: Optional
ADDRESS: Parliament, 105 Stefan cel Mare Str.,

Chisinau 277073
TELEPHONE: (373 2) 23 74 03
FAX: (373 2) 23 32 10

A resolution on legislative elections was approved by the presidium of the Supreme Soviet in October 1993 to replace a 380-member legislature elected in February 1990 with a new 104-member unicameral legislature. The elections were held on February 27, 1994, and were based on proportional voting, with a party required to receive at least 4 percent of the national vote to win legislative representation. Thirteen parties fielding more than one thousand candidates contested the elections, along with twenty independents, in voting judged by international observers as generally free and fair.

Four major parties emerged from the elections. The Agrarian Democratic Party (ADP) won a majority of seats (fifty-six), followed by the Socialist Party / Unity bloc (twenty-eight seats), the Peasants and Intellectuals List (eleven seats), and the Christian Democratic People's Front (CDPF; nine seats). The ADP supported the policies of President Mircea Snegur and slow economic reform. The Socialist Party / Unity bloc represented the Russian-speaking majority in Moldova and was composed mainly of former Communist Party members. The Peasants and Intellectuals List was composed of a splinter faction of the Moldovan Popular Front (PFM) and other groups that advocated an independent Moldova with close ties to Romania. The CDPF was composed mainly of the Christian Democratic Party and the PFM and supported reunification with Romania.

The PFM suffered a major loss in the elections. It initially had held the largest number of seats in the former legislature (145 of 355 seats), but its increasingly unpopular advocacy of quick reunification with Romania caused its legislative faction to dwindle to around two dozen by late 1993.

The new legislature approved a new constitution that went into effect in August 1994. It provides for a dual executive consisting of a president and prime minister and a strong legislature whose members serve four-year terms. Former chair of the Supreme Soviet Petru Lucinschi was elected speaker.

TAJIKISTAN

OFFICIAL NAME: Republic of Tajikistan (Respublika i Tojikiston)
CAPITAL: Dushanbe
POPULATION: 5,916,000 (1996 est.)
DATE OF INDEPENDENCE: September 9, 1991 (from the Soviet Union)
DATE OF CURRENT CONSTITUTION: Adopted November 6, 1994
FORM OF GOVERNMENT: Parliamentary democracy
LANGUAGES: Tajik (official), Russian
MONETARY UNIT: Tajik ruble
FISCAL YEAR: Calendar year
LEGISLATURE: Supreme Assembly (Oliy Majlis)
NUMBER OF CHAMBERS: One
NUMBER OF MEMBERS: 181
PERCENTAGE OF WOMEN: 2.8
TERM OF LEGISLATURE: Five years
MOST RECENT LEGISLATIVE ELECTION: February 26 and March 12, 1995
MINIMUM AGE FOR VOTING: 18
MINIMUM AGE FOR MEMBERSHIP: 18
SUFFRAGE: Universal and direct
VOTING: Optional
ADDRESS: Supreme Assembly, Dushanbe
TELEPHONE: (737 72) 23 19 33
FAX: (737 72) 21 51 10

Tajikistan was one of the most volatile of the post-Soviet republics. In September 1992 Tajikistan's longtime communist ruler, Rakhmon Nabiyev, was ousted by opposition militia forces. But communist loyalists fought back, escalating the conflict into a civil war that combined ethnic and territorial issues with political ideology. The communists ultimately prevailed under the leadership of Imomali Rakhmonov.

The legislature was the center of the power struggle in mid- to late-1992. Opponents of Nabiyev and the communist regime held more than a dozen legislators hostage in April, successfully demanding the resignation of the hardline Communist speaker, Safarali Kenjayev. Escalating violence between communist and opposition forces led Nabiyev to declare a state of emergency in May 1992, with the opposition demanding that he resign and a new legislature be elected. A few days later the sides agreed on the formation of an interim legislature, to be composed of seventy members, half belonging to the opposition and half to government supporters, until new legislative elections were held in December 1992. A draft constitution was unveiled at the end of May 1992 setting forth the structure of the new legislature, called the National Assembly (Milli Majlis).

In early September 1992 the legislature expressed no confidence in Nabiyev's rule and removed him from power. Executive powers were assumed by the chair of the Supreme Soviet, communist Akbarsho Iskanderov. His attempts to conciliate with the opposition failed, and the hardline communist legislators moved their meetings away from the strife-torn capital, Dushanbe, to the redoubt of Khodzhent. These hardline legislators abolished presidential rule and created a parliamentary system, naming Tajik Communist

Party official and paramilitary supporter Imomali Rakhmonov as speaker. The legislature returned to Dushanbe with the victorious communist forces at the end of 1992.

In mid-1993 legislative by-elections were held to replace many deputies who were killed or fled during the civil war. Several opposition political parties were formally banned and any of their officials still in the country were arrested, including some deputies who were stripped of their mandates and immunity from prosecution.

A new constitutional draft was unveiled in mid-1994 calling for resurrecting the presidency and creating a new legislature, the Supreme Assembly (Oliy Majlis). The constitution was adopted on November 6, 1994, after approval in a popular referendum. According to the new constitution, the legislature enacts and amends laws; interprets the constitution; determines basic directions of domestic and foreign policy; sets dates for referendums and elections; and approves the appointment of the prime minister, ministers, and the heads of the National Bank and the constitutional, supreme, and supreme economic courts. The Supreme Assembly also approves the state budget, addresses budget deficits, determines tax policy, specifies the monetary system, ratifies treaties, and approves a state of war or emergency as decreed by the president.

The constitution also calls for creation of a presidium of the legislature to organize its work; the presidium is to be elected by the legislators and to be headed by the speaker, or chair. The chair signs the decisions of the Supreme Assembly and represents the legislature inside the country and abroad. A legislator is forbidden from holding any other legislative or government post or to be engaged in entrepreneurial activity, although he or she may be active in scientific and creative activities. Laws are required to be passed by a two-thirds majority of the total number of deputies, and a presidential veto may be overridden by the same margin. Legislators are elected for a five-year term.

Rakhmonov was elected president of Tajikistan in a popular election in November 1994, and he stepped down as chair of the Supreme Soviet. First deputy speaker Abulmadjid Dostiyev was named interim chair until new legislative elections could be held in February 1995.

On December 1, 1994, the Tajik legislature passed a law on legislative elections and announced that elections would take place on February 26, 1995, to choose a 181-seat legislature. This law and other procedures and practices further ensured Rakhmonov's hold on power. There was a narrow window of time for nominations, from late December 1994 to mid-January 1995, hindering opposition participation. Four parties were approved to compete in the elections—the Communist Party, the Popular Party, the Popular Unity Party, and the tiny Economic and Social Revival Party. The Communist Party was headed by Rakhmonov client Shodi Shabdolov. The Popular Party, registered in mid-December 1994, was headed by first deputy legislative chair Abdulmajid Dostiyev, another Rakhmonov client. Although the four parties nominated some candidates that were registered by the Electoral Commission, two-thirds of the 354 candidates were nominated by work collectives and local administrations. During December 1994 Rakhmonov had appointed a series of local administrators, who stood as local candidates. Restrictive nomination procedures ensured that about 40 percent of candidates ran unopposed. The Popular Unity Party pulled out of the elections at the last moment, citing harassment and dubious electoral procedures.

Although a massive turnout was officially recorded, many in opposition-dominated localities, as well as government opponents in exile in Afghanistan, boycotted the elections. After runoff votes were held in mid-March in some constituencies where less than the required 50 percent turnout had occurred, the Communist Party emerged with the largest number of seats in the new legislature (sixty), followed by the Popular Party. Another major legislative bloc consisted of local administrators. The Popular Unity Party won two seats because two candidates defied the party's directive to boycott the elections.

In sessions during 1995, the Supreme Assembly conducted some open rather than staged debate, despite being elected in less than a "free and fair" manner. Legislators heatedly debated the government's economic program. Speaker Safarali Rajabov appeared skilled at explaining draft legislation and points of order. Sessions were also open to media and diplomats, allowing some accountability. While debate occasionally appeared freewheeling, this was belied by Rakhmonov's presence at sessions. Although not a member of the legislature, he sat above the speaker and freely entered debates. He forcefully defended the government's economic reform program, terming critics "backward thinking deputies," and the legislators dutifully approved it. The legislature also stripped one deputy of immunity, allowing his prosecution on vague charges.

Rakhmonov also interceded in debate over a draft law requiring government ministers to appear before the legislature to answer questions. Although the Supreme Assembly State-Building Committee endorsed accountability of ministers to the legislature as important for the legislature's control and monitoring of the executive, Rakhmonov opposed the committee-endorsed draft. After apparent coaxing by the Rakhmonov government, the two-thirds majority necessary to pass a constitutional law (a law fleshing out constitutional provisions) was assembled to pass the government version, which called for ministers to submit information in writing when requested. The legislature also easily assembled large majorities to pass other constitutional laws, reminiscent of earlier "rubber stamping" in the Soviet era.

TURKMENISTAN

OFFICIAL NAME: Republic of Turkmenistan (Tiurkmenostan Respublikasy)
CAPITAL: Ashgabat
POPULATION: 4,149,000 (1996 est.)
DATE OF INDEPENDENCE: October 27, 1991 (from the Soviet Union)
DATE OF CURRENT CONSTITUTION: Adopted May 18, 1992
FORM OF GOVERNMENT: Presidential
LANGUAGES: Turkmen, Russian, Uzbek
MONETARY UNIT: Manat
FISCAL YEAR: Calendar year
LEGISLATURE: Assembly (Mejlis)
NUMBER OF CHAMBERS: One
NUMBER OF MEMBERS: 50
PERCENTAGE OF WOMEN: 18.0
TERM OF LEGISLATURE: Five years
MOST RECENT LEGISLATIVE ELECTION: December 11, 1994
MINIMUM AGE FOR VOTING: 18
MINIMUM AGE FOR MEMBERSHIP: 25
SUFFRAGE: Universal and direct
VOTING: Optional
ADDRESS: Parliament, 17 Gogol Street, Ashgabat 744000
TELEPHONE: (736 32) 25 31 25
FAX: (736 32) 29 42 42

A 175-deputy unicameral Supreme Soviet was elected in January 1990. Only the Turkmen Communist Party (TCP) and affiliated bodies were allowed to field candidates, and most candidates ran unopposed. Local TCP officials prevented Agzybirlik (Unity) popular front activists from registering as candidates. About 90 percent of the elected deputies were TCP members. When the Supreme Soviet convened, it elected TCP first secretary Saparmurad Niyazov as its chair. In October Niyazov was popularly elected to the new post of president, relinquishing his post as chair of the Supreme Soviet. In late 1991 the TCP was renamed the Democratic Party of Turkmenistan (DPT), though Niyazov remained its head.

In May 1992 Turkmenistan became the first Central Asian republic to enact a postindependence constitution. It set up a secular democracy embracing a strong presidential system of rule, granting Niyazov wide powers as head of state and government and even certain legislative functions. The latter included Niyazov's unchecked powers to issue edicts that had the force of law and to appoint and remove judges and local officials. The legislature, the Supreme Soviet, was to be replaced by a fifty-member Assembly (Mejlis) whose members serve for five years. The sitting Supreme Soviet legislators continued to serve, however, pending elections to the new Assembly. Sakhat Myradov became the Supreme Soviet chair. The lame-duck Supreme Soviet acted as an old-style rubber stamp for Niyazov's policies, meeting only a few days each year. Nine of the deputies worked full-time on legislative affairs. There were five standing committees, with a total legislative staff of about ninety.

The constitution also created a People's Council (Khalk Maslakhaty) as a supreme advisory and quasi-ruling body, consisting of the president, ministers, fifty legislators, sixty "people's representatives," and others. The People's Council was to deliberate and decide important political and economic questions and was empowered to demand constitutional changes or even, in theory, to express no confidence in the president. The people's representatives were elected by district in virtually uncontested votes in November–December 1992. A Council of Elders, also hand-picked by Niyazov, was created to advise the president and choose presidential candidates.

Opponents complained that both the People's Council and the Council of Elders were designed to stifle dissent. Niyazov was simultaneously president, supreme commander of the armed forces, first secretary of the DPT, head of the People's Council, and chair of the Council of Ministers and the National Security Council. The constitution forbade the formation of ethnic or religious parties.

An Assembly of fifty members was elected on December 11, 1994. The candidates were all nominated by Niyazov and ran unopposed, and most were members of his DPT. Many voting irregularities were reported. Agzybirlik was supposedly offered the opportunity to register as a party and contest the elections, but the Central Electoral Commission reported that it could not muster the one thousand signatures necessary to register.

Convening on December 26, 1994, the Assembly elected former speaker Sakhat Myradov as legislative chair. On December 28 the new deputies, as members of the People's Council, met to rubber stamp the 1995 state budget. Lacking real power, the Assembly has little legislative initiative.

UZBEKISTAN

OFFICIAL NAME: Republic of Uzbekistan (Ozbekiston Respublikasy)
CAPITAL: Tashkent
POPULATION: 23,418,000 (1996 est.)
DATE OF INDEPENDENCE: August 31, 1991 (from the Soviet Union)

DATE OF CURRENT CONSTITUTION: Adopted December 8, 1992
FORM OF GOVERNMENT: Parliamentary democracy
LANGUAGES: Uzbek, Russian, Tajik
MONETARY UNIT: Som
FISCAL YEAR: Calendar year
LEGISLATURE: Supreme Assembly (Oliy Majlis)
NUMBER OF CHAMBERS: One
NUMBER OF MEMBERS: 250
PERCENTAGE OF WOMEN: 6.0
TERM OF LEGISLATURE: Five years
MOST RECENT LEGISLATIVE ELECTION: December 25, 1994; January 8 and 22, 1995
MINIMUM AGE FOR VOTING: 18
MINIMUM AGE FOR MEMBERSHIP: 25
SUFFRAGE: Universal and direct
VOTING: Optional
ADDRESS: Supreme Assembly, Mustakillik sq. 5, 700 008 Tashkent
TELEPHONE: (737 12) 39 87 49
FAX: (737 12) 39 41 51

Upon independence, Uzbekistan's legislative structure was similar to that of other former Soviet republics. Its unicameral legislature, the Supreme Soviet, had been elected in February 1990 and consisted of five hundred members. The Birlik (Unity) popular front movement, founded in 1989 and the largest opposition party, was forbidden to field candidates, and in many constituencies Uzbek Communist Party (UCP) candidates ran unopposed.

Upon convening, the Supreme Soviet elected Communist Party head Islam Karimov to the new post of president. In November 1991 the UCP renamed itself the People's Democratic Party of Uzbekistan (PDPU), retaining Karimov as its head. About forty deputies worked full time on legislative affairs. There were fifteen standing committees or commissions, with a total legislative staff of about 120.

A new constitution was adopted by the Supreme Soviet on December 8, 1992, by unanimous vote after two months of public discussion. It provides for a strong president who oversees the government and for a weaker, 250-member unicameral legislature, called the Supreme Assembly (Oliy Majlis), whose members serve five-year terms. Although a multiparty system was proclaimed, the Supreme Assembly, shortly after enacting the constitution, banned Birlik as a subversive organization and removed the legislative mandate from a prominent human rights activist.

As detailed in the constitution and a law on the legislature approved in September 1994, the Supreme Assembly adopts laws and amendments to the constitution, determines the direction of domestic and foreign policy, approves the budget, determines taxes, schedules legislative and presidential elections, elects the constitutional court, supreme court, and arbitration court, ratifies the president's choices for prime minister and other members of the cabinet, ratifies a presidential declaration of a state of emergency, and ratifies treaties, among other powers. A council comprising the speaker, the speaker's deputies, the chairs of committees and the credentials commission, and representatives of factions propose the legislative agenda, organize work on drafting laws, and oversee members' behavior. A legislator may belong to only one committee or commission. If involved in full-time work in the legislature, a deputy may not hold another paid post or engage in entrepreneurial activity. The Supreme Assembly may be dissolved by the president and new elections held with the concurrence of the Constitutional Court.

A law on elections was approved in late September 1994. It required parties planning to take part in the December 25, 1994, legislative election to garner fifty thousand signatures, no more than 10 percent in any one region or area, in order to prevent the emergence of regional parties. No opposition party succeeded in becoming eligible. At the same time, the government put a chill on opposition activities through arrests, harassment, and charges of treason. Two parties contested the elections: the National Democratic Party of Uzbekistan (NDP) and the Homeland Progress Party (HPP). In September 1991 the Uzbek Communist Party (UCP) had renamed itself the NDP at Karimov's urging and remained the ruling party with Karimov as its head. The HPP was founded by an adviser to Karimov in June 1992 and supported Karimov's policies.

Legislative elections were held on December 25, 1994, with run-off ballots held in January 1995. Candidates were nominated by two parties—the NDP and the HPP—and by local administrations. There were 634 candidates vying in 250 electoral districts. NDP candidates won 69 seats, and HPP candidates won 14 seats. Candidates nominated by local administrations were elected to 167 seats. Most of these were also NDP members.

The winning NDP members met before the legislative session opened to form a faction, decide on a legislative program, and elect faction leaders. Convening on February 23, the legislature followed NDP head Karimov's recommendation and elected Erkin Khalilov, former legislative chair, to head the Supreme Assembly. Factions were registered, including those of the NDP, the HPP, government officials, and a new forty-seven-member faction of Justice Party deputies (which had not been an officially registered party during the elections). Shukrulla Mirsaidov, former Uzbek vice president and Karimov opponent, proclaimed the formation of the Justice Party in the wake of the election. He stated that the new party would seek registration and would function as a legislative opposition to the NDP.

In his speech to the opening session of the Supreme Assembly, Karimov called for the legislature to develop as an effective law-making institution. He urged "a struggle of opinions and ideas" in the legislature to solve such problems as private land ownership, freeing him to attend to executive branch affairs. He emphasized that legislative factions and parties should rely on various occupational and social strata for input into law making. He called for the selection of committee chairs and other critical personnel who could work as professional politicians and not have outside occupational distractions.

Jim Nichol

BIBLIOGRAPHY

Bhavna, Dave. "A New Parliament Consolidates Presidential Authority," *Transition* (March 22, 1996): 33–37.

Commission on Security and Cooperation in Europe. *Elections in the Baltic States and Soviet Republics: A Compendium of Reports on Parliamentary Elections Held in 1990.* Washington, D.C.: Government Printing Office, 1990.

———. *Report on the March 7, 1994 Parliamentary Election in Kazakhstan.* Washington, D.C.: Government Printing Office, March 1994.

———. *Report on the Moldovan Parliamentary Elections: February 27, 1994.* Washington, D.C.: Government Printing Office, April 1994.

Inter-Parliamentary Union. *Chronicle of Parliamentary Elections and Developments, 1 July 1993–30 June 1994,* vol. 28. Geneva: Inter-Parliamentary Union, 1994, 113–114, 127–128.

Kiernan, Brendan. *The End of Soviet Politics: Elections, Legislatures, and the Demise of the Communist Party.* Boulder, Colo.: Westview Press, 1993.

Remington, Thomas E., ed. *Parliaments in Transition: The New Legislative Politics in the Former USSR and Eastern Europe.* Boulder, Colo.: Westview Press, 1994.

Woehrel, Steven. *Soviet Federal Crisis.* Washington, D.C.: Library of Congress, Congressional Research Service, August 12, 1991.

COMOROS

OFFICIAL NAME: Federal Islamic Republic of the Comoros (Jumhuriyat al-Qumur al-Ittihadiyah al-Islamiyah, Arabic; République Fédéale Islamique des Comores, French)
CAPITAL: Moroni
POPULATION: 569,000 (1996 est.)
DATE OF INDEPENDENCE: July 6, 1975 (from France)
DATE OF CURRENT CONSTITUTION: Approved October 20, 1996
FORM OF GOVERNMENT: Transitional democracy
LANGUAGES: Arabic (official), French (official), Comoran
MONETARY UNIT: Comoran franc
FISCAL YEAR: Calendar year
LEGISLATURE: Federal Assembly (Assemblée Fédérale)
NUMBER OF CHAMBERS: One
NUMBER OF MEMBERS: 43
PERCENTAGE OF WOMEN: 0.0
TERM OF LEGISLATURE: Four years
MOST RECENT LEGISLATIVE ELECTION: December 1 and 8, 1996
MINIMUM AGE FOR VOTING: 18
MINIMUM AGE FOR MEMBERSHIP: 21
SUFFRAGE: Universal and direct
VOTING: Optional
ADDRESS: Assemblée Fédérale, B. P. 447, Moroni
TELEPHONE: (269) 74 40 00
FAX: (269) 74 40 11

The Federal Islamic Republic of the Comoros, located off the coast of southern Africa between Mozambique and Madagascar, comprises three of the four islands in the Comoro Archipelago (see map, p. 665). The fourth island, Mayotte, is administered by the former colonial ruler, France. Marked by political turbulence since independence, and a de jure one-party state from 1979 until 1989, the Comoros adopted a multiparty constitution in 1992.

Each island under the 1992 constitution had some autonomy in matters not assigned to the central government, and each had a council which acted as the local legislature in nonfederal matters. The forty-three-member Federal Assembly met twice a year, in April and October, for not more than forty-five days per session. Matters subject to federal legislation included defense; posts and telecommunications; civil, penal, and industrial law; external trade; federal taxation; planning; education; and health.

The president could initiate legislation and assume emergency powers. The constitutionality of laws was determined by the Constitutional Court. Bills vetted by the Constitutional Court, the president of the republic, island governors, and presidents of island councils were sent to the appropriate standing committees. Voting was by show of hands or ballot, and a simple majority was sufficient for passage. Amendments could be moved and debated at all stages of a bill's passage.

The constitution of 1992 also created a second chamber, the Senate (Sénat), to have fifteen members (five from each island) indirectly elected to six-year terms. But no Senate elections were ever held.

For election purposes, Comoros was divided into forty-three constituencies, each of which returned one member. Grand Comore had twenty constituencies, Anjouan had seventeen, and Moheli had six. Temporary vacancies under the 1992 constitution were filled by substitutes who were elected concurrently with regular Assembly members, who had to secure an absolute majority to be elected in an initial round of voting or a simple majority in a second round. By-elections were conducted to fill permanent vacancies.

The 1992 constitution was replaced in October 1996. The December 1996 elections were boycotted by opponents of the ruling National Rally for Development (RND), who had sought the establishment of an independent electoral commission and scrutiny of the electoral registers. The opposition also objected to certain constitutional provisions regarding political parties. In consequence of the boycott, the ruling RND won thirty-six of forty-three seats.

George Thomas Kurian

CONGO, DEMOCRATIC REPUBLIC OF THE

OFFICIAL NAME: Democratic Republic of the Congo (formerly Zaire)
CAPITAL: Kinshasa
POPULATION: 46,499,000 (1996 est.)
DATE OF INDEPENDENCE: June 30, 1960 (from Belgium)
DATE OF CURRENT CONSTITUTION: Constitution abrogated
FORM OF GOVERNMENT: Transitional
LANGUAGES: French, Lingala, Swahili, Kingwana, Kikongo, Tshiluba
MONETARY UNIT: New Zaïre
FISCAL YEAR: Calendar year
LEGISLATURE: —
NUMBER OF CHAMBERS: —
NUMBER OF MEMBERS: —
PERCENTAGE OF WOMEN: —
TERM OF LEGISLATURE: —
MOST RECENT LEGISLATIVE ELECTION: September 1987
MINIMUM AGE FOR VOTING: —
MINIMUM AGE FOR MEMBERSHIP: —
SUFFRAGE: —
VOTING: —
ADDRESS: —
TELEPHONE: —
FAX: —

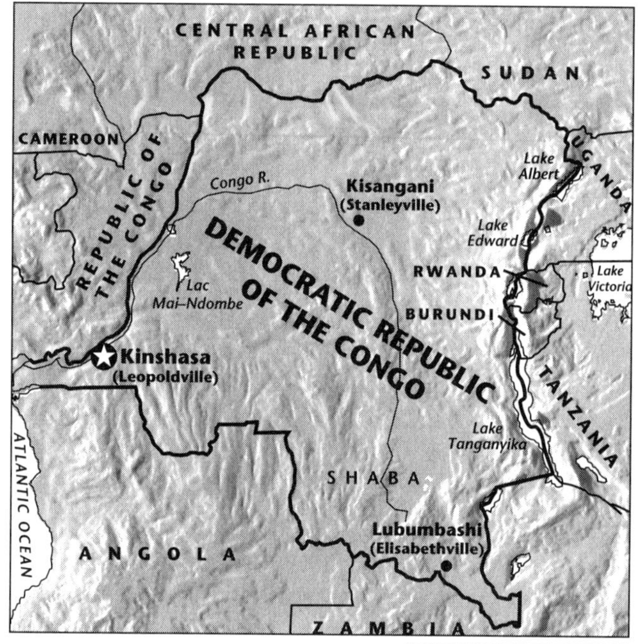

In the Democratic Republic of the Congo (formerly Zaire), located in central Africa, antigovernment forces in May 1997 overthrew long-time dictator Mobutu Sese Seko. The new government, headed by Laurent Kabila, professed the intention of creating a stable constitutional democracy, but its initial steps—abolishing the parliament and banning political parties—were not inspiring.

BACKGROUND

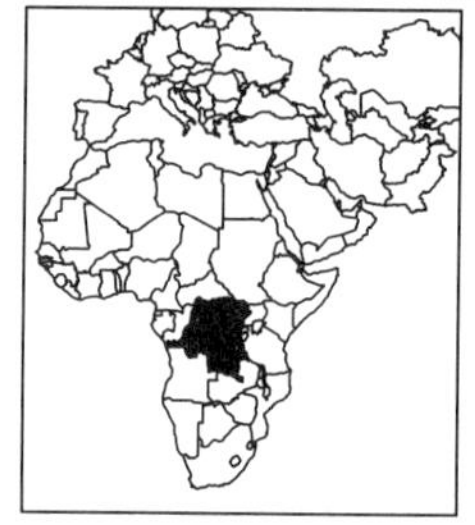

The Democratic Republic of the Congo, then known as the Republic of the Congo, became independent of Belgium in 1960. Its Belgian-based constitution established a bicameral legislature with significant powers—including the power to name the president. Independence, however, also brought a long period of turmoil marked by regional secessionist attempts, intervention by the United Nations, and the assassination of Prime Minister Patrice Lumumba. A 1964 constitution retained the bicameral legislature, but in November 1965 Mobutu, then an army colonel, seized power and suspended parliament.

In 1970 a 420-member unicameral legislature, later named the National Legislative Council, was elected under a 1967 constitution, but the body had no real power and Mobutu continued to rule by decree. In that same year, Mobutu's Popular Movement of the Revolution was made the sole legal party, and in 1974 "Mobutuism" became the official ideology. In 1977 Mobutu permitted multiple candidates, all drawn from his party, for legislative seats. This modest reform began to breathe some life into the parliament; however, legislators who aroused Mobutu's ire were subject to arrest or exile.

Political repression and economic decline led to mounting domestic opposition in the 1980s, and as the cold war ended Western donors began to press for political reforms. In April 1990 Mobutu made a number of concessions, announcing the creation of a three-party system, but protests continued. The government's often violent response to these protests brought criticism from human rights organizations and Western governments. In October 1990, consequently, Mobutu announced that a full, multiparty system would be created. Over the next seven years Mobutu and his parliamentary opposition sparred, to the advantage of neither side, over the implementation of democratic reforms.

THE 1990S

During much of 1991 Mobutu and the opposition struggled over the terms for the convening of a national political conference to resolve the political crisis, but when the body finally met in August, with 2,850 delegates, it was suspended amid disputes over the accreditation of delegates. After further unrest, the Sovereign National Conference finally met in April 1992. Declaring itself the sole legislative body, it quickly became a lively center of political debate. In August 1992 the conference named Etienne Tshisekedi wa Mulumba, a leading opposition figure, as transitional prime minister, and in November it adopted a draft constitution establishing a federal system and restoring a powerful bicameral legislature.

Although Mobutu seemed to be yielding to the decisions of the conference, the November draft constitution provoked a confrontation. When Mobutu attempted to dismiss Tshisekedi in December, the prime minister refused to acknowledge the legality of the action. The conference, meanwhile, created a 453-member High Council of the Republic with power to adopt and implement the new constitution; in January 1993 the council found Mobutu guilty of high treason for corruption. In retaliation, Mobutu named his own prime minister, in March, and reconvened the old National Legislative Council in order to undermine the High Council of the Republic.

The 1993 political stalemate, accompanied by urban unrest, ethnic tensions, and near economic collapse, threatened the existence of the state. To avert chaos, major elements of the opposition accepted a compromise with Mobutu in September that would lead to the convening of a new transitional parliament combining the National Legislative Council and the High Council of the Republic. Despite Tshisekedi's refusal to participate, the High Council of the Republic–Parliament of Transition (HCR-PT) convened in January 1994. The HCR-PT was an unwieldy body of well over 700 members, but in April 1994 it approved a fifteen-month transition program to include a constitutional referendum as well as legislative and presidential elections.

In June 1994 the HCR-PT selected a prime minister, Joseph Léon Kengo wa Dondo, who was acceptable to Mobutu, experienced in government, and widely regarded as a pragmatist and technocrat. Tshisekedi's supporters bitterly opposed the selection as illegitimate, but in succeeding months Western governments showed signs of accepting Kengo in the hope that he could prevent the breakup of Zaire.

The political situation did not stabilize under Kengo. In fact, it worsened. The 1994 upheaval in neighboring Rwanda had brought more than a million refugees into Zaire, which further strained the social fabric, economy, and political stability of the country. A constitutional referendum and presidential and legislative elections, all scheduled for July 1995, were postponed due to squabbling and factionalism in Kinshasa, and the fifteen-month transitional period was extended by two years. The referendum was rescheduled for December 1996, and the elections for May 1997. But neither was held, as the government was thrown into disarray by ethnic warfare.

In May 1996 hundreds of Zairian Tutsis were killed, allegedly by Rwandan Hutu refugees assisted by Hutu Zairian troops. Over the ensuing months the atrocities committed within Zaire mounted. Armed Tutsi rebel factions coalesced in November to form the Alliance of Democratic Forces for the Liberation of Congo-Zaire (AFDL), under the leadership of Laurent Kabila. Kabila, who is not a Tutsi, had been fighting the Mobutu regime since the 1960s. Over the first five months of 1997 the Zairian army melted away in the face of rebel assaults. Kabila's AFDL entered Kinshasa on May 17. Mobutu, who had been out of the country for much of the year convalescing from cancer surgery performed in August 1996, went into exile.

Kabila professed a desire to rebuild democratic institutions from the ground up. Within days of entering the capital he appointed himself president, named an interim government, changed the name of the country to the Democratic Republic of the Congo, dissolved parliament, abrogated the constitution, abolished political parties, and banned demonstrations. By the end of May he had announced plans for a December 1998 referendum on a yet-to-be-drafted constitution and for April 1999 presidential and parliamentary elections. In view of the past failures of parliamentary democracy in the country, the success of this transition is in question. The social, economic, ethnic, and factional issues that had hobbled the state under Mobutu remain largely unchanged.

Raymond Copson

CONGO, REPUBLIC OF THE

OFFICIAL NAME: Republic of the Congo (République du Congo)
CAPITAL: Brazzaville
POPULATION: 2,528,000 (1996 est.)
DATE OF INDEPENDENCE: August 15, 1960 (from France)
DATE OF CURRENT CONSTITUTION: Approved March 15, 1992
FORM OF GOVERNMENT: Parliamentary democracy
LANGUAGES: French (official), Lingala, Kikongo, other African languages
MONETARY UNIT: CFA franc
FISCAL YEAR: Calendar year
LEGISLATURE: Parliament (Parlement)
NUMBER OF CHAMBERS: Two. National Assembly (Assemblée Nationale); Senate (Sénat)
NUMBER OF MEMBERS: National Assembly, 125 (directly elected); Senate, 60 (indirectly elected)
PERCENTAGE OF WOMEN: National Assembly, 1.6; Senate, 3.3
TERM OF LEGISLATURE: National Assembly, five years; Senate, six years (one-third of the membership elected every two years)
MOST RECENT LEGISLATIVE ELECTION: National Assembly, May–October 1993; Senate, October 6, 1996
MINIMUM AGE FOR VOTING: 18
MINIMUM AGE FOR MEMBERSHIP: National Assembly, 25; Senate, 50
SUFFRAGE: Universal
VOTING: Optional
ADDRESS: National Assembly, B.P. 2106, Brazzaville; Senate, BP 1128, Brazzaville
TELEPHONE: National Assembly, (242) 83 08 14; Senate, (242) 83 53 32
FAX: National Assembly, (242) 83 19 50; Senate, (242) 83 04 47

The Republic of the Congo, an equatorial country on the Atlantic coast of Africa *(see map, p. 261)*, came under French rule in the nineteenth century as part of French Equatorial Africa. It gained independence from France on August 15, 1960, under the leadership of Fulbert Youlou, who became the first president of the Republic of the Congo. Youlou, an advocate of centralized government, resigned in 1963 in the wake of antigovernment rioting, possibly averting a civil war. Alphonse Massamba-Débat, elected as provisional president in December 1963, soon established relations with the Soviet Union and transformed the country into a Marxist-Leninist single-party state in 1964. Civilian rule abruptly ended in 1968 after a military coup staged by Capt. Marien Ngouabi.

Ngouabi, continuing to follow Marxist-Leninist ideology, established the Congolese Labor Party as the state party and dissolved the National Assembly, which he replaced with the National Council of the Revolution. In 1973 President Ngouabi introduced a new constitution and reestablished the National Assembly with delegates elected from the single party. Ngouabi was assassinated in 1977, and political power was assumed by an eleven-member Labor Party military committee headed by Col. Joachim Yhombi-Opango. Yhombi-Opango was later replaced by Denis Sassou-Nguesso after an internal struggle and leadership changes within the ruling military committee. In March 1979 Sassou-Nguesso organized a presidential election, which, in the absence of any challenger, he easily won. Sassou-Nguesso again faced no opposition in 1989, and he was reelected president for a third five-year term.

On January 1, 1991, Sassou-Nguesso bowed to accusations levied against his and previous governments and accepted responsibility for mismanagement. He also embraced the concept of political pluralism and abandoned Marxism. Under pressure from various political activists and the international community, the military regime organized an all-party National Conference in February 1991 that was attended by representatives of a broad segment of civil society. Elections were scheduled for 1992, and a transitional prime minister was appointed by the conference members to conduct most of the affairs of state during the period before the election.

The first round of the presidential election took place on August 1. Pascal Lissouba and Bernard Kolelas qualified to compete in the second round. Lissouba, leader of the Pan African Union for Social Democracy (UPADS), won the election with 61 percent of the vote and appointed Stéphane Maurice Bongho-Nouarra, a member of the Pan African Union, as the new prime minister.

CONSTITUTIONAL PROVISIONS AND PARLIAMENTARY OPERATIONS

The constitution of the Republic of the Congo, approved by popular referendum in March 1992, provides for a bicameral Parliament composed of a National Assembly (the lower house) and Senate (the upper house). Deputies of the 125-seat National Assembly are elected directly for five-year terms from single-member districts. If one candidate for the National Assembly does not win a majority of votes, a second round of elections is scheduled for the two candidates receiving the most votes in the first round. Members of the 60-member Senate are elected indirectly by local and regional councils for six-year terms. Elections for one-third of the Senate's seats occur every two years. The constitution provides for a mixed presidential-parliamentary form of government with executive authority vested in a directly elected president who appoints the prime minister and cabinet.

Sessions and powers

Parliament has three ordinary sessions each year lasting no longer than two months each. The first session begins on March 2, the second on July 2, and the third, during which Parliament debates the national budget, begins on October 15. Parliament may be called into extraordinary session at the request of the president of the republic, the prime minister, or one-third of each of the two chambers. While the plenary sessions of Parliament are open to the public, as provided in Article 99 of the constitution, committee meetings of the National Assembly are closed and attendance at them is mandatory.

The Senate ensures that local and community interests are represented on the national level. The Senate has full legislative powers and, according to Article 116 of the constitution, all bills must be examined by both chambers of Parliament whereby an identical text would be adopted into law. In addition, both chambers convene to elect members of the Supreme Court and other magistrates. In many cases, however, the National Assembly's authority takes precedence over that of the Senate. For example, if the two chambers cannot reach consensus on an identical text for a bill, the prime minister assembles a mixed commission from both the National Assembly and the Senate; if a compromise bill is not adopted, the government gives the National Assembly the authority to make a final ruling. Moreover, only the National Assembly has direct powers of overseeing the executive branch, such as passing a vote of no confidence.

Leadership and staff

The leadership of the National Assembly is elected by secret ballot for the duration of each legislature unless there has been a change in majority party, in which case a new Assembly president is elected. The leadership of the Senate is elected after each renewal of one-third of its members, with elections occurring every two years. The leadership of the National Assembly is composed of a president; three vice presidents, whose party affiliations must reflect the political configuration of the Assembly; two secretaries; and a bursar, who is responsible for the Assembly's finances.

In the Republic of the Congo, as in most African nations, deputies do not have their own staff on whom they may rely for access to information or to conduct research on a policy issue. As is the case with most African parliaments, Congo's lack of funds requires that a secretary general, who is under the authority of the president of the National Assembly, preside over a staff that is at the disposal of all members of Parliament.

Committee structure

The National Assembly has six permanent committees: Economy and Finance; Judicial Affairs; Foreign Affairs and Cooperation; Defense and Security; Education, Culture, Science, and Technology; and Health, Social Affairs, and Environment. Each deputy may choose to belong to one committee. In case of dispute or for reasons of faithfully representing the political configuration of the legislature, the Assembly leadership may adjust committee membership. The secretary of each committee takes attendance and is supposed to record the reasons for the absence of a deputy, who may, in case such absence is unavoidable, delegate voting rights to another deputy. A quorum consisting of a majority of deputies must be present in a committee meeting for its decisions to be binding. Presiding over each committee is a president, vice president, reporter, and secretary. The president and vice president of each committee are elected during plenary session of the National Assembly; the reporters and secretaries are elected by their respective committee members. Each committee has the power to create subcommittees.

Ad hoc committees, reflecting the political configuration of the Assembly, can be formed in plenary session to address a specific issue. The Congolese Assembly, in fact, formed an ad hoc committee to work toward the peaceful resolution of political conflict and the restoration of peace. Such a committee was deemed necessary because of armed militia fighting in the capital of Brazzaville precipitated by a political crisis surrounding legislative elections in 1993. Violence erupted sporadically in 1994 and 1995. Composed of twelve deputies evenly split between the parliamentary majority and opposition groups, the committee influenced Parliament to adopt directives concerning the disarmament of militia and the installation of a credible national police force capable of controlling all residential areas of the capital.

Relations with the executive

Government officials have full access to committee meetings. Deputies may question the prime minister or other government officials by transmitting questions to the president of the National Assembly, who in turn poses them to the government. Deputies may also question government officials during plenary sessions. Two question periods are allocated during each ordinary session of Parliament. All questions, along with the government's response to them, are published in an official journal. In addition to questioning government ministers or other officials, deputies may form investigative committees to review government activities; conduct "information missions" as a means to oversee the implementation of legislation; or exercise a vote of no confidence.

Parliamentary groups

Based on Western European models, parliamentary groups are caucuses of deputies who align themselves by political affiliation or ideology to advance a common agenda. Certain advantages are accorded to parliamentary groups. For example, they have a representative who sits in the President's Conference, which makes important administrative decisions about the Assembly as an institution. At least fifteen deputies are required to form a parliamentary group in the National Assembly. Parliamentary groups must submit to the president of the Assembly a list of their members as well as the name of the group's president. Any modification in the membership of a parliamentary group must also be submitted to the president of the Assembly and published in the official journal.

According to various sources, there currently are three parliamentary groups in the National Assembly. The parliamentary majority, or Presidential Tendency, still includes President Lissouba's Pan African Union and several other minor political parties. The opposition includes two parliamentary groups. The first is the Union for Democratic Renewal, which includes Bernard Kolelas's Congolese Movement for Democracy and Integral Development and the Rally for Democracy and Social Progress. The second group in the opposition is the United Democratic Forces, consisting of the Congolese Labor Party and several minor political parties. It supported the candidacy of Sassou-Nguesso, the former president under one-party rule, for the 1997 presidential election.

ELECTIONS

After the 1992 legislative elections, seven parties, including the Congolese Labor Party, the former state party, formed the Union for Democratic Renewal, constituting a parliamentary majority. This move precipitated a no-confidence vote in Lissouba's UPADS government, which resulted in the resignation of his prime minister. Unable to form a new government, Lissouba dissolved Parliament and called new legislative elections for May 1993.

Official results from the May elections showed pro-Lissouba parties to have won 62 of 125 National Assembly seats. Opposition parties contested the results and accused President Lissouba's UPADS of rigging the polling in some electoral districts. Opposition parties boycotted the second round of legislative elections, which were held in June, and continued the debate over first-round results. Meanwhile, Lissouba appointed a new cabinet with former president Gen. Yhombi-Opango as prime minister. Brazzaville was paralyzed by violence through parts of 1993 and early 1994. Nevertheless, deputies continued to meet. Opposition and government Assembly members used the meetings to argue over which group of parties controlled the parliamentary majority.

Diplomatic efforts to resolve the electoral dispute led to a repeat of the second round of legislative elections, which were held in October 1993. Presidential Tendency secured sixty-five seats and thus retained a majority in the National Assembly. During early 1995 by-elections were held for seven seats in the National Assembly that had been annulled after the May 1993 legislative elections. Opposition parties won five seats and Lissouba's UPADS won two.

General elections for all sixty seats in the Senate took place without incident on July 26, 1992. On October 6, 1996, elections were held for one-third of the Senate seats (twenty) as required by the constitution. Lissouba's UPADS won a majority of these seats, with eleven.

Benjamin Feit

COSTA RICA

OFFICIAL NAME: Republic of Costa Rica (República de Costa Rica)
CAPITAL: San Jose
POPULATION: 3,463,000 (1996 est.)
DATE OF INDEPENDENCE: September 15, 1821 (from Spain)
DATE OF CURRENT CONSTITUTION: Adopted November 7, 1949; effective November 9, 1949
FORM OF GOVERNMENT: Parliamentary democracy
LANGUAGE: Spanish (official)
MONETARY UNIT: Costa Rican colon
FISCAL YEAR: Calendar year
LEGISLATURE: Legislative Assembly (Asemblea Legislativa)
NUMBER OF CHAMBERS: One
NUMBER OF MEMBERS: 57
PERCENTAGE OF WOMEN: 15.8
TERM OF LEGISLATURE: Five years
MOST RECENT LEGISLATIVE ELECTION: February 6, 1994
MINIMUM AGE FOR VOTING: 18
MINIMUM AGE FOR MEMBERSHIP: 21
SUFFRAGE: Universal and direct
VOTING: Compulsory
ADDRESS: Asemblea Legislativa, Apdo 74-1013, San Jose
TELEPHONE: (506) 243 24 41
FAX: (506) 243 24 44

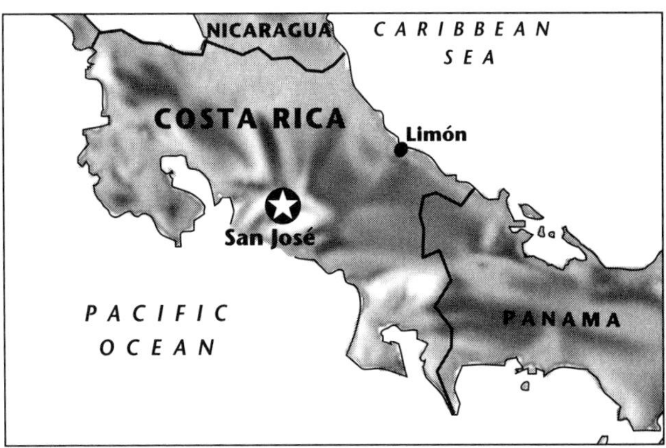

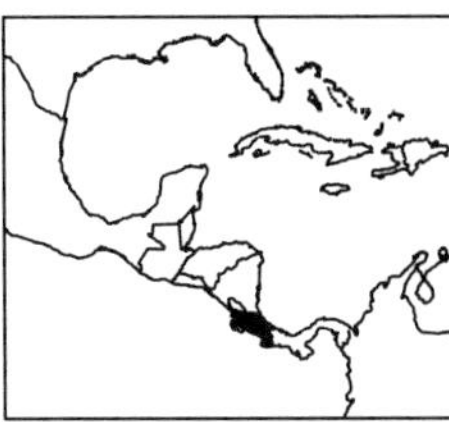

The wealthiest country of Central America, Costa Rica has the longest history of political stability and constitutional rule in the region. Costa Ricans take great pride in the democratic tradition that has been an important part of their history. Although heavily influenced by powerful, economically elite families, Costa Rica can claim to possess a competitive political system that dates to 1889. Since 1948 the country has witnessed an unbroken string of two-party democratic elections in which, with but one exception, the governing party has been defeated and replaced by the opposition party.

BACKGROUND

The origins of the Costa Rican Legislative Assembly go back to the 1824 constitution, which created a bicameral legislative branch consisting of a Senate and a Congress. The 1847 constitution abolished the Senate, and the participation of the executive in creating legislation was established. The current constitution, adopted November 7, 1949, has continued the unicameral tradition of the Legislative Assembly of Costa Rica. The most important powers of the Assembly include the power to formulate, amend, and repeal legislation; appoint, by a two-thirds vote, the comptroller general and members of the Supreme Court and their substitutes; approve international agreements and treaties; suspend, by a vote of no less than two-thirds of the members, certain individual constitutional rights and guarantees; approve regular and extraordinary national budgets; levy national taxes and contributions and approve municipal taxes; create courts of justice; and nominate the public defender and alternate public defender.

Despite its democratic tradition, the Costa Rican Legislative Assembly has only in the past decade begun to emerge as a significant force in the country's system of governance. The Assembly traditionally has been controlled by the party of the president, and more often than not the president has dominated the legislative branch through his control of the political party in power. Because partisanship historically has been very intense in Costa Rica, party discipline has been strong in the Assembly. Not only does the president of the country, who typically is the leader of the majority party in the Assembly, exercise strong control over his or her party's Assembly members, but so too the leader of the minority party has exercised significant discipline over minority-party members in the Assembly.

Presidential control of the Assembly is also facilitated by the fact that members of the Legislative Assembly and the president are elected for coterminous periods, and neither is allowed by the constitution to be reelected for a second term. The result is that as the president takes office, all members of the Assembly are taking office as well, and there is no established leadership to assume control of the Assembly, a circumstance that in turn enables the president to exercise considerable influence in determining party leadership in that body. Furthermore, unlike legislative personnel in many other countries, Legislative Assembly staff members are afforded the advantage of civil service protection and job security, in that their positions are a part of the National Civil Service System. However, since that system is operated by the executive branch, the potential exists for significant problems in terms of the autonomy of staff vis-à-vis the leadership of the Assembly.

Another important factor in accounting for the traditional weakness of the Legislative Assembly relative to the executive branch has been that each year, as it begins its annual session, the Assembly elects an entirely new leadership team. Most notably, the president of the Assembly and the chairs of all commissions are by tradition replaced. This practice has made it even more difficult for the body to maintain any degree of continuity or to build real institutional memory and strong policy-making capacity.

During the 1990s, however, the Legislative Assembly, which frequently has served as a training ground for future presidents, began to assert a higher degree of autonomy and independence from the executive branch. These tendencies have been enhanced by the Assembly's energetic pursuit of technical assistance from other countries, including the United States and several European nations, in order to strengthen itself as an institution of democratic governance.

One important element in strengthening the role of the legislative branch in democratic governance in Costa Rica has been a broadening of citizen involvement in the country's political parties. As party involvement has become more inclusive, and party competition even more intense, the legislative branch has emerged as an increasingly important forum for resolving partisan conflict. Whereas a decade ago the influence of the Legislative Assembly in the shaping of public policy had been nil, today one can point to several areas of Costa Rican life, including banking and agriculture, where policy shaped in the Assembly has significantly affected the country and its people.

PARTIES AND ELECTIONS

The fifty-seven-member Legislative Assembly is organized to represent proportionally the country's seven provinces. The National Electoral Board establishes before each election—according to population—the number of representatives to be elected in each district. San Jose, the capital and largest population center, has the largest legislative delegation, with twenty-one members. To be elected, a candidate must be Costa Rican-born or naturalized, have ten years of continuous residence in the country, and be twenty-one years old at the time of the election.

The dominant feature of voting and policy making in the Legislative Assembly is the preeminent role of the political parties. Because party discipline is strong, virtually every important vote splits along party lines unless prior agreement has been worked out by the parties, in which case votes are nearly unanimous. In recent times political pacts negotiated between the principal parties have led to periods as long as two years in which legislation in the Assembly was approved by consensus. At other times, however, partisan divisions have been very strong, and partisan conflict has sometimes served to immobilize the Assembly.

Almost always, the party of the president has the largest membership in the legislative body. For example, from 1990 to 1994 the presidency was held by the Social Christian Unity Party (PUSC), which also held twenty-nine seats in the Assembly. The minority National Liberation Party (PLN) held twenty-five seats in the Assembly. The February 1994 elections brought the PLN to power in the executive branch and to the majority in the Assembly, where it won twenty-eight seats, while PUSC took twenty-five seats and four minor parties each won one seat.

Despite the fact that both partisanship and party discipline are high, the distinction between the two parties is not as great as one might expect. In general, PUSC is oriented toward free-market, probusiness policies, while the PLN tends to be labor- and protectionist-oriented. Many observers, however, would argue that the differences between the parties have more to do with historic elite family rivalries than with significant political or ideological positions.

PARLIAMENTARY PROCEEDINGS

The Assembly meets in regular session every year from May 1 through July 31 and again from September 1 through November 30. Extraordinary sessions can be called by the Assembly or the president of the republic from August 1 to August 30 and again from December 1 to April 30.

The Costa Rica Legislative Assembly is housed in a small, two-story renovated historic building located on the edge of downtown San Jose. The building also contains various commission and staff offices and conference rooms. Several nearby buildings house offices for deputies and commissions and space for support and administrative staff.

The legislative process in Costa Rica is divided into four phases: introduction; preparation and deliberation at the commission (committee) level; deliberation and resolution at the plenary level; and promulgation and publication. This last phase is the responsibility of the executive branch, where legislation is sanctioned and then published in the official newspaper. During regular sessions of the Legislative Assembly, any representative or the president of the country can initiate legislation. During extraordinary sessions, however, only the executive can initiate bills. A constitutional amendment can be initiated by a petition signed by 33 percent of the members of the Assembly or by the president of the country. A new constitution can be requested only by a majority of the members of the Assembly. A two-thirds affirmative vote is required for approval.

In the introductory phase, legislation is submitted to the president of the Legislative Assembly. The president of the Assembly informs the plenary of the proposed legislation and assigns it to the appropriate commission for study. The deliberative process in commission begins with a reading of the legislation; discussion of the legislation and any motions to modify it follow. A vote is taken on motions to modify proposed legislation, and, if any motions are approved, the president of the Assembly assigns the draft law to a subcommittee to incorporate the amendments. Finally, the legislation is voted on in commission and a report is issued. If there is disagreement over the legislation in the commission, both a majority and a minority report are issued and forwarded for presentation in the plenary session. Commission sessions, as well as the plenary sessions, are open to the public.

The report (or reports) issued in commission is debated in the plenary on two separate occasions. The first debate begins with the reading of the commission report. Any further motions to modify the legislation are heard. After discussion and vote on these motions to modify, the plenary votes on the draft law. After the draft law is approved in the first debate, it is sent to the Drafting Commission to be written in its final form. The Supreme Court must be consulted on legislative proposals that involve international treaties or constitutional reform. Following such consultation, the proposed legislation is debated a second time and a final vote is taken. If approved, the legislation is signed by the president and secretary of the Assembly and sent to the executive branch for promulgation.

The executive branch sanctions the proposed law with the signatures of the president of the country and the respective minister and publishes it in the official newspaper, the *Gazette.* The president can partially or totally reject a bill within fifteen days of receiving it from the Assembly. A bill vetoed by the president is returned to the Assembly, which can accept or reject the veto. A two-thirds vote of the membership (thirty-eight votes) is needed in the Assembly to override the executive veto. However, since the party of the president is almost always in control of the legislative branch, presidential vetoes are unusual.

The Assembly can ask officials of the executive branch to testify on pertinent issues. Assembly representatives may request in writing that ministers, vice ministers, and the presidents or directors of governmental entities furnish information in writing to the Assembly. A minimum of five representatives must sign this written request. The president of the Assembly must ask the president of the country to instruct the officials to testify before the Assembly. The Assembly can send a report to the president recommending the continuation in office or the removal of the person asked to testify. However, the role of the executive branch in the Legislative Assembly is very powerful. Consequently, the Assembly has not developed a strong capacity for significant executive oversight. The one exception seems to be that when some major controversy or scandal emerges as a significant public issue, the Assembly, through the holding of commission hearings, can influence how the executive branch carries out particular activities. Within the past few years, one of the investigative commissions looked into a major financial system scandal. As a result, significant reform proposals were enacted which had a substantial impact on the performance of the executive branch.

In case of international war or serious internal upheaval, the president—with the approval of the Council of Ministers and the approval of the Assembly—can declare a state of emergency for a specified period, which can be extended for a specified period.

An official record of the sessions and debates is kept by the secretary of the Assembly. Each representative expresses publicly his or her vote. One of the Assembly's secretaries is charged with keeping notes and recording the vote. In some cases, and by prior agreement of the majority and minority party leaderships, the voting can be secret.

For the most part, the Legislative Assembly has not adopted an aggressive role in developing the country's annual budget, which has tended to be very much an executive branch initiative. The typical budget process in Costa Rica begins when the various government ministries present their proposals to the minister of finance, who in consultation with the president prepares a proposed budget, which is then presented to the Finance Commission of the Legislative Assembly. Normally the commission hearings are pro forma, and then the Finance Commission advances the annual budget to the full chamber of the Assembly. The Assembly typically approves the Finance Commission's recommendation.

Although in general the finance minister's recommendations are not changed by the Finance Commission or by the deputies on the floor, there is one area in which the deputies do have significant influence on the budget. By tradition, 2 percent of the annual budget is set aside to be divided among the deputies for local projects. This has in recent years amounted to about US$700,000 per year per deputy, which is used to support projects within the district of the individual Assembly member.

The Assembly can impeach—under certain circumstances—Supreme Court judges, the nation's general controller, and the members of the National Electoral Board. A majority of deputies is needed to request impeachment. Once the request is made in the Assembly and approved by the Executive Board of the Assembly, the request is assigned to commission for consideration and recommendation. The commission's recommendation is read in plenary session. Two-thirds of the vote in the Assembly is needed for approval.

The media, both print and television, cover the Assembly extensively. Debate on significant legislation receives considerable attention. There is some attempt to cover the most controversial issues, and the media is regarded as relatively independent and objective.

ORGANIZATION AND STRUCTURE

The commission system has evolved into a very important aspect of the Costa Rican legislative process. The commissions, which by Latin American standards have substantial staff, serve as a place where serious deliberations on proposed legislation can occur. In addition, they also often engage in the drafting or redrafting of proposed legislation.

The Legislative Assembly has three types of permanent commissions, and from time to time investigatory and ad hoc commissions are also established. Each commission elects a president, a vice president, one secretary, and one vice secretary. Deputies can change commissions during the month of May as long as the commission's political party representativeness is not violated.

The three types of permanent commissions include commissions with "legislative authority," permanent ordinary commissions (which are the principal commissions of the Assembly), and "special" permanent commissions. The three commissions that possess "legislative authority" are unique in the sense that when they act, they do so in the name of the entire Assembly, and thus their decisions automatically become law if not vetoed by the president of the country. Each of the three commissions with legislative authority is composed of nineteen members, with the political parties being proportionally represented in terms of membership on the commissions. No member of the Assembly may serve on more than one of these commissions, and consequently each member of the Assembly serves on one. These commissions—known as "Plenaries 1, 2, and 3"—are atypical of the normal pattern of commission arrangements that exist in most Latin American countries. They tend to focus on technical aspects of extant law and on important but noncontroversial legislation.

The most important Assembly commissions are in fact the six permanent ordinary commissions, which focus on crucial legislative areas: governance and administration; public finance; economic policy; social welfare; judicial matters; and agriculture and natural resources. Their work is preparatory to bringing legislation to the plenary. Nine deputies serve on each of these commissions. The president of the Assembly assigns deputies to the six commissions. An effort is made to make the commissions representative of the political make-up of the Assembly; however, this procedure is somewhat discretionary, and partisan issues come into play.

In addition to the permanent ordinary commissions, the Assembly has six special permanent commissions, in the areas of judicial consulting; public expenditures; international relations; honors; bill drafting; and library and documents. From three to seven deputies sit on each of these commissions. They are structured in the same manner as the six permanent ordinary commissions.

The Costa Rican Legislative Assembly also has two other types of commissions: investigative commissions, as required by the constitution, and ad hoc commissions, appointed by the Assembly leadership to carry out a specific task. Three to five deputies are assigned to each of these commissions, but no deputy can be a member of more than one. Investigative commissions are created for a specific time period, at the end of which a report must be submitted by the commission. Investigative commissions have the power to call anyone, public official or private citizen, to testify. However, the oversight capacity of these commissions is limited to public organizations and officials. Ad hoc commissions are named to study special legislation or legislative issues.

Finally, it should be noted that public hearings are an important part of the commission process in Costa Rica; testimony is routinely taken from executive branch officials and representatives of relevant organizations.

The president of the Assembly has considerable power—both formal and informal. In addition to the president's role as political leader of the Assembly, he or she acts as administrative leader and chief representative of the Assembly. These roles require directing and organizing floor debates; establishing the order of votes; opening, convening, or suspending sessions; ordering the procedures and resolution of issues; nominating, promoting, or removing administrative personnel; presenting the proposed annual budget for the Assembly; authorizing the expenses of members and staff and the payment of salaries to members and support personnel; and putting his or her authorized signature and seal, along with those of the appropriate corresponding commission secretaries, to the manuscripts of the sessions of the Assembly, including the laws, resolutions, declarations, and official correspondence.

The Assembly has an Executive Board, which is chaired by the president of the Assembly and includes the three vice presidents and three secretaries of the Assembly. It has considerable formal power over the day-to-day activities of the Assembly, since most Assembly presidents tend to seek the support of the Executive Board. In addition, each party has a caucus which typically meets once every week to sort out party positions on issues that are going to come before the Assembly in the following week. As noted above, party positions for the most part tend to be strongly adhered to once determined in the caucus. The one exception to this general rule tends to be when it comes time for the parties to nominate their candidates for president of the country and more than one individual within the Assembly seeks a party's nomination. Then, factionalism based on individual presidential ambitions will on occasion break out.

STATUS OF MEMBERS

Members of the Assembly cannot be detained unless they are caught committing a criminal act. Representatives can lose their seats by violating provisions of the constitution or by proof of inappropriate use of their influence. However, they cannot be accused for opinions expressed while exercising their functions. A two-thirds-majority vote is needed to be ousted from the body. If an accusation is found to have basis and the member is expelled, he or she can be brought to trial.

When a member of the Assembly dies, resigns (resignations are accepted by simple majority), is declared physically or mentally unable to serve by the Supreme Court, or asks for leave, he or she is replaced by a substitute named by his or her party or political movement.

As of 1995 the salary of a representative was US$2,100 per month. In addition, each deputy receives a representation allowance and is provided with an office and three staff members who are responsible to him or her. When Assembly members travel to the interior or outside the country, they receive extra per-diems. Representatives cannot receive municipal or state pay or work in other public enterprises. Medical personnel and teachers are exempted from this regulation. Other than the references to appropriate conduct found in the Assembly's internal regulations, there is no ethics statute or code of ethics.

In the 1990s the National Assembly has begun to develop a much more substantial parliamentary library, research capability, and legislative record-keeping system, in large part as a result of technical assistance provided by external donors including the United States and Great Britain.

Allan Rosenbaum and Alejandro Rodriguez

BIBLIOGRAPHY

Edelman, Mark, and Joanne Kenan, eds. *The Costa Rica Reader.* New York: Grove-Atlantic, 1989.

Yashar, Deborah J. *Demanding Democracy: Reform and Reaction in Costa Rica and Guatemala, 1870s–1950s.* Stanford, Calif.: Stanford University Press, 1997.

CÔTE D'IVOIRE

OFFICIAL NAME: Republic of Côte d'Ivoire (République de Côte d'Ivoire)
CAPITAL: Abidjan. Capital-designate: Yamoussoukro
POPULATION: 14,762,000 (1996 est.)
DATE OF INDEPENDENCE: August 7, 1960 (from France)
DATE OF CURRENT CONSTITUTION: Adopted October 31, 1960
FORM OF GOVERNMENT: Parliamentary democracy
LANGUAGES: French (official), sixty local dialects
MONETARY UNIT: CFA franc
FISCAL YEAR: Calendar year
LEGISLATURE: National Assembly (Assemblée Nationale)
NUMBER OF CHAMBERS: One
NUMBER OF MEMBERS: 175 (maximum)
PERCENTAGE OF WOMEN: 8.3
TERM OF LEGISLATURE: Five years
MOST RECENT LEGISLATIVE ELECTION: November 26, 1995
MINIMUM AGE FOR VOTING: 21
MINIMUM AGE FOR MEMBERSHIP: 23
SUFFRAGE: Universal and direct
VOTING: Optional
ADDRESS: Assemblée Nationale, 01 B.P. 1381, Abidjan 01
TELEPHONE: (225) 21 09 88
FAX: (225) 22 70 43

The Republic of Côte d'Ivoire is a small nation on the Atlantic coast of West Africa *(see map, p. 447)*. Formerly known as Ivory Coast, the area became a French protectorate in the mid-nineteenth century and gained independence from France in 1960. For thirty years it remained a single-party state under the authoritarian rule of Félix Houphouët-Boigny. Houphouët was one of the founders of the nationalist Democratic Party of the Ivory Coast, established in 1946 and a branch of the transnational African Democratic Rally. Consequently, the National Assembly, which was entirely in the hands of Houphouët's party, had only marginal influence.

The country's economic difficulties and the absence of legitimate channels for dissent brought mounting domestic demands for political reform in the 1980s, and as the cold war faded the Western donor states also pressed for democratization. Thus in 1990 Houphouët reluctantly permitted the formation of multiple parties, and some seventeen parties fielded almost five hundred candidates in the November 1990 parliamentary elections. The opposition, led by Laurent Gbagbo's Ivorian Popular Front, alleged massive fraud by the government, and indeed Houphouët's party won 163 of the 175 seats. Nonetheless, the election of nine Popular Front deputies and three other opposition members gave new life to the National Assembly as a national political forum.

The Assembly played an important stabilizing role in December 1993, when the nation was shocked and disoriented by Houphouët's death. The constitution designates the president of the Assembly, who at the time was Henri Konan-Bédié, as successor until the next election, but for a time there was concern that Prime Minister Alassane Ouattara would challenge Bédié for national leadership. Nudged by France and other countries, however, Ouattara decided to stand down in favor of the constitutional process.

In 1994 a new political party, the Rally of Republicans, appeared to be drawing at least tacit support from younger, technocratic members of the Assembly, even though most remained formally aligned with the Democratic Party. Thus the 1995 parliamentary elections were a genuine contest among the Democratic old guard, a politically centrist Rally of Republicans, and the more social democratic Popular Front.

The legislative election of November 26, 1995, was preceded by the presidential balloting of October 22, in which President Bédié was elected to a full five-year term. The presidential election was marred by an opposition boycott over the electoral lists. The issue was resolved shortly after the presidential election, with the government agreeing to opposition demands to revise the lists, and the opposition participated in the legislative balloting.

The legislative elections were held at the normal expiration of the legislature's five-year term. The 175-member body was elected from 154 constituencies, some of them single member and some multimember, on the basis of a simple majority vote. In generally peaceful and fair elections, the ruling Democratic Party of the Ivory Coast won 150 seats. The Rally of Republicans and Ivorian Popular Front combined won 25 seats.

Although Houphouët-Boigny ostensibly moved the capital to Yamoussoukro, his birthplace, the National Assembly, along with other institutions of government, is to be found in Abidjan, Côte d'Ivoire's principal city.

Raymond Copson

CROATIA

OFFICIAL NAME: Republic of Croatia (Republika Hrvatska)
CAPITAL: Zagreb
POPULATION: 5,004,000 (1996 est.)
DATE OF INDEPENDENCE: Declared June 25, 1991 (from Yugoslavia)
DATE OF CURRENT CONSTITUTION: Adopted December 22, 1990
FORM OF GOVERNMENT: Parliamentary democracy
LANGUAGE: Serbo-Croatian
MONETARY UNIT: Croatian dinar
FISCAL YEAR: Calendar year
LEGISLATURE: Assembly (Sabor)
NUMBER OF CHAMBERS: Two. House of Representatives (Predstavničke Dom); House of Counties (Županije Dom)
NUMBER OF MEMBERS: House of Representatives, 127 (directly elected); House of Counties, 68 (63 directly elected; 5 appointed)
PERCENTAGE OF WOMEN: House of Representatives, 7.9; House of Counties, 4.4
TERM OF LEGISLATURE: Four years
MOST RECENT LEGISLATIVE ELECTION: House of Representatives, October 29, 1995; House of Counties, April 13, 1997
MINIMUM AGE FOR VOTING: 18
MINIMUM AGE FOR MEMBERSHIP: 18
SUFFRAGE: Universal
VOTING: Optional
ADDRESS: Assembly, Trg sv. Marka 6-7, 10000 Zagreb

TELEPHONE: (3851) 456 94 20
FAX: (3851) 44 35 22

Croatia, a state bordering the Adriatic Sea which formerly was a constituent republic of the Socialist Federal Republic of Yugoslavia, gained its independence in 1991 *(see map, p. 749)*. Under the constitution of December 1990, legislative authority is vested in a bicameral Assembly.

HISTORICAL BACKGROUND

The Balkan Peninsula, settled during the Slavic migrations of the sixth and seventh centuries, was divided geographically and administratively between Croats, Serbs, and Bulgars following a series of invasions by tribes with competing territorial ambitions. Though the peninsula was organized largely according to the tribal traditions of its peasant inhabitants, the growth of a Croatian noble class throughout the northwest and coastal parts of the region helped to integrate Croat-populated lands. When Tomislav was crowned king in the tenth century, the Croatian kingdom extended south more than halfway down the coast of the Adriatic and east across the Pannonian Plain as far as the confluence of the Danube and Sava Rivers. The medieval Croatian kingdom had its political center on the northern Adriatic and included the lands of Dalmatia, the Banate Croatia (inner Croatia), and Slavonia.

The Sabor (originally an assembly of nobles) traces its origins to this period and in fact has functioned as an administrative body, with varying degrees of power, to the present day. In the twelfth century, when Croatia was incorporated under the Hungarian Crown, the Sabor continued to represent the Croatian provinces and sent delegates to the Hungarian diet. Although Croatia remained a subject of the Hungarian Crown until the sixteenth century, the continued local jurisdiction of Croatian nobles allowed the region to maintain a distinct character and substantial autonomy.

In the fifteenth and sixteenth centuries a series of important shifts in power occurred throughout the region as the Austrian Empire expanded its control over Dalmatia and the Ottoman Empire began making incursions into Bosnia-Herzegovina, both at the expense of the Hungarian Empire. As Croatia's nobility subsequently moved north, away from the Ottoman Turks, their landholdings diminished, leading to the contraction of Croatian territory and the growth of Zagreb as a new political center. In 1526, when King Louis II of Hungary was defeated by the Turks at the Battle of Mohács, a struggle over succession resulted in the transfer of power to the Habsburg monarchy seated in Vienna. As the Ottoman Empire continued to push north, the Habsburgs established a military frontier along the Sava River across southern Croatia. To defend this largely uninhabited frontier *(krajina)*, the monarchy offered Serbs fleeing their Ottoman-occupied homeland special concessions to settle in the district. Croatia's Serbian population thus expanded dramatically, and the southern Croat districts were cut off from Zagreb's administrative reach.

Croatia historically has stood at the fringe of great empires. As a result, its borders, which have expanded and contracted through the centuries—especially along the southern periphery—have long represented important cultural and political demarcations. Straddling the Latin territories of Europe and the Orthodox strongholds of the east, Croatia's crescent-shaped territory divided the Balkan Peninsula into the Catholic west and the Orthodox east. Following the establishment of the military frontier, Croatia also served as a buffer between Vienna and the encroaching Ottoman Turks. To many, the Krajina was Europe's last stronghold against Islam. At the same time, however, Croatia absorbed both the peoples and the traditions of its neighbors. Borders within the Balkans remained remarkably fluid, and the resulting population shifts, plus the widespread incidence of intermarriage, cultural assimilation, and religious conversion, resulted in a complex tapestry of people and traditions.

By the eighteenth century the centralizing reforms of the Habsburgs had severely eroded Croatian autonomy. Furthermore, Hungary had since been restored to the monarchy, and the Magyars sought to enhance their own influence in the region. In 1769 the Hungarian monarchy established the Croatian Royal Council, which effectively usurped all remaining authority held by the Sabor. The council was soon abolished, but it was replaced by an alternative Hungarian body, and the Sabor never regained its former influence.

With the European revolutions of 1848, Croatian intellectuals played upon the growing tension between the Magyars and the monarchy in Vienna. To counterbalance Hungarian nationalism, the Habsburgs lent support to Croatia's budding nationalists. Croats and Slavonian Serbs called for Croat and Serb autonomy within the context of a federated union with the Austrian Habsburgs. When in 1881 control over the Krajina reverted to the Croatian diet, Croatian nationalists expected to gain the support of the Krajina Serbs. Instead, they faced strong opposition, which would color Serb-Croat political relations for the next hundred years.

Following World War I and the dismemberment of the Austro-Hungarian Empire, Croatia joined the Kingdom of Serbs, Croats, and Slovenes, newly constituted under the Serbian Karadjordjevic dynasty. Serbia, however, maintained a disproportionate share of power, and Croatia continued to push for regional autonomy within the context of a federated union. This prompted King Aleksandar to impose a royal dictatorship, rename the kingdom the Kingdom of Yugoslavia, and vigorously suppress all sectarian nationalist expression. In 1934 Croatian extremists assassinated the king in France.

In 1941 the fascist Ustaša regime came to power in Croatia and allied itself with Adolph Hitler and Benito Mussolini. On April 9, 1941, the Ustaša severed its ties with the Kingdom of Yugoslavia and proclaimed Croatian independence. The Ustaše massacred thousands of Jews, Serbs, and Gypsies in Croatian concentration camps and were infamous for their brutality. Ustaše atrocities rallied Serbian resistance and contributed to the ethnic division and hatred that cripples the region today.

Josip Broz Tito, a native Croatian who led the partisan resistance to Nazi occupation during World War II, after the war reunited the South Slavs into the Socialist Federated Republic of Yugoslavia (SFRY). Tito was a strong, charismatic ruler and led the Communist Party for thirty years. In his efforts to stabilize the country and to centralize authority within the Communist Party, Tito reinforced and manipulated ethnic divisions to create a complex balance of power between the republics. Since Serbs and Croats were the largest national groups, the effects of Tito's maneuvering were felt most acutely by them. Serbs occupied the majority of Croatian government posts and wielded disproportionate power in Croatia. Croatian representation at the federal level was thus offset by Serbian representation at the republic level.

A rise in nationalist sentiments in Croatia in the 1960s and 1970s led to a harsh crackdown from Belgrade. In 1974 Tito introduced a new constitution and a series of reforms designed to placate nationalist tendencies. In a clear reversal of the Communists' centralizing tendencies, the new Yugoslav constitution significantly enhanced republican autonomy.

The reemergence of ethnic tensions and nationalist sentiments in Yugoslavia may be explained in part by the death of Tito in 1980. The other contributing factor seems to have been Slobodan Milošević's rise to power in Serbia in 1987.

When Croatia held its first multiparty elections in 1990, Franjo Tudjman campaigned on a platform calling for the expansion of Croatian territory (including into sections of Bosnia), an end to Serb political dominance in Croatia, an abandonment of communism, and an end to Yugoslavia as a federation. The elections, colored by a strong upsurge of nationalism, resulted in an overwhelming victory for Tudjman and the Croatian Democratic Union (HDZ). In the aftermath of the elections, Tudjman launched a vigorous effort to nationalize Croatian cultural symbols. He also removed Serbs from government and security posts and replaced them with Croats, breeding resentment and recalling memories of the fascist regime. A pronounced political insensitivity toward the Serb population of Croatia heightened ethnic tension both in and outside the republic.

On June 25, 1991, Croatia declared its independence of Yugoslavia. Croatia's sizable Serb population was unwilling to accept minority status inside an independent Croatian state. That summer, local Serbs, who comprised roughly 12.2 percent of Croatia's population, began an armed insurrection in the Krajina. They were supported in their efforts by the regime in Belgrade and by independent vigilante forces of the Yugoslav army. The self-declared Republic of Serbian Krajina (RSK), constituting approximately one-third of Croatian territory, won de facto independence from Croatia in 1991. The RSK held its own parliamentary elections on December 12, 1993, and elected Milan Martić as president of the self-proclaimed republic. Despite its refusal to recognize the RSK, the Croatian government continued negotiations in hopes of creating a special protected minority status for the Serbs in exchange for official recognition of Croatian sovereignty in the Krajina.

While Serbs and Croats battled inside Croatia, war erupted in neighboring Bosnia-Herzegovina in June 1991 and quickly involved fighting among all three ethnic groups. Unwilling to remain in a Serbian-dominated federation without Croatia and Slovenia, Bosnia declared itself an independent state. Although Croatia quickly recognized Bosnia's independence, secret meetings between Croatian president Tudjman and Serbian president Milošević suggested a willingness to divide Bosnia into ethnic spheres of influence.

In 1995 the Dayton Peace Agreement was signed by the governments of Serbia, Croatia, and Bosnia-Herzegovina. It provides a comprehensive system for maintaining peace in the region and also resulted in a final agreement on territorial matters over which the war had been fought. This agreement permits the continuance of a single Bosnia-Herzegovina state.

There has also been unrest in the Istria region of Croatia. In 1991 the Italian Union of Croatia and Slovenia was created, uniting Istrian Italians across the Croatian-Slovenian border. The Union maintains an "independent assembly" of eighty-five elected deputies. Though the assembly serves a primarily cultural function, in 1994 it called for special autonomous status within the Croatian Republic and promulgated a statute calling for self-government. The statute was harshly criticized in Zagreb and, according to Croatian officials, contained several provisions that are unconstitutional and violate Croatian law.

THE PARLIAMENT

The Croatian constitution, enacted on December 22, 1990, and amended on June 25, 1991, became fully effective following the October 8, 1991, parliamentary decision to terminate all legal relations with the Socialist Federal Republic of Yugoslavia. Legislative power rests with parliament (the Sabor), a bicameral body made up of the House of Representatives and the House of Counties (the lower house). Representatives to both houses are elected through a mixed system of majoritarian and proportional representation. Voting is conducted by direct, secret ballot, and representatives serve a term of four years.

The House of Representatives has 127 members. The Law on Voting Units of the House of Representatives of the Parliament of the Republic of Croatia was enacted in 1995. The law establishes twenty-eight voting (electoral) districts that are responsible for electing 28 of the 127 representatives on the basis of majority representation. Voters are given a ballot, or "single-constituency list," for specific candidates in each of the twenty-eight electoral districts. Eighty representatives are elected from the Republic of Croatia as a whole, in which all voters are given the same ballot, or "state list," of eligible political parties or coalitions. Until a population census takes place in Croatia, four representatives in the House of Representatives shall be elected to represent ethnic and national communities, one each by the Hungarian; Italian; Czech and Slovak; Russian, Ukrainian, German, and Austrian communities, in special geographically defined electoral units. Districts are established where these minorities reside. The Serbian minority elects three members. Since Serbs are not concentrated geographically, Serb candidates do not run in a special district; rather, they are listed at all polling stations.

The 1995 election law also provides Croatian citizens living outside of the Republic of Croatia the right to vote in Croatian elections. Consequently, 110,000 nonresident Croatians voted in the 1995 elections, of which 90 percent cast votes for the HDZ. The vast majority of voters were ethnic Croats from Bosnia-Herzegovina. This enabled the HDZ to capture an additional twelve seats in the House of Representatives.

The House of Representatives is divided into fourteen working committees, presided over by a secretary and one or two senior advisers. The House of Representatives, as well as the House of Counties, has a president and one or more vice presidents. The speaker of the House of Representatives is also the chair of the parliament. The House of Representatives has the authority to pass laws and state budgets, make amendments to the constitution, pass resolutions on declarations of war or border changes, call referenda, and oversee the government and other public officials. The House of Representatives is also responsible for electing the members of the State Judicial Council, a body responsible for appointing all court judges except for those presiding over the Constitutional Court, and state and assistant state prosecutors. The State Judicial Council is responsible for electing twenty-five judges to the Supreme Court, the highest judicial body in the country, upon the recommendation of the House of Representatives.

The House of Counties is made up of three deputies from each of twenty-one Croatian provinces, plus up to five members appointed directly by the president of the republic. The House is divided into four working committees and acts as an advisory body on issues of local government and the constitutionality of laws. The House of Counties may propose laws, which are then sent to the House of Representatives for a vote, but most legislation originates in the House of Representatives. It also has the right of suspensive veto (the right to return bills to the House for reconsideration), but any veto may be voided if the law is passed by a majority vote in the House of Representatives.

The explicit duties and responsibilities of the House of Counties include providing the House of Representatives prior opinion on the enactment of laws that, among other things, regulate national rights and the responsibilities and operation of government bodies.

ELECTIONS AND PARTIES

Elections are governed by the Law on the Parliamentary Elections of the Republic of Croatia (1993) and its amendment, the Law on Voting Units of the House of Representatives of the Parliament of the Republic of Croatia (1995). Elections are called by the president and may be held after thirty days.

In November 1992 the House of Representatives approved legislation that divided Croatia into 21 administrative provinces, 420 municipalities, and 61 towns. The 21 administrative provinces are also electoral units for the House of Counties. Any Croatian citizen at least eighteen years of age may vote in an election or run for office.

Candidates for the House of Representatives are elected from voter lists including all parties registered prior to an election. Candidates for the twenty-eight district seats are selected through a "single-constituency list." Candidates may run for the House of Counties by a simple declaration of candidacy with four hundred supporting signatures (one hundred for minority candidates) or be nominated by a party or coalition. Candidates running in the twenty-eight specified districts must only reach a plurality of the votes in order to obtain a seat. For proportional seats, a party must gain at least 3 percent of the vote to obtain a seat in parliament; a joint list of two parties must receive 8 percent, and a coalition of two or more parties must gain 11 percent.

According to basic conflict of interest guidelines, candidates may run for either house but may not hold office in both. In addition, representatives to either house are forbidden, while in office, to hold the position of judge, public prosecutor, public attorney, public defender, or director of a state institution. All candidates, as well as parties that have proposed candidates, are granted time on the state radio and television channel. Campaigning is forbidden twenty-four hours prior to a vote. Furthermore, candidates who receive at least 3 percent of the vote are entitled to state reimbursement for campaign expenses.

The first elections held under the new constitution for the House of Representatives and the presidency were held August 2, 1992. In the presidential election, Franjo Tudjman of the Croatian Democratic Union (HDZ) won a clear majority (56 percent) out of a field of eight candidates. Tudjman was sworn in as president on August 12, 1992, for a five-year term. In the August 1992 parliamentary elections, the HDZ won more than half of the majority-race seats and a plurality of the proportional-based seats in a race with thirty-seven political parties, to claim 85 of the total 138 House of Representatives seats. Elections for the House of Counties were held on February 7, 1993. The HDZ won a majority of the seats. The most recent elections for the House of Representatives were held in October 1995. The HDZ won 45 percent of the seats.

The 1992 elections were conducted under the regulation of the republic's Electoral Commission. According to observers, the electoral process was free and fair but suffered under its failure to explain decisions and provide information. The Commission on Security and Cooperation in Europe observed the 1995 elections along with the republic's Electoral Commission. The 1995 elections were characterized as suffering from bias due to the government's control of television access for the opposition parties. The elections were further marred by the government's failure to correct polling problems that had occurred in the previous elections.

The constitution guarantees the right of free association, and citizens may freely form political parties, labor unions, and other associations. A political party may register if its membership includes at least five hundred eligible voters. Political parties may not be formed in firms, the army, police, state organs, and other similar organizations. Parties may be denied registration if their programs or actions violate the "democratic constitutional order, independence, unity or territorial integrity of the Republic of Croatia."

As of January 1997 there were approximately fifty-eight political parties registered in the republic. The HDZ is by far the strongest represented party in both houses of parliament. The opposition parties of the left are relatively ineffective as a bloc. In 1993 the socialist parties attempted to unite, but personal interests and incompatible agendas resulted in the polarization rather than unification of the parties.

The HDZ was formed in late 1989, shortly before the April 1990 elections, and commands a majority in parliament. It was the best organized and financed of the opposition parties formed to challenge one-party rule. President Tudjman, founder of the party, is its chair. Tudjman is considered to be a communist dissident and was an army general. Party membership spans the breadth of the political spectrum, including both national extremists and liberals. The party was originally formed as a mass political organization to oversee the transition from communist rule. At the party's convention in October 1993, the Tudjman faction undermined support for a mass political movement and focused the party along the lines of a centralized Christian democratic platform.

Although the party holds a strong majority in both parliament and the government, the HDZ has encountered strong opposition at the local level. The party's response to local opposition has been vigorous. The party publishes the weekly *Glasnik* (The Herald) at its headquarters in Zagreb.

The Croatian Social-Liberal Party is the second-largest party in the republic, led by Dražen Budiša. Budiša was imprisoned for a time by the communist regime because of his political activities as a student leader in the "Croatian Spring" reform movement of 1971. In his 1992 bid for the presidency, Budiša captured only 21.9 percent of the vote and lost to Tudjman.

The Croatian Party of the Right won 5.4 percent of the popular vote for its presidential candidate, Dobroslav Paraga, in the 1992 elections and won four seats in the House of Representatives in 1995. The party dates to the mid-nineteenth century, when it supported the independence of Croatia from Vienna and Budapest. The fascist Ustaša regime after coming to power in the 1930s utilized the party's name for its ideological platform. Still today the party advocates for an expanded Croatian Republic reaching into the territory of Bosnia-Herzegovina. Some members began wearing black clothing to represent their neofascist orientation and have formed vigilante paramilitary troops. The party's strongest base of support came from among the Croatian youth. The Croatian Party of the Right (HSP) split in mid-1995 into two separate parties, the HSP and the HSP 1861.

The Croatian People's Party advocates a plan that would maintain the territorial integrity of Bosnia-Herzegovina yet grant Croats a degree of independence in certain Bosnian territories. The party was organized in 1990 by Communist dissidents Savka Dabčevic-Kučar and Miko Tripalo, both leaders of the suppressed democratic movement, Croatian Spring.

The Serbian People's Party represents Serbs and promotes cultural and human rights for Serbs living in Croatia. As a minority party, it is guaranteed representation in parliament. The party has approximately five thousand members.

Other parties that have significant roles in Croatia include the Social Democratic Party of Croatia, the Croatian Peasant Party, and the Istrian Democratic Assembly. The Social Democratic Party of Croatia, formerly a communist party, has gained significantly in popularity since the 1995 elections. It may be considered one of the strongest opposition parties to the HDZ. The Croatian Peasant Party is the oldest party in Croatia, with over a hundred years of tradition. It was the leading party during the early part of the twentieth century. The Istrian Democratic Assembly is the only Istrian Party currently to hold a seat in parliament. Moreover, it has the largest support base in the region, receiving between 70 percent and 80 percent of votes in Istria.

PARLIAMENTARY ORGANIZATION AND PROCEEDINGS

In May 1994 a crisis in parliament left Croatian lawmakers deadlocked for several weeks. The situation was precipitated when Stepen Mesić, speaker of the House of Counties, and Josip Manolić, speaker of the House of Representatives, resigned from the ruling HDZ to form a new party. In an overnight session several days after the resignations, deputies of both houses dismissed the men from their posts as speaker. Members of the opposition called the move illegal and anticonstitutional, and they boycotted the parliamentary session. On May 20, 1994, the HDZ and opposition parties reached a compromise over the terms of party representation and agreed to vote on successors to the Office of Speaker. It was stipulated that the Office of Speaker in each house would be held by the ruling party, and the Office of Deputy Speaker would be shared by the opposition and the ruling party. One deputy speakership is to be reserved for minorities, and committee chairs are to be divided among the HDZ and the opposition parties. Until the 1995 elections, the HDZ held an absolute majority in all committees in the parliament. Since then, the HDZ has maintained the majority in most committees but is matched by the opposition in some.

According to the constitution, the Croatian parliament is in session twice annually. The first session begins January 15 and ends June 30, and the second session begins September 15 and ends December 15. The first session must be held within twenty days after elections, or in the event of dissolution, not more than sixty days. Sessions are open to the public.

Both houses of parliament may dissolve themselves if a majority of deputies so decides. The president of the republic may dissolve the House of Representatives in accordance with the constitution and may call an emergency session of both houses.

Both the House of Representatives and the president may call referenda. The House of Representatives may call a referendum on an amendment to the constitution, a bill, or any other issue falling within its competence. The president may, with the countersignature of the prime minister, call a referendum on an amendment to the constitution or any other issue that he or she considers to be "important for the independence, unity, and existence of the republic." A referendum is passed by majority vote, provided that a majority of the electorate participates.

The government and representatives to both houses have the right to propose laws. Ordinarily, bills originate in the House of Representatives, from the respective work committees, and are sent to the House of Counties with attached opinions. The House of Counties may pass the bill or return it for reconsideration to the House of Representatives. If a bill is returned, the House of Representatives must pass the bill by a majority vote, unless the law requires a two-thirds vote. The law provides a limit of three discussion sessions for a proposed bill. The president shall promulgate a law within eight days of its passage by parliament.

The House of Representatives may authorize the government to issue decrees for a maximum period of one year on individual issues falling within its competence and limited by article 88 of the constitution.

The present parliamentary procedure heavily favors the HDZ majority. New regulations were proposed at the end of 1995 to insure a system of negotiation and formal debate. The proposal establishes rules for relations between parliament and the government, parliament and its committees, and parliament and the president, as well as more clearly defines the respective powers of parliament and the president.

A quorum of more than half the deputies to either

house must be present to hold a vote. Decisions in both houses are made by majority vote. However, the House of Representatives must pass national-rights legislation by a two-thirds majority vote.

The parliament's Informational and Documentation Service is responsible for minutes of the sessions and all record keeping. For information regarding parliament activities, the Public Relations Service organizes press conferences and also publishes a parliamentary newsletter.

THE EXECUTIVE BRANCH

The president of the republic is the most powerful figure in Croatia. The Croatian presidency is designed on the model of the Fifth French Republic. The president represents the country at home and abroad and is responsible for upholding the constitution, guaranteeing the existence and unity of the republic, and overseeing all state functions. The president is elected directly by the people for a five-year term and may not serve more than two terms. According to the constitution, the president is granted life tenure in the House of Counties upon expiration of his or her term. While in office, the president may nominate to the House of Counties as many as five representatives. The president may not hold any other office but may maintain a party affiliation. According to the Law on the Election of the President of the Republic of Croatia, eligibility for the presidency extends to Croatian citizens at least eighteen years of age. Candidates may be nominated by political parties, individuals, or groups and must receive at least ten thousand signatures of endorsement. The declared winner of the election must have the majority of all votes regardless of the number of candidates. The current president, Franjo Tudjman, was elected by parliament on May 30, 1990, and reelected by popular vote on August 2, 1992.

One of the most important powers of the presidency is the ability to dissolve the House of Representatives should it vote no confidence in the government or if it does not approve the state budget on schedule. Under provisions of the constitution, however, the president must first have the cosignature of the prime minister and must "consult with the chair of the House." The president may not dissolve the House again for a period of one year.

Other powers of the president include the right to call elections to the parliament and to propose referenda. The president also appoints and dismisses the prime minister, the deputy prime ministers, members of the government, and diplomatic representatives. He or she is the supreme commander of the army and, in the event of war or imminent danger to the republic, may issue decrees that carry the full force of law. On the basis of a decision of parliament, the president may declare war and conclude peace. The president may convene and preside over any ministerial session or governmental meetings. The president chairs both the Presidential Council and the Defense Council. The opposition parties object to these bodies because of the president's constitutional power to convene them as his personal counselors.

The president may be impeached for any violation of the constitution committed in the performance of his or her duties. The House of Representatives may, by a two-thirds majority vote, initiate impeachment proceedings. A decision to impeach the president must be reached by a two-thirds vote of the Constitutional Court. If the Constitutional Court sustains the impeachment, the president ceases to perform his or her duties, pursuant to the constitution.

Executive power in Croatia is vested in the president, the prime minister, deputy prime ministers, and ministers. The government is responsible to the president and to the House of Representatives. Following an election, the president nominates a prime minister, and the prime minister, in turn, proposes cabinet ministers to the House of Representatives no later than fifteen days from the prime minister's nomination. The nomination of the prime minister and members of the government is deemed accepted if a vote of confidence is carried by a majority of all the members of the House of Representatives. The government proposes the state budget, enforces laws and regulations passed by parliament, and may introduce bills and issue decrees.

An ombudsman is elected by the House of Representatives for an eight-year term. The ombudsman is charged under article 93 of the constitution with protecting the constitutional and legal rights of all Croatian citizens.

STATUS OF MEMBERS

All members of the Croatian parliament enjoy near total immunity under the Croatian constitution. A member may not be detained or charged with criminal conduct without the approval of the House in which he or she sits. The only exception is in the event that a member is caught engaging in a criminal activity that carries with it a penalty of at least five years.

The Administrative and Professional Services perform technical and administrative tasks for both houses. The service is headed by parliament's secretary, who is also the secretary to the House of Representatives. The service is divided into three organizational units, including the Secretariat (consisting of the secretariat of both houses), Office of the President and Vice President of the House of Representatives, and Office of the President and Vice President of the House of Counties.

JUDICIAL FUNCTIONS AND EMERGENCY POWERS

The Law on the State Judicial Council provides that the House of Counties nominate the candidates for the president and the fourteen members of the State Judicial Council. These candidates are proposed by the Supreme Court, the State Attorney's Office, faculties of law, and the Croatian Bar Association. The president and seven members of the council are selected from among the candidates suggested by the Supreme Court. Four members are selected from the state attorney's list of candidates. One member of the council is selected through the Bar Association, and two from recommendations provided by the law faculties. Council members serve a term of eight years. The council is responsible for appointing judges in the republic.

Judges can only be relieved of their duties if they request to be removed, become permanently incapacitated, or have been sentenced for a criminal offense that makes them unworthy to hold office. The Croatian judicial system comprises municipal courts, misdemeanor courts, county courts, commercial courts, the High Commercial Court, the Administrative Court, the Supreme Court, and the Constitutional Court.

Eleven judges are elected to the Constitutional Court by the House of Representatives upon recommendation of the House of Counties. Judges serve an eight-year term. The court's primary duty is to ensure that all laws passed by the House of Representatives comply with the constitution. In addition, the court protects the constitutional freedoms of citizens; resolves jurisdictional disputes between the legislative, executive, and judicial branches; rules on the impeachability of the president; oversees the constitutionality of elections; and rules in the case of an electoral dispute. Interestingly, the court is entrusted with determining the constitutionality of political party platforms and may place a ban on party activities if they are deemed to conflict with the constitution.

The constitution provides that individual freedoms and rights guaranteed by the constitution may be restricted in the event of "war or an immediate danger to the independence and unity of the republic, or in the event of natural disaster." The parliament has the power to invoke such emergency powers by a two-thirds majority vote of all representatives. If parliament is unable to convene, this power resides with the president.

PARLIAMENT AND THE MEDIA

The ruling HDZ has been attacked both at home and abroad for its control and domination of the press. This control was particularly evident during the October 1995 election campaign.

Croatian Radio and Television (HRT), controlled by the state, is run by a council of thirty-five members, fifteen of whom are appointed by parliament according to party representation. The directors of HRT also are chosen by parliament and by selected government officials.

Although the print media are subject to less direct government control than broadcast media, they too suffer from a lack of independence and often reflect sympathy toward the HDZ.

Mark S. Ellis

BIBLIOGRAPHY

Congressional Research Service. "Croatia: Background and Current Issues." Washington, D.C.: U.S. Government Printing Office, December 3, 1992.

Commission on Security and Cooperation in Europe. "Human Rights and Democratization in Croatia." Washington, D.C.: U.S. Government Printing Office, 1993.

McGregor, James. "The Presidency in East Central Europe." *RFE/RL Research Report* (January 14, 1994).

CUBA

OFFICIAL NAME: Republic of Cuba (República de Cuba)
CAPITAL: Havana
POPULATION: 10,951,000 (1996 est.)
DATE OF INDEPENDENCE: May 20, 1902 (from Spain)
DATE OF CURRENT CONSTITUTION: Adopted February 16, 1976
FORM OF GOVERNMENT: Communist dictatorship
LANGUAGE: Spanish
MONETARY UNIT: Peso
FISCAL YEAR: Calendar year
LEGISLATURE: National Assembly of People's Power (Asamblea Nacional del Poder Popular)
NUMBER OF CHAMBERS: One
NUMBER OF MEMBERS: 589
PERCENTAGE OF WOMEN: 22.8
TERM OF LEGISLATURE: Five years
MOST RECENT LEGISLATIVE ELECTION: February 24, 1993
MINIMUM AGE FOR VOTING: 16
MINIMUM AGE FOR MEMBERSHIP: 18
SUFFRAGE: Universal and direct

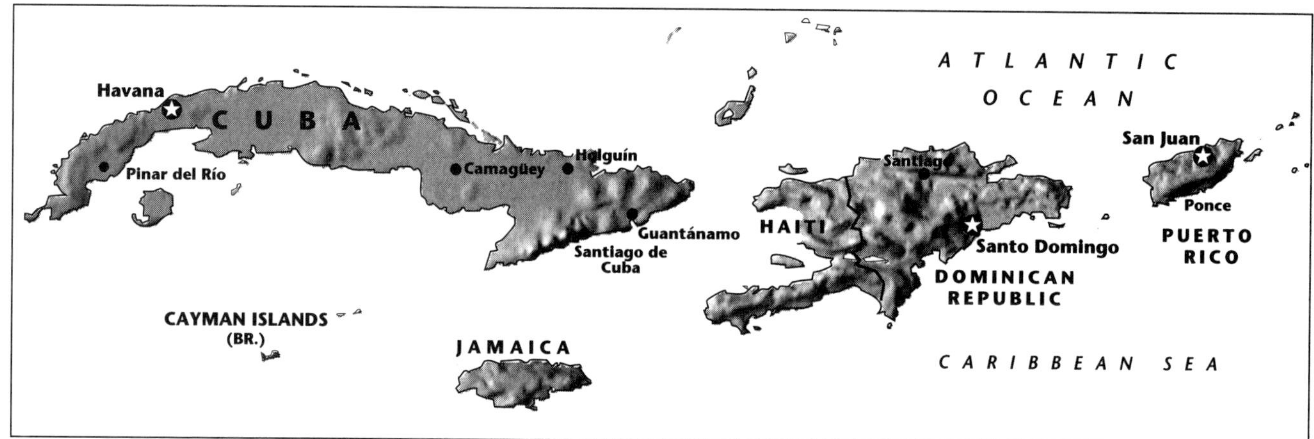

VOTING: Optional
ADDRESS: Asamblea Nacional del Poder Popular, 42 No. 2308, Playa, Havana
TELEPHONE: (537) 29 0451
FAX: (537) 33 1087

The 1976 constitution of Cuba, an island nation in the Caribbean, ended seventeen years of revolutionary rule and created what was for Cuba a unique institution, the National Assembly of People's Power. The locus of power remains in the Communist Party, the Council of Ministers, and the military, but the National Assembly is designed to serve as a channel of communication with the masses and to confer some measure of legitimacy on an essentially authoritarian regime.

The National Assembly is described in the constitution as "the supreme organ of state authority," a meaningless statement common to most communist constitutions. In theory the Assembly has the power to make laws, amend the constitution, rule on the constitutionality of laws, develop economic and social plans, approve the state budget, supervise elections, appoint justices of the Supreme Court, approve commissions, and oversee the Council of Ministers and the Council of State.

The Assembly meets in two regular sessions a year, and extraordinary sessions may be called by one-third of its membership or the Council of State, a thirty-one-member body elected by the Assembly from among its members to direct the Assembly's operations. The legislative powers of the Assembly devolve upon the Council of State when the former is in recess. The chair of the Council of State is also the head of state and the head of government, thus combining legislative and executive powers in one person.

Deputies receive allowances in lieu of salaries and also free travel and medical and travel services. A quorum is one-half of the membership plus one, and a simple majority is sufficient for regular motions and bills. All bills have to be approved before debate by the relevant permanent committee and the Committee on Constitutional and Legal Affairs. Balloting is by show of hands or roll call. Deputies speak from their seats. The deliberations of the Assembly are published in the *Official Gazette.*

Political groups are not permitted in the Assembly. The permanent and ad hoc committees of the Assembly have the right to summon officials. Legislation may be initiated by deputies, the Council of State, the Council of Ministers, trade unions, mass organizations, the Supreme Court, the attorney general, or any group of ten thousand citizens. The Assembly has the right to call referendums.

Candidates are selected by the National Candidate Commission from nominations submitted by social organizations representing workers, youth, women, and other groups. One candidate is selected per Assembly seat. Deputies are elected directly in an absolute majority ballot. If a candidate fails to win an absolute majority in the constituency, a new round of balloting is conducted. Voting is optional according to the constitution, but the regime reported a turnout of 99.6 percent in the February 1993 elections. Delegates may be recalled by the voters.

George Thomas Kurian

CYPRUS

OFFICIAL NAME: Republic of Cyprus (Greek, Dimokratia Kyprou; Turkish, Kibris Cumhuriyeti)
CAPITAL: Nicosia
POPULATION: 745,000 (1996 est.)
DATE OF INDEPENDENCE: August 16, 1960 (from the United Kingdom)
DATE OF CURRENT CONSTITUTION: Effective August 16, 1960
FORM OF GOVERNMENT: Parliamentary democracy
LANGUAGES: Greek (official), Turkish (official), English
MONETARY UNIT: Cyprus pound
FISCAL YEAR: Calendar year
LEGISLATURE: House of Representatives (Greek, Vouli Antiprosópon; Turkish, Temsilciler Meclisi)
NUMBER OF CHAMBERS: One
NUMBER OF MEMBERS: 80 (only the 56 Greek Cypriot seats are currently filled; 24 seats reserved for Turkish Cypriots are vacant)
PERCENTAGE OF WOMEN: 5.4 (3 of 56 sitting members)
TERM OF LEGISLATURE: Five years
MOST RECENT LEGISLATIVE ELECTIONS: May 26, 1996
MINIMUM AGE FOR VOTING: 21
MINIMUM AGE FOR MEMBERSHIP: 25
SUFFRAGE: Universal and direct
VOTING: Compulsory
ADDRESS: House of Representatives, Nicosia
TELEPHONE: (357 2) 30 34 51
FAX: (357 2) 36 66 11

Cyprus is an island nation in the eastern Mediterranean that is considered by some geographers as part of Asia and by others as part of Europe *(see map, p. 677)*. Culturally and historically, it is part of Greece, with which it shares a rich heritage encompassing religion, language, ethnic origins, and many social mores. Politically it is a parliamentary democracy with a presidential form of government.

BACKGROUND

Cyprus was ruled for much of the first half of the twentieth century by the United Kingdom. One of the legacies of British rule was a strong respect for parliamentary supremacy and rule of law. When Cyprus became independent in 1960 the majority Greeks and the minority Turks were joined by a bicommunal constitution (drafted by British, Greek, and Turkish constitutional experts) which prohibited union with any other country or the partition of the island and guaranteed the civil and political rights of both groups. Elaborate safeguards for the minority Turks were built into the constitution. The vice president was required to be a Turk; Greek and Turkish were designated as co-official languages; the Turkish vice president was given veto power over certain laws and decisions affecting Turkish affairs; and fifteen of fifty seats in the House of Representatives were reserved for Turks. Separate majorities were required in the House from Greek and Turkish Cypriot members for imposing taxes or duties and modifying electoral laws. In addition to the House, the constitution authorized the establishment of Greek and Turkish communal chambers composed of representatives elected by each community. The communal chambers had the right to impose taxes, and their jurisdiction extended to religious, educational, and cultural affairs and matters of personal status in their respective communities. (Both the Greek and Turkish communal chambers have since been dissolved; the powers and competence of the Greek chamber were transferred to the House of Representatives.) The bicommunal structure also extended to the judicial system, the bureaucracy, and the police force. Separate Greek and Turkish municipal authorities were established in the five main towns.

The fragile constitutional balance did not last long, and communal violence flared in 1964, precipitating the withdrawal of Turkish Cypriots from the government and the deployment of United Nations peacekeepers, who remain on the island to this day. Turkish Cypriots established a provisional government on the northern one-third of the island in 1967. A coup that temporarily brought down the Greek Cypriot government in July 1974 precipitated an invasion by mainland Turkish troops, who occupied the northern portion of the island. The provisional government redesignated the territory under its de facto control as a Turkish Federated State in early 1975, and the so-called Turkish Cypriot Legislative Assembly declared the full independence of the "Turkish Republic of Northern Cyprus" in November 1983. Turkey is the only state to have recognized the self-declared state's sovereignty.

The 1974 Turkish invasion of the island made the bicommunal provisions of the constitution moot. But the 1960 constitution itself has never been abrogated, and many people hope that Cyprus will one day be reunited and the provisions now in abeyance will be reactivated. The profile of the government and the House of Representatives that follows refers to the working of parliament in a divided country.

THE CONSTITUTIONAL STRUCTURE

Cyprus has a presidential system. Members of the government may not be members of the House of Representatives. The two offices are incompatible, and a member of the House appointed by the president as a minister must relinquish his or her seat in the House. The president and vice president of the republic may address the House personally or by message or convey their views to the House through the ministers. (The vice presidency is vacant, there having been no vice presidential election since 1973.) The ministers may follow the proceedings of the House or of any committee of the House and may make a statement to, or inform, the House or any committee of the House on any subject within their competence. Ministers are not constitutionally bound to appear before the House or before any committee of the House at the request of the House. In practice, however, no minister has declined to appear when requested to do so by the president of the House or by the chair of a committee.

The term of office of the president of the republic is constitutionally set at five years. Ministers hold office at the president's pleasure, and the House, under the principle of separation of powers that permeates the Cyprus constitution, has no power to determine the term of office of the government, just as the government has no influence over the term of the House.

The president of the republic and the vice president have the right of final veto on any law passed by the House that concerns certain specified issues of foreign affairs, defense, and security. This power may be exercised either jointly or separately by the president and vice president. As far as other types of legislation are concerned, the president and the vice president jointly or separately have only delaying power. They may return a law or other decision to the House. In such a case the House must again vote on the law within fifteen days or, if it concerns the budget, within thirty days. If the House reaffirms its decision, then the president and vice president are bound to promulgate the law or decision in question by publishing it in the normal way in the gazette of the republic.

PARLIAMENTARY FORMATION

The legislative power of the republic is exercised by the House of Representatives. The term of office of the House of Representatives is five years. A general election must be held on the second Sunday of the month immediately preceding the month in which the term of office of the outgoing House expires. The outgoing House continues in office until the newly elected House assumes office, but during this time the outgoing House does not have the power to make laws or to take decisions on any matter, unless in exceptional or unforeseen circumstances. These circumstances would have to be specifically stated in any law or decision approved during this time.

The House may dissolve itself before its term of office expires. Such a decision must specify the date of the general elections, which must not be fewer than thirty or more than forty days from the date of the dissolution decision, and must also specify the date of the first meeting of the newly elected House, which must not be later than fifteen days after the general elections.

Members of the Cypriot House of Representatives have immunity from civil or criminal proceedings in respect of anything they may say, or the way that they cast their vote, in the House. A representative may not be arrested or imprisoned without permission of the Supreme Court, unless he or she is caught in the act of committing specified grave offenses.

By a 1985 resolution of the House of Representatives, the size of that body increased to eighty members. Fifty-six representatives are elected by the Greek-Cypriot community and twenty-four by the Turkish-Cypriot community, separately, from among their respective members, by universal suffrage of adults over the age of twenty-one. Elections are by direct and secret ballots which should be held on the same day for both communities.

Turkish-Cypriot members have not attended the House since December 1963, nor have elections been held according to the constitutional provisions among the Turkish-Cypriot community since that time. Also in 1963 the Turkish-Cypriot vice president and the Turkish-Cypriot ministers and officials withdrew from the government. Although this abnormality has now lasted for more than three decades, and although 37 percent of the territory of Cyprus has been under Turkish occupation since the Turkish invasion of 1974, the House has kept the seats allocated to the Turkish-Cypriot community vacant, these remaining at the disposal of Turkish-Cypriot representatives once they are elected according to the constitutional provisions.

The electoral law provides for proportional representation. The number of seats in each of six constituencies is determined by law. The constituencies coincide with the administrative districts. Each voter may vote for a party or an independent candidate but may not select candidates from different parties. The parliamentary seats are then distributed according to the electoral strength of each party.

Candidates for election to the House must be citizens of the republic, must have attained the age of twenty-five, must not have been convicted for any offense involving moral turpitude or dishonesty, and must not be incapacitated for reasons of mental health. A seat becomes vacant if its occupant dies, resigns, or becomes disqualified due to conviction for an offense falling under the disqualifying categories or upon a representative becoming a minister, a member of a municipal council, a member of the security forces of the republic, or a public or municipal official.

The president of the House is Greek-Cypriot and is elected by the representatives of the Greek-Cypriot community. The vice president is a Turkish-Cypriot elected by the representatives of the Turkish-Cypriot community. In case of the temporary absence of the president or vice president of the House, the absent official's functions are performed by the eldest representative of the respective community unless the representatives of the respective community decide otherwise.

Five parties were represented in the House following the elections of May 26, 1996: Democratic Rally, a right-wing party, with twenty seats; Progressive Party of the Working People—Left—New Forces, a left-wing party, with nineteen seats; the Democratic Party, a centrist party, with ten seats; the Unified Democratic Union of Cyprus—Socialist Party, with five seats; and the United Democrats, with two seats.

PROCEDURES OF THE HOUSE

The ordinary session of the House of Representatives begins in September and ends in July of the following year. The meetings of the House take place once or twice a week, usually on Thursdays and Fridays. The meetings of the House are open to the public, and verbatim records of its debates are published. Extensive extracts of the debates are broadcast by radio.

The House is in quorum when at least one-third of the total number of its members are present. The laws and the decisions of the House are passed by a simple majority vote of the representatives present and voting.

The agenda must be distributed to the representatives at least twenty-four hours prior to the meeting. The agenda of a normal meeting of the House consists of four parts: legislation, introduction of bills and documents, questions and answers, and subjects raised by representatives.

Legislation

Legislation is the first order of business of any ordinary meeting of the House. Every bill on being introduced in the House is referred by the president for examination by the appropriate committee of the House. The introduction of the bill in the House is a formal stage, intended only to give the House notice that the bill has been introduced. This is considered to be the first reading of the bill.

With the exception of those bills that are declared to be of an urgent nature by a majority of the representatives, no bill that has passed the committee stage may be debated in the House before the lapse of forty-eight hours after it has been distributed with the report of the committee to the representatives.

A committee, when considering any bill referred to it, examines all memoranda, appeals, recommendations, and suggestions submitted on the subject by any organization or corporate body or by any citizen. The committee also considers all proposals for amendments put forward by representatives. A committee may, during its deliberations, hear any person or representative of any organization on any matter relating to the subject of a bill or a decision before it. Any member of the committee may question such persons for the purpose of elucidating statements made by him or her or for the purpose of obtaining further information. Committee meetings are open to journalists and other representatives of the mass media unless otherwise decided by the committee depending on the nature of the subjects under discussion.

When the committee completes its deliberation on a bill, it prepares a report for distribution to the representatives. The report usually contains the main provisions, in summary form, of the bill; the amendments suggested by the committee, if any, and the reasons for such amendments; the texts of all amendments recommended by members of the committee; and the observations of the committee on the bill and any recommendations as to points that the committee wishes the House to consider or convey to the government. When the committee has not decided unanimously on a bill, that fact is stated in the report, and the points on which there is a divergence of opinion are indicated, as are the positions taken by the majority and the minority. Any representative disagreeing with the decision of the committee, or any part of it, may address the House and explain his or her views.

When the committee reports back to the House, the latter considers the bill and the report of the committee and debates the bill, first on general issues raised by the bill as a whole and then clause by clause. This is considered to be the second reading of the bill. At this stage verbal alterations are allowed, or, on the House so deciding, the bill may be referred for further consideration to one or more committees.

The final stage in the House is the third reading, when the House considers the bill as a whole and whether it should become a law. A law of the House comes into force on its publication in the *Official Gazette* of the republic unless another date is provided for by such a law.

Introduction of bills

Both representatives and ministers have the right to introduce bills in the House. Representatives are limited in only one way in their ability to introduce bills to the House: they are constitutionally barred from introducing any bill that increases budgetary expenditure. The budget is introduced in the House by the minister of finance at least three months before the day fixed by law as the commencement of the financial year. If the budget has not been adopted by the House by the first day of the financial year to which it relates, the House may, by a resolution, authorize the meeting of any expenditure required by the government for periods not exceeding one month at a time or two months in aggregate, from the consolidated fund. Such authorizations may not exceed the sums voted for each service for an equivalent period during the preceding financial year.

During the financial year the government may, if necessary, introduce a supplementary budget for the approval of the House. In this case the House may approve or refuse to approve any expenditure proposed, but it may not vote an increase in the amount of expenditure or alter its purpose.

Questions and answers

Questions and answers are the third order of business on the daily agenda. Questions must conform to the standing orders, must be brief, and shall not contain any offensive expressions. Questions are sent by representatives to the Office of the House, and when it is established that the questions are in conformity with the standing orders, they are conveyed to the relevant ministry. The questions of representatives and the answers of ministers to whom they were directed are read by the clerks of the House.

Subjects raised by representatives

During the final order of business, discussion of a general nature takes place on topics raised by representatives with the approval of the House, or that arise from a question that has not been answered, or from a reply received from the appropriate minister that is unsatisfactory. A representative may register a subject for debate without the approval of a majority of the House if the subject arises from a question.

After the end of each meeting, the agenda of the next meeting is announced. The agenda is established with the consent of the House. Any member may move an addition or amendment to the agenda. Such a motion is decided upon by the House.

Debate and voting

Speeches in the House are made from the rostrum and are addressed to the House. Points of order may be raised by a representative from his or her seat. Interruption of a speech, personal attacks, and abuse by a representative are prohibited.

Voting in the House is by raising of the hand. The clerks of the House are responsible for counting the votes. Voting does not take place on a topic unless there is an objection to unanimous approval. Usually, the president asks whether there is an objection. If there is no objection, the article is approved.

ORGANIZATION OF PARLIAMENT

The clerks of the House are appointed by the president of the House. Their functions consist of determining whether there is a quorum, counting the votes, reading the questions and answers, reading the articles and the short title of bills, and reading the titles of the bills or other documents that have been introduced. They also keep a register of the members present at each meeting of the House.

The parliamentary committees are set up by the Committee of Selection, which consists of the president of the House as chair, the vice president of the House as vice chair, and eight other members elected by the House. On appointing the members of the parliamentary committees, the Committee of Selection also appoints, at the same time, the chair of each committee as well as the member who will replace him or her in case of temporary absence or incapacity.

Political parties are represented on the committees in proportion to the total number of their seats in the House. The parliamentary committees generally correspond to the ministries of the government and are set up to consider every bill or private bill or any other particular matter that may be referred to them by the House. On the completion of deliberations on a bill or other matter, every committee prepares a report and sees to its immediate distribution to all members of the House.

Ministers can be present at the debates of the committees of the House and express their views; the committees themselves have a right to summon any interested party, authority, organization, association, trade union, person, or corporate body to give information and evidence, and they have a right to express and explain an opinion or view on any bill or subject under consideration.

The decisions of the committees are taken by majority vote. In case of a tie, the chair or the member serving in the chair's capacity has a second or casting vote. Any disagreement by a member of the committee and the reasons therefor can be briefly entered, at his or her request, in the report of the committee.

The minutes of committee proceedings are kept in summary form, and copies of them are distributed to all members of the committee. The quorum of the committees consists of at least one-half of the total number of their members.

Takis Hadjioannou

BIBLIOGRAPHY

Arnold, Percy. *Cyprus Challenge. A Colonial Island and Its Aspirations: Reminiscences of a Former Editor of the* Cyprus Post. London: Hogarth Press, 1956.

Hitchens, Christopher. *Hostage to History: Cyprus from the Ottomans to Kissinger.* New York: Farrar Straus and Giroux, 1989.

Koumoulides, John T. A., ed. *Cyprus in Transition, 1960–1985.* London: Trigraph, 1986.

CZECH REPUBLIC

OFFICIAL NAME: Czech Republic (Česká Republika)
CAPITAL: Prague
POPULATION: 10,321,000 (1996 est.)
DATE OF INDEPENDENCE: Founded January 1, 1993
DATE OF CURRENT CONSTITUTION: Approved December 16, 1992; effective January 1, 1993
FORM OF GOVERNMENT: Parliamentary democracy
LANGUAGES: Czech, Slovak
MONETARY UNIT: Koruna
FISCAL YEAR: Calendar year
LEGISLATURE: Parliament of the Czech Republic (Parlament České Republiky)
NUMBER OF CHAMBERS: Two. Chamber of Deputies (Sněmovna Poslanců); Senate (Sénate)
NUMBER OF MEMBERS: Chamber of Deputies, 200; Senate, 81
PERCENTAGE OF WOMEN: Chamber of Deputies, 15.0; Senate, 11.0
TERM OF LEGISLATURE: Chamber of Deputies, four years; Senate, six years (one-third of members elected every two years)
MOST RECENT LEGISLATIVE ELECTION: Chamber of Deputies, May 31–June 1, 1996; Senate, November 1996
MINIMUM AGE FOR VOTING: 18
MINIMUM AGE FOR MEMBERSHIP: Chamber of Deputies, 21; Senate, 40
SUFFRAGE: Universal and direct
VOTING: Optional
ADDRESS: Chamber of Deputies, Snemovni 4, 118 29 Prague 1; Senate, Valdstejnské Námestí 4, 118 11 Prague 1
TELEPHONE: Chamber of Deputies, (42 2) 571 75 111; Senate, (42 2) 570 71 111
FAX: Chamber of Deputies, (42 2) 539 905; Senate, (42 2) 539 853

A central European nation formerly part of the Soviet bloc, the Czech Republic was created when Czechoslovakia split in January 1993. The Czech Republic is a multiparty, parliamentary democracy with a bicameral legislature and a dual executive led by the president, who is head of state, and the prime minister, who is head of government. The president is elected by parliament, and the prime minister is appointed by the president but accountable to the Chamber of Deputies.

HISTORICAL BACKGROUND

In the early Middle Ages the Czechs, who belonged to the western group of the Slav family, lived in the central European regions called Bohemia, Moravia, and Czech Silesia. In the ninth century a Slavic prince, Mojmir I, and his successors, Rastislav and Svatapluk, established a kingdom known as the Great Moravian Empire in this territory. The empire also incorporated the western part of Slovakia, where the neighboring Slovaks lived. In the thirteenth century the Czech territories came under the control of the Holy Roman Empire, while the Slovaks found themselves under the influence of the Magyars. In the second half of the fourteenth century Bohemia, one of the Czech regions, enjoyed a period of glory, when Prague under the reign of Charles IV became the capital of the empire. During the fifteenth and sixteenth centuries the Czechs endured religious wars and were incorporated into the Habsburg Empire after the Thirty Years War (1618–1648). Czech domains remained part of the Austrian Empire until its disintegration after World War I. The war drew the Czech and Slovak nationalist movements closer together, resulting in the formation of Czechoslovakia in October 1918.

In November 1918 a provisional constitution was promulgated. This constitution was replaced by the definitive constitution of February 1920. The 1920 constitution borrowed heavily from the French constitution of the Third Republic. The preamble defined Czechoslovakia as a "cultured, peace loving, democratic, and progressive" republic. Legislative power was vested in a bicameral parliament, elected on the basis of universal and equal suffrage by a direct and secret ballot on the principle of proportional representation. Executive powers were entrusted to a strong president, analogous to the French president, elected by the National Assembly (a joint session of both chambers); the president, in turn, appointed the prime minister and a cabinet. The constitution created an independent judiciary and established a Constitutional Court that followed the Austrian "centralized" type of judicial review; the power to review the constitutionality of laws was confined to a single judicial body.

The Munich pact of 1938 allowed Germany to annex the western territories of Czechoslovakia, known as the Sudetenland, in return for Hitler's pledge to leave the rest of Czechoslovakia independent. This annexation precipitated the fall of the First Czechoslovak Republic. President Eduard Beneš, denouncing the Munich agreement as a betrayal by France and Great Britain, resigned under pressure from Berlin on October 5, 1938, and left the country. The Second Republic yielded to Slovak demands for self-government and was officially renamed Czecho-Slovakia, to emphasize the confederative association. Soon after, Germany annexed the remaining Czech lands as the Protectorate of Bohemia and Moravia, while Slovakia was proclaimed a separate state under German protection, although some portions were annexed by Hungary. World War II led to tightened German control over the Czech and Slovak territories.

With the end of the war in 1945, as in other east central European countries, Soviet "liberating" maneuvers placed the communists of Czechoslovakia into the government for the first time and solidified their rule in 1948. A new Soviet-style constitution was promulgated on June 7, 1948. On July 11, 1960, Czechoslovakia adopted its second socialist constitution, which upgraded the country's status from a people's democracy to a socialist republic. The 1960 constitution was promulgated primarily for propaganda value, allowing the Communist Party to claim that Czechoslovakia was the second country to achieve socialism. The Soviet Union had made this claim for itself in 1936. The 1960 constitution was amended by six constitutional laws. The most important of these was that of October 1968, which created a Czechoslovak federation consisting of the Czech Socialist Republic and the Slovak Socialist Republic.

Czechoslovakia had a bicameral parliament (the Federal Assembly), comprising a 150-member House of the People and a 150-member House of the Nations. Following the 1968 federation amendment, the Czech and Slovak representatives in the House of the Nations voted separately. The amendment provided that a bill was approved only if it was passed by a majority of the total number of the representatives of each republic. This voting procedure resulted in the creation of a de facto three-chamber Federal Assembly consisting of the House of the People and the Czech and Slovak parts (called "councils") of the House of the Nations. Constitutional acts and amendments, declarations of war, and the election of the president required a three-fifths majority of the deputies of each house. In practice, thirty-eight votes of either the Czech or Slovak portion of the Chamber of Nations could block any ordinary law, and thirty-one votes in either section could block constitutional acts and amendments.

THE VELVET REVOLUTION

The dissolution of communist power in Czechoslovakia began at the end of 1989 with mass proreform protests in Prague and other cities, the formation of the opposition group Civic Forum, and the hasty resignation of the thirteen-member Politburo and the Communist Party general secretary, Miloš Jakeš. The initial stages of the communist retreat looked so mild that Western commentators termed the Czech revolution the "gentle" or "velvet" revolution.

After President Gustáv Husák resigned on December 10, 1989, a new coalition government of communists and noncommunists was sworn in. The main objectives of the interim government, under the direction of Prime Minister Marián Čalfa, were to lead the country to its first free elections since 1948 (to be held in June 1990) and to revive the stagnant economy.

Further signs of hope for reform in Czechoslovakia came with the elections of Alexander Dubček as chair of the Federal Assembly on December 28, 1989, and Václav Havel as president of the country on the following day. Dubček had been out of politics since 1968, when his attempt to introduce reform to Czechoslovakia was crushed by the Soviet Union. Havel, a playwright and activist who was jailed several times during the communist era for his subversive views and controversial plays, had the respect and support of the Czech people, who desperately needed reliable political leadership. Havel was unanimously elected the first noncommunist president of Czechoslovakia since 1948 by the 323 members of the still predominantly communist Assembly.

The first postwar free elections in Czechoslovakia took place in June 1990. They were based on an electoral law that limited participation to those parties that were able either to show proof of having ten thousand members or to collect ten thousand signatures. The law further limited representation in the Federal Assembly to those parties able to secure at least 5 percent of the popular vote. The turnout at the polls was overwhelming, with 96 percent of the 11.2 million eligible voters casting ballots. The Czech group Civic Forum, and its Slovak counterpart Public Against Violence, dominated the elections. Together they received 46.3 percent of the national vote and secured 170 seats in the 300-member Federal Assembly. Reelected as president, Havel asked Čalfa to form a new government.

CONSTITUTIONAL REFORM AND FAILURE

The major focus of Havel's 1990–1992 presidential term was constitutional reform. After the beginning of the Czechoslovak revolution in November 1989, several amendments had been passed to purge the 1960 constitution of its Stalinist legacy. The amendments eliminated the provisions on the leading role of the Communist Party and provided for an interim parliament and president pending adoption of a new constitution. One year later, in November and December 1990, parliament succeeded in passing additional piecemeal amendments to the constitution, most notably the Bill of Rights and Freedoms and an act on the mutual relations between the two republics. In March and July 1991 the Assembly adopted constitutional acts on the judiciary. But attempts to advance work on an all-new constitution brought frustration and disappointment.

The balance of political power between the Czech Civic Forum and the Slovak Public Against Violence in the interim Federal Assembly resulted in a failure of constitutional progress. In the 1990 elections neither party had secured the three-fifths support necessary to push through constitutional changes. And after the elections the winning parties in both republics suffered from internal factional wars and split into rival groups. The fractionalization of the political movements doomed chances for further constitutional development at the federal level. At the beginning of 1992 the Federal Assembly considered adopting an interim constitution, fashioned after Poland's so-called Small Constitution, which would regulate relations between the president, the federal parliament, and the federal government. However, the law did not pass.

As the country headed into the 1992 elections, dissolution of the seventy-four-year-old federation became an issue. Whereas in the 1990 elections the choice had boiled down to "anybody but the communists," in the 1992 elections the voters were deciding on the future existence of their country. The winners of the 1992 elections in the two republics espoused programs that were in exact opposition. In the Czech Republic, the Civic Democratic Party, led by Václav Klaus, won the most votes; Klaus advocated the maintenance of a common state and a swift transformation to a free-market economy. In Slovakia, the Movement for a Democratic Slovakia, led by Vladimír Mečiar, who advocated slowing the reform process and independence for Slovakia, won the most votes.

The emphasis shifted from the preparation of a constitution to the dissolution of the federation. In the summer of 1992 Czech and Slovak leaders worked out an agreement by which, on January 1, 1993, the country would divide into two separate and independent states with two currencies and two constitutions.

The Slovak parliament approved a draft constitution on September 1, 1992, providing for the dissolution of the federation, with the two republics cooperating only in customs and monetary matters. On December 16, 1992, the Czech National Council also adopted a new constitution. By January 1, 1993, the velvet divorce of the Czechs and Slovaks was an accomplished fact.

THE CZECH CONSTITUTION OF 1992

The Czech constitution of 1992 recognizes the principle of division of powers and provides for a parliamentary system with a double executive comprising the president as the head of state and the prime minister as the head of government. The parliament of the Czech Republic is bicameral, comprising a Chamber of Deputies and a Senate.

Parliament

The Chamber of Deputies consists of two hundred members elected for four-year terms by a two-tier system. In the lower tier, elections are held in eight multimember districts with seats allocated pursuant to proportional representation based on a Droop Quota system. The upper tier comprises one nationwide, multimember district with seats allocated pursuant to proportional representation. Candidates for the Chamber of Deputies must be twenty-one years of age.

The Senate has eighty-one members, one-third of whom are elected every two years on the basis of a majority system. Candidates for the Senate must be at least forty years old. After the adoption of the 1992 constitution, creation of the Senate became the center of controversy. Although the Chamber of Deputies repeatedly rejected amendments to the constitution to eliminate bicameralism, the Senate was not elected until 1996, and its functions had been taken over by the Chamber of Deputies. Finally, the 1996 elections established the second chamber of the Czech parliament, in which the Civic Democratic Party won thirty-two seats out of eighty-one constituencies.

All citizens eighteen years of age or older who reside permanently in the Czech Republic have the right to vote. Those who have been deprived of their legal rights or imprisoned by a decision of the court or whose freedom of movement has been restricted for protection of public health are disqualified. People under arrest retain the right to vote.

Parties submitting lists of candidates must have representation in the Czech parliament, have at least ten thousand registered members, or collect ten thousand signatures. A 5 percent threshold requirement was introduced to prevent excessive fragmentation of the Chamber of Deputies. Campaigns begin twenty-three days before the election and end forty-eight hours prior to the election. Public opinion polls may not be published during the seven days preceding elections. During a campaign, every party has equal access to the state media and to other services of state administration.

The constitution guarantees the immunity of deputies and senators. If a member of parliament is guilty of a misdemeanor, the member is subject to disciplinary action in the chamber to which he or she belongs. Criminal proceedings may not go forward against a member without the consent of his or her chamber. Members may be detained if caught in, or immediately following, a criminal act. The detainment must be reported immediately to the chair of the chamber; the member must be released within twenty-four hours if the chair does not consent to the detainment.

The executive

The president of the republic is elected for a five-year term by a majority of the deputies and senators at a joint meeting of both chambers of parliament. If no candidate receives an absolute majority, a second round of elections is held to which the two candidates who received the greatest number of votes in the Senate and Chamber of Deputies advance. If more than two candidates receive the same number of votes and no candidate receives a majority of votes of the present, voting deputies and senators, a third round is held; if it also fails to elect a president, new elections are held.

A candidate for the office of president must be a Czech citizen, at least forty years old, eligible to be elected as a senator, and nominated by at least ten deputies or senators. The president is not criminally liable but is constitutionally liable and may be removed from office for high treason upon a suit filed to the Constitutional Court by the Senate.

The president appoints generals and high officials of the state, such as the president of the Supreme Control Office, members of the Banking Council, judges, and justices of the Constitutional Court with the consent of the Senate. The president's control over the government is very limited. The president appoints the prime minister and, at the prime minister's proposal, other ministers.

In addition to ceremonial and representative functions, the president has some legislative and executive duties. The president may participate in the meetings of the government and request reports from its members. The president also has the right to address parliament and to return laws for reconsideration to the Chamber of Deputies, with the exception of constitutional laws. Adoption of a bill requires the vote of a simple majority of the deputies present, with a quorum of one-third of the deputies. Therefore, with a quorum of 67 deputies, at least 34 votes are required to pass a bill. A bill returned by the president is deemed adopted if it is affirmed by a majority of all deputies. In other words, to be passed, a bill opposed by the president requires a vote of at least 101 deputies, rather than the 34 deputies required in the initial stage.

The president can dissolve the Chamber of Deputies in four instances: if it does not pass a vote of confidence in a newly appointed government whose prime minister was appointed by the president at the proposal of the chair of the chamber; if the chamber does not act within three months on a government-sponsored bill to which the government attached the question of confidence; if the chamber is adjourned for a period longer than 120 days in one year; and if the chamber has not had a quorum for more than three months. The chamber cannot be dissolved in the three months prior to the end of its term.

CALENDAR AND CONTROL OF GOVERNMENT

The chambers' sessions are called by the president of the republic. The first session of parliament starts no later than the thirtieth day after the election. Sessions can be interrupted by a resolution, but the recess may not exceed 120 days per year. Joint meetings of the chambers are governed by the rules of procedure established by the Chamber of Deputies. The main organizational components of the chambers are the chair of the chamber, the Organizational Committee, the Mandate and Immunity Committee, and the Investigative Commission. Both chambers elect and recall their chairs and deputy chairs from among their members.

The chambers have a quorum if at least one-third of the members are in attendance. The adoption of resolutions requires an absolute majority of the deputies and senators present at the meeting. Declarations on a state of war and agreements on the presence of foreign troops in the territory of the Czech Republic require the votes of an absolute majority of all deputies and senators. Constitutional laws and international treaties on human rights and fundamental freedoms require the votes of a three-fifths majority of all deputies and a three-fifths majority of present senators to pass. Deputies have the right to interpellate the government or its members on matters within its or their jurisdiction. The government or member must reply to the interpellation within thirty days.

The government is composed of the prime minister, deputy prime ministers, and ministers. The government is accountable to the Chamber of Deputies, and its program must be submitted to the chamber within thirty days of its appointment. If the newly appointed government does not win the confidence of parliament, a new prime minister is appointed by the president, at the proposal of the chair of the Chamber of Deputies. The Chamber of Deputies can pass a vote of no confidence in the government at any time. The motion is considered by the chamber only if it is submitted in writing by at least fifty deputies, and to pass it must be supported by an absolute majority.

THE LEGISLATIVE PROCESS

The law on rules of procedure was originally adopted by the Czechoslovak Federal Assembly in 1989, before the state split. It was amended several times in 1990 and 1991 and was substantially amended in 1993.

Bills may be submitted to the Chamber of Deputies by the Senate, the government, a representative body of a higher territorial self-administrative unit, a deputy, or a group of deputies. The government has the right to express an opinion on all bills. If the government does not express an opinion within thirty days, the bill is considered as having the support of the government. The government may link a vote on a government-sponsored bill with a vote of confidence and request the discussion of the bill within three months of its submission. The single-reading system provides that bills, after an initial discussion of principles, are sent to the committees. The committee report at the plenary session is followed by discussion during which the deputies may propose amendments. Voting follows the discussion.

A bill approved by the Chamber of Deputies is submitted to the Senate; the Senate must discuss it and pass a resolution within thirty days. The Senate may approve, reject, or return the bill to the Chamber of Deputies or, alternatively, express an intent not to deal with it, in which case the bill is deemed adopted. A bill rejected by the Senate requires a second approval by a majority of all deputies to pass. If the Senate returns a bill with proposals for amendment, the deputies will vote on the new version, and the bill is adopted by a resolution of the deputies. If the deputies do not approve the new version, and reaffirm the previous version by a majority of all deputies, the bill is adopted in its original form.

If the Chamber of Deputies is dissolved, its legislative functions are taken over by the Senate. The government alone may propose the adoption of a legal measure to the Senate. These proposals may not concern the constitution, the state budget, the state budgetary report, electoral law, or international treaties regarding human rights and fundamental freedoms. The laws adopted by the Senate are signed by the president, the prime minister, and the chair of the Senate. Laws adopted by the Senate must be approved by the newly elected Chamber of Deputies at its first session.

Bills on the state budget and on the state closing account are presented by the government. They are subsequently discussed at a public meeting and are decided only by the Chamber of Deputies.

Judicial review of the constitutionality of laws is guaranteed by the constitution, clearly adhering to the Austrian model of constitutional enforcement. The constitution vests the right to review laws in one central Constitutional Court, which comprises fifteen judges appointed by the president, with the approval of the Senate. The court is an institution of final review, and no legal recourse against its rulings exists. The Constitutional Court also decides on the constitutionality of administrative acts, the legality of electoral proceedings, and lawsuits filed by the Senate accusing the president of high treason. The court settles jurisdictional disputes between the central government and local administrative agencies and hears complaints against decisions that allegedly violate constitutionally guaranteed rights and freedoms.

The procedure of the Czech Constitutional Court is not clearly explained by the constitution. The chapter on constitutional review was hastily drafted and leaves a number of important matters, such as initiation of legal proceedings before the court or execution of the court's decisions, to further regulation.

Rett R. Ludwikowski

BIBLIOGRAPHY

Ash, Timothy Garton. *The Magic Lantern.* New York: Random House, 1990.

Janyska, Petr. "Czechoslovakia: No More of That." *East European Reporter* (July–August 1992).

Judt, Tony R. "Metamorphosis: The Democratic Revolution in Czechoslovakia." In *Eastern Europe in Revolution,* ed. Ivo Banac. Ithaca, N.Y.: Cornell University Press, 1992.

Ludwikowski, Rett R. *Constitution-Making in the Region of Former Soviet Dominance.* Durham, N.C., and London: Duke University Press, 1996.

Mathernova, Katarina. "Czecho? Slovakia: Constitutional Disappointments." *American University Journal of International L. and Pol'y* 7 (1992): 471ff.

Schoenhoff, Steve, and Mark Hanna. "Czechoslovakia's Quest for Recovery." *New Dimensions* (March 1991): 60–65.

DENMARK

OFFICIAL NAME: Kingdom of Denmark (Kongeriget Danmark)
CAPITAL: Copenhagen
POPULATION: 5,250,000 (1996 est.)
DATE OF CURRENT CONSTITUTION: Adopted June 5, 1953
FORM OF GOVERNMENT: Constitutional monarchy
LANGUAGE: Danish
MONETARY UNIT: Danish krone
FISCAL YEAR: Calendar year
LEGISLATURE: Parliament (Folketing)
NUMBER OF CHAMBERS: One
NUMBER OF MEMBERS: 17
PERCENTAGE OF WOMEN: 33.0
TERM OF LEGISLATURE: Four years
MOST RECENT LEGISLATIVE ELECTION: September 21, 1994
MINIMUM AGE FOR VOTING: 18
MINIMUM AGE FOR MEMBERSHIP: 18
SUFFRAGE: Universal and direct
VOTING: Optional
ADDRESS: Folketing, Christiansborg, DK—1240 Copenhagen K
TELEPHONE: (45) 33 37 55 00
FAX: (45) 33 32 85 36

Denmark is a multiparty, West European constitutional monarchy with a unicameral parliament, the Folketing *(see map, p. 639)*. The prime minister serves as head of government, and the monarch as head of state.

HISTORICAL BACKGROUND

The Danish parliament was created in 1849 by the first democratic constitution of the country after a long period of royal autocracy ended in a bloodless revolution. The constitution was framed according to the contemporary nineteenth-century European idea of separation of powers. By modern standards it was not democratic; for example, the nonelected government, in which the king retained some power, was not responsible to parliament.

In 1866, after the country suffered a disastrous war against Prussia and Austria (1864) that resulted in a severe territorial loss, the Danish constitution was made even less democratic by the aristocratic and conservative forces. A protracted constitutional struggle between liberal and conservative parties ended in 1901 (without formal constitutional amendments) with the introduction of the principle of cabinet responsibility to the lower, or popular, chamber (Folketing) of the then-bicameral parliament (Rigsdagen). A new and more democratic constitution, which among other advances introduced women's suffrage, was adopted in 1915 during World War I, in which Denmark stayed neutral. The constitution was amended in 1920 after the return to Denmark of some of the territory lost in 1864.

Danish democracy was consolidated between the world wars, and in 1953 a thoroughly revised constitution was adopted, introducing a unicameral parliament (Folketing) and formalizing cabinet responsibility.

THE CONSTITUTION

The 1953 constitution is still in force and is in fact extremely difficult to change. Constitutional amendments require completion of the following steps: adoption by parliament of a bill amending the constitution, election of a new parliament, adoption of the same constitutional bill once again, and passage of a referendum on the bill, which requires that a majority of those participating vote in favor of the bill and that the majority constitutes at least 40 percent of the electorate.

The constitution is brief. In addition to establishing the principles of universal and equal voting and human rights, it declares that the parliament, consisting of no more than 179 members (including two elected in Greenland and two in the Faroe Islands), shall be elected by proportional representation with, as determined by election law, rather low thresholds for representation of political parties. According to the constitution, the government and any member of parliament may propose bills and other measures. The parliament adopts its own rules of procedure.

Although Danish democracy is basically representative, the constitution requires or allows referendums in various situations. Referendums, at least of the consultative type, may by law be arranged on almost any issue and have in recent decades been used to settle Denmark's relationships with the European Union (in 1972, 1986, 1992, and 1993). Since the adoption of the current constitution in 1953, ten referendums have been held.

Although Denmark is formally a constitutional monarchy, the monarch politically is virtually powerless. The queen, however, still retains an important ceremonial and symbolic function in the political system.

The present parliament building was inaugurated in 1918. The site of parliament, however, dates to medieval times. The parliament building is referred to as the "third Christiansborg," as two previous castles were destroyed by fire in 1794 and 1884, respectively. The present Christiansborg Castle is interesting in several ways. It accommodates and thus physically unites (in what is formally a separation of powers system) the legislative, executive, and judicial branches. Furthermore, it is possible to see the remains of the previous buildings, the oldest of which dates to the twelfth century.

According to the constitution, elections to parliament have to be held at least every four years. However, the prime minister is empowered to call for new elections at almost any time, the only exception being that elections may not be called by a new government until the prime minister has appeared before parliament. No fewer than ten elections have been held in the past twenty-five years. This reflects the balance of power: A government needs the confidence of parliament, which can dismiss any government; on the other hand, the government can dissolve parliament by calling new elections.

A session of the Danish parliament lasts a full year (if not interrupted by an election), from the first Tuesday in October to the first Tuesday in October of the next year. In a way, parliament is therefore always in session. But of course meetings are not held every day. An annual calendar indicates the days on which plenary sessions are planned, usually Tuesdays through Fridays, and the weeks in which parliament will not meet (normally there are no meetings in the months of July, August, and September, for example). But the speaker of parliament can convene a meeting at any time and has to do so if the prime minister or two-fifths of the MPs request a meeting be held. Usually, about one hundred plenary sessions are held during each parliamentary session. On average, a plenary session lasts about four hours.

According to the constitution the parliament elects a speaker (president) at the beginning of each session and after each election. In addition, four vice presidents are elected. The speaker and the four vice presidents comprise the Presidium of the parliament. The speaker also chairs the Standing Orders Committee, which consists of the members of the Presidium and sixteen ordinary members. The considerable powers of the speaker are listed in the standing orders. In general, it may be said that the speaker is responsible for the planning of parliamentary work, for the proper conduct of parliamentary debates and other activities, and for the internal administration of parliament. The speaker traditionally acts in a neutral and nonpartisan way in close cooperation with representatives of the various parliamentary parties.

LAW MAKING

The constitutional rules on the ordinary legislative process are very few: Government bills as well as private members' bills must be read three times in parliament before they can be passed; two-fifths of the MPs may demand that the third reading of a bill (with some exceptions) may not take place until twelve weekdays after the second reading; all bills not passed before a new election or at the end of the parliamentary session are void. More detailed rules are in the standing orders of parliament.

The standing orders determine how the three readings are to be conducted, when amendments may be moved, and how and when votes are to be taken. The orders stipulate that bills and other proposals may be subjected to the scrutiny of a committee at any stage during its reading.

At the first reading, a bill is debated in principle, without going deeply into details. Amendments cannot be moved. Toward the end of the first reading, parliament decides whether the bill shall be passed on to the second reading and, if so, whether it shall be referred to a committee before the second reading. Normally both decisions are in the affirmative.

After deliberations the committee submits its report on the bill to parliament. At the second reading the debate concerns the bill in general as well as its individual sections and any amendments moved by committee members, other MPs, and the government ministers concerned. When debate is concluded, votes are taken, if needed, on the amendments moved. As is generally the case for parliamentary decision making in Denmark, be that on the floor or in the committees, more than half of the members must be present for a vote to be taken. The second reading is concluded by a decision on whether the bill, amended or not, shall be passed on to the third reading, which usually happens. Sometimes, however, the bill is referred to the same committee before the third reading for further scrutiny, in which case the committee submits a supplementary report to parliament.

At the third reading amendments can be moved in the same way as at the second reading. The amendments are debated and decided upon, then the bill as a whole is discussed. At the end a vote is taken on final adoption of the bill. If the bill is adopted, it is signed by the speaker and forwarded to the prime minister.

A bill passed by parliament becomes a law if the monarch and a minister sign it within thirty days of its final adoption. However, if the government should decide not to sign the bill (the monarch has to follow suit), the bill technically is vetoed. A veto cannot be overruled, but the government would probably have to resign or call an election, as a vote of no confidence would almost surely be proposed and passed in parliament, unless the government veto was for some narrow, technical reason. A real veto, therefore, has no place in the Danish constitutional system.

In constitutional practice, but not in the letter of the constitution, the Supreme Court has the power to exercise judicial review. However, that power has always been used with extreme caution. No major political issue has ever been settled by such a procedure. The constitution grants the government the power to issue provisional laws in emergency situations, provided they are not at variance with the constitution and they are submitted to parliament for approval or rejection as soon as possible. That power has not been used in the twentieth century.

In addition to bills, parliament may pass draft resolutions introduced by the government, a committee, or MPs. If such proposals are recommended by a committee, they are dealt with according to the rules for second and third readings of bills. If they are initiated by the government or MPs, they are dealt with according to the rules for first and third readings of bills.

COMMITTEES

Until the 1960s the Danish parliament set up ad hoc committees to deal with particular legislative matters. After some experimentation with permanent, specialized committees in the 1960s, the committee system was completely reformed in the early 1970s. It is still possible to use ad hoc committees, and a few are set up every year, but since 1972 specialized, permanent committees have been the backbone of the committee structure. Today, twenty-four standing committees are set up at the opening of each parliamentary session and after each election. Apart from the Standing Orders Committee, the Scrutineers Committee, and the European Affairs Committee, the jurisdictions of the permanent committees basically mirror the division of competence among the government ministries.

The committees are composed of seventeen members, with the exception of the Standing Orders Committee, which has twenty-one members. Committee members are appointed by the parties in parliament according to their shares of the seats in parliament. The parties may also appoint one or two substitutes for their members on a committee. Substitutes may take part in the negotiations of the committee but are not allowed to vote or to make statements in the committee reports. However, since the work of a committee is usually disposed of in a pragmatic fashion, that formal rule is of no major importance. Usually the parties form coalitions to maximize their number of seats on committees. Such coalitions also make it possible for the smallest parties to obtain representation on at least some of the committees.

The committees have only a small staff of one or two secretaries, and in some cases a single secretary works for more than one committee. However, the Finance Committee and the European Affairs Committee are served by a couple of staffers. The modest staffs reflect the fact that Danish committees have traditionally been heavily dependent on the ministries for information.

Each committee appoints a chair and a vice chair. Usually the parties make deals in such a way that opposition parties, which recently have had a majority of the seats in the committees because Danish governments in recent decades have tended to be of the minority type, receive their share of the chairmanships.

Committee members tend to stay on their committees for several years and, if reelected to parliament, even for several election periods. They also tend to get committee assignments to match their policy interests and previous educational and work experiences. For these reasons committee members tend to be the policy specialists of their parties.

The committees are important in the decision-making process. Their main source of information on bills and draft resolutions is the responsible minister. The minister may be asked to answer any written question on a proposal. Formally speaking, the committee asks the questions, but in reality any individual committee member can usually put a question through the committee secretary at any time. Committee members may also request the presence of a minister before the committee to answer questions orally in what is called a "consultation." This is often done in matters considered important or urgent. The committees are not obliged to report on the proposals submitted. In effect they can kill a proposal by inaction, and they often do so.

When the committee system was reformed in 1972, it was decided that the new specialized committees would be allowed to put questions to the responsible minister even if no specific proposal was under consideration. Since then the agenda of committee meetings has had two main parts: one concerning specific bills and proposals under consideration, and another concerning any other matter or issue that committee members want to investigate or discuss. The latter has developed into an important instrument of parliamentary control. In the 1993–1994 session, the committees asked ministers about six thousand questions and had about six hundred consultations with ministers. Studies have shown, perhaps not surprisingly, that the questions are to an overwhelming degree put by members of the opposition parties.

The committees, except the Finance Committee, may also receive communications from individuals, organizations, institutions, firms, and other private interests. In the 1993–1994 session the committees received more than two thousand written communications. Individuals and groups of all sorts may even ask for an opportunity to meet with the committee to present their views on matters of concern. In 1993–1994 that happened on more than three hundred occasions.

Committee proceedings normally are not open to the public, but at the end of a meeting a committee may decide to forward statements to the public. The committees are allowed to hold hearings on proposals or on specific public matters. Except for ministers of government, a committee can only invite, not force, officials and private citizens to give evidence. The hearings are open to the public if the committee so decides. Open hearings have become more common in recent years. In 1995, for example, hearings open to the public (but not to television), were held by an ad hoc committee investigating a possible bank scandal involving ministers of government and public servants.

Two of the Danish committees have unique powers. The Finance Committee can grant expenditures at any time during the year on behalf of the whole parliament. Such additional appropriations are then included in the yearly Supplementary Appropriation Act, passed in the spring of the following year. The European Affairs Committee is parliament's watchdog in matters relating to the European Union. The government must receive a bargaining mandate from the European Affairs Committee before committing Denmark in the European Council of Ministers, and if need be the government must return to the committee to get a new mandate. The committee also reviews the decisions of the European Union in various matters.

The annual budget proposal has to be introduced by the government at least four months before the beginning of the financial year, that is, no later than August 31. The draft budget is technically a bill, albeit a rather big and special one. In principle it is handled as any other bill. However, according to the standing orders the government may introduce the budget bill in writing without convening parliament. In that case the speaker refers the bill to the Finance Committee, which can then start working on it even if no first reading has taken place.

In the Finance Committee, work is divided in an informal and nonpartisan manner among the members, each of whom is responsible for examining a part of the budget proposal. But the final adoption of the budget bill after the third reading in December is certainly not a purely technical matter. It at times develops into high-level party politics, especially when minority governments are in power, as opposition parties test whether the government can mobilize a majority in parliament. A government needs a budget, and rejection of the budget bill is interpreted as a vote of no confidence. In 1983, for example, the government called elections when it was defeated in the final vote on the budget. A provisional appropriation act then had to be passed (according to the constitution) before the end of December.

The public accounts must be submitted to parliament no later than the end of June of the following year. To examine the accounts parliament elects six auditors, who need not be MPs. The auditors, assisted by a special auditing unit staffed by civil servants, report to parliament, which eventually approves the accounts.

GOVERNMENT FORMATION

The constitution states that a government must leave office if a motion of censure is adopted unless the government calls elections. The government administration then functions as a caretaker until a new government has been appointed. The same applies if a government decides voluntarily to resign. There are no constitutional rules on how a new government is to be formed, but constitutional lawyers argue that a government cannot be formed if it is known that it will immediately be defeated in a no-confidence vote.

The actual practice of government formation has developed since the early twentieth century and may be summarized in the following informal rules:

- If there is uncertainty about the appointment of a new government, each of the parliamentary parties shall advise the monarch.
- If the recommendations made by the parties support the formation of a majority government, or a minority government with assured support from a majority in parliament, such a government shall be appointed.
- If no such majority is possible, the minority government most likely to survive shall be appointed.
- A "royal informateur" may be appointed to investigate the possibilities of forming a new government.
- The parties are not restricted by any norms with respect to the advice given.
- The acting prime minister, not the monarch, is responsible for interpreting any unclear advice given by the parties.

Since several parties follow these informal rules, the process of government formation can be complicated, but a new government is usually formed after a few weeks of interparty negotiation.

Governments fall for various reasons. All four majority

coalitions since 1953 lost their majority in the next election. Apart from the somewhat unusual minority coalition of 1978–1979, which broke down because of internal disagreements, the minority governments fell because they were defeated in important matters, could not enact their policies, or had their support from opposition parties withdrawn or critically reduced because of election results.

CONTROL OF GOVERNMENT

Danish MPs and opposition parties have numerous opportunities to monitor governmental actions. First, they may demand answers from ministers to pertinent questions in floor debates. Such debates are arranged on government and private members' bills and draft resolutions, budget proposals, and ministerial statements. An appendix to the standing orders lists the time (in minutes) allotted to ministers and MPs in debates on different kinds of items. Ministers are allotted more time than spokespersons for the parties, who in turn receive more time than do ordinary members. However, the speaker is empowered to allow deviations from the time limits and to call on members to address parliament by short remarks. The debates are recorded and printed in *Folketingstidende,* which also contains all bills (proposed and adopted), committee reports, and other documents and information.

All floor debates, except those on ministerial statements on public matters, may be ended by a vote. Voting requires a quorum consisting of more than half of the MPs. Members present but abstaining are considered as valid participants in the vote. A simple majority is sufficient for a positive decision on a proposal. If there is a tie in voting, the status quo prevails. Normally, votes are taken by use of an electronic voting machine. If that machine cannot be used, the speaker calls on the members to rise from their seats to indicate whether they vote for or against a proposal or whether they abstain. Roll call votes may also be taken if the speaker so decides, or if seventeen members so request with the approval of the speaker.

Aside from general debates, more specialized procedures are available for questioning ministers on the floor: short questions and interpellations. If an MP asks for an oral answer to a short question put before noon on Friday, the minister will answer during the question time the following Wednesday afternoon. The speaker may permit a few other MPs to join the debate. If a written answer is requested by an MP, it should be provided by the minister within one week of having received the question. Both questions and answers are printed in *Folketingstidende.* The number of questions requiring written answers increased dramatically during the 1970s and 1980s. In the late 1960s there were four to five hundred questions (requiring oral and written answers) per year, whereas the total in the 1993–1994 session was almost nineteen hundred, including about two hundred orally answered questions.

Questions from committees and short questions are important instruments of control, but for the government the interpellation procedure is politically more dangerous. Any MP may, according to the constitution, address an interpellation to one or several ministers. Parliament decides on its admissibility, which nowadays is almost a formality. In the past two decades, thirty to forty interpellations have been made each year. The importance of interpellations derives from the fact that during the debate a proposal may be made to pass on to the next matter on the order-paper. By adopting such a proposal for a resolution on the order of business, parliament can influence the behavior and policy of the government. In an extreme case, such a decision amounts to a vote of censure, sacking the government or forcing new elections to be held.

There are still other instruments for controlling the government. Parliament may force the government to establish ad hoc, quasi-judicial bodies to investigate certain matters in which ministers have been involved. This has happened quite a few times in recent years. Further, the old impeachment procedure, generally thought to have become obsolete after the introduction of cabinet responsibility, was recently revived when parliament decided to impeach a former minister of justice for illegal administration of the law regulating the rights of refugees. The High Court of the Realm, consisting of up to fifteen Supreme Court judges and an equal number of members elected by (but not of) parliament, tries such cases. A former minister of justice was convicted in 1995.

Finally, an ombudsman was established in the mid-1950s according to the constitution. The ombudsman is elected by parliament, to which he or she reports. Over the years the ombudsman has received an increasing number of complaints from citizens. In 1993 the complaints numbered almost three thousand, but fewer than 10 percent of them resulted in criticism or suggestions.

PARTIES IN PARLIAMENT

Political parties organized in parliamentary groups are crucial for understanding the organization and function of parliament, even though parties are not mentioned in the constitution. MPs are elected on party tickets, and party groups appoint members of committees and form and control governments.

After each election and at the beginning of the yearly session, each party organizes itself in parliament by electing a chair, an executive committee, a secretary, and a spokesperson in general political affairs. Party meetings are usually held each sitting day before the floor meeting of parliament. Attendance at party meetings is very good—a testament to the importance of parties in legislative politics.

The parties and their leadership decide party policy on a daily basis. They divide tasks and coordinate the activities of members, including their strategies, what positions to take, and possible compromises to agree to in committee work. MPs specialize in legislative areas and are to a considerable extent the policy experts of their respective parties on the relevant subjects. Nevertheless, they consider themselves primarily as representatives of their parties, although some of them certainly also pay attention to constituency interests.

The parties, of course, work in different ways, since they differ from one another in size and status (whether government or opposition). The smallest party may have only four MPs, whereas the largest, which since 1924 has been the Social Democratic Party, may have as many as seventy. Internal institutionalization and specialization increase with the size of the party, and if the party is in government, the party leadership is also in government. Government ministers may also be members of parliament, and they usually are. Since the Danish party system is fairly factionalized, there is no "official" leader of the "opposition" or "minority."

Party discipline is very high in Denmark by any comparative measure. Deviations from the party line in important matters are usually not tolerated, and the party leadership may apply sanctions if MPs defect in cases where deviations have not explicitly been permitted. MPs know that they are dependent on the party organization to get renominated, and even if they posses a strong local base ensuring nomination and perhaps election, they still have to consider that advancement in the party hierarchy presupposes party loyalty.

Members of disciplined parties vote uniformly. Voting in parliament, therefore, is almost always predictable. The secretary of the party is also the whip, ensuring that votes are delivered. The whips agree among themselves on "pairing systems," which ensure that the "proper" balance between government and opposition parties is maintained in cases of illness or other forms of nonattendance of MPs. Basically, the clearing system is an accepted rule of fair play.

STATUS OF MEMBERS

Constitutionally, individual MPs are bound solely by their own conscience, but, as indicated above, they are really party members with consciences. However, they enjoy all the traditional parliamentary privileges and immunities granted to parliamentarians in the advanced Western democracies, which restrains party control of their behavior. Members of parliament cannot be recalled, but in extreme cases of deviation from party proscriptions they may be expelled from the parliamentary party and thereby denied renomination for parliamentary office. Danish MPs may resign at any time but rarely do so.

The standing orders of parliament prescribe civilized behavior in parliamentary affairs. The few formal rules are supplemented with a great number of informal codes of conduct that have evolved over more than 150 years. The standing orders do contain rules on dealing with members who are not behaving properly, but they are used rarely because Danish MPs tend to behave in the prescribed manner. Only now and then must the speaker remind an MP not to use improper expressions.

In heated debates, when television is covering the proceedings (which rarely is the case because parliamentary debates are considered dull by most journalists and observers), MPs and particularly party leaders and spokespersons may try to attract public attention, but generally they are not that successful.

The status of Danish MPs is rather low in terms of pay, perquisites, and secretarial support, compared with a number of other economically advanced countries. Some progress has been made in recent years, however, and in 1995 a major reform introduced substantial improvements in several respects.

Erik Damgaard

BIBLIOGRAPHY

Arter, David. *The Nordic Parliaments: A Comparative Analysis.* London: C. Hurst, 1984.

Damgaard, Erik. "The Strong Parliaments of Scandinavia: Continuity and Change of Scandinavian Parliaments." In *Parliaments in the Modern World: Changing Institutions,* ed. Gary W. Copeland and Samuel C. Patterson. Ann Arbor: University of Michigan Press, 1994, 85–103.

Damgaard, Erik, ed. *Parliamentary Change in the Nordic Countries.* Oslo and Oxford: Scandinavian University Press, 1992.

Döring, Herbert, ed. *Parliaments and Majority Rule in Western Europe.* New York: St. Martin's, 1995.

Wiberg, Matti, ed. *Parliamentary Control in the Nordic Countries.* Helsinki: Finnish Political Science Association, 1994.

DJIBOUTI

OFFICIAL NAME: Republic of Djibouti (Arabic, Jumhuriyah Djibouti; French, République de Djibouti)
CAPITAL: Djibouti
POPULATION: 428,000 (1996 est.)
DATE OF INDEPENDENCE: June 27, 1977 (from France)
DATE OF CURRENT CONSTITUTION: Approved September 4, 1992
FORM OF GOVERNMENT: Limited democracy
LANGUAGES: Arabic (official), French (official), Somali, Afar
MONETARY UNIT: Djiboutian franc
FISCAL YEAR: Calendar year
LEGISLATURE: National Assembly (Assemblée Nationale)
NUMBER OF CHAMBERS: One
NUMBER OF MEMBERS: 65
PERCENTAGE OF WOMEN: 0.0
TERM OF LEGISLATURE: Five years
MOST RECENT LEGISLATIVE ELECTION: December 18, 1992
MINIMUM AGE FOR VOTING: 18
MINIMUM AGE FOR MEMBERSHIP: 23
SUFFRAGE: Universal and direct
VOTING: Optional
ADDRESS: Assemblée Nationale, B.P. 138, Djibouti
TELEPHONE: (253) 35 20 37
FAX: (253) 35 55 03

The National Assembly of Djibouti, a state in eastern Africa at the entrance to the Red Sea *(see map, p. 234)*, has no substantive powers. Although the constitution of 1992 legalized limited pluralism, the ruling Popular Rally for Progress won all sixty-five seats in the December 1992 elections.

George Thomas Kurian

DOMINICA

OFFICIAL NAME: Commonwealth of Dominica
CAPITAL: Roseau
POPULATION: 83,000 (1996 est.)
DATE OF INDEPENDENCE: November 3, 1978 (from the United Kingdom)
DATE OF CURRENT CONSTITUTION: Effective November 3, 1978
FORM OF GOVERNMENT: Parliamentary democracy
LANGUAGES: English (official), French patois
MONETARY UNIT: East Caribbean dollar
FISCAL YEAR: July 1–June 30
LEGISLATURE: House of Assembly
NUMBER OF CHAMBERS: One
NUMBER OF MEMBERS: 31 (21 elected representatives; 9 senators; president, ex officio)
PERCENTAGE OF WOMEN: 9.4
TERM OF LEGISLATURE: Five years
MOST RECENT LEGISLATIVE ELECTION: June 12, 1995
MINIMUM AGE FOR VOTING: 18
MINIMUM AGE FOR MEMBERSHIP: 21
SUFFRAGE: Universal
VOTING: Optional
ADDRESS: House of Assembly, Victoria Street, Roseau
TELEPHONE: (1809) 448 2401
FAX: (1809) 449 8353

The Commonwealth of Dominica, or Sunday Island (*Dominica* is the Latin word for "Sunday"), was named for its discovery by Christopher Columbus on Sunday, November 3, 1493, on Columbus's second trip to the West Indies. The island is part of the Windward group in the eastern Caribbean *(see map, p. 303)*.

Spanish efforts to settle the island were successfully resisted by the Carib Indians. In 1635 France took advantage of Spanish weakness and claimed Dominica. By the end of the eighteenth century the French and the English openly fought over the island. In 1805 the British took control, and their plantation system dominated.

In 1831 the House of Assembly of Dominica enacted the Brown Privilege Bill, which allowed propertied free blacks to vote and to seek political office. In 1832 three black men were elected to the House of Assembly, and by 1838 the House had a black majority. Dominica was the only British Caribbean colony in the nineteenth century to have a black-controlled legislature.

In 1967 Dominica became an associated state with the United Kingdom, in essence exercising domestic self-government but leaving the United Kingdom with the power to regulate defense and foreign policy in the area. In November 1978 Dominica became independent; it remains part of the British Commonwealth.

Unlike most of the other Commonwealth nations in the Caribbean, Dominica is a republic. The president, who is head of state, is elected by the legislature for a five-year term, upon joint nomination by the prime minister and the leader of the opposition, or by secret ballot in the event of a disagreement between the two. The president may not hold office for more than two terms. As is the case in the other Commonwealth nations, however, the head of state is primarily a figurehead, and the real power of the nation lies in the hands of the prime minister. If the president resigns or dies, parliament is required to meet to elect a successor president, by majority vote, either openly or by secret ballot.

The parliament consists of the House of Assembly, which includes one representative from each of the twenty-one constituencies (electoral districts) and nine senators who are either elected or appointed (if they are appointed, five are appointed on the advice of the prime minister and four on the advice of the leader of the opposition), depending upon the will of the House. The president is ex officio a member of the House of Assembly. Whereas most of the legislatures of the Commonwealth Caribbean have two separate chambers, the legislature of Dominica is a combined legislature in which the House of Assembly and the Senate sit together.

The head of government is the prime minister, who is the leader of the majority in the House. The constitution provides that the president has the right to remove the prime minister from office if, following a vote of no confidence, he or she does not resign or request a dissolution of the House of Assembly and new elections.

The House must meet at least once each six months, although generally it meets at least once a month. The constitution specifies that the parliament can continue to sit for a maximum of five years from the date of the first sitting of the House after any dissolution. Its term can be extended for no more than twelve months at a time, for no more than five years. Elections must take place within three months of a dissolution.

To be eligible to vote in an election individuals must be at least eighteen years of age, be citizens of Dominica or of the British Commonwealth, and meet the residence or domicile requirements of the law. Candidates for elective office must be twenty-one years of age, have Dominican citizenship (only Commonwealth citizenship is required for Senate candidates), have residence in Dominica for twelve months immediately before nomination, and have the ability to speak and read English. Individuals are ineligible to be candidates if they owe allegiance to a foreign state, have undischarged bankruptcy, have been documented as being insane, or are under a sentence of death or of imprisonment exceeding twelve months. Elected representatives also cannot be ministers of religion or government contractors. Candidates must deposit the equivalent of US$184, which is reimbursed if the candidate obtains at least one-eighth of the valid votes cast in the district.

The British Westminster model of government is the best single characterization of the legislative arena in Dominica. There is strong party discipline in the legislature, and the concept of party discipline explains most legislative behavior for both the government and the opposition sides of the House. Legislators describe virtually all activity, including committee work, parliamentary question time, debates, and the legislative process itself, in terms of party discipline.

The legislative process follows the British system closely: bills are introduced and read a first time, then read a second time, sent to committee (often a committee of the whole house), read a third time, and finally voted on. Since senators sit with members of the House of Assembly, there is no parallel second-house procedure. Bills approved by a majority of the thirty members of parliament are sent to the president for approval.

Gregory S. Mahler

DOMINICAN REPUBLIC

OFFICIAL NAME: Dominican Republic (República Dominicana)

CAPITAL: Santo Domingo

POPULATION: 8,089,000 (1996 est.)

DATE OF INDEPENDENCE: February 27, 1844 (from Haiti)

DATE OF CURRENT CONSTITUTION: Effective November 28, 1966

FORM OF GOVERNMENT: Parliamentary democracy

LANGUAGE: Spanish

MONETARY UNIT: Dominican peso

FISCAL YEAR: Calendar year

LEGISLATURE: National Congress (Congreso Nacional)

NUMBER OF CHAMBERS: Two. Chamber of Deputies (Cámara de Diputados); Senate (Senado)

NUMBER OF MEMBERS: Chamber of Deputies, 120; Senate, 30

PERCENTAGE OF WOMEN: Chamber of Deputies, 11.7; Senate, 3.3

TERM OF LEGISLATURE: Chamber of Deputies, four years; Senate, four years

MOST RECENT LEGISLATIVE ELECTION: May 16, 1994

MINIMUM AGE FOR VOTING: 18
MINIMUM AGE FOR MEMBERSHIP: 25
SUFFRAGE: Universal and direct
VOTING: Compulsory
ADDRESS: Congreso Nacional, Centro de los Heroes, Santo Domingo
TELEPHONE: Chamber of Deputies, (1809) 535 2626; Senate, (1809) 532 5561
FAX: Chamber of Deputies, (1809) 532 7012; Senate, (1809) 542 7582

The Dominican Republic, a nation in the Caribbean Ocean *(see map, p. 194)*, became democratic with the constitution of 1966, after many decades under the dictatorship of Rafael Leónidas Trujillo Molina. This constitution incorporates many of the features of the Institutional Act of 1965 and certain sections of the constitutions of 1962 and 1963.

The Dominican National Congress consists of two chambers: the Senate and the Chamber of Deputies, both elected by direct vote. Each province and the National District are represented by a senator, elected to a four-year term. Senators elect the judges and members of the Accounts and Electoral Councils and approve the nomination of diplomats.

Each deputy represents fifty thousand inhabitants or fraction over twenty-five thousand. Decisions in Congress are taken by simple majority, but urgent matters require a two-thirds majority. Each house normally meets on February 27 and August 16 to begin sessions of ninety days, extendible by another sixty days. Only the Chamber of Deputies may impeach public officials, by a vote of three-fourths of the total membership.

The legislative powers of the National Congress are spelled out in the constitution and include taxation, approval of the national budget, regulation of the national debt, sale of public property and acquisition of private property, creation of new provinces and abolition of existing ones, determination of their boundaries, determination of the number of courts of appeal, amendment of the constitution, proclamation of a state of siege or national emergency, approval or rejection of treaties, and grant of authorization to the president of the republic to leave the country for more than fifteen days.

Legislation may be initiated by senators and deputies, the president of the republic, the Supreme Court (in judicial matters), and the Electoral Board (in electoral matters). Each bill is subject to two periods of discussion in the chamber in which it originates. Upon approval, it is forwarded to the other chamber. Amendments passed in the second chamber must be approved by the first. Presidential vetoes may be overridden by Congress during its next session by a two-thirds majority.

Members of the Chamber of Deputies are elected on the basis of a closed party-list system with proportional distribution of seats according to the D'Hondt method. Senators are elected by simple majority. Seats that fall vacant between general elections are filled by substitutes elected in the general elections.

George Thomas Kurian

E

ECUADOR

OFFICIAL NAME: Republic of Ecuador (República de Ecuador)
CAPITAL: Quito
POPULATION: 11,466,000 (1996 est.)
DATE OF INDEPENDENCE: May 24, 1822 (from Spain)
DATE OF CURRENT CONSTITUTION: Approved January 15, 1978; effective August 10, 1979
FORM OF GOVERNMENT: Parliamentary democracy
LANGUAGES: Spanish (official), Quechua, other Indian languages
MONETARY UNIT: Sucre
FISCAL YEAR: Calendar year
LEGISLATURE: National Congress (Congreso Nacional)
NUMBER OF CHAMBERS: One. National Chamber of Representatives (Cámara Nacional de Representantes)
NUMBER OF MEMBERS: 82 (70 elected by provincial vote; 12 elected by national vote)
PERCENTAGE OF WOMEN: 3.7
TERM OF PARLIAMENT: Provincial deputies, two years; national deputies, four years
MOST RECENT LEGISLATIVE ELECTION: May 19, 1996
MINIMUM AGE FOR VOTING: 18
MINIMUM AGE FOR MEMBERSHIP: Provincial deputies, 25; national deputies, 30
SUFFRAGE: Universal and direct
VOTING: Compulsory
ADDRESS: Palacio Legislativo, Piedraita y 6 de Diciembre, Quito
TELEPHONE: (593 2) 526 183
FAX: (593 2) 220 933

Bestriding the equator on the Pacific Ocean in northwestern South America, the mainland of the Republic of Ecuador encompasses three distinct physical areas—the coast, the high country (or Sierra), and the tropical eastern area—which differ politically and culturally from one another *(see map, p. 536)*. The country is a presidential republic divided administratively into twenty provinces. The system of government is tripartite, with the executive, legislative, and judicial branches sharing power. The president is head of state and government.

Elected to a four-year term by direct popular vote, the president cannot serve consecutive terms. The president enforces the constitution, approves laws, maintains domestic order and national security, determines foreign policy, and assumes emergency powers during crises. The president can also share in forming, executing, and applying laws.

The unicameral legislature, the National Congress, has the constitutional authority to amend or make laws, amend and interpret the constitution, establish taxes and tariffs (although it may not adopt legislation that will increase public spending), approve the government budget, and approve or reject international treaties and conventions. The Congress also appoints a number of public officials and has the power to review and censure senior public officials.

HISTORICAL BACKGROUND

After gaining independence from Spain in 1822, Ecuador joined with Colombia and Venezuela in the confederation of Gran Colombia. It seceded in 1830, and its first constitution established a unicameral Congress with deputies elected by indirect suffrage. With the constitution of 1835, the Congress became bicameral, with a Senate and Chamber of Deputies whose members served four-year terms. The most common form of legislative organization has been bicameral. The 1843 constitution established direct election of senators, although it retained economic requirements for voting and stipulated that the Congress meet only every four years. The constitution of 1861 broadened the democratic nature of the Congress by abolishing all economic requirements for suffrage and by introducing direct, secret elections for legislators. With the constitution of 1929, Ecuador became the first Latin American country to grant the franchise to literate women twenty-one years of age and older. The Senate was also reorganized to provide functional representation to specific interest groups, such as workers, industrialists, farmers, and educators.

Ecuador saw five presidencies overthrown between 1944 and 1970, when a military government was installed. Civilian rule was restored in 1979. Before the military governments of the 1970s, a few powerful parties dominated Ecuadorean politics. Historically, the strongest electoral vehicles were the Conservative and Radical Liberal Parties, although since the 1940s these had been overshadowed by *velasquismo*, a populist movement founded by five-time president José María Velasco Ibarra that made direct appeals to rural and urban lower class voters for the first time in Ecuadorean politics.

After the return to democracy in 1979, parties multiplied rapidly until no fewer than seventeen contested the presidential election of the following year. By the late 1980s a large number of parties remained; the center-left Democratic Left and Popular Democracy, the center-right Social Christian Party, and the populist Roldosist Party of Ecuador were dominant. Delegates have not identified strongly with the parties under which they gained election, and subsequent shifts in allegiance have been common enough to have given rise to the popular term *cambio de camisetas* (literally, changing T-shirts).

Since 1979 the legislature has been unicameral. The constitution that took effect in August of that year contains other reforms that affect the Congress, including extending the franchise to illiterates (who, unlike literates, are not required to vote), requiring candidates in popular elections to be affiliated with a political party, and establishing four legislative commissions that operate with certain powers when the Congress is not in session. This constitution also abolished functional representation, in which various groups are represented in government.

In February 1997 Congress exploited a questionable provision in the constitution that allowed it to remove a president from office on grounds of "mental incapacity." President Abdalá Bucaram Ortiz had faced mounting opposition from virtually all sectors of society because of increasing levels of corruption, protest over his economic austerity policies, and what many viewed as his outrageous personal behavior. Despite protests from Bucaram and others that the vote had been unconstitutional, the legislature chose an interim president, but not before changing its mind twice within the same week. It first selected Fabián Alarcón, president of Congress, then later approved an agreement elevating Bucaram's vice president, Rosalía Arteaga, to a limited caretaker presidency. Arteaga became the first female president in Ecuador's history, serving three days in office. Before the week was over, the legislature had settled on its original choice, Alarcón, who was elected to a one-year term. Subsequently, Congress's actions were ratified in a popular referendum, but the crisis highlighted the fact that Ecuador's constitution does not delineate a clear line of presidential succession. Furthermore, it demonstrated that in the absence of such a guideline, Congress may select an interim president to serve until a national presidential election can be held. Following the crisis, legislators vowed to address the questionable constitutionality of the selection and of Bucaram's removal by passing whatever laws necessary to establish constitutional justification for their actions, thereby cementing the role of Congress in the presidential succession process.

THE LEGISLATURE AND ITS MEMBERS

Power is disproportionately concentrated in the executive branch, but regional interests and attempts to contain the excesses of populist leaders have given Ecuador's legislature relatively more power than that held by legislatures in many other countries in the region. But a weak party system and the lack of modern means of research or of tracking legislation have meant that congressional deliberations are slow and cumbersome. Most congressional actions are reactions, and the Congress initiates little legislation of its own. In recent years, tensions between the executive and legislative branches have been high, frequently erupting into political crises. Increasingly, the executive branch has sought to legislate through executive decree.

Congress holds both ordinary and extraordinary sessions in the Legislative Palace in the capital city, Quito. The ordinary congressional session runs sixty days, from August 10 until October 9. Congress may also be called into extraordinary session by the president of the republic, by a two-thirds vote of the Congress, or, as most often happens, by the president of the Congress. Congress is called into extraordinary session only to consider specific issues and is dissolved when it has resolved them.

There are both national and provincial representatives (deputies) to Congress, and all must be Ecuadorean by birth. Twelve national deputies are chosen in national elections. They serve four-year terms and must be at least thirty years old when elected. Provincial deputies must be natives of the province in which they stand for election or must have lived there for three uninterrupted years immediately before the election. They must be at least twenty-five years old, are chosen in provincial elections under a system of proportional representation, and serve a two-year term.

To run for election as either a national or provincial deputy, candidates must be members of a political party legally recognized by the Supreme Electoral Tribunal. Parties are prohibited from forming alliances. Legally recognized parties that receive at least 5 percent of the votes in elections with several candidates are eligible for state financial aid, 60 percent of which is allocated equally among all legally recognized parties, and 40 percent according to votes obtained in the last national election.

Once elected, congressional deputies may not hold any other public post except a university teaching position. Deputies are also prohibited from exercising their professions while Congress or its commissions are in session. Reelection is possible only after an absence of one term, although former national deputies may run for immediate reelection as provincial deputies and the converse.

Ecuadorean political scientist Simon Pachano (in *Los Diputados: Un Elite Politica)* describes the most common characteristics of deputies who held office between 1979 and 1988. Most were university graduates, with law the most common field of study. Most studied in Quito or Guayaquil or lived in one of those cities. Most of these delegates were born and lived a while in one of the provincial capitals, however, and it was typically their native province from which they were elected. Nearly 60 percent of all deputies had pursued private sector careers, but there were notable differences between the coastal region and the Sierra. Just under 80 percent of delegates from the coast had private sector backgrounds; this was true for only about 40 percent of those from the Sierra. About 95 percent of national deputies had held public office before election, but this was characteristic of only about 75 percent of provincial delegates. With the exception of delegates from coastal provinces other than Guayas (Guayaquil), more than two-thirds had held positions in the parties with which they were affiliated. Fewer than 25 percent of all deputies had held union positions. About half of all deputies had held leadership positions in provincial sports organizations.

Nearly all Ecuadorean delegates are male. Although women's participation in politics has grown since 1978, their access to elected office remains relatively restricted. Women have never accounted for more than 6 percent of all deputies. In 1978 there were no women deputies; in 1984 four deputies were women; in 1986 there was one; in 1988 and 1997 there were three. Women also occupy few leadership positions in the political parties.

LEGISLATIVE OPERATIONS AND POWERS

After convening on August 10, Congress elects from among its members a president and vice president, each of whom serves a one-year term. Within seven days the Congress must constitute from among its members four legislative commissions: the Civil and Penal; the Labor and Social; the Tax, Fiscal, Banking, and Budget; and the Economy, Agriculture, Industry, and Commercial. Each commission has seven members and seven alternates who serve two-year terms and who may be reelected.

These commissions function throughout the year. When the Congress is not in session, the legislative commissions may be called together in plenary session by the president of the Congress to debate and approve bills brought before it. The plenary also has the authority to rule on treaties and international agreements and to decide on the constitutionality of laws brought before it by the Tribunal of Constitutional Guarantees.

Despite the formal separation of powers among the three branches of government, the Congress exercises considerable control over the activities of both the executive and judiciary. It appoints the comptroller general, the attorney general, the fiscal minister, and the superintendents of banks and companies from lists submitted by the president. It also makes appointments to the principal judicial institutions: the Supreme Court, the Fiscal Tribunal, and the Contentious Administrative Tribunal. And the Congress appoints three of the seven members of the Supreme Electoral Tribunal, the institution charged with supervising and certifying elections. Two of the remaining four members are chosen by the Congress from a list submitted by the president, and two from a list submitted by the Supreme Court.

The Tribunal of Constitutional Guarantees interprets and monitors compliance with the constitution. Because the Congress is involved in making appointments to this tribunal and has power over its decisions, however, it in fact exercises considerable control over determinations of constitutionality. The Congress appoints three of the eleven members of the Tribunal of Constitutional Guarantees and selects the eight others from lists submitted by the president, the Supreme Court, the mayors and provincial prefects, the legal labor unions, and the chambers of production. The tribunal must submit its decisions on the unconstitutionality of laws, decrees, accords, resolutions, ordinances, or resolutions to the Congress (or to the plenary when it is in session) for final resolution.

PATRONAGE, POWER, AND CONFLICT

Although patronage has always been the means with which any Ecuadorean government has attempted to consolidate and legitimize its authority, those appointments controlled by the legislature took on increased importance as tensions between the legislature and the executive branch escalated. Since the return to democracy in 1979, the growth in the number of parties and the weak ties between them and many delegates have made constructing and sustaining legislative majorities particularly difficult. Opposition parties in Congress could use congressional appointments to encourage switching of party loyalty and affiliation.

The initial step in this direction took place in 1979, shortly after the election of Jaime Roldós Aguilera as president. Although Roldós ran on the Concentration of Popular Forces ticket, a rift had developed between him and the party's leader, Asaad Bucaram, who had been elected as a delegate. Intent on realizing his frustrated presidential ambitions by governing from Congress, Bucaram drew on the resources available to him as leader of the largest legislative bloc to fashion an opposition majority that would give him leadership. Appointments to the Supreme Court figured prominently in his successful efforts to forge an alliance with the Conservative and Liberal Parties.

In August 1983 Congress, then under the control of a coalition of center-left parties led by Raúl Baca of the Democratic Left Party, amended the constitution to reduce the terms of Supreme Court justices from six to four years to increase patronage opportunities.

León Febres Cordero of the center-right Social Christian Party assumed the presidency in August 1984 after a bitter campaign against the Democratic Left candidate, Rodrigo Borja. As soon as he took office, the new president faced an opposition majority in Congress. Led by the Democratic Left, which held twenty-four seats, the opposition coalition interpreted the previous constitutional amendment changing the terms of the Supreme Court justices from six to four years as taking effect retroactively. Thus, since four years had passed since the sitting justices had been installed, the new Congress moved to appoint a new court.

This move set off a dispute between the president and the Congress that threatened to rupture Ecuador's fragile democracy. Febres Cordero declared the action to appoint a new Supreme Court unconstitutional and ordered the police to prevent the new court from being installed. Several months of conflict ensued. The president and the Congress eventually reached an agreement, and a new court was named. Twelve of the new justices were appointed from the opposition coalition parties.

With the election of Rodrigo Borja as president in 1988, a new Congress controlled by the Democratic Left was installed. As one of its first acts, this Congress further amended the constitution to stipulate that the terms of all government officials appointed for four years (notably the justices of the Supreme Court, the Fiscal Tribunal, and the Court of Administrative Disputes; the procurator general; the comptroller general; the superintendent of banks; and the superintendent of companies) would be conterminous with the presidential term, further increasing opportunities for patronage by congressional leaders.

The Tribunal of Constitutional Guarantees, which had been silent throughout most of the constitutional conflict, pronounced this decision unconstitutional. Congress, however, exercised its constitutional prerogative to overturn the tribunal's decision, and a new Supreme Court was installed.

CENSURE AND LEGISLATIVE-EXECUTIVE RELATIONS

Through interpellation, the Congress can censure senior public officials for failure to discharge their duties while in office and for up to a year after they have left office. The president and vice president may be censured only for treason, bribery, or other actions that severely affect national honor.

Each deputy has the right to initiate interpellation against a public official by drawing up a list of questions. The secretary of the Congress must deliver the list of questions to the official at least five days before his or her scheduled appearance before the Congress. Members of Congress question the official and then debate and vote. If an official is found guilty, Congress may remove that individual from office with a simple majority vote.

Congressional use of interpellation to obstruct the president is not new. In the 1961 congressional session four ministers were summoned. In recent years, however, interpellation has been used with increasing frequency, as the struggle for power has escalated. For example, in 1986 the Congress dismissed Febres Cordero's minister of finance for alleged abuse of tariff, exchange, and public spending laws and forced his minister of mines and energy to resign for alleged improprieties in negotiating an oil trade agreement.

Escalating tensions have spurred the president to make increased use of legislative powers that the constitution allocates to the executive branch. When the president brings economic legislation to Congress and characterizes it as urgent, the Congress (or the plenary when the full congress is not in session) must approve, reject, or modify it within fifteen days. If Congress fails to take such action in the time allotted, the legislation passes into law with the designation "decree law." At this point, the full Congress (not the plenary) still has the authority to reject or modify the decree law. Should Congress reject the legislation, the president may not then overturn its decision.

David W. Schodt

BIBLIOGRAPHY

Chinchilla, Laura, and David W. Schodt. *The Administration of Justice in Ecuador.* San Jose, Costa Rica: Center for the Administration of Justice, Florida International University, 1993.

Pachano, Simon. *Los Diputados: Un Elite Politica.* Quito: Corporación Editora Nacional, 1991.

Pyne, Peter. "Legislatures and Development: The Case of Ecuador, 1960–1961." *Comparative Political Studies* 9 (April 1976): 69–91.

Schodt, David W. *Ecuador: An Andean Enigma.* Boulder: Westview Press, 1987.

EGYPT

OFFICIAL NAME: Arab Republic of Egypt (Jumhuriyat Misr al-ʿArabiyah)
CAPITAL: Cairo
POPULATION: 63,575,000 (1996 est.)
DATE OF INDEPENDENCE: February 28, 1922 (from the United Kingdom)
DATE OF CURRENT CONSTITUTION: Adopted September 11, 1971
FORM OF GOVERNMENT: Parliamentary democracy
LANGUAGES: Arabic (official), English, French
MONETARY UNIT: Egyptian pound
FISCAL YEAR: July 1–June 30
LEGISLATURE: People's Assembly (Majlis al-Sha'ab)
NUMBER OF CHAMBERS: Two. People's Assembly (Majlis al-Sha'ab); Consultative Assembly (Majlis al-Shura)
NUMBER OF MEMBERS: People's Assembly, 454 (444 elected and 10 presidentially appointed); Consultative Assembly, 258 (172 elected and 86 presidentially appointed)
PERCENTAGE OF WOMEN: People's Assembly, 2.0; Consultative Assembly, —
TERM OF LEGISLATURE: People's Assembly, five years; Consultative Assembly, six years
MOST RECENT LEGISLATIVE ELECTION: November 29 and December 6, 1995
MINIMUM AGE FOR VOTING: 18
MINIMUM AGE FOR MEMBERSHIP: 30
SUFFRAGE: Universal and direct
VOTING: Optional
ADDRESS: Majlis al-Sha'ab, Cairo
TELEPHONE: (202) 354 31 30
FAX: (202) 354 89 77

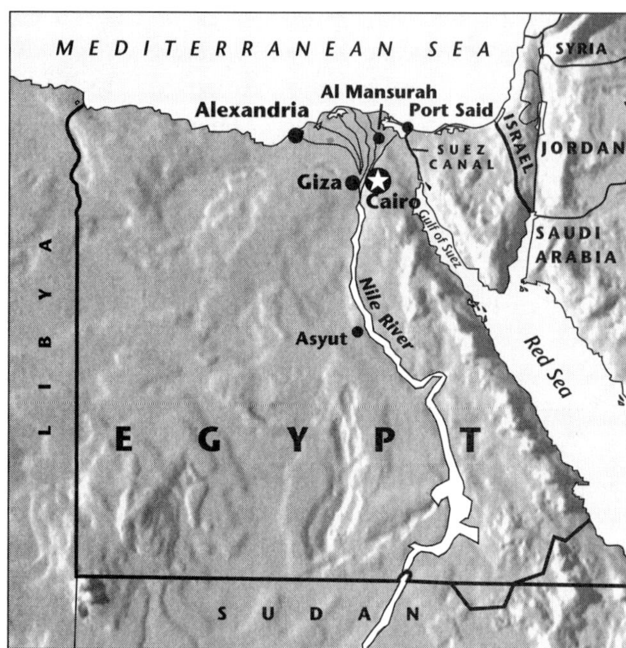

Located in the northeastern corner of Africa, Egypt has been the Arab world's political and cultural leader for most of the twentieth century. Its preeminence reflects the country's strategic location, geographic size, large population, and long history of modernization. The current constitution, adopted in 1971, and its various amendments concentrate power in the presidency. Thus, while the role of the legislature is politically significant, it is circumscribed constitutionally. For instance, the lower house can be dissolved by the president but cannot force the cabinet to resign through a vote of no confidence.

The legislature is divided into a People's Assembly (lower house) and a Consultative Assembly (upper house), but only the People's Assembly plays a truly meaningful role. The function of the Consultative Assembly, created in May 1980 by President Anwar al-Sadat, remains unclear. For example, is it a representative institution (two-thirds of its 258 members are elected, the others being appointed by the president), or is it an advisory organ to the president (its opinions are not binding)? In short, the rules of the political game within which the Egyptian legislature operates favor the executive and in some instances remain poorly delineated.

HISTORICAL BACKGROUND

The first assemblies in modern Egypt—the council established by Napoleon during his short-lived occupation of the country (1798–1801) and the Advisory Council created in 1829 by Muhammad Ali (the founder of the dynasty that ruled Egypt from 1805 until 1952)—were purely consultative bodies that had no legislative powers or executive oversight functions. In 1866 Khedive Ismaʿil—Egypt's hereditary ruler, who nominally was a governor accountable to the Ottoman sultan but was in practice independent—convened an Assembly of Delegates. He intended the Assembly to be a docile gathering of rural notables that would blindly approve his actions, thus helping him diffuse domestic criticism of his profligate expenditures while enhancing his standing with Western creditors. Instead, the Assembly grew increasingly vociferous in its criticism of the khedive, becoming in the late 1870s a focal point for mobilization against him and against Western interference in Egypt's internal affairs. For the first time in Egyptian history, the Assembly provided members of the rural elite with a forum to examine and criticize the policies of the ruler. It enabled them to express publicly their concerns over issues such as taxation and government expenditures. Inspired by both nationalism and economic considerations, the Assembly of Delegates steadily imposed more constitutional constraints on the executive branch. It agitated for greater popular representation and governmental accountability and for mobilization against foreign penetration.

Great Britain's occupation of Egypt in 1882 reversed this trend toward constitutionalism and the restriction of monarchical absolutism. The British contained the Assembly by controlling access to it through property restrictions on voters and by establishing an upper house, the members of which were appointed. In 1919, however, a nationalist uprising broke out, which three years later compelled the British to proclaim Egypt's formal independence, with important restrictions that actually left Britain an important player in Egyptian political life.

In 1923 King Fuad promulgated the country's first constitution, which was a product of negotiations between the three dominant forces in the country at the time: the monarch, the British, and the nationalist movement, represented principally by the Wafd Party. Fearful of the nationalist movement, the British stood by the king in his demands for extensive constitutional powers. Accordingly, the 1923 constitution gave the king the right to appoint the prime minister, dismiss the cabinet, delay legislative sessions, and disband the bicameral legislature (which consisted of a Senate and a Chamber of Deputies). In addition, all bills had to be approved by the king, who was also responsible for appointing the president of the Senate and one-fifth of its members.

Even though the 1923 constitution gave overwhelming power to the king, the latter repeatedly violated its provisions or suspended it (with the tacit or active support of the British) whenever he felt constrained by it. As a result, the Wafd, which originally had condemned the constitution as anti-democratic, came to be its major defender. Still, because of preponderant executive power and continued political manipulation by the British, the Wafd held government for only seven years between 1923 and 1952, even though it was far and away the country's most popular political party.

Executive-legislative relations established during that period are mirrored in contemporary practices. To subordinate parliament to his will, the king utilized not only the constitutional and even unconstitutional methods described previously, but he also rigged elections and created several small, palace-dependent parties to do his bidding in parliament or in the cabinet. He relied on executive patronage to ensure his electoral control over the countryside and on gerrymandering of electoral districts to perpetuate the subordination of the more radical urban centers to conservative rural areas. These abuses of power undermined the credibility of the legislature and gave democracy and parliamentary politics bad names in Egypt. They also eroded support for the political system, which was overthrown by a group of army officers on July 26, 1952. That coup created the regime that rules Egypt today. From 1954 until 1970 the regime was dominated by Gamal Abd al-Nasser.

THE NASSER ERA

A new constitution, adopted in 1956, substituted a presidential for a parliamentary system of government. It made the president responsible for appointing and dismissing ministers. It also established a single political party and empowered that party to approve all candidates for parliament, which was a unicameral National Assembly of 350 members. When these constitutional constraints on parliamentary independence failed to prevent MPs from criticizing executive performance, they were further tightened in the 1964 constitution, which was decreed by the government two weeks before the new parliamentary session was to commence.

The 1964 constitution required that half the members of the National Assembly be workers or peasants. This provision guaranteed executive control over those seats, since "workers" were drawn from the civil service and public sector and thus were more or less nominated by the executive branch, while "peasant" MPs were typically enmeshed in the government rural patronage network and hence beholden to it. In addition, the 1964 constitution stipulated that the president would not be directly elected but would be nominated by the National Assembly and then confirmed in a popular referendum.

These lopsided constitutional arrangements were supplemented by executive practices intended to further subordinate the legislature. Principal among these was the selection of candidates by the ruling party, itself a creature of the executive. The high turnover of deputies was also critical. Then, as now, high turnover results from the executive strategy of rotating political patronage within the ruling party. This enables the executive to derive maximum political control from patronage and to prevent the emergence of a cadre of skilled, experienced parliamentarians.

Still, the legislature proved intermittently feisty in the face of executive power. On occasions, it even was able to force the cabinet to retreat. Such partial successes stemmed primarily from the president's political calculations. By permitting certain constituencies to use parliament to voice their opposition to specific policies, Nasser gained a measure of legitimacy and support for himself and his regime, and he provided a relatively safe outlet for the expression of grievances. In addition, parliamentary criticism of cabinet ministers created a check on the ministers' political ambitions and a means of stimulating and monitoring their performance. Finally, attacks on ministers or their programs in parliament gave Nasser justification for jettisoning these individuals or their policies whenever he needed to do so.

Rivalries within the elite also contributed to parliament's occasional ability to stand up to executive power. During the Nasser era, leftists congregated in the only party, the Arab Socialist Union. Meanwhile, their opponents often relied on the National Assembly to mobilize support for their views. Significantly, the speaker of the Assembly from 1961 to 1969 was Sadat, who was strongly antagonistic to the left and its leadership. Sadat recruited Sayed Marei, a veteran politician and member of parliament during the *ancien regime,* as his deputy speaker. The two skillfully drew upon the material and political resources of the Assembly in their ongoing struggle with the left. Thus factionalism within the elite provided opportunities for the assertion of authority by the legislature.

In the wake of the 1967 Arab-Israeli war, which had significantly weakened the regime, the Assembly managed to circumvent the provision that the Arab Socialist Union screen all candidates to parliamentary seats. As a result, opponents of the left became ensconced in the Assembly, and their interests were served by strengthening the power of the legislature. That the Assembly played a role in the succession struggle that pitted Sadat against leftists is testament to the fact that it managed not only to survive but to prosper in the Nasser era.

NASSER'S SUCCESSORS

Nasser died in September 1970. His successor, Sadat, relied on parliament—the institution within which he had the greatest support—to legitimize and to some extent orchestrate his "Corrective Revolution" of May 1971, which amounted to a purge of his political enemies. Within months a new constitution was adopted. The 1971 constitution remains in force today, though with several amendments. Like the constitution it replaced, the 1971 constitution concentrates power in the presidency. It gives the president the right to rule by decree and to disband the legislature, which was renamed the People's Assembly. In addition, it grants the president extensive powers over legislation and makes him or her responsible for appointing and dismissing ministers and the vice president.

Subsequent events illustrate a recurrent theme in executive-legislative relations in Egypt: parliament asserts itself in times of executive weakness only to be subdued after the executive consolidates power. Having yet to establish fully his personal legitimacy and control of the state apparatus, Sadat remained in a precarious position until the October 1973 Yom Kippur War broke out. In the meantime, the People's Assembly was invigorated by new elections held in November 1971 and by the president's announced intention of creating "a state of institutions."

In its first postelection session (1971–1972), the Assembly considered and passed three times as many bills as it had in its last session (1970–1971). In addition, it rejected more than a quarter of the legislation introduced by the government. Executive oversight, in the form of questions, requests for information, and creation of special and fact finding committees, doubled. The ratio of bills introduced by MPs increased from one in ten to five in ten (although of all bills that passed, those introduced by members rose only from 7 to 18 percent). These data suggest that in the immediate wake of the Corrective Revolution the Assembly was becoming a significant counterbalance to executive authority and was even moving, albeit tentatively, into the domain of lawmaking. In sum, it was leading a political liberalization over which the president had only partial control. Following the October 1973 war, however, the Assembly's influence plummeted as the president brought the process of liberalization under his control and thereafter regulated its direction and progress. After 1973 the number of MP-initiated bills dropped dramatically, as did oversight activities.

Still, the decline of parliament did not trace a straight downward path. Confident that he had consolidated sufficient power to contain serious challenges, Sadat in 1976 embarked on a controlled liberalization that included new parliamentary elections in which candidates did not have to be approved by the Arab Socialist Union. Instead, candidates were allowed to run under the pseudo-party labels of left, center, or right or as independents. From this last category, forty-eight candidates were elected, making them a principal opposition force and inaugurating the conflict between independents and government that has continued through the present. The center, which inherited the structure and executive support of the Arab Socialist Union and which within three years evolved into the National Democratic Party, won four-fifths of the seats. The right won ten seats and the left three.

Sadat, however, soon felt forced to abort his controlled liberalization process. His trip to Jerusalem in November 1977, followed by negotiations that resulted in a peace treaty with Israel in March 1979, stimulated domestic criticism that he was not prepared to tolerate. Beginning in early spring 1978, he steadily tightened the screws on political activity. For criticizing Sadat's policies, several MPs were stripped first of their parliamentary immunity and then of their membership. Furthermore, a newly created party called the New Wafd provoked Sadat's ire, prompting him to push through Parliament Law 33 of 1978, which prohibited political parties "that did not espouse the principles of the July [1952] revolution." In this fashion, Sadat forced the New Wafd to dissolve one hundred days after it had come into existence. A few months later, he similarly rammed through Parliament Law 36 of 1979, which banned all parties that opposed the peace with Israel.

Shortly thereafter, Sadat dissolved the People's Assembly and held new elections. They were contested by four parties: the pro-government National Democratic Party; the left-wing National Progressive Union Party; the Liberal Party (the successor to the right wing of the former Arab Socialist Union); and the Labor Party, which Sadat had brought into existence with the intention of creating a credible "loyal opposition." Also taking part in the elections were some 1,192 independents. The National Democratic Party won an overwhelming 347 seats (200 of which were occupied by newcomers). Since no National Progressive Union Party candidate was elected, the Labor Party, with 29 seats, became the official opposition. Independents, who had been particularly outspoken in their criticism of Sadat, managed to win only 10 seats (in 1976, by comparison, 48 of 897 independent candidates had been elected).

Although Sadat must have believed that such an Assembly would be little more than a rubber stamp for his policies, that did not turn out to be the case. The first task of the new parliament was to ratify various laws that Sadat had decreed prior to the commencement of the session. The constitution states that the president can issue decrees in the absence of the Assembly under "conditions that cannot suffer delay." However, such decrees must then be approved by parliament when it reconvenes. The speaker provided MPs with copies of Sadat's decrees, now embodied in draft legislation, only minutes before they were called upon to vote on them. Several independent and Labor MPs objected, demonstrating thereby that even rigged elections do not guarantee the absolute quiescence of parliament. Sadat refused to brook even this limited criticism. He induced almost half of the Labor MPs to defect to the National Democratic Party, thereby reducing parliamentary opposition to a mere handful of deputies.

Because of his own experience as speaker during the 1960s, Sadat knew that even a weak parliament could be used by opposition forces to further their agenda. This may explain why much of the energy he devoted to domestic politics in the last three years of his life focused on subordinating the People's Assembly to his will. Ultimately, he more or less succeeded in that effort. This strategy, however, left him isolated and contributed to the tense political atmosphere that prevailed until his assassination on October 6, 1981.

Three characteristics of the relationship between the executive branch and parliament that became apparent during the Sadat era have become yet more pronounced under his successor, Hosni Mubarak. The first is that access to parliament is the principal point of contention between the government and opposition. The second is that the political centrality of parliament varies inversely with the degree to which the executive has consolidated power. The final characteristic is that presidential legitimacy is largely a function of the representation of the opposition within parliament: the fewer opposition MPs in parliament, the lower the level of presidential legitimacy.

Mubarak prepared the ground carefully for the 1984 elections, as he has done for subsequent ones in 1987, 1990, and 1995. In the lead up to the 1984 elections, opposition spokespersons (including those for the Wafd Party, which had been brought back to political life by a 1983 decision of the Supreme Constitutional Court) demanded that Egypt's longstanding constituency-based, multimember, simple majority, winner-take-all electoral system be changed to a proportional representation system. With this demand, the opposition unwittingly played into the hands of the executive and leadership of the National Democratic Party. A proportional representation, party-list system was bound to give the National Democratic Party leadership much greater control over candidate selection. It also would prevent independents from even contesting the elections. Not surprisingly, the government accepted the demand and then incorporated into the electoral law additional provisions designed to screen out opposition candidates. One such stipulation was that a party could enter parliament only if it captured a minimum of 8 percent of the vote nationwide.

The 73 percent of the vote won by the National Democratic Party translated into 391 seats, or 87 percent of the total. No independents were elected. Ultimately the courts ruled that the complex and largely unfair formula for distribution of votes had been fraudulently applied in several districts and that those National Democratic Party deputies elected as a result should be unseated. Parliament, however, refused to comply: its speaker, supported by more than four-fifths of the National Democratic Party majority, contested the courts' jurisdiction over the legislative branch. The electoral coalition of the Muslim Brotherhood and the Wafd, which had won fifty-eight seats, became the principal parliamentary opposition and proceeded to use its limited presence to good effect. In the 1984–1985 session, for example, MPs associated with the Wafd–Muslim Brotherhood alliance submitted 22 percent of all bills.

In December 1986 the Supreme Constitutional Court ruled that the electoral law was unconstitutional because it prevented independent candidates from contesting elections. Accordingly, new elections were held the following year. The revised election law passed by the People's Assembly stipulated that independents could compete for one seat in each of the forty-eight districts. That this concession to independents was so limited reflected governmental apprehension about their potential role in parliament. Three years later the Supreme Constitutional Court ruled that this revised electoral law was also unconstitutional, thereby precipitating the 1990 elections, for which the party-list system was abolished.

Despite the constraints of the electoral law, the opposition managed to capture 92 of the 448 seats in the 1987 Assembly. Eight independents (not including those more or less aligned with the National Democratic Party) also won. Still, opposition parties were unable to capitalize on their enhanced position. In 1990 they overplayed their hand when, with the exception of the National Progressive Union Party, they announced that they would boycott the upcoming elections unless supervision was to be conducted directly by the judiciary, as opposed to the Ministry of Interior. After the government refused to give ground, the National Progressive Union Party was the only significant opposition party to contest the elections, and it won a mere six seats. The National Democratic Party, including independents aligned with it, captured 385 seats, or 86 percent of the total. Able to martial at most twenty-five votes on important bills (most of which after 1991 were intended to further constrict political participation), the opposition lost the capacity it previously had enjoyed to utilize parliamentary procedures to embarrass the government and occasionally induce it to change its approach.

The Islamist insurgency that broke out in 1992 raised political tensions to a level with which Egypt's fragile institutions for representation and protection of the rule of law could not cope. Meanwhile, the legal opposition began to regroup. The government responded to this mounting challenge by embarking on a massive crackdown. The thrust of governmental measures was to make no distinction between the legal opposition and the Islamic underground. From 1993 through 1995 the severity of government measures steadily increased. In February 1993, alarmed by the growing influence of the Islamist movement within professional syndicates, the government rammed through parliament the so-called Law to Guarantee Democracy within Professional Syndicates, the impact of which was to place most syndicate elections directly under government control.

In October of that year the government tightened pressure on journalists, amending the Journalists Syndicate law to facilitate state control over all promotions. In March 1994 parliament passed legislation to terminate the century-old practice of electing village mayors and deputy mayors, a step the government apparently deemed necessary because the opposition (especially the Muslim Brotherhood) had performed comparatively well in the 1992 local government elections. Less than a month later, parliament extended the Emergency Law for a further three years, with only twelve dissenting votes being cast. In May 1995 the government forced the legislature to pass in a matter of hours Law 93, which drastically increased penalties on journalists accused of libeling government officials. In the summer of 1995 the government moved to close down human rights organizations in Egypt.

THE 1995 ELECTIONS

The November–December 1995 elections were marred by electoral fraud, administrative interference, and other irregularities. The National Democratic Party took 417 of 444 seats, with opposition parties winning but 14. Only one candidate representing political Islam, a Muslim Brother running as an independent, succeeded in winning a seat. The leader of the opposition became the Wafd Party, with a mere 6 seats. All opposition MP stalwarts had been removed from parliament.

Still, although neither free nor fair, the 1995 elections paradoxically demonstrated that substantial potential exists for a negotiated transition to democracy in Egypt. All legal parties participated actively in the campaign. The Muslim Brotherhood defied government intimidation, its leaders risking lengthy prison sentences, in order for some of its members to contest seats as independents or to run in alliance with the Labor and Liberal Parties. The poor showing of the opposition reflected in part the sharp divisions in its ranks. Rivalry between secularists and Islamists was intense in districts where both fielded candidates. Fierce as well was the competition between candidates who subscribed to opposing economic philosophies, with the Wafd and Liberals endorsing neoliberalism, and the Nasserists and National Progressive Union Party adhering to various versions of Arab socialism. Such competition suggests the maturation of the political system into one in which parties provide voters with choices between reasonably coherent political-economic philosophies.

The government's heavy-handed tactics in the mid-1990s

resulted not only from the threat posed by an Islamic insurgency, which by fall 1995 had been at least temporarily contained. They also stemmed from the ruling elite's concern about the legal opposition, which seeks access to power through the ballot box. The electoral base of the ruling party is fragile and in decline. The strongest organized political tendency in the country is Islamism. Were free and fair elections to be held, the Muslim Brotherhood would very likely win more votes than any other party. The regime, therefore, has felt that it has no choice but to turn its back on democracy and impose its will by physical coercion and by electoral fraud and interference. The resulting popular discontent, however, has contributed to growing public support for political change, which in turn has brought increased political pressure to bear on the ruling party.

The consequences of that pressure manifested themselves during and after the election. The large number of former National Democratic Party stalwarts who contested seats as independents was due in part to their awareness of the unpopularity of the ruling party. Indeed, some 140 candidates running as independents won, with the overwhelming majority of them then joining the NDP bloc in parliament. However, because of its lack of popularity, the NDP has only a limited capacity to enforce discipline among its members in the People's Assembly. This explains why the NDP parliamentary majority has been so critical of the government in areas of "low policy," especially policies connected to service delivery. Far from being a monolithic organization, the NDP is so fragmented that its various factions compete actively against one another, especially in parliament.

In short, extensive electoral abuse in the 1995 parliamentary elections reflected the relative weakness of the ruling party. Electoral irregularities also detracted from the government's legitimacy, thus further weakening it vis-à-vis the opposition. Because the People's Assembly produced by the elections does not accurately reflect public opinion, it cannot legitimize the government. In this context, factionalism within the National Democratic Party will encourage sniping at governmental policies and performance, thereby further weakening both the party and the government. In sum, Egypt in the mid- to late 1990s suggests that elections and parliaments—even when thoroughly subordinate to the executive branch—can propel a transition toward more democratic forms of government.

STRUCTURE AND PROCEDURES OF THE PEOPLE'S ASSEMBLY

The People's Assembly is composed of 454 members, 444 of whom are elected by direct and secret ballot under the supervision of the Ministry of Interior. At least half the members are required to be workers and farmers. Two representatives are elected from each of the 222 constituencies into which the country is divided. The president of the republic appoints 10 members. The term of the Assembly is five years from the date of its first meeting. Elections take place within sixty days of the end of the term.

By law, a member of the Assembly must be an Egyptian, registered on the electoral rolls, at least thirty years old, and literate in Arabic. He or she should have completed military service unless exempted.

The annual session of the People's Assembly lasts seven months, from the second Thursday in November to the end of June. The Assembly is in recess for the next five months but may be reconvened for extraordinary meetings in case of an emergency. The president of the republic cannot dissolve the People's Assembly without issuing a decree suspending the legislature and holding a referendum within thirty days. If the voters approve the dissolution, the presidential decree takes effect. Within sixty days of the dissolution, new elections must be held, and a new Assembly will convene within ten days of the elections.

Law Making

The president of the republic or a member of the Assembly may propose laws. They are called bills in the former case and initiatives in the latter. In practice, all major legislation originates with the executive and is transmitted to the legislature for approval. The speaker refers the bill or initiative to the competent committee for consideration and report. At the committee stage, amendments may be introduced, and each provision is voted upon. Ministers or their representatives often appear in front of the committee or the plenary to defend their proposals. The committee then submits its report to the plenary session, where further amendments may be proposed. Only a simple majority is required for ordinary measures, but in special cases the constitution and the standing orders require a two-thirds majority. On passage, bills are sent to the president of the republic for promulgation in the official newspaper. Every member of the Assembly receives a complete legislative record.

Proposed legislation referred to the People's Assembly often deals with general policies and directions. The ministers are often left to draw up the details and to provide implementation guidelines and standards. These are often issued through executive or ministerial orders and are not subjected to legislative approval.

Committees

The People's Assembly has eighteen standing committees, each charged with the oversight of a particular ministry. Committee membership is allocated by the Assembly Bureau at the commencement of each ordinary session. Each committee examines the constitutionality of bills, their effect on public welfare, and their budgetary impact.

Each committee selects its chair, two deputy chairs, and a secretary from among its members. Committees are allocated professional staff from the Secretariat of Committees. They are also entitled to seek the assistance of hired outside experts.

Beside the all-important function of approving the annual state budget, the People's Assembly monitors the general plan of economic development and exercises control over the executive. The People's Assembly may withdraw confidence in any minister or the prime minister. Ministers are expected to answer interpellations on the floor of the Assembly.

The president of the republic has the right to the executive veto. He or she may refer a bill passed by the People's Assembly back to it within thirty days. If the veto is overridden by a two-thirds majority, it becomes law without the presidential signature.

The speaker is an influential figure in the Egyptian parliamentary system. He or she opens the sessions, presides over them, announces their adjournment, conducts debates, determines the subject of discussion, allots time to individual members, and puts matters to vote and announces the results. The speaker may also call for special committee meetings. A speaker is elected by the People's Assembly at the beginning of every legislative session. There is no limit on the number of times a person may be reelected speaker. All communications between an Assembly committee and the executive or other bodies are conducted through the speaker or according to his or her instructions.

Electoral system

The electoral system is designed to favor the government. Candidates are screened and vetted by the Security Department, which formally certifies their eligibility. Elections are decided by a simple majority, but if no candidate obtains an absolute majority, a second round is held among the four candidates with the greatest number of votes.

Status of members

Members of the Assembly enjoy parliamentary immunities and, except when caught in the act of committing a crime, cannot be subject to criminal prosecution without the consent of the Assembly. Membership may not be revoked except by a two-thirds vote. Members receive a monthly remuneration of seventy-five Egyptian pounds. They also receive free air and rail travel, free medical treatment, and reimbursement of their expenses incurred in the conduct of their legislative duties.

Architecture

The People Assembly building was erected in 1924 under the monarchy. It consists of a main round hall topped by a round, highly ornamented dome. The main hall consists of two floors, each with a balcony. The main entrance to the building is to the south and is ascended by a marble staircase leading to a circular corridor surrounding the main hall. The hall has many annexes, of which the most impressive is the Pharaonic Hall. Another annex is devoted to committee meetings and contains offices of committee staff. Near the Assembly building, a ten-story building constructed under Sadat contains the parliamentary library and computer center.

Abdo Baaklini, Guilain Denoeux, and Robert Springborg

BIBLIOGRAPHY

Ansari, Hamied. *Egypt: The Stalled Society.* Albany: State University of New York Press, 1986.

Binder, Leonard. *In a Moment of Enthusiasm: Political Power and the Second Stratum in Egypt.* Chicago: University of Chicago Press, 1978.

Brown, Nathan, and Roni Amit. "Constitutionalism in Egypt." In *Political Culture and Constitutionalism: A Comparative Approach,* ed. Daniel P. Franklin and Michael J. Baun. London and New York: M. E. Sharpe, 1994.

Cooper, Mark N. *The Transformation of Egypt.* Baltimore: Johns Hopkins University Press, 1982.

Vatikiotis, P. J. *The Modern History of Egypt.* London: Weidenfeld and Nicolson, 1969.

Waterbury, John. *The Egypt of Nasser and Sadat: The Political Economy of Two Regimes.* Princeton: Princeton University Press, 1983.

EL SALVADOR

OFFICIAL NAME: Republic of El Salvador (República de El Salvador)
CAPITAL: San Salvador
POPULATION: 5,829,000 (1996 est.)
DATE OF INDEPENDENCE: September 15, 1821 (from Spain)
DATE OF CURRENT CONSTITUTION: Adopted December 6, 1983; effective December 20, 1983
FORM OF GOVERNMENT: Parliamentary democracy
LANGUAGES: Spanish, Nahua
MONETARY UNIT: Colon
FISCAL YEAR: Calendar year
LEGISLATURE: Legislative Assembly (Asamblea Legislativa)
NUMBER OF CHAMBERS: One
NUMBER OF MEMBERS: 84
PERCENTAGE OF WOMEN: 11.0
TERM OF LEGISLATURE: Three years
MOST RECENT LEGISLATIVE ELECTION: March 16, 1997
MINIMUM AGE FOR VOTING: 18
MINIMUM AGE FOR MEMBERSHIP: 25
SUFFRAGE: Universal and direct
VOTING: Optional
ADDRESS: Palacio Legislativo, Centro de Gobierno, Apartado Postal 2682, San Salvador
TELEPHONE: (503) 271 32 65
FAX: (503) 271 32 69

El Salvador, located in the heart of Central America *(see map, p. 526)*, is a constitutional, multiparty democracy with an executive branch headed by a president, a unicameral Legislative Assembly, and a separate, politically appointed judiciary. The Legislative Assembly is vested with authority by the 1983 constitution (as revised in 1994). The members of the legislature, or deputies, are elected to three-year terms with the possibility of unlimited reelection. Elections are held through secret ballot with universal suffrage for those eighteen years of age and older. The Supreme Electoral Tribunal, comprising five magistrates appointed by the Legislative Assembly, organizes each electoral process.

BACKGROUND

In the nineteenth century the government of El Salvador came increasingly under the influence of landed proprietors as coffee cultivation dominated the economy. For much of the twentieth century the economic elite ruled El Salvador in conjunction with the military. From Gen. Maximiliano Hernández Martínez's 1932 coup until 1980, every president, with the exception of one provisional executive who served four months, was an army officer. Periodic presidential elections were seldom free or fair. El Salvador's social, economic, and political situation reached crisis proportions in the 1970s, as the successive military-led governments had been unable to resolve the problems associated with overpopulation and an inequitable social and economic system. Discontent with the government led to the widespread violence the country endured throughout the 1980s.

El Salvador's civil conflict between a right-wing government and left-leaning guerrilla insurgency further increased the political polarization between the wealthy elite and the impoverished and excluded majority. Despite sincere reform efforts by President José Napoleon Duarte, a moderate elected to a five-year term in 1984, the civil war continued to rage and the nation's economy failed to improve. Duarte's inability to bring about improvements contributed to the victory of the right-wing National Republic Alliance (ARENA) in the 1988 legislative elections and the 1989 presidential election.

Upon his inauguration in June 1989, however, President Alfredo Cristiani called for direct dialogue between the government and the guerrillas. In 1990, following a request from the governments of Central America, the United Nations became involved in an effort to mediate between the two sides, eventually leading to a formal end to the conflict.

On January 16, 1992, after twelve years of civil conflict, the government and the Farabundo Martí National Liberation Front (FMLN) guerrilla movement signed a peace agreement in Mexico City. The agreement, the Accords of Chapultepec, established a two-year timetable for implementing certain elements of the peace accords, including the demobilization of the Salvadoran military and guerrilla forces and the holding of national elections.

The 1994 elections, referred to as the "elections of the century," were an important element in El Salvador's transition toward democracy. Although ARENA kept both the presidency and a working majority in the Legislative Assembly, the FMLN—participating for the first time as a political party—garnered enough votes to become the main opposition party.

PARTIES AND ELECTIONS

Based on the most recent population census, the Supreme Electoral Tribunal establishes the number of deputies to be elected in each of the fourteen departments of El Salvador. Deputies are elected by proportional representation in closed party-list voting using a national and departmental list procedure.

The department with the largest population (San Salvador) is entitled to sixteen legislative representatives, whereas the least populated department (Cabañas) has three representatives. The number of deputies elected from the national list is fixed at twenty. In the elections of March 1997, eighty-four deputies were elected to serve in the legislature: twenty correspond to the national list and sixty-four correspond to the fourteen departments.

There are no special elections to fill vacancies. Alternate candidates, equal in number to the directly elected members, are chosen during the national balloting. To be elected, a candidate must be Salvadoran by birth, child of a Salvadoran mother or father, and twenty-five years of age. Those who have served in high-profile public positions (for example, the president or vice president of the republic or Supreme Court justice) within the past three months, government contractors, and near relatives of the president of the republic may not serve in the Assembly.

Thirteen political parties participated in the March 1997 legislative and municipal elections, the second nationwide balloting since the end of the country's civil conflict. ARENA captured twenty-eight of the eighty-four legislative seats (a loss of eleven seats from the elections of 1994), and the FMLN secured twenty-seven seats (a gain of six). The far-right National Conciliation Party captured eleven seats, while the Christian Democrats slipped from third to fourth place, with ten seats. The remaining seats were filled by the Social Christian Renovation Party, the Unity Movement, the Democratic Party, Democratic Convergence, and the Liberal Democratic Party.

PARLIAMENTARY PROCEEDINGS

The Legislative Assembly of the Republic of El Salvador is located in a large, eight-story building in downtown San Salvador near the Supreme Court of Justice and several buildings of the executive branch. The Assembly convenes on May 1 of every election year and does not have an official recess. Extraordinary sessions may be called by the ruling body *(Junta Directiva)* of the Assembly.

Every session begins with the verification of a quorum—a simple majority of the deputies—after which the session is declared open by the president of the Assembly. Thereafter, discussion, approval, or modification of the order of the day is commenced in the plenary.

Legislative proposals may be introduced by any member of the Assembly and by the executive branch. The Supreme Court of Justice and municipal councils may also introduce legislative proposals related to matters within their jurisdiction. Any amendment to the constitution is considered solely within the Assembly. The proposal may only be introduced by at least ten deputies. To be passed into law, the amendment must be approved by a two-thirds majority vote.

All proposed bills are presented to the Junta Directiva of the Assembly before being introduced to the plenary. After the bill is introduced, it is delegated to the appropriate committee for its consideration. All legislative proposals must be presented to the appropriate committee for analysis unless the full Assembly agrees by a simple majority vote that the matter requires urgent consideration.

The appropriate committee analyzes the bill, deliberates, and renders a recommendation. All recommendations must be approved by an absolute majority of the members of the committee. Although there is no time limit in which the committee must submit its opinion to the full Assembly, each committee must submit a quarterly report to the plenary listing the total number of bills it has pending and the number of recommendations it has delivered.

The recommendations of the committee usually fall within one of four categories: in favor; not in favor; recommend; or reject. Once the committee has issued its recommendation, it sends the bill and recommendation back to the plenary, where the proposal is discussed and either approved or rejected. The full Assembly may vote against the committee's decision, with a simple majority. The Assembly, however, rarely votes against a committee's recommendations, since committee members usually follow party lines.

If a bill passes the Assembly with a simple majority, the Junta Directiva is required to send the bill to the president of the republic within ten days for his or her consideration. The president has fifteen days to approve or reject the bill. The president may also send the bill back to the Assembly with objections that do not merit a veto. The Assembly will either accept or reject the president's suggestions and return the bill to the president, which he or she is obligated to ratify and publish into law.

If the bill is vetoed, it must be sent back to the Assembly with an explanation. The Assembly may override the president's veto upon a two-thirds majority vote. If the Assembly succeeds in doing so, the president must promulgate and publish the law within eight days. If no action is taken by the president in the time allotted, the Assembly may publish the law. A bill is not considered a law until it has been published in the *Official Diary.*

If the president of El Salvador receives a bill that he or she considers to be unconstitutional, the bill is presented to the Supreme Court for its consideration. The Supreme Court must rule on the bill's legality within fifteen days of its submission. If the court rules that the bill is constitutional, the president must immediately sign the bill into law.

The annual budget is prepared by the Council of Ministers (comprising the president and vice president of the republic and cabinet members). The council presents the budget to the Assembly at least three months before the end of the fiscal year. The proposal is sent to the Budget and Finance Committee of the Assembly for review and comment before being considered by the plenary.

According to the constitution, the legislature may declare by an absolute majority vote the president or vice president of the country, the Supreme Court justices, or any other public officials chosen by the Assembly to be mentally or physically incapable of performing their duties. The declaration must be supported by an ad hoc committee of five medical specialists appointed by the full Assembly.

ORGANIZATION AND STRUCTURE

The president and members of the Junta Directiva are elected by a simple majority on the opening day of a new Assembly. The Junta Directiva, the governing body of the Assembly, comprises the president of the legislature, four vice presidents, and five secretaries. The Junta regulates the day-to-day activities of the Assembly.

The legislature is currently divided into fourteen working committees. Other committees may be created upon a two-thirds majority vote of the Assembly. Ad hoc committees may be created to address specific temporary issues. The Junta Directiva assigns an unspecified number of deputies to each committee based on each individual's area of expertise and party affiliation—the committees proportionally reflect the political parties represented in the full Assembly. Each committee elects its own president, delegate, and secretary.

On May 1, 1997, upon the opening of the new Assembly, members of the Junta Directiva and the legislative committees were selected quite differently from previous years. Since the March elections had failed to produce an absolute majority, the FMLN and ARENA signed a postelection agreement in an effort to avoid complications in assembling the legislature. In the pact, both parties agreed not to occupy the presidency of the Assembly, leaving the office to one of the minor parties.

Discussions over the selection of a new president, however, proved to be more difficult than either side had anticipated, causing ARENA to take back its offer. Two days after the official opening of the Assembly, an ARENA candidate was chosen by the full Assembly. All political parties, however, reached an agreement that added an eleventh position to the Junta Directiva and allowed the minor parties to fill the top position on six of the fourteen working committees.

Deputies are allowed to form political alliances within the Assembly, which are generally based on party affiliation. Each alliance is provided with an office and the necessary material and monetary resources for its effective operation.

The members of the Assembly, as representatives of the public and dignitaries of the nation, enjoy complete immunity (except under extreme circumstances) and may not be accused of crimes based on opinions expressed while exercising their functions. In 1997 the remuneration of the deputies was 21,000 colons, or approximately $2,400, per month.

Amy J. Standefer

BIBLIOGRAPHY

Dunkerley, James. *The Long War: Dictatorship and Revolution in El Salvador.* Rev. ed. New York: Routledge Chapman and Hall, 1985.

Haggerty, Richard A., ed. *El Salvador: A Country Study.* Area Handbook Series. Washington, D.C.: U.S. Government Printing Office, 1990.

Russell, Philip L. *El Salvador In Crisis.* Austin, Texas: Colorado River Press, 1984.

EQUATORIAL GUINEA

OFFICIAL NAME: Republic of Equatorial Guinea (República de Guinea Ecuatorial)
CAPITAL: Malabo
POPULATION: 431,000 (1996 est.)
DATE OF INDEPENDENCE: October 12, 1968 (from Spain)
DATE OF CURRENT CONSTITUTION: Approved November 17, 1991
FORM OF GOVERNMENT: Dictatorship
LANGUAGES: Spanish (official), Fang, Bubi, Ibo
MONETARY UNIT: CFA franc
FISCAL YEAR: April 1–March 31
LEGISLATURE: House of Representatives of the People (Cámara de Representantes del Pueblo)
NUMBER OF CHAMBERS: One
NUMBER OF MEMBERS: 80
PERCENTAGE OF WOMEN: 8.8
TERM OF PARLIAMENT: Five years
MOST RECENT LEGISLATIVE ELECTION: November 21, 1993
MINIMUM AGE FOR VOTING: 18
MINIMUM AGE FOR MEMBERSHIP: 45
SUFFRAGE: Universal and direct
VOTING: Compulsory

ADDRESS: B.P. 51, Malabo
TELEPHONE: (240 9) 21 22
FAX: —

Equatorial Guinea, located in western Africa and bordering the Atlantic Ocean, is the only Spanish-speaking black African state (*see map, p. 261*). Despite a new constitution, which restored the House of Representatives to legislative prominence, Equatorial Guinea continues to be a dictatorship under Teodoro Obiang Nguema Mbasogo. The ruling party controls sixty-eight of the eighty seats in the legislature, which functions as a rubber stamp.

George Thomas Kurian

ERITREA

OFFICIAL NAME: State of Eritrea
CAPITAL: Asmara
POPULATION: 3,910,000 (1996 est.)
DATE OF INDEPENDENCE: May 27, 1993 (from Ethiopia)
DATE OF CURRENT CONSTITUTION: May 19, 1993 (provisional)
FORM OF GOVERNMENT: Transitional
LANGUAGES: Tigre, Arabic
MONETARY UNIT: Ethiopian birr
FISCAL YEAR: Calendar year
LEGISLATURE: National Assembly (Hagerawai Baito)
NUMBER OF CHAMBERS: One
NUMBER OF MEMBERS: 150
PERCENTAGE OF WOMEN: —
TERM OF PARLIAMENT: Four years
MOST RECENT LEGISLATIVE ELECTION: February 1, 1994
MINIMUM AGE FOR VOTING: —
MINIMUM AGE FOR MEMBERSHIP: —
SUFFRAGE: —
VOTING: —
ADDRESS: National Assembly, P.O. Box 242, Asmara
TELEPHONE: (291 1) 11 97 01
FAX: (291 1) 12 51 23

Eritrea, bordering the Red Sea in east Africa and one of the world's newest nations (*see map, p. 234*), became independent in 1993 on the conclusion of a civil war in the former Ethiopian province of the same name. A transitional government took power on independence, and it gave itself four years to draft a formal constitution and establish the foundations of a democratic state.

The basis of the transitional government is Decree No. 37, which defines the powers of the transitional government as well as the interim National Assembly, which will perform legislative functions pending free elections. The National Assembly consists of the Central Committee of the People's Front for Democracy and Justice (PFDJ), thirty members from the provincial assemblies, and thirty members (of whom ten are women) nominated by the PFDJ Central Committee. The functions of the National Assembly are purely nominal and include election of the president, approval of the budget, and confirmation of presidential appointments. The National Assembly holds regular sessions every six months under the chairmanship of the president. A draft constitution was tabled in July 1996.

George Thomas Kurian

ESTONIA

OFFICIAL NAME: Republic of Estonia (Eesti Vabariik)
CAPITAL: Tallinn
POPULATION: 1,459,000 (1996 est.)
DATE OF INDEPENDENCE: Declared August 20, 1991 (from the Soviet Union)
DATE OF CURRENT CONSTITUTION: Adopted June 28, 1992; effective July 4, 1992
FORM OF GOVERNMENT: Parliamentary democracy
LANGUAGES: Estonian (official), Latvian, Lithuanian, Russian
MONETARY UNIT: Kroon
FISCAL YEAR: Calendar year
LEGISLATURE: State Assembly (Riigikogu)
NUMBER OF CHAMBERS: One
NUMBER OF MEMBERS: 101
PERCENTAGE OF WOMEN: 12.9
TERM OF PARLIAMENT: Four years
MOST RECENT LEGISLATIVE ELECTION: March 5, 1995
MINIMUM AGE FOR VOTING: 18
MINIMUM AGE FOR MEMBERSHIP: 21
SUFFRAGE: Universal and direct
VOTING: Optional
ADDRESS: Riigikogu, Lossi plats 1A, EE 0100 Tallinn
TELEPHONE: (372 6) 316 331
FAX: (372 6) 316 394

Located on the Baltic Sea between Sweden and Russia *(see map, p. 421)*, Estonia is a parliamentary democracy founded August 20, 1991. The president is head of state and the prime minister is head of government.

HISTORICAL BACKGROUND

After centuries of domination by Germans, Poles, Swedes, and Russians, an independent Estonia was established during the Russian Revolution and was officially recognized by the Russian-German treaty of Brest-Litovsk on March 3, 1918. It was also recognized by the major Western states and joined the League of Nations in 1921.

Estonia adopted three constitutions in the interwar period. The first democratic constitution, of June 1918, was followed by the authoritarian constitution of March 1934. The second constitution created a legal framework for the dictatorship of Konstantin Pats. In 1938 a new constitution introduced a presidential system and established a bicameral parliament.

Estonia survived as an independent political entity until 1940, when, under Russian tutelage, the Estonian Soviet Socialist Republic was proclaimed. Estonia remained within the Soviet federation until October 1989, when the Congress of the Estonian Popular Front voted to restore Estonian independence. In November 1989 the Estonian Supreme Soviet annulled its predecessor's 1940 decision to join the Soviet Union. After some attempts by the Soviet government to invalidate this declaration on the basis of its alleged violation of the Soviet constitution of 1977, the independence of Estonia was finally recognized in August 1991 by several European countries and on September 6 by the State Council of the Soviet Union.

THE CONSTITUTION

Shortly after declaring its independence, Estonia initiated work on a new constitution. The Constituent Assembly, a sixty-member commission, was formed to prepare a draft. It was composed of thirty members of the Supreme Council (the former Soviet-established parliament) and thirty members of the Congress of Estonia (an interim, independent quasiparliament).

The Constituent Assembly considered four drafts and discussed the possibility of using the 1938 constitution of Estonia as the model for a new basic law. As in other republics of the former Soviet Union, the drafters focused on two major problems: the limits of presidential power and the method of electing the president. After the initial rejection of two drafts, which clearly favored the presidential system, the Constituent Assembly took up the proposal of the Estonian National Independence Party to reactivate the 1938 constitution and considered two new drafts, one prepared by former Estonian minister of justice Juri Raidla and the other prepared by the drafting committee of the Assembly, led by Juri Adams. The 1938 constitution, the model favored by the Assembly, provided for election of the president by parliament.

The Assembly compromised, however, under pressure from that portion of the population favoring direct election of the president by the people. It was decided that the first president would be popularly elected, but successors would be elected by parliament. The Constituent Assembly clearly favored a parliamentary system. In the end, all drafts proposing a strong presidential power, including the draft based on the 1938 constitution, were rejected. The Assembly introduced to the electorate a modified draft by Adams that envisaged Estonia as a parliamentary republic. The draft constitution was adopted by a national referendum on June 28, 1992. Approximately two-thirds of eligible voters voted, and more than 91 percent accepted the draft. The constitution, the first adopted by a former Soviet republic, took effect July 4, 1992.

Presidential elections

The constitutional rules on presidential elections are complicated. The Law on Presidential Elections, adopted April 10, 1995, provides for three possible rounds of elections in the State Assembly *(Riigikogu)*, a 101-member unicameral parliament, and two rounds in the Electoral Assembly. Candidates for the office of president can be nominated by at least one-fifth of the deputies of the State Assembly. The candidates must be at least forty years old and Estonian citizens by birth. To be elected in one of the first three rounds, a candidate must receive two-thirds of the votes of all State Assembly deputies. If the president is not elected in the first round, new candidates may be nominated for the second round. In the third round, only the two leading candidates will remain. If neither candidate receives two-thirds of the total number of votes, a fourth round is held within one month by the Electoral Assembly, which consists of members of the State Assembly and representatives of local governments. The two candidates who participated in the third round in the State Assembly can be joined at this stage by other candidates nominated by at least twenty-one members of the Electoral Assembly. To be elected in the fourth round, a candidate requires the support of a majority of the members of the Electoral Assembly. If a president is not elected in the fourth round, the fifth round, held the same day, will elect the president with a plurality of votes.

The president is elected for a five-year term, cannot serve for more than two terms, and must relinquish any affiliation with political groups. The Constituent Assembly decided that the term of the first popularly elected president would be four years.

Legislative elections

The constitution vests supreme legislative power in the State Assembly. The law on election provides for two tiers, both based on a proportional system. The lower tier comprises twelve multimember districts with seats allocated pursuant to the Hare formula. To win a seat in parliament, it is necessary to get a one quota (quota = votes / seats). The upper tier comprises one nationwide multimember district with seats allocated pursuant to the d'Hondt system, which is a highest-average system favoring large parties. The threshold for parties to introduce representatives to parliament is 5 percent.

All citizens who are at least eighteen years old and not disqualified by a court decision have the right to vote. Citizens who are twenty-one years old and have the right to vote are eligible to run for the Assembly.

Parties may present only a single list of candidates. Candidates presented on the district lists for the first tier must be included on the national list. A party is not required to meet the 5 percent threshold requirement for the national list if three of its candidates gain seats in the territorial districts. A deputy is not bound by instructions from his or her constituency and cannot hold any other governmental position.

Presidential powers

The president, as the head of state, has functions typical of presidents in western European parliamentary republics. Notably, the president plays the role of arbiter in interparty disputes and represents the state in international relations.

Within limits, the president performs legislative functions. The president has the right to initiate constitutional amendments and issue decrees. Presidential decrees cannot, however, affect the constitution or any laws implementing the constitution. Decrees may be issued only if the State Assembly cannot convene, and they must be cosigned by the chair of the State Assembly and the prime minister and submitted to parliament for approval or rejection in a timely manner. The president may delay the promulgation of laws for fourteen days if he or she requests reconsideration of a statute or asks the National Court to review its constitutionality. If the State Assembly reaffirms a law returned for reconsideration, or if the National Court rules that it is constitutional, the president must promulgate the law.

ELECTIONS OF 1992

Presidential prerogatives remained a hot issue during the legislative and presidential elections held on September 20, 1992. Direct presidential elections did not result in a majority of votes for any of the four participating candidates. As a result, the next round of elections was held in the State Assembly. Two candidates ran in the second round of elections: Arnold Rüütel, leader of the Secure Home Alliance and chair of the former parliament (the Supreme Council), and Lennart Meri, a former minister of foreign affairs who was supported by Fatherland, the leading party. Meri was elected president of Estonia by a vote of 59 to 31. In October the president nominated a coalition government led by Prime Minister Mart Laar.

The relationship between the president, parliament, and the coalition government deteriorated soon after the constitution took effect. As a result, on May 5, 1993, the State Assembly passed a law regulating relations between the president and parliament. Under the law the National Court is empowered to supervise the president and parliament. For example, if the issue is whether the president should sign a law and the court finds that the law is contrary to the constitution, the president must abide by the decision of the court. In the beginning of 1994 the relationship between the president and the government deteriorated further when President Meri attempted to block the governmental reshuffling recommended by the prime minister. During several sessions, the Assembly debated whether the vagueness of the constitutional provisions on presidential powers would require the adoption of a new law "On the Order of the Work of the President."

The tensions led to the early dissolution of the Assembly and the new elections held on March 5, 1995. The election brought victory to the left-of-center Coalition and Rural People's Union, an alliance comprising the Estonian Coalition Party, led by former prime minister Tiit Vahi, and the Estonian Rural People's Party, led by Arnold Rüütel. The alliance won 32 percent of the vote, which translated to 41 of the 101 seats in parliament. On April 5 the Assembly approved Vahi's nomination as prime minister.

The parliamentary elections were followed by the presidential race, which concluded on the fifth ballot in the electoral college in September 1996. By a 372 to 206 vote, the incumbent president, Lennart Meri, was chosen for a second term, which was to run five years.

THE LAW ON CITIZENSHIP

Russians comprise some 40 percent of the population. There are 475,000 Russians in Estonia in a total population of 1.5 million, and the "Russian question" is still at the forefront of Estonia's politics. Relations between Estonians and Russians have been strained.

On February 28, 1992, the Estonian parliament enacted the Law on Citizenship, which denied the Russian-speaking minority automatic citizenship and the right to vote. According to the law, Estonian citizenship is granted only to those who were citizens prior to June 16, 1940, to their direct descendants, and to those who provide particularly valuable service to the state.

Many in the Russian-speaking minority were denied the opportunity to vote in the parliamentary and presidential elections of September 1992. And the Estonian language requirements imposed by the law made it difficult for Russian speakers to become naturalized, jeopardizing their voting rights indefinitely. A new citizenship law, adopted January 19, 1995, increased the obligatory period of residence required before one could apply for naturalization from three years to six. Applicants also must pass a language examination and show adequate knowledge about the country and its constitution. The requirements of this law have caused consternation within the Russian-speaking community and provoked human rights monitoring groups to comment that Estonia cannot create a modern democratic country without addressing the Russian question.

ORGANIZATION AND OPERATIONS OF THE STATE ASSEMBLY

The Assembly is clearly the predominant power in Estonia. The regulations of the Assembly—the Law on the State Assembly Standing Orders and the Law on State Assembly Procedure—have the status of law. The Assembly adopts laws, elects the president, authorizes referendums, ratifies and denounces foreign treaties, authorizes the candidate for prime minister to form the government, and makes major governmental appointments. Additionally, the Assembly has the power to appoint, on the proposal of the president, the chair of the National Court and the power to appoint, on the proposal of the chair, the members of the National Court.

In Estonia, members of the Assembly may form factions of at least six members. Parties are policy-making bodies, not strictly legislative structures. For this reason, they are not commonly mentioned in constitutions. They implement their political goals through factions, which are important organizational units of parliament. Usually, all party members combine to establish a faction, although some smaller parties may not be allowed to form a faction and, as a result, may have little impact on the legislative process. For this reason, members of smaller parties may form factions that are not necessarily party oriented. Each member may belong only to one faction. Affiliations of members are decided by the faction. A member may resign from a faction by application or by the decision of the faction. Each faction that is registered in the board of the Assembly elects its own chair and vice chair. Factions larger than twelve members may have more than one vice chair. Factions have the right to initiate laws and resolutions.

Members of the State Assembly are immune from criminal prosecution unless the prosecution is proposed by the legal chancellor and a majority of the members of the Assembly approve. The authority of a member terminates upon a criminal conviction. Members are not obliged to serve in the national defense forces.

Parliament is in session from the second Monday of January through the third Thursday of June, and from the second Monday of September through the third Thursday of December. Extraordinary sessions of parliament may be called by the president of the republic, the government, or at least one-fifth of the members of parliament.

If parliament fails to select a prime minister, the president may dissolve parliament and declare a new election. Parliament will dissolve after four failed attempts to form a government. The president must declare early elections if a referendum held on the decision of parliament fails. Additionally, the president may, on the proposal of the government, declare early elections after a no-confidence vote.

THE LEGISLATIVE PROCESS

Initiation of laws may be proposed by members of the Assembly, its factions, committees, or the government of the republic. The president or one-fifth of the deputies may propose constitutional amendments. Majority approval by the members of parliament on two separate votes is required to change the constitution. Amendments may also be made through referendums, but three-fifths of the members of parliament must first approve the initiative.

Bills, resolutions, and other legislative matters are considered by the standing committees. Their jurisdiction is provided by the Assembly's standing orders. Ad hoc supervisory committees may also be formed to monitor the executive structures.

The first reading of a draft law is not followed by a vote if the committee responsible for the draft consents and if other factions have not submitted proposals to reject the bill. After a second reading, amendments may be presented by a faction or by a standing committee. A proposal to subject a draft to a third reading may be made by the committee that drafted it, a faction, or a member of the Assembly. During the third reading, only one authorized representative of each faction or the standing committee may make comments.

With a few exceptions, all legal acts of the Assembly require a simple majority of affirmative votes from those deputies present. The adoption of more important laws, listed in the constitution, requires the vote of the majority of all deputies. These laws concern citizenship; elections; the State Assembly Standing Orders and Procedure in the State Assembly; remuneration of the president and deputies; the government; court proceedings against the president and members of the government; cultural autonomy for minorities; the state budget and state control laws; court structures and procedures; foreign and domestic loans; state financial obligations; states of emergency; and peacetime and wartime national defense.

The president may, within fourteen days, refuse to proclaim a law adopted by parliament and send it back for debate and decision, along with his or her reasons for rejecting it. If parliament readopts the law, the president must proclaim it a law or propose to the National Court that the law is unconstitutional. If the National Court deems the law constitutional, the president must proclaim it a law.

The legal chancellor is charged with monitoring whether legal acts of the Assembly are in accordance with the constitution. If the chancellor decides the regulations or laws completely or partially contradict the constitution, he or she will propose that the Assembly bring the law or regulation within the boundaries of constitutionality within twenty days. If such action is not taken by the Assembly, the chancellor will propose to the National Court that the regulation or law be declared null and void.

Some legislative procedural mechanisms were borrowed from the French constitutional model. For example, the government can attach confidence to a particular bill; it may stake its life on a particular bill. If the Assembly rejects the draft, the government will resign. In France, a motion of confidence fails if it does not receive a majority of the total membership of parliament, not just a majority of those present. The rationale of this provision is that if the motion of confidence passes, the bill passes without the separate vote. This consequence is not clearly provided, however, in the Estonian constitution; it seems to deprive the whole mechanism of its original rationale.

The Assembly has the authority to adopt the state budget and approve the report on its implementation. The Assembly approves a budget for all state incomes and expenditures for each year, following a draft budget submitted by the government. If parliament fails to approve a budget within two months of the beginning of the budget year, the president may call special elections.

Several features of the procedure for selecting the government appear to be borrowed from the German Basic Law. The president nominates a candidate for prime minister, who is expected to submit an "exposé," a proposal outlining the basics of forming the future government, to parliament within fourteen days. If two successive candidates for prime minister fail to form a government or fail to obtain parliament's approval for their exposés, the right to submit a candidate for prime minister reverts to parliament.

Article 90 of the Estonian constitution provides that the president can change the members of the government at the suggestion of the prime minister. The interpretation of this article led to clashes between President Meri, who claims that the final decision to change the composition of the government is vested in the president, and Prime Minister Laar, who maintains that the president exceeds his constitutional prerogatives by changing the government.

The legal chancellor (ombudsman) investigates violations of constitutional rights and liberties and oversees the constitutionality and legality of legislative and executive actions. The president is constitutionally liable and can be held criminally liable on a motion of the legal chancellor and upon the decision of a majority of the members of the State Assembly. In turn, the chancellor can be charged with a legal offense on the proposal of the president, with the consent of the State Assembly. The legal chancellor is an independent official, appointed for seven years by the Assembly, upon the recommendation of the president.

Parliament may vote the government down in a no-confidence action by a resolution carried by a majority vote of the Assembly. The vote may be initiated by one-fifth of the members through a written motion. In response to a no-confidence vote, the president has, at the suggestion of the government, the option of dissolving parliament and holding a new election. The right to dissolve parliament in times of governmental crisis seems to give the Estonian president a somewhat stronger position than that enjoyed by presidents in other Baltic states.

Members of parliament have the constitutional right to interpellate the government, its members, and various other officials. The member must be answered within twenty session days. Members of parliament may also be interpellated. A member cannot refuse to respond. If necessary, a closed-door session of the Assembly may be called to deal with the interpellation.

THE JUDICIAL SYSTEM

The court system comprises rural and city courts, district courts, and the National Court. The National Court appears to have the power of judicial enforcement of constitutional provisions. The constitution provides that all courts, in the course of their proceedings, should refrain from applying laws or legal measures if they are in conflict with the constitution. The power to invalidate unconstitutional legal acts is vested in the Constitutional Review Chamber, a division of the National Court.

In the fall of 1994 the Supreme Court, which had been established during the Soviet era, was liquidated and a new twelve-member National Court became fully operational.

The court immediately issued an important decision invalidating as unconstitutional two local autonomy referendums in the provinces of Narva and Sillamae.

Rett R. Ludwikowski

BIBLIOGRAPHY

Blaustein, Albert P., and Gisbert H. Flanz, eds. "Constitution of Estonia of June 28, 1992." In *Constitutions of the Countries of the World*. Dobbs Ferry, N.Y.: Oceana Publications, 1994.

Commission on Security and Cooperation in Europe. "Human Rights and Democratization in Estonia." Washington, D.C.: Commission on Security and Cooperation in Europe, 1993.

Dawisha, Karen. *Eastern Europe, Gorbachev, and Reform: The Great Challenge*. 2d ed. Cambridge: Cambridge University Press, 1990.

Ludwikowski, Rett. "Constitution Making in the Countries of Former Soviet Dominance: Current Development." *Georgia Journal of International and Comparative Law* 23 (1993): 155–267.

———. "Searching for a New Constitutional Model for East-Central Europe." *Syracuse Journal of International Law and Commerce* 17 (spring 1991): 91–170.

ETHIOPIA

OFFICIAL NAME: Federal Democratic Republic of Ethiopia
CAPITAL: Addis Ababa
POPULATION: 57,172,000 (1996 est.)
DATE OF INDEPENDENCE: Independent for at least 2,000 years
DATE OF CURRENT CONSTITUTION: Adopted December 8, 1994
FORM OF GOVERNMENT: Transitional parliamentary democracy
LANGUAGE: Amharic (official), Tigrinya, Orominga, and others
MONETARY UNIT: Birr
FISCAL YEAR: July 8–July 7
LEGISLATURE: Parliament
NUMBER OF CHAMBERS: Two. House of People's Representatives (Yehizib Twekayoch Mekir Ena); House of Federation (Yefedereshn Mekir Bet)
NUMBER OF MEMBERS: House of People's Representatives, 550 (directly elected); House of Federation, 120 (either directly or indirectly elected)
PERCENTAGE OF WOMEN: House of People's Representatives, 2.0; House of Federation, —
TERM OF LEGISLATURE: Five years
MOST RECENT LEGISLATIVE ELECTION: May 7 and June 18, 1995
MINIMUM AGE FOR VOTING: 18
MINIMUM AGE FOR MEMBERSHIP: 21
SUFFRAGE: Universal
VOTING: Optional
ADDRESS: Parliament, P.O. Box 80001, Addis Ababa
TELEPHONE: (251 1) 55 30 00
FAX: (251 1) 55 09 00

In June 1995 Ethiopia, an ancient country situated in northeastern Africa, completed a four-year transition from a Marxist military regime to a federal republic of ethnic states functioning according to nominally democratic procedures. The constitution of the new Federal Democratic Republic of Ethiopia (adopted by a Constituent Assembly on December 8, 1994) established a bicameral legislature that includes a directly elected lower house, the House of People's Representatives, and an upper house representing the country's various ethnic groups (or "nations, nationalities, and peoples" in the language of the constitution), called the House of Federation. This legislature embodies an unusual approach to nation building in which ethnic groups (or "nations, nationalities, and peoples") form the fundamental building blocks of a federal state. Significant rights and privileges are explicitly accorded to these constituent nations, including the right to secede from the federation.

The first elections to the lower house were held amidst controversy, boycotts, and complaints of harassment of the opposition. The governing coalition, the Ethiopian People's Revolutionary Democratic Front, won a substantial victory, gaining 90 percent of the seats.

HISTORICAL BACKGROUND

Some trace the origin of the Ethiopian kingdom to the liaison in 1000 B.C. of King Solomon and the queen of Sheba, who is viewed traditionally as an Ethiopian queen. Early Ethiopian rulers established the kingdom of Aksum, which flourished in what is now the Tigray region in northern Ethiopia from the first to the seventh centuries A.D. Until the revolution of 1974, direct descent from King Solomon was an important source of prestige and authority for Ethiopian monarchs. Equally important was the sense among Ethiopians of their status as a chosen people who had been selected to safeguard the Ark of the Covenant after it was taken from Jerusalem. Others, however, point to a more recent starting point for Ethiopia's national identity:

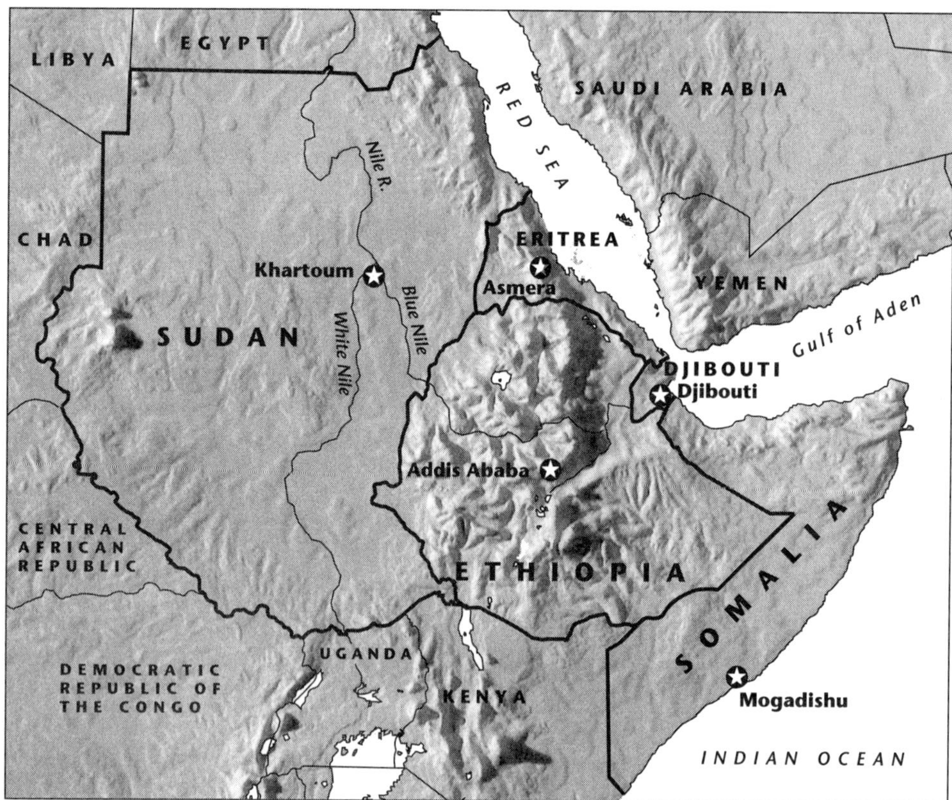

the late-nineteenth-century conquest of the lands and peoples to the south, east, and west of the traditional Ethiopian highland kingdom.

About A.D. 330 Emperor Ezena converted to Christianity, making Ethiopia one of the world's oldest Christian centers. The country's Orthodox (Coptic) Church has since been an important source of culture, tradition, and, through a belief in the divine sanction of the emperor, political authority. Today, the Christian and Muslim populations of Ethiopia are roughly equal in number, but until recently Islam remained on the margins culturally and politically.

Despite Ethiopia's strong imperial and religious traditions, much of the country's history has been marked by power struggles between the imperial center and regional principalities, particularly those in the northern portion of the country. The vast land mass of highland Ethiopia, crisscrossed by canyons and mountain ranges, made central authority difficult to impose. It was not until the reign of Emperor Tewodros (1855–1868), who modernized the army and the imperial bureaucracy, that a centralized state began to emerge. Tewodros and his successor, Yohannes, brought many of the northern principalities under tighter imperial control. Expansion to the south, east, and west was to follow under Yohannes's successor, Menelik II. Menelik conducted a series of military campaigns that by 1897 had expanded the country to its present borders. In so doing, he conquered a wide range of different peoples, creating the ethnic mosaic that is a distinctive feature of modern Ethiopia. Many of these areas were administered by northern military leaders (the *neftegna,* or "gun carriers") who established feudal control over the conquered lands.

Virtually alone among countries on the African continent, Ethiopia escaped European colonialism relatively unscathed. During "the scramble for Africa" in the late nineteenth century, Italy conquered and colonized the coastal territory of Eritrea. However, in 1896 at the battle of Adowa, just south of Eritrea, the Ethiopian army routed the invading Italians and thus secured protection for Ethiopia from further European incursion. The Italians returned during World War II, occupying the country from 1935 to 1941, until British and Ethiopian troops liberated all of Ethiopia, including Eritrea. In 1952, under a United Nations accord, Eritrea was federated with Ethiopia. A decade later Emperor Haile Selassie abrogated this agreement and annexed the region, igniting a thirty-year separatist insurgency led by the Eritrean People's Liberation Front (EPLF).

Haile Selassie, who ruled from 1930 to 1974, was the last emperor of Ethiopia. He succeeded in preserving Ethiopia's territorial and political integrity throughout the Italian occupation and decades of internal strife. In so doing, he brought Ethiopia to prominence on the world scene, symbolized by the location of the headquarters of the Organization of African Unity in Addis Ababa in commemoration of the country's long history as an independent African state.

BREAKUP OF THE FEDERATION AND TRANSITIONAL GOVERNMENT

Haile Selassie was less successful in bringing the feudal empire in step with the modern world. Although he presided over substantial achievements in strengthening education, he ignored concerns about the country's exploitative land tenure system and the corrupt, nepotistic imperial administration. Toward the end of his reign, Haile Selassie lost the allegiance of the intellectual community, which grew increasingly socialist in orientation—as did, eventually, the military. After he failed to respond to a massive famine in northern Ethiopia, the emperor was deposed, in September 1974, by rebel officers, who quickly formed the Armed Forces Coordinating Committee (known commonly as the Dergue, the Amharic word for "committee") to administer the country. In December of that year Ethiopia was declared a socialist state and Mengistu Haile-Mariam eventually emerged as the de facto head of state, as chair of the Provisional Military Government of Socialist Ethiopia.

Shortly after the revolution several opposition fronts began challenging the Dergue, some demanding civilian rule and democracy within a unified Ethiopia, while others called for the independence of particular regions of the country. In response, the government initiated an antiopposition campaign, the "Red Terror," which over several years killed tens of thousands of Ethiopians and drove thousands more into exile. Other repressive policies—such as the forced relocation of villages, collectivization of farms, nationalization of property, and aggressive military recruitment—strengthened resistance and fueled separatist movements in several parts of the country.

Of the several separatist or liberation movements, the strongest by the 1980s were the Eritrean People's Liberation Front and the Tigrayan People's Liberation Front (TPLF). Noting their separate evolution and the abrogation of the confederal arrangement mandated by the United Nations, Eritreans argued that they had no legal ties to Ethiopia. The TPLF also fought initially for independence from the repressive central state.

Despite massive military support from the Soviet Union, the Dergue army failed to suppress the rebellions, and eventually a demoralized army conceded Eritrea and Tigray regions. Anticipating defeat, Mengistu fled to Zimbabwe in May 1991, allowing the TPLF (which had now joined with rebel Amhara and Oromo groups to form the Ethiopian People's Revolutionary Democratic Front, EPRDF) to march toward the capital with little resistance. An eleventh-hour agreement brokered by the United States laid the framework for the peaceable entry of the revolutionary armies into Addis Ababa and established the terms for a transition to democracy in Ethiopia and independence for Eritrea.

The EPRDF began Ethiopia's transition to multiparty politics by organizing a relatively broad-based national conference held in Addis Ababa in July 1991. Attending the conference were more than twenty political and ethnic organizations from throughout the country. Some political organizations were excluded, however, including certain rival rebel factions and organizations associated with the Dergue regime. These groups remain outside and opposed to the transition process, mostly operating from exile. The national conference adopted a transitional charter and established an eighty-seven-member House of People's Representatives to oversee the transition period. The House elected TPLF leader Meles Zenawi as president of the transitional government.

During the transition period, the EPRDF initiated a process to convert Ethiopia to a federation of ethnic states. The internal map of the country was redrawn to establish new boundaries between areas occupied by the major ethnic groups, and some power was devolved to regional administrations. The language of various regional groups replaced Amhara in schools and in local courts. The policy of ethnic federalism has many critics in Ethiopia, but EPRDF officials argued that under all previous regimes ethnic groups had been forced militarily into living together and that only a voluntary union could endure. This concept of voluntary participation in the state has been incorporated into the constitution in a controversial article that accords all nationalities the right of self-determination up to and including secession. In May 1993, following a UN-supervised referendum, Eritrea became an independent state.

The first step in the transitional government's program to democratize the country and to devolve power to the regions was a series of regional and local elections that took place in June 1992. Five days before the election, several major opposition parties withdrew, alleging electoral irregularities and intimidation from EPRDF soldiers. A second source of concern was the expansion of the EPRDF coalition through the creation of roughly twenty new parties representing different ethnic groups. The boycotting parties also withdrew from the House of People's Representatives, beginning a protracted impasse in multiparty politics in Ethiopia. Major opposition parties have boycotted the two subsequent elections—for the Constituent Assembly in June 1994 and for the lower house of the federal legislature in May and June of 1995.

CONSTITUTIONAL PROVISIONS FOR PARLIAMENT

The constitution establishes a parliamentary system of government with two legislative chambers. The prime minister is the head of government. Ethiopia's president has mostly ceremonial functions.

The House of People's Representatives is the principal legislative body with "the power of legislation in all matters assigned by the constitution to federal jurisdiction." Most representatives are elected in single-member districts by plurality vote, for five-year terms. An additional group of no fewer than twenty members represent minority ethnic groups and are elected in special minority districts. The constitution stipulates that the House shall not exceed 550 members.

While it remains to be seen how the legislature will function in practice, it nominally has broad legislative power over federal matters and issues that involve more than one state, such as interstate commerce. Article 54 of the constitution declares that the representatives are to "represent the Ethiopian Peoples as a whole" and that members may lose their mandate of representation "upon loss of confidence by the electorate." This clause appears to refer not only to the possibility that a representative could be voted out of office at the end of the five-year term but also that a recall process could be invoked to remove a representative during his or her term. There is no specification in law yet about how this loss of confidence would be determined. Regarding immunity, the constitution stipulates that members shall not be charged with a crime without the permission of the House and that no administrative action may be taken against a member on account of statements made in Parliament.

The House also has power of legislation over, among other things, electoral laws and procedures; national defense and public security; international agreements; declarations of war and states of emergency; social and economic development; fiscal and monetary policy; and federal taxes and the federal budget. In addition, it approves the appointments of federal judges and other officials.

The constitution stipulates that the House will have one annual session from September to June. It may adjourn for one month of recess during its annual session. During recess, the speaker or a majority of its members may call a meeting. The two offices established by the constitution—speaker and deputy speaker—are elected by the House.

The government of Ethiopia is formed from the leading party or coalition in the House. The prime minister is elected by the House from among its members. The prime minister submits for approval by the House nominees for ministerial posts, who do not need to be members of the House.

The House of People's Representatives has the right "to call and to question" the prime minister, other ministers, and other federal officials to ensure that executive responsibilities are being adequately performed. Article 60 states that the president may invite political parties to form a new coalition government if a previous coalition loses its majority in the House and is dissolved. It is not clear whether this provision would allow for votes of no confidence against the prime minister or the government. The prime minister, with the House's consent, has the right to dissolve the House before its term expires. Again, it is not clear in what circumstances the prime minister would wish to dissolve the House and in what circumstances the House would consent.

The House of People's Representatives is also responsible for nominating the president of the republic, although the president is elected by a two-thirds vote of a joint session of the two parliamentary chambers. The president serves a six-year term.

Both the House of People's Representatives and the Council of Ministers have the right to initiate laws, although in the special cases of the declaration of war and the declaration of a state of emergency, the initiative is reserved for the executive. Laws are adopted by majority vote of members present. The presence of more than half the members constitutes a quorum. Laws adopted by the House are submitted to the president, who must sign them within fifteen days, after which time they take effect without the president's signature.

The House of People's Representatives formed nine standing committees during its first session, from October 1995 to June 1996. The committees cover the following jurisdictions: economic affairs, budget, social affairs, defense and security, foreign affairs, parliamentary administration, legal affairs, women's affairs, and culture and communication. Committee consideration of draft laws is a mandatory stage in the legislative process. Several committees have conducted public hearings on draft legislation. The majority coalition appoints the chair and secretary of each committee and also determines members' committee assignments. Of the 546 sitting members, 120 currently serve on a committee.

The second chamber of the legislative branch, the House of Federation, is composed of representatives of Ethiopia's "nations, nationalities, and peoples." A nation, nationality, or people is defined in the constitution as "a group of people who have or share a large measure of a common culture, or similar customs, mutual intelligibility of language, belief in a common or related identities, and who predominantly inhabit an identifiable contiguous territory." There are approximately eighty recognized nations in Ethiopia. Each is represented in the House of Federation by one representative, and each has an additional representative for each million people in its population. The election of House of Federation members is directed by the respective state councils, which may elect them directly or may hold general elections. Members of the House of Federation serve five-year terms and enjoy the same immunities as members of the House of People's Representatives.

The principal function of the House of Federation is to interpret the constitution and to mediate disputes among states. In addition, it determines how federal and state tax revenues are allotted to the states. In its power of constitutional interpretation, the House of Federation is assisted by recommendations from a Council of Constitutional Inquiry, a body of legal experts led by the president and vice president of the Supreme Court.

The constitution also states that the House of Federation "shall decide on claims based upon the right of nations, nationalities and peoples to self-determination, including their right to secession." This provision does not mean that the House has the last word on secession claims. The constitution elsewhere specifies the requirements for seceding from the country: a two-thirds vote in the legislative council of the "nation" and a majority vote in a popular referendum.

There are two joint functions requiring both the House of Federation and the House of People's Representatives. As mentioned previously, the president of the republic is elected by a joint session of the two chambers. The constitution also specifies that, on the initiative of the House of People's Representatives, a joint session may be called "to take appropriate measures when State authorities are unable to arrest violations of human rights."

Both houses meet in a parliamentary building constructed during the reign of Emperor Haile Selassie. The building is known as "Sedist Kilo," a reference to the distance (six kilometers) from Parliament to the emperor's palace.

RESULTS OF THE 1995 PARLIAMENTARY ELECTIONS

Elections were conducted on May 7, 1995, for the House of People's Representatives in most regions of the country. In some areas, elections were delayed for logistical and administrative reasons until June 18. The EPRDF coalition won 493 of the seats. The coalition consists of twenty-nine parties, the most important of which are the Tigray People's Democratic Organization (182 seats) and the Amhara Nation's Democratic Movement (144 seats). In addition thirteen independent parties won a total of 45 seats, and eight independent candidates were also elected. On August 21 the House of People's Representatives elected Meles Zenawi, who had been president of the transition government, as prime minister. Dr. Negasso Gidada was elected president.

The election results reflect the fact that substantial political competition within the framework of the new constitution has not yet developed in Ethiopia. The country hosts a large number of political parties; however, almost all of these parties belong to one of two groups: those that belong to or support the EPRDF coalition and those that reject the constitution, oppose the EPRDF-directed transition, and boycott elections. More than 90 percent of the parties in Ethiopia are associated with, and are named for, individual ethnic groups.

Kevin Johnson

BIBLIOGRAPHY

Harbeson, John. *The Ethiopian Transformation: The Quest for the Post-Imperial State.* Boulder, Colo.: Westview Press, 1988.

Zewde, Bahru. *History of Modern Ethiopia.* Addis Ababa: Addis Ababa University Press, 1991.

FIJI

OFFICIAL NAME: Republic of Fiji (Kai Vakarairai ni Fiji)
CAPITAL: Suva
POPULATION: 782,000 (1996 est.)
DATE OF INDEPENDENCE: October 10, 1970 (from the United Kingdom)
DATE OF CURRENT CONSTITUTION: Promulgated July 25, 1990
FORM OF GOVERNMENT: Parliamentary democracy
LANGUAGES: English (official), Fijian, Hindustani
MONETARY UNIT: Fijian dollar
FISCAL YEAR: Calendar year
LEGISLATURE: Parliament
NUMBER OF CHAMBERS: Two. House of Representatives (Vale); Senate (Seniti)
NUMBER OF MEMBERS: House of Representatives, 70; Senate, 34
PERCENTAGE OF WOMEN: House of Representatives, 4.3; Senate, 8.8
TERM OF LEGISLATURE: House of Representatives, five years; Senate, four years
MOST RECENT LEGISLATIVE ELECTION: House of Representatives, February 18–25, 1994; Senate, nonelective
MINIMUM AGE FOR VOTING: 21
MINIMUM AGE FOR MEMBERSHIP: 21
SUFFRAGE: Universal
VOTING: Compulsory
ADDRESS: Parliament Chambers, Government Buildings, P.O. Box 2352, Suva
TELEPHONE: (679) 30 58 11
FAX: (679) 30 53 25

The Republic of Fiji comprises more than eight hundred islands, of which about one hundred are inhabited, located about 1,200 miles south of the equator in the Pacific Ocean. From 1874 to 1970 it was a British possession.

The 1990 Fijian constitution declares Fiji to be a sovereign democratic republic. It elevates as the supreme arbiter of the nation the Great Council of Chiefs (Bose Levu Vakaturaga), a traditional body of some seventy members comprising the hereditary chiefs of every Fijian clan. The Great Council appoints the president and selects the twenty-four Fijian nominees to the Senate.

Legislative power is vested in the bicameral Parliament, comprising a nominated Senate and an elected House of Representatives. The term of the House is five years. The Senate has thirty-four members appointed by the president for four-year terms. Of these, twenty-four are ethnic Fijians nominated by the Great Council, one is a Rotuman (inhabitant of the island of Rotuma) appointed on the advice of the Rotuma Island Council, and nine are appointed by the president to represent minority ethnic groups, of whom East Indians are the most numerous. The Senate is a house of review with some power to initiate nonfiscal legislation. The Senate is the principal bulwark of protection for ethnic Fijians, and its consent is indispensable for any bill dealing with ethnic Fijian interests, especially land, customs, and traditions.

The House of Representatives has seventy elected representatives, who elect the speaker and deputy speaker from outside the membership. Voting is conducted on communal lines, but suffrage is universal for all citizens over twenty-one. In general elections, ethnic Fijians vote in five single-member urban constituencies and fourteen rural constituencies to elect thirty-seven representatives in all. There are twenty-seven seats on the East Indian electoral roll, one for Rotumans, and five general electoral seats for other races. Elections are administered by an independent supervisor of elections, and constituency boundaries are demarcated by the independent Boundaries Commission.

George Thomas Kurian

FINLAND

OFFICIAL NAME: Republic of Finland (Finnish, Suomen Tasavalta; Swedish, Republiken Finland)
CAPITAL: Helsinki
POPULATION: 5,105,000 (1996 est.)
DATE OF INDEPENDENCE: Declared December 6, 1917
DATE OF CURRENT CONSTITUTION: Adopted July 17, 1919
FORM OF GOVERNMENT: Parliamentary democracy
LANGUAGES: Finnish (official), Swedish (official)
MONETARY UNIT: Markka
FISCAL YEAR: Calendar year
LEGISLATURE: Parliament (Finnish, Eduskunta; Swedish, Riksdag)
NUMBER OF CHAMBERS: One
NUMBER OF MEMBERS: 200
PERCENTAGE OF WOMEN: 33.5
TERM OF LEGISLATURE: Four years
MOST RECENT LEGISLATIVE ELECTION: March 19–20,1995
MINIMUM AGE FOR VOTING: 18
MINIMUM AGE FOR MEMBERSHIP: 18
SUFFRAGE: Universal and direct
VOTING: Optional
ADDRESS: Parliament, 00102 Helsinki
TELEPHONE: (358 0) 43 21
FAX: (358 0) 432 35 60

The Republic of Finland is a parliamentary democracy situated in northeastern Europe *(see map, p. 639)*. Legislative power is shared by the president of the republic and the unicameral Parliament of two hundred members elected by universal suffrage. Headed by the prime minister, the Council of State, or cabinet, is responsible for the country's general administration. The president is head of state.

HISTORICAL BACKGROUND

From about the twelfth century to 1809, Finland was an "eastern province" of the Swedish empire. In 1362 Finns were granted the right for the first time to send a representative to participate in the election of the Swedish king; the political rights of the eastern province were officially recognized. In the fifteenth and especially the sixteenth centuries the political power of the Swedish government became increasingly centralized. This trend became even stronger in the 1600s, culminating in the 1670s when steps were taken toward uniform legislation, taxation, and administration for the Swedish empire. The domination of the Roman Catholic Church was terminated during the sixteenth century by the Lutheran Reformation, and considerable advances occurred in the eastern province, including the beginning of a written Finnish language. With passage of the act regulating the first Diet in Sweden and the Government Act of 1634, Finland was represented centrally as part of Sweden. Provincial assemblies were held, however, when matters of great importance to Finland were under discussion.

The first order of Parliament was promulgated in 1617 and is still considered one of the bases of the constitutional laws of Finland. During the latter part of the seventeenth century, tensions arose in the Swedish empire between the monarchy and the Parliament, and the idea of national unity was strengthened. General dissatisfaction with the power of Parliament and the monarchy led to constitutional changes in 1772 and 1789. The new constitutions formed a basis for the Grand Duchy of Finland, as Finland was called beginning in 1809 when it was ceded to Russia.

When the four estates (nobility, clergy, burghers, and peasants) of Finland convened in March 1809, after the occupation by Russia, they acted in accordance with the Swedish tradition. The Russian emperor considered the estates to be the official representatives of the Finnish nation (the relationship with Russia was partly one of subordination, partly a personal union for the Russian emperor). After the Crimean War (1853–1856) a lively public debate began in Finland over demands for new legislation. For the first time since 1809, a new Diet was held in Finland in 1863, and it began to reform the legislation. Hardly any field of law remained untouched by the extensive, and often revolutionary, reforms carried out. One reform, adopted in 1906, was the most radical in Europe at that time: the right to vote became universal and women obtained full suffrage and the right to stand in parliamentary elections. Finally, the system of the four estates was abolished, and a unicameral system was established. The current Parliament (*Eduskunta* in Finnish; *Riksdag* in Swedish) held its first session on May 23, 1907.

After the October Revolution of 1917 in Russia, Finland began the process of separation from Russia. On December 6, 1917, Parliament declared Finland's independence, which was recognized by Russia on January 4, 1918. After the ensuing civil war in 1918, a constitutional debate began, and it ended on July 17, 1919, with the signing of the Constitution Act. The constitution was a compromise between the monarchical and republican traditions because it called for a separation of powers and provided the president of Finland with substantial power in legislation, administration, and official appointments.

CONSTITUTIONAL PROVISIONS

The central constitutional provision for Parliament, set down in the Constitution Act of 1919, states: "Sovereign power in Finland shall belong to the people represented by their representatives assembled in Parliament." This statement contains two significant premises: the source of all political power is the people, and the power of the people is exercised by Parliament in session. Parliament, which is unicameral, is therefore at the center of the Finnish political system. The power of Parliament is based on and limited by law and thus contingent on rules and regulations. The most important of these are contained in the Constitution Act of 1919 and the Parliament Act of 1928.

Since the promulgation of those acts, constitutional amendments have extended the election term to four years (1954), gradually lowered the voting age to eighteen (1944, 1976), and shifted the power to end a parliamentary session before "dissolution elections" from the president to Parliament (1987). These amendments have made the constitution more specific and complete, but the status of the jurisdiction of Parliament has not been amended significantly since the constitution's enactment.

Finland's membership in the European Union, which became effective in 1995, will not be mentioned in the Constitution Act and will not change Finland's status as an independent and sovereign state. Some adjustments will be made to the Parliament Act, however, to reflect the de facto changes in the mutual relationships of the governmental organs resulting from European Union membership. The most important statement will be that the Council of State shall inform the speaker of Parliament of any proposal that has come to its notice for an act, agreement, or other measure to be decided by the European Union. The speaker shall then submit the information to the Grand Committee, through which all legislative proposals must pass except the budget, and to one or more specialized committees which shall deliver an opinion on the matter. The Speaker's Council also may take up a matter for debate in a plenary sitting, but Parliament shall make no decision on the matter.

ELECTIONS AND PARTIES

Elections for the two hundred members of Parliament are held every four years at the same time throughout the country. The president of the republic may, however, order new elections before the regular mandate period has expired if he or she deems it necessary. For elections, which are direct and proportional, the country is divided into a minimum of twelve and a maximum of eighteen electoral districts. The elections are conducted according to the d'Hondt system in which candidates receive a certain number of the votes in relation to the total number of votes cast for the party they are representing. For example, the most successful candidate is allotted the equivalent of the total number of votes for the party, the second candidate is allotted half of that number, the third a third of the number, and so on. The final order of all candidates is then based on these figures.

Every Finnish citizen who is at least eighteen on the day before the election has the right to vote, regardless of his or her place of residence, unless convicted of certain improper acts related to voting. Every citizen who is entitled to vote also may be elected as a representative. The chancellor of justice, the assistant chancellor of justice, a member of the Supreme Court or of the Supreme Administrative Court, the parliamentary ombudsman, the assistant parliamentary ombudsman, and soldiers cannot be representatives, however.

Members of Parliament must be elected from registered parties. The parties compile their lists based on the candidates who have been elected in local election districts. Frequently, different parties establish election alliances and run the same candidates for Parliament. This arrangement is usually for tactical reasons because smaller parties and "nonparties" have a better chance of getting their candidates elected in this way.

In Finland the custom of forming governments based on a majority of the parliamentary votes, on the one hand, has made the political opposition weak. On the other hand, the majority governments have been vulnerable to diverging opinions. This has led to many parliamentary crises in which governments have resigned, especially from the 1940s through 1980. In recent years the parties have been better able to cooperate, and during the 1980s and 1990s the same governments usually have functioned throughout a particular parliamentary term.

Parliamentary and party discipline to some extent depend on each other since party discipline is required for the general functioning of Parliament. This implies that members of Parliament are not obliged to adhere to the opinions of those who elected them. Much more important is members' loyalty to their parties and parliamentary groups, since it is there that most of the parliamentary attitudes are molded. Voting by members in the plenary sessions largely follows the preliminary decisions of the party groups. Both individual and group discipline are therefore important for the functioning of Parliament despite the lack of any specific laws on this form of discipline. The only legislation concerning these questions is that requiring representatives to abide by the law.

The distinction between the majority and the opposition

may at times become unclear depending on the importance of the decision, party discipline, and the regional interests of different members. The major part of the work of Parliament, however, follows the division between the opposition and the majority. In the legislative election held in March 1995, the Social Democrats won the election with fifteen new mandates in Parliament for a total of sixty-three mandates. The Center Party captured forty-four seats, National Coalition thirty-nine seats, Leftist Alliance twenty-two seats, Swedish People's Party twelve seats, Green League nine seats, Christian League seven seats, Progressive Finnish Party two seats, Rural Party and Ecology Party one seat each. The voter turnout was 71.1 percent, a normal figure.

ORGANIZATION AND OPERATION OF PARLIAMENT

Parliament is organized to carry out various levels of decision-making and preparatory work. Parliament as decision maker is the plenary session.

Sessions

Each parliamentary term begins on February 2 (or the next workday) and continues with or without interruption until the next regular session. The annual calendar of Parliament is divided into spring and autumn sessions, with recesses usually held in the summer and in December–January, depending on the number of questions Parliament has to handle in each term. Public sessions of Parliament are held on Tuesdays at 2:00 p.m. and on Fridays at 11:00 a.m.

The president of the republic has the right to call extraordinary sessions of Parliament if specific questions demand, but this presidential right has been used only on four occasions (the last in 1932).

Leadership

On the first day of the yearly parliamentary session Parliament elects by closed ballot from among its members a speaker and two deputy speakers to serve for the year. In the unofficial state hierarchy, the speaker is the second in command to the president of the republic. (This is reminiscent of Finland's days as a grand duchy under the Russian empire.) The speaker chairs the plenary sessions, decides on the agenda, and indicates when the sessions start and end. The speaker also oversees the legality of the procedures of Parliament. For example, if the speaker regards some items on the agenda as contradictory to some legislation, he or she may refuse to allow the plenary session to discuss the items. These refusals are not rare; between 1907 and 1977 on 831 occasions speakers disallowed discussion of an item in the plenary session. When forming new governments after parliamentary elections, the president of the republic is obliged to consult the speaker about the parliamentary basis before following the necessary procedures to form a new government.

Although the formal supervision of parliamentary sessions belongs to the speaker alone, in practice a Speaker's Council is available for assistance, which usually is given in the speaker's preparatory work. The main task of the council is to plan and manage the work of Parliament. The council consists of the speaker, the two deputy speakers, and the chairs of all the committees. Customarily, the chairs of the committees are chosen from as many parties as possible in order to create proportionality among the political groups in Parliament.

Debates

Members wishing to question the government by addressing an interpellation to the government must submit it to the speaker, who presents it to Parliament and then places it on the table until the next session. This form of interpellation must be supported by a minimum of twenty members. The member of the government receiving the interpellation must respond to it within fifteen days. The plenary session then votes on whether the answer is satisfactory and on whether the member of the government has Parliament's confidence. "Questions" are the second kind of interpellation, in which a member of Parliament may ask a member of the Council of State about a matter. (The Council of State shares power with the president of the republic and is composed of the ministers heading the branches of government administration.) Members of the Council of State have thirty days in which to deliver their answers. There is no debate or voting in the plenary session on this type of interpellation, as its purpose is usually to obtain information from the government and draw attention to an important matter. For the third kind of interpellation—oral questions—a member, in plenary session, may directly ask a member of the government short questions. This form of interpellation comes close to ordinary parliamentary debates.

In the plenary sessions members are given opportunities to express their opinions in a general discussion. The speaker also may allow a member to reply to a matter prior to speeches if a request to have the floor has been made. In a speech of reply, a member of Parliament is permitted only to clarify or correct someone's speech. If the member deviates from the subject, the speaker of Parliament reminds the member of this. If this does not help, the speaker forbids the member to continue. It is recommended that members speak no longer than fifteen minutes; in an official presentation or a speech on behalf of a parliamentary group, the maximum is thirty minutes.

Debates frequently are closed with a vote, the outcome

of which is indicated on a voting board. Ballot voting is used for matters concerning individuals and in resolving ties. Parliamentary voting procedure calls for a yes or no vote on two alternatives. The speaker of Parliament decides which alternatives will be put to a vote, and the plenary session approves or disapproves the suggestion. The debate in parliamentary sessions is recorded electronically and also is partly transcribed in shorthand. It also is published in the Finnish and Swedish languages and distributed regularly. Members may speak in either Finnish or Swedish since, constitutionally, Finland is a bilingual country.

Committees

The opinion of Parliament takes shape in the committees. The positions and tasks of parliamentary committees have remained the same since 1906. The Grand Committee, which holds a special position, was established to take the place of the second chamber that is found in many parliaments. The Grand Committee has twenty-five members. In addition to the Grand Committee, the following permanent committees are mentioned in the Parliament Act: Constitutional, Legal, Foreign Affairs, and Finance. The Constitutional, Legal, and Foreign Affairs Committees shall have no fewer than seventeen members. The Finance Committee is to have no fewer than twenty-one members. Other permanent committees are: Administration, Transport and Communications, Agriculture and Forestry, Defense, Culture, Social Affairs and Health, Economy, Labor Affairs, and Environment. They shall have no less than seventeen members. Parliament may appoint a temporary committee for the preparation of a specific matter. A temporary committee has a minimum of eleven members. The members of committees are appointed for a whole parliamentary term (four years), and they convene unofficial sessions usually one to four times a week.

In their work on proposed legislation, reports, statements regarding bills, and petitionary motions, committees question experts and other committees. Each matter coming before a permanent committee is taken up in two stages. In the first stage the committee makes a preliminary decision on the content of the matter; in the second stage the committee makes the final decision about the matter based on a final draft of a report or a statement.

The Grand Committee handles all bills proposed by the other committees and formulates necessary amendments to the proposed bills. The Grand Committee also takes into account any political compromises necessary for its work. The Grand Committee and the committees that report to it handle any matters dealing with Finland's membership in the European Union that fall within the purview of Parliament.

Parliament and the media

The work of Parliament is carried out in both official and unofficial sessions. Committee meetings, where most of the actual work of Parliament is undertaken, are unofficial and cannot be broadcast live. The plenary sessions, held on Tuesdays and Fridays, are public and are televised and broadcast on radio if important questions are being discussed. The government's question hour, held on the first Thursday of each month, is broadcast on television and radio. About one hundred accredited correspondents are permanently assigned to cover the operations and decisions of Parliament. About thirty of these correspondents are in Parliament every day.

LAW MAKING

The Constitution Act of 1919 grants to Parliament the power to approve laws, while the power to ratify them is bestowed on the president of the republic. Legislation may be introduced by a member of Parliament or the president of the republic, although the Council of State actually drafts all bills of the government.

In Finland the legal norms are on different hierarchical levels. Constitutional laws and ordinary laws are passed by Parliament; decrees are issued by the president of the republic; and decisions are made by the Council of State. The statutes at a level lower than acts of Parliament are, in general, stipulations about the enactment of laws, or they are based on legislative power delegated by Parliament.

To pass, legislative laws (constitutional acts, ordinary acts) must proceed through three readings. After a bill has been handled in the plenary session as a submission debate, it goes to a special committee, which discusses the proposed bill, hears experts on its subject matter, and makes a report. The first reading of the bill then takes place in Parliament as a general debate. Next, the proposed bill is passed to the Grand Committee, which may amend the proposal presented by the special committee. The report by the Grand Committee is the basis for the second reading, in which the plenary session decides on the content of the bill. If the proposal by the Grand Committee is approved as such, the second reading ends. But if there are further amendments, the plenary session sends the proposal back to the Grand Committee. In the third reading of the proposed bill, the plenary session can no longer amend the proposal; it can decide only whether to approve or reject the bill. Generally, a simple majority is required either to approve or reject a legislative bill in the third reading. Approval of special legislation such as tax laws requires a two-thirds majority.

At the end of the process, constitutional acts follow a slightly different procedure: a law may be approved at a third reading by a simple majority and then left in abeyance until the first regular session following an election, where it must be approved by a two-thirds majority. Alternatively, it may first be declared urgent by a five-sixths majority and then approved by a two-thirds majority at the same reading; it is not left in abeyance until after the election. Whatever the case, it must be stated explicitly that a law has been enacted in accordance with the procedure for enactment of a constitutional law.

The president of the republic has the right to veto bills passed by Parliament. In such a case, the law is returned to Parliament and if Parliament approves it again, thus overriding the president's veto, the bill becomes law without the president's signature.

Private bills

Bills proposed by members of Parliament take three forms: a legislative motion that contains a proposal, put into the form of law, for amendments to and specifications of existing laws; a money matter motion that contains proposals to include certain appropriations in the state budget; and a petitionary motion that contains a proposal that Parliament present its petition to the government so that it will undertake certain measures. These kinds of bills, in practice, are unlikely to be approved by Parliament since most of the legislation approved is initiated by the government.

Budget bills

Parliament approves all taxation and appropriations measures. A permanent taxation law requires a two-thirds majority, whereas temporary taxation laws, to be in force no longer than a year, require only a simple majority. State revenues are used to finance, for example, education, health care, road construction, and defense.

Each year the government proposes a new budget. At the first reading in Parliament, the minister of finance opens the general discussion by providing an outline of the main parts of the budget. The leaders of each political group of Parliament then make general political statements for or against the proposed budget. After the first reading the budget is passed on to the Finance Committee, which is divided into sessions because of the large number of budget items to be discussed in detail. Experts on taxes and finance also are heard at this stage of the process. After the sessions have discussed and analyzed the proposed budget, the Finance Committee takes over and discusses the budget in detail, possibly calling in more experts. The Finance Committee finishes by producing a proposal for the plenary session that includes all amendments and corrections to the budget. At the next, and last, reading in the plenary session a general discussion is opened by the chair of the Finance Committee, who explains the changes and compares the amended budget proposal with the first one presented by the government. In the detailed discussion that follows, members of Parliament may put forth changes in the proposal by the Finance Committee. If changes are approved by Parliament, the revised revenues or expenditures are returned to the Finance Committee, which provides a statement about the changes, either approving or rejecting the proposals. If the proposals are approved, a vote is not required, but if they are rejected, the plenary session decides on the final form of the budget. Changes seldom are made in the plenary session, however, because the government usually is supported by a majority of Parliament's votes and therefore presents a budget proposal that has been approved beforehand.

If, once the budget has been approved, changes are absolutely necessary, a supplementary budget may be submitted to Parliament for approval. In recent years supplementary budgets have been submitted three to five times annually.

Emergency powers

Two kinds of emergency powers apply to Finnish legislation. First, the general rights bestowed by law on the citizens of Finland may not prevent the prescribing by law of any restrictions that are necessary in time of war or rebellion. Second, restrictions may be prescribed for persons in the military service at any time. These emergency powers may be handled the same way as ordinary laws. The Finnish constitution specifies that the government is not to receive any exceptional emergency powers since these always are handled by Parliament.

MEMBERS OF PARLIAMENT

The Parliament Act of 1928 specifies that members of Parliament are obliged to obey the law and the constitution. No other regulations are binding.

Members of Parliament may not be charged or deprived of their liberty because of any opinion they expressed in a parliamentary session. A member of Parliament may, however, be prosecuted for a criminal offense if a court has passed sentence or if he or she was caught perpetrating a criminal offense punishable by a minimum of six months' imprisonment. If a member is arrested for some other reason, Parliament may set the member free. The principle behind this immunity is to enable members to execute their mandate without unnecessary disturbances. If a member has been sentenced to prison for a deliberate crime, Parliament may investigate whether he or she should be permitted to continue as a member of Parliament. If the nature of the crime is such that the member does not deserve the confidence and respect due the position of member of Parliament, the Parliament, through a decision supported by at least a two-thirds majority, may terminate the member's mandate. This has happened once, in 1993.

By law, a member of Parliament receives an annual salary that is seven salary categories below that of a member of the government. These categories are adjusted according to general wage agreements for all public employees. Members also receive compensation on the basis of the location of the district they represent: the farther a district is from Helsinki, the capital, the higher the amount of compensation. Travel in the course of parliamentary duties is free on buses, railways, and scheduled domestic flights. Members also receive compensation for travel to and from plenary sessions. Members who have turned sixty years of age or who have fewer than seven years left until age sixty, dating from the end of their parliamentary term, are entitled to a pension.

RELATIONS WITH THE EXECUTIVE AND THE OMBUDSMAN

Relations between Parliament and the president of the republic and the executive are regulated in the Constitution Act of 1919, which states that the legislative power shall be exercised by Parliament together with the president of the republic. The supreme executive power is vested in the president of the republic, and the general governing of the state is undertaken by the Council of State (government). The power to pass constitutional acts is vested in Parliament, which makes the final decisions on these acts. The president has the right to veto these acts and thereby to extend the process, but Parliament has the supreme power, as it may approve the acts, without the approval of the president, after a second reading in a plenary session. Parliament also has the supreme power over finances since it approves the central revenues and expenditures of the republic. If "unsolvable" conflicts arise between the president of the republic and Parliament, the power to make the final decision rests with Parliament. Major conflicts of this type, however, have never arisen.

As for the general governing of the state, the principle of parliamentarism prevails: the government must enjoy the confidence of Parliament. All members of the government are politically responsible to Parliament for their official actions. The implication is that each member or the whole government must resign if Parliament so demands. In practice, the principle of parliamentarism has meant that, in making decisions, the government has to take into account the general opinion of the parties and their interests, thereby providing Parliament with an indirect influence on the work of the executive.

The primary responsibility for the preparation of matters related to the European Union lies with the Council of State. The Council of State also is responsible for executing the European Union decisions, unless a decision requires approval by Parliament or an act to be given.

The ombudsman is elected by Parliament for four consecutive calendar years. Along with the chancellor of justice, the ombudsman is the supreme guardian of the law. The difference between the two is that the chancellor of justice supervises the actions of the Council of State, while the parliamentary ombudsman is a guardian of the law, on behalf of the Parliament, and reports to it on the legal functioning of the administrative machinery. The main purpose of this supervision is to ensure that the legal status of ordinary citizens is not neglected. The ombudsman, whose only power is that of supervising the work of officials and administrators, has the right to be present at meetings of the Council of State, the courts of law, and government agencies, and to see all the documents of officials and administrators. The ombudsman also has the right to inform the Parliament if a member of the Council of State has acted against the law, as well as to bring charges against members of the Supreme Court for offenses arising from their duties.

If the chancellor of justice or a member of the Council of State, Supreme Court, or Supreme Administrative Court has proceeded contrary to the law in the conduct of his or her office, the matter shall be handled in a special tribune, the High Court of Impeachment, for which specific constitutional law provisions shall be in force. If Parliament decides to raise the charge, it shall be prosecuted by the ombudsman of Parliament. This has been the case on four occasions—in 1933, 1953, 1961, and 1993.

THE HOUSE OF PARLIAMENT

The House of Parliament, in Helsinki, was built between 1926 and 1931 and designed by the architect Johan Sigfrid Sirén. The building has an external architectural style of classicism and an internal style influenced by functionalism. Because the cost of the building was no object, the materials used in its construction were of the best quality. The House of Parliament was extended and renovated during the 1970s in keeping with the original idea of Sirén. Completed in 1985, the renovation provided all members of Parliament with their own offices and extended conference possibilities.

The Central Office of Parliament comprises the Registration Office, Swedish Office, Documents Office, and Information Service. These offices handle tasks of preparation and implementation, as well as other service functions. The Administrative Department, which comprises the Administrative Office, Accounts Office, and Real Estate Office, arranges meetings of the Parliamentary Office Committee. The Committee Secretariat provides secretarial services for the committees and undertakes preparatory work on matters to be dealt with by the committees. The Information Service assists the work of Parliament by obtaining the information required by that body. The Parliamentary Office, which has a staff of about 350, also has an information unit which handles practical matters related to interparliamentary cooperation.

Located in the House of Parliament, the Library of Parliament is not restricted to parliamentary operations but nevertheless operates in conjunction with Parliament as a public institution under its care and supervision. The library contains the archives of Parliament as well as all documents from the parliamentary sessions and committees. In addition to serving Parliament, the library also serves as the main library in Finland for research in jurisprudence and political science.

Roger Bobacka

BIBLIOGRAPHY

Finnish Parliament. *The Finnish Parliament.* Helsinki: Government Printing Center, 1983.

Hakala, Liisa-Maria, and Pekka Suhonen, eds. *The Finnish Parliament.* Helsinki: Parliament of Finland, 1990.

Hidén, Mikael. "How the Finnish Parliament Functions." In *The Finnish Parliament. Its Background, Operations, and Building.* Helsinki: Parliament of Finland, 1990.

Ministry of Justice. *Making and Applying Law in Finland.* Helsinki: Valtion Painatuskeskus, 1983.

FRANCE

OFFICIAL NAME: French Republic (République Française)
CAPITAL: Paris
POPULATION: 58,040,000 (1996 est.)
DATE OF CURRENT CONSTITUTION: Adopted September 28, 1958
FORM OF GOVERNMENT: Parliamentary democracy
LANGUAGE: French
MONETARY UNIT: Franc
FISCAL YEAR: Calendar year
LEGISLATURE: Parliament (Parlement)
NUMBER OF CHAMBERS: Two. National Assembly (Assemblée Nationale); Senate (Sénat)
NUMBER OF MEMBERS: National Assembly, 577 (directly elected); Senate, 321 (indirectly elected)
PERCENTAGE OF WOMEN: National Assembly, 10.9; Senate, 5.6
TERM OF LEGISLATURE: National Assembly, five years; Senate, nine years (one-third of senators renewed every three years)
MOST RECENT LEGISLATIVE ELECTION: National Assembly, May 25 and June 1, 1997; Senate, September 24, 1995
MINIMUM AGE FOR VOTING: 18
MINIMUM AGE FOR MEMBERSHIP: National Assembly, 21
SUFFRAGE: Universal
VOTING: Optional
ADDRESS: Assemblée Nationale, Palais Bourbon, 126 rue de l'Université, 75355 Paris; Sénat, Palais du Luxembourg, 15 rue de Vaugirard, 75291 Paris Cédex 06
TELEPHONE: National Assembly, (33 1) 40 63 60 00; Senate, (33 1) 42 34 20 00
FAX: National Assembly, (33 1) 42 60 99 03; Senate, (33 1) 42 34 26 77

The largest country in Western Europe, the Republic of France is a multiparty democracy with a strong executive. The republic is composed of mainland France and Corsica, a large island in the Mediterranean Sea off the coast of Italy. This land area is divided administratively into ninety-six departments. France also has four overseas departments and six overseas territories. The departments are divided into some 36,000 communes headed by elected mayors. The present constitution provides for a president, elected by direct popular vote, and a bicameral Parliament *(Parlement),* consisting of a Senate elected indirectly by an electoral college and a National Assembly elected directly by the people. The president is head of state and the prime minister is head of government.

HISTORICAL BACKGROUND

The French Parliament originated in a revolutionary act. On May 5, 1789, the States General *(Etats généraux),* France's legislative body comprising representatives of the clergy (first estate), the nobility (second estate), and the bourgeoisie (third estate), gathered in Versailles in response to a request by King Louis XVI to help him improve the situation in France, particularly the country's finances. Six weeks later, on June 17, 1789, the States General, acting on the initiative of its representatives from the third estate, suddenly declared itself to be a National Assembly *(Assemblée Nationale).*

The States General reasoned that, having been called to act as a consultative assembly, it represented the nation and

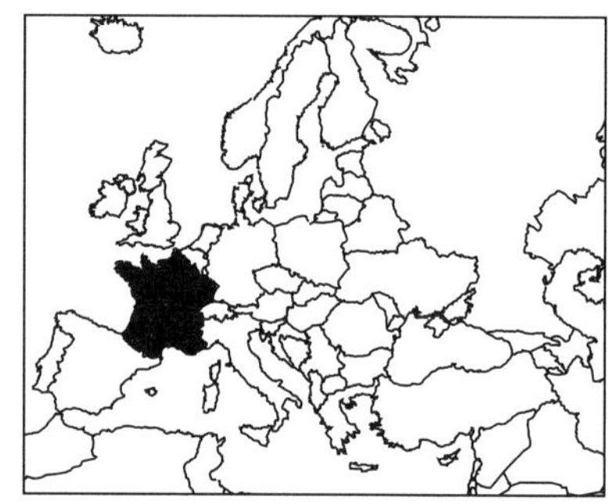

embodied the popular will. This legal and political *coup de force,* which founded the modern French constitutional system, was expressed in the famous Declaration of the Rights of Man and the Citizen of August 16, 1789. Article 3 of the declaration states: "The essential basis of all sovereignty is the Nation. No entity or individual may exercise authority unless it emanates expressly from the Nation." Article 6, one of the most famous articles of French public law, completes the declaration: "Laws are the expression of the general will. Every citizen is entitled to contribute personally or through their representatives to their drafting." Events of the summer of 1789, then, brought an end to the old juridical and political order based on royal sovereignty. The monarchy of the Old Regime permanently gave way to parliamentary representation, whose vocation it was to express the national will.

Since 1789 France has had fifteen constitutions and about twenty political regimes. Although with each constitution the institution of Parliament has evolved differently, over time a parliamentary tradition has been formed, based first and foremost on parliamentary sovereignty. At times, however, its exaggerated demands have threatened its existence.

An expression often used but rarely defined, "parliamentary sovereignty" symbolizes the type of political regime in which all sovereignty is exercised, some would even say monopolized, by Parliament. From the Revolution (1789–1799) to the Fourth Republic (1946–1958), Parliament, embodied in successive constitutional regimes, became ever more powerful. The first French constitution, dated 1791, established a unicameral parliament known as the Legislative Body *(Corps Législatif)*. The first republican constitution, which followed in 1793, also retained the principle of one chamber, but it was never implemented. Not until 1795 and the first "moderate" constitution of the revolutionary period did the bicameral parliament appear, in the form of the Council of Five Hundred and the Council of Elders. Since then, with a few exceptions (the Second Republic, 1848–1851, or periods in which there was a provisional government), the French parliamentary system has been bicameral.

In 1799 the governing executive body of five men *(Directoire)* established by the 1795 constitution gave way to the

Consulate and then to the First Empire (1799–1814). Parliament's powers were severely curtailed, its only function finally being to support Emperor Napoleon Bonaparte, who ruled France from 1804 to 1815.

The downfall of the First Empire in 1814 reinstated the monarchy. Although he would have liked to revive the practices in vigor before 1789, King Louis XVII had to include in the 1814 charter a bicameral parliament composed of the Chamber of Deputies and the Chamber of Pairs. Following the brief episode of Napoleon's return during the "Hundred Days" in the spring of 1815, the restoration period (1814–1830) saw a flowering of parliamentary life. This continued from 1830 to 1848, after a popular uprising in July 1830 led to the Bourbon king's abdication and Louis-Philippe's succession to the throne. During Louis-Philippe's "July Monarchy" the bicameral Parliament had real juridical powers and increasing political influence.

The downfall of Louis-Philippe in 1848 saw the beginning of the Second Republic. Its new constitution instituted a unicameral parliament, the National Assembly. Then, for reasons both political and constitutional, the Second Republic ended in a coup d'état on December 2, 1851, and was followed by the establishment of the Second Empire under Napoleon III. In a new constitution the emperor began by limiting considerably the power of the once again bicameral legislature. The Senate, as the second chamber was now called, played but a modest role. Gradually, however, between 1860 and 1870 the legislature assumed more power; by the fall of the Second Empire in 1870 a sort of parliamentary regime existed.

The Third Republic (1875–1940), which followed the Franco-Prussian War, was the epitome of French parliamentary sovereignty. The result of a compromise between moderate monarchists and hesitant republicans, the 1875 constitution established a two-chamber Parliament consisting of a Chamber of Deputies and a Senate. The Chamber of Deputies was elected by direct universal suffrage every four years; members of the Senate were elected by an electoral college for a nine-year term with one-third of the membership up for reelection every three years. Together these bodies constituted the heart of French public life.

Under the Third Republic, France's longest political regime since the Revolution, the power of the parliament was based on total equality of power between the Chamber of Deputies and the Senate and the gradual weakening of presidential prerogatives. The 1930s saw great political instability and an important deregulation of parliamentary life. Yet after the liberation of France by the Allies in 1944, Gen. Charles de Gaulle, who became head of the provisional government, attempted to strengthen the executive in vain.

The constitution of the Fourth Republic (1946–1958) established a bicameral Parliament in which power was shared unequally. On the one hand, the National Assembly, heir to the Chamber of Deputies, received complete legislative power and exercised daily control over a government that lacked a true political majority, a deficiency that contributed to its weakening. On the other hand, the Council of the Republic, a pale successor to the pre-1940 Senate, lost its main power, legislative equality. From then on, laws could be passed by the Assembly without the Senate's consent.

Thus the Third and Fourth Republics were characterized by government instability and procedural difficulties in the legislature. Indeed, the Third Republic had 111 governments with an average life span of less than eight months. Under the Fourth Republic, from December 1946 to January 1959, twenty-two presidents of the council held office, and the average government life span was only about six months.

Much of the government instability of this period—which often was compensated by the long tenure in office of political leaders—can be attributed to the lack of constitutional provisions that would allow the government to force the parliamentary majority to assume its responsibilities. Under the Third Republic the government's responsibility was not codified in any precise way. Any minister, at any time, could call for a vote of confidence. The Chamber of Deputies voted without allowing the head of the government time to dramatize the debate and rally his supporters. Under the Fourth Republic various procedures were implemented to strengthen government stability, but they were either diverted from their purpose or ignored.

Legislative procedures were at the heart of the French Parliament's difficulties. Under the Third Republic the complete equality between the Chamber of Deputies and the Senate made compromise an ongoing necessity to avoid stalemates on important issues such as the need for an income tax or the vote for women. Under the Fourth Republic various mechanisms were used to try to overcome this situation, and the National Assembly was given responsibility for legislating alone in the event of opposition from the Council of the Republic. The ensuing state of confusion, however, led to laws not being voted, budgets being adopted several months late, or Parliament abandoning its legislative function to the government by a procedure that the Third and Fourth Republics called law decrees.

At the end of the Fourth Republic the situation was so bad that certain ministerial crises lasted more than a month and a recently empowered government could not obtain the necessary parliamentary support for its legislation. In these circumstances, it is not surprising that several proposals for reform were drawn up by politicians and jurists. Indeed, after both of the world wars many suggestions were made to strengthen the power of the government, thereby structuring Parliament's role more successfully. None of these attempts came to anything until the 1958 crisis, brought about by a revolt in French colonial Algeria, when the Fourth Republic fell and General de Gaulle returned to power on May 31. A new constitution was promulgated on October 4, 1958, giving birth to the Fifth Republic.

THE MODERN CONSTITUTION AND PARLIAMENT

Within forty-eight hours of its investiture on June 1, 1958, de Gaulle's government was mandated to prepare a new constitution and put it to a referendum (constitutional law of June 3, 1958). The entire constitution was oriented toward making the state once again efficient and providing a new status for Parliament. When the government and its collaborators drafted the constitution, they were determined to end the way the previous Parliament had functioned, but they also wanted to preserve its basic structure. It would be a mistake to think that criticism of Parliament's exaggerated use of its sovereignty led the drafters to move closer to a presidential regime. Michel Debré, minister of justice and the principal author of the constitution, President de Gaulle, as well as all the other political figures who worked with him as ministers, rejected the idea of a presidential regime based on the American model. Rather, they sought a well-balanced parliamentary regime based on a stable government and an efficient Parliament.

At the heart of this determination were the classical provisions created by the British Parliament. First, the government must be responsible to Parliament (especially the National Assembly), but this responsibility must be limited by precise constitutional provisions such as the number of signatures needed to submit a motion of no confidence and the number of votes required to adopt it. Second, the threat of dissolution must hang over at least one of the two chambers—that is, the head of state, in this case the president of the republic, must be able to turn to the people if a disagreement between the National Assembly and the government were to block the country's decision-making process.

A reading of the constitution of October 4, 1958, reveals an almost perfect model of what might be called rational parliamentarianism. For the first time in the history of the French Republic, Parliament was no longer the central institution, the power around which all the others revolved; there now was a president. The president was not elected by universal direct suffrage until 1962, but from the beginning those holding the office had a permanent status and effective powers—for example, that of appointing the prime minister and dissolving Parliament—and this constituted a counterweight to Parliament's supremacy.

The many articles in the constitution that dealt with the organization of Parliament and the relations between Parliament and the government reflected the experience gained during the Fourth Republic. They also reflected the determination of those who wrote the constitution to establish an efficient parliamentary regime that would be capable of saying no to the government—that is, to overthrow it and risk dissolution—but that would be organized in such a way that Parliament could not wage an ongoing battle with the government. In addition, the constitution provided for new constitutional laws on the organization and competencies of Parliament to be drawn up by the government. The rules governing the internal functioning of Parliament, and intended to limit its status and functions, were to be submitted to the Constitutional Council so that the chambers could not disregard them.

The adoption of the new parliamentary statute raised only limited objections among politicians and jurists. There was such basic agreement on the need to remedy the situation that existed under the Fourth Republic that the provisions established in 1958 seemed wise and efficient. The constitution was adopted by the French people on September 28, 1958, by an 80 percent majority of votes cast. The new institutions were established in late 1958 and early 1959.

Since 1958 politics under the Fifth Republic have been marked by strict limitations on the powers of Parliament and the existence in the National Assembly since 1962 of a stable, coherent, and homogeneous parliamentary majority. These two phenomena, the second of which could not have been foreseen in 1958, together with the legitimacy that the election of the president of the republic by direct universal suffrage gives this office, often have caused politicians and commentators to consider strengthening and developing Parliament's role. Indeed, there is a permanent political and constitutional discourse that laments the fact that the French Parliament does not play a more important role in political life. For the past ten years the idea of strengthening Parliament's power, whether in terms of drafting laws, controlling government policy, or participating in European policy, has become a must for all those whose task it is to reflect on how the French Republic operates.

There also has been an ongoing debate on the question of whether the existence of a Senate corresponds to a veritable constitutional requirement. Article 24 of the constitution declares that "Parliament consists of the National Assembly and the Senate." This formula expresses one of the most tangible constitutional realities: the determination to have a two-chamber system. But in 1969 General de Gaulle, who was still president of the republic, tried to diminish the role of the Senate and transform the deliberative assembly into a consultative assembly. In a public referendum on the issue, 52.4 percent voted against such a step, thereby confirming the role of the Senate. President de Gaulle resigned.

Successive presidents of the National Assembly all sought ways and means to make Parliament more efficient. In January 1994 the National Assembly rules were significantly revised with the aim of better organizing its activities without affecting the constitution. The Senate also has sought to make its voice heard and, in particular, to underline the specificity of its role. Without going back to the all-powerful pre-1958 Parliament, there is certainly room for thought on how Parliament, dominated by a homogeneous majority that supports the government, can once again have true freedom of movement and thus become a platform for the grassroots expression at the heart of the republic.

PARTIES AND ELECTIONS

According to Article 25 of the 1958 constitution, an "organic enactment shall lay down the term for which each House is elected, the number of its members, their emoluments, the conditions of eligibility, and the system of ineligibility or incompatibility."

National Assembly

The constitution specifies that deputies to the 577-member National Assembly are to be elected by direct universal suffrage. All citizens age twenty-one and older are entitled to run for the Assembly, and all those age eighteen and over may vote. The constituencies represented by members are parts of metropolitan and overseas departments and overseas territories. Each department or territory is divided into electoral districts according to its population.

French electoral laws, which are not part of the constitution, determine the way elections for deputies are carried out. In France there always has been an important debate on how parliamentary elections should be run. Under the Third Republic, voters elected a single candidate on a majority basis with two rounds, except for the legislative elections of 1885, 1889, and 1919. In the first round, which was held on a Sunday, a candidate who obtained a majority of the votes cast was elected. If no candidate obtained a majority, a runoff was held on the following Sunday. The candidate with the most votes was elected. All the elections held from 1945 to 1958 were by proportional representation. This system, which is advantageous when there are many parties, and when there are well-structured parties, was abandoned in 1958, when the country returned to the previous electoral mode, the majority vote for one candidate with two rounds. Since 1958 this electoral method has been used for all legislative elections, except in 1986, when a law passed the year before reestablished proportional voting. Majority voting was reestablished immediately afterward by the right-wing majority that won the 1986 elections.

Although majority voting is not used commonly, the French find that it offers them a large choice for the first round, with each political party able to present its candidate. In the second round it allows for a regrouping according to traditional French political behavior, which generally results in one group on the right and one on the left. The underlying logic of majority elections leads to the belief in a majority bonus that boosts the political party in the lead. In present-day France, this system is favorable to the Socialist Party and the alliance of the Gaullist Rally for the Republic and the Union for French Democracy. It is unfavorable to the small political parties or to the extremes such as the left-wing French Communist Party, the right-wing National Front, and the Ecologists.

The circumscriptions, or electoral districts, were delimited most recently in 1986. The 1986 law was verified by the Constitutional Council, which declared there was no manifest abuse in terms of the delimitations, which are reviewed every twelve years. Deputies are elected for five years, generally in March. Their term is shortened if Parliament is dissolved. Under the constitution, after consulting with the prime minister and the presidents of the National Assembly and the Senate, the president of the republic can pronounce the dissolution of the National Assembly. No legal justification is needed to dissolve the Assembly; it is a question of political expediency or constitutional equilibrium. Under the Fifth Republic, Parliament has been dissolved five times: in 1962 the government was overthrown by the National Assembly, and the disagreement had to be settled by the country at large; in 1968 Parliament was dissolved in order to end the student and labor strikes that had paralyzed a large part of the country; the dissolutions of 1981 and 1988 followed the election each time of a left-wing president of the republic (François Mitterrand), who was confronted with the election of right-wing Assemblies in 1981 and 1986. The president, elected or reelected, had to obtain a parliamentary majority more in tune with his ideas. And Parliament was dissolved the fifth time in April 1997.

Senate

The present constitution specifies that the 321-member Senate "ensures the representation of the territorial units of the Republic." This formulation also was used to designate the Senates of the Third and Fourth Republics. The Senate is not elected by direct universal suffrage but by colleges of elected representatives in each department. The electoral assemblies are made up of the mayors of communes, National Assembly deputies, members of the general councils (the departmental assemblies), and the regional councilors (members of the regional assemblies) elected in the departments. Delegates from municipal councils also are appointed to the electoral assemblies, the number depending on the population of each commune. These rather complicated rules give the senatorial electoral college more of a rural than urban cast, and undoubtedly more of a conservative than progressive slant.

The way in which senators are designated also is complicated by the fact they are not all elected in the same way. In the smaller departments they are elected individually by a majority vote with two rounds, while in the larger departments where there are more than five senatorial seats they are designated by proportional representation according to the highest average number of votes. An ongoing debate about the Senate has focused on whether the composition of the electoral college should be modified to achieve greater balance between urban and rural areas, and whether senators should all be elected in the same way, or in any case whether greater importance should be given to proportional representation. This debate will be difficult to resolve since the moderate Senate majority would have to agree to these modifications.

Senators serve nine-year terms, with one-third of the seats up for election every three years. Since the Senate cannot be dissolved, the system gives the impression that the Senate goes on forever and remains above the political fray.

Contested votes

A contested vote, whether for a deputy or senator, can be settled only by the Constitutional Council—that is, an independent jurisdiction—and not by the assemblies themselves. This was also the rule before 1958.

MEMBERS OF PARLIAMENT

In France members of Parliament enjoy special legal privileges that allow them to exercise their mandate to express the general will. They also are subject to limitations on outside activities that may adversely affect their representation.

Incompatibility

In the French system, an incompatibility is a situation in which members of Parliament cannot exercise their parliamentary mandate and another activity at the same time. Over the years, legislation has progressively strengthened the system of incompatibilities. At this time, there is absolute incompatibility between a parliamentary mandate and a nonelected public function, whether it be civil service, military service, or membership in the government. The latter was an important innovation of the 1958 constitution—parliamentary tradition previously had permitted members of the government to serve in the Assembly. Determined to cut the umbilical cord between Parliament and government, General de Gaulle sought to oust members of the government from their seats in Parliament. They were replaced by substitutes elected at the same time for the purpose. (When deputies or senators are appointed as members of government, they lose their mandate in Parliament and are replaced by others, elected at the same time on the same ballot, for this specific purpose. As most members of government previously were members of Parliament, this situation happens rather frequently.)

For elective public functions, there has been a strong trend in favor of a member being able to hold several offices at once. Until 1985 there had been no limits to the practice. A member of Parliament could at the same time be mayor of a commune, president or member of a departmental or regional assembly, or member of the European Parliament. Since 1985 the number of elective offices that can be held at one time has progressively been limited so that now a member of Parliament can fulfill only one other important function such as mayor of a large city. The underlying idea is that a parliamentary mandate should be a full-time job, yet it is useful for members of Parliament to have some experience in local government, either within a city or in a lower-level assembly.

This question continues to be debated, and various proposals have been made to reduce even further the possibility of a member of Parliament holding several offices at once. Members are free to engage in most private professional activities. Some activities are forbidden, however, to avoid situations in which deputies or senators confuse their parliamentary mandates with leadership functions in companies that receive government subsidies or are otherwise dependent on the state.

Immunities

To be able to express their opinions and exercise their parliamentary mandate freely, members are granted two immunities. The immunity of nonliability prevents deputies and senators from being sued for declarations, acts, or votes carried out as part of their function. They can say what they want as long as their declarations are related directly to the exercise of their parliamentary function.

The other immunity is inviolability, which protects members of Parliament from being arrested or having their freedom restricted without the authorization of the bureau of the relevant chamber. Since a constitutional amendment of 1995, a member of Parliament can be prosecuted without any intervention of the chamber to which he or she belongs. Contrary to an oft-heard opinion, this immunity does not prevent members of Parliament from answering to the judiciary for penal offenses that they may commit in the course of their personal or professional activities. The immunity simply avoids an abuse of penal cases brought with the intent of preventing members from fulfilling their mandates. In recent years the spate of financial cases involving politicians has induced Parliament to pronounce itself frequently on the lifting of parliamentary immunity—that is, to authorize prosecution and even arrests. On the whole, decisions by both the National Assembly and the Senate were made with the intent of allowing justice to pursue its investigations and not give the impression that members of Parliament enjoyed unreasonable protection.

Compensation

Since 1848 members of Parliament have been compensated for their services (about $8,000 a month in 1996). Under provisions in effect since 1958, members' salaries are calculated in relation to the salaries of the highest-paid employees of the French civil service. The amount is reviewed regularly and automatically as civil service remuneration evolves. In addition to the basic compensation, members receive remuneration to cover staff salaries (each deputy and senator has three assistants and two secretaries) and certain professional expenses. Various credits also are available for traveling from Paris, where Parliament sits, to a deputy's home district, and for telephone calls and faxes.

Since 1988 deputies and senators have had to declare their assets. These declarations are drawn up at the beginning and the end of each term. They are not made public but are registered with an independent commission of high court judges. The declarations allow verification of any assets that may have been gained through corruption.

LEADERSHIP

Each Assembly elects its own president, who has a special constitutional status and is an important political figure.

The president of the National Assembly is elected on the first day the new deputies convene. He or she serves for five years—the term of the entire legislature—unless the Assembly is dissolved. The president presides over the debates and represents the Assembly in public events. In addition, this leader plays an important constitutional role by advising the president of the republic when the latter is considering dissolving the Assembly or by using his or her exceptional constitutional powers when dramatic circumstances warrant. Traditionally the president of the Assembly has been a majority political figure, who must combine a personal political commitment with the necessity of representing the entire Assembly.

The president of the Senate is elected every three years following each partial renewal of the chamber. In addition to having powers identical to those of the president of the National Assembly, the president of the Senate has the important honor of serving as interim president when the presidency of the republic falls vacant—because of illness, death, or resignation of the president—until a new president is elected. While away, the head of the Senate is replaced by a temporary president. This situation, which gives the Senate added prestige, occurred in 1964 after the death of President Georges Pompidou and in 1969 after de Gaulle's resignation. The presidency of the Senate is a very stable function; since 1958 only three people have served in the position, the longest for twenty-four years.

The presidents of each chamber are assisted in their administrative functions by a bureau composed of six vice presidents, as well as secretaries and treasurers. In each chamber the bureau is elected by all the members so that all political parties are represented according to their respective weight. The bureau serves as the superior administrative organ of each body and the political organ in charge of solving problems, whether they be improvements in work methods or—rarely—authorizing the arrest of members of Parliament.

Alongside the elected organs, each assembly has a considerable number of high-level administrative personnel. Parliamentary civil servants, who form one group, are recruited through competitive examinations, and their political independence of successive majorities is guaranteed. They respect a very strict code of ethics that allows them to assist all the deputies and senators, whatever their political label, competently and efficiently and allows the Assembly and the Senate to carry out their duties under the best conditions.

WORK STRUCTURES OF PARLIAMENT

In the French Parliament two work structures exist side by side: political groups, which generally are formed along political party lines, and permanent commissions, the workhorses of law making.

Parliamentary groups

Parliamentary groups of senators and deputies having the same political affinities are formed according to the provisions of each chamber. These political groups, which have taken shape progressively and developed uniformly, constitute important structures in the daily life of Parliament.

In the National Assembly, under rules modified in 1988, a

group must have at least twenty members. Since 1959 a group in the Senate need have only fifteen. Political groups are constituted by a political declaration to the president of the Assembly (in the Senate to the president of the Senate) signed by all members of the group and including the principles on which they agree.

Political groups in the Assembly and to a lesser extent in the Senate reflect the main political tendencies in the country. The Assembly is home to groups of Communists, Socialists, and members of the Rally for the Republic and Union for French Democracy; the group called Republic and Liberty is composed of twenty-some deputies who are highly attached to their individualism.

The large political groups, which are occupying an increasingly important place in both chambers, use proportional representation in establishing the working structures and procedures of the chambers. The presidents of the groups have special prerogatives, not only because they are ex officio members of the presidents' conference that determines the parliamentary agenda, but also because they can implement certain procedures in terms of how a session is run. For example, they can ask that a session be adjourned or request a public vote. The discipline that exists more and more within the groups constitutes an essential phenomenon of the political functioning of Parliament, particularly since the number of individual initiatives by deputies and senators is decreasing.

Permanent commissions

Permanent commissions are Parliament's basic work organs. Before 1958 each chamber had about fifteen commissions, and the commission heads (presidents) had considerable political clout. The framers of the 1958 constitution, determined to reduce the influence of the commission heads, limited the number of permanent commissions to six in each chamber. The number of members in each is proportionate to the weight of each political group. Because all bills must be discussed in their relevant commissions before being deliberated in public sessions, the presidencies of the commissions represent huge stakes. (Occasionally, ad hoc commissions are established to discuss a specific bill.)

Permanent commissions also have an important control function. They do not enjoy the same status as investigative commissions, but they can hold hearings and inquiries, questioning members of the government or experts, and produce reports on specific subjects. The control activities of the permanent commissions have grown considerably. Nonetheless, not everyone agrees on the commissions' usefulness, in particular because they are unavoidably subject to majority voting and, given the balance of power between the government and the two chambers of Parliament, their political nature is clearly affirmed.

SESSIONS

Before 1958 Parliament was in session almost all year. From 1958 to 1995 the new constitution distinguished between two ordinary sessions—one in the fall (October 2–December 20) and one in the spring (April 2–June 30)—and a restrictive regime of extraordinary sessions. In the minds of the framers of the constitution, the political calendar was to be distributed harmoniously among the four quarters of the year to prevent the government from being under permanent surveillance and pressure from Parliament. But the regime of ordinary sessions soon turned out to be insufficient, and extraordinary sessions began to be called on the initiative of the prime minister and, more rarely, at the request of a majority of deputies. Since 1960, under de Gaulle, the decision to call an extraordinary session and set the agenda has been made by the president of the republic on the basis of a rather broad interpretation of Articles 29 and 30 of the constitution. So that these sessions do not become false ordinary sessions, the constitution provides that the decree calling the sessions include the agenda. Should an emergency arise, the agenda can be modified.

Extraordinary sessions have been on the rise since 1981—the alternations in governing majority in 1981, 1986, 1988, and 1993 contributed to an increase in legislative work. A constitutional amendment adopted in 1995 in response to the situation created one nine-month ordinary session stretching from the beginning of October to the end of June. The agenda is distributed throughout the week in such a way that deputies can devote Tuesday, Wednesday, and Thursday to their legislative work in Paris and the rest of the time to their professions, their local offices, and other activities in their electoral districts.

The Assembly and Senate presidents or one of the vice presidents (there are six in each chamber) preside over meetings of their respective chambers. Those presiding over meetings can control how the meetings run by granting or refusing the floor and by adjourning when need be. But at the same time they must remain detached from their own political preferences, ensuring that the debates run smoothly and that images of the Assembly and Senate are preserved.

The opening of meetings of each chamber is accompanied by certain rituals. The president of the chamber enters after reviewing the military guard. Because of the secular nature of the republic, there is no prayer or moment of silence at the beginning of the meeting. The formal nature of the opening, however, creates a certain climate of serenity—which later may be troubled by the vivacity of the debates.

Although gradually adapting to the evolution of society, the behavior of deputies and senators is still quite formal, and they tend to be highly conscious of the importance of their utterances. As specified in the constitution, the sessions of both the Assembly and the Senate are open to the public. Everything said during the debates is transcribed stenographically in the *Journal officiel (Official Gazette),* the historical record of what is said and what decisions are made by the deputies and senators.

RULES AND AGENDA

Until 1958 the rules governing the work of the two chambers included most of the rules of parliamentary law. They were written without any control and interpreted by the internal body of each chamber. As part of the rationalization of Parliament in 1958, two important phenomena changed this state of affairs. First, a number of rules that previously were part of the parliamentary regulations are now part of the constitution. For example, provisions specifying the length of Assembly and Senate presidents' terms, the number of commissions, the texts to be discussed in public sessions, and the ways in which the agenda is determined are no longer part of the internal rules but of the constitution. Parliament is therefore less autonomous.

Second, it was mandated that, before taking effect, Assembly rules had to be submitted to the constitutional court, known as the Constitutional Council. Since its inception, the Constitutional Council has developed a strict jurisprudence to ensure that neither the original rules of 1958 nor their modifications contradict the constitution. Several times the Constitutional Council has won out on a strict interpretation of the constitution over attempts to enlarge the chambers' powers. Thus the two chambers are no longer as autonomous or as sovereign as they were under the preceding regime.

The list of subjects, or agenda, to be discussed during a given session of Parliament reflects both the hierarchy of concerns and the length of time to be spent on each. Before 1958 agenda setting had been a veritable political battle, at times leading to the government's downfall. Article 48 of the 1958 constitution completely reversed the situation. Now the list of subjects the government wants discussed by the National Assembly and the Senate has priority.

Although there are a few differences in the ways the two chambers handle agendas, both agendas basically include the list of projects and bills and the days on which they are to be discussed. As much as possible the government tries to set the priority agenda in cooperation with the chambers' entities—that is, the commissions in charge of preparing the debate and the majority political groups. But, in the end, only the government can impose its will or modify the agenda.

An additional agenda may be developed, decided in agreement with the government or decided in the remaining time periods by the chambers themselves after a proposal of the presidents' conference. This conference, which meets every week, is chaired by the president of either the National Assembly or the Senate and includes the presidents and vice presidents of the commissions, as well as a representative of the government. Its task is to inform the government of Parliament's views on the draft priority agenda, to define a few practical rules for the upcoming debates, and, eventually, to adopt proposals for the additional agenda.

The government's prerogatives in terms of the priority agenda were slightly reduced in 1995. A new amendment to the constitution gives to the chambers the right to introduce once a month a specific agenda, composed of either legislative works or control initiatives, decided by the presidents' conference.

LEGISLATION

At first sight, and according to a tradition based on British constitutional practice, it appears that the area of action of Parliament and therefore of the laws should be unlimited. In reality, however, under the Fifth Republic two types of limitations are applied to parliamentary law making. One tends to distinguish subjects that by their nature come under the law from those that come under the regulatory area that is left to the government. The other limitation, which grew out of increased constitutional control, tends to limit the area of the law in relation to the existence of a constitutional area.

Laws and regulations

The framers of the 1958 constitution, looking back at the experience of the Third and Fourth Republics, noted that Parliament tended to accumulate many laws in minor areas or to include in its laws provisions that need not have been debated by the representatives of national sovereignty and could have been left to the initiative of the government. With this thought in mind, the framers sought to distinguish between a list of matters for which laws would continue to set the rules or basic principles, and other, less important matters for which, under Article 37, the government would be competent under common law to set the legal standards.

This "distinction between the areas of law and regulation," which is contained in Articles 34 and 37, runs contrary to the French legal and parliamentary tradition under Article 6 of the Declaration of the Rights of Man and the Citizen of 1789, which states that "the law is the expression of the general will." Thus the "distinction" provoked severe criticism in 1958 and 1959. Members of Parliament and jurists who favored the traditional interpretation reacted strongly to a situation in which, in theory, Parliament could no longer legislate in all areas.

In reality, however, beginning in 1958 Parliament found that its legislative work would cover a wide area. The framers of the constitution had been careful to include in the parliamentary area all questions dealing with freedom, individual status, company law, the basic principles of social relations, labor law, the national education system, sovereignty (including the minting of money), national defense, the organization of justice—in fact almost all the questions on which there can be a political debate.

The text of the 1958 constitution also had set up mechanisms for distributing competencies. But in case of doubt, the State Council, for pre-1958 laws, and the Constitutional Council, for those passed after that date, would decide whether the questions dealt with came under the domain of the law or that of regulation, so that the correct procedure would be used in making subsequent modifications. Very quickly, however, experience showed that the distinction was much less important than some had thought, and many factors led to the frontier becoming almost transparent. First, governments tended increasingly to include regulatory provisions in their bills. Second, often amendments within the regulatory domain were not defeated. Finally, the Constitutional Council declared that a law that included regulatory provisions was not contrary to the constitution. Thus more than three decades later a distinction that was considered very rigid in 1958 was attenuated to the point of no longer being the subject of passionate debate.

Laws and the constitution

Just as the French constitutional tradition considered that the area of laws was unlimited, it refused to admit that, after parliamentary debates, a judge could conceivably exercise further control. Every time a law's conformity with the constitution was raised, either in front of an administrative judge or a judiciary judge, the answer always was the same: because a law adopted by Parliament is the expression of national sovereignty, it cannot be contested by the judiciary. This tradition was partly abolished in 1958 when the Constitutional Council was created.

The council has nine members appointed for nine years. Three are appointed by the president of the republic, three by the president of the National Assembly, and three by the president of the Senate. Among other things, the council reviews laws and treaties for conformity with the constitution and judges the most important elections. In the area of the constitutional control of laws, Article 61 provides that organic laws—special laws for the organization of public powers and directly related to the application of the constitution—must be submitted to the Constitutional Council between the time they are adopted by Parliament and their promulgation by the president of the republic. Although verification of the conformity of ordinary laws with the constitution is not required, the president of the republic, the prime minister, or the president of the Assembly or the Senate can request that an ordinary law be submitted to the Constitutional Council for verification.

For both political and legal reasons, it was not until 1971, when the Constitutional Council reviewed a law on freedom of association, that an efficient constitutional review became part of French political life. Three years later, the right to refer an ordinary law to the Constitutional Council between the time of its adoption and its promulgation was conferred on the parliamentary minority—that is, about sixty deputies or senators.

Since 1971 an abundant jurisprudence has developed. All laws that are politically important, or very controversial politically or juridically, are referred to the Constitutional Council. The council has developed a jurisprudence that, on the whole, protects fundamental rights and individual freedom. Basing its standards of reference on a constitutional block consisting of the Declaration of the Rights of Man and the Citizen, the preamble to the 1946 constitution (that of the Fourth Republic), the basic principles recognized in the laws of the republic, and certain principles embodied in the 1958 constitution, the council has given rise to a homogeneous, harmonious, and well-balanced jurisprudence. The effect, however, has been a limit placed on Parliament's legislative autonomy. Article 6 of the Declaration of the Rights of Man and the Citizen states that "statute law is the expression of the general will." But in its decision of August 23, 1985, on the evolution of New Caledonia, a French overseas territory, the Constitutional Council stated that "the law only expresses the general will so long as it respects the constitution." The possibility that laws voted by parliament may be controlled by the Constitutional Council forces the government, which drafts bills, and the members of the Assembly and the Senate, who debate them, to pay special attention to the juridical quality of the texts they propose or adopt. It is easy to see that when big political controversies arise, such as immigration or France's role in the construction of Europe, the political debate is now supplemented by a very important constitutional debate.

The question posed is no longer that of returning to the

past and doing away with the constitutionality of laws but, on the contrary, of extending the notion. In contrast to what occurs in most European countries and the United States, the question of contradiction between a law and the constitution cannot be raised for a law already in force. President Mitterrand presented a proposal to this effect in 1990, but at that time the Senate was opposed and it was not adopted. It probably will be raised again in coming years, and a solution will be found to enable laws already in force to be examined for conformity with the constitution.

THE LEGISLATIVE PROCEDURE

The legislative procedure is the set of rules that enables Parliament to examine a bill. The 1958 constitution considerably refined and detailed the legislative procedure while maintaining its main traditional aspects.

Normal procedures

Article 39 of the constitution specifies that only the government and members of Parliament may propose a law. Government initiatives are taken by the prime minister after an opinion by the Council of State, the government's legal adviser, on the legal quality of a bill and discussion by the Council of Ministers, which usually adopts the bill in a show of government solidarity. The bill submitted to Parliament is not just the text drafted by a minister but the text reflecting the views of the government as a whole. Once adopted by the Council of Ministers, a bill can be referred for examination either to the National Assembly or the Senate, except for finance laws which, according to the constitution, must be referred first to the Assembly.

Bills initiated by deputies or senators must be submitted to the bureau of the chamber to which their authors belong. The constitution specifies that bills submitted by members of Parliament must not threaten the equilibrium of the public finances; otherwise, they are declared null and void.

Once a bill is registered and published, the Assembly or Senate, whatever the case may be, can begin its work. First, the bill is examined by one of the body's six commissions by means of gathering information and opinions, holding hearings, and discussing the bill article by article. Upon completion of the process, the commission votes a report which generally includes proposed modifications in the form of amendments. The work of the commission is especially important in that it allows specialists on the question to give their opinions.

When the commission's work is over, the government requests that the bill be placed on the priority agenda for debate in public session. The debate in public session is divided into two parts. The first part, the general discussion, consists of a global debate on the advantages and disadvantages of the proposed legislation. Both the government, represented by the relevant ministers, and members of Parliament give their opinions on merits of the bill. In the second part of the public session the bill is examined in detail, article by article, and any amendments, either proposed by the commission or discussed on the initiative of deputies or senators, are taken up. Rules in both the constitution and the chambers' regulations specify in detail how the articles and amendments are to be discussed. Each specific discussion terminates with a vote adopting or rejecting the article or amendment. Various rules of procedure allow the government to oppose an amendment on the grounds that it would threaten the country's financial equilibrium, or to request that the chamber in question vote only once on one or several amendments or articles. The latter practice, known as a "blocked vote," has the advantage of avoiding certain sensitive votes and allowing a global debate of both the technical and political aspects of the issue.

Only in the National Assembly can the government engage its responsibility on the vote of a bill (Article 49). When this happens, the Assembly must either adopt the text or adopt a motion of censure, indicating its lack of faith in the government, which then falls. Often considered too brutal, this procedure enables deputies to accept their responsibilities in difficult times and either side with the government or accept its fall and the consequent risk of dissolution. In any case, in both assemblies debates end with a vote, whether in the standard manner or under Article 49.

The constitution provides that laws be approved in identical form by both chambers. A procedure known as the "shuttle" allows a bill to be discussed and voted successively by both chambers until they are in agreement on all the provisions. When both chambers are dominated by the same political majority, this is likely to happen. But when there are different majorities in each chamber, there is a real risk of the procedure coming to a dead end. To avoid blockages such as those that occurred under the Third Republic, in particular on the part of the Senate, Article 45 of the constitution provides a procedure for reconciling the positions of the Assembly and the Senate, as well as, if necessary, an ultimate procedure favorable to the Assembly.

When after two readings in each chamber (only one in emergencies) the government sees that a disagreement is persisting, it can form a commission composed of seven representatives from each chamber; the commission will seek to draft a text likely to satisfy both chambers. When it succeeds, which is generally the case when the majority is the same in both chambers, the text is submitted for ratification by the two bodies. But when there is profound political disagreement between the two chambers, the joint commission may fail to draft a satisfactory text, or the text it does draft may not be ratified by both chambers. When this occurs, after another reading by the National Assembly and the Senate the prime minister may request the Assembly to decide alone in a final reading. In this case the right to amend is limited so that the text cannot be completely rewritten.

With this system, the statistically more frequent situation is that of the Assembly and the Senate both agreeing to a law, either before action by a joint commission or with its agreement. It may happen, however, especially when there is a strong opposition such as in 1981, 1986, and from 1988 to 1993, that the government is forced to ask the Assembly to override the Senate's objections and adopt a law. The 1958 constitution ensures that the legislative mechanism is efficient and that any hostility on the part of the Senate would not block the political agreement between the government and the National Assembly majority.

When the law is finally adopted, either by an agreement between the two chambers or after a last reading and vote in the National Assembly, it is transmitted to the president of the republic; the president must sign and promulgate it within fifteen days. During this time the law may be referred to the Constitutional Council to be examined for conformity with the constitution. When the law is not referred for conformity, or when it is declared totally or partially conformed, it is promulgated by the president of the republic and published in the *Journal officiel* throughout the country.

Special procedures

In addition to the course just described for ordinary laws, several special procedures exist for finance laws, social security laws, organic laws, constitutional revisions, delegation laws, treaty ratification laws, and referendums.

Finance laws, which mainly concern budget provisions, come under a special regime designed to avoid blockages that would threaten the smooth functioning of the state. Special procedures govern the debate on finance laws, which must be submitted to the National Assembly every year in early October to be adopted with the next year's budget. In adopting the budget, Parliament must respect a seventy-day deadline. If Parliament fails to adopt the finance law, the government is authorized to put it into force by ordinance so there is no interruption in tax collecting and public spending on January 1. Should Parliament vote down the finance law—which has never happened—emergency provisions would be adopted to ensure continuity in tax collecting and minimal payment of expenditures.

A constitutional amendment (Article 47-1) adopted in February 1996 set forth a new procedure for passing bills on financing social security. Such new bills, introduced by the government, should determine the general conditions of the financial stability of the social security. If Parliament does not make a decision on such a bill within fifty days, the bill may be implemented by government order.

The 1958 constitution (Article 46) created a special category of legislation—organic laws—related to the application of constitutional provisions. These laws, which are considered important because they affect the functioning of constitutional bodies, must be submitted to the Constitutional Council for verification of conformity before they take effect.

The 1958 constitution describes two ways in which the constitution can be revised. In the first procedure (outlined in Article 89) revisions must be approved in identical forms by the Assembly and the Senate before being submitted for ratification either by popular referendum or through a joint session of the Assembly and the Senate called a Congress. In the latter case, there must be a three-fifths majority vote. The second procedure, used in 1962 and 1969 by President de Gaulle, is based on a direct referendum organized under Article 11 of the constitution. In 1962 this procedure yielded a positive result on the question of the election of the president of the republic by direct universal suffrage. But in 1969 there was a negative vote on the regionalization of France and the modification of the Senate's powers, resulting in de Gaulle's resignation. All other revisions of the constitution have been carried out according to the procedure outlined in Article 89—a positive vote of the two chambers, followed by a Congress. A constitutional and political debate continues on whether it is possible and wise to propose a constitutional revision directly to the French people through a referendum that is not preceded by a parliamentary debate and vote.

In an original way, the constitution (Article 38) allows Parliament to delegate to the government for a given period and in a given area the right to issue ordinances on measures that normally fall within the area of law. The purpose of these delegation laws, which are not subject to the strict control of the Constitutional Council, is to authorize the government to adopt measures that might be unpopular or to adopt rapidly measures that would require long parliamentary debates. Their political meaning can be important in certain cases.

The ratification of major treaties by the head of state requires a vote by Parliament. The constitution (Article 53) defines the cases in which ratification must be authorized by a vote of the Assembly and the Senate. A law authorizing ratification is proposed by the government and debated by Parliament (in general according to a simplified procedure). Once the law is adopted, the treaty can be explicitly ratified.

Article 11 of the constitution provides in detail for the adoption of a law without a vote of Parliament. In a limited number of cases applying to the organization of government or the ratification of treaties, the president can, on a proposal by the government or Parliament, during parliamentary sessions, organize a referendum for the approval of a law. This procedure, which is rarely used yet important, allowed President de Gaulle to have his Algerian policy directly approved by the people during the early years of the Fifth Republic; in 1992 it allowed President Mitterrand to have the Maastricht treaty, which constituted a basic transformation of the European Union, ratified directly.

PARLIAMENTARY CONTROL

The expression "parliamentary control" includes all the instruments that enable members of Parliament to form an opinion on the government's action and to pronounce themselves on its responsibility. In addition to the two traditional aspects of parliamentary control—information and investigative techniques and mechanisms for questioning the government's responsibility—a recently formulated series of mechanisms enables Parliament to take an interest in European policy.

Information and investigative techniques

In carrying out its oversight function, Parliament uses a mix of questioning procedures, investigative commissions, and information missions.

In their investigations, members of Parliament can pose their questions for government officials in the more formal written and oral forms, or they may question officials spontaneously in British Parliament fashion. Written questions and answers—more than twenty thousand a year—are published in the *Journal officiel*. In theory the answer is transmitted to the questioner within two months, but in reality it often takes longer. The rate of answers to written questions is 90–100 percent.

The procedures for oral questions and oral responses are different in the Senate and the Assembly, but the spirit is the same. A list of questions is included on the agenda of the day by the presidents' conference. The inquirer outlines the question briefly and one of the government ministers answers it immediately. In some cases, particularly in the Senate, several oral questions may be grouped together for a debate. Although the oral questions procedure attracts only moderate interest, it enables members of Parliament to draw the government's attention to specific issues.

Finally, to allow regular spontaneous control of the government's activity by deputies and senators, a procedure for questioning the government modeled on the British system was adopted in 1974. On Wednesday afternoon in the Assembly and one Thursday a month in the Senate members can question the government very quickly on current affairs issues. These question sessions have been highly successful politically (they are aired live on television) and have become the political rendezvous of the week during parliamentary sessions.

Inquiry commissions gather information and carry out investigations on a given question. To avoid situations in which investigative commissions become almost permanent institutions, leading to extra-jurisdictional procedures, the 1958 statute establishing commissions limited their term to four months and also considerably limited their powers. Since 1958 several legislative reforms have allowed them to develop and play an important role in parliamentary life, but without giving them a constitutional status. Present-day investigative commissions are created by a vote in the chamber concerned, and they may carry out their investigations for a period of six months. At the end of their work they adopt a report which is made public. Recent modifications allow public commission hearings. Although the commissions' results have been mixed, they are being used more and more frequently and are considered as a non-negotiable right for the opposition. They are, however, subject in terms of their composition and final decisions to the will of the majority—that is, at least for the Assembly, to its determination not to hinder government action. But when the Senate is in the opposition, or when the commissions are critical of the previous majority's handling of affairs, they can become a powerful instrument of opposition strategy.

Information missions, which are being employed increasingly by the Assembly and the Senate, have a simple legal framework allowing them to seek information, hold hearings, and publish reports. These information missions can touch on a variety of subjects; more especially, they serve as a place for discussions, or even confrontations, and at times for efforts to reach an agreement between the political partners.

Finally, sometimes the government or deputies or senators organize debates on a given subject or make declarations that give rise to a debate. Such declarations allow members either to voice their opinions on important national debates or to make them more widely known than during question time on a current issue. On the whole, these debates and declarations, which are of considerable interest within Parliament, are not reflected with the same passion in the media.

The government's responsibility

According to Article 20 of the constitution, the government is responsible to Parliament, which means that the National Assembly, but not the Senate, can threaten the government's existence. This essential rule puts the French constitutional regime in the parliamentary category. The government's responsibility is organized under Article 49 according to several provisions.

Article 49, paragraph 1, provides that the government may engage its responsibility vis-à-vis the National Assembly on a declaration of general policy or on its program. To do either, the prime minister must first obtain the agreement of the Council of Ministers, then ask the deputies to vote. In this case, an absolute majority is required for the government to obtain confidence. Article 49, paragraph 1, can be used in two types of situations: when a new government has just been formed and when, during its existence, the government considers it necessary either to verify that there is general agreement on policy or to solicit the Assembly's support on a particularly delicate problem.

The Fifth Republic has moved away from the pure theory of parliamentary regimes in that only half of all new governments have requested a confidence vote when taking power. Actually, the constitution does not include a formal obligation for a new government to engage its responsibility, and juridically it may govern as soon as it has been appointed by the president of the republic. From 1988 to 1993, when there was only a relative majority (275, versus the 289 needed for an absolute majority) in support of socialist governments, socialist deputies dared not request a positive vote, knowing it would be difficult to obtain. Yet it was almost certain they would not get a negative vote through a motion of censure.

The constitution provides a second way in which the government can engage its responsibility. When the government recognizes that a bill it deems essential to the conduct of its policy may not pass, the prime minister can, after consulting the Council of Ministers, engage the government's responsibility on the bill under Article 49, paragraph 3. In that case, the debate in the National Assembly is interrupted and the deputies have only two choices. First, one-tenth can ask for a motion of censure, which, if approved, means rejection of the bill and the fall of the government. Or, second, no motion of censure is requested—or if requested it is voted down—and the bill is adopted and the legislative process continues. The procedure outlined in Article 49, paragraph 3, which is brutal but effective, has at times been criticized for abuse. It is very difficult, however, to put precise limits on a procedure intended for politically delicate cases, which are by definition impossible to foresee.

Article 49, paragraph 2, specifies how the deputies can propose to censure the government and try to make it fall. After a motion of censure is signed by at least 10 percent of the deputies, a waiting period of forty-eight hours follows before a vote can be taken. A majority vote by the members of the Assembly is needed for censure. This requirement ensures that at least one deputy out of two is unfavorable to the government and wants it to fall. Yet it also counts together those who explicitly support the government and those who hesitate. These requirements make it difficult to overthrow the government, particularly when there is a coherent, homogeneous majority in the Assembly. Since 1958 only one government has been overthrown with this procedure: that of Pompidou on October 5, 1962, when he attempted to revise the constitution so that the president of the republic would be elected by direct universal suffrage. Since then, although there have been many motions of censure on important issues, none has been adopted.

The motion of censure also is a means by which deputies can respond to attempts by the government to link the vote on a bill to its existence. The rules relative to the submission and vote on a motion of censure are the same as under Article 4, paragraph 2. Since 1958 none of the motions of censure submitted in response to the government's engaging its responsibility on a text has ever been voted.

The 1958 constitution clearly states that the government is not responsible to the Senate, but Article 49, paragraph 4, does allow the prime minister, using a simpler procedure, to ask the Senate to approve a general declaration of policy. Since there is no obligation nor any possibility for senators to request a motion of censure, there is no risk of the government being overthrown by the Senate. When on rare occasion the prime minister seeks and obtains from the Senate approval of a general declaration of policy, it is possible in certain political contexts, particularly when there is agreement between the government and the Senate, to request the second chamber to render a positive vote, thereby expressing the solidarity of the two chambers in favor of the government.

Parliament and Europe

The growing importance of European matters in the political life of the member countries of the European Union, especially since the Maastricht treaty of 1992, has led France and other countries to strengthen, and even create, mechanisms that allow Parliament to follow and control the government's European policy. In this spirit, the constitutional revision of 1992, which enabled France to ratify the Maastricht treaty and enter the European Union as a full-fledged member, instituted Article 88-4, which gives both the Assembly and the Senate the power to vote resolutions—that is, to give an orientation or an opinion on projects submitted to the European Council of Ministers.

The insertion of Article 88-4 into the constitution marks the end point of several attempts since the 1970s to enable the French Parliament to be associated with European policy making. So far, the results of its application are positive, and the Assembly and the Senate have demonstrated their determination to follow almost daily the evolution of normative projects drafted by European Union policy makers. In their resolutions, the Assembly or the Senate ask the government to adopt a positive, negative, or nuanced attitude, depending on what is at stake in the text in question.

In the coming years, the development of this resolution procedure may lead to stiffer control of government action, forcing the government to take significant account of Parliament's desires during European negotiations. In terms of the spirit of the Fifth Republic, these resolutions constitute a novelty that is somewhat contrary to the strict separation of competencies between the government and Parliament intended in 1958.

THE ROLE OF PARLIAMENT

The question of whether the French Parliament is useful arises regularly in the national political and constitutional debates, and it is not easy to answer. First, it is obvious that Parliament under the Fifth Republic is not the center of French political life as it was under the Third or Fourth Republics. In this respect, Parliament has lost part of its influence and importance.

Second, the framers of the 1958 constitution intended to limit precisely the role of Parliament, yet the history of the Fifth Republic has seen a regular increase in its prerogatives and power. Whether it is a question of control procedures, the quantitative and qualitative development of amendments, or access to European questions, today's Parliament is very different and much more active than that of 1958.

Finally, the greatest account should be taken of the existence, previously unknown in French political life, of a true majority in the Assembly. One must compare the French Parliament's role not with what it was before 1958, or with that of the Italian Parliament, but with those of parliaments in comparable majority regimes such as Great Britain, Germany, or Spain. From this point of view, the function of the French Parliament is first of all to support the government. There is cohesion between the government and the majority in the Assembly, at times even with the president of the republic. It is nonetheless true that implementation of an important political program, particularly after a change of majority, requires Parliament's cooperation. Given their constraining aspects, the mechanisms in the French constitution enable a new majority or government to have its legislative measures adopted after a democratic debate and under the control of the opposition and the public. From this point of view, the French Parliament plays a similar role to those of other majority-regime parliaments.

Didier Maus

BIBLIOGRAPHY

Ameller, Michel. *L'Assemblée nationale.* Paris: Presses Universitaires de France ("Que sais-je?" collection), 1994.

An Introduction to French Administration. Paris: La Documentation française, 1996.

Assemblée nationale. *Connaissance de l'Assemblée.* 7 vols. Paris: La Documentation française, 1992.

Avril, Pierre, and Jean Gicquel. *Droit parlementaire.* Paris: Montchrestien, 1988.

Bell, John. *French Constitutional Law.* Oxford: Clarendon Press, 1992.

Fears, John. "The French Parliament: Loyal Workhouse, Poor Watchdog." *West European Politics* 13 (July 1990): 32–51.

Huber, J. "Restrictive Legislative Procedures in France and the United States." *American Political Science Review* 86 (1992): 675–687.

Maus, Didier. "Parliament in the Fifth Republic." In *Policy-Making in France, from de Gaulle to Mitterrand,* ed. P. Godt. London: Pinter, 1989.

Money, Jeannette, and Georges Tsebelis. "The Political Power of the French Senate: Micromechanisms of Bicameral Negotiations." *Journal of Legislative Studies* 1 (summer 1995): 192–217.

Sénat. *Pour mieux connaître le Sénat.* Paris: La Documentation française, 1993.

Stevens, Anne. *The Government and Politics of France.* London: Macmillan, 1992.

Tsebelis, Georges, and Jeannette Money. "Bicameral Negotiations: The Navette System in France." *British Journal of Political Science* 25 (January 1995): 101–129.

Wright, Vincent. *The Government and Politics of France.* 3d ed. London: Routledge, 1989.

G

GABON

OFFICIAL NAME: Gabonese Republic (République Gabonaise)
CAPITAL: Libreville
POPULATION: 1,193,000 (1996 est.)
DATE OF INDEPENDENCE: August 17, 1960 (from France)
DATE OF CURRENT CONSTITUTION: Adopted March 14, 1991
FORM OF GOVERNMENT: Parliamentary democracy
LANGUAGES: French (official), Bantu dialects
MONETARY UNIT: CFA franc
FISCAL YEAR: Calendar year
LEGISLATURE: Parliament (Parlement)
NUMBER OF CHAMBERS: Two. National Assembly (Assemblée Nationale); Senate (Sénat)
NUMBER OF MEMBERS: National Assembly, 120 (directly elected); Senate, 91 (indirectly elected)
PERCENTAGE OF WOMEN: National Assembly, 6.3; Senate, 8.9
TERM OF LEGISLATURE: National Assembly, five years; Senate, six years
MOST RECENT LEGISLATIVE ELECTION: National Assembly, December 15 and 29, 1996; Senate, January 26 and February 9, 1997
MINIMUM AGE FOR VOTING: 21
MINIMUM AGE FOR MEMBERSHIP: National Assembly, 28; Senate, —
SUFFRAGE: Universal
VOTING: Compulsory
ADDRESS: National Assembly, B.P. 29, Libreville; Senate, B.P. 7513, Libreville
TELEPHONE: National Assembly, (241) 76 22 64; Senate, (241) 73 16 77
FAX: National Assembly, (241) 72 61 96; Senate, (241) 73 16 82

Gabon, a small country on the Atlantic coast of west central Africa, gained independence from France on August 17, 1960. Like its neighbor Congo to the east and south, it had been part of French Equatorial Africa since the nineteenth century.

BACKGROUND

Two main political parties, the Gabon Democratic Bloc, led by Léon M'ba, and the Gabonese Democratic and Social Union, led by Jean-Hilaire Aubame, existed at the time of independence. M'ba was elected the first president of Gabon in February 1961. He subsequently outlawed the rival party and established a one-party state in 1964. Following his death in 1967, M'ba was succeeded by Vice President Albert-Bernard Bongo.

Bongo created a new party, the Gabonese Democratic Party, through which he maintained the single-party rule initiated by his predecessor. By the early 1980s, however, Bongo faced organized political opposition from the National Rectification Movement, which advocated the establishment of a multiparty system in Gabon. Amid protests by students and other groups, Bongo in 1990 announced a program of social and political reform. A national conference was convened and attended by approximately two thousand delegates representing political parties, civic organizations, and professional groups. The conference legalized multiparty political activity and formed a twenty-nine-member transitional government, headed by Casimir Oye M'ba.

Presidential elections were held December 5, 1993. President Bongo was elected in the first round with just over 51 percent of the vote. Father Paul M'ba-Abesole, the National Rally of Woodcutters candidate, won approximately 27 percent of the vote. Serious charges of fraud and other irregularities were made by international observers and opposition parties. Claiming that he had won the election outright, M'Ba-Abessole formed a High Council of the Republic and a parallel government that included a majority of opposition presidential candidates. The entity soon changed its name to the High Council of Resistance. Civil unrest followed, and the Gabonese government cracked down on opposition parties by imposing a curfew and banning public assembly.

The High Council of Resistance demanded that President Bongo's government hold negotiations aimed at normalizing the political situation and reviewing the electoral process. An agreement between the opposition and government, reached in Paris in September 1994, lessened tensions in Gabon by allowing the formation of a coalition government in which the High Council was allotted several ministerial posts.

THE CONSTITUTION AND PARLIAMENT

The constitution of the Gabonese Republic, which was ratified in March 1991 and modified in March 1994, creates

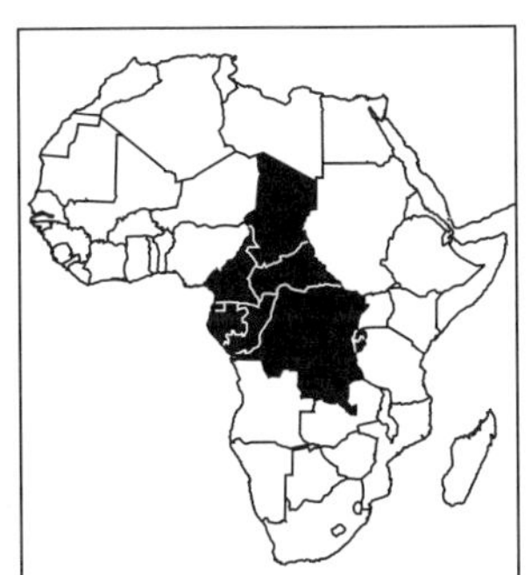

for the first time in the country's history a bicameral parliament composed of a National Assembly and a Senate. The National Assembly comprises 120 deputies elected for five-year terms from single-member districts. If no candidate wins a majority of votes, a second round of elections is scheduled for the two candidates receiving the most votes in the first round. The Senate is made up of ninety-one seats with senators indirectly elected for six-year terms. The constitution, originally providing for a "multiparty" system, was amended to provide for a "pluralist" system vesting executive power in the president, who appoints a prime minister as head of government. The prime minister, in consultation with the president, appoints the Council of Ministers.

Parliament meets in two sessions each year. The first session begins on the third Tuesday of March and ends no later than the fourth Friday of June. The second session opens the first Tuesday of October and finishes no later than the third Friday of December. Parliament may be called to extraordinary session by the president of the republic or by a majority of its members. Parliamentary debates in plenary session, which may take place only in the presence of a majority of members, are open to the public and are published in an official journal. At the request of the president of the republic, the prime minister, or one-fifth of the deputies or senators, closed parliamentary sessions may be held.

The Senate has coequal legislative powers. All bills must be debated in both chambers and must result in an identical bill to be ratified into law. Financial bills and proposals to revise the constitution first pass through the Assembly, while bills dealing with local issues must be debated first in the Senate.

PARLIAMENTARY OPERATIONS

The leadership of the National Assembly comprises a president, six vice presidents, six secretaries, and two bursars. The president of the Assembly is elected by a two-thirds majority of deputies in the first round of voting or by absolute majority in the second round; in the third and final round only a plurality of votes is necessary. Other members of the leadership are elected by majority vote in the first round and by plurality vote in the second round. Members of the Assembly leadership are elected every thirty months. According to the rules of procedure of the Gabonese National Assembly, the president represents the leadership and ensures the execution of its decisions. In addition, the president presides over all debates and directs the Assembly staff. The vice presidents perform the duties of the president in his or her absence. The secretaries oversee the recording of minutes and the voting procedure. The bursars, as in other countries of the region, manage the Assembly's finances. Any member of the leadership may be dismissed at any time by a majority vote.

The National Assembly staff, totaling about eighty members, is composed of the cabinet of the Assembly president, the services of the bursar, and the General Secretariat. The cabinet comprises a civil cabinet and a private cabinet, whose members are chosen specifically by the president. These staff members assist in protocol and the general flow of information to and from the president's office. The bursar staff is charged with social and medical services, accounting procedures, transportation, and various other housekeeping duties. The General Secretariat, under the direction of the secretary general, coordinates the professional activities of the Assembly, including the writing of reports and minutes of legislative proceedings, and implementation of legislative procedure—including transmissions of all bills to the executive branch or to the Supreme Court.

Under Article 59 of the constitution, all bills must be reviewed by the general committees of each chamber of parliament before debate takes place in plenary session. In the National Assembly deputies are divided into seven general committees: Finance, Budget, and Public Accountability; Administrative Affairs; Social Affairs; Economic Affairs and Development; Territorial Planning; Communications and Human Rights; and Foreign Affairs, International Cooperation, and National Defense. These committees are composed of a minimum of fifteen deputies; deputies are required to sit on at least three committees.

Every thirty months the committee leadership (a president, vice president, reporter, and alternate reporter) is elected by members of each committee. The president presides over all committee meetings. Attendance at committee meetings is mandatory. A committee member may, however, be excused for absence by transferring voting rights to another deputy, who cannot vote more than twice. At least half the committee members plus one must be present for any decisions to be considered binding. Committee members may call anyone to give testimony during the proceedings. Ad hoc committees, addressing a specific issue that may transcend the focus of any one general committee, may also be instituted.

Responsibility for setting the agenda resides in a "presidents' conference" comprising the president of the Assembly; the vice presidents of the Assembly; the presidents and vice presidents of each general committee; and the presidents of all registered parliamentary groups. Although the secretaries and the bursars of the Assembly leadership may participate in the meeting, they do not have a vote. The government may send a representative to any meeting of the presidents' conference.

Deputies may at any time pose oral or written questions to a government minister or the prime minister concerning any governmental policies. Oral questions may be posed either with or without debate. Deputies must notify the Assembly president of their intent to pose an oral question, which must be included on the plenary agenda within eight days of this request. In addition to questioning government ministers or other officials, deputies may form investigative committees to review government activities or control committees to review the administration and management of public services. Finally, they may pass a vote of no confidence in the prime minister and government with an absolute majority of votes.

At least five members are required to form a parliamentary group—a caucus of deputies who align themselves to advance a common agenda. According to the rules of the Assembly, parliamentary groups may not form around religious, ethnic, provincial, or professional identities. Three major parliamentary groups exist within the National Assembly. The Gabonese Democratic Party, the sole legal party until 1990, when the national conference resulted in President Bongo's accepting multiparty activity, retains an absolute majority of 84 seats in the 120-seat National Assembly. The Gabonese Progress Party and the National Rally of Woodcutters represent the major parliamentary opposition, with 8 and 5 seats, respectively, following the December 1996 elections. Political parties tend to have few distinguishing characteristics in terms of policy or ideological differences.

ELECTIONS

Legislative elections were held in September 1990 amid violent protests by those claiming that electoral irregularities were taking place in favor of the Gabonese Democratic Party. Nonetheless, President Bongo's party won an absolute majority in the National Assembly. In May 1996, after its normal mandate of five years was extended by six months as part of a constitutional referendum, the National Election Commission set dates for the new legislative elections. The dates were continually pushed back because of problems with logistical preparations.

The first round of elections was finally held on December 15. A second round held on December 29 secured the ruling party's continued absolute majority in the Assembly. Bongo's prime minister retained his portfolio and assembled a new cabinet of ministers, which was expanded to forty members. Overtures were made to include opposition parties in the cabinet. Only one opposition member accepted, however, thus creating some speculation about the opposition's ability to remain unified.

The opposition fared better in the indirect Senate elections of January–February 1997. In that ninety-one member body, the ruling Gabonese Democratic Party held fifty-two seats, the National Rally of Woodcutters held nineteen, and the Gabonese Progress Party held four. Three other parties also gained representation in the Senate as did a number of independents.

Benjamin Feit

GAMBIA, THE

OFFICIAL NAME: Republic of The Gambia
CAPITAL: Banjul
POPULATION: 1,205,000 (1996 est.)
DATE OF INDEPENDENCE: February 18, 1965 (from the United Kingdom)
DATE OF CURRENT CONSTITUTION: Adopted August 8, 1996; effective January 16, 1997
FORM OF GOVERNMENT: Transitional
LANGUAGES: English (official), Mandinka, Wolof, Fula
MONETARY UNIT: Dalasi
FISCAL YEAR: July 1–June 30
LEGISLATURE: National Assembly
NUMBER OF CHAMBERS: One
NUMBER OF MEMBERS: 49 (45 directly elected; 4 nominated)
PERCENTAGE OF WOMEN: 2.0
TERM OF LEGISLATURE: Five years
MOST RECENT LEGISLATIVE ELECTION: January 2, 1997
MINIMUM AGE FOR VOTING: 18
MINIMUM AGE FOR MEMBERSHIP: 21
SUFFRAGE: Universal
VOTING: Optional
ADDRESS: Parliament Buildings, Independence Drive, Banjul
TELEPHONE: (220) 228 305
FAX: (220) 225 123

The Republic of The Gambia is a narrow strip of land in West Africa on both banks of the Gambia River. It is shaped like a finger poking into the nation of Senegal, which surrounds it on three sides *(see map, p. 589)*. The Gambia is an anglophone enclave in a region that is overwhelmingly francophone. Formerly a British dependency under Sierra Leone, it became a separate colony in 1888. The first elections were held under the 1946 constitution, and political parties were formed in the 1950s. The nation became independent in 1965. A relatively stable democracy until 1994, Gambia experienced a military coup; constitutional government was restored in late 1996 and early 1997 amid opposition charges that the new political structures were weighted in favor of the ruling regime.

Under the 1979 constitution legislative power was vested in a unicameral House of Representatives with fifty members, of whom forty-one were voting members. Of the voting members, thirty-six were elected by universal adult suffrage and five were chiefs elected by the Assembly of Chiefs. Eight nonvoting members were nominated by the president, and the attorney general served ex officio.

The Gambia's long history of political stability came to an end in 1994 when junior army officers seized power and suspended the constitution and the legislature. The new regime almost immediately announced a four-year timetable for reestablishing civilian, constitutional rule, and shortly thereafter it shortened the time frame to two years under popular pressure.

The new constitution, which allegedly was crafted in such a way as to all but guarantee the continued rule of Yahya Jammeh, was adopted by referendum in August 1996. Jammeh was elected as president in September 1996.

Elections to the new legislature, the National Assembly, were held in January 1997. The forty-five elected members are chosen by majority vote in single-member districts. Some 107 candidates participated. Jammeh's Alliance for Patriotic Reorientation and Construction won thirty-three seats, five of them in uncontested districts. The return to civilian rule was completed when the nation's chief justice swore in the members of the National Assembly on January 16. The Assembly's first act was to ratify the constitution that had been adopted in August, thereby putting it into effect.

George Thomas Kurian

GEORGIA

See Commonwealth of Independent States, Non-Slavic

GERMANY

OFFICIAL NAME: Federal Republic of Germany (Bundesrepublik Deutschland)
CAPITAL: Berlin
POPULATION: 83,536,000 (1996 est.)
DATE OF INDEPENDENCE: January 18, 1871 (German Empire unification)
DATE OF CURRENT CONSTITUTION: Adopted May 23, 1949
FORM OF GOVERNMENT: Parliamentary democracy
LANGUAGE: German
MONETARY UNIT: Deutsche mark
FISCAL YEAR: Calendar year
LEGISLATURE: Federal Parliament (Parlament)
NUMBER OF CHAMBERS: Two. Federal Diet (Bundestag); Federal Council (Bundesrat)
NUMBER OF MEMBERS: Bundestag, 662 (directly elected; 598 beginning in 2002); Bundesrat, 68 (indirectly elected)
PERCENTAGE OF WOMEN: Bundestag, 26.2; Bundesrat, no fixed membership
TERM OF LEGISLATURE: Bundestag, four years
MOST RECENT LEGISLATIVE ELECTION: October 16, 1994
MINIMUM AGE FOR VOTING: 18
MINIMUM AGE FOR MEMBERSHIP: 18
SUFFRAGE: Universal
VOTING: Optional
ADDRESS: Federal Parliament, Bundeshaus, 53113 Bonn. (The Bundestag is scheduled to move to Berlin in 1999. The address will be: Bundestag, Unter den Linden 69-73, 10117 Berlin.)
TELEPHONE: Bundestag (49) 030 39 772133; Bundesrat (49) 228 91000
FAX: Bundestag (49) 030 39 47501; Bundesrat (49) 228 91 00400

The Federal Republic of Germany is the largest nation in western Europe and the largest economy in the European Union. In October 1990 East and West Germany—which had been formally divided since 1949—were reunited under the West German constitution, or Basic Law, of 1949.

German citizens are represented through elected parliamentary assemblies at three main levels: the sixteen federal-state diets at the subnational level, the federal parliament (Bundestag) at the national level, and the European Parliament at the supranational level. The elected representative bodies at the local level resemble parliaments in their organization and proceedings but do not have significant independent law-making powers. This article will focus on the national parliament.

HISTORICAL BACKGROUND

The history of representative assemblies in Germany, which can be traced back to the Middle Ages, has been characterized by frequent systemic changes and discontinuities. The medieval German empire was a highly fragmented federation of hundreds of autonomous principalities, ecclesiastical territories, and free cities. Little is known about the rights, rules, procedures, and activities of the medieval imperial diet, or Reichstag. Not a representative body in the modern sense, the Reichstag was irregularly convened in different cities and composed of delegates from the politically independent territories and free cities. A final consensus on the composition, rights, and procedures of the Reichstag did not emerge until the imperial reforms of the 1480s and 1490s. From 1489 the Reichstag consisted of three *collegia:* the collegium of electors entitled to elect the emperor, the collegium of the secular and ecclesiastical princes, and the collegium of the cities under the immediate jurisdiction of the Reich. Reichstag decisions required unanimity of the three collegia. Final decisions took the form of contracts between the emperor and the collegia.

More important than the developments on the Reich level were the parliamentary traditions at the territorial level. The estates of the territories represented the nobility, the clergy, and the cities. Taxes in the territories could be raised only with the estates' assent. The importance of the estates, or *Landstände,* declined from the middle of the seventeenth century onward, especially in the larger territories, as the power of monarchs grew.

The French Revolution and the subsequent occupation of parts of Europe by Napoleon's troops destroyed the old Reich and led to the establishment of new, larger states, especially in the southwest and south of Germany. In 1803 dozens of small territories, ecclesiastical states, and free cities were integrated into larger territories through an imperial decision made under French and Russian influence, a process that required a fundamental constitutional and ad-

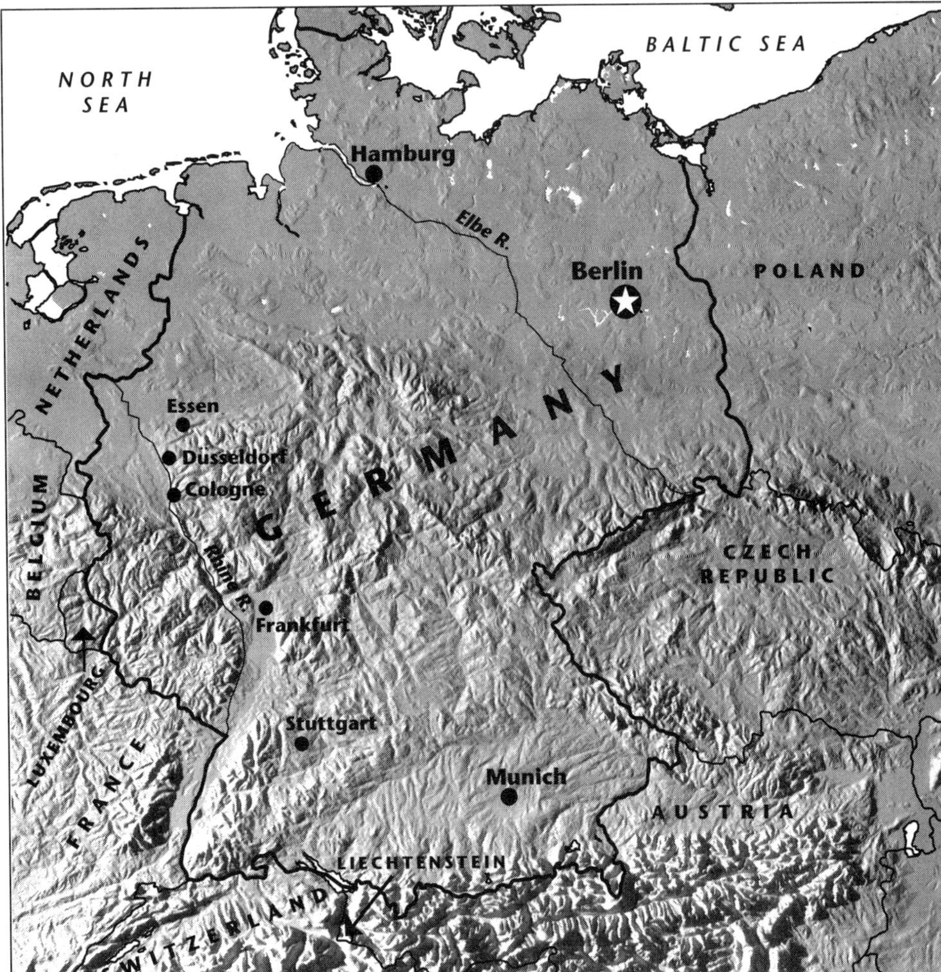

ministrative reform of the larger territories as well. The new constitutions imposed by the sovereign princes of what came to be known as the German federation were largely modeled after the French *charte constitutionelle* of 1814. Elected parliamentary assemblies were a means of consolidating the autonomous principalities of the German federation, but the suffrage remained restricted by property requirements. The representative assemblies were granted rights to participate in the territories' legislative process.

The federal Bundestag remained powerless as a regular lawmaking body. After 1819 the princes attempted to restore the prerevolutionary, absolutist order in their territories and to revoke many of the liberal concessions made under the impact of the French occupation and fears of a revolutionary spillover from France.

The development of constitutional government and parliamentarism in the German territories gained momentum after the July Revolution in France (1830) and constitutional developments in Belgium (1831). The first modern, national parliament was convened in Frankfurt in 1848 as a legislative and constituent assembly. It drafted a constitution for a German national state in which the central government would be responsible to a popularly elected parliament. After a year of deliberations, the Prussian king, Frederick William IV, scornfully refused to accept the crown offered to him by the national assembly, and the Frankfurt parliament had to succumb to the military forces deployed by the major German monarchs who opposed its aims.

Between 1849 and 1871 the institutional conditions for national unification were created: A customs federation with a "customs parliament" was established, and a national party system emerged. The Northern German Federation anticipated many institutions of the 1871–1918 empire. The empire that emerged after 1871 was a federal state dominated by Prussia. The emperor, who was also the Prussian king, appointed the head of government, or chancellor, who was responsible to him and not to the Reichstag. The chancellor then appointed his cabinet ministers.

Otto von Bismarck was the first chancellor, serving from 1871 to 1890. The Reichstag's role was restricted to assenting to new legislation, using its powers of appropriation, and exercising the right of petition. The development of parliamentarism in the empire did not follow the example set by the British model, in which sovereignty is exercised not by the monarch alone, but by the "crown in parliament." In Germany, the traditional dualism between the monarch and his government on the one hand and the assembly on the other remained intact and without political fusion between cabinet and the parliamentary majority. Thus, despite the comparatively progressive universal male suffrage in elections to the Reichstag, a genuine parliamentary system did not develop at the federal level or at the level of the principalities that made up the empire. The suffrage in many states remained grotesquely unequal. Under Prussia's indirect three-class suffrage (1849–1918), for example, 15 percent of the male population elected approximately 85 percent of the members of the Prussian second chamber.

The upper house of parliament, or Bundesrat, represented the interests of the principalities. Important legislation required its approval. It was dominated by Prussia, the largest state. The Prussian delegation was usually headed and instructed by the Prussian prime minister, who was also chancellor of the Reich.

The prospect of military defeat toward the end of World War I precipitated the development of a parliamentary system of government within the Reich. Anticipating defeat, the military leadership in 1918 advised Kaiser Wilhelm II to abdicate and urged the parliamentary leadership to proclaim a republic and negotiate peace with the Western democracies. The emperor fled the country and eventually abdicated the throne. In October a cabinet was formed under Prince Max of Baden, and the constitution was amended. Ministerial responsibility to parliament was established, and the chancellor could no longer govern without parliamentary confidence.

The postwar Weimar constitution of 1919 introduced universal suffrage and created a dual executive. As head of government the chancellor was appointed by the president but required the confidence of the lower house. The directly elected president was chief of state. Under Article 48 the president had the power to issue decrees in lieu of legislation if a state of emergency existed. The constitution could, therefore, be characterized as providing a semiparliamentary system of government with strong presidential reserve powers.

The Weimar Republic fell for a variety of reasons, but it is generally held that several defects of its parliamentary system contributed to the weakness of German democracy in the period. Strict proportional representation favored an extreme fractionalization of the party system. With growing divisions in the electorate and polarization between the parties, it was difficult to form stable parliamentary majority governments in the Reichstag. Referendums were repeatedly misused by anti-democratic parties as a platform for their agitation. The powers of the president, meanwhile, were formidable. He appointed the government and could dissolve the Reichstag. The two Weimar presidents, Friedrich Ebert (1919–1925) and Paul von Hindenburg (1925–1934), could and did suspend the parliamentary decision-making process temporarily by the use of decrees. Hindenburg used presidential powers to the detriment of parliamentary democracy when the Reichstag seemed unable or unwilling to form viable majority governments in the face of the economic depression of 1929–1932.

By 1932 Adolf Hitler's National Socialists had become the strongest party in the Reichstag. Together with the Communist Party they had a "negative" majority of anti-democratic forces in the chamber, with the democratic parties of the center caught between these extremes and plagued by internal divisions. In January 1933 President von Hindenburg appointed Hitler chancellor of a new conservative-nationalist coalition government. The Reichstag's majority approved the new government's enabling act of March 1933 which, in effect, allowed the government to suspend the constitution. By the end of 1934 all major social, economic, and political institutions had been suppressed, dissolved, or brought under the control of the National Socialist Party. The Reichstag was radically and brutally purged of all opposition forces and continued to exist only as a puppet parliament under National Socialist control.

The National Socialist Third Reich collapsed at the end of World War II. In May 1945 the Allies defeated the German armies and occupied the Reich. Soon thereafter Germany was divided into four occupation zones. With growing tension between the western Allies on the one hand and the Soviet Union on the other, the Allies began to envision a West German state composed of the American, British, and French zones. Democratic political institutions were gradually reintroduced at the local and federal levels under Allied supervision. In 1948 the three western Allied military governors met with the prime ministers of the federal states in their zones and called for a constituent assembly to draft a constitution for the western zones. The states then convened an assembly, which completed its work in May 1949. The new Basic Law was soon ratified by the state parliaments in the western zones.

In the same year a second German state, the German Democratic Republic (GDR), was proclaimed in the Soviet zone. Initially it had a bicameral parliament: a lower People's Chamber (Volkskammer) and an upper chamber representing the interests of the five *länder,* or states, making up the GDR. The upper chamber was abolished together with the *länder* in 1952.

The People's Chamber included representatives of all authorized political parties as well as members of so-called mass organizations such as the communist youth and trade-union organizations. Thus, nominally, the GDR had a multiparty system. However, there was no free electoral competition between political parties. Instead of choosing among parties or candidates, voters were allowed only to approve or reject—usually in less than secret circumstances—a "unity list" of candidates drawn from all parties and mass organizations which were controlled by the communist Socialist Unity Party (Sozialistische Einheitspartei, SED) and its allied mass organizations in the Volkskammer. In 1952 the noncommunist parties formally recognized the leading role of the SED, which dominated the personnel and policies of the other parties and groups. One indicator of the Volkskammer's subordinate role was the low number of plenary meetings (three to four sessions per year) and the low number of laws enacted. At all levels of government the leading role of the SED was evident. In 1968 that role was enshrined in the constitution.

REUNIFICATION

The SED regime began to disintegrate in the autumn of 1989. Under the pressure of soaring migration from eastern to western Germany and protests against flagrant electoral fraud in the 1989 local elections, the regime opened the borders in November 1989. The Berlin Wall, built in 1961, fell. For the first time since 1949, eastern Germans could travel to the West without restrictions. The first and last free elections to the Volkskammer, in March 1990, resulted in a Christian Democratic victory (if not an overall majority) and the formation of a coalition government that included all major noncommunist parties. In East Germany the main task of the government of Lothar de Maizière was to negotiate the terms of unification with the Federal Republic.

A treaty between West and East Germany establishing a monetary, economic, and social union came into force on July 1, 1990. That same month the Volkskammer passed a law reconstituting the five *länder* abolished in 1952. In addition, a new *Land* of Berlin was created. Unification came on October 3, 1990, when the five *länder* of the GDR and Berlin formally declared their full political accession to the Federal Republic.

Parliamentary elections were held in the new *länder* and in Berlin on October 14, 1990. Upon unification, 144 delegates of the Volkskammer joined the Bundestag until regular elections to the Bundestag were held on December 2. Soon after, the Federal Republic's Basic Law was adopted in the five new *länder.*

In June 1991 the Bundestag decided by a vote of 337 to 320 that Berlin, the nominal capital, should become the seat of government and of the Bundestag in ten to twelve years (the move will occur sooner than originally planned). The Bundesrat chose to remain in Bonn for the foreseeable future.

In November 1991 the Bundestag set up a joint constitutional commission of sixty-four members, thirty-two Bundestag deputies and thirty-two delegates of the federal states, to make recommendations for constitutional reform in the light of unification. The commission made its report in October 1993. As one of the major constitutional reforms, the role of Bundesrat and Bundestag in the policy process of the European Union was strengthened in the new Articles 23 and 45.

ELECTIONS AND THE "BASIC LAW"

The Basic Law provides for two lawmaking bodies. The Bundestag is directly elected and represents the principle of parliamentary government. The chancellor is chosen by, and responsible to, the democratically elected Bundestag. The Bundesrat upholds the interests of the *länder.* It is not directly elected but consists of delegates sent and instructed by the state governments.

One of the major concerns of the constituent assembly that drafted the Basic Law in 1948–1949 was to avoid the constitutional defects that were believed to have contributed to the breakdown of the Weimar Republic. Unlike the Weimar Republic's Reichstag, the Bundestag was created as the only national institution capable of conferring direct democratic legitimacy.

The Basic Law is pronounced in its emphasis on representative government. It restricts referendums to boundary changes between federal states. Legislation is the sole responsibility of the Bundestag and Bundesrat. Unlike the president of the Weimar Republic, the federal president is not elected directly by the people but by a federal assembly consisting of the members of the Bundestag and an equal number of representatives appointed by the state parliaments (Article 5). Lacking the emergency powers and control over the armed forces conferred by Article 48 of the Weimar constitution, the federal president is a ceremonial head of state who can be reelected for a second five-year term.

The Bundestag also elects half of the judges of the federal constitutional court through a special selection committee. (The rest of the judges are elected by the Bundesrat.)

Similarly, the sixteen state ministers of justice, an equal number of Bundestag representatives, and the federal minister of justice form an electoral college that chooses the judges of most other federal courts (Article 95). The Bundestag elects the parliamentary commissioner for the armed forces (Article 45b), Germany's representatives to several supranational bodies, and members of supervisory bodies in the cultural, social, and economic sectors. Thus, in its capacity as an electoral college, the Bundestag gives indirect democratic legitimacy to a host of constitutional and other political bodies.

In times of peace, parliaments have three main functions: making and unmaking the government, making the government behave, and making laws. The Basic Law allocates all three functions to the Bundestag. Making and unmaking the government is one of the characteristic functions of legislatures in parliamentary, as opposed to presidential, systems of government. The Bundestag elects the federal chancellor in a secret vote (Article 63). Once elected, the chancellor appoints the cabinet and has the sole power to appoint and dismiss ministers, who are individually responsible to the chancellor and not to the Bundestag. The chancellor and cabinet can be dismissed only by the Bundestag through a vote of "constructive no confidence" (Article 67) in which a majority of the Bundestag members must be willing not only to depose the chancellor and the cabinet but also simultaneously to elect an alternative candidate. This constitutional device was designed to prevent the Weimar experience whereby a chancellor could be toppled by a purely "negative" majority that subsequently could not agree on a successor, inviting presidential government by decree. The chancellor can request a vote of confidence to consolidate parliamentary support in critical situations. If the chancellor loses the confidence of the majority, he or she may ask the president to dissolve the Bundestag (Article 68).

Through the political fusion of cabinet and parliamentary majority the Bundestag sustains the government in office, thus securing stability and effectiveness. The role and discipline of political parties is central in this context. As a response to the traditional hostility toward political parties in Germany, the Basic Law explicitly acknowledges their role as indispensable elements of parliamentary democracy. The acknowledgment of parties in Article 21 is often said to clash with Article 38, which safeguards the independence of individual members of parliament. According to Article 38, members of the Bundestag are representatives of the whole people, not bound by any orders or instructions and subject only to their conscience. There is widespread consensus, however, that the Basic Law generally acknowledges the overriding importance of parties in parliamentary life, and that Article 38 has to be seen as a safeguard against excessive disciplining of members of the Bundestag.

The flip side of the fusion of cabinet and parliamentary majority is the government's dependence on the majority party's or parties' willingness to support its policies. This provides the members of the governing parties with an important lever in their attempt to influence government policy. Despite a high degree of party discipline, the government cannot take majority support for granted. Because Article 38 of the Basic Law protects individual parliamentarians from undue pressures, the government occasionally has to make major concessions to recalcitrant members within the majority parties to secure their support.

The Basic Law is also concerned with parliamentary rights that permit the opposition to keep the government on its toes. According to Article 43, the Bundestag and its committees have the right to demand the presence of any member of the federal government at any time. This provision implicitly includes a right of the Bundestag members to ask questions and request information. One of the decisive levers of the parliamentary minority is its ability to appeal to the public in a kind of permanent election campaign. The possibility of public clashes with the government is, therefore, an important precondition of the opposition's effectiveness. Article 42(1) provides that the public can be excluded from sessions of the Bundestag only by a two-thirds majority, that is, usually only with opposition consent.

According to Article 44 the Bundestag has the right to appoint investigative committees. The parliamentary minority's rights are enhanced by the provision that such committees have to be established upon a motion supported by one-fourth of the Bundestag's members.

The parliamentary commissioner for the armed forces elected by the Bundestag is not merely a military ombudsman monitoring respect for civil rights in the armed forces. He or she has the additional duty of assisting the Bundestag in monitoring civil rights in the Bundeswehr (Article 45b).

Committees are the most important tool of parliamentary scrutiny of the executive. The number and function of most committees in the Bundestag are laid down in the Bundestag's rules of procedure. The Basic Law explicitly requires the Bundestag to set up at least four committees: a Committee on Foreign Affairs, a Defense Committee (Article 45a[1]), a Committee on European Union Affairs (Article 45), and a Petitions Committee dealing with citizens' complaints (Article 45c). The powers of the Defense Committee go beyond the powers of an ordinary parliamentary committee in that it, like investigative committees, has the right to apply the rules of criminal procedure.

The Bundestag's powers to make laws are laid down in the Basic Law's section on federal legislation (Articles 70–82). The role of the Bundestag is stated in Article 77(1): "Federal laws are enacted by the Bundestag. After their enactment they shall without delay be transmitted to the Bundesrat by the president of the Bundestag." Bills can be initiated by the federal government, the Bundestag, or the Bundesrat (Article 76[1]). Although most bills are initiated by the federal government, the Bundestag has the final say over legislation. Since much of the government's policy is no longer laid down in acts of parliament but in delegated legislation and directives, circumvention of the Bundestag is prevented by Article 80 of the Basic Law, which stipulates that government directives cannot be issued unless the government is empowered to do so by an act of the legislature. The Bundestag's powers of appropriation are secured in Articles 110–115 of the Basic Law.

PARLIAMENT BUILDINGS

Between 1949 and 1989 Bonn was the provisional capital of the Federal Republic of Germany, while East Berlin was proclaimed as the capital of the German Democratic Republic. The Bundestag met in Bonn. As the number of members and staff grew, the seat of the legislature had to be expanded several times. In 1981 the Bundestag decided to expand and completely rebuild the plenary chamber. The new chamber's design breaks with the traditional shape of German parliaments, which is a semicircular arrangement of deputies' seats facing the rostrum, the Bundestag president's chair, the government benches, and the seats provided for Bundesrat representatives. In the new chamber, deputies' seats are arranged in a full circle. The government benches are no longer raised above the level of the rest of the house.

In June 1991 the Bundestag voted to move to Berlin once the old Reichstag building could be restored and suitable office space provided. The circular shape of the Bonn Bundestag's plenum is to be retained. The Bundestag will begin working in Berlin in the summer recess of the year 1999. The Bundesrat will remain in Bonn.

ELECTIONS, POLITICAL PARTIES, AND COALITIONS

The Bundestag is elected for a four-year term. Elections can be held sooner if the government loses its majority and the federal president assents to the chancellor's request to dissolve the house. The Bundestag's legislative term ends with the assembly of a new Bundestag. The Basic Law grants universal suffrage and the right to hold public office to Germans eighteen years of age or above.

For elections to the Bundestag, the Federal Republic is presently divided into 328 single-member constituencies, or electoral districts. The legislature consists of at least 656 members, half of whom are elected by plurality vote in the aforementioned districts. The other half are elected by proportional representation from state party lists. Each voter casts two votes—the first for a constituency candidate and the second for a party. There is no requirement of consistency and, since the early 1970s, there has been a significant increase in the number of "tactical" voters splitting their ticket—that is, supporting a candidate of one party with their first vote and the list of a different party with the second. Effective with the fifteenth Bundestag (which is to convene in 2002), the number of electoral districts will be reduced from 328 to 299. Hence the number of seats in the Bundestag will drop to 598.

The party vote is decisive for the outcome because it is used to determine the number of seats a party will receive. After the seats won in the district contests are deducted from this total, the party's remaining seats are filled with candidates from the state party lists. If a party wins more direct mandates than it would be entitled to under proportional representation, it retains these extra seats, and the size of the parliament is increased. Therefore, the number of seats in the Bundestag is often larger than twice the number of constituencies.

The formula used to calculate the number of parliamentary seats assigned to each party is the Niemeyer system of mathematical proportionality. Germany's electoral law does not ensure strict proportionality, however. The experience of a highly fractionalized Reichstag in the Weimar Republic encouraged the major parties to agree on a 5 percent threshold: Since 1953 a party has had to win at least 5 percent of the federal total or three direct district mandates to be represented proportionally. Because of a ruling of the federal constitutional court, this rule did not apply in the first all-German election of 1990. Instead, separate 5 percent thresholds were applied, for this election only, in the former areas of West and East Germany. The purpose was to give the smaller eastern German parties a better chance to win seats in the Bundestag.

The German party system underwent a process of concentration between 1949 and 1961. By 1961 a three-party system had emerged, with two major parties (the Christian Democratic Union, or CDU, and the Social Democratic Party, or SPD) and one smaller party (the Free Democratic Party, or FDP). In the elections of 1983 a fourth party (the Greens) straddled the 5 percent threshold and has been represented in the Bundestag most of the time since. Unification made remarkably little difference to the pattern of party representation in the Bundestag. The only additions were the eastern German Green Party, which merged with the western Greens in 1993, and the successor party of the former ruling communist party of the GDR, the Party of Democratic Socialism/Left List (PDS/LL). The 1994 Bundestag was characterized by a five-party system with the Christian Democratic Union/Christian Social Union (CDU/CSU) and SPD as the dominant parties.

Coalitions have been a characteristic feature of government formation and policy making in the Bundestag. Only once in the history of the Federal Republic has a single party managed to win an overall majority in the Bundestag. The 270 seats gained by the CDU/CSU in the 1957 elections gave it a majority of 54.3 percent of the seats in the Bundestag. Nevertheless, it formed a government coalition with the conservative German Party. The dominant pattern since 1961 has been a minimum winning coalition between one of the two major parties and the small FDP.

The Christian Democratic Union combines the social doctrines of the Roman Catholic Church with a conservative stress on authority and support for traditional institutions such as church and family. Internal factionalism notwithstanding, the CDU is united behind a set of political goals favoring a free-enterprise economic system restrained by a socially responsible government ("social market economy"). The party has traditionally advocated a Western orientation in its foreign policy, meaning reconciliation with France, European integration, and membership in NATO. The CDU has been considered as a right-of-center "catch-all party" appealing to a wide spectrum of the electorate. It is a national party, running in every state except Bavaria, where it is allied with the CSU. Despite occasional political and strategic differences between the leaderships of CDU and CSU, the two so-called Union parties generally function as one in matters of national politics. The two parties campaign together under the CDU/CSU banner, form a single parliamentary party in the Bundestag, and have always entered the government as a coalition.

The Social Democratic Party is a center-left catch-all party. During the 1960s and 1970s the SPD was often portrayed as a model of successful transformation from a traditional socialist party emphasizing class conflict and economic planning to a modern social democratic party advocating the extension of the welfare state, social policy, and increased worker benefits in return for acceptance of the free market economy and capitalist production. Since the end of the 1970s, however, the SPD has found itself wedged between the CDU's emphasis on market reforms and economic growth and the Green Party's dedication to environmental protection. In trying to appeal to both a working-class and a new middle-class, center-left constituency, the SPD has been torn repeatedly by conflicting interests. The party's cohesiveness under the chancellorship of Helmut Schmidt (1974–1982) was undermined accordingly, and the strategic conflict has not been resolved. While in opposition at the federal level, the SPD has entered government coalitions at the state level with the CDU, the FDP, and the Green Party. The Green Party is the SPD's predominant coalition partner in those states where the Social Democrats are in government.

The FDP consists of two major wings. The progressive faction stresses the protection of secular values in education and social life as well as civil liberties. The more conservative wing is an advocate of private enterprise and a free market economy. The party draws much of its electoral support from business interests, the Protestant middle class (especially the professions), and farmers. Although the FDP is the smallest of the parties that have been represented in the Bundestag without interruption since 1949, its influence in the party system greatly outweighs its share of the popular vote. With its strategic, centrist ideological position, the FDP normally controls enough votes to play a pivotal role in forming government coalitions and directing the course of German politics. In addition to helping other parties form majority coalitions, its most characteristic functions in the Bundestag are those of ideological balancer in government coalitions and agent of transition. In 1969 and 1982 major government changes took place as a result not of electoral swings but of a change of partners by the FDP.

The western Green Party was formed in 1980. It developed out of the environmentalist, peace, and other civic movements of the 1970s. It is opposed to nuclear energy and highly skeptical of economic growth, which is seen as the main agent of environmental degradation. The eastern Greens remained independent until the two parties merged in 1993. The eastern Greens have their roots in the civil rights opposition to communist rule in the GDR. The party's positive attitude toward economic growth is an issue that divides the western and eastern factions of the party. The eastern Greens consider strong economic growth as a vital precondition of recovery in the East. A strong pacifist element and an emphasis on women's and civil rights are shared by the two wings of the party.

The West German Greens cleared the 5 percent hurdle in the elections of 1983 and 1987 and were thus represented in the Bundestag between 1983 and 1990. The party had not merged with its eastern German counterpart before the first all-German elections in 1990 and failed to clear the 5 percent threshold in western Germany, but the eastern Greens were successful. The merger of the two Green Parties in 1993 secured their return to the Bundestag in 1994 with 7.3 percent of the total vote.

The PDS/LL is the successor to the former ruling communist party of the GDR. It is an alliance of reform communists and old hard-liners in the SED. Showing surprising resilience, the party gained more than 11 percent of the eastern vote in 1990 and more than 16 percent in 1994. With just 4.4 percent of the national vote in 1994, the party failed to clear the 5 percent threshold but did manage to secure proportional representation in the Bundestag because it won direct mandates in four East Berlin constituencies. Since 1990 the PDS/LL has had some success in attracting support from those sectors of eastern German society that have felt most affected by the painful transformation of the eastern German economy. In its program the PDS/LL portrays itself as a radical socialist party standing to the left of the SPD and emphasizing anticapitalist and "radical democratic" positions. In its economic and social policies it appeals primarily to eastern German protest voters by promising decisive action against unemployment, protection of property rights of eastern Germans against the claims of those whose property was expropriated between 1945 and 1989, expansion of the welfare state, women's rights, and the creation of a political body representing eastern German interests to the federal government and the Bundestag.

ORGANIZATION AND OPERATIONS OF PARLIAMENT

According to Article 39(2) of the Basic Law, the Bundestag "shall assemble at the latest on the thirtieth day after the election." Its term of office ends after a maximum of four years. "The new election shall be held at the earliest forty-five, at the latest forty-seven, months after the beginning of the legislative term. When the Bundestag is dissolved, the new election shall be held within sixty days" (Article 39[1]).

The Bundestag does not have the power to dissolve itself. Moreover, the federal chancellor lacks the British prime minister's power to dissolve parliament. The federal president may dissolve it under two conditions, which are clearly set out in the Basic Law: (1) If none of the candidates nominated for the office of federal chancellor has secured an overall majority of the votes in the house after three ballots, the president can either appoint a candidate who obtained a relative majority or dissolve the Bundestag within seven days of the third ballot (Article 63[4]). (2) "If a motion of the federal chancellor for a vote of confidence is not assented to by the majority of the members of the Bundestag, the federal president may, upon the proposal of the federal chancellor, dissolve the Bundestag within twenty-one days" (Article 68[1]). The same article stipulates that the right to dissolve lapses as soon as the Bundestag, with a majority of its members, elects another federal chancellor (for example, under Article 67). Between 1949 and 1994 the Bundestag has been dissolved only twice before its term had come to an end: in September 1972 and in January 1983. In both these instances the presidents used the second route for dissolution.

The Bundestag's annual calendar is highly flexible. Its working rhythm is determined by the Senior Council, a collective steering body comprising the president of the Bundestag, the four vice presidents, and the whips of all parliamentary parties and groups. Decisions of the Senior Council are usually taken unanimously. The Bundestag is not permanently in session. Usually, one or two weeks in which the Bundestag is in session alternate with two weeks without parliamentary business.

Weeks in which the Bundestag is in session have a relatively fixed structure. The week usually begins on Monday afternoon with meetings of the executive council and other bodies of the parliamentary parties. On Tuesday mornings the parliamentary parties' working groups meet, usually followed by party caucuses on Tuesday afternoon. On Wednesdays there are parliamentary committee meetings and question time on the floor of the Bundestag. The Bundestag allocates a maximum of 180 minutes per week to question time, during which members of the federal government answer questions put by individual members. Each member is allowed to submit up to two short questions each week to be answered orally. In the 1991–1994 Bundestag, 4,215 such questions were submitted. A further 16,665 questions were submitted for written answers from the government. Since 1995 question time may be extended if called for by the Bundestag's president and agreed to by the parliamentary parties. The plenary sessions of the Bundestag are usually held on Thursdays and Fridays. On Friday afternoon, members return to their constituencies.

As part of the parliamentary reforms of 1995, the Bundestag introduced a "core time" of four to six hours per week during which debates on "fundamental issues" were to be scheduled and no other parliamentary business could take place. The purpose of the reform was to enable members to attend plenary debates and avoid the publicly damaging image of a vast number of empty chairs in the chamber. Speeches are limited to ten minutes to encourage debate. The president or presiding vice president may interrupt the debate in consultation with the parliamentary parties if attendance appears to be dropping below one-quarter of the members. A recorded vote can be taken to monitor attendance.

Article 42 of the Basic Law stipulates that the Bundestag meets in public. The public can be excluded on a motion from the federal government or from one-tenth of the members provided the motion is supported by two-thirds of the Bundestag deputies. Proceedings in the plenum may be broadcast and televised.

Whereas plenary sessions of the Bundestag are public unless a qualified majority decides otherwise, the committees generally meet in private (Paragraph 69 [1] and [2] of the Rules of Procedure). Since 1995 visitors and media representatives have been allowed to attend committees' concluding sessions on a particular bill or issue. Deliberations preceding the concluding session generally are still closed, although the public may be admitted if a majority of the committee so decides. Committee meetings are never broadcast even when the public is admitted.

LAW MAKING

The Basic Law distinguishes among three types of laws: constitutional amendments, "simple laws," and "consent laws." Constitutional amendments require a two-thirds majority in both Bundestag and Bundesrat. A simple law is resolved by the Bundestag subject to the suspensory veto of the Bundesrat; that is, the Bundesrat can delay a bill's passage by lodging an objection. Such an objection can be overturned by an absolute majority of the Bundestag. If a two-thirds majority of the Bundesrat objects to a simple bill, this veto can be overturned only if at least two-thirds of the Bundestag members present and at least 50 percent of the total number of Bundestag members dismiss the veto (Article 77[4]). Consent laws require the consent of the Bundesrat; that is, they are subject to an absolute veto that cannot be overturned by the Bundestag. Most consent laws affect the interests of the states. They include amendments to the Basic Law, all laws affecting the federal relationship with the states (including state finance), the relationship between the federal and state governments, declaration of states of emergency and war, and legislation delegated to Germany by the European Union. In practice, more than half of all federal laws, and the vast majority of important domestic laws, are consent laws.

The federal government, the Bundesrat, a parliamentary party, or 5 percent of the members of the Bundestag from different parties are entitled to introduce bills in the Bundestag. Individual members of the Bundestag do not have the right to introduce bills.

Before a *government bill* is formally introduced, it passes through numerous phases of drafting, revision, consultation, and deliberation involving civil servants and ministers at the federal and state levels, affected interest groups, and the chancellor's office. Bills initiated by the government are submitted first to the Bundesrat as they clear the cabinet. The draft is then sent to the Bundestag, together with the Bundesrat's opinion. Bills initiated by the Bundesrat go first to the federal government, which sends them to the Bundestag, together with its opinion. Bills initiated by at least one parliamentary party ("nongovernment bills") are introduced in the Bundestag first.

The Bundestag considers bills in three readings. In most cases the first reading merely consists of the Bundestag president's referring the bill to a specialized standing committee for examination. Unlike parliamentary practice elsewhere, debate on the merits of a bill rarely takes place before the bill is sent to a committee. After detailed examination, the committee reports back to the plenum and the bill receives its second reading. It is possible for the bill to be sent back to committee before being voted on by the plenum at the third reading.

In practice the second and third readings are often fused, and the committee's report is usually accepted. The impact of the committee's work may be significant. Detailed scrutiny of a bill usually begins in the committees—and among the specialists within each party—rather than in the chamber as a whole. This leaves the Bundestag primarily in command of committee referral in the initial stage of deliberation. It is not uncommon for committees to substantially rewrite bills referred to them, and it is the committee version that the house considers in the second reading.

The discussion of bills by party experts in committee favors a consensual relationship between government and opposition in legislating. Nevertheless, there has been a relative decline of consensual law making since the mid-1960s. Whereas in the four Bundestag terms between 1961 and 1976 seven out of ten acts were passed unanimously in the third reading, this percentage had declined to about 50 percent by 1983. The parliaments of 1983–1987 and 1987–1990 witnessed extremely low levels of consensualism, with less than 20 percent of all acts being passed unanimously in the third reading. This extraordinary development in the 1983–1987 and 1987–1990 parliaments is largely a result of the Green Party's adversarial style in opposition.

If the Bundesrat rejects a bill or parts of it, it will usually be referred to the Conference Committee, which consists of thirty-two members, sixteen drawn from the Bundesrat and sixteen from the Bundestag. The Conference Committee is an autonomous constitutional body with its own rules of procedure. Its Bundesrat members are not bound by their state governments' instructions. The Conference Committee's purpose is to agree on a compromise acceptable to both assemblies so that it is unnecessary for the Bundesrat to use its veto powers. In the case of a simple law, only the Bundesrat can convene the Conference Committee. In the case of a consent law, either chamber or the federal government can initiate the mediation process. If the Conference Committee proposes amendments to the bill, the Bundestag must again vote on it. In times when the federal government has no majority in the Bundesrat, the Conference Committee is one of the key players in the policy process.

A bill comes into force by being signed by the federal president and promulgated in the federal statutes. The federal president has the right and duty to review the formal constitutionality of the law. If the president decides that a law is materially unconstitutional or that the process of law making has been unconstitutional, he or she has to veto it. Presidential vetoes have been extremely rare. Between 1949 and 1990 only 6 of 4,389 federal laws were vetoed by the president. Once a law has come into force, the federal constitutional court must, on the motion of a party entitled to bring such proceedings, review the material constitutionality of the law.

The number of bills introduced and acts passed did not increase in a linear fashion between 1949 and 1994. Cyclical ups and downs did occur, however. The Bundestag passed a very high number of laws in the phase of postwar reconstruction (1949–1957). After this phase the number of laws declined, increasing again when the first SPD-FDP coalition had a secure majority in the 1972–1976 Bundestag and continued its ambitious reform program. The subsequent decline came to an end in the 1983–1987 Bundestag, which saw a new CDU/CSU-FDP coalition. Legislative output increased in the 1990–1994 Bundestag because of unification.

While the number of federal laws varied in a cyclical pattern, legislation produced by the European Community (now European Union) increased dramatically. Directives of the Council of Ministers must be incorporated into national law by the national parliaments. The number of European laws referred, or "delegated," to the Bundestag increased from just 13 in the 1957–1961 Bundestag to 2,413 in 1987–1990. In 1990–1994, there was a slight decline to 2,070 European laws brought before the house.

In the first twelve parliamentary terms (1949–1994), 59 percent of legislative initiatives had their origin in government departments. Of all bills enacted, 76.2 percent were government bills. Laws initiated by the Bundesrat have been few—490 in 1949–1994, or 6.6 percent of all bills introduced in the Bundestag. Between 1949 and 1994, 34.4 percent of all bills were initiated by nongovernment actors such as a parliamentary party or 5 percent of the members, whereas only 18.5 percent of all bills enacted by the Bundestag were initiated by such means. In practice, the vast majority of successful "nongovernment" initiatives have been bills initiated by the governing majority parties. For example, ninety-seven out of ninety-nine successful nongovernment laws enacted by the Bundestag between 1990 and 1994 were sponsored by one or more of the government parties.

COMMITTEES

Most Bundestag members' parliamentary timetables are dominated by committee work—not only in the formal Bundestag committees, but also in parallel working groups within their parliamentary parties. In the period 1949–1994 the Bundestag held 2,487 plenary sessions with an average duration of approximately six hours. In the same period more than 32,000 committee meetings were held. At least four different kinds of parliamentary committees can be distinguished: standing committees organized by subject and area of government, special ad hoc committees, investigative committees, and commissions of inquiry. A residual category comprises committees like the Committee on Election Validation, Immunity, and Rules; the Petitions Committee; and the Senior Council. The role of committees in legislation and executive oversight is discussed elsewhere in this essay.

In the 1990–1994 Bundestag there were twenty-two specialized standing committees, one special ad hoc committee, three investigative committees, and four commissions of inquiry. According to the Bundestag's rules of procedure, the committees are "organs of the Bundestag," the purpose of which is to prepare subjects for its consideration. They can make recommendations to the Bundestag in matters expressly referred to them and examine any other subject in their area of specialization, but they have no independent legislative powers. In matters concerning European Union legislation, the Bundestag may delegate its powers to the Committee on European Union Affairs to speed up deliberations. The house can, however, revoke these powers at any time.

In practice, committees have a great deal of autonomy and exercise a good deal of control over their own jurisdictions. They determine their own calendar of meetings and set their own agenda. Only the Appropriations Committee, however, has blanket permission to meet during debates on the floor of the house; other committees require the Bundestag president's approval to meet while the legislature is in session. Complaints about the increasing tendency of Bundestag committees to meet on Thursdays and Friday mornings during plenary debates led in 1995 to the introduction of "core time" for plenary debate, as discussed previously. Committee chairs and deputy chairs together exercise great power over committee organization and procedure.

The number of committee seats to which each parliamentary party is entitled is determined by proportional representation. The committees' composition reflects the strength of the parties in the house. According to paragraph 57 of the Rules of Procedure, the parliamentary parties nominate committee members. Individual members not belonging to a party can be nominated by the Bundestag president if the need arises. They do not have the right to vote in committee, however. Once party quotas are established, the appointment of committee members, as well as the recall and replacement of committee members, is the sole responsibility of the parliamentary parties. Appointments need merely to be communicated to the president of the house. Likewise, committee chairmanships are distributed among the parties by proportional representation, and the parties fill the positions falling to them. The assignment of specific committee chairmanships is negotiated in the Senior Council.

APPROPRIATIONS AND BUDGET

The Bundestag makes annual appropriations to fund the operations of the federal government. The financial year corresponds to the calendar year. According to Article 110(2) of the Basic Law, the Bundestag must pass the budget for the next year before the end of the current year. In fact, however, never since 1949 has the budget been passed on time. In this situation the transitional arrangements provided for by Article 111 of the Basic Law take effect. Until the budget is passed, the government may continue to make payments and borrow money necessary to maintain the status quo. Under this time pressure, the Bundestag has empowered its Appropriations Committee to authorize transfers within the budget as eventually enacted, or to make new appropriations in advance of, or in place of, the action of the full house.

The sole right to introduce the appropriations bill rests with the federal government. By early summer the individual government departments submit their estimates to the Ministry of Finance, which is in charge of organizing interdepartmental negotiations and ensuring that the departmental estimates remain within the limits of the government's medium-term finance plan. The Ministry of Finance has to ensure that revenue and expenditure are balanced or, if necessary, additional expenditure is covered by borrowing. Disputes between spending departments and the ministry are usually settled before the budget plan reaches the cabinet, where remaining differences are settled and a final, collective decision is made by the government.

The appropriations bill usually receives its first reading in the Bundestag after the summer recess. Unlike ordinary bills it is sent to the Bundestag and the Bundesrat at the same time (Article 110[3] of the Basic Law). After a first reading in the plenary, the bill is referred to the Appropriations Committee, which receives reports and recommendations from the specialized committees that oversee each ministry.

The most influential committee of the house, the Appropriations Committee is by custom chaired by a senior opposition member. Despite the considerable experience and expertise of members, the government majority in the committee is relatively cohesive; thus the committee has little scope for major changes. It can, and usually does, change the government's plan in some details, hear civil servants, and make suggestions for the following years. In the second and third reading of the appropriations bill, the recommendations of the Appropriations Committee are usually accepted. The debates at second and third reading have the character of a clash between government and opposition over broad policy matters rather than details of the budget.

LEADERSHIP AND "PARLIAMENTARY PARTIES"

The presidency of the Bundestag is the highest office in the organization of the house. The president is also the chief of the Bundestag's administrative staff. The president and four vice presidents are elected by an absolute majority of the members of the Bundestag or, failing that on two ballots, by a plurality on the third. The rules of procedure charge the president with representing the Bundestag, chairing its sessions in a fair and nonpartisan manner, and maintaining order.

As a matter of protocol, the president of the Bundestag stands second only to the federal president. In practice, presidential influence is severely limited. For the employment of many of his or her formal powers, the president requires the consensus of the parties or the support of a majority. The exceptions are few. The president has discretion in the acceptance of points of order and of supplementary oral questions from the floor, may call members to order, and may expel members for using "unparliamentary language" or for other disruptive behavior. In case of disorder the president may suspend the session. All other powers can be employed only with party support. The 1995 procedural reforms strengthened the president's powers somewhat.

The president or presiding vice president may now extend debates, provided the parliamentary parties agree.

In the appointment, promotion, dismissal, and supervision of the staff of the Bundestag and in the general administration of the house, the president must work closely with the four vice presidents, who, with the president, make up the Bundestag's presidium. In chairing sessions, the president must follow agreements reached in the Senior Council on the agenda, the order of recognition of the main speakers, and the format of the debate.

The "parliamentary parties" are the key organizing agents in the house. A parliamentary party is defined by the rules of procedure as a group of members all belonging to the same party or to different parties with concomitant political goals that do not compete against each other in the same *land* (such as the CDU/CSU). Opportunistic combinations of members hoping to gain the privileges of party status are thus precluded. A group will be recognized as a parliamentary party only if it makes up at least 5 percent of the members of the Bundestag. At the discretion of the Bundestag majority, smaller groups can be granted a special group status with at least some of the parliamentary parties' rights in the plenum and committees. The size of a parliamentary party determines the number of seats accruing to it in committees, the number of committee chairs it can name, the amount of office space and clerical staff it receives, and its representation on the Bundestag's most important steering body, the Senior Council.

Considerable amounts of money are appropriated to the parliamentary parties in support of their work. In fiscal year 1991 the Bundestag spent more than DM100 million on the parliamentary parties. As official organs of the Bundestag, parliamentary parties can directly appeal to the federal constitutional court under Article 93(1) of the Basic Law. Most rights of initiative and participation in the legislative process accrue to the parliamentary parties rather than individual members. The most important instruments of parliamentary interpellation, for example, can be initiated only by the parliamentary parties or by groups of Bundestag members from different parties that meet the minimum size required of a parliamentary party in the rules of procedure. Parliamentary parties have the right to nominate and recall their members of committees.

Compared with the powers of the parliamentary parties, the rights of individual members are circumscribed. They may propose amendments at the second reading of bills, participate in debates, speak on points of order, demand amendments to the daily agenda, and see all documents presented to the Bundestag or one of its committees. The rights to participate in regular debates and ask parliamentary questions are further restricted by the rules of the individual parliamentary parties. Members without a party whip cannot be denied a place on committees, but they are not allowed to vote within the committee. Bundestag deputies have to work through, and find majorities within, their parliamentary parties rather than acting individually.

The parliamentary parties are complex organizations. Interest groups, ideological factions, and regional groups exist within them, yet three key organizational elements—caucuses, working groups, and leadership—are common to all of them. A parliamentary party's leadership consists of a chair, deputies, the elected members of the executive committee, the chairs of the working groups, and the party whips. The party meeting, or caucus, is the highest decision-making body of the parliamentary party. Members of the parliamentary party are bound by its decisions unless they declare their disagreement in advance. In practice, however, the caucus is an organ of ratification rather than a decision-making body.

The function of producing party agreement has fallen to the elected executive committees and, in particular, to the working groups. The latter are the most important bodies in the parliamentary parties' day-to-day work. In the two large parliamentary parties, CDU/CSU and SPD, these working groups usually shadow one or more standing committees of the house. Their chairs are part of the parliamentary parties' leadership, and their members are usually simultaneously members or deputy members of the appropriate Bundestag committees. The interlocking system of specialized committees and party working groups allows the Bundestag to obtain the advantages of division of labor and specialization while simultaneously reducing the risk of an overly segmented decision-making process.

Bundestag members vote with their parties most of the time. One of the most commonly used indexes of the voting consistency of parliamentary parties is the Rice index of cohesion. It ranges from 0 (completely divided) to 100 (perfectly cohesive). Data on recorded votes, which constitute only a minority of all votes taken in the Bundestag, tend to overestimate the general cohesion of the parliamentary parties. Recorded votes are usually taken when an issue is highly contentious, when at least one party wants to signal its position to the public, or when the party whips need to ensure members' attendance. Pressure on individual members is particularly high. Nevertheless, there is some interesting variation across time and parties. During the first four legislative terms of the Bundestag (1949–1965), the SPD was the most cohesive party in the house. The period between 1965 and 1972 was a phase of transition. The 1965–1969 Bundestag witnessed a major drop in the SPD's

Rice index, reflecting the strong intraparty tensions during the time of the "grand coalition" between Social Democrats and Christian Democrats. The same phenomenon can be observed for the CDU/CSU, for which the cohesion index also dropped. By contrast, the FDP stabilized its voting cohesion on a high level, which it has maintained since then.

SPD-FDP coalitions under chancellors Willy Brandt and Helmut Schmidt characterized the period between 1969 and 1982. The slim majorities these coalitions usually had and the competitive attitude of the CDU/CSU opposition, especially in the early 1970s, favored a high degree of voting cohesion on both sides of the house. The CDU/CSU, in particular, achieved much higher levels of cohesion than it had during the 1950s and 1960s. Since 1983 the SPD's voting cohesion has dropped slightly. Whereas the SPD had been by far the most cohesive party in the first four legislative terms of the Bundestag, it was the least cohesive between 1983 and 1990.

DEBATES, INTERPELLATIONS, AND VOTING PROCEDURES

Surveys have shown that for most members of the Bundestag committee work and legislation are more important than debates or constituency work. In an average session, the British House of Commons spends at least three to four times as many hours on the floor of the house as does the Bundestag. One frequent criticism of the Bundestag is, therefore, that it devotes too much time and energy to committee work and fails as the "grand inquest of the nation" in the plenum. This is partly a consequence of the relatively consensual relationship between government and opposition.

Nevertheless, the nature of debate on the floor has grown more adversarial since the 1970s. This adversarial quality is reflected in the growing number of "interpellations" initiated by the opposition. These instruments are of major importance because, unlike debates on occasions such as the second reading of bills or the chancellor's "government declarations," they do not have to be agreed upon in the interparty bargaining processes of the Senior Council. Nor do they require a majority vote in the chamber. Interpellations must simply be proposed by an opposition party. They enjoy preferential treatment in the Bundestag's timetable. Although they may on occasion serve the majority by allowing it to plant questions and help the government advance its own views, they are predominantly opposition instruments.

Voting procedures in the Bundestag can be grouped into three categories according to the degree of information each method discloses about the positions taken by individual deputies: closed or secret voting, "semi-open" or anonymous voting, and open or public voting (recorded votes). Completely closed voting is restricted to instances in which the Bundestag elects the federal chancellor, its own officers, or its representatives in other bodies. Secret votes are carried out with ballot papers bearing the names of candidates. Most votes are taken by semi-open or anonymous voting. Voting of this type is open in the sense that it occurs in the presence of people who have come to listen to speeches. It is closed in the sense that the voting position of individual members of parliament is not revealed because the votes of individual deputies are not recorded. In open voting, the individual positions of deputies are recorded in the minutes. The Bundestag votes by a combination of roll call and paper ballot: Members identify themselves and their voting positions on slips of paper. The members, as their names are called, place their voting slips in a ballot box.

The official record of the Bundestag is published at regular intervals. It is divided into two main sections: debates and papers. It is available in many public libraries and has a very detailed index of members' speeches.

EXECUTIVE-LEGISLATIVE RELATIONS AND OVERSIGHT

The government has no formal veto over Bundestag legislation, but it usually controls a parliamentary majority in the house. If it loses its majority, it must resign or be replaced by another government through a vote of constructive no confidence. All legislation involving federal expenditure requires government approval (paragraph 96[4] of the Rules of Procedure). The suspensory veto of the Bundesrat in the case of simple bills, and its absolute veto in the case of consent bills, comes close to an executive veto by the state governments, whose interests are represented in the Bundesrat.

The Bundestag's principal instruments of executive oversight are its standing committees. Most of these twenty or so committees parallel a government ministry. Only the Appropriations, Justice, and European Union Committees' terms of reference cut across all ministries. All committees are entitled, under the Basic Law, to compel the attendance of ministers, as is the whole house. Most committees regularly question ministers and civil servants on issues within their terms of reference.

The opposition typically uses investigative committees to inquire into instances of alleged government wrongdoing. Such committees are appointed at the request of at least one-fourth of the Bundestag members. Between 1949 and 1990 twenty-one of twenty-seven investigative committees were initiated by the opposition. Their effectiveness as fact-finding bodies is limited, however. The committees' terms of reference are, in effect, defined by the Bundestag's majority. (The Defense Committee is the only standing committee that has the power to constitute itself as an investigative committee for the purpose of holding inquiries. Between 1949 and 1990 it used that power eleven times.)

Due to the extraordinary salience and contentiousness of most of the issues dealt with by investigative committees, the relationship between majority and minority in committee is highly adversarial, with very little scope for interparty agreement. The committees can hear witnesses and experts and have the power to apply the rules of criminal procedure when hearing witnesses. However, governments of all parties have repeatedly used the rules of criminal justice (or claims of national security) to justify their refusal to permit civil servants to give evidence. Frequently, committees cannot agree on a single report, in which case a majority report and one or more minority reports are produced.

The adversarial style of investigative committees stands in strong contrast to the working of commissions of inquiry. These commissions are appointed ad hoc to inform house and public on issues of fundamental political importance. Whereas all other committees of the house consist solely of Bundestag deputies, commissions of inquiry have the power to appoint outside experts as full committee members. These experts are included to match the superior expertise of executive or private sector bodies. Commissions have dealt with issues such as constitutional reform, technology assessment, and long-term social problems. Their reports have often been of high academic value, yet their recommendations have had only limited influence.

The Petitions Committee can be approached directly by citizens who complain of instances of misadministration. The committee does not have the power to investigate a matter that is not the subject of a specific complaint. The committee is explicitly mentioned in the Basic Law (Article 45c) and has to be reappointed with each parliamentary term. It has the right to see government records, visit all federal institutions, and hear witnesses and experts. Courts and the administration have the duty to support the Petitions Committee. It can make recommendations to the house but has no power to redress grievances.

The office of the parliamentary commissioner for the armed forces is influenced by the model of the Scandinavian ombudsman. According to Article 45b of the Basic Law the commissioner assists the Bundestag in its exercise of parliamentary oversight. He or she is elected by the Bundestag for a five-year term. Although the office is incompatible with Bundestag membership, most incumbents have been former Bundestag members. The commissioner is assisted by a small staff and acts on behalf of the Bundestag or its Defense Committee as an investigator, with the right to initiate inquiries on his or her own authority and to receive complaints directly from members of the armed forces who feel that their legal rights have been violated.

The Bundestag gives relatively little importance to the after-the-fact scrutiny of expenditure. Spending audits are conducted by the Federal Audit Office, an independent body that receives the government's accounts and assesses the economic efficiency of government spending. Its reports are sent to the government first. Eventually the Appropriations Committee or its audit subcommittee receives the reports together with the government's response. The Appropriations Committee's subsequent reports to the Bundestag usually receive very little parliamentary or public interest.

Oversight of the three secret services in the Federal Republic is extremely difficult. The Parlamentarische Kontrollkommission (PKK), a consultative body, is not a proper committee of the house. Its members (there were eight in 1990–1994) are senior parliamentarians drawn from the CDU/CSU, SPD, and FDP. According to the terms of the secret service oversight legislation, the federal government must keep the commission up to date on the general activity of the services and alert it to issues of particular importance. The initiative lies with the government. The commission's rights do not affect the powers of other parliamentary committees to carry out investigations within their respective jurisdictions. The commission does not have the right to make recommendations to the house. The budget of the secret services is dealt with by a small subgroup of the Appropriations Committee. Similar rules apply to the G-10 Commission, whose five members (in 1990–1994) are to be informed by the government in cases where civil liberties are violated by the secret services for reasons of national security. (G-10 refers to Article 10 of the Basic Law, which protects the privacy of mail and telecommunications.)

RELATIONS BETWEEN CHAMBERS AND WITH THE *LÄNDERDE*

The Bundesrat is not a parliamentary body. It represents the state governments and is, in effect, part of the executive branch. Its sixty-eight representatives are delegates who vote as instructed by their respective state governments. Each state, or *land*, has between three and six seats, in proportion to its population. The Bundesrat rarely initiates legislation. Its real source of power is its veto power in matters that affect the material interests of the states. As members of the Bundesrat, the "minister presidents" (the official title of most states' head of government) and cabinet ministers of the *länder* are entitled to attend Bundestag meetings and speak in its debates. They make frequent use of this right.

Under the Basic Law (Articles 70–75), the legislative powers of the federation and the *länder* are clearly defined. The federation has exclusive legislative powers over foreign affairs, defense, citizenship, passport matters, immigration, currency matters, customs and free movement of goods, and posts and telecommunications. The *länder* have exclusive powers in cultural affairs (including broadcasting), education, and police. However, there are many areas with overlapping competences, especially "framework" laws and areas in which the powers of federation and *länder* are concurrent. With framework laws (for example, laws relating to public services, the principles of higher education, or the press and media), the federation lays down basic conditions, leaving the *länder* to legislate particular requirements and details. For areas covered by concurrent legislation (including criminal law, criminal justice, judicial procedures, the rights of association and assembly, firearms, and rights of residence for foreigners, among others), the *länder* may legislate only if, and to the extent that, the federation does not exercise its right to legislate. In addition, there are joint tasks—such as the expansion or establishment of institutions of higher education, the improvement of regional economic structures, and preservation of the coasts—where the federal government participates financially in responsibilities that are defined in the constitution as being prerogatives of the *länder* (Article 91a). In the event of conflict, federal law takes precedence over state law.

More than 50 percent of all federal bills, and virtually all important domestic bills, are subject to an absolute veto by the Bundesrat. Constitutional amendments need a two-thirds majority in the Bundestag and the Bundesrat. The party majority in the Bundesrat need not correspond to that in the Bundestag because coalitions in the *länder* need not be the same as the governing coalition at the federal level. Indeed, during much of the last two decades and a half the federal government has had no majority in the Bundesrat. Even if a *land* is ruled by the same party or coalition as the cabinet, its delegation will often serve its *land* rather than partisan interests. The federal government has no direct way of ensuring that its legislation will meet approval even by those state governments that consist of the same party or parties as the federal government. Nevertheless, suspensory and absolute Bundesrat vetoes are rare, and disagreements between the two chambers are usually resolved in the Conference Committee.

MEMBERS OF PARLIAMENT

The Bundestag and the area around its buildings are treated as inviolable precincts where demonstrations and other mass rallies are not allowed. Exceptions have to be approved by the federal minister of the interior in agreement with the president of the Bundestag.

Immunity

Members of the Bundestag enjoy legal immunity. According to Article 46 of the Basic Law members of the Bundestag must not be subjected to legal prosecution or disciplinary action for their votes or speeches in parliament except for cases of slander. If members of the Bundestag are suspected of having committed a legal offense, they may be prosecuted or arrested only with the consent of the Bundestag. Any limitation on a member's personal freedom or civil liberties requires Bundestag approval. Court trials infringing on the civil liberties of members of the Bundestag and other limitations of their personal freedom can be stopped at the Bundestag's request.

According to the body's rules of procedure, a request to lift a member's immunity must be addressed to the president of the Bundestag, who must convey it to the Committee on Election Validation, Immunity, and Rules. The committee determines whether sufficient grounds exist for a referral to the chamber. It does not examine evidence. In the case of trivial offenses the committee makes a recommendation, which is sent to all Bundestag members. The recommendation is considered as adopted by the house if no member files an objection within seven days. In all other cases the committee's recommendation will be placed on the Bundestag's agenda. If, in a new Bundestag, the Committee on Election Validation, Immunity, and Rules has not yet been appointed and there is an urgent application to lift a member's immunity, the president of the Bundestag may make a recommendation to the house.

Seizure

If a member's belongings are searched or seized in the Bundestag precincts, the president can request another member of the Bundestag to be present on behalf of the affected member. According to Article 47 of the Basic Law deputies may refuse to give evidence concerning persons who have confided facts to them in their capacity as deputies, or to whom they have confided facts in such capacity, as well as concerning these facts themselves. To the extent that this right to refuse to give evidence exists, no seizure of documents is permissible.

Expulsion, resignation, and recall

As free associations, the parliamentary parties may expel recalcitrant members from their ranks. By so doing, they do not in any way affect the electoral mandate held by the expelled member. (Loss of mandate for withdrawal or expulsion from a parliamentary party would violate Article 38.) Yet expelled members may lose some parliamentary privileges such as the right to vote in committees. The practice of the Communist Party in the first Bundestag (1949–1953), which required its candidates to sign a blank letter of resignation that could be used by the party leadership at any time, is unconstitutional. However, Article 38 of the Basic Law does not protect deputies against the loss of their mandates in the event that the party to which they belong is declared unconstitutional by the Federal Constitutional Court.

Members of the Bundestag who resign their seats are replaced by the next candidate on the appropriate state party list. Recalls by the electorate are not possible.

Pay and perquisites

According to Article 48(3) of the Basic Law, members of the Bundestag are entitled to a salary and allowances sufficient to ensure their independence. In 1994 the taxable monthly salary was DM10,366. (In 1995 an attempt to link members' salaries to the salaries of high court judges failed to achieve the necessary two-thirds majority in the Bundesrat.) In addition, members received a tax-free monthly allowance of DM5,978 to cover expenses for accommodation in the capital, travel, stationery, mail, telephone, office space in their electoral district, contributions to party funds, and general representation. Members of the Bundestag may use the federal railways and the federal mail free of charge. Finally, members receive an allowance of DM13,616 per month to employ secretaries, research assistants, and staff for offices in their constituency.

Ethics

A binding code of conduct is appended to the Bundestag's rules of procedure. Members provide information on their professional activities before and after election, including consulting work, directorships, and memberships of executive or supervisory boards. They must also report significant stock holdings. These data are published in the official handbook of the Bundestag. Members are not allowed to enter into contracts or to receive money to represent or promote the interests of those paying. The president of the Bundestag must be notified of all paid outside positions and of donations in excess of a certain amount. Members have to account for all donations they receive. There are no formal sanctions against deputies who violate the code. If violations occur, however, the deputy in question can be called before the Bundestag presidium. If the allegations are sustained, the presidium can inform the chair of the deputy's parliamentary party and ask for a response. The opinion of the presidium may be published.

Rules for the registration of interest groups and lobbyists are found in the Bundestag's rules of procedure. The Bundestag keeps a list of interest groups that have officially registered. The representatives of these groups may apply for and receive permits to enter the Bundestag precincts. The list of registered lobbyists is published annually in the official journal.

Staffing and offices

In 1991 the 662 members of the Bundestag employed 4,008 full- and part-time staff, including 909 graduate research assistants. The Bundestag provides members and their staff with office space. Deputies who have been members of the Bundestag for at least one year receive a transitional allowance when they leave the Bundestag. Under certain conditions, members are entitled to receive a pension.

Library and research facilities

The Bundestag has a large research division—the world's third largest after that of the U.S. Congress and the Japanese Diet. The research division is part of the Bundestag's administrative structure and is organized into four subdivisions. The documentation department includes the Bundestag archive, the press documentation center, the registry responsible for editing and referencing parliamentary debates and documents, the Bundestag library (which in 1991 held about 1,145,000 volumes), and the computer center. The two research services include the clerks and secretariats of the standing committees. These two departments also employ specialist research staff assisting individual Bundestag members. Finally, the petitions department provides research support for the work of the Petitions Committee.

CONSTITUTIONALITY OF LAWS AND EMERGENCY POWERS

The federal constitutional court has the last word on the constitutionality of laws enacted by the Bundestag. Unlike the U.S. Supreme Court, the German constitutional court is not a court of appeal in civil or criminal cases but rather a watchdog for the Basic Law. Its mission is to defend individual liberty and civil rights and to see that the courts apply legislation correctly.

The court is the final arbiter of contradictions and disputes between the federal executive and the Bundestag, between the federal government and the states, between states, and between other courts. It may hear complaints by private parties who believe that their constitutional rights have been violated. In 1952 and again in 1956 the court outlawed neo-Nazi and communist parties that espoused principles that the court found to contradict and undermine the Basic Law.

The court's sixteen members are divided into two senates, or chambers. The first senate's jurisdiction includes all cases dealing with basic rights covered by Articles 1–20 of the Basic Law as well as constitutional complaints involving these articles. The second senate is responsible for constitutional conflicts between different levels of government and a variety of political matters relating to political parties, election disputes, anticonstitutional activity, and international law. Between 1980 and 1990 the court nullified laws or parts of laws in sixty-four cases.

In the case of an external or internal emergency, the federal government has special powers. The provisions relating to internal emergencies such as a natural disaster or breakdown of order are—in the shadow of their abuse in the Weimar Republic—modest. They enable one state to request the assistance of the emergency services of other states. An external emergency is defined as a state of tension or state of war. If a state of tension is established by a two-thirds majority in the Bundestag, the federal government acquires additional powers in the fields of conscription and restriction of freedom of movement (Article 80a[1] of the Basic Law).

A state of war is declared in principle by a resolution of the Bundestag or by the fact of an armed attack on the Federal Republic (Article 115a of the Basic Law). Once a state of war exists, command of the armed forces passes from the minister of defense to the federal chancellor. If the Bundestag is unable to convene, legislative power is transferred to a joint committee consisting of thirty-two members of the Bundestag and sixteen delegates of the Bundesrat under the chairmanship of the president of the Bundestag. The federal government obtains extensive powers to issue emergency decrees. Either the Bundestag or Bundesrat can at any time declare the emergency to be at an end.

Thomas Saalfeld

BIBLIOGRAPHY

Conradt, David. *The German Polity.* 6th ed. New York: Longman, 1996.

Ismayr, Wolfgang. *Der Deutsche Bundestag: Funktionen, Willensbildung, Reformansätze.* Opladen: Leske und Budrich, 1992.

Johnson, Nevil. "Committees in the West German Bundestag." In *Committees in Legislatures: A Comparative Analysis,* ed. John D. Lees and Malcolm Shaw, 102–147. Oxford: Martin Robertson, 1979.

Loewenberg, Gerhard. *Parliament in the German Political System.* Ithaca, N.Y.: Cornell University Press, 1967.

Paterson, William E., and David Southern. *Governing Germany.* Oxford: Blackwell, 1991.

Saalfeld, Thomas. "The German Bundestag: Influence and Accountability in a Complex Environment." In *Parliaments and Governments in Western Europe,* ed. Philip Norton. London: Frank Cass, 1997.

———. "The West German Bundestag after 40 Years: The Role of Parliament in a 'Party Democracy.'" *West European Politics* 13 (1990): 68–89.

Schindler, Peter. *Datenhandbuch zur Geschichte des Deutschen Bundestages, 1983 bis 1991.* Baden-Baden: Nomos, 1994.

Schmidt, Manfred G. "Germany: The Grand Coalition State." In *Political Institutions in Europe,* ed. Joseph M. Colomer, 62–98. London: Routledge, 1996.

Schneider, Hans-Peter, and Wolfgang Zeh, eds. *Parlamentsrecht und Parlamentspraxis in der Bundesrepublik Deutschland.* Berlin and New York: Walter de Gruyter, 1989.

Schüttemeyer, Suzanne S. "Hierarchy and Efficiency in the Bundestag: The German Answer for Institutionalizing Parliament." In *Parliaments in the Modern World: Changing Institutions,* ed. Gary W. Copeland and Samuel C. Patterson, 29–58. Ann Arbor: University of Michigan Press, 1994.

Thaysen, Uwe, Roger H. Davidson, and Robert G. Livingston, eds. *The U.S. Congress and the German Bundestag.* Boulder, Colo.: Westview Press, 1990.

GHANA

OFFICIAL NAME: Republic of Ghana
CAPITAL: Accra
POPULATION: 17,698,000 (1996 est.)
DATE OF INDEPENDENCE: March 6, 1957 (from the United Kingdom)
DATE OF CURRENT CONSTITUTION: January 7, 1993
FORM OF GOVERNMENT: Limited parliamentary democracy
LANGUAGES: English (official), Akan, Moshi-Dagomba, Ewe, Ga, and others
MONETARY UNIT: New cedi
FISCAL YEAR: Calendar year
LEGISLATURE: National Assembly
NUMBER OF CHAMBERS: One
NUMBER OF MEMBERS: 200
PERCENTAGE OF WOMEN: 9.0
TERM OF LEGISLATURE: Four years
MOST RECENT LEGISLATIVE ELECTION: December 7, 1996
MINIMUM AGE FOR VOTING: 18
MINIMUM AGE FOR MEMBERSHIP: 21
SUFFRAGE: Universal and direct

VOTING: Optional
ADDRESS: National Assembly, Parliament House, Accra
TELEPHONE: (233 21) 664 181
FAX: (233 21) 669 159

Located on the Gulf of Guinea in northwestern Africa, Ghana has functioned formally as a republic since July 1, 1960, three years after its independence from Britain. Rule in the Republic of Ghana has changed not at the polls but rather at the hands of the military, which has overthrown civilian governments three times. Indeed, military rulers have governed Ghana for longer periods of time than have civilian governments. The history of elected parliaments in Ghana is a weak one, with the legislature having little role under civilian governments and none under military governments. Ghanaian political parties, on the other hand, have a rich history.

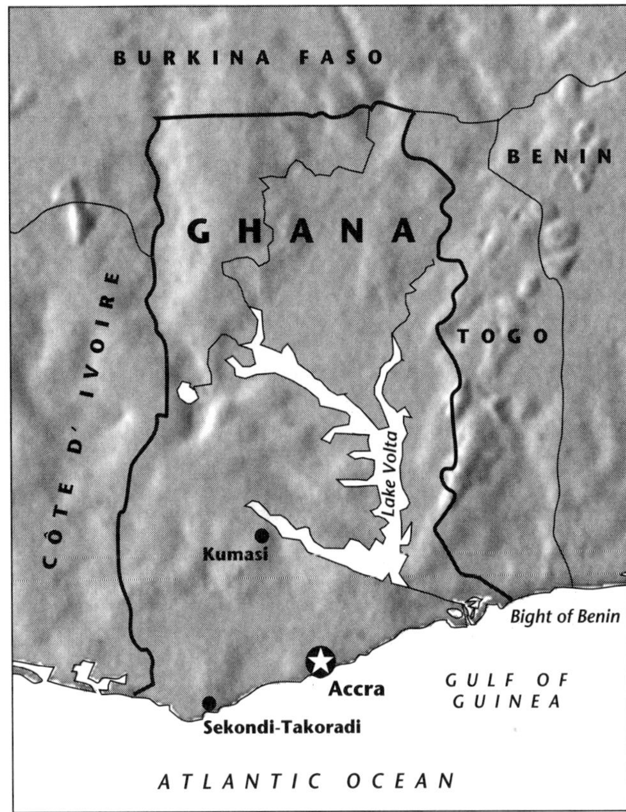

HISTORICAL BACKGROUND

Ghana's First Republic lasted from independence in 1957 to 1966 under the leadership of President Kwame Nkrumah. The opposition in the immediate postindependence era was vociferous and occasionally violent. Arguing that opposition posed a threat to stability and unity in the country, Nkrumah cracked down on internal rivals with the passage in 1958 of the Private Detention Act, which allowed the government to imprison individuals without trial for up to five years. In 1964 the Convention People's Party, which held a majority in the parliament, banned all other political parties. With Nkrumah as its head, the party subsequently appointed the 1965 parliament. Ghana's First Republic came to an end when the military seized power from Nkrumah in 1966.

The Second Republic followed three years of military rule and lasted less than three years. The military government had planned a quick return to civilian rule and duly held elections in 1969. It banned the Convention People's Party from participating, however, favoring instead the Progress Party, led by Kofi Busia, which had its roots in the opposition to Nkrumah. This marked the beginning of the two political groupings that dominated Ghanaian politics.

Unable to jump start a flailing economy, the Busia government lost the confidence of the military, which again seized power in 1972, this time under the leadership of Col. Ignatius Kutu Acheampong. Acheampong did not promise a return to civilian rule, but his successor, Lt. Gen. Frederick Akuffo, acceded to popular demands to do so following a failed referendum and a wave of strikes in 1978. Two weeks before the scheduled elections, Flight Lieutenant Jerry Rawlings took power. He allowed the elections to go forward but indicated that he would be watching from the sidelines.

The Third Republic, led by President Hilla Limann of the Nkrumist political grouping, ushered in a new era of tolerance that lasted less than two years. Rawlings assumed power again in December 1981 and this time gave no promise for a return to civilian rule. He and the Provisional National Defense Council (PNDC) government remained in power from 1982 to 1993, longer than any other Ghanaian government, military or civilian. Donors and analysts credit Rawlings with reversing decades of economic decline. Adopting the draconian austerity measures recommended by the International Monetary Fund caused short-term pain, but many saw the free-market policies as the principal factor behind five years of economic growth.

With changes occurring in neighboring countries, Rawlings conceded to internal and external pressures for political liberalization but managed to control the agenda and timetable for liberalization. He first appointed a committee to draft a new constitution incorporating aspects from the three previous versions. The committee's product was similar to the constitution adopted in 1979, retaining a presidential system with a parliament elected through single-member constituencies. In the second stage, Rawlings appointed a National Consultative Assembly to debate and ratify the draft. In a referendum in April 1992 the people voted by a 10 to 1 margin to accept the new constitution. The final stage began in May 1992, when Rawlings lifted the ban on political parties that had been in place since shortly after he had returned to power. Rawlings subsequently won the presidential election of November 1992. His inauguration ushered in Ghana's Fourth Republic.

The opposition contested the outcome of the 1992 presidential balloting and boycotted the subsequent legislative contest. Opposition parties did, however, participate in the December 1996 elections, in which they gained significant minority representation in the National Assembly. The December 1996 elections marked the first time in Ghanaian history that an elected government succeeded itself.

CONSTITUTIONAL PROVISIONS ON PARLIAMENT

The National Consultative Assembly was composed of 260 representatives, of whom 117 were elected representatives of district assemblies and 121 were from interest groups, including the National House of Chiefs, the Trade Union Congress, the Ghana Journalists Association, and committees for the defense of the revolution. Many complained that the body was heavily dominated by Rawlings's supporters. The Assembly pushed through the most important provisions with virtually no debate, including a controversial measure indemnifying PNDC members from prosecution for crimes committed under PNDC rule.

The constitution stipulates that parliament shall have no fewer than 140 members. There shall be a speaker and two deputy speakers. The deputy speakers may not be members of the same party. A quorum consists of one-third of all members. The Ghanaian constitution does not require that all ministers be sitting members of parliament. Although a majority of all ministers must be members of parliament (under Article 78), most senior cabinet ministers are not.

Article 106 states that bills must be accompanied by an explanatory memorandum setting out in detail the policy and principles of the bill, the defects of the existing law, the remedies proposed to deal with those defects, and the need for the bill. The bill must be published in the government gazette at least fourteen days before being introduced into parliament. Bills affecting the institution of the chieftaincy may not be introduced without first being referred to the National House of Chiefs.

A bill is referred to committee after its first reading. The committee examines the bill in detail and makes inquiries as it deems necessary. The committee reports the bill to parliament, and the full body then debates and votes on the legislation.

The president has seven days to accept or veto a bill. If the bill is vetoed, the president must explain the decision in writing to the speaker within fourteen days and set forth provisions he or she would support if the bill were reintroduced or amended. The president must then inform the speaker if the bill is being sent to the Council of State for consideration. Parliament then reconsiders the bill, taking into account comments made by the president or the Council of State. Parliament may override a presidential veto or ensure that a bill will be veto-proof by passing it by a two-thirds majority.

Article 112 specifies that a session shall be held at least once per year such that the time between sessions shall be no more than twelve months. Fifteen percent of the members may request a meeting of parliament, which the speaker must convene within seven days. When a vacancy occurs, a by-election must be held within thirty days, but it cannot be held within three months of a general election. Article 113 stipulates that parliament shall continue for no more than four years from its first sitting.

COMMITTEES

Article 103 gives parliament the right to appoint standing committees and other committees as necessary to discharge its functions. This gives parliament the incentive to set up committees without specifically mandating them. Specialized committees were first introduced in the Third Republic because the general committees did not allow members to develop sufficient expertise or effectively critique government actions.

Every legislator is to be a member of at least one committee, and, according to the constitution, the composition of the committees should "reflect the different shades of opinion in parliament." This could be interpreted to refer to ethnicity, region of origin, or political parties.

Committees have the same rights and privileges as the high court with regard to enforcing the attendance of witnesses, examining them under oath, and compelling the production of documents. Their power to subpoena persons or documents is not without limitations, however. Article 121 states that persons appearing before a committee have the same rights as they would in any courtroom.

The speaker may determine that a document need not be presented if it would adversely affect the public interest, and the National Security Council may do the same if a document would adversely affect national security.

Committees have specific duties, but they also operate within specific restrictions. When a bill is referred to committee, for example, the committee issues a report, which the full body takes into consideration during its deliberations, along with the memorandum submitted by the president. Article 106 stipulates that a committee may not delay a bill introduced by or on behalf of the president for more than three months, thereby preventing a committee from killing the president's agenda by inaction.

RELATIONS WITH THE EXECUTIVE BRANCH

Though given the power to make legislation, the Ghanaian parliament faces significant restrictions. Article 108 of the constitution provides that only the president, or a member of parliament acting on the president's behalf, has the right to introduce a bill or amend a bill to raise taxes or public expenditures. Members acting individually are prohibited from altering the structure of taxation and public expenditure unless the modification would reduce one or the other. This measure gives legislators very little leverage in negotiating with the executive branch. In practice, parliament has been unable to exert significant authority over the executive branch, though it has shown signs of life in its short existence.

The government must submit to parliament its annual budget, and opinions vary as to whether or not the parliament has any real effect on budget decisions. For example, the 1994 budget was submitted only a few days before the session concluded, leaving little time for substantive debate or changes.

Parliament also has the right to scrutinize ministerial appointees, and here, too, opinions differ as to the body's effectiveness. In 1994 parliament rejected two ministerial appointees, one because of his failure to disclose his assets as required by law and the other because he was not registered to vote. Rejecting a ministerial nominee effectively cripples a ministry.

ELECTIONS

In preparation for national elections, the PNDC established the parameters for political party organization. The law gives political parties the freedom to organize provided they are registered by the National Electoral Commission. Some have argued that the law is intrusive in several ways. First, before it can register, a party must provide extensive information on its founding members, its financial resources, and its contributors. Second, the electoral commission supervises internal elections of party officers. The commission was appointed by Rawlings, and some have questioned its independence.

The 1992 elections marked a return to elected government but were not universally accepted as legitimate within Ghana. Rawlings won election as president, but opposition parties challenged his victory and decided to boycott the ensuing legislative elections. Consequently, Rawlings's National Democratic Congress swept the legislative race, winning 188 of the seats. The National Convention Party and the Every Ghanaian Living Everywhere Party, both of which were allied with the National Democratic Congress, won 8 and 2 seats, respectively. Two independents took the last 2 seats.

During preparations for the 1996 elections, several steps were taken to involve and engage opposition parties. The Inter-Party Advisory Committee was established in March 1994 to serve as a nonstatutory advisory body to the elections commission. By including representatives of the opposition parties, the new committee helped to overcome suspicions of the government and fostered opposition participation in the electoral process. One of the opposition's complaints in 1992 was that the voter registry had not been updated since 1989. To address that concern, a national voter-registration campaign was conducted to create a new registry.

Simultaneous residential and legislative elections were held in December 1996. The ruling National Democratic Congress won a significant majority, gaining 134 of 200 seats. The New Patriotic Party won 60 seats, the People's Convention Party won 5, and the People's National Convention took 1 seat. Although the ruling party still controls the legislature, the opposition has at least gained representation, giving it a greater role in governing the country.

PARTY CAUCUSES AND GROUPS

The absence of an opposition does not mean that the National Assembly is a meaningless body. In his opening speech in April 1993, Rawlings called upon the body to discharge its duties as outlined in the constitution, specifically noting that it was expected to establish new institutions, including the National Electoral Commission and the Commission on Human Rights and Administrative Justice. He also called upon the ruling alliance in parliament to accommodate the opposition parties in legislative discussions, since they were not able to participate in floor debates.

Party discipline within the National Democratic Congress is somewhat lax because the party's majority is so substantial. Not all members feel obliged to vote with the executive branch, and some have challenged the government from within the party.

Kimberly Mahling Clark

BIBLIOGRAPHY

Gyimah-Boadi, E. "Ghana's Uncertain Political Opening." *Journal of Democracy* 5 (April 1994): 75–86.

Haynes, Jeff. "Sustainable Democracy in Ghana? Problems and Prospects." *Third World Quarterly* 14 (1993): 451–467.
Jeffries, Richard, and Clare Thomas. "The Ghanaian Elections of 1992." *African Affairs* 92 (1993): 331–366.
Kludze, A. K. P. "Ghana." In *Constitutions of the Countries of the World*, ed. Albert P. Blaustein and Gisbert H. Flanz. Dobbs Ferry, N.Y.: Oceana Publications, 1993.
Ninsin, Kwame, and F. K. Drah, eds. *Political Parties and Democracy in Ghana's Fourth Republic.* Accra: Woeli Publishing Services, 1993.

GREECE

OFFICIAL NAME: Hellenic Republic (Elliniki Demokratia)
CAPITAL: Athens
POPULATION: 10,539,000 (1996 est.)
DATE OF INDEPENDENCE: 1829 (from Ottoman Empire)
DATE OF CURRENT CONSTITUTION: Adopted June 11, 1975
FORM OF GOVERNMENT: Parliamentary democracy
LANGUAGES: Greek (official), English, French
MONETARY UNIT: Drachma
FISCAL YEAR: Calendar year
LEGISLATURE: Parliament (Vouli)
NUMBER OF CHAMBERS: One
NUMBER OF MEMBERS: 300
PERCENTAGE OF WOMEN: 6.3
TERM OF LEGISLATURE: Four years
MOST RECENT LEGISLATIVE ELECTION: September 22, 1996
MINIMUM AGE FOR VOTING: 18
MINIMUM AGE FOR MEMBERSHIP: 25
SUFFRAGE: Universal and direct
VOTING: Compulsory for ages 18–69
ADDRESS: Parliament Palace, Palaia Anactora, 10021 Athens
TELEPHONE: (301) 331 00 12
FAX: (301) 331 00 13

The Hellenic Republic is a southeastern European country, situated at the southern tip of the Balkan peninsula, that includes numerous islands in the Aegean Sea between the Greek mainland and Turkey. Since 1967, when the military took control of the government and later deposed the king, the country has managed to restore civilian government, in 1974, and reconstitute itself as a republic with a president as head of state and prime minister as head of government.

HISTORICAL BACKGROUND

The Greek city-states—in particular, Athens—were the birthplace of Western democracy and the origin of the concepts of liberty and rule by the people. But democratic impulses died in the land of their birth in the fourth century B.C., when Philip of Macedon subjected the city-states to Macedonian control. For many centuries Greece was under the heels of alien conquerors—from the Romans in the second century B.C. to the Ottomans beginning in the fifteenth century A.D. It was not until the war for independence in the 1820s that the modern Greek nation was born and the framework for parliamentary government was established.

A number of constitutions followed during the years after the revolution. Those of 1822 and 1823, which were influenced by the political precepts of the French Revolution, established a national legislature. The constitution of 1827, which was influenced by that of the United States, created an absolute separation of powers under which the legislative power belonged to the Vouli (Parliament). The recognition of the independence of the modern Greek state by Great Britain, France, and Russia led to the establishment of a monarchy with a Bavarian prince, Otto, as absolute monarch without any legislature. Otto's autocratic rule was somewhat restrained in 1844, when Greece's fourth constitution established a limited monarchy. An important feature of this constitution was the introduction of two legislative bodies: the Parliament, which was composed of no fewer than eighty members elected for office every three years by means of a quasi-universal ballot, and the Senate, which was composed of no fewer than twenty-seven members appointed by the king.

The elected Parliament held only limited power and could be overridden by the Senate and the king. As a result, Otto continued to rule autocratically until he was forced to abdicate in 1862 in favor of a Danish prince, who reigned as George I. The constitution of 1864 proclaimed the principle of popular sovereignty and prepared the way for the legislative supremacy of Parliament. The Senate was abolished, universal suffrage was introduced, the exercise of the duties of deputies was declared incompatible with the office of civil servant, and the right of the king to dissolve Parliament was tempered by the requirement that the decree of dissolution should bear the signatures of members of the cabinet. However, the constitution did not tamper with the royal right to appoint and dismiss cabinet members and did not require formally that the cabinet and the prime minister should enjoy the confidence of Parliament. As a result, during the latter part of the nineteenth century, many of the

cabinets did not enjoy parliamentary support and many that did were forced to resign at the behest of the king. Further, the king could threaten to dismiss Parliament in order to intimidate the legislators. Between 1864 and 1911 nineteen Parliaments were elected, but only three ran the course of their full three-year terms. Over time, the king became less active in politics and accepted the principle that cabinets should enjoy the "expressed confidence of Parliament," as stated by King George in 1875.

The early twentieth century was marked by important sociopolitical changes culminating in a coup d'état by the Military League in 1909. The Military League, a reform group, found an ally in Eleuthérios Venizelos, a prominent political figure with a large popular following. His first act was to call a convention to revise the constitution and make parliamentary government effective. The new constitution, of 1911, introduced important innovations in the organization and functions of Parliament. The legislative process was simplified so that consideration of urgent bills and ratification and codification of laws were easier than they had been in the past. The eligibility for members of Parliament was lowered to twenty-five years of age. Officers serving in the army and contractors doing business with the state were excluded from membership. A new court was set up to determine the validity of elections.

The defeat of the Greek army in Asia Minor and economic crises in the 1920s caused strains in the constitutional framework. In 1924 army officers deposed George II and established a republic with a new constitution that came into effect in 1927. The new constitution introduced two legislative bodies. The Parliament had between 200 and 250 members elected for four-year terms. The Senate was composed of 120 members; of these 90 were elected by the people, 10 were honorary senators appointed by a joint session of Parliament, and 20 were appointed by professional organizations. Senators were elected for nine-year staggered terms. When Parliament and Senate disagreed, Parliament prevailed.

The constitution of 1927 lasted eight years. A plebiscite in 1935 called overwhelmingly for the return of the king. In the parliamentary elections of 1936, neither the royalists nor the republicans won a clear majority. To resolve the deadlock, the king called on Gen. John Metaxas, who first adjourned Parliament and later dissolved it. Parliamentary institutions languished under the dictatorship of Metaxas, who modeled his government on fascist principles.

Greece was occupied by Axis powers in 1941, and when World War II ended a bitter civil war followed (1946–1949). It was not until 1952 that a new constitution was drafted restoring full parliamentary government. The new constitution specified a legislature with between 150 and 300 members; it extended the right to vote and the right to stand for elections to women. But this constitution was reactionary in that it empowered the government to issue legislative decrees without the consent of Parliament when Parliament was in recess. Governments resorted to issuing cabinet decrees to evade prior parliamentary scrutiny even though the decrees were submitted for ratification by Parliament after the fact.

Following a constitutional crisis in 1965, the military seized power once again in 1967, this time for seven years. After the collapse of the military junta in 1974, a plebiscite was held on the future of the monarchy. An overwhelming majority voted in favor of the republic. The constitution of 1975 was concerned primarily with decreasing the powers of the elected president, especially the power to dissolve Parliament and appoint the cabinet. Political differences resulted in the constitution being opposed by the left. These differences simmered until 1985–1986, when, with the left in power, the constitution was revised to abolish most of the regulatory powers of the presidency.

THE CONTEMPORARY PARLIAMENT AND ELECTIONS

The Greek Parliament is a unicameral body currently comprising 300 members. Of these, 288 are elected from single or multimember constituencies, and 12 "country members" are elected in a nationwide constituency in proportion to the electoral strength of each party to represent the nation as a whole. Members serve for four years except in times of war. Vacancies are filled by special elections, except during the last year of a regular term, when they are left unfilled.

The constitution does not establish a particular electoral system, nor does it designate the electoral districts. These are determined by laws that also set the maximum and minimum number of members. All Greek citizens at least eighteen years of age and in full possession of their civil rights are entitled to vote. Electoral rolls are compiled at the local level and are revised annually. Voting is compulsory under the age of seventy. Deputies are elected from fifty-six constituencies according to the Hagenbach-Bischoff system of proportional representation. Under this system, the leading party obtains an absolute majority in Parliament if it obtains at least 46 percent of the vote and leads the second leading party by at least seven percentage points. Voters cast ballots for a party list and, within that list, rank the candidates of their choice.

Parliament constitutes itself as a body with the election of a standing committee elected from among its own members and composed of the speaker, five deputy speakers, three deans, and six secretaries. The speaker is elected by an absolute majority at the beginning of each parliamentary term by secret ballot. A significant innovation introduced by the standing orders of 1987 is the presidents' meeting, presided over by the speaker and attended by the deputy speakers, chairs of the various ad hoc and standing committees, presidents of the parliamentary groups, and one independent member. The presidents' meeting examines the legislative business for the coming week, determines the overall duration of debates, and decides which issues are to be debated.

Article 41 of the constitution lays down the conditions for dissolution of Parliament by presidential decree before its full four-year term is completed. Parliament may be dissolved when the formation of a cabinet enjoying the confidence of a parliamentary majority is impossible or when Parliament is unable to elect the president of the republic after three ballots. In both cases the decree of dissolution must be countersigned by the prime minister. Parliament also may be dissolved on the initiative of the cabinet in order to renew its popular mandate on a critical national issue.

OPERATIONS, SESSIONS, AND COMMITTEES

The building that houses Parliament was initially constructed as the palace of Otto I. Work on the building began in 1836 under the direction of Friedrich Gartner, who had designed the royal palace of Munich and the Hermitage in St. Petersburg. The facade is in the Doric style, with impressive pediments and stately colonnades; the interior is decorated in the Ionic order. In 1884 the north section of the building was destroyed by fire, and in 1909 a second fire burned the main section of the palace. Renovations begun in 1930 under architect Andreas Kriezis were completed in 1934.

Each year Parliament convenes in regular session on the first Monday in October. The duration of each regular session is not less than five months, but it may be extended until the state budget is passed. Extraordinary sessions may be convened by the president of the republic, and special sessions may be convened by Parliament itself.

Parliament holds both public and private sittings. Ministers and undersecretaries are free to attend the sessions, and they have the right to be heard when they request the floor. Parliament and its committees may summon officials to be present and to provide information requested by members.

Parliament decides on the basis of an absolute majority of the members present, in no case less than one-fourth of the total membership.

Parliament sits either in plenary session or in sections, which are select groups that are charged with particular tasks. Certain functions are assigned by the constitution to the plenary session: among these are parliamentary standing orders and elections, church-state relations, religious freedom and individual liberties, operation of political parties, delegation of legislative authority to the president or a minister, and authorization of the state budget. Two sections are created at the beginning of each session. In addition, a section formed when Parliament is in recess exercises normal legislative business.

Much of the legislative work is done by standing committees whose composition reflects the strength of the various political parties in Parliament. There are six standing committees; the speaker determines who will be on each committee. In addition, there are special committees and four committees for Public Enterprises, Banks, and Public Benefit Organizations; National Matters or Matters of General Interest; Internal Matters of Parliament, such as standing orders, finance, and the parliamentary library; and International Relations.

CONSTITUTIONAL FUNCTIONS OF PARLIAMENT

The functions of Parliament are specified in the constitution. These include revising the constitution, passing laws, declaring a state of emergency, proclaiming referendums, electing the president of the republic, forming a government and maintaining oversight of its activities, passing the state budget, and exercising certain quasi-judicial powers.

Parliament has the sole right to revise the constitution, except constitutional provisions that designate the nation as a parliamentary republic and those that define certain fundamental rights and establish the principle of separation of powers. Revision of the constitution requires a proposal by at least fifty members and three ballots. The first two ballots, which ascertain the need for revision and define the provisions to be revised, are held at least one month apart. The third ballot concerns only the provisions to be revised; it takes place after a general election. The passage of the revision requires only an absolute majority of the total membership.

The right to pass laws is vested in Parliament. Both deputies and cabinet members may propose amendments and additions; government bills may be submitted only by cabinet members, while deputies may submit only private law proposals. Both bills and law proposals are accompanied by justification reports setting forth the scope of the provisions. Any bill or law proposal that will incur a charge on the state budget must be accompanied by a report from the General Accounting Office. Once introduced, bills and law proposals are referred to the appropriate standing or special committees, which eventually return them with recommendations.

Debate and voting take place in three stages: in principle, by specific article, and as a whole. Urgent and very urgent bills and law proposals may be voted without debate or with limited debate. Bills rejected by either section or by the plenary cannot be reintroduced in the same session. There are special procedures spelled out in the standing orders for certain types of legislation, including judicial codes and international treaties. Laws passed by Parliament are promulgated by the president and are published within one month of the vote. The president may return the law without signing, in which case Parliament may reintroduce the bill in its plenary session. If it is passed again by an absolute majority of the total number of members, it becomes law without the president's assent.

Parliament may declare a state of emergency in case of war, immediate threat against national security, or armed insurrection. The emergency may be declared for the whole country or for parts of it. In declaring a state of emergency, Parliament may establish certain tribunals and suspend certain constitutional provisions guaranteeing basic human rights. The duration of the emergency may be no longer than fifteen days. If Parliament is in recess and unable to meet, the president of the republic may issue a decree with the cabinet's approval, to be ratified by Parliament within fifteen days.

Parliament may proclaim a referendum for national issues and for bills regulating important social issues. These are decided by a three-fifths majority of the total number of members upon proposal by two-fifths of the members.

The president of the republic is elected for a five-year term in a special session called by the speaker of Parliament at least one month before the expiration of the tenure of the incumbent. The president is elected by a two-thirds majority of the total number of deputies. If this majority is not achieved by any candidate on the first round, successive ballots are held with decreasing majority requirements: three-fifths, absolute, and relative. Should even the third ballot fail to enable any candidate to win, Parliament is dissolved and new general elections are held.

The government of Greece is responsible and accountable to Parliament and is based on its command of the support of a majority of deputies. If no party has an absolute majority, the constitution provides for a special exploratory procedure. If these exploratory mandates prove unsuccessful, the president of the republic may bring together party leaders in a last-ditch effort to form a government. Should this effort also fail, Parliament is dissolved and a caretaker government is appointed for holding the elections.

The constitution also provides for motions of confidence and motions of censure as means of confirming the majority support of the government in Parliament. The government is obliged to seek a vote of confidence within fifteen days of the swearing in of the prime minister. The government also has the right to seek a vote of confidence for its own reasons at other times. Votes of confidence require a majority of the members present, but no less than two-fifths of the total membership. Motions of censure, on the other hand, require an absolute majority of the total membership and, if passed, bring down the government. Only one censure motion may be introduced every six months.

Parliament controls the government as a whole and each of its members. Parliamentary control is exercised in plenary sessions through one or more of the following means: petitions delivered to ministers through the speaker, requests for official documents, oral questions to which ministers must respond in writing, current questions (on Fridays only), and current interpellations (on Tuesdays only). Subsidiary parliamentary control is exercised by the standing committees and their subcommittees, which may conduct hearings, and by investigation committees set up by the plenary sessions. Twice every session, discussions are held before the actual legislative business, in which the prime minister, cabinet members, and presidents of parliamentary groups discuss national issues.

Parliament votes on the state budget, the financial statement, and the general balance sheet. The finance bill is introduced on January 1 each year.

Parliament may impeach the president of the republic (for high treason or violation of the constitution) and the prime minister and members of the cabinet. Parliament also is empowered to pardon those convicted by the Special Supreme Court, raise the immunity of its members in cases where members are indicted in a criminal court, and grant amnesty for political crimes.

CONCLUSION

The consolidation of Greek democracy and the maturing of political processes since the fall of the military junta have strengthened Parliament but have also led to a virtual monopoly of law making in the hands of the ruling parties. Of the nearly two thousand bills voted since 1974, only one originated from a nongovernment deputy. The adoption of bills has been somewhat informal, with the committee stage seldom lasting more than five to eight days. Committee deliberations are regarded as mere formalities. In the plenary sessions, deliberation and voting on bills generally occupy less than one day. The average annual number of laws passed by Parliament has declined from a high of 251 during 1974–1977 to about 70 in the early 1990s. Partisan conflicts, the growth of obstructionism, and the use of omnibus bills containing several provisions account for this trend.

There is also an increasing tendency to transfer legislative activity from Parliament to the executive, although the constitution permits such transfer in times of emergency only. Whole sections of government activity, such as defense, escape parliamentary control. Interpellations, which call the executive to account, and other devices of parliamentary scrutiny have become perfunctory, and questions are answered by ministers vaguely and briefly. Motions of confidence and censure have become infrequent because of the certainty of their outcome in a partisan chamber. No parliamentary investigation has been launched in recent years because a majority vote is required for the purpose.

The Greek Parliament thus is a talking parliament rather than a working parliament. The structure of parliamentary proceedings encourages long-winded speeches as well as symbolic protests by the opposition, such as walkouts during critical debates. Party discipline has helped to diminish the role and independence of individual deputies, who are dependent on the party whips. The abolition of the preferential vote in 1982 and the introduction of the closed list make the deputies subservient to the leadership, which can deny an erring deputy a place on the ticket in the next general election. Organized discussions introduced by the 1987 standing orders of the Parliament also restrict the right of individual deputies to speak during any discussion without leave of the leadership.

George Thomas Kurian

BIBLIOGRAPHY

Clogg, Richard, ed. *Greece, 1981–1989: The Populist Decade.* New York: St. Martin's, 1993.

Clogg, Richard. *Parties and Elections in Greece: The Search for Legitimacy.* Durham, N.C.: Duke University Press, 1988.

GRENADA

OFFICIAL NAME: State of Grenada
CAPITAL: St. George's
POPULATION: 95,000 (1996 est.)
DATE OF INDEPENDENCE: February 7, 1974 (from the United Kingdom)
DATE OF CURRENT CONSTITUTION: Effective February 7, 1974
FORM OF GOVERNMENT: Constitutional monarchy
LANGUAGES: English (official), French patois
MONETARY UNIT: East Caribbean dollar
FISCAL YEAR: Calendar year
LEGISLATURE: Parliament
NUMBER OF CHAMBERS: Two. House of Representatives; Senate
NUMBER OF MEMBERS: House of Representatives, 15 (directly elected); Senate, 13 (appointed)
PERCENTAGE OF WOMEN: House of Representatives, 20.0; Senate, —
TERM OF LEGISLATURE: Five years
MOST RECENT LEGISLATIVE ELECTION: June 20, 1995
MINIMUM AGE FOR VOTING: 18
MINIMUM AGE FOR MEMBERSHIP: 18
SUFFRAGE: Universal
VOTING: Optional
ADDRESS: Houses of Parliament, P.O. Box 315, St. George's
TELEPHONE: (1809) 440 3456
FAX: (1809) 440 4138

Grenada, the most southerly of the Windward Islands in the West Indies *(see map, p. 303)*, was a British colony until 1958, when it joined the Federation of the West Indies, an undertaking that was not as successful as many had hoped. In 1967 it became an associated state of the United Kingdom, a status that granted self-government in all domestic issues, while permitting the British government to control international and foreign policy issues that might affect Grenada. It achieved full independence in February 1974 and remains a member of the Commonwealth.

A coup d'état in March 1979 led to violence that ended in the death of the prime minister, Maurice Bishop. The Marxist People's Revolutionary Government, which took power after the coup, revoked the constitution adopted in 1973, ruling instead by decree. A multinational force, primarily composed of U.S. troops, invaded the country in October 1983 and deposed the Revolutionary Military Council; the constitution was later restored by the governor general. During all the commotion, Grenada never broke its ties with Britain nor its membership in the Commonwealth.

THE CONSTITUTION AND POLITICAL AUTHORITY

The 1973 constitution provides for a parliamentary system of government based on the British Westminster model. The head of state is the British monarch, whose authority is represented on the island by a governor general. When a Parliament is in place, the governor general has little real power and few official duties; the role is similar to that of the monarch in the United Kingdom. The real power lies with the prime minister, who is leader of the majority party in Parliament.

The power of the prime minister rests substantially on the authority to name a cabinet composed of members who assume responsibility for the administration of the government. The prime minister frequently assumes direct control over important government portfolios or over ministries of personal or political interest, such as finance, home affairs, or security.

Even when an elected Parliament is in place, the governor general retains a degree of potential constitutional authority. For example, Section 52 of the constitution says that the governor general may at any time prorogue (discontinue) Parliament or dissolve it. The governor general appoints both the prime minister and the leader of the opposition. The governor general has the power to dismiss members of Parliament under some circumstances (for nonattendance or criminal conviction, among other reasons), even though in practice this action is taken only at the urging of the prime minister or the leader of the opposition. The governor general also has the power to declare a state of emergency, a declaration that has the effect of dissolving Parliament. A final example of the governor general's potential power is described in Section 63 of the constitution, which states that "the Prime Minister shall keep the Governor General fully informed concerning the general conduct of the government of Grenada" and shall furnish him "with such information as he may request with respect to any particular matter relating to the government of Grenada." Thus the position is certainly not without potential power and influence.

Parliament clearly is the major governmental institution in Grenada. It is composed of two houses, a lower house called the House of Representatives and an upper house called the Senate. No more than six months can pass without a meeting of Parliament. The maximum term of Parliament is five years from the date of the first sitting; this period can be extended for not more than twelve months at a time, for not more than a total of five years.

PARLIAMENTARY ELECTIONS AND OPERATIONS

Since senators are appointed by the governor general on the advice of the prime minister and the leader of the opposition, the only legislative elections are for members of the House of Representatives. Elections for the fifteen members of the House take place in single-member constituencies; representation is based on population, and each of the fifteen seats in the House represents a specific constituency. The winners are the individuals who receive the most votes in each constituency—what is referred to as a "first past the post" system, which does not require individuals to receive a majority of the votes cast. Vacancies arising between general elections are filled through special elections.

To vote for House members, individuals must be citizens of Grenada or citizens of a Commonwealth nation who have been in the country for at least twelve months immediately before the election. The law disqualifies people from voting who have undischarged bankruptcies, who owe allegiance to a foreign state, who have been declared insane, who are under a sentence of death or imprisonment exceeding one year, or who are government contractors. To run for office, candidates must be at least eighteen years of age and must be nominated by at least six registered voters in the constituency. Candidates must pay a deposit (approximately US$100), which will be returned if the candidate receives at least one-eighth of the votes cast.

The leader of the party securing the majority of the fifteen seats in Parliament is named prime minister by the governor general. The leader of the party winning the next largest bloc of seats is named leader of the opposition. The thirteen senators are appointed by the governor general, seven on the advice of the prime minister, three on the advice of the prime minister after the prime minister holds discussions with "organizations or interests which the prime minister considers the senators should be selected to represent," and three on the advice of the leader of the opposition.

The constitution of Grenada includes the same clause found in many Commonwealth constitutions that gives Parliament the power to "make laws for the peace, order and good government" of the country. In a manner similarly typical of Commonwealth parliaments, the House of Representatives has the power of the purse, in that it alone may introduce legislation dealing with taxation or money bills. The Senate has the power to delay money bills for only one month; then they go to the governor general without a second passage by the House of Representatives.

The daily operation of parliament in Grenada closely follows the Westminster model. Bills may be introduced in either chamber (with the exception of money bills). Given its small size, the House conducts most of its business as a Committee of the Whole, and while legislative committees occasionally meet, they do not play a significant role in the legislative process. The institution of a "question period" is central to the House, and lively interrogations of government ministers take place on a daily basis when Parliament is in session. The typical Westminster-model three-reading procedure for legislation is closely followed.

CONCLUSION

Grenada has a flourishing system of political parties, with several parties represented in Parliament. In the years following the 1990 general election, a period of economic instability developed as a result of strikes by public-sector and port workers demanding better wages. This economic disruption, combined with general dissatisfaction with the government of Nicholas Brathwaite of the National Democratic Congress, led Brathwaite to resign in February 1995. He was succeeded by George Brizan, a former minister of finance. Major issues in the campaign included unemployment and the idea of a national income tax. In the election of June 1995, the opposition New National Party won eight of the fifteen seats in the legislature, primarily on the issue of doing away with the income tax.

Since the political instability of the early 1980s, democratic political institutions in Grenada have been regaining the legitimacy and stability that they had established in the decade prior to the period of violence. Parliament has played an important role in that relegitimation of government, and with each election and each peaceful transition from one government to another it continues to contribute to the country's institutionalization of democratic government.

Gregory S. Mahler

BIBLIOGRAPHY

Archer, Ewart. "Gairyism, Revolution, and Reorganisation: Three Decades of Turbulence in Grenada." *Journal of Commonwealth and Comparative Politics* 23 (July 1985): 91–111.

Maingot, Anthony P. "Politics Caribbean Style." *Caribbean Review* 14 (spring 1985): 5–6.

Menon, P. K. "The Organization of Eastern Caribbean States—An Important Milestone in Sub-Regional Integration." *Inter-American Law Review* 17 (winter 1986): 297–311.

St. Clair-Daniel, W. "Caribbean Concepts of Parliament." *Parliamentarian* 66 (October 1985): 211–213.

GUATEMALA

OFFICIAL NAME: Republic of Guatemala (República de Guatemala)
CAPITAL: Guatemala City
POPULATION: 11,278,000 (1996 est.)
DATE OF INDEPENDENCE: September 15, 1821 (from Spain)
DATE OF CURRENT CONSTITUTION: Adopted May 31, 1985; effective January 14, 1986
FORM OF GOVERNMENT: Parliamentary democracy
LANGUAGES: Spanish, many Indian dialects
MONETARY UNIT: Quetzal
FISCAL YEAR: Calendar year
LEGISLATURE: Congress of the Republic (Congreso de la República)
NUMBER OF CHAMBERS: One
NUMBER OF MEMBERS: 80
PERCENTAGE OF WOMEN: 12.5
TERM OF LEGISLATURE: Four years
MOST RECENT LEGISLATIVE ELECTION: November 12, 1995
MINIMUM AGE FOR VOTING: 18
MINIMUM AGE FOR MEMBERSHIP: 18
SUFFRAGE: Universal and direct
VOTING: Compulsory
ADDRESS: Congress of the Republic, 9a Avenida 9-44, Zona 1, Guatemala City
TELEPHONE: (502) 232 1260
FAX: (502) 232 1286

Since gaining independence from Spain in 1821, Guatemala, located between Honduras and Mexico *(see map, p. 526)*, has experienced a long series of dictatorships, coups, and military rule, with only occasional periods of representative government. Public participation in politics and government has been limited, with political parties tending to respond to the interests of a ruling elite rather than to the demands of civil society. The armed forces have played a leading role in the political history of Guatemala, often using the pretext of public safety and national stability as justification for interference in the affairs of state. The swearing-in of a new, reform-minded Congress in January 1996 has renewed hope for an independent and stable legislative authority.

The Congress of the Republic of Guatemala is a unicameral body vested with authority by the 1985 constitution (as revised in 1993). Members of the Congress are elected to four-year terms through secret ballot and universal suffrage for those eighteen years of age and older, with the possibility of unlimited reelection.

RECENT POLITICAL DEVELOPMENTS

Guatemala was the scene of Latin America's longest-running and bloodiest civil war. More than three decades of strife followed the 1954 coup, organized by the U.S. Central Intelligence Agency, that ousted left-leaning president Jacobo Arbenz Guzmán. Arbenz's alliance with local communists and expropriation of land belonging to U.S.-owned United Fruit Company had threatened Washington's political and economic hold on Guatemala.

The CIA recruited Carlos Castillo Armas, an exiled Guatemalan military officer, to lead the invasion that ousted the so-called communist sympathizer Arbenz. Subsequent U.S. funding and support of ultra-rightists helped sustain military rule throughout the 1960s and 1970s, increasing Guatemala's economic, political, and social polarization. As the pressures in society increased, so did the violence of protest and repression; terrorism perpetrated against successive military regimes begot equally vicious retaliation from the government. From 1954 to 1985 only one civilian government held office—between 1966 and 1970—and even that government was dominated behind the scenes by the army. By the late 1980s all major parties recognized that political negotiations and a return to civilian government were essential.

The first tentative steps toward civilian government were taken in 1984, when the National Constituent Assembly adopted a new constitution, and in 1985, when the Guatemalan public elected its first civilian president in two decades. The administration of Marco Vinicio Cerezo Arévalo, however, did not effectively rein in the military, nor did the National Congress elected on November 3, 1985. Only with the election of Jorge Serrano Elias in 1990, completing the transition from one democratically elected civilian to another, did the situation begin to stabilize. Under pressure from domestic religious leaders and international bodies, the Serrano government commenced formal negotiations with the Guatemalan National Revolutionary Unity (URNG), the main guerrilla organization.

In 1993, however, Serrano illegally dissolved Congress, dismissed the Supreme Court of Justice, and assumed near dictatorial powers in an alleged effort to combat corruption. Strong protest from the Guatemalan citizenry and the international community and the military's subsequent refusal to back the so-called self-coup lead to Serrano's forced exile on June 1, 1993. Four days later, Congress reestablished constitutional order by declaring the presidency vacant and naming Solicitor for Human Rights Ramiro de León Carpio to serve out the remaining presidential term.

Within a few months a series of corruption scandals shook the Congress. A national referendum resulted in a resounding vote of no confidence and led to the ouster of all members of Congress. In August 1994, special elections were held to choose new deputies to serve the remaining term of their predecessors. Although voter turnout was low (46 percent), the elections produced a majority of two conservative anticorruption parties—the Guatemalan Republican Front and the Party of National Advancement.

The subsequent elections of November 1995, supported by both the military and the international community, served to consolidate democracy further and brought to power a reform-minded president, Alvaro Enrique Arzú Irigoyen and the most representative Congress in Guatemalan history. The inclusion of the New Guatemala Democratic Front (FDNG), women, and indigenous leaders made this Congress unique, as did its commitment to work on a nonpartisan basis to rebuild the Congress as a model democratic institution.

Finally, in December 1996 the Guatemalan government and the URNG guerrilla group signed a formal peace accord, ending a brutal civil war that left at least 100,000 dead and 40,000 "disappeared." The peace agreement comprises eleven separate accords, which outline the procedures and timetable for the demobilization of the Guatemalan military and guerrilla forces and the reconstruction of civil society based on democratic principles.

PARTIES AND ELECTIONS

Congressional elections coincide with presidential and municipal elections. Members of the armed forces and the police are not eligible to vote. Every four years the Supreme Electoral Tribunal determines the election date and publicizes the date at least ninety days before the election. The constitution, however, obligates the Congress to hold national elections on the date stipulated by the law if the Supreme Electoral Tribunal is unable to do so.

The Supreme Electoral Tribunal establishes the number of deputies to be elected in each of the twenty-two departments and the capital city on the basis of the most recent census. Members of Congress are elected by proportional representation on closed party lists using a departmental and national list procedure. Each department of Guatemala constitutes an electoral district, with the exception of the Department of Guatemala, which is divided into two districts: the Central District, comprising Guatemala City, and the District of Guatemala, consisting of the other municipalities of the department.

The number of deputies for each district is based on population—one deputy for every 80,000 residents—with each district having at least one congressional representative. The number of deputies elected from the national list equals 25 percent of the number of departmental seats. In the elections of November 1995, eighty deputies were elected to serve in the legislature: sixteen from the national list and sixty-four from the twenty-three electoral districts.

There are no special elections to fill vacancies. Each political party is responsible for presenting one alternate for each congressional candidate presented. In the case of the national list, the alternate is the candidate who received the next highest number of votes during the national balloting. To be elected, a candidate must be a Guatemalan citizen and eighteen years of age. Active-duty military personnel, government contractors, those previously convicted of a crime, and near relatives of the president and vice president of the republic may not serve in the legislature.

In the national elections of November 1995 (and subsequent runoff elections of January 1996), Arzú was elected president of Guatemala with 51.2 percent of the vote. Final legislative results released by the Supreme Electoral Tribunal on November 25 gave the center-right National Advancement Party an absolute majority, with forty-two seats. The party on the extreme right, the Guatemalan Republican Front, which had held a majority previously, was left with twenty seats. The elections also marked the re-entrance of the left into Congress, with the New Guatemala Democratic Front winning six seats. The remainder of the seats were filled by the Christian Democratic Party, National Centrist Union, Democratic Union, and the National Liberation Movement.

PARLIAMENTARY PROCEEDINGS

The Congress of the Republic of Guatemala is housed in a two-story building in downtown Guatemala City near the National Presidential Palace. The Congress meets in regular sessions every year from January 14 to May 15 and from August 1 to November 30. Extraordinary sessions may be called by the Congress's Permanent Committee, the executive branch, or by a majority of the members of Congress.

Every session begins with the verification of a quorum—a simple majority of the deputies—after which the session is declared open by the president of the Congress. Thereafter, the order of the day is discussed, modified, and approved in the full Congress. All sessions of the legislature are open to the public with the exception of those concerning military operations, national security, or the investigation of crimes involving minors.

Legislative proposals may be introduced by any member

of Congress, the executive branch, the Supreme Court of Justice, the University of San Carlos in Guatemala, and the Supreme Electoral Tribunal. No law may contradict the constitution. Any amendment to the constitution must be approved by the Guatemalan Constitutional Court and requires a two-thirds majority vote by the members of Congress.

All bills initiated by deputies are presented to the secretary of Congress before being read to the plenary of Congress. After the reading, the proposal is passed to the appropriate committee for its consideration. Any legislative proposal presented to the Congress by the executive branch, the Supreme Court of Justice, the University of San Carlos in Guatemala, or the Supreme Electoral Tribunal is immediately passed to the appropriate committee after its presentation to the plenary.

The committee analyzes the bill, deliberates, and renders an opinion. The committee is required to submit an opinion, including any reservations, within sixty days of the bill's submission. All opinions must be approved by an absolute majority of the committee and signed by all its members. The bill and the committee opinion are then discussed in three separate plenary debates held on different days. The bill will not be voted on until it has passed all three sessions, unless the matter requires urgent consideration as so deemed by a two-thirds majority vote of the full Congress.

During the first two plenary sessions the proposal is discussed in general terms, and the members and pertinent public officials debate its constitutionality, importance, and overall purpose. During the third and final debate the proposal is discussed one article at a time. If the bill is complex, members may discuss and vote on each major section rather than each article.

Once a bill has been approved by a simple majority, the ruling body *(Junta Directiva)* must send the bill to the executive branch within ten days for its consideration. The president has fifteen days to approve or reject the law. If the law is vetoed, it must be sent back to Congress with an explanation. Laws may not be partially vetoed.

Congress may override the president's veto by a two-thirds majority vote. If it succeeds in doing so, the president must promulgate and publish the law within eight days. If no action is taken by the president in the time allotted, Congress may publish the law. A bill is not considered a law until it has been published in the *Official Diary.*

Decisions of considerable political importance are sometimes submitted to the citizenry for a vote. Popular referendums are held by the Supreme Electoral Tribunal when requested by the president of the country or the president of the Congress.

The volume of legislation varies from year to year. In 1994, 230 legislative proposals were presented to the legislature, 79 of which Congress approved. In 1995, 169 proposals were presented, of which 85 were approved. The current Congress faces a large backlog of legislation left unattended by previous legislatures. Over 70 percent of the reforms occasioned by the adoption of the new constitution in 1986, for example, have yet to be fully translated into law.

The annual budget is presented to the president of Guatemala by the minister of finance. The minister, acting on the president's behalf, presents the budget to the Congress by September 30 of each year. The proposal is sent to the Committee of Public Finance and Currency for its review and comment. Two days before the first debate of the full Congress, copies of the proposed budget, including any amendments or recommendations made by the committee, are given to all deputies. Motions by individual deputies to amend the proposed budget must be submitted in writing to the Congress. If the new budget has not been passed by the beginning of the fiscal year, the past year's budget is reinstated with any modifications or alterations approved by the Congress.

Ministers of the executive branch and other public officials are obligated to give testimony or provide explanations on any matter under their jurisdiction when called upon by the Congress. Vice ministers may be sent in place of a minister when the latter is unable to attend.

According to the constitution, Congress may declare the president of the country to be mentally or physically incapable of performing his or her duties by a two-thirds majority vote. The declaration must be supported by five members of the National Medical Board. Congress also has the power to impeach the president or vice president, Supreme Court justices, officials of the Supreme Electoral Tribunal, the attorney general, and its own members by a two-thirds majority vote.

In Guatemala the activities of the Congress are covered extensively by the media. Each major newspaper selects as many as three correspondents to cover legislative debates. The television stations also provide coverage of floor debates.

ORGANIZATION AND STRUCTURE

The president of the Congress is elected by a two-thirds majority vote of the deputies at the beginning of each annual session. Any member of Congress is eligible for consideration. The powers of the president include opening, convening, or canceling sessions; establishing and modifying the legislative agenda; organizing debates and setting speaking time; examining the admissibility of bills and amendments; appointing committees and their presiding officers; authorizing expenses; recruiting, assigning, and promoting staff; and playing a specific role in the conduct of foreign affairs or defense matters.

The Junta Directiva, the governing body of the Congress, is elected each year by a vote of all deputies. It comprises the president of the legislature, three vice presidents, and five secretaries. The members of the Junta may be reelected and serve for one year. The Junta is charged with regulating the day-to-day activities of the legislature. Before recessing, the Congress must elect a Permanent Committee to preside over the Congress during the absence of the members of the Junta Directiva. This committee comprises the president of the Congress, two secretaries, and two acting members.

The legislature is currently divided into twenty-five working committees. Congress may create other committees upon a two-thirds majority vote. Ad hoc committees may also be created to address specific temporary issues. Each of the current committees comprises five-to-eight representatives, with at least one from each of the political parties represented in Congress. A committee may exceed eight members under special circumstances but may never exceed eleven.

Committee presidents are elected by a simple majority vote of the full Congress. The members of the committee choose their own vice president and secretary. In every case, the committee president, vice president, and secretary must be from different political parties. Each committee may request information and reports from national, public, and private entities, as well as contract a permanent adviser to assist in the analysis and writing of reports.

Members of Congress are allowed to form political alliances within the Congress; they generally are based on party affiliation. Each political alliance elects a president who meets once a week with the president of the Congress and the presidents of the other alliances to discuss legislative and administrative issues. Each alliance receives an office and the material and monetary resources necessary for its effective operation.

The members of Congress enjoy complete immunity (except under extreme circumstances) and may not be accused of crimes based on opinions expressed while exercising their functions. In 1997 the remuneration of the deputies was 17,500 quetzals (before taxes), or approximately US$3,000, per month.

Amy J. Standefer

BIBLIOGRAPHY

Barry, Tom. *Central America inside out.* New York: Grove Weidenfeld, 1991.

Booth, John A. "Socioeconomic and Political Roots of National Revolts in Central America." *Latin America Research Review* 26 (1991): 33–73.

Gleijeses, Piero. *Shattered Hope: The Guatemalan Revolution and the United States, 1944–1954.* Princeton, N.J.: Princeton University Press, 1991.

Goodman, Louis, William M. LeoGrande, and Johanna Mendelson Forman, eds. *Political Parties and Democracy in Central America.* Boulder, Colo.: Westview Press, 1992.

Kinzer, Stephen, and Stephen E. Schlesinger. *Bitter Fruit.* New York: Doubleday, 1983.

GUINEA

OFFICIAL NAME: Republic of Guinea (République de Guinée)
CAPITAL: Conakry
POPULATION: 7,412,000 (1996 est.)
DATE OF INDEPENDENCE: October 2, 1958 (from France)
DATE OF CURRENT CONSTITUTION: Approved December 23, 1990
FORM OF GOVERNMENT: Partial parliamentary democracy
LANGUAGES: French (official), Soussou, Malinké, other tribal languages
MONETARY UNIT: Guinea franc
FISCAL YEAR: Calendar year
LEGISLATURE: National Assembly (Assemblée Nationale)
NUMBER OF CHAMBERS: One
NUMBER OF MEMBERS: 114
PERCENTAGE OF WOMEN: 7.0
TERM OF LEGISLATURE: Five years
MOST RECENT LEGISLATIVE ELECTION: June 11, 1995
MINIMUM AGE FOR VOTING: 18
MINIMUM AGE FOR MEMBERSHIP: 25
SUFFRAGE: Universal
VOTING: Optional
ADDRESS: Assemblée Nationale, Palaise du Peuple, BP 414 Conakry
TELEPHONE: (224) 41 11 17
FAX: —

The Republic of Guinea is a small country situated in western Africa where the great bulge of the continent stretches into the Atlantic Ocean *(see map, p. 447)*. The country was under French colonial control from the end of the nineteenth century until 1958, when the people of Guinea voted for independence. A republic was established with Ahmed Sékou Touré, one of the independence leaders, becoming president.

Under Touré's dictatorial rule opposition was suppressed, and the unicameral National Assembly, which had no real power, was in the hands of the sole legal party, Touré's Democratic Party of Guinea. Touré died in March 1984, and the military, led by Col. Lansana Conté, seized power in April, forestalling an attempted transition by Touré loyalists. The political institutions of the Touré era were abolished, and Conté ruled as president through a Military Committee for National Regeneration. His political and economic reforms initially were popular, but in the late 1980s, as democratic forces grew stronger throughout Africa, opposition began to mount. He was also forced to deal with the threat of coups against his regime.

In 1989, under pressure from Western aid donors as well as from opposition at home, Conté announced that a new constitution providing for a five-year democratic transition would be drafted. A referendum on the constitution was held in December 1990, and the government announced that it had been overwhelmingly approved. The opposition, however, objected to many aspects of the document, including the long transition period and the two-party system it mandated. In October 1991 Conté conceded that multiple political parties would be permitted to register. In December, as stipulated in the new constitution, the Transitional Council for National Recovery was installed, replacing the Military Committee for National Regeneration. This body is two-thirds civilian and one-third military, but in practice it was chosen by Conté and by no means constitutes a parliament.

President Conté had first promised parliamentary elections for late 1992, but he resisted opposition demands for the convening of a national conference to oversee the voting. In December 1992 the government postponed the election, claiming that it lacked the necessary funds. Conté then scheduled the parliamentary vote for December 1993, to follow presidential elections. Opposition parties objected to this arrangement and demanded that the legislature be elected before the president. Conté responded, amid widespread protests, by postponing the parliamentary vote a second time.

The opposition failed to present a united front in the 1993 presidential election, and Conté won with a 51.7 percent majority. Opposition parties rejected this outcome, alleging irregularities in the conduct of the election. Outside observers also questioned the results. Parliamentary elections were rescheduled for December 1994, but in October the government said that preparations were not complete and delayed the vote indefinitely. Organizing elections in Guinea's remote rural regions is indeed a difficult and expensive challenge, but the repeated postponements raised concerns about the regime's commitment to a democratic transition.

Elections to the new unicameral National Assembly were finally held in June 1995. The ruling Party for Unity and Progress won 71 of the 114 seats in balloting marred by the boycott of the Union of Democratic Forces and allegations of voting irregularities. Although other opposition parties won seats in the legislature, their influence was muted.

Raymond Copson

GUINEA-BISSAU

OFFICIAL NAME: Republic of Guinea-Bissau (República da Guiné-Bissau)

CAPITAL: Bissau

POPULATION: 1,151,000 (1996 est.)

DATE OF INDEPENDENCE: September 10, 1974 (from Portugal)

DATE OF CURRENT CONSTITUTION: Approved May 16, 1984

FORM OF GOVERNMENT: Parliamentary democracy

LANGUAGES: Portuguese (official), Criolo

MONETARY UNIT: Guinea-Bissau peso

FISCAL YEAR: Calendar year

LEGISLATURE: National People's Assembly (Assembléia Nacional Popular)

NUMBER OF CHAMBERS: One

NUMBER OF MEMBERS: 100

PERCENTAGE OF WOMEN: 10.0

TERM OF LEGISLATURE: Five years

MOST RECENT LEGISLATIVE ELECTION: July 3, 1994

MINIMUM AGE FOR VOTING: 18

MINIMUM AGE FOR MEMBERSHIP: 21

SUFFRAGE: Universal and direct

VOTING: Optional

ADDRESS: Assembléia Nacional Popular, Apartado 219, 1021 Codex Bissau

TELEPHONE: (245) 20 19 91

FAX: (245) 20 28 23

Guinea-Bissau is a small West African country between Senegal and Guinea (see map, p. 447). Until independence in 1974, it was West Africa's oldest Portuguese colony, settled in the fifteenth century, and it still remains a lusophone outpost in a French-dominated region.

The country's first constitution, that of November 10, 1980, was suspended four days after its adoption, following a military coup led by Maj. João Bernardo Vieira. The new regime in 1984 adopted the country's second constitution, making Guinea-Bissau a de jure one-party state and vesting legislative power in the National People's Assembly, an indirectly elected body of 150 representatives. Electors of the National People's Assembly were the regional council members, who were directly elected. The National People's Assembly, in turn, elected a fifteen-member Council of State to which its powers were delegated between Assembly sessions. The Assembly also elected the president of the Council of State, who was the head of state.

Under pressure at home and from abroad to liberalize, the National People's Assembly in May 1991 approved constitutional amendments authorizing direct, multiparty elections for the first time in the history of Guinea-Bissau. The amendments also called for universal adult suffrage and reduced the size of the Assembly to one hundred members.

The first elections held under the constitution took place in July 1994. The elections, judged generally free and fair by outside observers, returned to power the ruling African Party for the Independence of Guinea-Bissau and Cape Verde. (The party's name remains unchanged from the era of struggle for independence from Portugal.) Vieira won the presidential race on August 7, 1994, in second-round balloting.

George Thomas Kurian

GUYANA

OFFICIAL NAME: Co-operative Republic of Guyana
CAPITAL: Georgetown
POPULATION: 712,000 (1996 est.)
DATE OF INDEPENDENCE: May 26, 1966 (from the United Kingdom)
DATE OF CURRENT CONSTITUTION: Adopted February 11, 1980; effective October 6, 1980
FORM OF GOVERNMENT: Parliamentary democracy
LANGUAGE: English
MONETARY UNIT: Guyanese dollar
FISCAL YEAR: Calendar year
LEGISLATURE: National Assembly
NUMBER OF CHAMBERS: One
NUMBER OF MEMBERS: 65 (53 directly elected, 12 indirectly elected)
PERCENTAGE OF WOMEN: 20.0
TERM OF LEGISLATURE: Five years
MOST RECENT LEGISLATIVE ELECTION: October 5, 1992
MINIMUM AGE FOR VOTING: 18
MINIMUM AGE FOR MEMBERSHIP: 18
SUFFRAGE: Universal
VOTING: Optional
ADDRESS: Parliament Office, Public Buildings, Georgetown
TELEPHONE: (592 02) 61 465
FAX: (592 02) 51 357

Guyana, a member of the Commonwealth located on the northern coast of South America (see map, p. 91), is a young democracy in which efforts are under way to strengthen the role of the National Assembly. On October 5, 1992, after more than two years of delays and an arduous process of electoral reform, the Co-operative Republic of Guyana held general elections to fill the presidency and most of the seats in the National Assembly. For the first time in Guyana's history, ballots were counted in the open at voting stations, while the international community—including a Commonwealth delegation and another group led by former U.S. president Jimmy Carter—monitored the process. Although there were some disturbances and threats of greater violence, the 1992 elections, which returned the People's Progressive Party to power and party leader Cheddi Jagan to the presidency, represented a departure from decades of polling marked by complaints of electoral fraud. Moreover, the elections imbued the National Assembly with new prestige and legitimacy. While long-promised constitutional reform has not been realized through mid-1997, debate continues about possible reforms that would diminish the considerable authority of the executive president and correspondingly enhance the power of the National Assembly.

HISTORICAL BACKGROUND

This English-speaking country is ethnically complex, reflecting in its small population of African and Asian descent not only the extent and diversity of the British Empire in its heyday but Dutch, Portuguese, and French influence as well. About half of the country's inhabitants are Indo-Guyanese descendants of indentured servants brought to Guyana between the 1830s and 1920. Afro-Guyanese, descendants of slaves brought from West Africa in the eighteenth and early nineteenth centuries, make up more than a third of the population. The remaining population consists of indigenous Amerindians (about 5 percent), who live primarily in the Amazonian interior, and smaller percentages of Guyanese who claim English, Portuguese, Dutch, or Chinese ancestry. Guyana also is religiously diverse: about 50 percent of the population is Christian (Roman Catholic, Anglican, Methodist, or other Protestant sects), 33 percent Hindu, and 10 percent Sunni Muslim.

At the time the first Europeans sailed along the northern coast of South America (Amerigo Vespucci's first map-making expedition to the New World in 1499 traced this coastline) the territory that would become Guyana was inhabited by several indigenous tribes. The best-known to European writers were the Caribs, Warraus, and Arawaks. The seventeenth and eighteenth centuries saw the English, French, Portuguese, Spanish, and Dutch vying to establish trading posts and mercantilist colonies along the northern coast of South America. The most successful was the Dutch West India Company, which crafted rudimentary governing institutions sturdy enough to survive for a century after the departure of the Dutch.

The British secured permanent control of the Dutch possessions in 1814, and in 1831 the separate territories of Demarara, Essequibo, and Berbice were united in the single colony of British Guiana. Its governance was based on an unusually liberal compact—not typical for a Crown colony—that allowed the local assembly, the Combined Court, to reduce or refuse expenditures proposed by the governor, but not to increase or initiate expenditures. This meant that the local business community could reduce or eliminate the salaries of officials whose performances displeased them, prompting the British to search for ways to increase the authority of the Crown.

The principal constitutional innovations occurred in 1891, 1928, and 1943. Ordinance 1 of 1891 broadened the franchise by reducing the income qualification, and it consolidated the Combined Court into one body whose fourteen members would be elected. In 1896 secret voting was introduced, which appears to have accelerated the rate of electoral success for candidates of African and Asian ancestry. By the 1920s all fourteen of the elected members of the Combined Court were locally born, and they included men of Chinese, East Indian, Portuguese, African, and mixed origin. After the general election of 1926, when the voting population of less than 10,000 men (predominantly of African origin) brought the Popular Party to power, British concern about the inability of the government to balance its budget led to the imposition of a less representative colonial government. In 1928 the British Guiana Act created a colonial government with a unicameral Legislative Council, a majority of whose members were appointed by the governor. While the voters continued to select fourteen representatives, the appointment of thirteen members, plus the ex officio membership of the governor and two other colonial officials, meant that this legislature was distinctly less representative than its predecessors. The British Guiana Act also extended the franchise to women (although they were obliged to satisfy the income and property qualifications independently of their spouses).

As the Great Depression spread throughout the world in the 1930s, labor unrest in the British territories in the Caribbean led in 1938 to the appointment of the West India Royal Commission headed by Baron Moyne. The commission addressed the structures of governance in the region and concluded that more representative government was needed. In 1943 the constitution of British Guiana was finally amended by the British Parliament to reflect the recommendations of the Moyne Commission. A local commission recommended modest extension of the franchise in the next legislative elections, which, delayed by the Second World War, finally took place on November 24, 1947.

The elections held on April 27, 1953, to select all twenty-four members of the colonial House of Assembly—the first based on universal adult suffrage—were won by the People's Progressive Party. The party had been established in 1950 as a socialist, pro-independence party by Dr. Cheddi Jagan, an Indo-Guyanese dentist trained in the United States, and Forbes Burnham, an Afro-Guyanese barrister who received his professional education in Britain. Alarmed by the leftist agenda of the new government at the height of the cold war, the British suspended the constitution on October 9, 1953, deposing Dr. Jagan's government after just 133 days in office, and appointed a new legislature.

The colony's constitution was further modified in London, so that by the 1957 elections, again only fourteen of the twenty-four seats were elected. Six seats were filled by members nominated by the colonial government, three were filled by executive officials acting in an ex-officio capacity, and the speaker was named by the governor from outside the parliament. Although Burnham by this time had formed a new party, Jagan's People's Progressive Party won the elections, winning nine seats to Burnham's three. Jagan's party remained the most popular political organization thereafter.

Guyana became an independent nation and a member of the Commonwealth on May 26, 1966. Since then, the country has formally maintained a modified parliamentary form of government, although before the 1992 national elections Guyana's status as a democratic polity was questionable. The People's National Congress (PNC), which maintained power from independence to 1992, was continually accused by opposition parties and international observers of manipulating the electoral process. The steady decline in the economy was so grievous during the PNC's tenure that in 1989 a Commonwealth advisory group on the situation noted in the *McIntyre Report* that Guyana had fallen below Haiti to rank as the poorest country in the Western Hemisphere. Yet with each parliamentary election through 1985, the PNC's official margin of victory grew, as did complaints about the integrity of the electoral process.

THE MODERN CONSTITUTION AND PARLIAMENT

The 1980 constitution specifies that the parliament of Guyana "shall consist of the President and the National Assembly." The National Assembly is a unicameral body comprising sixty-five elected members and other nonelected members, whether by virtue of election as speaker or appointment as a cabinet minister in the government. In 1997 eight nonelected government officials were accordingly entitled to participate in the work of the National Assembly. Because the president is elected by virtue of being at the head of the list of the party receiving the most votes (even if it is a plurality), there is no effective separation of powers between the executive and the legislature.

LEADERSHIP OF PARLIAMENT

The president has the authority to name the prime minister, who also is considered a vice president. According to the constitution, the prime minister is the leader of government business in the National Assembly. In this capacity, the prime minister is generally referred to unofficially as the "leader of the house." Through most of the 1992–1997 Sixth Parliament, however, the senior minister of agriculture usually acted as leader of the house rather than the prime minister.

The speaker is chosen by vote of the newly elected National Assembly before any other business is conducted and need not be an elected member of the Assembly. A speaker elected from outside the Assembly becomes a member upon election to the speakership. Nevertheless, the speaker's power to cast tie-breaking votes is expressly not extended to speakers who are elected from outside the legislature. In such circumstances the motion fails on a tie vote. The prime minister, the leader of the house, and the speaker have somewhat overlapping responsibilities, but they always have been members of the majority.

The president also may select other vice presidents (President Forbes Burnham appointed his wife, Viola, a vice president in the 1980s) and is permitted to name the leader of the opposition, without any provision for votes of confirmation. In addition, members of the cabinet are appointed by the president. They too become nonvoting members of parliament.

ELECTIONS AND POLITICAL PARTIES

All Guyanese citizens age eighteen or older who are present in Guyana on election day are permitted to vote, provided they have properly registered in a process that is conducted prior to each election.

Of the sixty-five elected members of the National Assembly, fifty-three are directly elected in general elections according to a system of strict proportional representation in which the entire country is considered a single electoral district. The constitution expressly permits, but does not require, the election of up to twenty-six of the fifty-three members from single-member districts. The electoral law has never been amended to provide for this, although the constitution also provides that if this were to be done for twenty-six seats, the remaining twenty-seven would be filled on a compensatory basis so that the partisan composition of parliament would continue to reflect the national voting preference. The electoral law specifies that after the elections the party leader decides which of the names on the list of fifty-three will actually sit in the Assembly.

Twelve members of the National Assembly are elected indirectly. On the same day the national elections are held, voters also elect on a proportional basis Regional Development Councils in each of Guyana's ten regions. They vary from twelve to thirty-five members and are responsible for numerous administrative and development tasks. Each council then elects one person from its ranks to serve as a member of parliament. Each also elects two members to constitute the National Congress of Local Democratic Organs. While this twenty-seat body has failed since its creation in 1980 to perform virtually any of its constitutionally envisioned functions, it has managed (most recently in December 1992) to elect two of its number to the National Assembly.

Vacancies occurring among the fifty-three national seats are filled by the leader of the party whose member has departed, while the indirectly elected members are replaced by the relevant Regional Development Council or the National Congress of Local Democratic Organs. Unless the parliament is dissolved earlier by the president, the term of office is five years.

Guyana's electoral law ensures that political parties are the central institution of the legislature, and the country's political history has produced disciplined parties. In part because the constitution permits party leaders to fill parliamentary seats after the elections, Guyana's legislature is rather representative in terms of ethnic background and gender. Of the sixty-five elected members, thirteen are women (including two ministers). The present ruling People's Progressive Party, with thirty-six elected members, is generally viewed by most voters as representing the Indo-Guyanese community, while the People's National Congress, with twenty-six members, is identified as representing the Afro-Guyanese community. Both parties, however, boast members from the two major ethnic groups.

Because of the nature of the electoral system, only the ten members elected from the regions can be said to have constituents, but the major parties make a practice of assigning members to party-defined "constituencies." Often these are areas with which members have personal or family ties, and some members do offer limited constituency service to their assigned areas.

Party discipline is quite strong. In fact, party leaders obtain undated letters of resignation from members at the commencement of their legislative service. With the exception of the 1995 vote on abortion law revisions, there have been no instances in which a member has voted contrary to his or her party's majority. Crossing party lines is not explicitly prohibited by law or regulation, and on at least two occasions since independence members have left their party and continued to sit in the Assembly as independents.

ORGANIZATION OF THE NATIONAL ASSEMBLY

The constitution provides that the National Assembly will determine its own schedule but specifies that "the Assembly shall sit every day except Saturdays and Sundays." In fact, however, the Assembly meets irregularly and infrequently as issues arise and as the government calls it into session. Through the end of 1996 the Sixth Parliament had met eighty-five times since its election in late 1992, an average of about two days a month. Sittings begin at 2:00 p.m. and end at 10:00 p.m., after a thirty-minute break at 4:00 p.m. and a ninety-minute break at 6:30 p.m.

Since 1986 the Assembly has recessed from August 10 to October 10 each year unless "special reasons" arise for a sitting. When the speaker convened sessions at the government's request on August 10, 17, and 24, 1995, a member of the opposition who opposed the legislation then pending filed suit in the High Court requesting a restraining order to prevent the Assembly from meeting. While the High Court did not act on the suit, the speaker declared that his judgment was sufficient to determine whether "special reasons" existed for a sitting during the otherwise envisioned recess period.

Parliament may be dissolved at any time by the president, but its general stated term is five years. If parliament is dissolved, the legislative elections may be postponed by the president up to a total of ten years following the previous election.

LAW MAKING

Any member of the National Assembly may introduce a bill or propose any motion for debate to the Assembly. Bills, however, are introduced almost exclusively by the government and are drafted by the attorney general's office. Bills of certain kinds, such as those relating to taxation or some other financial matters, may be introduced only by the government.

The fiscal year begins January 1, although successive administrations have yet to present the government's budget to the Assembly by that date. Most years, Articles 218 and 219 of the constitution are invoked, which permit the government to spend money through the fourth month before enactment of the budget. Parliamentary debate on the budget therefore occurs typically in February or March.

Unless otherwise specified in the constitution (as in the case for amendments to the constitution itself), all questions proposed for decision in the National Assembly are determined by a majority of the votes of the members present during the voting process. A quorum of one-third of the elected members is required. Nominal voting is conducted by the calling of the roll by the clerk. Through 1996 only twenty-eight such recorded votes had been taken in the four years of the Sixth Parliament.

A bill can become a law only if the president assents. If the president withholds assent, the bill is returned to the Assembly with a message stating the reasons for presidential disapproval. If two-thirds of the Assembly agrees to return the bill to the president, the chief executive must assent to it within twenty-one days or dissolve the parliament before that time. Thus, a legislative override of a presidential veto would prompt new elections of both the president and the legislature. While it is possible under the present constitution that a president could fail to command a majority in the legislature, allowing the legislature to amend a government proposal to such an extent that the executive could not abide it, this political situation has not yet arisen and no bills have ever been returned.

COMMITTEES

In 1996 the National Assembly created its first two standing committees: the Committee on Foreign Affairs and the Committee on Natural Resources. Each has fourteen members and is chaired by the corresponding minister in the government. By year's end the Committee on Foreign Affairs had met twice; the Committee on Natural Resources had yet to convene. There also are six sessional select committees. The Committee of Supply, which comprises the entire Assembly, meets to consider the budget. A subcommittee recommends the allocation of time for budget debates to the various parties. The next most important committee is the Public Accounts Committee, which examines how public monies have been spent. Following Westminster tradition, the chair of this committee is selected by the leader of the opposition, while the chair of all the other sessional select committees is the speaker of the Assembly. Other committees in the Assembly include: the Standing Orders Committee, to consider changes in the standing orders; the Committee of Selection, to select the membership of other committees; the Committee on Privileges, to consider various matters referred to it by the National Assembly; and the Assembly Committee, to deal with matters of member comfort and convenience.

In addition to these committees, special select committees may be appointed to consider particular pieces of legislation or other topics as designated by the Assembly. If so authorized, these committees can hear outside witnesses. The best-known committee of the Sixth Parliament was concerned with a controversial government proposal to liberalize access to abortion. It heard witnesses, met about twenty times, and prepared a report. Its report and the form of legislation it recommended were adopted by parliament in May 1995 in the only instance to date in which members were explicitly permitted by party leaders to vote their conscience rather than obliged to respect the party's whip. Other select committees have dealt with public utilities, a proposal to create an Integrity Commission, and legislation concerning Amerindian issues. A special select committee to consider amendments to the constitution was created in 1994 and began work in the summer of 1996. It set a precedent by creating a staff secretariat of four persons to support the committee's work.

OVERSIGHT

The permanent secretary or accounting officer of any ministry may be called before the Public Accounts Committee to respond to members' questions about the expenditure of funds, and this is done frequently. Overall, however, there has been very little systematic oversight of the executive by the legislature because of the inactivity of committees and the dearth of professional staff or investigators.

The constitution provides for the presidential appointment of an ombudsman. Matters subject to investigation include any action taken by any department of the government, or by the president, ministers, officers, or members of such a department. This investigative power may not be applied to international relations, the protection of state security, and any actions taken in relation to appointments to government offices. The ombudsman is obliged to present an annual report to the Assembly that describes work undertaken during the previous year, although in most recent years no such report has been submitted.

OFFICIAL RECORD AND MEDIA COVERAGE

Minutes are taken for every sitting (daily session) of the plenary, and Standing Order 6 requires that printed copies be available to the members, public, and press before the next sitting. This usually is done in a timely fashion. Since independence in 1966, the *Hansard,* the official record of parliamentary debates, has been printed only occasionally. Verbatim transcripts of most of the Sixth Parliament's plenary proceedings have been published, however, through an arrangement with a private company that makes them available for sale to the public.

The speaker determines what media coverage will be allowed of all sessions of the National Assembly. In fact, the news media have full access to plenary proceedings. Newspapers report extensively on parliamentary proceedings and politics. Privately owned and state-owned television are given free rein to record debates and frequently broadcast excerpts. Occasionally, sessions are broadcast live by radio. Most proceedings of committees, however, are closed to the press and the public.

PARLIAMENTARY FACILITIES

The National Assembly meets in the Public Buildings, a painted yellow, brick, two-story structure located in the center of the nation's capital, Georgetown. Construction was completed in 1832 according to the plan of architect Joseph Hadfield and was turned over to the colonial legislature, the Combined Court, in 1834. The parliament chamber is housed on the top floor of the east wing. There also are offices for the speaker, the clerk, and the staff of about thirty-five. The Assembly chamber is arranged Westminster-style with government and opposition front rows facing each other across wooden tables and the ceremonial mace. The public gallery at floor level behind a rail opposite the speaker's chair seats seventy-two persons. Seating also is available for the press and for special guests of the Assembly. There is at present only one committee meeting room.

The clerk and deputy clerk, who act as staff to all committees, are appointed by the president upon the recommendation of the speaker of the Assembly. They are supported by a civil service staff. No members have personal offices or mailboxes in the Public Buildings, including the leader of the opposition. In addition, there are no facilities for party caucuses.

PARLIAMENTARY LIBRARY AND RESEARCH

In 1996 funding for construction and staffing of a parliamentary library was appropriated as part of the national budget—an important institutional step forward for the legislature. Four full-time library staff were hired and trained in 1997.

PARLIAMENTARY PRIVILEGES, PAY, AND ETHICS

The National Assembly determines the privileges and immunities granted to its members. No civil or criminal proceedings may be conducted against a member for words spoken or written to the Assembly or to a committee. During the session, members of the Assembly are free from arrest for civil debt. In addition, no process issued by any court shall be served or executed within the precincts of the Assembly while the Assembly is in session.

Guidelines for the tenure in office of members of the National Assembly are listed in the constitution. A member of the Assembly shall vacate his or her seat if the member resigns in writing to the speaker; is absent from more than six sittings of the Assembly without permission of the speaker; ceases to be a citizen of Guyana; is disqualified for election; or is judged to be of unsound mind or convicted of a crime. Members also must vacate their seats when parliament is dissolved.

In 1997 the base annual salary of a member of parliament was G$248,400 (US$1,733). The speaker and senior ministers are paid G$1,059,840 (US$7,418) a year, while the minority leader and ordinary ministers earn G$927,360 (US$6,491). The prime minister's annual salary is G$1,242,000 (US$8,613).

In addition to their taxable salaries, members receive a number of tax-free allowances for entertainment, travel, telephone, and subsistence while in the capital for meetings of the Assembly. Legislative leaders and ministers also receive housing and chauffeur allowances. Subsidies for the importation of a personal automobile and exemption from bridge tolls also are extended to all members. There are no rules on outside income, and most members have other jobs.

There are virtually no rules or statutory provisions relating to ethics or conflicts of interest. Standing Order 78 states that "no member of the Assembly shall appear before the Assembly or any committee thereof as counsel or solicitor for any party or in any capacity for which he is to receive a fee or reward." Although a law providing for the presidential appointment of an Integrity Commission was enacted in 1991, it has never been appointed.

Thomas O. Melia

BIBLIOGRAPHY

Daly, Vere T. *A Short History of the Guyanese People.* London: Macmillan, 1975.

Narain, Frank A. *A Handbook for Members of the National Assembly.* Georgetown: Parliament of Guyana's Assembly, 1992.

Rose, James. "The Coming of Crown Colony Government to British Guiana in 1928." *Guyana Historical Journal* 11 (1990): 47–67.

Sallahuddin. *Guyana: The Struggle for Liberation, 1945–1992.* Georgetown: Guyana National Printers, 1994.

H

HAITI

OFFICIAL NAME: Republic of Haiti (République d'Haiti)
CAPITAL: Port-au-Prince
POPULATION: 6,732,000 (1996 est.)
DATE OF INDEPENDENCE: January 1, 1804 (from France)
DATE OF CURRENT CONSTITUTION: Approved and effective March 29, 1987
FORM OF GOVERNMENT: Transitional parliamentary democracy
LANGUAGES: French (official), Creole
MONETARY UNIT: Gourde
FISCAL YEAR: October 1–September 30
LEGISLATURE: National Assembly (Assemblée Nationale)
NUMBER OF CHAMBERS: Two. Chamber of Deputies (Chambre des Députés); Senate (Sénat)
NUMBER OF MEMBERS: Chamber of Deputies, 83; Senate, 27
PERCENTAGE OF WOMEN: Chamber of Deputies, 3.6; Senate, 0.0
TERM OF LEGISLATURE: Chamber of Deputies, four years; Senate, six years
MOST RECENT LEGISLATIVE ELECTION: June 25 and September 17, 1995
MINIMUM AGE FOR VOTING: 18
MINIMUM AGE FOR MEMBERSHIP: Chamber of Deputies, 25; Senate, 30
SUFFRAGE: Universal and direct
VOTING: Optional
ADDRESS: Chamber of Deputies, Palais Législatif, Port-au-Prince; Senate, Avenue Marie Jeanne, Port-au-Prince
TELEPHONE: Chamber of Deputies, (509) 22 41 29; Senate, (509) 22 30 76
FAX: Chamber of Deputies, (509) 22 17 17; Senate, (509) 22 89 02

Haiti, located in the northern Caribbean Sea, is the poorest country in the Western Hemisphere and has a long history of political instability. Founded in 1804 after the world's only successful slave revolt, Haiti has witnessed extensive U.S. involvement in the twentieth century in response to its chronic instability. The politics of the country are complicated by racial tensions between the majority black population and the mulatto minority.

HISTORICAL BACKGROUND

Haiti shares the island of Hispaniola with the Dominican Republic. The Spanish, who were the first to colonize Hispaniola, formally ceded the western third of the island—corresponding roughly to present-day Haiti—to France in 1697. Under French administration, a highly stratified social structure emerged in the colony, comprising French, Creoles, mulattos, free blacks, and slaves. A mulatto revolt against French and Creole dominance at the end of the eighteenth century destroyed the structure of Haitian society and set the stage for the overthrow of French rule and, ultimately, independence in 1804. The nineteenth century was characterized by black-mulatto political and social friction and ever worsening economic conditions.

U.S. troops landed in Haiti in 1915 to protect American property and investments in the wake of a local uprising and remained nearly two decades. After the troops left in 1934, the U.S. government continued to control Haitian customs receipts until 1947. The decade following was characterized by continued governmental weakness. In 1957 François "Papa Doc" Duvalier was elected president. He quickly consolidated his power and, naming himself president for life in 1964, ruled until his death in 1971, at which time his son Jean-Claude ("Baby Doc") became president.

Jean-Claude Duvalier was forced into exile by a popular uprising in 1986, and Haiti descended into political chaos, with civilian governments falling in military coups with regularity. The Organization of American States, with the United States in the lead, took action following a military coup in September 1991 that deposed President Jean-Bertrand Aristide. After a trade embargo failed to force the military regime to restore Aristide to power, troops from the United States and several other nations of the hemisphere landed in Port-au-Prince.

Following the restoration of constitutional government under U.S. auspices and the return of deposed president Aristide in 1994, the legislative system of Haiti entered a transitional state.

THE NATIONAL ASSEMBLY

Historically, the legislature has been subservient to the executive, and its status is not likely to change dramatically in the near future. Most elections held in the twentieth century were rigged, and members of parliament were tied to or controlled by patrons belonging to the elite. As a result, true democratic traditions have never taken root in the country.

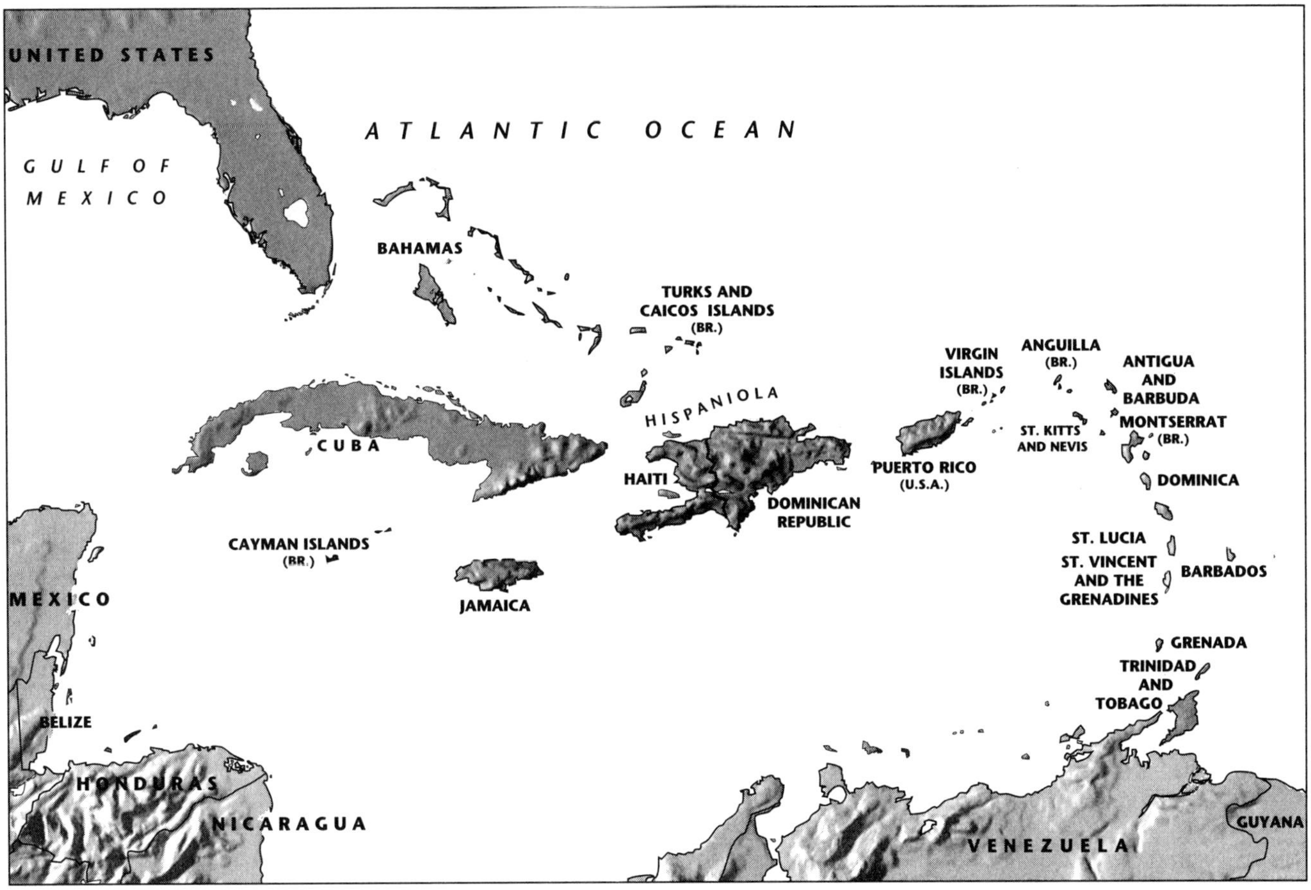

The Haitian legislature is bicameral. The last three constitutions, those of 1950, 1957, and 1987, provided that the two chambers—the Senate and the Chamber of Deputies—would become the National Assembly when meeting in joint session. Senators serve six-year terms, with one-third of the members up for election every two years. Deputies serve concurrent four-year terms. The Senate comprises twenty-seven members, and the Chamber of Deputies, eighty-three members.

The legislature meets in April of each year, and the session lasts three months. Senators are elected in nine three-member constituencies which correspond to the country's nine departments, whereas three deputies are elected by each of the twenty-seven *arrondissements* into which the departments are divided; two additional deputies are elected from Port-au-Prince. Both the Chamber of Deputies and the Senate elect speakers (known as presidents) from among their membership.

The constitution endows legislators with a wide range of powers and privileges, although few of the powers were used during the many years of dictatorship under the Duvaliers and their military-backed successors. They could in theory initiate legislation, declare war, approve treaties, revise the constitution, and act as a court of justice.

The age of suffrage is eighteen. The eighty-three deputies are selected by absolute majority in two rounds of voting. A second round is held in districts where no candidate obtained an absolute majority of the valid votes cast. Only the two candidates with the largest number of votes qualify for the second round. Senators also are elected by majority vote.

George Thomas Kurian

HONDURAS

OFFICIAL NAME: Republic of Honduras (República de Honduras)
CAPITAL: Tegucigalpa
POPULATION: 5,605,000 (1996 est.)
DATE OF INDEPENDENCE: September 15, 1821 (from Spain)
DATE OF CURRENT CONSTITUTION: Adopted January 11, 1982; effective January 20, 1982
FORM OF GOVERNMENT: Parliamentary democracy
LANGUAGE: Spanish
MONETARY UNIT: Lempira
FISCAL YEAR: Calendar year
LEGISLATURE: National Congress (Congreso Nacional)
NUMBER OF CHAMBERS: One
NUMBER OF MEMBERS: 128
PERCENTAGE OF WOMEN: 7.8
TERM OF LEGISLATURE: Four years
MOST RECENT LEGISLATIVE ELECTION: November 28, 1993
MINIMUM AGE FOR VOTING: 18
MINIMUM AGE FOR MEMBERSHIP: 21
SUFFRAGE: Universal and direct
VOTING: Compulsory
ADDRESS: Congreso Nacional, Palacio Legislativo, P.O. Box 595, Tegucigalpa, D.C.
TELEPHONE: (504) 32 22 81
FAX: (504) 38 60 48

A Central American state that gained its independence of Spain in 1821, Honduras has had a long history of dictatorial government and oligarchic rule *(see map, p. 526)*. Between the end of World War II in 1945 and the return to a competitive electoral system in 1982, every government came to power through a coup. Since the adoption of the new constitution in 1982, governments have come to power through elections.

The National Congress of Honduras is a unicameral body vested with authority by the 1982 constitution. The members of Congress and the president of the country are elected for four-year terms. In the November 1993 elections, which brought Carlos Roberto Reina Idiaquez to power as president, the Liberal Party of Honduras (PLH) won seventy-one seats, the National Party (PN) gained fifty-five seats, and the National Innovation and Unity Party–Social Democratic (PINU), two seats.

Since 1982 the PLH has won the presidency three times: in 1982, 1986, and 1993. In fact, the two dominant parties—the Liberal and the National—are both relatively conservative political parties. Both cut across class lines; they tend to be differentiated not so much by ideology as by family and regional traditions. Both parties have historically been dominated by oligarchic family elites. In addition to the two main parties, there are two minor parties—PINU and the Christian Democratic Party of Honduras—but they generally have little influence on Honduran politics.

Congress has increasingly asserted its power through both legislative action and oversight of the executive. It is growing more responsive to the citizenry of the country and more supportive of democracy and economic development. Some of the most important and more controversial legislation recently approved by the National Congress include the National Merchant Marine Law and the Intellectual Property Law. In both instances, congressional leaders opposed powerful interest groups without the support of the executive branch. Congress also demonstrated its legislative independence by vetoing an executive decree that had allowed the state-owned electric company to increase charges on household energy consumption. Congress proceeded to pass a law that reduced the prices to their original levels.

The introduction and approval of important bills over the past few years have created the opportunity for Congress to serve as a focal point for reaching compromise agreement on some of the fundamental issues facing the country. In so doing, the Congress has begun to be seen as a locus of social conflict resolution and as a body with a growing capacity for policy initiation and formulation.

As has traditionally been the case, the central issues facing Honduras are the eradication of poverty and the creation of jobs. The country has taken modest steps forward by encouraging the diversification of its economy. In addition to the exportation of bananas, coffee cultivation and textiles assembly are now important parts of the economy. Likewise, as is true in many countries, Honduras faces a growing crime rate and the problem of how to improve the performance of the judiciary.

Members of Congress are elected to four-year terms in national elections coinciding with the presidential and municipal elections. These are held on the last Sunday of November during election years. Congress is organized to represent the country's eighteen departments. It has 128 members and the same number of alternates. Although elected on the basis of closed party-list proportional balloting, members are designated to represent districts. Prior to each election, the National Electoral Board establishes—according to population criteria—the number of representatives to be elected in each department. Candidates must be Honduran and twenty-one years of age at the time of the election.

PARLIAMENTARY PROCEEDINGS

The Honduran National Congress is housed in a medium-size, six-story, modern building located in downtown Tegucigalpa. Congress meets in regular sessions every year from January 25 through October 31. The legislative session can be extended by majority vote of Congress at the request of one or more of its members or the executive. Congress is in recess during the month of May. Extraordinary sessions can be called at the request of the president of the republic, Congress's Permanent Committee, or a majority of Congress members. Congress cannot be dissolved under any circumstance.

Every session of Congress begins with the verification of a quorum (half of the members plus one), after which the session is declared open. The last session's minutes are read, discussed, and approved. Following this, correspondence and reports are read, and legislative proposals are presented. The Congress's opinion on the proposals is taken and motions begin.

Proposed legislation can be introduced by any representative and by the president of the country. The Supreme Court and the National Electoral Board can initiate bills on matters within their jurisdiction. A constitutional amendment can be initiated by a simple majority of the members of Congress or by the president. A two-thirds affirmative vote of Congress is required for approval of an amendment.

Bills initiated by representatives are first presented to the Congress's Office of the Secretary and are read in the plenary of Congress. After the first reading, the president of Congress assigns the bill to the appropriate committee. The committee (all committees comprise seven members) analyzes the bill, deliberates, and renders an opinion on the bill. There is no time limit by which committees have to reach their determination on a bill. The opinion is presented to the plenary for its consideration. A minority opinion may also be presented to the plenary.

Bills are discussed in three separate plenary debates held on different days unless Congress, by simple majority, approves the urgent consideration of a particular bill. In such cases, up to two debates may be eliminated. The first and second debate represent general readings of the proposed legislation. During the third and final debate, the bill is discussed one article at a time. If the proposed bill is approved by Congress, it is delivered to the executive for approval and promulgation within three days of the vote. A bill is not considered law unless it is approved, promulgated, and published. If the executive does not act on or publish a law within ten days, it can be approved and published by Congress. The executive can partially or totally reject a bill within ten days after the bill is received from Congress. A bill vetoed by the executive is returned to Congress accompanied by a statement of the reasons for its rejection. A majority of two-thirds is needed in Congress to override an executive veto.

The volume of legislation varies from year to year. From January 25, 1994, to December 22, 1995, 203 bills were approved by Congress and sent to the executive. An official record of the sessions and debates is kept by the secretary of Congress. Each representative expresses publicly his or her vote. One of Congress's secretaries is charged with keeping notes and recording the vote. In some cases, and by prior agreement, the voting can be secret.

Congress can ask representatives of the executive branch, military personnel, or any other public or private person to testify on pertinent issues. Representatives may request in writing that ministers, vice ministers, and the presidents or directors of governmental entities furnish information in writing to Congress. There is no minimum number of representatives that must sign these written requests. The president of Congress notifies the president of the country, who instructs the officials requested to testify to appear before the Congress. Congress subsequently can send a report to the president recommending the continuation in office or the removal of the person asked to testify.

The annual budget law is presented to Congress by the president of the country within the first fifteen days of September every year. The president of Congress sends the proposed law to the Finance and Public Credit Committee, and copies are furnished to all representatives. Motions to amend the proposed budget law must be submitted by representatives in writing to the Finance and Public Credit Committee within twenty days of receipt of the proposed law. The report of the committee must address all motions to amend that were received within the allowed time period. The plenary first discusses the proposed law in general terms, then each motion presented is discussed, and finally the bill as amended and in all its details is debated.

Congress can impeach the president, Supreme Court judges, the nation's controller general, the members of the National Electoral Board, and armed forces officers. They can be impeached for mismanagement while performing their activities, crimes committed in the performance of their duties, or for common crimes. Any such accusation must be made by the president or by a majority of Congress. Once the request is made in Congress and approved, the president of Congress must assign the request to committee for its consideration and recommendation. Congress publicly judges the cases and decides, by a vote of two-thirds of its members, if there is culpability.

The media, both print and television, cover Congress extensively. Debate on significant legislation receives a lot of media coverage and attention. There is some attempt to cover the most controversial issues substantively, and the media are regarded as relatively independent and objective.

In case of international war or serious internal upheaval, the president—with the approval of the Council of Ministers—can declare a state of emergency (with justification) for a specified time period and scope. A state of emergency cannot exceed forty-five days. Congress must be notified within thirty days of the declaration for its approval or modification.

ORGANIZATION AND STRUCTURE

The president of Congress is elected from among the members of Congress for a period of four years. The president of Congress has considerable formal power. This includes the power of directing and organizing legislative debates; ordering of votes; opening, convening, or suspending the sessions; authorizing the presence of the public in the session; ordering the procedures and resolution of issues; nominating, promoting, or removing administrative personnel; and presenting the proposed annual budget of the Congress; authorizing the expenses of the representatives, the payment of their salaries, and the salaries of support personnel; and putting his or her authorized signature and seal, along with those of the appropriate corresponding committee secretaries, to the manuscripts of the sessions of Congress, including the laws, resolutions, declarations, and official correspondence. Basically, the president of Congress has a great deal of authority and acts as the administrative leader and chief representative of the body.

Congress's Office of the Secretary is in charge of coordinating the relationships between the presidency and Congress. Congress is beginning to exercise much more significant oversight of the activities of the executive branch by requiring its officials to give information on the agencies they represent.

Congress has organized itself into fifty-four subject-area committees. It also creates ad hoc committees to deal with specific transitory issues. Each political party selects members to represent it on the committees. Proposed committee members are then presented to the plenary, which ratifies the party nominees. In each case, the committees must proportionally reflect the political parties as they are represented in Congress.

Each committee has a president, a vice president, a secretary, and four other members. Committees can request information and reports from national, public, and private entities to help them in analyzing and rendering opinions on proposed legislation. In the case of investigating committees, all authorities called to testify are under obligation to do so.

Public hearings are a frequent parliamentary practice in Honduras, but there are no regular procedures or established mechanisms for holding public hearings. They are called in an ad hoc fashion for sensitive issues and as a means to gain popular support for controversial proposals, rather than for public consultation and feedback.

The political parties represented in the Honduran Congress maintain a high degree of solidarity.

STATUS OF MEMBERS AND PARLIAMENTARY RESOURCES

The Computer Information and Legislative Studies Center of the Office of the Secretary is in charge of the Parliamentary Library. This library is not very large and is mostly a depository for archives and Congress documents.

Members of Congress cannot be detained unless Congress first finds judicial cause for their arrest. They cannot be accused of crimes based on opinions expressed while exercising their functions. Representatives can lose their seats and face criminal charges if they are found to be violating provisions of the constitution, or if proof is found of the inappropriate use of their influence. A two-thirds majority vote is needed to expel a member from the body. If the accusation is found to have basis and the member is expelled, he or she then can be brought to trial.

When a member of Congress dies, resigns, is declared physically or mentally unable to serve, or asks for leave, he or she is replaced by an alternate.

As of 1995, the remuneration of a representative was 15,000 Lempiras, or approximately US$1,500 per month. This includes salary of approximately US$1,200 per month and representation expenditures of approximately US$300 per month. When Congress members travel to the interior or outside the country they receive extra per-diems. Representatives cannot receive pay from or work for other public enterprises or agencies. Professional social work, cultural activity, and education are exempted from this regulation.

Beyond the references to appropriate conduct found in Congress's internal regulations, there are no established ethics statutes or codes of ethics.

Allan Rosenbaum and Alejandro Rodriguez

BIBLIOGRAPHY

Barry, Tom. *Central America inside out.* New York: Grove Weidenfeld, 1991.

Goodman, Louis, William M. LeoGrande, and Johanna Mendelson Forman, eds. *Political Parties and Democracy in Central America.* Boulder, Colo.: Westview Press, 1992.

HUNGARY

OFFICIAL NAME: Hungarian Republic (Magyar Köztársaság)
CAPITAL: Budapest
POPULATION: 10,003,000 (1996 est.)
DATE OF INDEPENDENCE: November 16, 1918 (from Austro-Hungarian Empire)
DATE OF CURRENT CONSTITUTION: Approved October 18, 1989
FORM OF GOVERNMENT: Parliamentary democracy
LANGUAGE: Hungarian
MONETARY UNIT: Forint
FISCAL YEAR: Calendar year
LEGISLATURE: National Assembly (Országgyülés)
NUMBER OF CHAMBERS: One
NUMBER OF MEMBERS: 386
PERCENTAGE OF WOMEN: 11.4
TERM OF LEGISLATURE: Four years
MOST RECENT LEGISLATIVE ELECTION: May 8 and 29, 1994
MINIMUM AGE FOR VOTING: 18
MINIMUM AGE FOR MEMBERSHIP: 18
SUFFRAGE: Universal and direct
VOTING: Optional
ADDRESS: National Assembly, Széchenyi rkp. 19, 1358 Budapest
TELEPHONE: (361) 268 4000
FAX: (361) 268 4800

Hungary, located in east central Europe, was among the first European nations to create a liberal constitution (the April Laws of 1848) based on the full sovereignty of the parliament. This constitution became the basis of all succeeding democratic constitutions: of 1918, 1946, and 1989. The constitution promulgated after the Compromise with the Habsburg empire (1867) also retained the decisive role of the Hungarian parliament in political life. The communist 1949 constitution, however, reduced parliament to a "rubber stamp" in a one-party state.

In 1983 a new electoral law made electoral competition mandatory; in each constituency there was to be more than one candidate. The parliament elected in 1985 under this law had some non-Communist Party MPs and was much more active and critical than earlier parliaments had been. In fact, between 1985 and 1990 parliament played a very important role in nurturing the democratization process, including drafting the 1989 constitution.

The new, fully democratic constitution was adopted by the old parliament in October 1989. The 1989 constitution was amended following the spring 1990 election—the so-called founding election—to change the rights and duties of the government. Specifically, the amendments incorporated into the Hungarian constitution the (West) German model of positive no-confidence vote with a strong prime-ministerial government. This constitution is still in force today, although the 1990–1994 parliament (the National Assembly) elaborated some additional legal provisions. In all of Central and Eastern Europe during the democratization of the 1990s, only Hungary maintained the same parliament and government for a whole four-year cycle, and this stability helped the passage of extensive legislation promoting both democratization and marketization.

In the 1994 election, however, the government failed to retain a parliamentary majority, and two former opposition parties formed the government. The new governing coalition passed new standing orders and reorganized the system of parliamentary committees.

THE CONSTITUTION

The 1989 constitution as amended has determined the basic nature of the Hungarian parliamentary system and outlines the functions of the National Assembly in detail. The National Assembly enacts laws; approves the state budget and oversees its implementation; determines the program of the government; enters into international agreements; declares war and concludes peace; declares a state of exigency and sets up a Council of Defense in the event of war or imminent danger of an armed attack; declares a state of emergency in the event of armed actions aimed at overthrowing the constitutional order, grave acts of violence, or natural or industrial disaster; elects the president of the republic, the prime minister, the members of the Constitutional Court, the National Assembly commissioner of national and ethnic minority rights, the president and vice presidents of the State Audit Office, the president of the Supreme Court, and the chief public prosecutor; dissolves any local body of representatives whose activity is contrary to the constitution, on the recommendation of the government, submitted with the opinion of the Constitutional Court; and grants amnesty.

The mandate of the National Assembly commences with its inaugural sitting, and the National Assembly may declare its own dissolution before the expiration of its mandate. The president of the republic, appointing the day of elections at the same time, may dissolve the National Assembly if the National Assembly during the term of its

mandate withdraws confidence from the government at least four times within twelve months or if the National Assembly does not elect the person proposed by the president of the republic as prime minister within forty days from the proposal. Prior to dissolving the National Assembly, the president of the republic must obtain the opinion of the prime minister, the speaker of the National Assembly, and the leaders of the parliamentary parties. Within three months of the expiration of the National Assembly's mandate or the declaration of its dissolution, a new National Assembly must be elected. The National Assembly shall continue to function until the inaugural sitting of the new National Assembly has been held.

The neo-Gothic building of the Hungarian National Assembly was designed by Imre Steindl and built between 1885 and 1902. It is an elongated building situated along the Danube. The symmetrical building was designed to accommodate two chambers, one for the representatives, the other for senators, with four hundred seats each. Since Hungary now has a unicameral parliament, the Senate hall is used for ceremonial sessions. The Hungarian parliament has a second building nearby for the offices of MPs. The Hungarian parliament building is considered one of the most beautiful in the world.

PARTIES AND ELECTIONS

Hungary has a four-year electoral cycle. According to the 1989 electoral law, 176 members (45 percent) are elected in individual constituencies (in two rounds if no candidate receives an absolute majority in the first round), and 210 are chosen from party lists (twenty county lists and a national list). Each voter casts two ballots, one for an individual candidate and one for a party list. Actually, almost all MPs on the lists also run in the individual constituencies and thus have a local connection. If they fail in their individual constituencies, they may still receive seats through the party lists.

The first plenary meeting of the National Assembly following the elections of spring 1990 was held on May 2, 1990. The government of József Antall was elected on May 24, 1990, as a coalition of the center-right Hungarian Democratic Forum (MDF), the radical-right Independent Smallholders' Party (FKgP), and the center-right Christian Democratic People's Party (KDNP), having a 59.6 percent majority. Antall died on December 12, 1993, and the minister of interior, Péter Boross, was elected as his successor on December 21, 1993.

During the first National Assembly term, twenty-nine MPs left (nine died and twenty resigned) and were replaced (five in by-elections in individual constituencies and twenty-four from the party lists). Altogether, fifty-nine parliamentarians changed factions over the course of the four-year term, including twelve MPs from the right wing of the ruling MDF, whose defection in mid-1993 weakened the ruling coalition.

The elections of May 8 and 29, 1994, were won by two former opposition parties, the Hungarian Socialist Party (MSzP; formerly the communist party) and the Federation of Free Democrats (SzDSz). The elections marked the first peaceful change of government for the young Hungarian democracy. There were six parliamentary parties after the 1994 elections, the same as in the former parliament. The two biggest parties, the SzDSz and MSzP, together hold 279 of the 386 seats (72 percent). The parliament held its first plenary meeting on June 28, 1994. The government of Gyula Horn was elected on July 15, 1994, as a coalition of MSzP and SzDSz, having a 72.5 percent majority.

PARLIAMENTARY PROCEEDINGS

The Hungarian National Assembly has two regular sessions annually, from February 1 to June 15 (the spring session) and from September 1 to December 15 (the fall session). Parliament may hold extraordinary sessions as well; from 1990 to 1994 it had both summer and winter sessions because of a legislative backlog. The Assembly usually has plenary meetings on Monday afternoons and Tuesdays, and sometimes also on Wednesdays; committee meetings are held on Wednesdays and Thursdays, and party caucuses on Monday and Wednesday mornings. The sittings of the National Assembly can be attended by the press and by a few members of the public as well.

The president of the republic may adjourn parliamentary sittings once in a four-year session, for thirty days, and he or she has to convoke parliament upon the written request of one-fifth of the MPs.

The legislative procedures of the Hungarian National Assembly are determined in part by the constitution. Legislation may be initiated by the president of the republic, by the government, by any committee, and by any National Assembly representative. Draft bills are submitted to the speaker and go first to the relevant committees; after discussion in committee, the House Committee puts the bills on the parliamentary agenda. The first reading in the plenary session deals with general matters, and MPs may propose amendments. After this general debate, the relevant committees meet again to discuss the amendments and reformulate the draft bills. Then the committees return them to a plenary session of the entire Assembly for a second reading, which is a detailed debate conducted only within the framework of the already accepted amendments. Most acts can be passed by the National Assembly with a simple majority, but some important laws require a two-thirds majority of those present, and amendments of the constitution need a two-thirds majority of all MPs.

Acts passed by the National Assembly must be signed by the speaker of the National Assembly, before being sent to the president of the republic. The president of the republic must promulgate the act in the *Official Gazette* within fifteen days of its receipt, or, upon the request of the speaker of the National Assembly for urgency, within five days. If the president of the republic does not agree with the act or any provision thereof, he or she may return it, together with comments, to the National Assembly within the five- or fifteen-day time period. The National Assembly then debates the act once more, and if passed again, the act is sent by the speaker of the National Assembly to the president, who must sign and promulgate the law within five days. The president of the republic, before signing the act, may send it to the Constitutional Court if he or she deems any of its provisions unconstitutional. If the Constitutional Court declares the act unconstitutional, the president of the republic returns it to the National Assembly; otherwise the act shall be signed and promulgated within five days.

Between 1990 and 1994 the Hungarian National Assembly passed more than eight hundred measures. Among them were very important acts of systemic change (democratization and marketization). But the legislative process is not yet efficient; many important laws had to be amended several times.

The draft law on the next year's budget is submitted to the National Assembly by September 30. The National Assembly decides on amendments concerning the major chapters of the draft budget, establishing broad policy priorities, by November 30; after that date debates concern only the internal division of each chapter. The budget act must be passed by December 31 and cannot be discussed under the urgency procedures. In the 1990–1994 parliamentary session the biggest clashes between government and opposition concerned the budget.

MPs submit interpellations to the members of government and to the chief public prosecutor in writing four days before a plenary session. At the plenary meeting, the MP repeats the interpellation in an oral presentation which is followed by an answer from the person concerned and a vote on the answer. A negative vote by a majority of MPs does not lead, however, to the dismissal of the minister concerned. Additionally, questions can be submitted to ombudsmen, the president of the State Audit Office, and the president of the Hungarian National Bank. In these instances there is no vote on the response provided.

Voting is public, although secret votes may be requested

in special situations; the National Assembly votes on these requests without debate. In most cases an electronic voting system is used, with the aggregate results appearing on a display in the chamber. There is an *Official Record of Parliament* containing all speeches, actions, and documents. It is available to parliamentarians, civil servants, and researchers.

Most plenary meetings of the Hungarian National Assembly are broadcast live by radio and television, and long summaries of the debates appear every day in both media. Parliamentary committee meetings have not yet been broadcast live; they are seen only later in short summaries. Daily and weekly newspapers report on the National Assembly regularly and extensively. The journalists who specialize in parliamentary affairs have formed their own independent association. There has been significant public interest in parliamentary meetings; as a result, the debates are followed closely and critically by both the public and the press.

PARLIAMENTARY ORGANIZATION AND STRUCTURE

The Hungarian parliament has an extensive system of nineteen standing committees, which handle long-term issues, and a varying number of special committees, which are convened ad hoc to handle particular short-term issues.

The committees express opinions, make proposals, and control the organs of parliament. All members of the standing committees must be MPs. The heads of authorities, offices, and institutes, as well as individual citizens, make available the information required by the committees of the National Assembly and testify before them, provide them with information, and make declarations.

The standing committees may, on their own initiative, deal with all significant issues in a given field. They can submit their proposals directly to parliament, the president of the republic, the government (to the competent minister or head of an administration with national competence), the ombudsman, the parliamentary commissioner of national and ethnic minority rights, the State Audit Office, the chief public prosecutor, and (in accordance with a separate law) the Constitutional Court. The concerned state organs have to examine the merits of the committee proposals and inform the committees about the results; however, the committees may not restrict the competence and responsibility of the state organs. The standing committees are entitled and obliged to prepare for debate the drafts and bills in their sphere of operation, to oversee the parliamentary debate on these measures, and to study and discuss matters submitted to them by the National Assembly and the speaker.

According to the standing orders of parliament, the speaker of the National Assembly convokes the sessions and meetings of the Assembly; convokes and chairs the meetings of the chairpersons of the committees and the leaders of the standing groups of representatives; submits to parliament the planned annual work program of parliament at the first session of the year for the purpose of discussion and approval; makes proposals on the agenda of the session; maintains relations with the groups of representatives; directs the formulation and execution of the budget; and determines the duties and the internal structure of the administrative staff of parliament and appoints its leaders.

As appropriate, the speaker may be assisted in performing his or her duties by one of the deputy speakers. At plenary meetings of the National Assembly, the speaker and the three deputy speakers (chosen from the largest parties) chair the meetings in a rotating order, assisted by two recorders. There are altogether eight recorders, most of them MPs from the smaller party factions.

The parties in parliament can form parliamentary factions if they have at least fifteen members. The faction leaders, along with the speaker and three deputy speakers, are members of the House Committee, which manages the operations of the National Assembly; the committee allots office space, secretarial assistance, and special funds for supporting the activities of the MPs to the party factions. As of early 1997 there were six factions, two comprising the government and four in opposition. Party voting discipline and participation in voting was rather low in the 1990–1994 parliamentary session, but it was higher for the governing factions than for the opposition MPs.

THE EXECUTIVE

The government has no veto power over the decisions of the National Assembly, but the president of the republic can return an act once, before signing it, to the National Assembly for further debate. If the Assembly reconfirms the act under its usual procedure, the president must sign it. The president also may send the act to the Constitutional Court, which has on several occasions ruled proposed acts unconstitutional. If the Constitutional Court declares an act or any part of it unconstitutional, the act is annulled and has to be reformulated accordingly. The president of the republic and Constitutional Court play a fundamental role in the checks and balances of legislation and in limiting the power of the government.

The prime minister is elected by the National Assembly upon the nomination of the president of the republic on an affirmative vote by a majority of MPs. This election and the acceptance of the program of government proceed jointly.

The other members of the government are appointed by the president of the republic upon the proposal of the prime minister. A motion of no confidence can be submitted against the prime minister by one-fifth of the MPs. In the so-called positive no-confidence vote procedure, a new prime minister has to be proposed, and only if he or she gets a parliamentary majority is the previous prime minister dismissed. This arrangement makes the prime minister very strong and stable, and an executive with a simple parliamentary majority is very difficult for the National Assembly or its committees to control, although the constitution envisages a series of controls by the Assembly, the president of the republic, and the Constitutional Court.

As a further check on the executive, the 1989 constitution established the position of ombudsman (called the National Assembly Commissioner of Human Rights) and also that of a commissioner for national and ethnic minority rights. These two ombudsman positions (joined by a third, that of a commissioner for personal data protection) are designed to control the activities of the government and parliament (as does the State Audit Office in financial matters), and they report to the National Assembly at least once a year.

Members of the National Assembly may not serve as president of the republic; members of the Constitutional Court; the National Assembly commissioner for civil rights; the president of the State Audit Office, its vice presidents and auditors; judges; procurators; employees of the organs of state administration, with the exception of the members of the government and the political undersecretaries of state; staff members of the armed forces; or police or other law enforcement officers. The National Assembly has declared some political roles compatible with Assembly membership, including positions in local government, such as mayor.

STATUS OF MEMBERS

Hungarian MPs cannot be held liable for their political activities and votes during their term of office. They have immunity from arrest and prosecution. The chief public prosecutor may ask for the cancellation of parliamentary immunity in order to start a legal procedure against an MP if deemed necessary. In this case, however, the National Assembly decides the issue by a two-thirds majority.

The constitution stipulates that National Assembly representatives receive remuneration adequate to ensure their independence and that they receive other defined benefits and reimbursement of expenses incurred. The MPs receive monthly pay of 60,000 forints (about US$600), which is 50 percent of a minister's pay. Travel costs inside the country are reimbursed. MPs who are not from the capital city, Budapest, receive their accommodation costs. Chairs of committees get an extra stipend equal to the monthly pay of parliamentarians, and all other MPs who are members of committees get some additional pay. To pass a law on the amounts of remuneration and reimbursement as well as on Assembly member benefits, the vote of two-thirds of the attending representatives is required.

All MPs may have one personal secretary, with pay equal to half of the MP's salary; in addition, they receive offices, secretarial assistance, and some budgetary support for expert assistance through their factions.

There are provisions in the standing orders that the speaker can warn an MP during his or her speech about inappropriate behavior and expressions. The speaker also can stop an MP from speaking and even exclude him or her from the plenary meeting on that given day. The parliament votes on this motion without debate.

The parliamentary library, located in the parliament building, provides parliamentarians with an information service. The library itself specializes in the social sciences, especially in legal studies and documents, and comprises approximately 700,000 volumes.

There are two supporting institutions of parliament. The first is the Secretariat, headed by the general secretary of parliament who, with a staff mostly of legal experts, assists with all the legal-administrative workings of the parliament. The second, the Office of the Parliament, comprising a director and staff, is responsible for all other financial and technical activities of the Assembly.

In cooperation with the Office of Parliament and the parliamentary library, the Hungarian Center for Democracy Studies has published every year since 1988 the *Political Yearbook of Hungary* (partly in English), providing data and analyses of the year's parliamentary activities.

JUDICIAL AND EMERGENCY POWERS

The Hungarian parliament has no judicial functions, except that the impeachment of the president of the republic on a charge of violating the constitution may be proposed by one-fifth of the MPs. When such a charge is made, the National Assembly debates the issue, and a two-thirds majority vote on a secret ballot is necessary to impeach the president of the republic.

The Constitutional Court is a very important institution of the checks and balances system controlling the activities of the National Assembly and government. It has the responsibility of interpreting the constitution and annulling all unconstitutional provisions. During the 1990–1994 parliamentary session, it reviewed 260 legal decisions (among them 21 acts of the National Assembly and 12 decrees of government) and ultimately found 80 of them (31 percent) unconstitutional, and thus the court annulled them. This high percentage shows that in the first parliamentary cycle (1990–1994) there were major problems concerning the implementation of the new democratic constitution.

Attila Ágh

BIBLIOGRAPHY

Ágh, Attila. "The First Democratic Parliament in Hungary." *Budapest Papers on Democratic Transition,* no. 96. Budapest: Hungarian Center for Democracy Studies, 1994.

———. "Democratic Parliamentarism in Hungary: The First Parliament and the Entry of the Second Parliament." In *The New Parliaments of Central and Eastern Europe,* ed. David Olson and Philip Norton. London: Frank Cass, 1996.

Ágh, Attila, and Gabriella Ilonszki, eds. *Parliaments and Organized Interests in Central Europe: The Second Steps.* Budapest: Hungarian Center for Democracy Studies, 1996.

Ágh, Attila, and Sandor Kurtan, eds. *Democratization and Europeanization in Hungary: The First Parliament, 1990–1994.* Budapest: Hungarian Center for Democracy Studies, 1995.

Hibbing, John, and Samuel Patterson. "A Democratic Legislature in the Making: The Historical Hungarian Elections of 1990." *Comparative Political Studies* 24 (January 1992): 430–454.

Kerekes, Zsuzsa. "Reflections on the First Four Years of the Constitutional Court: A Review in Figures." In *Political Yearbook of Hungary,* ed. Sándor Kurtán, Péter Sándor, and Vass László. Budapest: Hungarian Center for Democracy Studies, 1994.

Mishler, William, and Richard Rose. "Support for Parliaments and Regimes in the Transition toward Democracy in Eastern Europe." *Legislative Studies Quarterly,* 19 (February 1994): 5–32.

Soltész, István. "Controlling the Government by the Parliament." *Budapest Papers on Democratic Transition,* no. 100. Budapest: Hungarian Center for Democracy Studies, 1994.

I

ICELAND

OFFICIAL NAME: Republic of Iceland (Lydhveldidh Island)
CAPITAL: Reykjavík
POPULATION: 271,000 (1996 est.)
DATE OF INDEPENDENCE: June 17, 1944 (from Denmark)
DATE OF CURRENT CONSTITUTION: Effective June 17, 1944
FORM OF GOVERNMENT: Parliamentary democracy
LANGUAGE: Icelandic
MONETARY UNIT: Icelandic Króna
FISCAL YEAR: Calendar year
LEGISLATURE: Althing
NUMBER OF CHAMBERS: One
NUMBER OF MEMBERS: 63
PERCENTAGE OF WOMEN: 25.4
TERM OF LEGISLATURE: Four years
MOST RECENT LEGISLATIVE ELECTION: April 8, 1995
MINIMUM AGE FOR VOTING: 18
MINIMUM AGE FOR MEMBERSHIP: 18
SUFFRAGE: Universal and direct
VOTING: Optional
ADDRESS: Althing, 150 Reykjavík
TELEPHONE: (354 1) 56 30 500
FAX: (354 1) 56 30 520

The Republic of Iceland is an island country in the North Atlantic Ocean *(see map, p. 639)*, which operates under a parliamentary system with a president as head of state and prime minister as head of government. The Icelandic Althing, established in A.D. 930, is arguably the world's oldest parliament. Although Iceland did not achieve full national sovereignty until 1944, and the Althing's legislative functions were periodically suspended by various Danish and Norwegian monarchs, a history of the Althing's annual meetings stretches back almost continually for better than a thousand years.

HISTORICAL BACKGROUND

With no indigenous people to conquer, Iceland's early Viking settlers were able to stake large tracts of land for distribution among their kin and followers. As the large claims of the first landholders were divided into smaller lots, the original settlers and their descendants emerged as both spiritual and secular leaders of their respective clans. The laws that evolved through informal meetings among these local leaders *(godars)* were institutionalized in the form of local assemblies *(things)*, which arbitrated disputes and made the rules.

Rapid population growth and increased commerce produced demands for more general laws, resulting in A.D. 930 in the first meeting of the Althing in what is now Iceland's Thing Valley National Park. Blending the roles of high court and legislature, the Althing developed a tradition of judicial precedents, resembling a common law system, and a legal code recorded in the famous *Jonsbok* of 1281. During the era of what is known as the Free State (930–1262), Iceland was an almost purely legislative and judicial polity.

Whether its Althing was a true parliament is a question of both definition and methodology. Although there is nothing in the written history of the period nor in the early law books to challenge the Althing's claim to fame, the most convincing evidence on the point derives from the rich literary heritage of poems and sagas. Neither folktales nor chronicles, the sagas are, at base, family histories of everyday life that, considered in conjunction with "harder" data, provide fascinating insights in much the same sense that the novels of Anthony Trollope augment our understanding of nineteenth-century British politics. The sagas—read in conjunction with extant legal documents—make a convincing case that the early Althing was a true parliament in three respects: it was neither convened by nor beholden to a single sovereign, it was responsive to its constituents in some representative sense, and it had the power to make laws.

Absent an interested monarch, landed aristocracy, or established church, Iceland's Free State expanded the traditional Norse rights of freemen to create a system of law unusually isolated from monarchic or aristocratic rule. It was indeed a political system void of executive authority. Law enforcement was regarded essentially as a private concern in which the contending parties were expected themselves to implement the terms of settlements reached in assembly. These agreements were, as a rule, negotiated among the *godars* representing their respective clients. Unlike medieval lords, who frequently performed similar "representative" functions on the Continent, the Icelandic *godars* were neither a hereditary caste nor royal appointees. Indeed, there are frequent instances recorded in the sagas and in some early law books of peasants who changed from one *godar* to another. It is something of a reach to equate these changing affiliations with free elections, but it was an unusually fluid representative system for the times.

Remote, thinly populated, and without an indigenous population to subdue, Iceland had no need for a military or for the systems of taxation and conscription that armies tend to generate. Thus the early Althing was not summoned, constituted, or dismissed by a monarch. Its organizational structure, self-determined rather than ordained, was almost literally the product of a social contract. And, until Denmark tightened colonial control in 1380, its role extended considerably beyond that of parleying with the king or queen. Occasional instances of deference to the monarchy or the Catholic Church aside, the Althing was for nearly four hundred years a continuously functioning, essentially autonomous institution.

Each annual session of the Althing began with a recitation of the basic law. Some students of medieval parliaments, drawing analogies to speeches from the throne, have classified the early Althing as a pre-parliament, a body convened to discuss and approve of royal decrees. The Icelandic "lawgiver," however, had no independent powers and was more a neutral speaker of the house than a monarch. The imposition of royal control in the fourteenth century was a blow both to the nation's independence and to this tradition of parliamentary omnipotence. For most Icelanders, consequently, the concepts of home rule and the authority of the Althing have become one and the same. Not surprisingly, the present system embodies a weak, largely ceremonial president, and the cabinet remains as much the creature of parliament as its master.

THE MODERN CONSTITUTION AND PARLIAMENT

Iceland's contemporary parliamentary system dates formally from the establishment of true independence in 1944. The constitution adopted then has its roots both in ancient history and in the 1845 reestablishment of the Althing as the first semi-autonomous provincial assembly in the Kingdom of Denmark. In 1848, when the Danish king renounced absolute power, Iceland was granted a form of limited autonomy. An 1874 constitution proclaimed by the Danish monarch was never formally accepted by the Althing, though it served as the de facto national charter until 1918, when an Act of Union granted substantial home rule. An Icelandic constitution adopted in 1920 codified Danish control over foreign policy and territorial waters but granted effective autonomy in domestic affairs. This agreement quieted the independence movement until the Nazi takeover of Denmark in 1940. On the day following the fall of Copenhagen, the Althing passed two resolutions, one investing the cabinet with the functions previously ceded to the Danish crown and the other declaring Icelandic autonomy in foreign affairs. Years of parliamentary debate and consultation with the nation's wartime allies resulted in the formal establishment of the republic on June 17, 1944.

The 1944 constitution, amended four times by majority vote of the Althing, retains the essential character of the original charter of 1874. It consists of seven chapters, most deriving from the essential proposition of Chapter 1 that "Iceland is a republic with a parliamentary government." Before the establishment of home rule, the Althing was a bicameral body with an upper house in which half the members were appointed by the Danish monarch and half were elected by the members of the lower house. In 1915, when the royal seats were abolished, the bicameral structure was retained with the members of the United Althing dividing themselves into the two houses. This system—variously described as modified unicameral, mixed bicameral, and even tricameral (since bills had to be passed by both houses separately as well as by the United Althing)—was abolished in 1991. The Althing is now unicameral.

The Althing building, completed in 1881, was designed to house the National Museum, the National Library, and the parliament. What may have been an imposing building in the tiny fishing village of Reykjavík is today rather lost in the quiet old-town section of a modern city of 100,000 residents. Its stark, rectangular, dark gray volcanic stone front seems almost to recede into its surroundings, and is overwhelmed by its 1990 neighbor housing the municipal government. Even with the museum and library long moved to new locations, the Althing building is crowded. In the main meeting room, members sit in sixty-two assigned seats arranged in three rows along three walls. They face a dais seating the elected speaker and a podium for those addressing the body. Two clerks flank the dais, and a row of eight ministers face their colleagues from along the front wall. There is no room for staff, but then again, there is not much staff: by a generous estimate, the staff of the Althing, including janitors, librarians, and stenographers, numbers fewer than one hundred. The ground floor houses the conference rooms of three parliamentary parties. The second floor includes the main meeting room, the meeting room of the old upper house—now used as a member lounge—and a fourth party conference room. The third floor houses the galleries and most of the permanent staff. Several buildings in the vicinity of the Althing provide additional office space. Offices of the ministers are scattered throughout the downtown area. Despite its rather stark exterior and crowded quarters, the Althing is a remarkably open institution.

PARTIES AND ELECTIONS

The constitution provides for a system of universal suffrage for citizens over the age of eighteen. Turnout in national elections is typically in the 85 to 90 percent range. Iceland is a small country, and its politics reflect that fact. It is a rare citizen who is not related to, or well acquainted with, at least one member of parliament. For electoral purposes, the country is divided into eight districts that choose, by a modified d'Hondt method of proportional representation, between five and eighteen members each. In addition, bonus seats are allocated to reward high voter registration and to make parliamentary seats more reflective of the parties' shares of the national vote.

Iceland's system of proportional representation has two distinctive characteristics. First, the districts are skewed against Reykjavík and its surrounding communities; the capital area houses nearly 60 percent of the nation's citizens but holds fewer than half the seats. And, second, the system has an unusually low threshold for small parties. In the eastern constituencies, to use the extreme example, a candidate can be elected with as few as 750 votes. Not surprisingly, the Althing has almost invariably included a handful of members elected without the support of major parties.

Parliamentary members are elected for terms of four years. During this term, the Althing can be dissolved at any time. The tradition, however, when governments lose the confidence of the legislature, has been more one of forming new alliances among existing members than of going to a new election. Voters choose members from party lists that rank the candidates. According to the party's proportion of the vote, the candidates with the most votes become full members; those ranked next on the list become alternate members. Alternate members may occupy the seat of a full member who is absent for two weeks or more.

As more local party organizations follow the lead of the Social Democratic Party in establishing their slates through a primary election, control over party lists, long a key source of power, is less a factor than it has been. Open primaries, virtually unknown in parliamentary systems because of their supposed incompatibility with party discipline, are too new in Iceland to provide reliable evidence on the point. There have been few major surprises to date; but these changes in slate-making procedures seem certain to challenge the stability of a traditional party system already under stress from an increasingly volatile electorate.

From independence until the emergence of a Women's List in the 1980s, control of the Althing was essentially contested by four parties, none of which ever held a majority. From 1942 through 1967, the Independence Party—the oldest and most conservative of the major parties—averaged nearly 40 percent of both popular votes and seats in the Althing. The more moderate, rurally based Progressive Party usually finished second, some 10 percent or so ahead of the Social Democrats and the left-leaning People's Alliance. Although governing coalitions were fluid—involving almost every possible permutation except one including both the People's Alliance and the Independence Party—the dividing lines in voting behavior were reasonably clear.

Since the 1970s, this rather stable system of power relations has shown increasing signs of disintegration. Four minor parties—most enduringly the Women's List—have achieved major electoral breakthrough; the Independence Party saw its share of the vote dip as low as 27 percent (in 1987) before rebounding in 1995; and the electoral fortunes of the Social Democrats have gone as high as 22 percent in 1978 from less than 10 percent in 1974. The Progressive Party, under the dynamic leadership of Steingrímur Hermannsson, used television and other "modern" campaign techniques to extend beyond its largely rural electoral base, but it slipped badly in the countryside. The ideological and demographic bases of the traditional parties are no longer easily delineated, and each has seen an electoral faction split off to run its own campaign. The success of the Women's List—which does not allow male members—has compounded this confusion and further destabilized the existing parties by forcing them more seriously to consider gender balance in devising their election lists.

PARTY STRUCTURE AND LEADERSHIP

In the Althing, the parliamentary parties caucus regularly from four to eight hours a week. Norms encouraging party unity are strong, especially among Women's List members and in the People's Alliance, and team players tend to advance more rapidly to leadership positions than do mavericks. Sanctions are seldom applied, however, and party cohesion is below average for a cabinet system. Dissent within a party usually manifests itself in a vote of "present" on the Althing floor, but every party, except the Women's List, has had at least one serious split in recent years.

The four traditional parties elect separate sets of leaders for their parliamentary and national organizations. Generally speaking, the national party leader is the individual most likely to serve as prime minister should his or her party be asked to form a government, and the national leader's deputy is usually assured an important ministry. Even among government parties, the chairs and vice chairs of the parliamentary blocs are not likely to be high-ranking ministers.

Although Iceland's parties have the formal structural characteristics of traditional parties with open membership, Ólafur Ragnar Grímsson's term "network politics" is more descriptive of their operating reality. Grímsson, Iceland's president, who took office in 1996, and first ever professor of political science, argues that formal structure in a society as small as Iceland almost invariably gives way to a network of intimate personal relations. Even the Women's List, which claims not to be a party at all and eschews formal organization, appears in reality to be effectively sustained by a national network of some seventy to eighty friends and neighbors.

ORGANIZATION AND PROCEDURES

Regular sessions of the Althing begin in October, typically convening at 2:00 p.m. four days a week. Following a ceremony in the Lutheran State Church across the street, members convene to examine each other's credentials (each arbitrarily selected one-third of the members examining the next third), swear in new members, and elect a speaker. The second day's session is usually given over to the election of committees, unless it is a year following an election and a government has not yet been formed. At the close of a session, typically in May, the speaker delivers a farewell speech and invites the president of the republic to dismiss the assembled members.

All bills must be introduced as draft laws accompanied by explanatory memorandums. After the first reading they are either assigned to committee or, in unusual cases, voted directly to a second reading, which cannot be in the same calendar day. Amendments in committee and on the floor are accepted by majority vote and must be printed in advance unless they are government bills offered by a minister. On average, about 80 percent of the bills passed are government bills, but quite a few of these are amended, especially in committee, and a surprisingly high percentage of government bills (about 25 percent) do not become law. Although the number (and the proportion) of bills adopted that were introduced by private members is small and getting smaller, an average of some 20 percent—high for a parliamentary system—become law. In round numbers, the contemporary Althing processes between 250 and 300 bills a year; of these, about 100 (including budget bills) become law.

Except in emergencies, all bills in the contemporary Althing must be referred to one of its twelve standing committees. Although these committees do not have the power to kill a bill, they are not required to report a bill out of committee, and discharge proceedings forcing them to report have never been invoked. In marking up the details of legislation, the committees of the Althing play a significant role, surprisingly so, because, by and large, they lack the resources and expertise often associated with strong committee systems. Except for a single clerk assigned to the Finance Committee and another who works for all other committees, they have no staff.

Individual members sometimes bring to their committee work, or develop over time, a great deal of substantive knowledge. As in most committee systems, members of the Althing gravitate toward assignments that reinforce constituency interests, and the steering committees of all parties try their best to honor such requests. Thus, by way of example, not a single member of the Agriculture Committee is from Reykjavík, and membership in Foreign Affairs is heavily skewed toward the area surrounding the American naval base in Keflavík. Parties, however, hinder the development of subgovernment networks by rotating committee assignments; in two of the larger parties, rotation is not just encouraged but required. In most cases, moreover, it would tend to reflect badly on a member to bypass formal channels and establish independent sources of intelligence at the lower levels of a ministry. It is highly unusual for a committee to take any kind of formal action without consulting the concerned cabinet member.

The more important direction of information exchange is between the committees and the party caucuses. Each party attempts to place at least one member on each committee, and to use that individual—in the absence of a minister—as its resource person on the topic. In many cases this objective is achieved, though in a small country like Iceland informal networks of intelligence and information play a vital role. Committees may serve as the formal eyes and ears of the parliamentary party groups, and they may work largely through formal channels in dealing with their respective ministries, but informal communications are clearly the norm. Formal committee hearings are rare, and although ministers are often invited to meet with committee members, public questioning of the cabinet usually takes place during the weekly "question period" of the full Althing.

The cabinet presents its budget proposal, formally drafted by the minister of finance as the finance bill, in early October. It is given three readings in the Althing. Between readings it is referred to the Budget Committee, where it frequently undergoes considerable change before final passage in December. The fiscal year coincides with the calendar year. The minister of finance is generally considered to carry the cabinet's most prestigious portfolio, next to that of the prime minister, because of the finance minister's role in the budgetary process. Among backbenchers, membership on the Budget Committee is similarly valued, with Foreign Affairs following closely behind. The Althing's other standing committees are Agriculture; Commerce and Trade; Education; Environment; Fisheries; Health and Insurance; Industry; Social Affairs; and Transportation and Communications. A General Committee deals mainly with the Ministry of Justice and local governments.

DEBATES AND VOTING

No matter how thoroughly bills are examined in committee and in the party caucuses, floor debates in the Althing are lively and well attended, particularly when they are broadcast on state television and radio. Each party is formally allocated debate time, which is regulated by the speaker. Floor proceedings, both on legislative issues and during formal question periods, can be unusually lively in part because cabinet meetings are relatively rare. Legally, the cabinet does not act on a collegial basis, and the minister with jurisdiction has the power to make the relevant decision. The degree to which a minister consults with or informs other ministers of an impending decision is a matter of politics, not custom or law. With coalition government the norm, it is not uncommon for the floor of the Althing to become the laundry room for linens that other parliaments would wash privately in cabinet.

Half the membership of the Althing constitutes a quorum, and voting may be by unanimous consent, a show of hands, or roll call (conducted, since 1992, electronically). All amendments and budget bills require simple majorities, as do most votes on procedure and resolutions. A vote of "present" counts toward a quorum, but not a majority, and is frequently used by members who oppose a bill but do not wish to vote against their party's positions. On occasion an entire party bloc, unable to achieve consensus, will vote "present," allowing a bill to pass without openly supporting it. The Women's List in particular has frequently used this tactic. All recorded votes and debates in the Althing are recorded in the Althing journal *(tithindi)*, available in the United States in the libraries of Harvard and Cornell Universities and the Library of Congress.

MEMBERS OF PARLIAMENT

The 1994 salary of a member of parliament was the equivalent of approximately $3,000 in U.S. dollars, with increments for travel and housing. Ministers and other officials receive supplements. The office carries few perquisites: simple offices, phones, and basic office supplies are provided, but secretarial help, postage, and travel are funded by the party organizations. Despite low salaries, many members consider their parliamentary jobs a full-time occupation, though there are few legal constraints on outside employment and the concept of conflicts of interests is not well developed. In a rare, if not unique, instance of discipline, the Independence Party in 1988 asked its minister of commerce to relinquish his position in the cabinet (though not his seat in parliament) for what—in most Western democracies—would have been deemed a major scandal. Within a matter of days, the disgraced minister formed his own party, put together a slate of candidates that qualified in three districts, and won nearly 10 percent of the seats in the next election. While the Icelandic tolerance for its politicians' economic peccadilloes is unusually high, there is a remarkably clear focus, in the nation's press and politics, on substantive issues. Real corruption—the selling of votes, office, or influence—is virtually unknown.

The 110th Althing, which took office in October 1991, included a record number of new parliamentarians (twenty-one of sixty-three) and of women (fourteen). Turnover was almost as high in 1995, and the number of women increased to sixteen. The percentage of female members has thus increased to more than twenty-five from the 5 percent in office when Vigdís Finnbogadóttir became Iceland's first woman president in 1980. This is still a relatively low proportion for Scandinavia, however, and the "typical" member of the Althing remains a fifty-year-old, native-born, male university graduate. His profession was likely to be a supervisory position in government, industry, or academia, not law. As is generally true in the Nordic parliaments, a sharp distinction between law and politics is characteristic of Iceland.

THE EXECUTIVE AND JUDICIAL BRANCHES

Iceland's elected president, though strong in the constitution, has a largely ceremonial role. Few of the potential powers granted by the constitution (for example, the right to refer a statute to a referendum) have ever been used. Should a president so much as hint at the possibility of dusting off some unused capacity, as Vigdís Finnbogadóttir once did with the veto power, both press and parliament would be filled with dire warnings of imminent crisis. The power of ritual aside, the president is likely to play an active role in Icelandic politics only when there is difficulty in forming a government. Any presidential decision about who to ask what and when can markedly slant the tilt of the governing coalition.

The Supreme Court of Iceland has eight judges, technically appointed for life by the president, though in reality by the minister of justice. Ruling on questions of both law and fact, the Supreme Court typically decides nearly two hundred cases a year, mostly on appeal from a complex system of district and special jurisdiction courts. The principal source of Icelandic law is the written statutes of the Althing; but custom, precedent, the constitution, and general legal principles are recognized sources of law. The courts have the power to declare acts of parliament unconstitutional, an outcome that has happened on a few occasions.

CONCLUSION

Demographically, Iceland is among the world's most homogeneous countries; yet it sustains five ideologically diverse political parties. Although Iceland is geographically isolated and fiercely independent, its autonomy—whether economic or military—has never been secure. Few if any countries, however, have longer traditions of domestic tranquillity. The face-to-face nature of Icelandic democracy encourages cohesion and dampens conflict; and a deeply ingrained habit of and respect for the norms of parliamentary democracy has survived colonialism, military occupation, and economic crisis. Both as a historic model of near-mythic dimensions and as a functioning institution of governance, the Althing is a paradigmatic parliament.

Edward Schneier

BIBLIOGRAPHY

Arter, David. *The Nordic Parliaments: A Comparative Analysis.* London: C. Hurst, 1984.

Elder, Neal A., Alastair H. Thomas, and David Arter. *The Consensual Democracies? The Government and Politics of the Scandinavian States.* Rev. ed. New York: Blackwell, 1988.

Grímsson, Ólafur Ragnar. *Network Parties.* Reykjavík: University of Iceland, 1979.

Hardarson, Ólafur Th., and Gunnar H. Kristinsson. "The Icelandic Parliamentary Election of 1987." *Electoral Studies* 6 (1987): 219–234.

Pencak, William. *The Conflict of Law and Justice in the Icelandic Sagas.* Atlanta, Ga.: Rodopi Value Inquiry Book Series, 1995.

Schneier, Edward. "Icelandic Women on the Brink of Power." *Scandinavian Studies* 64 (1992): 417–438.

INDIA

OFFICIAL NAME: Republic of India (Bharat)
CAPITAL: New Delhi
POPULATION: 952,108,000 (1996 est.)
DATE OF INDEPENDENCE: August 15, 1947 (from the United Kingdom)
DATE OF CURRENT CONSTITUTION: Effective January 26, 1950
FORM OF GOVERNMENT: Parliamentary democracy
LANGUAGES: Hindi (official), Bengali (official), Telugu (official), Marathi (official), Tamil (official), Urdu (official), Gujarati (official), Malayalam (official), Kannada (official), Oriya (official), Punjabi (official), Assamese (official), Kashmiri (official), Sindhi (official), Sanskrit (official), Konkani (official), Manipuri (official), Nepali (official), Hindustani, English
MONETARY UNIT: Indian rupee
FISCAL YEAR: April 1–March 31
LEGISLATURE: Union Parliament
NUMBER OF CHAMBERS: Two. House of the People (Lok Sabha); Council of States (Rajya Sabha)
NUMBER OF MEMBERS: House of the People, 545 (543 directly elected; 2 nominated by the president); Council of States, 245 (233 indirectly elected; 12 nominated by the president)
TERM OF LEGISLATURE: House of the People, five years; Council of States is a permanent body, with one-third of membership retiring every second year
MOST RECENT LEGISLATIVE ELECTION: House of the People, April–May 1996
MINIMUM AGE FOR VOTING: 18
MINIMUM AGE FOR MEMBERSHIP: House of the People, 25; Council of State, 30
SUFFRAGE: Universal
VOTING: Optional
ADDRESS: House of the People, Parliament House, New Delhi 110001; Council of States, Parliament House, New Delhi 110001
TELEPHONE: House of the People, (91 11) 301 74 65; Council of States, (91 11) 303 46 95
FAX: Council of States, (91 11) 379 29 40; House of the People, (91 11) 301 55 18

Democratic institutions and some sort of representative bodies existed in India as early as the Vedic period, circa 3000–1000 B.C. The *Rigveda* and the *Atharvaveda*—two of the four holy books of Hindus—mentioned the "Sabhas" and the "Samitis," elected bodies closely associated with the affairs of the state. The king's administrative actions were not legitimized without their approval.

The Vedic monarchy was not hereditary. The king was chosen by the people and ruled over them with their con-

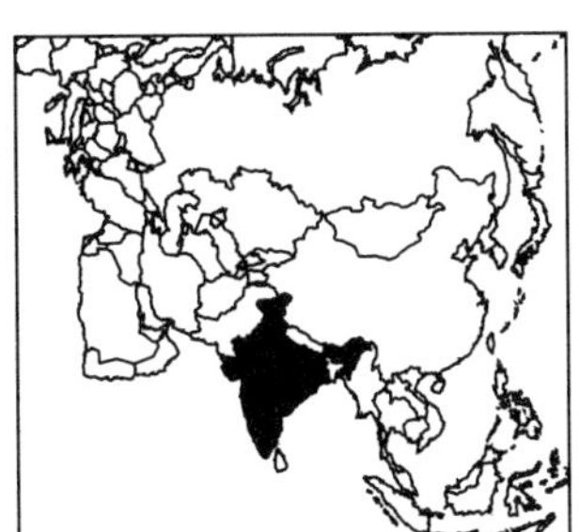

sent. The Sabhas and the Samitis ceased to function around 600 B.C. But a number of popularly elected republics, conversant with many rules similar to those of modern parliamentary procedure, were functioning around this time.

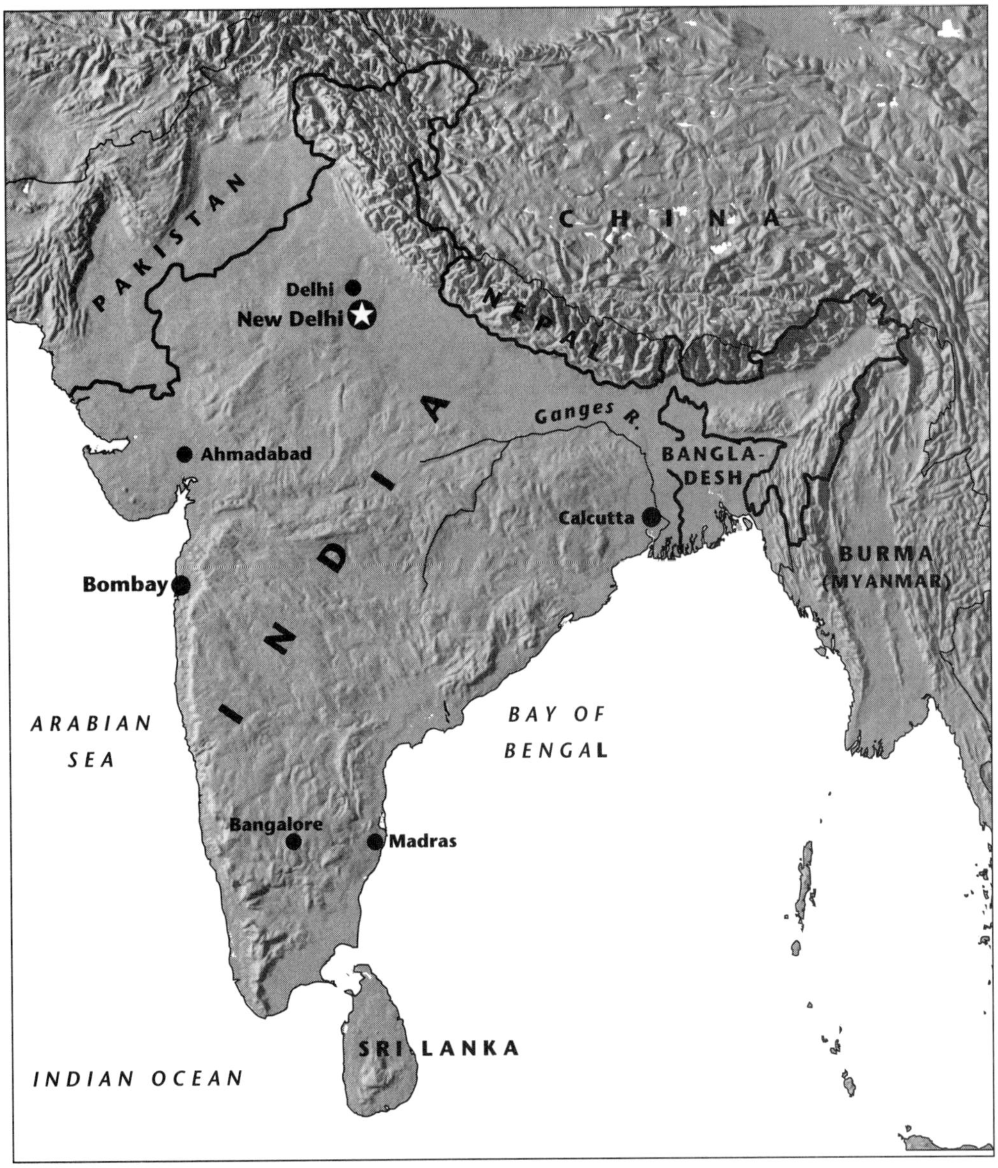

One of the remarkable political institutions that evolved in India at the village level was the *panchayat* system. Literally, *panchayat* meant governance by a council of five. The *panchayats* were elected bodies of the village folk and performed a number of administrative and judicial functions. Unlike the Sabhas, the Samitis, and the republics, the *panchayats* had an unbroken continuity throughout India's history.

Establishment of parliamentary government and legislative institutions in their modern connotation began during the British rule over India. They grew through the struggle for freedom from foreign rule and the successive constitutional reforms conceded by the British.

Until 1853 there was no legislative body distinct from the executive. The Charter Act of 1853 for the first time provided for some sort of a separate legislature in the form of a twelve-member Legislative Council, which included the governor general, four members of the Executive Council, the chief justice and another judge of the Supreme Court, and others.

The British Crown assumed the power of direct governance over India from the East India Company under the Government of India Act of 1858. The powers of the Crown came to be exercised by the secretary of state for India, assisted by a council composed exclusively of people from England. The secretary of state, who was responsible to the British Parliament, governed India through the governor general, who in turn was assisted by an Executive Council consisting of officials of the government.

Under the Indian Councils Act of 1861, the governor general's Executive Council—which was long composed exclusively of individuals who were in the civil or military service of the Crown in India—could include certain members not in the service of the Crown while transacting its business as a Legislative Council. The act, however, did not promise a representative legislative body for India. The Legislative Council was expressly forbidden to transact any business other than the consideration and enactment of legislative measures introduced. It had no authority to call for information or examine the conduct of the executive. The number of nonofficial members in the Legislative Council of the governor general as well as in Provincial Councils was further increased under the Indian Councils Act of 1892.

The Morley-Minto reform proposals of 1908, which were given effect through the Indian Councils Act of 1909, raised the number of members in the Indian Legislative Council from sixteen to sixty (excluding the executive councilors, who were ex-officio members). The size of the legislative councils in the provinces was more than doubled, and an element of election was also introduced in comprising the legislative councils. Members of the Indian Legislative Council from 1909 on had the power to move resolutions on the budget and on any matter of public interest. But the government was not bound to accept them.

A bicameral legislature was established for the first time under the Government of India Act of 1919, which gave effect to the Montague-Chelmsford reforms. It consisted of a Council of State (upper house) and a Legislative Assembly (lower house), each with an elected majority. Elections to both houses, however, were conducted on a much-restricted franchise based on property, tax, or education qualifications. The first Legislative Assembly constituted under the 1919 act came into being in 1921. The normal term of the Council under the act was five years, whereas that of the Assembly was three years. The governor general could dissolve either house before the expiration of its full term.

The governor general-in-council, however, continued to remain responsible to the secretary of state for India and through the secretary to the British Parliament. The powers of the central legislature in the field of legislation and financial control were limited and subject to the overriding powers of the governor general.

The act of 1919 also provided for the appointment of a royal commission at the expiry of ten years to report on the working of the act and to recommend further development of representative institutions for British India. As a result, the Simon Commission was appointed in 1927. The report of the commission was considered by a roundtable conference consisting of the delegates of the British government and of British India as well as of the rulers of the Indian states. The result was the Government of India Act of 1935.

The act of 1935 prescribed a federation taking the provinces and the Indian states as units. The governor general was to have a Council of Ministers to aid and advise in the exercise of his or her functions, except where the governor general was required to exercise personal discretion. The Federal Legislature was to consist of the British Crown, as represented by the governor general, and two chambers, to be known as the Council of State (upper chamber) and the Federal Assembly (lower chamber). The Council of State was made a permanent body not subject to dissolution, but one-third of its members were to retire every third year. The Federal Assembly, unless sooner dissolved by the governor general at his or her discretion, was to continue for five years.

Each house of the central legislature was given the power to regulate, subject to the provisions of the act, its own procedures and business. The governor general was empowered to summon and prorogue the legislature. No bill would become law unless agreed to by both houses and assented to by the governor general or, in the case of a bill reserved for the Crown, by the monarch. Even an act assented to by the governor general could be disallowed by the Crown.

The federal part of the 1935 act, however, never went into operation, as the princely states could not be persuaded to accede to the federation. In effect, the constitution of the central government of India remained almost the same as it had been under the act of 1919, with such modifications as were necessitated by the introduction of autonomy in the provinces. No Council of Ministers, responsible to the legislature, was appointed at the center, and the powers and functions of the central legislature, as provided in the 1919 act, remained in a way unchanged until the Indian Independence Act of 1947.

Under the Indian Independence Act of 1947, the Government of India Act of 1935 was modified to make it the provisional constitution of the dominion, until other provisions were made by the Constituent Assembly. With this act, the governor general became the constitutional head of the country. A Council of Ministers was constituted to aid and advise the governor general and was made collectively responsible to the popularly elected house of the legislature. The discretion of the governor general to dissolve the lower house was done away with. The act declared the Constituent Assembly of India to be a fully sovereign body, which assumed full powers of governance for the country. A distinction was also made between the constitution-making function of the Constituent Assembly and its functions as a legislature.

The republican constitution of independent India came into force on January 26, 1950, and a full-fledged parliamentary system of government with a modern institutional framework was established. The Constituent Assembly became the provisional parliament of India and functioned until after the first general elections, based on adult franchise, were held during 1951–1952. Thus the first Union Parliament was constituted in 1952.

THE CONSTITUTION

Under the constitution, Parliament consists of the president of India, the Council of States (Rajya Sabha), and the House of the People (Lok Sabha).

Though a constituent part of Parliament, the president does not sit or take part in the discussions in either house of Parliament. Yet, the president performs a number of constitutional functions in respect of Parliament, such as summoning and proroguing the two houses; addressing members of the houses; nominating twelve members to the Council of States and two members to the House of the People; assenting to bills; and dissolving the House of the People.

The Council of States consists of not more than 250 members. Of these, 12 are nominated by the president for their special knowledge or practical experience in such matters as literature, science, art, and social service. The remaining seats are allocated to the twenty-five states and seven union territories, roughly in proportion to their population; however, each state is represented by at least one member. The members from each state are elected by the elected members of the state legislative assembly, and those from a union territory are elected by an electoral college for that territory. The elections, held every second year, are by proportional representation and the single transferable vote. (Under the single transferable vote system, each voter casts only one ballot irrespective of the number of seats to be filled, but that single vote is transferred from the candidate indicated as a first preference, to the candidate indicated as the second preference, and so on if a candidate obtains more preference votes than are required for election, or if a candidate obtains so few votes that election is impossible.)

The Council of States was constituted for the first time April 3, 1952. It is a permanent body not subject to dissolution, but one-third of its members retire every second year by rotation and are replaced by newly elected members. The term of an individual member of the Council of States is six years. The total number of seats in the Council of States at present is 245.

The maximum strength of the House of the People envisaged by the constitution is 552: 530 members to represent the states, up to 20 members to represent the union territories, and not more than two members of the Anglo-Indian community to be nominated by the president if in the president's opinion that community is not adequately represented in the House. The total elective membership is distributed among the states such that the ratio of seats to population is, as far as practicable, the same for all states.

Election to the House of the People is direct and through single-member constituencies. The election is conducted on the basis of universal adult suffrage, and any citizen of India who is not less than eighteen years of age and is not otherwise disqualified on grounds of unsoundness of mind, crime, or corrupt or illegal practice(s) is entitled to vote at any election.

The House of the People is subject to dissolution, and unless sooner dissolved it continues for five years from the date appointed for its first meeting. However, while a proclamation of emergency is in effect, its term may be extended by Parliament by law for a period not exceeding one year at a time and not extending in any case beyond six months after the proclamation has ceased to operate. Dissolution of the House of the People may be effected before the expiry of its term by an order made by the president on the advice of the Council of Ministers, headed by the prime minister. At the end of its term, the House of the People stands automatically dissolved even if no formal order of dissolution is issued by the president.

The First House of the People was constituted April 17, 1952. Elections to the Eleventh House of the People were held in 1996. The effective strength of the Eleventh House of the People is 545, including two nominated members from the Anglo-Indian community. Under the Representation of the People Act of 1950 as amended, the number of members to be elected from the states is 530, and from the union territories, 13.

The highest proportion of women in the popularly elected House has been 8.1 percent, in the Eighth House of the People. The highest proportion of women in the indirectly elected Council of States has been 11.8 percent, in 1980. The First House of the People was the youngest, with the average age of its members being 46.5 years, whereas the Sixth House of the People had 52.1 years as the average age for its members, making the Sixth the oldest House thus far. Agriculturists have constituted a majority of the members in the House of the People since the Third

House, aptly reflecting the agrarian structure of the Indian economy and society.

PARTIES AND ELECTIONS

The preparation of electoral rolls for and conduct of all elections to Parliament, the state legislatures, and the offices of the president and vice president of India are vested in an independent authority called the Election Commission of India. From independence in 1947 to 1997, eleven free and fair elections were held at the national level and some three hundred at the state level.

The Election Commission lists 485 parties in its records, only a few of which are national. The major players are the Indian National Congress, the Bhartiya Janata Party, and the United Front, a center-left alliance of thirteen parties. The Indian National Congress has been defeated only three times: in 1977, 1989, and 1996. In all three instances, a loose coalition of other parties came together to form a government. The two earlier coalition governments lasted only for brief periods: the Janata governed 1977–1979, and the National Front, 1989–1990. In 1996 the United Front formed the government.

The president is elected by an electoral college comprising the elected members of both houses of Parliament and elected members of the legislative assemblies of the states. In the case of the vice president, the electoral college comprises members of both houses of Parliament.

To be eligible for election as president a person must be an Indian citizen, not less than thirty-five years of age, and qualified for election as a member of the House of the People. To be elected vice president, a person must be a citizen of India over thirty-five years of age and qualified for election as a member of the Council of States. A candidate for election to either office should not hold a paid office under the government of India or a state government or under any local or other authority subject to the control of any of the said governments.

The president and vice president hold office for five years from the date on which they enter office. Under the constitution, notwithstanding the expiry of their term, both continue to hold office until their successors enter office. The president may resign before the expiry of his or her term by writing to the vice president. The vice president can also resign by writing to the president. The president may also be removed from office before the expiry of the term by impeachment, on grounds of violation of the constitution, subject to a resolution passed by not less than two-thirds of the total membership in each house. The vice president can be removed from office by a resolution of the Council of States passed by a majority of all the members of that house and agreed to by the House of the People.

To be a member of Parliament a person must be a citizen of India; not less than thirty years of age for a seat in the Council of States and not less than twenty-five years for a seat in the House of the People; and an elector for any parliamentary constituency in India, but to be eligible for a seat in the Council of States, a candidate must be registered as an elector in the state or union territory from which he or she is to be chosen. Additional qualifications may be prescribed by Parliament by law.

CALENDAR

The constitution stipulates that the president shall, from time to time, summon each house of Parliament to meet at such time and place as he or she thinks fit. It also stipulates that six months shall not intervene between its last sitting in one session and the date appointed for its sitting in the next session.

Normally, the House of the People has three sessions in a year: the budget session, from February to May; the monsoon session, from July to August; and the winter session, from November to December. In the Council of States, however, the budget session is split into two sessions, and thus the Council of States has four sessions in a year.

From the First to the Tenth House of the People there was an almost steady decline in the total number of sittings. As a result, the total time spent on various kinds of parliamentary business in the House of the People also declined.

The time spent on legislation has also come down over the years. The decrease was very sharp from the First to the Second House of the People, from 48.8 percent of the total time to 28.2 percent. The decline continued during subsequent terms. For many years now, on average, the House has devoted about one-fourth of its time to legislation and three-fourths to other kinds of business.

The practice of referring government bills to select or joint committees for in-depth examination, which was quite pronounced during the First, Second, and Fourth Houses of the People, has steadily declined. From 1979 to 1993 it has been negligible. However, under the new procedure, since 1993 all important government bills after introduction have been referred to the concerned departmentally related standing committee for examination and making report thereon.

The practice of circulating government bills for eliciting opinion was in vogue only during the very early years (1952–1961), and then only in very rare cases. Subsequently, this practice has been disregarded.

LAW MAKING

The constitution provides for a threefold distribution of legislative power between the union and the states: the union list enumerates topics in respect to which Parliament has exclusive power to make laws; the state list enumerates topics in respect to which the legislature of a state has exclusive power to make laws; and the concurrent list enumerates topics in respect to which both Parliament and the legislature of a state have power to make laws. The residuary power of legislation is vested in Parliament.

All legislative proposals are initiated in Parliament in the form of bills. Bills can broadly be categorized as ordinary bills, money bills, and constitution amendment bills.

Ordinary bills

All bills that are not constitution amendment bills and money bills are ordinary bills, that is, draft proposals for ordinary legislation. Ordinary legislation can be initiated either by the government or by any private member. A government bill can be introduced in either house of Parliament by the minister concerned with a minimum of seven days' notice. Each bill undergoes three readings in each house before being presented to the president for assent.

The first reading involves the "motion for leave" to introduce the bill, which is generally requested after the Question Hour on the appointed day. Generally, the leave is granted by a voice vote and is rarely opposed. By convention there is no discussion at this stage. But, if the introduction of a bill is opposed on the ground that the proposed legislation is outside the legislative competence of Parliament, the chair may permit a full discussion in which the attorney general may also participate. The question is put to a vote of the house thereafter. There is no restriction on the number of government bills that may be introduced on a particular day; a minister may introduce as many bills as he or she wants.

After a bill has been introduced, it is published in the *Official Gazette of India*. If a bill has been published in the *Official Gazette* before its introduction, no motion for leave to introduce the bill is necessary. After introduction, the presiding officer of the concerned house can refer the bill to a departmentally related standing committee for examination. The committee considers the general principles and clauses of the bill. The committee can take expert opinion or take the opinions of public persons who are interested in the measure. After due consideration, the committee submits its report to the house. The report of the committee is treated as considered advice given by the committee.

The second reading is the most elaborate stage in the processing of a bill. First, discussion of a very general nature on the principle underlying the bill is taken up. At this stage, the house may refer the bill to a select committee of the house or to a joint committee of the two houses; may circulate the bill to elicit opinion thereon; or may straightaway take the bill up for consideration. If a bill is referred to a select committee, the house in turn considers the bill as reported by the committee. If a motion to circulate the bill is adopted, the secretariat of the house sends letters to all state and union territory governments asking them to publish the bill in their gazettes for inviting the opinion of local bodies, associations, individuals, or institutions concerned with the bill. After the opinions have been received, they are submitted to the house, followed by a motion to refer the bill to a select or joint committee. The bill again passes through the committee stage, and the bill, as reported, is presented to the house. A motion is then moved that the bill as reported by the select or joint committee be taken into consideration. At this stage, the bill is taken up for consideration clause-by-clause, and amendments are moved. Amendments, if accepted, become part of the bill.

In the third reading, when all the clauses and schedules, if any, of the bill have been considered and voted upon by the house, the minister can move that the bill be passed. On a motion, the chair puts the question and invites those in favor to say "aye" and those against to say "no." Opinion with regard to whether the "ayes" or the "noes" have it is then conveyed from the chair. If the opinion of the chair is challenged, the chair directs that the votes be recorded through the automatic vote recorder (AVR) or by using the "aye," "no," and "abstention" slips in the house. Slips are used in the house only when the AVR machine malfunctions or when seats and division numbers are not allotted to the newly elected members in the house.

After the bill has been passed in one house, it is transmitted to the other house for its concurrence. Here, again, the bill goes through all three readings. The house that receives the bill can reject it altogether, giving rise to a deadlock between the two houses; or pass the bill as it is or with amendments. If it passes the bill as transmitted by the originating house, the bill goes to the president for assent. If, on the contrary, the bill is passed with amendments, the bill is returned to the first house. If the originating house agrees to the amendments proposed by the second house, the bill is deemed to have been passed, as amended, by both houses. If, however, the originating house does not agree to the amendments proposed by the second house, the bill is sent again to the latter to get its concurrence. If this house continues to insist on its amendments, the result is a deadlock.

A house, upon receiving a bill from the originating house, also may take no action on the bill. In such a case, if more than six months elapse from the date it received the bill, a deadlock is deemed to have taken place.

A deadlock between the two houses on a bill is resolved by both houses sitting together. At the joint sitting, no amendment can be proposed to the bill apart from those necessitated by the delay in passage of the bill and those necessary to bridge the differences between the two houses. The decisions at such sittings are taken by majority vote of the total number of members of both houses present and voting. So far, there have been only two occasions when a joint sitting of the two houses had to be convened, namely, in regard to the Dowry Prohibition Bill of 1959 and the Banking Service Commission (Repeal) Bill of 1978.

After a bill has been passed by both houses, either separately or at a joint sitting, it is presented to the president. The president may assent to the bill, withhold assent, or return the bill (if it is not a money bill) with a message for reconsideration. The president may also recommend amendments. If the president assents, the bill becomes an act from the date of assent. If the president returns the bill and the houses pass the bill a second time, with or without amendments, the president must assent to the bill.

Money bills

The constitution defines a money bill as a bill containing provisions dealing with all or any of the matters relating to the imposition, abolition, remission, alteration, or regulation of any tax; regulation of the borrowing of money or the giving of any guarantee by the government of India, or amendment of the law with respect to any financial obligations undertaken or to be undertaken by the government of India; custody of the Consolidated Fund or the Contingency Fund of India and the payment of moneys into or the withdrawal of moneys from any such fund; the appropriation of moneys out of the Consolidated Fund of India; charging any expenditure on the Consolidated Fund of India or increasing the amount of any such expenditure; the receipt of money on account of the Consolidated Fund of India or the public account of India, the custody or issue of such money, or the audit of the accounts of the union or of a state; or any matter incidental to any of the matters specified above.

But a bill shall not be deemed to be a money bill by reason only that it provides for the imposition of fines or other pecuniary penalties or provides for the payment of fees for licenses or fees for services rendered, or by reason that it provides for the imposition, abolition, remission, alteration, or regulation of any tax by any local authority or body for local purposes. With regard to any question whether a bill is a money bill or not, the decision of the speaker of the House of the People is final.

A money bill can be introduced in the House of the People only on the recommendation of the president. After its passage in the House of the People, it is transmitted to the Council of States for its recommendation, with a certificate by the speaker that it is a money bill. The Council of States cannot reject a money bill nor can it amend a money bill. It must, within a period of fourteen days from the receipt of the bill, return the bill to the House of the People with its recommendations, if any. The House of the People may accept or reject all or any of the recommendations of the Council of States. On acceptance of the recommendations of the Council of States, the money bill shall be deemed to have been passed by both houses. If the House of the People does not accept any of the recommendations of the Council of States, the bill shall be deemed to have been passed by both houses in the form in which it was passed by the House of the People. Further, if a money bill transmitted to the Council of States for its recommendations is not returned to the House of the People within fourteen days, it shall be deemed to have been passed by both houses at the expiry of that period. There is no provision of a joint sitting in the case of a money bill.

The president may either give or withhold assent to a money bill. Under the constitution, a money bill cannot be returned to Parliament by the president for reconsideration.

Financial bills

Financial bills differ from money bills. While providing for any of the matters specified in the constitution for a money bill, financial bills provide for other matters also. Financial bills are of two categories. Financial bills of category "A" provide for any of the matters specified in Article 110 of the constitution but do not contain solely those matters. For example, a bill that contains a taxation clause but does not deal solely with taxation would be in category "A." Financial bills of category "B" contain, along with other matters, provisions involving expenditure from the Consolidated Fund of India.

A financial bill of category "A" has two features in common with a money bill: it cannot be introduced in the Council of States and it cannot be introduced except on the recommendation of the president. But the Council of States has the power to reject or amend a financial bill, as it does an ordinary bill subject to the restriction that an amendment other than for reduction or abolition of a tax cannot be moved in either house without the recommendation of the president. In case of disagreement between the two houses, the provision of joint sitting is also available.

A financial bill of category "B" is treated as an ordinary bill and as such can be introduced in either house. The Council of States has full power to reject or amend it. This type of bill does not require the recommendation of the president for its introduction. However, the recommendation of the president is essential for its consideration by either house, and unless such recommendation has been received neither house can pass the bill. In all other respects, such a bill is governed by the same procedure as for an ordinary bill, including the provision of a joint sitting in case of disagreement between the two houses.

Constitution amendment bills

Parliament has the power to amend the constitution, and the procedure for doing so has been laid down in the constitution. A bill seeking amendment of the constitution can be initiated in either house of Parliament. A bill to amend the constitution can be brought by a private member after it has been examined and recommended for introduction in the House of the People by the Committee on Private Members' Bills and Resolutions. In the Council of States no such committee exists. However, constitution amendment bills are examined by the concerned bills section in the Council of States, as is done for ordinary bills.

A bill to amend the constitution must be passed in each house of Parliament by a majority of the total membership of that house and also by a majority of not less than two-thirds of the members of that house present and voting. Bills to amend the provisions of the constitution relating to election of the president; the extent of executive power of the union and the states; the Supreme Court and the high courts; the distribution of legislative powers between the union and the states; representation of states in Parliament; or the procedure for amending the constitution itself must also be ratified by the legislatures of not less than one-half of the states.

The bill is finally presented to the president, who must give his assent before the constitution stands amended in accordance with the terms of the bill.

There is no provision for a joint sitting in the case of constitutional amendment bills.

Private member bills

A bill moved by any member other than a minister in Parliament is known as a private member bill. Two and a half hours are allotted on alternate Fridays during a session for transaction of business relating to private member bills, the other Friday being devoted to private member resolutions.

A private member bill proceeds on the same lines as a government bill except that for the former, a slight difference exists with regard to the period of notice for introduction, restriction on the number of bills that can be introduced in a session by a member, bills seeking amendment to the constitution, and relative precedence for discussion.

Many bills are introduced by private members in Parliament, but very few—only fourteen since 1952—have been enacted. It is difficult to get such bills enacted for want of support in the houses of Parliament. But such bills serve a very good purpose inasmuch as they bring to the attention of the government and the public the need to amend an existing law or to enact a new law in light of changing conditions.

Constitutionality of laws

Under the constitution, the legislature is the supreme lawmaking body. However, the power of legislation so conferred on the legislature is within a periphery demarcated by the constitution itself. Thus there is latitude for review of legislation. The power of review has been vested in an independent and integrated judiciary. The judiciary has the final say in interpreting the constitution and can, therefore, declare a particular piece of legislation unconstitutional. But the scope of judicial review is demarcated. The judiciary can determine only if a particular law is within the power conferred by the constitution on Parliament or within the legislative competence of Parliament. It cannot enter into an examination of what the law should be. Further, the Parliament in India has constituent power and can amend any provision of the constitution. But this power is subject to limitations imposed by the Supreme Court of India in its decisions, that the basic structure or framework of the constitution must not be altered. However, the judiciary has yet to define what constitutes the "basic structure."

ORGANIZATION AND STRUCTURE

The quorum to constitute a sitting of either house is one-tenth of the total number of members. If at any time during a sitting of a house there is no quorum, it is the duty of the presiding officer either to adjourn the house or suspend the sitting until there is a quorum.

Committees

There are two types of parliamentary committees: standing and ad hoc. Standing committees are elected or are nominated by the speaker of the House of the People or by the chair of the Council of States every year or from time to time, as the case may be, and are permanent in nature. Ad-hoc committees are constituted by a house or by the speaker or chair to consider and report on specific matters, and they become defunct as soon as they have completed their work.

The standing committees (and certain joint committees) may be further categorized in terms of their functions as follows: financial committees (for example, Committee on Estimates, Committee on Public Accounts, and Committee on Public Undertakings); house committees, that is, committees relating to the day-to-day business of the house (for example, Committee on Absence of Members from the Sittings of the House, in the House of the People only; Business Advisory Committee; Committee on Private Member Bills and Resolutions, in the House of the People only; and Rules Committee); enquiry committees (such as Committee on Petitions and Committee of Privileges); scrutiny committees (Committee on Government Assurances, Committee on Subordinate Legislation, Committee on Papers Laid on the Table, and Committee on the Welfare of Scheduled Castes and Scheduled Tribes); and service committees, that is, committees concerned with the provision of various services and facilities to members (such as General Purposes Committee, House Committee, Library Committee, and Joint Committee on Salaries and Allowances of Members of Parliament).

The ad-hoc committees may broadly be put into two categories: the select or joint committees on bills, which are appointed to consider and report on particular bills, and committees that are constituted to enquire into and report on specific subjects.

In order to further strengthen the committee system, seventeen departmentally related standing committees were set up in 1993: Agriculture; Communications; Commerce; Defense; Energy; External Affairs; Finance; Food, Civil Supplies, and Public Distribution; Home Affairs; Human Resource Development; Industry; Labor and Welfare; Petroleum and Chemicals; Railways; Science and Technology, Environment, and Forests; Transport and Tourism; and Urban and Rural Development. Each of these committees has forty-five members drawn from the House of the People and the Council of States in a 2:1 proportion. These committees have under their jurisdiction almost all the ministries and departments of the union government. These committees consider, among other things, the demands for grants of the concerned ministries and departments; national long-term policy documents presented to the house; annual reports of the concerned ministries and departments; and bills pertaining to these ministries and departments as are referred to them for review and comment. The committees, however, do not consider matters relating to the day-to-day administration of the concerned ministries and departments.

The biggest achievement afforded by these standing committees is that the demands for grants of most of the ministries and departments of the government are scrutinized by at least forty-five members of Parliament before they are put to a vote of the house. This ensures greater participation of members in deliberating the policies, programs, plans, projects, and underlying philosophies of the government and in evaluating the progress made in their implementation by the government. Previously, because of a paucity of time, Parliament was able to scrutinize the demands for grants of only a few ministries every year, and thereafter demands for grants had to be voted whether they had been debated or not.

The departmentally related standing committee system is a path-breaking step in parliamentary surveillance over administration. By concentrating on long-term plans and policies and the underlying philosophies of the executive, these committees are in a privileged position to provide the direction and guidance necessary for broad policy formulation and achievement of a long-term national perspective by the executive.

The members of parliamentary committees are appointed or elected by the house on a motion, or are nominated by the speaker of the House of the People or chair of the Council of States. A select or joint committee on a bill is appointed on a motion adopted by the house. Members of all financial committees (Public Accounts Committee, Estimates Committee, Committee on Public Undertakings), the Committee on the Welfare of Scheduled Castes and Scheduled Tribes, and the Joint Committee on Offices of Profit are elected every year by members, according to the system of proportional representation by means of single transferable vote. Members of other committees are nominated by the presiding officer of the house concerned. As far as possible, different parties and groups are represented on each parliamentary committee in proportion to their respective strengths in the house.

The chair of a parliamentary committee is appointed from among the members of the committee by the presiding officer of the house to which it belongs. If the presiding officer is a member of the committee, he or she is invariably its chair. Where the presiding officer is not a member, but his or her deputy is, the latter is appointed the chair. A parliamentary committee exists for a period not exceeding one year, for a specified period, or until a new committee is nominated.

The committees hold their meetings in Parliament House or in Parliament House Annex, in New Delhi. But in special cases, with the permission of the presiding officer of the house, meetings may be held elsewhere. A committee has the power to take oral or written evidence. It may send for persons, papers, and records in this regard. If any question arises as to whether the evidence of a person or the production of a document is relevant for the purposes of the committee, the question is referred to the presiding officer of the house, whose decision is final.

The sittings of a committee are held in private and are largely conducted in the same manner as sittings in the house. All questions are determined by a majority of votes of the members present and voting. In case of an equal division of votes on any matter, the chair has a casting vote. All committee reports are presented to the House.

Parliamentary leadership

The Office of Speaker of the House of the People dates to 1921, when the Legislative Assembly (the lower house) was constituted for the first time under the Montague-Chelmsford reforms of 1919. Before that, the governor general had presided over the sittings of the Legislative Council. Under statutory provisions of the Government of India Act of 1919, the speaker of the Legislative Assembly was to be elected by the membership, except for the first four years, when the speaker was to be appointed by the governor general. Accordingly, only in 1925 was the speaker elected for the first time.

Under the constitution of 1950, the speaker and deputy speaker of the House of the People are elected by the House from among its members. The speaker holds office from the date of his or her election until immediately before the first meeting of the next House of the People. The speaker is eligible for re-election. The Office of the Speaker becomes vacant earlier if the speaker ceases to be a member of the House, resigns in writing addressed to the deputy speaker, or is removed from office by a resolution passed by a majority of all the members of the House.

In the Warrant of Precedence, which rank orders officers of the government, the speaker has a very high place. His or her salary and allowances are charged on the Consolidated Fund of India and as such are not voted on by Parliament. The speaker's conduct cannot be discussed except on a substantive motion. The speaker is the conventional and ceremonial head of the House of the People and as such has varied functions. His or her powers and duties are laid down in the *Rules of Procedure and Conduct of Business in the Lok Sabha* and to some extent in the constitution.

The speaker presides over the meetings of the House and over joint sittings of the two houses. He or she does not vote in the first instance but has and exercises a casting vote in the case of tie votes. The speaker has the final power to interpret the rules of procedure and to maintain order in the House, and his or her conduct in regulating the proceedings is not subject to the jurisdiction of any court. All committees of the House function under the direction and control of the speaker, who appoints committee chairs and issues such directions to them as he or she may consider necessary pertaining to the organization of work and the procedures to be followed by them. A committee cannot hold a meeting outside of Parliament House or Parliament House Annex without the speaker's permission, nor can a committee call government officials to give evidence before it without the speaker's prior approval. Appeals from members of a committee against the decisions of its chair are decided by the speaker.

The speaker also determines whether a member of the House has become subject to disqualification on grounds of defection from his or her party. No question involving a breach of privilege of a member, of the House, or of a committee thereof can be raised in the House without the speaker's consent. The speaker determines whether there is a *prima facie* case of a breach of privilege or contempt of the House. He or she can, of course, refer any such question to the Committee of Privileges for examination, investigation, and report.

The presiding officer of the Council of States is the vice president of India, who is the Council's ex-officio chair. Though not a member of the Council of States, the vice president presides over its sittings. A deputy chair is elected by the Council of States from among its members.

Parliamentary parties

A well-developed party system is yet to emerge in the country, which has witnessed periods of one-party dominance and periods in which a multiplicity of political parties competed.

To be officially recognized, a parliamentary party or group should have a distinct ideology and program of action, whether in the political, social, or economic field, which is announced by it at the time of general elections and on which its members have been returned to the house; should have an organization both inside and outside the house that is in touch with public opinion on all important issues before the country; and should at least be able to command a strength that would enable it to keep the house in session, that is to say, its number should not be less than the quorum fixed to constitute a sitting, which is one-tenth of the total membership. A political party that satisfies the first two conditions but fails to command the minimum one-tenth of the total membership of the house is recognized as a parliamentary group, provided its minimum strength is at least thirty.

The prime minister, who is the leader of the majority party in the House of the People, functions as the leader of that house except when he or she is not a member of that body. In the latter case, the prime minister may appoint a minister who is also a member of the House as the leader of the House. The prime minister also appoints the seniormost minister of the Council of States who is also a member of the Council of States as the leader of that house.

The leader of the house is an important functionary and exercises direct influence on the course of business in the body. The arrangement of government business is the ultimate responsibility of the leader of the house, and it is the leader who proposes the dates of summoning and proroguing the house for the approval of the presiding officer. The leader is generally consulted when a motion for suspension of a member from the service of the house is moved or a question involving breach of privilege of a member, of the house, or of a committee is raised. In his or her day-to-day activities, the leader acts as leader of his party, but at times acts as the spokesperson and representative of the whole house.

The leader of the largest recognized opposition party in the house is given the status of the leader of the opposition in the house. The leader of the opposition has the rank of cabinet minister and as such enjoys certain facilities. On matters such as foreign relations and defense policy, the prime minister may at times consult the leader of the opposition. And in times of grave national crisis, the leader of the opposition usually underlines the unity of the nation on a particular issue by identifying with the government policy. At the same time, while eschewing obstructionism as such, the leader of the opposition can rightfully demand debate on an issue if he or she feels that the government is trying to slide over an important issue or shun parliamentary criticism.

Whips are chosen from among the members of the parties themselves. In fact, the efficient and smooth working of Parliament depends to a very large extent on the whips of the party in power and the whips of parties in opposition. The main function of the whips is to keep members of their parties informed of the possibility of important divisions in the house and when a vote will possibly take place and request them to be in attendance at that time. The whips also play a significant role in sending lists of members from their respective parties to the chair for participation in debates and for nomination on parliamentary committees. They keep members supplied with information about the business of the house and enforce party discipline. The whips act as intermediaries between the leaders and the rank and file of their parties. The whips also operate as channels of communication whereby one party negotiates with other parties about topics for debate or the conduct of business in the house.

With the adoption of the Constitution Act of 1985 (fifty-second amendment), popularly known as the antidefection law, political parties were recognized in the constitution itself. Under the law, a member of a house who belongs to a political party becomes disqualified from being a member if he or she voluntarily gives up membership of such political party, votes or abstains from voting contrary to the direction of the party without prior permission, or, in case of such action, the voting or abstention has not been condoned by the party within fifteen days. Similarly, an independent member becomes disqualified if he or she becomes a member of a political party. On the other hand, a nominated member shall not be so disqualified upon joining a political party within six months of taking a seat in Parliament. Disqualifications on the grounds of defection do not apply to members changing their original party through split or merger. A party split, under the law, is recognized to have taken place if one-third of the members of a legislative party leave their original party. A merger occurs when two-thirds of the members of an original party join another party.

The antidefection law has made party discipline much more rigid, and the role of party leaders and whips particularly important.

Relations between the houses

Under the constitution both houses have certain powers unto themselves and have certain coequal powers.

The House of the People has a number of powers exclusive to itself:

- A money bill can be introduced only in the House of the People. Even a bill having like financial provisions has to be introduced in the House of the People. The Council of States has no power either to reject or amend a money bill
- The speaker of the House of the People has the sole and final power to decide whether a bill is a money bill
- The House of the People has the power to assent or refuse to assent to any demand for grant of expenditure or even to reduce the amount sought by government. In the Council of States, only a general discussion is held on the annual financial statement. The Council of States has no power to vote on the demands for grants
- The Council of Ministers is responsible only to the House of the People and not to the Council of States. The House of the People has the power to vote no confidence in the Council of Ministers

Similarly, the Council of States has certain exclusive powers:

- Under the constitution, if the Council of States passes a resolution supported by not less than two-thirds of the members present and voting that it is necessary or expedient for Parliament to make laws with respect to any matter enumerated in the state list, it would be lawful for Parliament to make laws for the whole or any part of the territory of India with respect to that matter while the resolution remains in force
- Also under the constitution, if the Council of States passes a resolution supported by not less than two-thirds of the members present and voting that it is necessary or expedient to do so, Parliament may create one or more All-India Services common to the union and the states

The houses have coequal powers in respect of most other subjects, including the impeachment of the president, removal of the vice president, constitutional amendments, and removal of the judges of the Supreme Court and the high courts. Presidential ordinances, proclamations of emergency, and proclamations of the failure of constitutional machinery in a state must be placed before both houses of Parliament. Disagreement between the houses on a bill, other than a money bill or constitution amendment bill, is resolved at a joint sitting.

The relationship between the houses has generally been cooperative and harmonious, with hardly any occasion of friction and conflict.

BUDGET PROCEDURES

The budget is the annual financial statement of the government showing the estimated receipts and expenditures for one financial year and giving the estimates for the ensuing year. The expenditures embodied in the budget are twofold: the sums required to meet the items of expenditure charged on the Consolidated Fund of India; and the sums required to meet expenditures proposed to be made from the Consolidated Fund of India. Expenditures in the first category can be discussed in both houses but are the nonvotable part of the budget. The expenditures falling in the second category are presented in the form of demands for grants to the House of the People.

The budget is presented to Parliament in two parts, namely, the "railway budget," pertaining to railway finance, and the "general budget." By convention the railway budget is presented to the House of the People by the minister of railways in the third week of February every year, and the general budget is presented by the minister of finance on the last working day of February at 5 p.m. A copy of each is submitted to the Council of States at the conclusion of the speeches in the House of the People by the minister of railways and finance minister. Soon after the presentation of the general budget, the finance minister introduces the finance bill, which contains the taxation proposals of the government. There is no discussion on the budget on the day on which it is presented.

The discussion on the budget starts a few days after its presentation and involves two stages. The first stage entails discussion of a very general nature, during which members deal only with the general aspects of fiscal and economic policy of the government and do not go into details of taxation and expenditure. The second stage entails a detailed discussion and voting on the demands for grants. Under a procedure that has been followed since 1993, after the general discussion on the budget is over, the House of the People adjourns for a fixed period (of about one month), and the departmentally related standing committees consider the demands for grants of the concerned ministries and departments during this recess. The demands for grants are thereafter considered by the whole House in light of the reports of the committees. The House might confine itself to discussing specific points or recommendations made by the committees and thus might be able to discuss the demands of a larger number of ministries and departments before voting on them than would have been possible under the pre-1993 procedures.

During the discussion on the demands for grants in the House of the People, as in almost all other parliaments, motions may be moved by a member to reduce the amount of a demand. Such a motion is called a "cut motion." It is only a form of initiating discussion on the demand, so that the attention of the House is drawn to the matter. It is not obligatory that discussion begin with a cut motion. Cut motions—classified into three categories—may disapprove a policy pursued by a ministry or department, suggest measures for economy in the administration, or focus the attention of the ministry on specific local grievances. Cut motions have, in fact, only symbolic value, for they have no chance of being carried unless the government loses the support of the majority. Cut motions are generally moved by members of the opposition, and if carried amount to a vote of censure against the government.

The Business Advisory Committee fixes a time limit for voting on the demands for grants. As soon as the time limit for a demand has been reached, "closure" is applied and the demand is put to vote. On the last day of the days allotted for all the demands, at the appointed hour, the speaker puts forth every question necessary to dispose of all the outstanding matters in connection with the demands for grants, whether they have been discussed or not. This process is known as the "guillotine." The guillotine concludes the discussion on the demands for grants.

After the demands for grants are voted by the House, they, along with the expenditures charged on the Consolidated Fund, are incorporated in the appropriations bill, which is introduced in the House. The appropriations bill is considered and passed in the House in the same manner as any other bill except that the debate is restricted to those matters not covered during the debate on the demands for grants. After the bill is passed by the House, the speaker certifies it as a money bill. The bill is then transmitted to the Council of States, which, as stated earlier, has no power to amend or reject the bill. The bill, thereafter, is presented to the president for assent.

All financial proposals of the government for the following year are incorporated in the finance bill, which ordinarily is introduced in the House of the People every year immediately after the budget is presented. It seeks to give effect not only to the following year financial proposals of the government but also to supplementary financial proposals for any period. Discussion on the bill covers matters relating to general administration and local grievances within the sphere of responsibility of the union government. This bill has to be considered and passed by Parliament and assented to by the president within seventy-five days after it is introduced.

The entire budgetary process, beginning with the presentation of the budget and ending with discussion and voting of demands for grants and adoption of the appropriation and the finance bills, extends beyond the start of a financial year. This requires the government to keep enough finance to run the administration of the country until the demands are voted by Parliament. A special provision, therefore, has been made called the "vote on account," which empowers the House of the People to make any grant in advance for a part of a financial year, pending the completion of the budgetary process. Normally, the vote on account is taken to provide for two months a sum equivalent to one-sixth of the estimated expenditure for the entire year under various demands for grants.

EXECUTIVE-LEGISLATIVE RELATIONS

The relationship between the executive and the legislature is intimate. The two have not been envisaged as competing organs of the state but as inseparable partners in the business of government. The Council of Ministers is drawn from and remains part of Parliament. It is like an executive committee of Parliament charged with the responsibility of governance on behalf of the parent body. Their relationship, therefore, is that of a part with the whole.

However, a clear distinction exists between the functions of the executive and those of the Parliament. Parliament legislates, advises, criticizes, and ventilates public grievances. The executive governs the country and has almost unlimited right to initiate legislative and financial proposals in Parliament and give effect to policies approved by Parliament. Parliament can discuss, scrutinize, and approve the proposals made by the executive. Parliament exercises political and financial control over the executive and ensures parliamentary surveillance over the administration.

Under the constitution, the Council of Ministers is collectively responsible to the House of the People. It remains in office so long as it enjoys the confidence of the House. The House can express its lack of confidence in the government by passing a motion of no confidence in the Council of Ministers, by defeating the government on a major issue of policy, or by refusing to vote supplies. It can also censure the government by passing an adjournment motion.

There are a number of procedural devices through which the executive is made subject to the scrutiny of Parliament. Questions, "calling attention notices," half-an-hour discussions, short duration discussions, motions, resolutions, discussions on the motion of thanks on the president's address, the railway and general budgets, and other vehicles all provide ample opportunities to members to scrutinize the performance of the executive. Besides, the well-defined and elaborate committee system also helps in monitoring the performance of the government.

In India, an authority similar to an ombudsman is to be found at the state level in some states. The "Lokayukta" in a state basically deals with grievances of individuals against the administration—both bureaucratic and political. At the union level, however, no such authority exists, though efforts have been made from time to time to create one in the Indian Parliament.

JUDICIAL FUNCTIONS OF PARLIAMENT

Impeachment is a quasijudicial procedure in Parliament. Under the constitution, the president of India may be removed from office by Parliament before the expiry of his or her term by the process of impeachment on grounds of violation of the constitution; and for this purpose, a resolution has to be passed by not less than two-thirds of the total membership in each house.

Subject to the provisions of the constitution, Parliament has the power to make laws regulating the make-up, organization, and jurisdiction of the Supreme Court and various high courts in the country. A judge of the Supreme Court or a high court is removable, on grounds of proven misbehavior or incapacity, by the president on an address by each house of Parliament supported by a majority of the membership and by a two-thirds majority of the members present and voting in the same session. Only one such motion for the removal of a sitting judge of the Supreme Court had been moved by 1996, and that motion failed.

The comptroller and auditor general of India and the chief election commissioner can also be removed from office in like manner and on like grounds as a judge of the Supreme Court.

STATUS OF MEMBERS

Privileges and immunities

The privileges provided for in the constitution for each house of Parliament and its members and committees are freedom of speech in Parliament; immunity from court proceedings in respect of anything said or any vote cast in Parliament or any committee thereof; and immunity from proceedings in court in respect of the publication of any report, paper, vote, or proceeding by or under the authority of either house of Parliament. The constitution further provides that in other respects, the powers, privileges, and immunities enjoyed by each house of Parliament shall from time to time be defined by Parliament by law, and until so defined shall be those of that house and of its members and committees immediately before the coming into force of the Constitution Act of 1978 (forty-fourth amendment). The act omitted reference to the British House of Commons. But in the absence of a law defining these privileges, they in effect remain the same as those of the British House of Commons at the commencement of the constitution.

In addition to the immunities mentioned above, each house also enjoys certain privileges collectively. These are the right to publish debates and proceedings and the right to restrain publication by others; the right to exclude strangers; the right to regulate its procedure and conduct of its business and to decide matters arising within its walls; the right to commit persons, whether members or not, for breach of privilege or contempt of the house; and the right to compel the attendance of witnesses and to send for persons, papers, and records.

Pay and perquisites

The members of Parliament are moderately paid. A member of Parliament is entitled to a monthly salary of fifteen hundred rupees. In addition, each member is entitled to a constituency allowance of three thousand rupees per month, an office allowance of one thousand rupees per month, and a daily allowance at the rate of two hundred rupees during any period of residence on duty. A member having a minimum service of four years to the Parliament, either continuous or not, is entitled to a pension of fourteen hundred rupees per month. A member having a service of more than five years is entitled to an additional pension of two hundred fifty rupees per month for every year in excess of five years. Every person who served for any period as a member of the provisional parliament is entitled to a pension of fourteen hundred rupees per month.

The spouse or dependent of any member who dies while in office is entitled to a pension of five hundred rupees per month for a period of five years from the date of the member's death.

Each member is entitled to twenty-eight one-way airline tickets per year, with a companion or spouse. Every member is entitled to free railway travel anywhere in India during the term of office. Travel facilities by rail are also available to the spouse and a companion of the member as per rules. Besides, each member is entitled to fifty thousand free telephone calls per year, license-fee-free accommodation (with water and electricity to a certain extent), medical facilities, and an advance for the purchase of a car to a maximum fifty thousand rupees.

Member resources

Library and research facilities are provided to members of Parliament through an organized and integrated service known as Library and Reference, Research, Documentation and Information Service (LARRDIS).

The service maintains an up-to-date and well-equipped library backed by prompt and efficient research and reference support. Parliament Library is one of the richest repositories in the country, with holdings of more than one million volumes of printed books on various subjects, reports, governmental publications, United Nations reports, debates, and other material. About eight hundred journals and periodicals are received in the library regularly. Books and other publications for the library are selected and acquired on many subjects, keeping in view the legislative requirements of members. The library also regularly acquires about two hundred Indian and foreign newspapers for the use of members.

The service provides research and reference material on legislative measures as well as on a variety of other subjects coming before the houses. The service endeavors to keep members informed on a continuing basis about national and international issues in various fields by regular publication, in English and Hindi, of brochures, background notes, information bulletins, fact sheets, monographs, current information digests, and other formats. It publishes books on eminent national leaders and on various subjects of parliamentary interest with a view to promoting interest in parliamentary studies. The service also publishes the *Journal of Parliamentary Information* (quarterly); *Digest of Central Acts* (quarterly); *Digest of Legislative and Constitutional Cases* (quarterly); *Abstracts of Books, Reports and Articles* (quarterly); *IPG Newsletter* (quarterly); *Diary of Political Events* (monthly); *Public Undertakings: Digest of News and Views* (monthly); *Science and Technology News Digest* (monthly); and *Parliamentary Documentation* (biweekly).

A computer-based information service known as Parliament Library Information System (PARLIS) has been functioning since 1985. There are also proposals to develop a national on-line network to link the databases of PARLIS with the databases of state legislatures and parliaments of other countries having access to international networks.

A Microfilming Unit has been set up for preservation of holdings. Facilities for the computer-assisted retrieval of information from the microfilm also exist.

Parliamentary facilities

Designed by Sir Edwin Lutyens and Sir Herbert Baker in tune with Indian traditions, the Parliament House building was constructed by Indian labor with indigenous material. The foundation stone of the building was laid February 12, 1921, by the Duke of Connaught. The formal opening ceremony was performed January 18, 1927, by the governor general of India, Lord Irwin. The first meeting of elected members in Parliament House was held January 19, 1927, when the Central Legislative Assembly met for its third session.

In the center of the building is the circular edifice of the Central Hall. Originally used as the library, the hall was remodeled in 1946 for the meetings of the Constituent Assembly. At present, the Central Hall is used for joint sittings of the houses whenever necessary, including for the president's address and addresses by foreign dignitaries. The president-elect may also take the oath of office in the Central Hall.

On the three axes leading from the Central Hall are the chambers of the House of the People and the Council of States and the Library Hall. Open garden courts lie between them. A three-story circular structure surrounds the chambers, accommodating the offices of presiding officers, ministers, chairs of parliamentary committees, recognized political parties and groups, branches of the House of the People and the Council of States Secretariats, and the Ministry of Parliamentary Affairs.

The chamber of the House of the People is semicircular, with a seating capacity for 550 members. The speaker's chair is at the center of the diameter connecting the two ends of the semicircle. Seats to the right of the speaker are occupied by the members of the ruling party, and to the left by members of the opposition and unattached members.

The Official Gallery, meant for the use of officials required to be in attendance, is located to the right of the speaker's chair. To the left of the chair is the Special Box, reserved at the discretion of the speaker for the family and guests of the president, governors of states, heads of foreign states, and other high personages. In the pit of the chamber, just below the speaker's chair, is the table of the secretary general (clerk) of the House.

The Council of States chamber is also of a horseshoe shape and is almost on the same pattern as that of the House of the People, but it is smaller in size, having a seating capacity for 250 members.

The Library Hall, like the two chambers, is also in the shape of a horseshoe. Originally designed as a conference hall for the rulers of the various states of India, it used to be known as the Princes' Chamber. After independence it was used as a courtroom for the Supreme Court of India until August 1958. Thereafter, the design of the chamber was slightly altered to serve the purpose of a reading room as part of the library. In the wooden panel of the Hall are 102 gilded designs, which represent the emblems of the various states of the preindependence era.

To meet the manifold increase in the activities of Parliament after independence, and especially to cope with the demand for space for parliamentary parties and groups, committee rooms, offices for the chairs of parliamentary committees, and the Secretariats of the two houses, a separate building known as the Parliament House Annex was constructed. The foundation stone of the building was laid August 3, 1970, and the building was completed in October 1975.

To meet the growing demand for space for the collections and to accommodate the latest devices required of a modern library and information service system, construction of a new Parliament Library Building was taken up in the area between the Parliament House and its Annex. This building was expected to be commissioned by September 1997.

All persons other than members are regarded as strangers, with the exception of the officials on duty. Admissions of strangers to the galleries are made in accordance with the orders of the presiding officer, who may, whenever he or she thinks fit, order the withdrawal of strangers from any part of the house. Admission to the galleries is by cards that are issued by an order of the secretary general. In the case of the Speaker's Gallery, however, cards are issued by the speaker at his or her discretion.

Entry to the various galleries in both houses of Parliament—the Distinguished Visitors' Gallery, the Official Gallery, the Press Gallery, the Special Gallery, the Diplomatic Gallery, the Public Gallery, and the House of the People or the Council of States Gallery—is restricted to specific categories of people for whom these galleries are exclusively meant.

The admission of press correspondents to the Press Gallery is generally regulated on the basis of the advice given by the Press Advisory Committee, which is reconstituted every year from among the representatives of the press having Press Gallery cards. Applications from foreign correspondents for the issue of Press Gallery cards are considered only if they are accredited to the government of India and if requests to that effect are received in the Secretariat through the Press Information Bureau of the government of India.

Between sessions, visitors are permitted to see the Parliament House during specified hours. Such visitors are escorted by a security assistant in convenient batches of forty to fifty persons at a time, every half hour on the authority of sightseers' permits issued by the Reception Offices of the House of the People and the Council of States Secretariats.

OFFICIAL RECORD AND THE MEDIA

The daily proceedings of both houses of Parliament are published in the form of printed reports, which constitute the permanent official record of the proceedings in the houses. In the case of the House of the People, at present three versions of the official record are prepared. The original, uncorrected version is kept in the Parliament Library, and the English and Hindi versions are generally printed. In the Council of States, only two versions—original and Hindi—are prepared and printed.

Media coverage of parliamentary proceedings exists in India as a necessary corollary to the right to freedom of speech and expression guaranteed in the constitution. In both the House of the People and the Council of States a Press Gallery facilitates press coverage. A beginning in the direction of televising and broadcasting parliamentary proceedings was made when the president's address to members of both houses of Parliament was broadcast live by Doordarshan (the official television company) and All India Radio (the official organization for national broadcasting) on December 20, 1989. Since 1992, besides the president's annual address to Parliament, the presentation of annual railway and general budgets has also been broadcast live on the national channel every year. The complete proceedings of the House of the People are now being videotaped. The recordings are kept for archival purposes. The recorded proceedings of important debates are also telecast in the form of capsules of two-to-three hours. Two one-hundred-watt VHF transmitters have been installed in Parliament House. With them, the House of the People and the Council of States proceedings have been broadcast live since August 25, 1994, within a radius of ten to fifteen kilometers of New Delhi. Also, the Question Hour in the House of the People and the Council of States has been broadcast live throughout the country in alternate weeks.

R. C. Bhardwaj

BIBLIOGRAPHY

Belavadi, S. H. *Theory and Practice of Parliamentary Procedure in India*. Bombay: N. M. Tripathi, 1988.

Bhardwaj, R. C. *Legislation by Members in the Indian Parliament*. New Delhi: Allied Publishers, 1994.

Jain, R. B. *Indian Parliament: Innovations, Reforms, and Developments*. Calcutta: Minerva Associates, 1976.

Kashyap, Subhash C. *The Parliament of India: Myths and Realities*. New Delhi: National Publishing House, 1988.

———. *Our Parliament: An Introduction to Parliament of India*. New Delhi: National Book Trust, 1989.

Kaul, M. N., and S. L. Shakdher. *Practice and Procedure of Parliament*. New Delhi: Lok Sabha Secretariat, 1991.

Mukherjee, A. R. *Parliamentary Procedure in India*. 3d ed. Calcutta: Oxford University, 1983.

Rama Devi, V. S., and B. G. Gujar. *Rajya Sabha at Work*. New Delhi: Rajya Sabha Secretariat, 1996.

Shakdher, S. L. *Glimpses of the Working of Parliament*. New Delhi: Metropolitan Books, 1977.

INDONESIA

OFFICIAL NAME: Republic of Indonesia (Republik Indonesia)
CAPITAL: Jakarta
POPULATION: 206,612,000 (1996 est.)
DATE OF INDEPENDENCE: Proclaimed August 17, 1945; independence recognized December 27, 1949 (from the Netherlands)
DATE OF CURRENT CONSTITUTION: Effective August 18, 1945; restored July 5, 1959
FORM OF GOVERNMENT: Military-backed regime
LANGUAGES: Bahasa Indonesia (official), Dutch
MONETARY UNIT: Indonesian rupiah
FISCAL YEAR: April 1–March 31
LEGISLATURE: People's Representation Council (Dewan Perwakilan Rakyat)
NUMBER OF CHAMBERS: One
NUMBER OF MEMBERS: 500 (425 directly elected, 75 appointed)
PERCENTAGE OF WOMEN: —
TERM OF LEGISLATURE: Five years
MOST RECENT LEGISLATIVE ELECTION: May 29, 1997
MINIMUM AGE FOR VOTING: 17 (younger if married)
MINIMUM AGE FOR MEMBERSHIP: 21
SUFFRAGE: Universal
VOTING: Optional
ADDRESS: People's Representation Council, Jalan Jenderal Gatot Subroto, Jakarta 10270
TELEPHONE: (62 21) 571 55 15
FAX: (62 21) 573 48 04

The Republic of Indonesia comprises the world's largest island group, more than 13,000 islands stretching 3,000 miles from west to east. In population, its 6,000 inhabited islands make up the largest country in Southeast Asia and the fourth largest in the world. Most of the population resides on the five main islands: Sumatra, Java, Celebes, Borneo (one-third of which is part of Malaysia), and the western half of New Guinea (Papua New Guinea includes the eastern half). In July 1976 East Timor was formally incorporated into Indonesia.

The government is a presidential-style republic; its branches include the president and cabinet, the Supreme Advisory Council (Dewan Pertimbangan Agung), the legislature (Dewan Perwakilan Rakyat, or the People's Representation Council), the People's Consultative Assembly (Majelis Permusyawaratan Rakyat), the state auditor (Badan Pemeriksa Keuangan), and the High Court (Mahkamah Agung).

HISTORICAL BACKGROUND

The Indonesian archipelago has been settled since prehistoric times. Trade routes between China and India passed through the region, and Java and Sumatra had become important commercial centers by the ninth century. The Hindu and Buddhist legacy of the early traders was gradually supplanted by the Islam of Persian and Gujarati traders in the thirteenth through fifteenth centuries. Portuguese spice traders arriving in the sixteenth century encountered a number of Islamic kingdoms in the region; the Portuguese established colonies in the islands.

In the late 1500s the Netherlands became a dominant sea power, having warred with Portugal and Spain. In 1602 the Dutch East India Company was established and took over the islands. This powerful economic monopoly established coerced production and maintained control of Indonesia's politics and economy throughout the seventeenth and eighteenth centuries. From 1799 to 1816, the territory's ownership reflected European instability, as the French, English, and Dutch balance of power shifted. In 1816 the territory returned to Dutch control as the Netherlands East Indies.

In 1918 the colonial government established the first legislative body, the Volksraad. The Netherlands appointed a Dutch official to head the body, and local representation never exceeded 50 percent of the members. By 1927 Sukarno had founded the Indonesian Nationalist Party, which was an expression of the nationalism born of the people's reaction both to the corruption and abuses of the colonial state and to the disruption caused by an influx of Chinese earlier in the century.

World War II effectively ended the colonial period. While Germany occupied the Netherlands, Japan occupied the islands, and the Volksraad was disbanded in 1942. At the end of the war, in 1945, Sukarno proclaimed independence and established a constitution, although the Netherlands did not recognize the new nation. The constitution of 1945 established a legislature, the Komite Nasional Indonesia Pusat. The arrangement was temporary; elections were not held because the war had made them impossible.

The Dutch fought unsuccessfully to regain control. A new constitution in 1949 established an independent federation of states, with a Netherlands-style parliament, consisting of the 32-member Senate and 146-member People's Representation Council. Sukarno was president. The Netherlands relinquished all territory except the western half of New Guinea (in 1963, after a two-year military campaign by Sukarno, that province was returned to Indonesia as Irian Jaya).

In 1950 the legislature voted to return to a unitary government, and a provisional constitution went into effect (it was finally approved in 1955). A 235-member temporary

legislature (Dewan Perwakilan Rakyat Sementara) was convened. At this point, Indonesia was a constitutional democracy. In 1955 free elections were held to select a new legislature and to select members of a constitutional assembly, which had the task of creating a new constitution to replace the provisional constitution of 1950. Using proportional representation—with the whole country, in effect, one district—the 1955 elections yielded fragmented bodies without clear majorities. The constitutional assembly was unsuccessful, and civil unrest spread.

In 1959 Sukarno, with the support of the armed forces, declared martial law and reinstated the 1945 unitary constitution by decree; this act marked the beginning of "guided democracy." The legislature was dissolved; Sukarno established a new legislature, but this body lasted only a year before the president responded to a budget conflict by disbanding the legislature.

Sukarno revised the party system that had been in effect. In 1960 he banned the largest Muslim party, the Consultative Council of Indonesian Muslims, as well as the Indonesian Socialist Party, for having backed the rebels in the civil war. But three other parties were incorporated into the new system: the Indonesian National Party, the Islamic Scholars' Revival, and the Indonesian Communist Party. Sukarno appointed the entire assembly, which included 130 members of these and five other parties as well as 152 representatives of functional groups, such as the military, factory and farm workers, young people, and women; 1 additional member represented Irian Jaya (at the time not recognized as a legal part of Indonesia). The chair of the legislature was also one of the president's ministers. The president declared that the legislature did not control the government, and his policies toward neighboring states and foreign companies went unchallenged. No elections were held under Sukarno's guided democracy.

Sukarno had established a dictatorship. In 1963 he had himself named president for life; in 1964 he declared that the revolution required his involvement in judicial matters—thereby ending the independence of the judiciary.

Meanwhile, the communists were building support, and the president acquiesced in their efforts to arm the party's backers. Senior army officers reacted against the leftward movement of the government and the downward spiral of the economy; Golkar, the formal party-type organization of the functional groups, was launched as part of the effort to combat communism.

The pressure cooker exploded in the fall of 1965, when communists killed seven army officers in an attempted coup. In the last three months of 1965 and the first three months of 1966, many thousands of communists and suspected communists throughout the country were killed by soldiers and citizens. The party was nearly eradicated. Sukarno was not successful in restoring order, and he also refused student demands to dissolve the Communist Party. In March 1966 Sukarno was forced to hand over key powers to General Suharto, who took credit for turning back the communists. In 1967 the People's Consultative Assembly formally named Suharto to a five-year term as president.

Suharto's system was called the New Order (Sukarno's guided democracy now became known as the Old Order). Suharto decided to keep the constitution of 1945 in force, with its wide-ranging presidential powers. He also subscribed to, and eventually imposed on all social and political organizations, Sukarno's *pancasila,* or the five principles: monotheism, humanitarianism, unity, democracy, and justice.

A major difference between the two presidents can be seen in the elections: Suharto reinstated regular elections to the contested seats in the People's Representation Council, and elections were held in 1971, 1977, 1982, 1987, 1992, and 1997.

The 1971 elections, the first under the New Order, selected 360 of the 460 members; the government appointed 75 members from the military (active officers) and filled the remaining 25 seats with other government supporters. Golkar ended up with 261 seats in the Council.

Golkar, which represents the functional groups—including, prominently, retired military officers—has dominated all of the elections under Suharto, usually garnering about two-thirds of the seats. The 1977 elections were preceded by student unrest, partly in protest of the dominance of Golkar.

PARTIES

The party system was sharply reduced under the two presidents. In 1955 twenty-eight parties won seats in the Assembly. Sukarno chose eight parties for the Assembly that he appointed in 1960, and eight won seats in the 1971 elections. Suharto continued to rearrange the parties: in 1973 he amalgamated the Muslim parties into a United Development Party, and the nationalist and Christian ones into an Indonesian Democratic Party. Only Golkar and these two sponsored opposition parties were allowed subsequently to compete in national elections.

In conjunction with elections, references to and symbols of Islam are not allowed, and the United Development Party may not advocate an Islamic state. From 1982 to 1992 the party's share of the vote fell from 28 percent to 17 percent; in 1997 it rebounded slightly to 23 percent. The Indonesian Democratic Party gained seats, moving from 8 percent of the vote to 15 percent in the same period, then falling to 3 percent in 1997.

The parties that remain are dependent on the government, which completely funds them. Thus, their autonomy is very limited. Any party member whose actions offend the government can be forced out of office. In this way the president has even more power behind the scenes.

CONSTITUTION

The day after Indonesia declared independence from the Netherlands, in August 1945, a constitution that bears the stamp of Sukarno went into effect. Although this constitution was replaced by others in 1949 and 1950, Sukarno reinstated it by decree in 1959, and it has been in effect ever since.

In the preamble the goals of the state are set forth: to be free, united, sovereign, just, and prosperous. Sukarno's *pancasila* are also listed: "belief in the one and only God; just and civilized humanity; the unity of Indonesia; democracy guided by the inner wisdom of deliberations among representatives; and the realization of social justice for all of the people of Indonesia." The first article establishes that "sovereignty shall be vested in the people" and shall be exercised by the People's Consultative Assembly.

The president, as head of state and head of government, holds the most power. According to the constitution, only the People's Consultative Assembly (much of which is appointed by the president) can check the president's power. In addition to a judiciary, which does not review legislation, the constitution provides for a Supreme Advisory Council. This body advises the president and cabinet, answering questions and making recommendations.

PEOPLE'S REPRESENTATION COUNCIL

The legislature, the People's Representation Council, is a unicameral body. The majority (425) of its current 500 members are elected from regions at five-year intervals. All Indonesian citizens who are at least seventeen years of age (younger if married) and who have no criminal record are eligible to vote. Other members of the Council are appointed from the military and by provisional assemblies of functional groups. The Council has a chair and five vice chairs. The legislature enacts laws in conjunction with the president. Members receive a monthly salary and are eligible for a pension at the end of a five-year term.

The election system used to determine the contested seats in the People's Representation Council has been questioned in recent years. The multimember district system is used, with proportional representation; the twenty-seven provinces are the electoral districts. Councils of party leaders determine all the candidates for all the districts. Hence, many candidates are national figures who are not familiar in the districts and who owe their candidacy to the party, not to the district's voters. Questions of legitimacy arise, and members of the public are more likely to turn to local bureaucracies than to their legislators. President Suharto has asked the Indonesian Institute of Sciences to try to determine whether a different election system would better address Indonesia's needs.

The People's Representation Council meets in Jakarta for ten months of the year. Bills may be introduced by either the executive or the legislature but must be supported by both. A quorum is two-thirds of the total membership. Deliberations are held behind closed doors; bills are read at four deliberative sessions and may be passed by consensus or, rarely, by majority vote.

There have been criticisms of the Council. In part because the body has no power to conduct investigations, it is sometimes characterized as a rubber stamp for the president. But the body deliberates behind closed doors, and the public cannot witness the serious debates that take place. Only the last meeting of the session, when consensus has been established, is open to the public. Furthermore, questions may be framed for the executive only if at least twenty members from at least two factions sign the proposal. Thus, it is nearly impossible for the Council to exercise oversight.

Administratively, the Council faces a serious need for better staff support. For a brief period, from 1990 to 1993, the University of Indonesia staffed an information center, but that program was discontinued for lack of funds.

PEOPLE'S CONSULTATIVE ASSEMBLY

The highest state organ is the People's Consultative Assembly. Symbolically, the body is the incarnation of the Indonesian peoples, and all other government branches are accountable to it. Its one thousand members include all the members of the People's Representation Council and a like number of representatives from functional groups and geographic regions (proportional to population). Generally, 80 percent of the members are from government-supportive groups (primarily Golkar). The Assembly meets at least once every five years.

Although the body rarely meets, its functions are essential to the state. The People's Consultative Assembly has the power to amend the constitution or to replace it. The Assembly also determines the "broad outline of state policies," which the president is bound to implement. Last, the Assembly selects (or removes) the president and vice president. All decisions must be unanimous.

The first People's Consultative Assembly met in 1959, when Sukarno decreed a return to the 1945 constitution. The body met in 1960, 1963, and 1965. Under Sukarno, the Assembly chair was also a cabinet minister. The president reserved the power to make decisions if consensus could not be achieved, which in effect kept Sukarno in charge. After the 1965 coup attempt, however, a temporary assembly was convened. This body removed Sukarno from office in 1967, holding him accountable for the troubles that surrounded the attempted communist takeover. The new People's Consultative Assembly returned to the constitutional stipulation that its chair be independent of the president.

Golkar's majority has varied in size, but the functional groups continue to dominate the Assembly. This arrangement has kept Suharto in office since 1971.

NEW DIRECTIONS?

The government under Suharto has been more willing to allow differences in opinion, although the relationship between the military-dominated state and citizens has not always been comfortable. In the 1970s, inflation, the domination of foreign capital in certain sectors of the economy, and the continued importance of the military in government led to expressions of discontent. To some extent Suharto responded. For example, he ordered about 30,000 political detainees released in 1978.

Political stability has contributed to economic and social progress in Indonesia. Educational levels have risen, and foreign interests have been willing to invest. Suharto has improved the economic climate by lowering taxes and improving conditions for trade and foreign investment.

On the other hand, some citizens, especially middle-class city residents, have demanded more individual freedom and democracy; some leaders of the Democratic Party have cautiously supported moves in this direction. The government has accommodated some of the demands by allowing more freedom of expression since the mid-1980s—even to the point of criticism of the government. At times, however, the state retreats, as it did in a crackdown on the media in 1994.

Groups and individuals that advocate more democracy are not by and large part of the government, however. Most of those in government have not advocated change, and many see democracy as foreign to Indonesian ideals. Yet it remains possible that further democratization will come through other channels, especially in conjunction with industrial development.

Amir Santoso

BIBLIOGRAPHY

Crouch, Harold. *The Army and Politics in Indonesia.* Rev. ed. Ithaca, N.Y.: Cornell University Press, 1988.

Reeve, David. *Golkar of Indonesia: An Alternative to the Party System.* Singapore: Oxford University Press, 1985.

Schwarz, Adam. *A Nation in Waiting: Indonesia in the 1990s.* Boulder, Colo.: Westview Press, 1994.

IRAN

OFFICIAL NAME: Islamic Republic of Iran (Jomhori-e-Islami-e-Iran)
CAPITAL: Tehran
POPULATION: 66,094,000 (1996 est.)
DATE OF INDEPENDENCE: April 1, 1979 (Islamic Republic proclaimed)
DATE OF CURRENT CONSTITUTION: Adopted December 2–3, 1979
FORM OF GOVERNMENT: Theocratic Islamic republic
LANGUAGE: Persian (Farsi), Turkic, Kurdish, Luri
MONETARY UNIT: Rial
FISCAL YEAR: March 21–March 20
LEGISLATURE: Islamic Consultative Assembly (Majles-e Shawra-ye Islami)
NUMBER OF CHAMBERS: One
NUMBER OF MEMBERS: 270
PERCENTAGE OF WOMEN: 4.0
TERM OF LEGISLATURE: Four years
MOST RECENT LEGISLATIVE ELECTION: March 8 and April 19, 1996
MINIMUM AGE FOR VOTING: 16
MINIMUM AGE FOR MEMBERSHIP: 26
SUFFRAGE: Universal and direct
VOTING: Optional
ADDRESS: Islamic Consultative Assembly, Imam Khomeini Avenue, Tehran
TELEPHONE: (98 21) 646 4334
FAX: (98 21) 646 6724

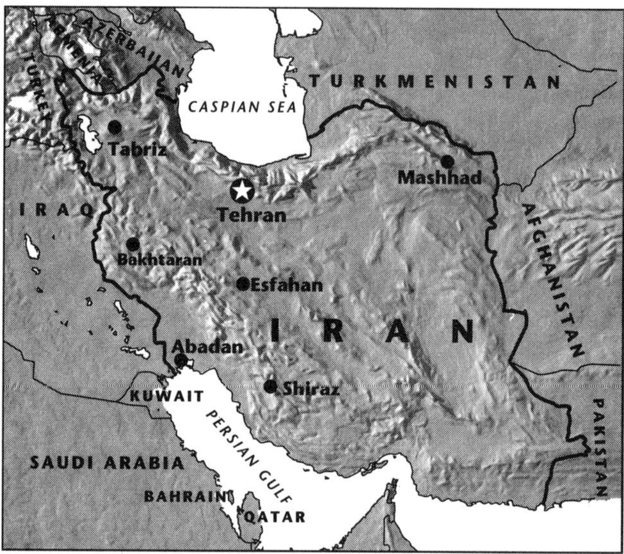

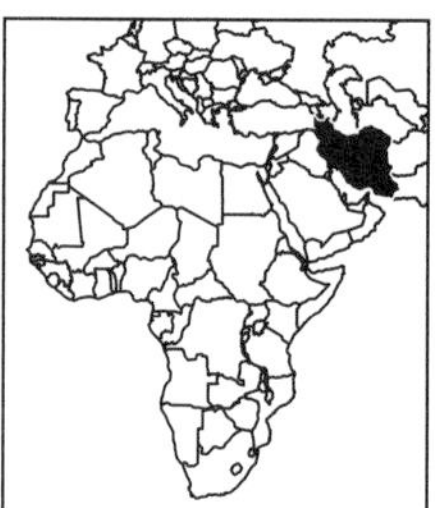

The Islamic Republic of Iran lies between Iraq and Pakistan in the Middle East. This theocratic republic is governed by an executive branch, consisting of a religious head and a head of state, and a unicameral parliament.

The Assembly (Majles) plays an important role in contemporary Iran and has a rich history reaching back to the constitutional revolution of 1905–1909. From 1905 until the Islamic revolution of 1979, when the ruling shah was overthrown, its full designation was National Consultative Assembly (Majles-e Shawra-ye Melli); its present name is Islamic Consultative Assembly (Majles-e Shawra-ye Islami).

The constitutional and the Islamic revolutions—two popular uprisings of modern Iran—necessitated the establishment of an institution that would, at least in theory, legislate, represent the public, and recognize the concept of popular sovereignty. From 1949 until 1979 Iran also had a Senate (Sena), half of whose members were appointed by the shah. It now has an Assembly of Religious Experts (Majles-e Khebregan) composed of clerics chosen by the general electorate. The main Majles, however, continues to be the chief legislative body.

From 1905 to 1996 the Majles had twenty-nine legislative sessions: twenty-four under the monarchy and five under the Islamic Republic. These years can be divided into five periods: the first constitutional era (1905–1925), Reza Shah's reign (1926–1941), the second constitutional era (1941–1953), Mohammad Reza Shah's autocracy (1953–1979), and, since 1979, the Islamic Republic. The role of the Majles has been different in each period.

HISTORICAL BACKGROUND

The 1905 constitutional revolution forced the ruling Qajar dynasty to accept a parliamentary form of government. The constitutional laws of 1905–1909 were modeled on those of Belgium. The shah remained the titular head of state, but the Majles was declared the representative of all the people and became the country's central institution. It could determine all laws, decrees, annual budgets, treaties, loans, monopolies, and concessions. Indeed, it had the right to propose any measure that it believed was required for the well-being of the government and the people. It also could appoint, investigate, and dismiss all cabinet ministers, including the premier and the war minister. So that they could fulfill their mandates without interference, deputies were given immunity from arrest. A bill of rights gave citizens protection of life, property, honor, religious worship, and political expression.

The main limitation on the parliament would have been a proposed Guardian Council of senior clerics. This body would have had the authority to veto parliamentary bills it deemed contrary to the *Shari'a* (divine law). No Guardian Council, however, was convened until after the 1979 revolution.

At first the electoral law confined the vote to the propertied classes, but later the vote was extended to all adult males. This strengthened the position of the large landowners and tribal chiefs who could herd their peasants and retainers to the polling booths. The recognized religious minorities were given seven seats in the Majles: four seats for the Jews, two for the Christians (Armenians and Assyrians), and one for the Zoroastrians.

Although the constitutional revolution was greeted with enthusiasm, the parliamentary system failed in the next decade from a combination of ills: foreign armies occupied parts of the country, especially during World War I; tribal revolts disrupted the countryside; the government lacked the institutional machinery to collect taxes and enforce law and order; and the Majles had become an upper-class club divided between reformers and conservatives, clerics and secularists, centralists and federalists, pro-British and pro-Russian landlords.

In 1921 Col. Reza Khan, the main military commander, carried out a coup. He arrested the leading politicians, and, while remaining behind the throne, consolidated power in his own hands. In 1926 he deposed the Qajars, established his Pahlavi dynasty, and crowned himself shah in the style of his hero, Napoleon. He proceeded to rule the country with an iron fist for the next sixteen years.

During his reign, Reza Shah used the Majles to hide his military autocracy. Elections were held every four years, and deputies had regular sessions with all the trappings of parliamentary government—rules of order, regulations, and elaborate committee systems. The constitution was observed to the letter of the law. But in reality the shah informed the police chief whom he wanted in the Majles. The police chief informed the interior minister. The interior minister informed the provincial governors. And the provincial governors, who supervised the elections, made sure that the right names came out of the ballot boxes. Handpicked assemblies then rubber-stamped all the shah's bills, decrees, and appointments. When the occasional deputies failed to do his bidding, they found themselves in jail.

The Majles regained much of its power in 1941, when the Anglo-Soviet invasion forced Reza Shah to vacate the throne in favor of his young son Mohammad Reza Shah. From 1941 to 1953, when a coup supported by the U.S. Central Intelligence Agency established Mohammad Reza Shah's autocracy, the Majles played a central role in drafting laws, passing budgets, and choosing cabinet ministers, including prime ministers. It failed, however, to exert influence on the War Ministry. The shah, as commander in chief of the armed forces, claimed the prerogative to appoint not only the chiefs of staff but also the war ministers. This precipitated a constitutional crisis in 1951–1953, when Dr. Mohammad Mosaddeq, the popular prime minister, cited the fundamental laws to argue that the duly elected head of government had the authority to choose all the ministers, including the war minister. This constitutional crisis helped to pave the way for the 1953 coup.

After 1953 Mohammad Reza Shah re-created his father's autocracy. As before, the shah handpicked the deputies, told them how to vote, and determined which bills were to be debated and which ones were to be passed without further discussion. Occasionally, he permitted a second party to function as the loyal opposition. One was dubbed the "Yes Party"; the other, the "Yes Sir Party." To further strengthen his hand and reward compliant politicians, the shah assembled the Senate that had been promised in the laws of 1949. Land reform in 1963, however, changed the social composition of the Majles by breaking up the large holdings and thereby undermining the old upper class. The new handpicked deputies were mostly civil servants, managers, professionals, and business executives linked to the royal palace.

THE ISLAMIC REPUBLIC

Immediately after the 1979 revolution against the shah, Ayatollah Ruhollah Khomeini, the cleric who had headed the revolt, convened a constituent body, the Assembly of Religious Experts (Majles-e Khebregan) to draw up an Islamic constitution. This body tried to synthesize popular sovereignty with Khomeini's theory of the "clergy's guardianship" *(Velayat-e Faqih)*. This theory argued that society should be regulated by the *Shari'a* and that the senior clerics had the divine mandate to oversee the government as well as to interpret and implement the *Shari'a*. The present constitution, together with amendments ratified in 1989 after Khomeini's death, tries to combine theocracy with democracy.

The constitution gives the general electorate—defined as all adults, including women—the right to choose every four years a Majles formed of 270 deputies. The balloting is direct and secret. The electoral law gives the vote to those over age sixteen and introduces a double-balloting system. If the leading candidate does not win more than 50 percent of the votes cast in the first round, the two leading candidates must run in a second round; the top vote-getter wins. The country is divided into 196 constituencies. The capital, Tehran, has thirty-seven seats. The religious minorities have five seats: Armenians two, and Jews, Assyrians, and Zoroastrians one each.

As the "Representative of the Nation" and "Legislative Branch," the Majles has extensive prerogatives. Among other things, it can investigate at will all cabinet ministers, affairs of state, and public complaints against the executive and the judiciary; remove cabinet ministers—with the exception of the president—through a parliamentary vote of no confidence; and block annual budgets as well as economic projects and all foreign loans. It also holds closed debates when it decides national security is at stake. Regular sessions are covered by the main national newspapers and the radio-television network.

The Majles regulates its internal operation through its own by-laws and committee system. It elects its own speaker, two deputy speakers, twenty-eight permanent committees, and a standing committee that determines which bills are brought to the floor. Moreover, the Majles, as the chief legislative branch, can draft statutes so long as they do not contradict the *Shariʿa.*

Although the Majles representatives have considerable power—as well as immunity from arrest—ultimate authority resides with the clergy in conformity with Khomeini's concept of *Velayat-e Faqih.* The 1979 constitution named Khomeini the supreme cleric, the supreme leader, and the *imam* (infallible leader) for life. It also stipulated that if no single cleric emerged after his death, all his authority would be passed on to a Leadership Council composed of two or three senior religious jurists. After his death in July 1989, however, his disciples so distrusted the surviving senior jurists that they did not set up a Leadership Council. Instead, the Assembly of Religious Experts elected one of their own, Hojjat al-Islam Khamenei, a medium-ranking cleric, to be the new supreme leader. Khamenei inherited all of Khomeini's constitutional powers and titles—except that of *imam.* Constitutional amendments approved in 1989 transformed the eighty-three-man Assembly of Religious Experts into a permanent body with the power to elect the supreme leader and to depose him if they deemed him "mentally incapable of fulfilling his arduous duties." In effect, then, the Assembly of Religious Experts has become a second-chamber equivalent to a clerical upper house above the regular Islamic Consultative Assembly.

The supreme leader can mediate among the legislative, executive, and judicial branches. Moreover, he can "determine the interests of Islam," "supervise the implementation of general policy," and "set political guidelines for the Islamic Republic." In his role as commander in chief he can declare war and peace, mobilize the armed forces, and make all the senior military appointments to both the regular forces and the revolutionary guards. The supreme leader also has the power to dismiss the president, who is chosen by the general electorate for a four-year term; nominate the main urban preachers, the heads of the large religious foundations, and the director of the national radio-television network; and appoint the chief judge, the district circuit judges, and, most important of all, six clerics to the important twelve-man Guardian Council. The other six members of the Guardian Council are elected by the Majles from a list of clerics drawn up by the chief judge.

The Guardian Council has the authority to ensure that all statutes voted by the Majles conform to the *Shariʿa* and the Islamic constitution. Moreover, it has the authority to supervise the elections for both the Majles and the Assembly of Religious Experts—it regulates electoral campaigns, allocates airwave time, decides which issues can be debated, and scrutinizes the qualifications of all candidates. It can—and often does—bar candidates whom it deems inadequately committed to Islam, the Islamic revolution, the Islamic constitution, the concept of *Velayat-e Faqih,* and the authority of the supreme leader. Thus the Islamic Republic has a parliament and parliamentary elections, but both are closely regulated by a small circle of clerics.

Because the clergy control access to the Majles, most of the successful candidates have been either clerics or laymen sponsored by the same clerics. In the last Majles before the revolution, less than 2 percent of the deputies were clerics. In the First Islamic Majles (1980–1984) after the revolution, more than 50 percent were clerics—the highest representation until then in Iran's history. The other 50 percent were mostly either white-collar employees with some seminary training or high school teachers with parents who had been medium-ranking clerics. In the Second Islamic Majles (1984–1988), the clerical representation increased further, to 54 percent; another 10 percent had studied in seminaries. In the Third (1988–1992) and Fourth (1992–1996) Islamic Majleses, the clerical representation fell to 32 percent. In the Fifth (1996–), it fell further, to 19 percent. But in all these assemblies, the laymen, without exception, continued to be sponsored by clerical organizations sanctioned by the regime—particularly by the supreme leader and the Council of Guardians. Without this sanction, they would have been unable even to enter the parliamentary elections. This narrow control, however, has led the public to lose interest in parliamentary elections. In the 1980 campaign as much as 80 percent of the electorate voted. In 1992 less than 40 percent voted.

MAJLES FACTIONS

Even though the supreme leader and the Guardian Council control access to the Majles, the five postrevolution parliaments have been divided mainly into two factions—

factions rather than parties because their membership is fluid and their activities are limited to the Majles. The factions differ mainly on economic issues, a subject that Khomeini at the height of the revolution had dismissed as "suitable for donkeys."

One faction has been formed of statists advocating government regulations, deficit financing, economic planning, price controls, rationing, subsidies for social programs, job-creation projects, low-income housing, antipoverty and anti-illiteracy campaigns, nationalization of industry, land reform, redistribution of wealth, and national self-sufficiency. The other faction has been formed of free-marketeers favoring small government, balanced budgets, business incentives, open markets, relaxation of price controls, an end to rationing, privatization of industry, free-trade zones, removal of red tape and trade restrictions, tax holidays for wealthy entrepreneurs, and the attraction of foreign capital, including from western Europe and North America. In short, one faction favors typical statist strategies; the other prefers conventional trickle-down economics. The former have described the latter as "medievalists," "rightists," and "pro-American Muslims." The latter have countered by describing the former as "extremists," "leftists," "pro-Communist Muslims," and "betrayers of the revolution." The statists are supported by the Association of Militant Clergymen, the Islamic Workers Councils, the Islamic Student Association, the ministries dealing with mines and heavy industries, the large foundations (particularly the Foundations for the Dispossessed), the Crusade for Rural Reconstruction, and some contingents of the Revolutionary Guards. The free-marketeers receive support from the Society of Militant Clergymen, the Teachers of the Qom Seminaries, the monetarist Central Bank and Finance Ministry, the chambers of commerce, the more prosperous farmers, and, most important of all, the richer merchants, especially their Islamic Association of Bazaar Guilds.

In this conflict the Guardian Council often has sided with the free-marketeers since most of its twelve members have been conservative jurists staunchly committed to the proposition that private property is sanctified by God and the *Shari'a*. In 1987 this conflict created constitutional gridlock, with the Guardian Council vetoing more than one hundred bills passed by the Majles on crucial issues such as land reform, nationalization of foreign trade, and confiscation of urban real estate. To break the gridlock, Khomeini set up an Expediency Council for Determining the Public Interest of the Islamic Order. He declared that the council could mediate between the Majles and the Guardian Council, and that the Islamic state could in special circumstances suspend even the central practices of Islam in order to safeguard its own long-term interests. Khomeini packed the Expediency Council with clerics, including six from the Guardian Council. Just after Khomeini's death in 1989, constitutional amendments institutionalizing the council were approved. They allowed the supreme leader to choose all its members and permitted the council to decree laws as well as to modify those passed by the Majles. Thus the Majles now has to contend with an appointed body that not only modifies parliamentary bills but also initiates legislation.

Although the Majles has lost much legislative power, it continues to retain some political influence. From 1992 to 1994 it rejected a number of candidates proposed by the president for the cabinet; forced the government to replace the director of the national radio-television network; and lobbied successfully to change the five-year plan, allocating more revenue to projects favored by influential deputies. After a series of urban riots against economic hardships, the Majles forced the president, Ali Akbar Hashemi Rafsanjani, who had sided with the free-marketeers, to backtrack on his economic reforms. He restored subsidies for food, medicine, and fuel; printed more money to avoid further budget cuts; and slowed down the privatization of industry to prevent more layoffs and unemployment. In short, the deputies, even the free-marketeers, were persuaded by their constituencies to preserve the welfare safety net.

To complicate matters further, the free-marketeers who had dominated the Fourth Islamic Majles began to divide in 1994 into two factions—those favoring cultural liberalization and those fearing any such relaxation, especially on the question of women and the veil. The cultural conservatives, drawing closer to Khamenei, the supreme leader, warned that Western influences, especially those emanating from films, videos, and satellite dish transmissions, would undermine Islamic values. The cultural liberals, supporting Rafsanjani—whose two-term tenure ended in 1997—argued that such reforms were necessary to attract back to Iran technicians and wealthy emigrés who had fled the country during the revolution.

Thus the 1996 elections for the Fifth Islamic Majles became a three-way fight among the cultural liberals, the conservative economic free-marketeers, and the radical statists who had survived from the early years of the republic. The supreme leader and the Guardian Council intervened at crucial times in the elections to eliminate outsiders, especially secular liberals, and to ensure that the conservatives obtained a majority but not a monopoly in the Fifth Majles. Consequently, the Fifth Majles was composed of three fluid but identifiable blocs: some one hundred conservatives who opposed any form of cultural relaxation; some seventy cultural liberals who supported Rafsanjani; and some forty economic statists who on many issues sided with the president against the conservatives. The Majles also contained thirty independent deputies whose votes shifted according to the immediate issue. Some describe this as political pluralism. Others describe it as political pluralism controlled by the small clerical elite. The "Yes" versus "Yes Sir" parties of yesteryear have been replaced by the "Allah" versus "Allah Akbar" (God is Great) factions of the Islamic Republic.

Ervand Abrahamian

BIBLIOGRAPHY

Abrahamian, Ervand. *Iran between Two Revolutions.* Princeton: Princeton University Press, 1982.
Azimi, Fakhreddin. *Iran: The Crisis of Democracy, 1941–1953.* New York: St. Martin's, 1989.
Bakhash, Shaul. *The Reign of the Ayatollahs.* New York: Basic Books, 1984.
Sarabi, Farzin. "The Post-Khomeini Era in Iran: The Elections of the Fourth Islamic Majlis." *Middle East Journal* 48 (1994): 89–107.
Siavoshi, Sussan. "Factionalism and Iranian Politics: The Post-Khomeini Experience." *Iranian Studies* 25 (1992): 27–50.

IRAQ

OFFICIAL NAME: Republic of Iraq (al-Jumhuriyah al-ʿIraqiyah)
CAPITAL: Baghdad
POPULATION: 21,422,000 (1996 est.)
DATE OF INDEPENDENCE: October 3, 1932 (from League of Nations mandate under British administration)
DATE OF CURRENT CONSTITUTION: Issued September 22, 1968 (provisional)
FORM OF GOVERNMENT: Totalitarian dictatorship
LANGUAGES: Arabic, Kurdish
MONETARY UNIT: Dinar
FISCAL YEAR: Calendar year
LEGISLATURE: National Assembly (Majlis al-ʿUmma)
NUMBER OF CHAMBERS: One
NUMBER OF MEMBERS: 250
PERCENTAGE OF WOMEN: 6.4
TERM OF LEGISLATURE: Four years
MOST RECENT LEGISLATIVE ELECTION: March 24, 1996
MINIMUM AGE FOR VOTING: 18
MINIMUM AGE FOR MEMBERSHIP: 25
SUFFRAGE: Universal and direct
VOTING: Optional
ADDRESS: National Assembly, Hamourabi Building, Karkh, Baghdad
TELEPHONE: (964 1) 885 35 24
FAX: (964 1) 537 82 09

Iraq, a Middle Eastern country whose history stretches back to the early civilization of Mesopotamia, became a British mandate under the League of Nations after World War I *(see map, p. 743)*. It gained full independence in 1932. Since 1958, when a military coup overthrew the Iraqi monarchy, the country has been a republic, though its leaders have maintained tight control over all aspects of government and the country in effect is a dictatorship.

The country's first constitution, the Organic Law of 1925, created a bicameral parliament with a Senate and a Chamber of Deputies. Until a modification of the electoral law in 1952, elections for the Chamber of Deputies were held in two steps, with the public choosing the electors who chose the deputies. By 1956 there had been fifteen different chambers, of which only two had completed their constitutionally mandated terms. The others were dissolved by the rulers because the deputies were growing critical of the administration.

The 1925 constitution was scrapped in 1958 with the overthrow of the monarchy. The new constitution of 1958 was replaced by another in 1964, only to be superseded by yet another in 1968, two months after Gen. Ahmad Hasan Al-Bakr seized power and established a Revolutionary Command Council (RCC) with absolute executive and legislative powers. Bakr's Arab Socialist Renaissance (Baath) Party, an Arab nationalist party founded in 1947, has remained the ruling party.

Although the 1968 constitution provided for a unicameral National Assembly, no elections were held until after Saddam Hussein succeeded Bakr in 1979. Hussein, through a decree of the Revolutionary Command Council which he headed, reactivated the National Assembly. Elections were held in June and September 1980, and the Arab Baath Socialist Party has maintained an overwhelming majority in the largely moribund National Assembly since that time. In the most recent elections of March 1996, the Arab Baath Socialist Party won 161 of 250 seats.

In 1989 Hussein unveiled a draft of a new constitution.

The new constitution, which has never been adopted or implemented, would abolish the RCC and establish a fifty-member Consultative Assembly. The new constitution also left in limbo the fifty-member Kurdish Legislative Council, created in 1980 to give voice to the country's Kurdish minority.

Only sketchy details are available on the working and leadership of the National Assembly. Standing committees in the National Assembly deal with petitions, administration, defense, finance, foreign affairs, economic matters, legal matters, and education.

For electoral purposes Iraq is divided into fifty-nine multimember electoral districts. Deputies are elected by absolute majority vote.

George Thomas Kurian

IRELAND

OFFICIAL NAME: Republic of Ireland (Éire)
CAPITAL: Dublin
POPULATION: 3,567,000 (1996 est.)
DATE OF INDEPENDENCE: December 6, 1921 (from the United Kingdom)
DATE OF CURRENT CONSTITUTION: Adopted July 1, 1937; effective December 29, 1937
FORM OF GOVERNMENT: Parliamentary democracy
LANGUAGES: Irish (Gaelic), English
MONETARY UNIT: Irish pound
FISCAL YEAR: Calendar year
LEGISLATURE: Parliament (Oireachtas)
NUMBER OF CHAMBERS: Two. House of Representatives (Dáil Éireann); Senate (Seanad Éireann)
NUMBER OF MEMBERS: House of Representatives, 166 (directly elected); Senate, 60 (49 directly elected, 11 appointed)
PERCENTAGE OF WOMEN: House of Representatives, 12.0; Senate, 13.3
TERM OF LEGISLATURE: Five years
MOST RECENT LEGISLATIVE ELECTION: House of Representatives, June 6, 1997; Senate, February 1, 1993
MINIMUM AGE FOR VOTING: 18
MINIMUM AGE FOR MEMBERSHIP: 21
SUFFRAGE: Universal
VOTING: Optional
ADDRESS: Parliament, Leinster House, Kildare Street, Dublin 2
TELEPHONE: (353 1) 678 99 11
FAX: (353 1) 676 25 82

The Republic of Ireland occupies four-fifths of the island of Ireland, which lies in the Atlantic Ocean adjacent to Great Britain. Closely but not always harmoniously linked with Britain from the twelfth century, Ireland gained substantial independence from the United Kingdom in December 1921 following the signing of a treaty between representatives of the Irish independence movement and the British government. Six of the nine counties of the historic northern province of Ulster remained a part of the United Kingdom as Northern Ireland.

HISTORICAL BACKGROUND

The origins of the contemporary Irish Parliament lie in the actions of the seventy-three Sinn Fein ("ourselves alone" in Gaelic) representatives elected to the British parliament in the general election of December 1918. They met in Dublin on January 21, 1919, and declared themselves to be the Dáil Éireann, or Irish Parliament. Claiming to have established an independent Irish parliament and state, the Dáil adopted a constitution and appointed a revolutionary government. Its practical achievements and authority, however, were limited by the circumstances of its creation: many of its members were in jail; it was soon declared an illegal assembly; and during three years of violent conflict between the British authorities and the Irish independence movement its leaders were in hiding and in constant fear of arrest. Dáil Éireann nevertheless had an unarguable electoral legitimacy deriving from the freely conducted 1918 election, and this in turn lent legitimacy to the militant wing of the independence movement.

The war of independence came to an end on December 6, 1921, with the signing of a treaty between representatives of the British government and plenipotentiaries of the Dáil government. The treaty was subsequently ratified by the British Parliament and by the Dáil. The outcome was a form of qualified independence within the British Commonwealth for the twenty-six counties of southern Ireland; the six counties of Northern Ireland, already provided with local political and administrative structures under the Government of Ireland Act of 1920, remained part of the United Kingdom.

The 1922 constitution that flowed from the treaty specified a legislature in the Westminster style. The bicameral parliament comprised a popularly elected lower house, the Dáil, and an indirectly elected upper house, the Seanad. All bills had to be passed by both houses and then signed by the governor general, the representative in Ireland of the British Crown, before becoming law. Members of the Oireachtas, as the parliament is known, also had to take an oath of allegiance to the British Crown. Most members of the Dáil were to be elected by proportional representation. Each voter cast a single transferable vote in his or her multiseat electoral district. In addition, graduates of the two established universities, Dublin University and the National University of Ireland, could each elect three members of the Dáil.

Acceptance of the treaty by a narrow majority in the Dáil was followed by a civil war between pro-treaty and republican forces, in which the latter were decisively defeated in the summer of 1923. Between 1922 and 1932 the government of W. T. Cosgrave demonstrated that, notwithstanding residual trappings of empire, the treaty did indeed give southern Ireland substantive independence. Many republicans, under the leadership of Eamon de Valera, gradually shifted toward a grudging acceptance of the practical legitimacy of the new state and switched their energies from subversion to political organization. De Valera's Fianna Fail party, founded in 1926, proved a spectacular electoral success. Since 1927, the year in which it dropped its policy of abstention from the Dáil, it has been the largest Irish political party.

On March 9, 1932, Eamon de Valera took office after his party's victory in a bitterly contested general election. This peaceful transfer of power was a watershed in Irish political development. Those who had won the civil war in 1923 accepted the verdict of the people and vacated office, while those who had lost it reaped the benefits of their conversion to strictly electoral politics. Only a small rump of committed republicans now denied the legitimacy of the new state.

The 1922 constitution could, for an initial period of eight years, be revised simply by legislation. In 1930, when that period was almost up, the Cosgrave government yielded to temptation and renewed the provision for a further eight years. This opened the door for de Valera, once he won power in 1932, to overhaul the constitution radically and quite legally without the trouble and uncertainty of a referendum. He removed the oath of allegiance and other symbols of imperial subordination, and in 1936 abolished the Seanad.

On December 29, 1937, a new constitution known as Bunreacht na hÉireann came into operation after its enactment by referendum. It provided for a bicameral parliament consisting of the Dáil and a greatly weakened Seanad. The duty of signing legislation now fell to a popularly elected president, who became the third part of the Oireachtas in place of the British Crown. The legislative process, the machinery of government, and the electoral system remained substantially the same as in the 1922 constitution.

On May 10, 1972, the electorate approved by referendum Irish accession to the European Community and the consequent subordination of Irish law to European law under the treaties of accession.

THE CONSTITUTION AND PARLIAMENT

The constitution provides a national parliament—the Oireachtas—consisting of two houses, the Dáil and the Seanad. The president, considered a member of the Oireachtas insofar as a bill becomes law only upon his or her signature, cannot be a member of either house. Under the constitution the Oireachtas is the sole lawmaking body in the state, subject to the important qualification that it shall neither invalidate a law enacted or action taken by the state pursuant to Ireland's membership in the European Union, nor prevent laws enacted or actions taken by the European Union from having legal effect in Ireland.

On receipt of a bill the president must either sign it into

law within seven days or, if she or he so decides, refer the bill to the Supreme Court for a definitive judgment as to its constitutionality. The president may not so refer a bill without first consulting an advisory body, the Council of State, whose advice is nevertheless not binding. On receipt of a petition signed by a majority of the Seanad and at least one-third of the Dáil, the president may decline to sign a bill on the grounds that the measure is of such importance that the will of the people should be ascertained, whether by referendum or through the election of a new Dáil. Again, the president may make such a decision only after consulting with the Council of State.

Although all legislation must be passed by both houses of the Oireachtas, the two chambers are of very unequal power. The Dáil predominates in the constitution as the popularly elected house and the one to which the government is responsible. Constitutionally and in practice, the Seanad is a very weak chamber. The Dáil has exclusive power in the making and breaking of governments, in financial matters, and in declaring war.

The constitution stipulates that the government must contain no fewer than seven and no more than fifteen ministers, all of whom must be members of the Oireachtas. The prime minister, deputy prime minister, and finance minister must all be members of the Dáil. Other ministers may be members of either house, but no government may include more than two members of the Seanad. Ministers may attend and speak in both houses of the Oireachtas, but the government is collectively responsible solely to the Dáil for all its activities. The government as laid down in the constitution is usually described as the cabinet to distinguish it from the wider set of government office holders. The pressure of public business has led to the creation of a subordinate tier of ministers termed ministers of state, who are also known as junior ministers. The maximum number of these is fixed by law at seventeen, all of whom must be members of the Oireachtas.

The prime minister is appointed by the president on the nomination of the Dáil. He or she nominates cabinet ministers for the approval of the Dáil, and these are then appointed by the president. Acting on the advice of the prime minister, the president also accepts or declines to accept the resignation of a minister. A minister who declines to resign when invited to do so by the prime minister may have his appointment withdrawn by the president on the prime minister's advice. A prime minister may resign at any time, and once having lost a vote of confidence must do so. When this happens, all members of the cabinet are deemed to have resigned also.

The prime minister advises the president on the dissolution of the Dáil and the consequent calling of a general election. The president, however, need not be bound by the advice of a prime minister who has ceased to command the confidence of a majority of the Dáil. No prime minister has ever been refused a dissolution. New elections to the Dáil must be held within thirty days of the dissolution, and the new Dáil must meet within thirty days of the polling date. A general election for the Seanad must be held within ninety days of the dissolution of the Dáil, and the first meeting of the new Seanad is determined by the president acting on the advice of the prime minister.

In December 1994 frenzied interparty negotiations after the collapse of Albert Reynolds's Fianna Fail–Labour coalition government eventually resulted in the formation of John Bruton's "Rainbow Coalition," which brought together the Fine Gael, Labour, and Democratic Left parties. This was the first occasion in the history of the state on which there had been a substantive change of government without a general election. It is unlikely to be the last.

The Oireachtas meets in Leinster House, a Georgian mansion completed in 1748 for the Earl of Kildare, later first Duke of Leinster. In 1815 the house was sold to the Royal Dublin Society, which gave it to the new state in 1922. Leinster House is flanked by buildings presently occupied on the north by the National Library and the National Museum, and on the south by the National Gallery and the National History Museum. This dignified setting has its disadvantages: the Oireachtas has long suffered from an acute lack of space for offices for members, committees, and staff.

The Dáil is housed in a chamber within Leinster House built in 1897 as a lecture theater by the Royal Dublin Society. It is semicircular in layout, with the leader of the house presiding from a raised dais situated at the center point of the back wall. The government and its supporters occupy the seats to the left of the chair, the opposition those to the right. Proceedings can be observed from the press and public galleries.

The Seanad chamber was formerly an ornate picture gallery running the length of one side of Leinster House. The shape of the room required the adoption of a transverse seating plan, with the chair facing the seats of the sixty senators arranged in semicircular rows. As in the Dáil, members who support the government sit to the chair's left, and members of the opposition parties and independent senators to the right.

The Dáil generally sits between January and July, and from October to December. In recent years it has met on average for a little under one hundred days per calendar year, which represents a gradual increase from the historic pattern. Its usual sitting days are Tuesdays, Wednesdays, and Thursdays. Friday sittings are unpopular with many members, who argue that they hamper constituency activities, but they are becoming more common. There is a rhetorical consensus among the political parties that the Dáil should meet more frequently and that it should discharge its business more efficiently.

The Seanad's sittings are largely determined by the timing and volume of draft legislation sent from the Dáil. In recent years it has met on average for about seventy days per year. It may sit on any weekday other than Monday.

Proceedings may be conducted in either the Irish or the English language, or in both. The proceedings are recorded by note takers and published. Members' statements are privileged; that is, members have complete legal immunity for anything said or written in the course of parliamentary proceedings.

Voting procedures are as laid down in standing orders. In the first instance members vote orally through the medium of the Irish language, replying *tá* (yes) or *níl* (no) to questions put by the chair. Any member may then call for a division, whereupon tellers will be appointed. Each member's vote is then recorded and published in the official record.

Since its foundation the state has faced an armed threat to its legitimacy from militant republicanism. Its response has routinely included draconian legislation conferring upon the police wide powers of arrest and detention, allowing the internment of suspects without trial, and providing for special nonjury courts to try cases of alleged offenses against the state. To legalize such provisions the state set aside normal constitutional protections, as permitted in the 1922 and 1937 constitutions. Following the ceasefire in Northern Ireland in the autumn of 1994, the government dispensed with some of its formidable battery of antiterrorist laws.

PARTIES AND ELECTIONS

The constitution provides that elections for the Dáil must be held at least once every seven years, whereas the electoral law lays down a five-year limit. Every citizen who has reached the age of eighteen years and is not disqualified by law (for example, those serving a prison sentence) is eligible to vote. So, too, are British citizens resident in the state, under a reciprocal arrangement. The constitution stipulates that elections must be conducted by secret ballot of those eligible to vote.

Any citizen of Ireland twenty-one years or older and eligible to vote may seek election. Candidates may nominate themselves or seek nomination from a voter in the constituency they wish to represent. They may indicate a party allegiance or declare themselves independent.

There are presently 166 seats in the Dáil, distributed among forty-one geographic electoral districts, or constituencies, as follows: thirteen have three seats, thirteen have four seats, and fifteen have five seats. Using a variant of proportional representation, each voter casts a single "transferable" ballot on which he or she ranks the candidates according to preference. When the ballots are tallied, votes may be transferred from candidates who do not need them (for example, because they already have enough votes to be elected or because they have no chance of being elected) to another who might benefit from the transferred vote.

There must be one member for not less than twenty thousand and not more than thirty thousand of the population. The Oireachtas must revise constituencies at least every twelve years to take account of changes and shifts in population. This has become a politically sensitive matter in recent decades because of a general drift of population from countryside to towns and cities and from the west to the east of Ireland. Since 1974 the detailed work of such revisions has been entrusted to an independent boundary commission headed by a high court judge, but the Oireachtas is under no obligation to accept that body's recommendations.

The Irish electoral system of proportional representation with a single transferable vote and multiseat constituencies was imposed at British insistence. It was expected to produce a myriad of small parties and consequently a strong legislature and a weak executive that would have to negotiate and compromise to get bills through. Nothing could be further from the case: Although the electoral system has indeed always provided a number of small parties, it also has sustained two large ones, Fianna Fail and Fine Gael. Fianna Fail governed on its own for forty-two of the sixty-two years after it first won office in 1932, and between 1989 and November 1994 it governed in coalition with other parties. Following the elections of June 1997, Fianna Fail held seventy-seven seats in the Dáil, and Fine Gael held fifty-four. The other parties represented were Labour (seventeen seats), Progressive Democrats (four), Democratic Left (four), the Green Alliance (two), and Sinn Fein (one).

There has been a considerable fragmentation of electoral support for the main parties during the last two decades. This is reflected in the fact that since 1987 no single party has won an overall majority of Dáil seats. Furthermore, two new small parties at different points on the political spectrum have succeeded in generating significant electoral support in some areas. The Progressive Democrats are liberal on social issues and conservative on economic issues. The

Democratic Left is an avowedly left-wing party that was formed following a breakaway from a hard-left socialist group.

Party leaders generally accept the unlikelihood of a single party winning an overall majority again under the present electoral system. The pattern of coalition governments seen since 1989 is likely to persist.

Women are grievously underrepresented in Irish politics in general, and in the Dáil, although there have been gradual increases in the numbers of women seeking election (from 6.6 percent in 1977 to 18.5 percent in 1992), and in the numbers successful (from 4.1 percent in 1977 to 12 percent in 1992). In June 1997, after the elections, women held 12.0 percent of Dáil seats.

The number of Seanad seats is fixed at sixty under the constitution. General elections to the Seanad must take place not later than ninety days following a dissolution of the Dáil. Eleven seats are filled on the nomination of the prime minister, a provision clearly intended to guarantee the government a working majority in the upper house. The remaining forty-nine seats are filled by election. The electorate is limited by the constitution, as described below. Election to the Seanad is by secret mail ballot, using proportional representation with a single transferable vote. In June 1997 women held 13.3 percent of Seanad seats.

Forty-three of the forty-nine elected senators are elected from five slates, or panels, of candidates: the administrative panel, the agricultural panel, the cultural and educational panel, the industrial and commercial panel and the labor panel. To compete for election on a panel, a candidate must be nominated either by one of several recognized nominating bodies or institutions or by four members of the Oireachtas.

Despite its vocational ethos and structure, which are rooted in the constitution, the Seanad's electoral process reflects wider electoral realities: the entire electorate for the forty-three panel seats are, after all, themselves elected politicians, members of county councils and county boroughs, outgoing members of the Seanad, and incoming members of the Dáil.

The remaining six seats filled by election are less the prisoners of national party politics. They are equally split between two university constituencies: the National University of Ireland and the University of Dublin. Graduates vote in their respective university constituencies. These arrangements are anomalous in modern circumstances, as they take no account of the existence of two other independent universities created in 1989 or of other educational institutions that confer degrees approved by the National Council for Educational Awards.

The Dáil and Seanad have a maximum life under the law of five years. Since 1922, general elections have been held on average every three years.

THE LEGISLATIVE PROCESS

The Irish legislative process follows that of the British Parliament very closely. Successive governments have exercised an extraordinary monopoly on legislation since the foundation of the state, almost always bringing their proposals to the Oireachtas fully formed and completed to the last detail, and have been markedly unwilling to accept any changes, however minor or innocuous, put forward by members of either house. In recent years, however, a combination of government insecurity, procedural reform, and some growth in members' expertise has produced a gradual change, with ministers somewhat more disposed to accept points and suggestions made during debate.

A bill goes through five stages, or readings, in the house in which it is introduced. It is then passed to the other house for consideration; there it is exempt from the first stage. The key stages are the second, where the broad principles of the measure are discussed, and the third or committee stage, where its provisions are examined and voted on section by section. Bills other than money bills, which must originate in the Dáil, can be initiated in either house. Amendments to bills may be introduced at the second, third, and fourth stages in either house. Each house may accept or reject amendments inserted into a bill by the other, but in the event of disagreement the Dáil prevails. Although the Seanad has no blocking power, it can delay general legislation for up to ninety days, and money bills for up to twenty-one days.

The Dáil's annual legislative output has tended to decline somewhat as the number of sitting days has increased in recent decades. In the five years from 1991 to 1996 an average of thirty-four bills became law each year. The increased use of legislative committees since the spring of 1993 may result in the speedier passage of a greater volume of laws.

The constitution provides that quorums for each house should be fixed in their standing orders. Although the Oireachtas normally meets in public session, in cases of special emergency it can conduct business in private if two-thirds of members present agree. Party discipline has always ensured that sufficient members are on call within the precincts of the Oireachtas, if seldom visible in the chamber, at times when their votes may be needed. On the other hand, committees of the Oireachtas often have had difficulty securing a quorum to begin business.

Private bills may be initiated in either house by members of the legislature who are not members of the government or ministers of state. Only ten such bills have become law since the present constitution was enacted in 1937. The device of a private bill can, however, be very useful in attracting publicity for an issue or in obliging the government to take action to address the problem highlighted.

Historically, the Oireachtas has made very little use of committees other than for certain procedural and housekeeping functions. Committees lapsed with each dissolution and might or might not be constituted afresh in a new Oireachtas. Almost all draft legislation that reached the third stage was dealt with by the whole house sitting in committee, rather than by a smaller group with more specialized interests and knowledge. The one committee with significant power, authority, and administrative support was the Committee of Public Accounts. Served by the comptroller and auditor general and his or her department, the committee was a byword for ineffectiveness because most members put little sustained effort into its work.

The last two decades have seen considerable changes. In 1978 opposition pressure led to the establishment of a joint committee to review the performance of state-owned commercial enterprises. Aided by a capable secretariat and advisers, it proved very useful in highlighting the strategic and operational dilemmas facing many state-owned firms.

Between 1983 and 1987 the Fitzgerald coalition sponsored a number of new committees. Experience was to show that too many were created, with rather incoherent charges that covered some but by no means all policy areas. For example, there was a committee on overseas development cooperation, but none on foreign affairs or on Northern Ireland, and there was one on small businesses but none on agriculture, the country's largest and most politically sensitive industry. Although these committees did give members greater opportunities to study some policy issues and facilitated interest-group submissions to the Oireachtas on policy issues, they did not result either in a significant strengthening of parliamentary scrutiny of the executive or in greater input from the Oireachtas into legislation. The majority of the new committees were not reconstituted after the 1987 general election.

Significant changes have been made to the Oireachtas's committee system since April 1993. Most important, committees on foreign affairs, enterprise and economic strategy, social affairs, finance and general affairs, and legislation and security are now charged with reviewing the entire range of government activity and departments. They also normally deal with the committee stage of bills in their specialist areas, an arrangement that has already facilitated far more give and take between ministers and Oireachtas than was usual under the old practice. The new committees also inquire into policy issues and routinely hear evidence and submissions from outside bodies and individuals. Although the current initiative has encountered some problems with attendance and scheduling—most members of the Oireachtas are on more than one committee—it appears to mark an important change in how the Oireachtas works, facilitating the build-up of expertise and specialization among members and increasing parliamentary influence in the legislative process.

Committees may take evidence and may deliberate in public or in private. In recent years committees have actively sought submissions on policy issues from the general public as well as from recognized interest groups through advertisements in the national media. Nevertheless, committees of the Oireachtas remain hamstrung by doubts about their powers to compel witnesses to attend and to give evidence.

The constitution requires the government to lay before the Dáil estimates of receipts and expenditures for each financial year. In addition, the government now publishes other financial data in the days leading up to the annual budget speech of the minister for finance in late January. In that speech, the minister sets out the means by which the government intends to meet the financial obligations implied in the estimates. The budget is given effect through the provisions of the Finance Act, while the estimates are adopted through the passage of an appropriation act for each of the fifty or so votes into which they are divided.

The procedures for debating government spending have long been criticized as archaic and artificial. For example, all the estimates must be passed by July, and, because of a shortage of time, many have to be passed without any prior discussion. Discussion of the estimates for a particular vote, if one takes place at all, may occur many months after the money has been committed. Successive governments since the early 1980s have acknowledged that the existing system is unsatisfactory, but undertakings to make radical improvements have not yet been honored. There has been a marked increase, however, in the breadth and quality of financial data published.

RELATIONS WITH THE EXECUTIVE

Since 1922 Irish governments have dominated the legislature to a degree unusual even in other Westminster systems. As a party accustomed to government, Fianna Fail has never shown much enthusiasm for strengthening the legislature in relation to the executive. Other parties, in opposition most of the time and handicapped by outmoded parliamentary procedures, have naturally taken the contrary view. Pressure for reform, including a more effective committee system and better scrutiny of the machinery of state, has come mainly from them.

The Dáil has always had one key instrument of accountability—an independent comptroller and auditor general prescribed by the constitution—but until recently few paid any attention to the auditor's findings. The state had existed for forty-six years before an audit was discussed in either chamber. In 1993, however, after lengthy negotiations, powers of audit were considerably expanded and modernized under new legislation.

In 1980, under pressure from the opposition, a Fianna Fail government introduced an Ombudsman Act, but it was only after an anti–Fianna Fail coalition came into office in 1983 that an ombudsman was actually appointed to investigate and report to the Oireachtas on citizens' grievances against the administrative system. The office is now firmly rooted and has received considerable support from members of the Oireachtas, despite the fact that it arguably threatens to replace much of the individual constituent casework that occupies so much of the time of elected politicians.

The use of parliamentary questions to ministers, in a Westminster system one of the most telling weapons in a member's armory, has grown considerably in the last decade. Although procedures were changed in the mid-1980s to enable the asking of "priority questions" on matters of current public interest, opposition deputies continue to complain about constraints in the system. Critics of the Oireachtas point out that the vast majority of questions asked relate to the real or alleged difficulties of individual constituents in getting their due from the administrative system, not to substantive issues of policy and governance. On the other hand, questions provide a useful spot check on the myriad activities of the civil service, and they also cause an occasional explosion. The coalition government of Albert Reynolds collapsed in November 1994 essentially because ministers had given misleading and incomplete answers to parliamentary questions put to them over the preceding weeks about delays in bringing extradition proceedings against a pedophile priest.

The government has no power to veto legislation passed by the Oireachtas. In practice, however, it has always had a virtual monopoly on legislation of every kind, and it would be difficult to envisage circumstances in which a government could stay in office if a measure to which it was strongly opposed became law. As noted above, the president may, after consulting the Council of State, refer a bill to the Supreme Court for a judgment as to its constitutionality before signing it into law. This important presidential power has been exercised fewer than ten times in the lifetime of the constitution. If the court finds a bill to be constitutional, it cannot revisit its own judgment in the light of experience or of changing values.

LEADERSHIP, PROCEDURE, AND PRIVILEGE

The speaker of the Dáil chairs its proceedings, controls the administration of its affairs, and exercises supervisory and disciplinary powers over its members. Although chosen from sitting members, and therefore a political partisan by background, the speaker must act with the utmost impartiality once in the chair. When the Dáil is dissolved, the outgoing incumbent is automatically reelected if he or she wishes to continue in office.

The functions of the speaker are broadly analogous to those of the speaker of the British House of Commons. The speaker may neither make a deliberative speech nor vote, except to break a tie. Convention dictates that on an issue of confidence he or she will vote in favor of the government to maintain the status quo, but that on other matters he or she will vote in such a way as to allow the house to revisit the issue under dispute. The speaker is assisted by a deputy, also elected by the Dáil. Analogous powers and conventions apply in the Seanad.

The pattern of Irish electoral politics has ensured the operation of relatively powerful parliamentary parties in the Oireachtas. Discipline, the responsibility of the party whips, is tightest within the two largest parties, Fianna Fail and Fine Gael. Belonging to a parliamentary party brings considerable benefits, because the business of the Dáil and Seanad is largely dictated by agreements between the party whips on procedural matters. Members have the opportunity to impress their views on colleagues and thereby to help set party policy. In addition, because they attract some state funding in proportion to their numerical strength, parliamentary parties can provide some policy-research resources for members as well as additional administrative support. What members give up in agreeing to toe the party line is the right to take each issue on its merits. Independent members, and political parties with fewer than seven members in the Dáil or five in the Seanad, are not recognized as parliamentary groups for procedural purposes under existing standing orders. Affected members complain that they lose out in terms of state funding, parliamentary time, nominations to committees, and other matters because they are excluded from the interparty negotiation process.

Party discipline is enforced by a range of sanctions, of which expulsion from the parliamentary party is the most extreme. In practice, expulsion has tended to be of short duration: either the recalcitrant member shows some signs of penitence and is readmitted to the fold, or he or she is left to fight the next election without party support and is therefore unlikely to hold on to the seat.

In addition to acting as police officer of the parliamentary majority, the government chief whip attends cabinet meetings but is not a member of the cabinet.

Relations between Dáil and Seanad have been very good since the present constitution was adopted in 1937. By contrast, in 1936 de Valera's government actually dissolved the Seanad because of what it saw as a pattern of deliberate obstruction of the Dáil's will. The present constitution was drafted so as to ensure that the redrawn Seanad would not operate in the same manner.

The Dáil is unequivocally the dominant house of the Oireachtas, to a greater degree even than implied in the constitution, and the Seanad is its procedural prisoner. For example, only two senators have ever been appointed as ministers. The likelihood of the Seanad exercising its powers of legislative delay is hedged in by other arrangements and circumstances, the most important of which are the reality that the government will almost certainly have a built-in majority and the tendency of governments to manipulate the flow of legislation so as to leave the Seanad underemployed for much of the year before being overwhelmed by a rush of bills toward the close of a parliamentary session.

The Seanad has, however, commanded respect in Irish parliamentary politics for a number of reasons. First, it is generally held that the quality of debate there is higher than in the Dáil. Second, in the last quarter century it has been an important outlet for the discussion of social and moral issues that the Dáil has avoided for fear of political embarrassment. Obvious examples are contraception, divorce, and gay rights. In the last decade coalition governments have shown a slightly greater willingness to introduce noncontroversial legislation in the Seanad. Furthermore, the gradual increase in the activities of Oireachtas committees has enabled some senators to participate in investigative and deliberative work.

The televising of its relatively dignified, if sedate, proceedings has, arguably, also increased the Seanad's public standing. The major power, however, continues to lie in the Dáil.

The nature and extent of parliamentary privileges and immunities under the Irish constitution are somewhat uncertain, as developments since 1970 have shown. This is so with regard both to members and to the rights of the two houses themselves. The uncertainties arise from potentially conflicting provisions of the constitution, notably those dealing with the legislature and those protecting the individual.

Under the constitution, members enjoy an untrammeled right of free speech within the Oireachtas and are answerable only to the house itself "in respect of any utterance in either House." This privilege has been extended by legislation to include what members say during committee proceedings. The Dáil and Seanad each have a committee on procedures and privileges, headed by the leader of each body. This is a potentially unsatisfactory arrangement. Some years ago the Seanad committee found against a senator whose alleged offense had been to make accusations against the leader of the Seanad. The senator claimed that this was an elementary breach of his constitutional rights and sought high court intervention. The penalty was then withdrawn and an apology issued to the senator by the chair, and the court action did not proceed. The episode suggested that the Oireachtas's right to discipline its own members was subject to review by the courts in the light of other provisions of the constitution.

The 1970 "arms crisis" revealed considerable limitations in the Oireachtas's powers. An act to extend parliamentary privilege to members of and persons appearing before an investigative Dáil committee and to give the committee the power to subpoena witnesses was found to be unconstitutional. The finding has restricted the Oireachtas's investigative capacity ever since. After the "Whelehan affair," which brought down the Reynolds government in November 1994, an act was passed to extend parliamentary immunity to witnesses and to the proceedings of an Oireachtas committee. Doubts remain about its constitutionality. Similar problems may arise if, as long promised, the Oireachtas grants committees the power to compel witnesses to appear before them and to give evidence. A bill dealing with these matters was introduced in 1995 but has not yet become law.

Members are "privileged from arrest" while in or traveling to or from the Oireachtas "except in case of treason . . . felony or breach of the peace." There is, however, nothing to prevent their prosecution for any offense. In a controversial case in 1990, a senator facing a charge of driving while drunk reportedly threatened to invoke his parliamentary immunity if the charge were not withdrawn, on the grounds that he had been on his way to the Oireachtas (in the early hours of the morning). Because the state withdrew the charges, the senator's putative claim was not tested in the courts.

The constitution does not provide any mechanism for the recall or expulsion of a member of the Oireachtas. Members of the Oireachtas may resign at any time. It is a source of recurrent irritation that once a Dáil seat has been vacated through resignation or death the constitution sets no deadline for the holding of an election to fill it.

Parliamentary pay and perquisites remain sensitive matters in Irish politics despite reforms in the last decade aimed at providing an impartial system for setting rates of pay and at rationalizing the tax-exempt benefits and entitlements of members. In 1996 the basic annual salary of a member was 33,900 Irish pounds (approximately $55,600); that of a senator was 21,500 pounds ($35,260). Members are allowed unlimited use of telephones in the Oireachtas, as well as generous mailing privileges. Since 1981 each deputy has been allowed to employ one full-time secretary or administrative assistant at state expense. A member can claim a maximum allowance of 5,195 pounds ($8,520) toward the cost of establishing a constituency office if the member's secretary is based there. The member can claim telephone costs of up to 2,000 pounds ($3,280) per year for constituency business. Members receive allowances for travel to and from the Oireachtas from their homes, and those outside easy traveling distance also receive fixed subsistence allowances. The chairs of several committees receive taxable allowances, as do the leaders of both houses and their deputies. All such charges are met from the annual appropriation for the houses of the Oireachtas. Members of the cabinet are paid additional salaries from departmental funds. Former members are entitled to a pension for their parliamentary service based on their years of service.

The library and research facilities available to members of the Oireachtas have long been recognized as inadequate. The library has suffered decades of underinvestment. In recent years demands on the library have grown considerably, as members and their assistants devote more time to research. A new library is planned. The use of dedicated research assistants is a very recent development for members of the Oireachtas, reflecting a shift in parliamentary culture away from the government-versus-opposition paradigm that has characterized parliamentary life for many decades, toward a somewhat more consensual, participatory pattern of law making. Although members of the Oireachtas do not receive any allowance or staff allocation explicitly for research purposes, members of the larger parties may receive some research support from their organizations. An established intern system places students from several Irish and American universities with members and senators as administrative and research assistants.

As the focus of national political life, the Oireachtas is the object of continual media attention. Journalists are accorded privileged access to both houses. Discovery of the improper tapping of two journalists' telephones in 1982 led eventually to the resignation of Prime Minister Charles Haughey a decade later. The crisis that brought down the Reynolds government in November 1994 was fueled by an extraordinary succession of press revelations about the actions and inactions of several ministers in a case involving the extradition of a pedophile priest to Northern Ireland and the appointment of the legal officer responsible for extradition, the attorney general, to the presidency of the high court.

Radio broadcasts of Oireachtas proceedings began in 1981, and television broadcasting in 1991. Live broadcasts have been made on important ceremonial occasions such as the annual budget speech and the election of a prime minister. Broadcast coverage of Oireachtas committees is an important development as it brings the committees into the public eye and thus provides a greater incentive to members to participate in their work.

For decades the Oireachtas relied entirely on the honor and probity of its members to ensure high ethical standards in public life. In recent years public and parliamentary unease about the lack of a clear ethical framework has forced the major parties to respond. In 1992 the incoming prime minister, Albert Reynolds, took the unprecedented step of making a public declaration of his personal assets. A subsequent government headed by John Bruton sponsored the 1995 Ethics in Public Office Act, under which politicians and certain other public office holders must register their personal interests. Ironically, the Bruton government itself endured controversy about ministerial behavior that resulted in unprecedented resignations. One junior minister had to resign in 1995 for prematurely disclosing budget details, and in 1996 two members of the cabinet were obliged to resign after evidence emerged of potential conflicts of interest and other possible irregularities. These embarrassments prompted the Bruton government to announce its intention in December 1996 to introduce legislation restricting the making of private contributions to parties and individual politicians and instead providing state funding for parties in proportion to their general election performance.

Eunan O'Halpin

BIBLIOGRAPHY

Chubb, Basil. *The Government and Politics of Ireland*. 3d ed. London: Longman, 1992.

———. *The Politics of the Irish Constitution*. Dublin: Institute of Public Administration, 1991.

Coakley, John, and Michael Gallagher, eds. *Politics in the Republic of Ireland*. 2d ed. Dublin: PSAI Press, 1993.

Farrell, Brian, ed. *The Creation of Dáil Éireann*. Dublin: Blackwater Press, 1994.

Lee, J. J. *Ireland 1912–1985: Politics and Society*. Cambridge: Cambridge University Press, 1989.

Morgan, David Gwynn. *Constitutional Law of Ireland*. 2d ed. Dublin: Round Hall Press, 1990.

ISRAEL

OFFICIAL NAME: State of Israel (Medinat Yisra'el)
CAPITAL: Jerusalem (official); Tel Aviv (in diplomatic use)
POPULATION: 5,422,000 (1996 est.)
DATE OF INDEPENDENCE: Declared May 14, 1948 (from League of Nations mandate under British administration)
DATE OF CURRENT CONSTITUTION: Unwritten
FORM OF GOVERNMENT: Parliamentary democracy
LANGUAGES: Hebrew (official), Arabic, English
MONETARY UNIT: New shekel
FISCAL YEAR: Calendar year
LEGISLATURE: Assembly (Knesset)
NUMBER OF CHAMBERS: One
NUMBER OF MEMBERS: 120
PERCENTAGE OF WOMEN: 7.5
TERM OF LEGISLATURE: Four years
MOST RECENT LEGISLATIVE ELECTION: May 29, 1996
MINIMUM AGE FOR VOTING: 18
MINIMUM AGE FOR MEMBERSHIP: 21
SUFFRAGE: Universal and direct
VOTING: Optional
ADDRESS: Knesset, 91950 Jerusalem
TELEPHONE: (972 2) 75 33 33
FAX: (972 2) 61 92 27

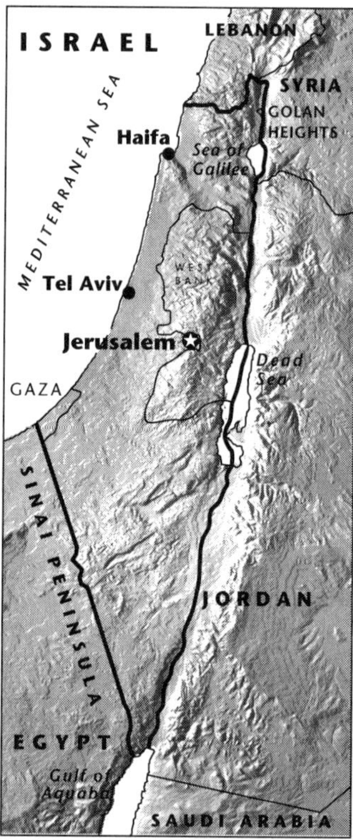

The State of Israel is a parliamentary republic at the eastern end of the Mediterranean Sea. Its government comprises a president, whose role is primarily nonpolitical and ceremonial; a prime minister and cabinet; a unicameral legislature, the Knesset; and a judicial system headed by a Supreme Court.

HISTORICAL BACKGROUND

Although Israel declared independence on May 14, 1948, its modern history begins in 1897 with the Zionist movement begun by Theodor Herzl in Basel, Switzerland. Israel's basic ideology, many of its political institutions and parties, and the people who established it came from the Zionist movement, which had as its goal creation of a Jewish homeland in Palestine.

Israel's history since its 1948 war of independence has been tumultuous. Full-scale wars in 1956 (the Sinai War), 1967 (the Six-Day War), and 1973 (the Yom Kippur War), and significant military action from 1968 to 1970 (the War of Attrition), in 1983 (Operation Peace for Galilee in Lebanon), and in 1991 (the Gulf War) have kept the concept of physical security high on its citizens' agenda. Politically and economically, Israel has struggled in the international community to be accepted, being admitted to the United Nations in 1949, becoming an associate member of the European Common Market in 1975, and signing a free trade agreement with the United States in 1985.

During these years the concept of peace has been elusive, although in recent years true progress has been made. In 1978 the Camp David accords were signed, leading to a peace treaty with Egypt the next year. Peace treaties with the Palestine Liberation Organization and the Hashemite Kingdom of Jordan were signed in 1994. The peace process has continued, in fits and starts, since that time.

CONSTITUTIONAL PROVISIONS

The Israeli constitutional system is an amalgam of several models. It has been characterized as following the British Westminster model of government, with a head of state chosen independently of the legislature, a prime minister, votes of confidence, and so on. But there are aspects of Israeli constitutionalism—such as a commitment to have a written constitution, for example—that are clearly non-Westminster. Students have argued that there are features of many constitutional systems to be found in the Israeli order, including the American, Russian, German, and French, to name but a few.

In 1948 the Provisional Council of Government decided against writing a constitution for the newly formed state of

Israel in part because of the imminence of war and in part because of a lack of a clear consensus on several issues central to the character of the state (the role of religion in the state, for example). In place of a single document, a system emerged in which a constitution would be written, chapter by chapter, over the years. Thus far, twelve chapters have been written, each of which is called a basic law. The basic laws cover the Knesset (1958); Israel lands (1960); the president (1964); the government (1968); the economy (1975); defense forces (1976); Jerusalem (1980); the judiciary (1984); the state comptroller (1988); direct election of the prime minister, freedom of occupation, and human dignity and freedom (all in 1992).

In addition to the basic laws, other pieces of legislation have appeared over the years as what might be called paraconstitutional doctrines: laws that are not designated as basic laws but are perceived by many to be equally broad and fundamental in scope. Included among these major statutes are the Law of Return (1950); the Equal Rights for Women Law (1951); the National Law (1952), regulating among other things the naturalization of non-Jews; the Judges Law (1953); the Courts Law (1969); and the Contracts Law (1970). Since judicial review has already been established in Israel, the Israeli constitution will undoubtedly continue to be interpreted as being a mixture of basic laws, major statutes, and judicial interpretation of law rather than solely a product of the Knesset.

The first of the basic laws, which dealt with the Knesset, described the relationship among the various branches of the government. The Knesset elects the head of state, the president, for a five-year term. The president is responsible to the Knesset and can be removed from office for misconduct or incapacity. Election and removal of a president require special majorities in the Knesset. One of the duties of the president is to sign legislation—a duty that cannot be refused. That is, the president has no veto power, although the situation has never arisen in which a president has refused to sign an act of the Knesset. Presumably this would precipitate a major constitutional crisis since the basic law on the Knesset is ambiguous in this matter.

Just as the head of state is chosen by the Knesset, so too does the Knesset vote to approve the government or governing coalition formed by the directly elected head of government, the prime minister. The president cannot dissolve the government; the Knesset may do so if it so wishes. With the leader of the government also the leader of the Knesset, there is a lack of separation of powers between the executive and legislative branches of government.

This practice implies the principle of legal continuity of government practiced in Israel: A government is always in existence. One Knesset does not dissolve, nor does a government fall, until its successor has been installed. If a government fails to win a vote of confidence, it stays in power as an interim government until some other coalition, or perhaps the same one, can show that it has the necessary support to maintain a majority in the Knesset. If no new coalition can be formed with a majority supporting it, new elections may be ordered, but the interim government remains until the new government is installed.

The cabinet draws its power directly from the Knesset. Several links exist between the Knesset and the cabinet, all of which help to blur the separation of powers between the executive and legislative branches of government. First, the new government must secure a vote of confidence before assuming office. Secondly, the government is collectively responsible to the Knesset. Finally, the Knesset may at any time move a vote of no confidence in the government.

THE ELECTORAL SYSTEM

The electoral system of any country is important in terms of both its role in selecting political leaders and its influence on the nature and style of political discussion and activity. In Israel the prevailing electoral system promotes such diverse and even contradictory phenomena as a splintering of established political parties, strict party discipline, and close control of individual legislators within party organizations.

Indeed, the nature of the Israeli electoral system is often credited with the existence of so many political parties. There are few institutional incentives for factionalized parties to remain together and many for groups with a moderate amount of support to break away from parent political organizations and run for office under their own banners.

Israeli elections must be held at least every four years. Although the maximum term of any single elected Knesset is four years, the Knesset may vote to dissolve itself before its term expires and call for new elections. Unlike in other parliamentary systems, the Knesset alone, not the head of state, has the power to dissolve the body before the expiration of its legislated term of office. On a number of occasions in Israeli history the term of a Knesset has been less than four years; twice (1949–1951 and 1959–1961) it was less than three years. In recent years, however, the general pattern has been to approach the end of the four-year term before calling for new elections.

The basic law on the Knesset says that "the Knesset shall

be elected in general, national, direct, equal, secret, and proportional elections." This means, in practice, that all citizens eighteen years of age or older can vote. The electoral system employs a single-ballot, national-constituency, proportional-representation electoral framework. The whole country is considered a single electoral district, and each voter casts his or her vote for the party whose platform and candidates he or she most prefers. The percentage of votes received by each party in the national election determines the percentage of seats it will receive in the Knesset.

Parties receiving at least 1.5 percent of the vote (1 percent until the 1992 elections) are entitled to representation. Parties receiving less than this threshold receive no Knesset representation. Total votes in the election (minus the votes going to parties that receive less than the 1 percent threshold) are divided by 120, the total seats in the Knesset, thereby establishing a key.

Seats remaining in the Knesset after the initial assignment are distributed among parties with high numbers of surplus votes. The process used in Israel since 1973 is the d'Hondt system, named after the Belgian who devised it. For many years seats were awarded based on the size of the remainders. This system, in fact, sometimes permitted parties that had won not even a single seat to win a surplus seat because they had higher remainders (in this case, a remainder after no seats and before one seat) than the more established parties (perhaps with more votes than needed for thirty-two seats but not enough votes for thirty-three seats).

Significant modifications to the Israeli electoral system drafted before the 1996 elections took effect with that election. Nomination and election of Knesset members remained unchanged, but a complex new primary structure added substantial uncertainty to the electoral process. Other modifications established direct election of the prime minister, something totally alien to the Westminster model of government.

In the new electoral system, political parties nominate candidates for prime minister in addition to their lists of candidates for the Knesset. The electorate votes directly for a prime minister while voting proportionally for Knesset members. A majority of the votes is required for victory, and the law provides for runoffs if needed. Once a prime minister has been elected, he or she is still required to assemble a cabinet that the newly elected Knesset will support. This means political coalitions will still be needed in the Knesset. The new electoral system makes it possible that the people could elect a prime minister from one party but elect a Knesset in which it would be very difficult for the party of the prime minister-elect to assemble a coalition.

CAMPAIGNS AND PARTY LISTS

During the preelection period, the amount and degree of campaigning intensifies dramatically. When the Knesset passes the act dissolving itself and calling for new elections, it sets the duration of the campaign. There is no legally mandated period, although campaigns generally last eight to ten weeks. Election expenses of Israel's political parties through the 1960s had been among the world's highest. Reform in 1969 led to limits on overall campaign expenses and increased government oversight of party spending during the election period. Since 1973 Israeli parties have been prohibited from receiving corporate contributions. Parties are given free time on television and radio for campaigning, and those that already control seats in the Knesset are given substantial allowances for the electoral campaign based on the number of seats they control in the Knesset at the time.

The role of the media merits some discussion. During the last month of the campaign in 1988, each party list was allocated ten free minutes of television prime time six nights a week, and parties already represented in the Knesset received an additional four free minutes per seat they controlled in the previous Knesset. There is no doubt that the television campaign added an extra dimension to the race. The question is, was it positive or negative?

Lists of candidates for elections may be submitted either by a party that is already represented or by a group of 15,000 qualified voters. In 1948 a group of 250 qualified voters was needed. This requirement was raised to 750 in 1951, and it has steadily increased ever since. Individuals whose names are on party lists must write to the Central Elections Committee and accept their nominations. To submit lists of candidates to the voters, new parties must deposit a sum of money with the Central Elections Committee. If a new party wins at least one seat, its deposit is returned; if not, it forfeits a portion of the money. This requirement is designed to discourage truly unrealistic parties from campaigning, but it is clear from the number that compete in Knesset elections that this rule does not stop new parties from forming.

Many of the serious parties submit lists with 120 names on them, one for each possible seat in the Knesset, even though they know that none will win 100 percent of the vote. Smaller parties, and the unrealistic parties, often submit lists with fewer names, realizing that there is no point in their putting forward 120.

There is no official law regulating how parties may assemble their lists of candidates. Some procedures are relatively complex. For example, in the 1992 election the Labor Party elected its head by using a primary system; twenty-two candidates were selected in general primaries, and twenty-two in regional primaries. The Likud Party list was assembled in two parts: in the first round, fifty names were selected by plurality voting; another round of voting determined the position of the first twenty-eight of those names, and positions twenty-nine through fifty were placed according to the votes received in the first vote.

The official assignment of seats in the Knesset is determined purely by position on a party list. If a party wins 25 percent of the national vote and is allotted thirty seats in the Knesset on the basis of that result (25 percent multiplied by 120 seats equals 30 seats), the seats are awarded to the first thirty names on the party list. If a member of Knesset dies during the term, or if a member resigns for some reason, the seat is passed to the next person on the list. The importance of rank order for an individual candidate on the party electoral list immediately becomes clear. Since most parties will put a great number of names on their lists that have no realistic chance of being elected, it is of crucial importance to a serious candidate that he or she be placed in a high position on the party list.

The Knesset is the ultimate arbiter of election results. The Knesset Committee has jurisdiction over election appeals, election irregularities, and any issue related to elections.

LEGISLATION

In addition to debate and discussion, probably the most important function of legislatures is that of passing laws. The legislative process in the Knesset follows the standard parliamentary model fairly closely; only a brief discussion of the process is needed here. An initial distinction must be made between government bills and private members' bills (the latter are so named because they are introduced by private members, not members of the government). Government bills are introduced by members of the cabinet. These bills are not all drafted by members of the cabinet, of course, but tend to be written somewhere in the ministries in the relatively vast governmental bureaucracy. These bills are passed up through the ministry involved eventually to reach the director general, the ministry's highest ranking civil servant. He or she would then pass the proposal along to the minister responsible for that department, who would then take the bill to the cabinet and, after receiving cabinet approval, would introduce the bill in the Knesset as a government bill.

Private members' bills are introduced by noncabinet members, whether they are members of parties belonging to the government coalition or members of opposition parties. Private members' bills are a small minority of the total number of bills the Knesset processes each year. This situation has changed somewhat over the years, but not as much as most legislators would like. Private members' bills still account for somewhat less than 9 percent of all legislation introduced and passed in the Knesset.

Private bills in the Knesset are apportioned to the parties by a key; each party is allowed to introduce approximately three private bills per seat it holds for each Knesset session. Quotas added up to nearly 2,000 bills and motions in recent years. This means that private members who want to introduce legislation must have their proposals screened by their parties or parliamentary bloc. If their party leaders do not give them permission, private members cannot introduce their own legislative proposals. After clearing, proposals still must go over several more legislative hurdles than government bills do before they become law.

The bulk of the Knesset's output comes from government-sponsored legislation. After being approved by the cabinet, government bills are submitted in the Knesset and are entered as items for the agenda. The bills must be available for examination for at least forty-eight hours before discussion on them begins. As with many other procedural rules, the Knesset Committee may waive this forty-eight hour rule if it so wishes.

The first stage in the legislative process is called the first reading. The minister in charge of the bill begins with a summation of the contents of the bill and then proceeds with a line-by-line reading. After the minister has finished presenting the bill, debate begins. This first reading debate is usually a general one. When the vote comes at the end of the debate, government bills almost invariably are passed and sent to committee. Private members' bills rarely meet with the same results.

The bill is then sent to whichever committee has jurisdiction. If more than one committee is involved, the bill goes to the committees one after another, in a sequence determined by the speaker. The committee in question may deal with a bill for three months or three hours, depending on the importance of the bill, the committee's workload, and the willingness of the committee to cooperate with the government's manager of the legislation. The committee has the power to revise a bill, even to the extent of virtually rewriting it, if necessary. The government retains the power to recall a bill to the Knesset floor in the exact form in which it was sent to committee if it believes that the committee has significantly altered the bill from its intended direction.

At this stage the second reading takes place. This is the final major hurdle the bill must pass because bills that pass the second reading almost invariably pass the third reading. Another debate takes place at this point, but only members of the committee may participate; all other members are in attendance only to vote on the bill, section by section.

If no amendments to the committee report are adopted, the third reading follows immediately after the conclusion of the second. If there are amendments, the third reading is postponed for one week to allow members time to consider the amendment. Even if amendments have been proposed, however, if the government requests an immediate third reading, it takes place immediately after the second. Following the third reading, the bill is voted on as a whole. Since the Israeli parliamentary system is unicameral, bills passed by the Knesset go immediately to the president to be signed.

COMMITTEES

Chairmanships are apportioned much as are the deputy speakerships, with the major parties sharing control. Seats on committees are given to parties, not to individuals, and the parties assign their own members to the committee seats. For example, the Finance Committee might have nineteen members, representing only three large parties—Labor, Likud, and the National Religious Party—and these parties in turn would assign their own members to the Finance Committee. Here again, not only is there competition for positions between parties but within parties as well. Even though it might be decided that the Labor Alignment would receive five positions on the Finance Committee, for example, the way the various factions of the Labor party would divide up these five positions might remain in dispute.

Committees provide Knesset members with an opportunity to specialize in their areas of interest and to keep in touch with government ministers and high-ranking civil servants in a variety of areas. The committees also play a role in the legislative process, although this fluctuates with the willingness of the government to accept proposed legislative changes.

As a general rule, there are between twelve and twenty members on each of the ten permanent standing committees, which are appointed for the full term of a Knesset. In addition to the ten permanent standing committees, temporary committees are appointed from time to time as deemed necessary by the Knesset speaker and deputy speakers. Committees made up of members from more than one permanent standing committee are sometimes appointed when legislation crosses the jurisdictions of more than one permanent standing committee.

Committee meetings are usually closed to the press and public. Some committees are seen as more important than others in the legislative process. Committee members are divided over what the true role of the committee is, with many saying that its role depends on the legislation that is before it at a given time. Most members agree, however, that tight party discipline combined with a government majority on each committee and the government's insistence that its agenda be supported limits committee roles.

But some committees are effective nonetheless. The Finance and the Labor Committees have a great deal of authority to write laws in their own spheres of expertise. They are considered powerful and influential, and positions on these committees are highly sought. The Foreign Affairs and Security Committee has few powers, and it is involved mainly in oversight and debate, devoting little time to drafting legislation. But since foreign affairs and security are priorities, and since members of the Knesset who are on this committee are privy to more classified information than are, say, members of the Agriculture Committee, positions are in greater demand.

When a member bolts the party line in a committee or speaks out of turn too often, he or she may be limited to participation in the general assembly, having been either reassigned from one committee to another or, in more extreme cases, having been stripped of all committee memberships. In fact, members may have no committee memberships if their party leaders feel they do not deserve such positions.

THE BUDGET

Control over the budget is, of course, a legislature's ultimate source of influence over the government of the day, and this is true in the Knesset as much as in other parliamentary legislatures. The Knesset is guaranteed at least sixty days to examine the government's budget before the beginning of a new fiscal year, and in recent years even this has resulted in such pressure on the body that suggestions have been made for more time. The basic law on the state economy says that the government has the right to introduce an interim budget bill if it feels that the budget will not be adopted before the beginning of the fiscal year.

The procedure for approving the budget is similar to the general legislative process, including a first reading debate, substantial hearings by the Finance Committee, and detailed discussion and examination in the Knesset when the budget is reported out of the Finance Committee.

Supplemental budget bills are permitted if the government believes them to be necessary, and in the past—especially in times of runaway inflation—these became frequent and almost common. More recently, the finance minister has been authorized to update the budget quarterly, a procedure that involved notifying the Finance Committee about how well targets were being reached. It was not necessary to report to the full Knesset; only the Finance Committee needed to be consulted.

CABINET SUPREMACY AND COALITION GOVERNMENT

In Israel, *government* refers to the prime minister and his or her cabinet. The principle of cabinet supremacy is relatively easy to express in its basic form. Individual members of the Knesset are expected to follow the instructions of their party leaders. Because the leaders of the majority party or the majority coalition are invariably members of the cabinet, the legislature, which is technically in command in the governmental structure, actually takes its orders from the leaders of the executive branch, the cabinet.

Because of the many political parties active in the Israeli political system, no single party has ever had an outright majority in the Knesset. It has been necessary for political parties to form coalitions, and traditionally there has been less latitude for individual legislative behavior than might otherwise be the case. Party discipline—the practice of having members of Knesset vote together and support party policy—becomes the norm, and coalition lines are rigidly enforced.

The cabinet meets weekly—usually every Sunday—to discuss those issues that have found their way onto the national political agenda. The cabinet operates under the principle of collective responsibility: once a decision is reached, that decision must be supported by all members of the cabinet. An individual cabinet member's only alternative to supporting a cabinet decision is to resign.

The office of prime minister itself has not traditionally had the same relative weight as in Britain, for example, primarily because of the coalition nature of Israeli cabinets. On occasion the prime minister has made political suggestions to his or her cabinet colleagues that were voted down by a majority of members of the cabinet (with the prime minister voting in the minority), leaving the prime minister with only two choices: support the views of the majority of the cabinet or resign—something that would not happen in Britain.

The changes reflected in the 1996 election have dramatically affected the power of the Israeli prime minister—some say presidentializing it—and only time will tell what the effect will be on Israeli politics. But the prime minister's new power is unlikely to diminish in the near future.

LEADERSHIP POSITIONS AND PARTY VOTING

Although one classic study of Israeli politics referred to the position of the speaker as nonpartisan, in reality the position of speaker has often been a highly partisan one, and speakers in the past have been defeated in their bids for reelection because of their overly partisan behavior.

The office of deputy speaker is equally partisan, with the number of deputies to be chosen varying with party distributions in the Knesset. Deputy speakerships are distributed among the major parties when a new Knesset is organized. The speaker and the deputy speakers as a group are called the presidium, a very important body in internal organization and behavior. Government coalition parties always control a majority of the positions in the presidium.

Members of Knesset almost never vote against their parties; in this respect Israel is very much like other parliamentary systems. A member who feels very strongly against his or her party's position on a particular issue is most likely to go to the Knesset restaurant for a long cup of coffee in the middle of a roll call to miss the roll-call vote. This practice can sometimes be effective, although occasionally absence in itself can be a sufficient act of insubordination to warrant punishment. If the vote is close, the party leader will pull in reluctant members—sometimes literally—from the restaurant or elsewhere to make sure that they vote on a given issue in the party's direction. With a narrow coalition majority, a government could fall as a result of only one or two undisciplined members.

DEBATE, PARTY DISCIPLINE, AND LEGISLATIVE SCRUTINY

In the Knesset debates are either personal or party. Personal debate, which is the less significant, usually is employed either in nonpolitical matters that are not related to pending legislation or in matters of legislation on which opinions are not divided along party lines. Party debate, on the other hand, constitutes the bulk of Knesset debate and takes place with respect to votes of confidence or no confidence, foreign policy, the budget, and other matters that the government regards as significant (which means virtually any bill introduced by the government). When this kind of debate takes place, the Knesset Committee decides how much time to allow for the debate; it then divides that time by the total number of members of the Knesset, yielding a time-per-member figure.

Party leaders may choose to permit everyone in their party to speak for the allotted time per member, or they may choose to pool all the time into one long speech. In many cases the party leader will speak, or the entire party time will be given to a senior party member who is considered the spokesperson on the given issue. Here again, the individual is vulnerable to pressure from party leaders. Should an individual behave (vote, speak) in a way that the party leader considers not supportive of the party, that party member may not be allowed to introduce legislative proposals or speak out in debates.

The Knesset has elaborate organizational and behavioral rules in addition to the more formal structures of the presidium and committees. A period of time is set aside for individual legislators to ask questions of the government—the so-called question time. This serves both to bring new issues to the attention of the government and to remind the government that the public is watching its behavior.

Since the government controls the daily calendar and thereby controls what and for how long subjects will be debated in the Knesset, there is a procedure to bring subjects the government may not want to talk about to the agenda for public scrutiny. "Motions to add to the agenda" and "urgent motions to add to the agenda" give members a potentially significant role in deciding what issues are and are not discussed in the Israeli political world. For example, after demonstrations by Israeli Jewish settlers on the West Bank against the *intifadah,* the West Bank Arab uprising, some Arab Knesset members sought to introduce a motion to add to the agenda so that they could have the Knesset debate the government's policy on the settlers and the way it was handling the Arab demonstrators.

MEMBERS OF THE KNESSET

Citizens who are twenty-one and older are eligible to stand for election to the Knesset. In return for their legislative responsibilities, members are entitled to certain immunities, salaries, and perquisites. Members also perform the role of ombudsman for their constituents.

Members of the Knesset are afforded substantial degrees of parliamentary immunity to guarantee the freedom to perform their legislative duties without fear of possible governmental persecution. This immunity is discussed in the Immunity, Rights, and Duties of Members of the Knesset Law passed in 1951, which was based on an ordinance dating to 1949. The protection afforded is extremely broad. The law states that a member of the Knesset "shall not be held civilly or criminally responsible, and shall be immune from legal action," for most types of behavior, including votes cast and any oral or written expressions of opinion, either in or out of the Knesset, provided that such vote, opinion, or act "pertains to, or has as its purpose, the fulfillment of his mandate as a member of the Knesset." Phrases such as "or any other act performed in or out of the Knesset" and "mandate as a member of the Knesset" are so broad that they give individual members a great deal of latitude in terms of their behavior.

The act protects members beyond their legislative behavior. Only customs officials may search members or their property. While they hold office, members of the Knesset are absolutely immune from arrest, unless they are caught committing a crime or an act of treason. If a member is arrested, the authorities must notify the speaker immediately, and the member may not be detained for more than ten days unless the Knesset has revoked his or her immunity.

The Knesset Members Remuneration Law was originally passed in 1949, although it has been amended a number of times. All members of the Knesset receive the same salary, except the speaker, whose salary is the same as that of the prime minister. Members receive a wage slightly in excess of three times the average national wage. Members' salaries are pegged to a consumer price index; as prices have increased in recent years, the salaries of legislators have automatically increased as well. Members may not accept salaries from any other source.

In addition to their salaries, members receive free bus and rail travel, a substantial number of free telephone calls (in a recent study this number was cited as being in excess of two thousand local calls per month, or their equivalent in long-distance calls), free postage (except immediately before an election), and reimbursement for official expenses. Members of the Knesset who do not live near Jerusalem are allowed a housing and travel budget in addition to their other reimbursable expenses.

Members of the Knesset perform much ombudsman work, speaking or acting on behalf of the people to help resolve their problems. This is often the aspect of the job on which members spend most of their time and receive most of their glory (or scorn). Citizens write, telephone, or visit individual Knesset members and complain that they need help. Members contact the appropriate ministers, who are in the Knesset daily; the ministers in turn contact the directors general of the ministries involved, and sooner or later the problem is usually resolved.

THE KNESSET BUILDING

As with other national legislatures, the Knesset building has immunity. Under the Knesset Buildings Law of 1952, the building and grounds are under the control of the speaker and sergeant at arms. This law, too, is designed to free members from extralegislative pressures and distractions, such as demonstrations and other interruptions.

The Knesset office building has five floors, with committee meeting rooms, offices of committee chairs and their staffs, and the printing office on the first floor. The second floor is referred to as the government's floor and has offices for cabinet members away from their ministry offices, rooms for conferences, and extra rooms that are used by coalition parties when the Knesset is in all-night session. The third floor includes a public cafeteria, the members' restaurant, the library, a small post office, the offices of the speaker, and the Plenary Hall. The fourth floor includes the spectators' gallery and room for official banquets, plus space for the public relations office and press. The fifth floor is made up entirely of party offices, caucus rooms, and rooms for party members to use for rest breaks during all-night sessions.

A ceremonial hall, used for state receptions, was designed by the Russian-born artist Marc Chagall. Three tapestries, twelve floor mosaics, and a wall mosaic can be viewed by the public.

The Knesset library provides research support for individual legislators' needs. It has a limited staff, however, and most Knesset members would like an American-style legislative research service or a staff of trained individuals who can draft legislation.

JUDICIAL FUNCTIONS AND EMERGENCY POWERS

The principle of judicial review is well established in Israel. There is a clear separation of powers between judicial and legislative functions. The Israeli Supreme Court has consistently refused to rule in areas that are political in nature, regarding these questions as nonjusticiable.

The Knesset does have what can be called parajudicial powers over its own members. It can lift the parliamentary immunity that members of Knesset possess. And it can decide to remove the president of Israel and the state comptroller from office.

There is a constitutional provision for emergency regulations in the Law and Administration Ordinance of 1948. Under this law, ministers may be empowered to make emergency regulations at their discretion "for the purpose of national defense, public security, or the maintenance of supplies and essential services." A state of emergency was proclaimed by the Provisional State Council on May 19, 1948, early in the war of independence, and has yet to be rescinded. Because this state of emergency continues, emergency regulations have from time to time been promulgated by individual ministers. These regulations expire three months after declaration unless they have been extended before their expiration by statute of the Knesset.

Because of a general concern about the unlimited scope of potential emergency regulations, some bodies of law are immune from emergency regulations—the Knesset, the president, the government, and the Knesset Elections Law.

Gregory S. Mahler

BIBLIOGRAPHY

Arian, Asher. *Politics in Israel: The Second Generation.* Chatham, N.J.: Chatham House, 1985.

Bin-Nun, Ariel. "The Borders of Justiciability." *Israel Law Review* 5 (1980): 569–579.

Mahler, Gregory. "Coalition Formation in a Quasi-Parliamentary Setting: The Israeli Election of 1996." *Israel Affairs* (forthcoming).

———. *Israel: Government and Politics in a Maturing State.* New York: Harcourt Brace Jovanovich, 1991.

———. *The Knesset: Parliament in the Israeli Political System.* Rutherford, N.J.: Fairleigh Dickinson University Press, 1981.

Penniman, Howard, ed. *Israel at the Polls, 1981: A Study of the Knesset Elections.* Washington D.C.: American Enterprise Institute, 1986.

Sager, Samuel. *The Parliamentary System of Israel.* Syracuse, N.Y.: Syracuse University Press, 1985.

Ya'acobi, Gad. *The Government of Israel.* New York: Praeger, 1982.

ITALY

OFFICIAL NAME: Italian Republic (Repubblica Italiana)

CAPITAL: Rome

POPULATION: 57,460,000 (1996 est.)

DATE OF INDEPENDENCE: March 17, 1861 (unified Kingdom of Italy proclaimed)

DATE OF CURRENT CONSTITUTION: Effective January 1, 1948

FORM OF GOVERNMENT: Parliamentary democracy

LANGUAGES: Italian (official); German (official in Trentino–Alto Adige)

MONETARY UNIT: Lira

FISCAL YEAR: Calendar year

LEGISLATURE: Parliament (Parlamento)

NUMBER OF CHAMBERS: Two. Chamber of Deputies (Camera dei Deputati); Senate (Senato)

NUMBER OF MEMBERS: Chamber of Deputies, 630 (directly elected); Senate, 325 (315 directly elected, 8 appointed, 2 ex officio)

PERCENTAGE OF WOMEN: Chamber of Deputies, 11.1; Senate, 8.0

TERM OF LEGISLATURE: Five years

MOST RECENT LEGISLATIVE ELECTION: April 21, 1996

MINIMUM AGE FOR VOTING: Chamber of Deputies, 18; Senate, 25

MINIMUM AGE FOR MEMBERSHIP: Chamber of Deputies, 25; Senate, 40

SUFFRAGE: Universal

VOTING: Optional

ADDRESS: Chamber of Deputies, Piazze Montecitorio, 00186 Rome; Senate, Piazze Madama, 00100 Rome

TELEPHONE: Chamber of Deputies, (39 6) 67 601; Senate, (39 6) 67 061

FAX: Chamber of Deputies, (39 6) 67 83 082; Senate, (39 6) 67 06 28 92

The Republic of Italy, a boot-shaped peninsula in southern Europe that stretches from the Alps in the north to the Mediterranean Sea, also includes two major islands, Sardinia and Sicily. Until 1861, when Italy was unified as a constitutional monarchy, the Italian peninsula comprised several small states, some under the control of Austria, some independent kingdoms or duchies, and some ruled by the pope.

In 1946, after World War II, Italian citizens voted in a referendum to abolish the monarchy and establish a republic. The new constitution of 1948 provided for a multiparty parliamentary democracy with a president as head of state, a prime minister as head of government, a bicameral legislature, and a separate judiciary.

Since the formation of the republic, Italy's numerous political parties and shifting coalitions have resulted in more than fifty-five governments. The dominant party until 1994 was the Christian Democratic Party, which was not strong enough to form a majority government but was forced to form coalition governments with other parties. In the 1990s, damaged by charges of political corruption and the public's disgust with the country's electoral politics, the Christian Democrats lost ground. Referendums held in 1991 and 1993 changed the electoral laws from a system based on proportional representation to one that, while including elements of proportional representation, was more majoritarian. In the April 1996 parliamentary elections two new blocs came to power: the center-left Olive Tree, which won a near-majority and formed the government, and the center-right Freedom Alliance, which formed the opposition.

HISTORICAL BACKGROUND

As in the rest of Europe, many Italian states from medieval times had some form of assembly more or less representative of the citizenry. In Sicily, the parliament gained political prestige and authority after Federico of Aragon permitted the constitution of 1296. Parliamentary authority increased when the Trastamara dynasty, a Spanish house, came to power in 1412.

The parliament in the Kingdom of Naples, after a few sporadic meetings of baronial assemblies in the mid-1300s (under the French Anjou dynasty), gained strength under the Aragonese dynasty in the fifteenth century. A similar development occurred in Sardinia, also under Spanish domination, in the early sixteenth century. The second half of the seventeenth century was not particularly favorable to these representative institutions, however.

In northern Italy, the Piedmontese Council of the Three States, after a number of assemblies were held in the late fifteenth century, succeeded in increasing its political power so that by the beginning of the sixteenth century it had become the arbiter of state policy. This development was abruptly curtailed in 1560, with the coronation of Emmanuel Philibert, of the House of Savoy, who rarely convoked the council.

Parliaments fell silent in the eighteenth century. After the French Revolution and the ascent of Napoleon Bonaparte in the latter part of the century, the constitutions of the Italian republics followed the French model of 1795. After the restoration, the Kingdom of Naples acquired in 1820 a true representative parliament, which, although brief (only nine months) in duration, marked a significant achievement in the political development of the people of southern Italy.

Another significant moment in Italian parliamentary history came with the revolutionary disturbances of 1848, which led to the promulgation of constitutions in several Italian states (the Kingdom of the Two Sicilies, which included Sicily and Naples; the Papal States; the Grand Duchy of Tuscany; the Duchy of Parma; and the Kingdom of Sardinia). These constitutions had taken their model from France's Charte Octroyé of 1814 and the subsequent French constitution of 1830. (The Belgian constitution of 1831 also had some influence.) The only exceptions to this institutional uniformity were the constitution of the Kingdom of Sicily (created by a parliament convoked in Palermo against Naples's wishes) and the democratic constitution of the short-lived Roman Republic of 1849, drafted by a constituent assembly on the French model of 1848.

In the wake of the failure of the revolutions of 1848 and increasing pressure for reform, Charles Albert, the king of Piedmont-Sardinia, reluctantly granted a constitution. The Statuto Albertino, which provided for a bicameral legislature, became the institutional point of reference for Italian patriots, whose aim was to unify Italy's separate states into a single country.

In 1861 the Italian states were unified as the Kingdom of Italy under Victor Emmanuel II, Charles Albert's son, and the Statuto Albertino became the new country's first constitution. Piedmontese electoral legislation, founded on the single-member constituency with census-based balloting and suffrage, was extended throughout Italy. The broadening of this legislation in 1882 quadrupled the number of voters from 2 to 8 percent of the general population. Universal male suffrage was not achieved until 1913. Liberal parliamentarism came to an end in 1919, with the adoption of a proportional electoral law and the advent of mass political parties.

The fascist regime, which came to power under Benito Mussolini in 1922, while still retaining the Statuto Albertino, in practice annulled the parliamentary system. After the collapse of Mussolini's regime, the parliament came back to life as the National Council (1944–1946) and then as the Constituent Assembly (1946–1948), when women voted for the first time.

CONSTITUTIONAL PROVISIONS CONCERNING PARLIAMENT

A referendum on June 2, 1946, abolished the monarchy and established Italy as a republic. Nearly all parties in the Constituent Assembly favored a parliamentary system for a number of historical, political, and legal reasons. The constitutional charter therefore reflects the assembly's selection of a parliamentary system. The first three titles of Part II of the constitution are dedicated, respectively, to Parliament, the president of the republic, and the government, whose roles and functions are distinctively parliamentarian. The legislative function is carried out collectively by the two chambers of Parliament (Parlamento), while political guidance is provided by the government. A formal relationship of trust exists between the two organs, on which the nation's general policy is based.

Moreover, the Italian constitution includes a number of other provisions that in total make the system less than a purely parliamentary one. The first adds a fourth body—the Constitutional Court—to the three primary organs. The second authorizes the use of the referendum, which allows the electorate to express its will directly. For example, in 1974 and 1981 referendums were used to abrogate and confirm legislation allowing divorce and abortion. The third measure is the institution of a regional governmental system and the guarantee of a degree of political autonomy granted to some minor territorial organizations (municipalities and provinces).

Political expediency lay at the foundation of the bicameralism adopted by the Italian constitution in the vote of confidence or no confidence in the government as well as in the prerogatives of deputies and senators. The two separate chambers were to carry out identical functions, in this respect modeling the bicameral legislature on traditional nineteenth-century parliamentary theory. The only difference lay in the provision for a third body, the assembly of the two chambers in joint session. But fears that this provision could weaken the bicameral system led the Constituent Assembly to list in detail the cases in which the chambers were to meet in joint session.

The constitution dedicates twenty-eight articles, divided into two sections, to defining the structure, formation, and powers of its representative organs. Parliament consists of the Chamber of Deputies (the lower house) and the Senate (the upper house). The two chambers meet in joint session only in the cases established by the constitution. Articles 56–62 set down the procedures for forming and convoking the houses and their duration. Articles 63–69 regulate the internal organization, status, and parliamentary guarantees.

Section II covers the drafting of laws (Articles 70–82). It deals with the fundamental power of the houses (Articles 70–72), the power to promulgate laws granted to the president of the republic (Articles 70, 74), and the government's regulatory power (Articles 76, 77). Article 75 defines the legislative power of the people, while declarations of a state of war, amnesty and pardon, and authorization to ratify international treaties are regulated by Articles 78–80. Finally, Articles 81 and 82 are concerned with Parliament's power to approve the national budget and with inquiries on matters of public interest.

THE RULES OF PARLIAMENT

Within the Italian constitutional system, Parliament is an expression of and a direct participant in popular sovereignty. Each house adopts its own rules by absolute majority vote of its members. Drafts of all laws submitted either to the Chamber of Deputies or the Senate are examined by committee and then by the chamber, article by article, before a final vote is taken. Internal matters are reserved to parliamentary rules. Otherwise, the internal constitutional guarantee of an absolute majority for the approval of rules designed expressly to protect minorities would be compromised. Parliamentary rules, unlike laws, cannot be tested for constitutionality by the Constitutional Court since the constitution guarantees the independence of Parliament as a sovereign body.

The rules of parliamentary functions therefore are of great importance and are decided upon by absolute majority in each chamber, upon proposal of the Select Rules Committee. The rules of 1971 strengthen the position of the two chambers as against the government, emphasizing the powers of political guidance, control, and intervention in procedures that previously had been reserved for the executive. (The constitution did not describe the procedures for the relationship between Parliament and the government.)

Of particular importance are five rule changes introduced by the Chamber of Deputies between 1981 and 1990; these were intended to bring greater rationalization to scheduling and regulation of parliamentary functions as well as to put into practice a new procedure for converting decree laws and European Community regulations. In 1988 the Senate also approved substantive changes in its rules regarding the scheduling of its functions and the procedures linked to the activities of European Community institutions.

THE ARCHITECTURE OF PARLIAMENT

The building that houses the Senate *(the Palazzo del Senato)* rose on the ancient Roman site of the Baths of Nero and the Stadium of Domitian. A palace built on the site later was purchased, in 1505, by Giovanni de' Medici, the future pope Leo X. Margaret of Austria, called the "Madama," inherited the palace, and it became known as the Palazzo Madama. It later reverted to the Medici family. Palazzo Madama remained Medici property until 1737, when it passed to the House of Lorraine, and then to the popes, who made it the seat of papal government. In 1871 the building was chosen for use by the Senate of the new Italian state.

The Chamber of Deputies assembles in Montecitorio. In the first part of the sixteenth century, Cardinal Nicolò Gaddi built a palace on the hill called Monte Citorio, a name that some scholars believe derives from the Latin *mons citatorius,* that is, the hill of Rome where electoral assemblies were held in ancient times. After a number of property transfers, the palace ended up in the hands of the family of Pope Innocent X, who entrusted the renovation and enlargement to the great baroque sculptor and architect Bernini. After the pope's death in 1655, these works were suspended because of the excessive cost of Bernini's grandiose vision. Montecitorio became, during the papacy of Innocent XII, the house of the papal tribunals (the Apostolic Curia). When Rome became the capital of the Kingdom of Italy, in 1871, the papal tribunals were expelled from Montecitorio and part of the palace was adapted for use as assembly sessions. This hall was the seat of the Chamber of Deputies until the beginning of the twentieth century. During the next renovation only the facade of the old Bernini palace was retained. The new palace was inaugurated in 1918. A series of offices and services for the deputies surround the assembly hall. The second story houses the Chamber's most important offices, including those of the president and the secretary general.

Many buildings in the surrounding area have been purchased by the administrations of the Chamber of Deputies and the Senate, thus establishing a "political city" in the very heart of Rome. Besides Montecitorio and Palazzo Madama, the vicinity includes the residences of the president of the republic, the president of the Council of Ministers, and the president of the Constitutional Court.

ELECTIONS

Since the late 1980s there has been bitter criticism of the system known as *partitocrazia,* or "party rule"—a semiofficial arrangement in which the control of various parts of government is informally distributed among the political parties and which has brought discredit to the postwar political system. The referendum of June 9, 1991, abolished the multiple-preference slate (a practice in which voters could list up to four choices for a seat in order of preference). This practice had been entrenched in the *partitocrazia,* and its abolition was the first move toward transforming the old, proportional electoral system into a mixed system with a majoritarian prevalence.

The referendum of April 18, 1993, significantly changed the Senate's electoral law. The old proportional electoral system was replaced by a predominately "first past the post" system in which the candidate with the most votes won. The new electoral regulations for both the Senate and the Chamber of Deputies, approved with the laws of August 4, 1993, were preceded by an intense legal and political debate, carried out in the previous year by a bicameral committee for institutional reforms.

Under the new electoral law, for the purposes of Senate elections each of Italy's twenty regions is divided into a number of subregional districts corresponding to three-fourths of the electoral seats available to that region. Only people living in a particular district may vote for its representative. Voters vote for only one candidate, and the candidate who receives the greatest number of votes wins. (This is sometimes called a majoritarian/uninominal system of election.) The remaining seats are divided among the political parties in proportion to the votes received in the region's districts by the nonelected candidates. (This is the d'Hondt method of proportional representation.)

The new law provides for a broadly majoritarian mixed-type electoral system for elections to the Chamber of Deputies. In each of the regions and subregional districts, three-fourths of the electoral seats are chosen under a majoritarian system with a single round of votes. The remaining seats are chosen by the proportional method and the use of scrutiny of competing lists. Each voter casts one vote in two separate ballots: one vote is cast for a candidate in the uninominal district under the majoritarian method, and the other is cast under the proportional method in lists presented at the district level. (Several uninominal bodies form one district.) In the uninominal districts, those candidates who obtain a relative majority of the votes cast (in a single round of voting) are elected.

PARLIAMENTARY OPERATIONS AND PROCEDURES

Parliamentary groups are formed around political parties. At the beginning of each legislature the Office of the President of the Chambers assigns to each political group its seats inside the hall. Generally, this formality is carried out quickly with no major problems.

The parliamentary mandate, which is for five years, can be extended only in a state of emergency (a declaration of war or similar political or legal crisis). The number of elected members of Parliament is set at 315 for the Senate and 630 for the Chamber of Deputies.

Agenda and calendar

Parliamentary work is regulated by three instruments: the plan, the calendar of sittings, and the agenda. The plan refers to issues that each house wishes to discuss in a given period of time (three months for the Chamber of Deputies, two for the Senate). The calendar establishes the days in which various measures are discussed, the length of time to be dedicated to their consideration, and other issues concerning the houses. (The calendar is three weeks for the Chamber and one month for the Senate.) The agenda specifies the daily themes of the sittings on the calendar. Time quotas, where necessary, establish the length of time devoted to examination of a given project.

The plan and calendar are approved unanimously by the Conference of Group Chairmen. If unanimity is lacking, the president of the assembly makes a decision based on the proposals from the government and the parliamentary groups. The government has a fundamental role in this process: it indicates the provisions it considers politically important to be inserted into the calendar of assembly functions. Therefore, the degree of a government's influence on Parliament is clearly demonstrated by its ability to present its proposals in Parliament. (This task is generally entrusted to the minister for parliamentary relations.)

Dissolution

The maximum duration of the legislature is five years. The legislative term begins on the day of its first convocation and ends at the first meeting of the new houses after the five-year term has expired, or, as has frequently happened since the beginning of the republic, after a decree to dissolve Parliament early.

A dissolution decree is countersigned by the president of the Council of Ministers and in general is derived from the political parties' inability to form a new government. The president of the republic thus entrusts to the electoral body the choice of a new majority that will be capable of establishing a relationship of confidence with the executive. Whether the houses are dissolved early or serve out their full term, their powers are extended for the period of time between the dissolution decree signed by the president of the republic and the first meeting of the new houses (which, according to the constitution, must take place no later than twenty days after elections). Because of this institution, known as *prorogatio,* the two houses in the republic are permanent organs, and not temporary as they were under the Statuto Albertino. This "caretaker" power of prorogatio is not to be confused with the extension of parliamentary terms, which can be carried out "only by law and in cases of war" according to the constitution.

The normal vacation periods of members of Parliament are subordinate to the demands of legislation, but generally members are given one week at Easter, two at Christmas, and one month, August, during the summer.

LAW MAKING

Under the Statuto Albertino, law made by the legislature was preeminent. In the current republic laws may have to pass the test of constitutional validity.

Legislative initiative

The constitution allows the following legal entities to propose new laws: the government, any member of Parliament, or the general public through a process in which at least fifty thousand signatures of voters are collected. A more restricted legislative initiative is vested in the individual regional councils and in the National Council for Economy and Labor. Of these ways in which new laws are proposed, governmental initiative is the most common: the government has a high probability of being able to carry through its initiatives because it enjoys the support of the parliamentary majority.

The government—through one or more ministries involved in the area to be regulated—submits a bill, first for the approval of the Council of Ministers and then for the authorization of the president of the republic. (If new expenses are anticipated, the assent of the Ministry of the Treasury is also necessary.) After the bill has passed these two examinations, it is submitted to Parliament. It is drawn up into articles and accompanied by a report explaining the bill's purposes and effects. In cases of extraordinary urgency, the government may issue "temporary provisions with the force of law" (Article 77 of the constitution), but they expire unless Parliament converts them into law within sixty days.

Any member of Parliament may present proposals on any matter, except those regarding the budget and related issues, and may do so independently or together with other members. Again, the proposal must be drawn up into articles and accompanied by an explanatory report. An individual deputy can in theory bring a matter forward for a vote without help from other members, but in practice such a proposal is not likely to become law. For this reason, laws proposed by an individual member are symbolic acts expressing the member's concern with a situation and generally are connected with protecting the interests of the voters in the member's home district.

Article 71 of the constitution establishes the procedures by which citizens outside Parliament may initiate legislation. The signatures of fifty thousand voters are required to start such a process. Popular initiatives follow the same procedure as other new legislation except that they do not expire at the end of a legislature.

Finally, the abrogative referendum, a piece of direct democracy unique to Italy, can be introduced at the request of 500,000 voters or five regional councils, after the Constitutional Court has ruled on its legality. Some laws are not subject to abrogative referendum—in particular, those regarding taxes or the budget, amnesty or pardon, and the ratification of international treaties.

Committee work

The Italian constitution provides for specialized parliamentary committees in the Chamber of Deputies and the Senate. These committees are empowered to study each bill and to carry out oversight activities. At present, the composition of the members in the committees reflects the strength of the various parliamentary groups. Each committee usually numbers about fifty members in the Chamber of Deputies and twenty-five in the Senate. Each committee elects a chair, two vice chairs, and two secretaries. There are fourteen standing committees in the Chamber of Deputies and thirteen in the Senate, covering the following areas: constitutional affairs; justice; foreign and community affairs; defense; budget, treasury, and planning; finance; culture, science, and education; environment, national territory, and public works; transportation, post, and telecommunications; production, commerce, and tourism; public employment and labor; social affairs; agriculture; and a special committee for community policies.

The constitution provides for three major types of proceedings, based on the kind of business before the committees. First, the "regular" type of proceeding consists of two phases: an examination phase in which a committee studies the bill and a decision-making phase that takes place in the assembly. The second type, which must have the consent of the government, takes place entirely in what the Chamber of Deputies calls the "legislative" and the Senate the "deliberating" committee; this procedure combines the examination and the decision-making phases. In this case, the opinions of the Committees on the Budget and Constitutional Affairs are binding. If the committees do not approve a measure, it is sent back to the assembly. Indeed, in the legislative or deliberating phases, the committee, after studying the project, approves it definitively. The third procedure is a hybrid. The bill is prepared by a drafting committee and is submitted to the assembly for approval with no opportunity to introduce amendments.

The chair of the assembly decides which procedure is to be assigned to each bill. Bills pass through four phases: study, examination of general principles, examination of specific articles, and final approval.

Readings of bills

A bill becomes a law only after it has been approved by the Chamber of Deputies and by the Senate. It is therefore necessary to have two readings of the same text. If the text is modified by one of the houses, the bill must be returned to the house that had first approved it so that deliberation can be made on the changes introduced.

In ordinary proceedings, once the committee has concluded its examination phase, study passes to the assembly in four stages: general discussion of the bill, examination of articles and amendments, voting on articles and amendments, and final voting.

A time limit is set for general discussion, with presentations limited to the reporter of the law, to minority reporters, if any, and to a speaker for each parliamentary group. If no obstructionist obstacles are raised, a request is made to close discussion (the so-called guillotine).

Amendments to bills can be suppressive, substitutional, or additional (there are also amendments to amendments, and sub-amendments). Once the speakers registered to speak on each article and the related amendments have finished their presentations, the reporter of the proposal under discussion and the government pronounce themselves in favor of or opposed to each amendment proposed.

Quorum and official reports

Voting must take place in the presence of a majority of the members of the assembly (that is, 50 percent plus one). This number will be verified by the president only when so requested; otherwise, a quorum is assumed to exist. Curiously, abstentions are considered "present" in the Senate and "absent" in the Chamber of Deputies, with differing effects on the numerical count.

The assembly has two kinds of official reporting: a shorthand record and a summary form. The former is a complete transcript of what was said; it provides detailed information concerning the assembly debate. A provisional version is printed immediately after each sitting, and a final version is prepared some days afterward. A provisional summary record is available thirty to forty minutes after the proceedings to which it refers, and the final version is available the following day.

A shorthand record is also prepared for the work of the committees in their legislative and drafting functions. In addition, shorthand records are prepared for examinations of budget documents and during inquiries (with hearings). All other cases require only the summary record.

VOTING

At the end of 1988, after long debate, the parliamentary rules of the Chamber of Deputies were changed. Until then a secret ballot had been used, but it had given rise to "snipers" who secretly voted against the government, although openly expressing their support. At present, in both the Chamber and the Senate the open ballot is the normal method of voting. The open ballot is obligatory for members voting on the revenue bill, budget laws, and all decisions with any financial consequences. The secret ballot is still used for votes involving persons or, upon request by a minority, for issues of "conscience" or for votes related to the state's constitutional bodies and electoral laws. The Senate requires open voting on electoral laws as well.

The four procedures for open balloting are by a show of hands; electronically, without recording of names; electronically, with recording of names; and by roll call, with the declaration of the vote (used only for votes of confidence or of no confidence in the government). The procedures for secret balloting are by electronic procedure or by filling out a paper ballot.

Before the final vote on a bill, the so-called vote declaration gives an overall evaluation of how the bill has been changed with the introduction of amendments. If the bill is approved in the final vote, it will be transmitted to the president of the chamber where it was initiated and to the president of the other assembly if it has not yet been considered there. If this approval has already taken place, the new law will be forwarded to the president of the republic for promulgation.

NONLEGISLATIVE ROLE OF COMMITTEES

Permanent committees have duties beyond their legislative role. They help guide government policy, for example, by urging adoption of certain measures. They supervise the government's activity and serve an inquiry function, for example, by requesting clarification of various government initiatives.

For some matters the permanent committees rely on subcommittees with more specialized areas of responsibility. The most important of these are the standing committees, which are composed of a limited number of deputies with particular specializations.

The Italian legislative system also provides for joint committees, through which the assemblies exercise their supervisory and guidance functions. Members are drawn from both houses. The constitution provides directly for only one joint committee, for regional issues. The other committees, called investigatory committees, are created to investigate specific important events (for instance, the kidnapping and assassination of Prime Minister Aldo Moro, in 1978). After completing their task, these committees cease to exist. Other committees, called vigilance and control committees, deal with specific, well-defined issues and are limited in duration.

Joint committees have increased in number over the years, and their political importance has become correspondingly more significant. Today joint committees have duties in areas ranging from regional issues to the Mafia. The two houses of Parliament can also create special committees to examine specific issues, with an indefinite or limited duration (for example, the Special Committee for European Community policies was set up in 1990 by the Chamber of Deputies, and the Select Committee for European Affairs was created by the Senate in 1968).

Standing parliamentary committees have three major roles: examination, deliberation, and drafting (their decision-making role follows the same procedure as that of the plenary assembly). Committees debate issues regarding the legislative committees, independently of the examination of the bills. In this case, the rules of the houses provide for various forms of collaboration between parliamentary committees and the ministers. Committees that are set up to gather information can carry out wide-ranging research on which they subsequently report their conclusions.

Within the framework of the general principle of cooperation between government and Parliament, the committees may obtain information and clarifications from ministers and undersecretaries through hearings and other means of communication. Hearings may also involve directors in public administration or public bodies. Informal hearings also may deal with regulations of a given area (trade unions and trade associations, for example).

THE BUDGET

Under the constitution, Parliament approves the budget and expenditure accounts submitted by the government. If the budget is not approved by December 31 (the end of the fiscal year), all functions of government come to a halt, an event that has particularly serious consequences in Italy where much of the social expenditure and the economy is managed by the state. Therefore, examination of the numerous documents connected with the annual budget is the activity with the highest priority in Parliament.

Several stages mark the parliamentary marathon to approve the budget within the required time periods. If it is not approved in time, a provisional budget is passed to prevent state operations from ceasing altogether until April 30 of the next year. The process for the approval of the budget law begins May 30, when the government transmits to the Chamber of Deputies and the Senate an economic and financial plan setting out the basic estimates for financial expenditure for the following year. This plan, after examination by both houses simultaneously, with modifications introduced where necessary, is approved and becomes binding on the government.

By July 31 the government submits the budget to both houses—that is, the estimates for revenue and expenditure for the following year, accompanied by a three-year budgetary plan. By September 30 the government submits revenue and related bills to both houses; these are subject to legislative scrutiny. There is a special session of Parliament, designed to approve the budget within a fixed period. During this session the examination of financial and economic documents takes precedence over other parliamentary work. The revenue bill is also sent to the individual committees, which have ten days in which to offer a consultative opinion. A report is prepared for the budget committee, listing any amendments introduced (provided for and limited by law) as well as proposals for modifications to the revenue bill (a minority report is also provided for). After this procedure is completed, but before the budget is submitted for the assembly's approval, its general features must be approved by the budget committee in its examination role. The budget committee must interpret the modifications proposed to the revenue bill to the assembly, accompanied by the reports from the relevant committees, thereby giving the assembly the opportunity to make informed decisions.

The budget sitting goes through the following stages. First, the budget bill, including the expenditures of the various ministries, is approved for the following year by ordinary ballot. Then the revenue bill is discussed and approved in its entirety. Subsequent ballots will not change the overall amount of the expenditure estimates but may change their distribution. After the revenue bill has been approved, the government prepares a document showing the variations from the original of the state budget, introducing into the budget the modifications made by the revenue bill. This document is discussed and voted on immediately by the assembly, which is already conducting its debate on the budget. The final vote on the budget, as modified by the revenue bill (after the bills connected with it have also been approved), is set to meet rigid deadlines.

RELATIONS WITH THE EXECUTIVE

The most politically significant act in the relations between the government and the two houses of Parliament is the "motion of confidence" in the government, without which the government cannot survive. The procedure for the vote of confidence is established by the constitution: a roll-call vote with each member of Parliament "taking the walk" to the bench of the president of the assembly, pronouncing his or her vote by voice (a vote of confidence cannot be voted by division).

Political support accorded to the government may be withdrawn by a motion of no confidence. Because of its political and institutional significance (at times leading to the fall of the government in office), a no-confidence motion is subject to particular procedural guarantees. First, a no-confidence motion cannot be debated more than three days before its presentation, and it must be signed by at least one-tenth of the members of one of the two houses (again, voting by division is prohibited). The no-confidence motion, unlike the motion of confidence, need be approved by only one of the two houses. The motion of no confidence is usually presented by opposition forces to test whether the government still has support in Parliament for its program to continue.

In 1986 the Chamber of Deputies introduced the motion of "individual no confidence" for dealing with a single member of the government. It required the same procedures as those for no confidence in the government as a whole. Voting on the question of confidence takes place twenty-four hours after the request is made, following the procedures established for the motion of confidence. Votes of confidence and no confidence are an important part of Italian parliamentary practice. Votes of confidence are often used to provide an extra measure of support for a bill. They are frequently political maneuvers (for example, to clear up the government's doubts regarding the attitude of some majority deputies).

Monitoring executive performance

The most important tools the houses have to monitor the executive are motions, resolutions, and agendas. A motion is not intended to acquire information but to promote a decision of the assembly. It may contain a political guideline (directive), or it may sanction responsibilities emerging from inspection procedures (censure) or establish ad hoc parliamentary agencies and procedures. A motion sets forth a debate, and a resolution is the outcome of that debate. An agenda is a request made by a parliamentary body to commit the government to a specific interpretation dealing with some legal or administrative matters.

Parliamentary inquiries are also used to monitor the activities of the government and public administration.

Questions and interpellations

Among its fact-finding tools, the legislature also has the right to bring questions and interpellations before the government. Questions presented in written form and submitted by one or more members of Parliament about the motives and intentions of the government in policy matters are called interpellations. An interpellation is not a simple request for information or particular documents but a request for clarification on the government's behavior regarding issues of a general nature. "Cluster interpellations" are presented by a number of groups on the same issue. In addition, there are urgent interpellations regarding important and sudden events in the nation and abroad.

Questions are precisely worded and are addressed to the government concerning a fact or specific situation. They require an equally precise answer. The question can be presented in writing, and the government may respond in one of three ways: orally, in assembly, through the minister (or undersecretary with responsibility in this area); orally, in committee; or in writing to the questioner. Since the 1980s there have been provisions for questions to be asked with an immediate answer mandatory—a practice modeled after the British "question time."

Interpellation does not deal with specific facts but is a question about the government's activities as a whole, a request to justify policy. Like questions, an interpellation can be submitted by a single member of Parliament, and the government is obliged to respond orally since the answer is likely to be of general interest. The originator of the interpellation may declare satisfaction or dissatisfaction with the government's response.

Vetoes

The Italian constitution does not provide for explicit powers of executive veto over parliamentary actions that are comparable to those in other nations. The nearest thing to an executive veto—really a power of postponement—belongs to the president of the republic, who before promulgating a law approved by Parliament can send it back to the houses with a message outlining his or her reasons and requesting a new debate. The president can reject a bill on its merits or from a belief that it is unconstitutional. If the two chambers pass the bill once more, the president of the republic is required to promulgate it.

LEADERSHIP

The top leadership of the Italian Parliament is made up of the president of the Chamber of Deputies and the president of the Senate. The president of the Chamber of Deputies presides when the two chambers meet in joint session. The Italian constitutional system attributes great importance to these offices (which are second only to the president of the republic). Behind the importance given these two positions is the conviction that they are the highest-level offices of the two institutions that directly represent the people.

Duties

Under the constitution (Article 86), the duties of the president of the republic in all cases in which he cannot carry them out are exercised by the president of the Senate. The president of the Chamber of Deputies has the important function of calling and presiding over Parliament in joint session. The president of the republic must consult with the presidents of the two chambers in cases of early dissolution of the chambers or in the event of government crisis.

Contrary to practice in nations with a presidential system, where the president of the legislature exercises considerable political power as majority leader, in states with a parliamentary system, like Italy, the president of the assembly must bring together both the majority and the opposition parties. The president ensures the efficient working of the political process, both as regards the application and interpretation of the rules of each house and as regards its internal administration (with the assistance of the Office of the Presidency). The president recognizes the members who are to speak, directs and moderates debates, preserves order, states the questions for votes, establishes the order of voting, clarifies the significance of the vote, and announces the result of the vote.

These functions can be divided into four categories:

- Convening and assigning functions: the president calls the assembly and the numerous bodies over which he or she presides, including the Office of the Presidency, the Conference of Group Chairmen, and the Rules Committee, and assigns legislative provisions to various committees.
- Appointment functions: the president appoints the members of the Select Rules Committee, the Select Elections Committee, and the Select Committee for Authorizations to Proceed.
- Direction and organization functions: the president establishes the plan and calendar of work, if the parliamentary group chairs cannot agree; conducts assembly sittings with the broadest decision-making and discretionary powers, including disciplinary and police powers necessary to preserve order; and resolves questions of interpretation of rules.
- Control and disclosure functions: the president oversees the regular production and distribution of documentary materials, attests to the approval of laws, and represents the whole chamber. In addition, the president is the political chief of the administration—that is, of the entire bureaucratic organization created as a function of parliamentary work. The president enjoys wide power to issue decrees, through which he or she makes executive decisions. In this function, the president proposes the appointment of the secretary general, the chief of administration.

Elections of the presidents

The presidents of the two houses are elected by the members of these bodies. For the election of the president of the Chamber of Deputies, the requirement is a supermajority on the first three ballots (a two-thirds majority of members on the first ballot, a two-thirds majority of voters—including any blank ballots—on the second and third ballots), and an absolute majority thereafter. For the election of the president of the Senate, an absolute majority is required for the first four ballots. After this, a simple plurality is enough to elect one of the two candidates who obtained the most votes.

Office of the Presidency

The Office of the Presidency is composed of four vice presidents, who act for the president in cases of the president's absence or inability to perform the duties of office. They have full presidential powers. In addition, three quaestors assist the president in the internal administration of the chambers, in particular as concerns the application of the rules and the directives of the president. Eight secretaries supervise the keeping of minutes, with the task of verifying the result of each vote. All members of the Office of the Presidency are elected, in a secret ballot, by the respective chambers in order to guarantee representation of all parliamentary groups.

The Office of the Presidency issues rules for administration and internal accounting of the chambers, for office regulations, and for the management of employees of the chamber. The Office of the Presidency also appoints, at the proposal of the president of the assembly, the secretary general, the chief of the chamber's offices and services. The secretary general takes part in meetings of the Office of the Presidency.

PARTY CAUCUSES AND GROUPS

The Statuto Albertino gave no legal status to political parties. Rather, various groups organized around conservative or liberal leanings. After the introduction of a proportional electoral system in the elections of 1919, the Chamber of Deputies divided into political groups, an arrangement that continued with the elections of 1921. This development was cut short when Mussolini came to power, and after the elections of 1924 parliamentary groups were suppressed. When the Italian Republic was founded after World War II, the existence of parties was established by the constitution. Since then, the parties have organized in territorial networks headed by national directorates in which the dominant figure is the party secretary.

On the institutional and parliamentary levels, party influence is ensured by parliamentary groups, whose existence is to some degree recognized by the constitution. Under the rules of the Senate and the Chamber of Deputies, each senator and deputy belongs to a parliamentary group. In the first days of each new legislature, senators and deputies must declare which group they intend to be part of. The adherence of each member of Parliament to a specific group is essential to the chamber's ability to carry out its other operations. Generally, there is convergence between the political party and the parliamentary group (with the exception of "mixed" groups), although this agreement is not obligatory since deputies are free to enroll in the group they prefer or to pass from one group to another during a given legislature, without ceasing to be a member of Parliament.

A parliamentary group must have at least ten senators and twenty deputies. The Office of the Presidency can authorize these numbers to be lowered, but only when the group represents a nationally organized party.

Parliamentary groups are fundamental for the formation of almost all the assemblies' constituent bodies, in which they are represented in proportion to their numbers. The Conference of Group Leaders is called at regular intervals by the president of the assembly to plan legislation.

PARTY DISCIPLINE

In the absence of a whip and majority and minority leaders in the Italian political system, group discipline is exercised by the executive board. The executive board directs the work of individual deputies, imposing on them the rules established by their respective regulatory bylaws, especially as regards voting (with the exception of cases of conscience or moral and ethical issues). This principle of party group discipline stands in contrast with Article 67 of the constitution, which states that "each member of Parliament represents the nation and carries out his duties without constraint of mandate." Thus respect for group discipline must be considered to be completely voluntary, since the measures adopted against a dissenting member of Parliament affect only the relationship between that member and the group or party and in no way invalidate the member's status in Parliament. Appeals, fines, and censures that may be brought against "disobedient" members of Parliament can at most force them to change the group (and, where necessary, the party) to which they belong.

RELATIONS BETWEEN CHAMBERS

Today, Italy's two assemblies carry out very much the same functions. Indeed, it has been said that the two houses are actually a form of monocameralism, in the sense that they may be considered two sessions of a single Parliament. It is therefore not by chance that a complex interchamber relationship between the two assemblies is growing steadily. In addition to the joint sittings of both houses provided for in the constitution, bicameral activity flourishes in the joint committees that carry out various important tasks.

The constitution provides for joint sittings of the two chambers on the following occasions: the election and swearing in of the president of the republic (Article 91); the election of one-third of the members of the High Council of the Judiciary (Article 104); the election of five judges of the Constitutional Court and forty-five citizens (from whom sixteen are chosen by lot to complete the Constitutional Court), who hear impeachment proceedings against the president of the republic (Article 135); and impeachment of the president of the republic for high treason or plots against the constitution (Article 90).

In recent years, a number of proposals to modify the bicameral structure have been debated in Parliament. The Senate in particular has been the target of various reform plans.

MEMBERS

Election as deputy involves the right to enjoy a series of immunities and prerogatives as well as the obligation to abide by certain duties and limitations. The status of members is regulated by the constitution, laws, and regulations aimed at ensuring each member free exercise of the parliamentary mandate.

Prerogatives

Parliament itself verifies the legality of the electoral status of its members. Election committees evaluate the legality of the electoral proceedings as well as the existence of causes for ineligibility or incompatibility. This important prerogative is motivated by the fear of external influence in some way limiting the full sovereignty of the assemblies (Article 66 of the constitution).

Another important prerogative of members of Parliament is the legal immunity of the opinions and judgments they express. As Article 68 of the constitution states, "members of Parliament may not be prosecuted for opinions expressed and votes cast in the exercise of their duties." Article 68, modified by constitutional law on October 29, 1993, has limited the parliamentary immunity originally established for every criminal trial (to which a member of Parliament could not be subjected without the authorization of the house to which he or she belonged) exclusively to cases of personal or home search and arrest (unless apprehended in the act of committing a crime), as well as interception of conversations, messages, and mail. For these purposes, there is a Committee for Authorizations to Proceed in the Chamber of Deputies (composed of twenty-one members appointed directly by the president of the assembly in proportion to the numerical size of the groups). The Senate entrusts these tasks to a single Select Committee for Elections and Parliamentary Immunity, which is composed of twenty-three senators. As regards ministerial crimes, the constitutional modifications of 1989 have entrusted to the ordinary courts final judgment on crimes committed by ministers in the exercise of their duties, with the houses retaining the power to deny authorization to proceed against them.

Recall, expulsion, and resignation

The Italian system does not include a provision for recall of members. Article 67 of the constitution states that "each member of Parliament represents the Nation and carries out his duties without constraint of mandate." Should a member of Parliament fail to respect the discipline of the party group to which he or she belongs or the wishes of the constituency regarding a given vote, there is no legal "punishment" for the member.

A member of Parliament may be expelled from his or her party or group for reasons satisfactory to the party. But expulsion does not mean that the individual is no longer a member of Parliament. Members may be expelled temporarily from the house by the president for incorrect behavior to colleagues or members of the government. There is also the possibility of the use of censure in cases where a deputy incites disorderly conduct or seriously offends the institutions. The member is denied access to the assembly for a period of time ranging from two days to fifteen days.

It is common parliamentary practice to reject resignations, at least the first time a resignation is submitted. If the resignation is repeated, it may again be rejected because, in theory, the parliamentary assemblies are not required to accept them.

Pay and perquisites

A 1965 law established that the salary (called the "allowance") of members may not exceed the maximum gross pay of a section president of the Court of Cassation. Each member of Parliament also receives an allowance for the days they are present in the hall, a fixed lump-sum refund of telephone and mail expenses, free use of transportation throughout the national territory, a contribution toward the maintenance of one or more assistants, and an office. Also included are some forms of insurance and refund of health expenses for members and their families. The Office of the Presidency accords an additional allowance to members who carry out certain roles within the assembly. A member's salary cannot be withheld or seized. Each member usually contributes a portion of the salary to his or her parliamentary group.

At the end of the parliamentary mandate, each member receives a final check in proportion to the duration of the mandate and a pension, also proportional to the duration of the mandate, to be enjoyed generally after the age of sixty.

Ethics

Oversight of parliamentary ethics is entrusted to the president for less serious offenses and to the Office of the Presidency for more serious ones. The most serious offenses directly affect the status of the member of Parliament, who can be prohibited from taking part in the house for some days. Disciplinary measures also include the following: a call to order for a member of Parliament who disturbs the proceedings by using improper language, and short-term or long-term censure—that is, prohibition from entering the hall. When necessary, a member may be removed forcibly from the hall. Committee chairs have disciplinary powers concerning internal order of their committees, but they cannot take further measures in this regard.

All deputies and senators are expected to attend proceedings as frequently as possible. Toward this end, the daily allowance is decreased by a sum commensurate with the number of absences from parliamentary sittings, and an even larger amount is subtracted for missed votes.

Each member of Parliament must provide a statement detailing his or her assets, with the following documents: the family's assets and a liability statement; the most recent tax return; and documentation of the total expenditures for the election campaign, with the major contributors listed. Members are required to update these reports annually. The information is accessible to anyone who requests it.

JUDICIAL FUNCTIONS OF PARLIAMENT AND IMPEACHMENT

The constitutional law of January 16, 1989, established that the president of the Council of Ministers and the ministers are subject to normal justice for crimes committed in the exercise of their duties, provided that authorization is given by the Senate or the Chamber of Deputies. Judicial proceedings are regulated first by a select committee and then in assembly, which must decide the case by absolute majority.

The same law also changed the procedures concerning crimes of high treason and plots against the constitution committed by the president of the republic. Only after a report from a committee composed of members from the two Select Committees for Authorization to Proceed can Parliament, in a joint sitting chaired by the president of the Chamber of Deputies, impeach the president, with an absolute majority (Article 90). In this case, the president will be judged by the Constitutional Court in its enlarged form.

THE PARLIAMENTARY LIBRARY AND RESEARCH FACILITIES

The library of the Chamber of Deputies has holdings of 800,000 volumes and 5,000 periodicals. Open to the public, it is accessible with a permit issued upon request. A Study Service prepares the documentation necessary for the work of the individual committees, as well as for the parliamentary groups and for deputies, when they so request. The historical archives at the Chamber of Deputies keeps all data concerning parliamentary activity beginning with the first sittings of the Parlamento Subalpino, in 1848.

The Senate library, founded in 1848, holds approximately 500,000 volumes and 3,500 periodicals. Strong in law, history, and political and social science, it is known for its collection of the statutes of Italian municipalities, corporations, universities, and hospitals from medieval times to the eighteenth century. It is reserved for senators and Senate staff, but scholars may be authorized to use it.

The Senate's Study Office carries out the tasks of documentation, research, and consulting for the standing parliamentary committees. At the request of individual senators and the public, the Study Service provides copies of the most important parliamentary speeches. A Budget Service provides committees with documentation on request.

The Senate archives has a special information service for members of Parliament concerning assembly work and other material. Connected to the archives is the Parliamentary Information Division, which provides data and information on the two houses' activities. The archives also reproduce the reports of parliamentary debates from 1848 onward (on microfilm and optical disks).

PARLIAMENT AND THE MEDIA

Modern mass communication has helped to bring Italy's Parliament closer to the people. In addition to shorthand and summary reports, there is some radio and television coverage of assembly proceedings. An internal closed-circuit radio system connects all the offices of each of the chambers with the assembly. The president can allow live television coverage of assembly proceedings, and question time is broadcast live.

In the case of committee proceedings, the reports (summaries for the Senate) are also accompanied by the shorthand record for drafting and legislation sittings, as well as those dedicated to inquiries. In addition, live, closed-circuit television covers drafting and legislation sittings, as well as those dedicated to policy and inquiries, when so requested. (Journalists are able to watch committee functions by closed circuit.)

In 1971 regulations established that assembly proceedings could be covered live on television upon authorization by the president (in practice, live TV coverage takes place in the Senate, although it is not provided for under Senate rules). The rise of private television networks has broadened the audience of potential viewers interested in parliamentary proceedings, which are no longer carried only on state-run television.

CONSTITUTIONALITY OF LAWS

The government's frequent use of the decree law—beginning in particular at the end of the 1970s and increasingly used to skirt the constitutional requirement of necessity and urgency—has given rise to a series of problems in the relationship between the legislative and executive branches. In fact, a decree, which must be converted into law within sixty days, is placed in a "privileged lane" on the calendar of the two chambers and therefore forces the assemblies to revise their work plan. The Chamber of Deputies (since 1981) and the Senate (since 1982) have had rules to ensure that the constitutionally established prerequisites of necessity and urgency have been met by the government in issuing a decree law.

In Italy, judgments concerning the constitutionality of laws and acts that have the force of law of the government and the regions are entrusted to the Constitutional Court. The Constitutional Court is made up of fifteen judges, five appointed by the president of the republic, five by Parliament in a joint sitting, and five by the ordinary and administrative supreme courts.

According to the constitution, a law declared unconstitutional "ceases to have effect from the day following publication of the decision in the *Gazzetta Ufficiale* [the official gazette]." Parliament therefore has the responsibility of bridging the legislative gap thus created, an occurrence that has given rise to frequent complaints concerning the lack of official links between the activities of the court and those of Parliament.

The Rules of the Chamber of Deputies establish that the decisions of the Constitutional Court are sent to the Committee on Constitutional Matters as well as to the committee responsible. Within thirty days these committees set forth in a final document their opinion about what legal changes are necessary. This document is sent to the president of the Senate, the president of the Council of Ministers, and the president of the Constitutional Court. Senate rules provide that, after a declaration of unconstitutionality, the text of the court's decision is sent to the committees responsible. If they decide that the abolished regulations must be substituted by a new provision of law, they ask the government to proceed in that direction. The president of the Senate then communicates to the president of the Council of Ministers the approved resolution, giving notice to the president of the Chamber of Deputies. As a rule, the Senate examines only declarative decisions of unconstitutionality, whereas the Chamber automatically passes all Constitutional Court decisions through the committees.

EMERGENCY POWERS

Article 78 of the constitution establishes that "the houses decide on states of war and confer the necessary powers on the Government." Only if there is a state of war can the five-year parliamentary mandate be extended. The prohibition on extending terms, sanctioned by Article 60 of the constitution, may not be broken "except by law and only in cases of war."

An extension lasts as long as the situation that provoked it. Under an extension, members retain their full powers. The period of extension may not continue beyond one legislature.

Maria Sofia Corciulo

BIBLIOGRAPHY

Adams, John Clarke, and Paolo Barile. *The Government of Republican Italy.* 3d ed. Boston: Houghton Mifflin, 1972.

Di Ciolo, Vittorio, and Luigi Ciaurro. *Il diritto parlamentare nella storia e nella pratica.* 3d ed. Milan: Giuffré, 1994.

Furlong, Paul. *Modern Italy: Representation and Reform.* London and New York: Routledge, 1994.

Manzella, Andrea. *Il Parlamento.* Bologna: Il Mulino, 1991.

Mazzoni, Honorati L. *Lezioni di diritto parlamentare.* Turin: Giappichelli, 1993.

Pasquino, Gianfranco, and Patrick McCarthy, eds. *The End of Post-War Politics in Italy: The Landmark 1992 Elections.* Boulder, Colo.: Westview Press, 1993.

IVORY COAST

See Côte d'Ivoire

J

JAMAICA

OFFICIAL NAME: Jamaica
CAPITAL: Kingston
POPULATION: 2,595,000 (1996 est.)
DATE OF INDEPENDENCE: August 6, 1962 (from the United Kingdom)
DATE OF CURRENT CONSTITUTION: Effective August 6, 1962
FORM OF GOVERNMENT: Constitutional monarchy
LANGUAGES: English, Creole
MONETARY UNIT: Jamaica dollar
FISCAL YEAR: April 1–March 31
LEGISLATURE: Parliament
NUMBER OF CHAMBERS: Two. House of Representatives; Senate
NUMBER OF MEMBERS: House of Representatives, 60 (directly elected); Senate, 21 (appointed)
PERCENTAGE OF WOMEN: House of Representatives, 11.7; Senate, 14.3
TERM OF LEGISLATURE: Five years
MOST RECENT LEGISLATIVE ELECTION: House of Representatives, March 30, 1993
MINIMUM AGE FOR VOTING: 18
MINIMUM AGE FOR MEMBERSHIP: 21
SUFFRAGE: Universal
VOTING: Optional
ADDRESS: Houses of Parliament, P.O. Box 636, Kingston
TELEPHONE: (500 809) 92 20 200
FAX: (500 809) 96 70 064

Jamaica is the third-largest island in the Caribbean, lying between Cuba and Haiti *(see map, p. 194)*. It was the first British colony acquired by conquest and also the first colony to have a representative legislative body.

The Jamaican House of Assembly was organized on January 20, 1664, and met in the Spanish Town under Speaker Robert Freeman. The House of Assembly was one of the first legislative bodies in the Western Hemisphere. The powers of the House of Assembly were gradually enlarged after adoption of the 1944 constitution, which introduced adult suffrage and restored the legislature to its original bicameral structure. The first elections contested by formal political parties were held in 1944. Independence came to the island under a new constitution in 1962.

The bicameral legislature consists of a Senate and a House of Representatives. The Senate consists of twenty-one senators, of whom thirteen are appointed by the governor general on the advice of the prime minister and eight are appointed by the governor general on the advice of the leader of the opposition. The House of Representatives consists of sixty elected members called members of Parliament. The term of Parliament is five years. Parliament meets in the George William Gordon House, erected in 1960. It is a modern structure in Kingston.

Following the British Westminster model, the Senate is the less important of the two branches of the legislature. It may delay money bills for one month and other bills for seven months. Senate votes may be overridden if the lower house passes the bill by majority vote three times in succession. Senate concurrence, however, is essential for a constitutional amendment. The cabinet generally includes two or three senators, and other senators may serve as parliamentary secretaries.

The House initiates all money bills; other bills may be introduced in either house. Government bills are generally introduced by a cabinet member. The standing orders cover the dates and hours of sitting, petitions and papers, questions, motions and amendments, rules of debate, rules of order, voting, procedure of bills, financial procedures, and select committees. In most cases, the rules follow those prevailing in Westminster. After election to office, the speaker is expected to be nonpartisan, but he or she enjoys considerable prestige and influence. Standing committees have relatively little investigative power and tend to shore up rather than scrutinize government actions.

The quorum is eight in the Senate and sixteen in the House, but there is widespread absenteeism during all but the most important sittings. The constitution requires parliamentary sessions to be not more than six months apart.

Members of Parliament are immune from arrest and protected from prosecution for the discharge of their duties. They are expected to disclose their interests, but drug money has corrupted the integrity of many members of the legislature as well as members of the executive.

George Thomas Kurian

JAPAN

OFFICIAL NAME: Nippon
CAPITAL: Tokyo
POPULATION: 125,450,000 (1996 est.)
DATE OF INDEPENDENCE: c. 660 B.C.
DATE OF CURRENT CONSTITUTION: Effective May 3, 1947
FORM OF GOVERNMENT: Constitutional monarchy
LANGUAGE: Japanese
MONETARY UNIT: Yen
FISCAL YEAR: April 1–March 31
LEGISLATURE: Diet (Kokkai)
NUMBER OF CHAMBERS: Two. House of Representatives (Shugi-in); House of Councillors (Sangi-in)
NUMBER OF MEMBERS: House of Representatives, 500; House of Councillors, 252
PERCENTAGE OF WOMEN: House of Representatives, 4.6; House of Councillors, 13.9
TERM OF LEGISLATURE: House of Representatives, four years; House of Councillors, six years
MOST RECENT LEGISLATIVE ELECTION: October 20, 1996
MINIMUM AGE FOR VOTING: 20
MINIMUM AGE FOR MEMBERSHIP: House of Representatives, 25; House of Councillors, 30
SUFFRAGE: Universal and direct
VOTING: Optional
ADDRESS: Kokkai, 7-1 Nagatacho 1, Chiyodaku, 100 Tokyo
TELEPHONE: House of Representatives, (813) 3581 5111; House of Councillors, (813) 3581 3111
FAX: House of Representatives, (813) 3581 2900; House of Councillors, (813) 5512 3895

Japan, a constitutional monarchy in the northwestern Pacific Ocean to the east of mainland Asia, comprises an archipelago of four main and many lesser adjacent islands. A modern democracy with a long imperial legacy, the country traditionally traces its history to the founding of the first imperial house by Emperor Jimmu in 660 B.C.

In 1889 Japan became the first constitutional state in Asia. With the constitution of 1947 the emperor became the ceremonial head of state. The government is led by a prime minister and cabinet, and the country's legislature is bicameral.

HISTORICAL BACKGROUND

During the ninth century A.D. the emperors began to retire from public life, delegating affairs of government to subordinates. By the tenth century the *samurai*, or warrior class, had supplanted the central authority of the emperor, and Japanese society evolved along feudal lines.

Beginning in the seventeenth century the Tokugawa *shoguns* (military rulers) asserted control over a newly reunified Japan and closed the country to outside influence. When Japan was reopened to the West in the mid-nineteenth century, traditional political, military, and economic systems were no match for powerful foreign intruders, and the shogun's government failed. It was replaced by a new oligarchy of strong regional leaders who brought about the Meiji Restoration, ostensibly reinstating imperial power in 1868.

The Meiji rulers carried out wholesale reform, importing thousands of foreigners to teach modern science and mathematics and sending students and envoys to Europe and North America. They returned to combine foreign ideology and modern methods with Japanese traditions, devising a uniquely Japanese governmental and economic system. The emperor emerged as a symbol of national unity.

A privy council was established in 1888 to evaluate the forthcoming constitution and to advise the emperor. The Meiji constitution, when it was finally granted by the emperor as a sign of his sharing of authority and granting of rights and liberties to his subjects, provided for an imperial Diet, with two houses and a cabinet responsible to the emperor and independent of the legislature. Party participation was recognized.

THE IMPERIAL DIET

The imperial Diet, which first met in 1890, consisted of the House of Peers and House of Representatives. Members of the House of Peers were chosen from the imperial family, the aristocracy, high-ranking officials, career officers, and top taxpayers and were appointed by the emperor. Initially, members of the House of Representatives were elected by voters who were at least twenty-five years old and who paid at least a certain amount in taxes each year. The powers of the two houses were fairly equal, but only the House of Representatives had the right to debate on the budget.

The Diet could approve government legislation and initiate laws, make representations to the government, and submit petitions to the emperor, but its sphere of legislation and power of deliberation were limited. Sovereignty still resided in the emperor, who had the right to open or close a session or dissolve or recess the Diet. The Diet could not remove budget items without the consent of the government. If the Diet rejected the budget bill, the government could enforce the budget of the previous year.

The emperor's powers included supreme command of

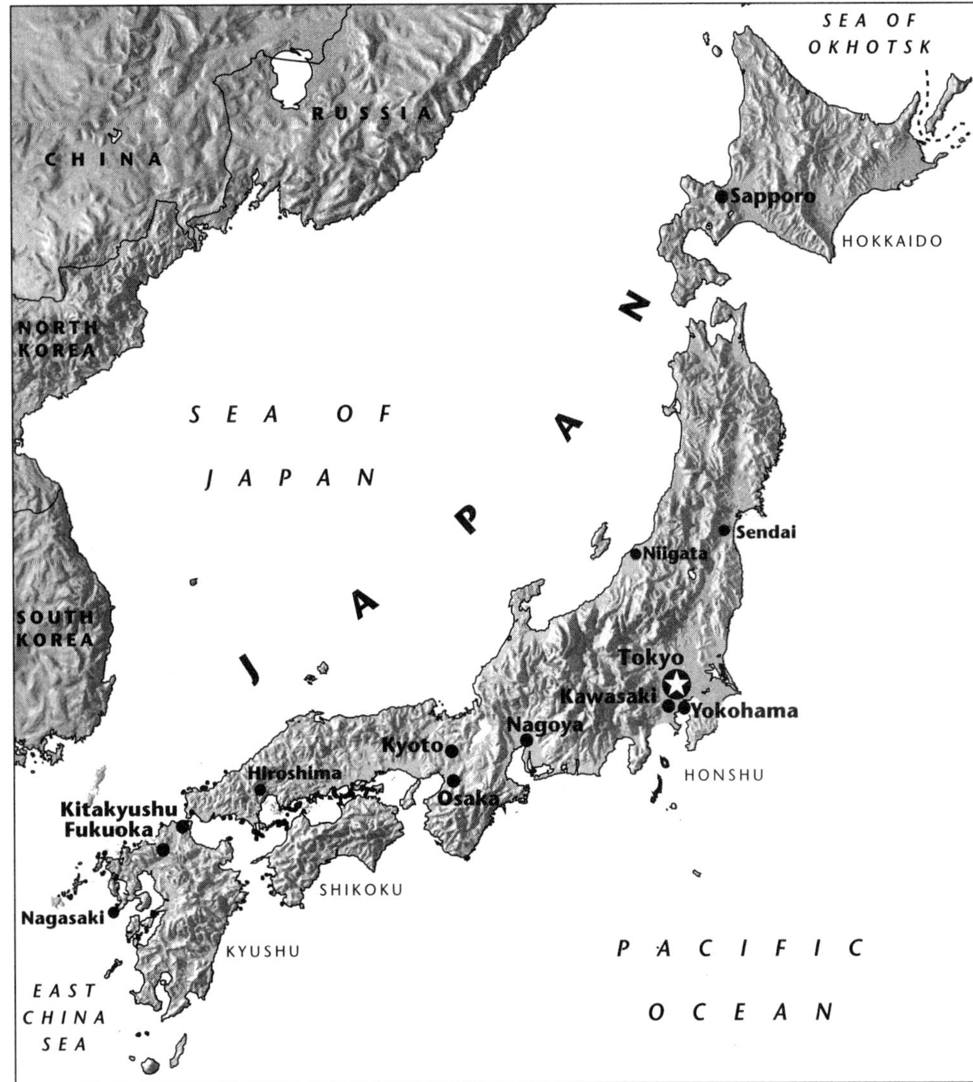

the army and navy, declaration of war, and the conclusion of treaties. The Diet had difficulty influencing government and military decisions on military actions and diplomatic problems, and its powers were largely limited by the prerogatives of the emperor and the cabinet.

The first session of the imperial Diet was convened on November 25, 1890, with an opening ceremony in the House of Peers; the emperor was in attendance. In this session the Liberal Party and the Reform-Progress Party tried to reduce the budget plan proposed by the government, but the plan finally was approved in a compromise. The main issues were reducing the land tax and revising foreign treaties. The House of Representatives soon became the arena for disputes between the politicians and the government bureaucracy over large issues, such as the budget, the ambiguity of the constitution on the authority of the Diet, and the desire of the Diet to interpret the will of the emperor versus the oligarchy's position that the cabinet and the administration should transcend all conflicting political forces.

The outbreak of the First Sino-Japanese War (1894–1895) brought all parties into line behind the government. After the war the Liberal Party and the Progress Party, formerly the Reform-Progress Party, shared power by turns. The landowning class objected to a government proposal for a tax increase on land to cover the costs of the war. The successive cabinets of Masayoshi Matsukata and Hirobumi Ito resigned. The Liberal and Progress Parties later united in the Constitutionalist Party, and the two leaders formed a cabinet. The military leaders and bureaucrats opposed this cabinet, which was dissolved when the House of Peers proposed a vote of no confidence.

Although the political parties had become stronger, they were not yet able to establish a government. Unstable political conditions continued, and in 1900 Hirobumi Ito organized the Constitutional Political Friends Party, which was important in amending the electoral law. The reformed law relaxed the qualifying conditions for voters and favored men of commerce and industry in urban districts. The po litical parties now represented not only landowners but also a part of the bourgeoisie.

The rise of party politics

When the Russo-Japanese War (1904–1905) was nearing an end without considerable results, the cabinet of Taro Katsura needed the support of the Political Friends Party to avoid trouble after conclusion of the peace treaty. Katsura promised to transfer the power of government to Kinmochi Saionji, president of the Political Friends. The importance of political parties was thereby established, though the bureaucracy and the military still stood in the way of universal suffrage and the development of party politics. In 1913 the third cabinet of Katsura was overthrown.

Only in 1918 was the first party cabinet realized under Takashi Hara, president of the Political Friends. Considering it premature to adopt universal suffrage, Hara enlarged the pool of qualified voters by reducing the amount of tax necessary to vote, and he introduced electoral reforms that contributed to the victory of the Political Friends in the following election. But in 1921 Hara was assassinated by a disgruntled railroad worker, the party split, and Hara was followed by a succession of nonparty prime ministers and coalition cabinets. The House of Peers was charged with organizing the cabinet, and in 1924 Keigo Kiyoura, president of the privy council, succeeded in filling his cabinet with members of the House of Peers, except for the seats of the ministries of army and navy. Amid a growing sense of crisis, three political parties—the Constitutionalist and Political Friends Parties and the Reformist Club—organized a movement to defend the constitution and regained political power after the election.

This cabinet established the law of universal suffrage in 1925. The political reform was not perfect, but the Japanese Diet had its first party government. In 1932 a group of junior naval officers and army cadets assassinated the prime minister. Although the assassins were tried and sentenced to fifteen years' imprisonment, the popular view was that they had acted out of patriotism. Bureaucrats again took over politics, though they did give some cabinet positions to party members. The military's power increased in the 1930s. In 1931 the Japanese army took over Manchuria without the approval of the Japanese government; in 1936 about 1,500 troops went on a rampage, assassinating the current prime minister and former ministers. The military took the lead in politics, although there was still some resistance from political parties.

Military might

In 1937 Fumimaro Konoe, a member of the imperial family, formed a cabinet with only one minister of each party, the People's Government Party and the Political Friends. In the same year the Second Sino-Japanese War began, and the two houses of the Diet decided to cooperate with the government. They passed without amendment the Law of General Mobilization of the State. Thereafter, the Diet's role was merely to support the government. The last evidence of party resistance was in 1940, when Takao Saito, leader of the People's Government Party, made an antimilitary speech and was punished. From then on the Diet had only one party, called the Serving and Supporting Association of the Imperial Rule, which replaced all other political parties.

With the outbreak of war in the Pacific in 1941, the Diet approved an enormous war expenditure. Prime Minister Hideki Tojo used the Association to Support the Emperor's Reign—a kind of superparty comprising not only most Diet members but also figures influential in politics, economics, finance, and culture—to support his position. As the war escalated and the Japanese were forced to retrench, Tojo's cabinet was obliged to resign, and in 1944 Kuniaki Koiso formed a cabinet, of which three members were elder statesmen of the former parties.

At the end of the war in 1945, the United States promoted democracy in Japan; many political parties were restored, and women gained the right to vote and to run for office. In the April 1946 general election, the Liberal Party gained the majority, and party leader Shigeru Yoshida became prime minister. On November 3, 1946, the revised Japanese constitution was promulgated; it became effective on May 3, 1947. With the end of the 92d session, the imperial Diet turned the last page of its fifty-seven-year history.

THE NATIONAL DIET UNDER THE NEW CONSTITUTION

Under the Meiji constitution of 1889 the imperial Diet was merely an advisory organ to the emperor, but Article 14 of the 1947 constitution states that the Diet "shall be the highest organ of state power and shall be the sole lawmaking organ of the state." Under the new constitution, sovereignty resides with the people, and the emperor is the symbol of the state, deriving his position from the will of the people.

The national Diet based on the 1947 constitution is also composed of two houses, the House of Representatives (the lower house) and the House of Councillors (the upper house). The House of Representatives has priority in decisions on legislation and the budget; it recognizes treaties and nominates the prime minister. It alone has the right to pass a vote of no confidence in the cabinet.

Democratic parliamentary politics began when the new

Diet convened, with old parties reemerging and new ones being founded. In the 1947 general election the Social Democratic Party of Japan won 143 seats; the Liberal Party, 131; the Democratic Party, 124; the Cooperative Party, 31; and the Japan Communist Party, 4. The Social Democrats, Democrats, and Cooperative Party formed a coalition government. Tetsu Katayama, the Social Democratic party leader, became prime minister, but his cabinet did not last long. In 1955 the Liberal and the Democratic Parties were united as the Liberal Democratic Party. This conservative party and the Social Democratic Party were distinguished by their numbers and power. The two big parties, conservative and progressive, were expected to dominate by turns, but the Liberal Democratic Party remained in power for more than thirty years.

Struggle for power

The late 1950s were marked by ideological opposition between the Liberal Democrats and the Social Democrats. Under the cabinet of Nobusuke Kishi, the two parties argued over various issues, including a treaty of mutual cooperation and security between Japan and the United States (ratification was approved). This bill in particular caused violent anti-U.S. demonstrations, and Prime Minister Kishi's cabinet resigned.

In the early 1960s the opposition's struggle against the U.S.-Japan treaty continued. Hayato Ikeda and his cabinet adopted a policy of putting economics before politics but respecting the dialogue between the government party and the opposition. After Ikeda's death, Eisaku Sato formed a cabinet that lasted nearly eight years. The one-party rule of the Liberal Democrats seemed firm, and the Social Democrats were resigned to being the perpetual chief opposition party. Other opposition parties multiplied, and the Japanese Communist Party developed a considerable following. In 1972 Kakuei Tanaka formed a cabinet with the slogan, "a plan for remodeling the Japanese archipelago," proposing industrial expansion in the provinces. With the overwhelming power of the Liberal Democratic Party, Tanaka was able to pass important bills, but his most brilliant achievement was in 1972, when he normalized diplomatic relations with the People's Republic of China. The oil shortage of 1973 put an end to the period of high economic growth, and Tanaka's plan to remodel Japan failed.

Scandal

In the late 1970s a major scandal was uncovered during the administration of Takeo Miki, implicating some members of the Liberal Democratic Party, including former prime minister Tanaka. Tanaka was arrested in July 1976 and indicted the following month on the charge of having accepted, while prime minister, about $2 million in bribes from Lockheed Aircraft Corporation to influence All Nippon Airways to buy Lockheed jetliners. The Liberal Democrats did not win a majority in the general election in 1976. The next two cabinets were the products of factional power struggles, with Masayoshi Ohira's cabinet resigning in 1980 after a vote of no confidence. The election of both houses in 1980 put the Liberal Democrats back in power, but in the 1983 election they had to request the cooperation of the New Liberal Club, a Liberal Democratic offshoot.

Prime Minister Yasumasa Nakasone came to power in the 1986 election, and the Liberal Democrats succeeded in maintaining stable political strength, taking over the New Liberal Club. In 1988 another major scandal surfaced, revealing the political corruption that long-term, one-party rule can occasion. The scandal—which involved influential leaders of the Liberal Democratic Party and a smaller number of opposition party figures in an insider trading deal—was not strictly illegal, but it caused public outrage at a time when the ruling party was considering a highly controversial consumption tax.

Because the successive cabinets of Noboru Takeshita and Sosuke Uno were unpopular, the Liberal Democratic Party suffered heavy losses in the election of 1989, especially in the House of Councillors. In the 1990 general election the Liberal Democrats gained enough seats to keep an overwhelming majority under the cabinet formed in August 1989 by Toshiki Kaifu, who pledged to make political reforms. But the Persian Gulf War in 1991 and the dissolution of the Soviet communist system highlighted the inability of Kaifu's cabinet to keep up with international crises and changes. Kaifu put three bills for political reform before the Diet, but they were rejected because of disorder within the party. Kiichi Miyazawa succeeded Kaifu in 1992. The arrest of an elder member of the Liberal Democratic Party on charges of graft and Miyazawa's passive attitude toward political reforms invited severe criticism. A vote of no confidence in the cabinet forced Miyazawa to dissolve the Diet.

In the history of the Japanese Diet, 1993 was an epoch-making year. The July election ended the Liberal Democratic Party's thirty-eight-year monopoly. Morihiro Hosokawa, leader of the Japan New Party, formed a coalition cabinet with the Social Democrats, the Cleaning Government Party, the Japan Renewal Party, the New Party Harbinger, and the Democratic Socialist Party. Advocating radical reform, Hosokawa managed to pass proportional representation as one of the reforms. But the weakness of the coalition cabinet did not make his position as prime minister stable, and on April 8, 1994, he suddenly made known his intention to resign. Tsutomu Hata, leader of the Japan Renewal Party, tried to keep the Liberal Democratic Party from succeeding to the prime minister's post, but it combined with the Social Democrats to form a cabinet, and Social Democrat leader Tomiichi Murayama was chosen prime minister. In the October 1996 elections, however, the Liberal Democrats won a near majority, and Ryutaro Hashimoto became prime minister.

ELECTIONS TO THE DIET AND SESSIONS

Members of both houses of the Diet are elected by universal suffrage. Members of the House of Representatives are elected for four-year terms. Under the 1994 reforms the number of members was reduced to 500, to take effect in 1996, the first elections after the reform. (Under the old system, the lower house had 511 members elected from multiseat districts, with an average of four or five members representing each district.) Of these, 300 members are from new single-seat districts, and the other 200 are determined by proportional representation, with each party receiving seats according to the proportion of overall votes. The minimum age requirement for voters is twenty, and that of candidates, twenty-five.

The 252 members of the House of Councillors are elected at the national and prefectural levels. One hundred members are elected from the whole nation, and 152 members are elected from forty-seven prefectures, each constituting an electoral district. The term of office is six years, and half the members are elected every three years. The minimum age requirement for the House of Councillors is thirty. Voters cast two ballots, one under the proportional representation system and one in the electoral district to which the voter belongs.

The House of Representatives, but not the House of Councillors, may be dissolved. The councillors close their session when the House of Representatives is dissolved. In times of national emergency, the cabinet may convoke the House of Councillors, but measures taken are provisional and become null and void unless they are agreed to by the House of Representatives within ten days after the opening of the next session of the Diet.

There are three kinds of Diet sessions. An ordinary session of the Diet is convoked once a year in January and lasts 150 days. The cabinet calls extraordinary sessions in response to demands from a quarter or more of all the members of either house. One or two extraordinary sessions are usually convened from summer to autumn each year. An extraordinary session must also be called after a general election when the term of office of the members of the House of Representatives expires and after an ordinary election of the members of the House of Councillors.

A special session must be convoked within thirty days after a general election of the members of the House of Representatives following dissolution. Because the cabinet must resign en masse when a special session is called, the prime minister is chosen from among the members of the Diet during the session. The term of an extraordinary or special session is determined by a concurrent vote of both houses and may be extended when both houses agree by a concurrent vote. If the two houses do not agree on these matters, or if the House of Councillors fails to decide, the determination of the House of Representatives prevails. The term can be extended twice for these two sessions, but only once for an ordinary session.

During a session the House of Representatives usually sits in plenary session at 2:00 p.m. on Tuesdays, Thursdays, and Fridays; the House of Councillors usually sits at 10:00 a.m. on Mondays, Wednesdays, and Fridays. The speaker of the House of Representatives and the president of the House of Councillors have power to hold a plenary on any other day should he or she consider it necessary.

HOW LAWS ARE MADE

Both the House of Representatives and the House of Councillors can initiate bills. Members initiating bills present their drafts to the speaker or the president, respectively, of the house to which they belong. Presenting members must secure the support of at least twenty members in the House of Representatives and at least ten members in the House of Councillors. If a bill affects the budget, the member must secure the support of at least fifty members in the House of Representatives and at least twenty in the House of Councillors. A member may initiate a bill alone or with other members. The prime minister presents cabinet bills to the presiding officer of either house.

Since the opening of the first session of the Diet, the number of bills the cabinet has introduced has been overwhelmingly greater than that of bills introduced by members of either house. A committee, standing or special, can also present a bill concerning matters under its jurisdiction to the speaker or the president in the name of its chair. Bills can be presented any time the Diet is in session. The cabinet introduces bills in the same way that members do.

Bills affecting the budget, other important bills, and treaties are usually submitted to the House of Representatives first. Amendments to the constitution are submitted to a national referendum, after they are initiated by the Diet through a concurring vote of two-thirds or more of all members of each house.

The second stop for bills is committee deliberation, though the houses may decide to omit this step. The speaker or the president refers the bill introduced to the house to an appropriate committee. The work of committees includes explanations of the bill, questions, public hearings, joint committee investigations, hearing of witnesses, debate by party representatives, and voting. The time taken to examine a bill in committee is generally much longer than the time taken in the plenary session. A committee may amend or shelve a bill referred to it and may reject it as unworthy of submission to a plenary session, provided that the bill is not one sent from the other house. The decision of a committee does not bind a plenary meeting, but the decisions of a committee and a plenary session are usually the same because the membership of a committee is in proportion to the numerical strength of political parties and groups in the house.

On the completion of the committee's work the chair of the committee that examined the bill reports to the speaker, who in turn puts the bill on the order of the day of a plenary session. When a bill comes up for consideration in the plenary meeting of the house after the committee examination, the chair first makes a report on the course of deliberation and the results. Questions may be addressed concerning the bill, and debate then follows. With the close of the debate, the house votes.

Generally, a bill becomes law if both houses pass it—in other words, establishing the intention of the Diet requires a concurrent decision of both houses. When a bill passes the House of Representatives and goes to the House of Councillors, it becomes a law if the councillors pass it, and vice versa. If the House of Councillors amends the same bill, it is referred to the House of Representatives, and it becomes a law when the House of Representatives agrees to the amendment. When the House of Councillors rejects a bill passed by the House of Representatives, the bill is sent back to the representatives and becomes a law only when it is passed again by the house by a two-thirds majority of the members present. This provision also applies if the House of Councillors fails to take final action within sixty days after receipt of the bill, time in recess excepted. The constitution gives the House of Representatives final authority when the two houses cannot agree on the budget, treaties, or designation of a prime minister.

It is up to each of the two houses, if they disagree on the text of a bill, to call for a conference committee of both houses. The conference committee is composed of twenty members, each house electing an equal number. A quorum of the committee is two-thirds of the members from each house, and approval requires a two-thirds majority of the members present. When no agreement can be reached even through a conference committee of both houses, the decision of the House of Representatives becomes that of the Diet.

DEBATES

The deliberations of each house are, as a rule, open to the public, and business cannot be transacted in either house unless one-third or more of the total membership is present. At least half of the committee members must be present.

Members who wish to speak in a plenary session or a committee must give prior notice, except in unavoidable circumstances. Question, debate, points of order, and all speeches must be invited by the speaker, the president, or the chair of the committee. Before a plenary session, the Rules and Administration Committee arranges the number of speakers, the order of speeches, and the amount of time for each speech in proportion to the numerical strength of each party or group.

All matters are decided by a majority of those present, except as elsewhere provided for in the constitution. In case of a tie, the speaker, the president, or the chair of the committee decides a matter.

There are three ways of voting: oral, standing, and open ballot. Oral voting is used when a question seems neither to be grave nor to arouse strong opposition. A standing vote is taken in similar cases. In requesting those in favor of a question to rise, the speaker or the president compares the number of those who are standing with the number of those who are seated and declares the result to the house. An open ballot is frequently used for important bills. A vote by open ballot is taken when it is difficult to ascertain whether the members standing are in the majority; when one-fifth or more of the members have taken exception to the declaration of the speaker, president, or the chair; or when members demand it. While open voting is taking place, all entrances to the chamber are closed. Members in favor of the bill cast white ballot slips with their names on them into the ballot boxes, and those in opposition cast blue ballot slips. Names of the members who vote pro or con are entered in the minutes of the house.

As a rule, the deliberations of each house are open to the public, so the press, radio, television, and other media can cover a plenary session. Radio and television broadcast all deliberations during a session—ordinary, extraordinary, or special—convoked in each house. Although committee meetings are, as a rule, closed to the public, members of the press, radio, and television and other media may be admitted to meetings at the discretion of the chair.

THE DIET COMPLEX

The neoclassical building that houses the Diet stands on a hill at Nagata-Cho in the ward of Chiyoda in Tokyo. Completed in November 1936, the complex has been in use since 1937. In the center of the main block is a tower, with a central entrance at the foot. This entrance is used only for the emperor on the opening day, for members on the first convocation day, and for state guests. Facing the central entrance is a central hall. At the top of the grand staircase that leads from the hall is the room used for the emperor's visits to the Diet.

The north wing of the main building is occupied by the House of Councillors; the south wing, by the House of Representatives. The chamber of the House of Councillors can seat as many as 460. The chamber of the House of Representatives can seat 512 members. The chambers of the two houses are about the same size.

The throne on which the emperor sits for the Diet's opening ceremony and the royal box provided for the emperor and empress when they visit the Diet in session are in the House of Councillors. Each chamber has offices for the president and the vice president, drawing rooms for their guests and for meetings of the Rules and Administration Committees, and several committee rooms. The largest is used mainly for meetings of the Budget Committees. There is also a dining hall for the members. Each Diet member has an office.

Surrounding the Diet building are the Parliament Museum, the National Diet Library, and the Diet Reporter's Building. Also in the vicinity are joint ministerial buildings, the headquarters of some political parties, and the official residences of the prime minister, the speaker, and the president of the two houses.

The National Diet Library stands across the road to the north of the Diet Building. It was established in 1948 to assist Diet members and provide library services for the executive and judicial branches of the national government and the general public.

COMMITTEES

In each house there are standing committees and special committees. The House of Representatives has twenty standing committees, each with twenty to fifty members; the House of Councillors has seventeen, each with ten to forty-five members. House of Representatives committees are on the cabinet; local administration; judicial affairs; foreign affairs; finance; education; health and welfare; agriculture, forestry, and fisheries; commerce and industry; transport; communications; labor; construction; security; science and technology; environment; budget; audit; rules and administration; and discipline. The House of Councillors has committees on the cabinet; local administration; justice; foreign affairs; finance; education; social and labor affairs; agriculture, forestry and fisheries; commerce and industry; transport; communications; construction; budget; audit; rules and administration; and discipline. Since 1986 committees have been set up to conduct long-term, comprehensive investigations into fundamental matters of state administration.

A special committee may be appointed by either house to examine matters that are deemed necessary by the house or that do not come under the jurisdiction of any standing committee. The house appoints members of special committees, who serve until the house decides on the business referred to the committee. The chair of a special committee should be elected from among its members but in practice is selected by a motion of recommendation in the committee.

In preparation for a plenary meeting, committees examine law bills, budgets, treaties, and petitions in detail. They also investigate those aspects of government within their jurisdiction. Sometimes committees establish subcommittees. Membership on committees is allocated to various political parties and groups in proportion to their respective numerical strength. Every Diet member has to serve on at least one standing committee. A committee must hold public hearings on the general budget and important revenue bills and may do so on important bills of public interest. A committee may, if it is deemed necessary, summon a witness for evidence. No business may be transacted in a committee unless at least one-half of its members are present. All the decisions in a committee are made by a majority of the members present.

Chairs of standing committees are nominated by each house, but their selection in practice is entrusted to the speaker of the House of Representatives or the president of the House of Councillors. Committee chairs preside over the meetings, arrange the proceedings of the committee, maintain order and represent the committee, and have the right to call committee meetings, to make decisions by casting vote, to report to the house about matters examined by the committee, to explain in the other house bills initiated by the house to which they belong, and to give an opinion at other committee meetings.

THE BUDGET

The fiscal year begins on April 1. The national budget is, therefore, presented to the Diet at the beginning of an ordinary session convoked in January. The cabinet initiates the budget, which is first introduced into the House of Representatives. The budget is referred to the Budget Committee, which has the largest committee membership. This committee may request the prime minister and other ministers of state to be present at its meetings so that it can ask them questions on the national administration in general. The proceedings on the budget frequently provide opportunities for members to criticize the administration.

When a motion of amendment to the budget is placed on the order of the day in a plenary meeting, at least fifty members in the House of Representatives or at least twenty members of the House of Councillors must support it. When the House of Councillors makes a decision on the budget different from that of the House of Representatives and no agreement can be reached (even through a conference committee of both houses), or when the House of Councillors fails to take final action within thirty days (recesses excluded) after receiving the budget passed by the House of Representatives, the decision of the House of Representatives becomes that of the Diet.

SELECTION OF THE EXECUTIVE AND OVERSIGHT

The prime minister is designated from among the Diet members by a resolution of the Diet. He or she is elected by a simple majority of representatives. If any single party holds a majority, it elects the prime minister. Otherwise, parties negotiate to form a governing coalition and choose a prime minister. If the two houses disagree, and if no agreement can be reached even through a conference committee, or if the House of Councillors fails to make a designation within ten days (excluding recesses) after the House of Representatives has made a designation, the decision of the House of Representatives prevails. Most cabinet ministers are chosen from among the members of the House of Representatives.

When the House of Representatives passes a no-confidence resolution or rejects a confidence resolution, the cabinet resigns en masse, unless the House of Representatives is dissolved within ten days. A member of either house who wishes to introduce a resolution of confidence or no confidence in the cabinet makes a draft with reasons attached, signed by at least fifty supporters. This resolution is submitted to the speaker or the president.

When members of either house wish to address questions to the government, they must submit them in writing to the speaker or the president for approval. The speaker or the president then transmits to the cabinet the approved written questions. The cabinet must answer questions so put within seven days after receipt. If cabinet ministers cannot respond during this period, they must give the reason and state a time at which a reply can be made. Urgent questions may be posed orally in the chamber with the concurrence of the house.

Each house may investigate the government and may demand the presence and testimony of witnesses and the presentation of records. Such investigations are usually conducted in committee meetings. A standing or special committee may investigate government matters that fall under its own jurisdiction.

In 1980 a commission for the study of the ombudsman system was founded in the Administrative Management Agency (now the Management and Coordination Agency). In 1986 the commission proposed the introduction of an ombudsman system attached to an administrative office rather than to the Diet, but this project has not yet been carried out.

POWERS OF THE SPEAKER AND THE PRESIDENT

The speaker of the House of Representatives and the president of the House of Councillors have similar powers. The speaker and the vice speaker are elected by secret ballot. Their term of office coincides with their term of office as members.

The speaker has the power to maintain order in the House. When members disturb the order of the chamber or impair the dignity of the House, the speaker warns or restrains them or orders them to retract their remarks. If members refuse to obey the order, the speaker may prohibit them from speaking until the sitting is over, make them leave the chamber, or—according to circumstances—refer the case to the standing committee on discipline. When visitors in the public gallery obstruct the proceedings of the House, the speaker may make them leave the House or, if necessary, hand them over to the police. The speaker may order the gallery to be cleared in case of a disturbance.

The speaker has the power to arrange the business of the House—that is, to refer a bill to an appropriate committee after it is introduced; to determine the order of the day; to call a plenary meeting when he or she deems it urgent, announcing the date and time of the sitting through the official bulletin of the House; to limit the length of time for questions, debates, or other speeches, unless otherwise decided by the House; to allow a member to put a written question to the cabinet; to call members of the House, ministers of the state, and government delegates to speak; and to adjourn or suspend the House.

The speaker also supervises administration of the House. When the House negotiates with the House of Councillors, the cabinet, and others, the speaker represents it. Through the speaker, members can demand an extraordinary session, and a committee can request the presence of ministers of state, government delegates, or the president and members of the audit board at its meeting. Government delegates are appointed by the cabinet with the approval of the speaker.

The speaker may attend and address committee meetings. With the consent of the speaker, a committee may hold a public hearing and dispatch committee members for the purpose of examination or investigation. Minutes are recorded under the speaker's supervision. The speaker exercises police power to maintain discipline in the House. Guards perform police duty inside the House, and police officers do so outside the House. But the speaker may call police officers inside the House building when he or she deems it necessary.

PARTY FACTIONS AND CONTROL

The Liberal Democratic Party—the largest political party in Japan—has almost always succeeded in having its chair named prime minister. Among the factions there is a constant struggle for leadership, but in 1993 the Liberal Democrats organized a coalition cabinet with their ancient rivals, the Social Democrats, and with the New Party Harbinger. In Japanese politics, factions may dissolve and new factions or nonpartisan groups are organized.

The Social Democratic Party also has factions and groups ranging from left wing to right, each of which has a different opinion about the political line that their party is taking. Under the cabinet of Tomiichi Murayama, who formed a government in 1994, these factions seemed to be making every effort to keep the party together by compromising with one another.

The election reform of 1994 was based on a belief that it would advance a two-party system. With power alternating between two strong parties, many in Japan hoped there would be more action on government deregulation, market reform, and relief for Japanese consumers. But, as noted above, the 1996 elections returned the Liberal Democrats to power.

MEMBERS OF THE DIET

The members of each house are paid no less than the maximum salary of a regular government official. They may also have a government subsidy to employ two secretaries. Members of each house can use the Japan Railway free of charge, and they receive financial aid for correspondence.

The constitution states that no member of either house can be arrested during a session of the Diet, except for a case prescribed by law. A member who is arrested before a session is set free for the session if the house he or she belongs to so requests.

Each house can permit the resignation of a member during a session; outside a session the speaker or the president can give such permission. When a member of one house becomes a member of another house, or when a member loses the qualification given by law, he or she retires. When there is disagreement about a member's qualification, the house to which he or she belongs decides after a committee investigation. Members may be defended by two counselors and can continue to work as a member until it is proved that they are not qualified. But they cannot participate in any decision concerning their status.

In 1985 a deliberative council that would handle ethical matters related to members' activities outside the Diet was established in each house. Both houses also approved principles of political ethics and standards of conduct. In the House of Representatives the Council on the Parliamentary System functions as an organ to discuss parliamentary ideals and problems connected with the Diet.

A motion for disciplinary measures, which can be proposed by forty or more supporters in the House of Representatives or by twenty or more supporters in the House of Councillors, is always referred to the committee on discipline. There are four degrees of discipline: reprimand, apology, suspension, and expulsion.

Tatsunori Isomi

BIBLIOGRAPHY

Beasley, William G. *The Rise of Modern Japan.* New York: St. Martin's, 1990.

Curtis, Gerald L. *The Japanese Way of Politics.* New York: Columbia University Press, 1988.

Ike, Nobutaka. *A Theory of Japanese Democracy.* Boulder, Colo.: Westview Press, 1978.

Uchida, Kenzo. *Gendai Nihon no Hshu Seiji: The Conservative Politics of Contemporary Japan.* Tokyo: Iwanami Shoten, 1989.

JORDAN

OFFICIAL NAME: Hashemite Kingdom of Jordan (al-Mamlakah al-Urduniyah al-Hashimiyah)

CAPITAL: Amman

POPULATION: 4,212,000 (1996 est.)

DATE OF INDEPENDENCE: May 25, 1946 (from League of Nations mandate under British administration)

DATE OF CURRENT CONSTITUTION: Adopted January 8, 1952

FORM OF GOVERNMENT: Constitutional monarchy

LANGUAGE: Arabic (official)

MONETARY UNIT: Jordanian dinar

FISCAL YEAR: Calendar year

LEGISLATURE: National Assembly (Majlis al-ʿUmma)

NUMBER OF CHAMBERS: Two. Chamber of Deputies (Majlis al-Nuwwab); Chamber of Notables (Majlis al-Aʿyaan)

NUMBER OF MEMBERS: Chamber of Deputies, 80 (directly elected); Chamber of Notables, 40 (appointed)

PERCENTAGE OF WOMEN: Chamber of Deputies, 1.3; Chamber of Notables, 5.0

TERM OF LEGISLATURE: Four years

MOST RECENT LEGISLATIVE ELECTION: November 8, 1993

MINIMUM AGE FOR VOTING: 19

MINIMUM AGE FOR MEMBERSHIP: Chamber of Deputies, 30; Chamber of Notables, 40

SUFFRAGE: Universal

VOTING: Optional

ADDRESS: Parliament House, P.O. Box 72, Amman

TELEPHONE: (962 6) 664121

FAX: (962 6) 685970

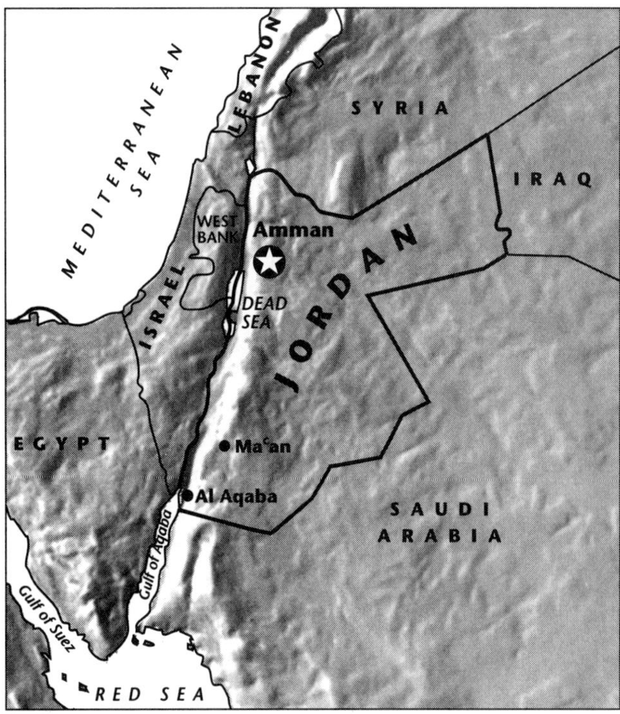

The Hashemite Kingdom of Jordan, a nearly landlocked state in the Middle East, is a constitutional monarchy. The bicameral National Assembly comprises an elected Chamber of Deputies and a Chamber of Notables, the members of which are appointed by the king.

BACKGROUND

Created by Great Britain in 1922, the Emirate of Transjordan was carved out of the ruins of the Ottoman Empire. Until it achieved independence in 1946, the emirate was a British mandate, ruled by Emir ʿAbdallah ibn Hussein. Almost from the moment Transjordan came into existence, its ruler faced calls for the establishment of a representative institution. For years such demands were resisted by the British, who feared that an elected assembly might challenge their control over the country's affairs. In the late 1920s, however, plans were made for the election of a Legislative Assembly in order to give the regime a constitutional character.

The 1928 organic law, which defined the prerogatives of the Assembly, subordinated it to the palace and the British resident general. Members of the Executive Council (that is, the cabinet) continued to be chosen and appointed by the emir and were not made accountable to the Assembly. The emir was given the power to convene, adjourn, suspend, or dismiss the Assembly at will. Bills adopted by the Assembly had to be ratified by the emir and the British resident general. All six members of the Executive Council were ex-officio members of the twenty-two-member Assembly. Two Assembly seats reserved for the nomadic tribes were to be filled by individuals chosen by two separate tribal commissions appointed by the emir. The fourteen remaining members were to be elected indirectly to represent geographical constituencies. The head of the Executive Council would chair the Legislative Assembly and thus be in a position to shape its agenda and the course of its debates. Finally, through a system of quotas, the electoral law ensured that the Christian, Circassian, and Chechen minorities, which were seen as natural allies of the palace, would be over-represented in the Assembly.

Despite these restrictions, the first Legislative Assembly, elected in April 1929, turned out to be quite assertive and critical of the executive branch. In fact, it so often embarrassed the government that the emir finally disbanded it on February 9, 1931. Moreover, from the moment the organic law was issued, the Legislative Assembly became the focus of widespread demands that it be made more representative and influential. This suggests that it was seen as a credible institution, capable of providing an effective counterweight to the executive. In 1928, for instance, a national conference brought together 150 notables, tribal leaders, and intellectuals who adopted resolutions protesting the electoral law and the Assembly's insufficient power. Their grievances were formally conveyed to the emir, the British resident general, and the League of Nations. Similar conferences were held in 1929, 1930, 1932, and 1933. In short, the Assembly's very limitations had triggered within Transjordan a debate over the need for more representative institutions. That by itself was a considerable achievement. The election of five successive Assemblies between 1929 and 1946 also served as a valuable apprenticeship with the practice of representative government.

Shortly after it became independent in 1946, Transjordan adopted its first constitution. That constitution and an electoral law issued the following year provided for a bicameral legislature made up of a directly elected, twenty-member Chamber of Deputies and a ten-member Chamber of Notables appointed by the king. Criticism of this constitution was voiced by those who wanted the cabinet to be responsible to the elected lower house, not to the monarch.

During the Arab-Israeli war of 1948 Transjordan seized the West Bank. After it formally annexed the West Bank in 1950, the country came to be known as Jordan. Emir ʿAbdallah was assassinated in July 1951, and a new and far more liberal constitution was promulgated in January 1952. For the first time, the cabinet was made constitutionally responsible to an assembly elected by the people. Although the prime minister was still chosen and appointed by the king, the prime minister and his cabinet now had to secure a vote of confidence from the Chamber of Deputies before they could formally assume their functions. Prior to the vote, the prime minister had to present his program to the Chamber. Once the prime minister was invested, a two-thirds majority in the Chamber was required to force the government to resign. In addition, deputies could impeach ministers. No bill originating in the executive branch could become law without being submitted to the Chamber, which had the power to amend or reject bills. Although the king could veto legislation adopted by parliament within six months of its passing, deputies could override this veto with a two-thirds majority vote.

The 1952 constitution also eliminated several provisions that previously had enabled the executive branch to control the legislature's agenda. Moreover, it granted the lower house greater authority over financial and foreign affairs, including the power to ratify treaties. This represented a substantial encroachment on what until then had been considered the king's "reserved domain." Although it was amended in 1974, 1976, and 1984, the constitution of 1952 remains in place today.

In May 1953, at the age of eighteen, ʿAbdallah's grandson Hussein ascended the throne. (ʿAbdallah's son Talal, who had ascended the throne upon his father's assassination in July 1951, was deposed in August 1952 for medical reasons; since Hussein was not yet eighteen—and therefore, under the constitution, could not be crowned king—a regency council directed the country's affairs until May 1953.) From the beginning of his reign Hussein was under considerable domestic and external pressure. Since the addition of the West Bank to the kingdom in 1950, a majority of the country's population was of Palestinian origin. Many if not most of these Palestinian-Jordanians were unwilling citizens of the state. They opposed the institution of the monarchy and did not recognize Jordanian sovereignty over the West Bank. They espoused various Arab nationalist and leftist ideologies such as communism, Baathism, and Nasserism. The native Transjordanian population itself featured a young and radicalized intelligentsia that was highly critical of the regime's pro-Western policies and of its generally conservative orientation. Meanwhile, outside powers were interfering in the kingdom's domestic politics. The Jordanian Baath Party was actually run from Damascus, Syria. Other groups were professing allegiance to Egyptian president Gamal Abd al-Nasser.

In this highly volatile and polarized atmosphere characterized by a lack of agreement on the rules of the political game, the legislature could hardly discharge its functions effectively. A crisis seemed inevitable, and one arose in the wake of the parliamentary elections of October 1956. These elections resulted in a strong showing for the pan-Arab National Socialist Party (NSP) led by Sulayman Nabulsi. With eleven deputies, the NSP emerged as the largest party in the lower house. Altogether, candidates sympathetic to pan-Arab and leftist ideas controlled twenty seats, or one-half of the Chamber. Appointed prime minister by King Hussein, Nabulsi formed a government that represented a coalition of the "progressive" forces in parliament. Meanwhile, the Chamber developed for itself a strong nationalist agenda. It abolished the Anglo-Jordanian Treaty in February 1957, ratified the Arab Union between Iraq and Jordan, and asserted itself on a number of legislative matters. Most important, the Chamber of Deputies succeeded in holding the cabinet accountable. To some observers, Jordan seemed to be moving toward a constitutional monarchy with a representative, accountable parliamentary system. By early April 1957, however, the Nabulsi government was engaged in a showdown with the monarchy.

PARLIAMENTARY GOVERNMENT WEAKENED

Some members of the Nabulsi government suggested publicly that the king become a mere figurehead or that he resign and the monarchy be abolished. Defying the king, the cabinet dismissed several of his protégés who occupied key positions in the state bureaucracy. At about the same time, King Hussein faced a coup attempt by military officers. On April 10, 1957, the young ruler stood up to what seemed like a frontal attack on the monarchy, and he fired Nabulsi. Soon afterward, a gathering of prominent leftist leaders issued a "proclamation to the people" that challenged not only the king's authority but the very existence of Jordan as a separate entity. That proclamation bore the signature of twenty-three deputies and was coauthored by the NSP, which was still the main party in the cabinet and the Chamber. King Hussein reacted swiftly. On April 25 he imposed martial law, banned all political parties, cracked down on the press, and arrested several hundred well-known opponents of the regime. Although he allowed the legislature to complete its term, he did so only after expelling nine deputies and forcing six others to resign their seats. This ensured that the legislature would be far more compliant and would no longer provide a power base for politicians who opposed the legitimacy of the country's institutions and borders. By these steps, the representativeness and authority of the Jordanian legislature were greatly reduced.

Between 1957 and 1967, elections (specifically those of 1961) were marred by administrative interference. Opposition candidates and their supporters were frequently intimidated or harassed. In addition, the electoral law was altered in 1960 to favor the government. And when all these measures failed and the Chamber of Deputies still adopted a defiant attitude, it was dissolved. This was the case when the Chamber denied a vote of confidence to the new government in April 1963. The king responded by disbanding it and calling for new elections.

In November 1974, seven years after Jordan lost the West Bank to Israel, King Hussein dissolved the upper and lower houses and decided to rule without a parliament. His decision was prompted by the Israeli occupation of the West Bank, which prevented new elections to the Chamber of Deputies, and by an Arab League summit resolution adopted in October 1974 which declared the Palestine Liberation Organization (PLO) to be the sole representative of the Palestinian people, thus implicitly denying the Jordanian monarch the right to speak for West Bank Palestinians (who at the time still accounted for half the members of both houses). By the mid-1970s, however, Jordan's tradition of representative government had become so rooted that calls were heard almost immediately for the establishment of an institution that would provide popular input into the policy-making process. In response to these demands, the king created the National Consultative Council in 1978.

The Council's sixty members were all appointed by the monarch, and their narrowly defined mandate was to provide the cabinet with advisory opinions on specific bills and policies upon request by the prime minister. The Council could not approve, amend, or reject a bill and could not pass motions of no confidence against the cabinet. Despite its limited representativeness and power, the Council, which sat until 1983, proved to be a valuable institution. Its members took their responsibilities seriously and endeavored to make the most of their prerogatives. The Council facilitated contacts between the bureaucracy and the population and provided a forum in which important bills and policies were debated. The questions with which it dealt were often sensitive, including civil liberties and the future of the West Bank. Discussion of these issues in the Council ensured a wider reporting of different opinions about them in the press.

RESURGENCE OF PARLIAMENTARY POLITICS

In 1984 King Hussein recalled parliament. Within four years, however, he was forced to deal with the ramifications of the Palestinian uprising, or *intifada,* which had erupted in the Israeli-occupied territories in December 1987. The monarch was quick to realize that the *intifada* had dealt a lethal blow to the pro-Jordanian notables who had been his main allies on the West Bank. He also had grown tired of fruitless efforts to develop with PLO leader Yasir Arafat a common position on the peace process. Accordingly, in July 1988 he severed all administrative and legal ties between Jordan and the West Bank. Having done so, he no longer could keep a parliament in which half the members came from the West Bank, and he therefore dissolved the legislature. The legislature was reconvened in November 1989, seven months after serious riots had rocked Jordan, forcing the king to address mounting political and economic discontent by democratizing political life. This marked the beginning of the resurgence of parliamentary politics, which has been one of the main manifestations of the democratization process that has been unfolding in Jordan since 1989.

The November 1989 election was the first in twenty-two years and the first national contest in which women were able to vote. The election was held on the East Bank only.

Although the ban on political parties remained in place and forced all candidates to run as independents, these candidates' ideological orientations—which ran from Islamic fundamentalism to Baathism and communism—were well known. The campaign was lively and remarkably free of governmental interference.

The outcome of the election surprised many observers. Politicians affiliated with the religious movement known as the Muslim Brotherhood captured twenty-two seats, and Islamic fundamentalists altogether won thirty-four seats in the eighty-seat lower house. The secular left also did relatively well, as twelve candidates known for their communist, Baathist, Arab nationalist, or pro-Palestinian sympathies were elected. The remaining thirty-four members fell in two main categories: tribal or traditionalist candidates, who were the regime's strongest backers; and independent, centrist politicians whose reformist tendencies put them at some distance from the government but whose moderate and pragmatic outlook led them to reject both the fundamentalists' and the left's messages.

The new legislature quickly asserted itself. From the moment it met, it debated such sensitive topics as corruption, economic reform, and civil liberties. Its proceedings were widely reported in the press, which provided the citizenry with an opportunity to witness heated exchanges on public policy. Leftist as well as Islamic fundamentalist deputies criticized the structural adjustment program sponsored by the International Monetary Fund. A Committee on Public Freedoms was formed to investigate alleged violations of public liberties. That committee also launched highly publicized inquiries into corruption by government officials, some of whom were very close to the palace. Former prime minister Zaid al-Rifa'i narrowly escaped parliamentary indictment for misuse of public funds.

The lower house also debated regional and international issues in which Jordan had an interest. Shortly after Iraq invaded Kuwait on August 2, 1990, parliament became a rallying point for condemnation of the Western coalition against Saddam Hussein, thus putting pressure on the king to move from his initially neutral stance to a decidedly pro-Iraqi position. Finally, the National Assembly made important contributions to law making. During the meetings of specialized parliamentary committees, ministers were pressed to explain their proposed legislation, and changes suggested by committee members were often incorporated into the bills. In a clear indication that the regime was forced to take the legislature's opinion seriously, several of the main parliamentary blocs were represented in successive cabinets nominated by the monarch. Meanwhile, King Hussein's policy of distancing himself from the day-to-day decisions of the government had a profound effect on the legislature. Criticism of the cabinet could no longer be automatically interpreted as attacks on the monarchy or the regime. This in turn spurred the National Assembly to become more assertive in its oversight of governmental policies and the actions of specific ministers.

New elections were held in November 1993. By then political parties had been legalized, but approximately 90 percent of the 536 candidates campaigned as independents. As a result of a change in the electoral law, widespread disenchantment with ideological politics, and somewhat greater administrative interference than in 1989, the contest resulted in a victory for traditionalist and middle-of-the-road notables closely associated with the palace. Liberals and center-left figures also did reasonably well. By contrast, Islamists and leftist candidates suffered a relative setback, the former capturing only eighteen seats, as opposed to thirty-four in 1989. The elections, however, did not produce a rubber-stamp legislature. Islamists remained a force to be reckoned with in a lower house that also included Baathists, leftists, and pan-Arabists. Liberal and centrist deputies also showed themselves to be vocal. Even MPs frequently described as representing the "tribal" and "traditionalist" vote did not want to be taken for granted by the regime and were quick to assert their prerogatives.

When parliament met for its regular session in November 1994, its agenda was dominated by the peace treaty that Jordan had just signed with Israel on October 26. After heated debates, the lower house ratified the treaty by a comfortable 55–24 vote. This endorsement was instrumental in helping the regime legitimize the normalization of relations with the Jewish state. A few months later, the Chamber repealed the laws providing for an economic boycott of Israel, but only after including several amendments designed to limit Israeli investment in Jordanian companies and real estate.

In 1995 and 1996 parliament passed important legislation to boost domestic and foreign investment, and it revamped the taxation system. In addition, it adopted measures intended to facilitate the privatization of the energy and telecommunications sectors. At the same time, the Chamber provided an outlet for the expression of opposition to the rapid transformation of relations with Israel. Islamist and leftist deputies repeatedly expressed their concern that the government was restricting public liberties and clamping down on dissident voices. These and other parliamentary attacks on the cabinet and its policies made it clear that this supposedly conservative legislature was determined to force the government to account for its actions.

CONCLUSION

In summary, Jordan features an old legislative tradition. The assertion of parliament after 1989 did not take place in a historical vacuum; rather, it had deep roots in the country's past. The 1952 constitution, which endowed parliament with significant powers, was never suspended. Certainly, the legislature often led a precarious existence and was disbanded on several occasions. But that is no more significant than the fact that it was restored every time. Whenever parliament was not in place, voices called for its reconvening or for the establishment of some other representative institution. Most important, since the early 1990s Jordan's democratic experiment has been predicated on a central role for the legislature. The National Assembly has become more representative of the political forces in the country. It has gained in autonomy relative to the executive branch and has exercised greater influence over government formation and policy making. This process can be expected to continue as the country enters the twenty-first century.

Abdo Baaklini, Guilain Denoeux, and Robert Springborg

BIBLIOGRAPHY

Abu Jaber, Kamel S. "The Jordanian Parliament." In *Man, State, and Society in the Contemporary Middle East,* ed. Jacob M. Landau. New York: Praeger, 1972.

Freij, Hanna Y., and Leonard C. Robinson. "Liberalization, the Islamists, and the Stability of the Arab State: Jordan as a Case Study." *Muslim World,* 86, no. 1 (January 1996): 1–31.

Khoury, Nabeel A. "The National Consultative Council of Jordan: A Study in Legislative Development." *International Journal of Middle East Studies,* 13 (1981): 427–439.

Robins, Philip J. "Politics and the 1986 Electoral Law in Jordan." In *Politics and the Economy in Jordan,* ed. Rodney Wilson. London: Routledge, 1991.

K

KAZAKSTAN

See Commonwealth of Independent States, Non-Slavic

KENYA

OFFICIAL NAME: Republic of Kenya (Jamhuri ya Kenya)
CAPITAL: Nairobi
POPULATION: 28,177,000 (1996 est.)
DATE OF INDEPENDENCE: December 12, 1963 (from the United Kingdom)
DATE OF CURRENT CONSTITUTION: Effective December 12, 1963
FORM OF GOVERNMENT: Parliamentary democracy
LANGUAGES: Swahili (official), English, many indigenous languages
MONETARY UNIT: Kenyan shilling
FISCAL YEAR: July 1–June 30
LEGISLATURE: National Assembly
NUMBER OF CHAMBERS: One
NUMBER OF MEMBERS: 202 (188 elected, 12 appointed by the president, 2 ex officio)
PERCENTAGE OF WOMEN: 3.0
TERM OF LEGISLATURE: Five years
MOST RECENT LEGISLATIVE ELECTION: December 29, 1992
MINIMUM AGE FOR VOTING: 18
MINIMUM AGE FOR MEMBERSHIP: 21
SUFFRAGE: Universal
VOTING: Optional
ADDRESS: Parliament Buildings, P.O. Box 41842, Nairobi
TELEPHONE: (254 2) 221 291
FAX: (254 2) 336 589

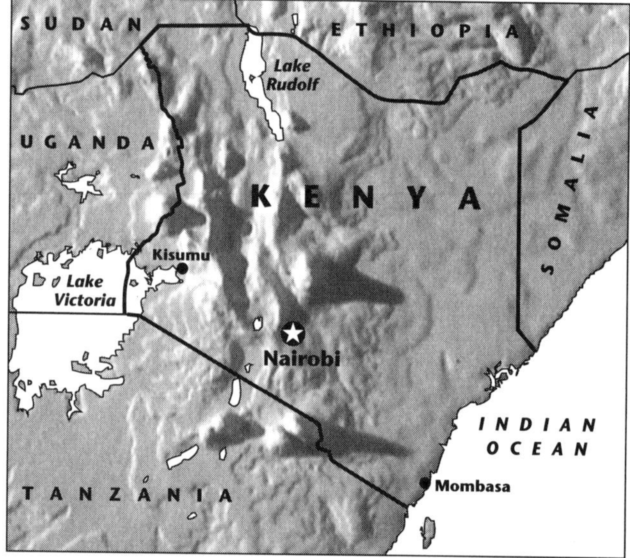

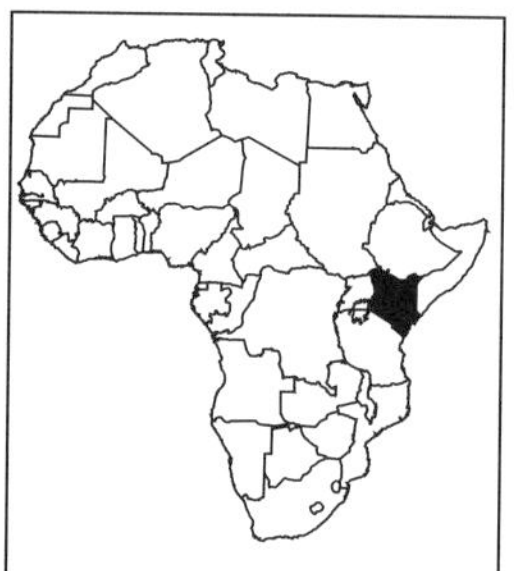

A former British Crown Colony in East Africa, Kenya is struggling to establish a multiparty system after many years of one-party government. The president, who is elected directly by the people, also sits in Kenya's unicameral National Assembly.

HISTORICAL BACKGROUND

After several years of Portuguese rule, Kenya came under British rule in 1895 as the East African Protectorate. In 1920 it became a British colony and in 1963 gained independence, though remaining a member of the Commonwealth. The country became the Republic of Kenya in 1964, although its nationalist movement began in 1944 with the formation of the Kenya African Union (KAU). The country's first president, Jomo Kenyatta, came on the national scene in the late 1940s as the president of the Kenya African Union. In 1953 the British banned the Union, as they associated it with the guerrilla uprisings of the time, and Kenyatta was imprisoned. By the time of Kenyatta's release in 1961, the 1960 constitutional conference held in London had installed a transitional constitution. Political parties were now permitted to form—resulting in the appearance of the Kenya African National Union (KANU) and Kenya African Democratic Union (KADU)—and Africans were given the majority in the Legislative Council, formed originally for white settlers in 1907. By the second constitutional conference in 1962, legislative and executive councils representing Africans, Europeans, and Asians separately had been established.

In 1964, a year after independence, Kenya was declared a republic, with Kenyatta as president. The basis for this new government was, and remains, the 1963 constitution and its amendments. Within the year, Kenyatta merged the Kenya African Democratic Union into the Kenya African National Union; a 1966 constitutional amendment merged the Senate and the House of Representatives into a unicameral National Assembly.

Upon Kenyatta's death in 1978, Vice President Daniel arap Moi inherited the presidency. By 1982 Moi had become increasingly intolerant of the opposition forces within Kenya, and the National Assembly declared Kenya a de jure one-party state. Later that year, during a coup attempt by the air force, Moi invoked the 1966 Preservation of Public Security Act for the first time since Kenyatta's rule. This act allows the president to take drastic measures to maintain public security, including indefinite detention without charge or trial. Moi began taking control of Kenyan society by banning independent associations at all levels. In 1986 the National Assembly amended the constitution to transfer control of the civil service from the Assembly to the president and to allow the president to dismiss the attorney general and auditor general. Two years later this authority was extended to judges.

In 1990 Kenyans began calling for the return of multipartyism, as was occurring in many other African nations. But Moi argued that such competition would result in ethnic wars throughout the country and refused their demand. By December 1991 threats from foreign donor states to cut off aid to Kenya had forced Moi to compromise by repealing the section of the constitution that made Kenya a one-party state. But the opposition parties lacked unity, and Moi won the 1992 elections with just over a third of the votes. Even now, Moi continues to stand firm on his belief in a one-party government.

THE CONSTITUTION AND THE LEGISLATURE

Kenya's unicameral National Assembly comprises 188 members elected by universal adult suffrage, 12 presidential appointees, the speaker, and the attorney general. The Assembly is primarily responsible for deliberating, legislating, and overseeing the government's use of public monies. The constitution gives the National Assembly the power to legislate on all matters, including those of the ministries, but it prohibits Assembly debate of the issues being handled in the courts and any related to the president's conduct.

Cabinet members, who with one exception are elected members of the Assembly, play a direct role in legislative deliberations and the drafting of legislation. The cabinet also includes the president, the vice president, and government ministers. The attorney general is the only member of the cabinet who is not required to be selected from the National Assembly. The cabinet is collectively responsible to the National Assembly.

As an elected member of the Assembly, the president is entitled to attend its meetings and vote on bills but has no veto power. The president must command a majority vote in the National Assembly. A president who loses a vote of confidence must either resign or dissolve the Assembly and call new elections. The National Assembly can force the resignation of the entire cabinet by a simple vote of no confidence in one or more of the cabinet's members. Although this rarely has occurred, in April 1989 Vice President Josephat Karanja received a unanimous parliamentary vote of no confidence because of his alleged use of his position to further personal and tribal interests. Although he denied the allegations, he soon resigned.

Kenyan law is derived from the constitution, legislative acts of the National Assembly, English common law, specific acts of the British Parliament before the establishment of the Republic of Kenya, and doctrines of equality in force at the beginning of colonial rule. Empowered by the constitution, the courts may judge the constitutionality of laws passed by the National Assembly and all subsidiary legislation and enforce the provisions of the Bill of Rights. The courts also have the final authority on disputes arising from national elections.

PARTIES AND ELECTIONS

Members of the National Assembly are elected for five-year terms. If the Assembly is dissolved, new elections take place within three months.

Kenya is divided into constituencies, each of which has a registration officer. Each constituency is divided into polling areas and stations. A voter must be a Kenyan citizen at least eighteen years of age, with no criminal record, no record of mental illness, and no record of bankruptcy or successful prosecution for an electoral offense within the previous five years. Voting is conducted by secret ballot, and the winner is the candidate with the most votes.

To run for a seat in the Assembly, a candidate must meet voting requirements and be registered to vote, though not necessarily in the constituency in which he or she is running. A candidate may not be a citizen of another country, be under sentence of death or imprisonment, or be employed by the local government.

The transitional constitution adopted in 1960 enlarged

the Legislative Council to sixty-five members. Part of the membership was apportioned by race, with the remaining appointed by the colonial governor. In 1961, with 12 percent of the eligible voting population participating, the Kenya African National Union won nineteen seats in the legislature, the Kenya African Democratic Union eleven, and independents three. This was the first time the majority of the members were elected by the African population, but KADU representatives refused to participate until the British released Kenyatta from prison. After Kenyatta's release in December 1961, a constitution providing for a federal government and a bicameral legislature composed of a Senate and House of Representatives was adopted.

The level of voter participation in the 1963 parliamentary elections rose to 33 percent, and the respective strength of the two political parties remained the same. Although the two parties still lacked substantive policy differences, KANU promised to remove constitutional provisions for the federal system of government, given adequate support. By independence, KANU held ninety-six seats in the House and KADU twenty-six, allowing KANU to follow through on its promise of returning Kenya to a unitary form of government.

The Assembly elections of 1969 followed a one-party format, repeated in 1974, 1979, and 1983. In 1988 the electorate rejected 65 percent of the incumbents, indicating that Presidents Kenyatta and then Moi had been able to incorporate a small measure of accountability through the electoral system.

In February 1991 Jaramogi Oginga Odinga and eight other people formed the Forum for the Restoration of Democracy (FORD). As other opposition parties began to form after the repeal of party ban in December 1991, each took on ethnic characteristics. In early 1992 FORD split into two factions primarily because of personal rivalries: the Asili ("original") faction, which kept most of the original FORD leaders, and the FORD-Kenya faction, which followed Odinga and was composed of younger, more radical professionals. In February 1992 Mwai Kibaki formed the Democratic Party, further splintering the opposition.

More than five million Kenyans, 53 percent of the eligible voters, participated in the 1992 elections, deemed largely free and fair by the 160 international observers on hand despite irregularities. The opposition's disunity contributed tremendously to Moi's victory with 36.4 percent of the vote. In the Assembly elections, only 26 percent of the incumbents and 39 percent of the ministers won reelection. Even so, the Kenya African National Union won 100 of the 188 elected seats. Moi appointed 12 KANU members to the National Assembly, giving it a narrow majority. KANU currently has 118 seats, having increased its majority through constant pressure on opposition Assembly members to defect to its ranks. The constitution requires that a by-election be held when an Assembly member changes party affiliation, and the Kenya African National Union has won many of these by-elections.

REGULATING THE OPPOSITION

Although the Bill of Rights guarantees freedom of political association, the government has the power to regulate and restrict political activity and has used this power to its advantage since the advent of multiparty politics. The Public Order Act prohibits unregistered meetings of ten or more people; the government reserves the right to refuse registration of meetings at its discretion. The FORD-Kenya Party was refused registration six times in 1994. Even when registered, some gatherings are still disbanded by police. Government employees are warned against supporting the opposition.

The Societies Act governs freedom of association, including registration of political parties. By 1994 ten parties were registered: KANU, FORD-Kenya, FORD-Asili, Democratic Party, Social Democratic Party, Kenya National Democratic Alliance, Kenya National Congress, Labor Party Democracy, Kenya Social Congress, and Party of Independent Candidates of Kenya. The Islamic Party of Kenya was refused registration even though the Societies Act does not prohibit religious parties.

Government officials have little tolerance for opposition activities, subjecting their leaders and supporters to harassment, detention, and arrest. Thirty-six opposition Assembly members were detained in 1993. The number dropped to fifteen in 1994, thirteen of whom were charged with sedition and subversion.

ORGANIZATION AND OPERATIONS OF THE NATIONAL ASSEMBLY

The National Assembly meets in a building dating from 1954 on City Square in the capital of Nairobi. The building has four committee rooms, a speaker's room, and a Commonwealth Parliamentary room (where new members take their oaths) adjoining the library. The National Assembly chamber, which seats 150–200 people, is arranged in traditional British style.

Sessions

The constitution requires that the National Assembly meet annually and that there be fewer than twelve months between sessions. Each session lasts generally from early

March until early December. At the end of each session the president announces the opening date for the next session.

Of the 202 members of the National Assembly, 30 are needed for a quorum, not including the speaker. If the speaker sees that there is not a quorum at any time during the proceedings, he or she may ring the division bell, summoning other members to the chamber. Absence from the proceedings for eight consecutive days results in the permanent loss of the seat. (A member also loses his or her seat if elected speaker.) If a quorum cannot be reached after the bell is rung, the speaker will adjourn until the following day.

Legislative procedure

Each proposed bill is assigned to a minister, who is responsible for guiding it through the Assembly. The bill is published in the government's *Kenya Gazette,* and the first reading to the Assembly may take place no sooner than two weeks. At the second reading the bill is examined and debated clause by clause. A vote on the bill is taken at the third reading, and, if the bill passes, it is presented to the president for concurrence.

Two kinds of bills are considered by the Assembly: public and private. Public bills are designed to alter the law on public policy. They originate as campaign promises or recommendations from the ministries. A private bill is promoted by a member of the Assembly who is not a member of the government so that the interests of individuals and localities are addressed.

In 1969 a constitutional amendment mandated that both Swahili and English be used in conducting Assembly business. Thus it is now required that public petitions be handwritten in Swahili.

The government submits a development plan to the Assembly every five years to outline political and economic considerations. The Assembly must approve the government's budget annually and must legislate all appropriations. As a result, appropriations are specific in sum and purpose. The treasury is responsible to the Assembly for maintaining financial order and regularity in government accounting.

Committee system

The National Assembly has two kinds of committees: committees of the whole house and select committees. Committees of the whole house—Ways and Means, Supply, and "in Relation to a Public Bill"—are composed of the entire Assembly but sit "in committee" under the control of the chair of committees and require no quorum. Select committees are composed of no fewer than five and no more than fifteen members unless otherwise ordered by the Assembly. These committees debate new legislation in detail and investigate what the Assembly as a whole is not suited to do. Standing select committees are reappointed every session, while ad hoc select committees are established to inquire into and report on a particular issue; they disband after their report is made to the Assembly.

Four standing select committees deal with financial procedures. The Estimates Committee considers budgetary policy, and the Public Accounts Committee audits and reviews expenditures. These committees are appointed by the Assembly at the beginning of every session. The Committee of Ways and Means handles the policy aspects of taxation proposals, authorizing the government to implement new taxes or increase existing ones. Finally, the Committee of Supply authorizes the allocation of funds not otherwise addressed during the session, therefore handling some policy aspects of the spending program.

Committees have taken on new meaning with the presence of opposition Assembly members, whose participation has been hotly contested. For example, in July 1994 opposition Assembly members angrily withdrew from the Public Accounts Committee and the Public Investments Committee after the Sessional Committee ignored the representatives the opposition parties had chosen, appointing those of their choice.

MEMBERS

Members of the National Assembly have the right to speak freely in the Assembly, and they are free from arrest for any civil debt that does not constitute a criminal offense. They may not, however, publish false or scandalous material, use improper means to influence people, or falsify information with the intent to deceive.

Housing allowances are provided to members of the National Assembly when low-cost housing for government officials is not available. Members may borrow funds to purchase vehicles in the absence of official transportation and are provided allowances for up to twenty-six business trips outside Nairobi a year. Life insurance is made available to members and their dependents.

Zoey L. Breslar

BIBLIOGRAPHY

Barkan, Joel D. "The Electoral Process and Peasant-State Relations in Kenya." In *Elections in Independent Africa,* ed. Fred M. Hayward. Boulder, Colo.: Westview Press, 1987.

———. "Kenya: Lessons from a Flawed Election." *Journal of Democracy* 4 (July 1993): 85–99.

Gicheru, H. B. Ndoria. *Parliamentary Practice in Kenya.* Nairobi: Transafrica Publishers, 1976.

KIRIBATI

OFFICIAL NAME: Republic of Kiribati (I Kiribati)
CAPITAL: Bairiki, on Tarawa Atoll
POPULATION: 81,000 (1996 est.)
DATE OF INDEPENDENCE: July 12, 1979 (from the United Kingdom)
DATE OF CURRENT CONSTITUTION: Effective July 12, 1979
FORM OF GOVERNMENT: Parliamentary democracy
LANGUAGES: English (official), Gilbertese
MONETARY UNIT: Australian dollar
FISCAL YEAR: —
LEGISLATURE: House of Assembly (Mwaneaba ni Maungatabu)
NUMBER OF CHAMBERS: One
NUMBER OF MEMBERS: 41 (39 elected, 1 nominated, 1 ex officio)
PERCENTAGE OF WOMEN: 0.0
TERM OF LEGISLATURE: Four years
MOST RECENT LEGISLATIVE ELECTION: July 21–29, 1994
MINIMUM AGE FOR VOTING: 18
MINIMUM AGE FOR MEMBERSHIP: 21
SUFFRAGE: Universal
VOTING: Optional
ADDRESS: House of Assembly, P.O. Box 52, Bairiki, Tarawa
TELEPHONE: (686) 21 053
FAX: (686) 21 278

The Republic of Kiribati comprises thirty-three atolls in three principal groups in the Pacific Ocean midway between Hawaii and Australia. Formerly known as the Gilbert Islands, Kiribati was a protectorate of the United Kingdom from 1892 to 1979, when it achieved independence.

The current 1979 constitution vests all legislative power in the House of Assembly, a unicameral body consisting of thirty-nine elected members most of whom stand for election as independents. There are no organized political parties in the country, but there are loose groups that form and re-form before every election. Members of the Assembly are elected by universal adult suffrage for four-year terms in twenty-three electoral districts (some single-member and some multimember). In addition, there is one nominated member from the island of Banaba and the attorney general, who sits as an ex-officio member. The constitution also provides for a Banaba Island Council to protect the rights of Banabans.

The speaker of the House of Assembly is elected by the members from outside the Assembly membership.

George Thomas Kurian

KOREA, NORTH

OFFICIAL NAME: Democratic People's Republic of Korea (Chosŏn Minchu-chui In Min Konghwa-guk)
CAPITAL: Pyongyang
POPULATION: 24,000,000 (1996 est.)
DATE OF INDEPENDENCE: September 9, 1948
DATE OF CURRENT CONSTITUTION: December 27, 1972
FORM OF GOVERNMENT: Communist dictatorship
LANGUAGE: Korean
MONETARY UNIT: Won
FISCAL YEAR: Calendar year
LEGISLATURE: Supreme People's Assembly (Choe Ko In Min Hoe Ui)
NUMBER OF CHAMBERS: One
NUMBER OF MEMBERS: 687
PERCENTAGE OF WOMEN: 20.1
TERM OF LEGISLATURE: Four years
MOST RECENT LEGISLATIVE ELECTION: 1994 election canceled due to presidential succession problems
MINIMUM AGE FOR VOTING: 17
MINIMUM AGE FOR MEMBERSHIP: 17
SUFFRAGE: Direct and universal
VOTING: Compulsory
ADDRESS: Supreme People's Assembly, Mansudong Central District, Pyongyang
TELEPHONE: (850) 23 9322
FAX: (850) 81 4410

The Democratic People's Republic of Korea (North Korea) is a communist state in East Asia, located between China and Japan *(see map, p. 141)*. In the People's Republic the highest organ of state power and the exclusive legislative authority is the Supreme People's Assembly. It is elected by direct, equal, secret, and universal ballot for a term of four years. Its principal functions are to adopt or amend the constitution; to elect the president, vice president, secretary, and members of the Central People's Committee; to elect members of the Standing Committee of the Supreme People's Assembly, the premier of the Administrative Council, the president of the Central Court, and other legal officials; to approve the state plan and budget; and to decide on matters of war and peace. It holds both regular and extraordinary sessions, the former twice a year and the latter at the request of at least one-third of the deputies. The Standing Committee is the permanent body of the Supreme People's Assembly. It examines and decides on bills and amends legislation in force when the Supreme People's Assembly is not in session.

The Supreme People's Assembly elects the members of the Central People's Committee, also for four-year terms. The majority of the latter are also members of the Politburo of the Korean Workers Party. The principal functions of the Central People's Committee are to direct the work of the Administrative Council as well as local government organs, to establish or abolish ministries, and to appoint ambassadors and defense chiefs. It is assisted by a number of commissions.

Each electoral constituency represents thirty thousand people. Elections are stage-managed by the Korean Workers Party, which prepares a single slate of candidates for the electorate. Candidates are elected by a simple majority in single-member constituencies. Voter turnout is always 100 percent, and candidates are generally elected unanimously. Electoral registers are compiled at the constituency and subconstituency levels. Voting is compulsory.

George Thomas Kurian

KOREA, SOUTH

OFFICIAL NAME: Republic of Korea (Taehan Min'guk)
CAPITAL: Seoul
POPULATION: 45,482,000 (1996 est.)
DATE OF INDEPENDENCE: August 15, 1948
DATE OF CURRENT CONSTITUTION: Approved October 27, 1987; effective February 25, 1988
FORM OF GOVERNMENT: Presidential
LANGUAGE: Korean
MONETARY UNIT: Won
FISCAL YEAR: Calendar year
LEGISLATURE: National Assembly (Kukhoe)
NUMBER OF CHAMBERS: One
NUMBER OF MEMBERS: 299
PERCENTAGE OF WOMEN: 3.0
TERM OF LEGISLATURE: Four years
MOST RECENT LEGISLATIVE ELECTION: April 11, 1996
MINIMUM AGE FOR VOTING: 20
MINIMUM AGE FOR MEMBERSHIP: 25
SUFFRAGE: Universal and direct
VOTING: Optional
ADDRESS: National Assembly, 1 Yeoido-dong, Yeongdungpo-ku, Seoul
TELEPHONE: (822) 784 3561
FAX: (822) 788 3385

The Republic of Korea, an East Asian country often called South Korea, occupies the southern part of the Korean peninsula to the east of the People's Republic of China and west of Japan. South Korea was established in 1948 after Japan's defeat in World War II. It made a transition from an authoritarian system to democracy in the late 1980s, and today the country has a unicameral legislature—the National Assembly *(Kukhoe)*. The president is head of state and government, and the prime minister is deputy head of government.

The history of the National

Assembly has been short but turbulent. In the wake of various regime changes, it was dissolved several times but has never been abolished.

HISTORICAL BACKGROUND

The Yi dynasty, which had governed Korea for more than five centuries, was overthrown in 1910. Japan then ruled Korea until 1945, when the country was liberated by the Allied powers at the close of World War II. During the cold war that followed, military and ideological conflicts between the United States and the Soviet Union hindered the emergence of Korea as a unified nation. In the south, a U.S. military government ruled for three years, and elections for a Constituent Assembly were held on May 10, 1948. Members of the Assembly, elected for a two-year term, adopted a democratic constitution that contained a mixture of presidential and parliamentary features. Syngman Rhee was elected by the legislature as the first president of the republic.

Despite the optimism of those who drafted the constitution, the goal of democracy and constitutionalism was elusive in Korea. Friction developed between Rhee and the National Assembly. The president and his supporters ruthlessly suppressed political opposition and dominated the legislature. In 1952, while the country was mired in a war against the Soviet Union and communist North Korea, Rhee proposed a constitutional amendment providing for direct popular election of the president. This proposal was initiated primarily because Rhee's chance of reelection in the legislature was slim. The president used physical intimidation to coerce legislative members into approving the proposal. Many opposition members were arrested on charges of conspiracy with the communists.

In the general election held in May 1954, Rhee's Liberal Party manipulated the election to win nearly a two-thirds majority in the Third Assembly. The governing party passed another constitutional amendment that removed the two-term limit on presidential incumbency. Flagrant election rigging in the 1960 presidential election triggered the student uprising that led to the downfall of the First Republic and the suspension of the Fourth Assembly.

The new constitution of the Second Republic instituted a parliamentary type of government and a bicameral legislature. The Democratic Party, an opposition party in the previous republic, emerged victorious in the election for the Fifth Assembly and formed a new government led by Premier Chang Myon. The legislature was strengthened and was able to exercise considerable power in shaping major policy decisions. Prospects for parliamentary democracy notwithstanding, the Democratic regime was seriously undermined by strife between two big intraparty factions. One faction eventually broke away from the Democratic Party. Consequently, the governing party was incapable of providing effective leadership for coping with increasing demands from the people after the fall of Rhee's government. The Democratic regime and the Fifth Assembly lasted only nine months before a military coup, in May 1961, overthrew the government.

The military junta under the command of Gen. Park Chung Hee ruled South Korea for two and a half years. In 1963 the military leaders decided to maintain their rule by "civilianizing" themselves. They successfully amended the constitution to replace the existing parliamentary system with a presidential system. General Park was elected president of the Third Republic, and his Democratic Republican Party won a majority in the Sixth Assembly. The regime focused on economic development. In pursuing this goal, the legislature played a minimal role and remained weak relative to the executive throughout the Third Republic. A constitutional amendment designed to lift the two-term restriction on the presidency was passed in the midst of a bitter partisan confrontation. President Park was narrowly elected to a third term in 1971. His narrow margin portended serious difficulty for the president in retaining arbitrary rule through direct popular election.

In October 1972 Park launched a series of measures to perpetuate his rule. He proclaimed martial law on October 17, justifying this measure as necessary for reform. The Eighth Assembly was dissolved suddenly, and several months later the Ninth Assembly was convened under the new constitution of the Fourth Republic.

President Park announced as his overriding political goal the establishment of a Korean democracy that would be appropriate to the social conditions peculiar to Korea. Under this concept of democracy, the power of the legislature became further weakened. The presidentially appointed members, in combination with the Democratic Republican Party members, ensured the president automatic approval of his programs in the Ninth and Tenth Assemblies.

The Fourth Republic was on the verge of collapse when Park was gunned down in October 1979. In the months after the assassination, South Korea witnessed a brief period of political realignments and popular demands for a new democratic government. However, in the maelstrom of disorder and uncertainty, the military under the leadership of Gen. Chun Doo Hwan took over the government. The Tenth Assembly was disrupted. The junta leaders closely followed the steps taken by their predecessors two decades before. A referendum in October 1980, held in no free political climate, endorsed the Fifth Republic constitution, which established the indirect election of the president through an electoral college.

RETURN TO CIVILIAN GOVERNMENT

In the Fifth Republic the Eleventh Assembly completed its four-year term, but the Twelfth Assembly served only three years because of another constitutional change. In June 1987 President Chun was forced to concede to opposition forces, who demanded a revision of the constitution to allow for direct popular election of the president. A three-way presidential election followed in December 1987: Two prominent civilian leaders split the opposition vote, and Roh Tae Woo of the Democratic Justice Party squeezed out an electoral victory.

The Sixth Republic started off with the inauguration of Roh's government in February 1988. In the election for the Thirteenth Assembly in April 1988, the Democratic Justice Party failed to secure an overall legislative majority. Instead, the opposition, divided into three parties, obtained a majority. During the early part of the Thirteenth Assembly (May 1988–January 1990), Korean legislative politics could be characterized as a politics of coalition building. In order to pass the governing side's legislative proposal, the Democratic Justice Party had to seek support from at least one opposition party. Amid the checks and balances provided by the multiple parties, some party leaders gradually became uneasy about the inherent fluidity of partisan alignments and cleavages in the legislature. The governing party found it both time-consuming and difficult to build working majorities and make compromises. Not only President Roh but also two opposition leaders, Kim Young Sam of the Reunification Democratic Party and Kim Jong Pil of the New Democratic Republican Party, could take little comfort in the four-party system.

Party politics underwent a sudden reshaping when President Roh and the two Kims made a surprise announcement of their agreement to merge the three parties on January 22, 1990. Thus the Democratic Liberal Party, a motley gigantic coalition, emerged on the governing side. In the general election held in March 1992, however, the legislative strength of the Democratic Liberal Party was reduced to a much more modest majority than before in the Fourteenth National Assembly. After winning a plurality in the presidential election of December 1992, Kim Young Sam installed a true civilian government for the first time since 1960.

In Korean party politics, personalities loom larger than ideologies or policy programs. Political parties rally around particular leaders, and the fate of a party, including a split or the formation of a new party, hinges on the actions of its leaders. This makes Korean political parties highly fluid. In January 1995 Kim Jong Pil and his followers bolted from the Democratic Liberal Party when he was pressured to resign from his leadership position, second only to that of Kim Young Sam within the governing party. Kim Jong Pil subsequently founded the United Liberal Democrats. In the summer of 1995, Kim Dae Jung, who had declared his withdrawal from politics after his unsuccessful presidential bid in 1992, suddenly returned to the political stage. He drew his followers away from the Democratic Party, then the main opposition, and organized the National Congress for New Politics. Furthermore, the governing party changed its name from the Democratic Liberal Party to the New Korea Party four months before the election of the Fifteenth National Assembly in April 1996. In the current National Assembly, the New Korea Party controls 53 percent of the total membership; the Liberal Democrats hold 15 percent.

THE NATIONAL ASSEMBLY BUILDING

The Korean National Assembly has met in its current compound since 1975. It accommodates the National Assembly Building, the Members' Building, and the National Assembly Library. The National Assembly Building, a six-story structure, includes large chambers for plenary sessions, committee meeting rooms, and the offices of the National Assembly leaders. The architectural style, though modern, incorporates Korean cultural tradition. Twenty-four octagonal pillars on four sides support the building, and it is capped by a dome. The ceiling of the rotunda hall is made up of several tiers of concentric round shapes. This symbolizes the parliamentary political process through which varying opinions are brought forth, debated, and eventually accommodated into a collective decision.

The Members' Building is situated at the right front of the National Assembly Building. On the left front of the National Assembly Building is located the National Assembly Library.

CONSTITUTIONAL POWERS OF THE NATIONAL ASSEMBLY

The formal powers given to the National Assembly in the present constitution can be categorized into four types: legislation, fiscal control, check over the executive branch, and house autonomy.

Legislative power is vested in the National Assembly. This does not mean that the national legislature substantively monopolizes the right to enact laws, but that the enactment of formal laws is possible only by passage through the legislature. Not only the members of the National Assembly but also the government (executive branch) can introduce legislative bills. The president is empowered to influence the legislative process by the use of or the threat of using the veto power. The Constitutional Court may also affect the legislative power of the National Assembly by reviewing the constitutionality of a law passed by it. Furthermore, the law defined in a broad substantive sense may take various alternative forms such as emergency decree, executive order, and local government by-law or ordinance. These can bypass the legislative process in the National Assembly. Apart from the enactment of formal laws, the National Assembly can propose and deliberate a constitutional amendment and give its consent to the conclusion and ratification of treaties.

The National Assembly also deliberates and decides upon the national budget, which is proposed by the government. A budget proposal is not the same as a legislative bill. Strictly speaking, it does not attain the status of a formal law even after it has passed through the legislature. It has no power to amend or repeal a law. The Assembly determines the types and rates of taxation. When the government proposes to issue national bonds or to conclude contracts incurring the financial obligations of the nation, it must have the prior consent of the Assembly. In addition, the legislature is invested with the power to examine the settlement of public revenue and expenditure accounts.

The constitution authorizes the National Assembly to oversee the decision making and policy implementation of the executive branch in various ways. It may inspect all aspects of government operations during every annual regular session. Also, the legislature is given the power to investigate specific matters when deemed necessary. The Korean constitution provides the Assembly with leverage usually unavailable to a legislature under a presidential system. The consent of the Assembly is required for the appointment of the prime minister by the president. The prime minister, ministers, and other government representatives must appear before the plenary session or committee meetings to answer questions from the members of the Assembly, if such requests are made. Additionally, the legislature has the right to pass a nonbinding but politically significant recommendation for the removal of the prime minister or any state council (cabinet) member. The other checks over any possible abuse of presidential prerogatives include the passage of a motion for impeaching the president, approval of emergency orders, concurrence in the declaration of war, and consent to a general amnesty.

Finally, the National Assembly has autonomy to establish its own rules and regulations for its internal operation, as long as they are not in conflict with the constitution and laws.

MEMBERS

Each member of the Korean National Assembly serves a four-year term of office. The current Assembly is composed of 299 members, who include 253 district representatives and 46 at-large members. District representatives are those members who are elected from single-member districts, and at-large members are chosen under nationwide party lists. The latter seats are divided in proportion to each party's nationwide vote share among those parties that win at least five district seats or that receive 5 percent or more of the total valid votes. Each voter casts one vote to choose a single district candidate, and that vote is also counted as the choice of the candidate's party list for nationwide proportional representation.

About 46 percent of the members are freshmen. The members of the Korean National Assembly, like their counterparts in other countries, are a highly select group in terms of their social backgrounds. The incumbents are predominantly male (97 percent) and in their fifties (53 percent). They are well educated with college degrees or more (far more than 90 percent).

Members of the National Assembly are entitled to certain parliamentary privileges and immunities under the constitution. Members are not held legally responsible outside the National Assembly for opinions expressed or votes cast in the Assembly. During sessions of the Assembly, no member can be arrested or detained without the legislature's consent except when actually caught in the act of misconduct.

The constitution and the rules of the National Assembly explicitly stipulate the privileges as well as the duties of the member. The constitutional duties encompass maintaining high standards of integrity, performing the job conscientiously while putting national interests above all else, restraining oneself from engaging in influence peddling and from using the office improperly to seek material compensation, and holding no other political office. A member must submit an explanatory note in case of absence from a National Assembly meeting. Members should abide by formal rules controlling proceedings. And they are expected to observe the code of ethics, which was set up in May 1991.

The National Assembly may take disciplinary action against a member who neglects parliamentary duty and violates the rules. If a member is subject to disciplinary action, the speaker of the Assembly refers the case to the Committee on Ethics. The committee investigates the case and reports to the plenary session for disciplinary action. The Assembly may issue a warning to the violator or receive a public apology from him or her. In serious cases the violator may be suspended for a period not exceeding thirty days or expelled. Any member expelled is prohibited from standing for the by-election to fill the vacancy resulting from the expulsion.

The average annual compensation paid by public funds to a member of the National Assembly amounts to about 59.2 million won (approximately US$4,000), including salaries and allowances for personal expenses. The salary of a member is equivalent to that of a minister in the executive branch. Other major perquisites are allowances for office and car maintenance, mail and telephone charges, and costs for printing pamphlets; allowances for domestic and foreign official travel; free passes on national ships, airplanes, and trains; free office space; and five personal staffers.

ORGANIZATION

The National Assembly has always been unicameral except for a brief period during the Second Republic. Key officials of the Assembly are the speaker, two vice speakers, partisan floor leaders, and committee chairs. The speaker and vice speakers are elected by secret ballot in the plenary session. Elections require the concurrence of a majority of the entire membership. Each officer serves for a two-year term. The position of the speaker is controlled by the majority party. As a courtesy, one of the two vice speakerships is assigned to the opposition party, although there is no formal requirement to do so. In the absence of the speaker, a vice speaker designated by the speaker is in charge. If the speaker and vice speakers are all absent, the Assembly elects a speaker pro tempore.

The speaker

The speaker represents the National Assembly, presides over its proceedings, maintains order in the Assembly, and supervises its administrative affairs. An example of the speaker's power to act for the national legislature is that he sends a bill passed by the legislature to the government in his name. The speaker has wide-ranging powers to regulate parliamentary proceedings. His or her permission is necessary when a member wishes to take the floor. The speaker may change the opening hour of the plenary session, which normally begins weekdays at 2:00 p.m. He prepares the agenda, which includes the date and hour of the opening of the plenary session. He can also limit the period of examination of a proposal by a committee. In exercising these powers, the speaker consults with partisan floor leaders. To keep order when the National Assembly is in session, the speaker has the authority to ensure security in the legislature. If disruptive behavior occurs at committee or plenary meetings, the speaker may mobilize security guards to restore order.

Bargaining groups

A bargaining group, called *kyosop danche* in Korean, refers to an intraparliamentary party caucus that is formally established within the National Assembly. This group can be formed whenever a political party has secured at least twenty seats. In the present Assembly, only the Democratic Liberal Party, the National Congress for New Politics, and the United Liberal Democrats have mustered enough members to form a bargaining group. Each bargaining group is represented by its floor leaders, who sit on the Steering Committee of the legislature and engage in the give and take of parliamentary politics. The floor leaders of a bargaining group include a whip, a senior deputy whip, and several deputy whips.

Floor leaders

The purpose of floor leaders is to whip up support among the rank and file in order to maintain strong party discipline. At every stage of decision making, members follow the instructions of their floor leaders. In Korea's presidential system of government, an underlying principle is checks and balances between the executive and legislative branches. Furthermore, about 85 percent of the members of the National Assembly are elected in single-member districts where individual candidate appeal is instrumental in determining electoral success. Although one may conclude that party discipline is weak in the Assembly, in reality there are good incentives for members to follow the directives from above. The top leaders of a Korean party, in or out of power, hold a firm grip on the process of nominating candidates for Assembly seats. Candidates are legally allowed to run without party nomination. Yet a member who fails to obtain renomination faces a much smaller chance of being reelected as an independent candidate than in running with the party label. Also, the central party's financial and organizational support is crucial for activities related to representing constituencies and in electoral campaigns. Party discipline is especially strong in the president's party (always the majority or largest party in the Assembly) because the chief executive in effect controls the legislative members of his party through rewards and sanctions.

Committees

The National Assembly has two types of committees, standing and special. Currently, there are sixteen standing committees, including the Steering Committee, and fifteen committees that oversee specific areas. The jurisdictions of these subject committees are parallel to those of government ministries and agencies: legislation and justice; administration; finance and economy; national unification and foreign affairs; home affairs; national defense; education; culture, sports, and information; agriculture, forestry, and fisheries; trade and industry; communication, science, and technology; environment and labor; health and welfare; construction and transportation; and intelligence.

Special committees are appointed to examine special matters as deemed necessary by the Assembly. In particular, the Special Committee on Budget and Accounts reviews the budget proposal and statement of accounts. This committee dissolves automatically when the plenary session decides on the budget proposal and accounts. Two other special committees, on ethics and on women, are permanently established.

Of all committees, the Special Committee on Budget and Accounts—with fifty members—is the largest. The other committees vary in size from twelve to thirty members. A member can sit on only one of the standing committees (except for Steering and Intelligence). Formally, the speaker is responsible for committee assignments. In practice, the party whips play a key role in committee assignment. The partisan composition of each committee reflects the legislative strength of each party in the Assembly.

Chairs of standing committees are elected by secret ballot in the plenary session. Chairs of special committees are elected in committee meetings. The chair presides over meetings, maintains order, and supervises management affairs concerning the committee.

Committees have a central role in the parliamentary process. Legislative bills and petitions are first reviewed by the relevant committee. The committee may make amendments to legislative proposals, and the plenary session usually upholds the committee's decision. The committee may hold public hearings, request explanatory remarks of high-level executive officials, and question them about important matters.

The bureaucracy

The National Assembly's support staff consists of roughly three thousand people, several hundred of whom have research or administrative responsibilities. The secretariat manages administrative affairs and provides support for the members of the Assembly. It is headed by the secretary general, equivalent in rank to a government minister. The secretary general is appointed and dismissed by the speaker in consultation with the floor leaders and with the consent of the Assembly.

The National Assembly's library assists members with their legislative activities by supplying reference materials.

PARLIAMENTARY SESSIONS

The National Assembly meets either in regular or special sessions. The regular session opens annually on September 10 or the next day if it is a holiday. A special session may be convened at the request of the president or at least one-fourth of the total membership. If the president requests convocation of a special session, its duration and the reason for the request must be specified. Before January 10 each year, the speaker draws up a basic framework of the legislative schedule for the calendar year in consultation with the Steering Committee.

The duration of a session, except for that requested by the president, is determined by a vote immediately after the opening of the session. The period of the regular session may not exceed one hundred days; a special session may not exceed thirty days. During a session the National Assembly may decide to adjourn for a fixed number of days. Committee meetings may be held when the Assembly is not in session. The Assembly must terminate adjournment and resume its plenary session if the president, the speaker, or at least one-fourth of the entire membership asks for a continuation because of an urgent matter. Recently, the Assembly has averaged 170 days or so a year in session. The plenary session, however, has met only for an average of 45 days a year, meaning that approximately three-fourths of a session is usually spent on committee work and intermittent recess.

The quorum for opening the plenary session is at least one-fourth of the whole membership. Unless otherwise stipulated in the constitution or other laws, a decision in the plenary session requires the presence of a majority of the total members and concurrence of a majority of those present. A tie vote means that the matter has been rejected. To open a committee meeting, one-third of the membership or more forms a quorum. A decision is made in the committee if a majority of the committee members are present and a majority of those present affirm the decision.

Generally, sessions in the National Assembly are open to the public, but they may be closed if a majority of those present decides to close the session or if the speaker invokes a national security reason. Thus the Intelligence Committee holds executive sessions. There are some other principles concerning the sessions of the National Assembly. A matter submitted for deliberation should not be dropped on the ground that it was not acted upon during the session in which it was submitted (unless the term of the members has expired). A matter defeated in a vote may not be proposed again during the same session.

A member who wishes to speak in the plenary session must gain prior permission from the speaker. Normally, members may speak for no more than fifteen minutes; they must further limit their speech to five minutes if it concerns a point of order or personal matter, or if it supplements a committee report. Members who speak on a topic of their own choice during the first hour immediately after the opening of the plenary session are given only four minutes. The time can be extended up to forty minutes when a representative of a bargaining group makes a speech on its behalf.

The number of members of each bargaining group who address a matter on the agenda is based on the total length of time available for speeches and each group's share of seats in the Assembly. In addition, there are further constraints on the speeches made in the plenary session so that members have equal opportunities to take the floor. For example, a member normally is prohibited from making a speech that is not relevant to the subject on the agenda and from speaking more than twice on the same subject. But these kinds of limitations are almost nonexistent when it comes to speeches made by members in committee. This lack of restriction is conducive to in-depth deliberation in the committees.

LEGISLATION

The government as well as members of the National Assembly may introduce a legislative bill. When a member introduces a bill, he or she must obtain at least twenty cosignatures. A committee can introduce a bill concerning a matter under its jurisdiction in the name of the chair. If the bill requires budgetary measures, it must be accompanied by a financial statement. Once a bill is introduced to the Assembly, the speaker has it printed and distributed to each member. After reporting the bill to the plenary session, the speaker refers it to the relevant committee before placing it on the agenda of the plenary session.

Committee examination and report

Before examining a referred bill, the committee is given an explanation of the purpose of the bill by the bill's sponsor and a report from a senior committee staff member. Following a period of general debate, an ad hoc subcommittee may be established for reviewing the bill and reporting the result to the full committee. The committee may hold public hearings by summoning interested parties and experts as witnesses to hear their opinions. The committee must also hear from the government about any budgetary matters. The committee then examines the bill article by article (a process that may be superseded by a vote). Finally, the committee votes on the bill. Once the bill is approved, it is referred to the Committee on Legislation and Justice; this committee checks the legal formalities, including the organization and wordings of the bill.

The committee reports to the plenary session noting whether it approved or rejected the bill either in its original or amended version. The plenary session usually does not act further on a bill that has been rejected in committee. In unusual cases, however, the bill can be placed on the agenda of the plenary session if thirty or more members make such a request within seven days, excluding the times between sessions or intermittent recesses in the middle of a session, from the date of the committee report.

Debate and amendment

Further debates and amendments regarding a bill reported by the committee can take place in the plenary session. Members who wish to debate must notify the speaker in advance. The speaker gives alternate turns to members who oppose and support the bill, while taking into consideration the order of notice and the strength of each bargaining group. The speaker ensures that the member opposing the bill takes priority in speaking. Once the debate has finished, the speaker declares it closed.

A motion for amending a bill in the plenary session should be submitted in advance together with the reasons stated and accompanied by at least thirty cosignatures. When multiple amendments are submitted for the same subject, the speaker determines the order of voting as follows: the amendment proposed last is first voted on, an amendment proposed by an individual member is voted on before that submitted by the committee, and the amendment differing most from the original proposal is the first voted on among the amendments submitted by members. When all the amendments have been voted, voting on the original proposal takes place.

Voting

After the speaker's announcement of a vote, no member may speak on the subject at hand. A member who is not present at the time of voting cannot participate in the voting. When a vote is taken by ballot, members may participate in the voting up to the time the ballot box is closed. When the speaker asks members if there are any objections and sees that none are raised, he or she declares the matter passed. If, however, there is an objection, the speaker takes the vote by asking members to stand or to cast ballots. Until recently, other voting methods have rarely been used in the National Assembly. An open-ballot vote has been used only for deciding on a proposal to amend the constitution. And a secret-ballot vote has been limited to a few instances such as the decision about a bill vetoed by the president. But now the National Assembly law stipulates that the recorded vote (open ballot, electronic vote, or roll call) or the secret-ballot vote can be applied to any important matter at the speaker's proposal, at the request of at least one-fifth of the total membership, or by a decision in the plenary session.

Promulgation

A bill passed by the National Assembly is sent to the government, and the president signs the bill and promulgates it within fifteen days. The president may return the bill to the Assembly for reconsideration. The president cannot request the legislature to reconsider some part of the bill, nor can he or she propose an amendment to it. If the Assembly, with at least a majority of the total members present, passes the same version of the bill as before by a two-thirds majority, the bill becomes law. There have been seven presidential vetoes exercised over the bills approved by the Assembly in the past fifteen years (during the period from the Tenth Assembly to the present). All of these occurred in the first two years of the Thirteenth Assembly, when the ruling Democratic Justice Party did not hold the majority status and hence could not dominate the legislative process. The vetoed bills died or were significantly modified to obtain presidential approval.

During the period of the Fourteenth Assembly, an average of 226 bills per year were introduced in the legislature, and some 164 pieces of legislation were passed. About 64 percent of the introduced bills were proposed for consideration by the government, while the remaining bills were introduced by members. The passage rate of the government bills was 92 percent, whereas that of members' bills was 37 percent. These figures for both introduction and passage of bills suggest that the executive dominates in the lawmaking process.

THE BUDGET

The fiscal year in South Korea is the calendar year. At least 120 days before the beginning of the next fiscal year, the Board of Audit and Inspection, an executive organ under the direct control of the president, submits to the National Assembly the accounts of revenue and expenditure of the previous year, with the audit findings. The accounts are reviewed in each standing committee, then are examined in the Special Committee on Budget and Accounts, and finally are approved in the plenary session. In general, this deliberative process is perfunctory.

The budget proposal is considered more important than the accounts report. The Finance and Economy Board performs a central clearance function in the formulation and execution of the government budget. The agency draws up an overall budget proposal on the basis of the estimates done by each government ministry and submits it to the Assembly ninety days before the next fiscal year, that is, October 2. In the course of its examination, the Assembly hears the budget statement from the government and then refers it to each standing committee for preliminary review. Each standing committee examines the portion of the budget that concerns that committee's jurisdictional counterpart in the executive branch.

At the next stage, the Special Committee on Budget and Accounts embarks on an overall examination. The minister in charge of finance and economy gives a briefing on major features of the budget; the briefing is followed by questions and answers. The Budget and Accounts Committee is divided into several subcommittees, which work on specific parts of the budget. Another task force subcommittee, with approximately eleven members, is set the task of adjusting budget figures. The full Special Committee on Budget and Accounts convenes to adopt the modified budget proposal and reports it to the plenary session for final approval.

There is a significant constitutional constraint on the deliberation of the budget by the National Assembly. If the legislature wants to increase the amount of any item of expenditure or create any new item in the budget, it must obtain the consent of the executive branch in advance. In addition, the Assembly states that a motion for amending the budget proposal requires the support of at least fifty members. The budget for the National Security Planning Agency is subject only to the preliminary review by the Intelligence Committee in a closed session; it bypasses a comprehensive review by the Special Committee on Budget and Accounts. Consequently, the Assembly exercises little fiscal control. Since its inception, the legislature has only twice altered the budget proposal by more than 3 percent. In the past twenty years, with the exception of only one year (fiscal 1990), changes came within just 1 percent of the original proposal.

OVERSIGHT AND ACCOUNTABILITY

At the outset of the annual regular session, the National Assembly establishes a twenty-day period for conducting inspections of state administration. Each standing committee oversees government ministries and agencies under its jurisdiction. Also, the Assembly may request that a standing or special committee investigate a specific matter. One-third or more of the total membership may request this investigation, but the plan for carrying it out must be approved in advance by a majority in the plenary session. Investigative hearings may be held as a way of obtaining evidence and testimony.

The plenary session may request the presence of the prime minister, ministers, or government representatives for interpellation, a procedure through which a legislative body calls the government to account. The member who wishes to question a minister or government representative submits to the speaker in advance a summary of questions and the length of the time needed. The speaker transmits the summary to the government at least forty-eight hours prior to the interpellation. The speaker is also responsible for deciding, in consultation with the floor leaders, the length of an interpellation period, the number of interpellators in each bargaining group, and their order. An interpellator is normally given no more than fifteen minutes. The National Assembly may also have a question time for a specific matter of urgency in the plenary session. In addition, the member may submit written questions through the speaker to the government.

To redress constituents' grievances, members of the National Assembly can introduce petitions to the legislature. Once a member has filed this formal petition, the speaker refers it to a standing committee for examination. The committee decides whether or not to report the petition for further consideration. If the plenary session, upon the committee's report, adopts the petition and considers it appropriate for the executive branch to dispose of the petition, the Assembly transfers the case to the executive branch together with its written opinion. The Assembly's adoption rate for such petitions is remarkably low—less than 2 percent in the Fourteenth Assembly.

The National Assembly publishes the verbatim records on the proceedings of the plenary session as well as of committees. The records are distributed to the members and to the public. Proceedings within the Assembly can be covered live or recorded as long as the Assembly or a committee does not decide to hold a closed session.

Although the National Assembly has less policy-making power than the executive branch, it remains a meaningful representative body. The Korean people have opportunities for political participation in regular legislative elections. By providing their constituents with various types of services, members of the National Assembly can be made to be responsive.

Chan Wook Park

BIBLIOGRAPHY

Kim, Chong Lim, and Seong-Tong Pai. *Legislative Process in Korea.* Seoul: Seoul National University Press, 1981.

Kim, Kwang-woong, and Chan Wook Park. "Public Attitudes toward the National Legislature and Its Members." *Korea Journal* 31 (1991): 78–82.

Park, Chan Wook. "Constituency Representation in South Korea: Sources and Consequences." *Legislative Studies Quarterly* 13 (1988): 225–249.

———. "The Fourteenth National Assembly Election in Korea." *Korea Journal* 33 (1992): 5–16.

———. "Legislators and Their Constituents in South Korea: The Patterns of District Representation." *Asian Survey* 28 (1988): 1049–1065.

———. "The 1988 National Assembly Election in South Korea: The Ruling Party's Loss of Legislative Majority." *Journal of Northeast Asian Studies* 7 (1988): 59–76.

———. "The Organization and Workings of Committees in the Korean National Assembly." *Pacific Focus* 11 (1996): 57–77.

———. "Partisan Conflict and Immobilism in the Korean National Assembly." *Asian Perspective* 17 (1993): 5–37.

KUWAIT

OFFICIAL NAME: State of Kuwait (Dawlat al-Kuwayt)
CAPITAL: Kuwait City
POPULATION: 1,950,000 (1996 est.)
DATE OF INDEPENDENCE: June 19, 1961 (from the United Kingdom)
DATE OF CURRENT CONSTITUTION: Effective November 16, 1962
FORM OF GOVERNMENT: Nominal constitutional monarchy
LANGUAGE: Arabic (official)
MONETARY UNIT: Kuwaiti dinar
FISCAL YEAR: July 1–June 30
LEGISLATURE: National Assembly (Majlis al-Umma)
NUMBER OF CHAMBERS: One
NUMBER OF MEMBERS: 50
PERCENTAGE OF WOMEN: 0.0
TERM OF LEGISLATURE: Four years
MOST RECENT LEGISLATIVE ELECTION: October 7, 1996
MINIMUM AGE FOR VOTING: 21
MINIMUM AGE FOR MEMBERSHIP: 25
SUFFRAGE: Limited and direct
VOTING: Optional
ADDRESS: National Assembly, P.O. Box 716 -Safat, 13008 Kuwait
TELEPHONE: (965) 245 42 02
FAX: (965) 245 09 53

Kuwait's long experience with parliamentary politics is one of the features that has set this emirate apart from its neighbors in the Persian Gulf. Since achieving independence of the United Kingdom in June 1961, Kuwait has been without a legislature for only two relatively brief periods: 1976–1981, and 1986–1992. Furthermore, since it was reestablished in October 1992, the Kuwaiti parliament has been one of the most assertive in the Arab world.

EARLY PARLIAMENTARY EXPERIENCE

The roots of Kuwaiti parliamentary experience go deep into the country's past. As early as 1938, when Kuwait was still a British protectorate, a fourteen-member National Legislative Council (Majlis al-Umma al-Tashri'i) was established to act as a check on the power of the ruling al-Sabah family. The Council came about as a result of two decades of pressure by the country's leading merchant families, and it accomplished much over the course of its short existence

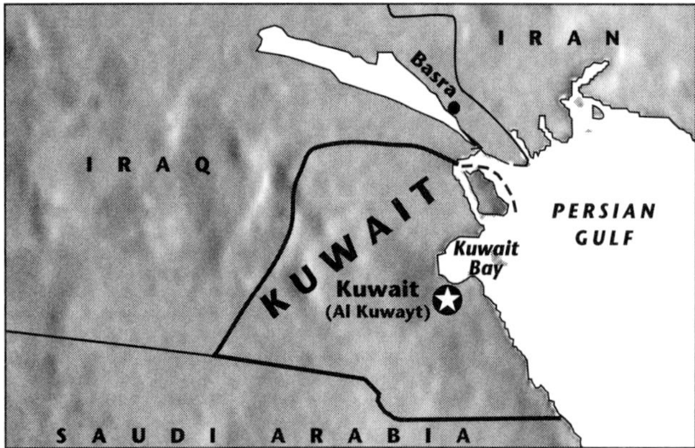

(June through December 1938). Its most important act was to draw up a basic law, which stipulated that the people are the source of all authority and that they should be represented by an elected assembly authorized to legislate on all matters of concern to the country, including security, foreign policy, the budget, and social affairs. It further stated that internal concessions, leases, monopolies, as well as all agreements and treaties with foreign powers, could not be considered legal and binding unless approved by the Council.

The Council also passed far-reaching legislation. It revamped the tax and the judicial systems, launched important construction projects, expanded educational facilities, and introduced public health regulations. In December 1938, however, it overreached when it requested that it, rather than the emir, should decide how oil revenues should be allocated. The emir responded by disbanding the Council. When the members of the Council resisted, the ruler resorted to force. Ultimately, the Council speaker was executed for calling for the overthrow of the regime. The remaining members either fled or were arrested.

Despite its short existence, the National Legislative Council established a precedent for an elected representative body, and its memory inspired Kuwaiti reformers during the 1940s and 1950s. In November 1962—fewer than eighteen months after the country had achieved independence—the emirate adopted the constitution that remains in place today. This constitution provides for a unique blend of hereditary rule and representative government. With respect to the former, it stipulates that the ruling family chooses the head of state from among the male descendants of Mubarak al-Sabah (Kuwait's ruler at the turn of the century, who is also known as Mubarak the Great). Under normal circumstances, the emir cannot be forced to step down. He selects and appoints the prime minister, who by convention has always been the crown prince. He also chooses the entire cabinet, which is responsible for day-to-day policy making. However, side by side with these characteristics of hereditary rule, the constitution also provides for a fifty-member National Assembly.

THE NATIONAL ASSEMBLY

Elected every four years, the Assembly is endowed with significant constitutional prerogatives. It is in charge of passing the country's laws. Although the emir can veto legislation approved by the Assembly by refusing to sign it, the parliament can override the emir's veto by a two-thirds vote. The Assembly is given particular authority in matters related to the budget and foreign affairs. Under the constitution, the Assembly must debate the budget and approve all government expenditures, and it must ratify treaties related to war and peace, alliances, the use of natural resources, and financial obligations. The Assembly is allowed to discuss any issue it deems appropriate, including the cabinet's policies and actions. To that end, Kuwaiti legislators are granted numerous constitutional protections against arrest or prosecution by the government. No member can be prosecuted unless the Assembly has suspended his immunity.

Any member of parliament can request specific information from a minister, and the answer must be forthcoming within a week. If unsatisfied by the government's explanation, MPs can express their objections and ask for clarification. At the initiative of only five of its members, the legislature can even call for a general debate on the issue. Although the National Assembly cannot pass a vote of no confidence in the cabinet, it can do so for ministers individually. Parliament's ability to request the resignation of ministers is in part a by-product of its ability to question them and investigate their conduct. Upon the request of ten of its members, the Assembly can ask that a specific minister be interpellated. Finally, although the emir is empowered to designate his successor, his choice must be ratified by the Assembly through a majority vote.

Although it has undergone several modifications over the years, the electoral law has always provided for very limited participation. Only male citizens who can trace their family roots in the emirate to 1920 are allowed to vote. Thus, about half of the population is disenfranchised on the basis of gender, and several hundred thousand men who were born in Kuwait and have spent their entire lives there cannot vote because their ancestors did not reside in the emirate prior to 1920. In addition, political parties are illegal (although they exist in practice), and the boundaries of electoral districts have been drawn and redrawn to favor the government.

Despite these serious restrictions, the National Assembly has played a crucial political role since the first parliamentary elections were held on January 29, 1963. It has provided an avenue through which a broad array of social forces—bedouins, intellectuals, professionals, and the business community—have been able to express themselves on the issues facing the country. It has contributed to the emirate's stability by working as a controlled forum for the expression of dissent by constituencies—including Sunni fundamentalists and members of the Shi'ite minority—that otherwise might have resorted to extralegal means for airing their grievances.

Through its questioning of government policies or the actions of individual ministers, the Assembly has been able to hold the cabinet accountable (even though criticism of the emir or of the prerogatives and legitimacy of the ruling family have remained beyond the pale). By publicizing instances of corruption, anticonstitutional behavior, misuse of public funds, violation of due process, and abuse of authority, the Assembly has provided a vital check on arbitrary rule.

Side by side with its oversight functions, the National Assembly has made significant contributions to policy making. It has initiated and passed laws and weighed heavily at times on the government's foreign policy choices. For instance, during the 1960s and 1970s, pressure from Arab nationalist MPs contributed to the government's repeated expressions of support for the Palestinian cause. Such pressure also explains why throughout that period the emirate refrained from policies that could be characterized as too pro-Western and why it sought to distance itself from British and U.S. positions in the region. Similarly, in the early 1970s opposition MPs helped bring about a radicalization of the government's oil policy. Parliamentary proceedings convinced the cabinet to put a ceiling on oil production in 1972 and to nationalize the Kuwait Oil Company two years later.

The National Assembly has also served to educate the public about domestic and foreign policy issues, regional developments, and the policies of the superpowers in the region. Its often acrimonious debates have been widely reported in Kuwait's relatively free and independent-minded press, which in turn has contributed to a more informed population. In many instances, had parliament not existed important topics likely would never have become part of the public agenda. Most important, through the very act of circumscribing the authority of the ruling family and the cabinet, the Assembly has helped the former legitimize its rule by projecting the image of a polity that has been far more open and participatory than most others in the Arab world.

DISBANDED AND RECONSTITUTED

The assertiveness of the legislature explains Kuwait's tormented parliamentary experience. On two occasions—in 1976 and 1986—the vigorous criticisms of government policies emanating from the Assembly prompted the emir to suspend it, leaving the government in sole control of national affairs. Significantly, however, in both instances the regime eventually reconvened parliament. This suggests that the Assembly had performed important political functions that no other body had been able to assume after the Assembly had been dissolved. These functions included co-opting or appeasing critical constituencies and facilitating communication among members of the political elite as well as between them and the population as a whole.

When, on July 3, 1986, the emir disbanded parliament for the second time in a decade, he also clamped down on the press, suspended parts of the constitution, outlawed public meetings of more than five people, and ruled by decree. This authoritarian turn encountered strong resistance from important segments of Kuwaiti society. In the months that followed the August 1988 cease-fire that ended the Iran-Iraq war, a coalition of prominent merchants, professionals, intellectuals, former parliamentarians, and even government officials began to agitate for political reforms. As in the previous instance when the Assembly had been dissolved, the demands of this nascent pro-democracy movement centered on the restoration of parliament, which was widely seen in the emirate as the one institution capable of ensuring a degree of governmental accountability and popular input into decision making.

In April 1990 the emir attempted to deflect the growing call for reconvening the legislature by announcing the establishment of an advisory National Council (Majlis al-Watani) of seventy-five members (fifty of whom were to be elected, with the remaining twenty-five to be appointed by the ruler). However, the opposition's boycott of the June 1990 elections to this consultative council deprived the new institution of the legitimacy it would have needed to be effective. Turnout was unusually low, and since only pro-government tribal leaders had been willing to compete for the elected seats, the Council was completely dominated by forces sympathetic to the regime. Fewer than two months later, on August 2, 1990, Iraq invaded a country that had become so caught up in its internal battles that it had failed to appreciate the magnitude of the threat posed by its powerful neighbor.

While in exile during the Iraqi occupation, the emir struck a deal with representatives of all major Kuwaiti political groupings, including opposition figures who had long been at odds with the regime. The leaders of the opposition reaffirmed their loyalty to the ruling family and acknowledged the emir as the legitimate ruler of the country. In exchange, the emir promised that liberation would be followed by far-reaching political reforms, including the restoration of the Assembly.

On October 5, 1992, eighteen months after the emirate was freed, legislative elections were finally held (after much hesitation by the emir and despite the strong ambivalence of many members of the ruling family toward democratization). That day, 67,724 Kuwaiti men (83.2 percent of the eligible voters) went to the polls to elect 50 representatives from 278 candidates in the country's twenty-five electoral districts. Campaigning was lively and vigorous. Numerous public meetings were held every day, and candidates discussed vital issues free of governmental interference. Only about 81,400 men were allowed to vote, but a very large number of those not eligible (including women and naturalized citizens) made their voices heard throughout the campaign. Although parties remained forbidden, most candidates were affiliated with loosely organized factions that had clear political platforms. These political groupings voiced the concerns of a broad spectrum of Kuwaiti society, including former Arab nationalists, independents, prodemocracy advocates, the business community, moderate Sunni fundamentalists relatively close to the regime, religious activists hostile to the government, and Shi'ites. The intensity and quality of the public debate suggested that the reconvened parliament would be the main vehicle for the democratization of political life in the emirate.

The elections resulted in a major political upset. Opposition and independent candidates captured thirty-five of the fifty seats in the National Assembly. Several progovernment candidates who were believed to be shoe-ins were defeated, whereas most of the prominent personalities in the prodemocracy and Islamic opposition camps were elected. This outcome came as a shock to the al-Sabah and as a surprise even to the most optimistic members of the opposition. For the first time since independence, the government would be unable to rely on a majority in the Assembly.

Shortly after reconvening, parliament elected as its speaker the outspoken Ahmad al-Sa'adun, who had held the same position in the Assembly that had been suspended in 1986. Soon afterward, al-Sa'adun and the prime minister (who is also the crown prince) repeatedly clashed. On several occasions, the crown prince—who made no mystery of his disdain for the Assembly—tried to circumvent it, but his efforts were thwarted by al-Sa'adun.

AN ASSERTIVE NATIONAL ASSEMBLY

The new legislature was quick to tackle some of the most sensitive issues facing the country. It launched several investigations into matters related to the use of public funds and the management of the country's overseas investments. These highly publicized probes unearthed evidence of embezzlement, incompetence, and corruption. Several of those accused of wrongdoing belonged to the ruling family. Prior to the Iraqi invasion, the regime would have regarded such developments as unacceptable parliamentary questioning of the ruling family's "discretionary spending" and as an interference in its internal affairs. Its response might have been to disband parliament. This time, instead, the National Assembly was allowed to perform its constitutional role as watchdog over public investments.

More generally, the Assembly asserted its control over financial and budgetary matters. After relentless efforts, it won access to the accounts of public sector companies. In 1993 and 1994 it passed several laws that enable it to review all expenditures by state-owned enterprises. One such law requires corporations in which the government holds 25 percent or more of the shares to report to official auditors changes in investment policies or portfolios. Delays in reporting can lead to prosecution. Under the same law, officials of state-owned companies who are convicted of misusing public funds can receive stiff sentences, including life in jail. Considering that the top decision makers in Kuwaiti public corporations have usually been al-Sabah, the law imposes additional constraints on the ruling family's freedom of maneuver. Not surprisingly, the law had been staunchly opposed by the crown prince and the finance minister. In the end, however, neither could prevent the passing of legislation that forced the government and the ruling family to become more transparent in the management of emirate assets. The Assembly also made headway toward forcing the cabinet to disclose fully all revenues and expenditures in the official budget.

Beyond budgetary and financial matters, the Assembly elected in 1992 drew attention to the structural weaknesses of the national economy (including the absence of a tax base, the existence of a bloated and unproductive public sector, and the widening gap between state revenues and expenditures) and made proposals to address them. It investigated the rearmament policy of the government and issued a well-publicized report that questioned the preferential treatment given to British companies. It also kept alive controversies such as the regime's responsibility for the Iraqi occupation and the ineptitude displayed by members of the ruling family in the days leading up to the invasion. It even contributed to an old polemic surrounding the government's bailout of investors following the crash of an informal stock market in 1982.

Finally, cultural themes featured prominently in the debates of the 1992–1996 Assembly. In late 1994 fundamentalist

MPs tried to mandate the separation of men and women in educational institutions. Some even suggested that a new state organization be created, the purpose of which would be "to direct the public to do good and refrain from evil." In these and other such instances, the proposed legislation was easily defeated; discussion of the relevant bills did not go beyond the appropriate committee, since there was not enough support for a debate in the plenary. Nevertheless, these examples illustrate the determination of Islamist MPs to push for legislation that would "Islamicize" Kuwaiti society (particularly in the areas of family affairs and education) and inevitably curtail personal freedoms.

Assembly rules and procedures are similar to those found in most parliamentary systems. When a bill reaches the Bureau of the Assembly, it is referred to the appropriate committee. There are currently eleven committees, the membership of which varies between five and nine representatives. After studying the bill, the committee will send a report to the plenary, where the real debate over the bill takes place. To pass, the bill requires a simple majority of the quorum.

New elections took place on October 7, 1996. Despite the tense regional situation that prevailed at the time (six weeks earlier, the regime of Iraqi president Saddam Hussein had sent troops to the Kurdish "safe haven" in northern Iraq, and the United States had retaliated with missile attacks on military installations in southern Iraq), the campaign was remarkably free of government interference, and the election was fair. More than 80 percent of the 107,000 men eligible to vote showed up at the polls. Candidates had debated vigorously, both in meetings and in the media. The 1992–1996 parliament came under strong criticism, and several politicians ran against what they denounced as its poor performance. They argued that the Assembly elected in 1992 had failed to live up to expectations, and that it had wasted precious time and energy on peripheral issues while ignoring the more serious ones facing the country.

The results of the 1996 elections suggested that many voters agreed with these claims. Turnover was high, as half of the elected members were newcomers. Several well-known parliamentary figures—particularly among liberals, reformists, Arab nationalists, and supporters of Speaker al-Saʿadun—lost their seats. For its part, the Islamist bloc slightly increased its overall strength, with twenty MPs. Overall, the opposition emerged significantly weaker. Close to half of the Assembly was made up of representatives from tribal areas, who were generally supportive of the regime. Nevertheless, the new legislature was not expected to be docile. Independents, liberal reformers, and the Islamist opposition were bound to question and criticize the government and force it to account for its policies. Even MPs described as "pro-regime" were expected to distance themselves from the government on critical issues. As a representative institution broadly reflective of the diversity of Kuwaiti society, the 1996 National Assembly seemed likely to assert itself as its predecessors had.

In summary, since 1963 the Kuwaiti parliament has operated as a critical channel for the airing of competing views on the rules that should govern the emirate's political life. It has been in the Assembly that the ruling family and the opposition have tested each other and have succeeded or failed in hammering out the necessary compromises. Consequently, the Assembly has been the arena in which Kuwait's defining struggle—the tug-of-war between a ruling family jealous of its prerogatives and a broad array of political forces pushing for greater governmental accountability and increased political participation—has played itself out most clearly. Since 1992, furthermore, the Kuwaiti Assembly has been reinvigorated. While it has been careful not to engage in the posturing and rhetorical excesses that in 1976 and 1986 led to its disbanding, the Assembly has proved to be one of the most assertive legislatures in the Arab world.

Abdo Baaklini, Guilain Denoeux, and Robert Springborg

BIBLIOGRAPHY

Aarts, Paul. "The Limits of Political Tribalism: Post-War Kuwait and the Process of Democratization." *Civil Society* (December 1994): 17–22 (pt. 1); (January 1995): 16–18 (pt. 2).

Baaklini, Abdo. "Legislatures in the Gulf Area: The Experience of Kuwait, 1961–1976." *International Journal of Middle East Studies* 14 (1982): 361–379.

Crystal, Jill. *Kuwait: The Transformation of an Oil State.* Boulder, Colo.: Westview Press, 1992.

Ghabra, Shafeeq. "Democratization in a Middle Eastern State: Kuwait, 1993." *Middle East Policy* 3 (1994): 102–119.

Khalaf, Jassim Muhammad. "The Kuwait National Assembly: A Study of Its Structure and Function." Ph.D. diss., State University of New York at Albany, Graduate School of Public Affairs, 1984.

KYRGYZSTAN

See Commonwealth of Independent States, Non-Slavic

L

LAOS

OFFICIAL NAME: Lao People's Democratic Republic (Sathalanalat Paxathipatai Paxaxôn Lao)
CAPITAL: Vientiane
POPULATION: 4,976,000 (1996 est.)
DATE OF INDEPENDENCE: October 23, 1953 (from France)
DATE OF CURRENT CONSTITUTION: Adopted August 14, 1991
FORM OF GOVERNMENT: Communist dictatorship
LANGUAGES: Lao (official), French, English
MONETARY UNIT: New kip
FISCAL YEAR: July 1–June 30
LEGISLATURE: National Assembly (Sapha Heng Xat)
NUMBER OF CHAMBERS: One
NUMBER OF MEMBERS: 85
PERCENTAGE OF WOMEN: 9.4
TERM OF LEGISLATURE: Five years
MOST RECENT LEGISLATIVE ELECTION: December 20, 1992
MINIMUM AGE FOR VOTING: 18
MINIMUM AGE FOR MEMBERSHIP: 21
SUFFRAGE: Direct and universal
VOTING: Compulsory
ADDRESS: National Assembly, National Assembly Building, 1 That-Luang Square, P.O. Box 662, Vientiane
TELEPHONE: (856 21) 41 35 18
FAX: (856 21) 41 35 13

Laos is a communist state in Southeast Asia ruled by the Lao People's Revolutionary Party *(see map, p. 735)*. The 1991 constitution modernized the political system without permitting political pluralism. The National Assembly is the legislative organ, but in theory it also oversees the executive and the judiciary. Members of the National Assembly are elected for a term of five years by universal adult suffrage.

The National Assembly elects a Standing Committee from among its members. Ordinary sessions are held twice annually, and extraordinary sessions may be convened by the Standing Committee. The National Assembly is empowered to amend the constitution; to make, amend, or abrogate laws; to elect or remove the president and the vice presidents of state; to elect or remove the president of the Supreme Court; and to pass motions of no confidence in the cabinet or any of its members. There is one deputy for every fifty thousand citizens.

George Thomas Kurian

LATVIA

OFFICIAL NAME: Republic of Latvia (Latvijas Republika)
CAPITAL: Riga
POPULATION: 2,469,000 (1996 est.)
DATE OF INDEPENDENCE: Declared August 21, 1991 (from the Soviet Union)
DATE OF CURRENT CONSTITUTION: Adopted May 1, 1922
FORM OF GOVERNMENT: Parliamentary democracy
LANGUAGE: Latvian (official), Lithuanian, Russian
MONETARY UNIT: Lat
FISCAL YEAR: Calendar year
LEGISLATURE: Parliament (Saeima)
NUMBER OF CHAMBERS: One
NUMBER OF MEMBERS: 100
PERCENTAGE OF WOMEN: 10.0
TERM OF LEGISLATURE: Three years
MOST RECENT LEGISLATIVE ELECTION: September 30 and October 1, 1995
MINIMUM AGE FOR VOTING: 18
MINIMUM AGE FOR MEMBERSHIP: 21
SUFFRAGE: Universal and direct
VOTING: Optional
ADDRESS: Parliament, 11 Jekaba Str., Riga LV 1811
TELEPHONE: (371 2) 32 29 38
FAX: (371 2) 21 16 11

A country on the eastern littoral of the Baltic Sea *(see map, p. 421)*, Latvia operates under a parliamentary system with a president as head of state and prime minister as head of government.

After achieving independence from Russia following

World War I, Latvia convened its parliament, the Saeima, for the first time in 1922. It was dissolved twelve years later subsequent to a bloodless coup d'état. After the Soviet Union annexed Latvia during World War II, a Soviet-style legislature was created. Latvia regained its independence in 1991. In 1993 the country chose a new Saeima in its first free and fair election in more than sixty years.

HISTORICAL BACKGROUND

The territory that is present-day Latvia was subjugated by foreign powers for most of the past eight hundred years. Invaded by crusading German knights in the thirteenth century and the object of various imperial expansion schemes, Latvia did not win self-rule and establish deliberative bodies until the twentieth century.

Pre-World War I development

Latvian self-government was made possible by the emergence of an educated Latvian elite in the mid-nineteenth century that gave birth to the very concept of a Latvian nation. The vast majority of Latvians in the nineteenth century were peasants living in the countryside and working in agriculture. They were governed by the Baltic German nobility, the descendants of the conquering knights, who maintained their economic and social dominance even after the Russian empire conquered the area in the eighteenth century. Late in the nineteenth century, Latvian nationalism became intertwined with the socialist movement. The emerging Latvian elite reacted against both the privileges enjoyed by the Baltic Germans and the Russification policies being pursued by the tsar.

The Revolution of 1905 flared suddenly and violently throughout Latvia. In the cities, workers rose up against their political and economic masters. In the countryside, the revolution gave peasants the opportunity to settle scores with the landed nobility, who were chiefly Baltic Germans. As central authority collapsed, local groups took matters into their own hands. One thousand delegates from throughout Latvia met in Riga in November 1905. They resolved that local parish councils should be elected to oversee local affairs, the privileges of the nobles should be abolished, and an elected national assembly should be established. But those gathered stopped short of demanding independence, calling instead for a Russian Constituent Assembly to work out plans for self-governance. Tsarist authorities crushed the revolution in 1906, however, and all these plans went unrealized.

Several Latvians were elected to the Russian Duma (1906–1917), where they generally allied themselves with the Constitutional Democrats and sought to reform the agricultural system, which favored the large landowners. Although the Duma had no real power, these individuals gained experience in government and politics, and many played prominent roles in the crucial years to come.

World War I visited untold devastation upon Latvia. In 1914 Latvia's population exceeded 2.5 million; by 1920 it was less than 1.6 million. Upwards of 850,000 refugees—one-third of Latvia's population—fled to Russia. The chaos of the war, however, provided Latvians with the opportunity to organize. Latvian refugee assistance committees sprang up to fill the void left by an increasingly ineffective tsarist bureaucracy. These committees provided refugees with all essential services, schooling their leaders in self-governance and indirectly promoting Latvian national consciousness. The Latvian Central Refugee Committee in Petrograd (present-day St. Petersburg), which coordinated the 260 local committees, is sometimes called the first Latvian parliament because it included leaders representing the entire Latvian political spectrum.

With the collapse of the Russian empire in 1917, Latvian demands for autonomy grew. Representatives of leading Latvian groups met in Riga on July 30, 1917, and unanimously adopted a resolution demanding the right of self-determination for the Latvian nation, Latvia's autonomy within a Russian republic, and a legislature, the Saeima, to be elected by adults on a general, direct, and secret basis according to proportional representation rules. In September 1917 leaders of all major parties except the Bolshevik Party met in Riga to form the Democratic Bloc. They all shared a commitment to an independent Latvia.

In Latvia, as elsewhere in Russia, people elected local councils ("soviets," in Russian). The Social Democrats, particularly the Bolsheviks, proved themselves very popular in these elections; in rural areas the Farmers' Union also ran well. The measurable popularity of the Bolsheviks crested with the elections to the Russian Constituent Assembly, held within weeks of the October Revolution. The delegation representing Latvia at that short-lived assembly consisted overwhelmingly of Bolsheviks and a handful of Farmers' Union members. Meanwhile, Latvian nationalists living outside Riga went underground to form the Latvian Provisional National Council. In November the National Council brought together representatives from most large Latvian organizations at its first congress. The congress decreed that Latvia was an autonomous entity uniting all Latvian-speaking people, and that a Constituent Assembly should decide upon the form of Latvia's government and its foreign relations. Thus, by November, two major groups were working for a new order in Latvia. The German army still occupied most of Latvia, however, so they made little headway.

In November 1918 the Democratic Bloc and the National

Council merged to form the People's Council of Latvia. On November 18, 1918, the People's Council declared Latvia independent and announced that the Council would serve as Latvia's provisional government until the people of Latvia elected a Constituent Assembly.

The interwar years

The Treaty of Brest-Litovsk partitioned Latvia between Germany and Russia. Despite this agreement, both countries tried to assert control over Latvia. Germany withdrew its forces from Riga before the city could be adequately defended and obstructed the Latvian provisional government in its efforts to defend western Latvia. The Red Army entered Riga in January 1919 and proclaimed a Soviet republic. In spring and summer 1919, Latvian, Estonian, and German forces successfully expelled the Bolshevik forces. German, Bolshevik, and White Russian attempts to crush the newly founded Latvian state by military means and political subversion failed. In 1920 Latvia signed peace treaties with both the German and Russian governments. International recognition followed, and Latvia finally became a sovereign state.

From November 17, 1918, to April 30, 1920, the People's Council functioned as Latvia's legislature. The state of war that prevailed for most of this period forced the Council to be itinerant, as it sought to avoid being captured by foreign armies. Along with the task of drawing up the rules to govern the Constituent Assembly, the Council had to oversee the effort to repel foreign invaders, establish new administrative structures, and manage the more mundane affairs of the new country.

All three cabinets appointed under the Council, each headed by Prime Minister Karlis Ulmanis, comprised well-educated younger men, mostly in their forties, who were capable and prominent. The high caliber of these early leaders enhanced the prestige of the Council and government in the public's perception. The Council's broad composition—one-third representing farm and business interests, one-third selected by socialist parties, and one-third selected by parties of the democratic center—also provided a cushion of popular support. The violent attacks on the nascent Latvian state by German, Bolshevik, and White Russian forces, coupled with the unpopular programs each offered, rallied Latvians and local minorities to the Council's side.

The Council handled its business through twenty-two standing committees, each of which included representatives from all of the political parties represented in the People's Council. The Council also appointed special investigative committees to review individual matters, particularly those concerning government actions. The Council actively oversaw the provisional government but began to interfere in its actions only as election day for the Constituent Assembly approached.

The People's Council put off elections for the Constituent Assembly until no foreign troops remained on Latvian soil. In April 1920 Latvia's voters elected 150 constitutional delegates. The country was divided into five voting districts: the city of Riga and the provinces of Kurzeme, Latgale, Vidzeme, and Zemgale. Mandates were allocated to each district in proportion to district population as recorded in the 1897 census. Delegates were selected by a proportional representation system. The turnout of almost 85 percent meant that more than 700,000 voters had chosen from among fifty-seven party lists. The Social Democrats made the strongest showing by far with 275,000 votes and fifty-seven mandates. The Farmers' Union won 126,000 votes and received twenty-six mandates, and the Farmers' Party of Latgale won 73,000 votes and seventeen mandates. Thirteen parties divided the remaining fifty mandates. The fractionalization of this body foreshadowed the political problems independent Latvia would face. For the next two years the Constituent Assembly served as Latvia's parliament.

On May 1, 1922, the Constituent Assembly adopted the *Satversme*, Latvia's constitution. The government created by this document, which is the basis of the post-Soviet Latvian state, was a parliamentary democracy patterned after the French and German post–World War I governments. It created a highly democratic political system with a strong parliament, called the Saeima, elected through proportional representation. The Saeima elected a president, who served as head of state. Although this office was more than ceremonial, it lacked a great variety of powers.

The constitution's single greatest flaw was that it contained no provisions to minimize the centrifugal effects of a proliferation of political parties based on narrow interests. Any group of voters could propose a list of candidates for the Saeima in any of the five voting districts. On average, in each of four interwar elections, voters had 113 candidate lists from which to choose; of these, an average of twenty-five lists succeeded in electing at least one candidate. Many of those elected were more interested in protecting their own narrow interests than in pursuing broader goals, giving rise to obstructionism and irresponsibility. Prime ministers formed thirteen governments during the first four Saeimas, each lasting an average of only eleven months.

Some viewed Latvia's parliamentary system as ineffective and chaotic. They feared that politics would deteriorate into street battles between extremists on the left and the right. Upon becoming prime minister in March 1934 for the fifth time in sixteen years, Ulmanis concluded that decisive action needed to be taken. He declared a state of emergency, suspended parliament, banned political parties, and arrested political opponents. Ulmanis presided over a mildly authoritarian regime; nevertheless, he did smother Latvia's democratic institutions.

The Soviet era

Ulmanis ruled until June 1940, when the Soviet Union invaded Latvia and installed its own government. In July Soviet authorities held a rigged election for a puppet legislature, the People's Parliament. That parliament's first act was to declare Latvia a socialist republic and to request annexation into the Soviet Union. In August 1940 the People's Parliament adopted a constitution for the Latvian Soviet Socialist Republic patterned after the 1936 Soviet constitution.

Following World War II, the Latvian Supreme Soviet, consisting of 325 deputies elected by citizens over age eighteen, became the highest legislative body in Latvia, at least formally. Deputies were elected from single-member districts of equal populations for four-year terms, until 1975, when terms were extended to five years. In theory, the Supreme Soviet was the center of political power in the republic. It wrote the laws, elected the government and judges, approved republic budgets and development plans, and monitored their execution. The chair of the Supreme Soviet served as head of state. In reality, however, the Supreme Soviet was virtually powerless. The Communist Party carefully selected the one candidate nominated in each election district. Although voters could cast their ballots against a candidate, nominees rarely failed to win a majority of votes. Communist Party leaders and ministry officials in Moscow made virtually all decisions of any consequence. The Latvian Supreme Soviet rubber-stamped those decisions at its occasional meetings.

TRANSITION TO INDEPENDENCE

The Supreme Soviet remained irrelevant to the political process until the era of Mikhail Gorbachev. As the Soviet political system opened up in the late 1980s, politicians began to act like politicians. Legislators felt pressure from constituents as well as from their political masters, and Latvians began to organize to pursue their interests. Suddenly, in 1988 the Latvian Supreme Soviet began to enact legislation on its own, not under orders from Moscow. Anatolijs Gorbunovs, appointed chair, used his position to rally republic governmental resources and the public to the rapidly growing autonomy movement.

The Latvian Supreme Soviet voted to reform itself in 1989. It reduced the size of parliament to 201 deputies and permitted more than one candidate to be nominated in each election district. In the 1990 Supreme Soviet elections, the Popular Front, a broad-based movement seeking Latvia's independence, successfully challenged the Communist Party. The Front and its allies captured a two-thirds majority in the new legislature. On May 4, 1990, the newly elected Supreme Soviet declared that the Soviet annexation of Latvia had been illegal; therefore the 1922 constitution remained valid. This parliament, which preferred to be known in the West by the more accurate translation "Supreme Council," served until 1993. Once under Popular Front control, the Supreme Council became the leading force in Latvia's drive for independence from the Soviet Union and formed the outlines of post-Soviet Latvian politics, economics, and society. The Supreme Council withstood Soviet pressure to disavow its independence declaration and, when the Soviet Union crumbled, Latvia became an independent state again.

During the difficult transition to independence, citizenship loomed as the most inflammatory issue facing Latvia. During the Soviet era, large numbers of workers and soldiers and their families had settled in Latvia. At the time of the 1989 census, Latvians constituted barely more than one-half the republic population; Russians made up one-third. The citizenship law the Supreme Council passed in 1991 granted automatic citizenship only to those who had been citizens of the Republic of Latvia as of the day the Soviet Union invaded and their descendants. Others would have to apply for naturalization, but the Council did not set down rules for that process. Thus, when the first post-Soviet elections took place in the spring of 1993, the overwhelming majority of eligible voters (79 percent) were ethnic Latvians. Leaders of the disenfranchised objected. In 1994 the parliament approved procedures for naturalization that were deemed unreasonable by Western governments. The president, at the request of the prime minister, returned the bill to parliament for reconsideration. The parliament passed an amended law after removing the objectionable articles. The citizenship issue continues to be a hot political issue, however.

THE CONSTITUTION AND PARLIAMENT

At its first session, on July 6, 1993, the Saeima voted to restore the 1922 constitution. The constitution establishes a unicameral legislature called the Saeima, a term that connotes a gathering. The primary function of the Saeima is to write laws. The Saeima elects the president, known formally as the "state president," who is the head of state. The president invites a candidate to become prime minister, formally called the "minister president," who assembles a cabinet and serves as head of government. Although the Office of the President is largely ceremonial, it includes a few blunt instruments to influence policy.

The Saeima comprises one hundred deputies elected for

three-year terms by citizens eighteen years of age and older by universal, equal, direct, and secret ballot. The Saeima elects the president by secret ballot. To be elected, a candidate must receive at least fifty-one votes. The president is elected for a three-year term and may serve for a maximum of six years. The Saeima may dismiss the president by a two-thirds vote of all deputies.

The president is empowered to call extraordinary meetings of the cabinet to address specific issues. He or she may require the legislature to reconsider laws it has passed. The president may propose dissolving the Saeima, but to do so is a huge political gamble. Once the president has proposed dissolving the parliament, he or she must call a special referendum. If more than 50 percent of voters support the president, the Saeima is dissolved and elections for a new Saeima are scheduled; if less than a majority of voters support the president, the president is removed from office. This provision has never been exercised.

The president also serves as head of the armed forces, declares war in accordance with the decisions of the Saeima, appoints a commander in chief in time of war, and appoints diplomatic representatives. The president chairs the National Security Council, which supervises the Constitutional Defense Bureau—Latvia's intelligence agency—and which oversees security and defense policy.

The Saeima confirms the prime minister and the ministers he or she nominates. The cabinet, formally known as the Cabinet of Ministers, supervises all state administrative bodies. The cabinet is accountable to the Saeima. A vote of no confidence in the prime minister forces the entire cabinet to resign. An individual minister may be forced to resign if the Saeima expresses no confidence in him or her. In the event of serious domestic or international threat, the cabinet may proclaim a state of emergency and temporarily rule without the Saeima's involvement.

Ministers have the right to vote on all matters, whereas state ministers may vote only on matters related to their particular realm. As of April 1997 the cabinet consisted of the prime minister, two deputy prime ministers, thirteen full ministers (one of whom was also a deputy prime minister), and four state ministers. To coordinate legislation, three committees of the Cabinet of Ministers have been created: Foreign Affairs and Security; Economics and Finance; and State and Social Affairs. Cabinet ministers, including the prime minister, need not be members of the Saeima, though they usually are.

The judicial branch is independent of the rest of the government. The court system consists of three levels: district, appellate, and supreme. Judges are appointed for life by the cabinet on the recommendation of the justice minister and are confirmed by the Saeima. Judges may be removed from office against their will only by the Supreme Court. In 1996 the Saeima created a Constitutional Court, which comprises seven judges appointed for ten-year terms, to hear issues involving constitutional conflicts.

The constitution also establishes an independent State Audit Board. The board is appointed by the cabinet and confirmed by the Saeima for a fixed term. As an independent investigative body, the State Audit Board has the potential to play a significant role in assessing policies and investigating allegations of wrongdoing.

PARTIES AND ELECTIONS

The constitution stipulates that Saeima elections be held every three years on the first Sunday in October and the Saturday preceding it. The country is divided into five voting districts: the city of Riga (twenty-four mandates) and the provinces of Kurzeme (fourteen), Latgale (twenty), Vidzeme (twenty-six), and Zemgale (sixteen). The number of mandates apportioned to each district is determined by the population of eligible voters in that district. Parties assemble lists in each district. Voters may cast their ballots for only one list, but they may affix a plus or minus sign beside the names of certain candidates on that list, which may affect the final order of candidates. Mandates are disbursed according to a modified D'Hondt system. Rules for the 1993 Saeima elections required a party to win at least 4 percent of the total national vote to qualify its candidates for seats in the parliament. That threshold was raised to 5 percent in the 1995 Saeima elections.

Because of the confusion and uncertainty inherent in a transition, elections since the reestablishment of independence have been complex affairs. In the 1993 election, parties at the center-right won a plurality. In 1995 voters abandoned the center for more extreme parties but still snubbed the former communists. But the traditional labels of liberal and conservative can be misleading. The two top issues have been citizenship and economic transition. Some otherwise conservative nationalists desire retaining a strong state sector in the economy, whereas capitalist tycoons dominate some left-wing parties.

The large number of parties contesting for the Saeima—twenty-three in 1993 and nineteen in 1995—constitute one legacy of the interwar years. The 5 percent electoral threshold, however, reduced the extreme fractionalization that beset the interwar Saeimas.

To emphasize the legal continuity of the Latvian state, the body elected in June 1993 was called the Fifth Saeima; Karlis Ulmanis had dismissed the Fourth Saeima in 1934. Two-thirds of Latvia's adult population were eligible to vote in 1993, and turnout was high: nearly 90 percent. Eight parties won seats, and centrist groups dominated. Latvia's Way Alliance, an amalgam of former communist elites and emigré activists, won, capturing 32 percent of the vote and receiving thirty-six seats. Latvia's Way promised a moderate approach to the sensitive citizenship and privatization issues. It formed a coalition with the Farmers' Union, which won 11 percent of the vote and twelve seats. The Latvian National Conservative Party (13 percent, fifteen seats) and the Fatherland and Freedom Union (5 percent, six seats) were to the right of the governing coalition; both stressed protecting Latvia and Latvian culture from former communists, Russia, and the many non-Latvians living in Latvia. Another moderately conservative party, the Christian Democratic Union, won 5 percent of the vote and six seats.

The political left has been defined by its support for a less restrictive citizenship law and a strong role for the state in economic affairs, but the left has been split along ethnic lines. Whereas the Harmony for Latvia coalition (12 percent, thirteen seats) drew its supporters from all ethnic groups, Equal Rights (6 percent, seven seats) garnered its support from non-Latvians, chiefly ethnic Russians, who sought closer ties with Russia and rejected the legitimacy of an independent Latvia. The Democratic Center Party (5 percent, five seats), a center-left party, sent the smallest contingent. Significantly, the tattered remains of the two most powerful forces in Soviet Latvia at its twilight—the Democratic Labor Party (the successor to the nationalist wing of the Communist Party of Latvia) and the Popular Front—failed to win any seats in the new parliament.

Elections for the Sixth Saeima occurred on September 30 and October 1, 1995. Turnout dropped considerably, to 72 percent of eligible voters. The naturalization process, which had been in effect since 1994, boosted the proportion of eligible voters to three-fourths of all adult residents. The voters elected a parliament so evenly divided that forming a new government took months. Nine parties won seats in the parliament. Extremist parties on the left and right grew stronger at the expense of parties at the center. The left-of-center Democratic Party "Saimnieks" received the most votes, winning eighteen seats with 15 percent of the vote. The populist People's Movement won sixteen seats with 15 percent of the vote. Winning only seventeen seats with 15 percent of the vote, Latvia's Way Alliance lost more than half of its seats. Fatherland and Freedom Union, one of the most conservative parties, gained eight seats, capturing fourteen with 12 percent of the vote. The more moderate conservatives, the Latvian National Conservative Party–Green coalition and the Farmers' Union coalition lost ground, each winning eight seats with 6 percent of the vote. Latvian Unity party, emphasizing state intervention in the economy, came from nowhere to win 7 percent of the vote and eight seats. The Popular Harmony Party, promoting citizenship law liberalization, won six seats with 6 percent of the vote. Equal Rights reconstituted itself as the Socialist Party and held steady at 6 percent of the popular vote and five seats. Former nationalist communists ran as the Labor and Justice coalition with the support of trade union leaders of the obsolete industrial enterprises but received less than 5 percent of the vote and won no seats.

Stitching together a governing coalition proved difficult. The Saeima elected a speaker from the Democratic Party "Saimnieks" on a 51–49 vote, but it was not until Christmas that a cabinet could be formed. Before that happened, however, the Saeima rejected a right-wing cabinet by a 48–51 vote and a left-wing cabinet by a 50–50 vote. Except for the two extremist parties—the Socialists and the People's Movement—every party in parliament entered into this grand coalition, the broadest in Latvian history. Andris Skele, a business executive and former deputy agriculture minister, who was not a Saeima deputy, agreed to lead the cabinet. Despite fears that the unwieldy coalition would soon fall apart, Skele proved to be an effective leader. He is credited with performing what was thought to be an impossible feat: forcing the Saeima to approve a balanced budget for 1997.

After Saeima elections, parties and individual deputies maneuver for position. Parties split up, regroup, and realign. The rules of the Saeima recognize and provide material assistance to parliamentary parties and coalitions that declare themselves "factions." Five or more deputies may form a faction. The People's Movement split into two factions (neither of which is part of this governing coalition). Internal strife befell the Socialist Party; for a time the most vehement opponents of the Latvian state did not qualify as a faction. As of April 1997 eighty-seven Saeima deputies were organized into seven factions, leaving thirteen deputies classified as unaffiliated. Factions have sought to maintain voting discipline in the Saeima, something that they had failed to do in the Supreme Council.

ORGANIZATION AND PROCEDURES

The constitution stipulates that a newly elected Saeima convene for its first session on the first Tuesday in November following regularly scheduled elections.

The Saeima is administered by the Presidium, which consists of a speaker, two deputy speakers, a secretary, and a deputy secretary, all of whom are elected by the Saeima. The Presidium is responsible for convening the Saeima for regular and extraordinary sessions and for setting its agenda. The Presidium is required to convene the Saeima if the president, the prime minister, or more than one-third of Saeima deputies request it. The Saeima speaker serves as interim president of the state when the sitting president is unable to carry out his or her duties. The speaker serves as acting president when the president travels abroad.

The Saeima handles its business through sixteen standing committees. These committees draft legislation, conduct investigations, and monitor the implementation of legislation by the cabinet. As of January 1, 1997, the following committees were operating: Administrative; Audit; Budget and Finance; Citizenship Law Implementation; Defense and Internal Affairs; Economic, Agricultural, Environmental and Regional Development; Education, Culture, and Science; European Affairs; Foreign Affairs; Government Review; Human Rights and Public Affairs; Legal Affairs; Mandate and Submissions; National Security; Social and Employment Matters; and State Administration and Local Government.

The president, the cabinet, Saeima committees, five or more Saeima deputies, or 10 percent of the electorate may introduce draft laws. Most bills must be approved by a majority vote in three readings to become law. The Saeima approves the state budget, which the cabinet submits, and ratifies international agreements.

Minutes of Saeima plenary sessions are published in *Latvijas Vestnesis,* the official state newspaper, and they are available on the World Wide Web. Deputies are not allowed to profit directly from state contracts but are permitted to hold outside jobs and sit on corporate boards, leading to charges of conflict of interest.

ARCHITECTURE

The Saeima building stands in Old Riga, the medieval section of Riga. Built for the Livonian Order of Nobility in 1863–1867, the Saeima building was expanded in 1900–1903, renovated to meet the needs of the Saeima in 1922–1923, and restored after a fire in 1926. The architects, Janis Baumanis (the first Latvian architect with formal training) and Robert Pflug, designed it in the style of a Florentine neo-Renaissance palace, as interpreted by the Berlin school. It is characterized by its eclectic style and monumentalism. The granite facade is echoed in the building's interior space. Motifs from various historical styles decorate the interior. The western wing contains the main assembly hall and other meeting rooms, and the eastern wing contains administrative offices.

Andrejs Penikis

BIBLIOGRAPHY

Dreifelds, Juris. *Latvia in Transition.* Cambridge: Cambridge University Press, 1996.

Misiunas, Romuald J., and Rein Taagepera. *The Baltic States: Years of Dependence, 1940–1990.* Berkeley: University of California Press, 1993.

Plakans, Andrejs. *The Latvians: A Short History.* Stanford: Hoover Institution, 1995.

von Rauch, Georg. *The Baltic States: The Years of Independence, 1917–1940.* New York: St. Martin's, 1995.

Spekke, Arnolds. *History of Latvia: An Outline.* Stockholm: M. Goppers, 1957.

LEBANON

OFFICIAL NAME: Republic of Lebanon (al-Jumhuriyah al-Lubnaniyah)

CAPITAL: Beirut

POPULATION: 3,776,000 (1996 est.)

DATE OF INDEPENDENCE: November 22, 1943 (from League of Nations mandate under French administration)

DATE OF CURRENT CONSTITUTION: Effective May 23, 1926

FORM OF GOVERNMENT: Parliamentary democracy

LANGUAGE: Arabic (official), French (official)

MONETARY UNIT: Lebanese pound

FISCAL YEAR: Calendar year

LEGISLATURE: Chamber of Deputies (Majlis al-Nuwaab)

NUMBER OF CHAMBERS: One

NUMBER OF MEMBERS: 128

PERCENTAGE OF WOMEN: 2.3

TERM OF LEGISLATURE: Four years

MOST RECENT LEGISLATIVE ELECTION: August–September 1996

MINIMUM AGE FOR VOTING: 21

MINIMUM AGE FOR MEMBERSHIP: 25

SUFFRAGE: Direct and universal

VOTING: Optional

ADDRESS: Chamber of Deputies, Beirut

TELEPHONE: (961 1) 38 81 75

FAX: (961 1) 345 270

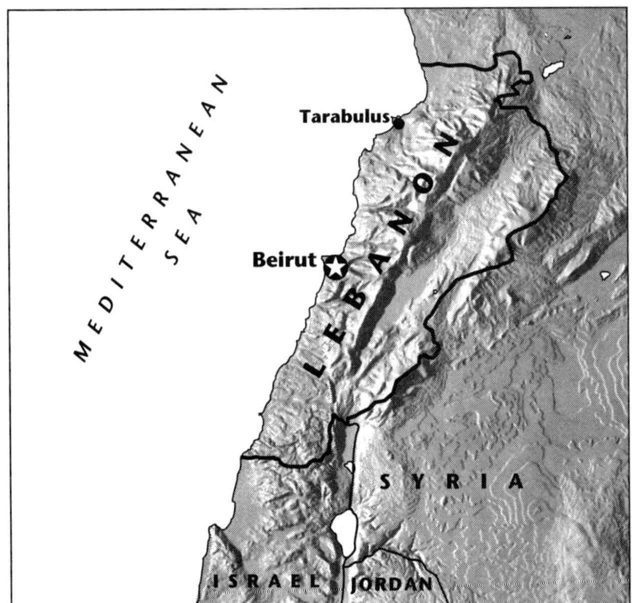

One of the features that sets Lebanon, a Mediterranean coastal state bordering Syria and Israel, apart in the Arab world is the influential role that the legislature has played in that country's political system since the 1920s. During the French mandate (1920–1943), the Chamber of Deputies made important contributions to the emergence of a sense of nationalism as well as to the struggle for independence. After 1943 it became the cornerstone of a consociational system designed to allow various communities to live together while preserving their unique identities and traditions. During the 1950s and 1960s the Lebanese took great pride in their legislature, which contributed to the atmosphere of freedom that so sharply distinguished Lebanon from its neighbors. Even after civil war broke out in 1975, the Chamber remained active, and in October 1989 its members played a crucial role in negotiating an end to the hostilities by establishing the foundations of a new political order. Since 1990 the political reconstruction that Lebanon has experienced has been accompanied by a strengthening of the Chamber's role in the political system and by an increase in its internal capacity.

FRENCH ADMINISTRATION

In 1922, two years after the League of Nations had given them a mandate over the newly created state of Lebanon, the French allowed the election of a Representative Council. This Council did not turn out to be the compliant body that the French had anticipated. In 1925 it moved to exercise its mandate for the election of the chief executive. Despite French objections, the Council was determined to elect Bishara al-Khuri, a Maronite Christian who enjoyed the support of many Muslim leaders opposed to the French presence. The French high commissioner, Gen. Maurice Sarrail, repeatedly applied pressure on the Council to choose France's preferred candidate, Emile Eddé. But the Council could not be swayed. In desperation, Sarrail dissolved it, and elections for a second Council were held.

From the moment it convened, the second Representative Council worked assiduously to muster opposition to France's decision to proceed unilaterally in drafting a constitution for Lebanon. Pointing to the League mandate, which called for the participation of the people of mandated territories in drafting their own laws, the Council requested that it be allowed to draft and ratify the constitution. Fearing unfavorable reactions from members of the International Committee of the League of Nations (which was supposed to supervise the way in which the mandatory powers were fulfilling the provisions of their mandates), France eventually complied. Accordingly, the Council acted as a constituent assembly, and in 1926 it wrote and promulgated the constitution that remains in place today, although with several amendments. A Council that many observers had initially dismissed as a "rubber stamp" forced France to back down. It also made a lasting contribution to Lebanese political life by establishing the formal framework that would govern Lebanese politics well after independence was achieved.

The legislature was initially divided into two houses, a Senate and a Chamber of Deputies, but the Senate was abolished in 1927. The constitution was amended again in 1929, at the initiative of the French, who wanted to strengthen the president at the expense of the Chamber of Deputies. Even after that amendment, however, the Chamber remained endowed with strong constitutional prerogatives, the most important of which was the election (by a two-thirds majority in the first round, and by a simple majority in the second round) of the chief executive, the president of the republic.

The Chamber also had strong oversight powers. It could force the cabinet to step down through a vote of no confidence. Its members were given immunity against arrest or prosecution while performing their duties, and members could not be prosecuted for opinions they had expressed during a parliamentary session. In addition, under normal circumstances, the president was bound to carry out the budget as passed by the Chamber. Finally, the Chamber's legislative powers were extensive. The president was bound constitutionally to promulgate the laws as it had passed them. He or she was not empowered to change laws or make special exceptions. Laws passed by the legislature had to be promulgated within one month after they had been referred to the cabinet. Any project bill (a proposed law initiated by the government) that had been rejected by the Chamber could not be submitted to it again during the same session.

As soon as the constitution was implemented, the French discovered that the Chamber often could prevent them from carrying out their policies, which were usually opposed by a majority of the deputies. Between 1926 and 1943 a constant tug-of-war existed between the high commissioner and the Chamber. In 1926, for instance, competition between the French-supported candidate for president and the candidate backed by the anti-French forces in the Chamber resulted in the selection of a compromise candidate, Charles Debbas, a Greek Orthodox. Compromise, however, was not always possible. In those instances, the French did not hesitate to suspend the constitution, dissolve the Chamber, and appoint the president. Yet, every time they resorted to such measures, they faced a hostile public and eventually had to agree to new elections, which usually yielded an even more defiant legislature.

One of the factors that allowed the Chamber to act as a catalyst for independence was its ability to integrate the many regions and sects that made up the country. When the French had created Greater Lebanon in 1920, they stitched together populations that differed greatly in outlook, temperament, and tradition. The core of the new country was Mount Lebanon, which in late Ottoman times had enjoyed a semiautonomous status. To Mount Lebanon, however, the French had added substantial territories to the north, south, and east (the Bekaa Valley). Unlike Mount Lebanon, these territories were politically, ideologically, and economically oriented toward Syria. If Lebanon were to survive, these people had to be tied to the central government in Beirut and had to develop a stake in the country's political system. No institution contributed toward this goal more than the Chamber, which brought together representatives of the various regions and sects and allowed them to cooperate in charting the path of their country.

PARLIAMENT AFTER INDEPENDENCE

After Lebanon became independent in 1943, the Chamber played an even greater role in enabling the country's diverse groups to be represented and to strike the necessary compromises with one another. This important function can be understood only within the context set by the so-called National Pact of 1943. According to the pact, political offices were to be divided among the various religious sects that made up the country. The distribution was to reflect each sect's share of the total population, as indicated by a census carried out in 1932. The president was to be a Maronite, the prime minister a Sunni Muslim, and the speaker of parliament a Shi'ite Muslim. Similarly, since the 1932 census had shown that Christians outnumbered Muslims by six to five, all parliamentary seats (and positions in the cabinet and bureaucracy) were to be apportioned accordingly. Thus, although the number of deputies changed significantly over the years, it was always a multiple of eleven, in order to preserve the fixed ratio of six Christian MPs for every five Muslim ones.

The country's mixed-list electoral system also contributed to the sectarian representation and intersectarian bargaining that sustained Lebanon's distinct form of liberal democracy. Each district was usually given several parliamentary seats, divided among the various sects according to their share of the district's population. For instance, three of the eight seats of the Shuf district, in Mount Lebanon, went to Maronite candidates, two to Sunnis, two to Druze Muslims, and one to a Greek Catholic. This system, which remains in place today, ensured that each of the competing lists would include politicians from different sects. It also compelled voters to select candidates according to the sectarian breakdown of their district. A Druze voter in the Shuf, for instance, was allowed to pick eight candidates, but only two of them could be Druze; the others had to be Maronites (three), Sunnis (two), and Greek Catholic (one). That voter could choose one of the existing lists (all of which were composed of three Maronites, two Sunnis, two Druze, and one Greek Catholic), or the voter could form his or her own list by picking candidates from among the various lists or by selecting independents.

The main strength of this mixed-list system was that it contributed to reducing intersectarian rivalries and promoting communal integration. It did so in four ways. First, in each district, competition for a given seat always occurred among members of the same sect. Second, since candidates usually faced the voters as part of a multisectarian list, intersectarian accommodation among politicians was encouraged. Third, aspiring deputies knew that they could win only by appealing to members of sects different from their own. Therefore, extremists campaigning on narrow, sectarian platforms were unlikely to prevail. Finally, the candidates elected on a given list would often continue to cooperate in the Chamber, thus creating cross-cutting linkages among deputies from different sects.

In addition to national and intersectarian integration, the Chamber made important contributions to Lebanon's political development. Through floor debates, question-and-answer sessions, votes of confidence, and committee requests for information and documents from the government, the

Chamber exercised significant oversight of the executive branch. Even the powerful office of the president could not ignore the legislature. Similarly, parliamentary leaders were instrumental in mobilizing opposition to the growing political influence of the military during the 1960s. When the Chamber elected Sulayman Franjiyah president in 1970, it succeeded in reasserting the influence of traditional politicians over a military institution that was attempting to usurp power.

The legislature also operated as a recruitment pool for important offices in the executive branch. Presidents, prime ministers, and ministers invariably came from the Chamber. Through the rotation of deputies in and out of the cabinet, the Chamber developed a political leadership with extensive executive branch experience; that, in turn, enhanced its influence in the political system. Constituency services were yet another strength of the Lebanese legislature, the members of which were known to maintain particularly close relations with their districts. Contributing to this phenomenon was the fact that an overwhelming majority of MPs (90 percent in the Chamber elected in 1968) were born in the district that they represented. Critical as well was the small size of the country and the ease of communications within it. Lebanese deputies operated as key intermediaries between individuals and the broader political system. In view of the competitive nature of Lebanese elections, deputies had to remain sensitive to their local bases in order to keep their jobs. Finally, successive chambers accumulated an impressive lawmaking record. They debated and decided on the bills submitted by the cabinet and usually made important amendments to them. The steady growth over time in the number and percentage of bills introduced by deputies also points to the Chamber's increasingly active part in initiating legislation.

Unfortunately, in the early 1970s Lebanon found itself caught in the midst of powerful internal, regional, and international forces that plunged the country into one of the most protracted and vicious civil wars in modern times. After they were ousted from Jordan in September 1970, Palestinian organizations relocated to Lebanon, which they proceeded to use as a base for launching attacks against Israel. Retaliatory raids by Israel had a devastating impact on southern Lebanon and polarized the country between supporters of the Palestinian resistance (found mostly among Muslim, Arab nationalist, and leftist groups) and right-wing Maronite Christian militias, which advocated reining in the Palestinian movement. Meanwhile, an alliance developed between Palestinian organizations and some Lebanese Arab nationalist and leftist groups that called for a more equitable distribution of power and wealth in Lebanon. In addition, several Arab governments and Israel stepped up their interference in Lebanese affairs. The massive external pressure exacerbated internal conflicts and eventually led to a full-blown civil war.

Even after the civil war had broken out in 1975, however, the Chamber of Deputies continued to meet periodically. Unlike the army or the Council of Ministers, it never split into contending factions. When, in 1976, the spread of hostilities made the election of a new Chamber impossible, the term of the 1972 legislature was extended. It continued to be extended until August 1992, less than two years after the end of the civil war. Throughout, the Chamber continued to perform many of its constitutionally mandated functions, including the election of the president of the republic (in 1976, 1982, and 1988).

CIVIL WAR AFTERMATH AND CONSTITUTIONAL CHANGES

Parliamentarians played a prominent role in arranging an end to the fighting. From September 30 to October 22, 1989, sixty-two of the seventy-one living members of the original ninety-nine-member Chamber elected in 1972 met in Taif, Saudi Arabia. This gathering, sponsored by the Arab League, was the last in a series of efforts to agree on a formula to rebuild a political system shattered by years of harrowing civil war. The reliance on parliamentarians to conduct the negotiations in Taif suggests that the Chamber was widely seen as the one institution entitled to work out the details of a new political system for the country, because it had been legally elected by the Lebanese people.

Out of the Taif meeting came a Document of National Understanding, better known as the Taif Accord. This pathbreaking agreement retained the basic structure of the Lebanese political system but redistributed power among the various sects and institutions in order to reflect more accurately the country's new demographic and political realities. The president would remain a Maronite, but his or her prerogatives would be significantly reduced, to the benefit of the Sunni prime minister and the cabinet. As a result, power within the executive branch would be exercised more collectively than before. Both the president and the prime minister would now have to act within the Council of Ministers, which was given ultimate responsibility for setting policy and overseeing its implementation. Major decisions of the Council of Ministers would require the approval of two-thirds of its members before they could be presented to the legislature.

Similarly, the Taif Accord redistributed power within the Chamber, dividing parliamentary seats equally between Christians and Muslims (instead of in a six-to-five ratio in favor of the Christians). In addition, the authority of the speaker was enhanced. The most controversial provision was that which called upon Syrian armed forces to assist the Lebanese government in extending its authority over the entire territory. Thus the process of political reconstruction was to take place under Syrian auspices, even though the Taif Accord also stipulated that after two years the Lebanese government would negotiate with its counterpart in Damascus the terms under which Syrian troops would be withdrawn.

Finally, the Taif Accord reaffirmed the secular nature of government and legislation, as well as the territorial unity of the country. This was significant considering that during the war some Muslim fundamentalist groups had called for a state that would enforce Islamic law, while some Christian leaders had advocated that the country be broken into autonomous cantons.

On August 21, 1990, the Chamber approved sweeping constitutional amendments based on the Taif Accord. Signed a month later by President Ilyas Hrawi, these amendments created what is often described as a "troika": a political system that can operate smoothly only if its three dominant figures—the president, the prime minister, and the speaker—cooperate and strike the necessary compromises with one another.

The constitutional changes strengthened the legislature in several respects. First, they mandated that the president, who formally appoints the prime minister, can choose the latter only after binding consultations with the parliamentary groups, in the presence of the speaker. The Chamber and its speaker thus were given de facto veto power over the selection of the prime minister. Second, the amendments specified that only the Chamber has the authority to remove the prime minister (whereas before 1990 the prime minister could be dismissed by the president). Third, the method under which the executive can present urgent legislation was amended. The constitution still enables the executive to declare a particular bill as urgent, but the legislature has forty days from the time it takes up the bill, rather than forty days from when the executive submits it, to act on the bill. If it fails to act within that period, the executive can promulgate the legislation as presented. In effect, the Chamber has been empowered to determine whether to give a bill the character of urgency. Finally, the speaker's role has been enhanced. The term has been lengthened from one to four years, which gives the speaker time to develop a power base within the Chamber and therefore increases his or her standing and bargaining power when negotiating with the prime minister or the president.

THE 1992 AND 1996 ELECTIONS

As the state consolidated its authority, parliamentary elections—the first in twenty years—were scheduled for August–September 1992. A new electoral law was promulgated which increased the number of deputies from 99 to 128, divided equally between Christian and Muslim sects. Unfortunately, these elections were marred by a boycott called by Christian Maronite leaders and a handful of their Muslim counterparts. Both groups objected to holding elections under the guns of the Syrian army and opposed several provisions of the electoral law. Most of the Christian electorate failed to show up at the polls. Nevertheless, voter turnout was reasonably high in many predominantly non-Christian districts, and the electoral process was fair.

Most important, the Chamber now included a substantial number of political figures who had risen to prominence during and after the war. These newcomers would sit in the legislature side by side with representatives of Lebanon's traditionally dominant families (the families that have played a leading role in Lebanese politics since the late nineteenth century). Eight candidates affiliated with the Shiʿite fundamentalist group Hizballah won seats. Overall, only 18 of the 128 deputies elected in 1992 had belonged to the previous Chamber. This figure highlights the extent to which the elections had contributed to a much needed renewal of the political class. Only 40 of the new MPs bore party labels (which was similar to pre–civil war trends). All remaining 88 members had run as independents.

As in the past, political parties had not played a major role in the campaign and were not expected to become a dominant force in the Chamber. Historically, Lebanese political parties mostly have been vehicles to promote the personal interests and agendas of their leaders. They have been defined less by adherence to a common program and ideology than by loyalty to the dominant personality around which they are built. Elections, furthermore, have always been fought predominantly over local issues, not national ones. Accordingly, even representatives affiliated with political parties usually owe their seats in the Chamber less to their party identification than to their membership in locally or regionally influential families.

The 1992 Chamber sat for its mandated term of four years, during which time it proved to be one of the most active and assertive legislatures in the Arab world. Its incorporation of a large number of previously excluded political elements, especially from among Shiʿite Muslims, enhanced its importance as an institution of political representation. Significantly, deputies affiliated with Hizballah and Sunni fundamentalist parties showed themselves willing to play by the rules of parliamentary politics. In this respect, the Chamber was instrumental in bringing into the formal institutional framework forces that until then had been operating outside it.

Moreover, capitalizing on its enhanced constitutional powers, the legislature succeeded in compelling the cabinet and individual ministers to account for their policies and in giving expression to public grievances. The government's economic policy was the target of constant criticism in the legislature. Hizballah also consistently used parliamentary debates to seek to embarrass and discredit the cabinet by pointing to the government's inability to force Israel to withdraw from its self-declared "security zone" in the south. The 1992–1996 Chamber promulgated the greatest number of laws (approximately four hundred) in Lebanon's parliamentary history. Furthermore, the percentage of proposed laws (bills submitted by a deputy or group of deputies) rose from 9 percent in 1992–1993 to 20 percent in 1995 (both figures being well above the world average of 5 percent).

During the August–September 1996 elections, voter turnout reached 44 percent, as opposed to 13 percent in 1992. The new legislature was thus far more representative than the one it replaced. The increase in participation as well as the outlook of the candidates who were elected demonstrated that a much larger percentage of the population, including people in predominantly Christian areas, was willing to play within the parameters of the Taif Accord and the Syrian-dominated political order.

The legislature that emerged was dominated by two large blocs led by, respectively, Prime Minister Rafiq al-Hariri and speaker of Parliament Nabi Berri (both of whom kept their positions). Three smaller coalitions were also expected to wield considerable influence: one comprised supporters of Druze leader and minister Walid Jumblatt, another comprised followers of former minister and Maronite leader Sulayman Franjiyah (grandson of the president who bore the same name), and the third was the Shi'ite Hizballah group. Each of these blocs had close relations with Syria, but, beyond that, their interests diverged significantly, and their leaders were political rivals.

Although al-Hariri seemed the dominant figure, he was not strong enough to dominate the Chamber. To push his policies through the Chamber, he was expected to have to compromise with other Syrian-backed leaders, particularly Berri. The need to compromise had already become clear by November 1996, when Hariri was beset by mounting opposition in the legislature, and when his supporters there won the chairmanship of only two of the seventeen commissions formed by the new Chamber.

Abdo Baaklini, Guilain Denoeux, and Robert Springborg

BIBLIOGRAPHY

Baaklini, Abdo. *Legislative and Political Development: Lebanon, 1842–1972*. Durham, N.C.: Duke University Press, 1976.

El-Khazen, Farid. "Lebanon's First Postwar Parliamentary Elections, 1992." *Middle East Policy* 3 (1994): 120–136.

Harik, Iliya F. "Voting Participation and Political Integration in Lebanon, 1943–1974." *Middle Eastern Studies* 16 (1980): 27–48.

LESOTHO

OFFICIAL NAME: Kingdom of Lesotho
CAPITAL: Maseru
POPULATION: 1,971,000 (1996 est.)
DATE OF INDEPENDENCE: October 4, 1966 (from the United Kingdom)
DATE OF CURRENT CONSTITUTION: Approved July 4, 1991; effective April 2, 1993
FORM OF GOVERNMENT: Constitutional monarchy
LANGUAGES: English (official), Sesotho, Zulu, Xhosa
MONETARY UNIT: loti
FISCAL YEAR: April 1–March 31
LEGISLATURE: Parliament
NUMBER OF CHAMBERS: Two. National Assembly; Senate
NUMBER OF MEMBERS: National Assembly, 65 (directly elected); Senate, 33 (nonelective)
PERCENTAGE OF WOMEN: National Assembly, 4.6; Senate, 24.2
TERM OF LEGISLATURE: Five years
MOST RECENT LEGISLATIVE ELECTION: National Assembly, March 27, 1993
MINIMUM AGE FOR VOTING: 21
MINIMUM AGE FOR MEMBERSHIP: 21
SUFFRAGE: Universal
VOTING: Optional
ADDRESS: National Assembly, P.O. Box 190, Maseru 100; Senate, P.O. Box 553, Maseru 100
TELEPHONE: National Assembly, (266) 323 503; Senate, (266) 323 660
FAX: National Assembly, (266) 310 438; Senate, (266) 310 438

The Kingdom of Lesotho is a landlocked country entirely surrounded by South Africa *(see map, p. 615)*. Formerly known as Basutoland, it was a dependency of the United

Kingdom from 1868. The colony's first legislative council was established in 1956, and the first general election on the basis of universal adult suffrage took place in 1965. The following year, Basutoland became independent as Lesotho.

The constitution that took effect on independence provided for a bicameral legislature consisting of a sixty-seat National Assembly and a thirty-three-member Senate. The 1966 constitution was suspended in 1970 and replaced by a new constitution in 1993. The membership of the National Assembly was raised to sixty-five, and the term of office remained five years. The Senate comprises twenty-two traditional chiefs and eleven members nominated by the king. Party political activity was banned from 1986 to 1991. Although the new constitution authorizes multiparty politics, the ruling Basotho Congress Party won all seats in the 1993 elections.

George Thomas Kurian

LIBERIA

OFFICIAL NAME: Republic of Liberia
CAPITAL: Monrovia
POPULATION: 2,110,000 (1996 est.)
DATE OF INDEPENDENCE: Declared July 26, 1847
DATE OF CURRENT CONSTITUTION: Adopted August 20, 1995
FORM OF GOVERNMENT: Transitional
LANGUAGES: English (official), various African languages
MONETARY UNIT: Liberian dollar
FISCAL YEAR: Calendar year
LEGISLATURE: Legislature
NUMBER OF CHAMBERS: Two
NUMBER OF MEMBERS: House of Representatives, 64; Senate, 26
PERCENTAGE OF WOMEN: —
TERM OF LEGISLATURE: House of Representatives, six years; Senate, nine years
MOST RECENT LEGISLATIVE ELECTION: July 19, 1997
MINIMUM AGE FOR VOTING: 18
MINIMUM AGE FOR MEMBERSHIP: House of Representatives, 25; Senate, 30
SUFFRAGE: Universal and direct
VOTING: Optional
ADDRESS: Capitol Building, Monrovia
TELEPHONE: (231) 226 311
FAX: (231) 226 000

The Republic of Liberia, a West African country north of Côte d'Ivoire, is the oldest African republic, having been established by former slaves from the United States in 1847 *(see map, p. 447)*. The constitution and governmental institutions are modeled on those of the United States.

Liberia enjoyed very stable governments until 1980, when President William R. Tolbert was assassinated in a military coup. The military-led government that seized power resorted to savagery and mass terror to remain in office. Public reaction against these excesses led to a civil war beginning in 1989.

Under the terms of the peace agreement signed in 1993, the Interim Government of National Unity, which had been established in 1991, was replaced by a Council of State, and the existing twenty-eight-member Interim National Assembly was replaced by a thirty-five-member Transitional National Assembly comprising representatives of the principal warring factions. A second Liberian National Transitional Government took office in 1995.

Originally scheduled for February 1997, elections to the new bicameral legislature were pushed back to July due to continuing hostilities. The National Patriotic Party (NPP), formerly known as the National Patriotic Front, won overwhelming majorities in both houses. NPP leader Charles Taylor, who had led the insurrection against the former military government, won the presidential election. But political stability and democratic consolidation are not yet evident.

George Thomas Kurian

LIBYA

OFFICIAL NAME: Great Socialist People's Libyan Arab Jamahiriya (al-Jamahiriya al-ʿArabiyah al-Libiyah al-Shaʿbiyah al-Ishtirakiyah al-Uzma)
CAPITAL: Tripoli
POPULATION: 5,445,000 (1996 est.)
DATE OF INDEPENDENCE: December 24, 1951 (from Italy)
DATE OF CURRENT CONSTITUTION: Proclaimed December 11, 1969

FORM OF GOVERNMENT: Military dictatorship
LANGUAGES: Arabic, Italian, English
MONETARY UNIT: Libyan dinar
FISCAL YEAR: Calendar year
LEGISLATURE: General People's Congress (Mutamar al-Sha'ab al-Aam)
NUMBER OF CHAMBERS: One
NUMBER OF MEMBERS: 750
PERCENTAGE OF WOMEN: —
TERM OF LEGISLATURE: Three years
MOST RECENT LEGISLATIVE ELECTION: None
MINIMUM AGE FOR VOTING: 18
MINIMUM AGE FOR MEMBERSHIP: 18
SUFFRAGE: Universal and indirect
VOTING: Compulsory
ADDRESS: General People's Congress, Sirt, Tripoli
TELEPHONE: (218 21) 333 00 51
FAX: (218 21) 60 67 03

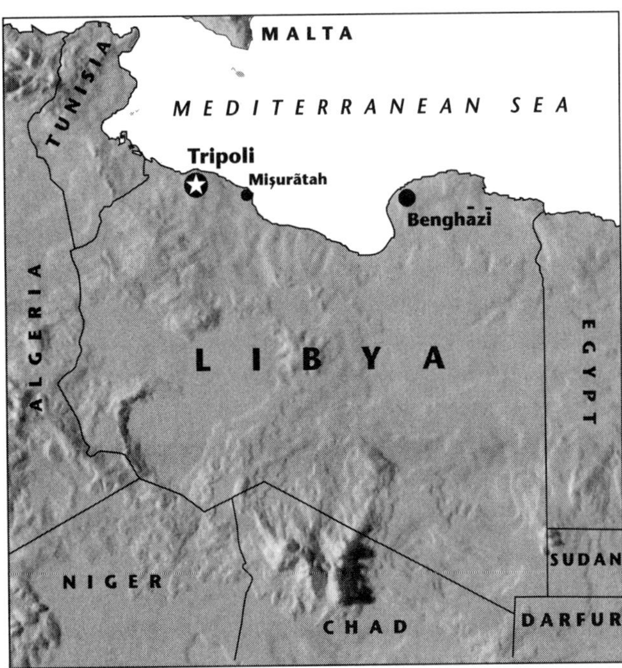

Libya extends along the North African coast between Egypt and Tunisia. Formerly an Italian colony, it was an independent federal state from 1951 to 1963. During that time the United Kingdom of Libya had three semiautonomous provinces and a bicameral parliament, but in 1963 Emir Muhammad Idris al-Sanussi instituted a unitary form of government. Idris was deposed six years later by a group of army officers led by Moammar Quadafi. The Great Socialist People's Libyan Arab Jamahiriya is now ruled by Quadafi and his Islamic fundamentalist regime.

The former Senate and House of Representatives were dissolved after the 1969 coup, and the provisional constitution of that year made no mention of a legislature or election. At the same time, all political parties other than the Arab Socialist Union were banned. In 1976 the 1,112-member General National Congress of the Arab Socialist Union met to approve a new constitution. Later, this assembly was converted into the General People's Congress. Because it has no constitutional status, it is not clear whether the Congress is a form of legislature or simply another of Quadafi's propaganda forums.

On paper, the General People's Congress has the power to declare war, ratify treaties, and consider general government policy and its implementation. It also chooses a presiding officer, a chair, who signs laws and accepts the credentials of foreign representatives. The Congress is the country's highest policy-making body and takes its membership from thirteen municipal people's congresses, the several popular committees that report to them, trade unions, and professional groups.

The municipal people's congresses bear ultimate responsibility for provincial and urban affairs. At the base of the Libyan electoral system are two thousand people's congresses located around the country. They appoint the popular committees and authorize them to execute policy at the local and provincial levels.

Members of the General People's Congress must be eighteen years old and citizens of Libya. They are chosen generally from among the leaders of a single party, the Arab Socialist Union.

The General People's Congress is assisted in its work by other government bodies, including the General Secretariat, the General People's Committee, and the courts. The General Secretariat consists of a secretary general, who serves as the titular head of state, and other secretaries who supervise the various sectors of state activity. Executive power is vested in the General People's Committee, a cabinet-like body presided over by an official resembling a prime minister. The judicial function is performed by a Supreme Court, courts of appeal, courts of the first instance, and summary courts. People's courts and a people's prosecution bureau were created in 1988 to replace the revolutionary courts, which had frequently acted without regard for judicial norms or safeguards for the accused.

George Thomas Kurian

LIECHTENSTEIN

OFFICIAL NAME: Principality of Liechtenstein (Fürstentum Liechtenstein)
CAPITAL: Vaduz
POPULATION: 31,000 (1996 est.)
DATE OF INDEPENDENCE: January 23, 1719
DATE OF CURRENT CONSTITUTION: Adopted October 5, 1921
FORM OF GOVERNMENT: Constitutional monarchy
LANGUAGE: German (official)
MONETARY UNIT: Swiss franc
FISCAL YEAR: Calendar year
LEGISLATURE: Diet (Landtag)
NUMBER OF CHAMBERS: One
NUMBER OF MEMBERS: 25
PERCENTAGE OF WOMEN: 4.0
TERM OF LEGISLATURE: Four years
MOST RECENT LEGISLATIVE ELECTION: February 2, 1997
MINIMUM AGE FOR VOTING: 20
MINIMUM AGE FOR MEMBERSHIP: 20
SUFFRAGE: Direct and universal
VOTING: Compulsory
ADDRESS: Landtagssekretariat, Kirchstrasse 10, 9490 Vaduz
TELEPHONE: (41 75) 236 65 70
FAX: (41 75) 236 65 80

The Principality of Liechtenstein, a landlocked country in western Europe between Switzerland and Austria, is a constitutional monarchy that was established as an independent state in 1719 *(see map, p. 650)*. The country's hereditary prince is head of state and holds legislative power with the unicameral Landtag, or Diet. The prime minister, appointed by the prince from the majority party, is head of government.

The Landtag meets for one or two days every four to five weeks. Extraordinary sessions may be held at the request of three members, three parish councils, or six hundred voters. The legislative calendar is established by the president of the Landtag in consultation with leaders of political party groups known as fractions. Each political fraction must consist of at least three members.

Decisions are taken by voice vote, show of hands, or ballot. The quorum is two-thirds of membership. The deliberations of the Landtag are published in the *Landtagprotokoll.* Preliminary review of legislation is conducted by three committees which meet in private and may summon officials, witnesses, and ministers. Ministers may be questioned by Landtag members for thirty minutes each sitting. Ministers respond to oral questions immediately and to written questions in the next session. The Landtag may establish committees of inquiry. The Permanent Parliamentary Audit Committee may investigate any aspect of state administration.

The legislative process begins with the introduction of a bill and a general debate on whether to proceed or refer it to a committee. If the bill proceeds, it goes through two more readings. Amendments may be introduced during either reading, and the bill may be referred to a committee. If the bill is passed, it goes to the prince for royal assent, is countersigned by the government, and is promulgated by publication in the *Landesgesetzblatt.* The law enters into force within thirty days of publication. Voters may participate directly in creating legislation by means of the initiative and the referendum. Legislative proposals may be initiated by three parish councils or six hundred voters, but any proposal that increases expenditures must be accompanied by a revenue proposal for generating a corresponding amount of money.

The twenty-five members of the Landtag are elected by proportional vote (according to the d'Hondt method) in two electoral districts: Unterland, which elects ten; and Oberland, which elects fifteen. To qualify for representation a party must obtain 8 percent of the votes cast in the whole country. Seats are distributed among the party lists by using the simple electoral quotient, with the remaining seats distributed on the basis of the greatest remainders. Seats that fall vacant between legislative elections are filled by the candidates next in line on the same party list. Members may be recalled by the electorate. Members of the Landtag enjoy constitutional immunity for their actions, and their salary is tax-free.

In the case of adjournment or dissolution, the Landtag is replaced by a National Committee consisting of the president of the Landtag and four deputies.

George Thomas Kurian

LITHUANIA

OFFICIAL NAME: Republic of Lithuania (Lietuvos Respublika)
CAPITAL: Vilnius
POPULATION: 3,646,000 (1996 est.)
DATE OF INDEPENDENCE: Declared March 11, 1990; recognized September 6, 1991 (from the Soviet Union)
DATE OF CURRENT CONSTITUTION: Adopted October 25, 1992
FORM OF GOVERNMENT: Parliamentary democracy
LANGUAGE: Lithuanian (official), Polish, Russian
MONETARY UNIT: Litas
FISCAL YEAR: Calendar year
LEGISLATURE: Parliament (Seimas)
NUMBER OF CHAMBERS: One
NUMBER OF MEMBERS: 141
PERCENTAGE OF WOMEN: 17.5
TERM OF LEGISLATURE: Four years
MOST RECENT LEGISLATIVE ELECTION: October 20 and November 10, 1996
MINIMUM AGE FOR VOTING: 18
MINIMUM AGE FOR MEMBERSHIP: 25
SUFFRAGE: Universal and direct
VOTING: Optional
ADDRESS: Seimas, 53 Gedimino Ave., 2026 Vilnius
TELEPHONE: (370 2) 22 47 89
FAX: (370 2) 22 74 34

Lithuania, a small country in northeastern Europe, was one of three Soviet Baltic republics, along with neighboring Estonia and Latvia, until the Soviet Union recognized the country's independence on September 6, 1991. The Republic of Lithuania is now a multiparty parliamentary democracy with a president as head of state and prime minister as head of government. Although the Lithuanian Democratic Labor Party, a faction of the former Communist Party, had been in power since 1992, the Homeland Union Party, successor to the Lithuanian Reform Movement, which was associated with Lithuania's bid for independence, took first place in the parliamentary elections held in the fall of 1996.

HISTORICAL BACKGROUND

In the early Middle Ages the Lithuanians formed a loose federation in the Baltic area. The first historical records of political activity in this region are found in the Quedlinburg Chronicle, a Prussian manuscript of 1009. In the middle of the thirteenth century the Lithuanians founded a dukedom, which in the fourteenth century embraced a vast territory of the future Ukraine and Belarus. The Grand Duchy of Lithuania had to defend its borders against Russian, Tatar, and German military encroachments.

In the late fourteenth century, under a permanent threat of invasion by an order of Teutonic Knights, the Lithuanians entered into union with Poland. Lithuanian grand duke Wladyslaw Jagiello became a Polish king, starting a new Polish-Lithuanian dynasty that ruled in both countries until 1572. In 1569 the links between the two states were solidified by the Union of Lublin, which formed a Polish-Lithuanian commonwealth reaching from the Baltic Sea to the Black Sea.

The commonwealth survived until 1795, when, at the third partition of Poland, Lithuania was incorporated into the Russian empire. At the end of World War I, after a period of German occupation, the Lithuanians managed to restore their own state and declared independence on February 16, 1918. Russian and Polish attempts to reclaim Lithuania resulted in a war that broke out in 1920 and was waged with varying degrees of success for both states. The peace treaty, which was signed in Riga on March 18, 1921, divided the disputed territories of Lithuania, Ukraine, and Belarus. Lvov and Vilnius were left with Poland, but Lithuania was recognized as an independent state. On August 1, 1922, Lithuania adopted the country's first constitution. The constitution declared a system of parliamentary democracy that lasted until December 17, 1926, when Antanas Smetona seized power following a military coup. The new authoritarian regime survived until 1940.

The German-Soviet pact of August 23, 1939, left Lithuania in the sphere of Soviet control. As a result of successive German invasions of Poland, and the annexation by the Soviets of the eastern Polish territories, Lithuania was forced to accept Soviet troops and a pro-Soviet puppet government. On August 3, 1940, the country was incorporated into the Soviet Union. Following a German attack on the Soviet Union in 1941, Lithuania was incorporated into Hitler's newly created Ostland (Eastland), which comprised the Baltic states and part of Belarus. The Germans were swept from Lithuania by the Russian offensive in 1944, and at the end of the war Lithuania was reclaimed by the Soviets.

The creeping disintegration of the Soviet Union in the 1980s strengthened the separatist movement in Lithuania. The Lithuanian Reform Movement (Sajudis) won electoral victory in March 1990, and, amid intense public debate on the legitimacy of the Soviet annexation of the state, the new Lithuanian parliament elected Vytautas Landsbergis, leader of Sajudis, as its chair and issued a declaration of Lithuanian sovereignty on March 11. Several attempts by the Soviet Union to regain control over Lithuania failed, and it recognized Lithuanian independence on September 6, 1991. A few days later similar statements were made by the United States and by several European governments. Finally, the establishment of the Commonwealth of Independent States, the successor to the Soviet Union, on December 8, 1991, and the termination of the central organs of the Soviet Union at the end of that year, confirmed Lithuania's split from Moscow.

THE CONSTITUTION-MAKING PROCESS

Lithuania began the process of constitutional reform in the early stages of the disintegration of the Soviet Union. The first draft of the new republic's constitution, dated March 7, 1991, was discussed at a constitutional workshop in Vilnius in January 1992. The workshop was followed by a visit of the Lithuanian delegation to Washington, D.C., in March 1992, during which the second draft, dated February 26, was deliberated. This draft was supplemented in May by a draft law on the court system.

Despite encouragement from the West, the process of adopting a new constitution in Lithuania progressed slowly. A significant problem was the establishment of a formal presidency. The debate centered on whether the president should be directly elected by the people and to what extent the president should share power with the prime minister, who headed the government. A referendum held in May 1992 failed to support an amendment to the provisional Basic Law (March 11, 1990) that was intended to bind the drafters to a final constitution by preordained constitutional provisions. In fact, 69.5 percent of those voting favored the amendment, but only 57.5 percent of eligible voters turned out, thereby denying the referendum the required approval of 50 percent of the electorate.

The parliamentary elections of October 25, 1992, were held under a new electoral law that provided for a mixed system of majority voting and proportional representation. The question of presidential powers was also put on the ballot. The voters approved the new constitution establishing presidential institutions, but the independence movement, Sajudis, was defeated by the Communists in the election. In the February 1993 presidential elections, Algirdas Brazauskas, the former Lithuanian Communist Party chief, was elected president after receiving 60 percent of the popular vote.

The new constitution established a dual executive system under which the executive branch is made up of the president, directly elected by the people, and the government, headed by the prime minister. The president appoints the prime minister, and the prime minister appoints a cabinet. The cabinet is subject to parliamentary approval. The parliament, or Seimas, may approve or reject the government program. The prime minister must present the ministers and the government program within fifteen days after being appointed.

The president is elected for a five-year term directly by the citizens of Lithuania on the basis of universal, equal, and direct suffrage by secret ballot. Candidates for the presidency must collect at least twenty thousand voter signatures. Candidates in the presidential election must be citizens by birth and at least forty years old; they must have resided in Lithuania for at least three years before the election. A president may serve for only two consecutive terms. The president may be removed from office by a three-fifths majority vote of all Seimas members for gross violation of the constitution, for breach of oath, or for the commitment of a felony.

DIVISION OF POWERS

The constitution is the result of a solid effort by its drafters to introduce into the Lithuanian system the basic principles of Western constitutionalism, such as sovereignty of the people, democratic and representative government, division of powers, and judicial review. The 1992 draft established a parliamentary system and attempted to create checks and balances among the three branches of the government. The concept of division of powers was, however, designed halfheartedly. On the one hand, the draft provided that full and absolute power may not be concentrated in any one state institution (Article 5); on the other hand, it declared that the Seimas is the "supreme and sole organ of state power representing the Lithuanian people" (Article 40).

The final 1992 constitution introduced some changes. The drafters dropped explicit references to the checks-and-balances doctrine, as well as phrases prohibiting the concentration of power in one organ. They also discarded the provision reserving supreme power to the Seimas. The constitution, in the final 1992 version, states that "the powers of the State shall be exercised by the Seimas, the President of the Republic, the Government, and the Judiciary" (Article 5). Recognizing that the powers should be balanced rather than equal, the drafters introduced a provision stating that the constitution shall define the scope of powers.

THE LEGISLATURE AND THE PRESIDENT

The legislative and controlling power of the parliament is meant to be balanced by Lithuania's dual executive system. The 1992 draft vested the president with the right to veto legislation. The veto could be overridden by two-thirds of all the Seimas deputies. The president, however, was stripped of the power to dissolve the Seimas, retaining only the right to form a provisional government for a period of six months if the Seimas failed to confirm two-thirds of all ministers and approve the government's program within thirty days of the nomination of the prime minister or to express confidence in the government within six months of its formation.

Some of the institutions the drafters tried to adopt resembled the features of the German constitution known as the "constructive vote of no confidence" and "legislative emergency." These institutions were incorporated into the German system to protect it from a deadlock resulting from a no-confidence vote that is not followed by the designation of a new chancellor by an absolute majority. The Lithuanian drafters sought to implant in their system a stability similar to that offered by the German system.

Still, the rationale for adopting the institution of the constructive vote of no confidence in the Lithuanian draft was not clear. The Seimas lacked the right of the German Bundestag to elect the prime minister by an absolute majority without presidential cooperation. The president and the prime minister also lacked the power to dissolve the Seimas, a power that might prevent a parliamentary impasse. The shortcoming of the Lithuanian arrangement was that, upon the expiration of the six-month term of the provisional government, the president still might not be able to resolve a stalemate.

The new constitution brought significant changes to presidential powers. The president now can return legislation to the Seimas for reconsideration, but the adoption of a bill questioned by the president requires only another affirmative vote by the Seimas. To implement the powers vested in him, the president issues decrees. Presidential decrees require the countersignature of the prime minister or a minister. Ministers are responsible to the Seimas for the decrees. Although the president was stripped of the power to appoint a provisional government in times of legislative crises, the new constitution vested in the president the right to dissolve the Seimas in three situations: if the Seimas fails to adopt a decision on the new program of the government within thirty days of its presentation, if it twice in succession disapproves the government program within sixty days of its initial presentation, or if it expresses no confidence in the government. If the president announces preterm elections to the Seimas—that is, elections before the conclusion of the full parliamentary term—the newly elected members may, within thirty days of the first session, announce a preterm election of the president by a three-fifths majority vote of all members. If the president chooses to run in the new election, he is automatically registered as a candidate.

The president convenes the first session of the Seimas and may call extraordinary sessions. The president, together with the government, composed of the prime minister and cabinet ministers, implements foreign policy. Diplomatic nominations require governmental countersignature. Additionally, important treaties, such as those involving realignment of state borders, political and long-term economic cooperation with other countries, renunciation of force, stationing of armed forces in foreign states, and participation in international organizations, must be submitted to the Seimas for ratification.

The Seimas is authorized to supervise the activities of the government. Members have the constitutional right to submit questions to the prime minister, individual ministers, or heads of other state institutions by a decision of one-fifth of the total number of members. Persons at whom these questions are directed must respond either orally or in writing at a session of the Seimas. If the Seimas decides a minister's response is unsatisfactory, it may, by majority vote, express no confidence in that minister. Under the 1992 constitution the government must resign if the Seimas rejects its program in two consecutive votes, or if the Seimas expresses a lack of confidence, by a majority vote, in it or in the prime minister.

ELECTIONS TO THE SEIMAS

Lithuanian citizens may freely form political parties, providing that they do not contradict the constitution and laws (the minimum threshold for a party to secure representation is 4 percent). The Communist Party was the only party banned in Lithuania on August 22, 1991. The reformist faction of the Communist Party became the Democratic Labor Party, which held a majority of seats in the Seimas until 1996. Sajudis, which was founded in 1988, governed Lithuania in the early 1990s. The Lithuanian Christian Democratic Party, founded in 1905, was reestablished in 1989. The Social Democratic Party, established in 1986 and once dissolved by the Communists, was also reestablished in 1989.

The parliamentary elections held in 1996 gave victory to the right-wing parties. The Homeland Union—the reshaped party of Landsbergis, leader of Sajudis—won seventy seats, and the Christian Democrats won sixteen seats. The Democratic Labor Party secured only twelve seats in the new parliament. The remaining seats were divided among smaller political groups.

The Seimas's 141 members are elected by secret ballot for a four-year term on the basis of universal, equal, and direct suffrage. All citizens at least eighteen years of age and not legally declared incapable by a court have the right to vote for members of parliament. Citizens of Lithuania are eligible for nomination to the Seimas who are at least twenty-five years old on election day and have resided in Lithuania permanently. (Some citizens are ineligible to be elected: members of the police force, the national defense service, the alternative service, and the internal affairs service and persons who have not completed a court-imposed sentence or who have been declared incapable by the court.) Nomination requires the signatures of one thousand citizens. Each national party list must include at least twenty candidates. A person may be placed on only one national list but may also be a candidate in a single-member district. Parties may enter only one coalition.

Candidates are required to make deposits in the amount of the average monthly wage. The deposits are forfeited if the candidate or party fails to win seats in the elections. The maximum campaign expenditure per candidate is twenty times the average monthly salary; for parties, the maximum is two hundred times the average monthly salary.

Elections for the Seimas are held in two rounds. During the first round, seventy-one members of the Seimas are elected from single-member districts. Several elections may be held until a candidate receives a majority of votes. The second round, during which the other seventy members are elected, is based on a proportional Droop quota system. To be elected, a candidate must reach one quota (a quota equals votes divided by seats plus one) or, alternatively, have the highest number of votes when only two candidates remain for one seat. The Droop quota is counted for the party list in the constituency, and those candidates who obtain the quota are elected. The votes received by winning candidates above the quota are transferred to other candidates on the list. Electoral districts are set up by the Central Election Committee, and the population in each district may not vary from that in others by more than 25 percent.

Once elected, parliamentary members are exempt from performing national defense duties. Members are immune from criminal prosecution, arrest, or any other form of restriction of personal freedom, unless the Seimas consents to such action. Members may not be prosecuted for speeches or voting in parliament, but they may be held liable for personal insult or slander. Questions of the ethical conduct of a member are considered by the Commission on Ethics and Procedure.

OPERATIONS OF THE SEIMAS

The Seimas convenes for two sessions annually: a spring session (March 10–June 30) and a fall session (September 10–December 23). A majority of the deputies can vote to extend the sessions; otherwise, the Seimas is in recess between sessions. Extraordinary sessions may be convened by the president or by a vote of at least one-third of the members of parliament. Sittings of the Seimas are presided over by the chair or the assistant chair. The first session following elections to the Seimas is opened by the oldest member of the Seimas.

The Seimas considers and enacts amendments to the constitution, enacts laws, imposes taxes and other obligatory payments, approves and supervises the implementation of the state budget, adopts resolutions for the organization of referendums, announces presidential elections, forms state institutions, and appoints and dismisses their chief officers. In addition to the right to approve the president's choice of prime minister and the right to monitor executive performance, the Seimas has the power to appoint judges to the Constitutional Court and to the Supreme Court; appoint and dismiss the state controller and the chair of the board of the Bank of Lithuania; and form the Central Election Committee. Additionally, the Seimas announces local government elections, establishes the administrative divisions of the republic, ratifies or denounces international treaties, considers other issues of foreign policy, establishes state awards, issues acts of amnesty, imposes direct administration and martial law, declares states of emergency, announces mobilizations, and adopts decisions to use the armed forces.

Groups are the key organizational units of the Seimas that bring together representatives of a party or a coalition of parties. Through groups, the political organizations in the parliament control its operation and influence the legislative process. The groups receive drafts of laws and necessary documents and other information. They participate in establishing the Assembly of Spokespersons, which collectively represents all the groups. The main function of the assembly is to resolve conflicts arising among the groups. Groups may suspend consideration of drafts, introduce amendments and modifications, express their opinion in discussions, and present conclusions. They also have the exclusive right to discuss the nominations for prime minister. Parliamentary groups must have at least three members. New groups must notify the speaker of the Seimas about the establishment of the group, the name of the group, and the names of its members, spokesperson, and deputy spokespersons. The speaker must announce the formation of a new group within one week.

Standing committees are appointed according to proportional representation by parliamentary groups. Although there is no constitutional provision for committees to act as supervisors of the activities of the government, committees do consider the programs submitted by the government and present their conclusions to the Seimas. Committees may question members of the government, invite them to committee meetings, and initiate proceedings for the dismissal of a government member. Additionally, committees consider reports on the implementation of the state budget.

THE LEGISLATIVE PROCESS AND THE BUDGET

The right of introducing legislation lies with the members of the Seimas, the president of the republic, and the government. Citizens may initiate a piece of legislation if they can get the support of fifty thousand persons who have the right to vote. Laws are adopted if a majority of the Seimas members participating in the "sitting vote" approve the law. Constitutional laws are adopted if more than half the members approve, and they are amended if at least three-fifths of all members approve.

The list of laws with constitutional status is established by the Seimas by a three-fifths majority vote of all members. The constitution may be amended if a proposal submitted to the Seimas is approved by at least one-fourth of the members of the Seimas or by at least 300,000 voters. Amendments are decided upon by the Seimas, with the exception of Article 1 of the constitution, describing the state as an independent democratic republic, which may be amended only by at least three-fourths of the participants of a referendum. The Seimas must vote twice, with at least three months between each vote. Each time, the required majority for amendments is at least two-thirds of all the deputies. A rejected amendment cannot be submitted for another vote for at least one year.

Within ten days of receiving an approved law from the Seimas, the president of the republic will either sign it or refer it back to the Seimas with reasons for reconsideration. The president may delay the implementation of a law but may not block it entirely. If a law is neither signed by the president nor referred back within ten days, the law will be signed by the chair of the Seimas and will be deemed to be in effect. The Seimas may reconsider and enact laws referred back by the president or accept the amendments and supplements suggested by the president by a majority of the members voting affirmatively. The president must sign the law within three days after it has been endorsed again by the Seimas. The president cannot resubmit for reconsideration an adopted law regarding an amendment to the constitution. This category of law must be signed within five days, or it will be signed and put into effect by the chair of the Seimas.

In Lithuania the calendar year is the budgetary year. The government prepares a draft budget and submits it to the Seimas for consideration not later that seventy-five days before the end of the budgetary year. The Seimas can increase the budget only after specifying financial resources for additional expenditures. If the budget is not approved at the beginning of the budgetary year, the government operates on the basis of monthly budgets, which cannot exceed one-twelfth of the state budget expenditures of the previous budget year. To amend the budget or to approve an additional budget, the government and Seimas must follow the same procedure.

CONSTITUTIONAL REVIEW

The 1992 constitution provides for the establishment of a Constitutional Court. The structure and functions of this court were clarified by the law on the constitutional court of February 3, 1993. The chair of the Supreme Court, the chair of the Seimas, and the president each nominate three justices whose appointments are subject to confirmation by the Seimas. Justices are appointed for nine years; one-third of the members of the court are replaced every three years.

The constitution follows a centralized, or concentrated, model of review, which reserves the right to evaluate the constitutionality of laws to one special judicial organ. The constitution provides that the Constitutional Court has the power to review statutes adopted by parliament, presidential decrees, and governmental directives and resolutions. The court, at the request of parliament, will review violations of electoral law, the constitutionality of international agreements, and the capacity of the president to continue his or her tenure. During impeachment proceedings the court will also present opinions concerning compliance with the constitution.

With the exception of international agreements, the Constitutional Court's decisions are final and cannot be appealed. The court's rulings on the constitutionality of international agreements are subject to the reconsideration of the Seimas, and it is not clear what majority is required to overrule a court decision. The status of international agreements in the hierarchy of Lithuanian law is not clear, either. Article 138 of the constitution states that international agreements are "the constituent part of the Lithuanian legal system." The Constitutional Court, however, will have to rule whether these agreements were given an equal footing with statutes or constitutional laws. The ruling will determine whether the Seimas will need a plurality or a three-fifths majority to overrule a court decision on the constitutionality of international agreements.

CONCLUSION

The drafters of the 1992 constitution received wide praise from Western commentators for their attempts to correct the major inconsistencies of earlier drafts. They borrowed less from the German model and more from classic parliamentary systems, in which legislatures are in control, presidents play the roles of senior statesmen, and governments are responsible to parliaments. As a result, the system of state governance established by the new constitution seems to be well balanced and fits the political needs and democratic traditions of Lithuania.

Rett R. Ludwikowski

BIBLIOGRAPHY

Lucky, Christian. "Table of Presidential Powers in Eastern Europe." *East European Constitutional Review* 2 (fall 1993–winter 1994): 89–91.

———. "Table of Twelve Electoral Laws." *East European Constitutional Review* 3 (spring 1994): 72–75.

Ludwikowski, Rett R. *Constitution Making in the Region of Former Soviet Dominance.* Durham, N.C., and London: Duke University Press, 1996.

LUXEMBOURG

OFFICIAL NAME: Grand Duchy of Luxembourg (Grousherzogdem Lëtzebuerg)
CAPITAL: Luxembourg
POPULATION: 416,000 (1996 est.)
DATE OF CURRENT CONSTITUTION: Adopted October 17, 1868
DATE OF INDEPENDENCE: 1867
FORM OF GOVERNMENT: Constitutional monarchy
LANGUAGES: Luxembourgisch, French, German
MONETARY UNIT: Luxembourg franc
FISCAL YEAR: Calendar year
LEGISLATURE: Chamber of Deputies (Chambre des Députés)
NUMBER OF CHAMBERS: One
NUMBER OF MEMBERS: 60
PERCENTAGE OF WOMEN: 20.0
TERM OF LEGISLATURE: Five years
MOST RECENT LEGISLATIVE ELECTION: June 12, 1994
MINIMUM AGE FOR VOTING: 18
MINIMUM AGE FOR MEMBERSHIP: 21
SUFFRAGE: Direct and universal
VOTING: Compulsory
ADDRESS: Chambre des Députés, 19 rue du Marché-aux-Herbes, 1728 Luxembourg
TELEPHONE: (352) 466 966-1
FAX: (352) 22 02 30

The Grand Duchy of Luxembourg, a landlocked country in western Europe which borders on Belgium, France, and Germany, was recognized as an independent state in 1867 *(see map, p. 265)*. It is a constitutional monarchy with the hereditary grand duke as head of state. The prime minister, appointed by the grand duke, is head of government.

The unicameral legislature, the Chamber of Deputies, meets once a year in ordinary session beginning the second Tuesday in October. Extraordinary sessions may be requested by one-third of the deputies. The legislative agenda is set by the president of the Chamber in consultation with the Business Committee, which includes all parliamentary group leaders. Recognized political groups must consist of at least five members. The administrative head of the legislature is the clerk *(greffier)*. Deputies enjoy constitutional immunity for their parliamentary actions, and half their salary is tax-free.

Legislative protocol is established by standing orders. Members may speak from the rostrum or their seats. In general debates, sixty minutes are allotted to groups and fifteen minutes to individual deputies, and in detailed discussions, fifteen minutes for groups and five minutes for deputies. Penalties for unparliamentary conduct include (in increasing order of severity) withdrawal of speaking rights, admonition, suspension for one sitting, and suspension for ten sittings. The quorum is a simple majority in general sessions and two-thirds for considering constitutional amendments. The proceedings of the Chamber are published in *Compte Rendu des Séances Publiques,* in Luxembourgisch and French.

The Council of State (Conseil d'Etat), consisting of twenty-one members nominated by the sovereign, fulfills certain legislative functions. It also advises the Chamber of Deputies on the constitutionality of laws and reviews draft bills submitted to the Chamber.

The legislative process differs for government bills and private bills. For the former, the process begins with the submission by the government of a draft bill accompanied by a statement of purposes to the Council of State. The government then submits the bill with the advice of the Council to the grand duke and requests authorization for its introduction in the Chamber of Deputies. The appropriate minister introduces the bill to the Chamber of Deputies, where the president of the Chamber refers it to a committee. After the committee has presented its report on the bill, general debate is conducted in plenary session, followed by detailed debate, amendment, if any, and vote. If amendments are adopted or any of the articles rejected, the advice of the Council of State must be sought again, followed in the Chamber of Deputies by a second debate and vote on changes and a second vote on the whole bill after the lapse of three months. On passage, the bill goes to the grand duke, upon whose signature it is published in the official gazette.

Bills from private members must be submitted to the president of the Chamber of Deputies and must be authorized by the Business Committee for introduction. The bill is then presented to the Chamber by the author, who reads it before the plenary session and explains its purposes. If the bill is supported by at least five members, the Chamber must consider it. It is then submitted to the Council of State for advice. On its return, the president refers the bill to a committee, and the procedure for government bills is followed after the committee completes its consideration. The grand duke may issue regulations having the force of law.

Ministers may be questioned by members for ninety minutes each Tuesday. Five minutes are allocated for each oral question, and written replies must be provided within two weeks.

For election purposes, the country is divided into four multimember constituencies: south, center, north, and east, which return twenty-three, twenty-one, nine, and seven deputies, respectively. The sixty deputies are elected by the Hagenbach-Bischoff method of proportional representation and preferential vote. A voter may cast a preferential vote (a vote for one party list only) or split his or her vote among different lists. Voters may vote either for a whole list or for particular names on any list. The number of seats each party list obtains is based on the sum arrived at by adding up its total number of votes (individual candidate and list). The remaining seats are allotted to parties with the highest average after the second count. Next-in-line candidates of the same party fill parliamentary vacancies arising between general elections.

George Thomas Kurian

GLOSSARY

Absolute majority. A vote requiring approval by a majority of all members of a house rather than a majority of members present and voting. *See also* Simple majority.

Act. The term for legislation once it has passed the legislature and has been signed into law by the executive or passed by the legislature over the executive's veto.

Ad hoc committee. Temporary committee assigned a specific, short-term matter for action.

Address-in-reply. The formal answer of the parliament, or each house of a bicameral parliament, to the speech made upon the opening of parliament by the monarch or the monarch's representative, such as the governor general.

Adjournment. In many parliamentary systems, the termination by a chamber of its own sitting within a session. Can be for any length of time. Often preceded by an "adjournment debate" at the end of each sitting day, during which members may raise matters of interest. Also refers to the period of time of the suspension. Precise definition and its relationship to recess vary from country to country. *See also* Dissolution; Recess.

Agenda. A prepared lists of items for legislative action in the order in which they will be addressed. Also referred to as the order of business or the order of the day.

Alternative vote. A form of majority electoral system combining single-member districts and preferential voting. Voters rank order the candidates, and a candidate must receive an absolute majority (one vote more than half the votes cast) to be elected. *See also* Electoral system; Majority system; Preferential vote.

Amendment. A proposal to alter the text of a bill, resolution, amendment, motion, treaty, or other document.

Appropriations bill. A type of money bill that gives legal authority, upon its passage into law, to spend or obligate money. Often called a supply bill.

Authorization. Basic, substantive legislation that establishes or continues the legal operation of a program or executive agency, either indefinitely or for a specific period of time, or that sanctions a particular type of obligation or expenditure. An authorization is often a prerequisite for an appropriation or other kind of budget authority.

Backbencher. A rank-and-file party member; a parliamentarian who is not a leader in his or her party. The term derives from the seating arrangement in the British House of Commons.

Backbench pressure. Opposition to the programs, actions, or policies of a party's leaders by its rank-and-file members.

Bar. Commonly, a barrier beyond which nonmembers may not pass.

Basic law. A state's constitution and constitutional laws—the laws from which all other laws are derived and which determine the legality of other laws and actions. A fundamental and supreme law that prescribes how a nation is to be governed. *See also* Constitution; Organic law.

Bell. A device for summoning members of parliament to the floor, either to vote (in which case often called a "division bell") or to achieve a quorum.

Benches. A term that refers to the seating arrangement of the British House of Commons: government parties to the right of the speaker, and the opposition to the left; government and opposition leaderships on the front benches, and rank-and-file members on the back benches.

Bicameral legislature. A legislature composed of two chambers. *See also* Lower house; Upper house.

Bill. A draft of proposed legislation, which can take different forms in different countries. *See also* Government bill; Money bill; Private bill; Private member's bill; Public bill.

By-election. An interim election conducted to fill seats that have become vacant.

Cabinet. In presidential systems, generally an advisory body to the head of government, usually comprising executive heads of departments and other appointed officials. In parliamentary systems, the cabinet is the government itself—that is, the executive officials or ministers selected by the ruling majority. Sometimes known as the Council of Ministers.

Calendar. Schedule of sessions, sittings, recesses, and adjournments; sometimes also refers to an agenda or list of business awaiting possible action by a legislative chamber.

Casework. Assistance given by members of the legislature and their staff to constituents who seek help in dealing with government agencies.

Cassation. The power to reverse the force and validity of a court judgment *See also* Court of cassation.

Casting vote. The right of a presiding officer to break a tie vote. Presiding officers who have an original vote may vote a second time.

Caucus. The official organization of a party in a legislative chamber. *See also* Political group.

Censure. An action taken by a legislature against one of its members or a member of the government for improper or disorderly behavior. Can take the form of a vote of censure and can lead to a reprimand, expulsion, or other sanctions. *See also* Cut motion.

Chair. The person presiding over a meeting.

Chamber. The place where a legislature meets; also refers to a house of a legislature. *See also* Bicameral legislature; Lower house; Unicameral legislature; Upper house.

Checks and balances. A principle of presidential government organization that, along with separation of powers, gives the branches of government responsibilities for overseeing (checking) each other's actions; it also requires that the powers of each branch be relatively equal (balanced) to prevent one branch from becoming dominant. *See also* Presidential government; Separation of powers.

Clerk. Chief administrative officer of a legislative body; sometimes goes by the title secretary general

Closure. *See* Cloture.

Cloture. The process by which a filibuster can be ended in legislatures that permit filibusters. The requirements for invoking cloture vary from legislature to legislature. Sometimes referred to as closure. *See also* Filibuster.

Coalition government. In parliamentary systems of government, the situation arising when no single party holds a majority of seats and as a result does not have the votes necessary to form a cabinet, thus necessitating the formation of an alliance of two or more parties.

Committee. A division of a legislative chamber (or of a legislative body, in the case of joint committees in bicameral systems) that prepares legislation for action by the parent chamber or legislature and that conducts investigations and performs other functions as directed by the parent body. Also called a commission. *See also* Ad hoc committee; Conference committee; Hearings; Joint committee; Oversight committee; Standing committee.

Committee of the whole. A body comprising all the members of the legislative chamber sitting as a committee. When meeting as a committee of the whole, the legislative body invokes different quorum requirements and procedures from those it would if sitting as a plenary body. *See also* Plenary session.

Common law. Legal precedents derived from the decisions of courts of law as opposed to those drawn from statutes. Common law countries are generally those that have derived their legal system from England.

Commonwealth. Often referred to as the British Commonwealth. A voluntary association of fifty-one sovereign states that recognize the British monarch as the symbol of their free association and as head of the Commonwealth. Many member states recognize the British monarch as their ceremonial head of state.

Compulsory voting. A legal requirement that citizens participate in elections, on threat of fines or imprisonment.

Confederation. A group of states united for a common purpose, similar to an alliance. Distinct from a federation in its lack of significant central government. *See also* Federation.

Conference committee. An ad hoc meeting between members of both houses in a bicameral system to reconcile differences between the two houses on provisions of a bill passed by the chambers in different versions. Also called a conciliation, mediation, or reconciliation committee. *See also* Navette system.

Consolidated fund. The account that receives all revenue raised by or granted to the state.

Constituency. *See* Electoral district.

Constitution. An organic, fundamental, basic, and supreme law that may be written or unwritten and, at the least, establishes a political regime with procedures for acquiring, wielding, and transferring political power through government officials and institutions. May also create rights and duties for the state and for its citizens. *See also*Entrenched provision; Organic law; Provisional constitution; Small constitution.

Constitutional. In accordance with or authorized by a constitution, thus legal; also, authority limited by a constitution, such as a constitutional monarchy.

Constitutional court. A special body, either within or outside the judicial system of a state, that exercises some degree of review over the constitutionality of laws and actions of government officials.

Constitutional law. In some countries, a category of legislation fleshing out constitutional provisions. Often requires a supermajority to be enacted.

Constitutionalism. Adherence to constitutional principles, not necessarily to a particular or even a written constitution. A law that is not in conflict with the express provisions of a particular constitution may nevertheless be unconstitutional in a broader sense because it is in conflict with accepted constitutional norms.

Constructive vote of no confidence. A requirement that a legislature select a new head of government before the present head may be removed. Also known as a positive vote of censure. *See also* No-confidence vote.

Council of Ministers. *See* Cabinet.

Coup d'état. A change in government by unconstitutional means, usually by force.

Court of cassation. In France and countries whose legal systems have been significantly influenced by France, the highest court of appeal. *See also* Cassation.

Crown. Originally, the sovereign; the term now also refers to the government under a constitutional monarchy, including the prime minister and other members of the cabinet, who are said to carry out their official duties on behalf of the crown.

Cut motion. A proposal of only symbolic value that has almost no chance of passing; moved by a member of the opposition to disapprove a policy pursued by the government, suggest measures for economy in the administration, or focus the attention of the government on specific local grievances. If passed, it amounts to a vote of censure against the government. *See also* Censure; Motion.

Decree law. An order by an officer of the executive branch of government that has the force of an enacted law and that in many cases must be authorized in advance or subsequently approved by the legislature.

Demands for grants. Departmental and ministry budget requests.

d'Hondt formula. *See* Party-list voting.

Direct democracy. The participation of citizens in the decision making of government without intermediaries; the antithesis of representative government. Participation by means of referendums, initiatives, and recall of representatives. *See also* Initiative; Recall; Referendum.

Discipline. *See* Party discipline.

Dissolution. Act generally taken by a monarch, governor general, or chief executive (president) to end a session of a parliament; results in a recess and is followed by general elections to a new parliament. Also referred to as prorogation. *See also* Recess.

District. *See* Electoral district.

Division. A vote in which the presiding officer first counts those in favor of a proposition and then those opposed to it, usually with no record made of how each member votes. The vote may be taken by show of hands, by standing and sitting in place (a "standing vote"), by segregating those for and against on opposite sides of the chamber, or by filing past tellers. A division usually occurs after the outcome of a voice vote is disputed. *See also* Standing vote; Voice vote; Voting.

Division bell. *See* Bell.

Dominion. Derived from the British North America Act of 1867, which created "one Dominion under the name of Canada." In the early 1900s the term also came to denote other countries in the British Empire that had a measure of self-government and that were not colonies, such as Australia, New Zealand, and South Africa.

Droop quota. *See* Party-list voting; Single transferable vote.

Electoral district. A geographic area represented in a legislative body by an individual (single-member district) or by individuals (multimember district) selected by eligible voters. Also known as a constituency or riding. *See also* Gerrymandering.

Electoral roll. Registry of eligible voters.

Electoral system. The means by which legislative seats are filled. Comprises three components: a districting system (single-member, multimember, or at-large); an electoral formula (plurality, majority, or proportional representation); and a balloting method (the number of votes each voter will cast and a determination of whether the voter will have an "either-or" choice or the option of rank ordering the candidates).

Electronic voting. A means of taking a recorded vote. The use of a computerized system for casting roll-call votes, in which the position of each legislator is ascertained and recorded. *See also* Roll-call vote.

Emergency powers. Extraordinary powers granted to a head of government in time of national emergency; certain individual rights may be suspended during a state of emergency. *See also* Martial law.

Entrenched provision. A section in a constitution or law that is protected from deletion or change by the ordinary process of amendment. Often applied to fundamental civil liberties and basic statements about the nature and structure of the political system. Sometimes used to protect minority rights. Also referred to as a reserved provision.

Estimates. Government expenditure plans submitted by executive departments and agencies to parliament for debate. Supplementary estimates are submitted as needed. *See also* Money bill.

Ex officio. By virtue of one's office.

Extraordinary majority. *See* Supermajority.

Extraordinary session. A convocation of a legislative body or some subset of the body, such as a committee, that is not regularly scheduled as part of the annual calendar.

Faction. *See* Political group.

Federal state. A state that distributes power vertically between a national government and state or provincial government units; the opposite of a unitary or completely centralized state. *See also* Unitary state.

Federation. A union of political entities that mutually agree to subordinate their authority, or some measure of their authority, to a central government.

Filibuster. The use of obstructive and time-consuming parliamentary tactics by a minority in an effort to prevent a vote on a bill or amendment that probably would pass if voted upon directly. Can be ended by cloture.

First-past-the-post system. Electoral system developed in Great Britain and adopted elsewhere that combines single-member districts and a plurality vote rule; the single candidate with the greatest number of votes (not necessarily a majority of the votes) in a given district wins that seat in the legislature.

First reading. *See* Readings of bills.

Fiscal year. The twelve-month accounting period of the government, which need not, and often does not, coincide with the calendar year.

Formateur. An individual appointed by the head of state to help negotiate the formation of a coalition government. Also referred to as informateur. *See also* Coalition government; Government formation.

Fraction. *See* Political group.

Franking privilege. The privilege of a legislator to send mail for official business postage-free.

Free vote. A vote on which party discipline is not imposed or expected.

Frontbencher. A member of parliament who is a leader in his or her party. The term derives from the seating arrangement in the British House of Commons, in which party leaders sit in front, near the speaker.

Gazette. A generic term used in many countries to refer to an official compilation of laws and transcripts of legislative proceedings.

General election. An election in which every seat of the legislative body is at stake. *See also* By-election.

German mixed-model system. *See* Mixed-member system.

Gerrymandering. The manipulation of the boundaries of an electoral district to benefit a particular party, politician, or group. *See also* Electoral district; Redistricting.

Government. Generally, the combination of political institutions, laws, and customs through which the function of governing is carried out. Also refers to (1) the executive branch of a presidential constitutional system, as opposed to the administration alone, which consists of the political officeholders from the president on down; and (2) the cabinet, which in a constitutional parliamentary monarchy includes political officeholders.

Government bill. In parliamentary government, draft legislation introduced by the prime minister or cabinet ministers, as distinct from legislation introduced by members of parliament who are not government ministers. *See also* Private member's bill.

Government formation. The process in a parliamentary system of government of selecting the prime minister and cabinet; the process is complicated if no one party has won a majority of the seats in parliament *See also* Coalition government; Formateur.

Government time. Originally a British practice, subsequently adopted elsewhere, in which a period of time is set aside each week for a ministry official to address the parliament and then respond to members' questions and answers. *See also* Question time.

Governor general. A ceremonial chief executive who represents the British monarch in countries proclaiming allegiance to the British Crown. Nowadays the position is generally reserved for residents of the countries in which they serve.

"Guillotine." A motion stipulating a timetable upon which deliberations on a bill or parts of a bill must be completed; a means of choking off a filibuster. Also the term for a process by which all demands for grants not yet voted upon are voted in quick succession whether or not they have been debated. *See also* Demands for grants.

Hagenbach-Bischoff method. *See* Party-list voting.

Hansard. A written record of parliamentary debates, named after T. C. Hansard, who took over the publishing of debates of the British Parliament in 1812. Specifically, a report of all activities of both houses of the British Parliament. The name subsequently has been appropriated by other national parliaments as the title of their official proceedings.

Hare formula. *See* Party-list voting; Single transferable vote.

Head of government. Usually a prime minister but may also go by the title premier, chancellor, or president of the Council of Ministers. Serves as the chief executive officer of a state, who ensures that laws are executed, that government programs are developed and presented to the legislature for action, and that government officials are appointed and supervised. In a parliamentary system, usually selected from among members of the parliament. In a presidential system, usually elected directly or indirectly by the voters and also fulfills the function of head of state.

Head of state. Usually a monarch or president; generally a ceremonial position unless combined with that of head of government.

Hearings. Committee sessions for taking testimony from witnesses. Hearings may be held on legislation or on special investigations.

Immunity. Grant of exemption from certain civil and criminal penalties accorded to parliamentarians for the duration of their service in the chamber, and sometimes beyond their service, in order to ensure their freedom to perform their duties as representatives. Often constitutionally granted; sometimes granted or extended by standing orders. *See also* Inviolability; Nonliability.

Impeachment. A criminal proceeding against a public official before a quasi-political court initiated by a written accusation called articles of impeachment.

Incompatibility. The notion that two positions may not be held simultaneously, such as member of parliament and court justice. Also, the ineligibility of certain persons for membership in a legislature or certain positions in the government because of their status, profession, or past actions.

Indirect election. Selection of members of a legislative body not by the voters but by an intermediary body, such as an electoral college or provincial or state legislature.

Informateur. *See* Formateur.

Initiative. The right of a citizen or group of citizens to propose legislation or amendments to legislation, such as constitutional amendments. *See also* Direct democracy; Referendum.

Interim constitution. *See* Provisional constitution.

Interpellation. A procedure by which members of a parliament may formally question a member of the government or cabinet about an official action, policy, or personal conduct. If the inquiry is not answered to the satisfaction of the parliamentary majority, it may lead to a vote of no confidence in the official or the government as a whole and to a consequent resignation. *See also* Parliamentary question.

Inviolability. One of two types of immunity that protects members of parliament from being arrested or having their freedom restricted without the authorization of the bureau of the relevant chamber. *See also* Immunity; Nonliability.

Joint committee. A committee comprising members of each house of a bicameral legislature. Also called a joint commission. May be ad hoc or permanent.

Joint session. A sitting of the two houses of a bicameral legislature. Sometimes called a plenary session.

Judicial review. The determination of constitutionality by ordinary courts of law. A principle at odds with parliamentary supremacy, in which supremacy of the parliament over the constitution is claimed.

Junta. A self-appointed body, generally of military officers, that often takes over after a coup d'état.

Laws. Bills that have been passed by the legislature and signed by the executive or that have been passed by the legislature over executive veto.

Lay on the table. *See* Table.

Legislative district. *See* Electoral district.

Lobby. A group seeking to influence the form, passage, or defeat of legislation or government action.

Lower house. Generally, the larger, more representative chamber of a bicameral legislature. Members usually are directly elected, and the lower house usually has the power to initiate money bills. In parliamentary systems the prime minister and members of the cabinet usually are selected from the lower house. *See also* Upper house.

Majlis. An Arabic term translated as assembly or council.

Majority system. An electoral formula in which the winning candidate must receive one more than half of the votes cast (as opposed to a plurality of the votes cast). Examples of majority systems include the alternative vote and second ballot. *See* Alternative vote; Electoral system; Plurality; Second ballot system.

Mandate. Generally, a delegation of authority, especially from the voters to their representatives; popular support for elected officials' policies or a general authorization to officials to carry out the will of the majority of the voters who put them in office. Specifically refers to authorization given by the League of Nations to a member country to administer a territory.

Martial law. A form of military government instituted primarily when the security of a nation is seriously threatened; often abused unconstitutionally as a means by which one group maintains power. A period during which ordinary law and civil liberties may be suspended and law may be enforced by the military. *See also* Emergency powers.

Minister. A government official responsible for overseeing the operations of one or more government departments or agencies. In many parliamentary systems, a member of parliament. *See also* Secretary.

Ministry in waiting. In a parliamentary system of government, the shadow cabinet, or leaders of the minority party who would presumably hold cabinet positions were their party to become the majority party. *See also* Opposition leader.

Minority government. In a parliamentary system, a government formed by a party or coalition of parties that does not hold a majority of the seats in parliament.

Mixed-member system. An electoral system in which some members of a legislative body are elected by means of proportional representation and some are elected in single-member districts. Also referred to as the German mixed-member model.

Monarchy. A government in which all power is vested in a single individual who may be called a king or queen, an emperor or empress, a sovereign, a monarch, or, in some Arab countries, an emir or amir. The monarch and his or her government may be referred to as *the crown*.

Money bill. A broad term referring to legislation that authorizes the expenditure of government funds or that seeks to raise funds for the government, generally by taxation; often treated specially by legislatures in accordance with provisions of the constitution. Money bills encompass estimates, revenue, finance, appropriations, and supply bills.

Motion. A formal procedure by which a lawmaker submits a proposal for consideration and action. *See also* Cut motion.

Multimember district. *See* Electoral district.

Naming. A disciplinary procedure employed by a presiding officer to maintain order in the chamber.

Navette system. A path that legislation might follow in a bicameral system in the event of disagreement between the two houses. The legislation moves back and forth from one chamber to the other until common ground is found. Can end in a deadlock, in a joint sitting, or in a conference committee.

No-confidence vote. A vote taken by parliament in a parliamentary system on the continuance in office of an executive officer or of the prime minister and Council of Ministers (cabinet) as a whole. *See also* Constructive vote of no confidence.

Nomenklatura. An instrument of communist party control in communist systems of government whereby appointments to all important political and administrative positions must be confirmed by the party.

Nomination. Executive appointment to office subject to legislative confirmation.

Nonliability. One of two types of immunity that allows members to express their opinions and exercise their parliamentary mandate freely. Prevents legislators from being sued for declarations, acts, or votes carried out as part of their official function. *See also* Immunity; Inviolability.

Ombudsman. A person with authority to receive citizens' complaints and to investigate wrongdoing or inefficiency on the part of government officials. Also refers to the office held by that person.

Opposition. The party or parties out of power. Also refers to the members of such parties.

Opposition leader. The member of parliament elected or selected by the opposition party or parties to shadow the head of government. Often the presumptive head of government should the opposition gain power through election. *See also* Ministry in waiting.

Order of business. The order in which certain types of issues are addressed in a legislative body; the organizing principle behind the order paper or agenda. *See also* Agenda; Order paper.

Order paper. Agenda of events. A term common to Westminster systems.

Organic law. Legislation affecting the organization of government or another entity. It may or may not have constitutional status, but it usually requires more than a simple majority vote in the legislature. *See also* Basic law; Constitution.

Oversight committee. A legislative committee, or designated subcommittee of a committee, that is charged with general oversight of one or more government programs, activities, or agencies. Often a standing committee.

Pairing. A voluntary, informal arrangement that two lawmakers, usually on opposite sides of an issue, make on recorded votes. In many cases the result is to subtract a vote from each side, with no effect on the outcome.

Parliamentary government. One of two major types of democratic governing systems (the other being presidential government), having an elected body of representatives (commonly but not necessarily bicameral); a government or Council of Ministers (cabinet) with a prime minister (head of government) approved by the majority of the members of the parliament (or one house of the parliament); a maximum period between elections, although the more representative house in a bicameral parliament may be dissolved earlier if the government originally approved by it loses the confidence of the majority of its members and is therefore forced to resign, initiating new elections; and a head of state (a monarch or president), who must, if only ceremonially, assent to bills passed by the parliament before they may become effective. The fundamental difference between a parliamentary government and a presidential system is that the head of government serves at the pleasure of the parliament and is often drawn from among the members of the parliament, thus parliamentary government is not characterized by a rigid separation of powers. *See also* Head of government; Head of state; Presidential government; Separation of powers.

Parliamentary group. *See* Political group.

Parliamentary question. Similar to an interpellation in that a query is put to a government minister for written or oral answer, but unlike an interpellation no debate or vote follows the question.

Party. A group of people, generally having a similar political philosophy, who are organized to nominate candidates for office and to contest elections.

Party discipline. The degree to which members of a political party in a parliament or legislature vote alike, for reasons of shared philosophy or pressure from the party leadership. *See also* Free vote; Whip.

Party-list voting. One of two major classifications of proportional representation electoral formulas (the other being the single transferable vote), which aims to achieve representation of parties proportionate to their share of the votes cast. Mathematical formulas for translating percentage of votes to number of seats are of two types: highest-average formulas (d'Hondt, St. Laguë, and Hagenbach-Bischoff) and greatest remainder formulas (Droop quota, Hare quota, and Imperial quota).

Permanent committee. *See* Standing committee.

Plebiscite. *See* Referendum.

Plenary session. A meeting attended by all qualified members of a body.

Pluralism. The notion that the state is just one of many centers of power in society and that a democracy can exist only as long as access to the political process is guaranteed to competing interest groups.

Plurality. A number of votes, in an election or other balloting, in excess of that received by the next-highest-achieving proposition or candidate. *See also* Majority system.

Politburo. Contraction of "political bureau." The most powerful institution of a communist party.

Political group. An organization of legislators or parliamentarians, often but not necessarily sharing political party affiliation, officially recognized by a legislative chamber and deriving institutional benefits such as the right to participate in agenda setting and leadership positions by virtue of their group status. Also referred to as a faction, fraction, or parliamentary group. *See also* Caucus.

Positive vote of censure. *See* Constructive vote of no confidence.

Preferential vote. A balloting method in which voters rank the candidates in order of preference. *See also* Alternative vote.

Premier. *See* Prime minister.

Prerogative. Discretionary power that is an attribute of sovereignty, such as the authority historically inherent in the British Crown.

President. Head of state (as in many parliamentary systems of government) or both head of state and head of government (as in many presidential systems of government). *See also* Head of government; Head of state; Parliamentary government; Presidential government.

Presidential government. One of two major types of democratic governing systems (the other being parliamentary government), in which the position and powers of both head of state and head of government are vested in a president whose election, duties, and powers are constitutionally independent of the legislature. Characterized by separation of powers and checks and balances. *See also* Checks and balances; Parliamentary government; Separation of powers.

Presidium. A permanent executive committee of a larger body, generally a legislature, often used in countries dominated by a communist party.

Prime minister. Head of government in a parliamentary system of government. Also referred to as premier, chancellor, or president of the Council of Ministers. *See also* Head of government.

Private bill. Draft legislation that if adopted would affect only one person or interest. Private bills often deal with an individual's claim against the government, immigration and naturalization questions, or land titles.

Private member's bill. In a parliamentary system, draft legislation introduced by a parliamentarian who is not a member of the government. Can be introduced by an independent, a member of the opposition, or a government backbencher. Often treated differently from legislation introduced by a parliamentarian who is a member of the government. *See also* Government bill; Public bill.

Privy council. Originally, an advisory body to the crown. In the United Kingdom, the term now refers to the Judicial Committee of the Privy Council, which consists of lords of appeal (law lords), who sit in the House of Lords and hear final legal appeals.

Procurator. A legal representative of the state in judicial, particularly criminal, matters. A term often used by communist governments.

Promulgate. To put a new law, ordinance, decree, or constitution into effect.

Proportional representation. A broad, generic term describing various electoral formulas in which parties win seats in a legislature in proportion to their share of the votes cast. There are two major types of proportional representation systems: party-list voting and single transferable vote (see those terms).

Prorogation. *See* Dissolution.

Provisional constitution. A basic law put into effect with the presumption that it will soon be superseded. Also referred to as an interim constitution.

Public bill. Draft legislation that deals with general questions and affects the general public, as distinct from a private bill. A public bill can take the form of a government bill or a private member's bill. *See also* Private bill; Private member's bill.

Question. *See* Parliamentary question.

Question time. A period allotted in many parliamentary systems for members to direct oral questions to government ministers. Sometimes referred to as question hour. *See also* Government time.

Quorum. The number of members whose presence is necessary for the transaction of business.

Readings of bills. The traditional parliamentary procedure by which bills are brought up for action three times before passage. Normally, a bill is considered to have its first reading when it is introduced and printed. The second reading often is followed by a debate on the bill's underlying principles and then by a vote to pass the bill to third reading, which involves clause-by-clause examination and debate and is followed by a final vote on adoption.

Recall. The right of citizens to remove the mandate from their elected representative in a legislative body. *See also* Direct democracy; Mandate.

Recess. In many parliamentary systems, the period between prorogation and the beginning of a new session. Colloquially used to refer to a long adjournment. Precise definition and its relationship to adjournment vary from country to country. *See also* Adjournment; Dissolution.

Recognition. The power of the presiding officer (speaker, president, chair, or some other title) to permit a member to address the body.

Recorded vote. A legislative ballot in which the position of each legislator is made known. Most often taken by electronic voting machine, but may be taken by roll call or signed paper ballot as well.

Redistricting. The redrawing of legislative constituency boundaries. *See also* Gerrymandering.

Referendum. The practice of submitting a proposed law—including a constitutional law, revision, or amendment, whether proposed or already in effect—to a direct popular vote. The vote itself. Also referred to as a plebiscite. *See also* Initiative.

Report. A formal record of a committee meeting's findings and recommendations on a measure after it has examined a bill referred to it by the parent chamber. The committee "reports" to the chamber when it returns the measure.

Reporter. A member who has the task of steering legislation through floor debate and the amendment process to a final vote in the plenary. Reporters, also sometimes called floor managers or rapporteurs, are often chairs or ranking members of the committee that reported the bill.

Reserved provision. *See* Entrenched provision.

Riding. *See* Electoral district.

Right of inquiry. The right to request and conduct an investigation; one means of controlling the executive. *See also* Interpellation.

Roll-call vote. A legislative ballot in which each member's position is ascertained and recorded.

Rule of law. A standard for holding government officials to the same substantive law to which all citizens are subject; generally, government by laws rather than by people.

Rules of procedure. The normative proscriptions by which a legislature of other government body conducts its business. Occasionally spelled out in a constitution but more often incorporated in a legislative body's standing orders.

St. Laguë method. *See* Party-list voting.

Second ballot system. A form of majority electoral system that employs single-member districts and a second round of balloting if no candidate wins an absolute majority of the vote in the initial round.

Second reading. *See* Readings of bills.

Secretary. A common appellation in presidential and semipresidential systems of government for the head of one or more government departments or agencies. Also referred to as cabinet secretary. Analogous to a minister in a parliamentary system but not a member of the legislature. *See also* Minister.

Secretary general. *See* Clerk.

Separation of powers. A constitutional principle that divides the power of government into three functions or branches: making the laws (legislative), interpreting the laws (judicial), and enforcing the laws (executive). Designed to prevent tyranny or a monopoly of government power in the hands of a single person or group.

Session. In many parliamentary systems, defined as the period between the opening of parliament and its dissolution. Sessions are divided into sittings. *See also* Extraordinary session.

Shadow cabinet. *See* Ministry in waiting.

Shadow minister. A member of the opposition party in a legislature or parliament who is given primary responsibility for examining a particular area of government policy and administration. *See also* Ministry in waiting.

Simple majority. A vote requiring approval by a majority of all members of a house who are present and voting. *See also* Absolute majority.

Single-member district. *See* Electoral district.

Single transferable vote. Also known as the Hare system, after Thomas Hare, a nineteenth-century British parliamentarian. One of two major classifications of proportional representation electoral formulas (the other being party-list voting). A type of preferential vote in which voters using a multiparty ballot rank various candidates first, second, third, and so on, without confining choices to one party. Mathematical formulas for translating votes to seats include the Hare formula and the Droop quota.

Sitting. The discrete segments, each ended by adjournment, into which a legislative session is divided. A sitting may last only a few minutes or extend over several calendar days.

Small constitution. An interim constitution, as that adopted by Poland in 1992, that sets forth the basic structure of government pending adoption of a comprehensive constitution.

Standing committee. A division of the legislative body that is permanently established for the duration of a session or longer, generally being assigned oversight and legislative review authority. Also referred to as a permanent committee.

Standing orders. Rules governing the conduct of legislative business and listed among the permanent rules of the chamber. Standing orders deal with such issues as duties of officers, the order of business, admission to the floor, parliamentary procedures on handling amendments, and voting and jurisdictions of committees.

Standing vote. A nonrecorded vote in which members in favor of a proposal stand and are counted by the presiding officer. Then members opposed stand and are counted. There is no record of how individual members voted. *See also* Division.

Supermajority. A term sometimes used for a vote on a matter that requires approval by more than a simple majority of those members present and voting; also referred to as an extraordinary majority. May be three-fifths, two-thirds, or three-quarters of the membership or some other fraction in excess of one-half.

Supply bill. Draft legislation to appropriate funds. *See also* Money bill.

Suspensive veto. The power of an executive to return bills to the legislature for reconsideration. Less than a right of absolute veto.

Table. In many parliamentary systems, literally a table in front of the speaker's chair at which the clerk sits; the place where documents are submitted for consideration of the chamber (whence derives the parliamentary term "to lay on the table," meaning to present for consideration). In U.S. congressional parlance, to table means to "kill" a bill or amendment.

Teller. A member or clerk who counts members in certain voting or quorum-call situations

Third reading. *See* Readings of bills.

Threshold. In party-list voting, the minimum percentage of the vote a party must receive to claim seats in the legislature.

Unicameral legislature. A legislature composed of one chamber.

Unitary state. A state in which sovereignty is not shared vertically with other units, such as states or provinces; not a federal state.

Upper house. Generally, the smaller, less representative chamber of a bicameral legislature. *See also* Lower house.

Veto. The refusal of an executive officer, generally the chief executive of a state, to assent to the passage of a law where the executive's assent is required for the law to become effective. *See also* Suspensive veto.

Voice vote. A ballot taken in a legislative body when the person presiding calls for the "ayes" and then the "noes" (or "yeas and nays," or "ayes and nays"). Members shout in chorus on one side of the proposition or the other, and the chair determines the result. If the outcome is in dispute, a division or roll-call vote may ensue.

Voting. Generally, the process of casting ballots and tallying the results. In the context of a legislature, voting may be by voice, by roll call, by general consent or acclamation, or by secret ballot.

Warrant of precedence. Ordering of government officials by rank.

Westminster system. Prototypical system of parliamentary government, as historically developed in the United Kingdom. Named for the site of the British Parliament in London. Characterized by strong cabinet government, majority rule, a two-party system, loyal opposition, and parliamentary supremacy. The term also encompasses the many formal and informal procedures of the British Parliament, such as the three-reading system. Also referred to as the Westminster model of government. *See also* Parliamentary government.

Whip. A member of the party leadership in a parliament or legislature charged with maintaining communications with backbenchers and ensuring party discipline.

Writ. A legal instrument to enforce obedience to an authority, generally a court of law.

INDEX

C

P